The Denmark Vesey Affair

Southern Dissent

University Press of Florida

Florida A&M University, Tallahassee
Florida Atlantic University, Boca Raton
Florida Gulf Coast University, Ft. Myers
Florida International University, Miami
Florida State University, Tallahassee
New College of Florida, Sarasota
University of Central Florida, Orlando
University of Florida, Gainesville
University of North Florida, Jacksonville
University of South Florida, Tampa
University of West Florida, Pensacola

The Denmark Vesey Affair

A Documentary History

EDITED BY DOUGLAS R. EGERTON
AND ROBERT L. PAQUETTE

Foreword by Stanley Harrold and Randall M. Miller

University Press of Florida
Gainesville · Tallahassee · Tampa · Boca Raton
Pensacola · Orlando · Miami · Jacksonville · Ft. Myers · Sarasota

Publication of this paperback edition made possible by a Sustaining the Humanities through the American Rescue Plan grant from the National Endowment for the Humanities.

First cloth printing, 2017
First paperback printing, 2022

27 26 25 24 23 22 6 5 4 3 2 1

Library of Congress Cataloging-in-Publication Data
Names: Egerton, Douglas R., editor. | Paquette, Robert L., 1951– editor. | Harrold, Stanley, author of foreword. | Miller, Randall M., author of foreword.
Title: The Denmark Vesey Affair : a documentary history / edited by Douglas R. Egerton and Robert L. Paquette ; foreword by Stanley Harrold and Randall M. Miller.
Description: Gainesville : University Press of Florida, [2017] | Includes index.
Identifiers: LCCN 2016030101 | ISBN 9780813062822 (cloth) | ISBN 9780813068992 (pbk.)
Subjects: LCSH: Vesey, Denmark, approximately 1767–1822. | Slaves—South Carolina—Charleston—Biography. | Charleston (S.C.)—History—Slave Insurrection, 1822. | Slave insurrections—South Carolina—Charleston.
Classification: LCC F279.C49 N417 2017 | DDC 975.7/91503092 [B]—dc23
LC record available at https://lccn.loc.gov/2016030101

The University Press of Florida is the scholarly publishing agency for the State University System of Florida, comprising Florida A&M University, Florida Atlantic University, Florida Gulf Coast University, Florida International University, Florida State University, New College of Florida, University of Central Florida, University of Florida, University of North Florida, University of South Florida, and University of West Florida.

University Press of Florida
2046 NE Waldo Road
Suite 2100
Gainesville, FL 32609
http://upress.ufl.edu

Subvention for this publication generously provided by
The Alexander Hamilton Institute for the Study of Western Civilization

CONTENTS

ILLUSTRATIONS

Figures

Maps

FOREWORD

Preparing and publishing scholarly editions of historical documents are major, time-consuming undertakings. Those who initiate and engage in such projects invest years of effort in identifying, locating, evaluating, transcribing, and organizing relevant materials. Their goals include making history's primary sources more accessible for scholars, students, and others who seek insight into the past.

Often scholarly editions focus on the correspondence of politicians, reformers, authors, and artists. Roy Basler's collection of Abraham Lincoln's writings and speeches, published during the 1950s, totals nine volumes, with supplementary volumes added afterward. There are six volumes in Walter M. Merrill and Louis Ruchames's *Letters of William Lloyd Garrison*, published between 1971 and 1981. The Thomas Jefferson papers project, which started in the 1950s, continues with many volumes in print and others in process. So, too, for other long-running multivolume papers projects of several Founding Fathers. More recently the collecting, editing, and publishing of the papers of such major nineteenth-century American leaders as Andrew Jackson, Frederick Douglass, and Elizabeth Cady Stanton have become well-funded, institutionalized projects conducted by large editorial teams at major American universities. They produce multiple volumes over long spans of time, and increasingly there are online versions.

The person at the center of Douglas R. Egerton and Robert L. Paquette's *The Denmark Vesey Affair: A Documentary History* stands in contrast with such major national politicians and reformers. Vesey, a free black resident of Charleston, South Carolina, neither carried on correspondence nor delivered public speeches. He lived much of his life as a slave in the Caribbean region. Upon gaining freedom in 1799, he worked as a carpenter and raised several families in Charleston. Vesey's 1822 conspiracy, centered in that city, ranks with Gabriel's 1800 conspiracy near Richmond, Virginia; the 1811 River Road Rebellion, led by Charles Deslondes in Louisiana; and Nat Turner's Southampton County, Virginia, revolt of 1831 as one of the important examples of black resistance to slavery in American history. Yet, like the leaders of these other conspiracies and revolts, Vesey became a public figure for just weeks during his lifetime, though his memory lived on as an inspiration for African Americans and a worry for white Americans. As Egerton and Paquette note, Vesey left few documents of any kind, and, until the slave revolt conspiracy that bears his name, he barely appeared in the public record. It took the exposure of the conspiracy and the rapid arrest, trial, and execution of Vesey and his fellow conspirators to bring him to prominence.

To understand the dynamics and implications of the Vesey conspiracy and contemporary responses to it in law and society, Egerton and Paquette's task has been to gather a wide variety of documents that pertain to Vesey and the conspiracy he led. These documents include private correspondence, diaries, transcripts of trial proceedings, an official report on the trial, other government publications, contemporary newspaper articles, and later public and private reflections on Vesey, the conspiracy, and their importance. In each case, Egerton and Paquette rely on their intensive and extensive knowledge of the Vesey conspiracy and its historical contexts—regional, national, and international.

As Egerton and Paquette write in their introduction, much of the importance of the Vesey conspiracy lies in white South Carolinians' and other white southerners' reactions to it. Discovery of the conspiracy intensified a long-standing fear of slave revolt. The conspiracy represented black dissent from an oppressive system of forced labor and race control. That dissent in turn increased a white southern defensiveness that led to tighter racial controls in South Carolina and elsewhere and to increasingly adamant demands aimed at strengthening the slave system in the nation. It contributed to later white southern moves to shore up slavery that brought on sectional discord, secession, and the Civil War. Both for its exhaustive presentation of Vesey documents and its linkage of Vesey to major national events, Egerton and Paquette's scholarly edition is a welcome addition to the Southern Dissent series.

Stanley Harrold and Randall M. Miller
Series Editors

ACKNOWLEDGMENTS

The Alexander Hamilton Institute for the Study of Western Civilization (AHI) in Clinton, New York, has never said "No" in supporting any aspect of this project over the years. We would like to thank in particular Carl Menges of the AHI's Board of Directors and President Richard Erlanger for approving the resources needed to turn an early draft of the manuscript into a polished finished product. Indeed, to Mr. Menges, whose unstinting generosity to the AHI has helped this project every step of the way, the editors wish to dedicate this book.

David Frisk and Mary Grabar, resident fellows at the AHI, kindly responded to our request to supply extra pairs of eyes in proofreading every section of the manuscript. They did so with a thoroughness and professionalism that would be hard to match. We would also like to thank the Watson-Brown Foundation of Thomson, Georgia, and its redoubtable leader, Tad Brown, for providing Paquette with support during the initial stages of the project. AHI interns Michael Adamo and Ami Elinski ran more errands for us during the summer of 2014 than they would care to remember. Marcia Wilkinson, secretary-for-hire extraordinaire, had the job of cleaning up messes left behind by two word-processing sophomores.

A good number of friends supplied us with documents that had escaped our notice. Both James O'Neil Spady of the Soka University of America, who has published major insights into the testimony of George Wilson, and Mark Fleszar, who recently completed his dissertation at Georgia State University on Florida planter and slave trader Zephaniah Kingsley, provided us with several key documents. Ethan Kytle of the California State University, Fresno, uncovered two post–Civil War newspaper stories that helped untangle Vesey's complicated marriages as well as a clue to the razing of the African Church. Judith Wellman, an authority on free blacks in New York State at SUNY Oswego, turned our attention to the later life of Prince Graham, who had been exiled to West Africa but relocated to Manhattan. Manuel Barcia helped track down documents related to the transportation of some convicted plotters to Cuba. Without this noteworthy scholarly generosity, the volume could make no legitimate claim of completeness.

Historian and archivist Harlan Greene has probably touched every document pertinent to early national Charleston, and he patiently answered all of our endless queries about missing manuscripts, relocated collections—even graveyards and dead bodies.

Harlan also read the entire manuscript, as did David Moltke-Hansen, and their advice proved invaluable. Nicholas Butler, currently with the Charleston County Public Library, performed similar kind tasks. Charles Lesser, now retired from South Carolina's Department of Archives and History, not only answered never-ending questions and pointed us in the direction of obscure documents, he provided detailed comments on the materials compiled here in Part I. At Le Moyne College, research librarian Wayne Stevens tracked down innumerable rare pamphlets and booklets, in one case locating a curious magazine piece that even the Library of Congress could not find.

Douglas Egerton's Le Moyne colleague, Leigh Fought, a veteran of both the Ulysses S. Grant and Frederick Douglass papers projects, advised us on a number of editorial issues and uncovered the fascinating reference to Vesey at Anna Murray Douglass's funeral. As ever, this editor is grateful to Leigh for help with this project—and for far more. At the University Press of Florida, series editors Stanley Harrold and Randall Miller performed their tasks perfectly. They read every page of the volume and were as wise as they were supportive, as well as endlessly patient with our chronic disregard for deadlines. Sian Hunter guided the manuscript through the editorial process with great professionalism, and Stan Ivester did a superb job as copyeditor. Stephanye Hunter took enormous care during the final stages of publication to ensure that what was being printed was an exact match to what had appeared in 1822 on the written page. Thanks also to Marthe Walters for putting the final coat of polish on the final version.

EDITORIAL STATEMENT

This documentary collection represents an exhaustive effort to reproduce and interpret all documents relevant to the Denmark Vesey affair. The discovery in 1822 by Charleston officials of an alleged revolutionary slave plot, masterminded by Vesey, a freed person of color, transformed the politics of South Carolina and, in so doing, helped set the slaveholding South on the course to secession. There is considerable debate as to the causes, content, and consequences of the plot. This volume contains the official narrative as well as documents that prove consistent or inconsistent with it, in whole or in part. We have used notes to add relevant information, correct errors, and remove confusion while providing our own considered judgment that the Vesey plot was one of the most sophisticated acts of collective slave resistance in the history of the United States. The volume consists of six sections, reflecting both chronology and subject matter in a way that will unfold for modern readers and scholars as they did for those witnessing the events of 1822. We have not segregated the documents by type. Correspondence and newspaper accounts, for example, may be found in each of the volume's sections.

Part I, Preconditions, includes documents that pertain to Denmark Vesey's early life in the Caribbean and Charleston. This section also contains documents regarding the founding of the city's African Methodist Episcopal congregation, initially known as the African Church, as well as materials detailing pre-1822 slave resistance in South Carolina and white responses and retribution. Part II, Proceedings, contains materials about the detection and collapse of the conspiracy, the authorities' description of the plot's unraveling, the initial arrest of leading rebels, and the debate among white elites as to what sort of legal protections, if any, should be granted to the accused.

Part III, Trials: The *Official Report* and the Senate Transcript, is the heart of the volume. Four types of courtroom documents for the Charleston trials of 1822 exist. Unfortunately, the original handwritten documents, upon which all four subsequent versions of the proceedings were based, no longer survive. The two courts that met during that summer acted in great haste, yet the extant handwritten trial documents in the state archives, prepared at Governor Thomas Bennett Jr.'s direction for presentation to the South Carolina House and Senate, proved uniformly neat and precise. No hurried scrawl mars the documents, each drawn by the same patient hand, undoubtedly, from fragmentary scraps of paper that were tossed away after transcription by one or more Charleston clerks. Lacking modern stenographic capabilities and uninterested in contemporary preservation techniques, the court evidently saw no reason to retain random bits of data that were subsequently rendered into several far more readable versions.

The trial transcripts requested by the governor appeared in two forms. The shorter version, which was presented to the House, ran from Wednesday, June 19, to Friday, July 26, 1822, and was docketed as "Document B House of Representatives." The longer Senate copy, docketed simply as "Evidence Document B," includes the trials covered in the House version but runs into August. It concludes with the lengthy sentences read to Denmark Vesey, Jack Pritchard, and "ten of the criminals." The Senate version also contains correspondence between the governor and South Carolina Attorney General Robert Young Hayne (which we have moved to Part II of this volume). Small variations, usually of punctuation or capitalization, exist between the two versions, just as the two versions surely varied slightly from the original and now missing fragmentary court documents.

After the adjournment of the second court in August, three white men involved in the previous summer's proceedings of the first court published two separate but related works that contained all or parts of the two courts' records. As early as mid-August, Charleston Intendant (Mayor) James Hamilton Jr. wrote *An Account of the Late Intended Insurrection among a Portion of the Blacks of the City*, a 48-page collection of court documents, together with a short biography of Denmark Vesey and a brief narrative of events. (In 1822 a northern edition appeared, published in Boston by J. W. Ingraham under the title *Negro Plot: An Account of the Late Intended Insurrection among a Portion of the Blacks of the City of Charleston, South Carolina*). In October, two magistrates, both attorneys, Lionel Henry Kennedy (1787?–1847) and Thomas Parker Jr. (1793?–1844), produced a far longer work, *An Official Report of the Trials of Sundry Negroes*. This 202-page volume includes some of the same material published by Hamilton, such as the brief biography of Vesey, which was almost certainly provided by Joseph Vesey, Denmark's aged former master.

The *Official Report* includes a longer narrative of events and detailed descriptions of the trials held inside the Charleston Work-House as well as an explanation of the state's laws pertaining to slaves and free blacks. All three authors had access to both original sets of documents. The *Official Report* includes minor details omitted from the versions presented to the House and Senate, such as the forenames of whites who accompanied their accused bondmen to the trials, and the rulings in some of the cases. Meant to calm public fears and demonstrate the reassertion of mastery by South Carolina's whites over the state's black majority, the *Official Report*, in turn, omitted information regarded as inflammatory. In a revealing moment of editorial honesty, Kennedy and Parker replaced Gullah Jack Pritchard's reference to the plotters' design to poison city wells with a series of asterisks. The *Official Report* also identified those slaves who were offered immunity in exchange for their testimony only by a number or a capital letter. By comparison, most of the slaves' names appear in the versions provided to South Carolina's House and South Carolina's Senate. The final trials in August by the Second Court of Magistrates and Freeholders, detailed in the Senate transcript but absent from the House version, receive mere summaries in the *Official Report.*

Since the original documentary scraps were destroyed, scholars will never know which of the four versions represents the most accurate version of events. Because Hamilton's pamphlet appeared only weeks after the August trials ended, his version and Kennedy and Parker's longer *Official Report*—which generally differ only in length—may be more accurate than the handwritten versions subsequently presented to the state assembly three months later. Thus, by the time a clerk had copied at the governor's request the original records in November, those manuscripts had already been used twice by three officials for two different publications. Clerks were chosen for their elegant handwriting rather than for their historical sense or archival ability. The messiness of the Senate and House versions most likely resulted from a disorganized stack of documents turned over by Kennedy and Parker for transcription rather than from the disorderliness of court sessions run the previous summer. Hamilton's *Account of the Late Intended Insurrection* and Kennedy and Parker's *Official Report,* in short, probably constitute the best record of the two courts' actions. Hamilton's *Account* has proved to be the superior source for providing specific trial dates; it also discusses a number of slaves questioned and released who were unmentioned elsewhere.

Because integration of the Senate report into the *Official Report* would violate the integrity of each, we have chosen to reproduce both reports in back-to-back versions, supplemented by occasional additions from Hamilton's *Account.* Because the October *Official Report* appeared one month before the Senate transcription, we have placed that publication before the legislative account. Footnotes indicate where we have relied on Hamilton's *Account.* They also identify differences between the various versions and, on occasion, discuss minor variations between the House and Senate versions. All editorial insertions into the transcribed texts—which we have used sparingly and only when the original document is unclear—appear in square brackets; because the printer of the *Official Report* used square brackets on occasion, we have changed the original brackets to parentheses to avoid confusion in Part III.

Fidelity to the original documents has guided our transcription. Given controversies in the historiography, in some cases related to the reading of texts, we have chosen to refrain from the use of an intrusive "[*sic*]" every time an archaic spelling, misspelling, or some idiosyncrasy or peculiarity appeared in the text. Our efforts at exactitude should leave readers confident that mistakes visible in the transcribed text are the fault of the document's author, not the volume's editors. When words are mistakenly repeated in either published or handwritten documents, we have removed the second word. Footnotes are used to supply context, to make connections, and to identify people and places mentioned in the documents, usually on their first mention. The symbols used by Charleston typesetters in 1822, such as an asterisk to indicate additional data added to footnotes in the pamphlets, are here retained, and what were footnotes here appear at the bottom of each corresponding paragraph.

Part IV, Eyewitnesses, chronicles those who watched and reported on the events of the summer of 1822, and Part V, Aftermath, the largest section, recounts the plot's major ripple effects, inside and outside of South Carolina, including the legislation inspired by the conspiracy, as well as the newspaper-and-pamphlet war that ensued as white Carolinians sought to justify not only their judicial behavior, but their way of life in a slave society. The documents in this part of the book make clear that no white notable in South Carolina in 1822—not Governor Bennett, not his brother-in-law Supreme Court Justice William Johnson Jr.—doubted the existence of an insurrectionary plot, although debate existed as to its precise content and magnitude. Part VI, Recollections and Memorializations, contains documents written years after the affair by those who experienced it. Subsequent generations of whites and blacks resurrected and reimagined Vesey and his conspiracy in quite different ways, creating a powerful symbol or myth that spoke to contemporary challenges of race and class.

INTRODUCTION

The Caribbean historian C.L.R. James prefaced his grand narrative of Toussaint Louverture and the Haitian Revolution by paraphrasing Karl Marx: "Great men make history, but only such history as it is possible for them to make."[1] James's maxim holds equally true for the man who would come to be known as Denmark Vesey. His life and actions reshaped the course of southern history, and hence the contours of American history as well, but not in the way he had hoped. As an elderly man in his fifties, Vesey sought to liberate his sons, his friends, and a good number of enslaved South Carolinians. He ended up hanging by the neck until dead, executed by Charleston officials along with thirty-four other Africans and African Americans. Yet Vesey, much like John Brown—another, later, abolitionist—did achieve a measure of success in death.

The Missouri debates of 1819 to 1821 over the place of slavery in the West had already begun to erode any post–War of 1812 nationalism that existed among white Carolinians. But, as William W. Freehling noted in his seminal 1966 study of the Nullification Crisis, Vesey's failed conspiracy spurred the development and articulation of a theory of state sovereignty that would define the state's politics for the following three decades, and in the process win over much of the slaveholding South. Before the Vesey affair, such leading lights of the nullification movement as James Hamilton Jr., Robert Young Hayne, and John C. Calhoun supported nationalist projects and stood outside the camp of the extreme states' rightists, represented in their own state by the firebrand William Smith. Indeed, the politics of Hamilton, Hayne, and Calhoun prior to the Vesey affair might be best characterized as neo-Federalist. If the course of the South to secession can be encapsulated by the extension of South Carolina's proslavery, states' rights principles to the other slaveholding states, then the events set in motion by Vesey and his followers played a crucial role in shaping South Carolina's political principles on the road to disunion. As journalist John Lofton put it in 1964, Vesey "lit the fuse to Fort Sumter." He precipitated a series of events that culminated at Appomattox Courthouse and ended slavery not just around Charleston but throughout the American South.[2]

For a man whose reputation terrified many white Americans while inspiring perhaps as many black Americans, the multilingual Vesey left behind few documents. No letters or diaries in his hand exist. State and city authorities made it their business to harass the city's free blacks, but there is no evidence that the imposing carpenter—unlike his third wife, Susan Vesey—ever paid the special tax imposed on free people of color. His name appears in occasional documents, stretching from Presbyterian Church records to the city's directory of free blacks, but never in his own hand. For most of his life, Vesey labored simply to survive. For roughly the first thirty-three years of his life, he was a slave, perhaps initially in the Gold Coast region of West Africa or in the Danish Caribbean colony of St. Thomas and then in the French colony of Saint-Domingue. Purchased by Captain Joseph Vesey in the fall of 1781 and then again in late April of 1782 after a buyer in the colony complained of the child's ill health, the boy was renamed Telemaque. When the captain settled in Charleston in the spring of 1783, Telemaque became Joseph's domestic servant; married a fellow slave, Beck; and remained the property of Joseph and Mary Clodner Vesey until winning the city lottery and buying his freedom on December 31, 1799. During the next two decades, the freedman calling himself Denmark Vesey married twice more and eked out a living as a carpenter while his third wife, Susan, took in laundry. In 1822 he was approximately fifty-five years old, twenty years past the average life expectancy for free blacks in antebellum America. His friends called him "the old man," and despite his age, he briefly considered emigrating to Sierra Leone or Liberia with Susan, their young daughter Diana, and his son John Anthony. But, as he told his friend, the slave Frank Ferguson, he "decided to stay, and see what he could do for his fellow creatures."[3]

Instead of abandoning his extended family, Vesey resolved to orchestrate a rebellion followed by a mass exodus from Charleston to Haiti, where rebellious slaves had declared formal independence from France in 1804 and where Haitian leaders, beginning with Alexandre Pétion (1770–1818), had been officially encouraging black migration from slaveholding areas to soil guaranteed free by Haiti's constitution. Although opposed to the American Colonization Society's repatriation of blacks to Africa, Richard Allen's African Methodist Episcopal (AME) Church, created in 1816, looked positively on their emigration to Haiti. Jean-Pierre Boyer, Haiti's president in 1822, had publicly encouraged black Americans to bring their skills and capital to his depressed republic. All of Charleston's major newspapers in the years immediately preceding the Vesey affair contained stories about Haiti, including the rise of Boyer, who as the head of an army of tens of thousands was not only uniting Haiti, but conquering the entire island of Hispaniola.

Vesey did not intend to tarry in Charleston long enough for white military power to present an effective counterassault. "As soon as they could get the money from the Banks, and the goods from the stores," conspirator Rolla Bennett insisted, "they should hoist sail for Saint Doming[ue]" and live as free men. Those recruited into the plot during the winter of 1822 were directed to arm themselves from their masters' closets. Vesey also knew that the Charleston Neck militia stored its three hundred muskets and bayonets in the back room of merchant Benjamin Hammet's King Street store, and that Hammet's slave, Bacchus, had a key. But, as few slaves had any experience with guns, Vesey encouraged his followers to arm themselves with swords or long daggers, which in any case would make for quieter work as the city bells tolled midnight. Vesey also employed several enslaved blacksmiths to forge "pike heads and bayonets with sockets, to be fixed at the end of long poles."[4]

The plot unraveled in June 1822 when two slaves, including Rolla's friend, George Wilson, a fellow class leader in the African Church, revealed the plan to their owners. Intendant James Hamilton Jr. called up the city militia and convened a special court to try the captured insurgents. Captured at the home of Beck, his first wife, on June 21, Vesey was hanged on the morning of Tuesday, July 2, together with Rolla, Peter Poyas, and three other rebels. According to Hamilton, the six men collectively "met their fate with the heroic fortitude of Martyrs."[5] In all, thirty-five men were executed. Forty-two others, including Denmark's son Sandy Vesey, were sold outside the United States; some, if not all, became slaves in Spanish Cuba. Another son, Robert Vesey, lived to rebuild the African Church after the fall of Charleston and the Confederacy in 1865.

In the aftermath of the Vesey conspiracy, Charleston authorities demolished the independent African Church and banished its clergy to Philadelphia. Although the Vesey plot, like that of the slave blacksmith Gabriel in Richmond, Virginia, in 1800, implicated few free persons of color, legislators seized the moment of slave unrest to enact repressive measures to restrict and marginalize them as a class. The South Carolina Assembly passed laws prohibiting the reentry of free blacks into the state, and Charleston officials enforced ordinances against teaching slaves to read. The city council also voted to create a permanent force of 150 guardsmen to patrol the streets around the clock at an annual cost of twenty-four thousand dollars. To deal with the problem of black mariners bringing information about events around the Atlantic into the state's ports, the legislature in December 1822 passed the Negro Seamen Act, which placed a quarantine on any vessel from another state or foreign port that employed blacks. Although US Circuit Court Judge William Johnson Jr.—a critic of the methods used by the magistrates who tried Vesey—declared the law unconstitutional in the case of *Elkison v. Deliesseline,* a defiant South Carolina Assembly renewed the act in 1823. It would be no coincidence that many of those who nullified federal law in 1832, including one of the nullifiers' prime movers, then-governor James Hamilton, were veterans of the two tribunals that tried Vesey and his men a decade before and thus had intimate knowledge of the plot's content and scope.

Vesey left behind a very thin paper trail before 1822, but his actions generated a wealth of comment in letters, diaries, and newspapers. Commentators, white and black alike, described the old carpenter, wrote about the plot, and hotly debated the conspiracy's lessons and legacy. Observers, editors, and ministers recounted what they knew about the events of 1822, some only after relocating to safer climes in the North. Some of these accounts appeared in earlier collections. In 1970, writer John O. Killens published *The Trial Record of Denmark Vesey* while working on his novella, *Great Gittin' Up Morning,* which appeared two years later. Also in 1970, historian Robert S. Starobin, the author of a groundbreaking study of industrial slavery, published *Denmark Vesey: The Slave Conspiracy of 1822.* Both volumes contained only a small portion of the documents pertaining to Vesey's world and the context that allowed for his conspiracy to emerge. Killens especially engaged in the sort of editorial policies—modernizing spelling, standardizing grammar, adding punctuation, and even merging documents—that are now avoided in modern documentary collections. Edward A. Pearson's somewhat larger 1999 collection of documents, *Designs Against Charleston: The Trial Record of the Denmark Vesey Slave Conspiracy of 1822*, after criticism by the archivist Charles Lesser and historian Michael Johnson, was deemed faulty by its publisher and removed from print.[6]

Perhaps because of inconsistencies in the official sources and the absence of testimony taken from Vesey himself, a handful of historians registered doubt about the reality of an organized plot in 1822 or, at least, a plot that amounted to much. In 1964, historian Richard C. Wade, then finishing a study called *Slavery in the Cities*, published an article in the *Journal of Southern History* which argued that the conspiracy was little more than angry "loose talk" on the part of enslaved Carolinians. In Wade's view, justifiable resentment on the part of blacks, together with equally justifiable anxiety on the part of the state's white minority, fed "a false alarm" that led Charleston authorities to arrest dozens of slaves whose only crime was to complain about their condition.[7]

Despite its publication in a leading journal, Wade's argument, for a variety of reasons, never attracted many adherents. Prominent critics found his fundamental contention at odds with the data presented in his own monograph, which demonstrated that the slave controls necessary to sustain unfree labor tended to break down in urban areas. More seriously, Wade supported his argument with faulty data. He misidentified key actors in the events of 1822 and, in one critical case, even fused the two men who helped to bring the plot down—William Penceel and George Wilson—into a single individual named "George Pencil." As William W. Freehling observed in a devastating rebuttal, Wade crafted his prose in such a way as to imply that important white contemporaries shared his "loose talk" thesis. Largely because of these errors, Wade's theory has been generally relegated to footnotes, and for most historians Vesey remained an antislavery activist. In the words of historians Michael P. Johnson and James L. Roark, he "plotted full-scale insurrection against white power."[8]

In 2001, however, Johnson retreated from his previous views. In a lengthy article in the *William and Mary Quarterly*, he built on Wade's argument to move the interpretation of the Vesey affair in a different direction. No longer was the Vesey plot the product of a fevered misunderstanding by whites of "angry talk" on the part of the enslaved, but rather Vesey and his friends had fallen victim to a Machiavellian contrivance "conjured into being" by Intendant Hamilton and a handful of other white politicians bent on advancing their careers and shutting down the city's African Church. Instead of the "revolutionary assassin" once described by Johnson and Roark, the Vesey redrawn by Johnson after reexamining the court records emerged as a kind of harmless loudmouth whose "flouting" of Carolina's social conventions "made him a target for whites' suspicion and black [court] witnesses who repeatedly testified against him."[9]

The question of the reality of this plot, or others like it that never reached the stage of open insurrection, cannot be established beyond peradventure, for the application of torture or inducement of reward may not make reliable slave witnesses. The documents presented in this volume demonstrate, however, that Carolina whites uniformly believed in the reality of a dangerous plot. Writing in 2001, historian Robert Gross claimed that "doubts" about the reality of the plot "were raised at the time," and Michael Johnson, aligning himself with Richard Wade, agreed, pointing to the "doubts about the plot expressed by Governor Thomas Bennett" and his brother-in-law, "United States Supreme Court Justice William Johnson." The Bennett–William Johnson correspondence reprinted here indicates, however, that the concerns of both Justice Johnson and Governor Bennett were about the two courts' *methods,* not about the reality of the plot. Bennett's letters allude to "the late conspiracy" and what he learned of the plan from his domestic slave Rolla Bennett, "one of the conspirators, whose veracity was unimpeached by the Court." Justice Johnson, on his part, acknowledged the existence of a "Cabal" to no less than Thomas Jefferson, although, to be sure, he downplayed the seriousness of the machinations.[10]

The documents collected here also depict an agitated and anxious society. At a time when South Carolina's elite stood at the forefront in articulating a paternalistic narrative to defend slavery from intensifying internal and external threats, numerous slaveholding planters, seeing around them the highest density of slaves in the country, believed that the bonds of control over the slaves had become dangerously loosened. Antislavery ideas and agents, they believed, were unsettling slaves like never before. Since the Vesey plot drew into it conspicuously privileged slaves, slaves who hired themselves out and performed domestic labors, and slaves owned by widows, elite South Carolinians had to think about regaining mastery by shoring up institutions and practices of management and control. Out of the Vesey affair came the South Carolina Association, the paradigmatic vigilance association of the antebellum South.

The Vesey affair, nine years before Nat Turner's bloody insurrection, also sparked considerable debate inside and outside the state about the Christianization of slaves and the responsibilities of masters in attending to their dependents' spiritual well-being. The Reverend Morris Brown's African Church implicitly challenged not merely white religious domination, but white social and political control as well. The section on the city's church in Part I of this volume shows the determination of black Charlestonians—free and enslaved—to manage their religious lives without white control. But because secular authorities regarded the black congregations as dangerous bastions of slave autonomy, the city government routinely disrupted the churches' services and harassed congregational leaders. White ministers played a more complicated role in this drama, as they devoutly believed in the importance of Christianizing the African population but in a way that would bolster the slave system by reforming it in accord with Christian precepts. Because many of the leading conspirators had attended white churches prior to the creation of the African Church, a number of white ministers knew the accused quite well and visited them in the Work-House shortly before their executions. The ministers' comments about what they heard there remain the hardest evidence for doubters of the conspiracy to dismiss.

Despite Lacy Ford's recent, carefully agnostic, but sympathetic reading of Johnson's argument, the majority view within the historical profession as of this writing continues to regard Vesey as a rebel leader. David Brion Davis, writing in 2006, stated that he remains "convinced that Denmark Vesey and a significant number of slaves were in all probability involved in a plot to rise in insurrection." Davis believes, as did both Governor Bennett and Justice Johnson, that white fear and panic led to "grossly exaggerated" figures for the number of slaves involved and that perhaps even some of the condemned were innocent. Sean Wilentz concurs that there is "sufficient evidence of a plot—not least the words of the original betrayer blacks—to conclude that *something* dangerous was afoot in Charleston in the summer of 1822." Blain Roberts, Erskine Clark, and Marcus Rediker simply describe the events of 1822 as "Denmark Vesey's conspiracy," and W. Scott Poole adds, "Unfortunately, too many have run to Johnson's interpretation too quickly." The three leading textbooks on African American history uniformly agree that Vesey and his lieutenants planned "a massive slave revolt." Philip F. Rubio, in a study of the four white men arrested for expressing sympathy with the hanged conspirators, alleges that Michael P. Johnson "relied on selective use of evidence including inconsistent and unjustified privileging of certain primary sources to fit his thesis." James O'Neil Spady, applying Johnson's own "criteria for evaluating the evidence," examines the confessions of George Wilson and Joe La Roche and argues that their testimony suggests the plotters "extended their reach into the countryside." The voices collected here, white and black alike, support that view.[11]

Notes

1. C.L.R. James, *The Black Jacobins: Toussaint L'Ouverture and the San Domingo Revolution,* 2nd ed. (New York: Vintage, 1963), x.

2. William W. Freehling, *Prelude to Civil War: The Nullification Controversy in South Carolina, 1816–1836* (New York: Harper & Row, 1966); John Lofton, *Insurrection in South Carolina: The Turbulent World of Denmark Vesey* (Yellow Springs, OH: Antioch Press, 1964).

3. Douglas R. Egerton, *He Shall Go Out Free: The Lives of Denmark Vesey,* 2nd ed. (Lanham, MD: Rowman & Littlefield, 2004), chaps. 1–4, quotation on 123.

4. Ibid., 136, 143.

5. Ibid., 190.

6. John O. Killens, ed., *The Trial Record of Denmark Vesey* (Boston: Beacon Press, 1970); Robert S. Starobin, ed., *Denmark Vesey: The Slave Conspiracy of 1822* (Englewood Cliffs, NJ: Prentice Hall, 1970); Edward A. Pearson, ed., *Designs Against Charleston: The Trial Record of the Denmark Vesey Slave Conspiracy of 1822* (Chapel Hill: University of North Carolina Press, 1999).

7. Richard C. Wade, *Slavery in the Cities: The South, 1820–1860* (New York: Oxford University Press, 1964), 240; Richard C. Wade, "The Vesey Plot: A Reconsideration," *JSH* 30 (1964): 143, 148.

8. Richard C. Wade, "The Vesey Plot: A Reconsideration," *JSH* 30 (1964): 152–53; William W. Freehling, *The Reintegration of American History: Slavery and the Civil War* (New York: Oxford University Press, 1994), 279; Michael P. Johnson and James L. Roark, *Black Masters: A Free Family of Color in the Old South* (New York: Norton, 1984), 37–38. One exception remains Winthrop D. Jordan, who in 2002 wrote "kudos for Richard C. Wade," as if Wade's conclusions could somehow be separated from his flawed research and scholarship. See Jordan's "The Charleston Hurricane of 1822; Or, the Law's Rampage," *WMQ* 59 (2002): 178.

9. Michael P. Johnson and James L. Roark, *Black Masters: A Free Family of Color in the Old South* (New York: Norton, 1984), 37; Michael P. Johnson, "Denmark Vesey and His Co-Conspirators," *WMQ* 58 (2001): 915–73, quotation on 971; Robert S. Tinkler, *James Hamilton of South*

Carolina (Baton Rouge: Louisiana State University Press, 2004), chap. 2, argues that "James Hamilton believed there was indeed a Vesey plot, and [that] he ruthlessly sought to root it out."

10. Robert A. Gross, "Forum: The Making of a Slave Conspiracy," Part I, *WMQ* 58 (2001): 913; Michael P. Johnson, "Denmark Vesey and His Co-Conspirators," *WMQ* 58 (2001): 919; see Thomas Bennett Jr. to Charles Cotesworth Pinckney, October 1, 1822, and William Johnson to Thomas Jefferson, December 10, 1822, elsewhere in this volume.

11. Lacy K. Ford, *Deliver Us from Evil: The Slavery Question in the Old South* (New York: Oxford University Press, 2009), 209–27; David Brion Davis, *Inhuman Bondage: The Rise and Fall of Slavery in the New World* (New York: Oxford University Press, 2006), 222; David Brion Davis, *The Problem of Slavery in the Age of Emancipation* (New York: Knopf, 2014), 78–79, 209–10; Sean Wilentz, *The Rise of American Democracy: Jefferson to Lincoln* (New York: Norton, 2005), 238–39; Blain Roberts, "Uncovering the Confederacy of the Mind: Or, How I Became a Belle of the Ball in Denmark Vesey's Church," *Southern Cultures* 19 (2013): 6–25; Erskine Clarke, *By the Rivers of Water: A Nineteenth-Century Atlantic Odyssey* (New York: Basic Books, 2013), 48; Marcus Rediker, *The Amistad Rebellion: An Atlantic Odyssey of Slavery and Freedom* (New York: Viking, 2012), 108; W. Scott Poole, *South Carolina's Civil War: A Narrative History* (Macon, GA: Mercer University Press, 2005), 172; Darlene Clark Hine, William C. Hine, and Stanley C. Harrold, *The African-American Odyssey,* 5th ed. (Upper Saddle River, NJ: Prentice Hall, 2011), 198–99; Clayborne Carson, Emma J. Lapsanksy-Werner, and Gary B. Nash, *African American Lives: The Struggle for Freedom, Combined Volume* (New York: Pearson Longman, 2005), 177–79; John Hope Franklin and Evelyn Brooks Higginbotham, *From Slavery to Freedom,* 9th ed. (New York: McGraw-Hill, 2011), 155–57. Eric Foner, *Give Me Liberty! An American History,* 3rd ed. (New York: Norton, 2011), 446, also depicts Vesey as a rebel. Philip F. Rubio, "'Though He Had a White Face, He Was a Negro in Heart': Examining the White Men Convicted of Supporting the Denmark Vesey Slave Insurrection Conspiracy," *SCHM* 113 (2012): 52; James O'Neil Spady, "Power and Confession: On the Credibility of the Earliest Reports of the Denmark Vesey Slave Conspiracy," *WMQ* 68 (2011): 287–304.

ABBREVIATIONS

ALS	Autograph Letter Signed
ANB	*American National Biography*
BDSCHR	*Biographical Directory of the South Carolina House of Representatives*, 5 vols. (Columbia: University of South Carolina Press, 1974–1992): vol. 2 (*The Common House of Assembly, 1692–1775*, Walter B. Edgar and N. Louise Bailey, eds., 1977), vol. 3 (*1775–1790*, N. Louise Bailey and Elizabeth Ivey Cooper, eds., 1981), vol. 4 (*1791–1815*, N. Louise Bailey, ed., 1984), and vol. 5 (*1816–1828*, Alexander Moore, ed., 1992)
CDSG	Abraham Motte, *Charleston Directory and Strangers' Guide for the Year 1816 including the Neck to the Six Mile House* (Charleston, SC, 1816)
CLS	Charleston Library Society
CPL	Charleston Public Library
CSCCD	William Hagy, *Charleston, South Carolina City Directories for the Years 1816, 1819, 1822, 1825, and 1829* (Baltimore: Clearfield, 1996)
CWH	*Civil War History*
DAB	*Dictionary of American Biography*
DSGCC	*The Directory and Stranger's Guide for the City of Charleston. Also a Directory for Charleston Neck between Boundary-Street and the Lines: Likewise for the Coloured Persons within the City, and Another for Coloured Persons Residing on the Neck, for the Year 1822* (Charleston, SC: Archibald E. Miller, 1822)
DUL	Duke University Library
FO	Foreign Office, British National Archives
GM	Governor's Messages
HSP	Historical Society of Pennsylvania

Hamilton, *Account*	James Hamilton Jr., ed., *An Account of the Late Intended Insurrection among a Portion of the Blacks of This City* (1822)
JER	*Journal of the Early Republic*
JNH	*Journal of Negro History*
JSH	*Journal of Southern History*
LC	Library of Congress
MHS	Massachusetts Historical Society
NA	National Archives, Washington, DC.
OR	Lionel H. Kennedy and Thomas Parker, eds., *An Official Report of the Trials of Sundry Negroes, Charged with an Attempt to Raise an Insurrection in the State of South-Carolina* (1822)
RGA	Records of the General Assembly
SCDAH	South Carolina Department of Archives and History
SCHGM	*South Carolina Historical and Genealogical Magazine*
SCHM	*South Carolina Historical Magazine*
SCHS	South Carolina Historical Society
SCL	South Caroliniana Library, Columbia
SHC, UNC	Southern Historical Collection, University of North Carolina
UNC	University of North Carolina
USC	University of South Carolina
WMQ	*William and Mary Quarterly*

TIMELINE

1740

South Carolina Assembly passes the comprehensive slave code, commonly known as the Negro Act.

1747

Joseph Vesey is born in Warwick, Bermuda.

1767?

Birth of Telemaque/Denmark Vesey, probably on the Danish sugar island of St. Thomas or the Gold Coast of West Africa.

1783

Joseph Vesey rents a house at 281 King Street and opens a business as ship chandler on East Bay Street.

1790

November 1. Charleston's mixed-race freemen organize an exclusive Brown Fellowship Society.

1791

August 22. Slaves led by Boukman torch cane fields in northern Saint-Domingue.

1799

November 9. Denmark wins East-Bay Lottery.

December 31. Denmark purchases his freedom.

1806

April. Ship carpenter Paul Pritchard purchases Gullah Jack in Charleston.

1816

Prince Saunders publishes the *Haytian Papers* in London.

April 11–27. Methodists of African descent hold a convention in Philadelphia under the leadership of Reverends Richard Allen and Daniel Coker.

1817

January 23. James Forten presides over a meeting in Philadelphia to protest colonization.

Camden Gazette publishes a story on Prince Saunders and the publication of his *Haytian Papers.*

April 13. Denmark Vesey is admitted for the first time to communion at the Second Presbyterian Church.

November 8. Solomon Bryan, a Methodist minister, writes a letter to the Charleston City Council expressing his concern about the secession of persons of color from the Methodist Church.

December 18. South Carolina legislature passes a law severely penalizing shopkeepers and other whites who trade with slaves without their masters' permission.

1818

May 9. Henry Drayton and Morris Brown attend Philadelphia Annual Conference of the African Methodist Episcopal Church.

June 7 (Sunday). One hundred forty-three free blacks and slaves belonging to the African Church are arrested by the City Guard and placed in the Guard-House.

June 8. Charleston City Council sentences five unnamed leaders of the African Church to one month's imprisonment or to give security to leave the state. Eight other ministers are sentenced to receive ten lashes or pay a five-dollar fine.

November. Grand jury presentment from the Kershaw District complains of the inadequacy of punishment to those who murdered slaves, saying that such murders had "occurred often."

December 8. Special state legislative committee, headed by John Blake White, reports on a bill to make changes in an act for the better governing of slaves and free persons of color.

1819

November. A grand jury presentment from the Kershaw District complains about murdered and abused slaves.

November 22. Governor John Geddes expresses concern to the state legislature about the inadequacy of existing punishments for whites who kill slaves.

1820

October 6. A Charleston grand jury complains of the number of free persons of color in the state as well as the light punishment for whites who murder slaves.

October 16. More than 140 whites, most of them leading planters, petition the South Carolina House of Representatives to suppress the black church near Charleston.

November. *The Panoplist, and Missionary Herald* publishes an issue that notes the angry response from white southerners, including South Carolinians, to the June issue, which discussed slavery.

November 27. Governor John Geddes, in the context of the Missouri debate, criticizes the presence of free people of color.

December 20. South Carolina legislature passes "An Act to restrain the emancipation of slaves," which forbids private manumissions by deed or self-purchase. The law also forbids any free person of color to migrate into the state after March 1, 1821.

1821

January 15. City Marshall John J. Lafar, in the name of the Charleston City Council, notifies "ministers of the gospel and others who keep night and *Sunday schools for slaves* that the *education of such persons is prohibited by law.*"

January 22. Merchant Benjamin Hammet files a complaint against Lorenzo Dow for libeling his father, William Hammet, a Methodist minister.

February 26. Charleston City Council ratifies an ordinance that taxes free males of color, age twenty-one to fifty, who are "carrying on a trade or art, or being a mechanic and residing within the city, or exercising his trade or art therein."

May 14. Trial of Lorenzo Dow begins. Samuel Prioleau acts as attorney for Dow; Robert Young Hayne, as attorney general, prosecutes the case.

May 24. Methodist minister Lorenzo Dow is found guilty of libel.

May 27. Planter George Ford, South Island, Georgetown District, is killed in an ambush by slaves who had been preying on his cattle.

September 17. Charleston City Council ratifies an ordinance regulating the City Guard. Instead of a drum being beaten, a bell is to be rung at 9 p.m. to indicate that all slaves and free persons of color should be in their homes and off the streets.

September 21. A complaint is published in the *Southern Patriot* about drunken blacks in dram shops who are repeatedly violating the Sabbath.

October 1. James Hamilton Jr., critical of the "strict and literal construction of the Constitution" and the doctrine of state sovereignty taken publicly by several Georgia Crawfordites, embraces George McDuffie's nationalist defense of popular sovereignty over states' rights.

October 3. James Creighton, a free man of color and a barber who has accumulated money and property in Charleston, sails with his family in the schooner *Calypso* for Sierra Leone.

October 13. A Charleston grand jury complains of the proliferation of grog shops populated by slaves.

October 22. Charleston City Council ratifies an ordinance "to suppress Riots and Disturbances in the vicinity of Disorderly Houses."

November 27. In a message to the state legislature, Governor Thomas Bennett urges reform of the legal process for slaves.

December 1. *Charleston Courier* reports that the South Carolina Senate will form a committee to investigate the question of slave "emancipation" (manumission).

December 18. *Charleston Courier* reports that a law that permits "emancipation" (manumission) will probably be passed and that the penal law will likely be changed to punish with death whites who murder slaves.

December 19. *Charleston Courier* reports that Dr. Philip Moser's bill to punish whites with the death penalty for "the willful murder" of a slave has been returned to the Senate with amendments.

December 20. State legislature passes a law providing that any free person of color who helps a runaway slave will suffer corporal punishment.

December 21. *Charleston Courier* reports that the state legislature "passed a Law, whereby they changed the mode of emancipating slaves."

December 25. *Charleston Courier* reports acts passed by the state legislature, including "Murder in the first degree, on the body of a slave, is to be punished with death, without the benefit of Clergy."

1822

February 9. Exhibit of Rembrandt Peale's "Court of Death" ends at the South Carolina Academy of Arts.

March. Monday Gell is said to have written a letter to Haiti asking for help, according to later testimony by John Enslow.

April 2. Charleston City Council ratifies an ordinance dealing with free-colored seafarers who are taken to the Work-House.

April 12. *Baltimore Patriot & Mercantile Advertiser* announces the arrival on the previous day of Richard Allen and "four Preachers from Charleston" for the beginning of the Conference of the AME Church.

April 27. Peter Poyas and four others come to Bulkley's farm "and sung and prayed until day light," according to later testimony by Billy Bulkley.

May 1. Frank, slave of James Ferguson, first hears of Vesey's plot.

May 2. Bacchus Hammet confesses that on or around this date he met Perault Strohecker, who persuades him to go to a meeting of the "Society."

May 9. Philadelphia Annual Conference of the African Methodist Episcopal Church convenes.

May 18. *Niles' Weekly Register* reports that President Boyer "has abolished slavery in the whole island of Haiti."

May 25. Peter Prioleau (later Peter P. Desverney), the slave of John Cordes Prioleau, is approached by the slave William Paul on a wharf below the fish market regarding the plot.

May 30. James Hamilton is informed at 3 p.m. on this Thursday afternoon about the plot. The Corporation of Charleston is summoned at 5 p.m. The male slaves of John Paul are arrested, and William Paul is identified and examined. In solitary confinement, William makes "some disclosures" to Captain William P. Dove that confirm what Peter has said.

May 31. William Paul is reexamined after spending the night in solitary confinement. Mingo Harth and Peter Poyas are implicated. Both are brought in by wardens Frederick Wesner and Thomas D. Condy for examination. Trunks are searched by the wardens. An "enigmatical letter" is found.

June 1. On or about this date Vesey visits Lot Forrester, who tells Vesey to leave because his master would not like him there.

June 8. William Paul, still in solitary confinement, confesses to Thomas Napier. Morris Brown returns to Charleston on or about this date after sojourning in the North. New York Conference of African Methodist Episcopal Church begins; Henry Drayton is in attendance, but not Morris Brown. Scipio hires a horse to mobilize slaves in the country for the coming revolt.

June 9. Bacchus Hammet goes to Monday Gell's house, where he meets Charles Drayton.

June 10. Coach driver Frank recruits slaves "with Vesey's stories" on the Ferguson plantation.

June 14. Governor Bennett is notified at 9 p.m. by Hamilton and John Wilson about the information given by Wilson's slave George. At 10 p.m. field officers of the Charleston militia convene on Bennett's order at Hamilton's house on the corner of Coming and Bull streets.

June 15. Governor Bennett issues Order No. 1, which places arms and munitions in the Charleston Arsenal. Monday Gell says he met Jacob Glen on the street with Benjamin Cammer. Jacob prepares for the rising the next day. Dr. John Ward McCall is found dead in his Meeting Street home, sparking rumors of his assassination by slaves.

June 16 (Sunday). At 10 p.m. militia corps rendezvous. Ringleaders of the plot meet at Vesey's house at 4 p.m. Gullah Jack tells Yorrick Cross that the revolt will not break out because the patrols are too strong. Rolla Bennett sees George Wilson on this night. Bacchus Hammet said that at Monday Gell's house he and Charles Drayton are told by Gullah Jack that they could not go to the farmhouse on Meeting Street Road because of the patrols. Governor Bennett signs Order No. 2, which places Robert Young Hayne in charge of a regiment of the Charleston Guard. James Hamilton writes William Lowndes that he has been investigating the cause of the public's concern during the previous day and is confident things are under control. George Thompson questions Pharo about the plot. A hastily impaneled jury of inquest finds that Dr. McCall killed himself when his pistol accidentally discharged.

June 17. Governor Bennett orders nightly patrols. Committee of Vigilance and Safety is formed. Yorrick testifies that John Horry repeated what he had said before on June 16, that as soon as the revolt broke out he would kill his master and his family.

June 18. Ten more slaves are arrested. Hamilton notifies Lionel Kennedy and Thomas Parker of the confinement of the alleged plotters. Process to form Court of Magistrates and Freeholders begins. Hamilton provides names of suitable jurors. Peter Prioleau (Desverney) is paid two hundred dollars by the City Council for "secret services rendered."

June 19. First Court of Magistrates and Freeholders assembles. Hamilton presents the court with "a calendar, containing the names of all the criminals then ascertained, the charges on which they had been committed, and the witnesses against them." William Paul testifies.

June 20. Joe La Roche, Bram Lucas, Richard Lucas, and George Wilson testify.

June 21. Robert Harth and William Paul testify.

June 22. Vesey is arrested by Captain Dove. Peter Bennett, March Bennett, Sampson Bennett, Joe La Roche, Isaac La Roche, and Polydore Bennett all testify. Elizabeth La Roche testifies about Joe La Roche. Jacob Axson cross-examines Joe La Roche and Polydore Bennett. James Hamilton defends the corporation and the court publicly after publication in the *Courier* of Justice William Johnson's essay, "The Melancholy Effect of Popular Excitement."

June 24. The court acquits free black men Samuel Guifford and Robert Hadden and slaves Matthias Bennett, Mungo Poyas, Robert Harth, Richard Lucas, and John Lucas. Sambo La Roche, John Woodworth (white), and Robert Herron (white) all testify.

June 25. Court examines, finds not guilty, and discharges slaves Jim Ancrum, Sandy Holmes, and Friday Rout. Governor Bennett later says that "positive proof" on Vesey is obtained on this day. Rolla Bennett, Sally Howard, Lot Forrester, and Syke Waring testify.

June 26. Abraham Poyas is tried and found not guilty. Batteau Bennett testifies. Frederick Wesner warns James Ferguson that his slaves Adam and Frank are involved. Ferguson accompanies Wesner to the Work-House to examine Jesse Blackwood.

June 27. Vesey is tried. Monday Gell is arrested. Frank Ferguson, Adam Ferguson, Jesse Blackwood, and Peter Poyas testify. Jesse Blackwood identifies Adam. James Ferguson brings his slaves Frank and Adam before the court. Governor Bennett says important testimony against Vesey is given by Frank Ferguson on this day.

June 28. The court sentences six plotters, Rolla Bennett, Denmark Vesey, Batteau Bennett, Ned Bennett, Peter Poyas, and Jesse Blackwood, to death. James Ferguson informs Governor Bennett that the plot "extended to my plantation."

June 29. James Ferguson returns to his plantation and punishes John and Pompey. Henry Drayton returns to Charleston from New York City on or about this date.

June 30. James Ferguson returns to Charleston without a confession from his inculpated plantation slaves.

July 1. Yorrick Cross testifies that he meets with Charles Drayton, who wants a "break out" to prevent the six from hanging. He tells Yorrick that the revolt would begin now on July 6 and that he commands a company of countrymen. Gullah Jack tells Yorrick that there will be a revolt on July 6 and that the arsenal will be taken. Governor Bennett writes Attorney General Robert Y. Hayne about the Court of Magistrates and Freeholders. Hayne responds to Bennett in a letter on the same day. Governor Bennett writes to the magistrates on the first court to seek the "mitigation of punishment" of Batteau Bennett.

July 2. Rolla Bennett, Batteau Bennett, Ned Bennett, Peter Poyas, Jesse Blackwood, and Denmark Vesey are executed. Charles Drayton is arrested. Harry Haig meets with Yorrick Cross, who tells him that the rebels are waiting for the "head man," a white man. Yorrick Cross meets Charles Drayton again and expresses sorrow that he had ever joined the plot.

July 3. Attorney General Robert Young Hayne responds again to Governor Bennett. Sixteen blacks, alleged runaways from Charleston, are seized in Columbia.

July 4. Pharo informs George Thompson that he had met with Perault Strohecker about the plotters' lack of response to the arrest of their "leaders." Thompson reports the details of Pharo's conversation to Intendant Hamilton.

July 8. Trial of Julius Forrest begins. Order No. 4 is signed by Jonathan Lucas Jr., aide de camp. Jury of inquest investigates the death of slave Beck of Lionel Kennedy and finds it is caused by a "visitation of God." Governor Bennett issues general orders on permanent regulations to be put in place once the extra guard has been discontinued in Charleston.

July 9. Monday Gell, Charles Drayton, John Horry, Harry Haig, and Gullah Jack Pritchard are sentenced. While in the Work-House, Charles Drayton sends for William E. Gordon, deputy keeper of the Work-House, and asks to see Intendant Hamilton. The Philadelphia *United States Gazette and True American* editorializes against the growing presence of fugitive slaves in their city.

July 10. Hamilton visits Charles Drayton in the morning at the Work-House. The court is informed of Charles's disclosures. Perault Strohecker is arrested. Prudence Bussacre and Harry Haig give testimony in the trial of Julius Forrest. Hamilton writes to Frederick Beard of the Charleston Alms-House that the suspects confined there may meet only with "their Wives, Masters, Children & such Clergymen as they may be desirous of communicating with."

July 11. Billy Bulkley testifies before the court. Benjamin Hammet commits his slave Bacchus to authorities, suspecting his involvement in the conspiracy.

July 12. Bacchus Hammet and Smart Anderson testify. Morning session is adjourned for "want of the presence of Witnesses." John Horry and Gullah Jack Pritchard are executed.

July 13. Court hears Monday Gell's confession. Bacchus Hammet testifies again. Julius Forrest is found guilty by the court and sentenced to hang. James Legaré withdraws from the court because of illness. The magistrates issue a warrant to call Henry Deas to serve. Monday Gell, Charles Drayton, and Billy Bulkley testify.

July 14. Vesey's first proposed date for the uprising coincides with Bastille Day. Charleston newspapers publish praise for the efforts of Hamilton and the court in investigating the plot.

July 15. Tom Russell, Louis Cromwell, Mingo Harth, Saby Gaillard, Joe Jore, and Jack Purcell are arraigned. Perault Strohecker is examined by the court and cross-examined by James Gray. Charles Drayton and Monday Gell are examined by the court. Marks and James Mall, two white men, testify. Perault gives testimony against Tom Russell, Louis Cromwell, and Joe Jore. Governor Bennett writes Secretary of War John C. Calhoun on the vulnerabilities of Fort Johnson and Fort Moultrie and requests that more federal troops be stationed there.

July 16. Frank Ferguson gives testimony. Smart Anderson pleads guilty; his confession is handed to the court. Monday Gell, Frank Ferguson, Perault Strohecker are examined about Smart Anderson. Pharo Thompson is put on trial. Charles Drayton, Monday Gell, and Perault Strohecker are examined about Pharo. Paris Ball and Sandy Vesey are tried. Robert, Adam, and John Robertson are arraigned, as are Cuffy Graves, Bounaparte Mulligan, Sandy Curtis, Butcher Gibbes, and Isaac Trapier. Trial of four slaves who fired on a mail carrier on Parker's Ferry Road begins in Jacksonborough.

July 17. Bacchus Hammet testifies again. William Colcock's confession to Thomas Jervey is provided to the court. Charles Drayton, Peter Ward, and Jack Glen are arraigned and plead not guilty. A letter to the *Charleston Courier* praises Captain Martindale for his patrols, which have broken up frequent nightly meetings of blacks.

July 18. Permanent order is issued to the regiment of artillery in Charleston on when and how to rendezvous in case of emergency. Julius Forrest, Tom Russell, Joe Jore, Mingo Harth, Smart Anderson, Paris Ball, Polydore Faber, Robert Robertson, John Robertson, Adam Robertson, Lot Forrester, Louis Remoussin, Pharo Thompson, Sandy Vesey, Jack Glen, and Jack Purcell are sentenced to death, to be carried out July 26.

July 19. Three slaves are executed in Jacksonborough for firing on a mail driver.

July 20. Bennett publishes a proclamation offering a two-hundred-dollar reward for the capture of William Garner.

July 22. Secretary of War John C. Calhoun issues orders for a company of soldiers to be sent from St. Augustine, Florida, to Charleston.

July 23. James McCord, Intendant of Columbia, writes to Hamilton that William Garner has been apprehended near Granby.

July 24. The Court of Magistrates and Freeholders writes two letters to Governor Bennett. One explains its sentencing according to degrees of guilt; the other recommends the pardoning of the inculpated slaves Monday Gell, Charles Drayton, and Harry Haig.

July 25. Job Palmer's letter to the court about the slave Billy Palmer is read. Governor Bennett writes to the court, adding Billy Palmer's name to that of Sandy Vesey, Paris Ball, and Louis Remoussin as slaves respited.

July 26. Twenty-two slaves, including Bacchus Hammet and Polydore Faber, are executed on the Lines. Sam, the teenage slave of William Peronneau, is accidentally killed by a carriage during the public hangings. First Court of Magistrates and Freeholders adjourns.

July 30. James Ferguson, having learned of the involvement of his driver, returns to his plantation to have him committed to the Work-House in Charleston. Governor Bennett expresses concern to Secretary of War John C. Calhoun about the dilapidated state of Castle Pinckney and the need for more regular troops to reinforce Charleston.

July 31. A Court of Magistrates and Freeholders in the Horry District sentences the slave Toney to death for "trying to raise an Insurrection."

August 2. William Garner arrives in Charleston as a prisoner.

August 3. Charleston newspapers announce the constitution of a second Court of Magistrates and Freeholders. William Garner is convicted and sentenced to death.

August 5. *New York Commercial Advertiser* publishes criticism of the execution of twenty-two slaves in Charleston.

August 6. Charleston City Council passes an ordinance that revises the so-called Negro Ordinance of 1816 by prohibiting all free persons of color from owning "any boat or other vessel" unless licensed by the Commissioner of Markets. Ministers Henry Drayton and Morris Brown are tried in the Court of Common Pleas, charged with illegally returning to the state. Major Abraham Eustis informs Secretary of War Calhoun that a company of soldiers is proceeding from St. Augustine to Charleston.

August 8. Second Court adjourns. *New York Commercial Advertiser* publishes additional criticism on the conduct of Charleston officials in handling the plot.

August 9. William Garner is executed on this day.

August 10. Bennett publishes a circular letter on the plot. Charleston *City Gazette* announces the resolution of the cases of August 6 against Brown and Drayton.

August 8. *Charleston Courier* pronounces that "tranquility of the city is now restored" and reports the departure aboard the *Dolphin* of Alexander Harleston, Prince Graham, and other unnamed "persons of color" for Cape Mesurado, Liberia.

August 13. City Council asks Intendant Hamilton to prepare for publication a detailed account of the plot. Hamilton announces in a public letter that investigations are over and that an account of events will be presented. Joel Roberts Poinsett, a judge on the second Court, writes President James Monroe that the national debate about Missouri's statehood contributed to the slaves' plotting.

August 15. A company of federal troops from St. Augustine under Captain Matthew Payne arrive in Charleston. *New York Commercial Advertiser* responds to criticism from the Charleston *Southern Patriot*.

August 17. Charleston City Council resolves to publicly thank Intendant Hamilton for his "unremitting attention to the public interest."

August 21. *Southern Chronicle and Camden Gazette* publishes the governor's circular of August 10.

August 23. Newspapers in Charleston report the apprehension of five runaway slaves who attempted to rob the Southern Mail in the Salketcher Swamp.

September 2. James Hamilton is reelected intendant of Charleston without opposition.

September 10. Justices of the peace in Savannah, Georgia, begin the examination of three slaves charged with plotting to poison their master and his family.

September 15. Thomas Parker writes to James Ferguson asking about the involvement of his slaves in the plot. Whites in Beaufort seize ten slaves for their alleged involvement in an insurrectionary plot.

September 22. In the Circular Church, Benjamin Morgan Palmer preaches a sermon about the plot.

September 23. Charles Cotesworth Pinckney, on behalf of the Charleston Bible Society, writes Governor Bennett, requesting a statewide day of thanksgiving.

October. Benjamin Pearson, captain of the *Dolphin*, arrives in Rio Pongo with black Charlestonians aboard.

October 1. Governor Bennett responds to the Charleston Bible Society.

October 2. Morris Brown meets with Richard Allen in Philadelphia.

October 10. Reverend Artemas Boies meets with other Presbyterians at the house of Thomas Flemming to discuss whether to admit to the Second Presbyterian Church persons of color who are members of the African Church.

October 11. A grand jury in Charleston complains of the inadequacy of the city jail, the expensive dress of free people of color, and "the frequent introduction and sale of slaves from other states in this state."

October 15. One of the convicted slaves sentenced to transportation is sold to a horse dealer. On being taken unsecured to Savannah by way of Beaufort, he is seized by a group of whites and brought back to the city.

October 22. Thomas Parker and Lionel H. Kennedy register the *Official Report of the Trials of Sundry Negroes, Charged with an Attempt to Raise an Insurrection in the State of South-Carolina,* with the district clerk.

November 7. Charleston City Council declares Thursday, November 7, a day of thanksgiving and prayer. Arthur Buist delivers a sermon in the First Presbyterian Church, the day devoted to thanksgiving, "humiliation, & prayer."

November 9. A gang of runaway slaves operating in the area of New Bridge robs whites.

November 14. Charleston newspapers announce that Intendant Hamilton has agreed to run for Congress.

November 16. Naomi Smith petitions the state senate for compensation for the loss of her slave Caesar, who was executed.

November 18. Governor Bennett orders the James Island Beat Company to muster "for the purpose of suppressing the depredations, and quelling the insurrectionary spirit of a gang of negroes."

November 20. Neill McNeill petitions the state senate for remuneration for the slave Jack, who is executed. Benjamin Hammet writes William Crafts, who is in charge of a memorial that Hammet signed, to recoup money for the loss of Bacchus. Richard Hart signs affidavit attesting to the value of Dick and Scipio Sims. Governor Bennett calls out the James Island Beat Company to suppress a gang of runaway slaves. The *Winyaw Intelligencer* reports that the wounded runaway slave Joe has left Clarendon in the Sumter District and returned to the area of Mrs. Horry's plantation.

November 21. David Haig and two other whites sign a statement placing the appraised value of the slaves Naphur, Adam, and Belisle, "prime young Negroes" under the age of thirty owned by the late cooper Joseph Yates, at six hundred dollars each. Jon Robertson, William M. Scott, Jacob Lankester, John Billing, William Harth, John S. Glen, Thomas Purse, William Wightman, and Paul Pritchard sign an affidavit about their slaves executed for involvement in the plot.

November 25. South Carolina state legislature convenes.

November 28. Governor Bennett addresses the state legislature about the plot.

November 29. South Carolina House of Representatives forms a committee of four, which includes James Hamilton Jr., to handle petitions of owners of slaves executed for involvement in the plot.

December 3. Charleston City Council petitions the legislature for compensation for expenses incurred in suppressing the alleged insurrection.

December 6. Committee on Claims of the state legislature recommends that the master of the Work-House be paid for expenses incurred in apprehending persons of color involved in the plot. Governor Bennett delivers Message No. 10 to the state legislature, which includes a concluding paragraph justifying his balancing of justice and mercy in dealing with the conspirators.

December 14. A state legislative committee issues a reply to a memorial from Charleston City Council on the expenses incurred as a result of dealing with the plot.

December 19. Harry Haig dies in the Work-House.

December 21. State legislature passes "An Act to establish for the better regulation and government of Free Negroes and Persons of Color"

December 24. Reverend Richard Furman begins writing his *Exposition of the Views of the Baptists, Relative to the Coloured Population in the United States,* to Governor John Lyde Wilson.

December 26. *Charleston Mercury* reports that alleged plotters sentenced to transportation are still confined in the Charleston Work-House.

1823

January 21. Charleston City Council repeals the prohibition on masters having free access to their slaves confined in the Work-House.

February 7. Masters of vessels in Charleston petition US Congress seeking federal relief from the state law that requires imprisonment of "free colored" seamen.

February 28. Joel Roberts Poinsett writes Secretary of State John Quincy Adams to explain the connection of the Negro Seamen's Act to the Vesey affair.

July 24. South Carolina Association is formed.

July 9. A slave of Charles Gray is executed for attempting to incite an insurrection.

August 22. Scipio Sims, sentenced to transportation for his involvement in the Vesey plot, is reported at large in Charleston.

August 25. Intendant John Geddes of Charleston issues a proclamation about Scipio and offers a reward of one hundred dollars for his capture.

November 18. John Girardeau petitions the state senate for remuneration on behalf of the James Island Boat Company after being called out by Governor Bennett the previous November to suppress a gang of runaway slaves. William Seabrook petitions the state house for incorporation of the Edisto Island Auxiliary Association.

November 27. Governor John Lyde Wilson appoints John Geddes, William S. Smith, and Francis G. Deliesseline to appraise the value of Peter, the slave of John C. Prioleau, and George, the property of John Wilson.

December 9. Black Swamp Association petitions for incorporation.

December 10. A state legislative committee recommends payment to the Charleston City Council for expenses incurred for the "Support & Maintenance" of slaves in the Work-House involved in the plot.

1826

April 6. In the US House of Representatives, James Hamilton Jr. delivers a scathing rebuke to those in the federal government who would support US participation in the Panama Congress by referring to the grave threat posed by Haiti.

1833

November 23. Joshua Coffin writes Amos Phelps on slave revolts; he mentions the 1822 plot without naming Vesey.

1843

August 16. Henry Highland Garnet, at the National Convention of Colored Citizens in Buffalo, New York, speaks of "Denmark Veazie" and "his plan for the liberation of his fellow men."

1849

Henry Bibb publishes a pamphlet on the Nat Turner revolt that contains seven pages on the Vesey plot, mostly excerpted from Hamilton's *Account*.

1850

January. A "Colored American" from Philadelphia writes a pamphlet on *The Late Contemplated Insurrection in Charleston*.

1854

December 7. In the South Carolina House of Representatives, J. Harleston Read, chairman of the Committee of Colored Population, attempts to amend the statute of 1835 that pertains to Negro seamen.

1855

William Nell publishes a few pages on "Denmark Veazie" and his plot to "overthrow slavery."

1856

Harriet Beecher Stowe publishes the novel *Dred,* about a rebellious son of Denmark Vesey. Volume one contains a lengthy excerpt from the *Official Report* about Vesey.

August 16. James McCune Smith proposes in *Frederick Douglass' Paper* that the day of Denmark Vesey's death be celebrated by blacks in the United States as a national day of freedom.

1859

June. J. Theodore Holly mentions Vesey in the *Anglo-African Magazine.*

November 5. In an editorial in *Weekly-Anglo-African,* Thomas Hamilton refers to Vesey.

November 19. In a letter on the death of John Brown to Governor Henry Wise of Virginia, published in *New-York Daily Tribune,* Lydia Maria Child mentions Vesey.

November 28. William Wells Brown lectures at the Joy Street Baptist Church in Boston on "Heroes of Insurrection."

1860

Joshua Coffin mentions Vesey in *An Account of Some of the Principal Slave Insurrections.*

January 6. The *New York Herald* publishes an article on slave insurrections that includes discussion of Vesey.

February 6. William Nell writes a letter to Thomas Wentworth Higginson, telling him of Bibb's work on Vesey.

March 17. Lydia Maria Child writes Thomas Wentworth Higginson, responding to his request for information about Vesey and slave insurrections.

1861

April 27. George Lawrence Jr. mentions Vesey in an editorial for the *Weekly Anglo-African.*

June. Thomas Wentworth Higginson publishes an essay on Vesey in the *Atlantic Monthly.*

1863

March 2. In a "call to arms for men of color," Frederick Douglass invokes the name of Denmark Vesey. William Wells Brown publishes *The Black Man,* which contains a short chapter on Vesey.

1865

April 14. Re-dedication ceremony at Fort Sumter includes Major Martin Delany, William Lloyd Garrison, and Robert Vesey.

May 12. Major Delany delivers a speech on Vesey to a packed house in Charleston's Zion Church.

October. Robert Vesey designs the new African Methodist Episcopal Church for Charleston.

1869

March 6. Henry Highland Garnet's essay on Morris Brown in the *Christian Recorder* mentions Vesey.

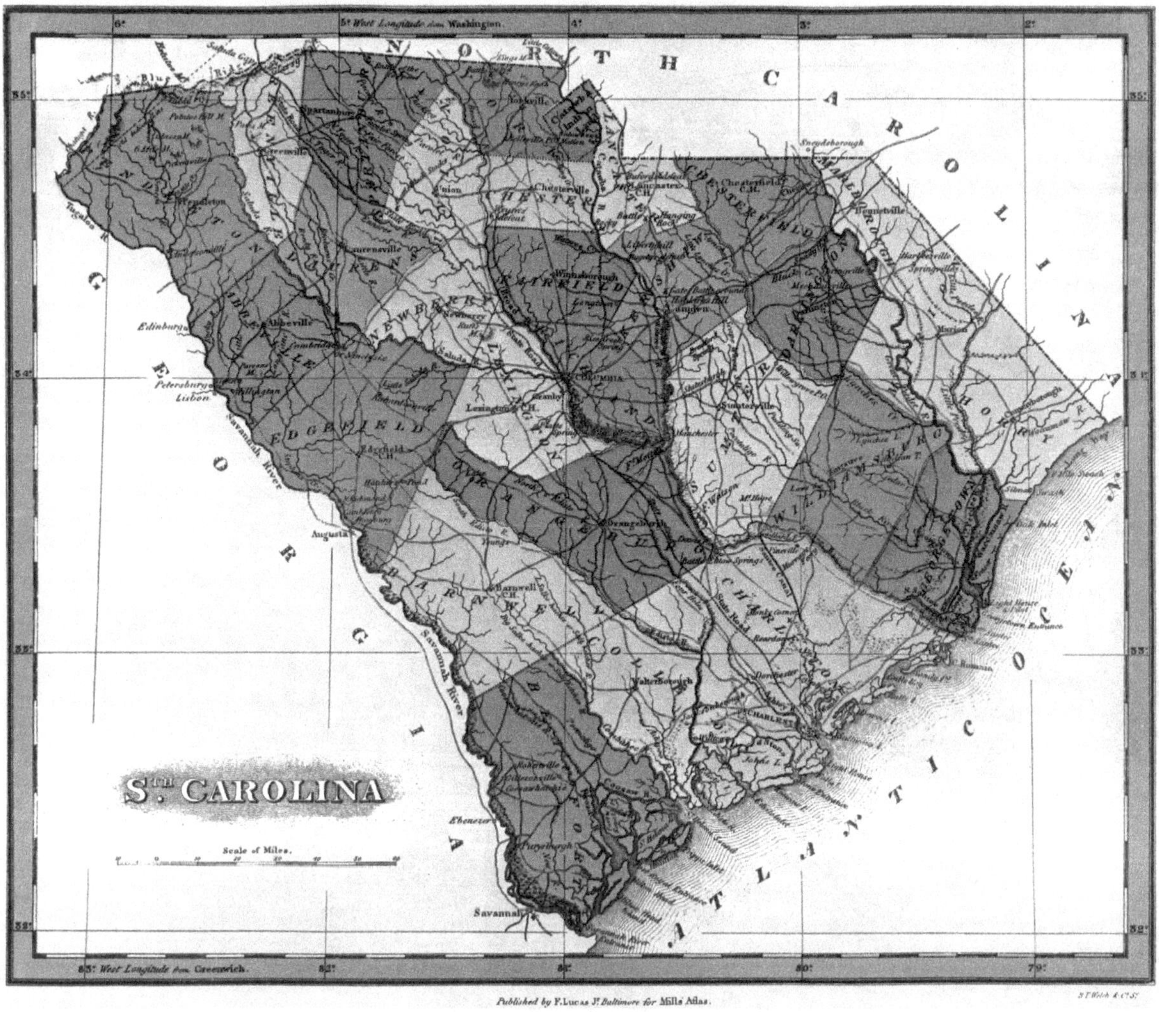

Map 1. State of South Carolina. From Robert Mills, *Atlas of the State of South Carolina* (1825).

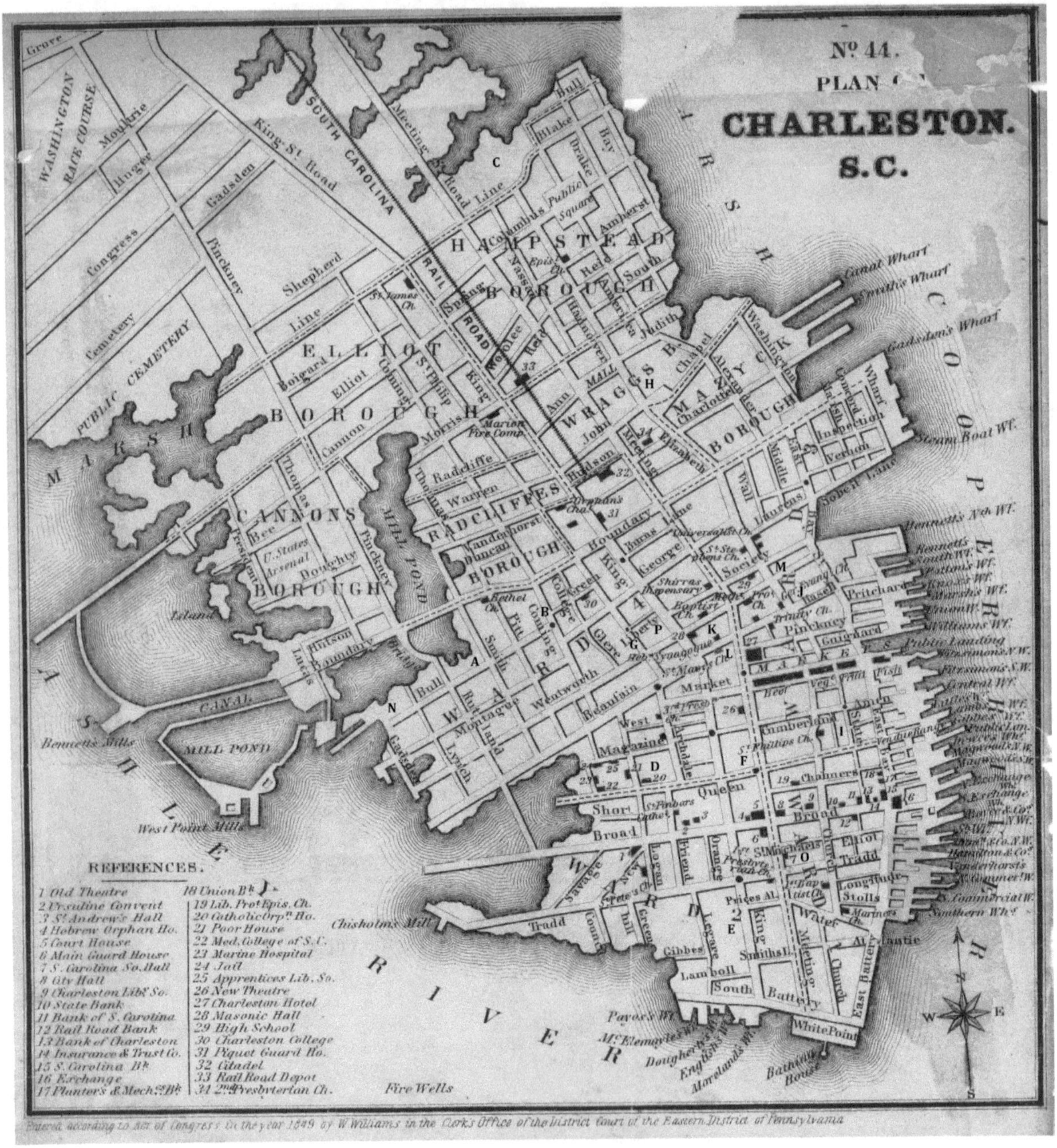

Map 2. Plan of Charleston, 1849. From Hoole Library Maps, University of Alabama Libraries.

I

Preconditions

Most of the slaves and free blacks involved in the conspiracy of 1822 had resided in Charleston for years, if not decades. These documents chart the arrival and subsequent lives of the key leaders of Vesey's plot. They also establish the context of the plot through their depiction of black life and culture in the Carolina lowcountry. The first of these documents, most of them newspaper accounts, pertain to the purchase, sale, and reacquisition of the enslaved child initially renamed Telemaque, or Telmack, who would later come to be known as Denmark and then Denmark Vesey. Since Denmark remained in Captain Joseph Vesey's possession after mid-1782, the documents reveal his location. After the British evacuation of Charleston in December 1782, the captain bought a house at 281 King Street and began to import goods and small numbers of slaves. Around 1796, he began a relationship with Mary Clodner.

This section also includes the brief biography of Vesey, reprinted here in chronological excerpts, which originally appeared as a lengthy footnote in Intendant James Hamilton Jr.'s pamphlet, *An Account of the Late Intended Insurrection Among a Portion of the Blacks of the City of Charleston, South Carolina*. Because the dates provided in the biography conform so closely to the newspaper accounts below, that information could only have come from the aged Captain Joseph Vesey (1747–1835), who lived in Charleston until his death. A Catholic Francophile slave-trading merchant with an active associational life in the city, Captain Vesey established businesses that formed close commercial ties with the French colony of Saint-Domingue.

Affiches Américaines

Wednesday, April 24, 1782

Le Navire *la Patience*, de Saint-Thomas, Capitaine Joseph Wesey,[1] est arrive dans ce Port la 23 de ce mois avec usie tres-belle cargaison de Negres de la Côte-di Or, à l' adresse des Sieurs Lory, Pombard & Companie.

1. Despite the misspelled surname, it clearly identifies Joseph Vesey, the Bermudan-born mariner who had invested in Charleston real estate as early as 1774.

Biography of Denmark Vesey, August 1822

As Denmark Vesey has occupied so large a place in the conspiracy, a brief notice of him will, perhaps, be not devoid of interest. The following anecdote will show how near he was to the chance of being distinguished in the bloody events of San Domingo.[1] During the revolutionary war, Captain Vesey, now an old resident of this city,[2] commanded a ship that traded between St. Thomas and Cape Francais (San Domingo.) He was engaged in supplying the French of that Island with Slaves. In the year 1781, he took on board, at St. Thomas', 390 slaves and sailed for the Cape; on the passage, he and his officers were struck with the beauty, alertness and intelligence, of a boy about 14 years of age,[3] whom they made a pet of, by taking him into the cabin, changing his apparel, and calling him, by way of distinction, *Telemaque.* (which appellation has since, by gradual corruption, among the negroes, been changed *to Denmark,* or sometimes *Telmak*).[4] On the arrival,[5] however, of the ship at the Cape, Captain Vesey, having no use for the boy, sold him among his other slaves, and returned to St. Thomas'. On his next voyage to the Cape, he was surprised to learn from his consignee that Telemaque would be returned on his hands, as the planter, who had purchased him, represented him unsound, and subject to epileptic fits. According to the custom of trade in that place, the boy was placed in the hands of the king's physician, who decided that he was unsound, and captain Vesey was compelled to take him back, of which he had no occasion to repent, as Denmark proved, for 20 years, a most faithful slave.

1. France received the western third of the island of Hispaniola by the Peace of Ryswick (1697). There was no French colony called "San Domingo." Yet even before the 1795 Treaty of Basle briefly ceded the Spanish colony of Santo Domingo, which occupied the eastern two-thirds of the island of Hispaniola, to France, Americans often used the term "San Domingo" or "St. Domingo" to refer to the French colony of Saint-Domingue or to the entire island.

2. The *DSGCC,* 84, indicates that the seventy-five-year-old Joseph Vesey then resided at 82 Anson Street. This biographical information, which is supported by the Saint-Domingue newspaper excerpted, p. 1, was surely provided by the captain, and this sentence suggests that Vesey spoke informally to the court.

3. Although Herbert Aptheker, *American Negro Slave Revolts* (New York: Columbia University Press, 1943), 268, claimed that Denmark was born in Africa, as do Raymond M. Hyser and J. Chris Arndt, *Voices of the American Past: Documents in U.S. History,* 3rd ed. (Belmont, CA: Thomson-Wadsworth, 2004), vol. 1: 218, no source precisely identifies the place of his birth. Most likely it was St. Thomas or the Gold Coast region of West Africa. No contemporaneous source identifies Vesey as mixed-race, the assertions of several modern scholars notwithstanding. Philip Morgan, "Conspiracy Scares," *WMQ* 59 (2002): 165–66, errs in insisting that reliable evidence exists to that effect. Morgan cites Archibald Grimké, *Right on the Scaffold, or The Martyrs of 1822* (Washington, DC: The Academy, 1901), 6, a page that makes no mention of Vesey's color. Grimké instead said on page 1: "He was black but comely. Nature gave him a royal body, nobly planned and proportioned, and noted for its great strength." Morgan also cites William Gilmore Simms, *The History of South Carolina* (Charleston, SC, 1840), 328, an unreliable source that incorrectly identifies Vesey as a native of Saint-Domingue who took part in the 1791 slave revolt. Magistrates Kennedy and Parker, *OR,* simply described him as "black," as did the Charleston *City Gazette and Commercial Daily Advertiser,* August 21, 1822, which appears in Part IV of this volume. Michael P. Johnson,

"Denmark Vesey and His Co-Conspirators," *WMQ* 58 (2001): 918, also errs in writing that "no source documents Vesey's physical size." Apart from Grimké, see Lydia Maria Child to Thomas Wentworth Higginson, March 17, 1860, in Part VI of this volume; Child quoted Thomas Cilavan Brown, a free man of color who had worked as a carpenter in Charleston at the time of the Vesey affair, as describing Vesey as "a Corromantee negro . . . brought from the [African] coast" and "a large, stout man." Enslaved Africans from the Gold Coast were often called, with variant spellings, Coromantee, after an English trading post created there in the seventeenth century. Among slaveholders in the circum-Caribbean region during the seventeenth and eighteenth centuries, Coromantees (also called "Minas" in some countries) acquired a well-earned reputation for insurrectionary behavior. Of the estimated 65,257 African slaves who debarked on the Danish Virgin Islands from 1751 to 1800, 45,399 (70 percent) derived from the Gold Coast (calculated from data in the Trans-Atlantic Slave Trade Database, http://www.slavevoyages.org/tast/assessment/estimates.faces, accessed August 5, 2014). Thus, a Gold Coast origin, membership in the Akan ethnolinguistic group, and transit at the end of the middle passage through the island of St. Thomas stand as distinct possibilities for Vesey's early life. See also John K. Thornton, "War, the State, and Religious Norms in 'Coromantee' Thought: The Ideology of an African American Nation," in *Possible Pasts: Becoming Colonial in Early America,* ed. Robert Blair St. George (Ithaca, NY: Cornell University Press, 2000), esp. 182.

4. Telemachus figures prominently in Homer's *Odyssey* as the wandering son of Odysseus and Penelope. He was shipwrecked on the deadly island of Ogyia until rescued by Calypso. Joseph Folker, *A Directory of the City and District of Charleston and Stranger's Guide for the Year 1813* (Charleston, SC, 1813), 81, listed Joseph Vesey as a schoolmaster who resided on King Street. The naming of Denmark thus suggests Joseph Vesey's interest in classical literature.

5. As the above notice in the *Affiches Américaines* indicates, Vesey returned to Saint-Domingue in April 1782.

[James Hamilton Jr.], *An Account of the Late Intended Insurrection among a Portion of the Blacks of the City of Charleston, South Carolina* (Charleston, SC, 1822), 17.

Charleston *Gazette of the State of South-Carolina*

Wednesday, September 24, 1783[1]

NEGROES. Just imported in the schooner POLLY Capt. Higgins, a Cargo of healthy young SLAVES, to be Sold on SATURDAY the 27th of September (instant) at Mrs. DEWEES'S, No. 43 Queen-street. The Sale to continue every fair day (Sundays excepted) until all be Sold.

The conditions will be made agreeable as possible to the purchasers.

J. VESEY & Co.
No. 27¼ Bay

NEGROES. On WEDNESDAY the first of October, at Mrs. DEWEES'S, No. 43, Queen-street, WILL be exposed for Sale, 104 Prime SLAVES, just imported in the schooner Eagle, Captain David Miller. The Sale will continue every fair day (Sundays excepted) until all be sold. The conditions will be made as convenient as possible to the purchasers.

J. VESEY & Co.
No. 27¼ Bay

1. A number of scholars, including Edward A. Pearson, ed., *Designs Against Charleston: The Trial Record of the Denmark Vesey Slave Conspiracy of 1822* (Chapel Hill: University of North Carolina Press, 1999), 28, speculate that young Denmark may have spent as many as "eight or nine years at sea" with the captain. But these newspaper accounts, together with Joseph Vesey's importation records (found in the Duties on Trade at Charleston, Manifests and Entries, SCDAH), place the master and his slave in Charleston during the 1780s and 1790s. Most likely, Denmark was a mariner for only one year, from the spring of 1782 to the early spring of 1783.

Charleston *South-Carolina Gazette, and General Advertiser*

Saturday, September 27, 1783

For Sale, the Schooner Dove, Bermuda built, about 230 barrels Rice burthen, KNOWN in the West Indies for a strong, fast-sailing Vessel, well calculated for that trade, And the Schooner Polly, Virginia built, burthen about 180 barrels.

JO. VESEY

Charleston *South-Carolina Gazette, and General Advertiser*

Saturday, March 13, 1784

FOR SALE

THE GOOD SNOW QUEEN, Joseph Lightburne, Master, now lying at COCHRAN'S Wharf; is a new Vessel, Virginia built, well sound, burthen about 360 barrels rice.

Inventory may be seen and terms known by applying to the Master on board, or at No. 35, Bay, to

J. VESEY

Charleston *South-Carolina Gazette, and General Advertiser*

Saturday, May 8, 1784

JOSEPH VESEY

REQUESTS the favour of those indebted to him for Negroes sold last year, to discharge their Bonds and Notes before next entering day, or he shall be under the necessity of lodging them with an Attorney, to be sued for without distinction. . . .

No. 35, Bay.

Charleston *State Gazette of South Carolina*

Thursday, July 1, 1790

. . . *Resolved,* That the elections to be had on the second Monday of October next, and on the day following, for senators and members of the house of representatives, shall be held at the following places, and conducted by the following persons, viz.

For Charleston, including St. Philip and St. Michael, at the city Exchange. Managers, Edward Trescot, Thomas Wright Bacot, Joseph Vesey, and John Beale . . .

Lease, Tuesday, July 26, 1796

Mary Clodner commonly called Mary Vesey a free East Indian now residing in the City of Charleston purchased three farm tracts of land called the Grove near Charleston from John Irving, lately of Charleston, now of St. James for £1200.[1]

1. The Grove, an estate of thirty-five acres on the Ashley River near the racecourse just north of Charleston, was known for the beauty of its grounds. It stands today as Lowndes' Grove. See Carl J. Vipperman, *William Lowndes and the Transition of Southern Politics, 1782–1822* (Chapel Hill: University of North Carolina Press, 1989), 26

Charleston Deeds, P-6, pp. 467–68, SCDAH.

When slaves in the French colony of Saint-Domingue, where Denmark had briefly labored in 1782, rose for their freedom in August 1791, South Carolinians of both races became aware of the very real possibility of servile revolt closer to home. Jacobinical France's adoption of black liberty in its Constitution of 1795 complicated Franco-American diplomacy. White southerners, particularly lowcountry Federalists, began to abandon the French cause two years earlier, when Edmond-Charles Genet, the French minister who had been sent by the Girondists to the United States, violated neutrality laws by recruiting support for revolutionary France. Captain Vesey continued to do business with Saint-Domingue for years after the outbreak of the slave insurrection that metamorphosed into a social revolution. The use of arson by rebellious slaves became a personal issue in the Vesey household in 1796 when an enslaved domestic named Molly set fire to Mary Clodner's house; Molly's death became Denmark's first brush with arson as a weapon and hanging as a punishment. Despite any doubts Joseph and Mary might have had about blacks as free and independent people, when Denmark won the city lottery in the fall of 1799, they allowed him to buy his freedom. Legally, they might simply have confiscated their chattel's winnings.

Jean-Jacques Dessalines formally declared the independence of Haiti in 1804. Haitian pleas for African Americans to relocate to the black republic followed from his successors and allowed men like Denmark to consider the country a haven for escaping rebels. Aware as he surely was of that nation's poverty, Vesey may have planned to take plunder from Charleston's banks less as a desire to achieve back pay for former slaves than to buy his and their way into Haiti, since serving as a refuge for rebellious black Carolinians would little help Haiti's already unfavorable standing among white politicians around the Atlantic.

Charleston *City Gazette & Daily Advertiser*

Thursday, April 25, 1793

COFFEE.

A quantity of excellent GREEN COFFEE, imported in the last vessels from St. Domingo, for sale, by NORTH & VESEY[1] April 25.

1. Captain Edward North (d. 1798), like Captain Vesey a ship chandler and merchant from Bermuda, partnered with Vesey until 1797. See Charleston *City Gazette & Daily Advertiser,* February 16, 1797, and August 22, 1798.

Charleston *City Gazette & Daily Advertiser*

Wednesday, October 9, 1793

STATE of SOUTH-CAROLINA.

At a meeting of the citizens in Charleston, on Tuesday, the 8th day of October, 1793, the intendant was called to the chair, and the following resolutions were unanimously agreed to:—. . . [1]

12. That his excellency the governor be requested to take immediate measures, that the two vessels which arrived in this harbour last week, from St. Domingo, and are, now lying under the guns of fort Johnston, with their crews, passengers, free negroes and people of color, do quit the harbour and state immediately; except such persons as, on full examination, may, in the opinion of the committee, be admitted without any danger to the community.

13. That any vessel that may arrive from St. Domingo with passengers, negroes, or people of color, shall remain under the guns of Fort Johnston, till such passengers as the committee may deem improper to admit, and the negroes and people of color be sent out of the state; and that such passengers whom the committee shall think improper to admit, and the negroes and people of color, be, on no account, suffered to land in any part of the state.

14. That the above resolutions be extended to all vessels, from any part of the world, bringing negroes and people of colour.

15. That the committee do take immediate measures to send out of the state all free negroes, and free people of colour, which have arrived from St. Domingo, or which have arrived within twelve months from any other place. . . .

17. That the following persons, viz. Jacob Read, Charles Cotesworth Pinckney, Thomas Cochran, Edward Rutledge, John Splatt Cripps, William Johnson, Nathaniel Russell, Anthony Toomer, Daniel Strobel, William Crafts, John Bee Holmes, Peter Faysoux, Thomas Morris, Edward Darrell, Henry William Desaussure, Edward Blake, John Blake, Joseph Vesey, Arnoldus Vanderhorst, and John Sandford Dart, be a committee to attend to the observation and enforcement of the above resolutions; and the citizens pledge themselves to each other, to support the committee in the execution of this trust. . . . [2]

1. The first eleven resolutions do not pertain to the rebellion in Saint-Domingue and so are omitted here.

2. Captain Vesey here appeared with his sometimes partner Captain John Blake (1752–1810), and with merchant William Crafts (1763–1820). William Crafts Jr. (1787–1826), a lawyer, would later defend accused rebel Billy Robinson. Supreme Court Justice William Johnson Jr. (1771–1834) would write a much-criticized essay condemning the 1822 court's legal methods. For Johnson's essay and the controversy it generated, see Part II of this volume.

Charleston *City Gazette & Daily Advertiser*

Saturday, November 9, 1793

We are informed, that Mr. S. Blakely,[1] merchant of this city, received, on Wednesday last, from a gentleman on Enoree river, in Ninety-Six district, a considerable quantity of flour, as a donation towards the relief of the unfortunate sufferers in this city who have arrived from St. Domingo, with instructions to deliver the same to capt. Joseph Vesey, treasurer of the fund collected for that purpose, and which was done accordingly.

1. "S. Blakely" refers to Samuel Blakeley (d. 1805), a merchant who owned a home in the 1790s on Sullivan's Island. In 1796, he and dozens of other Charlestonians suffered losses from a great fire that swept the city, allegedly sparked by an enslaved arsonist of Caribbean origin. See Charleston *City Gazette & Daily Advertiser,* August 17, 1797, and November 5, 1805; William L. King, *The Newspaper Press of Charleston, S.C.: A Chronological and Biographical History* . . . (Charleston, SC, 1872), 45.

Charleston *City Gazette & Daily Advertiser*

Thursday, November 21, 1793

Messrs. Markland & M'Iver,

WE have just now observed in your Gazette of to-day, a paper under the head of New-York, 9th Nov. said to be a "circular letter of citizen Genet,[1] minister plenipotentiary from the French republic, to the different committees of beneficence, established in the different towns of the United States, for the relief of the unfortunate people from St. Domingo." As the present acting members of the society established here, we owe it to our fellow-citizens to declare, that we have never received any letter from Mr. Genet and as it is therein mentioned "that, *a very considerable quantity of provisions were distributed at the expence of the republic at Charleston,* and implied to be to those unhappy sufferers, it is equally incumbent on us to assure our fellow-citizens, that such distribution has been entirely without our knowledge, nor do we believe any such has been delivered to the real objects of charity, now and for four months past, subsisted by the benevolent here, the greatest part being women and children."

NATHANIEL RUSSEL,[2]
JOSEPH VESEY,
EDWARD PENMAN.[3]

1. On the arrival in Charleston of Edmond-Charles "Citizen" Genet (1763–1834) as an agent of the Girondist government in revolutionary France, see Harry Ammon, *The Genet Mission* (New York: Norton, 1973), 44–45.

2. Born in Rhode Island, Nathaniel Russell (1738–1820) moved to Charleston in 1765 and made his fortune as an importer, mostly of Africans. In 1799 he purchased a lot at 51 Meeting Street, not far from Joseph Vesey's business office on East Bay Street. His widow, Sarah Hopton Russell (1752–1832) owned the enslaved blacksmith Tom Russell, who was executed in the plot. Given the connection between Nathaniel Russell and Captain Joseph Vesey, the slave Tom would likely have known Denmark Vesey quite well. See Walter J. Fraser Jr., *Charleston! Charleston! The History of*

a Southern City (Columbia: University of South Carolina Press, 1989), 181, and Sarah Russell to South Carolina House of Representatives, December 2, 1823, no. 133, Series # S165015, SCDAH.

3. Edward Penman (d. 1817) was a prominent merchant who helped organize in Charleston the Bank of South-Carolina. See Charleston *City Gazette and Commercial Daily Advertiser,* August 4, 1817; W. A. Clark, *The History of the Banking Institutions Organized in South Carolina Prior to 1860* (Columbia: Historical Commission of South Carolina, 1922), 42.

Charleston *City Gazette & Daily Advertiser*

Wednesday, May 6, 1795

Presentments of the Grand Jury of Beaufort District, at April Term, 1795. WE present, as a grievance of the most alarming nature, the assembling of large bodies of negroes together, under pretence of praying, preaching &c. where discourses are held and doctrines taught highly detrimental to the welfare and policy of the state, and attended with the most pernicious consequences to the interest of their owners. We recommend that a very heavy fine be inflicted upon those who suffer such proceedings on their plantations, or among those under their care; as the late shocking scenes in St. Domingo originated in the manner above mentioned. . . . [1]

1. On Sunday, August 14, a week before the uprising in Saint-Domingue, slaves, many of them foremen (*commandeurs*) on sugar plantations, assembled to plan a large-scale insurrection. See Laurent Dubois, *Avengers of the New World: The Story of the Haitian Revolution* (Cambridge, MA: Belknap Press of Harvard University Press, 2004), 97.

Charleston *City Gazette & Daily Advertiser*

Tuesday, March 22, 1796

Belvedere, the elegant seat of Thomas Shubrick, esq.[1] three miles from this city, was yesterday morning destroyed by fire. We are informed that all the furniture, except what was in the lower story, was consumed.

1. Thomas Shubrick (1756–1810) served as aide-de-camp to General Nathanael Greene during the American Revolution. Following the war, he received a land bounty of 640 acres to add to his already considerable inheritance. At his death on Belvedere plantation on Charleston Neck in St. Philip Parish, not far from the Grove, he owned 254 slaves. See John Howard Brown, *The Cyclopedia of American Biography* (Boston, 1903), vol. 7: 72.

Charleston *City Gazette & Daily Advertiser*

Wednesday, September 7, 1796

Yesterday was executed, pursuant to her sentence, a Mulatto Girl, named MOLLY, belonging to col. Shubrick, for robbing her master, and setting fire to capt. Vesey's house at the Grove. She confessed being guilty of these crimes, and also that she was the person who set fire to her master's house at Belvedere, which was burned in March last; that she was persuaded to the commission of these atrocious acts by a Frenchman, named *Renaud,* her master's gardener, former a servant to Mr. Michaud, at the Botanical Garden belonging to the French Republic, who prevailed upon her, (by promising to run away with her to New-York and there marry her) to commit the robbery, and then set fire to the house to prevent a discovery.[1]

1. Charleston suffered a rash of fires in 1796, prompting the intendant in August to issue a proclamation that offered rewards for the identification of arsonists. See "A Proclamation," Charleston *Columbian Herald, or, the New Daily Advertiser,* September 30, 1796. Charleston newspapers reported on multiple arsons during the previous year as well. See Charleston *City Gazette & Daily Advertiser,* January 13, October 7, November 4, and November 6, 1795.

Charleston *City Gazette & Daily Advertiser*

Tuesday, October 1, 1799

EAST-BAY LOTTERY. *The Commissioners of East-Bay-street Second Lottery, give notice, that on Monday next, the 7th October, the said Lottery will commence drawing. In the mean time, the Holders of Tickets of 6 dollars, will call on Mr. Roach, at the City Treasury, to have them exchanged for the Tickets of this Class.*

September 30.

Charleston *City Gazette & Daily Advertiser*

Saturday, November 9, 1799

EAST-BAY-STREET LOTTERY

THIRTEENTH DAY'S DRAWING

Prize of 1500 *dollars*—No. 1884.[1]

Prize of 250 *dollars*—No. 2768.

Prize of 50 *dollars*—No. 1024.

Prizes of 25 *dollars*—Nos. 246, 7.

Prizes of 8 *dollars*—2215, 2959, 729, 2022, 2097, 2726, 481, 784, 936, 3141.

BLANKS.

Nos. 1491, 223, 2283, 1129, 2949, 2337, 3215, 1279, 2771, 2994, 1962, 3182, 3183, 594, 488, 2582, 488, 1625, 2810, 2688, 2859, 1035, 1737, 3265, 581, 1800, 1477, 2335, 948, 38, 42, 1362, 2105, 2147, 1315, 2047.

The Commissioners of East-Bay-street Lottery give notice, that they will continue drawing every Monday, Wednesday, and Friday, until further notice.

Tickets to be had every day after the drawing, of the Commissioners, and of the City Treasurer.

On the close of the drawing of the lottery yesterday, the following prizes remained in the wheel:

Two of 500—two of 250—three of 200—three of 150—six of 100—fourteen of 50—seventeen of 25—twenty-five of 20—thirty of 15—sixty of 10—about six hundred of 8—first drawn last day 200—last drawn d[itt]o d[itt]o 450.

1. This was the only day in which a prize of $1,500 was given. According to the Charleston *City Gazette* of December 4, 1799, the top prize for the "TWENTY-THIRD DAY'S DRAWING" was

$200, and on Monday, December 9, the *City Gazette* announced that "the drawing of East Bay-street Lottery, will positively finish This Day." Two days later, on December 11, the *City Gazette* announced the final top prize had been $500. Harlan Greene, Harry S. Hutchins, and Brian E. Hutchins, *Slave Badges and the Slave-Hire System in Charleston, South Carolina, 1783–1865* (Jefferson, NC: McFarland, 2004), 72, discovered that the city made a net profit of $4,570.88 in the East Bay lottery of 1799.

Emancipation Deed, Tuesday, December 31, 1799

Know ye that I, the said Mary Clodner[1] for and in consideration of the Sum of Six hundred Dollars and for divers good causes in hereunto moving for one of my heirs for ever have manumitted, released and from the yoke of Servitude set free and discharged a certain negro man named Telemaque with all his goods and chattels by him already acquired or to be hereafter acquired and know ye also that I the said Mary Clodner, have forever quitted claim for me and my Heirs, Executors, and Administrators, and by this present writing do relinquish, release and for ever quit claim unto the said Telemaque and from all manner of actions, Real and Personal. In Witness whereof I have set my seal at Charleston, this seventh day of December, the year of our Lord one thousand and seven hundred and ninety-nine—and of the Independence of America, the twenty fourth. As Witnesses, Charles G. Core, J. Vesey of Charleston so personally appeared. Mr. Charles Core, being duly sworn made oath he was present and saw Mary Clodner sign, seal and deliver the written Manumission to and for the uses and purposes for the above-mentioned, and that he together with Joseph Vesey, signed their names. Sworn before me this 31st December 1799. Jas. Ravenel.[2] Recorded 31st December.

1. This deed indicates that, at some point, Joseph Vesey transferred ownership of his enslaved domestic, still known to whites as Telemaque, to Mary Clodner, his common-law wife. Although 1800 became Denmark's first full year of freedom, the agreement of sale came as early as December 7, 1799, and Denmark spent the last evening of 1799 as a free man. Both Walter C. Rucker, "'I Will Gather All Nations': Resistance, Culture, and Pan-African Collaboration in Denmark Vesey's South Carolina," *JNH* 86 (2001): 135, and Lacy K. Ford, *Deliver Us from Evil: The Slavery Question in the Old South* (New York: Oxford University Press, 2009), 213, incorrectly date the lottery prize to 1800. David Robertson, *Denmark Vesey: The Buried History of America's Largest Slave Rebellion and the Man Who Led It* (New York: Knopf, 1999), 40, theorizes that Denmark learned of his winnings "early in the year 1800." In his pioneering account of the affair, John Lofton, *Insurrection in South Carolina: The Turbulent World of Denmark Vesey* (Yellow Springs, OH: Antioch Press, 1964), 251, did not provide a firm date but correctly placed Vesey's liberation sometime in late 1799. Joanne Turner-Sadler, *African-American History: An Introduction* (New York: Peter Lang, 2009), 50, misdates Vesey's emancipation as decades later in 1822.

2. Members of the Ravenel family not only knew Denmark Vesey and his master, Captain Joseph Vesey, they figured conspicuously, as this volume reveals, in the events of 1822 and the related narratives to follow. Daniel James Ravenel (1774–1836), justice of the peace for St. John Berkeley Parish in 1799, who recorded Vesey's manumission, died unmarried. But his brother Rene Ravenel (1762–1822) was the grandfather of Henry Williams Ravenel (1814–1887), who took possession of the written testimony of the inculpated slave John Enslow (see Part III, Senate, pp. 326–27).

Miscellaneous Records, vol. 3M, pp. 427–28, SCDAH.

Biography of Denmark Vesey, August 1822

In 1800, Denmark drew a prize of $1500 in the East-Bay-street Lottery, with which he purchased his freedom from his master, at six hundred dollars, much less than his real value. From that period to the day of his apprehension, he has been working as a carpenter in this city, distinguished for great strength and activity. Among his colour he was always looked up to with awe and respect. His temper was impetuous and domineering in the extreme, qualifying him for the despotic rule, of which he was ambitious. All his passions were ungovernable, and savage; and to his numerous wives and children, he displayed the haughty and capricious cruelty of an Eastern Bashaw.[1]

1. Vesey appears to have married three times. The documents reprinted in this volume suggest he was first married to Beck, a possibly older woman who already had one child named Sarah. Once owned by a grocer named John Paul (1785–1846), Beck appears to have been sold numerous times. In 1822 she worked as a domestic for stonecutter James Evans (1772?–1849) in a house near Coming and Bull streets. Evans owned the slave George, who was inculpated in the Vesey plot and sentenced to transportation outside of the state. See James Evans to the Senate of South Carolina, December 4, 1822, no. 122, Series # S165015, SCDAH. Vesey's sons Sandy, Robert, and Polydore may have been hers, and Denmark also had a daughter who was old enough to be married in 1822.

Ten years after Denmark Vesey's death, Robert Vesey's wife, Patsey, gave birth to Robert A. Vesey Jr., who had four siblings, Randolph, Martha, Michael, and Susan. See Freedman's Savings Bank Papers, Series M816, Roll 23, page 277, NA. The Charleston Death Records for July 14, 1822, list the death of a ten-month-old child named "M. B. Vesey" of "Diarrhea" and identified as "M[ale] B[lack] F[ree]." No parents were listed. At this point, Robert Vesey Sr. was old enough to sire a child, and if so, this means that Denmark's grandson died the same month in which he was hanged. Robert Vesey did not again appear in a public record until 1865, and the Vesey family has always believed that he remained in slavery until war's end. His son Randolph, according to the 1900 US Census (Texas), NA, was born in Georgia in July 1827, which may be where Robert was sold to after the conspiracy collapsed. See letter of Venus Henry Vesey to Douglas Egerton, February 21, 2016.

According to the Freedman's Savings and Trust Company records, Denmark's grandson, Robert A. Vesey Jr., married Anna Crate. They had five daughters: Martha, who died young and was perhaps named for her aunt; May Magdalene; Anna; Ellen; and Martha Ann, named, evidently, for her deceased sister.

According to the Charleston City Death Records, 1821–1914, on January 15, 1874, a newborn boy, Robert A. Vesey, died of "spasms." He was buried in the "C.B.G.," or City Burial Grounds, a paupers' field. This was surely the child of Robert Jr. and Anna Crate Vesey.

Although it remains unclear as to when Denmark Vesey ended his relationship with Beck, their children all appear to have been born prior to his purchased freedom in 1799. His second wife was a Charleston woman named Dolly, the slave of Elizabeth Toomer (d. 1821). In 1825, Dolly and her four children were sold for $1,100 by Toomer's heirs to John and Thomas Gates. One of Dolly's children was a girl named Charlotte; the other three were boys, with Denmark the oldest, followed by London and Gabriel. The modest price for the five slaves suggests that the children were young and born between 1800 and approximately 1815. In later years, the eldest boy was known as Denmark Vesey, and publicly acknowledged to be "a son of the notorious Denmark Vesey." He married Hannah Vesey and was alive in 1866 but deceased by 1873; Hannah Vesey appeared in the 1870 census, which listed her as seventy years old and a black native of Charleston.

She died on January 1, 1872. See US Census, South Carolina, Charleston, series M593, roll 1487, p. 601, NA; the Charleston City Death Records, 1821–1914; and *Charleston Daily News*, March 28, 1873, which appears in Part V of this volume. For Dolly's purchase, see Bill of Sale, September 3, 1825, vol. 5A, p. 547, SCDAH.

Vesey's third wife, Susan, was born a slave sometime between 1788 and 1795, making her roughly two decades his junior. No manumission deed is extant, but in 1821 tax collectors found a "free negro" named "Susan Vesey" residing with Denmark at 20 Bull Street. (Although a sign on the house at 56 Bull Street identifies the home as that of the Veseys, archivist Wylma Wates demonstrated in 1980 that the house is too new and in the wrong spot by three lots. See her "Report on Research to Verify House at 56 Bull Street," August 29, 1980, in Denmark Vesey House File, National Register, SCDAH.) According to the American Colonization Society documents reproduced in Part V of this volume, Susan was forty-five when she briefly moved to Liberia in 1833, which would place her birth around 1788. Census takers in 1830, however, guessed her to be born around 1795. She took with her two children, Diana Vesey, born around 1819 and only three when her father was hanged, and John Anthony Vesey, born in 1809 and thirteen at the time of the conspiracy. John Anthony was listed in emigration records as a "House Carpenter," and so, like his half-brother Robert Vesey Sr., pursued his father's trade. Joseph Kelly, *America's Longest Siege: Charleston, Slavery, and the Slow March toward Civil War* (New York: Overlook Press, 2013), 142, characterizes the end of Denmark's marriage to Beck as the carpenter "effectively divorc[ing] his slave wife," although no record exists to detail the collapse of their relationship or who instigated its end, and at the time of his marriages, all three of his wives appear to have been enslaved. Only Susan's master, evidently, was willing to sell her to her husband.

In fiction, Harriet Beecher Stowe made Denmark Vesey the father of her protagonist in *Dred: A Tale of the Great Dismal Swamp* (Boston, 1856). Novelist Sue Monk Kidd, *The Invention of Wings* (New York: Viking, 2014), has Vesey practicing polygamy, but no contemporaneous document suggests that his three marriages overlapped.

Hamilton, *Account*, 17.

New-York Commercial Advertiser

Saturday, October 10, 1818

PEOPLE OF COLOR

The following official communication from the secretary General of the Haytian Republic, is highly interesting to all whom it may concern in the U. States. The communication was made in reply to an inquiry—*what privileges people of color might expect who should emigrate thither from America.*

The most interesting part of the answer is as follows:

"Liberty. Republic of Hayti. Equality.

Port au Prince, Nov. 21, 1817, 14th *year of Independence*

The Secretary General, near his Excellency the President of Hayti,[1] *to Mr. James Tredwell.*[2]

SIR—I have communicated to H.E. the President of Hayti, the verbal message which you brought me from your fellow countrymen, the black and colored men of the city of New-York, who groan under the dominion of a barbarous prejudice, and desire to become partakers of those blessings which the constitution we have given ourselves affords. This message, Sir, could not but be received with the greatest satisfaction by those who have sacrificed twenty-eight years of their life, in order to efface the traces of a yoke to which other men, who pretend to virtue and justice, too long enchained them.

The men of color, who may desire to become Haytians, will find but little difference in our manner of living from that of the places they shall leave. They who possess some capital will use it either in commerce or in cultivation, which produces ordinarily more than fifty per cent per annum beyond the original disbursement. Men of all arts—of all trades—smiths, braziers, tinmen, ship and house carpenters, millwrights, caulkers, coopers, cabinet makers, boot and shoemakers—can earn in this place from six to twelve dollars per week, and even more, according to their talents and activity. The cultivators of the soil can get from two to four dollars per week, besides board and lodging; those among the last class who have numerous families, can find portions of land already planted, either in coffee, sugar cane, or cotton, to work on shares with the proprietors. The result of these associations are very advantageous to those who undertake them. Others can raise stock, particularly horned cattle—Laborers are in great demand, and will easily gain a dollar per day, if industrious, besides boarding and lodging. Sailors will find employment, either in the coasting trade or long voyages. In a word, all such as will come with a resolution to establish themselves in this country, will be protected by the government, which, on its part, will grant bounties of land to those who wish it. Men, women and children, of our color, let them come, we will receive them with pleasure, and we wait for them with open arms.

I shall be flattered, Sir, if this statement of facts, this genuine picture, which you can present to our unhappy fellow countrymen, shall determine a great number of them to come and console themselves beneath the protection of our laws, from the cruel idea of being transported to the deserts of Africa, the land, it is true, whence we all derive our origin, but which our civilization has now rendered altogether a foreign country.

The character of the President, which you have been able to appreciate, guarantees to you, Sir, as well as to your fellow citizens, the good reception of those who desire to become our brethren and friends. The government will pay the passages of those who have no means, at the rate of forty dollars per head for men and women, and half that sum for children from three to twelve years of age. I have the honor to salute you.

(Signed) B. INGINAC[3]

1. Henri Christophe (1767–1820).

2. Tredwell, an African American from New York, moved to Haiti, along with thousands of other blacks in the 1820s after visiting there in 1817. See Sara Connors Fanning, "Haiti and the U.S.: African American Emigration and the Recognition Debate" (PhD diss., University of Texas, Austin, 2008), 47n56, 48. This story also appeared in *City of Washington Gazette,* October 13, 1818; *Niles' Weekly Register,* October 17, 1818; and Boston *Recorder,* October 17, 1818. Inginac's letter also appeared in *The Constitution of the Republic of Hayti to Which Is Added Documents Relating to the Correspondence of His Most Christian Majesty with the President of Hayti Preceded by a Proclamation to the People and the Army* (New York, 1818), 4–7.

3. Joseph Balthazar Inginac served as secretary-general under several Haitian rulers. See *Memoires de Joseph Balthazar Inginac . . . depuis 1797—jusqu'à 1843* (Kingston, Jamaica, 1843).

Washington (DC) *Gazette*

Saturday, February 24, 1821

Haytian company of Maryland.

This company consisting of free people of color and blacks, dispatched their agent George M'Gill to the Island of Hayti, for the purpose of conferring with President Boyer, on the emigration of a certain class from this country to Hayti. The President received the agent with the utmost cordiality, and conversed on the project with the most lively interest. On the 29th of April 1820, the Secretary general, Inginac, addressed an official letter to M'Gill,—after full consultation with the President. We extract the following.

"His excellency has been charmed to hear that the descendants of the African, form the project of coming here and of carrying their industry into a free country, which guarantees to them an honorable existence under the protection of a constitution, the liberality of which is known to you, and which asks no other return but love of industry, and obedience to our laws. His excellency charges me consequently, to tell you, that mechanics and agriculturalists will be received with open arms, and when landed upon the shores of this Republic they will enjoy all the rights of Haytien citizens—the former will enjoy peaceably the fruits of their industry, and the latter can make arrangements with the land holders to cultivate the land either on shares or workers for wages, that those who have means will be enabled to make themselves either farmers or land holders of estate which they will be able to cultivate. Interested more than any other in the fate of descendants of the Africans, whose blood runs in their veins, the Haytiens form at this time a society whose end is to favour the emigration of our American brethern into the Republic, and above all to render it useful is assuming an honorable employment, and consequently an existence to the emigrants, every thing makes us hope for an advantageous result."

Circular, 1823

[Translation.]

Port-au-Prince, 24th *December,* 1823.

Jean Pierre Boyer, President of Hayti, to the Commandants of the Districts.

Desirous to increase in the country the number of agriculturalists, and thus augment its population, I have decided, my dear General, that emigrants of colour to Hayti, who may wish to establish themselves in the mountains or vallies to cultivate with their own hands the public lands, shall be to cultivate the same for their own profit. These lands, after payment of the taxes established by the authority of the place, shall be ceded in fee simple, to those who open them and enhance their value, dividing them into suitable plantations for the produce of coffee and other productions which may yield a revenue to the state. You are therefore charged so far as your authority extends, to settle the people of colour who may arrive, or who may wish to disembark and establish themselves in the district which you command, and to send me a list of the names of all such persons, and a description of the land given them.[1]

It is understood, that this measure is not to change that prescribed by my circular of 2d December, 1822, in favour of the persons, who, anterior to the first of last January, should be established without title upon the state lands. Signed,

BOYER.

NOTICE.

In prosecuting an agency in behalf of the noble objects of the American Colonization Society, I found the public feeling generally was very favourable to the Emigration of the Coloured People to Hayti. Among the Coloured People themselves, a preference of Hayti over Africa was frequently expressed, and among the whites, there was not only an opposition to colonization in Africa manifested by many, but an assurance given of their ready aid to promote emigration to Hayti. The present peaceful state of the island, and the fair prospects before the Haytiens, of having their Independence acknowledged by other nations, indicated that the great obstacles in the way of emigration there, which had hitherto existed, were removed, and that the time had now come to aid our coloured population to plant themselves under the mild climate of that Island, were it encouraged by the Haytien government. On inquiry, I found very little was known definitely in this country, what the views of that government were, on this subject. There were some favourable reports brought by persons of colour who had been to Hayti; others gave discouraging accounts. Except some liberal offers, by the Secretary Inginac, which I had seen, the information obtained, was limited and uncertain. Under these circumstances, the letter with which the Correspondence commences, was addressed through the Secretary General, B. Inginac, to the President of Hayti. The generous reply of the President, together with the arrival in this country, of his agent, Citizen J. GRANVILLE, with ample means to carry into effect, the philanthropic overtures of President Boyer, shows what great good may now be hoped for our unhappy countrymen, who are the objects of his generosity.

I will add, that perhaps I did not write so explicitly as to leave no room for doubt, whether I wrote as the agent, and at the direction of the American Colonization Society, or not; yet, if more explicitness, (and the want of it was unintentional,) had prevented the reply of the President, few, probably will regret that the delinquency occurred, even though they may not excuse the delinquent.

L. D. DEWEY[2]
New-York, June 15, 1824.

1. Former president Alexandre Pétion (1770–1818) had been urging black Americans to emigrate to Haiti since early 1817. See New York *Columbian*, n.d., quoted in Boston *Recorder*, February 18, 1817.

2. Loring D. Dewey (1791–1867) was a New York–born Presbyterian minister who worked as agent for the American Colonization Society for the entire state. By early 1824, as funds for Liberian emigration began to dry up, Dewey shifted his attention to Haiti and contacted President

Boyer, who encouraged his efforts. See P. J. Staudenraus, *The African Colonization Movement, 1816–1865* (New York: Columbia University Press, 1961), 79–87; *Correspondence Relative to the Emigration to Hayti of the Free People of Colour, in the United States. Together with the Instructions to the Agent Sent Out by President Boyer* (New York, 1824).

Six years after Vesey purchased his freedom, the African woodworker and priest who would come to be known as Jack Pritchard was sold into slavery and arrived in Charleston, where he was purchased by Paul Pritchard Sr. (1779–1837), a ship carpenter who in 1822 resided at 6 Hasell Street. Pritchard arrived in the state just before the congressional ban on the importation of Africans took effect on January 1, 1808. Concerns about keeping the percentage of enslaved Africans and African Americans to a safe amount kept the debate about importations from other states a lively one, as the assembly sought to balance internal security with the demands of upcountry slaveholders. In November 1821, Pritchard lost his workshops on Gadsden's Wharf to a suspicious fire.

Zephaniah Kingsley[1] to William Allen, Monday, April 21, 1806

Tybee [Island, Georgia]

Sir,

We Anchored this day for Orders with 240 Negroes. Please to write me via Savannah the state of things. if my friend Mr. James Hamilton is about a line from him would be satisfactory as we are entire strangers & who is doing well and who ill. time does not permit me to mention particular compliments for Mr. Mason & my friend Mr. J. Ewing &

Yours & Z. Kingsley

1. Zephaniah Kingsley (1765–1843) was a wealthy planter and slave importer who owned a plantation in Spanish Florida just below the Georgia line. William Allen was a Charleston-based merchant. On Kingsley and his African wife, see Daniel L. Schafer, *Anna Madgigine Jai Kingsley: African Princess, Florida Slave, Plantation Slaveowner* (Gainesville: University Press of Florida, 2003). The editors are grateful to Mark Fleszar for this document.

ALS in James Hamilton Papers, Hargrett Rare Book and Manuscript Library, University of Georgia.

Biography of Jack Pritchard[1]

All the late insurrections of slaves are to be traced to (influential[1828, 1829]) (fanatical[1833, 1834]) preachers (of the gospel,[1828, 1829]) (as, for instance, at Barbadoes and Demerara,) (and [1833, 1834]) to white (preachers, [1828, 1828]) (missionaries) from England. Vesey, who instigated the Charleston plot, was an exhorting brother. (What regret need it give to a slave, an orthodox believer, to know that he is going to die, or be removed from under the power of a wicked master, and miserable state of penance and oppression in an unhappy world, where he has been unjustly held in bondage, and placed in a state of misery by a beneficent and just being, to prepare him for a happy world hereafter, which is promised to all sinners who repent and are true believers; where he is to have plenty of every thing that is good and pleasant, without work or master; but if he does not believe in whatever is told him, he must be eternally tormented with fire and brimstone. To refuse the offer of such an alternative would prove any one to be either a fool or an unbeliever.[1828]) (Gullah Jack or Jack the Conjurer was a (priest[1829]) (Conjurer[1833, 1834]) in his own country, M'Choolay Moreema, where a dialect of the Angola Tongue is spoken clear across Africa from sea to sea, a distance perhaps of three thousand miles: I purchased him a prisoner of war at Zinguebar.[2] He had his conjuring implements with him in a bag which he brought onboard the ship and always retained them.

1. Zephaniah Kingsley published, with slightly varying titles, four editions of *A Treatise on the Patriarchal, or Co-operative, System of Society as It Exists in Some Governments, and Colonies in America and in the United States, under the Name of Slavery,* in 1828, 1829, 1833, and 1834. Daniel W. Stowell, *Balancing Evils Judiciously: The Proslavery Writings of Zephaniah Kingsley* (Gainesville: University Press of Florida, 2000), 67–68, transcribes Kingsley's comments on Gullah Jack and the Vesey affair, showing changes made by Kingsley in the four editions. We have transcribed Stowell's edition verbatim for completeness of detail.

2. The port of Zinguebar was adjacent to the island of Zanzibar, where Swahili and Arab traders sold men and women from a broad region of central and eastern Africa to American and European traders. Kingsley was evidently buying woodworkers for his Florida plantation, but as the letter above indicates, when his ship, the *Gustavia,* reached Tybee Island, he sold some of the carpenters, including Jack, to Paul Pritchard Sr. (1779–1837), a ship carpenter who operated a shop at Gadsden's Wharf; Pritchard later told the 1822 court that he had owned Jack for approximately sixteen years.

Zephaniah Kingsley, *A Treatise on the Patriarchal, or Co-operative System of Society,* in Daniel W. Stowell, ed., *Balancing Evils Judiciously: The Proslavery Writings of Zephaniah Kingsley* (Gainesville: University Press of Florida, 2000), 67–68.

Charleston *Southern Patriot, and Commercial Advertiser*

Saturday, November 28, 1818

MESSAGE NO. 1

From his excellency the Governor, to the Legislature of South Carolina. . . . [1] The law, passed in December 1816, prohibiting the introduction of Negroes into this State, is again, with great reluctance, brought before you. It is believed that this law, which is thought so repugnant to the interests of so many of our fellow-citizens, is violated, in many instances, with impunity; as no one will incur the odium attached to the character of an informer. It is therefore made a question, proper for your determination, whether it would not be better to repeal it altogether, than it should remain a nullity, upon our own statute book, only as it presents a difficulty, to prudent and conscientious men, who would be valuable acquisitions to our society.

1. Governor Andrew Pickens Jr. (1779–1838) delivered this message on Tuesday, November 24, 1818.

An Act to Limit Slave Importations, December 1818

I. *Be it enacted,* by the Senate and House of Representatives, now met and sitting in General Assembly, and it is hereby enacted by the authority of the same, That from and after the passing of this Act, the Act of the legislature entitled "An Act to prohibit the importation of slaves into this State from any of the United States; and for other purposes therein mentioned," passed the nineteenth day of December, in the year of our Lord one thousand eight hundred and sixteen; also the Act entitled "An Act to amend an Act entitled an Act to prohibit the importation of slaves into this State, from any of the United States; and for other purposes therein mentioned;" passed the eighteenth day of December, in the year of our Lord one thousand eight hundred and seventeen, be, and the same are hereby repealed.

Thomas Cooper and David J. McCord, eds., *The Statutes at Large of South Carolina* (Columbia, SC, 1840), vol. 7: 458.

For Africans and African Americans living in an oppressive slave society, the solace of religion helped sustain body and soul. By the end of the War of 1812, black Methodists outnumbered their white counterparts in Charleston by ten to one. White ministers and church leaders defended efforts to Christianize the state's black majority—a crusade resisted by many planters—even as they promoted a proslavery theology. For a time, Vesey was a congregant in the city's Second Presbyterian Church. But like other black Carolinians, Vesey became increasingly interested in the Reverend Richard Allen's African Methodist Episcopal Church, founded in Philadelphia in 1816. Beginning a year earlier, Anthony Senter (1785–1817), a white Methodist minister stationed in Charleston, and his immediate successors attempted to reassert authority over the black Christians who formed a majority of congregants in his church. In early 1816, Morris Brown (1770–1849), a free "brown" man three years Vesey's junior, and Henry Drayton (d. 1837) journeyed north to confer with Allen (1760–1831) and be ordained for pastorates. James Osgood Andrew (1794–1871) succeeded Senter at the Trinity Methodist Church in 1816. More than a decade later, he recalled what he claimed was the "correct information" about why 4,367 black congregants ultimately withdrew from the white church to begin construction of an independent AME Church known as the "African Church." Andrew, who stood at the center of the North-South schism of the national Methodist Church in 1844 over the issue of slaveowning ministers, identified a struggle over power, money, and influence within Charleston's Methodist communion. Francis Asbury Mood (1830–1884), born and raised in Charleston and the son of a Methodist minister in the city during the Vesey affair, indicated that the precipitant for the withdrawal of black congregants in 1817 was the construction of a hearse house atop a black cemetery, which black Methodists regarded as a calculated act of desecration. Interestingly enough, Thomas Bennett Sr. (1754–1814), father of Governor Bennett, donated the land on which the Bethel Methodist Church and a new burial site were established.

The appearance and trial in Charleston of the eccentric itinerant antislavery Methodist minister Lorenzo Dow (1777–1834) agitated both whites and blacks. Dow, a man of "zeal and piety," preached, uninvited by masters, to slaves. Charleston merchant Benjamin Hammet (1794?–1826) filed suit against Dow in 1821 for libeling his father, William Hammet, who was also a Methodist minister. Benjamin's slave Bacchus, executed for involvement in the Vesey affair, referenced Dow's trial in his testimony, and whites claimed that, while in Charleston, the millennialist Dow had been preaching cryptic prophetic words against slavery. Charleston's Court of Sessions found Dow guilty. He was released from jail, fined one dollar, and sent on his way. His attorney, Samuel Prioleau (1784–1840), was the brother-in-law of James Hamilton Jr.

The Reverend Daniel Alexander Payne (1811–1893), as a boy in Charleston, heard uplifting stories of Haiti and the Haitians, and he "desired to become a soldier and go to Haiti." When white officials cracked down on free persons of color in South Carolina in the 1830s, Payne left Charleston for the North. He became a prominent AME minister, Morris Brown's private secretary, and the church's first historian. He knew intimately black and white principals in the Vesey affair.

Baltimore *American Commercial Daily Advertiser*

Thursday, May 2, 1816

Convention of the African Church. On the 11th inst.[1] the first Convention held in America by colored Ministers, and composed of Delegates from different African Methodist Churches, met in this city.[2]

On no similar occasion, since the Apostolical era of the church, has more Christian love and unanimity been manifested, than by the Convention.

Having finished other important business, on Thursday, the 25th instant, the reverend Richard Allen, of this city, and the reverend Daniel Coker, of Baltimore, were unanimously chosen by the convention to be ordained to the office of Elders, and the same day was set apart for that purpose, by the imposition of hands of one regularly ordained Elder, and three regularly ordained Deacons. And on the day following, the reverend Richard Allen was ordained to the General Superintendent or the imposition of hands of two regularly ordained Elders, and three regularly ordained Deacons.

On the 27th ult. the Convention adjourned.—*Philad. Pap.*

1. From the Latin "Instante Mense," meaning the current month.

2. The Baltimore paper was quoting from a Philadelphia journal, so the reference to "in this city" meant Philadelphia.

Petition for Burial Site, 1818

To the honorable, the Speaker and Members of the House of Representatives of the State of South Carolina—

The humble Petition of the subscribers Respectfully Sheweth,

That your Petitioners, who are free persons of color, on behalf of themselves and others of the religious sect or denomination called Methodists, in the City of Charleston, are desirous of purchasing two lots of land to be appropriated as a place of interment for themselves and their descendants; the present burial ground being inadequate for that purpose—That the said lots are situated in the Village of Wraggs-Borough in the vicinity of Charleston, adjoining each other, and contain each in front, on Judith Street, forty feet, and one hundred and twenty eight feet in depth, more or less—That these lots being beyond the limits of the City, your Petitioners are informed, that is necessary to obtain the sanction of your honorable body to appropriate the same for the purposes aforesaid—Your Petitioners therefore humbly pray, that they may be authorized and empowered to purchase and use the said lots, as a place of burial for themselves, and their descendants, under such regulations and restrictions, as your honorable body may think proper to prescribe—And your Petitioners as in duty bound will ever pray and so forth.[1]

Morris Brown	Henry Drayton
Charles Corr	William Eden
Marcus Brown	Abraham Ash
Malcom Brown	Amos Crukshank
Harry Bull	Smart Simpson
John Mathewes	Peter Mathewes
Jack Mathewes	Henary Mathewes
Water Hanes	John Ancrum
James Mack	Joseph Brown
Benjamin Berry	Jonny Holmes
Cato Mack	Aleck Harleston
James Savage	

We whose names are subscribed do recommend that the prayer of the Petitioners be granted.

Robert Wilson	Robert Howard
Charles Cotesworth Pinckney	W. S. Smith
Tho: W. Bacot	Simon Magwood

1. Of the twenty-three free persons of color whose names are on the petition, those of Marcus Brown, Abraham Ash, Amos Crukshank, Harry Bull, Aleck Harleston, and James Savage were written in by a third party above an "X" or some other mark to identify the signatory. Most of the free colored petitioners practiced skilled trades in the city. Morris Brown, for example, was a shoemaker; Charles Corr, a tailor; Smart Simpson, a carpenter; Aleck Harleston, a drayman. None of the free colored signatories to the petition number among the arrested identified in the calendar of the *OR*. In General Charles Cotesworth Pinckney (1746–1825) the petitioners had recruited to their cause one of the most eminent persons in South Carolina, delegate to the Constitutional Convention and the Federalist candidate for the vice-presidency in 1800. In 1818—and in 1822—Pinckney headed the Charleston Bible Society.

Petition no. 3997, n.d. [ca. 1818], series S165015, Petitions to the General Assembly, SCDAH.

Figure 1. The Reverend Morris Brown (1770–1849), second bishop of the African Methodist Episcopal Church. From Daniel Alexander Payne, *History of the African Methodist Episcopal Church* (1891).

Methodist History, 1830

. . . IN the year 1817, a serious division took place in the coloured society in this city, which has been more disastrous in its influence on the religious prosperity of the slave population, than any event which has occurred in the history of southern Methodism. On this subject we shall bestow some attention, and this may be the more necessary, as a correct history of this unhappy affair has never been presented to the public. It has been hinted in the preceding part of this sketch, that Methodism had acquired considerable influence among the coloured people. The ministrations of our preachers had been graciously owned of God, in the awakening and conversion of hundreds of them, in the city and in the surrounding country. Many active and useful exhorters had been raised up among them from time to time, who had gone by day and by night among the neighbouring plantations, to exhort those of their own colour to seek the salvation of their souls. Many classes were formed,—many of the white people too, who, at first opposed, had, at length, after witnessing the influence of religion among their slaves, begun to relent; and many had become favourable, and even encouraged the efforts which were making to impart religious instruction to them. The whole aspect of affairs portended a wider spread of the gospel among the coloured population of the southern country. So mighty had been its influence among this people, that at the close of 1816, there were more than four thousand of them connected with our society, in the city of Charleston and the surrounding country. In such a multitude it is not wonderful that there should have been discontented and ambitious individuals, whose element was discord. Among the leaders were several men of intelligence, and some of them of considerable property. The preachers, confiding in the intelligence and integrity of these men, committed a very large portion of the management of the coloured society to them. They made numerous collections among themselves, all of which, with the exception of the class and sacramental collections, they disbursed among themselves, either for the relief of their sick and poor, or for the purchase of the freedom of such as were to be sold. The natural tendency of these proceedings was to give to certain men an influence which could scarcely fail to injure both its possessors, and those over whom it was exerted. Such was the state of matters when, in the year 1815, the Rev. Anthony Senter[1] was appointed to the charge of this station. With him commenced a new era in the administration of discipline among the coloured people. From that time they were required to bring their love feast collections into the hands of the stewards of the church, agreeably to the provisions of the Discipline; and to bring all cases of the trial of members to be decided in the presence of the preacher in charge. These proceedings gave considerable umbrage, especially to many of the leaders, among whom there were not a few disciples of *Diotrophes.* These men commenced "*reformers,*" and sounded secretly among the people, that the preachers, whom they had hitherto regarded as their best friends, were their oppressors, who had not only injured them, but designed to rob them and their poor, to enrich themselves. These things were gradually and artfully insinuated into the minds of the people, until the leaders, who were to be the chief actors in this mighty scheme, found things ripe for the execution of their purpose. Preparatory to the full development of their plan, two men, who had stood high among them as class leaders and exhorters, had gone to Philadelphia, and had received ordination from Richard Allen. With these additional powers, they returned to Charleston, and waited a favourable opportunity to blow up to a flame the slumbering embers of discontent. A suitable pretext was not long delayed, and the storm which had been so long collecting, burst on the church with alarming violence. Almost all the leaders surrendered their class papers; whole classes followed their leaders; and, for awhile, it seemed doubtful whether the whole coloured society, the fruit of so many years of labour and reproach, was not to be taken from us at one fell swoop. Various arts were employed to lead the unsuspecting and well disposed astray. They were told that it was the same church still. They would still be *Methodists;* only they were to be under the charge of men of their own colour. By such arts, and others of a similar character, they succeeded in drawing off very many pious, but ignorant persons. Some of the leaders did not go, but seemed to be pondering for awhile what course to take. A short consideration decided them to *abide by the old ship.* And a few had, from the beginning, borne a decided and resolute testimony against the proceedings of the "*reformers.*" They had been converted to God under the ministry of the Methodist preachers. From them, also, they had been long accustomed to receive the bread of the kingdom. They knew that those preachers had been the instruments of making them a people who were no people. They remembered that on their account these men had borne reproach and persecution *in abundance.* They also saw among the active partisans of this division, not a few who owed their all, under God, to the labours of the very men whom they were now actively engaged in traducing. These few worthies served as a rallying point for such as were disposed to abide in the old paths. Desolate indeed, for some time, was the appearance of the churches. In the galleries, once crowded with attentive and prayerful hearers, now only a few faces were seen; and instead of the full chorus of happy voices, which used to hymn the praises of God, the preacher was called to witness a silent and mournful solitude. Gradually, however, the scene brightened. Many who had been deceived by designing men, returned; and many of the leaders, after cool reflection had dispersed the mists of passion and misrepresentation, saw their error, repented, and returned. But the great body of the leaders, whose pride and ambition had too deep a stake in the issue of the revolution, obstinately held on their course, even when it became obvious that their schemes could not be realized. It appears, indeed, that they had projected a plan of marked boldness. They seem to have contemplated the obtaining of legislative sanction to the establishment of a separate church; in which event they calculated to obtain, by legal process, one of our houses of worship, toward which the blacks had liberally contributed when it was built. This plan subsequent events compelled them to relinquish. They built a house, however, in which they continued to worship till the insurrection of 1822. Their separate establishment was then broken up, and the people scattered. Some of them returned to their former fold; many went into other churches; and not a few became identified with the ungodly world.

When the separation above mentioned took place, the preacher in charge communicated the fact to the intendant of the city, informing him that we no longer exercised over those people any pastoral care, and that the Methodist Church would not hold herself responsible for any of their doings. And yet when, some years afterward, an insurrectionary plot was discovered in which these people had a very considerable share, it was very confidently asserted that it originated in the Methodist Church; whereas the fact was that not a solitary member of this Church, in regular standing, had the slightest concern in the business. . . .

1. The Reverend Anthony Senter (1785–1817), a blacksmith, ministered to Methodists in Charleston from 1814 to his death. See "Obituary," *Methodist Magazine* 1 (1818): 199–200.

Letter II, James Osgood Andrew, January 1830, in "Letters on Methodist History," *Methodist Magazine and Quarterly Review* 12 (1830): 22–25.

Methodist History, 1856

. . . During the year 1815, under the administration of Anthony Senter, preacher in charge, a careful revision was had of the state of the colored society. They numbered at that time about four thousand. Upon a close investigation of the conduct and management of their monetary affairs, much corruption was found to exist.

Up to this time the colored official members were allowed a distinct Quarterly Conference, and their collections, taken up by their leaders and preachers, were held and disbursed by them. Mr. Senter, upon the discovery of the improper workings of this system, required of them to deliver the collections, according to Discipline, into the hands of the stewards. And their church trials, also, which had been hitherto entirely among themselves, were now conducted in the presence of the preacher in charge. His proceeding awaked considerable opposition among the leaders, particularly after the abolition of their Quarterly Conferences, and their opposition soon awakened quite an agitation among the colored membership. This agitation was secret in its character for a long time, and during the two years of this hidden movement the enormous increase of two thousand was reported.

It appears, as was afterwards developed, that a regular scheme, had been devised for the formal secession of the disaffected ones from the church; and, as a preparatory step, two of them had gone to Philadelphia and obtained ordination, with a view of assuming the pastorate over them. Measures were also commenced by them to obtain possession of Bethel Church by legal process, because, as they had heard by tradition, the colored members at the time of its erection had contributed liberally towards it.

For two years their plans were being matured, and they awaited a pretext for a demonstration. An occasion was afforded in the erection of a hearse house upon their burial lot on Pitt street. This lot, it will be remembered, was the gift of Mr. Bennet,[1] and it was only a benevolence to them in allowing them its use. Upon the trustees paying no heed to their protests against the erection of the house, great excitement ensued, and at the time fixed upon for the deploy, at one full swoop nearly every leader delivered up his class-papers, and four thousand three hundred and sixty seven of the members withdrew. . . . Comparatively a few, numbering thirteen hundred and twenty-three, who had hitherto found the Methodist preachers their best friends, hung bravely to the old side. . . .

The schismatics combined, and, after great exertion, succeeded in erecting a neat church building at the corner of Reid and Hanover Streets. Their organization was called the African Church. They, however, were never permitted to worship in their own building. They dragged out a miserable existence until the year 1822. In that year, upon the discovery by the authorities of an intended insurrection among the blacks, the church building was demolished by their order, and a deserted burial-place is all that is left to mark this singular movement. . . .

1. Thomas Bennett Sr. (1754–1814), a successful businessman, owned the Charleston mills and ended life as a prosperous planter.

F. A. Mood, *Methodism in Charleston: A Narrative of the Chief Events Relating to the Rise and Progress of the Methodist Episcopal Church in Charleston, S.C.*, ed. Thomas O. Summers (Nashville, TN, 1856), 130–33.

Daniel Alexander Payne, History of the African Methodist Episcopal Church, 1866[1]

. . . About 1817, Rev. Morris Brown, at the head of about 1,000 souls, resigned from the M.E. Church in South Carolina, and united with the Connection—now 1822, the number had swelled to 3,000, including Charleston, and the Circuit immediately surrounding it.

When we take into consideration the intolerant laws, and police regulations, which were made to restrain the movements of the slave and free colored people of South Carolina, that was a large increase. Among these were the eleven preachers whose names we have already given, who would, if they could, have been members of the Convention of 1816. [2]

This little band of Christians had to suffer great persecutions on account of their *independent spirit, their opposition to colorphobia,* and *their desire to worship God in their own house consecrated to His* service—in which no one could say, '*Away to the seats and galleries for Negroes,*'—for this simple desire, this determination, prompted by the purest motives, for which white men would have been commended throughout the country, they were *repeatedly arrested,* while *in the act of public worship,* and driven like a flock of sheep before the civil authorities, who punished them by fines and stripes according to their ability to pay or not pay, or their condition as free or bond. In the case of slaves, sometimes a humane master did interfere, and save the trembling flesh of his favorite servant from the bloodly lash.

After repeated arrests and punishment, they were allowed to worship God in their own house, but under the most humiliating restrictions, till 1822, when the civil authorities of the State, maddened by the incipient efforts of the heroic, but luckless Denmark Vesey, to overthrow the infernal system, ordered their organization to be suppressed. . . .

1. Daniel Alexander Payne (1811–1893), born free in Charleston, became the third bishop of the African Methodist Episcopal Church, following Richard Allen and Morris Brown. One of the founders of Wilberforce University in Ohio, he became its first president in 1863. See James T. Campbell, *Songs of Zion: The African Methodist Episcopal Church in the United States and South Africa* (New York: Oxford University Press, 1995), 37–39.

2. Methodists of African descent held a convention in Philadelphia, April 11–27, 1816.

Daniel A. Payne, *The Semi-Centenary and the Retrospection of the African Meth[odist]. Episcopal Church in the United States of America* (Baltimore, 1866), 23.

Second Presbyterian Church Records, Saturday, April 13, 1817

On the 2nd Sabbath in April 1817 the Sacrament of the Lord's Supper, was again administered in the Church, when the following persons, were admitted to Communion for the first time—Martha Robertson—and three people of Colour, viz. Marshall Groning—John Millar—Danmark Vesey—the two former Baptised.—[1]

1. Despite the misspelling of his first name, this was clearly Vesey. Located near the corner of Charlotte and Meeting streets, the church was dedicated in April 1811. The fact that Vesey was not baptized at the service suggests this was not his first visit to the church. After this date, however, Vesey vanished from the church records, reflecting the transfer of his religious allegiance to the African Church.

"Second Presbyterian Church, Charleston County, 1809–1837" (typescript), p. 15, SCL.

Charleston *Southern Patriot, and Commercial Advertiser*

Monday, June 8, 1818

One hundred and forty Free Negroes and Slaves, belonging to the *African Church,* were taken on Sunday afternoon by the City Guard, and lodged in the Guard-House. The City Council yesterday morning sentenced five of them, consisting of a Bishop and four Ministers, to one month's imprisonment, or to give security to leave the state. Eight other Ministers were also sentenced, separately, to receive ten lashes, or pay a fine each of five dollars.[1]

1. This story was reprinted almost verbatim in the *Charleston Courier,* June 9, 1818, and the Boston *Recorder,* October 30, 1818, but with the heading: "Impious! Disgraceful!" If Vesey were among those taken in this unusually large gathering of persons of color, the experience may have marked his first incarceration.

Charleston *Southern Patriot, and Commercial Advertiser*

Wednesday, June 10, 1818

We are authorized and we deem it our duty to give a fuller statement of the facts, than that contained in our paper of Monday last, in relation to the Free People of Color and Slaves, who were taken up on Sunday, whilst holding an unlawful meeting in the form of a distinct congregation; as from the hasty manner in which the paragraph was drawn up, erroneous impressions may go abroad. It is well known that in every Church in Charleston, and throughout the state, accommodations are provided for such of the Negroes and Free People of Color, as choose to attend Divine Service, and that large numbers of them are Communicants. By sundry Acts of the Legislature, it is positively forbidden that Slaves, or Free People of Colour should assemble "for the purpose of mental instruction," unless a majority of the assembly be composed of white persons. This law has been in force since the year 1800, and, until lately, has been so far observed, that the public authorities had no occasion to take measures under it—A few weeks since, some blacks constituted as Bishops and Preachers in one of the Northern cities came here, and endeavored to hold meetings of black congregations exclusively; and one of their congregations was taken up and confined, and the next day dismissed personally by the City Magistrates, who explained the law to them, and admonished them individually to abstain from a repetition of a like breach of the laws.[1] The Black Priests afterwards endeavored to get the City Council to grant a dispensation, and allow them to hold their meetings in the way they wished. It was fully explained again to them, that the law of the state was obligatory on the City Council, who not only, without the presence of a single white person, could not dispense with its provisions, but were also disposed to support so essential a part of the policy of this state. Notwithstanding all these lenient measures, the same Preachers, in open violation of the law, and in defiance as it were both of the state and city authorities, last Sunday held in a house in the suburbs of the city, a large and unlawful assemblage of Free People of Color and Slaves, as they had done before. This assembly was taken up by the City Guard, and although every individual was liable, by law, both to imprisonment and corporal chastisement, yet the penalty was mitigated, and inflicted only on a few of the ring-leaders.

1. This item appeared verbatim in the *Charleston Courier* one day later. Neither account identified the northern delegates, but the group almost certainly did not include the aged Richard Allen, who refused to travel into the lower South. See Richard S. Newman, *Freedom's Prophet: Bishop Richard Allen, the AME Church, and the Black Founding Fathers* (New York: New York University Press, 2008), 48.

Charleston City Ordinance, Thursday, June 11, 1818

. . . *And be it further ordained by the authority aforesaid,* That if any Negro or Person of Color shall be guilty of whooping or hallooing any where in the City, or of making a clamorous noise, or of singing aloud any indecent song, he or she shall, for each and every such offence, receive at the Work-House or Public Market such a number of stripes, not exceeding *twenty,* as any Warden of the City shall adjudge.

"*And be it further ordained by the authority aforesaid,* That no Negro or other Person of Color shall smoke a pipe or segar in any street, lane, alley, or open place in Charleston; or walk with a cane, club, or other stick, except such as may be blind or infirm. And every Negro or Person of Color who shall smoke a pipe or segar, or who shall walk with a cane, club or other stick, contrary to this Ordinance, shall receive such a number of lashes as any Wardens of the City shall adjudge, not exceeding twenty; and shall moreover forfeit every such pipe, segar, cane, club, or other stick, to any white person seizing the same."

Charleston Courier, June 15, 1818.

Boston *Recorder*

Tuesday, July 7, 1818

Treatment of Negroes in Charleston, S.C.

We gave in our last a short account of the persecution waged against the Blacks in Charleston, for assembling on the Sabbath day for Divine Worship. We have rarely recorded a deed that excited emotions so unpleasant. Tenderness for the reputation of our country—pity for the sufferers—abhorrence of their persecutors, or of the laws which decree such penalties—respect for the rights of conscience—dread of the vengeance of heaven on the land that nourishes a spirit so unchristian—conspired to produce in us a heart-sinking that we cannot describe. Whatever excuses may be offered, or whatever pleas may be urged in vindication of the course pursued, the *fact* can never be divested of its baseness and guilt. It is often said that slaves in this country are well treated;—allow that in many instances they are so; in many others are they not treated with more inhumanity than the beasts of the field? But in this case, not only slaves, but blacks *as free as any man in the country,* are taken up on the Sabbath, and committed to prison, and sentenced to continued confinement, to the whipping-post or a heavy fine, and to banishment from the state—for what? Because they assemble quietly to worship "the God of love and peace" on the day which he has expressly set apart, and required to be devoted to his worship! It will be said that such precautions are *necessary*—that large assemblages of Negroes cannot be permitted with safety to the country—*not even if assembled to serve God*! Admitting this to be true, we have no hesitation in saying, that the time is not far distant when signal judgments will be *necessary* to break the yoke of the oppressor and let the oppressed go free; or when assemblages of Negroes will be formed for less holy purposes than to serve Jehovah; and those men who deny them a privilege to which God has entitled the black and the white alike, will fall victims to *other* passions than those encouraged in the temples of the Lord.

We deprecate the retributions of incensed justice on our country; and are willing enough, for the ease of our own consciences, to admit that some portion of our guilt has been contracted in those "times of ignorance" which God may "wink at;" but those times are passed away—"we are now commanded to repent," "because God hath appointed a day in which he will judge the world in righteousness," when "the hire of the laborers who have reaped down our" Southern "fields, which is by us kept back by fraud," or even paid in stripes and imprisonment, shall enter the ears of the Lord of Sabaoth.

Some light gleams athwart the "darkness visible" in our future prospects. A reforming spirit arises even in the South. Thousands of our fellow-citizens feel the grievance of a vast mass of population, deprived of the rights of freemen in the bosom of a free country, and are seriously engaged to redress wrongs that have been inflicted, and relieve the nation from the guilt and apprehension under which it labors. Will not the fact that has occasioned these remarks, serve to stimulate their zeal yet more, and furnish them with new energy, in the prosecution of their benevolent designs? And will not the same fact serve to loosen those ties by which the free negroes have felt themselves attached to this *free* and *Christian* country, and remove out of the way one of the strongest objections to the Colonization Societies recently formed, viz. that "the blacks love this land of liberty too well, to be induced to return to the land of their fathers?" However *these* questions may be settled, of this we happily have *no* doubt, "that the wrath of man shall praise God, and the remainder of wrath, he will restrain."

Boston *Recorder*

Saturday, August 29, 1818

Treatment of Blacks in Charleston, S.C.

(The following Communication, offered for publication by a respectable gentleman from Charleston, is cheerfully admitted. We are happy to hear of the privileges the Blacks are allowed; we hope they are such as they can, and do improve. We are willing every thing should be said in palliation of the conduct of the whites, and we leave the public to judge how far the laws which sanction such conduct are consistent with the Gospel or the Constitution.)

To the Editor of the Recorder.

Sir,—I have read, with deep regret, in your paper of the 7th ult.[1] certain remarks upon the "*Treatment of Blacks, in Charleston, S.C.*" and being fully aware what impressions have been made upon the public mind, in this vicinity, by the account of the apprehension of persons assembled for public worship, I deem it proper to give such explanations as may be afforded by the disclosure of facts, within my personal knowledge. The writer in the Recorder, and others who have published animadversions upon this subject, seem to take it for granted, that the Blacks in Charleston enjoy very few Christian privileges; and that even those few are threatened to be wrested from them by an impious oppression.

The fact is, that the blacks enjoy equally with the whites, all the blessings of Christian instruction. There are seventeen churches in the City; and in these such ample provision is made for their accommodation, that they may all attend upon the regular ministry of the Gospel. All denominations freely receive them to the full enjoyment of Christian ordinances; and the actual number of black and colored communicants, united with the various churches in Charleston, is above Six Thousand!! Yes, Mr. Editor, of these people who are represented as the objects of stern and cruel persecution, six thousand constantly sit down at the table of the Lord with those who are held up to view as their religious oppressors.

This unexampled number of communicants, embracing more than a third of the whole colored population, includes as great a proportion of fervent, engaged Christians, as is ordinarily found among professors.

These, in common with all the other blacks, enjoy the same ministry and the same Christian liberty with the white people; and besides this, they enjoy peculiar privileges of their own.—They have more than an hundred Exhorters, or Class-leaders, who constantly meet with them, in rooms of their own, for prayer and Christian Instruction. These black preachers act under the permission, and with the advice of the Pastors of their churches and are generally very pious and sensible men, well instructed in the great doctrines of the Gospel, deeply engaged for the conversion of sinners, and capable of speaking usefully and impressively upon the great essentials of religion—They hold perhaps hundreds of prayer-meetings every week, for the instruction of their brethren. I have sometimes attended meetings of fifty or sixty of these black preachers, who had met to pray for an out-pouring of God's Spirit, and to devise measures for the advancement of vital religion among their brethren; and seldom have I seen in any Christian assembly, greater appearance of fervent devotion and earnest engagedness in the cause of the Redeemer. So that the real state of the case is, that the blacks attend upon the same ministry, and all church privileges, with the white people; and in addition to this, freely enjoy the instructions and admonitions of pious Exhorters of their own color. Now, I believe it would be difficult to point out any community equally numerous, in the Christian world, in the enjoyment of greater religious freedom, or more frequent opportunities of hearing the Gospel, or of which a larger proportion professedly embrace the offers of salvation—Such has long been, and still continues to be, the situation of the slaves and free people of color in that city, as it respects religious advantages.

But let me particularly refer to the immediate occasion of this outcry of persecution.

A few months ago, two or three black men arrived from the north, calling themselves Bishops and Ministers, stating that they had been ordained in Philadelphia. They immediately began to excite discontentment among the colored people, and persuaded them to separate from the churches and from a distinct congregation. Most of the pious black people were convinced that the plan was pernicious and therefore opposed it; but others less wise and prudent, warmly engaged in it. They began directly to hold unlawful and disorderly meetings on the Sabbath, and petitioned the City Council to sanction their proceedings. The Council calmly and patiently considered the subject for some weeks. They were disposed to do any thing, which might comport with the general good, for their gratification. At length they decided that it would be both unlawful and inexpedient to permit the formation of a distinct independent congregation of blacks. Unhappily the petitioners refused to submit to the prohibition, preserved in their resolution to have a church under their own control, and continued to hold unlawful and tumultuous assemblies.—Mild measures were pursued for some time without effect; and it was only, when all other means were exhausted, when the evil had assumed an alarming aspect, and when, in the judgment of Christians generally of every color, the intervention of authority became necessary; that the law was carried into effect, the assembly broken up, and the leaders committed and fined. Now let the candid Christian fairly examine this proceedure. Can it be supposed that the blacks would be benefitted by leaving the ministry and privileges of the regular churches, and confining themselves to teachers of their own color? May it not be expected, that the most ambitious and discontented among them, will be most forward in such a project; and will a community composed of such be likely to manage the affairs of a church judiciously or profitably? Who would be answerable for the character and designs and conduct of black men, who might go among them from the north calling themselves ministers? Is it not easily supposable, that one of the numerous villains who crowd the State Prisons of the Middle States, might come and announce himself to them as a Bishop, and kindle a flame, which would overwhelm them with ruin? Is it not moreover evident, that such an establishment would limit the privileges of the blacks, by confining them to preachers of their own color, while now they enjoy the ministry of the clergy and the instruction of their brethren besides? And finally will it not be admitted by every unprejudiced Christian, that it is better for the blacks to continue united with the white people in the regular churches, while they freely enjoy their own private meetings, than to attempt to support a separate communion?

Thus when the act of authority, which has excited such emotions of abhorrence, is correctly understood, it is found perfectly defensible in every point of view. And it is peculiarly desirable, that persons would first clearly understand events of this nature, before they proceed publicly to anathematize a whole community. Southern Christians are not the apologists of slavery. None can more deeply deplore the existence of such a system; none can be more sensible of the host of evils which accompany it; and none can more earnestly pray for its extirpation. Yet in the present case it is a general opinion among them, that it was right and proper, forcibly to arrest the progress of a plan, needless, injudicious, and fraught with evil consequences.

1. "Ultimo" or "Ultimo Mense" is a Latin expression that refers to an occurrence from the previous month.

Reminiscences of Reverend Abiel Abbot,[1] November 1818

. . . Nov. 22. Preached for Dr. Palmer[2] in the Circular Church, the most extraordinary building on some accounts, I presume to say, in the United States.[3] It has cost 60,000$ & *is not finished.* It was intended, it seems, to present to the eye a concave of a semi-globe, the diameter of which is 80 feet, the semi-diameter or height, of course, 40 ft. It is built of Carolina brick with a flagged pavement, the aisles broad to accommodate negro worshippers & carpetted to prevent echo—the pulpit at the East end, neat & convenient. The vast gulf of space before the speaker is filled by pews & galleries, the whole of the right hand space of the gallery being appropriated to black people. It is, beyond all comparison, the most difficult to fill with a human voice that I have ever seen & is said to be the *coldest* house in the winter in this city & the hotest in the summer. The house was well filled, above & below; the most interesting section of the whole globe to me being the dark cloud on my right. The negroes were decently & many handsomely dressed, still & attentive—appeared to sit by families—men, wives & children—& a considerable number had hymnbooks & sung quite as well, to say the least, as the fairer occupants of the singing gallery. I am informed by Dr. P. that the negroes in his congregation hold regular religious meetings where the performances are entirely by themselves & in a style perfectly astonishing as to the degree of excellence. Their music is sustained in the four parts & they perform some pieces of much taste & difficulty. The Dr. often attends these meetings to give them countenance, as a certain number of whites must be present to answer the demand of the law. . . .

1. Abiel Abbot (1770–1828), a Harvard-educated minister from Andover, Massachusetts, turned from Congregationalism to Unitarianism. He formed a close relationship with Charleston's Samuel Gilman (1791–1858), the antebellum South's most important Unitarian minister. See S. Everett, ed., *Sermons By The Late Rev. Abiel Abbot, D.D. of Beverly, Mass. with a Memoir of His Life* (Boston, 1831).

2. Benjamin Morgan Palmer (1781–1847), minister of Charleston's Circular (Congregational) Church, is often confused with his more famous nephew, a Presbyterian minister (1818–1902), of the same name. The elder Palmer edited Charleston's *Southern Evangelical Intelligencer.* Well known for his missionary outreach to the slaves, he knew intimately a number of the slaves accused of complicity in the Vesey affair, including Billy Palmer, who was owned by Benjamin's father, Job Palmer (1747–1845). See Doralyn J. Hickey, "Benjamin Morgan Palmer: Churchman of the Old South" (PhD diss., Duke University, 1962).

3. A number of conspirators involved in the Vesey plot attended Palmer's Circular (so called because of the shape of its 1804 sanctuary) Congregational Church. Destroyed by fire in 1861, it took twenty years to rebuild. See Walter J. Fraser Jr., *Charleston! Charleston! The History of a Southern City* (Columbia: University of South Carolina Press, 1989), 254, 291, and "Register of the Independent Congregational (Circular) Church of Charleston S.C. 1784–1815," *SCHGM* 33 (1932): 306–16.

John Hammond Moore, ed., "The Abiel Abbot Journals: A Yankee Preacher in Charleston Society, 1818–1827," *SCHM* 68 (1967): 70.

Regulation for Black Clergy, 1819

THE number of Coloured Members in the BAPTIST CHURCH in Charleston, being considerable, and they esteeming it a privilege to have Meetings for Religious Worship among themselves; from the enjoyment of which, also, advantages to Religion have heretofore apparently been derived—the Church, as a body, think proper to give encouragement to those Religious Meetings under proper Regulations. And as some unhappiness has arisen among the persons concerned, tending to division, and to prevent the good effects formerly produced by means of those Meetings; which, it is thought, may be greatly owing to the want of fixed and known Rules to direct and regulate the proceedings of those Members who attend at said meetings:—Therefore, the Church have thought proper to point out the following Rules, as being expressly or virtually contained in the sacred Scriptures, for the direction and assistance of the Coloured Members in the transactions referred to above.

1st. The meetings shall be held at suitable times and places, so as to suit best with the convenience of all concerned; and to avoid giving offence to the civil authority. This Regulation may, in common, take place by the general voice of the Coloured Male Members; but in case of any difficulty arising on the subject, shall be determined by the Church as a body. . . .

Rules and Regulations of the Coloured Ministers, Elders and Members of the Baptist Church, in Charleston, S.C. (Charleston, SC, 1819).

Petition, 1820[1]

South Carolina

To the honorable the Speaker, and Members of the House of Representatives of the said State—

The Petition of the subscribers respectfully sheweth—That your Petitioners are free persons of color, attached to the African Methodist Episcopal Church, in Charleston, called Zion, and have recently erected a house of worship, at Hampstead, on Charleston-Neck, at the corner of Hanover and Reed Street—That your Petitioners are very desirous of obtaining the permission of your honorable body to open the said building for the purpose of Divine worship, from the rising of the sun, until the going down of the same, under the following regulations and restrictions—that is to say—That the doors of the said building shall always remain open, and that all white ministers of the Gospel of every denomination shall be respectfully invited to officiate in the said Church, whenever disposed so to do, and that seperate seats shall be provided for such Citizens as may honor the congregation with their presence, either for religious instruction or to inspect their morals and deportment—That no minister of color, who does not reside in this State shall officiate for the said congregation nor shall any slave be admitted a member thereof, without the approbation of his or her owner, nor shall any person, who is a member of any other religious Society be admitted into the same, without a recommendation from the minister of such Society, and (if a slave) the written permission of his or her owner—That every exertion will be used by your Petitioners to preserve the utmost order and decorum in the said congregation, to inform against all evilly designed persons of color, and to bring them to condign and merited punishment—Your Petitioners are aware, that their motives and intentions have, and still may be much misrepresented, but they trust and hope that a strict and religious adherence to the above regulations, or to any others, that your honorable body may please to impose, will convince the Citizens of this State, how much they have been deceived, in supposing that your Petitioners had any other wish or design, than to worship the omnipotent ruler of the Universe "in spirit, and in truth"—

Your Petitioners therefore pray that their Petition be granted, and they, as in duty bound, will ever pray and so forth—

Morris Brown
Henry Drayton
Charles Corr
Harry Bull
Amos Cruckshanks
J. B. Mathewes
Peter B. Mathewes
A. Harleston
Marcus Brown
Malcom Brown
Sam Cochran
James [*illegible*]
James Eder
Robert Milner
J. B. Haig
Quash A Harleston
Cato Mack
London Turpin
Charles Drayton
Isaac A. Mathewes
Henery Mathewes
John Drayton
Samuel Brown
James Mack
Charles Rogers
Smart Simpson

We the subscribers having read
the forgoing Petition and
believing that the object therof is
highly laudable do therefore
grant the prayers of the same

Benjn M Palmer, Pastor of
the Congregational Church

Geo. Reid, Pastor pro tem
the First Presbyterian Church

John Buchan Pastor of St.
Andrews Presbyterian Church

A. W. Leland Pastor of the
Pres. Chh James Island

Israel Munds
Minister of the gospel

Artemas Boies
Pastor of the 2nd Pres
Church

C Dupré
H^{ry} A Bryce
Geo Logan
David Bell
Wm Thompson
J. H. Mitchell

John Dawson Jr.
Daniel Cruckshanks
John Hoff
Philip Gadsden
Joseph Young
Isham Williams
John M[c]Kee
Chas. Prince
Tho[s] Jones
J. A. Johnson
A. J. Browne
[*illegible*] Kirkwood
Jn. Lukens
Daniel Latham
Rob[t] R. Gibbes
Rob Howard
Thomas Paine
D. Crocker
Joseph Yates
James Evans

1. Twenty-six free persons of color and thirty-two whites signed the petition. Initiated by the African Church's black leadership, it was endorsed by some of the most prominent white ministers in Charleston. Artemas Boies (1792–1844) was the minister at the Second Presbyterian Church, of which Vesey was formerly a member; Reverend Boies and Reverend Benjamin Morgan Palmer (the elder), who also signed the petition, would visit a number of the condemned slaves on the nights before their executions.

Of these signatories of African descent, many, like Morris Brown (1770–1849) and his son Malcolm (also spelled "Malcom"), were mixed-race and may not have been trusted by leading black conspirators. Although white mobs wanted Morris Brown's head, the official proceedings implicated none of the nonwhite signatories to the events of 1822. Job Palmer (1747–1845), the father of Benjamin, owned William (Billy) Palmer, who was ultimately punished by transportation out of the state. Joseph Yates (1775–1822) owned three slaves—Bellisle, Naphur, and Adam—who were hanged on July 26. Jacqueline Jones et al., *Created Equal: A Social and Political History of the United States* (New York: Longman, 2003), vol. 1: 376, misidentifies the minister as "Moses" Brown.

Petition no. 1893, n.d. [ca. 1820], series S165015, Petitions to the General Assembly, SCDAH.

Boston *Christian Observer*

April 1820

To the Editor of the Christian *Observer.*
With a view to repel the charges of European journalists against the United States, as not being sufficiently alive to the interests of religion, a gentleman has been for some time engaged in collecting complete information respecting the number of places of worship

and charitable societies, and the state of religion in general, throughout the Union. To assist his efforts, a committee of gentlemen at Charleston, South Carolina, have instituted inquiry into this important subject in their own State, and have given the following particulars as the result of their researches. . . .

In the city of Charleston upwards of one-fourth of the communicants are slaves, or free people of colour; and it is supposed that in other parts of the State the proportion of such communicants may be estimated at about one-eighth. In every church they are freely admitted to attend on Divine service; in most of the churches distinct accommodations are provided for them; and the clergy in general make it a part of their pastoral care to devote frequent and stated seasons for the religious instruction of catechumen from amongst the black population. . . .

"Religious Communications," *Christian Observer* 19 (April 1820): 217.

Boston *The Panoplist, and Missionary Herald*

June 1820

ON THE CONDITION OF THE BLACKS IN THIS COUNTRY.

Editorial.

SINCE the decision of the Missouri question in Congress, we have been desirous of giving a brief history of that most important discussion, and a brief view of what the people of this country have to hope, and what to fear, from the present state of our laws on the subject of slavery, and the domestic slave-trade. . . .

Our southern brethren are extremely irritable on the subject of slavery; and are apt to be indignant, if any thing is said respecting it, by the people of the north. We could most gladly wish, that there were such evidence of an enlightened, humane, and persevering attention to the improvement of the blacks in the southern regions of the United States, as would justify a profound silence on the part of the northern people. But during the forty years which have elapsed since our nation became independent, what has been done by the legislatures of Virginia, the Carolinas, and Georgia, to elevate the character of the blacks, to secure their rights, and to fit them to become ultimately entitled to all the privileges of men and citizens. Let the statement be fairly made, and let all the laws, favorable and adverse to the happiness of the slaves, be duly considered: it will then appear, that the inhabitants of the non slave-holding states ought not to remain silent, on the ground that the southern people know best what is to be done, and that they are doing all they can, for the benefit of the blacks. Unquestionably the people at the north would not be able to legislate wisely and judiciously, with respect to the slaves of Carolina. But they might safely adopt some general principles on the subject. They might be able to say positively, that something ought to be done. They might without hazard assert the following positions as incontrovertible: viz. That slavery is an unnatural state of society;—that it brings with it innumerable and tremendous evils;—that the idea of a perpetuation of slavery in a country claiming to be free, and asserting that all men are "created equal," is a monstrous anomaly;—that the general countenance of such an idea would be supremely dishonorable to this country;—that all men, in every part of the world, ought to be taught to read the Bible;[1]—that withholding the Bible from any class of men, under any pretence whatever, is unchristian, and a daring opposition to the will of the Most High;—that the blacks of our country ought to be immediately furnished with the means of religious instruction—that the most persevering, public-spirited, and unremitted exertions of the best and wisest members of the community should be applied to the mitigation and gradual abolition of slavery;—that no time is to be lost in this business;—that the sooner the work is commenced the more rapid will be its progress, and the less arduous the conflict with prejudice, injustice, and selfishness;—and that no dictate of religion, or of an enlightened conscience, will permit a benevolent man to sit down contented with the present state and prospects of the negro population of this country. . . .

1. From September 12, 1804, to March 12, 1815, Joseph Vesey was hired by the Charleston Fellowship Society to teach reading, writing, arithmetic, and navigation to the children in the society's school, many of whom were orphans and the offspring of artisans. As many of the documents included in this volume indicate, Denmark Vesey possessed these very skills. See Fellowship Society Papers, Treasurer's Accounts, Special Collections, College of Charleston. The editors are grateful to James Spady for this citation.

Boston *The Panoplist, and Missionary Herald*

November, 1820

ON THE CONDITION OF THE BLACKS IN THIS COUNTRY.

Editorial.

Since the publication of our number for June, we have received from the south several complaints against the article, which bears the same title as the one we have now commenced; and though the subject is a delicate one, and requires great caution and prudence in the discussion of it . . .

A highly respected friend of ours has received letters from gentlemen in South Carolina, written with a view to be shown to us, which express regret that the article in question made its appearance, and dissatisfaction with the manner, in which the subject was treated. The letters evince a candid spirit; and the character of the writers entitles them to respectful consideration. One of these correspondents, a clergyman whom we greatly esteem, has intermingled other topics with his animadversions on us, so that we cannot, without obvious inconvenience and impropriety, quote his words. He would not wish us to quote them entire. The substance of his remarks is, 'that the article in the June Panoplist has produced a considerable ferment among those, who have seen it; that he fears the effect will be to diminish the patronage of that work, and to keep alive and increase those sectional prejudices, which have already done so much mischief, in our common country; that the article is regarded as an attack, not only on Virginia, but on the southern states generally and indiscriminately; and that some of the inferences, which it contains, are considered as illegitimate, and as exhibiting more of feeling, than of any other quality.'

In a subsequent part of the letter are some remarks, which we insert at large.

"If our northern brethren, in commenting on the state of slavery in this country, in terms sometimes severe and almost bitter, would look on the luminous as well as the dark side of the picture, and tell the world the good things that are going on, in relation to slaves, in several places, it would give more effect to their censures, where they are just, and take off the impression, which is too apt to be received by southern men, that in speaking and acting as they do, they are more under *northern* than *Christian* influence. Every thing which is now spoken or written by northern men, on the subject of slavery, whether good or bad, right or wrong, is apt to be referred, by southern folks, to the *Missouri Question*; and to be considered as the effusion of disappointment, or revenge, on account of the decision which took place in Congress, on that topic. Of this spirit many, or at least some, good Christians partake, to a degree greater than one is apt to be aware of; but perhaps not greater than, considering the habits, feelings, views, &c. to which they have been accustomed from their birth, is to be expected. Every reader of John Newton's life must be surprised at the fact of his continuing, even after his conversion, for some time in the *slave-trade,* without seeming to be aware, at the time, that there was any thing wrong in it.

"Besides, intercourse between many places at the north and many at the south is now so great, so frequent, or rather so constant, that there is ample opportunity for correcting the erroneous impressions, that may be taken up, in relation to each other. The religious privileges of the blacks, in Charleston particularly, are well known, or at least ought to be well known; and they are daily and I may say rapidly, on the increase. But this good influence must go on, in a quiet, retired way, and diffuse itself like leaven. Otherwise, without a miracle, (which we can hardly expect,) every good plan, in relation to the improvement of the colored population, must be frustrated. "The kingdom of God," in relation to the people in question, must not come "with observation; neither must we say, lo here, or lo there." A fact, with which I have been made acquainted, I would here mention. The blacks, belonging to what is called by themselves the African Society, consisting chiefly, if not exclusively, of Methodists, with one or two free blacks at their head, who it is stated, had received episcopal ordination in Philadelphia, and who announce themselves to be bishops here, have been for some time engaged in building, for themselves exclusively, a place of worship. They obtained, as I understand, the countenance of the Governor,[1] before the commencement of the undertaking. But, since the article in the Panoplist appeared, he has prohibited it, and the work is for the present suspended. You will not be surprised at the jealousy of people against religious meetings, consisting entirely of blacks, and particularly where the worship is to be conducted by them, when you are informed, that most of the incipient schemes of insurrection, &c. that have been detected, have taken place at *professedly religious meetings.*"

"Rejoicing in the extensive and various and efficient plans for doing good, now in operation among you, I should be sorry to see any of them curtailed, or cramped, or injured by injudicious or unseasonable publications, in any of your periodical papers, which circulate in the southern region. When I have more leisure, I should like to forward a complete account of the number of black members in the different churches;—of the schools for teaching children and adult blacks to read;—of classes led by black men, &c.

&c. to be published in the Panoplist or Recorder. Whether I shall ever get time, pressed as I am already on every side, is quite problematical."

The following extracts are taken from a letter, written by a South-Carolina planter, with whom we have not the pleasure of being acquainted, but whose character is distinguished for amiableness and piety. Both he, and the writer of the preceding letter, are natives of the state in which they live.

"This communication, my good sir, has been delayed by the protracted illness, and the death of [*blank*] which prevented my procuring a few documents to forward you, that, if expedient, in your judgment, might be submitted to the perusal of the Editor of the Panoplist,[2] to rectify some mistakes in the publication of the June number of that work, wherein he states, that nothing has been done in the way of bettering the colored people in the Carolinas. I have not procured the Reports of the Sunday School Societies in this city, as I intended, but was prevented; which contained information most conclusive; but I send to you the Report of the Harmony Presbytery, and the Constitution of the Charleston Protestant Episcopal Sunday School Society. In the first are expressed the feelings of the truly pious generally, as well as the facts of the uncommon religious attention of the slaves and people of color in this state, and the unexampled efforts, which have been made for their instruction. In the sixth article of the last, is a transcript of the privileges granted to the people of color, by every previously organized Sabbath School institution among us. And likewise there are very many schools in our city, conducted by colored teachers, for the tuition of colored children, as well as hundreds of other people in the country and city both, who read the Scriptures and other religious books to their fellow servants, and are daily teaching them to read. In short, I feel no hesitation in saying, it has been a subject of deep interest with me for years past; and that, as far as my influence extended, they have had all possible prudent means of instruction, and I conscientiously add, that there never was a more rapid change for the better in the state of any people, than in theirs for the last ten years. Indeed, subordination is losing ground too fast for their own happiness, and the safety of our domestic policy. There have been recent instances of unprovoked attacks from some of them, on respectable citizens peaceably walking our streets, and the perpetrators sentenced to severe punishment by our laws.

"I really fear, that such publications, with the consequence licentiousness of these people, will defeat the professed benevolent design of their authors, and paralyze the exertions of the pious of these states, by inducing their legislators to pass laws prohibiting any assemblages of them for instruction, as inconsistent with our internal safety; when, if we are left to the benign influences of the spirit of Christianity, that is spreading through the region, a little time will level all distinctions in one united effort for promoting the glory of God, and the temporal and eternal happiness of mankind. I do believe, that a respectable part of this community, as to numbers, as well as otherwise, would at this moment rejoice to see such a day, regardless of the pecuniary loss sustained by them, if the minds and state of our posterity were prepared by habits of more exertion for their temporal comfort, and the minds of these people by moral and political instruction.

"Surely it cannot be the disposition of any individual Christian among our eastern brethren, that these people should be let loose among us, with the character now belonging to so great a portion of them, while we are making every exertion, consistent with our own safety, to promote their happiness, both temporal and spiritual,—and are not at the same time, chargeable with the evil of their slavery, which, it is well known, is coeval with our existence; and its extirpation certainly calls for the union of moderation and prudence, on the part of its Christian advocates at least."

1. John Geddes (1777–1828).
2. Jeremiah Evarts (1781–1831).

Charleston Courier

Tuesday, December 5, 1820[1]

. . . DECEMBER 2. . . . The petition of the free persons of color, praying at Hampstead, was referred to the Charleston Delegation, who report, that in their opinion, the prayer should not be granted. . . .

1. This same issue reported Jean-Pierre Boyer's triumphs in Haiti.

Morristown (New Jersey) *Palladium of Liberty*

Thursday, April 19, 1821

An official notification from the City Council of Charleston, S.C. signed by "John J. La-Far City Marshall,"[1] has been handed to several of the Clergy and Laity of that city those Ministers and others, who keep *night and Sunday schools for slaves,* that the *education of such persons is prohibited by law* and that the city council feel imperiously bound to *enforce the penalty* against those who may hereafter forfeit the same."[2]

1. On John Joseph Lafar (1784–1849), see *Charleston Courier,* February 23, 1849, and Harlan Greene, Harry S. Hutchins, and Brian E. Hutchins, *Slave Badges and the Slave-Hire System in Charleston, South Carolina, 1783–1865* (Jefferson, NC: McFarland, 2004), 85, which has Lafar born in 1781.

2. This news was reprinted in the Boston *Commercial Gazette,* April 30, 1821, *Niles' Weekly Register,* April 21, 1821, *Genius of Universal Emancipation* 1 (September 1821) 3: 46, and the *Arkansas Gazette,* June 23, 1821.

Report of the Female Bible Society of Charleston, June 1821

. . . An old negro man walked seventeen miles from the country to get a larger Bible. He had a small duodecimo, much worn, which he could not see to read; and when he received an octavo, he raised his half blind eyes, and devoutly thanked God for so great a gift. . . .

Sixth Report of the American Bible Society, Presented May 9, 1822 (New York, 1822), 149–50.

The Reverend Lorenzo Dow in a Charleston Jail, 1821

Mr. EDITOR—In a kind of postscript to the trial of LORENZO DOW, lately distributed in this city, appears the following sentence which, he says, was written while confined in Charleston Jail:—"There is a cloud arising, though remote; the Quakers have seen it, and, are gone, retired beyond the river; and their worship-houses are monuments of mourning."—I should ask if this is not too probable reference to the late domestic occurrences in our city. Written May 24th, 1821. Should such men be countenanced by any community, however zealous their pretensions, or sanctified their demeanor?

A CITIZEN

"Communication," Charleston *City Gazette and Commercial Daily Advertiser*, September 3, 1822. See also "Lorenzo Dow," *Charleston Courier*, June 14, 1821, and Lorenzo Dow, *The Stranger in Charleston! or the Trial and Confession of Lorenzo Dow* (Philadelphia, 1822).

Baltimore Patriot & Mercantile Advertiser

Friday, April 12, 1822

COMMUNICATION.

The Rev. RICHARD ALLEN, Bishop of the African Bethel Episcopal Chu[r]ch arrived in this city yesterday morning, with four Preachers from Charleston, one from New York, three from Pittsburgh, three from Washington city, and three [f]rom Harrisburg circuit. Conference commences *This Day*, the 12th inst.[1] by divine permission.[2]

1. From the Latin "Instante Mense," meaning the current month.

2. Two of the four Charleston churchmen were Morris Brown and Henry Drayton, who were put on trial in August 1822 for leaving South Carolina and reentering its borders, a violation of a state law of December 20, 1820 (printed below). See August 13, 1822, trial of Drayton, and Charleston *City Gazette and Commercial Daily Advertiser*, August 10, 1822, both of which are reprinted on pp. 665–68 in Part V of this volume.

South Carolina, for much of its history as a colony and as a slaveholding state, had a black majority with a long history of slave resistance. In 1800, Vesey's first full year of freedom, he was one of only 3,185 free persons of color in the entire state, and many of them were the mixed-race offspring of white fathers and enslaved mothers. That group made up only 2.1 percent of the state's black population. (By comparison, 15.6 percent of Maryland's black residents were free by 1800.) By 1820, the year the state assembly passed a law banning private manumissions, South Carolina was home to 258,475 slaves—many of them, like Gullah Jack Pritchard, captured Africans who retained memories of freedom—but only 237,440 whites. Charleston newspapers after 1804 continued to publish news about Haiti. Its impact on the mind of the slaves, together with published offers of welcome for black emigrants who might move to the black republic, fostered dreams of freedom. Cycles of black rebellion and white oppression created a tradition of resistance that Vesey and those who served as his recruiters were able to make use of in 1822. In the years before the uncovering of the Vesey plot, newspapers published a number of stories about slaves found brutally murdered in and around Charleston. Stories and rumors were bruited about, and leading whites called for legal reform to address the problem. Recruiters such as Monday Gell, as some of the trial documents in Part III reveal, played upon the murder of slaves by their masters, such as the one described below, when trying to convince bondmen like Harry Butler to join the conspiracy.

Courtroom Speech of Judge Samuel Wilds,[1] 1806

THROUGH the politeness of a gentleman of the bar, on whose accuracy we rely, we have been favoured with the following impressive and eloquent *sentence,* passed on the inhuman SLATER, by Judge *Wilds,* which we have pleasure in communicating to the public, as doing no less honour to his head, as a sound and able Judge, than to his heart, as a virtuous and humane man.

JOHN SLATER! You have been convicted by a jury of your country, of the wilful murder of your own slave; and I am sorry to say, the short, impressive, uncontradicted testimony, on which that conviction was founded, leaves but too little room to doubt its impropriety.

The annals of human depravity might be safely challenged for a parallel to this unfeeling, bloody and diabolical transaction.

You caused your unoffending, unresisting slave to be bound hand and foot, and by a refinement in cruelty, compelled his companion, perhaps the friend of his heart, to chop his head with an ax, and to cast his body, yet convulsing with the agonies of death, into the water! And this deed you dared to perpetrate in the very harbour of *Charleston,* within a few yards of the shore, unblushingly in the face of open day. Had your murderous arm been raised against your equals, whom the laws of self-defence, and the more efficacious law of the land unite to protect, your crimes would not have been without precedent, and would have seemed less horrid. Your personal risk would at least have proved, that though a murderer you were not a coward. But you too well knew that this unfortunate man, whom chance had subjected to your caprice, had not, like yourself, chartered to him by the laws of the land, the sacred rights of nature; and that a stern, but necessary policy, had disarmed him of the rights of self-defence. Too well you knew, that to you alone he could look for protection; and that your arm alone could shield him from oppression, or avenge his wrongs; yet, that arm you cruelly stretched out for his destruction.

The counsel, who generously volunteered his services in your behalf, shocked at the enormity of your offence, endeavoured to find a refuge, as well for his own feelings, as for those of all who heard your trial, in a derangement of your intellect. Several witnesses were examined to establish this fact, but the result of their testimony, it is apprehended, was as little satisfactory to his mind, as to those of the jury, to whom it was addressed. I sincerely wish this defence had proved successful, not from any desire to save you from the punishment which awaits you, and which you so richly merit; but from the desire of saving my country from the foul reproach of having in its bosom so great a monster.

From the peculiar situation of this country, our fathers felt themselves justified in subjecting to a very slight punishment, him, who murders a slave. Whether the present state of society require a continuation of this policy, so opposite to the apparent rights of humanity, it remains for a subsequent legislature to decide. Their attention would ere this have been directed to this subject, but for the honour of human nature, such hardened sinners as yourself are rarely found, to disturb the repose of society. The grand jury of this district, deeply impressed with your daring outrage, against the laws both of God and man, have made a very strong expression of their feelings on the subject, to the legislature; and from the wisdom and justice of that body, the friends of humanity may confidently hope soon to see this blackest in the catalogue of human crimes, pursued by appropriate punishment.

In proceeding to pass the sentence, which the law provides for your offence, I confess, I never felt more forcibly the want of power to make respected the laws of my country, whose minister I am. You have already violated the majesty of those laws. You have profanely pleaded the law under which you stand convicted, as a justification of your crime. You have held that law in one hand, and brandished your bloody ax in the other, impiously contending, that the *one* gave a licence to the unrestrained use of the *other.*

But, though you will go off unhurt in person, by the present sentence, expect not to escape with impunity. Your bloody deed has set a mark upon you, which, I fear, the good actions of your future life will not efface. You will be held in abhorrence by an impartial world, and shunned as a monster, by every honest man. Your unoffending posterity will be visited for your iniquity, by the stigma of deriving their origin from an unfeeling murderer. Your days, which will be but few, will be spent in wretchedness; and, if your conscience be not steeled against every virtuous emotion, if you be not entirely abandoned to hardness of heart, the mangled, mutilated corpse of your murdered slave will ever be present in your imagination; obtrude itself into all your amusements, and haunt you in the hours of silence and repose.

But, should you disregard the reproaches of an offended world; should you hear, with callous insensibility, the gnawings of a guilty conscience; yet remember! I charge you remember! that an awful period is fast approaching, and with you, is close at hand, when you must appear before a tribunal, whose want of power can afford you no prospect of impunity; when you must raise your bloody hands at the bar of an impartial, omniscient Judge! Remember! I pray you remember! whilst yet you have time, that God is just, and that his vengeance will not sleep forever.

1. Samuel Wilds (1775–1810), a prominent and widely respected judge, was born in Darlington District, South Carolina, and died near Cheraw. He rendered his sentence in January 1806. John Slater had tied one of his slaves to a block and ordered a second bondman to chop off his head with an ax. See "For the Courier," *Charleston Courier,* January 28, 1806; John Calvin Metcalf, ed., *Library of Southern Literature* (New Orleans, 1917), vol. 16: 121; E. Warren Moise, *Rebellion in the Temple of Justice: The Federal and State Courts in South Carolina During the War Between the States* (Lincoln, NE: iUniverse, 2003), 85.

"Charge Delivered by the Honourable Judge Wilds of South-Carolina," *American Law Journal and Miscellaneous Repertory* 1 (1808): 67–69. See also *The British Cicero; or, A Selection of the Most Admired Speeches in the English Language* (London, 1808), vol. 3: 17–20.

Trenton (New Jersey) *Federalist*

Monday, July 3, 1809

From the account of the proceedings of the May Sessions, 1809, at Charleston, (S.C.) before his honor Judge Smith, we select, without comment, the two following articles.

"James Hutton, FOR KILLING A NEGRO, Fined 50 pounds!!!

"George Burrows and Robert Welch, *Negro Stealing*—TO BE HANGED!!! on Friday the 23rd day of June, between the hours of 12 and 2 o'clock."[1]

1. James Hutton, a Charleston resident who owned six slaves in 1800. See US Census, 1800, South Carolina, Charleston, roll 48, p. 114, NA. He may be the factor identified as living on South Bay Street in Richard Hrabowski, *Directory for the District of Charleston . . .* (Charleston, SC, 1809), 45. No South Carolina slaveholders named George Burrows or Robert Welch appear in the US Census.

New-York Evening Post

Friday, March 30, 1810

Apprehended Insurrection of the Blacks. The Editors of the Boston Patriot, have received from a correspondent in Augusta, Georgia, the following copy of a letter from General Thomas Blount,[1] of North Carolina, to the Hon. J. Milledge,[2] of Georgia. Mr. M. spread the information, and it excited much alarm, and occasioned great preparations for security. The communicator says, "the letter of "Captain James" is but a small evidence of the disposition of the blacks in this part of the country."

Tarborough, March 26, 1810

Dear Sir—I have this moment (8 o'clock at night) received a letter from a negro in Greene county, Georgia, to a negro in Martin county, North Carolina, calculated, if genuine, and so it appears to be, to induce a belief that a general insurrection is seriously contemplated. The letter is in the following words:

"Dear Sir—I received your letter to the forteenth of June, 1809, with great freedom and joy to hear and understand what great proceedance you have made, and the resolution your have in proceeding on in business as we have undertook, and hope you will still continue in the same mind. We have spread the ruse nearly over the continent in our part of the country, and have the day when we are to fall to work, and you must be sure not to fail on that day, and that is the 22d April, to begin about midnight, and do the work at home first, and then take the armes of them you slay first, and that will strengthen us more in armes—for freedom we want and will have, for we have served this cruel land long enuff, & be as secret convaing your nose as possabel, and be sure to send it by some cearfull band, and if it happens to be discovered, fail not in the day, for we are full abel to conquer by any means.—Sir, I am your captain James, living in the state of Jorgy, in Green county—so no more at present, but remaining your sincer friend and captain until death."

Directed to "Cornell Luces, North Carolina, in Martin county, near Roanoak river."

Exum Lewis, Esq. a gentleman of character, who conveyed this letter to me, informs

me, "that it was lately found in the road in Halifax county, near James Moore's store, and that another was found with it, dated in Tennessee, and directed to Brunswick county, Virgina, purporting nearly the same in substance, and agreeing exactly as to the time fixed on for the purpose of carrying the scheme into effect."—I have considered it my duty to give this information, and have only time to add, as the hour for closing the mail has already arrived, that I hope you will so use it as to prevent the meditated mischief.—I am your most obedient servant.
THOMAS BLOUNT.

1. General Thomas Blount (1759–1812) was a member of the Twelfth Congress at the time of his death. See Charles Rodenbough, *Governor Alexander Martin: Biography of a North Carolina Revolutionary War Statesman* (Jefferson, NC: McFarland, 2004), 158. Blount was incorrectly identified as a former governor of North Carolina by Justice William Johnson Jr. in his 1822 essay, *Melancholy Effect of Popular Excitement,* reprinted on pp. 131–33 in Part II of this volume.

2. John Milledge (1757–1818) served as Georgia's governor from 1802 to 1806 and in both the US House of Representatives and Senate.

Pittsfield (Massachusetts) *Berkshire Reporter*

Tuesday, March 26, 1811

"*All men are born free and equal.*—

"*Liberty and Equality forever,*" are the constant cries of the southern Jeffersonians. A late Charleston paper gives the following specimen of the kind of Liberty & Equality they mean—"At a late Court of Sessions, David Matthews was *fined 50l* for [only] KILLING A NEGRO."

Charleston *City Gazette and Commercial Daily Advertiser*

Monday, January 22, 1816

IN THE COURT OF GENERAL SESSIONS, CHARLESTON DISTRICT. . . .

The Grand Jury further present as a most serious evil, the many instances of *Negro Homicide,* which have been committed within the city for many years. The parties exercising unlimited control, as masters and mistresses, in the indulgence of their malignant and cruel passions in the barbarous treatment of slaves, using them worse than beast of burdens, and thereby bringing on the community, the state, and the city, the contumely and opprobrium of the civilized world.

John Cordes Prioleau, Foreman[1]
[15 other signatures]

1. John Cordes Prioleau (1772–1825) was the owner of Peter Prioleau, later Peter Desverney, who would be the first to reveal the plot to white authorities in May 1822. This grand jury presentment suggests one reason why Peter regarded his owner as a kind master.

Grand Jury Presentment, 1818

. . . We would also respectfully bring into view of the Legislature the inadequacy of the punishment attached to the crime in preventing persons of malignant dispositions from murdering slaves, it has of late occurred often—and in our opinion he that wilfully murders a slave is as bad and ought to be equally punished with him who murders a freeman.

Presentment, Kershaw District, 1818, no. 8, series S165010, SCDAH.

Charleston Courier

Tuesday, June 30, 1818
FOR THE COURIER

From the report of the committee appointed by the Legislature of this State, during the session of 1816, "to enquire if it be expedient to alter the penal code of this state, &c." it appears that the convictions in this state for "penitentiary offences," from the year 1810 to 1815, were in a decreased ratio to those of the ten preceding years. Knowing the high character of the gentlemen who composed that committee, the talents and indefatigable industry of the chairman, I have no reason to doubt the correctness of their report. But notwithstanding the convictions of the years included between 1810 and 1815 were in a *decreased* ratio to those of the ten years next preceding, I believe the *commission* of crimes was in an *increased* ratio. . . .

There are persons in the parish in which I reside, who, within a year, have killed negro slaves by severe whipping and other barbarous treatment—have stolen horses, cattle and hogs, and committed forgery; and are now running at large unapprehended. . . .

James Tallmadge,[1] Speech in Congress, Tuesday, February 16, 1819

. . . Sir, I have since received, through the post office, a letter, post marked in South Carolina and signed "A native of England," desiring that when I again had occasion to repeat my boast against England, I would also state that she had atoned for her original sin, by establishing in her slave colonies a system of humane laws, ameliorating their condition, and providing for their safety, while America had committed the secondary sin of disregarding their condition, and had even provided laws by which it was not murder to kill a slave. Sir I felt the severity of the reproof; I felt for my country. I have enquired on the subject, and I find such were formerly the laws in some of the slaveholding States; and that even now, in the State of South Carolina, by law, the penalty of death is provided for stealing a slave, while the murder of a slave is punished by a trivial fine. Such, sir, is the contrast and the relative value which is placed, in the opinion of a slaveholding State, between the property of the master and the life of a slave. . . .

1. James Tallmadge Jr. (1778–1853) was a New York attorney and politician. Elected to Congress to fill the uncompleted term of the deceased Henry B. Lee, Tallmadge served from June 6, 1817, to March 3, 1819. A Republican but a supporter of former governor George Clinton, Tallmadge agreed with those who believed southern slaveholders and agrarian interests unfairly dominated

his party, and in February 1819 he gave a fiery speech dedicated to keeping slavery from expanding into the proposed state of Missouri. His antislavery amendments to the enabling bill for Missouri's admission to statehood sparked the most momentous national debate on slavery since the founding. See Robert P. Forbes, *The Missouri Compromise and Its Aftermath: Slavery and the Meaning of America* (Chapel Hill: University of North Carolina Press, 2007), 35–53.

"Admission of Missouri," *Annals of Congress,* House of Representatives, Fifteenth Congress, Second Session, 1211–22.

Charleston Courier

Saturday, June 5, 1819

TO THE EDITOR OF THE COURIER.

SIR—On my way to this city, from a short tour through the interior of this state, a few days ago, 20 miles west of Columbia, I was suddenly attracted to a spot of earth, over which a respectable company of citizens were deeply intent, on witnessing the exhumation of the body of an animal, costing $1200;—but which its humane owner, (one Kelly) and three other persons like minded, had seized and tied to a tree at midnight—and each, in turn, wantonly whipt until sunrise, when, from incessant lashing, its bowels gushed out, and it expired, and was instantly buried in a private corner, on Sunday the 23d ult. But on enquiry, the said *animal* proved to be of the *Negro,* and by some was thought to be of the *human* species: and stood "guilty of having a skin not coloured like our own"—an offence, for which these arbiters of life and death, doomed it to die! To their honor it should be told that, when fainting, they threw cold water on its face, and poured whiskey down its throat, in order to *prolong* the sport—it, however, for several minutes before it was untied, became *speechless* and motionless as the tree to which it was bound—it could feel, and writhe, and smart under the merciless lash *no longer.*

Good God! exclaimed I, *where* am I? On the earth which thou hast created and didst once pronounce blessed? or in the Pandemonium of the heathen?—Heaven, I knew, it could not be, for a cruel task-master, his hands embrued in human blood, had just crossed my path! Is it then, continued I, *free* America, and an asylum for the distressed and oppressed of all other lands—the land of my adored Washington—the adopted country of my dearest friends—the *only* country on this huge cursed earth where liberty finds an ark, or rest for the sole of her pained foot—and the country to which I came with every fond prejudice and predilection. What, *free,* and yet offer up human sacrifice! Monstrous anomaly! Go, fly these hasty lines through the world. Challenge offended humanity to produce a spectacle more *genuinely hellish,* or so *purely demoniacal*! Did, Sir, ever a Sabbath sun dawn on a catastrophe so horribly abhorrent to your feelings, or those of, Sir, your most obedient servant.

W. FAUX.[1]

Planter's Hotel. Charleston, June 2, 1819.

1. William Faux, possibly the nom de plume of an antislavery English gentryman, arrived in the United States in 1819 and spent several weeks during the summer in Charleston. He visited again in 1820 and departed under the name "W. Faux" on board the ship *President,* Sunday, April 3, 1820.

He published a traveler's account: *Memorable Days in America: Being a Journal of a Tour to the United States*... (London, 1823), which, 73–91, discusses his inflammatory article in the *Charleston Courier* and the response by elite Charlestonians to it. See also *Charleston Courier*, April 4, 1820.

Charleston Courier

Wednesday, June 9, 1819

TO W. FAUX

To W. Faux, Planters Hotel.

The conclusions which will be drawn from your letter in the *Courier* of yesterday, in many parts of the world you have sent it forth to, are, that in the Southern states, negroes are not considered as human creatures, but that, as they are of a different complexion, they are looked upon in the same light with brute beasts—that is horses, mules, or horned cattle; and that as the brute creation are cruelly treated negroes are so likewise. Many will take pleasure in your publication, and give it as evidence, that the treatment of Kelly's negro is a common occurrence in South-Carolina. That we have amongst us men, and *women too*, capable of great cruelty, nobody will deny; but that animals of any description are, in general, cruelly treated, and particularly that negroes are often subject to such severity, neither you nor any other person can pretend to say.

You have been it appears in the interior of the state, and whatever may be your standing in your own country, must have had an opportunity of seeing the general mode of treating our slaves—Can you, sir, say that they fare worse than the lower orders of society, in many countries you may have traveled into? or, that they have not great means of comfort, and even happiness?

I call upon you, sir, to say whether you are or are not satisfied, that the negroes of this state and of all the Southern states, are on the whole *well treated*; and if you are, then to give an equal publicity to said declaration, as you have to your story of the animal, "guilty of having a skin not colored like our own!" If on the contrary, you think otherwise, and you will make your opinion public, the planters of this state will convince you, and the world, of your error, and that it is not necessary for strangers to take such steps as you have done, to bring to punishment the infamous perpetrators of such cruelty.

Many parts of the Northern states, (for one of which I depart to-morrow) are under strong prejudices on these heads, arising from misrepresentation. You, sir, may help to do them away, and that philanthropy which has induced you to come forward, with so little reflection may yet tend to shew you are a friend to justice as well as humanity.

A South-Carolina Planter. June 7.

Charleston City Ordinance, Tuesday, July 6, 1819

An ORDINANCE, entitled an Ordinance, amending the twenty-third section of an Ordinance, commonly called the Negro Ordinance. (Ratified 6th July, 1819)

WHEREAS, public decorum, and due observance of public decency, are at all times worthy of the attention of this Council; and, whereas, the twenty-third section of an

Ordinance, commonly called the Negro Ordinance, had been found inefficient to secure these objects:—

1. *Be it ordained,* That if any negro or person of colour shall be guilty of speaking aloud any blasphemous or indecent words, or crying out in a blasphemous, obscene, or indecent manner, such negro or free person of colour shall receive, at the Work House or Public Market, such a number of stripes, not exceeding twenty, as any Warden of the City shall adjudge.

2. That, from and after the passage of this Ordinance, it shall not be lawful for any slaves or person of colour whatsoever, assembled at the corner of the streets, or at other places, at any time, to make any loud or offensive conversations, under the pain of receiving for each offence, correction at the Work-House, of not more than twenty, nor less than five stripes, as may be ordered by the Committee of Council for the time being, attending at the Guard-House: *Provided,* That if the owner of such slave, or guardian of such free person of colour, shall pay the sum of not less than one, nor more than five dollars, for the use of the city; and that in such case, it shall be at the discretion of such Warden, to remit the corporal punishment of such slave or free person of colour.

Charleston City Ordinance, Ratified Monday, August 16, 1819

An ORDINANCE, entitled an Ordinance, to alter and amend so much of the 24th section of an Ordinance, entitled Ordinance, to define the power and duties of the Commissioners of STREETS and LAMPS, in the City of Charleston, and for other purposes therein mentioned, passed the 20th November, 1816, as relates to persons not permitted to game in any street, &c.

1. *Be it ordained,* That it shall not be lawful for any coloured person, or negro, whether free or a slave, to play at any place whatever within the City of Charleston, at any game or games, with cards or dice, or at any gaming table, commonly called ABC or EO, or at any gaming table known or distinguished by any other letters or any figures, or Roley Poley table, or at Rouge and Noir, or at any Faro Bank, or at any other table or bank of the same or the like kind, under any denomination whatever, or to bet on the sides or hands of such as do game, under the penalty of receiving any number of lashes not exceeding twenty, to be adjudged by two or more Wardens of the City: *Provided,* That the Wardens shall be authorised to commute the corporal punishment for a fine not exceeding fifty dollars. . . .

A Collection of the Ordinances of the City Council of Charleston: from the Twenty-Eighth of September, 1818, to the Twelfth of August, 1823 (Charleston, SC, 1823), 9–10, 12.

Charleston Courier

Saturday, October 9, 1819

A Jury of Inquest was held on the body of a female Negro Slave, about four miles above this place, on Sunday evening. After mature deliberation, the Jury returned a verdict of murder by her owner, Christiana Hornsby.[1]

If the decision of the Jury be correct, (and we have very little reason to doubt it) who will not say, let the murderer be brought to condign punishment? And yet we scarcely know how this could be done. Strangers must feel an indignant horror on being told that so glaringly and scandalously defective is the law of South-Carolina, on this point, that a murderer of the worst kind, who has destroyed his victim where there is no power of appeal or resistance, may escape with impunity, or at least by paying a paltry sum, which would scarcely defray the funeral expences of a man of ordinary standing. Shame on the framers of such a law! We repeat it, in behalf of justice and humanity—shame to the man, who could be so far influenced by interest and prejudice as to give his voice in favor of a law which would be a disgrace to any country! We could wish to hear this echoed, and loudly echoed, from one end of the state to the other, until those who have taken an active part in supporting this measure should blush at their proceedings, and hasten, as far as they are able, to consign to oblivion an act, which carries disgrace and infamy on the very face of it.

1. Probably Christina Hornsby (1770–1859), wife of Henry Hornsby of Richland District near Columbia. See 1850 US Census, District, Richland, South Carolina, roll M432-858, p. 74B, image 154.

Grand Jury Presentment, November, 1819

1st We the grand Jury in and for the district aforesaid do present as a grievance highly derogatory to the character of the State, and disgraceful to humanity, that murdering a slave is punished with a pecuniary fine only; & recommend to the consideration of the legislature the Propriety of making Capital such murder in the first degree, and of increasing the punishment in cases of murder in the second degree and of killing by undue correction, & in that of passion. . . . 8th We present as a grievance that the existing laws do not sufficiently protect the owners of Slaves from having that valuable part of their property wantonly abused and crippled by loose and Licentious men who very often do not possess sufficient property from which compensation can be obtained by law either for their being so maimed, or for the loss of their services whilst disabled. An Evil we find to be fast increasing, notwithstanding the many presentments of the Grand Juries of this district on this subject.

Presentment, Kershaw District, November (no date), 1819, no. 5, series S165010, SCDAH.

Charleston Courier

Saturday, November 27, 1819

Message from the Governor.[1]

. . . Our penal code, it is hoped, will not escape your notice. The experience which has been had of the penitentiary system is not so satisfactory as to justify me in recommending its adoption; and as our sister state, Georgia, is trying it, I think we shall act wisely in waiting the result of her experiment. In the mean time it is proper that we should give to our present system all the improvement of which is susceptible, taking care to preserve always a just proportion between crimes and punishments. I know of no law in which this proportion has been so much disregarded as in that for the killing of a slave by a white man—Its inflictions for this offence are so very inadequate to the demands of justice, that our state has suffered in its reputation for humanity. The rules of justice require that the punishment for murder should be the same in all cases; and it is to be observed, that a slave, being deprived of his natural right of self-defence against a white man, the killing of him by the latter receives from this circumstance additional aggravation. If, however, from considerations arising out of the situation of our country, it should be deemed inexpedient to apply these rules to the case of a slave, it is confidently believed there can be no well grounded objection to the annexing of other severer penalties to the commission of this barbarous deed.—The extension of the benefit of a trial by jury, to consist of citizens, to this class of persons, for offences affecting life or limb, seems practicable, and as conformable to the dictates of justice as it is in unison with the feelings of humanity. . . .

1. John Geddes (1777–1828) served as governor of South Carolina 1818–20 and as Charleston's intendant (mayor), 1824–25. See Yates Snowden and Harry Gardner Cutler, eds., *History of South Carolina,* 5 vols. (Chicago: Lewis Publishing, 1920), vol. 1: 550.

New England Galaxy & Masonic Magazine

Friday, March 3, 1820

MURDER. A Letter from Camden. S.C. dated 17th inst. mentions the following horrible transaction.

"We have had a murder committed in this place, which for atrocity, is unprecedented in the annals of villany. It was the act of John Harris, upon his own slave, a woman. It appears the slave was sick, confined to her bed and unable to work. He went to her hut at the lower end of the town, about 12 at night, dragged her from her bed, and beat her in a most unmerciful manner; then got a rope, one end of which he tied round her neck, and the other round the neck of his horse, and dragged her about the streets, till she was apparently dead. He then built a fire upon her and left her. The only witnesses of this diabolical act were two poor old women, who could do nothing in defence of the victim. The murderer was apprehended next morning, and bound over to make his appearance to next court." A bailable offence!![1]

1. Enslaved recruiter Charles Drayton later used such cases to convince other bondmen to join the 1822 conspiracy, telling potential rebels such as George Parker that Carolina whites planned "to make an alarm of fire and then to kill all the blacks." See Parker's trial in Part III of this volume.

Charleston Courier

Wednesday, May 3, 1820

Letters from Aux Cayes[1] mention, that President Boyer has completely quelled the insurrection occasioned by the revolt of Gen. Gomaz. . . . Boyer has an army of about

25,000 men, regularly officered and disciplined, who are eager to take the field. The finances of this Chief are also in a flourishing condition.

N.Y. Gaz. 24th *ult.*

1. A port town in southwestern Haiti.

Charleston Courier

Monday, August 7, 1820

COMMUNICATION.

Mr. Editor.—I wish to enquire, through the medium of your paper, by whose license or authority a gang of Negroes, or Mulattoes, are so frequently of late, permitted at all hours of the night, to disturb the peace and quiet of this community, under the pretence of *Serenading*!—Between two and three o'clock this morning, the neighborhood in which I reside, was assailed for nearly an hour, by one of these gangs, rending the air with their vile discordant attempts at *music*, accompanied by an obscene song, and the most boisterous talking and laughing. If a stop is not put to this annoyance, by those whose duty it is to attend to the quiet of the city, it is the determination of the residents in my neighborhood, to break the heads of these caterwaulers with their own instruments, should the imposition be repeated. A CITIZEN.

Sunday Morning, August 6, 1820.

Elizabeth A. Yates[1] to Harrison Gray Otis,[2] Saturday, September 30, 1820

Charleston

Respected Sir

What but a Subject of such great Magnitude & of so much Distress & Inquietude to the Humane & Benevolent as Slavery would excuse the Liberty of a Stranger addressing you & Intruding upon time which no Doubt has its alloted duty for every hour, but this great Subject which has engaged the attention of all good Great & Humane Men in the Union has given me much Concern & deep reflection. In our happy Republic each Private Individual must feel an Interest in the Question & it is in this Enlightened Age that Females know they are Equal & respected In Society, I am no Politician & pretend to know but Little of the Affairs of the Nations, but I am a Mother of four Sons & two Daughters whose Lot with that of their Excellent Father & my own has been cast in a Slave State, Your Great Philanthropy Honoured Sir with the Names of many other Worthy ones has not gone unnoticed, I feel convinced the Day is Coming & I sometimes flatter myself has come when all who feel for those oppressed wronged injured Human Beings must use every prudent exertion & Zeal in their Behalf. I must now inform you we own between 40 & 50 of those unfortunate fellow Mortals which Conscience has ever whispered to both my Husband & Self that it was & is Injustice & oppression of the greatest Magnitude we will & have allways owned & I flatter myself no Candid Honest Man but will do the Same, let Interest Say what it will Conscience will do its Duty, our Interest Relatives and all is Cast in a Southern State yet with a Large Family & Quite a

Moderate Competency we have made up our minds not to entail our Slaves which at a reasonable Calculation we estimate as having cost 25 or 30 Thousand Dollars & it is our great wish (& is now under the particular attention of our Attorney) to Cautiously Emancipate them, the accomplishment of which I can with Christian Candor Say is one of the first Wishes of my heart & you cannot Conceive the Dificulties our Laws have put in the way, & our next Legislature anticipate Passing Such Laws as will allmost Amount to an exclusion indeed they wish to exsclude all Free Poeple of Color from our State (may God in his Infinite Mercy Soften their hearts to those already Suffering Patient Poeple) Our Country Men at the North think they know the Evil of Slavery but be assured you cannot even Concieve them. If we who know & See it would disinterestedly & Candidly tell you half of them from what I Judge of you from Your Public Character you would Say Let my every exertion & every Talent be Zealously used against that hedious Monster Slavery, you must well know that it would take Volumes & the Pen of a ready Writer to Describe them, what then can a weak unimproved Female hope to do farther than Candidly if it meets your approbation as one of the Same great Family to Describe to you Some of their Sufferings, hoping that it may Interest the feelings of some Oh that it could be all of our great statesmen of each state to use their Abilities in forming Judicious Plans for a Gradual But General Emancipation, I am happy to Inform you that the Enlightened Male & Female now view it in a very Diferent light to what they did a few years ago & the rising Generation I anxiously hope will Wipe away Some of our foul Stains I have a Son of 16 years of age at the South Carolina Colledge who is now on a visit to us, who when I am Using my feeble exertions to Influence the Young & Tender Minds of my Children says 'Mother, I am Proud to tell you we are allmost unanimous at Colledge in allowing the Injustice of it—we see plainly the great Evil & the only Question we hope will soon be how & which is the way to remidy this great affliction.' But I can Say more I hear & Converse with some of our wisest men their opinion is generally that it is injustice & oppression & the greatest evil we could of ever had entailed on us, well if we acknowledge thus far will we still entail it & go on to Add Injustice to Injustice Injury to Injury Heaven forbid, I wish I could find words to Describe to you my anxious feelings on this great Subject, when I have conversed with some sensible good Man who gives me hope the Day is Rising of Emancipation, my Joy is beyond Description, on the other side if I hear it the Opinion of a Sensible Man that there is no Prospect of that happy period, I am as much Distressed nay more than I can Possibly paint, only Let us Conceive than Slave States have what we term Slave Laws, & will South Carolina ever forget a *Slater* a wicked wretched man, nay I cannot say Man, but rather Monster of that name that ordered his unfortunate Slave to put his head on a Block when the Master chopped it Off & when this inhuman Wretch was tried in our Supposed Court of Justice & found Guilty he turned Round took Coolly out his Pocket Book, gave the Judge the fine & no doubt would do the same again for he did not even hear as he should of done from a Virtuous Poeple the Hiss of Shame that happened only a few years ago, & only a very few Days ago & a few Miles from our City was found a Black Woman of Middle Age Dead in the woods with a *Mouth Piece* on & a pair of *hand Cuffs* the unfortunate Sufferer had Crawled from her oppressors Inclosure & expired in the woods, her owner is known he is of no

Respectability, but what is done Nothing but an endeavour to bury the Crime with the Body, & it is not even Bublickly noticed for fear it should be known at the North but the great Question is, is there not the Eye of an all seeing Just God upon us & does not our Land Mourn on account of such atrocious acts, I dare not use Language sufficiently Strong to paint this & many other Deeds arising out of the great evil Slavery, the great Injury to us I must with much more if it meets your approbation Leave for another opportunity, I am sorry to tell you that many Persons from the North when they come here & find it to their Convenience & Interest to own them they then do so & advocate the horrid Crime of Enslaving a set of men to whom we pretend no Right but that thay are a Defenceless Nation who have injured us but our Strenght can overcome their Right, Dreadfull unjust inhumane Conduct, I was wishing the other Day that I Dared Commence a Correspondence with some of our Enlightened States men in the North when Mr Coleburn to whom I addressed myself Mentioned that he could answer for it that you would reply to a Letter upon that all important & Benevolent Question & the Subject of this Letter is my Apology for this great Liberty if you should so far honour me, I would feel much Oblidged the Question is do you in your Sound Judgment & Deep Council see any hope & have you seen any plan that would give Light upon this Important Subject how the thing can be done Wisely, I have had from a very Respectable Wealthy Friend in Philadelphia several Phamplets against Slavery which have been carefully read & by some Deeply Interested in that Property, When I delight to tell you the Question is how can the thing be done, only put us in the way, dont throw us out of bread suddenly but we see the Injustice & evil of it & only want the Prudent Plan The Ideas of my Country Men are improving & getting much & happily Enlightened on the Subject, for Certainly as we get moral Improvement, we must abhor oppression, should you favor me with an opening I will say more to you, for I am a Native of S Carolina but cannot love its Laws, I love my Country its honour is Dear to me & will love my Native State when it acts Justly & loves Mercy, our evils are innumerable & although I must acknowledge in many Respects the Situation of our Slaves are ameliorated still much Cruelty exists & our Legislature is still going I fear to add to this already Distressed State, but it is what they Deam Nesessary for our Preservation only Conceive what a State we live in, you hear Nothing of our Slaves attemps to Rise which is Frequently the Case in the Country when 8 10 or 12 is hung gibbeted or Burnt for what, for what we would Commend in our Color Resisting oppression how must those men feel who Condemn them to awefull Deaths they can Certainly not think of a State of Final Retribution Many very Many never think on the Subject so does Interest Guide them but I hope our Wise Congress may Rouse them to think & feel too on this great Subject, of so much Consequence to the Whole Nation for such a Blot on a part ought to Interest the Whole, although the General feeling is that the Northern States should not Interfere but I think they are Bound to do good & must feel an Interest in the Republic Generally, I wish the Pieces Written on the Subject would be addressed to our Humanity Justice & Benevolent feelings for I flatter myself we possess many, & not in Reproaches I think the former mentioned mode would have the best effect, there was a Piece in the Panoplist some little time ago which gave great umbrage I did not myself disapprove of it for I think the Truth ought to be spread from Pole to Pole, but the Northern Papers or Phamplets are not Generally read I wish there could be some Prudent Devised Means used to address the State Generally in an Eloquent feeling Manner on the Subject I feel assured much Good could be Done, I am sorry to say that a Gentlemen Bearing the Name of a Clergyman from your State whose Name Delicacy forbids me Mention came here he was taken to one of our Sea Islands shewn one of the Drivers Houses & their situation Favorably represented to him he occationally Preached in a Unitarian Church in this City & really did much in favor of the Present State of things he gained Favor of a few Planters but be assured the Good of our Community Detest his Conduct he plainly shewed he wished to please Men, for not one that owns slaves have I ever heard sufficiently hard hearted as to say things were as they should be, & had that Gentleman reflected for a Moment did the same Planter that told their desirable situations tell or shew his Places of Correction shew his Stocks his Billows tell that at one season they work in the field untill dark & they Gin Cotton until 12 Oclock at night, or does any of our Nothern Visitors to our City know that we have a house of Correction w[h]ere Indelicate & severe Punishments go on Daily nay all Day, we own them we accuse them we Judge them we Punish them now can any Sincere Man, & Particularly a Pious Minister of the Gospell Compliment such a State of Society I hope he has poor Man repented I am sure the time will come when he will Lament his unmerited flattery, many of our Slaves are made Comfortably & kindly Treated but that is not the General Case, & Interest is our great Guide their Winter Cloths are generally given to Prevent Colds & plurisys but not one Planter in ten in twenty gives a summer Suit & as to under Garments they never get, a Jacket Trousers & Shoes in Winter every third year a Blanket & would God I could hope that that allways was given but I know to the Contrary, some few again receive more, but the General evil exceeds Description we will say nothing at Present of the seperation of Parent & Child Husband & Wife Brother & Sister, which Frequently takes Place, their Constant fear of a Change of Masters is sufficient Cause of misery the Death of a good Master is Distressing, if those who say Negroes as they are Generally call'd have no feeling could see them at the Death of a Benevolent feeling Owner, they would Change their opinions I have knwon them Grieve Longer than their Mistress & Longern than a son then Frequently to make a Division or to Pay Debts those unfortunates are sold seperated & get into Wicked hands, I must stop my feelings get too much exercised, I have Just read a Letter from Savannah they are in a Dreadfull State the City Deserted from the fear of an awefull Disease[3] & the Mortality has been great beyond what will be Puplished & the few that is Left under Dreadfull fear of insurrection Georgia a few years ago made cruel Laws & although I feel convin[c]ed this isnt the world of rewards & Punishments yet their Capital Savannah has & is Drinking Deeply of the Cup of Affliction I remain with sincere wishes for the wellfare of yourself & Family Your most Obedient Humble Servant

Elizabeth A. Yates

PS You will exscuse all errors for when I get upon this Subject I forget everything but the Distressing Subject, I often Lament being a Spoiled Child & of a Delicate Constitution so that my Education was almost entirely Neglected but if I could but be Instrumental in doing something for those unfortunates I shall not think I have lived in Vain, & no Days of my Life have given me so much pleasure as the Days that I have had my Carriage got at 6 in the morning & not returned home untill 4 to Dinner to get a Punishment remitted If you see any hope of a better Day your Communication will be Joyfully thankfully Received

1. Elizabeth Ann Saylor Yates (1787–1867) was the wife of Charleston native Joseph Yates (1775–1822). Both Elizabeth and Joseph were members of Benjamin Morgan Palmer's Circular (Congregational) Church. See "Register of the Independent Congregational (Circular) Church of Charleston S.C., 1784–1815," *SCHGM* 33 (1932): 306–16. He was also a member of the Charleston Grand Jury in 1809 and signed the 1820 petition in support of the African Church. Three of his slaves—Bellisle, Naphur, and Adam—were hanged on July 26, 1822.

2. When Elizabeth Yates sent her letter to Harrison Gray Otis (1765–1848), he was an antislavery Federalist serving Massachusetts in the US Senate. During the debate about the admission of Missouri to statehood, he had spoken conspicuously against the extension of slavery.

3. In 1820, Savannah suffered its first major outbreak of yellow fever. More than 600 died in a population of 7,500. See Joseph Waring, "The Yellow Fever Epidemic of Savannah in 1820," *Georgia Historical Quarterly* 52 (December 1968): 398–404.

Typescript letter, Yates Papers, SCHS.

Grand Jury Presentment, October 1820

. . . We present as a great Grievance the number of free Mulattoes & negroes now in this State; and the increasing numbers of such persons from other States: being induced thereto from the facility of settling amongst us & who generally are from their idle habits a bad example to our Domestics & a growing evil to our State; we would therefore recommend that a similar Law to that which exists in one of our stisters states be enacted for their better government.

We recommend that the Legislature pass a Law respecting the one now of force, making the punishment for murdering a negro slave only of a pecuniary nature & that they enact a Law instead thereof; more consistant with humanity & the dignity of the State. . . .

James Lowndes Foreman[1]

1. James Lowndes (1769–1839), trained in law, owned multiple properties and more than a hundred slaves in 1820. *CSCCD*, 88, identifies him in 1822 as a planter with a residence at 14 Meeting Street. See also *BDSCHR* 4: 356–57.

Presentment, Charleston District, October 6, 1820, no. 3, series S165010, SCDAH. See also *Camden Gazette and Mercantile Advertiser*, November 9, 1820.

Petition, October 1820[1]

South Carolina

To the honorable the Speaker and Members of the house of Representatives, The humble petition of the undersigned Respectfully, sheweth that,

Your petitioners have seen with anxious concern the number of Free Negroes and coloured people, who have migrated into this State from various quarters, and when the late Legislative Acts of Virginia and Georgia, are duly considered as relates to these people, your petitioners have every reason to apprehend a daily increase of this alarming evil, to prevent which Your petitioners pray Your honorable body to interdict by the most energetick Laws all free Negroes and coloured people from migrating into this State, hereafter from any neighboring State or slave state, such as have already migrated into this State from any neighbouring State whatever, or elsewhere within the last five years may be Banished. And your petitioners further pray your honorable Body to prohibit all persons whatever, hereafter, from emancipating his or her slave or slaves, unless such emancipated slave or slaves, shall within twelve months after such emancipation leave the State.

Your petitioners beg leave to invite the attention of the Legislature to other existing evils, in communicating which they have first to state, that a spacious Building has lately been erected in the immediate neighbourhood of Charleston for the *exclusive* worship of Negroes and coloured people, from means supplied them by Abolition Societies in the Eastern and Northern States, as your petitioners are credibly informed, this Establishment is no less impolitick than unnecessary in as much as ample accommodation is, and has always been provided and afforded the Negroes and coloured people in the numerous Churches and places of Publick worship in the City of Charleston and its neighbourhood.—Another evil equally impolitick, is that of permitting our free Negroes and coloured people, to visit the Eastern States for *Ordination* and other religious pretences and again returning. Your petitioners pray your honorable Body, that all free Negroes and coloured persons (seamen and servants excepted) who shall hereafter leave this State shall be prohibited by Law, from ever returning.

Another evil, and one of the greatest magnitude, is that of suffering Schools or assemblages of negroes slaves to be taught reading and writing, organised and conducted not only by Negroes and colored people and in some instances by white persons of this State, But it is well known, during the last Winter, that several *Missionary School-Master's* or teachers arrived in Charleston from Philadelphia amply furnished with pecuniary means by Abolition Societies of that State, for the avowed purpose of educating our Negroes. Your petitioners are aware that there is an Act of the Legislature of this State forbidding Negroes being taught to write, but th[e] Act is silent as to their being taught to read, which is easier attained, equally mischevious and impolitick and at variance with slavery. In communicating these serious evils, your petitioners forbear from accompanying these with observations which would be no less judicious than unnecessary, as they cause reflections that cannot escape Your honourable Body, they are briefly narrated in the confident expectation that the remedy will be no less prompt than ample.

And your petitioners as in duty bound will ever pray.

Charleston 16 October 1820

Micah Jenkins	W[m] Mathewes
Ja[s] Lowndes	John Axson
W. Dawson	R. W. Vanderhorst
Charles P. Dawson	E. Haskell

B Elliott
Thomas B. Seabrook
B. D. Roper
Thos Wigfall
J. J. Darrell
Benjn Seabrook
Robert J. Turnbull
Charles W. Bulow
States Gist
Jn Huger
Morton A. Waring
Jeremiah A. Yates
George Edwards
Thomas Barksdale
Ch^{s} Graves
Peter Gaillard Junr
J. H.Stevens
Thomas Ham
Jn Duffus
John Johnson
James D. Mitchell
James Jervey
D. Jennings Waring
George Rivers
Edwin C. Holland
Isaac Parker
Joseph Manigault
Wm Logan
Wm M. Smith
H. Smith
John S. Brisbane
Barnard E. Bee
J. C. Martindale
Elias Horry
John Horlbeck
David Deas
John Ashe
John Dawso
Robert Little
W Lee
Alex. Gillon
Richard B. North
R Osborn
States Rutledge
John Bryan
James F. Edwards
Robt Deas
Maurice Simons
Jn Harleston
J Drayton
Henry P. Holmes
Edward Blake Lining
Ch^{s} Lining
Henry M. Parker
John Parker Junr
Thomas Napier
John S. Cogdell
E. H. Bay
John Cordes Prioleau
John E. Poyas
James Poyas
Peter Smith
Philip Gendron Prioleau
Ben^{n} Fuller
W. Roper
Wm Dewees Junr
Richard A. Allan
Robert W. Mazyck
Benjn S. Dart
Isaac M. Wilson
John Holmes
Joshua Lockwood
Benj. B. Smith
Samuel Patterson
James Ferguson
Sam. Ferguson
Wm Warley
James Ross
James Rutledge
Arth^{r} G. Rose
John C. Duke
Sims White
Daniel Webb
Barnard Elliott
Chas Rowan
Geo. Perman

John E. Farr
W H Miller
William Elfe
Theodore Gaillard
B. Gaillard
William Mazyck Jr.
Richard W. Cogdell
Arthur Middleton

Ch. B. Cochran
Wm Price Junr
J. Righton
W B Minott
Ed Simons
Robt Bentham
Wm Hassell Gibbes
Henry Laurens
Joshua W. Toomer
Robt Hazlehurst
William Perroneau
Wm Drayton
J. H. Manigault
William Read
Josiah Taylor
Chas Kershaw
John Stoney
E. Thayer
A. B. Miller

Geo. Chisolm
Thomas Scott
Henry O'Hara
Henry H. Bacot
W. L. Smith
Tho. W. Bacot
James R. Pringle
Joseph Winthrop
A Henry
Richard Yeadon
William B. Foster
F. G. Deliesseline
W. F. Shackelford
Fredk Rutledge
John Woddrop
Thomas Morris
J. Mair
Edward Harleston
Tho Rogers
John J. Pringle
Geo Warren Cross
T Ford
Ed Mortimer
Jn Fraser
Thos Smith Jun
John Magrath
A. S. Willington

1. More than 140 whites, the majority of them slaveholding planters, signed this petition, calling for a crackdown on black liberties. The names, transcribed here as they appeared on the document, overlap considerably with the names of those individuals involved in the creation of the South Carolina Association in the aftermath of the discovery of the Vesey plot. (See Part IV for additional information.) George Cross (1783–1836), a French-speaking attorney who was then Vesey's landlord, would serve as defense counsel at Vesey's trial. Dr. John Earnest Poyas Jr. (1759–1824) owned Abraham, who would be transported, and James Poyas (1790–1872) owned Peter Poyas, who was hanged on July 2. As noted above on p. 44 n1, John Cordes Prioleau (1772–1825) owned Peter, the first slave to reveal the plot. Elias Horry (1773–1834) experienced trouble with his slave Jack in 1821, and his coachman John was executed in 1822. William Drayton (1776–1846) and Robert J. Turnbull (1775–1833) served together on the first court. John Stevens Cogdell (1778–1847) acted as assistant warden, and Edwin C. Holland (1794–1824) penned an 1822 pamphlet, defending the state's actions, which is excerpted later in this volume on p. 513.

Petition of the Inhabitants of Charleston, October 16, 1820, Petitions to the General Assembly, no. 143, series S165015, SCDAH.

Camden Gazette and Mercantile Advertiser

Thursday, November 9, 1820
THE STATE OF SOUTH-CAROLINA.

Presentments of the Grand Jury of Charleston District for October Term, 1820, *Judge Richardson presiding.*

. . . We recommend that the Legislature pass a law, repealing the one now in force, making the punishment for murdering a negro slave only of a pecuniary nature, and that they enact a law instead thereof, more consistent with humanity and the dignity of the state.

Petition, Tuesday, November 21, 1820

To the Honorable the President, and Members of the Senate

The Memorial of David P. Rodgers[1] of Williamsburgh District; Respectfully representeth, to your honorable Body, a loss which he has sustained, in getting a prime Negroe fellow[2] killed, during the Summer of 1819. Your Memorialist will farther state, to your honorable Body, the particulars of the untimely death of the Negroe; which statement, will be accompanied with corroborating testimony on the subject. During the Summer of 1819, a pretty large gang, to the number of sevin, Negroes, had associated and imbodied themselves together, committing depredations of various kinds, on the property of the Inhabitants.

Many attempts were made to detail the said Negroes; but all attempts proved abortive for some lapse of time. It was eventually thought to be, by the Colonel of the Regiment, indispensably necessary, that the People should turn out with Fire Arms; and quell the negroes in their nefarious Acts. This last, and only probable way of subduing the negroes, was agreed upon, and pursued for some time: Ultimately the negroes were found imbodied, and measurably in a state of rebellion, against the peace and welfare of the neighborhood. They manifested in their conduct, no pacifick disposition to surrender, when ordered to give up; but endeavored as far as possible to effect their escape. In doing which, this said negroe fellow, belonging to your Memorialist, was shot dead.—Your Memorialist will also state to your honorable Body, that the said Negroe was very valuable in many respects; he was a good Boat hand, a very prime field hand; a good sawyer; And was quite handy in the use of Mechanical Tools of different kinds. The said negroe, was between Forty and forty five Years of Age. And in all probability would have commanded at the time of being killed, at least Nine hundred, or one Thousand Dollars. He had sustained previous to being killed, uniformly, a good character, with the exception of running away once, or twice at farthest.

1. David P. Rodgers (1797–1824) owned more than six hundred acres in Williamsburg District, which is roughly sixty miles north of Charleston.

2. The slave's name was Pompey.

Petition of W. Salters and I. Nelson to the Senate of South Carolina, November 21, 1820, no. 1344, Series S165015, SCDAH.

Governor John Geddes, Message to the South Carolina State Legislature

Monday, November 27, 1820

. . . I must again state to you, gentlemen, that no law exhibits a greater disproportion of punishment, than that which relates to the Offence of killing a Slave by a white man. Its inflictions are so very inadequate to the demands of Justice, that the State has suffered in its reputation for humanity. The rules of reason Justice and religion, require that the punishment for wilful and deliberate murder should be the same in all cases; and it is to be observed, that a slave being deprived of his natural right of Self-defence against a white man, the killing of him by the latter, receives from this circumstance additional aggravation and demands at least equal punishment. If however, from considerations arising out of the Situation of Our Country such a punishment should be deemed inexpedient, there can be no well founded objection to the annexing of other severe penalties to the commission of this barbarous deed. The extension of the benefit of trial by Jury to this class of persons, for offences affecting life or limb, is imperiously called for, and seems as practicable and as conformable to the dictates of common Justice, as it is in unison with the principles of morality and the feeling of humanity. It would also be a source of great felicitation if cases of this description should be tried by tribunals whose legal Judgment would ensure the protection of the innocent and the conviction of the guilty. It cannot be expected, that those who have not made the law their Study, can always properly administer it; and the necessity of legislative interference is the more urgent, from the circumstance that the Constitutional Court has decided, that in trials of this nature before magistrates and freeholders there is no appeal.

The Missouri question, which was agitated during the last session of Congress, and may be revived at the present, has given rise to the expression of opinions and doctrines respecting this species of property, which tend not only to diminish its value, but also to threaten our safety. We cannot for a moment suppose that Congress will ever consent to be instrumental in disquieting the public mind, by legislating on the condition of Our Slaves, since it cannot do so, without a breach of good faith, and a violation of the Constitution, but it is not to be concealed, that in the discussion of that question, principles were advanced, which should put us upon our guard, and the mischeivous effects of which, we should counteract by the most efficient measures. I forbear, however, to enter into detail on this delicate subject—satisfied that your own discretion will readily suggest the proper course of conduct to be pursued.

In connection, however with this subject I deem it proper to inform you, that a number of free persons of colour have emigrated and are daily emigrating to and settling in this State. The policy of our country forbids the increase of this class of persons amongst us, and under existing circumstances imperiously calls for the adoption of the strongest measures to prevent it, and it may be deemed a duty to oppose at the threshold, every thing likely in its consequences to disturb our domestic tranquility. The restrictions on emancipation might be dispensed with, if persons emancipated should be obliged to depart the State within a limited time, and not be allowed to return to it afterwards, without your authority, on pain of seizure—But least such a condition annexed to emancipation should be deemed void, owners of Slaves might be allowed to release all right to their Services, provided they remove out of the state within a certain time, and the release to be in force only during their absence from the State, and a Slave to whom it may be given, to be liable to be seized as a Slave on his being found within the State at any time after the period fixed by law for his leaving the same. . . .

No. 1271, GM, series S165009, SCDAH. See also *Charleston Courier,* December 1, 1820.

Charleston Courier

Tuesday, December 5, 1820

MISSOURI QUESTION IN HAYTI!

A letter received by Mr. LYFORD,[1] from a respectable commercial house at Port-au-Prince. . . ." . . . At the same time I must mention to you, that it is expected this government will, in the course of the next year, adopt measures that will have a tendency to curtail American commerce, that is, to prevent vessels from coming to this Island from any State or place where negroes and people of colour held in slavery."

Norfolk Herald.

1. William Gilman Lyford (1784–1852) published the *Norfolk Herald.*

City Gazette and Commercial Daily Advertiser

Wednesday, December 20, 1820

HOUSE OF REPRESENTATIVES,

Wednesday, December 13.

. . . Mr. Prioleau,[1] from the judiciary committee. . . .

A bill to restrain the emancipation of slaves, and for preventing free persons of color from migrating into this State, and for other purposes, was read a second time, and ordered to be sent to the Senate.

1. Samuel Prioleau (1784–1840), the attorney for Lorenzo Dow and brother-in-law of James Hamilton Jr.

An Act to Restrain the Emancipation of Slaves, Wednesday, December 20, 1820

WHEREAS, the great and rapid increase of free negroes and mulattoes in this State, by migration or emancipation, renders it expedient and necessary for the Legislature to restrain the emancipation of slaves, and to prevent free persons of color from entering into this State.

I. *Be it therefore enacted,* by the honorable the Senate and House of Representatives, now met and sitting in General Assembly, That no slave shall hereafter be emancipated but by act of the Legislature.[1]

II. *Be it further enacted* by the authority aforesaid, That from and after the first day of March next, it shall not be lawful for any free negro or mulatto to migrate into this State;

and every free negro or mulatto who shall migrate into this State contrary to this Act, shall and may be apprehended and carried by any white person, before some justice of the peace of the district or parish where he or she shall be taken; which justice is hereby authorized and required to examine such free negro or mulatto, and to order him or her to leave this State. And every free negro or mulatto so ordered to leave the State, and hereafter remaining longer than fifteen days within the same, or having left the State, and thereafter returning to this State, (unless it be in consequence of shipwreck or some other unavoidable accident, or as a seaman on board or belonging to a vessel with which he shall depart, or as a servant to any white person travelling into this State,) upon proof thereof, made before any magistrate and three freeholders, and on conviction thereof, shall be subjected to a fine of twenty dollars, and in default of the payment thereof, shall be publicly sold, after ten days notice, for a term of time not exceeding five years; and if such free negro, mulatto, or mestizo, shall be found in this State after the lapse of ten days after paying such fine, or after such servitude under such sale, he, she, or they shall be liable to be proceeded against in like manner, and shall be sold for the like sum, and for a term not exceeding five years, until such slave or slaves shall depart the said State.

III. *Be it further enacted* by the authority foresaid, That every master of a vessel or other person, who shall bring into this State, by water or by land, in any vessel or land carriage, or otherwise, any free negro or mulatto, shall forfeit and pay for every such free negro or mulatto so brought, the penalty of five hundred dollars; to be recovered by action or debt, or by bill, plaint or information, in any court of record having jurisdiction of the amount; one moiety to be appropriated to the State, and the other to the prosecutor or person who shall inform thereof; and the defendant, in every such case, shall be required to give special bail. *Provided,* that this Act shall not extend to any masters of vessels bringing into this State any free negro or mulatto employed on board or belonging to such vessel, and who shall therewith depart; nor to any white person travelling into this State, having any free negro or mulatto as a servant; but if said servant shall remain longer than six months within the State, then such white person shall be subject to the penalty aforesaid, and the free negro or mulatto shall be dealt with in the manner before specified in this Act.

IV. *And be it further enacted,* That nothing herein contained shall effect any free person of color, being a native of this State, who shall return within the limits of this State two years after the passing of this Act; or who shall leave this State as a servant of any white person, and shall return with any white person in said capacity.

V. *And be it further enacted* by the authority aforesaid, That if any person or persons shall hereafter bring or cause to be brought into this State, any free negro or person of color, and shall hold the same as a slave, or sell or offer the same for sale to any person or persons in this State as a slave, every such person shall pay for every such free negro or free person of color, the sum of one thousand dollars, over and above the damages which may be recovered by such free negro or free person of color to any person or persons who will sue for and recover the same; which may be done either by indictment, or action in nature of ravishment of ward, established by law.

VI. *Be it further enacted,* That if any white person shall be duly convicted of having, directly or indirectly, circulated or brought within this State, any written or printed paper, with intent to disturb the peace or security of the same, in relation to the slaves of the people of this State, such person shall be adjudged guilty of a high misdemeanor, and shall be fined not exceeding one thousand dollars, and imprisoned not exceeding one year. And if any free person of color shall be convicted, in the mode provided for by law for the trial of such persons, of such offence, he or she shall, for the first offence, be sentenced to pay a fine not exceeding one thousand dollars; and for the second offence, shall be whipped, not exceeding fifty lashes, and be banished from the State; and any free person of color who shall return from such banishment, unless by unavoidable accident, shall suffer death without the benefit of clergy.[2]

1. John L. Bradley, "Slave Manumissions in South Carolina, 1820–1860" (master's thesis, University of South Carolina, 1964), 36, argued that "there seems to be no evidence that the 1820 law and the anti-manumission policy of the 1821 legislature played a role in the motivations causing the [Vesey] conspiracy." Although it is true that no deposition taken in 1822 made direct reference to the law, the fact that private manumissions or self-purchase became illegal only two years before suggests that bondmen who wished to someday be free understood that their only remaining recourse was to run away or rebel. As the 1832 petition from Eliza Smith Garner in Part V suggests, enslaved drayman William Garner, the last conspirator to be hanged in 1822, hired his time with an understanding that he could eventually buy his freedom. An anonymous pamphlet composed by "A Colored American," "*The Late Contemplated Insurrection in Charleston, S.C. with the Execution of Thirty Six of the Patriots* . . . (New York, 1850), reprinted in the present volume, Part VI, pp. 735–39, claims that the 1820 law had a devastating impact on Charleston's slave community, as their "prospects . . . for freedom were blasted; many of whom had toiled anxiously at night to earn sufficient means to purchase freedom for themselves; all of whom aspired to the manly boon of freedom, the declaration of their masters to the contrary notwithstanding. Freedom many of the slaves resolved to have at all hazards."

2. This clause suggests how concerned the state was about the dissemination of antislavery literature in the wake of the Missouri debates. As Jack Purcell's confession indicates, legislators were right to be concerned. Purcell's statement about New York's Rufus King appears in Part III of this volume.

Thomas Cooper and David J. McCord, eds., *The Statutes at Large of South Carolina* (Columbia, SC, 1840), vol. 7; 459–60

Samuel Sitgreaves Jr.[1] to Reverend Jackson Kemper, Sunday, January 7, 1821

. . . I had anticipated many long arguments upon the subject of Missouri with these hot-headed Carolinians, but I have managed to keep tolerably clear of the discussion. However I have made a few debates, and I got the better in them too, except with Mr. Heyward; but we have not finished yet. . . .

1. Samuel Sitgreaves Jr. (1798–1832) was an antislavery Episcopal clergyman, born in Easton, Pennsylvania. His interlocutor was most likely William Heyward (1779–1845), a wealthy planter in St. Luke's Parish and the nephew of Nathaniel Heyward (1766–1851) who served as one of the six freeholders on the first Court of Magistrates and Freeholders that tried Vesey and many of his

followers. James B. Heyward, "The Heyward Family of South Carolina," *SCHM* 59 (1958): 155. See Part IV, pp. 436–37, for a letter written by Harriott Pinckney Rutledge, who at the time of the Vesey trials recalled how Sitgreaves had unsettled elite lowcountry South Carolinians with his remarks about emancipation.

P. J. Staudenhaus, "Letters from South Carolina, 1821–1822," *SCHGM* 58 (1957): 213.

Hartford *Connecticut Courant*

Tuesday, January 30, 1821

St. Domingo.—Accounts are received by an arrival at Boston from St. Domingo, of the discovery of an extensive and deep-laid plot, by the blacks of that place, to massacre the whites and mulattoes, and pillage the city. The discovery was made but a few hours previous to the one fixed on for carrying their horrid project into execution, and the ringleaders were seized and are imprisoned. The conspiracy amounted, it is said, to upwards of 5000 blacks, all armed. On the first alarm being given of their intentions, the inhabitants were panic struck, and flew on board of the shipping in port for safety.—*N. York Even*[*ing*]. *Post.*

Boston *Columbian Centinel*

Wednesday, February 28, 1821

The Island of Hayti, to which we are sorry to perceive means are in activity to entice our free people of colour, will most probably become a renewed scene of carnage and proscription. The African race can never be reconciled with that which is mixed with the white. Of this the recent plot affords an example, in addition to those, which so many massacres have attested, in the Island.—Whilst it remained divided between the black and yellow chiefs, it enjoyed, for a number of years, a degree of tranquility which is now probably about to disappear. Why therefore are our emancipated natives to be precipitated into such an effervescing vortex? We can foresee no middle state for them, after arriving, but to assist in these exterminating scenes, or to become the passive victims of them. In the former case by becoming barbarians, and ceasing to be christians, it may be painfully experienced, that their annoyance will be much more inconvenient, at Hayti, than at home. The least consideration must, we think, convince every man, that the proposed emigration will be more destructive to their welfare, and pernicious to our interests, than almost any plan that could be adopted.—*Federal Republican.*

Hartford *Connecticut Courant*

Tuesday, March 20, 1821

The annexed communication has been on hand several days, and its publication delayed until we should hear from the author, relative to its authenticity. He is now in town, and ready to vouch for its correctness in every particular. Whilst our readers must, with us, shudder at the bloody recital; they must also rejoice, as we sincerely do, that few such monsters disgrace our state.—The arm of vengeance must, from the crying of this wretch's guilt, soon overtake him.

To the Editor of the Times.

SIR,—I was riding on Monday morning last, in the upper part of Prince William Parish, (Beaufort District) and saw a number of people assembled round a dead body, lying in a field near the road side. On enquiry, I found that they composed a jury of Inquest, called to investigate the cause and manner of the death of the body before them, which was that of a negro, shockingly mangled and disfigured.

It appeared, from the evidence of an aged lady, mother-in-law to the owner and murderer of the negro, that the unfortunate slave had been sick some days, and on the Saturday previous was in the kitchen; that on stepping out of doors, she saw her son-in-law dragging him, prostrate, into the kitchen, swearing that he would "finish the rascal;" that from the great effusion of blood in the yard, and the motionless insensibility of the negro, she believed he was already dead, and told his master so; that he swore it was nothing b[u]t stubborn hypocrisy, which he would soon force out of him—and calling for some boiling water, threw it into the face of his victim: finding all his endeavors to reanimate the body ineffectual, he crushed his skull with an axe!

The verdict of the Jury was, "That the deceased came to his death, in consequence of sundry blows of an axe, inflicted on his neck and head, by the hands of his master, SAMUEL LEWIS.[1]

My blood ran cold in my veins, as I cast a look on the helpless victim of infuriated arrogance. His fellow servants (perhaps his relatives) had prepared a rude coffin, and were mournfully proceeding to restore him to the dust, whence we are taken and to which we must all return.

Wretched, wretched man, his crime is traced in bloody characters, which years of penitence can scarce efface. An outcast from mankind, he leaves a mark of his crime on his forehead, he shrinks from the scrutinizing eye of innocence. CAIN had a Mahala to soften, in some measure, the gnawing of the worm that never dies, but that consultation is denied him.

She, who, perhaps, would have forsaken father and mother to have shared his sorrows: she, whose prayers, with his, might have gained peace to his soul, and pardon to his sins—may ere now be an inmate of thc tomb!

Even the mild pages of the gospel breathe vengeance against the murderer: and did not the sacred nature of my duties forbid my interference in political and legislative matters, methinks I could point out, a blameable lenity in our criminal code.

A PREACHER.

1. This story widely circulated in northern newspapers, such as the Salem *Essex Register*. A Samuel Lewis migrated in South Carolina from the Horry District to the Beaufort District in 1821. See Jerry Dale Lewis, *My Neck of the Woods: The Lewis Families of Southeastern North Carolina and Northeastern South Carolina*, 2nd ed. (Baltimore: Clearfield, 2005), 96.

Charleston *City Gazette and Commercial Daily Advertiser*

Monday, June 4, 1821

The Negro JACK, the property of Mr. Fonberg, of Lancaster District, was tried before a Court of Magistrates and Freeholders, at Georgetown, on Thursday last, for the murder of Mr. Ford, (the account of which we published on Friday).[1] He was found guilty, and sentenced to be hung on the 8th inst. It is stated, that "during the trial, he exhibited no mark of penitence or sorrow, but preserved the utmost stubbornness of feature and of manner. The trial of the other fellow, called JACK, the property of Mrs. Horry,[2] has been postponed, in order to have his testimony as to the identity of JOE, who is yet in the neighborhood of Lucas's plantation on Santee, and who it is supposed will be taken. He threatens to sell his life dearly, and declares that he will not be taken alive. Volunteer parties are still going out. . . .

His Excellency the Governor, has offered by Proclamation, a reward of Two Hundred Dollars, for the apprehension of JOE, and about $300 more have been already obtained for the same object, by subscription, among the Citizens of Georgetown and its vicinity.

1. George Ford (1776–1821) was a wealthy planter. See *Columbia* (SC) *Telescope*, June 12, 1821; *BDSCHR* 3: 240. On the eventual fate of Joe, and allegations that he harbored 1822 conspirator Scipio Sims, see Charleston *City Gazette and Commercial Daily Advertiser*, September 10, October 8, 1823, reprinted in Part V of this volume.

2. Possibly Mary Rutledge Shubrick Horry (1789–1852), the second wife of planter Elias Horry (1773–1834), a wealthy planter with properties in Georgetown. His enslaved coachman, John Horry, was among the Vesey conspirators hanged on July 12, 1822.

Washington (DC) *Gazette*

Thursday, June 7, 1821

A Mr. Ford of Georgetown, S.C. on the night of the 27th ultimo, with several other persons, started in search of a gang of negroes that he learned were killing his cattle: but the negroes hearing of the circumstance advanced some distance upon the road, and remained in ambush until the party came up when they fired and immediately killed Mr. Ford. The rest fled. The military have since apprehended several of the negroes.

Hartford *Connecticut Mirror*

Monday, September 24, 1821

From the Boston Gazette.

From Hayti—We have conversed with Mr. John Lewis, a respectable man of color, who has resided for many years in this town and who has recently returned from Hayti. He was induced to visit that growing country to ascertain what advantages and privileges the free blacks in this country would enjoy by emigrating to that island. He has returned perfectly satisfied with the stability of the government there established, and with perfect assurance that every facility will be extended to emigrants from this country; and in consequence, has determined immediately to remove his family there for a permanent residence.

The information we have derived from Mr. Lewis we can vouch for, as we have long known him for a man of honest habits, and of veracity. He informs that at Aux Cayes and Jacquemel, there are a number of resident white merchants, many of them American, who transact extensive business, and with perfect security; that no animosity subsists between the well informed part of the inhabitants towards the whites. The trade is represented to be highly flourishing in that section of the island. President Boyer has adopted a wise course of policy, in recently disbanding a part of the black troops, and distributing to them fertile spots of ground for the purposes of cultivation.—That every facility of this sort is and will be rendered by the government to those emigrants who are not able to purchase lands, and the most generous terms allowed. That President Boyer was very popular, and was evidently laboring, by every possible measure, to ameliorate the condition of his people—and induce them to facilitate by industry and enterprize, the growing happiness and prosperity of the country. This is the substance of our information, and we thus give it, anxiously hoping that it may produce some benefit towards that hitherto unhappy, but now rising nation.[1]

1. This story first appeared in the Boston *Commercial Gazette,* August 23, 1821.

Charleston *Southern Patriot, and Commercial Advertiser*

Thursday, September 20, 1821

We take this opportunity of apprizing the citizens that the new regulations made of force by the Ordinance of the 17th inst, will go into operation to night that the Drum will cease to be beaten in the street as has been customary at Tattoo, and that the Bell will be rung at nine as a signal for slaves or free persons of color to retire to their homes. It would be well for masters of families to explain this alteration to their servants. We call the attention of the former to the Ordinance published in our advertising department of to-day.

Charleston *City Gazette and Commercial Daily Advertiser*

Friday, September 28, 1821

FOR THE CITY GAZETTE.

It requires no ordinary foresight to perceive the difficulties that must at some future time accompany the discussion of the rights of that class of people termed "free persons of color." These rights, at present so imperfect and indefinite, and so little understood, must acquire strength by prescription, be more valuable to the possessors by gradual but continued accessions, and will eventually ripen to that perfect state, in which it may be hazardous to limit their extent, or to question their legitimacy. We witness the continual encroachments that are made by them—favours construed into privileges, and privileges matured to rights. And so numerous and extensive have those rights become, it should be a subject of enquiry, on what law or precedent they have been founded; and a question of policy, by what limits they should be restricted. Upon the mere exemption from involuntary servitude, which seems to be the sole consequence of emancipation contemplated by our laws, have been founded a pretext for unwarrantable assumptions. We would be persuaded, that the tenure of property, which must originally have been, in the hand of that description of people, a mere estate at will, or so encumbered with conditions and other contingencies, as to carry with it an inconsiderable interest, has matured into a freehold—and that the security of person, not more tenderly protected by our laws than our slaves, should be construed into a constitutional privilege. The period has almost passed, when these pretensions should be investigated; and our own security and domestic tranquility require a timely check to the progress of these dangerous encroachments. It will be perceived, by a reference to our laws, and by the construction of those laws, agreeably to the spirit which pervades them throughout, (and of necessity must pervade them;) that it was never intended to elevate, by the sanction of emancipation, the free persons of colour above the ordinary level of those continued in servitude; nor encourage, by extending to them extraordinary privileges, feelings of insubordination. . . .

Charleston *Southern Patriot, and Commercial Advertiser*

Saturday, September 29, 1821
COMMUNICATION.

Mr. Editor,

In the Council of our City, I was one, who for many years used my utmost exertion to have carried into effect, that Ordinance, by which the tranquility of our city is persevered on the Sabbath.

It is not to be supposed that my efforts were crowned with complete success, because the vigilance of an inferior officer could not be expected from me; but I considered it my duty, and the duty of my colleagues, to make such exertions and enquiries as were calculated to excite vigilance in the proper officers, and enforce an observance of the Ordinance.

It is with regret that I am compelled to notice a disgraceful violation of this Ordinance in one part of our town. Had I been informed that the sanctity of the Sabbath had been so signally violated in any part of this city, I would have withheld my belief; but what our senses inform us of we must believe. To my astonishment I saw last Sunday, in passing down South Bay, two dram shops open, yes *open,* Mr. Editor, filled with drunken Negroes, and surrounded by a drunken crowd, fighting, yelling and swearing. It must be admitted that this is a disgraceful scene—I am sorry to learn that it is to be witnessed every Sunday, on South Bay. . . .

Petition, November 1821

South Carolina—St. Georges Parish

I do hereby depose that in consequence of some run-away negroes being very offensive to the neighbours, in the vicinity of Dorchester, repeatedly committing depredations on their property, & jeopardizing the lives of some, the Governor of the State ordered the

Captn. of the Parish, to summons a body of men, for the express purpose of pursuing, taking, & killing such as would not surrender.—In pursuance of these orders Captn Seth T. Prior[1] collected a body of men, by legal summons, in the usual way, and patroled the country.—Some were routed in Doctor Brailsford's plantation,[2] and not stopping, they were fired upon, when a prime young fellow, named Absolum, was shot in the head, and expired a few hours after, who belonged to Doctor Brailsford.—In testimony of the above, I hereunto annex my seal & signature this Twenty first day of November in the year of our Lord one thousand eight hundred & twenty one.

Seth Prior
then Captain commanding
the Dorchester Company

1. Seth Thornton Prior (1781–1830) owned a plantation in St. George's Parish. See *Charleston Courier,* December 11, 1830.

2. In 1822, Dr. Edward Brailsford (1776?–1856) resided in Charleston at 57 Church Street. Two of his plantation slaves were killed. See *CSCCD,* 72.

Affidavit of Seth T. Prior, November 1, 1821, in Petition of Edward Brailsford, n.d., no. 1838, Series S165015, SCDAH.

Charleston Courier

Saturday, December 1, 1821

FROM COLUMBIA.

Extract of a letter, dated Nov. 27

Several petitions having been already presented for leave to emancipate slaves, the Senate has approved a special committee on the subject, consisting of five, with authority to report by bill. This committee will probably be joined by one of the House on the same subject. . . .

Charleston Courier

Wednesday, December 12, 1821

. . . The Legislature at their last session, passed a Law, whereby they changed the mode of emancipating slaves. It is believed they intended to do more, and before the session terminated they will be required to say what they did intend. In the Senate a bill has been reported to emancipate the slaves whose owners have petitioned, on security being given that they shall leave the State. The whole number applied for is less than 45, and consists chiefly of women and children. . . .

Charleston Courier

Tuesday, December 18, 1821

. . . On the subject of *Emancipation* an act will probably pass—permitting emancipation in cases where contracts for that purpose had been entered into previous to December last, and to restrain it in all other cases. In relation to the *Penal Code,* several important alterations will probably prevail. The murder of a slave is to be punished by death. . . .

Charleston Courier

Wednesday, December 19, 1821

From Columbia, Dec. 15. . . . Dr. Moser's Bill, for punishing with death the willful murder of a Slave, has been returned to the Senate, with amendments, from the House, and on motion, in Senate, for its indefinite postponement, the yeas and nays being called, were for the motion 10, against it 27.—. . . [1]

1. Philip Moser (1770?–1835), a physician, seems to have adopted the antislavery sentiments of his mentor, Dr. Benjamin Rush (1746–1813) of Philadelphia, arguably the foremost educator of the founding generation. A longtime member of the South Carolina state legislature, Moser left Charleston for his native Philadelphia in the 1830s. See *BDSCHR* 4: 415–16, and US Census, 1820, South Carolina, Charleston, series M33, roll 119, p. 102, NA.

An Act to Promote More Effectually Against the Offence of Harbouring Negro or Other Slaves

Thursday, December 20, 1821

1. *Be it enacted,* by the honorable the Senate and House of Representatives, now met and sitting in the General Assembly, and by the authority of the same, that if any white person shall harbour, conceal or entertain any runaway or fugitive slave, such person shall be liable to be indicted for a misdemeanor, or prosecuted in a civil action for damages, at the election of the owner or person injured: and in case any person, being indicted, shall be convicted of said offence, such person shall be fined and imprisoned at the discretion of the court, not exceeding one thousand dollars fine, nor one year's imprisonment.

II. *And be it further enacted* by the authority aforesaid, That if any free negro, mulatto or mestizo shall harbour, conceal or entertain any fugitive or runaway slave, and be convicted thereof before two justices and five freeholders, he shall suffer such corporal punishment, not extending to life or limb, as the said justices and freeholders who try such offender, shall, in their discretion, think fit.[1]

1. The law was reprinted verbatim in the *Charleston Courier,* Monday, January 7, 1822.

Thomas Cooper and David J. McCord, eds., *The Statutes at Large of South Carolina* (Columbia, SC, 1840), vol. 7: 460–61.

Philadelphia *United States Gazette and True American*

Tuesday, January 8, 1822

By an act of the legislature of South Carolina passed during its recent session, the murder of a slave (when the crime is of the first degree) is made punishable with death,—manslaughter with a fine of $500, and six months imprisonment.

Philadelphia *United States Gazette and True American*

Saturday, February 2, 1822

From St. Domingo.—Capt. Greenman, arrived at Newport, from Port au Plat, reports that the Haytien flag was hoisted at that place on the 1st of January. When Capt. G. sailed, the place was in a state of revolution, and the whites were in daily fear of a massacre from the blacks. The whole of the Spanish part of St. Domingo was in possession of the blacks.—*N. Y. Gaz.*

Charleston *City Gazette and Commercial Daily Advertiser*

Thursday, February 14, 1822

. . . The Grampus[1] touched at Cape Tiberoon (Hayti.) Seven thousand men had marched for the City of St. Domingo—it was reported that the advance had taken possession of the city, and that the whole Island was completely in possession of the blacks.

1. The United States schooner *Grampus* arrived at Tiburon, a port in southern Haiti.

Charleston Mercury, and Morning Advertiser

Wednesday, February 20, 1822

Hayti.—By the Ruby, arrived yesterday from Port-au-Prince, we learn that President BOYER had commenced his march, at the head of a strong force, towards the City of St. Domingo. There was no doubt of the surrender of that place upon his appearance before it, as the Haytian flag was flying in every other part of that quarter of the Island.

Charleston *City Gazette and Daily Commercial Advertiser*

Tuesday, April 2, 1822

. . . Arrivals from Santo Domingo bring accounts of the whole of the slave population of Spanish Santo Domingo having been emancipated. Nothing less could have been expected from the political change which so lately took place in that territory. It is perfect conformity with the constitution of Hayti. . . .

II

Proceedings

The conspiracy began to unravel on May 22, 1822, when minor recruiter William Paul spoke of the planned uprising to Peter, a mixed-race cook owned by Colonel John Cordes Prioleau (1772–1825). Prioleau, a prominent merchant and planter, resided in 1822 on Meeting Street and owned a large plantation in St. James Goose Creek Parish, north of the city. Peter took the news to his friend, William Penceel, a free member of the exclusive Brown Fellowship Society. Acting on Penceel's advice, Peter spoke to Prioleau about the conversation when he returned to Charleston on Thursday afternoon, May 30. In turn, Prioleau hurried the information along to Intendant (Mayor) James H. Hamilton Jr., who ordered Paul arrested and confined to the Work-House. Fearing for his life, Paul gave up the names of Mingo Harth, in whose company he served, and Peter Poyas. When questioned, both men retained their composure and were released. Hamilton had the two men watched, however.

On Sunday, June 9, two slaves, Joe La Roche, owned by the widow Mary La Roche (1749–1842), and Rolla Bennett, a domestic slave owned by Governor Thomas Bennett Jr., tried to recruit their friend George Wilson. Wilson, a blacksmith and founding member of the African Church, hired his time away from his master, Major John Wilson (1789–1833), who was employed as South Carolina's state engineer. George Wilson urged his fellow slaves to abandon the plan as unchristian and, after five sleepless nights, decided to reveal what he knew to his owner. Once again, Intendant Hamilton received the news, and this time he brought in Governor Bennett, who initially refused to believe that his slaves were involved. He responded, however, with military force once he heard that Rolla, his favored domestic slave, had confessed his own involvement in the plot. In October, magistrates Lionel H. Kennedy and Thomas Parker published their lengthy *Official Report*, which contained the following "Narrative" explaining how the conspiracy unraveled.

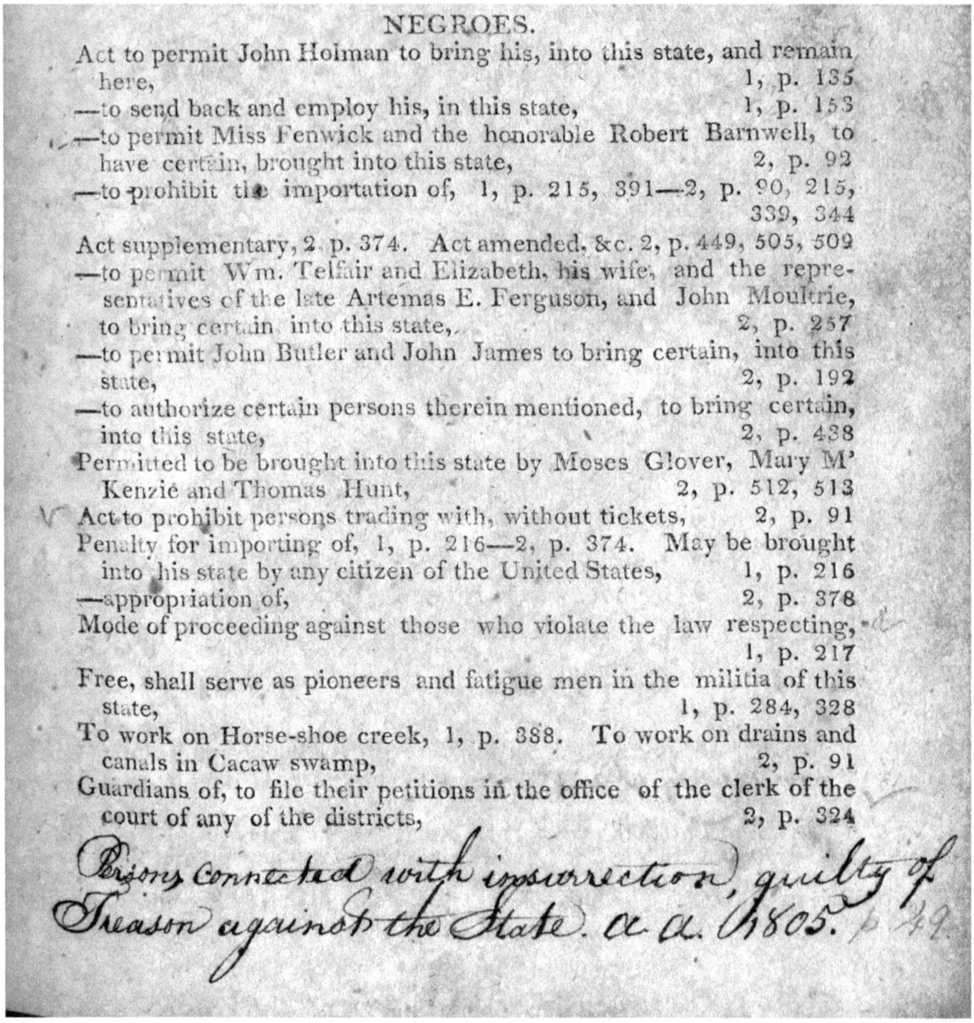

NEGROES.

Act to permit John Holman to bring his, into this state, and remain here, 1, p. 135
—to send back and employ his, in this state, 1, p. 153
—to permit Miss Fenwick and the honorable Robert Barnwell, to have certain, brought into this state, 2, p. 92
—to prohibit the importation of, 1, p. 215, 391—2, p. 90, 215, 339, 344
Act supplementary, 2, p. 374. Act amended, &c. 2, p. 449, 505, 509
—to permit Wm. Telfair and Elizabeth, his wife, and the representatives of the late Artemas E. Ferguson, and John Moultrie, to bring certain into this state, 2, p. 257
—to permit John Butler and John James to bring certain, into this state, 2, p. 192
—to authorize certain persons therein mentioned, to bring certain, into this state, 2, p. 438
Permitted to be brought into this state by Moses Glover, Mary M' Kenzie and Thomas Hunt, 2, p. 512, 513
Act to prohibit persons trading with, without tickets, 2, p. 91
Penalty for importing of, 1, p. 216—2, p. 374. May be brought into this state by any citizen of the United States, 1, p. 216
—appropriation of, 2, p. 378
Mode of proceeding against those who violate the law respecting, 1, p. 217
Free, shall serve as pioneers and fatigue men in the militia of this state, 1, p. 284, 328
To work on Horse-shoe creek, 1, p. 388. To work on drains and canals in Cacaw swamp, 2, p. 91
Guardians of, to file their petitions in the office of the clerk of the court of any of the districts, 2, p. 324

Persons connected with insurrection, guilty of Treason against the State. A. A. 1805. p 49

Figure 2. Lionel H. Kennedy (1787?–1847), judge on the First Court of Magistrates and Freeholders, glosses on "Negroes" in his volume *Acts of the General Assembly* (1808). Courtesy of Special Collections, Burke Library, Hamilton College.

Lionel H. Kennedy[1] and Thomas Parker,[2] "A Narrative of the Conspiracy and Intended Insurrection," October, 1822

At the head of this conspiracy stood Denmark Vesey, a free negro; with him the idea undoubtedly originated. For several years before he disclosed his intentions to any one, he appears to have been constantly and assiduously engaged in endeavoring to embitter the minds of the colored population against the white. He rendered himself perfectly familiar with all those parts of the Scriptures, which he thought he could pervert to his purpose; and would readily quote them, to prove that slavery was contrary to the laws of God; that slaves were bound to attempt their emancipation, however shocking and bloody might be the consequences, and that such efforts would not only be pleasing to the Almighty, but were absolutely enjoined, and their success predicted in the Scriptures. His favorite texts when he addressed his own color were, "Zechariah, chapter 14th, verses 1, 2 and 3*, and Joshua, chapter 4th, verse 21†; and in all his conversations he identified their situation with that of the Israelites.[3] The number of inflam[m]atory pamphlets on slavery brought into Charleston from some of our sister states, within the last four years,‡, (and once from Sierra Leone)[4] and distributed amongst the colored population of the city, for which there was a great facility, in consequence of the unrestricted intercourse allowed to persons of color between the different States in the Union; and the speeches in Congress of those opposed to the admission of Missouri into the Union, perhaps garbled and misrepresented, furnished him with ample means for inflaming the minds of the colored population of this state; and by distorting certain parts of those speeches, or selecting from them particular passages, he persuaded but too many that Congress had actually declared them free, and that they were held in bondage contrary to the laws of the land. Even whilst walking through the streets in company with another, he was not idle; for if his companion bowed to a white person he would rebuke him, and observe that all men were born equal, and that he was surprised that any one would degrade himself by such conduct; that he would never cringe to the whites, nor ought any one who had the feelings of a man. When answered, We are slaves, he would sarcastically and indignantly reply, "You deserve to remain slaves;" and if he were further asked, What can we do, he would remark, "Go and buy a spelling book and read the fable of Hercules and the Waggoner;"[5] which he would then repeat, and apply it to their situation. He also sought every opportunity of entering into conversation with white persons when they could be overheard by negroes near by, especially in grog-shops; during which conversation he would artfully introduce some bold remark on slavery; and sometimes, when from the character he was conversing with he found he might be still bolder, he would go so far, that had not his declarations in such situations been clearly provided, they would scarcely have been credited. He continued this course, until sometime after the commencement of the last winter; by which time he had not only obtained incredible influence amongst persons of color, but many feared him more than their owners, and one of them declared, even more than his God.

* "Behold the day of the Lord cometh, and thy spoil shall be divided in the midst of thee. For I will gather all nations against Jerusalem to battle; and the city shall be taken, and the women ravished; and half of the city shall go forth into captivity; and the residue of the people shall not be cut off from the city. Then shall the Lord go forth, and fight against those nations, as when he fought in the day of battle."

† "And they utter destroyed all that was in the city, both man and woman, young and old, and ox, and sheep, and ass, with the edge of the sword."

‡ As far back as the year 1809, several hundred pamphlets of an insurrectionary character were brought to Charleston, in the ship Minerva,[6] from New-York, by her steward, who was a black man. A citizen of Charleston, a passenger on board, immediately on her arrival informed the Intendant of the circumstance, who promptly repaired, with the City Marshal,[7] to the vessel; but did not arrive there in time to seize them before they were landed. The Steward was, however, committed to prison for trial, and a few of the pamphlets having been procured, he would have been tried for this life, had he not entered

> into an arrangement with the civil authorities of the city to leave the state, never to return therein; and what is a little remarkable, his counsel on that occasion was one of the presiding magistrates of the late court.

At this period he sounded Rolla and Ned, two slaves of his Excellency Thomas Bennett, and finding them ready to acquiesce in his schemes, he made the same proposals to Jack, belonging to Mrs. Purcell,[8] and Peter, belonging to Mr. Poyas,[9] who also consented with equal promptness. These men were his first four associates; three of whom, viz: Rolla, Ned and Peter, immediately became his most active agents. Some time after Christmas he was also joined by Gullah Jack, belonging to Mr. Pritchard,[10] and subsequently by Monday, belonging to Mr. Gell;[11] who soon proved themselves to be as fit men for his purpose, and as active as Rolla, Ned and Peter.—These constituted his five principal officers, by whose means, aided by some others whom he employed to go about and travel the country adjacent to Charleston, and amongst the latter of whom the principal agents were Lot Forrester[12] and Frank Ferguson,[13] he engaged great numbers to join in the intended insurrection. He also at his house held nocturnal meetings, for the purpose of interchanging opinions, maturing the plan, collecting and giving information, &c.; at which meetings numbers of the insurgents, both from country and town attended; and where collections were made for the purpose of providin[g] arms, ammunition, &c. and for defraying such expences as might be indispensibly necessary. He also attended meetings at other places appointed by him; at one place in particular on Charleston Neck, about two miles and a half from the city. Besides his five principal officers already mentioned, he had other recruiting agents, though on a smaller scale, amongst whom were William Palmer,[14] Wm. Garner,[15] Charles Drayton[16] and Peirault Strohecker.[17] In order to induce the colored population to join them, every principle which could operate upon the mind of man was artfully employed: Religion, Hope, Fear, Deception, were resorted to as occasion required. All were told, and many believed, that God approved of their designs; those whose fears would have restrained them, were forced to yield by threats of death; those whose prudence and foresight induced them to pause, were cheered with the assurance that assistance from St. Domingo and Africa were at hand; whilst those upon whom none of these principles operated, were excited from despair on being informed, that the whites, perceiving they were becoming too numerous, had resolved to create a false alarm of fire, and as they came out in the dead of the night to kill them, in order to thin their numbers. And strange as it may appear, yet vast numbers of the Africans firmly believed that Gullah Jack was a sorcerer; that he could neither be killed nor taken; and that whilst they retained the charms which he had distributed they would themselves be invulnerable. Add to all this, their belief that Congress had emancipated them, and we may readily credit the declaration of Monday Gell and Perault, that they never spoke to any person of color on the subject, or knew of any one who had been spoken to by the other leaders, who had withheld his assent. Vesey being a free man encountered none of those obstacles which would have been in the way of a slave; his time was at his own disposal, and he could go wherever he pleased, without interruption; qualifications and advantages absolutely necessary for the Chief in a Conspiracy, and which enabled him to travel so much about the country as he did.

On perusing the testimony, the declaration of one or two of the witnesses that this plot had been in agitation for four years will strike the observation of every one; but it must not be supposed therefrom, that recruiting or enlisting had been progressing for that time; or that, for that time there existed any direct proposal from Vesey or any one else for such a measure. Such was not the case. No active measures were taken until near last Christmas. In speaking of this attempt being in agitation for four years, allusion was had to Vesey's conduct and language during that time; and to the dissatisfaction which appeared since, to exist amongst the coloured population. This was about the time that the African congregation, (so called from its being composed wholly of persons of colour and almost entirely of blacks,) was formed, and their Church built in Hampstead;* of which Vesey had been a member, and of which his principal associates, Gullah Jack, Monday, Ned and Peter, were also members; and the two last, were class leaders. It was also about this time, that class meetings of the coloured people had become so common as they now are; each class having a coloured preacher or leader as they were termed, named by the Minister of the Church to which he belonged; at which meetings, held usually at night in some retired building, avowedly for religious instruction and worship, no white person attended. That inflamatory and insurrectionary doctrines, without any direct proposal for such an attempt, were inculcated at these meetings or some of them, was positively proved; and further, that they were to be used as places of rendezvous and rallying points, for communicating to all, the exact night and hour, on which the first blow was to be struck. The great impropriety of allowing meetings of any kind to be held solely by slaves, and at such times and places, must forcibly strike every reflecting mind. The African congregation above mentioned was not only composed altogether of coloured persons, but their Ministers were also coloured; and were stated to have been regularly ordained Bishops and Ministers of the Gospel. The influence which such men and class leaders must necessarily acquire over the minds of the ignorant blacks is evident; and if a disposition exists in them to obtain for their own colour and themselves, the freedom and privileges enjoyed by the whites, by enlisting into their cause perverted religion and fanaticism, that desperation is kindled in their hearers, the consequences of which are but too well known. Is it to be wondered at that, under all the foregoing circumstances, an attempt to create an insurrection should be contemplated!

* A part of the suburbs of Charleston.

Religious fanaticism has not been without its effect on this project, and as auxiliary to these sentiments, the secession of a large body of blacks from the white Methodist Church, with feelings of irritation and disappointment, formed a hot bed, in which the germ might well be expected to spring into life and vigour. Among the conspirators, *a majority* of them belonged to the *African church,* and among those executed were several who had been Class Leaders. It is, however, due to the late head of their church (for since the late events the association has been voluntarily dissolved) and their deacons, to say, that, after the most diligent search and scrutiny, no evidence entitled to belief, has been discovered against them. A hearsay rumour, in relation to *Morris Brown,*[18] was traced far enough to end in its complete falsification.[19]

Vesey perceiving that so far every thing had answered his most sanguine expectations, himself in possession of vast influence over his own colour, and their minds poisoned and embitterred against the white population, began about Christmas 1821, to probe those whom he had selected as leaders; and found as he expected a ready acquiescence in his measures by all of them except Monday Gell, who wavered for some time before he joined. In the selection of his leaders, Vesey shewed great penetration and sound judgment. Rolla was plausible, and possessed uncommon self-possession; bold and ardent, he was not to be deterred from his purpose by danger. Ned's appearance indicated, that he was a man of firm nerves, and desperate courage. Peter was intrepid and resolute, true to his engagements, and cautious in observing secrecy where it was necessary; he was not to be daunted nor impeded by difficulties, and though confident of success, was careful in providing against any obstacles or casualties which might arise, and intent upon discovering every means which might be in their power if thought of before hand. Gullah Jack was regarded as a Sorcerer, and as such feared by the natives of Africa, who believe in witchcraft. He was not only considered invulnerable, but that he could make others so by his charms; and that he could and certainly would provide all his followers with arms. He was artful, cruel, bloody; his disposition in short was diabolical. His influence amongst the Africans was inconceiveable. Monday was firm, resolute, discreet and intelligent.

With these men as his principal officers, amongst whom Peter and Monday was certainly the most active, Vesey began to seduce others at the commencement of the present year. Peter and Monday (and probably the other leaders) kept lists of those who had joined their company or band. As Monday did not join until the business of enlisting had considerably progressed, and proceeded very prudently himself, he had but few on his list, according to his own confession only forty-two; but Peter who had consented as soon as spoken to, and was bold and active in his exertions, had six hundred names on his list; whom he had engaged in Charleston, from that division of the city in which he resided, which was South-Bay. Peter also had in his possession another list of names, or as the witness afterwards explained himself, a memorandum of the whole number engaged, and who amounted as the witness was told to nine thousand, partly from the country and partly from the city. It is true that the witness who made these assertions did not see the lists himself; but he heard it from one who was in daily communication with Peter, and who was then endeavouring, and succeeded in inducing the witness to join; and as Peter wrote a good hand and was active throughout the whole affair, it is impossible to doubt but that he had such lists; but whether the numbers mentioned were really engaged or not, there is no mode of ascertaining; and it is more than probable that they were greatly exaggerated, and perhaps designedly so. That Peter was engaged in enlisting, was possibly proved; but so scrupulously and resolutely to the last did he observe his pledge of secrecy to his associates, *that of the whole number arrested and tried, not one of them belonged to Peter's company.* Monday acknowledged that he had kept a list, but had he not become state's evidence, but had died without disclosing as Peter did, as well might we have doubted that *he kept a list.* In the course of the trials it was also stated, that Vesey had a variety of papers and books relating to this transaction, *which he burnt when the discovery of the intended attempt was made.* Monday also burnt his list, *and probably so did Peter at the same time.*

As these leaders only communicated to each other the numbers, and not the names of those whom they had engaged, and who constituted their company; and as with the exception of Monday, none of them betrayed their associates; the companies of Vesey, Peter, Ned, Rolla and Gullah Jack have escaped detection and punishment; with the exception *of a few of Gullah Jack's band,* who were discovered in consequence of one of his men betraying such of his companions as he knew, together with his leader.

In enlisting men the great caution observed by the leaders was remarkable. Few if any domestic servants were spoken to, as *they* were distrusted; and all who were consulted were told, that death would certainly await them if they informed; and Peter whilst he urged one of his agents to speak to others and solicit them to join, at the same time gave him this charge, "but take care and don't mention it to those waiting men who receive presents of old coats, &c. from their masters, or they'll betray us; *I will speak to them.*" The enlistments appear to have been principally confined to Negroes hired or working out, such as Carters, Draymen, Sawyers, Porters, Labourers, Stevidores, Mechanics, those employed in lumber yards, and in short to those who had certain allotted hours at their own disposal, and to their neighbouring country negroes.[20] When the proposal was made to any one to join, such arguments or threats were made use of as would ensure success, and which the leaders had been cautious to prepare before hand, and suit to the different tempers and dispositions they would have to deal with.

As Vesey, from whom all orders emanated, and perhaps to whom only all important information was conveyed, died without confessing any thing, any opinion formed as to the numbers actually engaged in the plot, must be altogether conjectural; but enough has been disclosed to satisfy every reasonable mind, that considerable numbers were concerned. Indeed the plan of attack, which embraced so many points to be assailed at the same instant, affords sufficient evidence of the fact.

The extent of country around Charleston which was embraced in this attempt, has not been so precisely ascertained as to be traced on a map with as much certainty as a division line between two states; but enough has been discovered, to induce a belief, that it extended to the North of Charleston many miles towards Santee,[21] and unquestionably into St. John's Parish; to the South to James' and John's Islands; and to the West beyond Bacon's Bridge[22] over Ashley River. That all who inhabited this extent of country were engaged in the plot, will not be pretended; it was not necessary or perhaps adviseable; for at the season of the year in which the attempt was to be made, all the planters and their families are compelled to be absent from their plantations. If therefore a small number on a plantation or in the neighbourhood were engaged in the plot, and acquainted with the precise night and hour of its execution, it would be an easy matter for them in the course of the preceding day, or within a few hours of their taking their own departure, to induce many others whose minds were already poisoned to precede with them. In St. John's Parish four entire plantations of negroes were engaged by Frank Ferguson, as he declared to one of the witnesses; and his statement receives great strength, from the letter of his owner to one of the authors, in reply to one from him requesting certain information in writing.* It was principally for the attempt of Jesse,[23] (one of the conspirators) to go to Mr. Ferguson's plantation in St. John's, to inform the negroes of the night and hour they were to be in Charleston, that he was executed; though the declarations made by him independently of this act, shewed that he had heartily embarked in the plot. It was in testimony that the Insurgents *were trying all round the country, from Georgetown and Santee, round about to Combahee to get people,*" and subsequent to the determination of the trials, it has been distinctly ascertained, that Vesey had been in the country as far North as South Santee; and Southwardly from Charleston as far as the Euhaws;[24] which is between seventy and eighty miles from the city.

* Conclusion of Thomas Parker's letter of 15th September, 1822, addressed to James Ferguson, esq. If in this statement, I am incorrect, do furnish me with a full one of what it was you did, especially as to what passed between the Governor and yourself, in relation to the negroes in St. John's.

During the period that these enlistments were carrying on, Vesey held frequent meetings of the conspirators in his house; and as arms were necessary to their success, each night, a hat was handed round, and collections made, for the purpose of purchasing them, and also to defray other necessary expenses. A negro,[25] who was a blacksmith, and had been accustomed to make edged tools, was employed to make pike heads and bayonets with sockets, to be fixed at the ends of long poles and used as pikes. Of these pike heads and bayonets, one hundred were said to have been made at an early day, and by the 16th June, as many as two or three hundred, and between three and four hundred daggers. At one time, Gullah Jack was seen by several witnesses with six of the pike heads, which he said, he had just brought from the blacksmith's; and a bundle containing upwards of twelve well seclected poles, neatly trimmed and smothed off, and about nine or ten feet long, were found concealed on the farm on Charleston Neck, where several of their meetings were held; and which were carried there to have the pike heads and bayonets fixed on them. These were brought before the Court: how many more may have been carried there, and were afterwards removed, destroyed, or effectually concealed; or how many more would have been carried there had the plot not been discovered, is altogether a matter of conjecture; but certain it is, that twelve or twenty poles were more than were requisite for only six pike heads, and as those six pike heads have not been found, there is no reason for disbelieving the testimony of there having been many more made.[26] To presume that the Insurgents had no arms because none were seized, would be drawing an inference in direct opposition to the whole of the evidence. Bedsides, the arms above-mentioned, it was proved that Peter had a sword; that Cha's. Drayton had a gun & sword; that John Horry[27] had a sword; that Pharo Thompson[28] had a sythe converted into a sword; that Adam Yates[29] had a knife, such as are used by Riflemen as dirks, but which from its length was more properly a sword; that Monday had a sword; that Bacchus Hammett[30] gave Peirault a sword and carried another and a pistol to Vesey, together with a keg of powder, that was afterwards made up into fixed ammunition, and which he had stolen from his owner; and that some of the arms of the Revenue Cutter had been stolen, yet none of these arms were found. A dagger rudely made, was found in Rolla's trunk; a quantity of slow match which was suppose to have been stolen out of the Arsenal by Lot was found concealed on one of the wharves, with which the City was to have been fired; and a very considerable number of musket balls were accidently discovered, concealed under water in one of the docks. But the means which the insurgents had in their power of arming themselves were ample. On King-street road, beyond the limits of the city considerably, though within the lines, in a common wooden store, unguarded, were deposited the arms of the Neck Company of Militia, amounting to between two and three hundred muskets and bayonets, and a few swords; the door of which store was to have been opened by Bacchus Hammett immediately as the Insurgents appeared before it, which a party were to have done at the appointed hour. Mr Duqercron's store on King-street road,[31] also beyond the limits of the City, and but a short distance below the last mentioned store, were deposited for sale about five hundred muskets and bayonets; to which store a body of the same party were to have gone at the appointed hour and secured those arms. To assist in effecting their several purposes, Vesey had made a collection purposely to purchase dark lanthorns. Mr. Schirer's store in Queen-street,[32] and the other stores with arms, were noted by the chief as magazines of arms to which they could resort; especially the stores of those Gun Smiths, with whom the arms of some of the militia companies are deposited for the purpose of being kept in order. But in addition to these means, the Arsenal in Meeting-street opposite St. Michael's Church, in which the greatest proportion of the arms of the State are deposited, was to have been forced and the arms seized. Let it be remembered that this Arsenal is on the public street, without even a brick wall in front of it, with doors not stronger than those of many dwelling houses, and the difficulty of forcing it will not appear very great. The slaves who were enlisted in Charleston were to endeavour to purloin their owner's arms, and there appeared to be a confidence in the leaders, that a sufficient number in Charleston would from different sources be provided with arms to enable them in the first moments of surprise, and before the whites could possibly assemble, completely to succeed in their first attacks on the Guard House, and the unguarded Arsenals and Stores containing arms; after which they would be at no loss for arms. The negroes from the country were also to bring with them their hoes, hatchets, axes and spades, which might either be used as offensive weapons, or as instruments to break open doors. Had the plot not been discovered, and the Insurrection commenced at the appointed time, they would not have been found unarmed.

Vesey had originally fixed upon the night of the second Monday in July[33] for the attack, as about that time the number of the white inhabitants in the city would be much diminished; those who are either going to the North, or to Sullivan's-Island,[34] or into the upper parts of the State to spend the summer, generally before that time depart; a circumstance which had not escaped the observation of Vesey—However, in consequence of the discoveries made on the 30th May, and the apprehension of Peter and Mingo Harth[35] the day after, (but who after being examined were discharged) Vesey thought it prudent to fix upon an earlier day for the attack, and changed it some time after to the night of Sunday the 16th of June, which change, though he was able to communicate to his associates in the city, it would appear from his sending messengers into the country for that purpose, as late as the very day preceding the night on which the attempt was to be made, that he had not had sufficient time, or found some difficulty in communicating to his followers in the country; which accounts for their not generally appearing in the city on the night of the 16th of June. Twenty or thirty men however in a canoe did reach the city, and immediately had their arrival reported to Vesey; and with this view may many of those who came into the city on Saturday night and during Sunday have visited Charleston, on which day, great numbers, (certainly above a thousand as will presently be shewn) invariably repair to the city; but the preparations made by the whites, and the number of troops on duty that night, convinced him and his followers that their plot was discovered and the whites on their guard; and as their hope of success was founded on effecting a suppris, Vesey sent them word to depart from the city as soon as possible and wait for further orders; "and the conspirators finding the whole town encompassed at 10 o'clock by the most vigilant patrols, did not dare to shew themselves, whatever might have been their plans. In the progress of the investigation, it was distinctly in proof, that but for those military demonstrations, the effort would unquestionably have been made; and that a meeting took place on Sunday afternoon, the 16th at 4 o'clock, of several of the ringleaders at Denmark Vesey's, for the purpose of making their preliminary arrangements."

The plan of attack as originally formed was still adhered to, with the exception of the change of time before mentioned. It was to commence precisely at 12 o'clock on the night of Sunday the 16th of June; at which hour every one was to move, and the attack at every point to be made at the same moment.[36]—Peter was to lead a party which was to assemble on South-Bay, and to be joined by a force from James' Island;[37] he was then to march up and seize the Arsenal and Guard House opposite St. Michael's Church and secure the arms. From this force, a party was to be detatched, whose duty it would be to prevent the Citizens from assembling at their alarm posts, by cutting them off as they arrived. A second body consisting partly of negroes from the country and from the Neck, was to assemble on the Neck, under the command of Ned, and to seize the Arsenal there. A third to assemble at Bennett's Mills,[38] to be headed by Rolla, and, after murdering the Governor and Intendant, to march through the City, or take his station at Cannon's-Bridge, and thus prevent the inhabitants of Cannonsborough[39] from entering the City. A fourth, partly from the country, and partly from that portion of the city, was to rendezvous on Gadsden's-wharf,[40] march and attack the upper Guard-House. A fifth, of country and Neck negroes, for whom in particular the pikes which were made had been provided, was to assemble at Bulkley's farm, about two miles and a half from the City, and seize the powder magazine, three miles and a half from town, and then march into the City; and a sixth to assemble at Vesey's, and under his command, to march down to the Guard House. Whilst these attacks were going on, a number of them on horseback were to ride thorough the streets, and kill every person they might meet, and prevent them from assembling, or extending the alarm. Batteau was to join and march down with Vesey; and Gullah Jack with another body, which was to assemble in Boundary-street at the head of King-street, was to take possession of the arms of the Neck Company, which were deposited in a store as before-mentioned, and also those in

Mr. Duquercron's store. Arms being thus from these different sources provided, the City was to have been fired, and an indiscriminate slaughter of the whites to commence, and also of those of their own colour who had not joined them, or did not immediately do so. It was determined that no one should be neuter; "he that is not with me is against me."* was their creed. The leaders appeared to have no doubt but that those slaves who had not been particularly spoken to would join them, as soon as the Insurrection had fairly commenced, and the most partial success had been attained. "Let us assemble a sufficient number to commence the work with spirit and we'll not want men, they'll fall in behind us fast enough."[41]

* 11th Chapter of St. Luke, 23d verse.

Amongst those unacquainted with the employments, habits and customs of the inhabitants of Charleston and the country and Islands immediately surrounding it, a doubt might arise, how the Insurgents were to provide themselves with horses in the City; and how the negroes from the Islands and opposite sides of Ashley and Cooper rivers would find a conveyance to town. In neither of these respects however, was there the least difficulty. There were four sources from which they intended to obtain horses; the three first not only feasible but certain, the last more difficult, but by no means insurmountable. First, numbers of the draymen and carters of the city, who are all persons of colour, and many of whom have their horses both day and night under their controul, (those who are free keeping them in their own yards, and many of the slaves keeping their horses out of their owner's) were to act as horsemen; so were, secondly, some of the butcher's boy's, who could with ease provide themselves with horses; thirdly, the slaves at some of the public livery stables were engaged in the plot, and were a short time before the appointed hour to have the horses saddled, and at the hour to open the stable doors, and thus provide their comrades with horses; and fourthly, some of those whose owners were attached to either of the corps of cavalry in the city, were to endeavor to seize and bring of[f] with them their owners horses. As to the means which those on the Islands &c. would have to reach Charleston, they were abundant. The immense number of canoes of various sizes, (many of which could transport upwards of one hundred men) employed in bringing to the Charleston market, vegetables, stock of every kind and the staple of the country, would have afforded conveyance for thousands. As a matter of information and precaution, the Intendant of Charleston during the trials, and investigations of the plot, when negroes were rather fearful of coming into town, directed the numbers of those who came over in such boats on Sundays from the Islands to be counted, when even at that time, upwards of five hundred entered the city on one Sunday. From this statement some estimate may be formed of the number of negroes who ordinarily come into Charleston on Sunday from different parts of the country; of the facility of transportation afforded by these canoes to those on the islands and rivers, and the foresight of Vesey in fixing on Sunday night for the attack, as on that day the slaves might leave their owner's plantations and come into town without being particularly noticed, which would on any other day be just the reverse.

The attention of the leaders to the most minute particulars is worthy of observation.

In order to insure the assemblage of the Insurgents at the exact moment, the negroes who lived near the places of meeting, were requested for that night to conceal in their owner's premises one or more of their comrades; at least Gullah Jack was pursuing this plan, and as it was proved that the order emanated from Vesey, the same orders were no doubt extended to the others. A white man in this city who was a barber and hair dresser,[42] was employed to make a number of wigs and false whiskers of the hair of white persons for some of the Insurgents, with the assistance which, and by painting their faces, they hoped in the darkness of the night and in the confusion to be mistaken for white men. Such a plan as this would no doubt have assisted Peter in his bold determination to advance singly some distance ahead of his party, and surprise and put to death the sentinel before the Guard House. These wigs and whiskers were the only things by means of which Vesey was thrown off his guard during his imprisonment. The hair dresser who had been employed was carried by the Intendant into Vesey's cell, and Vesey was asked if he knew that man. With the greatest effrontery and composure he denied having ever seen him; at which moment, the Intendant took out of his pocket the very wig made for Vesey himself, which had such an effect upon him, that he exclaimed "good God[")—remained silent a moment or two, and then acknowledged that the wig was made for him and that he knew the man.

The principal features in the plan of attack above given were proved by most of the witnesses; but some of them omitted parts, and some stated other particulars, which it would perhaps be tedious and unnecessary to mention. In addition of the foregoing circumstances, it was proved and subsequently acknowledged by Monday, that Vesey had written two letters to St. Domingo on this subject of the plot;* but of the character, extent and importance of the correspondence, no satisfactory information has been obtained, and perhaps by no other person but Vesey could this have been given.

* Monday never acknowledged *to the Court* that he had written two letters to St. Domingo, but said that Vesey had, and that he in company with Pierault had carried them on board a vessel there bound.

What were the views and plans of the Insurgents after they had taken Charleston, had they succeeded in doing so, does not satisfactorily appear; and it is probable they had formed none, but intended to regulate themselves according to circumstances; but they appeared confident, that they would have been joined by such numbers from the country, as to have been able, at that particular season of the year, and with the fortifications on the Neck and around the Harbour, to have retained possession of the city, as long as they might deem it expedient. One or two of the Insurgents said, that Vesey, after robbing the Banks of species, and plundering the city of all that was most valuable, intended to sail for St. Domingo with his principal adherents; but the informants themselves spoke of it more as a suggestion, than a fixed plan.

The character and condition of most of the Insurgents were such, as rendered them objects the least liable to suspicion. It is a melancholy truth, that the general good conduct of all the leaders, except Gullah Jack, had secured to them not only the unlimited confidence of their owners, but they had been indulged in every comfort, and allowed every priviledge compatible with their situation in the community; and although Gullah Jack was not remarkable for the correctness of his deportment, he by no means sustained a bad character. Vesey himself was free, and had amassed a considerable estate for one of his colour;[43] he was in good business as a carpenter, and enjoyed so much the confidence of the whites, that when he was accused, the charge was not only discredited, but he was not even arrested for several days after, and not until the proof of his guilt had become too strong to be doubted.*

* The following sketch of his life is copied from the account of the intended Insurrection published by the authority of the Corporation of Charleston.[44] . . . He had nearly effected his escape, after information had been lodged against him. For three days the town was searched for him without success. As early as Monday, the 17th, he had concealed himself. It was not until the night of the 22d of June, during a perfect tempest, that he was found secreted in the house of one of his wives. It is to the uncommon efforts and vigilance of Mr. Wesner,[45] and Capt. Dove,[46] of the City Guard, (the latter of whom seized him) that public justice received its necessary tribute, in the execution of this man. If the party had been one moment later, he would, in all probability, have effected his escape the next day in some outward bound vessel.

It is difficult to conceive what motive he had to enter into such a plot, (unless it was the one mentioned by one of the witnesses, who said, that Vesey had several children who were slaves, and that he said on one occasion he wished to see them free;) as he himself artfully remarked in his defence on his trial; yet with him it unquestionably originated, and by him was headed. Rolla was the confidential servant of his master; so much so, that when his master's public duties required his absence from his family, they were left under the protection of that slave; and yet that very man, undertook to head a party, whose first act was to be, the murder of that master, who had reposed such confidence in him, and had treated him with great kindness. Ned was also a confidential servant, and his general good conduct was commendable. "Peter was a slave of great value, and for his colour, a first rate ship carpenter. He possessed the confidence of his master in a remarkable degree, and had been treated with indulgence, liberality and kindness." "Monday enjoyed all the substantial comforts of a free man; (he was) much indulged and trusted by his master; his time and a large proportion of the profits of his labour were at his own disposal. He even kept his master's *arms* and sometimes his money." "He is a most excellent harness-maker, and kept his shop in Meeting-street." "Monday is an *Ebo,* and is now in the prime of life, having been in the country 15 or 20 years." But not only were the leaders of good character and much indulged by their owners, but this was very generally the case with all who were convicted, many of them possessing the highest confidence of their owners, *and not one of bad character.*[47]

Another characteristic of this plot was, that a decided majority of the Insurgents, either did or had belonged to the African Congregation; amongst whom the inlistments were principally and successfully carried on. From the testimony, the presumptions of innocence are in favor of the Bishops and Ministers, (as they styled themselves,) of the Congregation; but two of them have left the state under strong suspicions of having favoured the plot. The class leaders appointed by them, certainly did; two of whom were principals, and Vesey their chief and a fourth leader though not class leaders, yet belonged to the congregation, Rolla being the only exception. . . . [48]

The whole number arrested were one hundred and thirty one, of whom sixty-seven were convicted.—From amongst those convicted, thirty-five were executed; the remainder will be sent beyond the limits of the United States, as well as some of those, who though not convicted, are morally guilty; and of those who suffered death, twenty-two were executed at the same time, on the same gallows. The object of punishment being effectually attained by these examples, and the ring-leaders being convicted, the arrests stopped here.

One who was not a member of the Court, cannot well conceive the effect produced by the threats used, in preventing a discovery of the plot. The enlistments had been going on and the preparations making actively since Christmas, yet it was not until the 30th May, that the least suspicion was entertained by the whites. Had it not been that one, not authorised by Vesey or the other leaders, and evidently unfit for such a purpose, undertook to enlist, no discovery might have been made; for though the information received on the 14th June, was infinitely more extensive and in detail, and from a very different quarter, yet the first communication and the excitement it occasioned, might have had considerable effect in eliciting the other. The information received on the 30th May, however, so far from leading to a discovery of the plot, was eventually disbelieved; so that the detection was not really made, until two nights preceding the intended exhibition of the dreadful tragedy. The discovery of the plot, however, in sufficient time, in this, as in every other instance, enabled the constituted authorities to crush it in the bud.

The information received on the 30th of May, was communicated to the Intendant of Charleston about three o'clock in the afternoon, by a gentleman of great respectability,[49] who that morning had returned from the country. This gentleman stated, "That a favorite and confidential slave of his[50] had communicated to him, on his arrival in town, a conversation which had taken place at the market on the Saturday preceding, between himself and a black man;[51] which afforded strong reasons for believing that a revolt and insurrection were in contemplation among a proportion at least of our black population. The Corporation was forthwith summoned to meet at 5 o'clock, for the purpose of hearing the narrative of the slave who had given this information to his master, to which meeting the attendance of His Excellency the Governor was solicited; with which invitation he promptly complied. Between however, the hours of 3 and 5 o'clock, the gentleman who had conveyed the information to the Intendant, having again examined his slave, was induced to believe, that the negro fellow who had communicated the intelligence of the intended revolt to the slave in question, belonged to Messrs. J. & D. Paul, Broad-street, and resided in their premises. Accordingly, with a promptitude worthy of all praise, without waiting for the interposition of the civil authority he applied to the Messrs. Paul, and had the whole of their male servants committed to the Guard-House, until the individual who had accosted the slave of this gentleman, on the occasion previously mentioned, could be identified from among them.

On the assembling of the Corporation at five, the slave of this gentleman was brought before them, having previously identified Mr. Paul's William as the man who had accos[t]ed him in the Market, he then related the following circumstances:

"On Saturday afternoon last[52] (my master being out of town) I went to market; after finishing my business I strolled down the wharf below the fish market, from which I observed a small vessel in the steam with a singular flag; whilst looking at this object, a black man, (Mr. Paul's William) came up to me and remarking the subject which engaged my attention said, I have often seen a flag with the number 76 on it, but never with 96, before. After some trifling conversation on this point, he remarked with considerable earnestness to me. Do yon know that something serious is about to take place? To which I replied no. Well, said he, there is, and many of us are determined to right ourselves! I asked him to explain himself—when he remarked, why, we are determined to shake off our bondage, and for this purpose we stand on a good foundation, many have joined, and if you will go with me, I will show you the man, who has the list of names who will take yours down. I was so much astonished and horror struck at this information, that it was a moment or two before I could collect myself sufficient to tell him I would have nothing to do with this business, that I was satisfied with my condition, that I was grateful to my master for his kindness and wished no change. I left him instantly, lest, if this fellow afterwards got into trouble, and I had been seen conversing with him, in so public a place, I might be suspected and thrown into difficulty. I did not however remain easy under the burden of such a secret, and consequently determined to consult a free man of colour named———[53] and to ask his advice. On conferring with this friend, he urged me with great earnestness to communicate what had passed between Mr. Paul's man and myself to my master, and not lose a moment in so doing.* I took his advice and not waiting, even for the return of my master to town, I mentioned it to my mistress and young master—On the arrival of my master, he examined me as to what had passed, and I stated to him what I have mentioned to yourselves.

* It would be a libel on the liberality and gratitude of this community to suppose that this man can be *overlooked* among those who are to be rewarded for their fidelity and principle.

"On this witness being dismissed from the presence of Council, the prisoner (William) was examined. The mode resorted to in his examination was to afford him no intimation of the subject of the information which had been lodged against him, as it was extremely desirable in the first place, to have the testimony of the other witness corroborated as to time and place, that, from the confessions of the prisoner himself, it might appear that he was at the fish-market at the period stated, and that a singular flag, flying on board of a schooner, had formed the subject of his observation. After a vast deal of equivocation, he admitted all these facts, but when the rest of his conversation was put home to him, he flatly denied it, but with so many obvious indications of guilt, that it was deemed unwise to discharge him. He was remanded for the night, to the Guard-House, it having been decided to subject him to solitary confinement in the black hole of the Work-House, where, on the succeeding morning, he was to be conveyed.

"On the morning of the 31st he was again examined by the attending Warden at the Guard-House (having during the night, made some disclosures to Capt Dove) on which occasion he admitted all the conversation which he had held at the fish-market, with the witness before mentioned, and stated that he had received his information from Mingo Harth, who was in possession of the muster-roll of the insurgents.

"With the hope of still further disclosures William was conveyed to the Work-House and placed in solitary confinement. The individuals (Mingo Harth and Peter Poyas) against whom he gave information, as those who had communicated to him the intelligence of the plot for raising an insurrection, were forthwith taken up by the Wardens, and their trunks examined. These fellows behaved with so much composure and coolness, and treated the charge, alledged against them with so much levity—(no writings being found in their chests, containing the smallest suspicion, excepting an enigmatical letter, which was then too obscure for explanation, and to which subsequent events only afforded a clue)—that the Wardens (Messrs. Wesner and Condy,) were completely deceived and had these men discharged;" but their movements were nevertheless watched, and measures of precaution taken. "Things remained in this state for six or seven days, until about the 8th of June, when William, who had been a week in solitary confinement, beginning to fear that he would soon be led forth to the scaffold, for summary execution, confessed, that he had for some time known of the plot, that it was very extensive, embracing an indiscriminate massacre of the whites, and that the blacks were to be headed by an individual,[54] who carried about him a charm which rendered him invulnerable."

"Three or four days now elapsed, and notwithstanding all our efforts, we could obtain no confirmation of the disclosures of William, on the contrary, they seemed to have sustained some invalidation, from the circumstance, of one of the individuals (Ned Bennett) whom he named as a person who had information in relation to the insurrection, coming voluntarily to the Intendant, and soliciting an examination, if he was an object of suspicion. In this stage of the business, it was not deemed advisable prematurely to press these examinations, as it might have a tendency to arrest any further developements.

"On the night, however, of Friday the 14th, the information of William was amply confirmed, and details infinitely more abundant and interesting afforded. At 8 o'clock on this evening, the Intendant received a visit from a gentleman, who is advantageously known in this community for his worth and respectability.

This gentleman, with an anxiety, which the occasion was well calculated to beget, stated to the Intendant, that, having the most unbounded confidence in a faithful slave belonging to his family, who was distinguished alike for his uncommon intelligence and integrity, he was induced to inform him, that rumours were abroad of an intended insurrection of the blacks, and that it was said, that this movement had been traced to some of the colored members of Dr. Palmer's church,[55] in which he was known to be a class leader.—On being strongly enjoined to conceal nothing, he, the next day, Friday the 14th, came to his master, and informed him, that the fact was really so, that a public disturbance was contemplated by the blacks, and not a moment should be lost in informing the constituted authorities, as the succeeding Sunday, the 16th, at 12 o'clock, at night, was the period fixed for the rising, which, if not prevented, would inevitably occur at that hour. This slave, it appears, was in no degree connected with the plot, but he had an intimate friend,[56] A——(one of his class) who had been trusted by the conspirators with the secret, and had been solicited by them to join their association; to this A——first appeared to consent, but at no period absolutely sent in his adhesion. According to the statement which he afterwards made himself to the Court, it would seem that it was a subject of great regret and contrition with him, that he had ever appeared to lend his approbation to a scheme so wicked and atrocious, and that he sought occasion to make atonement, by divulging the plot, which on the 14th he did, to the slave of the gentleman in question, his class leader."*

* Most of the black religious communities in this place, are divided into classes, over which a Leader is placed, having the confidence of the Pastor of the Church.

As the account given by this slave was remarkably coincident with the one given by William, with whom he had had no communication, and also coincided in its most material points with the plan of attack just given; such measures were taken by his Excellency the Governor, as the occasion req[u]ired. On the night appointed for the attack, the insurgents found a very strong guard on duty, and by 10 o'clock the whole town was surrounded by the most vigilant patrols; they therefore dared not shew themselves.

Notwithstanding the discovery which had been made, and the complete frustration of their plans, yet so true were they in observing their pledge of secrecy to each other, that of all those arrested up to the 22d June, only six of them were convicted.[57] The discovery which had been made and the conviction of those six, amongst whom was their chief and three of his principal leaders, together with Batteau,[58] who though not as principal a leader as the others, was yet an officer, did not however induce them to lay aside their design, for subsequent to these arrests and convictions, it was proposed to make the attempt early on the morning of the 2d July, immediately after the nightly Guards and Patroles had been discharged from duty, and which would be at the beating of the Reville; and some even had the boldness to propose a rescue and general attack, as the convicts were carried forth for execution. Their reason for fixing on so early a day was, their anxiety to save their Chief and Leaders, who were on that day to be executed; but the time between the day on which those six were sentenced, and that on which they were to be executed, was too short, to enable them to concert proper measures; especially as the whites where now on the alert and watchful; and moreover, one of their two remaining Leaders on whom they principally depended, was arrested the very day previous to the execution, a circumstance well calculated to disconcert and deter them. On the 5th July, further information was received from the slave of another gentleman,[59] who voluntarily came forward and offered to reveal all the information he possessed, on condition that his name should never be disclosed. In addition to naming several of his associates, and describing the sorcerer Gullah Jack, who was his leader, so as to lead to his apprehension, he mentioned that the Insurgents had by no means been induced to abandon their original design by the execution which had taken place on the 2d instant; and that their remaining leader Gullah Jack was actively extending the information, that he had resolved to rise and make the attack at day dawn on the morning of the 6th. Want of time to concert measures for this attack also, would probably have prevented its being made; but it was effectually stopped by the arrest of Gullah Jack on the day previous. . . . [60]

By the timely discovery of this plot, Carolina has been rescued from the most horrible catastrophe with which it has been threatened, since it has been an independent state; for although success could not possibly have attended the conspirators, yet before their suppression, Charleston would probably have been wrapped in flames—many valuable lives have been sacrificed—and an immense loss of property sustained by the citizens, even though no other distressing occurrences were experienced by them; whilst the plantations in the lower country would have been disorganized, and the agricultural interests have sustained an enormous loss.

1. Lionel Henry Kennedy (1787?–1847), an attorney, held a variety of public offices in South Carolina at both the municipal and state levels. A graduate of Yale University, he resided in 1822 at 7 St. Michael's Alley and was "brigade inspector" in the state militia. See *BDSCHR* 4: 329–30; H. P. Archer, *Local Reminiscences: A Lecture Delivered by Mr. H. P. Archer before the Mutual Aid Association, No. 1, of Charleston, S.C. in the Hall of the Mechanics Union, at Charleston, S.C. June 6th, 1889* (Charleston, SC, 1893), 12, and "Obituary," *Charleston Courier,* March 16, 1847.

2. Thomas Parker Jr. (1793?–1844) practiced law in Charleston and resided in 1822 on Meeting Street. President George Washington appointed his more famous father to serve as South Carolina's first US district attorney. See "Obituary," *Charleston Courier,* March 6, 1844, and John Belton O'Neall, *Biographical Sketches of the Bench and Bar of South Carolina . . . ,* 2 vols. (Charleston, SC, 1859), vol. 2: 4.

3. The symbols in this sentence appeared in Kennedy's and Parker's *OR* and were used as footnotes, to alert the reader to additional text at the bottom of the page. We have placed these footnotes at the end of the paragraph to which they correspond.

4. The *OR* may be referring to *Journal of Daniel Coker: a Descendant of Africa, from the Time of Leaving New York, in the Ship Elizabeth, Capt. Sebor, on a Voyage for Sherbro, in Africa, in Company with Three Agents, and about Ninety Persons of Colour* (Baltimore, 1820). Literate and religious Charleston slaves would have known of Sierra Leone and Coker's exploits there from numerous articles in Benjamin Morgan Palmer's *Southern Evangelical Intelligencer.* See, for example, "Sherbro," April 17, 1819, and "Foreign Intelligence," November 18, 1820. Coker (1780–1846), a freedman and Methodist minister, born in Baltimore, had participated in the founding of the AME Church.

5. One of the most popular of Aesop's Fables during the age of democratic revolution. The moral of the fable has a Christian variant: "God helps those who help themselves."

6. The *Charleston Courier,* December 21, 1809, reported the arrival of a variety of consumer goods from the ship *Minerva.*

7. James Browne (1760?–1817), an English immigrant who lived in Charleston for more than forty years, served as Charleston city marshal in 1809. See Charleston *City Gazette and Commercial Daily Advertiser,* July 30, 1817.

8. In 1801, Ann Smith Bonsell Purcell (1763–1836), the widow of Joseph Purcell (d. 1807), a surveyor and cartographer whom she had married in 1792, bought a family of slaves that included Jack. See Sale List, Estate of Joseph Purcell, Charleston District Court of Equity, Equity Bill, 1801, no. 64, SCDAH. *CSCCD,* 58, has the Widow Purcell residing in 1819 at the corner of Green and Bull streets, although the streets, as Harlan Greene has pointed out to this volume's editors, appear to be near each other rather than intersecting. The widow does not appear in the 1822 directory.

9. Peter belonged to James Poyas Sr. (1790–1872), who resided in 1822 at 49 King Street. James Poyas also owned a shipyard on South Bay Street that built coasting vessels involved in Caribbean trade. See *CSCCD,* 95, and *Charleston Courier,* October 14, 1829.

10. Paul Pritchard Sr. (1779–1837) was a ship carpenter who resided in 1822 at 6 Hasell Street.

11. Monday Gell belonged to John Gell Jr. (d. 1824), who in 1822 ran a Charleston livery stable at 127 Church Street. See *CSCCD,* 80.

12. Alexander J. G. Forrester, a minor, owned Lot Forrester. Alexander was probably the son of deceased parents Captain Alexander Forrester and Susannah Forrester, a seamstress, who married in 1802. See Petition of Jeremiah Yates, John R. Rogers, and A. W. Campbell to the South Carolina Senate, n.d. [ca. 1822] no. 1745, Series S165015, SCDAH; "Marriage and Death Notices from the City Gazette," *SCHGM* 27 (April 1926): 98; Richard Hrabowski, *Directory for the District of Charleston . . .* (Charleston, SC, 1809), 38.

13. Frank was the slave of Ann (Wragg) Ferguson (1756–1835), the widow of Thomas Ferguson (1726–1786), a wealthy planter.

14. William (Billy) Palmer belonged to Job Palmer (1747–1845), father of the Reverend Benjamin Morgan Palmer the elder (1781–1847). Job was deacon of Benjamin's Independent or Circular Church in Charleston. See George Howe, *History of the Presbyterian Church in South Carolina,* 2 vols. (Columbia, SC, 1870–1883), vol. 2: 585.

15. The slave William Garner, a drayman, belonged to Martha R. Garner (d. 1832).

16. Charles Drayton, a cook, was owned by Judge John Drayton (1766–1822), a rice planter and twice governor of South Carolina, 1800–1802 and 1808–10.

17. Both Perault and his master, John Strohecker (1776?–1849), were blacksmiths. Strohecker's shop in 1822 was located at 163 Meeting Street. See *CSCCD,* 100.

18. The Reverend Morris Brown (1770–1849), leader of Charleston's African Church, worked as a shoemaker. In 1822 he resided on Wentworth Street. See *CSCCD,* 72.

19. This paragraph appears in Hamilton, *Account,* 29–30. Michael P. Johnson, "A Conversation with Michael Johnson," Centre for the Study of the United States, University of Toronto, online newsletter, January 12, 2004, theorizes that "the mayor [Hamilton] has a big political agenda to make himself famous." Far more than Kennedy and Parker, however, Hamilton was determined to defend the reputation of the African Church's leaders, and unlike the *OR,* his *Account* mentioned the Reverend Morris Brown by name. As the AME materials in Part V of this volume reveal, Hamilton even risked his political career by hiding Brown in his home. See also Robert S. Tinkler, *James Hamilton of South Carolina* (Baton Rouge: Louisiana State University Press, 2004), esp. chap. 2.

20. See letter of James Ferguson to Thomas Parker Jr., September 16, 1822, pp. 108–9.

21. The bottomland of the south bank of the South Santee River, northeast of Charleston, contained thousands of slaves and the estates of some of South Carolina's most illustrious families such as Middleton, Horry, Rutledge, and Pinckney. See G. S. S., "Sketches of the Santee River," *American Monthly Magazine* 8 (October 1836): 313–20 and (November 1836): 431–43.

22. Bacon's Bridge crossed the upper Ashley River twenty miles northwest of Charleston, in the Colleton District, near Stono Swamp.

23. The slave Jesse was owned by Thomas Blackwood (d. 1837), president of the Planter's and Mechanics' Bank, who in 1822 resided at 18 Pitt Street. See *CSCCD,* 107.

24. "The Euhaws" refers to a tract of land, named after an Indian tribe, in the Beaufort District, southwest of Charleston, near the source of Broad River.

25. Hamilton, *Account,* 24, identifies the enslaved blacksmith as Tom Russell. He kept a shop on East Bay Street. Sarah Hopton Russell (1752–1832), widow of Nathaniel Russell (1730–1820), a wealthy merchant, owned Tom.

26. On the burial of arms, see Lydia Maria Child to Thomas Wentworth Higginson, March 7, 1860, in Part VI of this volume. In 1838, more than three hundred citizens from the Abbeville and Edgefield districts protested the choice of the Reverend Thomas D. Turpin (d. 1838) by the South

Carolina Methodist Conference to preach to South Carolina's slaves. The petitioners referenced the Vesey affair in complaining about the dangers posed by slave assemblages under the pretext of religious instruction and cited, among other things, "mock interments" used by slaves in 1822 to bury weapons. For the relevant passage see Part VI, p. 727, in this volume. For an analogous instance in Guadeloupe of rebellious slaves using burial grounds to secret weapons, see New York *Chronicle Express,* December 2, 1802.

27. John Horry, a slave coachman, belonged to Elias Horry (1773–1834), one of the largest slaveholders in lowcountry South Carolina. He owned hundreds of slaves and multiple rice plantations on and near the Santee River, fifty miles or so northeast of Charleston.

28. Pharo (also "Pharaoh") Thompson belonged to Jane Thompson (also spelled "Thomson"), an elderly widow. See Jane Thomson to the Senate of South Carolina, November 22, 1822, no. 132, Series S165015, SCDAH.

29. Adam's owner, the cooper Joseph Yates (1775–1822), died in February, four months before the plot was uncovered. His antislavery wife, Elizabeth Saylor Yates (1787–1867), wrote the letter to Harrison Gray Otis, transcribed in Part I of this volume.

30. Bacchus worked as a porter for the merchant Benjamin Hammet (1794?–1826). Benjamin's father, William, was the Methodist minister whom the antislavery Reverend Lorenzo Dow (see Part I, pp. 18–19) was convicted by a Charleston Court of Sessions of libeling.

31. The merchant Francis Duquercron (d. 1848), listed as a "grocer" in the 1819 Charleston directory, owned a store on King Street Road, Charleston Neck.

32. In 1822 John Schirer (d. 1827) worked as a gunsmith at 48 Queen Street. See *CSCCD,* 98.

33. July 8.

34. Sullivan's Island, home to Fort Moultrie, just northeast of Charleston Harbor, contained an African American burial ground where officials suspected the plotters had concealed weapons. Of the estimated 200,000 or so African slaves estimated to have entered the Carolinas and Georgia from 1710 to 1810, tens of thousands would have passed through Sullivan's Island. No site in what became the United States held more imported African slaves in quarantine, usually for ten to fourteen days. See Peter McCandless, *Slavery, Disease, and Suffering in the Southern Lowcountry* (New York: Cambridge University Press, 2011), 6, 48–50, 55.

35. Mingo, a domestic slave, belonged to William Harth, a prosperous lumber merchant, who in 1822 lived at 1 Gibbes Street. See *CSCCD,* 82.

36. Despite the precise date supplied here, mentioned again in the trial documentation, Richard C. Wade, "The Vesey Plot: A Reconsideration," *JSH* 30 (1964): 150, argued that "no cache of arms lay hidden about the city; no date for an uprising had been set." In addition to the reference above to arms being buried, see Part III, p. 222, for the testimony provided by Billy Bulkley at the July 16 trial of Polydore Fabor, in which a "bundle of pike poles found concealed on the farm [were] then in court." For a devastating dismantling of Wade's misuse of evidence, see William W. Freehling, "Vesey's Reality," in *New Perspectives on Race and Slavery in America: Essays in Honor of Kenneth M. Stampp,* ed. Robert H. Abzug and Stephen E. Maizlish (Lexington: University Press of Kentucky, 1986). On the question of arms, see Robert L. Paquette, "From Rebellion to Revisionism: The Continuing Debate about the Denmark Vesey Affair," *Journal of the Historical Society* 4 (Fall 2004): 306–11.

37. James Island, home to Fort Johnson, the oldest of the forts that guarded Charleston Harbor, lies to the south of Charleston, across Ashley River.

38. "Bennett's Mills" refers to a waterfront property, originally known as Bennett & Stone's Wharf, on the Ashley River where Thomas Bennett Sr. (1754–1814), father of Governor Bennett, conducted a successful rice and lumber business. See Charleston *City Gazette and Commercial Daily Advertiser,* March 3, 1816.

39. Cannonborough was a suburb north of Charleston near Coming's Creek. See Robert N. Rosen, *A Short History of Charleston* (Columbia: University of South Carolina Press, 1997), 86.

40. Gadsden's Wharf, located on the Cooper River, was a major landing for slaves entering Charleston when South Carolina reopened the Atlantic slave trade in 1804. See New York *Public Advertiser,* March 5, 1807; James A. McMillin, *The Final Victims: Foreign Slave Trade to North America, 1783–1810* (Columbia: University of South Carolina Press, 2004), 110.

41. As Eugene D. Genovese, *From Rebellion to Revolution: Afro-American Slave Revolts in the Making of the Modern World* (Baton Rouge: Louisiana State University Press, 1979), 10, aptly observes, Vesey "expected to force his people to choose not between revolution and safety but between revolution and counter-revolutionary violence." Severe restrictions on slave movements and assemblage made recruitment on the march an obvious tactic for leaders of slave rebellions throughout the Americas.

42. Most of the hairdressers in Charleston in 1822 were free persons of color, yet Vesey chose to approach instead a white hairdresser for the disguises. *CSCCD,* 40, 71, 77, identifies only two white hairdressers in 1822: Patrick Boyle and Leon Duplan. Given that John Potter in a letter to Langdon Cheves, July 5, 1822 (see Part IV, pp. 372–73), identifies the fellow as a "french man," Duplan is the likely witness against Vesey.

43. The Charleston *City Gazette and Commercial Daily Advertiser,* August 21, 1822, claimed that Vesey died a rich man worth nearly eight thousand dollars, but there is no evidence that he ever owned a single piece of property. His rented home on Bull Street, which is now gone, was first owned by attorney George Warren Cross (1783–1836), who defended Vesey during his trial, and toward the end of Vesey's life by Benjamin Ireland (d. 1821?), a white carpenter.

44. The "sketch" of Vesey's life that first appeared in Hamilton, *Account,* 17, was reprinted as a footnote to this paragraph in *OR.* The first parts of this brief biography are reprinted in Part I of this volume.

45. Frederick Wesner (1788–1848), a carpenter and architect, was a city warden in 1822 and a member of the vigilance committee that had formed in response to the Vesey affair. In its aftermath, Wesner designed the state arsenal that would become known as the Citadel. See William H. Buckley, *The Citadel and the South Carolina Corps of Cadets* (Charleston, SC: Arcadia, 2004), 9, and Beatrice St. Julien Ravenel, *Architects of Charleston* (Columbia: University of South Carolina Press, 1992), 137, 146.

46. William Pritchard Dove (1789–1828), a ship joiner, had served as captain of the City Guard in Charleston as early as 1818. See "Election of City Officers," Charleston *City Gazette and Daily Advertiser,* October 20, 1818. On the night of May 30–31, the slave William Paul "made some disclosures" about the Vesey affair to Dove. He captured Vesey on Saturday, June 22.

47. Kennedy and Parker took the descriptions of Monday Gell and Peter Poyas, which appear here in quotation marks, from Hamilton, *Account,* 14, 21. The word "Ebo," which has several variant spellings, to identify Monday suggests that he arrived in South Carolina from the Bight of Biafra in West Africa. See Alexander X. Byrd, "Violence, Migration, and Becoming Igbo in Gustavus Vassa's *Interesting Narrative,*" in *Constructing Borders/Crossing Boundaries: Race, Ethnicity, and Immigration,* ed. Caroline B. Brettell (Lanham, MD: Lexington Books, 2007), 47.

48. The descriptions here of "the conduct and behaviour" of Vesey and the other leaders at the time of their executions appear in Part III of this volume.

49. The reference here is to John Cordes Prioleau (1772–1825), merchant and planter.

50. Peter Prioleau, who would obtain freedom as a result of his testimony and become known as Peter Desverney.

51. William Paul, a slave owned by John Paul (1785–1846), a Scottish-born grocer, who in 1822 ran a business with his brother Dunbar (1792–1876) at 47 Broad Street.

52. May 22.

53. The unnamed free person of color is William Penceel, or "Pinceel." He appears in the *DS-GCC*, 105, as a "tin-plate worker" who lived at 81 Meeting Street. The *Rules and Regulations of the Brown Fellowship Society, Established at Charleston, S.C., 1st November, 1790* (Charleston, SC, 1844), 17, lists "William Pinceel" as a member. On June 10, 1868, his son William B., described as "Brown," opened an account with the Charleston branch of the Freedman's Savings Bank for his children, Evelyn and William H. Penceel, age seven. See Register of Signatures of Depositors in Branches of the Freedman's Savings and Trust Company, Reel 21, National Archives. Since the literate William B. Penceel in the years after the Civil War adopted that spelling, it was evidently the family's preferred spelling.

54. Gullah Jack Pritchard, slave of ship carpenter Paul Pritchard Sr. (1779–1837).

55. Benjamin Morgan Palmer's Congregational or Circular Church.

56. Joe La Roche.

57. Hamilton, *Account,* 43, writes that six of those "executed" were arrested by June 22. Jesse Blackwood was arrested on June 23.

58. Batteau (French for a shallow-draft, flat-bottomed boat used in American waters) was one of three slaves owned by Governor Bennett and sentenced to death for involvement in the plot.

59. This unidentified slave may have been Harry Haig, the slave of David Haig, (1783–1832), a Scottish immigrant who ran a cooperage at Craft's Wharf. According to Hamilton, *Account,* 45, Harry was arrested on July 5. The slave Yorrick Cross testified that Harry Haig was in Jack Pritchard's company, and his commuted sentence of transportation suggests that Haig proved useful to the court. See Petition of David Haig, November 22, 1826, no. 131, series S165015, Petitions to the General Assembly, SCDAH.

60. The ensuing discussion, which appeared in *OR,* 56–59, as to why the court decided on July 10 to pardon Monday Gell and Harry Haig, has been moved to the relevant section of the trials and appears here on pp. 202–4.

W. Hasell Wilson to Reverend Robert Wilson, no date[1]

In the early part of the year 1822, there were appearances of something unusual going on among the negroes, and suspicion was aroused as to insurrection, but nothing definite was ascertained until the latter part of May.

My grandmother Wilson owned a slave named George, who being a good blacksmith was allowed to work at his trade, paying to his owner a reasonable amount of wages; this was not unusual in cases where the personal services of slaves were not required by their owners. I remember George very well: he was a dark mulatto of large frame and good appearance, a class leader in the Methodist Church.[2] He could read and write and bore an excellent character among both whites and blacks. It appeared that overtures had been made to George by some of the leaders in a plot for an uprising and general massacre of the white population. He held the matter in abeyance long enough to gain knowledge of material points, and then communicated his information to my father,[3] who immediately conferred with the authorities of the city. I remember George coming to our house on two or three successive evenings, and holding mysterious conferences with my father, who then went to see Major Hamilton, the Intendant of the City. (corresponding to Mayor to which the title was subsequently changed). For several days consultations were being held by those in authority and prominent citizens. Information having been obtained as to the exact night upon which the uprising was to take place, preparations were made to meet it. The city guards were kept on duty all the time, and were re-inforced at night by detachments from the several volunteer military companies, all of whom were held under orders. The watchmen at the several signal stations were doubled, and for two or three days prior to the expected time, men were kept busy putting arms in order, preparing cartridges &c &c at the guard houses and arsenal.

I can never forget the feeling of alarm and anxiety that pervaded the whole community, from the time the danger became known, until all risk appeared to be over. On the night appointed for the consummation of the plot, no one not even the children ventured to retire. The passing of the patrols on the streets, and every slight noise, excited attention. When morning dawned without any alarm having been given, there was a general feeling of relief, but the anxiety and suspense were not dissipated for some time.

The negroes had become alarmed at the preparations that could not escape their attention, and feared to make the attempt; they had calculated upon the secresy of their plans for insuring success. As usual in such cases, as soon as it began to be realized that the plot had been discovered, there were enough of the weak hearted coming forward to testify in hopes of getting clear, and no difficulty was experienced in securing sufficient evidence for the conviction of the leaders. According to my recollection, about twenty were executed; the others who had been induced to join in the movement, were too ignorant and too thoroughly frightened to ensure any uneasiness as to a repetition. Nevertheless, a strict system of vigilance continued to be kept.

On account of the fidelity, uprightness and good judgement evinced by George, his freedom was purchased by the City of Charleston.

W. Hasell Wilson

1. William Hasell Wilson (1811–1902), a Charleston native, wrote this undated letter long after the fact. The author of *Reminiscences of a Railroad Engineer* (Philadelphia, 1896), Wilson evidently recovered this letter while drafting his autobiography, which Elizabeth Pharo edited and published in 1937 under the title *Reminiscences of William Hasell Wilson* (Philadelphia: Patterson & White, 1937). Wilson wrote on the bottom of this letter that the date was "now (June 1900)" and that he was eighty-nine. He added: "None of the names are mentioned in this book, as that would have led to the discovery of George's identity, kept secret to protect him from the vengeance of the negroes." Since his autobiography was to be published long after George Wilson's death in March 1848, Wilson may have been referring to the *OR*.

2. According to Kennedy's and Parker's "Narrative of the Conspiracy," which appears above, George Wilson was once a member of Reverend Benjamin Morgan Palmer's Congregational or Circular Church. As a devout Christian who regarded his friend Rolla Bennett's actions as ungodly, George Wilson was an unimpeachable witness who poses a problem for modern scholars who believe, as did historian Richard Wade, that the plot was "probably never more than loose talk by aggrieved and embittered men." In his "The Vesey Plot: A Reconsideration," *JSH* 30 (1964), 143, Wade fused William Penceel and George Wilson into a single individual named "George Pencil." On Wilson, who was freed by the state assembly in December 1825 and changed his name to George Watkins before dying in 1848, see Larry Koger, *Black Slaveowners: Free Black Slave Masters in South Carolina, 1790–1860* (Jefferson, NC: McFarland, 1985), 178, and James O'Neil Spady, "Power and Confession: On the Credibility of the Earliest Reports of the Denmark Vesey Slave Conspiracy," *WMQ* 68 (2011): 287–304.

3. Major John Wilson (1789–1833), who resided at 106 Broad Street, worked as the state's chief civil and military engineer.

ALS in CLS.

James Hamilton Jr. to William Lowndes,[1] Sunday, June 16, 1822

For the last week, I have been indulging myself with the hope that I should find time to ride to the Grove[2] and see you before your departure, but for several days I have been increasingly occupied both night & day in relation to a subject on which public anxiety has been astutely awakened. And I am sorry at the last moment I should be debarred this pleasure.

I must therefore by Letter wish you a prosperous voyage, and a safe return to us, with your health altogether reestablished.

Before I close this communication, I must observe to you, that the more I have investigated (within the last twenty four hours) the *cause* of the public's alarm the more satisfied I am of the little reason we have for apprehension. In either alternative we are safe, as the measures to be adopted assure to us, immediate security, and ample triumph.

I have taken it of course for granted that you must have heard of the rumor of a contemplated commotion among a certain part of our population. . . .

1. William Lowndes (1782–1822), planter and statesman, was a nationalist war hawk, considered presidential material by the lowcountry neo-Federalists like James Hamilton Jr., who surrounded Lowndes in 1822, shortly before his premature death. Lowndes had earned high marks in the

Figure 3. James Hamilton Jr. (1786–1857), intendant of Charleston in 1822. From a portrait, ca. 1815. Courtesy of Louis Round Wilson Special Collections Library, University of North Carolina at Chapel Hill.

US House of Representatives as chairman on both the Committee on Ways and Means and the Committee on Naval Affairs. Scorching national criticism of a contrived slave revolt before the presidential election of 1824 would not have served the interests of such men who were intent on elevating the first South Carolinian to the White House. In fact, during a meeting of South Carolina's state legislature in December 1821, members wasted no time in nominating Lowndes as their preferred candidate in the 1824 presidential election. See *BDSCHR* 4: 359–61; "Interesting Papers," *Charleston Courier*, July 18, 1853.

2. Lowndes, coincidentally, purchased the Grove estate from Captain Joseph Vesey, who inherited it following the death of Mary Clodner Vesey in 1802. See Mary Clodner Vesey, January 15, 1802, Letters of Administration, Probate, RR, p. 360, Charleston County, SCDAH.

ALS in William Lowndes Papers, folder 9A, SHC, UNC.

Thomas Bennett Jr. to Colonel George Cross,[1] Monday, June 17, 1822

Head Quarters
Charleston June 17, 1822.

Col. Com. Cross
Com. the 4th Brigade So. Ca. Militia
Sir

You are hereby required to detail from the Brigade which you command one or more Companies as a nightly guard; which detachment shall consist of not less than Sixty privates and non-commissioned officers, nor more than One Hundred and the requisite number of commissioned officers.

In the extension of this order, respect will be paid to that organizing a detachment in cases of alarm from fire; should their services be required in the capacity of a guard, the whole number of the detachment will be ordered out.

Those who have already performed that duty will not again be called out until that service shall have been performed by all the companies within your command.

From the general directions contained in this order, you will exempt the command of Capt Martindale,[2] whom you will separately require to furnish a sufficient guard for his beat or double his Patrol as he shall deem expedient.

You will concert measures with the city authorities to avoid collision between the guard hereby ordered and the *City Guard*; and between the guard which you shall organize within the corporate limits and that which shall be ordered by Capt. Martindale.

You will forthwith report to me the regulations which have been adopted for your Brigade in cases of extraordinary alarm as a meeting of the Field Officers of the Brigade will be immediately convened for their review and revision if necessary.

Reports will be made as usual and the details of the duty subjected to your discretion.

Very Respectfully Sir,
Your Obet St
Tho: Bennett

1. George Warren Cross (1783–1836), of Huguenot descent and a French-speaker, was a colonel in the state militia. He would later serve as Denmark Vesey's attorney. See *BDSCHR* 4: 137–38.

2. James C. Martindale (d. 1823), a planter, resided in 1822 on King Street in Charleston Neck. As a militia captain active on Charleston Neck in the aftermath of the discovery of the Vesey plot, he armed his corps at his own expense with muskets and bayonets purchased from Duquercron's store. See *CSCCD,* 89; Petition of Louisa Martindale to the South Carolina House of Representatives, November 20, 1823, no. 54, series S165015, SCDAH.

ALS in SCL.

City Gazette and Commercial Daily Advertiser

Monday, June 17, 1822

CORONER'S REPORT

A Jury of Inquest was impannelled yesterday morning, at No. 25 Meeting street, between the hours of 7 and 8 o'clock. to enquire into the cause or causes which led to the death of Dr. *John Ward M'Call,* aged about 29 years.[1] From the evidence adduced to the Jury, it appears that the deceased was in the act of putting away his pistol in the wardrobe of his chamber when it suddenly went off. The Jury, after being perfectly satisfied of the facts above mentioned, brought in the following verdict: That the deceased came to his death by an accidental discharge of a loaded Pistol which he was putting away in the wardrobe of his chamber. . . .

JOHN MICHEL, *Coroner*
For the Parishes of St. Philip and St. Michael

1. McCall (1793–1822) left behind a young wife, Mary (Ravenel) McCall (1800–1886), and a newly born child. She never remarried. According to Ravenel family lore, "During the negro insurrection in 1822, the gentlemen in Charleston kept arms about their bedrooms. Mr. McCall had arisen before his wife one morning, and she was aroused by the report of a pistol, to find him shot dead by his own weapon, the blood being sprinkled over the bed." Henry Edmund Ravenel, *Ravenel Records: A History and Genealogy of the Huguenot Family of Ravenel, of South Carolina* (Atlanta, 1898), 60. McCall's death caused rumors about foul play by slaves and precipitated Judge William Johnson's article on slave panic in the *Charleston Courier.*

Philadelphia *United States Gazette and True American*

Friday, June 28, 1822

The blacks of South Carolina, have lately manifested a disposition to revolt, and some preparations were made by the plantation negroes to attempt to take the city of Charleston. But prompt measures were taken to repel an attack and the fears of an insurrection are now dissipated.

Salem *Gazette*

Friday, June 28, 1822

NEW YORK, JUNE 25.

Blacks of South Carolina.—We have seen a letter from Charleston, of the 17th inst. of which the following is an extract:

"You will doubtless hear many reports, and exaggerated ones, respecting an insurrection among the negroes.—There certainly was a disposition of revolt manifested, and some preparations made, principally, as far as we have ascertained, by the plantation negroes, to attempt to take the city; but from the arrangements for defence made by us, there is now little *hopes* that the attempt will be made—and, if made, no fear of the result. I say *hopes,* because we did *hope* they would progress so far as to enable us to ascertain and punish the Ringleaders, in an exemplary manner. I was ordered on duty last night, but the orders were afterwards countermanded, we however got very little sleep.

"Assure my friends, and those who have friends here, that we feel in perfect security, although the number of nightly guards, and other demonstrations, may induce a belief, among strangers, to the contrary."[1]

1. This information was reprinted nearly verbatim in *The Genius of Universal Emancipation* 2 (July 1822): 15–16; Hartford *Connecticut Courant,* July 2, 1822; and Gettysburg *Republican Compiler,* July 3, 1822.

Charleston *Southern Patriot, and Commercial Advertiser*

Monday, July 1, 1822

COMMUNICATED. MR. EDITOR:—It was with much pain that we read in the "Courier" of this morning, a suggestion that our fellow-citizens, the members of the Court now assembled on an investigation, all important to the peace and security not only of our City but of our State, propose to retire. Through your excellent paper, Sir, permit us to express an earnest hope that no *consideration whatever* may at this momentous crisis be of weight sufficient to influence them to such a determination; the very apprehension of which has excited no common degree of anxiety and regret throughout the community. They have well deserved, and they must know that they possess the utmost respect and the fullest confidence of their fellow citizens, no small number of whom beg leave in this communication, to offer to the Members composing the Court to which we refer, not only collectively, but individually, every assurance of cordial esteem and heartfelt gratitude.

James Hamilton Jr. to Frederick Beard, Wednesday, July 10, 1822

Charleston 10th July 1822

Mr. Beard[1]

I have it expressly in charge from the Court to desire that you permit no person whatsoever to visit the prisoners in your custody excepting their Wives, Masters Children & such Clergymen as they may be desirous of communicating with.[2] Should the prisoners express a wish to see one of the Members of the Corporation in this event he is to be admitted not otherwise. By order of the Court.

J. Hamilton Jr. Intendant

While the Commissioners feel sensible at the arduous official duties you are called upon, at this Juncture to perform, and of the correctness of your motives they deem it due to their respectability to object to the course of proceeding adopted by you as far as the object & Policy of the order in question are concerned. They concur strictly in opinion with yourself & the Court, nor would any Member of the Board have complained of the measure, had it passed through the proper channel. Regarding themselves as the immediate guardians of the Institution, they could not but feel wounded by your order which invested the Master with a permanent authority, and placed them in a situation awkward & delicate in the extreme. We are authorized to assure you, Sir, that there is not a Member of the Board who feels any other disposition, than that which actuates your conduct in relation to the existing causes of Public excitement. They are disposed at all times, to countenance & defend the Measures of Public Policy, which may be resorted to by Council while they confidently trust that upon the recurrence of a case like the present you will in justice to their feelings direct your Instructions for the treatment of Prisoners to the Board, who will send every aid in their power to carry them into effect.

With Sentiments of Respect & Esteem
We have the pleasure Sir to
subscribe ourselves
yr obt St
J B Legare[3]
Chas Parker[4]

1. Because of the need to segregate prisoners and move those already condemned out of the crowded Work-House, the court began to place prisoners in both the city jail and the Charleston Poor-House, also known as the Alms House. Located at 4 Mazyck Street, just across from the jail, the three-story brick building was finished in 1771. See *CDSG*, 65, and Walter J. Fraser Jr., *Charleston! Charleston! The History of a Southern City* (Columbia: University of South Carolina Press, 1989), 193. *CSCCD*, 70, lists for 1822 three male Beards, two named Frederick and one named William. City Council of Charleston, "Petition and Supporting Papers Asking Compensation for Expenses Incurred in Putting Down the Late Slave Insurrection," December 3, 1822, series S165015, item no. 130, SCDAH, identifies an "F. Beard" owed $175 for the making of thirty-five coffins for the executed. Of the two Frederick Beards in 1822, one was a bank teller, the other a mill owner. The latter is the likely correspondent of James Hamilton Jr.

2. These exceptions suggest that Thomas C. Brown, a carpenter and lay minister, may have had contact with some of the accused before or after their trials. See Brown's reminiscences to Lydia Maria Child (1802–1880) in her March 17, 1860, letter to abolitionist Thomas Wentworth Higginson (1823–1911) in Part IV, pp. 749–53, of this volume.

3. The Charleston City Council had elected John Berwick Legaré (1794–1850), an attorney, to superintend the Poor-House.

4. Charles Parker (1797–1859), a surveyor and engineer, was elected in 1822 to superintend the Poor-House.

ALS in Minutes of the Charleston Alms House, 1822–1828, p. 29, CPL.

Governor Thomas Bennett Jr. to Secretary of War John C. Calhoun, Monday, July 15, 1822[1]

Executive Department
Charleston July 15 1822

The Hon: John C. Calhoun
Secty of the War dept. of the United States
Sir

The state of alarm which has for some time pervaded this community consequent on the discovery of insurrectionary movements, has directed anxious inquiry and awakened the most extraordinary vigilance. Among other facts the discovery of which is attributable to this state of the Public mind the following will deservedly attract your attention

The Local situation of Fort Johnson[2] and its immediate connection with a populous Island separated from the main only by a narrow creek fordable at low water is at present garrisoned by *five men.* At their post the Mystello Tower[3] erected during the late war has been converted into a magazine, and contains at present besides a few implements of War One hundred and forty Barrels of gun powder represented to be partially damaged

Application has been made to Major Bird[4] on this subject who proposes as a remedy the removal of the powder to the State Magazine; desirable as this change of position would be it is rendered impracticable while this establishment remains almost wholey occupied by the United States.

The Executive of this state was authorized previous to the cession of this post to the United States, to establish there a sufficient guard for the execution of the Health Laws. (You are aware that this commands the quarantine station). You may readily imagine with how much confidence his proclamation is issued when he is to rely on a garrison of five men to carry into effect its provisions.

The Effective force at Fort Moultrie[5] does not exceed an aggregate of Forty men—from which it is deemed inexpedient to augment the garrison at Fort Johnson. The alternative presented is to detail a Guard from the Militia for the protection of this post should it be requisite.

The peculiar character of a large proportion of our population, and the evidence of a temper hostile to the peace and welfare of society which has so recently been manifested, will continue for some time to exact vigilance, and elicit anxiety. At such a moment it is certainly to be deprecated that any causes should exist, remediable by the general government, which are calculated to perpetuate, the public alarm. Yet such is distinctly the fact, so far as it embraces the unprotected state of the several Forts in this Harbour. I pray you not to infer any charge of remissness or want of attention on the Part of the officer commanding at this station.

I would respectfully submit to your consideration the propriety of augmenting the number of men on this station. It will I trust be unnecessary to accede to the motives which should influence your decision, or urge the claims of their state on the General

Government for such a proportion of the Military force of the nation as the present exigency requires.

I have the honour to be
Very Respectfully and
with the highest esteem
your Ob. Servt
Tho. Bennett

1. John Caldwell Calhoun (1782–1850) served as secretary of war in the administration of President James Monroe. Like many white South Carolinians in the early 1820s, Calhoun was not yet a sectionalist or states' rights man, and his nationalist policies included support for protective tariffs. Elected to the House of Representatives in 1810, Calhoun became the nation's tenth secretary of war on October 8, 1817. See Irving H. Bartlett, *John C. Calhoun: A Biography* (New York: Norton, 1993), 69–104.

2. Fort Johnson, the oldest of the forts protecting Charleston harbor, was erected on James Island during the first decade of the eighteenth century. See Robert B. Roberts, *Encyclopedia of Historic Forts: The Military, Pioneer, and Trading Posts of the United States* (New York: Macmillan, 1988), 715.

3. A Martello tower is a circular fortification made of stones, popular during the Napoleonic era.

4. In 1822 Major John A. Burd (1784?–1827) commanded the US Army at the Charleston station.

5. On Sullivan's Island, Fort Moultrie, in its third incarnation, completed in 1809, consisted of masonry fortifications. It sits at the entrance to Charleston Harbor across from and to the north of Fort Johnson. See Robert B. Roberts, *Encyclopedia of Historic Forts: The Military, Pioneer, and Trading Posts of the United States* (New York: Macmillan, 1988), 716–17.

ALS in Letters Received by the Secretary of War. Registered Series, 1810–1860, roll 95, NA.

Joel Roberts Poinsett[1] to John C. Calhoun, Sunday, July 21, 1822

Charleston 21 July 1822

When the Commissioners were here to examine the defences of Charleston[2] they privately expressed an opinion, that the Lines[3] of our city were useless. I have been long impressed with the belief, that they are worse than useless and am anxious to have them removed. They retard the progress of our city; the ditches contain a great deal of stagnant water and render that part of the Neck unhealthy. By removing the Lines and cutting a canal from river to river a distance of three-quarters' of a mile, the land would be well drained, a water communication established for the upper part of our City, and a better line of defence formed than the present one.

I shall address the Legislature on the subject and would be glad to have the opinion of the Commissioners whether the Lines across the neck of Land above the City of Charleston are necessary for the defence of the City.

Joel R. Poinsett

1. Joel Roberts Poinsett (1779–1851) was one of five freeholders to sit in judgment of accused conspirators in the Vesey plot on the second Court of Magistrates and Freeholders. A Jacksonian

Figure 4. John C. Calhoun (1782–1850), secretary of war in 1822. From an engraving of a drawing in *The National Portrait of Distinguished Americans* by J. B. Longacre, part 15 (1834).

nationalist with British military training, diplomatic skills, and doubts about theories of racial superiority, Poinsett would lead South Carolina's Unionist Party in opposition to the nullification movement. See "Death of the Hon. Joel R. Poinsett," Macon *Georgia Telegraph,* December 23, 1851; J. Fred Rippy, *Joel R. Poinsett, Versatile American* (Durham, NC: Duke University Press, 1935).

2. The commissioners alluded to here served on the Charleston Board of Engineers.

3. The Lines were a string of earthen fortifications that ran above the city of Charleston from the Ashley River to the Cooper River. Major John Wilson, whose wife, Eliza (Gibbes) Wilson (1787–1853), owned George Wilson, a key witness in the Vesey proceedings, constructed the Lines at the beginning of the War of 1812. See Elizabeth Pharo, ed., *Reminiscences of William Hasell Wilson* (Philadelphia: Patterson & White, 1937), 8.

The Papers of John C. Calhoun, ed. W. Edwin Hemphill (Columbia: University of South Carolina Press, 1973), vol. 7: 219.

John C. Calhoun to James Bankhead,[1] Monday, July 22, 1822

Washington, Department of War

Upon the representation of the Governor of South Carolina requiring an additional military force to be stationed at Charleston, the enclosed order[2] has been given to Lieut Colonel Eustis[3] for the removal of one Company from St. Augustine to that place, with orders, on its arrival to report to you.

You will consult with the Governor of South Carolina upon the distribution to be made of the Company on its arrival and co-operate with him upon such measures as may be deemed adviseable in quelling the disturbances at Charleston.

John C. Calhoun

1. In 1822, Virginia-born Major James Monroe Bankhead (1783–1856) commanded an artillery regiment in Charleston. See "Distribution of the Army," *Portland* (ME) *Gazette*, May 29, 1821, and "Death of a Veteran," Washington *Daily National Intelligencer*, November 13, 1856.

2. Dated July 22.

3. Lt. Colonel Abram Eustis (1786–1843) commanded artillery at St. Augustine, Florida.

The Papers of John C. Calhoun, ed. W. Edwin Hemphill (Columbia: University of South Carolina Press, 1973), vol. 7: 219.

John C. Calhoun to Thomas Bennett Jr., Monday, July 22, 1822

Department of War, July 22d 1822

I have received your letter of the 15th instant in relation to the state of the Garrisons in Charleston Harbour, and have ordered without delay a reinforcement of one Company from St. Augustine, which I hope will be sufficient to remove the uneasiness in the publick mind on account of the inadequacy of the Garrisons. I would add another Company, but the Military Establishment is so reduced in proportion to the number of posts which we are compelled to occupy that it cannot be done with propriety. At no point on the Atlantic Coast is there more than one Company, except at Boston, New York, Norfolk, Charleston and St. Augustine, at the latter of which there are three, and at all the others but two each. To reduce the Garrison by withdrawing a Company from Boston, New York, or Norfolk, would I fear produce much excitement, and make an impression which ought if possible to be avoided. The recruiting depots, are, however now opened and the recruiting will be pushed with activity in the principal Northern Cities, and I have given orders to fill the Companies at Charleston Harbour so soon as the recruits are made. I have also ordered the Officer Commanding in the Harbour[1] to consult with you, and to co-operate to the extent of his means in such measures as may be thought advisable to be adopted. I enclose you a copy of the orders to him.

I hope these measures will be satisfactory. I wish you to be assured that if more ample means existed, it would have afforded me much pleasure to have added those which have been adopted.

John C. Calhoun

1. Major James Monroe Bankhead.

The Papers of John C. Calhoun, ed. W. Edwin Hemphill (Columbia: University of South Carolina Press, 1973), vol. 7: 220.

John C. Calhoun to Abram Eustis, Monday, July 22, 1822

Washington, Department of War

Orders, Lieutenant Colonel Eustis, or Officer Commanding at St. Augustine will cause to be embarked immediately from that place one effective Company of Artillery under the Command of a suitable subaltern Officer to proceed to Charleston South Carolina, and report for orders to Major Bankhead or Officer Commanding.

The Company on its arrival at Charleston, will be turned over to the command of Captain Payne[1] who is now at that place.

The Quarter Master's Department will provide the necessary transportation in the above case.

John C. Calhoun

1. Captain Matthew Mountjoy Payne (1787–1862) arrived on Sullivan's Island from St. Augustine on Thursday, August 15, with a company of troops. See *Charleston Courier*, August 16, 1822.

The Papers of John C. Calhoun, ed. W. Edwin Hemphill (Columbia: University of South Carolina Press, 1973), vol. 7: 220–21.

John C. Calhoun to Winfield Scott,[1] Monday, July 22, 1822

Department of War, July 22d 1822

You will perceive by the enclosed order[2] that one Company of Artillery at St. Augustine, has been directed to proceed to Charleston. The order was given direct from this Department, upon the urgency of the case, and upon the requisition of the Governor of South Carolina for an additional military force.

John C. Calhoun

1. Brigadier General Winfield Scott (1786–1866) then held regional command in the Division of the North. See Allan Peskin, *Winfield Scott and the Profession of Arms* (Kent, OH: Kent State University Press, 2003). 2. The order went to Abram Eustis.

The Papers of John C. Calhoun, ed. W. Edwin Hemphill (Columbia: University of South Carolina Press, 1973), vol. 7: 221.

John C. Calhoun to Joel R. Poinsett, Monday, July 29, 1822

Department of War, July 29, 1822

I have had the honor to receive today your communication of the 21st Inst upon the subject of the present lines for the defence of Charleston, & expressing a wish to have the opinion of the Board of Engineers whether the lines across the neck of land above the City are necessary for its defence. The Bd of Engineers have not yet reported their plans for the defence of the Coasts of So Carolina & Georgia, and it will be necessary to refer the subject of your communication to them. A Copy of your letter will be immediately dispatched to the Board, who are in New York with direction to make a report upon the subject thereof as soon as practicable, which will be transmitted to you without delay.

John C. Calhoun

The Papers of John C. Calhoun, ed. W. Edwin Hemphill (Columbia: University of South Carolina Press, 1973), vol. 7: 226.

Charleston Courier

Tuesday, July 30, 1822

We understand that, at the suggestion of the Executive of this State, orders have been received from the War Department, augmenting the force of the garrisons in this harbor.[1]

1. This information was reprinted verbatim in Charleston *Southern Patriot, and Commercial Advertiser,* July 30, 1822.

Governor Thomas Bennett Jr. to Secretary of War John C. Calhoun, Tuesday, July 30, 1822

Executive Department
Charleston July 30, 1822

The Hon: John C. Calhoun
Secy of the War Dept. of the U. States

Sir

Your Communication of the 22nd Inst: with copies of the order to Col: Eustis commanding the forces at St. Augustine; and the letter addressed to Col: Bankhead as officer commanding at this station, were duly received. The prompt attention given to my request, has proved highly gratifying to the Citizens of this place, and the arrival of the forces will no doubt contribute greatly, to allay the public excitement.

I, feel some reluctance, under existing circumstances to ask your attention to the military Works in this Harbour. Castle Pinckney[1] is in a state of rapid dilapidation, it would be impossible under any emergency to apply it to its appropriate uses. Having proposed to Major Bird[2] the removal of the Powder at Fort Johnson[3] to this insular spot; it was objected, that there was no safe or dry place of deposit within its walls. Permit me to suggest that a small magazine erected at this Post, would not only promote the convenience of the detachment here, but contribute to the General Safety. The State Magazine near Charleston is furnished with a very small and inefficient guard, and the Building is so impaired a State as to render it a very unsafe deposit for Powder.

Fort Johnson can no longer be regarded as a Military Post; except the officers' Quarters and the Barracks, no appearance of its having once been so, exists. Major Bird with a laudable zeal to give effect to our health laws, has constructed with materials from the spot and carpenters furnished by the Garrison a small platform, on which he has placed a couple of pieces of Ordnance. Understanding that another site has been selected by the Engineer Department, in which it is proposed to construct permanent and extensive works, I should be much gratified to learn at what time it is probable these will be commenced, and whether in time to anticipate a communication to the Legislature of this State, having for its object the adoption of efficient measures to enforce the Quarantine Regulations.

If it should be the intention of the General Government to abandon this Post, I am confident that the relinquishment of its jurisdiction to this State, will prove highly acceptable; a site for a Lazaretto and Ware Houses having long been anxiously sought after—and there is no spot beside, so well adapted to these uses.

I regret the necessity which prevents your increasing the force on this station to three companies; such an augmentation at this particular juncture would tend not only to tranquillize the public mind, but produce the happiest effects upon that class of persons who have caused the present excitement. I am very confident however that the causes of disappointment are very remote from any sentiment connected with your inclination to serve this community.

I have the honor to be
Very Respectfully
Your obt Sert
Tho: Bennett

1. Castle Pinckney was rebuilt as a masonry fortification before the War of 1812 on a small island in Charleston Harbor.

2. In this letter Bennett continued to misspell Major John A. Burd (1784?–1827), commander of the US Army at the Charleston station.

3. See p. 102 n2, above.

ALS in Letters Received by the Secretary of War, Registered Series, 1810–1860, roll 95, NA.

Major Abram Eustis to Secretary of War John C. Calhoun, Tuesday, August 6, 1822

St. Augustine, 6th August 1822

Sir.

I have this day received your order of the 22nd Ult. Capt. Payne being on duty at this station, I have in obedience to the spirit of your order, directed him to proceed with his Company to Charleston, S.—C. Fortunately a suitable vessel is now lying in this harbour. She has been engaged to transport this Company, & weather permitting, will sail from the port on Thursday the 8th inst. The weather at present indicates a storm which may detain the Company a few days longer.

I am with high respects
Your humble servt
Abram Eustis

ALS in Letters Received by the Secretary of War, Registered Series, 1801–1860, roll 95, March 1822–June 1823, NA.

James Ferguson to Thomas Parker Jr., Monday, September 16, 1822[1]

Charleston, 16th *September,* 1822.

To THOMAS PARKER, Esq.

Sir—As I perceive by your letter of yesterday, that your memory is not altogether correct with regard to my going up to my plantation on the business connected with the late attempt at insurrection, I shall endeavour to comply with your request, by relating transactions as they occurred.

About 26th or 27th June, Mr. Wesner,[2] one of the committee of vigilance, had the politeness to communicate to me, that he had received information that my servants Frank and Adam, were concerned in the insurrection; and asked me whether I had a fellow named John, and one named Pompey in the country! He then took me to the Work-House to examine Jesse Blackwood (then under sentence of death,) from whom the information was received: immediately upon leaving the room I told Mr. Wesner I was satisfied of the truth of Jesse's evidence. I directly brought Frank and Adam before the Court; you recollect that Frank was used as state's evidence and Adam discharged.

Jesse's evidence as regards the country negroes, was; that he was to have gone to summon them down; that on his arrival he was to have asked for John and Pompey, that John was called John O—and that one was a cooper; and that he was not to be seen by the driver: these directions were given him by Frank. Upon examining Frank a day or two after, he confirmed what Jesse had said; and said that John and Pompey and several others had agreed to come to town in case the insurrection began, or as he expressed it, "in case such things took place."

Thinking it was my duty to inform the proper public authorities of my knowledge of the insurgents, and being anxious that if my negroes were to be tried, they should have the benefit of such a Court as was then organized; on Friday, 28th June, I waited on the Governor and informed him that the insurrection had extended to my plantation, that two fellows were particularly named, and that if he thought proper to have them apprehended, I would assist personally any officers he might choose to send: he said it would be a great pity those poor wretches should suffer upon slight evidence: I then stated to him the evidence of Jesse and Frank; he said there was a Court organized which with the committees appointed, appeared to take the entire management of the business. He expressed some regret at a misunderstanding with the Court, by which he had been at first prevented, having such communication with some of the criminals as he could have wished. After this short conversation, I said explicitly to him, then, sir, you do not intend to apprehend those negroes. He replied he would not like to take upon himself the responsibility. From the Governor's house I went immediately to the Court Room, and formally gave to the Court and Intendant the same information I had given the Governor, they declined their interference only upon the ground that my plantation was beyond their jurisdiction.

On Saturday, 29th June, I went into the country and had John and Pompey severely corrected in the presence of the other negro men on the plantation; but neither from them, nor from the others could I get any confession that they were at all cognizant of the intended plot. I gave orders to my driver to press on them the inutility of denying what was so fully proved against them; and to inform me of any confession they might make. I returned to town the next day, and for the four succeeding weeks, to my great astonishment I could get no acknowledgment through the messenger who came to me weekly. I then sent up a confidential old negro who returned and told me, that, the negroes were ready to confess all to me, and had been so for some time past, but were prevented by the driver who was as much concerned as any of them. The next day (30th July,)[3] I went into the country and sent the driver to town to be committed to the Work-House, where he is now in confinement.

The confession of the negroes went to say, that when Frank drove me from George-town to the plantation, which was about 10th June, he told them Denmark Vesey's stories, and said they must come to town and assist. And although they would not acknowledge that they had actually consented to come, yet I am of opinion, that they were so thoroughly convinced that the negroes would succeed in their attempt, that they did intend to obey the summons of any messenger that should have reached them.

From the time I first heard that Frank had spoken of the intended insurrection, at my plantation, and from my knowledge of the means ordinarily used by negroes in communicating intelligence from one plantation to another; I was of opinion that it was well known thorough the neighbourhood, and my visit of two days on 30, and 31st July, gave me an opportunity of being confirmed in my opinion—and if it would not exceed the limits of a letter, I would willingly detail the minutiae by which I was so confirmed.

By the confession of some of my most intelligent negroes, it appears that reports of the emancipation had of late years been much in circulation; but they said, that until Frank told them, they had no idea it was to be effected in the manner proposed by Denmark Vesey. In various conversations with Frank he always persisted in saying he had no knowledge of Denmark Vesey's plot until 1st May, 1822; which assertion I could not reconcile with several conversations of his on freedom, which I had traced back to nine months before that time; but he explained it by stating that Billy Palmer was the first who told him of the rights of blacks, two summers ago.

The orderly conduct of the negroes in any district of country within 40 miles of Charleston, is no evidence that they were ignorant of the intended attempt. A more orderly gang than my own is not to be found in this state—and one of Denmark Vesey's directions was, that they should assume the most implicit obedience.

Very respectfully, I have the honor to be, your most obedient servant.

JAMES FURGUSON [*sic*].

1. James Ferguson (1784–1874) was a wealthy planter in St. John Berkeley Parish. Ferguson wrote to Thomas Parker Jr. (1793?–1844), one of the magistrates on the court, in response to a brief query Parker had mailed on September 15. Because this September 16 missive details the events in late June, we have placed the letter here. The original of this letter has not been found; it was printed in the "Narrative" section of the *OR*. On Ferguson, see *BDSCHR* 5: 90–92.

2. On City Warden Frederick Wesner, see p. 93 n45, above.

3. The date in parentheses was presumably added by editors Parker and Kennedy. It should read June 30, not July 30.

ALS in *OR*, 28–31.

The magistrates who tried the slaves and free blacks in 1822 relied on an eighty-two-year-old criminal code, commonly known as the "Negro Act," one of the most comprehensive slave codes in United States history. Passed in the aftermath of the bloody Stono slave insurrection (1739), this "Act for the Better Ordering and Governing Negroes" remained the foundation of slave law in South Carolina until the end of the Civil War. Acts codifying unfree labor in the colony dated to the first moments of South Carolina's history, but in the wake of the violent 1739 uprising near the Stono River, just south of Charleston, colonial legislators drafted a comprehensive code that, in fifty-three articles, covered all aspects of slave life. It made clear where all Africans and African Americans stood in the social order. The code drew few distinctions between bondpersons and free blacks; the preamble judged "negroes, Indians, mulattoes and mustizoes" to be "absolute slaves," although subject to qualification by "positive laws." So sure were planter-legislators that blacks were meant to be slaves that the lengthy code mentioned freed blacks only four times, with Article I insisting that "it shall be always presumed that every negro, Indian, mulatto and mustizo, is a slave" unless a court determined otherwise. Section XI established the Court of Magistrates and Freeholders for trying slaves accused of crimes. Despite South Carolina's comprehensive slave laws, considerable disagreement existed in 1822 during the legal proceedings among top state officials as to what rights slaves accused of involvement in the Vesey affair possessed. Governor Bennett's exchange with South Carolina Attorney General Robert Young Hayne and the firestorm ignited by the essay published anonymously by Supreme Court Justice William Johnson, Bennett's brother-in-law, speak to the point.

South Carolina Slave Code, 1740

AN ACT FOR THE BETTER ORDERING AND GOVERNING NEGROES AND OTHER SLAVES IN THIS PROVINCE.[1]

WHEREAS, in his Majesty's plantations in America, slavery has been introduced and allowed, and the people commonly called negroes, Indians, mulattoes and mustizoes, have been deemed absolute slaves, and the subjects of property in the hands of particular persons, the extent of whose power over such slaves ought to be settled and limited by positive laws, so that the slave may be kept in due subjection and obedience, and the owners and other persons having the care and government of slaves may be restrained from exercising too great rigour and cruelty over them, and that the public peace and order of this Province may be preserved: We pray your most sacred Majesty that it may be enacted,

I. *And be it enacted*, by the honorable William Bull,[2] Esquire, Lieutenant Governor and Commander-in-chief, by and with the advice and consent of his Majesty's honorable Council, and the Commons House of Assembly of this Province, and by the authority of the same, That all negroes and Indians, (free Indians in amity with this government, and negroes, mulattoes, and mustizoes, who are now free, excepted,) mulattoes or mustizoes who now are, or shall hereafter be, in this Province, and all their issue and offspring, born or to be born, shall be, and they are hereby declared to be, and remain forever hereafter, absolute slaves, and shall follow the condition of the mother, and shall be deemed, held, taken, reputed and adjudged in law, to be chattels personal, in the hands of their owners and possessors, and their executors, administrators, and assigns, to all intents, constructions and purposes whatsoever; *provided always,* that if any negro, Indian, mulatto or mustizo, shall claim his or her freedom, it shall and may be lawful for such negro, Indian, mulatto or mustizo, or any person or persons whatsoever, on his or her behalf, to apply to the justices of his Majesty's court of common pleas, by petition or motion, either during the sitting of the said court, or before any of the justices of the same court, at any time in the vacation; and by the said court, or any of the justices thereof, shall, and they are hereby fully impowered to, admit any person so applying to be guardian for any negro, Indian, mulatto or mustizo, claiming his, her or their freedom; and such guardians shall be enabled, entitled and capable in law, to bring an action of trespass in the nature of ravishment of ward, against any person who shall claim property in, or who shall be in possession of, any such negro, Indian, mulatto or mustizo; and the defendant shall and may plead the general issue on such action brought, and the special matter may and shall be given in evidence, and upon a general or special verdict found, judgment shall be given according to the very right of the cause, without having any regard to any defect in the proceedings, either in form or substance; and if judgment shall be given for the plaintiff, a special entry shall be made, declaring that the ward of the plaintiff is free, and the jury shall assess damages which the plaintiff's ward hath sustained, and the court shall give judgment, and award execution, against the defendant for such damage, with full costs of suit; but in case judgment shall be given for the defendant, the said court is hereby fully impowered to inflict such corporal punishment, not extending to life or limb, on the ward of the plaintiff, as they, in their discretion, shall think fit; *provided always,* that in any action or suit to be brought in pursuance of the direction of this Act, the burthen of the proof shall lay on the plaintiff, and it shall be always presumed that every Negro, Indian, mulatto, and mustizo, is a slave, unless the contrary can be made appear, the Indians in amity with this government excepted, in which case the burthen of the proof shall lye on the defendant; *provided also,* that nothing in this Act shall be construed to hinder or restrain any other court of law or equity in this Province, from determining the property of slaves, or their right to freedom, which now have cognizance or jurisdiction of the same, when the same shall happen to come in judgment before such courts, or any of them, always taking this Act for their direction therein.

II. *And be it further enacted* by the authority aforesaid, That in every action or suit to be brought by any such guardian as aforesaid, appointed pursuant to the direction of this Act, the defendant shall enter into a recognizance, with one or more sufficient sureties, to the plaintiff, in such a sum as the said court of common pleas shall direct, with condition that he shall produce the ward of the plaintiff at all times when required by the said court, and that whilst such action or suit shall be depending and undetermined, the ward of the plaintiff shall not be eloined, abused or misused.

III. And for the better keeping slaves in due order and subjection, *Be it further enacted* by the authority aforesaid, That no person whatsoever shall permit or suffer any slave under his or their care or management, and who lives or is employed in Charlestown, or any other town in this Province, to go out of the limits of the said town, or any such slave who lives in the country, to go out of the plantation to which such slave belongs, or in which plantation such slave is usually employed, without a letter superscribed and directed, or a ticket in the words following:

Permit this slave to be absent from Charlestown, (or any other town, or if he lives in the country, from Mr.———plantation,———parish,) for———days or hours; dated the———day of———.

Or to that purpose or effect; which ticket shall be signed by the master or other person having the care or charge of such slave, or by some other [person] by his or their order, directions and consent; and every slave who shall be found out of Charlestown, or any other town, (if such slave lives or is usually employed there,) or out of the plantation to which such slave belongs, or in which [such] slave is usually employed, if such slave lives in the country, without such letter or ticket as aforesaid, or without a white person in his company, shall be punished with whipping on the bare back, not exceeding twenty lashes.

IV. *And be it further enacted* by the authority aforesaid, That if any person shall presume to give a ticket or license to any slave who is the property or under the care or charge of another, without the consent or against the will of the owner or other person having charge of such slave, shall forfeit to the owner the sum of twenty pounds, current money.

V. *And be it further enacted* by the authority aforesaid, That if any slave who shall be out of the house or plantation where such slave shall live, or shall be usually employed, or without some white person in company with such slave, shall refuse to submit or undergo the examination of any white person, it shall be lawful for any such white person to pursue, apprehend, and moderately correct such slave; and if any such slave shall assault and strike such white person, such slave may be lawfully killed.

VI. *Provided always, and be it further enacted* by the authority aforesaid, That if any negro or other slave, who shall be employed in the lawful business or service of his master, owner, overseer, or other person having charge of such slave, shall be beaten, bruised, maimed or disabled by any person or persons not having sufficient cause or lawful authority for so doing, (of which cause the justices of the peace, respectively, may judge,) every person and persons so offending, shall, for every such offence, forfeit and pay the sum of forty shillings, current money, over and besides the damages hereinafter mentioned, to the use of the poor of that parish in which such offence shall be committed: And if such slave or slaves shall be maimed or disabled by such beating, from performing his or her work, such person and persons so offending, shall also forfeit and pay to the owner or owners of such slaves, the sum of fifteen shillings, current money, per diem, for every day of his lost time, and also the charge of the cure of such slave; and if the said damages, in whole, shall not exceed the sum of twenty pounds, current money, the same shall, upon lawful proof thereof made, be recoverable before any one of his Majesty's justices of the peace, in the same way and manner as debts are recoverable by the Act for the trial of small and mean causes; and such justices before whom the same shall be recovered, shall have power to commit the offender or offenders to goal, if he, she or they shall produce no goods of which the said penalty and damages may be levied, there to remain without bail, until such penalty and damages shall be paid; any law statute, usage or custom, to the contrary notwithstanding.

VII. *And be it further enacted* by the authority aforesaid, That it shall and may be lawful for every justice assigned to keep the peace in this Province, within his respective county and jurisdiction, upon his own knowledge or view, or upon information received upon oath, either to go in person, or by warrant or warrants directed to any constable or other proper person, to command to their assistance any number of persons as they shall see convenient, to disperse any assembly or meeting of slaves which may disturb the peace or endanger the safety of his Majesty's subjects, and to search all suspected places for arms, ammunition or stolen goods, and to apprehend and secure all such slaves as they shall suspect to be guilty of any crimes or offences whatsoever, and to bring them to speedy trial, according to the directions of this Act; and in case any constable or other person shall refuse to obey or execute any of the warrants or precepts of such justices, or any of them, within their several limits and precincts, or shall refuse to assist the said justices or constables, or any of them, when commanded or required, such person or persons shall forfeit and pay the sum of five pounds, current money, to be recovered by a warrant under the hand and seal of any other justice of the peace, in the same way and manner as is directed by the Act for the trial of small and mean causes.

VIII. *And be it further enacted* by the authority aforesaid, That if any person shall be maimed, wounded or disabled, in pursuing, apprehending, or taking any slave that is runaway or charged with any criminal offence, or in doing any other act, matter or thing, in obedience to or in pursuance of the direction of this Act, he shall receive such reward from the public, as the General Assembly shall think fit; and if any such person shall be killed his heirs, executors or administrators, shall receive the like reward.

IX. And *whereas,* natural justice forbids that any person, of what condition soever, should be condemned unheard, and the order of civil government requires that for the due and equal administration of justice, some convenient method and form of trial should be established; *Be it therefore enacted* by the authority aforesaid, That all crimes and offences which shall be committed by slaves in this Province, and for which capital punishment shall or lawfully may be inflicted, shall be heard, examined, tried, adjudged and finally determined by any two justices assigned to keep the peace, and any number of freeholders not less than three or more than five, in the county where the offences shall be committed, and who lives in the parts adjacent, and can be most conveniently assembled; either of which justices, on complaint made or information received of any such offence committed by a slave, shall commit the offender to the safe custody of the constable of the parish where such offence shall be committed, and shall without delay, by warrant under his hand and seal, call to his assistance and request any one of the nearest justices of the peace to associate with him, and shall, by the same warrant, summon such a number of the neighboring freeholders as aforesaid, to assemble and meet together with the said justices, at a certain day and place, not exceeding three days after the apprehending of such slave or slaves; and the justices and the freeholders being so assembled, shall cause the slave accused or charged, to be brought before them, and shall hear the accusation which shall be brought against such slave, and his or her defense, and shall proceed to the examination of witnesses and other evidences, and finally to hear and determine the matter brought before them, in the most summary and expeditious manner; and in case the offender shall be convicted of any crime for which by law the offender ought to suffer death, the said justices shall give judgment, and award and cause execution of their sentence to be done, by inflicting such manner of death, and at such time, as the said justices, by and with the consent of the freeholders, shall direct, and which they shall judge will be most effectual to deter others from offending in the like manner.

X. *And be it further enacted* by the authority aforesaid, That if any crime or offence not capital, shall be committed by any slave, such slave shall be proceeded against and tried for such offence in the manner hereinbefore directed, by any one justice of the peace and any two freeholders of the county where the offence shall be committed, and can be most conveniently assembled; and the said justice and freeholders shall be assembled, summoned and called together, and shall proceed upon the trial of any slave who shall commit any offence not capital, in like manner as is hereinbefore directed for trying of causes capital. And in case any slave shall be convicted before them of any offence not capital, the said one justice, by and with the consent of the said freeholders, shall give judgment for the inflicting any corporal punishment; not extending to the taking away life or member, as he and they in their discretion shall think fit, and shall award and cause execution to be done accordingly. *Provided always*, that if the said one justice and two freeholders, upon examination of any slave charged or accused before them for an offence not capital, shall find the same to be a greater offence, and may deserve death, they shall, with all convenient speed, summons and request the assistance of another justice and one or more freeholders, not exceeding three, which said justice and freeholders newly assembled, shall join with the justice and freeholders first assembled, and shall proceed in the trial, and unto final judgment and execution, if the case shall so require, in manner as is hereinbefore directed for the trial of capital offences.

XI. *And be it further enacted* by the authority aforesaid, That two justices and one freeholder, or one justice and two freeholders, of the said two justices and three freeholders, shall make a quorum, and the conviction or acquittal of any slave or slaves by such a quorum of them shall be final in all capital cases; but on the trial of slaves for offences not capital, it shall and may be sufficient if before sentence or judgment shall be given for inflicting a corporal punishment, not extending to life or member, that one justice and any one of the freeholders shall agree that the slave accused is guilty of the offence with which he shall be charged.

XII. *And be it further enacted* by the authority aforesaid, That so soon as the justice or justices and freeholders shall be assembled as aforesaid, in pursuance of the direction of this Act, the said justices shall administer to each other the following oath.

I, A B, do solemnly swear, in the presence of Almighty God, that I will truly and impartially try and adjudge the prisoner or prisoners who shall be brought before me, upon his or their trial, and honestly and duly, on my part, put in execution, on this trial, an Act entitled "An Act for the better ordering and governing negroes and other slaves in this Province," according to the best of my skill and knowledge. So help me God.

And the said justice or justices, having taken the aforesaid oath, shall immediately administer the said oath to every freeholder who shall be assembled as aforesaid, and shall forthwith proceed upon the trial of such slave or slaves as shall be brought before them.

XIII. And for the preventing the concealment of crimes and offences committed by slaves, and for the more effectual discovery and bringing slaves to condign punishment, *Be it further enacted* by the authority aforesaid, That not only the evidence of all free Indians, without oath, but the evidence of any slave, without oath, shall be allowed and admitted in all causes whatsoever, for or against another slave accused of any crime of offence whatsoever; the weight of which evidence being seriously considered, and compared with all other circumstances attending the case, shall be left to the conscience of the justices and freeholders.

XIV. And *whereas,* slaves may be harbored and encouraged to commit offences, and concealed and received by free negroes, and such free negroes may escape the punishment due to their crimes, for want of sufficient and legal evidence against them; *Be it therefore further enacted* by the authority aforesaid, That the evidence of any free Indian or slave, without oath, shall in like manner be allowed and admitted in all cases against any free negroes, Indians (free Indians in amity with this government, only excepted,) mulattoe or mustizoe; and of all crimes and offences committed by free negroes, Indians, (except as before excepted,) mulattoes or mustizoes, shall be proceeded in, heard, tried, adjudged and determined by the justices and freeholders appointed by this Act for the trial of slaves, in like manner, order and form, as is hereby directed and appointed for the proceedings and trial of crimes and offences committed by slaves; any law, statute, usage or custom to the contrary notwithstanding.

XV. *And be it further enacted and declared* by the authority aforesaid, That if any slave in this Province shall commit any crime or offence whatsoever, which, by the laws of England or of this Province now in force, is or has been made felony without the benefit of the clergy, and for which the offender by law ought to suffer death, every such slave, being duly convicted according to the directions of this Act, shall suffer death; to be inflicted in such manner as the justices, by and with the advice and consent of the freeholders, who shall give judgment on the conviction of such slave, shall direct and appoint.

XVI. And *whereas,* some crimes and offences of an enormous nature and of the most pernicious consequence, may be committed by slaves, as well as other persons, which being peculiar to the condition and situation of this Province, could not fall within the provision of the laws of England; *Be it therefore enacted* by the authority aforesaid, That the several crimes and offences hereinafter particularly enumerated, are hereby declared to be felony, without the benefit of the clergy, that is to say:—if any slave, free negro, mulattoe, Indian or mustizoe, shall wilfully and maliciously burn or destroy any stack of rice, corn or other grain, of the product, growth or manufacture of this Province, or shall wilfully and maliciously set fire to, burn or destroy any tar kiln, barrels of pitch, tar turpentine or rosin, or any other the goods or commodities of the growth, produce or manufacture of this Province, or shall feloniously steal, take or carry away any slave, being the property of another, with intent to carry such slave out of this Province, or shall wilfully or maliciously poison or administer any poison to any person, free man, woman, servant or slave, every such slave, free negro, mulattoe, Indian, (except as before excepted,) and mustizoe, shall suffer death as a felon.

XVII. *And be it further enacted* by the authority aforesaid, That any slave who shall be guilty of homicide of any sort, upon any white person, except by misadventure, or in defense of his master or other person under whose care and government such slave shall be, shall, upon conviction thereof as aforesaid, suffer death; and every slave who shall raise or attempt to raise an insurrection in this Province, shall endeavor to delude or entice any slave to run away and leave this Province, every such slave and slaves, and his and their accomplices, aiders and abettors, shall, upon conviction as aforesaid, suffer death; *Provided always,* that it shall and may be lawful to and for the justices who shall pronounce sentence against such slaves, by and with the advice and consent of the freeholders as aforesaid, if several slaves shall receive sentence at one time, to mitigate and alter the sentence of any slave other than such as shall be convicted of the homicide of a white person, who they shall think may deserve mercy, and may inflict such corporal punishment, (other than death,) on any such slave, as they in their discretion shall think fit; any thing herein contained to the contrary thereof in any wise notwithstanding; *Provided always,* that one or more of the said slaves who shall be convicted of the crimes or offences aforesaid, where several are concerned, shall be executed for example, to deter others from offending in the like kind.

XVIII. And to the end that owners of slaves may not be tempted to conceal the crimes of their slaves to the prejudice of this public, *Be it further enacted* by the authority aforesaid, That in case any slave shall be put to death in pursuance of the sentence of the justices and freeholders aforesaid, (except slaves guilty of murder, and slaves taken in actual rebellion,) the said justices, or one of them, with the advice and consent of any two of the freeholders, shall, before they award and order their sentence to be executed, appraise and value the said negroes so to be put to death, at any sum not exceeding two hundred pounds current money, and shall certify such appraisement to the public treasurer of this Province, who is hereby authorized and required to pay the same; one moiety thereof, at least, to the owner of such slave or to his order, and the other moiety, or such part thereof as such justices and freeholders shall direct, to the person injured by such offence for which such slave shall suffer death.

XIX. *And be it further enacted* by the authority aforesaid, That the said justices, or any of them, are hereby authorized, empowered and required, to summons and compel all persons whatsoever, to appear and to give evidence upon the trial of any slave; and if any person shall neglect or refuse to appear, or appearing, shall refuse to give evidence, or if any master or other person who has the care and government of any slave, shall prevent or hinder any slave under his charge or government, from appearing or giving evidence in any matter depending before the justices and freeholders aforesaid, the said justices may, and they are hereby fully empowered and required to, bind every such person offending as aforesaid, by recognizance with one or more sufficient sureties, to appear at the next general sessions, to answer such their offences and contempt; and for default of finding sureties, to commit such offender to prison.

XX. *And be it further enacted* by the authority aforesaid, That in case the master or other person having charge or government of any slave who shall be accused of any capital crime, shall conceal or convey away any such slave, so that he cannot be brought to trial and condign punishment, every master or other person so offending, shall forfeit the sum of two hundred and fifty pounds current money, if such slave be accused of a capital crime as aforesaid; but if such slave shall be accused of a crime not capital, then such master or other person shall only forfeit the sum of fifty pounds current money.

XXI. *And be it further enacted* by the authority aforesaid, That all and every the constable and constables in the several parishes within this Province where any slave shall be sentenced to suffer death or other punishment, shall cause execution to be done of all the orders, warrants, precepts and judgments of the justices hereby appointed to try such slaves; for the charge and trouble of which the said constable or constables, respectively, shall be paid by the public treasurer of this Province, upon a certificate produced under the hands of the said justice or justices before whom such negroes or slaves shall be tried; unless in such cases as shall appear to the said justices and freeholders to be malicious or groundless prosecutions, in which cases the said charges shall be paid by the prosecutors; for whipping or other corporal punishments not extending to life, the sum of twenty shillings; and for any punishment extending to life, the sum of five pounds current money; and such other charges for keeping and maintaining such slaves, as are allowed to the warden of the work house in Charlestown, for keeping and maintaining any slave, committed to his custody; for the levying of which charges against the prosecutor, the justice or justices are hereby empowered to issue their warrant. And that no delay may happen in causing execution to be done upon such offending slave or slaves, the constable who shall be directed to cause execution to be done, shall be, and is hereby, empowered to press one or more slave or slaves, in or near the place where such whipping or corporal punishment shall be ordered to be inflicted, to whip or inflict such other corporal punishment upon the offender or offenders; and such slave or slave so pressed, shall be obedient to and observe the orders and directions of the constable in and about the premises, upon pain of being punished by the said constable, by whipping on the bare back, not exceeding twenty lashes, which punishment the said constable is hereby authorized and empowered to inflict; and the constable shall, if he presses a negro, pay the said negro five shillings out of his fee for doing the said execution.

XXII. *And be it further enacted* by the authority aforesaid, That if any person in this Province shall, on the Lord's day, commonly called Sunday, employ any slave in any work or labour, (works of absolute necessity and the necessary occasions of the family only excepted,) every person in such case offending, shall forfeit the sum of five pounds, current money, for every slave they shall so work or labour.

XXIII. *And be it further enacted* by the authority aforesaid, That it shall not be lawful for any slave, unless in the presence of some white person, to carry or make use of fire arms, or any offensive weapons whatsoever, unless such negro or slave shall have a ticket or license, in writing, from his master, mistress or overseer, to hunt and kill game, cattle, or mischievous birds, or beasts of prey, and that such license be renewed once every month, or unless there be some white person of the age of sixteen years or upwards, in the company of such slave, when he is hunting or shooting or that such slave be actually carrying his master's arms to or from his master's plantation, by a special ticket for that purpose, or unless such slave be found in the day time actually keeping off rice birds, or other birds, within the plantation to which such slave belongs, lodging the same gun at night within the dwelling house of his master, mistress or white overseer; and *provided also,* that no negro or other slave shall have liberty to carry any gun, cutlass, pistol or other weapon, abroad from home, at any time between Saturday evening after sun-set, and Monday morning before sun-rise, notwithstanding a license or ticket for so doing. And in case any person shall find any slave using or carrying fire arms, or other offensive weapons, contrary to the true intention of this Act, every such person may lawfully seize and take away such fire arms or offensive weapons. But before the property of such goods shall be vested in the person who shall seize the same, such person shall, within forty-eight hours next after such seizure, go before the next justice of the peace, and shall make oath of the manner of the taking; and if such justice of the peace, after such oath shall be made, or if, upon any other examination, he shall be satisfied that the said fire arms or other offensive weapons shall have been seized according to the direction and agreeable to the true intent and meaning of this Act, the said justice shall, by certificate under his hand and seal, declare them forfeited, and that the property is lawfully vested in the person who seized the same: *Provided always,* that no such certificate shall be granted by any justice of the peace, until the owner or owners of such fire arms of other offensive weapons so to be seized as aforesaid, or the overseer or overseers who shall or may have the charge of such slave or slaves from whom such fire arms or other offensive weapons shall be taken or seized, shall be duly summoned, to shew cause, if any such they have, why the same should not be condemned as forfeited, or until forty-eight hours after the service of such summons, and oath made of the service of such summons before the said justice.

XXIV. *And be it further enacted* by the authority aforesaid, That if any slave shall presume to strike any white person, such slave, upon trial and conviction before the justice or justices and freeholders, aforesaid, according to the directions of this Act, shall, for the first and second offence, suffer such punishment as the said justice and freeholders, or such of them as are empowered to try such offences, shall, in their discretion, think fit, not extending to life or limb; and for the third offence, shall suffer death. But in case any such slave shall grievously wound, maim or bruise any white person, though it by only the first offence, such slave shall suffer death. *Provided always,* that such striking, wounding, maiming or bruising, be not done by the command, and in the defense of, the person or property of the owner or other person having the care and government of such slave, in which case the slave shall be wholly excused, and the owner or other person having the care and government of such slave shall be answerable, as far as by law he ought.

XXV. *And be it further enacted* by the authority aforesaid, That it shall and may be lawful for every person in this Province, to take, apprehend and secure any runaway or fugitive slave, and they are hereby directed and required to send such slave to the master or other person having the care or government of such slave, if the person taking up or securing such slave knows, or can, without difficulty, be informed, to whom such slave shall belong; but if not known or discovered, then such slave shall be sent, carried or delivered into the custody of the warden of the work-house in Charlestown; and the master or other person who has the care or government of such slave, shall pay for the taking up such slave, whether by a free person or slave, the sum of twenty shillings, current money; and the warden of the work-house, upon receipt of every fugitive or runaway slave, is hereby directed and required to keep such slave in safe custody until such slave shall be lawfully discharged, and shall, as soon as conveniently it may be, publish, in the weekly gazette, such slave, with the best descriptions he shall be able to give, first carefully viewing and examining such slave, naked to the waist, for any mark or brand, which he shall also publish, to the intent the owner or other person who shall have the care and charge of such slave, may come to the knowledge that such slave is in custody. And if such slave shall make escape through the negligence of the warden of the work-house, and cannot be taken within three months, the said warden of the work-house shall answer to the owner for the value of such slave, or the damage which the owner shall sustain by reason of such escape, as the cause shall happen.

XXVI. *And be it further enacted* by the authority aforesaid, That the said warden of the work-house shall, at the charge of the owner of such slave, provide sufficient food, drink, clothing and covering, for every slave delivered into his custody, and shall keep them to moderate labour, and advertise them in the gazette, in the manner aforesaid; and on failure thereof, shall forfeit all his fees due for such slave; and the said warden is hereby directed and required to cause every such slave delivered into his custody as a runaway, upon receipt of such slave, to be whipped on the bare back, not exceeding twenty lashes; and on failure thereof, shall forfeit all his fees due for such slave.

XXVII. *And be it further enacted* by the authority aforesaid, That any person who shall take up any runaway slave, and shall deliver such slave either to the master or other person having the care or charge of such slave, or to the warden of the work-house, shall be entitled to receive from the owner or warden of the work-house, upon the delivery, fifteen pence, current money, per mile, for every mile such slave shall have been brought of sent, to be computed from the place where such slave was apprehended. And if such slave shall be delivered into the custody of the warden aforesaid, the person delivering such slave shall give an account of his name, place of abode, and the time and place when and where such slave was apprehended; which account the said warden shall enter down in a book to be kept for that purpose, and shall give a receipt for any such slave which shall be delivered, as aforesaid, into his custody. And the said warden is hereby fully authorized and empowered to demand and receive from the owner or other person having the charge or care of any such slave, for negroes committed from the month of October to March, inclusive, for finding necessaries, clothing and covering, to be the property of the master, any sum not exceeding six pounds, and the several sums following and no other sum, fee or reward, on any pretence whatsoever, (that is to say,) for apprehending each slave, paid to the person who delivered such slave in custody, twenty shillings, current money; for mileage, paid to the same person, fifteen pence, like money; for a sufficient quantity of provision for each day, for each slave, three shillings and nine pence, like money; for advertising and publishing every slave, as directed by this Act, five shillings, like money, exclusive of the charge of printing; for receiving such slave, five shillings, and for delivering of him, five shillings, like money; for poundage on money advanced, one shilling in the pound, like money. And the said warden shall and may lawfully detain any slave in custody until the fees and expenses aforesaid be fully paid and satisfied; and in case the owner of such slave, or his overseer, manager, agent, attorney, or trustee, shall neglect or refuse to pay and satisfy the said fees and expenses, for the space of thirty days after the same shall be demanded by notice, in writing, served on the owner of such slave, or (if the owner is absent from this Province,) upon his overseer, agent, manager, attorney or trustee, the said warden shall and may expose any such slave to sale, at public outcry, and after deducting the fees and expenses aforesaid, and the charges of such sale, shall upon demand, return the overplus money arising by such sale, to any person who has a right to demand and receive the same.

XXVIII. And forasmuch as for want of knowing or finding the owner of any fugitive slave to be delivered to him, as aforesaid, the said warden may not be obliged to keep such slave in his custody, and find and provide provisions for such slave, over and beyond a reasonable time, *Be it therefore further enacted* by the authority aforesaid, That if the owner or owners of such fugitive slave shall not, within the space of eighteen months from the time of commitment, make his, her or their claim or claims, or it shall not be otherwise made known to the said warden, within the time aforesaid, to whom such committed slave shall belong, it shall and may be lawful for the said warden to sell such slave at public outcry, in Charlestown, he the said warden first advertising such sale six weeks successively in the public gazette, together with the reason of the sale of such slave, and out of the money arising by such sale, to pay, deduct or retain to himself what shall be then due for money by him disbursed on receipt of such fugitive slave, and for his fees and provisions, together with the reasonable charges arising by such sale, and the overplus money, (if any there shall be,) shall be rendered and paid by the said warden to the public treasurer for the time being, in trust, nevertheless, for the use of the owner or owners of such slave, provided the same be claimed by him, her or them within one year and a day after such sale, or in default of such claim, within the time aforesaid, to the use of the public of this Province to be applied as the General Assembly shall direct.

XXIX. *And be it further enacted* by the authority aforesaid, That if any free negro, mulatto or mustizo, or any slave, shall harbour, conceal or entertain any slave that shall run away or shall be charged or accused with any criminal matter, every free negro, mulatto and mustizo, and every slave, who shall harbour, conceal or entertain any such slave, being duly convicted thereof, according to the directions of this Act, if a slave, shall suffer such corporal punishment, not extending to life or limb, as the justice or justices who shall try such slave shall, in his or their discretion, think fit; and if a free negro, mulatto or mustizo, shall forfeit the sum of ten pounds, current money, for the first day, and twenty shillings for every day after, to the use of the owner of owners of such slave so to be harboured, concealed or entertained, as aforesaid, to be recovered by warrant, under the hand and seal of any one of his Majesty's justices of the peace, in and for the county where such slave shall be so harboured, concealed or entertained, in like manner as debts are directed to be recovered by the Act for trial of small and mean causes; and that in case such forfeitures cannot be levied, or such free negroes, mulattos or mustizoes shall not pay the same, together with the charges attending the prosecution, such free negro, mulatto or mustizo shall be ordered by the said justice to be sold at public outcry, and the money arising by such sale shall, in the first place, be paid and applied for and towards the forfeiture due, made payable to the owner or owners, and the charges attending the prosecution and sale, and the overplus, (if any,) shall be paid by the said justice into the hands of the public treasurer, to be afterwards paid and applied in such manner as by the General Assembly of this Province shall be directed and appointed.

XXX. *And be it further enacted* by the authority aforesaid, That no slave who shall dwell, reside, inhabit or be usually employed in Charlestown, shall presume to buy, sell, deal, traffic, barter, exchange or use commerce for any goods, wares, provisions, grain, victuals, or commodities, of any sort or kind whatsoever, (except as hereinafter particularly excepted and provided, and under such provisos, conditions, restrictions and limitations as are herein particularly directed, limited and appointed,) on pain that all such goods, wares, provisions, grain, victuals or commodities, which by any slave shall be so bought, sold, dealt, trafficked or bartered for, exchanged or used in commerce, shall be seized and forfeited, and shall be sued for and recovered before any one justice assigned to keep the peace in Charlestown, and shall be applied and disposed of, one half to him or them who shall seize, inform and sue for the same, and the other half to the commissioners of the poor of the parish of St. Philips, Charlestown; and moreover, that the said justice shall order every slave who shall be convicted of such offence, to be publicly whipped on the bare back, not exceeding twenty lashes; *provided always,* that it shall and may be lawful for any slave who lives or is usually employed in Charlestown, after such license and ticket as hereinafter is directed shall be obtained, to buy or sell fruit, fish and garden stuff, and to be employed as porters, carters or fishermen, and to purchase any thing for the use of their masters, owners or other person who shall have the charge and government of such slave, in open market, under such regulations as are or shall be appointed by law concerning the market of Charlestown, or in any open shop kept by a white person.

XXXI. *And be it further enacted* by the authority aforesaid, That no slave or slaves whatsoever, belonging to Charlestown, shall be permitted to buy any thing to sell again, or to sell any thing upon their own account, in Charlestown; and it shall and may be lawful for any person or persons whosoever, to seize and take away all and all manner of goods, wares or merchanize, that shall be found in the possession of any such slave or slaves in Charlestown, which they have bought to sell again, or which they shall offer to sale upon their own accounts, in Charlestown, one half of which shall be to the use of the poor of the said parish, and the other to the informer, and shall be adjudged and condemned by any justice of the peace in the said parish.

XXXII. *And be it further enacted* by the authority aforesaid, That if any keeper of a tavern or punch house, or retailer of strong liquors, shall give, sell, utter or deliver to any slave, any beer, ale, cider, wine, rum, brandy, or other spirituous liquors, or strong liquor whatsoever, without the license or consent of the owner, or such other person who shall have the care or government of such slave, every person so offending shall forfeit the sum of five pounds, current money, for the first offence, and for the second offence, ten pounds; and shall be bound in recognizance in the sum of one hundred pounds, current money, with one or more sufficient sureties, before any of the justices of the court of general sessions, not to offend in the like kind, and to be of good behaviour, for one year; and for want of such sufficient sureties, to be committed to prison without bail or mainprize, for any term not exceeding three months.

XXXIII. And *whereas,* several owners of slaves do suffer their slaves to go and work where they please, upon conditions of paying to their owners certain sums of money agreed upon between the owner and the slave; which practice has occasioned such slaves to pilfer and steal, to raise money for their owners, as well as to maintain themselves in drunkenness and evil courses; for prevention for which practices for the future, *Be it enacted* by the authority aforesaid, That no owner, master or mistress of any slave, after the passing of this Act, shall permit or suffer any of his, her or their slaves to go and work out of their respective houses or families, without a ticket in writing, under pain of forfeiting the sum of ten pounds, current money, for every such offence, to be paid the one half to the church-wardens of the parish, for the use of the poor of the parish in which the offence is committed, and the other half to him or them that will inform and sue for the same, to be recovered in the same way as debts are by the Act for the trial of small and mean causes. And every person employing any slave without a ticket from the owner of such slave, shall forfeit to the informer five pounds, current money, for each day he so employs such slave, over and above the wages agreed to be paid such slave for his work; *provided* that the said penalty of five pounds per diem, shall not extend to any person whose property in such slave is disputable; and *provided,* that nothing herein contained shall hinder any person or persons from hiring out by the year, week or day, or any other time, any negroes or slaves, to be under the care and direction of his or their owner, master or employer, and that the master is to receive the whole of the earnings of such slave or slaves, and that the employer have a certificate or note, in writing, of the time or terms of such slave's employment, from the owner, attorney or overseer of every such slave, severally and respectively.

XXXIV. And *whereas,* several owners of slaves have permitted them to keep canoes, and to breed and raise horses, neat cattle and hogs, and to traffic and barter in several parts of this Province, for the particular and peculiar benefit of such slaves, by which means they have not only an opportunity of receiving and concealing stolen goods, but to plot and confederate together, and form conspiracies dangerous to the peace and safety of the whole Province; *Be it therefore enacted* by the authority aforesaid, That it shall not be lawful for any slave so to buy, sell, trade, traffic, deal or barter for any goods or commodities, (except as before excepted,) nor shall any slave be permitted to keep any boat, perriauger or canoe, or to raise and breed, for the use and benefit of such slave, any horses, mares, neat cattle, sheep or hogs, under pain of forfeiting all the goods and commodities which shall be so bought, sold, traded, trafficked, dealt or bartered for, by any slave, and of all the boats, perriaugers or canoes, cattle, sheep or hogs, which any slave shall keep, raise or breed for the peculiar use, benefit and profit of such slave; and it shall and may be lawful for any person or persons whatsoever, to seize and take away from any slave, all such goods, commodities, boats, perriaugers, canoes, horses, mares, neat cattle, sheep or hogs, and to deliver the same into the hands of any one of his Majesty's justices of the peace, nearest to the place where the seizure shall be made; and such justice shall take the oath of such person who shall make any such seizure, concerning the manner of seizing and taking the same, and if the said justice shall be satisfied that such seizure hath been made according to the directions of this Act, he shall pronounce and declare the goods so seized, to be forfeited, and shall order the same to be sold at public outcry; and the monies arising by such sale shall be disposed of and applied as is hereinafter directed; *provided,* that if any goods shall be seized which come to the possession of any slave by theft, finding or otherwise, without the knowledge, privity, consent or connivance of the person who have a right to the property or lawful custody of any such goods, all such goods shall be restored, on such person's making oath before any justice as aforesaid, who is hereby impowered to administer such oath, to the effect or in the following words:

"I, A B, do sincerely swear, that I have a just and lawful right or title to certain goods seized and taken by C D, out of the possession of a slave named———; and I do sincerely swear and declare, that I did not, directly or indirectly, permit or suffer the said slave, or any other slave whatsoever, to use, keep or employ the said goods for the use, benefit or profit of any slave whatsoever, or to sell, barter or give away the same; but that the same goods were in the possession of the said slave by theft, finding or otherwise, or to be kept bona fide for my use, or for the use of E F, a free person, and not for the use or benefit of any slave whatsoever. So help me God."

Which oath shall be taken *mutatis mutandis,* as the case shall happen; *provided also,* that it shall be lawful for any person, being the owner or having the care or government of any slave who resides or is usually employed in any part of this Province, without the limits of Charlestown, to give a license or permission to sell, exchange, or barter in Charlestown, or elsewhere, within this Province, the goods or commodities of the owner, or other person having the care or government of such slave; *provided* that in such license or permission, the quantity or quality of the goods and commodities with which such slave shall be instructed, be particularly and distinctly set down and specified, and signed by the owner or other person having the charge and government of such slave, or by some other person by his, her or their order and direction.

XXXV. *Provided also, and be it enacted* by the authority aforesaid, That this Act shall not extend or be construed to extend to debar any of the inhabitants of Charlestown from sending any of their slaves residing therein, to sell in open market, any sort of provisions whatever, which the owner of such slave shall have received and brought from his or her estate in the country, to be sold at the first hand; nor shall such slaves be debarred from buying any kind of provisions for the use and consumption of their master's and mistress's of their families, and for which such slave or slaves shall have a license or permit from the master of mistress, or some other person under whose care such slave shall be; any thing in this, or any other Act, to the contrary notwithstanding.

XXXVI. And for that as it is absolutely necessary to the safety of this Province, that all due care be taken to restrain the wanderings and meetings of negroes and other slaves, at all times, and more especially on Saturday nights, Sundays, and other holidays, and their using and carrying wooden swords, and other mischievous and dangerous weapons, or using or keeping of drums, horns, or other loud instruments, which may call together or give sign or notice to one another of their wicked designs and purposes; and that all masters, overseers and others may be enjoined, diligently and carefully to prevent the same, *Be it enacted* by the authority aforesaid, That it shall be lawful for all masters, overseers and other persons whomsoever, to apprehend and take up any negro or other slave that shall be found out of the plantation of his or their master or owner, at any time, especially on Saturday nights, Sundays, or other holidays, not being on lawful business, and with a letter from their master, or a ticket, or not having a white person with them; and the said negro or other slave or slaves, met or found out of the plantation of his or their master or mistress, though with a letter or ticket, if he or they be armed with such offensive weapons aforesaid, him or them to disarm, take up and whip: And whatsoever master, owner or overseer shall permit or suffer his or their Negro or other slave or slaves, at any time hereafter, to beat drums, blow horns, or use any other loud instruments, or whosoever shall suffer and countenance any public meeting or feastings of strange negroes or slaves in their plantations, shall forfeit ten pounds, current money, for every such offence, upon conviction or proof as aforesaid; *provided,* an information or other suit be commenced within one month after forfeiture thereof for the same.

XXXVII. And *whereas,* cruelty is not only highly unbecoming those who profess themselves christians, but is odious in the eyes of all men who have any sense of virtue or humanity; therefore, to restrain and prevent barbarity being exercised towards slaves, *Be it enacted* by the authority aforesaid, That if any person of persons whosoever, shall wilfully murder his own slave, or the slave of any other person, every such person shall, upon conviction thereof, forfeit and pay the sum of seven hundred pounds, current money, and shall be rendered, and is hereby declared altogether and forever incapable of holding, exercising, enjoying or receiving the profits of any office, place or employment, civil or military, within this Province: And in case any such person shall not be able to pay the penalty and forfeitures hereby inflicted and imposed, every such person shall be sent to any of the frontier garrisons of this Province, or committed to the work house in Charlestown, there to remain for the space of seven years, and to serve or to be kept at hard labor. And in case the slave murdered shall be the property of any other person than the offender, the pay usually allowed by the public to the soldiers of such garrison, or the profits of the labor of the offender, if committed to the work house in Charlestown, shall be paid to the owner of the slave murdered. And if any person shall, on sudden heat or passion, or by undue correction, kill his own slave, or the slave of any other person, he shall forfeit the sum of three hundred and fifty pounds, current money. And in case any person or persons shall willfully cut out the tongue, put out the eye, castrate, or cruelly scald, burn, or deprive any slave of any limb or member, or shall inflict any other cruel punishment, other than by whipping or beating with a horse-whip, cow-skin, switch or small stick, or by putting irons on, or confining or imprisoning such slave, every such person shall, for every such offence, forfeit the sum of one hundred pounds, current money.

XXXVIII. *And be it further enacted* by the authority aforesaid, That in case any person in this Province, who shall be owner, or shall have the care, government or charge of any slave or slaves, shall deny, neglect or refuse to allow such slave or slaves, under his or her charge, sufficient cloathing, covering or food, it shall and may be lawful for any person or persons, on behalf of such slave or slaves, to make complaint to the next neighboring justice, in the parish where such slave or slaves live or are usually employed; and if there shall be no justice in the parish, then to the next justice in the nearest parish; and the said justice shall summons the party against whom such complaint shall be made, and shall enquire of, hear and determine the same; and if the said justice shall find the said complaint to be true, or that such person will not exculpate or clear himself from the charge, by his or her own oath, which such person shall be at liberty to do, in all cases where positive proof is not given of the offence, such justice shall and may make such orders upon the same, for the relief of such slave or slaves, as he in his discretion shall think fit, and shall and may set and impose a fine or penalty on any person who shall offend in the premises, in any sum not exceeding twenty pounds, current money, for each offense, to be levied by warrant of distress and sale of the offender's good, returning the overplus, if any shall be; which penalty shall be paid to the church-wardens of the parish where the offence shall be committed, for the use of the poor of the said parish.

XXXIX. And *whereas,* by reason of the extent and distance of plantations in this Province, the inhabitants are far removed from each other, and many cruelties may be committed on slaves, because no white person may be present to give evidence of the same, unless some method be provided for the better discovery of such offences; and as slaves are under the government, so they ought to be under the protection, of masters and managers of plantations; *Be it therefore further enacted* by the authority aforesaid, That if any slave shall suffer in life, limb or member, or shall be maimed, beaten or abused, contrary to the directions and true intent and meaning of this Act, when no white person shall be present, or being present, shall neglect or refuse to give evidence, or be examined upon oath, concerning the same, in every such case, the owner or other person who shall have the care and government of such slave, and in whose possession or power such slave shall be, shall be deemed, taken, reputed and adjudged to be guilty or such offence, and shall be proceeded against accordingly, without further proof, unless such owner or other person as aforesaid, can make the contrary appear by good and sufficient evidence, or shall by his own oath, clear and exculpate himself; which oath, every court where such offence shall be tried, is hereby empowered to administer, and to acquit the offender accordingly, if clear proof of the offence be not made by two witnesses at least; any law, usage or custom to the contrary notwithstanding.

XL. And *whereas*, many of the slaves in this Province wear clothes much above the condition of slaves, for the procuring whereof they use sinister and evil methods: For the prevention, therefore, of such practices for the future, *Be it enacted* by the authority aforesaid, That no owner or proprietor of any negro slave, or other slave, (except livery men and boys,) shall permit or suffer such negro or other slave, to have or wear any sort of apparel whatsoever, finer, other, or greater value than negro cloth, duffils, kerseys, osnabrigs, blue linen, check linen or coarse garlix, or calicoes, checked cottons, or Scotch plaids, under the pain of forfeiting all and every such apparel and garment, that any person shall permit or suffer his negro or other slave to have or wear, finer, other or of greater value than negro cloth, duffils, coarse kerseys, osnabrigs, blue linen, check linen or coarse garlix or calicoes, checked cottons or Scotch plaids, as aforesaid; and all and every constable and other persons are hereby authorized, empowered and required, when as often as they shall find any such negro slave, or other slave, having or wearing any sort of garment or apparel whatsoever, finer, other or of greater value than negro cloth, duffils, coarse kerseys, osnabrigs, blue linen, check linen, or coarse garlix, or calicoes, checked cottons or Scotch plaids, as aforesaid, to seize and take away the same, to his or their own use, benefit and behoof; any law, usage or custom to the contrary notwithstanding. *Provided always*, that if any owner of any such slave or slaves, shall think the garment or apparel of his said slave not liable to forfeiture, or to be taken away by virtue of this Act, he may apply to any neighboring justice of the peace, who is hereby authorized and empowered to determine any difference or dispute that shall happen thereupon, according to the true intent and meaning of this Act.

XLI. And *whereas*, an ill custom has prevailed in this Province, of firing guns in the night time; for the prevention thereof for the future, *Be it enacted* by the authority aforesaid, That if any person shall fire or shoot off any gun or pistol in the night time, after dark and before day-light, without necessity, every such person shall forfeit the sum of forty shillings, current money, for each gun so fired as aforesaid, to be recovered by warrant from any one justice of the peace for the county where the offence is committed, according to the direction of the Act for the trial of small and mean causes, and shall be paid to the church-wardens of the parish where the offence shall be committed, for the use of the poor of the said parish.

XLII. *And be it further enacted* by the authority aforesaid, That no slave or slaves shall be permitted to rent or hire any house, room, store or plantation, on his or her own account, or to be used or occupied by any slave or slaves; and any person or persons who shall let or hire any house, room, store or plantation, to any slave or slaves, or to any free person, to be occupied by any slave or slave[s], every such person so offending shall forfeit and pay to the informer the sum of twenty pounds, current money, to be recovered as in the Act for the trial of small and mean causes.

XLIII. And *whereas*, it may be attended with ill consequences to permit a great number of slaves to travel together in the high roads without some white person in company with them; *Be it therefore enacted* by the authority aforesaid, That no men slaves exceeding seven in number, shall hereafter be permitted to travel together in any high road in this Province, without some white person with them; and it shall and may be lawful for any person or persons, who shall see any men slaves exceeding seven in number, without some white person with them as aforesaid, travelling or assembled together in any high road, to apprehend all and every such slaves, and shall and may whip them, not exceeding twenty lashes on the bare back.

XLIV. And *whereas,* many owners of slaves, and others who have the care, management and overseeing of slaves, do confine them so closely to hard labor, that they have not sufficient time for natural rest; *Be it therefore enacted* by the authority aforesaid, That if any owner of slaves, or other person who shall have the care, management or overseeing of any slaves, shall work or put to labor any such slave or slaves, more than fifteen hours in four and twenty hours, from the twenty-fifth day of March to the twenty-fifth day of September, or more than fourteen hours in four and twenty hours, from the twenty-fifth day of September to the twenty-fifth day of March, every such person shall forfeit any sum not exceeding twenty pounds, nor under five pounds, current money, for every time he, she or they shall offend herein, at the discretion of the justice before whom such complaint shall be made.

XLV. And *whereas,* the having of slaves taught to write, or suffering them to be employed in writing, may be attended with great inconveniences; *Be it therefore enacted* by the authority aforesaid, That all and every person and persons whatsoever, who shall hereafter teach, or cause any slave or slaves to be taught, to write, or shall use or employ any slave as a scribe in any manner of writing whatsoever, hereafter taught to write, every such person and persons, shall, for every such offense, forfeit the sum of one hundred pounds current money.

XLVI. And *whereas,* plantations settled with slaves without any white person thereon, may be harbours for runaways and fugitive slaves; *Be it therefore enacted* by the authority aforesaid, That no person or persons hereafter shall keep any slaves on any plantation or settlement, without having a white person on such plantation or settlement, under pain of forfeiting the sum of ten pounds current money, for every month which any such person shall so keep any slaves on any plantation or settlement, without a white person as aforesaid.

XLVII. And *whereas,* many disobedient and evil minded negroes and other slaves, being the property of his Majesty's subjects of this Province, have lately deserted the service of their owners, and have fled to St. Augustine and other places in Florida, in hopes of being there received and protected; and *whereas,* many other slaves have attempted to follow the same evil and pernicious example, which, (unless timely prevented,) may tend to the very great loss and prejudice of the inhabitants of this Province; *Be it therefore enacted* by the authority aforesaid, That from and after the passing of this act, any white person or persons, free Indian or Indians, who shall, on the south side of Savannah river, take and secure, and shall from thence bring to the work house in Charlestown, any negroes or other slaves, which within the space of six months have deserted, or who shall hereafter desert, from the services of their owners or employers, every such white person or persons, free Indian or Indians, on evidence of the said slaves being taken as aforesaid, and the same certified by any two justices of the peace in this Province, shall be paid by the public treasurer of this Province the several rates and sums following, as the case shall appear to be; *provided always,* that nothing in this clause contained shall extend to such slaves as shall desert from any plantation situate within thirty miles of the said Savannah river, unless such slaves last mentioned shall be found on the south side of Altamahaw river; that is to say:—for each grown man slave brought alive, the sum of fifty pounds; for every grown woman or boy slave above the age of twelve years brought alive, the sum of twenty five pounds; for every negro child under the age of twelve years, brought alive, the sum of five pounds; for every scalp of a grown negro slave, with the two ears, twenty pounds; and for every negro grown slave, found on the south side of St. John's river, and brought alive as aforesaid, the sum of one hundred pounds; and for every scalp of a grown negro slave with the two ears, taken on the south side of St. John's river, the sum of fifty pounds.

XLVIII. *And be it further enacted* by the authority aforesaid, That the expense of taking and securing all slaves brought alive as aforesaid, shall be at the charge of the respective owners; and no such slave or slaves taken on the south side of Savannah river, and brought to the work houses of Charlestown, as aforesaid, shall be delivered out of the custody of the warden of the said workhouse, without a certificate to him first produced, from the public treasurer of this Province, that the money by him disbursed, for the taking and securing the said slave or slaves, is fully satisfied to the treasurer, besides the following fees, which the said treasurer is hereby required to allow, pay and charge for the trouble necessary to be taken concerning the place and manner of apprehending the said slaves, viz:—to the two justices who shall examine, take and certify the said evidence, for each slave brought alive, the sum of forty shillings; and to the treasurer for his trouble in executing this Act, for each slave brought alive as aforesaid, the sum of twenty shillings; and to the warden of the work house, the sum of three shillings and nine pence per diem, for his maintaining the same while in custody. And on the commitment of any slave or slaves to the custody of the said warden, where the public treasurer shall, by virtue of this Act, expend any money for apprehending the same, the said warden is hereby required to advertise in the public gazette of this Province for the space of three months, the best description he can form of all and every the said slaves, with the place and manner of their being taken; and in case the owner or employer of the said slave or slaves, shall neglect within that time, to redeem the said slave or slaves, by fully satisfying the public treasurer the changes he shall be at, in such manner and proportion as by this Act is directed, then, and in every such case, the said public treasurer shall be at liberty to dispose of every such slave or slaves to the best bidder at public auction, which sale shall be deemed good and effectual, to all intents and purposes, to such person or persons as shall purchase the same; and the produce of every such slave or slaves, shall first go towards satisfying the expense of the said public treasurer and warden of the work house, for the taking, securing and keeping the said slave or slaves, as aforesaid; and then the surplus, (if any,) shall be paid to the respective owner or owners.

XLIX. *And be it further enacted* by the authority aforesaid, That from and after the passing of this Act, where any slave or slaves shall be tried and condemned to be executed for deserting out of this Province, every such slave or slaves shall, before their execution, be valued by the tryers of the same; and in every such case the owner or owners of every such slave, shall be paid by the public of this Province, the full sum and rates at which such executed slave or slaves shall be valued as aforesaid, without being a charge to any particular owner or owners; any law, usage or custom to the contrary notwithstanding.

L. *And be it further enacted* by the authority aforesaid, That all charge of taking and bringing in slaves as aforesaid, shall be defrayed and paid by the public.

LI. *And be it further enacted* by the authority aforesaid, That if any constable or other person, directed to required to do or perform any matter or thing, required, commanded, or enjoined by this Act, who shall know or be credibly informed of any offence which shall be committed against this Act, within his parish, precinct or limits, and shall not give information thereof to some justice of the peace, and endeavor the conviction of the offenders according to his duty, but such constable or other person as aforesaid, or any person lawfully called in aid of the constable or such other person as aforesaid, shall wilfully and willingly omit the performance of his duty in the execution of this Act, and shall be thereof convicted, he shall forfeit for every such offence, the sum of twenty pounds current money. And in case any justice of the peace, warden of the work house, or freeholder, shall wilfully or willingly omit the performance of his duty in the execution of this Act, every such justice of the peace and warden of the work house, shall forfeit the sum of forty pounds current money; and every such freeholder shall forfeit the sum of fifteen pounds current money; which several penalties shall be recovered and disposed of as hereafter is directed; and *moreover,* the judges and justices of the court of general sessions or the peace, oyer and terminer, assize and general gaol delivery, are hereby commanded and required to give the offenders against this Act in charge in open court; and all grand juries, justices of the peace, constables, and other officers, are hereby required to make due and true presentment of such of the said offences as come to their knowledge.

LII. *And be it further enacted* by the authority aforesaid, That if any person shall be at any time sued for putting in execution any of the powers contained in this Act, such person shall and may plead the general issue and give the special matter and this Act in evidence; and if the plaintiff be nonsuit, or a verdict pass for the defendant, or if the plaintiff discontinue his action, or enter a *noli prosequi,* or if upon demurrer judgment be given for the defendant, every such defendant shall have his full double costs.

LIII. *And be it further enacted* by the authority aforesaid, That this Act, and all clauses therein contained, shall be constructed most largely and beneficially for the promoting and carrying into execution this Act, and for the encouragement and justification of all persons to be employed in the execution thereof; and that no record, warrant, process or commitment to be made by virtue of this Act, or the proceedings thereupon, shall be reversed, avoided, or any way impeached, by reason of any default in form.

LIV. *And be it further enacted* by the authority aforesaid, That all fines, penalties and forfeitures imposed or inflicted by this Act, which are not hereby particularly disposed of, or the manner of recovery directed, shall, if not exceeding the value of twenty pounds current money, be recovered, levied and distrained for, by warrant from any one justice of the peace, in the country or precinct where such offence shall be committed, according to the Act for the trial of small and mean causes; and in case such fine, penalty or forfeiture shall exceed the value of twenty pounds current money, the same shall be recovered by action of debt, bill, plaint or information, in any court of record in this Province, wherein no privilege, protection, essoign, wager of law, or *non vult ulterius prosequi,*[3] or any more than one imparlance, shall be admitted or allowed; and all the said fines, penalties and forfeitures, which shall be recovered by this Act, and are not before particularly disposed of, shall be applied and disposed of, one half to his majesty, his heirs and successors, to be applied by the General Assembly for the use of this Province, and the other half to him or them who will sue or inform for the same.

LV. *And be it further enacted* by the authority aforesaid, That his Majesty's part of the fines, penalties and forfeitures which shall be recovered by the virtue of this Act, shall be paid into the hands of the justices, or in the court where the same shall be recovered, who shall make a memorial and record of the payment of the same, and shall, without delay, send a transcript of such memorial or record to the public treasurer of this Province, from the said courts or justices who shall receive his Majesty's part of such fines and forfeitures; which memorial shall be a charge on the judges or justices respectively to whom the same shall be paid; and the public treasurer of this Province for the time being, shall and may, and he is hereby authorized and empowered to, levy and recover the same by warrant of distress, and sale of the goods and chattels of the said judges or justices respectively, who shall be charged with the same, in case they or any of them shall neglect or refuse to make such memorial or record as aforesaid, or send such transcript thereof, as before directed, or shall neglect or refuse to pay the same over to the treasurer within twenty days after the receipt of the same; *Provided always,* that no person shall be prosecuted for any fine, forfeiture or penalty imposed by this Act, unless such prosecution shall be commenced within six months after the offense shall be committed.

LVI. And *whereas,* several negroes did lately rise in rebellion, and did commit many barbarous murders at Stono and other parts adjacent thereto; and *whereas,* in suppressing the said rebels, several of them were killed and others taken alive and executed; and as the exigence and danger the inhabitants at that time were in and exposed to, would not admit of the formality of a legal trial of such rebellious negroes, but for their own security, the said inhabitants were obliged to put such negroes to immediate death; to prevent, therefore, any person or persons being questioned for any matter or thing done in the suppression or execution of the said rebellious negroes, as also any litigious suit, action or prosecution that may be brought, sued or prosecuted or commenced against such person or per[s]ons for or concerning the same; *Be it enacted* by the authority aforesaid, That all and every act, matter and thing, had, done, committed and executed, in and about the suppressing and putting all and every the said negro and negroes to death, is and are hereby declared lawful, to all intents and purposes whatsoever, as fully and amply as if such rebellious negroes had undergone a formal trial and condemnation, notwithstanding any want of form or omission what-ever in the trial of such negroes; and any law, usage or custom to the contrary thereof in any wise notwithstanding.

LVII. *And be it further enacted* by the authority aforesaid, That this Act shall be deemed a public Act, and shall be taken notice of without pleading the same before all judges, justices, magistrates and courts within this province.

LVIII. *And be it further enacted* by the authority aforesaid, That this Act shall continue in force for the space of three years, and from thence to the end of the next session of the General Assembly, and no longer.

C. PINCKNEY,[4] *Speaker.*

In the Council Chamber, the 10th *day of May, 1740.*

Assented to: WM. BULL.

1. The best recent discussion of the evolution of South Carolina's slave codes and the creation of the 1740 code, the tenth revision of the original and far briefer 1690 statute, is Christopher Tomlins, *Freedom Bound: Law, Labor, and Civic Identity in Colonizing English America, 1580–1865* (Cambridge, UK: Cambridge University Press, 2010), 431–52.

2. William Bull (1683–1755), one of the largest land and slave holders in colonial South Carolina, governed the colony from late 1737 to 1744. He participated in the suppression of the Stono rebels in 1739. See "The Bull Family of South Carolina," *SCHGM* 1 (January 1900): 76–79; *BDSCHR* 2: 120–22.

3. The Latin phrase *non vult ulterius prosequi* means agreement has been reached and that there will be no further prosecution. See Thomas Cooper and David J. McCord, eds., *The Statutes at Large of South Carolina* (Columbia, SC, 1840), vol. 7: 352–65.

4. Charles Pinckney (1699–1758) figured prominently in the public life of colonial South Carolina. See *BDSCHR* 2: 520–22. He was the father of Charles Cotesworth Pinckney (1746–1825) and Thomas Pinckney (1750–1828), both of whom would be attentive witnesses to events in Charleston in 1822. The older brother, a delegate to the Constitutional Convention, knew Morris Brown and numbered among the six white lay persons who supported Brown and twenty-two other free persons of color in their petition to the state house to buy land in Wraggsborough near Judith Street for a cemetery for black Methodists (see Part I, pp. 19–20). Thomas Pinckney, under the pseudonym "Achates," would write a perceptive analysis of the causes of the Vesey affair (See pp. 552–62).

Thomas Cooper and David J. McCord, eds., *The Statutes at Large of South Carolina* (Columbia, SC, 1840), vol. 7: 397–417.

Charleston Courier

Friday, June 21, 1822

COMMUNICATION.

Melancholy Effect of Popular Excitement.

The following anecdote may be relied on as a simple narrative of facts, which actually occurred within the recollection of thousands.[1]

In the year 1810 or 1811, Mr. BLOUNT[2] being Governor of North Carolina, Mr. MILLEDGE of Georgia,[3] and Mr. DRAYTON of South Carolina,[4] the two latter states were thrown into great alarm by a letter transmitted from Gov. Blount to Gov.

Milledge, and by the latter despatched by express to Gov. Drayton. The militia of the two states, in the counties adjacent to Augusta, were ordered to be held in readiness for action, *en masse,* and Guards and Patrols to scour the country. The sufferings of the inhabitants, particularly the females, from apprehensions painfully excited, induced a gentleman of this city, then a resident near Augusta, to call on the Governor, then residing near that place, and request a sight of the letter. At the first glance of the eye he pronounced it a hoax: for it bore date on the 1st *April,* and had been picked up in one of the country towns in North Carolina, where it had in fact been dropped by some thoughtless schoolboy. On the face of it also it bore such evidence of its origin, as must have struck any observer whose vision was not distorted by alarm. For it was dated Augusta, signed "Your loving brother Captain Jack," and purported to be directed to an associate, in Lewisville, North Carolina. But it was in vain that these suggestions were made. The Governor of Georgia could not brook the mortifying discovery of his having been duped, and the whole country, on the designated night was kept in agitated motion.

Happy had it terminated in nothing more than the suffering and disturbance communicated to the people of both states, and the useless expenditure of some thousands of public money. But another hoax gave it a most tragical termination.

The trumpeter of the Augusta Cavalry resided in the opposite district of Edgefield, and orders had been issued to him to attend the company that night. By some accident these orders did not reach him in time to make Augusta that evening, he halted at Moore's mills, on Chever's creek, in South Carolina. Here he and a companion were shown into a garret, where they were amusing themselves over their pint of whiskey, when the continual passing and repassing of the mounted militia drew their attention; and the half intoxicated bugleman resolved to try the effect of a blast of his music upon the fears of a party just gone by. The effect was electrical; it was deemed the expected signal; the detachments gallopped off in all directions in quest of the offender, and towards morning returned with a single poor half-witted negro, who had been taken crossing a field on his way home, without instrument of war or of music. But none else could be found, and he alone could have given the significant blast, which so many had heard. It was in vain that he denied it: he was first whipped severely to extort a confession, and then, with his eyes bound, commanded to prepare for instant death from a sabre, which a horseman was in the act of sharpening beside him.

He now recollected that a man named Billy, belonging to Capt. Key, had one of those long tubes which boatmen use on our rivers, and declared that he had sounded the horn, and done it at the command of Capt. Key's men; but still denied all sort of combination, and affirmed the innocence of the act.

An armed force was immediately detached to the house of Billy, and there found him quietly sleeping in the midst of a large family, in a degree of comfort very unusual for a slave—for Billy was a blacksmith, a fellow of uncommon worth, and indulged in such privileges by his master as his fidelity justly merited.

But in one corner of his house, exposed to the view of every one, was found the terrific horn, and he was hurried away to be tried for his life. The Court of Magistrates and Freeholders was selected from men of the first respectability in the neighbourhood; and

Figure 5. William Johnson Jr. (1771–1834), associate justice of the US Supreme Court. From an undated portrait. Courtesy of the Collection of the Supreme Court of the United States.

yet it is a fact, although no evidence was given whatever as to a motive for sounding the horn, and the horn was actually found covered and even filled with cobwebs, they condemned that man to die the next day!—and, what will scarcely be believed, they actually received evidence of his having been once charged with stealing a pig, to substantiate the charge upon which he then stood on trial. Respectable bystanders have declared, that his guilt or innocence as to the pig soon took the lead of every other question on the trial.—The owner, one of the worthiest men in all that country, thunderstruck at the sentence, entreated a more deliberate hearing; but not being listened to, hastened away to his friends, and among them a judicial character in the neighborhood, to unite their entreaties with his. They promptly attended to his solicitations, procured a meeting of the court, and earnestly pressed the injustice and precipitation of the sentence, and their right to time to solicit a pardon, but in vain. The presiding magistrate actually conceived his dignity attacked, and threatened impeachment against the judge, who, as an individual, had interfered only to prevent a legal murder; and interfered upon the witness, retracting all he had testified to.

Billy was hung amidst crowds of execrating spectators;—and such appeared to be the popular demand for a victim, that it is not certain a pardon could have saved him.[5]

1. William Johnson Jr. (1771–1834), was born in Charleston and read law under Charles Cotesworth Pinckney. He married Sarah Bennett, the sister of future governor Thomas Bennett Jr., and together they had a daughter, Anna Hayes Johnson (d. 1870), whose correspondence related to the Vesey affair can be found in Part IV of this volume. Following a brief career in the state assembly

as a Republican, Johnson served on the state supreme court. In 1804, President Thomas Jefferson nominated him as associate justice of the US Supreme Court, a position he held until his death in 1834. See Donald G. Morgan, *Justice William Johnson, The First Dissenter: The Career and Constitutional Philosophy of a Jeffersonian Judge* (Columbia: University of South Carolina Press, 1954).

2. David Stone (1770–1818) was governor of North Carolina from 1808 to 1810; Benjamin Smith (1756–1826) succeeded him and served until 1811. No man with the surname of Blount was governor of North Carolina during this period, but Major General Thomas Blount (1759–1812) was a member of the Twelfth Congress at the time of his death. Willie Blount, governor of Tennessee from 1809–1815, was born in North Carolina.

3. John Milledge of Georgia served as that state's governor from 1802 to 1806.

4. John Drayton of South Carolina served two terms as governor: 1800–1802 and 1808–10. See "Apprehended Insurrection of the Blacks," *New-York Evening Post,* April 30, 1810, for a verbatim transcription of the letter, Blount to Milledge, March 26, 1810, which sparked the panic that Justice Johnson recalled imperfectly.

5. This information was reprinted verbatim in the Hartford *Connecticut Mirror,* July 8, 1822; Philadelphia *United States Gazette and True American,* July 9, 1822; Washington *National Intelligencer,* July 10, 1822; Philadelphia *National Gazette and Literary Register,* July 10, 1822; Salem *Gazette,* July 15, 1822; and Louisville *Public Advertiser,* July 31, 1822. Judge Johnson's authorship of "Melancholy Effect" also became known nationally and was linked in northern newspapers to the fact that his brother-in-law Governor Bennett had three slaves condemned to death. See, for example, *Newburyport Herald,* July 19, 1822.

Charleston *Southern Patriot, and Commercial Advertiser*

Saturday, June 22, 1822

To the Public.

It is with great pain I am constrained, on the part of the civil authorities of this City, to notice and mark with the most pointed reprobation a Communication which appeared in the "*Courier*" of Friday, headed "*The Melancholy Effect of Popular Excitement.*" If it was intended as it would seem to make this moral, and the story which accompanies it applicable to a supposed existing state of things in our community, so that the advantages of the atrocious hoax at Augusta might be quoted for the especial benefit of the Corporation and the Court organized at their instance, I have only to remark that the *discretion* of the writer is altogether equal to the unjust libel he has insinuated against his Fellow-Citizens.

It was to have been hoped that the measures adopted by the corporation in a spirit of the most perfect justice and moderation, in arranging such a court for respectability and intelligence as has rarely been convened on any occasion in our country, would have screened them from the *salutary* monitions of a Mentor, however wise he may be, beyond the generation in which he lives, and who seems at least to want some of the qualifications of a *Dictator.*

On the part and behalf of the
Corporation of Charleston.
J HAMILTON, jun. *Intendant.*

John Potter to Langdon Cheves, Saturday, June 29, 1822[1]

private) Charleston

My Dear Sir,

I wrote you a few lines by James—who sailed here for New York—last Monday, and where I hope he has arrived—I adverted to Subjects, which he could better explain than I could do it by letter—a Circumstance which has Caused much agitation and extreme feeling with public mind—as such reports ever will keenly produce, among us—a Court of the most respectable individuals in the City have been patiently and laboriously investigating this business for 10 or 12 days past—and you will perceive by the newspapers I send you—that six wretches are to pay the forfeit of their worthless lives on tuesday—the plot was deeply laid, and a plan of insurrection (which a member of the court told me yesterday) was organised with an address & Cunning, as he said would much surprise the Community. at first Governor Bennett, Could not believe that his own negroes were implicated—but the subsequent investigation proved a Scene of Guilt, and murder, to be intended, unparalleled even exceeding if possible, the *Demons,* of St. Domingo!!!

His excellency it is Said, was to be the first victim by his favorite Servant *Rolla*—and his reward was to be miss B—the Governor's Daughter[2]—the very thought, makes my blood recoil in my Veins—I believe the plan was, that the white males were all to be Cut off—!!

Their meetings Commenced, and were held under the perfidious Cover of Religion—and I cannot doubt but they were aided by the black missionaries from *Your City*![3]

Judge Wm. Johnson put in the Courier of Yesterday[4] week a piece of as much imprudent tendency as were a man in his Sober Senses—Could write—it was a severe reflection on the Court Composed of members as highly respectable as he was—The Intendant Mr. Hamilton, in behalf of the Wardens made a reply on Saturday the day after[5]—both of which You Can See published—in the papers I now send you—You will See a severe recrimination and the Judges, by the members of the Court—(in which the whole Community Seems to Concur) and his short reply!!!

I believe he thought that Bennett's Negroes, were innocent & possibly His publication, was intended to have a bearing on this supposition—a moments reflection must have Shown, it would & must have had, a Contrary tendency.—

a White Villain[6] was apprehended the night before last—(a fellow lately tryed for piracy)—he had been endeavoring [to] Suborn a free Negro, into a plot, all he wanted he Said was 400 such fellows, to effect his purposes: the Negro discovered—and induced this fellow, to Cover at night & develop all his plans—when Major Hamilton (the Intendant & a Warden had him secreted & heard all that passed—when the mutiny broke up—& the fellow was going off—the [*illegible*] Clapped a pistol to his breast, when he was easily led to Jail & I hope will receive the gallows as he deserves—no doubt others are [*illegible*] implicated in the plot—which will be Constantly in agitation if we do not get rid of the *poison,* that has been too deeply & I fear successfully introduced into this plan—You are free from these unpleasant feelings I wished much that my wife & daughter would have gone with James—but it would not be lifting to be without them.

I am always yrs truly J. Potter

1. Born in Ireland, John Potter (1765–1849) migrated to South Carolina in 1784 and became a prominent merchant and banker. In 1822 he resided at 32 Society Street. See *BDSCHR* 4: 11–14, 458–59; *CSCCD*, 95. Potter's script makes the precise date of the letter difficult to decipher. Saturday, June 29, seems likely since the term "yesterday week" means a week ago yesterday, i.e., June 21. Since Potter was on the board of directors of the Charleston branch of the Bank of the United States along with Hamilton and James Reid Pringle, judge on the first court, he had ready sources of access to what officials thought was going on during the summer of 1822. See Charleston *City Gazette and Commercial Daily Advertiser*, December 6, 1821.

2. Governor Thomas Bennett Jr. had two daughters alive in 1822, Mary Hayes Bennett, born in 1804, and Anna Margaret Bennett, born in 1812. His son Thomas Benjamin Palmer—the second son of that name—was baptized in 1821 by the Reverend Benjamin Morgan Palmer. See Craig Miller Bennett, "Family Records of Governor Thomas Bennett Jr.," *SCHM* 51 (1850): 51–54.

3. Langdon Cheves (1776–1857) was a former Charleston alderman, state assemblyman, and member of Congress. He declined to run for reelection in 1814 and returned to South Carolina to practice law. On March 6, 1819, President James Monroe appointed him president of the Second Bank of the United States. Cheves held the position until October 1822 and received Potter's eight letters on the Vesey affair in Philadelphia, where the bank was located. On Cheves, see Archie Huff, *Langdon Cheves of South Carolina* (Columbia: University of South Carolina Press, 1977); "Death of the Hon. Langdon Cheves," *Charleston Mercury*, June 27, 1857; *BDSCHR* 4: 111–14; and Leigh Fought's biography of Cheves's daughter, *Southern Womanhood and Slavery: A Biography of Louisa S. McCord, 1810–1879* (Columbia: University of Missouri Press, 2003).

4. Potter here refers to Justice William Johnson's essay, "The Melancholy Effect of Popular Excitement," which appeared in the *Charleston Courier*, Friday, June 21, 1822. The essay appears on pp. 131–33.

5. See above, p. 134.

6. William Allen, one of the four white men later put on trial.

ALS in Langdon Cheves Papers, SCHS.

Charleston Courier

Saturday, June 29, 1822

The following Communication was handed for publication of the Gentlemen composing the Court to which reference is made, and its insertion required as an act of justice to them, which I was not at liberty to refuse. It is, as will readily be conceived, extremely painful to an editor to be thus situated.

The article which has caused such melancholy excitement, was brought to the Courier office by a gentleman whose standing in society is of such a commanding character, as is well calculated to impress upon any thing he might offer, the certainty of its usefulness; and under an impression of this kind, it was given out for publication, having been read over in a very hasty manner.

I trust it will be believed, that I would not, knowingly, give publicity to any piece, which could, by any possible implication vary from the expression of perfect respect which I feel, in common with the community, for the character and conduct of the gentlemen who compose the Court—nor would I, on any occasion, voluntarily admit into the *Courier*, a publication tending, in the remotest degree, to wound the feelings of any one in the community.

A. S. WILLINGTON.[1]

[COMMUNICATION.]

The Members of a Court now assembled, upon a very painful occasion, are compelled to notice a publication which appeared in the *Courier*, on the 21st inst. headed "*Melancholy effect of popular excitement.*" This piece, in their own opinions, and of all with whom they have conversed relative to it (the number of whom is very great,) contained an insinuation, that the Court, under the influence of popular prejudice, was capable of committing perjury and murder, and implied that the author if it possessed sounder judgment, deeper penetration, and firmer nerves, than the rest of his fellow citizens. The individuals constituting this humble tribunal, relying upon the purity of their motives, and their conduct through life, had hoped to have pursued their labors, important to the state and distressing to themselves, unassailed by suspicion or malevolence; and, notwithstanding the publication they have adverted to, they would never have addressed their fellow citizens, if the person who caused its insertion, had declared in the gazette, as he was required to do, that he "did not mean to imply any thing disrespectful towards the court, much less to insinuate that, under the influence of popular excitement, or of any other inducement, they were capable of departing from the course which was prescribed to them by their oaths and by their consciences." But this requisition, after first promising to comply with, he afterwards refused to perform.

Injured and defamed as the Court considers itself to be, they nevertheless owe it to themselves and to the community, not to degrade themselves by the use of epithets and expressions which the occasion would seem to require: they, therefore, leave it to the public to make their comments—and to the individual they will only say, that they are at a loss how to reconcile his conduct with that which ought to influence a gentleman respecting his solemn promise, and sensible of the obligations of decency and propriety.

TO THE PUBLIC.

You are respectfully requested to suspend your opinion of the subject of a publication of the Court of Magistrates and Freeholders, in this day's *Courier*. I pledge myself to satisfy all the world that it is one of the most groundless and unprovoked attacks ever made upon the feelings of an individual. An indictment shall bring it before an impartial tribunal, and a narrative of facts shall exhibit to the view of the public an instance of the most unprecedented pretension.

WILLIAM JOHNSON.

1. Aaron Smith Willington (1781–1862) was editor of the *Charleston Courier*.

Supreme Court Justice William Johnson Jr.'s Defense of *Courier* Essay, June 1822

TO THE PUBLIC OF CHARLESTON

It is not until I have composed my feelings from the severe attack of last Saturday, to a state which will enable me to address you with perfect calmness, that I undertake to redeem the pledge into which I have entered, to restore myself to your good opinion.

It has been, at all times, in my power to prove to your satisfaction, that I have never intended to interfere with the state authorities, much less cast censure upon the respectable men who have thought proper to treat me in so unceremonious a manner.—My misfortune is, that I have presumed too much upon the hope, that the censures cast upon me would be repelled, by a community with whom I was born and raised, among whom I have spent a life now looking downward in its course, whose confidence and kindness I have many reasons to be grateful for, and whom I can confidentiality say, I have faithfully served, and never dishonoured.

What interests have I that are not yours? What feelings, what opinions, but in common with you?

The bones of my forefathers rest among you; all my connexions are in the bosom of this city. Every thing that our industry has acquired for the sustenance of our families is under your protection.

But I will not complain; I shall be content if I succeed in convincing you, that I am still entitled to your confidence.

I shall ever most unaffectedly regret the agency that I had in the publication of the 21st ult. because it has been the subject of so much discussion; but I shall be able to satisfy you that I cannot possibly be charged with the views attributed to it, and hope to show myself not responsible for its appearing in print.

My furnishing the anecdote to the printer was altogether accidental, and the facts attending it, will furnish a complete vindication of its innocency.

Every one recollects the unhappy accident which threw a gloom over this city on Sunday the 16th ult.[1] By the time the rumour of it had reached the place of my residence, the story had acquired some mysterious connection with the cause of the very general alarm at that time prevailing. On my way to church, I met with Mr. William Crafts,[2] Colonel O'Hara,[3] and Mr. Henry O'Hara,[4] in Beaufain-street, and stopped to inquire of them what was the truth with regard to the incident. Upon ascertaining that it was altogether an accident, not the least ground for supposing it the act of an assassin, some hurried remarks were exchanged on the folly and wickedness of raising such stories, and as I drove away I observed to Mr. Crafts that I could give him an anecdote or two on that subject.

The next morning early I recollected my promise, and sat down and wrote the piece that appeared on the 21st ult. At that time I solemnly declare, that I did not believe there would ever be a necessity for holding a court at all. A night of alarm had passed over without furnishing an incident of any import; little was then known of the grounds of alarm; our constituted authorities had been prudent; for myself I can prove that I knew nothing; and I had no suspicion of the serious aspect which subsequent investigations have given to the affair.

The anecdote when written was thrown on my table before me, not deemed of sufficient importance to be sent by a servant; and on Thursday, probably the first time of my going into town afterwards, I put it into my pocket, expecting to see Mr. Crafts in the neighbourhood of the Bank or the Post-Office. Not seeing him, I stepped into the

Courier Office, and inquiring for him, Mr. Willington informed me he had gone over the bar with a party of friends. I left the office and proceeded some steps towards my chair, when recollecting how seldom it was I came to town, I returned back and put the piece in the hands of Mr. W. informing him that I had promised it to Mr. Crafts; that he could do what he pleased with it, or words to that effect; expressing at the same time an opinion, which I most solemnly entertained, that it contained an useful moral, and might check the causes of agitation which were then operating upon the public mind; or words of that import.

Every one knows that I never should have chosen the Courier to publish in, since my political and other relations have always estranged me from it.

The next morning I was somewhat surprised at seeing the piece in print, but I saw nothing in its early appearance, but a benevolent design; not dreaming that any other application could be made of it than a solemn warning to the fabricators of alarming rumours, from a view of the heavy responsibility in which it might unexpectedly involve them—and a precaution to the weaker sex against suffering their fears to be alarmed by every aggravated rumour that reached them.

For the publication of the anecdote I feel myself no farther responsible than for the opinion which (it now appears) I erroneously entertained of its utility; and that such was the view of the Editor, will appear from the following extract of a letter from Mr. Crafts, dated the 22d. "Mr. Willington, who is not easily to be intimidated, published the communication on his own responsibility. In my opinion, he was answerable for it had there been any occasion of censure, of which I solemnly believe there is none. As, however, a candid mind 'sibi conscia recti'[5] must always be ready to vindicate itself, I did think that an appeal to yourself was due to your character, and your reply to that appeal, if my opinion be of any avail, is equally frank and honourable."

It was not until Saturday afternoon, that I discovered, that while I sat unconsciously at home, never dreaming of having contributed to an act, that could give offence, a volcano had been kindling beneath my feet. The first intimation I had was in a letter from Mr. Crafts, in which he informed me, that two members of the Court, had called on Mr. W. to demand the author. In this letter Mr. Crafts observes, "It appears that much animadversion has taken place with regard to that piece. Its motives and views are misunderstood, and therefore easily misrepresented."

I thought the application to me very unnecessary, for I had imposed no injunction of secrecy, and did not hesitate about permitting him to name the author, at the same time intimating that I could not see what offence could be given by a piece which at its utmost, could only be construed into a call upon the reader to "pause and reflect." Wishing, however, to make atonement to all whom I may have unconsciously offended, I wrote, "Should that publication have indeed produced any excitement, or given any umbrage, I am sure nothing was further from my intentions;" and this letter I afterwards expressly requested should be sent to the Court.

When the Court was organised, I know not even now; but it certainly was not before the article of the 21st ult. was written, much less before it was promised.[6] And even when it was delivered to the Printer, it is in my power to prove that I knew nothing of the existence of the Court, by the very person who communicated it to me afterwards. The truth is, my habits of life throw me very little into the way of knowing these things.

The same evening the Intendant's denunciation appeared, and then first developed to me the extent to which the misapprehension had spread. But as soon as Major Hamilton understood that I was the author, a friendly communication was made to me, an explanation ensued, and I trust I have sustained no diminution in his confidence. I am sure my feelings towards him are as kindly as ever. Happy would it have been for me, and perhaps for others, had the same course been pursued by all who felt themselves aggrieved!

As I found no difficulty in answering the Intendant's publication, I sent a piece in reply to it on Monday morning, to be inserted in the Patriot.—This was returned to me, accompanied by many sensible observations of the Editor, from which I extract the following:

"I have to suggest to you the propriety of with drawing from publication the article sent by you this morning for insertion in the Patriot." "Personal feeling should be sacrificed to public considerations, and it would be an act of magnanimity, and the public would receive it as such, if an individual with your station and influence in society, were to forego, in this instance, the resentment of those wrongs, if any there are, to which you may have been subjected.

"Independently of these considerations, the agitation of the public mind is likely to be prolonged, not quieted by a controversy in the public prints, and to compose the feelings of the community there is but the one mode, namely, to let the subject sleep as easily as possible."

This appeared to me to be reasoning sensibly; I thought the Editor better acquainted with public sentiment than I was, and I resolved to let the matter rest; firmly trusting that nothing more would occur to force me into controversies in the public prints—to me the most disgusting of all necessities.

But I was not permitted to rest a moment, and in the course of that day received from the members of the Court, a note, the express object of which was to force me into the public prints; not to *elicit* explanation, but to *command* a public expurgation founded on their own views, and not addressed to me as a Court, but expressly as individuals: I will give the letter in its own terms.

"SIR—The members of a court now assembled upon a very painful occasion, have read your letter, to Mr. Crafts, in which you disclaim having intended any allusion injurious to them in your publication in the Courier, of the 21st inst. As that piece, however you may regard it, not only, in the opinions of the court, but of every individual, who has been heard to express his sentiments of it, (which has been the case with great numbers,) was calculated to produce, not only a distrust of our proceedings, but contained an insinuation, that, under the influence of popular excitement, we were capable of committing perjury and murder—we must *require* of you to insert in the Courier (the vehicle of your former communication) that you did not intend by your publication, to imply any thing disrespectful towards us, much less, to intimate, that, under the influence of popular prejudice, or of any other inducement, we were capable of departing from the course prescribed to us, by our oaths and our consciences."

I will make no comments on this letter. All men must feel alike upon it. It bears the stamp of command; its meaning is, comply or receive your punishment; not leaving an opening for honourable exculpation. And to shut the door against explanation, the note was signed abruptly, studiously refusing the ordinary civilities due from man to man. Such an omission furnished a commentary upon the whole letter.

It is not necessary to detail, the successive resolutions that I formed upon it; until upon the advice of a friend, I recurred to the prudent advice of the Patriot, and resolved to make another sacrifice to public peace. This was in complying for the present, by inserting in the Courier, an article, that should also contain my defence; and reserving the right of reviving the discussion at a more convenient season.

Accordingly, I addressed to the members of the Court my note of the 25th ult. in these words:

"GENTLEMEN,

"I have, to acknowledge the receipt of your note of yesterday. Had it assumed a less dictatorial style, I should have thought myself treated with candour. *If any ulterior calculations have been founded upon my being piqued to resistance, I will disappoint them by an unexpected acquiescence.*

"Prudence dictates that I should stoop until the storm which my enemies have raised against me, shall spend itself beyond me. The time may come when our respective rights and wrongs may be discussed on more equal terms."

The attention of the reader is particularly called to the passage of this letter marked in Italics, since upon it is founded the charge of a violation of promise. I insist that it is altogether hypothetical, and therefore, as well as from the nature of the case, retains the alternative of either complying or braving the penalty.

But it is immaterial to examine this question, for I did comply; and my accusers knew of it through the communication of a mutual friend. On the same day, (the 25th) in time for the next day, I sent an article to the Courier for insertion, into which were copied an acknowledgment in the very words of their mandate. It was not my fault that it was not inserted—I could not compel the Printer. It is true, the piece also contained my vindication, and it was perfectly consistent that it should contain it, and in fact the whole was such as I would cheerfully have conceded to the least intimation not communicated with insult.

On the evening of the next day this piece was returned to me from Mr. Crafts, with a suggestion of alterations, in a few points, which I had no objection to make. But when I sat down with the intention to copy it, such a view of the humiliation to which I was submitting rushed upon me, that I could not proceed.

For this state of feeling, I was then in a state of advanced preparation, by a new attack on my republican sensibilities, inflicted by my accusers on that day.

It was probably the first act that they did after the meeting of the Court on the morning of the 26th, to dispatch another mandate as unceremonious as the first, demanding why my publication had not appeared in that morning's paper. A friend to whose knowledge it happened to come, and who felt what ought to be the consequence of it, with a benevolence equally regardful to my feelings and honourable to his own, managed so as to turn aside this thrust, both at my candour and my independence; I suffered it to pass over, and the article still to remain with the printer; resolved not to send for it, but sensible how I ought to treat it if it came again into my hands. It did come without any act of mine, but still I was half turned from my purpose by my longing after peace, until I felt it impossible to go on.

I then sat down and wrote the following letter.

GENTLEMEN—From causes, which it is now unnecessary to explain, the communication which I sent to the Courier on the 25th, was yesterday evening returned to me; and it is an occurrence on which, I must ever felicitate myself, since it has saved me from an act of self-abasement, which I could never have justified to my family and friends. Every conjecture relative to your ulterior views, presented to me, the prospect of some event, that would still further agitate the public mind; and I was induced to adopt the measure of a temporary, though not abject submission, as a sacrifice to a community, which needed repose. But I now look back with self-reproach at having, for a moment, tolerated any other reply to your letter of the 24th, than a prompt refusal.

A polite suggestion, should have commanded from me, any thing in reason; to an imperious command, I owed nothing, but an indignant repulse.

I feel sensible, that I am the injured man. You have imputed to me, views and motives, which I am known to be incapable of; and even when acknowledging my prompt disclaimer of every allusion injurious to you, you require of me, a publication in a prescribed newspaper and in prescribed language, disavowing intentions which it is degrading to admit that I could be thought capable of; and this too, not in the language of my natural political and social equals, but that of dictators.

I have not injured you, gentlemen; on no rational principle can this piece, of which you complain, bear the construction or application that you have given it, and I am not responsible for any construction that is either forced or fancied; nor was the publication of the piece, any act of mine; I furnished it to the printer as any man I hope, may furnish an historical fact or reported case; but I neither put a signature to it, nor requested that it should be printed; I had promised it to Mr. Crafts, and delivered it to Mr. Willington, for him, merely to make what use he pleased of it. I did express an opinion that the publication of it, might have a good effect in deterring men from propagating false reports, and sporting with the fears of the people, and such it would have produced, had not this most unlooked for misconstruction of it got abroad. Thus circumstanced, your demand of a counter publication, is altogether arbitrary.

But I ought not to intrude these reflestions upon you: you have not invited discussion; you have exercised authority. Your address to me of the 24th, is that of men, on whom my misconduct had conferred a right to command me; I am to presume that you will persist in the stand you have taken; I shall therefore only expose myself to fresh indignity by suggesting that, a reference of our differences to judicious men, is a sacrifice due to public tranquillity; I am aware of the objections; such adjustments are the acts of equals.

I must apologize for having omitted in my answer of the 25th, those expressions of respect, which custom has prescribed to the intercourse of society; I was led into the error, by placing the claim upon the ground of reciprocity; my better judgment satisfies me that it is of indispensable obligation.

I have the honour of subscribing myself,

Gentlemen,

Your very humble servant,

WILLIAM JOHNSON.

In this letter, it will be perceived, I state my injuries, defend myself against those charged upon me, remark on the course of the court as precluding accommodation, and with a hesitation not without cause afforded by the previous demeanour of these gentlemen towards me, suggest the measure of a reference to judicious friends.

But still I did not send the letter; for a mutual friend had suggested, the previous day, that, perhaps the court would let the business drop where it was, and I was resolved to wait until their views were developed.

I had not to wait long; another mandate in the same unceremonious form, was handed me by a city constable, who sent for me out of my study, informed me he was ordered to deliver it to me personally, and to inform me that he was instructed to wait for an answer.

It was impossible to hesitate longer, and I sent my answer of the 27th; the consequence is known: the publication of the 29th appeared.

But let no one suppose the publication which did appear, was that against which my caution was sent to the printer. Had the article appeared, which, I am perfectly well informed, was ordered to be published (in the legal sense of the word, actually was published) my very enemies would have cried shame!

I mean not to investigate the question now, nor return "railing for railing." I am inculpating no body; I mean nothing but to defend myself; and having thus gone through the narrative of my case, I will dismiss the subject, by stating a string of impossibilities, and—

1st. It is impossible that under the circumstances of this case I could have intended to interfere with the state authorities; a bare reference to dates establishes this point.

2d. It is impossible that I could have intended any reflection upon men who, at the time I promised, and the time I wrote the anecdote, were still to be detailed; were no more likely to be summoned on such a Court, than any other magistrates or free-holders. Nay, I will put it on a different footing; no one but an idiot, would think of making such extravagant charges against men of their unqualified respectability. It is impossible to believe that any one, who has the standing in society to maintain that I have, would render himself so ridiculous as to to make such charges; or, since I am now unfettered, I will say, any, the slightest charges against them. Nay, I will go further and declare, that at any time before the 24th ult. had I been on my own trial for life or death, I would have rejoiced to have had them for my constitutional judges; and they knew it, or at least most of them knew it.

III. It was impossible for any man, who does not disgrace the name of a freeman, to tolerate being domineered over in the manner I was; I say nothing of age, station, character, or the claims which the honour of my country may have given me to consideration; I take the case of the humblest citizen among us, and make it my own. He would deserve to be disfranchised, who could submit to it. Who would dare to raise his face among you this day, with the consciousness of being thus degraded? I blush that I ever hesitated; but my reasons are before you.

4th. It is impossible for these gentlemen to support their reiterated charge against me, of a breach of promise. Besides the hypothetical tenor of my note (which is sure not a promise,) and my actual and honourable compliance with it, the very nature of the case, left me the choice of alternatives; it was the alternative offered by the conqueror, the sword or tribute. To the last moment, the victim might hide his wealth and bare his throat. On such a case the charge (and contumelious charge,) of "not respecting a solemn promise" could not be founded. It was a simple exercise of volition; a choice that I had a right to retract, not a promise creating a right in another.

Lastly. It is impossible upon any principle of law or logic, to deduce from the piece of the 21st, the inuendos which the publication of the 29th insists upon. The piece itself does not raise them, and the gentlemen were in the acknowledged possession of my solemn declaration, that nothing was farther from my intentions than making them. And how they will ever be able to extract defamation from a mere reported case, an historical fact, is to me inscrutable. Yet on this they must rest their justification for pursuing this novel mode of inflicting punishment for such an offence; of tyrannising over my feelings and attacking my fame.

The measure of the publication of the 29th, was, at least, a very unwise one. My reputation is the property of the United States. It is in safe hands, and defies scrutiny. But I wish to live in harmony with those who surround me. The smiles of my fellow citizens are dear to me. They will read and consider my defence; and though for a time a cloud may intercept the beams of their favour, I fear nothing. Persecution against an individual cannot triumph long: every one will feel that it may become his own turn next; and though misrepresentations may prevail awhile, the weapon finally recoils upon the hand that would have inflicted the wound. Man was not always the erring being he is now; there is a natural sympathy between his soul and truth, a tact by which he still discovers and instinctively delights in it.

"All the earth calleth upon the truth; and the heaven blesseth it: all works shake and tremble at it, and with it is no unrighteous thing."

WILLIAM JOHNSON.

1. Johnson refers here to the death of Dr. John Ward McCall by the accidental discharge of his own pistol.

2. William Crafts (1787–1826), a prominent criminal attorney as well as a brigade major in the state militia, resided at 52 Beaufain Street in 1822. See *CSCCD*, 75; H. P. Archer, *Local Reminiscences: A Lecture Delivered by Mr. H. P. Archer before the Mutual Aid Association, No. 1, of Charleston, S.C. in the Hall of the Mechanics Union, at Charleston, S.C. June 6th, 1889* (Charleston, SC, 1893), 12. Crafts would serve as legal counsel to Billy Robinson and Denbow Martin, slaves inculpated in the Vesey plot.

3. Colonel Charles O'Hara (1772?–1822), a prominent merchant, resided at 45 East Bay Street in

1822. He commanded a regiment of artillery in the Fourth Brigade of the South Carolina militia and died shortly after this incident on July 27. See *Charleston Courier,* July 29, 1822; *CSCCD,* 93; H. P. Archer, *Local Reminiscences: A Lecture Delivered by Mr. H. P. Archer before the Mutual Aid Association, No. 1, of Charleston, S.C. in the Hall of the Mechanics Union, at Charleston, S.C. June 6th, 1889* (Charleston, SC, 1893), 12.

4. *CSCCD,* 93, identifies Henry O'Hara (1775?–1833) as a broker and auctioneer who lived on Mazyck Street.

5. The Latin phrase means "conscious of its rectitude."

6. Johnson was in error; the first court was organized on June 19, 1822.

William Johnson, *To the Public of Charleston* (Charleston, SC, 1822).

Boston *New-England Galaxy*

Friday, July 12, 1822

CHARLESTON. From the tone of certain mysterious paragraphs and communications in the Charleston Courier, it might be supposed that the negroes of that city had been detected in an attempt at an insurrection, and that the decisions of the court of Magistrates and Freeholders had not given *entire* satisfaction. The Courier of the 29th June, states that six blacks, five of them slaves and one a free man, were found guilty and ordered to be executed on the second of July. The same paper contains a communication purporting to be from the Court, which is followed by another, signed "WILLIAM JOHNSON,["] who declares that the publication by the Court is one of the most groundless and unprovoked attacks ever made upon the feelings of an individual; and intimates that an indictment shall bring it before an impartial tribunal.

Charleston *Southern Patriot, and Commercial Advertiser*

Friday, July 12, 1822

COMMUNICATION.

Mr. EDITOR:—Permit me to express to the gentlemen composing the Court, who are now sitting on a very painful and distressing business, the thanks of I believe the whole community, for their unwearied labors and calm and discriminating investigation of the subject before them.

The combination of talents, respectability and integrity, which are found in those gentlemen, reconciles every man to the awful examples which are making.

To his Honor the Intendant, are justly due the undivided thanks and approbation of his Fellow-Citizens, for his able, faithful and zealous discharge of his high and responsible duties.

A Citizen of Charleston.

Philadelphia *National Gazette and Literary Register*

Saturday, July 13, 1822

We republished, a few days ago, the article which excited, in Charleston, so strong a sensation against Wm. Johnson, Esq. one of the judges of the Supreme Court of the

United States. He was supposed to have intended, by that article, to cast the most degrading and injurious reflections upon the Court of Freeholders and Magistrates formed to try the negroes, six of whom were recently executed, for planning an insurrection.—Judge Johnson has published, in the pamphlet form, an address to the public of Charleston, in which, we think, he exonerates himself fully from the charge of having meant to affect the reputation or feelings of the members of the court. He solemnly disclaims this intention.—He states, moreover, that when the article was written by him, the court was not organized, and that, when it was delivered to the printer some days after, he yet, as he has it in his power to prove, knew nothing of the existence of the court.

Justice William Johnson Jr. on Slavery, 1822

. . . Domestic Slavery must ever be a cause of national weakness.[1] The laboring classes of a country, furnish the materials for armies; and armies cannot be formed when the laboring classes cannot be trusted with arms. But the evil was not so great in the southern states, as is generally imagined. There exists nothing of that personal hostility between the master and slave, that theorists suppose must be the result of the relation they bear to each other. Mildly treated, reared up as the humble companion of the children of the whites, and accustomed from intimacy to look up to them for protection, it is generally found, that the slave in those states, bears a strong attachment to the master. Nothing but brutal conduct, on his part, or extraordinary corruptness on the part of the slave, produces an exception. Innumerable were the instances exhibited in the revolutionary war, of the most affecting fidelity of this class of people to their master and his family. The number who joined the British, was comparatively very small,[2] and consisted chiefly of the young and thoughtless, particularly of the female sex. In many instances, they would return, and with repentant tears, solicit to be again received into confidence.

But the number dispersed through these states, was very great. So great, as to render it impossible for the citizens to muster freemen enough to withstand the pressure of the British arms. This evil, it is generally asserted, has been entailed upon the southern states, by the introduction of rice. But, nothing was ever more erroneous. They had been introduced into Virginia, many years before the Carolinas were settled, and had spread into North Carolina, in considerable numbers.

In the original settlement of the Carolinas, it was contemplated to introduce negro slaves; as is obvious from an article in the fundamental constitution. And it was not that the culture of rice made the introduction of slaves necessary; but that a valuable staple, enabled the planters to purchase them. This was enough for the Liverpool merchant. As soon as he saw a prospect of a market, he was ready to furnish the article in demand. Before that time, as has already been observed, the inhabitant bought, or trepanned, the native savages; and either employed them himself, or shipped them off for sale. . . .

During the whole of the revolutionary war, it is clear that the slaves never once meditated any thing like insurrection. Indeed, it is not whilst their masters have arms in their hands that such an event is ever to be apprehended. . . .

1. Justice Johnson published these words on slavery a few months before the trial of Vesey and his coadjutors. While critical of slavery in the abstract, Johnson actually offered a rather revealing encapsulation of the evolving paternalistic narrative that white southerners were increasingly using to justify slavery. That Vesey's lieutenants came largely from the ranks of privileged slaves, including the household of his brother-in-law, Governor Bennett, appeared to make a mockery of Johnson's judgment on the benign nature of the master-slave relation. The fact that Johnson's paternalistic apology for slavery appeared shortly before the discovery of the Vesey plot meant that Johnson, a man quite touchy about honor and even more sensitive to criticism, would have felt formidably challenged to defend his position. Having previously made a conspicuously public intellectual commitment to paternalism, a defensive Johnson had reason to downplay the magnitude of the Vesey plot. See Robert L. Paquette, "From Rebellion to Revisionism: The Continuing Debate about the Denmark Vesey Affair," *Journal of the Historical Society* 4 (Fall 2004): 298–99.

2. Johnson's remarks on the docility of slaves during the American Revolution fly in the face of those of South Carolina's David Ramsay (1749–1815), who in his classic study *The History of the American Revolution*, 2 vols. (Philadelphia, 1789), vol. 2: 293, a work Johnson would surely have read in preparation for his biography of Nathanael Greene, spoke frankly about the desertion of southern slaves to British lines and asserted that, during the Revolution, "South-Carolina lost a great number of its citizens, and upwards of 20,000 of its slaves." Governor Bennett, Johnson's brother-in-law, adopted two children—Jean and Madeleine L'Engle—who were orphaned refugees from the slave revolution in Saint-Domingue. Yet, to justify slavery in the Old South, he and many other southern proslavery apologists would construct for the American Revolution a history that omitted the desertions of thousands of slaves to British lines. See Eugene D. Genovese and Elizabeth Fox-Genovese, *Fatal Self-Deception: Slaveholding Paternalism in the Old South* (Cambridge, UK: Cambridge University Press, 2011), 134–35.

William Johnson, *Sketches of the Life and Correspondence of Nathanael Greene, Major General of the Armies of the United States, in the War of the Revolution*, 2 vols. (Charleston, SC, 1822), vol. 2: appendix E.

Governor Thomas Bennett Jr. to Attorney General Robert Young Hayne, Monday, July 1, 1822

Executive Department
Charleston. July 1. 1822

Rob[t] Y. Hayne Esq.
Att[y] Gen[l]. of So. Ca.

Dear Sir

The very large amount of property involved, the extensive range which enquiry is taking and the number of lives which may yet be demanded to appease offended Justice induce to the request that you will favour me with your opinions on the subjoined questions.

Accustomed to regard the negative of each as the immutable rule of Courts exercising criminal jurisdiction; I feel a weight of responsibility arising from the course of proceeding which has been adopted, which I dare not assume. Whatever your opinion may be, it can produce no effect on the decisions of the court recently adjourned—but as it is my duty, so shall it govern my conduct in relation to others.

Can a Court of Justice, particularly in criminal cases, be held with *closed doors*?

Figure 6. Robert Young Hayne (1791–1839), attorney general of South Carolina in 1822 and judge on the Second Court of Magistrates and Freeholders. From a portrait, 1820. Courtesy of the South Carolina Governor's Mansion Collection. Photo by Sam Holland.

Can a prisoner be legally tried and convicted without being confronted by his witnesses and everyone of them?

Can a Corporation legally organize a court for the trial of Felons?

These enquiries are dictated by a sense of duty and an anxious desire to relieve my mind from great embarrassment; your immediate attention therefore to the subject is particularly desired.

I am Dear Sir with great esteem
Very truly yours
Tho: Bennett

ALS in Document D (copy), RGA, GM, 1328, SCDAH.

Attorney General Robert Y. Hayne to Governor Thomas Bennett Jr., Wednesday, July 3, 1822

Office of the Attorney General
Charleston 3rd July 1822

Dear Sir

The important questions suggested by your letter of the 1st inst. have commanded my serious attention & I shall now proceed to give you the result of my deliberations. The questions submitted are the following, which I shall answer in the order in which they are stated.

1st "Can a Corporation legally organize a Court for the trial "of felons"?

2nd "Can a Court of Justice particularly in criminal cases "be held with *closed doors*"?

3rd "Can a prisoner be legally tried and convicted without being *confronted by his witnesses* and every one of them?"

I distinctly understand from your letter, that these questions are not intended to relate to *Criminal Courts in general* organized for the trial of *Freemen*, but that they relate to *Courts of Justices and Freeholders* organized under our Acts of Assembly for the trial of *Slaves*;—and that they are intended to apply immediately to such a Court now actually engaged in the trial of certain slaves in this City and supposed to be organized by the City Council of Charleston.—In this view of the subject, I am of opinion on the *first question* submitted, that the proper mode of organizing a Court for the trial of slaves for capital offences is clearly pointed out by the Acts of 1740 and 1754 (2 Brevard's Dig. 245) which provide that upon information being received of an offence committed by any slave for which capital punishment may be inflicted, *a Justice of the Peace* "shall without delay by his warrant *call to his assistance* any one of the nearest Justices of the Peace to associate with him; and shall by the same warrant summon any number of the neighbouring Freeholders not less than three or more than five to meet at a certain day and place and so forth:—and finally hear and determine the matter brought before them in the most expeditious and summary manner." This mode I am informed has been strictly pursued in the case before us. That a warrant was issued a Justice to call to his assistance another Justice and five Freeholders, and as he had under the Law a right to summon any of his neighbours, it can afford no ground of exception to his proceedings that he was probably influenced by the wishes of the City Council in selecting the respectable individuals who now compose the Court. My answer to the first question therefore is, *that the Court must be organized by a Justice of the Peace, though I have no hesitation in adding that this appears to me to have been sufficiently done in the case under consideration.*

The 2d & 3rd Questions, I shall consider together as they relate to *the mode of proceeding in the trial* and my opinion on both results from the same train of reasoning. If I had been asked whether a *free white man* could be lawfully tried by a Court sitting with closed doors and without being confronted with his witnesses I should have had little difficulty in giving the answer. I would then have referred to the *Great Charter* of our *liberties* and the *established principles* of the *Common Law*, and from thence clearly have deduced those rules which now govern our criminal courts, giving such ample security to *all the rights of the Citizen*. But nothing can be clearer than that *slaves* are not entitled to *these rights*. Magna Charta & Habeas Corpus and indeed all the provisions of our Constitution in favor of Liberty, are intended for *freemen* only. If a Slave could possess these privileges, he would change his condition and becoming a freeman, could not be deprived of life, liberty or property but by the judgment "of his peers."

The same reasoning applies to *the mode of proceedings* in the trial of Slaves. It cannot be for a moment imagined *that all the rules of the Common Law* are obligatory in the trial of slaves. If any man will turn to Chitty's Criminal Law[1] and trace *the numerous forms necessary to be observed* in the trial of a freeman from the moment of his *arrest* to the *final sentence*, he would rise from the examination with a thorough conviction that it is impossible to apply these forms to the trial of Slaves by Courts of Freeholders organized as ours generally are. These Courts it is well known are not composed of Judges or

Lawyers and they are not attended by the Attorney General or Solicitor to prosecute in behalf of the State. It must be obvious therefore that the Legislature never intended that a Court of Freeholders should be governed by *the same rules* as *the Courts of General Sessions.* The rules of the Common Law on the single subject of the *form* of *Indictments* if applied to courts organized for the trial of Slaves would defeat almost every prosecution, commenced against them. Now if a Court of Freeholders are not *imperatively* bound by *all the rules* of the Common Law, *by which of them* I ask are they so *bound*? It will be admitted that it is not necessary that a slave should be formally indicted. No Grand Jury presents a bill against them—he has no right of challenge and the witnesses are not even sworn on his Trial. Now if *these great and established rules of the Common Law* are not regarded in his trial, by what authority can we say that *certain other rules must of necessity be* observed. The Legislature in establishing our criminal courts for the trial of Freemen declare that they shall be governed by *the practice of the Court of King's Bench,* but they make no such provision in relation to the Court of Freeholders and merely declare that "they shall finally hear and determine the matter in the most expeditious and summary manner." The *spirit* in which this act was framed, may be discerned from the 53d Section, which provides that: "This act and all clauses therein contained shall be construed most largely and beneficially, for the promoting and carrying into execution this act and for the encouragement and justification of all persons to be employed in the execution thereof, and no record, warrant, precept or commitment, to be made by virtue of this act or the proceedings therefrom, shall be reversed, avoided or any ways impeached by reason of any default in form." On the whole I conclude that Slaves (according to our Institutions) have no civil rights which are not derived from our statutes, that we must look into these statutes for the mode of organizing a Court for their trial as well as the rules of proceeding in such trial. In this Court (which must in capital cases consist of *two Justices* of the Peace (officers of trust answerable to the Legislature for their conduct) and of Freeholders (presented to be responsible men) *is confided* the task of hearing and determining all questions relating to Slaves. The punishment to be inflicted is in almost every case *fixed by the Statute* and the Court has little more to do than to ascertain the guilt or innocence of the accused. In making this enquiry, *no form of proceeding is prescribed*—but it is simply declared "They shall hear and determine the matter in the most summary manner." It is true that such a Court ought *in general* to observe (and I will add it is their usual practice to observe) in all their proceedings as many of the rules of the Common Law as are adapted to the nature of their Court and are *calculated to subserve the ends of Justice.* But I am not prepared to say that the observance of any one of these rules is indispensable in order to give validity to their proceedings. I know that it is usual and I cannot doubt that it is in general very just and proper that a Court of Freeholders should sit with open doors. Yet I can find no authority for declaring that their omitting to do so would vacate their judgments and I can easily perceive cases in which it would be indispensable to the public peace and safety that they should proceed with closed doors. Let us (by way of example) suppose that extensive combinations had been formed for the purposes of insurrection that the plot was but partially discovered and that the names of only a few of the parties concerned had been disclosed. It is obvious that the public trial of these individuals might be the means of effecting the escape of all the others; and this is still more obvious when we remember the provisions of the Law which (requiring that every slave shall be tried *within six days* after his arrest) precluded the possibility of extensive private investigations before trial. In such cases too it must be considered that the feelings of the community are greatly agitated and if the Public were day after day to be made acquainted with the partial proofs then adduced, without waiting for the result of the whole evidence, the most lamentable excitement would be the consequence. In every view of the subject I am satisfied *that circumstances may exist to justify and even recommend a trial with closed doors and as far as I am acquainted with the facts, such circumstances have recently existed and probably now exist.* But however that may be *I do not think the exercise of a sound discretion on the part of the Court with closed doors would vacate their proceedings.* The same reasoning applies to the 3d question as to "confronting the witnesses by the accused." This is certainly the usual course of proceeding. But in cases of Insurrection it might happen that a party to the Plot might be deterred from disclosing it without the protection afforded by a private examination. Indeed it might be an express stipulation on the part of such an informer that he should not be known. In this and other like cases which can be imagined, it would seem to be proper that the witnesses should be privately examined. *I cannot say therefore that such a proceeding would render void the sentence of the Court.* If it be asked where then we are to find protection for the slave, or security to the interests of his owner, I reply that the Legislature *have supposed* that these will be found in the *organization* of the Court itself;—the *obvious policy* of upright and humane decisions and the characteristic humanity of our fellow-citizens. I will add that I conceive *cases might exist* in which a Prohibition would issue from the Judges of the Court of Sessions to restrain the proceedings of a court of Freeholders. If these are not sufficient *guards* to afford protections, the Legislature can alone furnish the proper remedy. I think that in *practice* few evils have resulted from the present Law. I have had some experience in the administration of our criminal Laws and I have no hesitation in declaring my firm belief that *equal humanity* is in general displayed in the treatment of criminals whether *slaves* or *freemen.* Indeed it has several times happened within my knowledge that slaves have been *corporally punished* for offences, which would have cost white men their lives; and this arose from compassion for their ignorance and dependant condition. Wherever Slavery exists, this dependence is necessary and will always afford better protection *to the Slave* than the ineffectual effort of the Laws to confer half way privileges which can only serve to place him in hostility to his master. I will not deny however that some wholesome improvements might be made in our Laws both for the government and trial of slaves. I have not separately considered the case of *free persons of color,* because in relation to all the questions submitted to me, they are treated by the Laws in all respects in the like manner as slaves.

I fear I have trespassed on your patience in taking this general view of the subject. Its intrinsic importance and the deep sense you have expressed of "*the weight of responsibility* which has been thrown on you arising from the course of proceeding which has been adopted" must be my apology. On this last suggestion however you will permit me to remark (which I do with the utmost deference) that however your judgment may disapprove of the "course of proceeding" yet you ought not perhaps to consider any "responsibility" as thereby "thrown on you." The Executive is certainly not bound to examine into Judicial errors, nor is it his duty to correct them. In most cases the parties immediately concerned can obtain redress by appealing to a higher Judicial tribunal, but in no event could I regard any responsibility as resting with the Executive. I take the liberty of making the suggestion to relieve your mind from anxiety which might still be felt on this subject and am

Dear Sir with the highest
respect & esteem
Your most Obet. Sert.
Robt. Y. Hayne
Attorney General

His Excy Governor Bennett

1. Joseph Chitty, *A Practical Treatise on the Criminal Law . . .* (London, 1816).

ALS in RGA, GM, 1328, Document E, SCDAH.

Washington *National Intelligencer*

Tuesday, July 9, 1822

We copy the subjoined articles from the Charleston Courier of the 1st inst. It appears that the publication headed "Melancholy effect of popular excitement," to which reference is made, was ascribed to Judge Johnson, to whose brother in-law, Governor Bennett, three of the negroes condemned to death for an attempt to raise an insurrection, belonged. The culprits were tried, according to law, by a special court composed of Magistrates and Freeholders. The members of the court are all gentlemen of the highest respectability, and some of them are eminent for talents. We give their names:—Col. Wm. Drayton, J. R. Pringle, R. J. Turnbull, James Legare, Nathaniel Heyward. Magistrates—L. H. Kennedy, Thomas Parker.[1]

1. This information, together with Johnson's complete Communication of July 1, was reprinted verbatim in the Philadelphia *National Gazette and Literary Register,* July 9, 1822, and the *New-York Evening Post,* July 7, 1822. For information on the judges, see Part III, pp. 160–61.

Governor Thomas Bennett Jr. to William Peronneau, Friday, August 30, 1822

Executive Department
Charleston Augt 30, 1822

The Hon: William Peronneau[1]
Intendant pro tem: of the city of Charleston
Dear Sir

Deeming it essentially important and highly beneficial to the State that the particular causes which led to, and the means used to nurture, and extend the conspiracy lately projected within this City, should be fully investigated and all its particulars made known to the Legislature of this State; I requested several gentlemen of respectability to explore (if practicable) these subjects and furnish me the result of their enquiries.

It is with infinite surprise that I have been unofficially informed that the City Council have adopted measures to counteract this object; and that these gentlemen, acting as my agents will be subjected to a painful and indignifying repulse, by a subordinate City Officer, should they again meet for the accomplishment of my desires.

Beleiving it impossible that the City Council could attempt to abridge a power, the exercise of which is incidental and from obvious causes attached to the Executive; or that they could be induced to withhold from me the communication of a measure, the execution of which would necessarily involve sensations extremely painful; I must request from you, Sir, such information on this subject as will enable me (if the report be true) to avoid the consequences threatened by the absence of that comity to which I think myself entitled from the corporate authorities of this City and which I have uniformly tendered to them.

I have the Honor to be
Very Respectfully Your obt Sevt
Tho: Bennett

1. William Peronneau (1768–1848), a planter described in his obituary as a "gentleman of the Old School, distinguished for his affability and kind deportment," served as acting mayor of Charleston during absences by James Hamilton Jr. He lived in 1822 at 34 South Bay Street. During the executions at the Lines on July 26, an excited crowd caused the death of his teenaged slave Sam, who was accidentally struck by a carriage pole. See *CSCCD,* 94; "Coroner's Report," Charleston *City Gazette and Commercial Daily Advertiser,* July 27, 1822; Charleston *Southern Patriot,* June 19, 1848.

ALS in GM, no. 1328, SCDAH.

William Peronneau to Governor Thomas Bennett Jr., Friday, August 30, 1822

Charleston 30th August 1822

His Excellency
Governor Bennett
Dear Sir

As an individual, I hope you will do me the justice to believe, that no one can regret more than I do, that any difference of opinion should ever exist between your Excellency and the Council; but as the organ of that body, it has become officially my painful duty to inform you, that the Council have directed that no person but your Excellency, shall be permitted for the future to see any of the Culprits.

I have the honor to be
With the greatest respect
yr Excellency's most obt Servt
Wm Peronneau. I. P. T.

ALS in GM, no. 1328, SCDAH.

III

Trials

The *Official Report* and the Senate Transcript

The Editorial Statement that precedes Part I identifies the three white men who in 1822 published two accounts that contained all or parts of the records generated by the proceedings of the two courts of magistrates and freeholders formed to pass judgment on the accused plotters. As early as mid-August, Intendant (Mayor) James Hamilton Jr. printed *An Account of the Late Intended Insurrection among a Portion of the Blacks of the City,* a 46-page collection of court documents, together with a short biography of Denmark Vesey and a brief narrative of events. Two months later, magistrates Lionel Henry Kennedy and Thomas Parker Jr. produced a far longer work, *An Official Report of the Trials of Sundry Negroes.* Their 202-page tract included some of the same material published by Hamilton, such as the brief biography of Vesey. The authors of the *Official Report,* which is reprinted below, intended to give a more "full and complete" account of events to the public, both inside and outside of Charleston. All three authors had access to the original sets of clerk-produced documents that were also provided to the state House and Senate. The *Official Report* includes minor details omitted from the versions presented to the House and Senate, such as the forenames of white masters who accompanied their accused bondmen to the trials, and the rulings in some of the cases. Meant to calm public fears, justify the proceedings, and demonstrate the mastery of Carolina whites over the slave population, the *Official Report* omitted information regarded as inflammatory. Slaves offered immunity in exchange for their testimony were, for example, identified in the *Report* only by a number or a capital letter. (By comparison, most of the slaves' names appear in the versions provided to the House and Senate.) While the Senate transcript contains details of the final trials conducted in August by the second court, the House version ignores them completely and the *Official Report* provides merely a summary of the proceedings.

Because Hamilton's pamphlet appeared only weeks after the August trials ended, his version and Kennedy's and Parker's longer *Report*—which generally differ only in length—may be more accurate than the handwritten versions presented to the state assembly three months later. Hamilton's *Account,* in particular, proves the best at providing specific trial dates and discussed a number of slaves questioned and released who were unmentioned elsewhere. But because the *Official Report* is more complete,

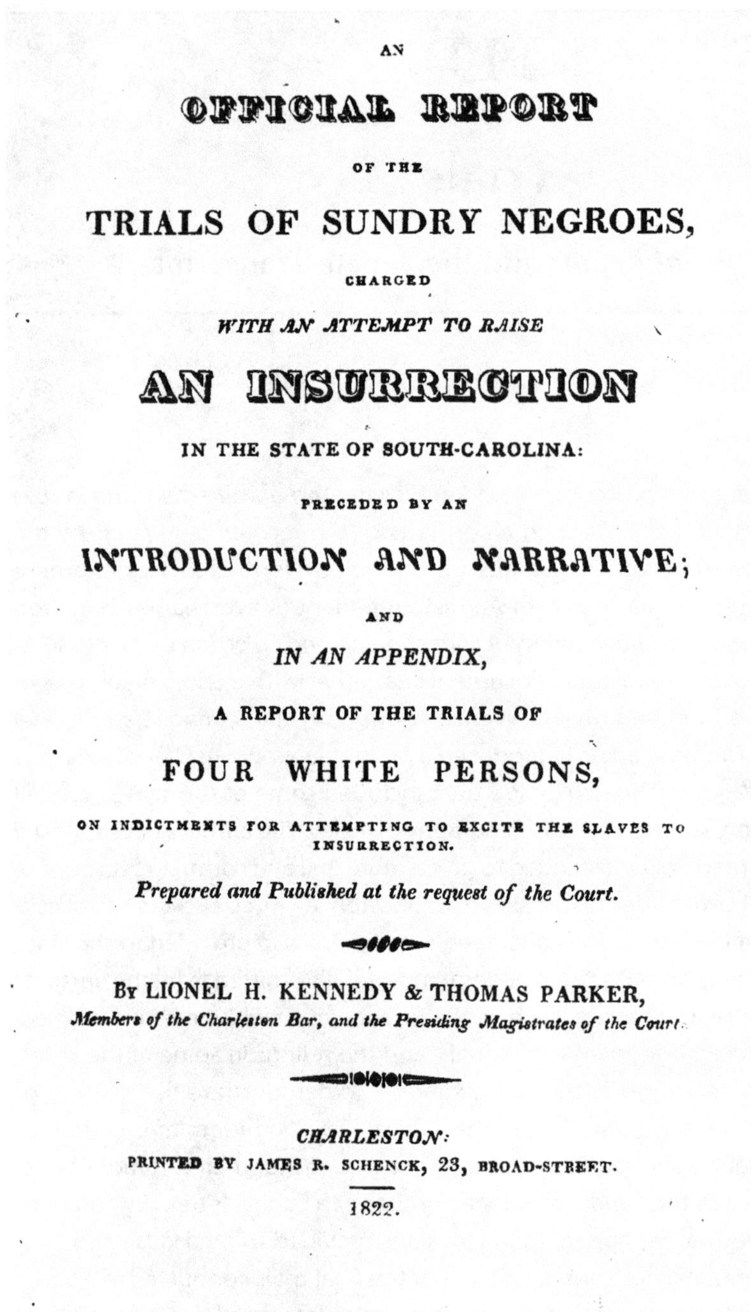

AN

OFFICIAL REPORT

OF THE

TRIALS OF SUNDRY NEGROES,

CHARGED

WITH AN ATTEMPT TO RAISE

AN INSURRECTION

IN THE STATE OF SOUTH-CAROLINA:

PRECEDED BY AN

INTRODUCTION AND NARRATIVE;

AND

IN AN APPENDIX,

A REPORT OF THE TRIALS OF

FOUR WHITE PERSONS,

ON INDICTMENTS FOR ATTEMPTING TO EXCITE THE SLAVES TO INSURRECTION.

Prepared and Published at the request of the Court.

BY LIONEL H. KENNEDY & THOMAS PARKER,

Members of the Charleston Bar, and the Presiding Magistrates of the Court.

CHARLESTON:

PRINTED BY JAMES R. SCHENCK, 23, BROAD-STREET.

1822.

Figure 7. Title page of Kennedy and Parker, *Official Report of the Trials of Sundry Negroes* (1822).

we have reproduced that pamphlet only, supplemented by occasional additions from Hamilton's *Account.* And because the October *Official Report* appeared one month before the Senate transcription, we have placed that pamphlet before the legislative account. Footnotes indicate where we have relied on Hamilton's *Account,* just as they identify differences between the various versions and, on occasion, discuss minor variations between the House and Senate versions.

District of South-Carolina.

BE IT REMEMBERED, That on the twenty-second day of October, Anno Domino 1822, and in the forty-seventh year of the Independence of the United States of America, LIONEL H. KENNEDY and THOMAS PARKER, Esquires, deposited in this office the title of a book, the right whereof they claim as authors and proprietors, in the words following, to wit:

AN Official Report of the Trials of Sundry Negroes, charged with an attempt to raise an Insurrection in the state of South-Carolina: Preceded by an Introduction and Narrative; and in an Appendix, a Report of the Trials of four White Persons, on indictments for attempting to excite the Slaves to Insurrection. Prepared and published at the request of the Court, by LIONEL H. KENNEDY and THOMAS PARKER, Members of the Charleston Bar, and the presiding Magistrates of the Court.

In conformity to the act of Congress of the United States, entitled, "An Act for the encouragement of learning, by securing the copies of maps, charts, and books, to the authors and proprietors of such copies, during the times therein mentioned;" and also, an act entitled, "An Act, supplementary to an Act, entitled, An Act for the encouragement of learning, by securing the copies of maps, charts, and books to the authors and proprietors of such copies, during the times therein mentioned, and extending the benefits thereof to the arts of designing, engraving, and etching historical and other prints."

JAMES JERVEY, *District Clerk*

WE, the subscribers, who, with LIONEL H. KENNEDY and THOMAS PARKER, Esquires, composed the first Court organized for the trial of Slaves and other Persons of Colour, charged with attempting to raise an Insurrection, do hereby certify, that the following Introduction, Narrative and Report were prepared for publication by request, at a meeting of the members of the said Court; that the same were submitted to us individually for our approbation, and that we unanimously approve of and sanction the publication of the same. We further certify, that the Report of the Trials contains the Evidence given in each case.

WM. DRAYTON,[1]
NATHL. HEYWARD,[2]
J. R. PRINGLE,[3]
JAS. LEGARE,[4]
ROBERT J. TURNBULL,[5]
HENRY DEAS.[6]

INTRODUCTION.

The account published by the authority of the City Council of Charleston,[7] presents the prominent features of the late contemplated insurrection, but it does not profess to be full and complete, and is ingenuously characterized, as furnishing "a very brief abstract of the testimony offered in the cases brought before the Court." As the public had not an opportunity of witnessing these proceedings, in consequence of the peculiar nature of the investigations, which occupied the attention of the Court; and as a very general desire has been expressed to be informed of the detail of the plot, as far, as it has been developed; the presiding Magistrates of the first Court, in whose possession are all the original documents, at the request and under the sanction of the whole Court, have undertaken the present publication. The whole evidence has been given, in each particular case, in the order of it's trial, and wherever any additional, or incidental testimony has been disclosed against any criminal subsequently to his conviction, sentence or execution, it has been duly noticed. The evidence is in most cases preserved, as it was originally taken, without even changing the phraseology, which was generally in the very words used by the witnesses.

Although a different style might have been more agreeable to the ear, it was supposed, that this report would be considered more authentic and satisfactory, if this method were adopted. It will be perceived, in several instances, that hearsay communications have been recorded, and it may be imagined, that they had some influence on the minds of the Court. Such communications were only admitted under the belief, that they might lead to further discoveries, but they had no effect whatever on the decision of the cases; and being preserved, it was thought adviseable, to lay before the public, the whole narrative, as it was given by the witnesses, *and not to suppress any part of it.*

It frequently happened, in the investigation of this plot, that information was communicated, which, as it did not involve the guilt or innocence of any of the criminals, was not recorded; but which in conjunction with various facts and anecdotes, not committed to writing, and within the knowledge, perhaps, of the Court alone, would be very interesting to the community. In addition therefore, to a mere report of the trials, and at the suggestion of many; an historical account of the intended insurrection, embracing all such information, is inserted in this publication, under a separate article. On Tuesday, the 18th of June, the Intendant of Charleston, informed the authors, that there were several colored persons, in confinement, charged with an attempt "to excite an insurrection among the blacks against the whites," and requested them to take the necessary steps to organize a Court for the trial of those criminals. The Intendant, at the same time, suggested the names of five gentlemen, as freeholders, who, possessing in an eminent degree, the confidence of the community, and being highly approved of, were immediately summoned, in the form prescribed by law, to assemble the next day, at 12 o'clock. The Freeholders convened at the time and place appointed, when the following oath, contained in the act "for the better ordering and governing negroes and other slaves," was first administered by the Justices to each other, and then to each Freeholder.—"You do solemnly swear in the presence of Almighty God, that you will truly and impartially, try and adjudge the prisoners who shall be brought before you upon their trials, and honestly and duly, on your part, put in execution, on these trials, an act, entitled an act for the better ordering and governing of negroes and other slaves, in this state, according to the best of your skill and knowledge. So help you God." After the Court had been thus organized, the Intendant briefly related the circumstances, which led to the detection of the plot, and the preliminary measures adopted, which are detailed in the account published by the authority of the City Council. He at the same time presented to the Court a callender, containing the names of all the criminals, then ascertained, the charges on which they had been committed, and the witnesses against them. Before the Court proceeded to any trial, they were engaged some time, in examining all the testimony they could obtain, in order to ascertain how far, a conspiracy had really been formed: being convinced by these means, of the existence of a plot, they laid down the rules and principles, on which, the trials should be conducted. As the Court had been organized under a statute of a peculiar and local character, and intended for the government of a distinct class of persons in the community; they were bound to conform their proceedings to its provisions, which depart in many essential features, from the principles of the common law, and some of the settled rules of evidence. The Court however, determined to adopt those rules, whenever they were not repugnant to, nor expressly excepted by that statute, nor inconsistent with the local situation and policy of the state; and laid down for their own government the following regulations:—First—That no slave should be tried, except in the presence of his owner, or his counsel, and that notice should be given, in every case, at least one day before the trial: Second—That the testimony of one witness, unsupported by additional evidence, or by circumstances, should lead to no conviction of a *capital* nature: Third—That the witnesses should be confronted with the accused, and with each other, in every case, except where testimony was given under a solemn pledge that the names of the witnesses should not be divulged, as they declared in some instances, that they apprehended being murdered by the blacks, if it was known that they had volunteered their evidence: Fourth—That the prisoners might be represented by counsel, whenever this was requested by the owners of the slaves, or by the prisoners themselves, if free: Fifth—That the statements or defences of the accused should be heard, in every case, and they be permitted themselves to examine any witness they thought proper.

The Court, on mature deliberation, determined that the public generally, or in other words those, who had no particular interest in the slaves accused, should not be present at their trials; but that the owners of all the slaves tried, and their counsel, as well as the owners of those, who were used as witnesses, should be admitted, if they desired it. The Court also extended the same permission to the Intendant and Wardens of Charleston. Among other reasons, which induced this course, were the following; because several witnesses had volunteered their testimony, under a solemn pledge of secrecy, and because the further detection of the plot, would be greatly impeded, if not entirely stopped, by the accused being apprized of the information against them, and being thus enabled to effect their escape before they could be apprehended.

It was also morally certain, that no colored witness would have ventured to incur the resentment of his comrades, by voluntarily disclosing his testimony in a public court. The court was likewise anxious to prevent the public mind from being excited by the exaggerated representations of the testimony which might have been circulated by auditors under the influence of misapprehension or terror.—In the progress of these trials, the propriety of these measures was completely verified, and they were also sanctioned by precedent, on a former occasion, under similar circumstances, at Camden,[8] in this state.

In the conspiracy of the blacks, at Antigua, in 1736,[9] the criminals were tried privately, and not even their owners admitted; and in the negro plot, at the city of New-York, in 1741,[10] the trials were in general conducted in a private manner.

After the execution of the first six criminals, and the conviction and passing sentence on five more, two of the latter made disclosures, which caused the arrest of such considerable numbers, that the court were induced to lay down certain rules of discrimination, in the guilt of the parties, and to adopt two classes of offences. Under the first class were included those who attended the meetings at Denmark Vesey's, at Bulkley's Farm, or at appointed meetings in Monday Gell's shop, for the purpose of obtaining and communicating intelligence of the progress of the conspiracy; all those, who aided and abetted in the contribution of money, arms or ammunition; all those, who persuaded others to join; all those, who were employed as couriers, to communicate intelligence, or convey orders; and generally, those, who, from their acts or declarations, indicated a hearty concurrence in the plot; and all those, who, after the condemnation of the first 6, endeavored to keep up the sprit of insurrection, to promote, or endeavored to promote or excite a party to rescue the prisoners to be executed. Those who were embraced in this class were, upon conviction, to be punished with death. Under the second class were included those, who had merely consented to join in the plot, without taking any active part.—Those, who were included under this class, were to be transported[11] beyond the limits of the United States, not to return therein, under the penalty of death.

As the Act of Legislature, under which the Court were organized, may not be generally known abroad, it is deemed adviseable to extract not only such parts of it, as relate immediately to these trials, but so much thereof, as may exhibit its general outlines. With this view the following sections are inserted: . . . [12]

1. William Drayton (1776–1846) was a prosperous attorney and close friend of both James Hamilton Jr. and Robert J. Turnbull. A Federalist who opposed war with Great Britain in 1812, he served Charleston in 1822 as a judge and court recorder. He resided at 6 Gibbes Street. See *BDSCHR* 4: 164–66; John Belton O'Neall, *Biographical Sketches of the Bench and Bar of South Carolina . . .*, 2 vols. (Charleston, SC, 1859), vol. 1: 305–23.

2. Nathaniel Heyward (1776–1851) was South Carolina's most prominent rice planter and one of the largest slaveholders in the antebellum South. He would eventually own more than two thousand slaves on seventeen plantations clustered along the Combahee River. When in Charleston in 1822, he resided at 275 East Bay Street. See James B. Heyward, "The Heyward Family of South Carolina," *SCHM* 59 (1958): 155; Eugene D. Genovese and Elizabeth Fox-Genovese, *Fatal Self-Deception: Slaveholding Paternalism in the Old South* (Cambridge, UK: Cambridge University Press, 2011), 37; *CSCCD*, 83.

3. At the time of his service on the court, James Reid Pringle (1782–1840) owned more than one hundred slaves in Prince Williams Parish and a townhouse in Charleston at 101 Tradd Street. He had served for years as collector of customs for the city and was elected president of the state senate. See *BDSCHR* 4: 461; *CSCCD*, 95.

4. James Legaré (1762–1830), a big planter in St. John Colleton Parish, worshipped at Benjamin Morgan Palmer's Circular Church. In 1822 he owned a home in Charleston at 7 New Street. Legaré

stepped down from the court because of illness on July 13, to be replaced by Henry Deas. See *BDSCHR* 3: 426–27; *CSCCD,* 87; Eliza C. K. Flood, *Biographical Sketches of the Huguenot Solomon Legaré and of his Family. . . .* (Charleston, SC, 1886), passim.

5. Robert J. Turnbull (1775–1833), planter and attorney, identified as a Federalist before becoming after the Vesey affair one of the prime movers behind the nullification movement. In 1822 he lived on 1 Logan Street. See O'Neall, John Belton O'Neall, *Biographical Sketches of the Bench and Bar of South Carolina . . . ,* 2 vols. (Charleston, SC, 1859), vol. 2: 604; *CSCCD,* 101.

6. Henry Deas (1770–1846), lawyer, planter, and politician, replaced James Legaré on the court on July 13, 1822. In 1822 Deas owned scores of slaves and multiple properties along the North Santee River as well as a townhouse in Charleston at 1 Friend Street. He married Margaret Horry (1771–1846), the sister of Elias Horry (1773–1834), whose coachman was involved in the Vesey plot.

7. This refers to Hamilton, *Account.*

8. In 1816, white officials in Camden, South Carolina, claimed to have uncovered a conspiracy of slaves who aimed to rise in rebellion on July 4. See Thomas J. Kirkland and Robert M. Kennedy, *Historic Camden,* 2 vols. (Columbia, SC: State Company, 1905), vol. 1: 187–89.

9. In 1736, British officials in Antigua, the largest of the British Leeward Islands, alleged that they had uncovered a plot by African and creole slaves to take over the entire island. Almost ninety slaves were executed during several months' investigation; the majority suffered death by burning. Although most of the leaders were creoles, the supreme commander was a "Coromantee," interestingly enough, the same "ethnic" identification used by Thomas Cilavan Brown (b. 1800), a free colored carpenter in Charleston who knew Susan Vesey, to describe her husband Denmark. See Lydia Maria Child to Thomas Wentworth Higginson, March 17, 1860, in Part VI, pp. 749–53, of this volume. "Coromantee" typically meant an Akan-speaker from the Gold Coast region of West Africa. The best book on the Antigua plot remains David Barry Gaspar, *Bondmen & Rebels: A Study of Master-Slave Relations in Antigua with Implications for Colonial British North America* (Baltimore: Johns Hopkins University Press, 1985). Jason T. Sharples, "Hearing Whispers, Casting Shadows: Jailhouse Conversation and the Production of Knowledge during the Antigua Slave Conspiracy of 1736," in *Buried Lives: Incarcerated in Early America,* ed. Michele Lise Tarter and Richard Bell (Athens: University of Georgia Press, 2012), 35–59, has questioned the reality of the plot.

10. About thirty slaves and three whites were executed in New York City as a result of investigations precipitated in 1741 by a destructive fire. See Jill Lepore, *New York Burning: Liberty, Slavery, and Conspiracy in Eighteenth-Century Manhattan* (New York: Knopf, 2005). Almost 20 percent of New York City's population was enslaved at the time.

11. "Where to stay the hand of the executioner is an important question," said Thomas Jefferson in replying to Governor James Monroe's letter on the punishment of slave rebels involved in Gabriel's plot (1800) in Richmond, Virginia. Authorities in South Carolina and other southern states followed Virginia's lead in using transportation as a more humane method of dealing with slaves convicted of capital crimes. See Monroe to Jefferson, September 15, 1800, and Jefferson to Monroe, September 20, 1800, in *The Papers of Thomas Jefferson,* vol. 32: *June 1800 to February 1801,* ed. Barbara B. Oberg (Princeton, NJ: Princeton University Press, 2005), 144–45, 160–61.

12. The *OR,* ix–xv, here reprints portions of the 1740 "Negro Act," which appears in its entirety in Part II of this volume, as does the material here listed as "A Narrative."

MEMORANDUM.

A Gentleman of respectability, the owner of one of the Slaves deeply engaged in the Conspiracy, stated to the Court, previously to his Servant's guilt being ascertained, that he was a Negro in whose honestly and veracity he confided, and whose attachment and fidelity to him had been great. That this Negro had been twice in the Northern States with him, where he had every reason to believe that attempts were made to induce this Slave not to return to Charleston. He further said he had owned him since 1806 or 1807, during all which time he had behaved himself well. It thus appears that even a Servant whose attachment to his owner was so great, that he refused to avail himself of the means of lawfully attaining his freedom, (the laws of the State, or the friendly feelings of its inhabitants, where he then was putting that in his power,) could not resist the arguments or threats of the Conspirators, even though he knew that they aimed at nothing less than the murder of his master and family.[1]

1. The unnamed slave appears to be Yorrick Cross, an African owned by George W. Cross (1783–1836), the Charleston lawyer who defended Vesey. Cross appears in the trials below as Witness No. 10.

THE TRIALS, &C.

THE COURT organized for the trial of sundry Negroes apprehended and charged "*with attempting to raise an Insurrection amongst the Blacks against the Whites,*" and of such others as might be brought before them on the same charge, met on Wednesday, the 19th June, 1822, and consisted of the following Gentlemen, viz:

LIONEL H. KENNEDY, Q.U. THOMAS PARKER, J.P.	Magistrates
WILLIAM DRAYTON, NATHAN HEYWARD, JAMES R. PRINGLE, JAMES LEGARE, ROBERT J. TUMBULL,[1]	Freeholders

The trial of ROLLA, a negro man, the slave of His Excellency, Governor Bennett—Jacob Axson, Esq.[2] attending as Counsel for his owner.

EVIDENCE.

WITNESS No. 1*—A negro man[3] testified as follows:—I know Rolla, belonging to Mr. Thomas Bennett, we are intimate friends; all that I know of the intended Insurrection I got from him. About three months ago he asked me to join with him in slaying the whites, I asked him to give me time to consider of it; a week after he put the same question to me, and at the end of another week he again came to me on the same subject. I told him "take care, God says we must not kill;" you are a coward he said and laughed at me. He said he would tell me how it was to be done. There are said he, white men who have come from off, and who say that St. Domingo and Africa will assist us to get our liberty if we will only make the motion first. I advised him to let it alone, and told him I would oppose them if they came to kill my owner, when he again laughed at me as a coward—He summoned me to go to their meetings where said he you will hear what is going on and be better informed; I told him yes, I would go—Friday night about three weeks ago he appointed to take me with him to their meeting; at that night he came to me and again summoned me to go to the meeting, I went away from him, I went out of

Figure 8. Colonel William Drayton (1776–1846), judge on the First Court of Magistrates and Freeholders. From a portrait, 1818. Courtesy of White House Collection, White House Historical Association.

his way. The next day he came to me and said the meeting had been expecting me and I must send my name to be put down as one of the Band—This thing has been going on for four months. He told me that at the meeting it was said that *some white men said Congress had set us free, and that our white people here would not let us be so,* and that St. Domingo and Africa would come over and cut up the white people if we only made the motion here first—that last Saturday night (the 15th June,) might be the last he had to live, as they were determined to break open the thing on Sunday night (the 16th June)—I told him it could not be done, it would not succeed, that our parents for generations back had been slaves, and we had better be contented—He desired me to tell—(Witness No. 2) to go up to him, that he wished to see him—No. 2 went in the evening—Rolla told No. 2 in my presence what he was going to do—No. 2 told him to let it alone, he would not succeed, and then turned away and wept—*Rolla replied 'tis now gone too far to stop it*—He told No. 2 to go out of town on Sunday night, as he did not wish him to be hurt—I told No. 2 to sound the alarm, and if he did not I would—I asked Rolla what was to be done with the women and children? he said, *"when we have done with the fellows, we know what to do with the wenches"*—He said *there are a great many involved in it in the country;* that Mungo from James' Island was to come over to Charleston with 4000 men, land on South-Bay, march up and seize the Arsenal by the Guard-House and kill all the City Guard; that another body was to seize upon the Powder Magazine, and another body to take the United States' Arsenal on the Neck, then march to town and destroy the Inhabitants, who could only escape by jumping into the river—*My Army he said will first fix my old buck and then the Intendant*—I asked him if he could bind his master or kill him; he laughed at me again; I then told him I would have nothing to do with him—He said he was going to John's Island to hasten down the country negroes, as he feared they would not come. I felt that it was a bad thing to disclose what a bosom friend had confided to me, and that it was wicked to betray him, and I suffered a great deal before I could bring myself to give information, but when I thought on the other hand that by doing so I would save so many lives *and prevent the horrible acts in contemplation,* 'twas overbalenced, and my duty was to inform—I refused to go to the meetings as Rolla wished, as I feared if I opposed them there, they might make away with me to prevent me from betraying them—I don't know where the meetings were held, but believe 'twas in Bull-street, in which street Denmark Vesey lives—Rolla said that Ned and Mathias[4] were concerned—I am well acquainted with Stephen, Mr. T. R. Smith's man; I believe him to be a worthy, good man, and in a conversation with him on this subject, he agreed with me that this was an abominable plot—I have not seen him for the last four weeks—I know Denmark Vesey—I was one day on horseback going to Market when I met him on foot; he asked me if I was satisfied in my present situation; if I remembered the fable of Hercules and the Waggoner whose waggon was stalled, and he began to pray, and Hercules said, you fool put your shoulders to the wheel, whip up the horses and your waggon will be pulled out; that if we did not put our hand to the work and deliver ourselves, we should never come out of slavery; *that Congress had made us free.* I know that he is intimately acquainted with Rolla—Rolla told me that there had been a sort of disagreement and confusion at their place of meeting, and that they meant to meet at Vesey's—Vesey told me that a large army from St. Domingo and Africa were coming to help us, and we must not stand with our hands in our pockets; he was bitter towards the whites. Sambo who lives on Mrs. La Roache's plantation (on John's Island) sent word down to Rolla that he would be in town on Sunday night last—Rolla said that they would have a countersign to be known to their friends, and in the action, those blacks who could not give it would be killed; that they would fire the town—Rolla's threats are that if any black person is found out giving information or evidence against them, they would be watched for day and night and be certainly killed—Even now the friends of those in prison are trying about the streets to find out who has given information—*If my name was known I would certainly be killed.* I advised Rolla to let it alone, but told him that if they persevered and commenced it, I had no arms, but that as they passed by my house, I would fall in behind with my fishing line and grains which was all that I had. Rolla did not tell to No. 2, all the particulars, but told him of the intended rising and the time.

* This witness came forward voluntarily, and gave information of the intended Insurrection, and of the places and those concerned, as far as his information extended, *previously* to the appointed day, and only asked that his name would not be divulged, which the Court

pledged themselves to conceal as far as it depended on them. His name is therefore suppressed—*He is in no way inculpated.*

WITNESS No. 2.* A negro man testified as follows:—The first I heard was from witness No. 1—he told me that such was the idea of the coloured people; that he was asked to join but that he asked for time to consider; that he was told to tell me to go out of town; that at 12 o'clock on Sunday (the 16th June,) the rising would take place.—I told him I would tell my master and he said he would do the same. On Friday (the 14th of June) witness No. 1, and myself told my master every thing. I went up to Rolla as he requested, and saw him, who complained of his hard living; I found that he was at something wrong and my heart got so full that I wept. Rolla never told me in express words that he was going to join in the rising to kill the whites. Witness No. 1, was present when Rolla and myself were speaking and heard most of what passed; Rolla's last words were "*'tis gone too far now to be stopped.*" Though Rolla said nothing expressly to me about insurrection, yet we seemed to understand each other perfectly, and that such was in contemplation—Rolla told me that on Sunday evening I must go out of town as he did not wish me to be hurt; he said words to the effect that he was going to join in the rising; he said that on Sunday night at 12 o'clock such and such a thing would take place. Witness No. 1, said that Rolla had told him they were to join and take the Powder Magazine and the Arsenal on the Neck, and that an army of 4,000 men from James' Island would land at South-Bay, march up and take the Laboratory in town and kill all the City Guard, and then they would kill the whites &c. Witness No. 1, and Stephen, Mr. T. R. Smith's man are truly good men.

* This witness as regards the concealment of his name, stands precisely in the same situation as No. 1.

THE OWNER OF WITNESS, No. 2.[5] testified as follows—What my servant has just said is substantially what he told me some days ago; he is a servant of the very best character, and, every word he says may be relied on. I never heard a complaint against him from white or black.

WITNESS No. 6,[6] a negro man belonging to his Excellency Governor Bennett, gave the following evidence—Rolla proposed to me to join with the blacks to rise against the whites, 'twas on last Saturday (the 25th of June); he asked me to join him to raise an army against the whites; I refused and went away; he said I was a fool.

WITNESS No. 7,[7] a negro man gave the following evidence—I reside on John's Island. About a month ago Rolla advised me to join the blacks against the whites, I told him it was vain; he told me to come to town on Saturday week last (the 15th of June). He said he would let me know what day to be down and sent me word last Friday week not to come down on the Saturday as the thing had been found out. He said the plan was to take the Guard House and the Magazine and then get arms and ammunition; that a great many were concerned but no name was mentioned to me; I mentioned it to no one on the Island.

The voluntary CONFESSION OF ROLLA* *to the Court,* made after all the evidence had been heard, but before his conviction—I know Denmark Vesey—On one occasion he asked me what news, I told him none; he replied we are free but the white people here won't let us be so, and the only way is to rise up and fight the whites. I went to his house one night to learn where the meetings were held. I never conversed on this subject with Batteau or Ned—Vesey told me he was the leader in this plot. I never conversed either with Peter or Mingo. Vesey induced me to join; when I went to Vesey's house there was a meeting there, the room was full of people, but none of them white. That night at Vesey's we determined to have arms made, and each man put in 12½ cents towards that purpose. Though Vesey's room was full I did not know one individual there. At this meeting Vesey said we were to take the Guard-House and Magazine to get arms; that we ought to rise up and fight against the whites for our liberties; he was the first to rise up and speak, and he *read to us from the Bible, how the Children of Israel were delivered out of Egypt from bondage.* He said that the rising would take place, last Sunday night week, (the 16th June) and that Peter Poyas was one.[8]

* Rolla on his arraignment and throughout his trial, until after the evidence closed denied his guilt, and pretended utter ignorance of the intended insurrection.

ON BEHALF OF ROLLA, five Witnesses[9] were introduced and examined prior to his confession to the Court, with a view to impeach the credibility of witness No. 1, but they rather strengthened it. The owner of that witness, (No. 1,) who was introduced as a witness on behalf of Rolla, amongst other things creditable to that witness, stated, that since he had given information against Rolla, he had been distracted, that being the first day he seemed composed; that he thought and said he had acted like a traitor to his friend.

Rolla when arraigned, affected not to understand the charge against him, and when it was at his request further explained to him, assumed with wonderful adroitness, astonishment and surprise. He was remarkable throughout his trial, for great presence and composure of mind. When he was informed he was convicted and was advised to prepare for death, though he had previously, (but after his trial,) confessed his guilt, he appeared perfectly confounded; but exhibited no signs of fear.[10]

THE COURT *unanimously* found Rolla GUILTY—After sentence of DEATH* had been passed upon him, he made a CONFESSION in prison *to the Rev Dr. Hall,*[11] who furnished the Court with it in writing, and in the following words: "I was invited by Denmark Vesey to his house, where I found Ned Bennett, Peter Poyas, and others, some were strangers to me, *they said they were from the country.* Denmark told us, it was high time we had our liberty, and he could shew us how we might obtain it. He said, we must unite together as the St. Domingo people did, never to betray one another; and to die before we would tell upon one another. He also said, he expected the St. Domingo people would send some troops to help us—The best way, said he, for us to conquer the whites, is to set the town on fire in several places, at the Governor's Mills, and near the Docks, and for every servant in the yards to be ready with axes and knives and clubs, to kill every man, as he came out when the bells began to ring. *He then read in the Bible where God commanded, that all should be cut off, both men, women and children, and said, he believed, it* *was no sin for us to do so, for the Lord had commanded us to do it.* But if I had read these Psalms, Doctor, which I have read, since I have been in this prison, they would never have got me to join them—At another meeting, some of the company were opposed to killing the Ministers, and the women and children, but Denmark said, it was not safe to keep one alive, but to destroy them totally, for you see, said he, the Lord has commanded it—When I heard this, master Hall, my heart pained me within, and I said to myself, I cannot kill my master and mistress, for they use me, more like a son, than a slave—I then concluded in my mind, that I would go into the country, on Saturday evening, before they were to commence on Sunday, that I might not see it—Some of the company asked, if they were to stay in Charleston; he said no, as soon as they could get the money from the Banks, and the goods from the stores, they should hoist sail for Saint Domingo, for he expected some armed vessels would meet them to conduct and protect them.

* The mode of execution ordered in this and the subsequent cases where the convicts were sentenced to death, was the Gallows.[12]

(*Note.*—Every possible care was taken by the Court throughout the trials, to prevent collusion between the witnesses, or either of them knowing what the others had testified to. Those in prison were confined in different rooms, or when, from their being wanted in Court it was necessary to bring them in the room adjoining that in which the Court was sitting, they were put together in one room, a confidential non-commissioned officer of the City Guard was placed in the room with them to prevent their communicating together. They were brought in and examined separately, none of them knowing against whom they were called, until they entered the Court Room; and the evidence given in the one room could not be heard in the next. Those who were not arrested, as they could not know who were to be the witnesses against a particular individual, or what individual was to be tried, could not well collude together.)

1. *CSCCD,* 101, identifies Robert James Turnbull (not "Tumbull") (1775–1833) in 1822 as a "planter" who resided at 1 Logan Street. Hamilton, *Account,* 12–13, states that the court assembled on the "morning of the 19th of June" and, "thus organized," proceeded to the trial of Rolla Bennett. The Senate transcript indicates that Rolla's trial took place on June 20, so the court may have spent the first day discussing process and gathering depositions. On Turnbull, see Raymond J. Krohn, "Antebellum South Carolina Reconsidered: The Libertarian World of Robert J. Turnbull," *Journal of the Historical Society* 9 (2009): 129–54.

2. Jacob Axson Jr. (1794–1843) lived in 1822 at 70 King Street. According to the *OR,* Axson served as attorney for seven accused slaves: Rolla, Batteau, Ned, Monday Gell, Naphur, Adam Yates, and Bellisle Yates. Attorney Robert Bentham, together with James Poyas, served as Peter Poyas's counsel. He also plied his legal skills as brigade judge advocate in the Fourth Brigade of the state militia. See *CSCCD,* 69; H. P. Archer, *Local Reminiscences: A Lecture Delivered by Mr. H. P. Archer before the Mutual Aid Association, No. 1, of Charleston, S.C. in the Hall of the Mechanics Union, at Charleston, S.C. June 6th, 1889* (Charleston, SC, 1893), 12. Attorney William Crafts Jr. (1787–1826) represented Billy Robinson and Denbow Martin. Attorney George W. Cross served as counsel for Vesey; attorney Joseph Clark represented Jacob Stagg. The *OR* reveals that twenty-seven of the accused were attended by their owners, an owner's friend (especially if the owner was a woman), as well as an attorney. Despite this, Michael P. Johnson, "Denmark Vesey and

His Co-Conspirators," *WMQ* 58 (2001): 942, asserts that it "is beyond doubt that the *Official Report* falsifies the record of testimony and court procedures documented in the [later] manuscript transcript." When the *OR* was widely published in October 1822, however, none of the attorneys or masters listed in the pamphlet—all of whom had lost valuable property with no guarantee of compensation—challenged, publicly or privately, the veracity and authenticity of the essentials of the Vesey plot as published in either pamphlet account.

Rolla, Ned, and Batteau were just 3 of the 51 slaves—36 men and 15 women—owned by Governor Bennett, most of whom evidently worked in his mills. See US Census, 1820, series M33, roll 119, p. 149, NA.

3. The Senate transcript identifies Witness No. 1 as Joe La Roche and Witness No. 2 as George Wilson. On their testimony, see James O'Neil Spady, "Power and Confession: On the Credibility of the Earliest Reports of the Denmark Vesey Slave Conspiracy," *WMQ* 68 (2011): 289–304.

4. Both Ned and Mathias were owned by Governor Thomas Bennett Jr.

5. Major John Wilson.

6. The Senate transcript identifies Witness No. 6 as Polydore, the slave of Thomas Bennett Jr.

7. The Senate transcript identifies Witness No. 7 as Sambo, the slave of the widow Mary La Roche (1749–1842), identified in 1819 as a "plantress," residing on Hudson Street in Cannonborough on Charleston Neck. See *CSCCD*, 49.

8. Rolla Bennett's courtroom confession was reprinted verbatim in the Hartford *Connecticut Mirror*, September 16, 1822.

9. The Senate transcript reveals these five men to be Peter, March, Sampson, and Polydore, all owned by Thomas Bennett Jr., and Isaac, the property of Mary La Roche.

10. This paragraph describing Rolla Bennett's courtroom demeanor appears in *OR*, 45–46, and has been moved here.

11. This was most likely the Reverend Daniel Hall, a Methodist minister who was appointed to Charleston in 1821 and 1822. He then was appointed to Wilmington, North Carolina, in 1823, and in 1824, transferred his conference membership to Mississippi after which time he disappeared from church records. See communication to editors, May 19, 2006, R. Philip Stone, archivist, Sandor Trezler Library, Wofford College. See also *Minutes of the Annual Conferences of the Methodist Episcopal Church, for the Years 1773–1828*, 2 vols. (New York, 1840), vol. 1: 369. This confession does not appear in the Senate transcript, which contains only the confession Rolla made to the court.

12. Although tradition holds that Vesey and the other slaves hanged before July 26 died on a "hanging tree" located near what is now Ashley Avenue and Fishburne Street, no contemporaneous source identifies the "gallows" as a tree. On the tradition, see Adam Parker, "Leaders Had Pivotal Role in Civil Rights," *Charleston Post and Courier*, January 17, 2010. The tradition was first challenged by Samuel Gaillard Stoney, "Exploding Myths About Oaks," *Charleston News and Courier*, October 31, 1948, although references to the "hanging tree" reappeared in the local press in 1969 during a hospital workers' strike, when the Reverend Ralph Abernathy promised to visit Charleston to "preach at the 'hanging tree' on Ashley Avenue." See *Charleston News and Courier*, May 12, 1969. Two months later, on July 19, the same newspaper discussed "the Ashley Oak in the center of Ashley Avenue where Denmark Vesey and 33 of his men were reputed to have been hanged in 1822." Thirty-five men, and not thirty-four, were hanged during the summer of 1822, but not all at the same time nor in the same location.

David Robertson, *Denmark Vesey: The Buried History of America's Largest Slave Rebellion and the Man Who Led It* (New York: Knopf, 1999), 103, supports the tree myth and asserts that the "trapdoor gallows of the later nineteenth century was not then in common use." As early as 1571, however, the London gallows at Tyburn featured a horizontal wooden platform supported by three legs, which allowed for the execution of more than one person at a time. See Alan Brooke and David Brandon, *Tyburn: London's Fatal Tree* (Gloucestershire, UK: Sutton, 2004). The city also paid for "erecting a Gallows," and since the twenty-two men who were hanged from the Lines on July 26 were shoved off low benches, this was most likely a reference to the gallows on Blake's Lands. See South Carolina Treasury Records, Journal C, 1814–1824, SCDAH. In 1877, William L. King, *The Newspaper Press of Charleston, S.C.: A Chronological and Biographical History, Embracing a Period of One Hundred and Forty Years* (Charleston, SC, 1872), 61–62, identified the spot as being "on a hill East of the Meeting Street road, about eight hundred yards North of the street, now known as Line Street." This information places the gallows near what is now Nassau and Line streets, well east of Ashley. Thomas Fleming, *A Disease in the Public Mind: A New Understanding of Why We Fought the Civil War* (New York: Da Capo Press, 2013), 96, erroneously reduces the number of those hanged from thirty-five to twenty-five.

THE TRIAL of BATTEAU, a Negro Man, the slave of His Excellency Governor Bennett.—Jacob Axson, Esq. attending as Counsel for the owner.[1]

EVIDENCE.

WITNESS No. 3*—A Negro, about 18 years of age testified as follows:—I know Batteau, he belongs to Mr. Bennett—Sunday before last he met me, stopped me and told me something very grevious—he asked me if I would go as one of the army—I told him I could not, as I was so bound to my father that I could not go out without his leave—nothing more then took place as I immediately left him—I have not seen him since—Cross-Examined—Batteau told me this army was to raise the blacks against the whites—he said the army was to act last Sunday night (the 16th June)—before he commenced speaking to me he took me one side and then spoke low to me—my brother (witness No. 4) and myself afterwards spoke together on this business, and he said that Batteau had likewise spoken to him about it.[2]

* Against this witness there was no charge in relation to the Insurrection—secrecy as to his name was pledged to him.

WITNESS No. 4†—A Negro about 20 years of age gave the following evidence:—I know Batteau, he belongs to Mr. Bennett, he once said to me that he wanted me to agree to join them with as many blacks as I could get to kill the whites—This was last Sunday week in the afternoon after Church—I said I could not attempt such a thing—he tried to pursuade me to join but I refused—he said he could raise armies directly—that he was one at the head—that they would put one force at the Bridge and another in town—that he expected some aid from the country—the last time I saw witness, No. 3, was last Saturday night—Batteau said the rising would be last Sunday night (the 16th June)—Cross-Examined.—On the Sunday afternoon I saw Batteau, 'twas near the Rev. Mr. Bachman's not far from Cannon's Bridge,[3] he was talking with a woman—he called to me and took me one side and began the conversation, speaking low so that no one could hear him—he said if I could raise men enough 'twixt Saturday and Sunday next to meet him to kill the white people—*he said they could get arms enough*—he is called Batteau and Botteau—My brother (witness No. 3) and myself afterwards spoke together on this subject, and he said that Batteau had spoken to him too.

†This witness is in the precise situation, and had the same pledge given him as No. 3.

THE COURT *unanimously* found Batteau GUILTY, and on the 28th June passed upon him the sentence of DEATH.

1. Hamilton, *Account,* 14, 47, confirms that Batteau Bennett, who was arrested on June 18, was the second slave to be tried.

2. The Senate transcript identifies Witness No. 3 as Bram, owned by Jonathan Lucas (1754–1822), and Witness No. 4 as his brother, Richard. The *CDSG,* 53, identifies Jonathan Lucas as "proprietor of the mills [in] cannonboro," which at the time was a suburb of Charleston near Coming's Creek, north of Harleston Village. See Robert N. Rosen, *A Short History of Charleston* (Columbia: University of South Carolina Press, 1997), 86. Jonathan Lucas was an English millwright who is credited with building the first rice-pounding mill in Charleston. See James Jonathan Lucas, "Built the First Rice Mill—the Work of Jonathan Lucas which Made the Rice Industry Practicable," *Louisiana Planter and Sugar Manufacturer* 32, no. 24 (1904): 407–8. According to his grandson, Lucas died in April 1822.

3. The Reverend John Bachman (1790–1874), the antebellum South's most prominent Lutheran minister, lived on the corner of Pinckney and Hudson streets in Charleston Neck. See *CSCCD,* 69.

On the first day of July, the following letter was received from His Excellency Governor Bennett:

Charleston, July 1st. 1822.

L. H. KENNEDY, Esq. Q.U.
THOS. PARKER, J.P. } Presiding Magistrates of the Court of Justices and Freeholders organized for the trial of slaves charged with attempting to raise an insurrection:

GENTLEMEN,

After a very attentive consideration of the evidence yesterday presented, permit me to request that the case of Batteau may be reviewed with a view to the mitigation of his punishment; such a power is vested in the Court by the provisions of the act for the better ordering and governing of slaves.

If guilty of an attempt to raise an insurrection, it does not appear from the evidence to extend beyond an invitation to two boys to join in the project: from no part of the evidence does it appear that he is further implicated.

It is known that one of the boys referred to, was charged with using improper threats, and therefore supposed to be involved in the general plot, for which he was arrested. As he states that he had subsequently a communication with his brother, and they both testify to a simple insolated fact, collusion may be inferred. And even admitting the truth of their evidence, it would not appear that he is equally guilty with the others. If so the benignant provisions of that act would sanction the request made.

I ask this Gentlemen, as an individual incurring a severe and distressing loss.

I am very respectfully,
Your obedient serv't,
THOMAS BENNETT.

The Court agreeable to the request contained in the above letter, reviewed their decision, but after having sent for and again interrogated witness No 3 and 4, came unanimously to the conclusion they had at first done. After his execution it was incidentally proved, in the course of the subsequent trials, that he attended the meetings of the conspirators at Vesey's.

STEPHEN, a negro man belonging to Mr. Thomas R. Smith,[1] was next brought before the Court, but there being no testimony against him, he was immediately discharged.

1. Thomas Rhett Smith (1768–1829) was a big slaveholder with multiple estates, who resided at 1 Meeting Street. See *BDSCHR* 4: 527–28; *CSCCD*, 99. Hamilton, *Account*, 49, places Stephen's arrest on June 18. Stephen was acquitted.

THE TRIAL of PETER, a negro man the property of Mr. James Poyas.[1]—Mr. Poyas with Robert Bentham, Esq.[2] as his counsel attending.

EVIDENCE.

WITNESS No. 5,* a negro man,[3] gave the following evidence:—I know Peter, he belongs to Mr. James Poyas—in May last Peter and myself met in Legare street, at the corner of Lambol-street, when the following conversation took place—he asked me the news—I replied none that I know of—he said by George we can't live so—I replied how will we do—he said we can do very well; if you can find any one to assist us will you join—I asked him how do you mean—he said, why to break the yoke—I replied I don't know—he asked me suppose you were to hear that the whites were going to kill you would you defend yourself—I reply'd I'd try to escape—he asked have you lately seen *Denmark Vesey,* and has he spoken to you particularly—I said no—well then he said that's all now, but call at the shop tomorrow after knocking off work and I will tell you more—we then parted. I met him the next day according to appointment, when he said to me, we intend to see if we can't do something for ourselves, we can't live so—I asked him where he would get men—he said we'll find them fast enough, we have got enough—We expect *men from country and town.* But how said I will you manage it—why we will give them notice said he, and they will march down and camp round the city—but what said I will they do for arms—he answered they will find arms enough, they will bring down their hoes, axes, &c.—I said that won't do to fight with here—he said stop; let us get candidates from town with arms, and we will then take the Guard-House and Arsenal in town, the Arsenal on the Neck and the upper Guard-House, and supply the country people with arms—how said I will you approach these Arsenals &c. for they are guarded—yes said he, I know that, but what are those guards, one man here and one man there, we won't let a man pass before us—Well said I but how will the black people from the country and those from the Islands know when you are to begin; or how will you get the town people together—why said he we will have *prayer meetings at night and there notify them* when to start and as the clock strikes 12 all must move—But said I, the whites in the back country, Virginia, &c. when they hear the news will turn to and kill you all, and besides you may be betrayed—Well said he what of that, if one gets hanged we will rise at that minute—We then left his shop and walked towards Broad-street, when he said *I* *want you to take notice of all the Shops and Stores in town with arms in them, take down the numbers and give them to me*—I said I will see to it and then we parted—About the 1st June I saw in the public papers a statement that the white people were going to build Missionary Houses for the blacks, which I carried and shewed to Peter and said to him, you see the good they are going to do for us—when he said, what of that, have you not heard that on the 4th July the whites are going to create a false alarm of fire, and every black that comes out will be killed in order to thin them[4]—Do you think that they would be so barbarous said I—Yes said he I do; I fear they have knowledge of an army from St. Domingo, and they would be right to do it, to prevent us from joining that army if it should march towards this land—I was then very much alarmed—we then parted and I saw no more of him 'till the Guards were very strict about a fortnight ago—at that time I saw Peter and Ned Bennett standing and talking together at the corner of Lambol and Legare-street—they crossed over and met me by Mrs. Myles, and Ned Bennet said to me, did you hear what those boys were taken up for the other day—I replied No, but some say 'twas for stealing—Ned asked me if I was sure I had never said any thing to the whites about what Peter Poyas had spoken to me about—I replied No—says Peter you never did—No I answered—says Ned to me how do you stand—at which I struck the tree box with my knuckles and said, as firm as this box, I'll never say one word against you—Ned them smiled and nodded his head and said, that will do, when we all separated—last Tuesday or Wednesday week Peter said to me you see my lad how the white people have got to windward of us—you won't said I be able to do any thing—O yes said he we will, by George we are obliged to—he said all down this way ought to meet and have a collection to purchase powder—what said I is the use of powder, the whites can fire three times to our once—he said but 'twill *be such a dead time of night they won't know what is the matter, and our Horse Companies will go about the streets and prevent the whites from assembling*—I asked him where will you get horses—why said he there are many butcher boys with horses, and there are the public Livery Stables, where we have several candidates and the waiting men belonging to the white people of the Horse Companies will be told to take away their master's horses—he asked me if my master was not a horseman—I said yes—has he not got arms in his house—I answered yes—can't they be got at—I said yes—then said he 'tis good to have them—I asked him what was the plan—why said he after we have taken the Arsenal and Guard Houses, then we will set the town on fire in different places, and as the whites come out we will slay them; if we were to set fire to the town first, the man in the steeple would give the alarm too soon—*I am the Captain said he, to take the lower Guard-House and Arsenal*—But, I replied, when you are coming up the centinel will give the alarm—he said he would advance a little distance ahead, and if he could only get a *grip at his throat he was a gone man,* for his sword was very sharp; he had sharpened it and had made it so sharp it had cut his finger, which he shewed me—as to the Arsenal on the Neck he said that is gone as sure as fate, *Ned Bennett would manage that with the people from the country, and the people between Hibben's Ferry and Santee would land and take the upper Guard-House.*—I then said, then this thing seems true—My man, said he, God has a hand in it, we have been meeting for four years and are not yet betrayed—I told him I was afraid after all of the white people from the back country and Virginia, &c.—He said that the blacks would collect so numerous *from the country* we need not fear the whites from other parts, for when we have once got the city we can keep them all out—He asked if I had told my boys—I said no—then said he you should do it, for Ned Bennett has his people pretty well ranged; but said he take care and don't mention it to those waiting men who receive *presents of old coats &c. from their masters or they'll betray us*; I will speak to them. We then parted and I have not since conversed with him—he said the rising was to take place last Sunday night (16th June)—*that any of the coloured people who said a word about this matter would be killed by the others—The little man who can't be killed, shot or taken* is named Jack,[5] a Gullah negro—Peter said there was a French company in town *of* 300 *men fully armed*—that he was to see Monday Gell about expediting the rising. I know that Mingo went often to Mr. Paul's to see Edwin, but don't know if he spoke with William—*Peter said he had a sword* and I ought to get one—he said he had *a letter from the country, I think from St. Thomas,' from a negro man who belonged to the Captain of a Militia Company, who said he could easily get the key of the house where the Company's arms were put after muster, and take them all out* and help in that way. This business originates altogether with the *African Congregation* in which Peter is a leader. When Bennett's Ned asked about those taken up, he alluded particularly to Mr. Paul's William, and asked me if I had said any thing to him about it.

* Against this witness the Court had not a tittle of testimony—he consented without hesitation to become a witness, and to give all the information he possessed, a pledge having been previously given him by the Court that he should not be prosecuted or his name revealed.

THE OWNER OF WITNESS No. 5,[6] testified as follows: My servant bears a good character. His general conduct is good. He was raised up in my family, and I would place my life in his hands.

WILLIAM, a negro man belonging to Mr. Paul, testified as follows:—Mr. Harth's negro man Mingo told me about the insurrection and referred me to Peter Poyas for further information, who he said had a list with 9,000 names upon it, and that he was still taking down names. On the week I was to see Peter I was apprehended. Mingo said that 600 men on the Bay were already down on the list in Peter's possession. I never had any conversation with Peter. Peter, Ned Bennett and Charles Shubrick are *class leaders in the African Church.* The African Association have also a Church in Anson-street and one in Cow-alley, where they have service. Mingo said that Peter would tell me when the rising would take place. He said that letters were passing between Peter Poyas and Ned Bennett and Charles Shubrick, and that all the orders he got, he got from Peter. My fellow servant Edwin brought the first news of the rising into our yard. He has a wife at Mr. Parker's near the lines. One Monday morning when he came from his wife's he told me there would be something shortly 'twixt the blacks and the whites—that he knew the parties and that the thing was going on, and *all the African Church were engaged in it,* and in particular mentioned Peter Poyas and Ned Bennett. Edwin told me generally about the matter—that Peter knew all, and that all who wants to know goes to him.

ROLLA in his confession said, that Denmark Vesey told him Peter was one[7]—(THE

COURT *unanimously* found Peter GUILTY, and passed upon him the sentence of DEATH.)

Not so with Peter, for in his countenance were strongly marked disappointed ambition, revenge, indignation, and an anxiety to know how far the discoveries had extended, and the same emotions were exhibited in his conduct. He did not appear to fear personal consequences, for his whole behaviour indicated the reverse; but exhibited an evident anxiety for the success of their plan, in which his whole soul was embarked. His countenance and behavior were the same when he received his sentence, and his only words were on retiring, "I suppose you'll let me see my wife and family before I die?" and that not in a supplicating tone. When he was asked a day or two after, if it was possible he could wish to see his master and family murdered who had treated him so kindly! he only replied to the question by a smile.[8]

Subsequently to Peter's trial, a good deal of testimony was given against him in the course of the succeeding trials. Amongst others, witness No. 10[9] testified that—Peter Poyas was the first man who spoke to me and asked me to join—I asked him what, the Church—he said no, have you not heard that the blacks were joining to try to take the country—I asked him if he thought he had men enough to do it—he said yes, a plenty of men and the Society will contribute money with which a white man would purchase guns and powder for them—He said he would call back, and I must consider if I would join them—He called back and asked me if I was willing now—why Peter said I you have not got force enough—he said if I did not join he would turn all my country people against me—said I, if so, I'll join you, but you must not put my name down, when you come out if I find you strong enough I'll join you—well said he if you don't join you'll be killed—Peter and Harry Haig called on me afterwards—I was not at home. Peter Poyas told me also that they had force enough, that some would come from James' Island and Johns' Island, and some from Christ Church Parish,[10] where he generally went over to a meeting to have a talk, and that he had some about and about in town, the number of which he would shew me from the Society Books if I would only come to the Society—he said they were to fight the whites and keep on fighting 'till the English came to help them—Harry Haig told me the same thing. (See also Frank Ferguson's testimony against Denmark Vesey, who told him that "himself, Ned, Peter and Monday Gell were the principal men, and himself the head man, &c.")

But confined as four of the convicts were in one room, they "mutually supported each other; and died obedient to the stern and emphatic injunction of their comrade, (Peter Poyas.") "Do not open your lips! Die silent, as you shall see me do."[11]

1. James Poyas (1790–1872) resided in 1822 at 49 King Street and owned a shipyard (at 35 South Bay Street) that built coasting vessels involved in Caribbean trade. See *CSCCD*, 95, and *Charleston Courier*, October 14, 1829.

2. Attorney Robert Bentham (1790–1843) lived at 10 Logan Street. James Poyas's marriage to Charlotte Bentham in 1817 may help explain the choice of Bentham to defend Peter Poyas.

3. The Senate transcript identifies Witness No. 5 as Robert Harth. His testimony against Poyas appeared verbatim in the *Baltimore Patriot & Mercantile Advertiser,* September 2, 1822, and the Hartford *Connecticut Mirror,* September 16, 1822.

4. According to the trial testimony in the case of Harry Butler, which appears only in the Senate transcript, Monday Gell also used the fear that whites would murder their slaves as a recruiting tool.

5. Jack Pritchard.

6. William Harth was a prosperous lumber merchant and active Episcopalian, who in 1822 lived at 1 Gibbes Street. He owned three slaves involved in the proceedings: Mingo, Isaac, and Robert. See *CSCCD,* 82. In 1826, Harth sat on the Charleston Grand Jury that recommended the use of a treadmill instead of whipping and branding for punishing slaves. See "In the Court of General Sessions," Charleston *City Gazette and Commercial Daily Advertiser,* October 13, 1826.

7. This reference to Rolla's confession to the court suggests that on occasion the magistrates simply read earlier statements into the record of later trials. It was published in the Hartford *Connecticut Mirror,* September 16, 1822.

8. This paragraph describing Poyas's courtroom demeanor appears in *OR,* 46, and has been moved here.

9. Witness No. 10 was Yorrick Cross. His testimony against Poyas appears verbatim in the Baltimore *American & Commercial Party Advertiser,* September 2, 1822; *Washington Gazette,* September 4, 1822; and *Baltimore Patriot & Mercantile Advertiser,* September 5, 1822.

10. Christ Church Parish, near Charleston, was surrounded by waterways and penetrated from end to end by the Great Northern Road.

11. This paragraph describing Poyas's Work-House behavior first appears in Hamilton, *Account,* 19, was republished in the *OR,* 46, and has been moved here.

AMHERST, a Negro Man belonging to Mrs. Lining, was next tried.[1] The strongest part of the testimony against him was, his requesting his class leader on Sunday, the 16th June to pray for him, as it might be the last day he had to live. Amherst admitted that he had said so, and that he alluded to the intended insurrection, which he had that day heard of; but denied that he was in any manner engaged in it, and only asked for the prayers of his class leader, as in the confusion, he would be in danger of losing his life whether he was engaged in it or not.

THE COURT *unanimously* found him NOT GUILTY and discharged him.

1. Amherst was the slave of Mary Blake Lining (1758–1836), "the widow of Charles" Lining (1753–1813), a Charleston banker. She lived at 17 Legare Street and had been previously married to Thomas Rose. See *CSCCD,* 87, and Mabel L. Webber, "Marriage and Death Notices from the South Carolina Weekly Gazette," *SCHGM* 19 (1918): 110. Hamilton, *Account,* 49, dated Amherst's arrest to June 18. No reference to this trial appeared in the Senate transcript, which again suggests that the printing of the *OR* predated the final handwritten version of the trials presented to the Senate.

THE TRIAL OF NED, a Negro Man the Slave of His Excellency, Governor Bennett—Jacob Axson, Esq. attending as Counsel for his owner.

EVIDENCE.

WITNESS No. 5,[1] testified as follows:—About the 7th June I saw Peter and Ned Bennett standing and talking together at the corner of Lambol and Legare-street—they crossed over and met me by Mrs. Myles, and Ned Bennett said to me, did you hear what those boys were taken up for the other day—I replied No, but some say 'twas for stealing—Ned asked me if I was sure I had never said any thing to the whites about what Peter Poyas had spoken to me about—I replied No—says Peter you never did—No I answered—says Ned to me how do you stand—at which I struck the tree box with my knuckles and said, as firm as this box, I'll never say one word against you—Ned then smiled and nodded his head and said, that will do, when we all separated. Peter told me that Ned Bennett with the people *from the country* would attack and take the Arsenal on the Neck. He asked me if I had told my boys—I said no—then said he you should do it; for Ned Bennett has his people pretty well ranged. When Ned Bennett asked about those taken up, he alluded particularly to Mr. Pauls' William, and asked me if I had said any thing to him about it.

WILLIAM, Mr. Paul's Slave testified as follows:—Mingo Harth told me that Ned Bennett knew all about it, and told it all to Mr. Bennett's people, and that letters were passing between Peter Poyas, Ned Bennett, and Charles Shubrick, and that Ned Bennett and Charles Shubrick, are officers. My fellow servant Edwin told me he knew the parties and that the thing was going on well—that all the African Congregation were engaged in it and Peter Poyas and Ned Bennett.

WITNESS No. 1,[2] testified, that Rolla said, Ned and Mathias were concerned.

FRANK a Negro Man, the slave of Mrs. Ferguson,[3] gave the following evidence:—Vesey told me that Ned Bennet and Peter Poyas were concerned with him, and that they were to go about and tell the blacks that they were free and must rise and fight for themselves. He said that himself, Ned Bennet, Peter Poyas and Monday Gell, were the principal men, and himself the head man—that they were the principal men to go about and inform the people, and fix them I have seen Ned Bennett at Vesey's—I met Ned Bennett, Monday Gell and others at Vesey's, where they were talking about this business.

THE COURT *unanimously* found Ned GUILTY, and passed upon him the sentence of DEATH.

In Ned's behaviour there was nothing remarkable; but his countenance was stern and immoveable, even whilst he was receiving the sentence of death: from his looks it was impossible to discover or conjecture what were his feelings.[4]

JESSE in his confession to the Rev. Dr. Hall said, "at another meeting at Denmark Vesey's, Ned Bennett and Peter Poyas["] and several others were "present, and in conversation" about this business, &c.

1. Robert Harth.

2. Joe La Roche.

3. Frank was the slave of Ann Wragg Ferguson (1756–1835), the widow of Thomas Ferguson (1726–1786), a wealthy and much older planter. She lived in 1822 at 5 Liberty Street. See *CSCCD,* 79. According to Hamilton, *Account,* 48, Frank was arrested on June 27. Although a major recruiter in the countryside—where Ferguson also owned a plantation—Frank was never put on trial and evidently gave testimony in exchange for transportation out of the state.

4. This paragraph describing Ned Bennett's courtroom demeanor appears in the *OR*, 46, and has been moved here.

THE TRIAL of JESSE,[1] a Negro Man, the Slave of Mr. Thomas Blackwood.[2]—His owner attending.

EVIDENCE.

SALLY, a Negro Woman, the Slave of Mr. Alexander Howard,[3] gave the following evidence:—I know Jesse and heard him speak several times about it—One day in particular he was anxious to see his brother who has my mother for his wife, and waited until he came, when they conversed together—Jesse said he had got a horse *to go into the country to bring down men* to fight the white people; that he was allowed to pass by two parties of the patrole on the road, but that a third party had brought him back and that if there were but five men like him they would destroy the city—this was on last Sunday week, (the 16th June)—he said that before 3 o'clock on that night all the white people would be killed—that if any person informed or would not join in the fight, such person would be killed or poisoned—he frequently came into the yard to see his brother, and I threatened to inform if he came there, and spoke in that way to get us all into trouble—We never had any quarrel.

LOT, a Negro Man, the Slave of Mr. Forrester,[4] testified as follows:—I know Jesse—he met me last Sunday week (16th June) at the corner of Boundary-street, as I was coming into town—he said he was going to get a horse *to go into the country*—From what my master had told me the Thursday before I distrusted his errand and gave him something of a caution when as I was going down into town towards Mr. Hibben's Ferry Slip,[5] and conversing with him, he said *you shall see to night when I come down what I am going up for, and if my own father does not assist I will cut off his head*—He said he was going *as far as Goose Creek Bridge,* and would get him a horse if it cost him nine dollars—the church bells were then ringing, and at half past 10 o'clock the same day I saw him at Mr. Howard's, and afterwards *understood from Sally that he had set off for the country and had been brought down by the Patrole.*[6]

SYKE, a Negro Man, the Slave of Mr. Waring, gave the following testimony:—Jesse asked me on Sunday week last, (16th June) before breakfast, where he could get a horse to go a little way *into the country with*—I told him I did not know—he then went away and did not return before 9 o'clock that night—he had a wife at Mr. Waring's.[7]

FRANK, Mrs. Ferguson's slave, testified as follows: On the 15th of June, Vesey gave to Jesse $2 to hire a horse *to go into the country to my Mistress' plantation in St. John's, to inform the people to be down* on the night of the 16th. Myself and Adam put in 25 cents each for it. Vesey told Jesse, if he could not go, he must send some one else.

The voluntary CONFESSION OF JESSE *to the Court,* made after all the evidence had been heard, but before his conviction.

I have had several conversations with Denmark Vesey, the first about four weeks ago (about 1st June) he asked me if I had heard about the rising, &c. and did I know that the coloured people were going to try to get their liberty—I then could stop no longer and he asked me to call and see him—I afterwards met him on Wednesday previous to the Sunday (16th of June) that the rising was to take place—we walked up St. Phillip-street and were joined by Frank Ferguson opposite Liberty-street, and we all three walked up to Vesey's house. Says Frank I am just from the country—well says Vesey and what success—says Frank I have got two fine men for our purpose on my Mistress' plantation, who must be sent up to and informed when the people are wanted in town—Vesey asked me if I would be the man to go—I said yes, but I don't know the way—says Vesey, Frank will tell you—Frank then told me how to go to Mrs. Ferguson's plantation, and that I must ask for John O and Pompey and gave me other directions—Vesey then gave me $2 to hire a horse and Frank and Adam threw down on the table 25 cents each, I dont know what for—this was about 1 o'clock P.M. on Saturday before last (15th June)—I promised to go that night. On Sunday I met Lot who betrayed me; the same day I told Vesey I had started but that the patrol turned me back; in fact I had not started and only told him so to deceive him—the same day I met Charles Drayton at Vesey's who said the business was postponed—Vesey asked Charles how he knew the business was postponed—Charles said Ned Bennett and Monday Gell told him so. But said Vesey, how could they know it was postponed as they have not seen me—Says Charles they said they had seen you and that you had told them so. Now, said I to Vesey, you see there, suppose I had gone into the country and brought those people down to night, we should all have been destroyed. As far as I know, I believe *Denmark Vesey and Monday Gell were the chief men.*

THE COURT *unanimously* found Jesse GUILTY, and passed upon him the sentence of DEATH.

Subsequently to his conviction, he made the following CONFESSION in prison *to the Rev. Dr. Hall*[8]—I was invited to Denmark Vesey's house, and when I went, I found several men met together, among whom was Ned Bennett, Peter Poyas, and others, whom I did not know. Denmark opened the meeting by saying, he had an important secret to communicate to us, which we must not disclose to any one, and if we did, we should be put to instant death. He said, we were deprived of our rights and privileges by the white people, and that our Church was shut up, so that we could not use it, and that it was high time for us to seek for our rights, and that we were fully able to conquer the whites, if we were only unanimous and courageous, as the St. Domingo people were—He then proceeded to explain his plan, by saying, that they intended to make the attack by setting the Governor's Mills on fire, and also some houses near the water, and as soon as the bells began to ring for fire, that they should kill every man as he came out of his door, and that the servants in the yard should do it, and that it should be done with axes and clubs, and afterwards they should murder the women and children, for he said, God had so commanded it in the scriptures—At another meeting at Denmark's, Ned Bennett and Peter Poyas, and several others were present, in conversation, some said they thought it was cruel to kill the ministers, and the women and children, but Denmark Vesey said, *he thought it was for our safety not to spare one white skin alive, for this was the plan they pursued in St. Domingo*—He then said to me, Jesse, I want you to go into the country to enlist as many of the country negroes as possible, to be in readiness to come down to assist us—I told him I had no horse and no money to hire one; he then took out two dollars, and gave them to me to hire a horse, and told me to enlist as many as possible. I got the horse the next Sabbath, and started, but the guard was so strict, I could not pass them without being taken up; so I returned, and told Denmark, at which he expressed his sorrow, and said, the business was urgent, for they wanted the country people to be armed, that they might attack the Forts, at the same time, and also to take every ship and vessel in the harbour, and to put every man to death, except the Captains. For said he, it will not be safe to stay in Charleston, for as soon, as they had got all the money out of the Banks, and the goods out of the stores on board, they intended to sail for Saint Domingo, for he had a promise that they would receive and protect them. This Jesse asserted to me, was the truth, whilst the tears were running down his cheeks, and he appeared truly penitent, and I have reason to hope, that he obtained pardon from God, through the merits of Christ, and was prepared to meet his fate with confidence and that he was accepted of God—At 4 o'clock, on the morning of the execution, I visited all the prisoners condemned, and found Jesse at prayers—he told me, his mind was placid and calm; he then assured me, that what he had told me was the truth, and that he was prepared to meet his God.[9]

1. Hamilton, *Account,* 43, states that Jesse Blackwood was arrested on Sunday, June 23, and that his sentence was read on Friday, June 28. Since Lot Forrester, who provided testimony, was not arrested until June 27, Jesse's trial and sentencing probably fell on the same day.

2. Thomas Blackwood (d. 1837), president of the Planter's and Mechanics' Bank, owned Jesse. In 1822 he resided at 18 Pitt Street. See *CSCCD,* 107.

3. *CSCCD,* 83, identifies Howard as a tax assessor, who lived at 236 Meeting Street. He had also operated a factorage business on Gadsden's Wharf. See *Charleston Courier,* September 15, 1809.

4. On Alexander J. G. Forrester, Lot's owner, a minor, see Part II, p. 91 n12.

5. Hibben's ferryboats ran out of Prioleau's wharf. See *CDSG,* 40.

6. The examinations of Sally and Lot in the case of Jesse Blackwood were reprinted verbatim in the *Washington Gazette,* September 3, 1822, and the Hartford *Connecticut Mirror,* September 23, 1822.

7. In 1822, Morton A. Waring (d. 1863), Charleston's federal marshal, had an office at 40 East Bay Street and a residence at 36 Meeting Street. See *CSCCD,* 102.

8. Michael P. Johnson, "Denmark Vesey and His Co-Conspirators," *WMQ* 58 (2001): 934, asserts that the *OR* "lies about the trials of Denmark Vesey and the five slaves sentenced to death at the conclusion of the June proceedings." One of the five was Jesse Blackwood, whose confession in the Work-House to Methodist minister Daniel Hall sustained the one previously made in court. Both were reprinted in the *OR,* and so if the report "lies," it enjoyed the active collusion of the Reverend Hall and many of the most prominent ministers in Charleston who also visited the accused slaves in the Work-House.

9. Jesse's second confession appeared verbatim in the Hartford *Connecticut Mirror,* September 23, 1822.

THE TRIAL of SAMUEL GUIFFORD,[1] a free Negroe, and ROBERT HADDEN,[2] a free Mulattoe; both of them boys.[3]

EVIDENCE.

JOHN WOODWORTH,[4] a white boy, testified as follows:—I am 14 years old. About a week ago, (subsequent to the 16th June) I heard Robert Hadden say to Samuel Guifford, he was going to join to set fire to the Town, take the Magazine, and kill every White Man who did not give up the country. I do not think he meant me to hear him. Robert Herron,[5] Jefferson Campbell, and Henry, were also present.

ROBERT HERRON, a white boy deposed as follows:—I am 12 years old. I heard Robert Haddon say, that on the night they raised they would kill the Governor, fire the Magazine, and kill every damn white man who would not give up the country to the Blacks—He spoke moderately loud, and did not seem to care who heard him. Samuel Guifford afterwards repeated to me what Hadden had said.

THE COURT were satisfied that the expressions charged had been used by the prisoners, but from their youth and other circumstances, they considered them as rather the effect of puerile boasting, than as evidencing a conspiracy on their part. The prisoners were therefore *unanimously found* NOT GUILTY, *but ordered* to be retained in custody *charged with a minor offence.* They were afterwards whipped in the Work House and discharged.

1. Samuel Guifford was a free person of color. Like Robert Hadden, his surname does not appear in either the city directories or the capitation records. One possibility is that both Hadden and Guifford were free colored mariners, the kind of transients who would be targeted after the Vesey proceedings by the Negro Seamen Act (1822).

2. Robert Hadden was a free person of color. No one with that surname shows up in either the Charleston city directories for the 1820s or in the relevant Charleston capitation tax records for free blacks.

3. Hamilton, *Account,* 15, places these two trials on Monday, June 24. Since Jesse Blackwood's trial did not take place until June 28, these trials clearly appeared out of order.

4. John Woodworth may have been a son of mariner George Woodworth, who resided in 1822 at 23 Boundary Street. See *CSCCD,* 104.

5. *CSCCD,* 83, lists two individuals with the surname "Herron" in 1822: the tailor Charles Herron and the widow of John Herron, both of whom resided at 40 Pinckney Street.

MATHIAS, the Slave of Governor Bennett; MUNGO the Slave of Mr. James Poyas; RICHARD and JOHN, the Slaves of Mr. I. Lucas; and SANDY, belonging to Mr. Holmes, were discharged by the Court as not Guilty. JIM, belonging to Mr. Ancrum; and FRIDAY, the property of Mr. Rout, were found NOT GUILTY, and discharged—Against them there was little or no testimony.[1]

1. Hamilton, *Account,* 15, places the trials of Mathias, Mungo, Richard, and John, as well as Harth's Robert—who is not listed in the *OR*—as Monday, June 24. The trials of Sandy, Jim, and Friday took place on Tuesday, June 25.

THE TRIAL of ABRAHAM, a Negro Man, the Slave of Dr. Poyas—His owner attending.[1]

EVIDENCE.

The following LETTER, found in the trunk of Peter Poyas, was acknowledged by Abram, to have been written by himself—

"*Dear Sir*—With pleasure I give you an answer. I will endeavour to do it. Hoping that God will be in the midst to help his own. Be particular and make a sure remark. Fear not, the Lord God that delivered Daniel is able to deliver us. All that I inform agreed. I am gone up to Beach-Hill."

(Signed) ABRAHAM POYAS.

Abraham for several days denied that the following words in that letter, viz:—"*fear not*"—"*All that I inform agreed*"—were written by him, saying, that they must have been added by some one—This, however, was evidently false, as he himself in a day or two afterwards admitted, but not before Peter Poyas had stated to the Court that every word in the letter was there when he received it. On Peter's being asked to explain the meaning of the letter, he said, it alluded to the Negroes in Abraham's neighbourhood, who had all agreed that Abraham should be permitted to change his Church and join theirs—Abraham, however, gave a different meaning to it, and said, it related to his having two wives. Dr. Poyas, however, stated to the Court, that Abraham had subsequently given to him the same explanation of the letter that Peter had done. Although this letter taken in connection with his conduct was extremely suspicious, yet there being no other testimony against Abraham, he was found NOT GUILTY.

1. Hamilton, *Account*, 15, places this trial on Wednesday, June 26.

THE TRIAL of DENMARK VESEY, a free black man[1]—Col. G. W. Cross attending as his Counsel.[2]

WILLIAM , the Slave of Mr. Paul, testified as follows:—Mingo Harth told me *that Denmark Vesey was the chiefest man, and more concerned than any one else*—Denmark Vesey is an old man in whose yard my master's negro woman Sarah cooks—he was her father in law,[3] having married her mother Beck, and though they have been parted some time, yet he visited her at her house near the Intendant's (Major Hamilton) where I have often heard him speak of the rising—*He said he would not like to have a white man in his presence—that he had a great hatred for the whites,* and that if all were like him they would resist the whites—he studies all he can to put it into the heads of the blacks to have a rising against the whites, and tried to induce me to join—he tries to induce all his acquaintances—this has been his chief study and delight for a considerable time—my last conversation with him was in April—he studies the Bible a great deal and tries to prove from it that slavery and bondage is against the Bible. I am persuaded that Denmark Vesey was chiefly concerned in business.

WITNESS No. 1,[4] gave the following testimony:—I know Denmark Vesey—I was one day on horseback going to Market, when I met him on foot—he asked me if I was satisfied in my present situation—if I remembered the fable of Hercules and the Waggoner whose waggon was stalled, and he began to pray, and Hercules said, you fool put your shoulders to the wheel, whip up the horses, and your waggon will be pulled out—that if we did not put our hand to the work and deliver ourselves we shall never come out of slavery—*that Congress had made us free*—I know that he is intimately acquainted with Rolla—Rolla told me that there had been a sort of disagreement and confusion at their place of meeting, and that they meant to meet at Vesey's—Ves[e]y told me that a large army from St. Domingo and Africa were coming to help us, and we must not stand with our hands in our pockets—he was bitter towards the whites.

See the CONFESSION of ROLLA in page 66, 67, 68.[5]

FRANK, Mrs. Ferguson's slave gave the following evidence—I know Denmark Vesey and have been to his house—I have heard him say that the negroe's situation was so bad he did not know how they could endure it, and was astonished they did not rise and fend for themselves, and he advised me to join and rise—he said he was going about to see different people, and mentioned the names of Ned Bennett and Peter Poyas as concerned with him—that he had spoken to Ned and Peter on this subject; and that they were to go about and tell the blacks that they were free, and must rise and *fight for themselves*—that they would take the Magazines and Guard-Houses, and the city and be free—that he was going to send *into the country* to inform the people there too—he said he wanted me to join them—I said I could not answer—he said if I would not go into the country for him he could get others—he said himself, Ned Bennet, Peter Poyas and Monday Gell were the principal men and himself the head man. He said they were the principal men to go about and inform the poople and fix them, &c. that *one party would land on South-Bay, one about Wappoo, and about the farms*—that the party which was to land on South-Bay was to take the Guard-House and get arms and then they would be able to go on—that the attack was to commence about 12 o'clock at night—*that great numbers would come from all about,* and it must succeed as so many were engaged in it—that they would kill all the whites—that they would leave their master's houses, and assemble together near the lines, march down and meet the party which would land on South-Bay—that he was going to *send a man into the country* on a horse *to bring down the country people* and that he would pay for the horse. He gave $2 to Jesse to get the horse on Saturday week last, (15th June) about 1 o'clock in the day, and myself and No. 8, also put in 25 cents a piece, and he told Jesse, if he could not go he must send some one else. I have seen Ned Bennett at Vesey's—I one night met at Vesey's a great number of men, and as they came in each handed him some money. Vesey said there was a *little man named Jack,* who could not be killed, and who would furnish them with arms, he had a charm and he would lead them—that Charles Drayton had promised to be engaged with them—Vesey said the Negroes were living such an abominable life, they ought to rise. I said I was living well—he said though I was, others were not and that 'twas such fools as I, that were in the way and would not help them, and that after all things were well he would mark me. He said he did not go with *Creighton to Africa,*[6] *because he had not a will, he wanted to stay and see what he could do* for his fellow-creatures—I met Ned, Monday and others at Denmark Vesey's where they were talking about the business. The first time I spoke with Monday Gell 'twas one night at Denmark Vesey's house, where I heard Vesey tell Monday that he must *send some one into the country to bring the people down*—Monday said *he had sent up Jack* and told him *to tell the people to come down and join in the fight* against the whites and also to ascertain and inform him how many people he could get. A few days after I met Vesey, Monday and Jack, in the streets, under Mr. Duncan's trees at night, where *Jack stated that he had been into the country round by Goose-Creek and Dorchester,* and that he had spoken to 6,600 persons who had agreed to join. Monday said to Vesey, that if Jack had so many men they had better wait no longer but begin the business at once, and others would join. The first time I saw Monday at Vesey's, he was going away early, when Vesey asked him to stay, to which Monday replied, he expected that night a meeting at his house to fix upon and mature the plan, &c. and that he could stay no longer—I afterwards conversed with Monday in his shop, where he asked me if I had heard that Bennett's and Poyas' people were taken up, that 'twas a great pity—he said he had joined in the business—I told him to take care he was not taken up. Whenever I talked with Vesey, he always spoke of Monday Gell as being his principal and active man in the business.[7]

ADAM a Negro Man belonging to Mr. Ferguson testified as follows:—Denmark Vesey one day asked me to walk to his house, and there asked me for 25 cents to hire a horse to send up into the country—I put down the money on the table and asked what he was going to send into the country for—he said 'twould be for my benefit—as he would tell me no more I took up the money and put it back into my pocket again—I afterwards met the man who was to go into the country, who told me he had set off, but had been brought back by the patrole; *that he was going up to bring down the black people to take this country from the whites*—I have been at Vesey's house and there it was I met the man who was to go into the country, he was a yellowish man—the witness pointing at Jesse said, that is the man who was to go into the country.

See the CONFESSION OF JESSE to the Court in p. 30.[8]

Benjamin Ford,[9] a white lad, about 15 or 16 years of age, deposed as follows:—Denmark Vesey frequently came into our shop which is near his house, and always complained of the hardships of the blacks—he said the laws were very rigid and strict and that the blacks had not their rights—that every one had his time, and that his would come round too—*his general conversation was about religion which he would apply to slavery,* as for instance, he would speak of the creation of the world, in which he would say all men had equal rights, blacks as well as whites, &c. *all his religious remarks were mingled with slavery.*

THE COURT *unanimously* found Denmark Vesey GUILTY, and passed upon him the sentence of DEATH. After his conviction, a good deal of testimony was given against him during the succeeding trials.—Amongst others

WITNESS No. 9, a negro man testified as follows:—Denmark Vesey has frequently spoken to me about the intended insurrection, and endeavoured to persuade me to join them—He enquired of me *if my master had not arms in his house, and tried to persuade me to get them for him.* The blacks stand in great fear of him, and I so much so, that I always endeavoured to avoid him.[10]

EDWIN, a negro man belonging to Mr. Paul, gave the following evidence:—Charles Drayton told me that Denmark Vesey and Monday Gell knew about the insurrection of the blacks, and that my fellow servant *William, in consequence of what he had said, would run great risque of his life if he went out*—I have heard every body, even the women say, when several were apprehended at first, that they wondered Denmark Vesey and Monday Gell were not taken up.

SEE CONFESSION of JESSE to the Rev. Dr. Hall, in page 81.[11]

When Vesey was tried, he folded his arms and seemed to pay great attention to the testimony given against him, but with his eyes fixed on the floor. In this situation he remained immoveable, until the witness had been examined by the Court and cross-examined by his counsel; when he requested to be allowed to examine the witnesses himself. He at first questioned them in the dictatorial, despotic manner, in which he was probably accustomed to address them; but this was not producing the desired effect, he questioned them with affected surprise and concern for bearing false testimony against him; still failing in his purpose, he then examined them strictly as to dates, but could not make them contradict themselves. The evidence being closed, he addressed the Court at considerable length, in which his principal endeavour was to impress them with the idea, that as his situation in life had been such that he could have had no inducement to join in such an attempt, that charge against him must be false; and he attributed it to the great hatred which he alleged the blacks had against him; but his allegations were unsupported by proof. When he received his sentence, the tears trickled down his cheeks.[12]

The three following Sentences were pronounced by LIONEL H. KENNEDY, Esquire, the presiding Magistrate of the first Court, organized for the trial of Slaves and other persons of colour, charged with attempting to raise an Insurrection in this State.—Several other sentences were delivered, but were not reduced into writing:[13]

Sentence on Denmark Vesey, a Free Black Man.

DENMARK VESEY—The Court, on mature consideration, have pronounced you GUILTY—You have enjoyed the advantage of able Counsel, and were also heard in your own defence, in which you endeavored, with great art and plausibility, to impress a belief of your innocence. After the most patient deliberation, however, the Court were not only satisfied of your guilt, but that you were the author, and original instigator of this diabolical plot. Your professed design was to trample on all laws, human and divine; to riot in blood, outrage, rapine and conflagration, and to introduce anarchy and confusion in their most horrid forms. Your life has become, therefore, a just and necessary sacrifice, at the shrine of indignant Justice. It is difficult to imagine what *infatuation* could have prompted you to attempt an enterprize so wild and visionary. You were a free man; were comparatively wealthy; and enjoyed every comfort, compatible with your situation. You had, therefore, much to risk, and little to gain. From your age and experience, you *ought* to have known, that success was impracticable.

A moments reflection must have convinced you, that the ruin of *your race,* would have been the probable result, and that years' would have rolled away, before they could have recovered that confidence, which, they once enjoyed in this community. The only reparation in your power, is a full disclosure of the truth. In addition to treason, you have committed the grossest impiety, in attempting to pervert the sacred words of God into a sanction for crimes of the blackest hue. It is evident, that you are totally insensible of the divine influence of that Gospel, "all whose paths are peace." It was to reconcile us to our destinies on earth, and to enable us to discharge with fidelity, all the duties of life, that those holy precepts were imparted by Heaven to fallen man. If you had searched them with sincerity, you would have discovered instructions, immediately applicable to the deluded victims of your artful wiles—"*Servants' (says Saint Paul) obey in all things your masters,' according to the flesh, not with eye-service, as men-pleasers, but in singleness of heart, fearing God.*" And again "*Servants' (says Saint Peter) be subject to your masters' with all fear, not only to the good and gentle, but also to the forward.*"

On such texts comment is unnecessary.

Your "lamp of life" is nearly extinguished; your race is run; and you must shortly pass "from time to eternity." Let me then conjure you to devote the remnant of your existence in solemn preparation for the awful doom, that awaits you. Your situation is deplorable, but not destitute of spiritual consolation. To that Almighty Being alone, whose Holy Ordinances, you have trampled in the dust, can you now look for mercy, and although "your sins be as scarlet," the tears of sincere penitence may obtain forgiveness at the "Throne of Grace." You cannot have forgotten the history of the malefactor on the Cross, who, like yourself, was the wretched and deluded victim of offended justice. His conscience was awakened in the pangs of dissolution, and yet there is reason to believe, that his spirit was received into the realms of bliss. May *you* imitate his example, and may *your* last moments prove like his! [14]

1. Hamilton, *Account,* 16, places the trial on Thursday, June 27.

2. Michael P. Johnson, "Denmark Vesey and His Co-Conspirators," *WMQ* 58 (2001): 971, suggests that it is possible that Vesey never actually stood trial, since that event, as well as "the presence in court" of "G. W. Cross attending as his counsel" was mentioned only in the *OR* and not clearly indicated in the later, far messier second-generation Senate transcript. Johnson's former colleague Jon Wiener agrees in "Denmark Vesey: A New Verdict," *The Nation,* February 21, 2002, 933: "There is nothing suggesting" that Vesey ever stood trial. Both the August *Account of the Late Intended Insurrection,* 17, and the October *OR,* however, confirm that he did, and certainly George Warren Cross, a highly regarded attorney whose practice specialized in defending members of Charleston's French-speaking elite, would know whether he had been present at a trial or whether he had been Vesey's attorney. If in fact there were no trial, would Cross have allowed his name to be used fraudulently in public by Hamilton in his *Account* and by Kennedy and Parker in their *Official Report*?

Wiener also errs in writing that "Virtually all historians before Johnson have relied on the *Official Report* of the trial." Most scholars who have written about Vesey, Charleston, and the subsequent Nullification Crisis have used *both* the trial transcripts and the *OR.*

3. William Paul was clearly confused on this point. When Vesey married Beck, he became step-father, and not father-in-law, to Sarah. Michael P. Johnson, "Denmark Vesey and His

Co-Conspirators," *WMQ* 58 (2001): 933, argues that Paul could not have given this testimony at Vesey's trial, since Vesey was arrested on June 22, and the Senate transcript indicates that Paul's initial deposition was given on June 19. The Senate version, at 883 words, is far longer than the 194 words given in Vesey's trial and so suggests only that Paul here repeated portions of his earlier statement on June 27.

4. Witness No. 1 was Joe La Roche. His numerical designation, and that of the other witnesses identified in this manner, did not change from trial to trial.

5. In this volume, Rolla Bennett's confession appears on pp. 165–66. It is unclear whether Rolla Bennett appeared in court during Vesey's trial. It is possible the magistrates simply read this confession into the record as evidence, since Justice William Johnson criticized the court on the grounds that defendants were not always able to confront their accusers. See his correspondence and pamphlet elsewhere in this volume on pp. 137–44, 587–88.

6. James (also "John") Creighton was an African-born freedman, Episcopalian, and prosperous barber. In 1819, he lived at 83 Anson Street and ran his shop at 197 East Bay Street. He sailed for Sierra Leone aboard the *Calypso* on October 3, 1821. See Charleston *City Gazette and Commercial Daily Advertiser,* October 3, 1821; *CSCCD,* 37; and "Missionary Zeal in a Negro," *Friendly Visitor* 15 (December 1833): 184–85. The State Free Negro Capitation Tax Book, Charleston, South Carolina, 1821, SCDAH, has the word "banished" in his entry.

7. This examination was reprinted verbatim in the *Washington Gazette,* September 3, 1822, and the Hartford *Connecticut Mirror,* September 23, 1822.

8. In this volume, Jesse Blackwood's confession appears on pp. 177–78.

9. Possibly the same Benjamin Ford who opened a boot-and-shoe business in Charleston in the 1840s. See *Charleston Courier,* September 12, 1844.

10. This testimony appears as undated evidence in the Senate transcript, which also indicates that Witness No. 9 was Bryan's Pompey. Since Pompey was arrested only on June 28, the day of Vesey's sentencing, this statement was, as Kennedy and Parker note above, material obtained later that the court regarded as corroborating evidence and inserted into their pamphlet to prove the correctness of their actions.

11. In this volume, Jesse Blackwood's confession to Reverend Hall appears on pp. 178–79.

12. This description appears in the "Narrative" section of the *OR,* 45, and has been moved here.

13. This judgment appears in the summary of the *OR,* 177–78, and has here been moved forward, since Hamilton, *Account,* 17, claims the "sentence of death" was read on Friday, June 28. The other two printed sentences mentioned are those of Jack Pritchard's and that read to nine of the defendants hanged on July 26.

14. On Vesey's demeanor during sentencing, see also the information that free black carpenter Thomas Cilavan Brown passed to Lydia Maria Child, who in turn passed the information along to abolitionist Thomas Wentworth Higginson in a letter of March 17, 1860. That letter, as well as excerpts from Higginson's *Black Rebellion,* appears in Part VI, pp. 749–53, 758–60. As a lay minister, Brown may well have been allowed into the Work-House courtroom, since the Poor-House regulations, reprinted in this volume on pp. 99–100, allowed for the visits of ministers and wives of the accused. On the character of Brown, his "intelligence, probity, and Christian forbearance" attested to by elite whites from South Carolina, see *Examination of Mr. Thomas C. Brown: A Free-Colored Citizen of S. Carolina, as to the Actual State of Things in Liberia in the Years 1833 and 1834* (New York, 1834), 4–8. Brown, a class leader in the Methodist Church, after leaving Charleston and emigrating to Liberia, returned to the United States, residing in Philadelphia in the early 1830s when Morris Brown was also living and preaching there. Like Vesey, a skilled carpenter, Brown had managed to accumulate property in Charleston worth several thousand dollars.

THE TRIAL of MONDAY, a Negro Man, the Slave of Mr. John Gell. Col. Wm. Rouse[1] as his friend, and Jacob Axon, Esq. Counsel for his owner attending.[2]

EVIDENCE.

Frank, belonging to Mrs. Ferguson, testified as follows:—The first time I spoke with Monday Gell, was one night at Vesey's house, where I heard Vesey tell Monday *he must send some one into the country to bring the people down*—Monday said *he had sent up* Jack, aud told him to bring the people down, and tell them to come down and join in the fight against the whites, and to ascertain and inform him how many people he could get. A few days after I met Vesey, Monday and Jack in the street, under Mr Duncan's trees at night, where Jack stated that he had been in the *country, round by Goose-Creek and Dorchester,* and that he had spoken to 6,600 persons who had agreed to join—At Vesey's the first time I saw Monday, he was going away, Vesey asked him to stay, when Monday said he expected that night a meeting at his house to fix upon and mature the plan, &c. and he could not stay. I afterwards conversed with Monday in his shop, where he asked me if I had heard that Bennett's and Poyas' people were taken up, that 'twas a great pity—he said that he had joined in the business—I told him to take care he was not taken up. Whenever I talked with Vesey he always spoke of Monday Gell as being his principal and active man in this business. I heard Gullah Jack say, he would pay no more wages, he was too busy in seeing about this insurrection; besides what would the white people want with wages they would soon be no more—Monday Gell said to Vesey, that if Jack had so many men they had better wait no longer, but begin the business at once and others would join.

See EDWIN's testimony, page 89.[3]

WITNESS No. 10,[4] a Negro Man gave the evidence following:—I saw Charles Drayton before the 16th at Monday Gell's—I was going to Market and Charles called to me—as I was crossing the street Joe who has a wife at Mr. Remoussin's, asked me if I did not know that Monday was at the head of the Ebo Company who are going to fight the white people—Monday is an Ebo—I asked Joe if he was one of that Company—he said yes he was—I asked him what he could do as he was an invalid—he said he would take Remoussin's sword and gun and tell him to lay down in his bed and be quiet—We parted.—Previous to the 16th of June, Monday Gell called me into his shop—I went in and said to him, I heard he was Captain of his countrymen's company the Ebo's—he said he was a sort of a one—I bid him good morning, when he said when you want to hear the news come here—I never saw him afterwards.—Monday and Charles were very often together.

See the *latter part* of JESSE'S CONFESSION, p. 81.[5]

WITNESS No. 5,[6] testified as follows:—Peter Poyas told me about the 10th of June, that he was to see Monday Gell about expediting the rising.

Monday's behavior was not peculiar. When he was before the Court his arms were folded; he heard the testimony given against him and received his sentence with the utmost firmness and composure.[7]

THE COURT *unanimously* found Monday GUILTY, and passed upon him the sentence of DEATH; after which he made the following Confession:—

Confession of Monday Gell.—I come out as a man who knows he is about to die—some time after Christmas Vesey passed my door, he called in and said to me, that he was trying to gather the blacks to try and see if any thing could be done to overcome the whites; he asked me to join; I asked him his plan and his numbers; he said he had Peter Poyas, Ned Bennett, and Jack Purcell; he asked me to join; I said no; he left me and I saw him not for sometime—About four or five weeks ago as I went up Wentworth-street, Frank Ferguson met me, and said he had four plantation's of people who he was to go for on Saturday, 15th June. How, said I, will you bring them down; he said through the woods; he asked me if I was going towards Vesey's to ask Vesey to be at home that evening, and he would be there to tell me his success. I asked Jack Purcell to carry this message, he said he would; that same evening at my house I met Vesey's mulatto boy,[8] he told me Vesey wished to see me, I went with him; when I went into Vesey's I met Ned Bennett, Peter Poyas and Frank Ferguson, and Adam, and Gullah Jack; they were consulting about the plan; Frank told Vesey on Saturday 15th, he would go and bring down the people and lodge them near town in the woods; the plan was to arm themselves by breaking open the stores with arms. I then told Vesey I would join them, after sometime I told them I had some business of my own and asked them to excuse me, I went away, and only then was I ever there. One evening, Perault Strohecker, and Bacchus Hammet brought to my shop a keg, and asked me to let it stay there till they sent for it; I said yes, but did not know the contents; the next evening Gullah Jack came and took away the keg; this was before the 16th June; since I have been in prison I learnt that the keg contained powder.

Pharo Thompson is concerned, and he told me a day or two after Ned and Peter were taken up, if he could get a fifty dollar bill, he would run away; about two Sunday's before I was brought here, he asked me, in Archdale-street, when shall we be like those white people in the Church; I said when it pleased God; Sunday before I was taken up, he met me as I came out of Archdale Church,[9] and took me into a stable in said street, and told me he told his master, who had asked him, that he had nothing to do in this affair; which was a lie. William Colcock came to my shop once and said a brother told him that five hundred men were making up for the same purpose. Frank said he was to send to Hell-Hole Swamp[10] to get men.

Perault Strohecker is engaged; he used to go of a Sunday on horse back up the road to a man he knows on the same errand. One Sunday he asked me to go with him; I went and Smart Anderson; we went to a small house a little way from the road after you turn into the ship yard road, on its left hand; they two went into the stable with an old man that lived there, I remained in the yard; they remained in the stable about half an hour; as soon as they came out, I and Peirault started to town to go to Church, and left Smart there; I was told by Denbow Martin, who has a wife in Mr. Smith's house, that Stephen Smith belonged to some of the gangs.

Saby Gailliard is concerned, he met me on the Bay, before the 16th June and gave me a piece of paper from his pocket; this paper was about the battle that Boyer had in St.

Domingo; in a day or two he called on me and asked if I had read it, and said if he had as many men he would do the same too, as he could whip ten white men himself; he frequently came to me to speak about this matter, and at last I had to insult him out of the shop; he and Paris Ball was often together. A week before I was taken up, Paris told me that my name was called.

Billy Palmer and Vesey were constantly together; there was once in my shop a long talk between them about this same matter; I begged them to stop it; Vesey told him to try to get as many as he could; he said he would.

John Vincent told me that Edward Johnson, a free man, has said, as he was a free man he would have nothing to do with slaves, but the night they began he would join them.

I told Charles Drayton what uproar there was about this business, and since we have been here we have talked together.

Albert Inglis came to me and asked if I knew any thing about it; I said yes. He asked me if I had joined; I said yes; he said he was one also: he said Adam, a free man wanted to see me, I went with him one night; Adam asked me how many men had joined; I told him what Frank Ferguson had said; he asked me if I believed it; I said yes; he said if he could only find men behind him he would go before. Previous to the 16th, Albert said to me quit the business; I told him I was too far into it, so I must stick to it.

I never wrote to St. Domingo or any where else on this subject, nor kept a list or books, nor saw any such things, but heard that Paul's William had a list, nor did I hear any thing about arms being in possession of the blacks. I don't know that Tom Russell made pikes, nor that Gullah Jack had any of them.

Lewis Remoussin called at my shop and asked me to call at his house, he had something to tell me, but I did not go; Jack Glen told me he was engaged.

I met Scipio Sims one Sunday, coming from the country, who said he had been near the Savannah's to Mr. Middleton's place; I heard afterwards that his errand was on this business.

I know John the cooper, who said he was engaged too in this business.

William Garner said he was engaged in it and had got twelve or thirteen draymen to join.

Sandy Vesey told me he belonged to it too.

At Vesey's house, Frank told Gullah Jack, to put one ball and three buck shot in each cartridge.

Mingo Harth acknowledged to me that he had joined, and Peter Poyas told me so too; he, Mingo, told me so several times; Mingo said he was to have his master's horse on the night of the 16th.

Lot Forrester told me frequently that he was one of the company, and I know that he had joined in the business myself. Isaac Harth told me once that he had joined, he knew I was in the business.

Morris Brown knew nothing of it, and we agreed not to let him, Harry Drayton, or Charles Corr, know any thing about it.———told me in my store that he was to get some powder from his master and give it to Peter Poyas; he seemed to have been a long time engaged in it, and to know a great deal—Joe Jore acknowledged to me once or twice that he had joined, he said he knew some of the Frenchmen concerned; he knew I was in it.[11]

1. The Colonel Rouse in attendance was probably William Rouse Sr. (1756–1829), an English immigrant who ran a tannery, although his son, Colonel William Rouse Jr. (1782?–1824), is also a possibility. Colonel Rouse commanded a cavalry squadron in the Fourth Brigade of the state militia. Both resided at 83 Market Street. Although *BDSCHR* 4: 492, dates "William, Jr. (1802–1824)," the *Charleston Courier,* July 22, 1824, contains the obituary of "Col. William Rouse, Jun. aged 42 years." The elder Rouse, a Revolutionary War officer, served as mayor of Charleston from 1808 to 1810 and held a number of state and local offices. A prominent Charleston Baptist, Rouse was close to the Reverend Richard Furman. See *BDSCHR* 4: 491–93; H. A. Tupper, ed., *Two Centuries of the First Baptist Church of South Carolina, 1683–1883* (Baltimore, 1889), 285, 308–9; H. P. Archer, *Local Reminiscences: A Lecture Delivered by Mr. H. P. Archer before the Mutual Aid Association, No. 1, of Charleston, S.C. in the Hall of the Mechanics Union, at Charleston, S.C. June 6th, 1889* (Charleston, SC, 1893), 12; and *CSCCD,* 87.

2. Hamilton, *Account,* 19, places Gell's trial on Monday, July 1.

3. Edwin's testimony appears on pp. 183–84.

4. Yorrick Cross.

5. This portion of Jesse's confession appears on p. 178.

6. Robert Harth.

7. This description of Monday Gell's courtroom demeanor appears in the *OR,* 46; on 56, the magistrates stated that Gell's sentence was read on July 9.

8. The "mulatto boy" presumably was Sandy Vesey, most likely Vesey's eldest son and one of the two old enough to be involved in the plot. If so, this reference suggests that Beck, Sandy's likely mother, was mixed-race.

9. The Archdale Church could refer to either the St. John's Lutheran Church, under the pastoral care of the Reverend John Bachman, or the Unitarian Church, also called the Second Independent Church, under the pastoral care of the Reverend Samuel Gilman.

10. Hell Hole Swamp today forms part of the Francis Marion National Forest. Some forty-five miles from Charleston, the marsh lay close to the estates of such planters as Elias Horry and Richard Withers Vanderhorst in St. James Santee Parish, on the south side of the Santee River, and thus close as well to thousands of slaves.

11. Gell's undated confession was reprinted verbatim in the *Washington Gazette,* September 5, 1822; *Baltimore Patriot & Commercial Advertiser,* September 6, 1822; and Hartford *Connecticut Mirror,* September 23, 1822. In newspaper accounts, Yorrick Cross's name appeared as two blank lines, as it did in the OR; the Senate transcript indicates this was Cross. Second Confession of Monday Gell

Subsequently to this confession, Monday was examined as a witness in a number of cases, during which, he stated many things he had not mentioned in his confession. The Court conceiving it all important to obtain from Monday, all the information he possessed, (believing him to possess more information on this subject than any man then alive) offered to recommend him to the Governor for a conditional pardon, or commutation of his punishment to banishment, if he would reveal all he knew in relation to this plot. He promised to do so, and made this SECOND CONFESSION:

The first time I heard of the intended insurrection, was about last Christmas, from Denmark Vesey, who called at my shop, and informed me of it. Vesey said he was satisfied with his own condition, being free, but as all his children were slaves, he wished to see what could be done for them. He asked me to join, but I then positively refused to do so—I inquired of him, how many he had enlisted, and he mentioned the names of Peter Poyas, Ned Bennett, Rolla Bennett, and Jack Purcell. I inquired if those were all and he replied "yes." He then departed, and had no further correspondence with me until about three months ago—I was then walking in Wentworth-street on my way to a man named Peet Smith, up King-street, and was accosted by Frank Ferguson, who told me, he had just returned from the country, and had *collected four plantations of Negroes.* He requested me to inform Vesey, that he would call on him that evening, and give him an account of his *operations in the country.*—I went to Jack Purcell and requested him to carry the message for me, being busy—On my return home, in the evening, I met Vesey's Son-in-law, at my door,[1] who said, that Vesey wished to see me—I accompanied him to Vesey's, and there found Peter Poyas, Ned Bennett, Gullah Jack, Frank and his fellow servant, Adam Ferguson. Frank then informed Vesey, he had collected four plantations of negroes, and said he would start on Saturday the 15th of June, to bring them to town, on the 16th. He said, he would conduct them into the woods, and place them, about three miles from town, until Sunday night. Vesey then again urged me to join, and I consented. This was about three months prior to the 16th of June. Vesey, from that time continued to visit the shop, in which I worked. Peter, Ned, Vesey, Frank, Rolla, Adam, Gullah Jack, Jack Purcell and myself were the party at Vesey's, and there agreed to enlist as many men as we could. Vesey *even ceased working himself at his trade, and employed himself exclusively in enlisting men,* and continued to do so until he was apprehended. Shortly afterwards Vesey said he would endeavour to open a correspondence with Port-au-Prince, in St. Domingo, to ascertain whether the inhabitants there would assist us. He said he would send letters there and I advised him to do so, if he could. Some time after this he brought a letter to me, which was directed to President Boyer, and was enclosed in a cover, which directed to the uncle of the cook of the vessel by which it was sent. The name of this cook was William—His uncle was to open the envelope, and present the letter to Boyer—this vessel, a schooner, had been repaired at the ship-yard, at Gadsden's Wharf, and was afterwards brought to Vanderhorst's wharf, where she was then lying—I walked with Vesey to the wharf—Pierault[2] was in company with us, at the time—Vesey asked William the cook, if he would carry the letter for him, and he consented to do so—We then returned, each of us to his respective home—nothing extraordinary took place after this, and I met no other band or association after this time, but Vesey's particular company—*Bacchus Hammett brought a keg of Powder to my shop, and said he would procure five hundred* (500) *muskets from his master's store on the night of the 16th June*—Bacchus also told me, that he could procure *more Powder,* but did not say where—the plan was to break open all the Stores where Arms were deposited, and seize them, after they had procured the five hundred muskets above mentioned—Vesey said he would appoint his leaders, and places of meeting, about one week before the 16th of June, but the meeting for this purpose was prevented by the capture of some of the principals before that period—Vesey determined to kill both women and children, but I opposed him and offended him in doing so—Peter and the rest agreed to the opinion of Vesey in the murder of all—some time before any discoveries or apprehensions were made, myself and Pierault wished to drop the business, but thought we had gone too far to retreat—I know personally of no arms, except six pikes, shewn to me by Gullah Jack, which were made by Tom Russell—I knew of no lists except the one which I kept, containing about forty names, and which, I destroyed after the first interruption and alarm—It was said that William Paul had a list, but I never saw it—William Garner told me that he was to command the Draymen, and that he had procured twelve or thirteen horses—Jack Purcell told me that *Scipio Sims had been at the Savannah's, in the neighbourhood of Bacon's Bridge, to obtain men*—Denbo Martin belonged to the party, and informed me that Stephen Smith acknowledged that he was one.

Charles Drayton and Perault have both seen Denbo at my shop—*Vesey originally proposed the second Sunday, or the 14th of July, as the day for rising,* but afterwards changed it to the 16th of June. After the plot was discovered, Vesey said, it was all over unless an attempt was made to *rescue those who might be condemned,* by rushing on the people, and saving the prisoners, or all dying together. Vesey said, that as Peter and Ned were accustomed to go into the country they must go there and recruit men. Vesey was in the habit of going to Bulkley's farm[3]—*William Palmer and Vesey were very intimate*—Jack Purcell knew of this conspiracy before myself—I do not recollect any person who refused when I applied to him. Some took time to consider, but they all finally agreed. Vesey was considered by the whole party, as a man of great capacity, and was also thought to possess a bloody disposition—He had, I am told, in the course of his life, several wives,[4] and had traveled through almost every part of the world, with his former master Captain Vesey, and spoke French with fluency[5]—Morris Brown, Harry Drayton, and Charles Corr, and other influential leaders of the African Church, were never consulted on this subject, for fear they would betray us to the whites—Vesey had many years ago a pamphlet on the slave trade—Vesey said that his eldest step-son was engaged in this affair.[6]

1. This was presumably the husband of Charlotte, Vesey's daughter with Dolly, his second wife; his daughter with Susan, named Diana, was only four years old in 1822. See Part I, pp. 11–12 n1.

2. This was Perault Strohecker.

3. Lax oversight probably made Bulkley's farm a good place for slaves to rendezvous unnoticed. Stephen Bulkley (1763–1841), an affluent merchant and banker who served as one of the officers in the Charleston branch of the Bank of the United States, spent much of his time in the city at his King Street residence. In his absence, Bulkley's farm became a common meeting place for bondmen who lived on the northern edge of Charleston. Located less than three miles north of the Lines and near Meeting Street Road, the farm's position near a fork in Town Creek also allowed slaves to approach by water. See W. A. Clark, *The History of the Banking Institutions Organized in South Carolina Prior to 1860* (Columbia: Historical Commission of South Carolina, 1922), 46–47, 69; *CSCCD,* 72; Charleston *City Gazette and Commercial Daily Advertiser,* March 13, 1823.

4. The Senate transcript reads "several" for the number of Vesey's wives. The extant record reveals three, Beck and then Dolly and then later the much younger Susan. Although it is unclear as to exactly when Vesey's relationships with Beck or Dolly ended, no contemporary source suggested that these relationships were polygamous, and the rough ages of his children indicate that the marriages did not overlap.

5. Given Vesey's ability to speak French and the considerable number of refugees in Charleston

from Saint-Domingue/Haiti, it is certainly possible, as Michael P. Johnson and James L. Roark argue in *Black Masters: A Free Family of Color in the Old South* (New York: Norton, 1984), 38, that Vesey "knew the ringing proclamations of the natural rights of freedom and equality found in the Declaration of Independence and the Declaration of the Rights of Man." But no source documents that theory. William Lloyd Garrison's *Liberator,* August 25, 1837, recalled a story (see Part VI, p. 726) of "a pious" slave, incarcerated during the Vesey affair, speaking the liberationist language of the American Revolution to the Reverend Benjamin Morgan Palmer, who knew and visited with jailed slaves inculpated in the Vesey plot.

6. Presumably this stepson was the husband of Beck's daughter Sarah, who was Vesey's stepdaughter.

The Court had, previously to this confession, twice applied for and obtained from the Governor a respite for Monday, Charles Drayton and Harry Haig, with a view to obtain from them the testimony and information they appeared willing to give. On the 24th day of July, after Monday had made his last confession, they addressed the following letter to the Governor.

Charleston, 24th *July,* 1822

SIR,

"We recommend that Monday Gell, Charles Drayton, and Harry Haig should be pardoned upon condition that they be sent out of the limits of the United States. We feel it our duty to state to your Excellency the reasons which have influenced us in this measure. These men are unquestionably guilty of the offences with which they have been charged; but under the impression that they would ultimately have their lives spared, they have made to us disclosures not only important in the detection of the general plan of the conspiracy, but enabling the Court to convict a number of the principal offenders. Having used these individuals as witnesses and obtained from them the knowledge they could communicate, we deemed it un[ne]cessarily harsh and amounting almost to treachery, afterwards to sacrifice their lives. In addition to this inducement, we regard it to be politic that the Negroes should know that even their principal advisers and ringleaders cannot be confided in, and that under the temptation of exemption from capital punishment they will betray the common cause."

On the next day they received an answer, in which the Governor declines pardoning conditionally, Monday, Charles and Harry, and says, "the cases of Monday Gell, Charles Drayton and Harry Haig, would produce me considerable embarrassment, were you not clothed with authority to carry your recommendation into full effect. . . ."[1]

1. By this date, Bennett had seen three of his slaves hanged and clearly had no wish to risk his political career by granting pardons to bondmen as deeply involved in the conspiracy as had been Rolla, Ned, and Batteau.

THE TRIAL of CHARLES, a Negro Man, belonging to the Honorable John Drayton—His owner attending.[1]

EVIDENCE.

EDWIN, Mr. Paul's Slave—For his testimony see page 89.[2]

PATRICK, a Negro Man belonging to Miss Datty, testified as follows:—I know Charles Drayton, who asked me in the streets about five months ago if I would join with him—I asked him what—He said we want to make up a company—I asked for what—he said for some respectable brown man coming here from abroad—I said I did not want death to take me yet.[3]

WITNESS No. 10,[4] gave the following testimony:—I met Charles Drayton before the 16th June at Monday Gell's shop; I was going to Market and Charles called to me. I afterwards met him on the 1st July in the streets, when he said now get ready, we must break out at once, for we will not let six lives be taken—I asked him where they would begin—He said at Boundary-street directly as the Patrole and Light-Horse turned in—I said had you not better wait 'till after the 4th July—he said no, because in the mean time the people will be hanged—Charles said they had force enough and we parted—I met him in Market, 'twixt 8 and 9 o'clock on 2d July and said to him, now the people are hanged I suppose you are sorry you joined in the business—He said yes and we parted. Monday and Charles were very great together. On Monday, 1st July, Charles Drayton told me that there would be an Insurrection on the *morning of the 6st July as soon as the Guard turned in—he said he commanded the country born company.* Charles Drayton said he had prepared for himself a gun and a sword.

GEORGE, a Negro Man belonging to Mr. Vanderhorst, testified as follows:—Gullah Jack is an enemy of the white people—Charles Drayton told me that he would die with Gullah Jack, this was about the time of the execution—I was in the company of Witness No. 10, who asked me to join, and carried me to Jack's house, where they met, and which is next to Monday Gell's—he said he was ready to join, and asked me to join—There I met Gullah Jack, Witness No. 10, John Horry, Harry Haig, Julius Forrest, and Charles Drayton, and others whose names I don't recollect or know—this was after the 16th June—there 'twas said they would come against the white people.[5]

JESSE'S CONFESSION* see latter part of it, p. 81.[6]

[*] The Court considered Jesse's confession good evidence, because it was voluntarily made under the conviction of approaching death, and because the court did not think the principle of the common law relative to the testimony of a convicted prisoner to be applicable to an individual in the situation of this witness. Moreover, the confession of Jesse and Rolla to the Court were made before conviction.[7]

THE COURT *unanimously* found Charles GUILTY, and passed upon him the sentence of DEATH.[8]

Subsequently to his conviction he made the following CONFESSION:—I have seen Pierault Stroheker talking with Monday Gell in his shop—Jack Purcell said to me just before I was taken up, that he had gone into the country to gather the people's mind on this subject, but the overseer was so watchful that he had no chance of speaking to the people.

I heard William Palmer say in Monday Gell's shop, that he was one. I met Pharo Thompson at Monday Gell's—he said what he would do when they commenced—that he had no sword, but that he had a part of a saw which he would have ground into a sword—that he was one—he bragged of what he would do with his sword. Mingo Harth came once to Monday Gell's when I was there, and he then spoke to the effect that he was one of them, but I can't recollect his words—his brother also told me that Mingo had joined. Lewis the mattrass maker said to me one day that he had something particular to say to me, of what was going to happen here, but that as he was a country born they did not choose him—I took his meaning.

Lewis Rewoussin[9] told me one day, that when it broke out he would be one, and in the mean time he would be leagued in it—this was before the 16th of June.

Sandy Vesey said he knew as much about this business as any one, and was engaged in it—this was after Jesse was taken up.

Miss Datty's cook, a Frenchman,[10] said to me, as I was a country born, I should not know any thing of what was going on till the horn blew and it broke out.

I heard Tom Russel say in Monday Gell's shop that he was to make the pikes—Monday at the same time was working, and may or may not have heard him.

The same reasons which induced the Court to alter Monday's sentence to transportation, induced them to alter Charles' to the same.

1. Hamilton, *Account,* 19, 45, dates Charles Drayton's arrest to Tuesday, July 2, and indicates that his trial followed soon after the July 1 trial of Monday Gell, probably on Wednesday, July 3.

2. Edwin Paul's deposition appears in this volume on pp. 183–84.

3. Patrick spoke French and was most likely Haitian. He lived with his owner, Julia Datty (1762–1836), a refugee from Saint-Domingue, who resided in 1822 at 94 Wentworth. See *CSCCD,* 76. Indeed, Datty's School in what is today the Hannah Heyward House specialized in training the young ladies of Charleston in the French language. See *Charleston Courier,* December 11, 1812, and Jonathan H. Poston, *The Buildings of Charleston: A Guide to the City's Architecture* (Columbia: University of South Carolina Press, 1997), 249. Datty became an intimate of the Catholic Bishop John England after his arrival in Charleston in 1820. She became mother superior of Charleston's Sisters of Charity of Our Lady of Mercy, an order established in December 1829. See "Bishop England's Institute of the Sisters of Mercy," *American Ecclesiastical Review* 20 (1899): 262; Jane H. Pease and William H. Pease, *Ladies, Women, & Wenches: Choice & Constraint in Antebellum Charleston & Boston* (Chapel Hill: University of North Carolina Press, 1990), 81, 121.

4. Yorrick Cross.

5. A far longer version of this examination appears in the Senate transcript. See p. 285 n2, for a discussion of how this deposition was merged with two others given by George Vanderhorst.

6. Identified in the *OR* with an asterisk, This portion of Jesse Blackwood's confession appears in this volume on pp. 177–78.

7. This paragraph appears as a footnote to Jesse Blackwood's confession.

8. In the "Narrative" section of the *OR,* 56, Kennedy and Parker state that Charles Drayton's sentence was not read until July 9, when they also passed sentence on Jack Pritchard and Monday Gell.

9. Louis Remoussin.

10. "Miss Datty's cook" was Patrick Datty, who was most likely Haitian rather than French, since Julia Datty, discussed above in note 3, most likely arrived in Charleston from Saint-Domingue between 1791 and 1795.

103

would slaughter them and what and what he would do. I have met John Horry with others at the meetings at Gullah Jack's.

THE COURT *unanimously* found John GUILTY, and passed upon him the sentence of DEATH.

THE TRIAL of GULLAH JACK a Negro Man, belonging to Mr. Pritchard—His owner attending.

EVIDENCE.

WITNESS No. 10, testified as follows:—Jack Pritchard also called on me about this business—he is sometimes called Gullah Jack. sometimes Cooter Jack; he gave me some dry food, consisting of parched corn and ground nuts, and said eat that and nothing else on the morning it breaks out, and when you join us as we pass put into your mouth this crab-claw and you can't then be wounded, and said he, I give the same to the rest of my troops—if you drop the large crab-claw out of your mouth, then put in the small one—said I, when do you break out and have you got arms—he said a plenty, but they are over Boundary-street, we can't get at them now, but as soon as the patrol was slack they could get them—this was previous to the 16th June, on which day he said they were to break out—On that day he came to me and said they would not break out that night as the patrol was too strong—he said he would let me know when they were ready—that Sunday fortnight, the 30th June, he came to me and said I must lay by still, they would not break out then, that he had been round to all his company and found them cowards. I said thank God then—he said give me back my corn and cullah (that is crab-claw) I said I would not and upbraided him for having deluded so many. He said all his country born promised to join because he was a doctor (that is a conjurer)—He said the white people were looking for him and he was afraid of being taken; that two men came to his

Figure 9. Page from Kennedy and Parker, *Official Report of the Trials of Sundry Negroes* (1822), that covers up the gruesome testimony related to John Horry's intended slaughter of whites.

THE TRIAL of JOHN, a Negro Man, the property of Elias Horry.—His owner attending.[1]

EVIDENCE.

WITNESS No. 10,[2] testified as follows:—John, Mr. Elias Horry's coachman, came to me one day and asked me what I thought; every one is ready said John to fight the whites are you ready? He said "I am ready"—this took place sometime before the 16th of June, and every day he asked me the same questions. He came to me very often, and once said he had a sword, and that as soon as it broke out he would go up stairs and kill his master and family—On the 17th of June, on his carriage box he expressed himself to me in the same manner that he had done previous to the 16th.

GEORGE, Mr. Vanderhorst's negro man slave gave the following evidence:—John Horry and myself have conversed on this subject—he said he would be ready with these men whenever they were ready, and spoke much against the whites, saying that he would slaughter them and what and what he would do.[3] I have met John Horry with others at the meetings at Gullah Jack's.

THE COURT *unanimously* found John GUILTY, and passed upon him the sentence of DEATH.

1. John Horry was owned by Elias Horry (1773–1834), mayor of Charleston in 1815–16, and again in 1820. He lived in 1822 on Meeting Street. See *CSCCD,* 83. Hamilton, *Account,* 43, dates John Horry's arrest to Friday, July 5. Since Hamilton dated the following trial, that of Jack Pritchard, to July 9, Horry's trial most likely took place on July 6 or 8, as the court stood adjourned on Sunday, July 7.

2. Yorrick Cross.

3. The curious reference "and what and what" John Horry intended to do appears not to have been a simple printer's error but a conscious masking by the court of the slave coachman's actual and gruesome courtroom testimony in front of his master Elias Horry on how John intended to dispose of Elias. Savannah resident Martha Proctor Richardson had access to events in Charleston through Charles Harris (1772–1827), a lawyer, family friend, and former mayor of Savannah. James Hamilton Jr. wrote Harris several letters on the Vesey affair. In a letter of July 6, 1822, to Doctor John Proctor Screven, Martha Richardson actually quoted Hamilton's words on the plot from one of his letters to Harris. In a letter of August 7, 1822, she spoke of John Horry's intention "to kill you [Elias Horry], rip open your belly & throw your guts in your face." Officials would not have wanted such language to reach the ears of Charleston's white women, who had already become unnerved by events. See Richardson's unusually detailed letter in Part IV, pp. 438–39, of this volume.

THE TRIAL of GULLAH JACK a Negro Man, belonging to Mr. Pritchard—His owner attending.[1]

EVIDENCE.

WITNESS No. 10,[2] testified as follows:—Jack Pritchard also called on me about this business—he is sometimes called Gullah Jack. sometimes Cooter Jack; he gave me some dry food, consisting of parched corn and ground nuts, and said eat that and nothing else on the morning it breaks out, and when you join us as we pass put into your mouth this crab-claw and you can't then be wounded, and said he, I give the same to the rest of my troops—if you drop the large crab-claw out of your mouth, then put in the small one—said I, when do you break out and have you got arms—he said a plenty, but they are over Boundary-street, we can't get at them now, but as soon as the patrol was slack they could get them—this was previous to the 16th June, on which day he said they were to break out—On that day he came to me and said they would not break out that night as the patrol was too strong—he said he would let me know when they were ready—that Sunday fortnight, the 30th June, he came to me and said I must lay by still, they would not break out then, that he had been round to all his company and found them cowards. I said thank God then—he said give me back my corn and cullah (that is crab-claw). I said I would not and upbraided him for having deluded so many. He said all his country born promised to join because he was a doctor (that is a conjurer)—He said the white people were looking for him and he was afraid of being taken; that two men came to his master's wharf and asked him if he knew Gullah Jack, and that he told them no—*he said his charms would not protect him from the treachery of his own colour.*—He went away and I have not seen him since. On the 16th June, Jack requested me to let twelve men sleep at my wife's, as they were to break out that night and he wanted them to be near Boundary-street, near to which in King-street my wife lives—on being refused he departed in anger and reproached me. Geo. Vanderhorst called on me yesterday morning and asked if I knew that Charles Drayton was taken up, and said he was afraid Charles would name him, not because he was on his list, for he had joined Jack's Company, but because Charles had met him at Gullah Jack's when they were consulting on the subject—that if he could hear that Charles had named him he would run off—on Monday, 1st July, Charles Drayton told me that there would be an Insurrection on the *morning of the 6th July, as soon as the Guards turned in—he said he commanded the country born company*—Jack told me on the 1st July the same thing, and in addition that they were to rush with their dirks, guns and swords, &c. they had got, kill the City Guard, and take all the arms in the Arsenal—he also said there were some arms in King-street beyond Boundary-street, in the possession of a white man which they intended to take—(alluding to the arms of the Charleston Neck Company, deposited at Mr. Wharton's in King-street.)[3]

The blacks would have risen on the night of the 16th June, had the Guards not been so strong—this I know from Gullah Jack and Harry Haig, who said, that if the Guards were not too strong they would get the arms near the Lines, but if the Guards were out, they could not get them to break out with—("Jack is a little man, a Gullah Negro, with small hands and feet and large whiskers, and belongs to Mr. Pritchard," was the discription given of him by this witness, and by which Jack was apprehended.)

GULLAH JACK when apprehended denied to the Court that he ever wore whiskers, although the map of a large pair of them was plainly discernable on his face, and continued to deny it stoutly until confronted with his owner—he also positively denied that he ever pretended to be a Doctor or Conjurer.

Mr. PAUL PRITCHARD deposed as follows:—My Slave Jack always wore a very large pair of whiskers which he prized very much, and which nothing could induce him to cut off, and which I often threatened to shave off as a punishment when he misbehaved—These whiskers I found he had cut off to my great surprise about three days ago, and wondered at the cause of it, little dreaming that it was to prevent his being apprehended by a description of him—I did hear some years ago that Jack was a Doctor or Conjurer—he is called Gullah Jack and Cooter Jack.

GEORGE, Mr. Vanderhorst's slave,[4] gave the testimony following:—Gullah Jack is an enemy of the white people. I attended a meeting of several at his house, and he was the head man there—all present agreed to join & come against the whites—Jack was my leader—he is the head of the Gullah Company—I heard that amongt them they had charms—Jack said if any man betrayed them, they would injure him, and I was afraid to inform—the little man standing before me is Gullah Jack, who had large black whiskers, which he has cut since I saw him last—If I am accepted as a witness and my life spared, I must beg the Court to send me away from this place, *as I consider my life in great danger from having given testimony.* I have heard it said all about the streets, generally, I can't name any one in particular, that whoever is the white man's friend, God help them; from which I understood they would be killed—I was afraid of Gullah Jack as a conjurer.*

* When this witness was about to the [be] examined in the presence of Gullah Jack, it was not without considerable difficulty that the Court satisfied him that he need no longer fear Jacks *conjurations,* (as he called them.) It was in the course of this witness' evidence that Jack laid aside the character of the fool he was counterfeiting, and shewed his real character.

WILLIAM, Mr. Paul's Slave, gave the following evidence:—Mingo Harth told me that he knows the little man who can't be shot, who told him that there was a Gullah Society going on which met once a month.

WITNESS, No. 5,[5] testified that "the little man who can't be killed, shot or taken, is" named Jack, a Gullah Negro.

FRANK, Mrs. Ferguson's Slave testified as follows: The first time I spoke with Monday Gell 'twas one night at Denmark Vesey's house, where I heard Vesey tell Monday that he must *send one into the country to bring the people down*—Monday said *he had sent up Jack* and told him *to tell the people to come down and join in the fight* against the whites, and also to ascertain and inform him how many people he could get—A few days after I met Vesey, Monday and Jack in the street, under Mr. Duncan's trees, at night, where *Jack stated he had been into the country round by Goose Creek and Dorchester,* and that he had spoken to 6,600 persons who had agreed to join.

THE COURT *unanimously* found Gullah Jack GUILTY, and passed upon him the sentence of DEATH.

"But no description can accurately convey to others, the impression which the trial, defence and appearance of Gullah Jack made on those who witnessed the workings of his cunning and rude address."—When arrested and brought before the Court in company with another African named Jack, the property of the estate of Pritchard, he assumed so much ignorance, and looked and acted the fool so well, that some of the Court could not believe that this was the Necromancer who was sought after. This conduct he continued when on his trial, until he saw the witnesses and heard the testimony as it progressed against him; when in an instant, his countenance was lightened up as if by lightening, and "his wildness and vehemence of gesture, and the malignant glance with which he eyed the witnesses who appeared him, all indicated the savage, who indeed had been *caught* but not *tamed.*" His courage, however, soon forsook him. When he received sentence of death, he earnestly implored that a fortnight longer might be allowed him, and then that a week longer, which he continued earnestly to solicit until he was taken from the Court Room to his cell; and when he was carried to execution "he gave up his spirit without firmness or composure." He was sentenced on the 9th July to be hung on the 12th.[6]

Sentence on Jack, *a Slave belonging to Paul Pritchard, commonly called* GULLAH JACK, *and sometimes* COUTER JACK.

GULLAH JACK—The Court after deliberately considering all the circumstances of your case, are perfectly satisfied of your guilt. In the prosecution of your wicked designs, you were not satisfied with resorting to natural and ordinary means, but endeavoured to enlist on your behalf, all the powers of darkness, and employed for that purpose, the most disgusting mummery and superstition. You represented yourself as invulnerable; that you could neither be taken nor destroyed, and that all who fought under your banners would be invincible. While such wretched expedients are calculated to excite the confidence, or to alarm the fears of the ignorant and credulous, they produce no other emotion in the minds of the intelligent and enlightened, but contempt and disgust. Your boasted charms have not preserved yourself, and of course could not protect others.— "Your Altars and your Gods have sunk together in the dust. The airy spectres, conjured by you, have been chased away by the superior light of Truth, and you stand exposed, the miserable and deluded victim of offended Justice. Your days are literally numbered. You will shortly be consigned to the cold and silent grave; and all the Powers of Darkness cannot rescue you from your approaching Fate!—Let me then, conjure you to devote the remnant of your miserable existence, in fleeing from the "*wrath to come.*" This can only be done by a full disclosure of the truth. The Court are willing to afford you all the aid in their power, and to permit any Minister of the Gospel, whom you may select to have free access to you. To him you may unburthen your guilty conscience. Neglect not the opportunity, for there is "no device nor art in the grave," to which you must shortly be consigned.[7]

1. Paul Pritchard Sr. (1779–1837) was a shipwright who in 1822 lived at 6 Hasell Street. See *CSCCD,* 95. Pritchard operated a shipyard on Gadsden's Wharf. Since Jack was a woodworker in Africa, Pritchard presumably purchased him in April 1806 to help with his business. Paul Pritchard appears to have been Jack's only master. Hamilton, *Account,* 47, 50, dates Jack's arrest to July 5 and his trial to July 9.

2. Yorrick Cross.

3. Samuel Wharton (1783–1827) was a merchant who resided on the corner of King and Mary streets, Charleston Neck. See *CSCCD,* 103.

4. Richard Withers Vanderhorst (1786–1832) owned multiple properties, including a large plantation in St. James Santee Parish, a home in the Charleston suburb of Mazyckborough, and, in 1820, more than two hundred slaves. See *CSCCD,* 102; *BDSCHR* 4: 577–78.

107

said Jack, we will have arms—he said he would have some arms made at the blacksmith's—Jack was going to give me * * * * *
* * * * * * *
* * * * * * *
* * * * * * *

I refused to do this as I considered it murder, and that God would never pardon me for it; 'twas not like fair fighting. Until Jack was taken up and condemned to death, I felt as if I was bound up, and had not the power to speak one word about it—Jack charmed Julius and myself at last, and we then consented to join—Tom Russel the Blacksmith and Jack are partners, (in conjuring) Jack learnt him to be a Doctor, Tom talked to Jack about the fighting and agreed to join, and those two brought Julius and myself to agree to it. Jack said Tom was his second and "when you don't see me, and see Tom, you see me." Jack said Tom was making arms for the black people—Jack said he could not be killed, nor could a white man take him."

THE TRIAL of HARRY, a Negro Man belonging to Mr David Haig.—James Haig, Esq. attending as Counsel for his owner.

EVIDENCE.

WITNESS No. 10, testified as follows :—After Peter Poyas had twice called on me about this business, he and Harry Haig called on me. I was not at home, but the next morning I met Harry who asked me for my name—I refused it—he said I would be killed if I did not join—I said I would join when they came out, if they were stronger than the whites---Harry called on me again, and asked me if I was willing, that the thing would break out soon--I asked him where he would begin---he said in Boundary-street---at what hour---he said at 12 o'clock at night or early

P

Figure 10. Page from Kennedy and Parker, *Official Report of the Trials of Sundry Negroes* (1822) that elides with asterisks testimony related to Gullah Jack's plan to poison whites.

5. Robert Harth.

6. This paragraph describing Pritchard's courtroom demeanor first appears in Hamilton, *Account,* 24–25, and was republished in the *OR,* 46.

7. The July 9 sentence of Jack Pritchard was reprinted verbatim in the Richmond *Enquirer,* September 3, 1822, and the Newbern (now New Bern, NC) *Carolina Centinel,* September 7, 1822. It appeared toward the end of the *OR,* 179, and has here been moved forward.

Subsequently to his conviction, HARRY HAIG, who received sentence of death at the same time that he did, made the following CONFESSION:[1]

"Julius Forrest and myself always worked together—Gullah Jack calls himself a Doctor Negro—he induced Julius and myself to join at last, but at first we refused—before the 16th of June, Jack appointed to meet us at Bulkley's farm—when we got there Jack was not there, but Peter Poyas came—we broke up at day light. Not quite a month before the 16th of June, Jack met us and talked about war—I asked Jack how he would do for arms—bye and bye, said Jack, we will have arms—he said he would have some arms made at the blacksmith's—Jack was going to give me *

I refused to do this as I considered it murder, and that God would never pardon me for it; 'twas not like fair fighting. Until Jack was taken up and condemned to death, I felt as if I was bound up, and had not the power to speak one word about it—Jack charmed Julius and myself at last, and we then consented to join—Tom Russel the Blacksmith and Jack are partners, (in conjuring) Jack learnt him to be a Doctor. Tom talked to Jack about the fighting and agreed to join, and those two brought Julius and myself to agree to it. Jack said Tom was his second and "when you don't see me, and see Tom, you see me." Jack said Tom was making arms for the black people—Jack said he could not be killed, nor could a white man take him.[2]

1. Hamilton, *Account,* 43, states that Julius Forrest was arrested on Monday, July 8, and the Senate transcript indicates that his trial began on July 10, which was presumably the date Haig made his confession.

2. Harry Haig's confession, complete with the asterisks designed to indicate that some material—the terrifying talk of poison—was omitted, was reprinted verbatim in *Washington Gazette,* September 4, 1822; *Baltimore Patriot & Mercantile Advertiser,* September 6, 1822; and Salem *Gazette,* September 23, 1822. Michael P. Johnson, "Denmark Vesey and His Co-Conspirators," *WMQ* 58 (2001): 934, asserts that "the *Official Report* is a document of advocacy, a public, retrospective statement of the prosecution's case" against the accused designed to calm the public mind. Although it was that, one also wonders why Kennedy and Parker simply did not omit the reference to poison completely, rather than to indicate that something incendiary had been cut from the pamphlet version. The asterisks appear also in Hamilton, *Account,* 39.

On the 9th July, sentence of death was passed upon five more, two of whom were Monday and Gullah Jack, and a third, Charles, the slave of the Honorable John Drayton;[1] who though not a leader, had taken so active a part in the business, as to be perhaps as much known in it as the leaders were. It was now thirty-nine days since the civil authorities had received information of this plot, and twenty during which the Court organized for the trial, of the Insurgents had been engaged (Sundays excepted;) and yet, so true were they to each other, that during all that time only fifteen had been discovered whose connection in the plot was clear, of whom four were used as witnesses. "After Monday Gell and Charles Drayton were convicted there appeared to be a pause in our further discoveries, and some prospect of the investigation closing with their execution and that of John Horry, Harry Haig and Gullah Jack" On the 9th of July, however, these five men, were called before the Court to receive sentence, and after it had been pronounced, with the most impressive solemnity, they were withdrawn to a common ward in the Work-House, for half an hour, until separate cells could be provided for them. It was at this moment that *Charles Drayton,* overwhelmed with terror and guilt, went up to *Monday* and reproached him with having induced him to join in a scheme which had placed him in such a miserable and perilous situation. To this appeal Monday not only confessed his guilt, but observed to Charles—that their present fate was justly and precisely what they had a right to expect, after their detected and defeated project. On which there immediately ensued between them a conversation on the extent of the guilt of others, in which Monday gave Charles the names of many accomplices whom he had not previously known in the plot; the arrival of the blacksmith to iron the convicts, and the turnkey to convey them to separate cells, interrupted the conversation.

Charles, during the night of the 9th, sent for Mr. Gordon, who has charge of the Work-House, and informed him that he was extremely anxious to see the Intendant, as he had some important disclosures to make. By day-light, on the morning of the 10th, this message was conveyed to the person for whom it was intended, and Charles was visited at sun-rise. He was found, in a state of the most lamentable depression and panic, and he seemed prepared to make the most ample declarations from the fear of death and the consequences of an *hereafter,* if he went out of the world without revealing all that he knew, in relation to the Conspiracy, in which he had been so active an agent. Before his narrative was received, he was most specially put on his guard, that no promises could be made to him of a reversal of his fate, but that he might rest satisfied, his condition could not be worse by his coming out with a full disclosure of all that he knew. He then stated many particulars, that had come to his own knowledge, proving a much wider diffusion of the plot than, at that period, was imagined; and, after giving up the names of several of his comrades, he mentioned the conversation which had been commenced and broken off, in the common ward of the Work-House, between Monday Gell and himself. As Monday, at this period, did not seem disposed to make any confessions to others, whatever he might be inclined to do to his friend Charles, it was considered important, that the conversation between them, should be renewed, and they were brought together in the same cell, and left for twenty four hours alone; but some little stratagem was employed, to divert the suspicions of Monday, that Charles was confined with him, merely for the purpose of getting information out of him.

On the morning of the 10th, the Court were apprized, generally, of these new disclosures, which Charles had made, but as he was still *closeted* with Monday, he could not be examined on that day, and the Court met and adjourned from day to day until the 13th; on which day Monday Gell's own confession was heard by them. Between the 10th and 13th, *Charles* and *Monday* were separated (having been respited by His Excellency, the Governor, at the request of the Court) and Charles, on his re-examination afforded much important information, which he had derived from Monday. On Monday's having all this brought to his view, he confessed his own guilt, as well as the truth of the statements which he had made to Charles. With the information obtained from Charles, arrests recommenced on the 10th, in the course of which day Peirault belonging to Mr. Strohecker[2] was arrested; whose additional information, with some further details obtained from Harry, belonging to Mr. Haig,[3] in conjunction with the disclosures of Charles and Monday, caused the arrest of upwards of sixty slaves in the course of three or four days. After the trial of these, and a few more subsequently arrested, the civil authorities conceiving that enough had been done to serve as an example, determined to pursue the investigation no further; but should any further information be communicated to them, to bring to trial such only as had taken an active part, and arrange with the owners of the others to send them out of the state.[4]

THE COURT then resolved to *reconsider the sentence* they had passed on Monday, Charles and Harry, *unanimously altered* their sentence, and passed upon them the following—"That they be imprisoned in the Work-House of Charleston, until their masters, under the direction of the City Council of Charleston, shall send them out of the limits of the United States, into which they are not to return under penalty of death."[5]

1. Charles belonged to John Drayton (1766–1822), not only a judge but a slaveholding rice-planter and prominent politician. Judge Drayton lived at 24 Friend Street. See *CSCCD*, 77, 94; David Dobson, *Directory of Scots in the Carolinas, 1680–1630*, 2 vols. (Baltimore: Clearfield, 1986–2004), vol. 1: 261. *BDSCHR* 4: 162–64.

2. On the blacksmith John Strohecker (1776?–1849), owner of Perault, see Part II, p. 91 n17.

3. Harry Haig was owned by David Haig (1783–1832), a Scottish immigrant who ran a cooperage at Craft's Wharf. He resided at 204 Meeting Street. See *CSCCD*, 82.

4. The above four paragraphs appear in the "Narrative" section of the *OR*, 56–59.

5. This paragraph appears in the *OR*, 99, above the trial of Charles Drayton. Because it refers to the magistrates' decision to alter Drayton's sentence of death, we have moved it to this section.

THE TRIAL of HARRY, a Negro Man belonging to Mr. David Haig.—James Haig, Esq.[1] attending as Counsel for his owner.

EVIDENCE.

WITNESS No. 10,[2] testified as follows:—After Peter Poyas had twice called on me about this business, he and Harry Haig called on me. I was not at home, but the next morning I met Harry who asked me for my name—I refused it—he said I would be killed if I did not join—I said I would join when they came out, if they were stronger than the whites—Harry called on me again, and asked me if I was willing, that the thing would break out soon—I asked him where he would begin—he said in Boundary-street—at what hour—he said at 12 o'clock at night or early in the morning as soon as the guard were discharged. Harry Haig has since seen me several times, and told me to hold myself ready—I said I'm ready when called on. He said all the draymen came to his master's Cooper-yard, and said they were ready, but he told them he was waiting for Gullah Jack—he said he would tell me when they were ready, that they were only waiting for the head man, who was a white man; but he, although asked, would neither tell me the white man's name, nor where the powder and arms were—this was last Tuesday,[3] the very day six negroes were hanged, about 6 o'clock, A.M.—This was the last time we spoke though I have seen him since.

GEORGE, Mr. Vanderhorst's[4] slave[,] gave the evidence which follows:—I have met Harry Haig at Gullah Jack's, where he and all agreed to join and come against the whites. I can't say *he* was afraid of Gullah Jack as a Conjurer—I was—I have often seen Harry with Julius Forrest.

THE COURT *unanimously* found Harry GUILTY, and passed upon him the sentence of DEATH.

After his conviction, *he confessed his guilt*—see page 106.[5]

The reasons which induced the Court to alter the sentences passed on Monday and Cearles[6] to transportation, induced them to alter Harry's to the same.

1. James Haig (1797–1835), brother of David, the owner of Harry, was a gifted attorney. He resided in 1822 at 204 Meeting Street. See *CSCCD,* 82, and "Obituary," *Charleston Courier,* July 25, 1835. Hamilton, *Account,* 48, places Harry's arrest on July 5.
2. Yorrick Cross.
3. This was Tuesday, July 3, two days before Haig's arrest.
4. On George's master, Richard Withers Vanderhorst, see p. 200 n4.
5. In this volume, Haig's confession appears on p. 202.
6. Charles Drayton, not Cearles.

THE TRIAL OF JULIUS a negro man belonging to Mr. T. H. Forrest.[1]—His owner attending.

EVIDENCE.

PRUDENCE, a Negro Woman, the property of Mr. Bussacre,[2] testified as follows:—The first time I conversed with Julius Forrest on this business was previous to the execution of the six negroes—'twas of a Sunday night about a fortnight ago, that he called at my house and said he had just come from the Island—that he had been looking for Harry Haig but could not find him—he said that he and Harry were to have gone up the road on Sunday the 16th June to meet the black people who were coming to fight in town, but that the white people having got wind of it turned out too strong, they were obliged to go away—he came again last Sunday night to my house and said Harry Haig was taken up for the same thing he had been talking to me about the Sunday night, and asked me if I had said any thing to any person about what he had been speaking to me about that Sunday night—as they have taken up Harry Haig, said he, I suppose my time will come next, but if Harry don't call my name I shall be safe—this was our last conversation.

Mr. T. H. FORREST, deposed that, Prudence is like a kind of mother to Julius, having raised or brought him up. Harry Haig and Julius are very intimate and are together at her shop almost every night.

GEORGE, Mr. Vanderhorst's Slave testified as follows:—I met Julius at Gullah Jack's meeting, where he, together with all, agreed to join and come against the white people. The man now standing before me is Julius Forrest, whom I have often seen with Harry Haig.

HARRY HAIG'S CONFESSION, see in page 106.[3]

THE COURT *unanimously* found Julius GUILTY, and passed upon him the sentence of DEATH.*

* At the conclusion of this trial on the 13th of July, Mr. James Legare, from feeble health and great exhaustion during the previous sittings of the Court, asked, and obtained, leave to withdraw; whereupon Mr. Henry Deas,[4] was summoned by the Magistrates, who took his seat and served until the adjournment of the Court.

1. Julius Forrest, according to *OR*, 183, was the slave of Thomas H. Forrest, who ran a cooperage on Chisolm's Wharf and resided at 83 Tradd Street. See *CSCCD*, 79. But "Inhabitants of Charleston, Petition and Supporting Papers Asking Compensation for Their Slaves Who Were Executed for Involvement in a Slave Insurrection," [n.d., ca. 1822], no. 1839, series S165015, SCDAH, contains an affidavit, dated November 21, 1822, that identifies Julius Forrest, "a Cooper aged 27," as the property of Charleston residents Thomas F. Purse and William Wightman (d. 1835). Wightman owned a rice plantation on the Savannah River, and upon his death, Purse acted as executor of Wightman's estate. See "Executor's Sale," *Macon Georgia Telegraph*, November 17, 1836. Hamilton, *Account*, 43, dates Forrest's arrest to July 8. The Senate transcript indicates that his trial took place on July 10 with his sentence read on July 13.

2. The *CDSG*, 14, identifies two Charles Bussacres. One was a grocer on "e. side state," and the other operated a dry goods store at 157 King Street. The 1822 directory identifies only one Charles "Bussaker," the proprietor of a dry goods store on King Street. See *CSCCD*, 73.

3. In this volume, Haig's confession appears on p. 202.

4. Henry Deas (1770–1846), lawyer and planter, was born in Edinburgh, Scotland, attended the College of New Jersey (Princeton), served in South Carolina's state legislature for decades, and held high-ranking positions in Charleston in a wide range of private associations. See *Southern Patriot*, December 8, 1848; Clare Jervey, *Inscriptions on the Tablets and Gravestones in St. Michael's Church and Churchyard, Charleston, S.C.* (Columbia, SC: State Company, 1906), 18; and *BDSCHR* 4: 151–52. After the Vesey affair, Deas, like James Hamilton Jr. and many other prominent Charleston planters, moved from neo-Federalist politics to states' rights. A lawyer and planter, he owned multiple properties, including a large plantation on the North Santee River. *CSCCD*, 76, identifies his Charleston residence in 1822 as located at 1 Friend Street. The abolitionist Theodore Dwight Weld singled out both Deas and Nathaniel Heyward, Deas's fellow freeholder on the first court, for denunciation as brutal slaveholders in *American Slavery as It Is: Testimony of a Thousand Witnesses* (New York, 1839), 174–75: "Another of the individuals chosen to constitute that court was Colonel Henry Deas, now president of the Board of Trustees of Charleston College, and a few years since a member of the Senate of South Carolina. From a late correspondence in the 'Greenville (S.C.) Mountaineer,' between Rev. William M. Wightman, a professor in Randolph, Macon, College, and a number of the citizens of Lodi, South Carolina, it appears that the cruelty of this Colonel Deas to his slaves, is proverbial in South Carolina, so much that Professor Wightman, in the sermon which occasioned the correspondence, spoke of the Colonel's inhumanity to his slaves as a matter of perfect notoriety." For this and other indictments of elite Charleston planters, Weld relied on his wife, Angelina Grimké, and her sister Sarah, both born and raised in South Carolina before moving north in the 1820s, converting to Quakerism, and joining the abolitionist movement.

Figure 11. James Legaré (1762–1830), judge on the First Court of Magistrates and Freeholders. Courtesy of the Walpole Family. Photo by Julia Lofton Walpole.

THE TRIAL of TOM, a Negro Man, the Slave of Mrs. Russel[1]—James Gray Esq. [2] attending for his owner.

EVIDENCE.

*PERAULT, a Negro Man belonging to Mr. J. Strohecker, testified as follows:—Tom told me at his shop that he had joined Gullah Jack's band—I know he belongs to this band—I belong to Monday Gell's—these bands were to rise against the whites, and Tom told me himself that he would rise with the band against the whites—I saw six pike heads at Monday Gell's shop, three of them were like spears, and three like bayonets, with holes in them to fix in poles—I met Tom at Vesey's house, where it was agreed that the 16th June should be the day for the rising, and where was also Gullah Jack—Monday had a list with forty-two names on it, mine was one—he burnt his list when Peter Poyas was taken up.

* Upon the testimony of this witness, the Court placed great reliance. His open, frank and blunt manner convinced every one who heard him that he was incapable of uttering a falsehood, and that he possessed many fine traits of character.—The following account of his

> life was politely furnished by his owner. Perault was born at Jumba in Africa, about a weeks travel from Goree. Mamadu his father, who is wealthy and owns about 60 working hands, trades to Hassou with Tobacco and Salt, in exchange for which he receives Gold; to which place Perault accompanied him six times. Perault was engaged in three battles against the people of Hassou, who do not cultivate their lands, but make predatory incursions into the cultivated territories of their neighbours. Perault also fought twice against the people of Darah, but in the second battle he was taken prisoner and carried to that place.[3] Here his brother-in-law saw him, and offered to the Captain of a Brig three slaves for him if he would wait his return from Jumba. The Captain, however, could not delay his voyage, and Perault was brought to Charleston in a Brig belonging to Mr. Delaire,[4] who kept him for his own service. In 1814, he was purchased by his present owner,[5] who is sati[s]fied with his conduct since he bought him. His master stated that he is very tenacious, whenever he conceives that he is right, and that he believes he would rather suffer death than deviate from the truth—that those who are not accustomed to his mode of expressing himself would be affronted by his bluntness, but that he does not mean to offend.

Cross-Examined by Mr. Gray, the Prisoner's Counsel—The first time I met Tom at Vesey's was on the 16th June—when I went to Vesey's I met him there—I knew him long before—Tom was willing to agree to all that was adopted there, but did not talk himself—I met Charles Drayton at Tom's shop—Smart Anderson was present when the spears were brought into Monday's shop.

Re-Examined—I saw Gullah Jack carry those spears to Monday Gell's.

CHARLES gave the following evidence:—Tom told me himself in Monday's shop that he was making the pikes for Gullah Jack.

Cross-Examined—I did not meet Peirault at Tom's shop, but at Monday's—I never was in company with Tom and Pierault together on this business.

MONDAY, testified as follows:—Tom and Charles Drayton talked together in my shop once, but I did not hear what they said—I had frequent conversations with Pierault, but not with Tom.

Mrs. MARK MARKS[6] deposed as follows:—Mrs. Russell the prisoner's owner told me that Gullah Jack was constantly with Tom at breakfast, dinner and supper, and that she cautioned Tom not to have so much to do with Jack or he would be taken up.

(*Note.* Mr. Gray consented to this testimony being received instead of sending for Mrs. Russel.)

JAMES MALL,[7] a White Lad, about 16 or 17 years of age, a witness on behalf of the prisoner, deposed as follows:—I was working with Tom in his shop from February to last of March—I then went into the country and received a message from him some time after to come down and work in his shop with him again—I came down about the last of May and he refused to employ me—one day when I went to his shop I saw him making something like a knife a foot long, out of a file which he had not yet finished—he makes edged tools.

Cross-Examined by the Court—when I was working with Tom I did not eat any meals at the shop but at home—Gullah Jack was frequently at Tom's shop, and they frequently talked together in Gullah, which I do not understand—Tom said, after the people were taken up, that he would not do as some had done, tell upon one another for money.

THE COURT *unanimously* found Tom GUILTY, and passed upon him the sentence of DEATH.

1. Hamilton, *Account,* 24, identifies Tom Russell (not Russel) as a blacksmith and a member of Gullah Jack's band. He kept a shop on East-Bay Street and was alleged to be the "armourer," that is, a maker of pikes and spears for the rebels. Sarah Hopton Russell (1752–1832), widow of Nathaniel Russell (1730–1820), a wealthy merchant, owned Tom. See Petition of Sarah Russell to South Carolina House of Representatives, December 2, 1823, no. 133, series S165015, SCDAH. In 1822 she resided at 11 Lynch's Lane. Captain Joseph Vesey and Nathaniel Russell came together in 1793 to form a society to benefit refugees from Saint-Domingue. Thus, Denmark Vesey and Tom Russell may have known each other for some time. See Charleston *City Gazette & Commercial Daily Advertiser,* November 21, 1793. Hamilton, *Account,* 47, says Russell was arrested on Wednesday, July 10; the Senate transcript indicates that his trial was held on Monday, July 15.

2. *CSCCD,* 81, identifies James W. Gray (1795–1870) as an attorney who in 1822 resided at 44 Meeting Street.

3. Gorée is a small island near the port of Dakar, capital of Senegal. Gorée's minor involvement in the Atlantic slave trade peaked under French auspices during the second half of the eighteenth century when Saint-Domingue became the world's leading producer of coffee and sugar. See James F. Searing, *West African Slavery and Atlantic Commerce: The Senegal River Valley, 1700–1860* (Cambridge, UK: Cambridge University Press, 1993), 106–13, and Anthony Todman, "Gorée Island," in *The Historical Encyclopedia of World Slavery,* ed. Junius P. Rodriguez (Santa Barbara, CA: ABC CLIO, 1997), 1: 308.

4. James Delaire (d. 1814) was an established merchant in Saint-Domingue's capital city of Cap François before the slave revolution sent him fleeing in the 1790s to Charleston, where he resurrected his business, which would include trading slaves. See *Charleston Courier,* April 5, 1814.

5. Monday Gell's owner was John Gell Jr. (d. 1824), owner of a livery stable. See Part II, p. 91 n11.

6. Mark Marks (1778?–1834), of Jewish descent, born in London, served Charleston as a deputy sheriff in 1822. He resided at 310 King Street. See *CSCCD,* 88; Barrett A. Elzas, *The Old Jewish Cemeteries at Charleston, S.C.: A Transcript of the Inscriptions on Their Tombstones, 1762–1903* (Charleston, SC: Daggett, 1903), 43.

7. No person with the surname "Mall" appears in any of the Charleston city directories published in the 1820s. The teenage boy in question may be, however, James G. Maull, born in 1806 to James Maull, a merchant, and Mary (Givhan) Maull. See Hayneville (AL) *Watchman,* April 6, 1860.

THE TRIAL of LOUIS REMOUSSIN,[1] a Negro Man, the Slave of Mr. Cromwell—His owner attending.[2]

EVIDENCE.

PERAULT testified as follows:—I know Louis—Louis and Joe and myself met in the street, and Joe said to me Louis was one to join against the whites; Louis did not deny it, this was on the 15th of June—Louis said he was ready to rise against the white people—Joe said the French Band had been ready a long time—this is all I know against Louis—the conversation was in Creole French, I understand it. *(The Court required Louis and Perault to speak together in French, which they did, and Perault evidently understood that language.)*

CHARLES testified as follows:—Louis met me one day as he came out of the Work-House. He one day said to me that he had not much to do with the business, but that on the night the attack commenced against the whites, he would be ready, and he told me to get ready—I understood from his conversation plain enough that he was one of them.

Cross-Examined—This was the Saturday before the thing was to break out—I met him at his own house—he told me at Monday Gell's, to come to his house to talk about this business—I have seen him often at Monday's.

MONDAY gave the following evidence:—Louis came to my shop and told me to go to his house that night, that he wanted to see me about something particular—I did not go though.

THE COURT *unanimously* found Louis Remoussin GUILTY, and passed upon him the sentence of DEATH, *but recommended* to the Governor to pardon him *upon condition* that he be transported out of the limits of the United States.

1. Louis Remoussin was a French-speaking slave whose forename was often spelled "Lewis" in the Senate transcript (which on occasion also identified him as Lewis Cromwell).

2. Samuel Cromwell (1775–1844), an English-born bricklayer who in 1822 resided at 7 Back Street, owned Louis. See *CSCCD,* 75. Hamilton, *Account,* 47, dates Samuel's arrest to Friday, July 12; the Senate transcript indicates that his trial fell on Monday, July 15.

THE TRIAL of JOE, a Negro Man belonging to Mr. Jore—His owner attending.[1]

EVIDENCE.

PERAULT testified as follows:—I met Joe at the corner of Boundary and Wall-streets; he said to me how does this business stand now—this affair—he said I don't want to go home before I see how this business, meaning the rising against the whites terminates—he was then a runaway and belonged to the man who keeps a Shoe Shop in King-street, by Mr. Hart's[2]—we parted, the next time we met it was at Monday Gell's, when the spears were on the table—Joe said to Monday Gell in my presence, that the French people would be ready when they were ready, and that he was one of them—the third time I met Joe was when we met Louis—after Louis parted, Joe said that his master's store in King-street was not yet open, and that there were plenty of arms at Mr. Duquercron's store,[3] near the Inspection, even to bayonets—he said that when we raised, we must all run in there, break the door open and get arms.

Cross-Examined by Mr. Jore—He told me that he had runaway, but I don't know it myself—this was about the 1st June—the second time was before any one was taken up on this business—the third time I met him was on 15th June—our meetings were accidental.

CHARLES gave the evidence following:—I met Joe three or four times at Monday's—he generally speaks like as in a parable—that is, gives hints, &c—he said the French Band was armed throughout, and were ready, and he was ready; but he did not know how to trust country borns; this he said in Monday's presence.

MONDAY testified as follows:—Joe has been often at my shop, and I and he talking of this concern—he said he knew the French who were to join, but as they did not speak to him he did not speak to them—that he was one of those who had joined—this was better than a month ago.

Cross-Examined by Mr. Jore—He comes to my shop as a friend to get me to do work for him—he insinuated that he would be an active man.

Mr. JORE and Col. CROSS testified that Joe's general conduct was good.

THE COURT *unanimously* found Joe GUILTY, and passed upon him the sentence of DEATH.

1. Peter Louis Jore (also spelled "Joor" and "Ioor") owned Joe. Hamilton, *Account,* 43, dates his arrest to Saturday, July 6; the Senate transcript indicates that his trial fell on Monday, July 15. He was hanged on Friday, July 26. Although the transcript identifies Joe's owner as a shoemaker on King Street, Peter Louis Jore does not appear in *CSCCD.* Together with William Sims, Benjamin Hammet, Robert Anderson, and James Mitchell, Jore petitioned the state senate asking for just remuneration for executed slaves. See William Sims et al., Petition Asking for Compensation for Slaves Executed for Participation in an Insurrection, n.d., no. 1743, series S165015, SCDAH.

2. Nathan Hart (1783–1840) owned a hardware store located in 1822 on 206 King Street. See *CSCCD,* 82; "Obituary," *Charleston Courier,* September 9, 1840.

3. On the grocer Francis Duquercron and his store, see Part II, p. 92 n31.

THE T[R]IAL of MINGO, a Negro Man, the property of Mr. William Harth—His owner attending.[1]

EVIDENCE.

MONDAY testified as follows:—Mingo told me in my shop that Peter Poyas had told him of this business, and that he was to take his master's horse and act as a horseman in the fight.

Cross-Examined by Mr. Harth—This was before Peter was taken up on the 2d June—he was often at my shop, and knows me well—he asked me if I knew Peter—I said yes, and that he had spoken to me, he said he had spoken to him too—I sometimes visit the society he belongs to—George Wilson is his class leader.

CHARLES gave the following testimony:—I have seen Mingo Harth at Monday Gell's—he was talking about the rising—he said expressly he was one.

Cross-examined by Mr. Harth—this was after William and Edwin were taken up.[2]

William, a negro man belonging to Mr. John Paul testified as follows:[3]—I have heard something about an insurrection of the blacks, but was not concerned in it—Mr. William Harth's Negro man Mingo told me about it, and referred me to Peter Poyas for further information, who he said had a list with 9,000 names upon it, and that he was still taking down names—on the week I was to see Peter I was apprehended. Mingo said that 600 men on the Bay was already down on the list in Peter's possession—Mingo would not before the Wardens own what he told me—I never had any conversation with Peter—Mingo said his name was not yet down, and he would not put it down 'till he knew all that was to be done—that Ned Bennett knew all about it, and told it to all Mr. Bennett's people, and that letters were passing between those concerned—I can read and count printed characters but not written. On a Saturday night Mingo told me as we were going towards his wife's house, that every day at 2 o'clock Peter went to Mr. Harth's lumber yard[4] and talked to the other men about this matter, to make them sensible of the plan. At Mingo's house I took up the Bible and read two chapters from the prophet Tobit[5]—Mingo said that *all those belonging to the African Church are engaged in the insurrection, from the country to the town—that there is a little man*[6] *amongst them who can't be shot, killed or caught, who was to be their general, and who would provide them with arms—that some arms were provided but he did not tell me where they were,* and he also said that Ned Bennett and Charles Shubrick are officers. Peter, Ned and Charles I know to be class leaders in the African Church—The African Association have also a Church in Anson-street near Boundary-street, and one in Cow-alley, where they have service. I believe that Mingo was endeavouring to get me to join them in the rising, and from his conversation I have no doubt but that he was engaged in the conspiracy, and that all he said to me was to get me to join them. *It was also told to me that our colour from the North to the South had combined together to fight against New-Orleans.* Mingo was no doubt satisfied that I would join—I never had any conversation with any one about the rising but with Mingo and Col. Prioleau's man[7]—Mingo said that Peter Poyas would tell me when the rising would take place—that Mr. Bennett's Ned was one of them—*that Denmark Vesey was the chief man and more concerned than any one else.* I beg you won't take up Sarah, for no woman knows any thing about it—Mingo said that letters were passing between Peter Poyas, Ned Bennett and Charles Shubrick. I am persuaded that Denmark Vesey was chiefly concerned in this business—Mingo said that the country places were engaged in the plot, and also the Islands—that he knows the little man who can't be shot, who told him that there was a *Gullah Society* going on which met once a month—that all the orders he got he got from Peter—Mingo always denied that he was engaged, and yet always talked to me as if he wanted me to join. Mingo said they would get horses, which were engaged at one, two or three *Livery Stables from the Stable Boys; two Stables he named in particular, viz:* Mr. Billing's[8] and the one behind the old Church—Mingo said a brown man, the steward of the cutter, had stolen some of the arms, and that Jim, a blacksmith of Mr. Bennett made arms.

GEORGE, a Negro man belonging to Mr. Wilson, *a witness on behalf of the prisoner,* testified as follows: I never saw Monday Gell at my Society[9]—he would not have been admitted, as he was a member of the African Association. Cross-examined—He might have been there and I not have known it, as there are sometimes 60 or 100 persons present.

PETER PARLER, a free black man, *a witness on behalf of the prisoner,* testified as follows:—I have never seen Monday Gell at my Society. Cross-examined—I am generally at the meetings unless I am sick.[10]

THE COURT *unanimously* found Mingo GUILTY, and passed upon him the sentence of DEATH.

1. On Mingo's owner, William Harth, see p. 175 n6. Hamilton, *Account,* 47, dates Mingo Harth's arrest to June 21. Despite being one of the first slaves arrested, the Senate transcript indicates that Harth was not put on trial until Monday, July 15, and 16. He was hanged on Friday, July 26.

2. Hamilton, *Account,* 45, indicates that William was arrested on May 31, and Edwin on June 24.

3. This deposition, which appears in two parts in the Senate transcript, was given in part at the earlier trial of Peter Poyas. Both Mingo and Poyas appear in the statement; most likely the magistrates took this statement, given on June 19, and read all or parts into the court record depending on who was on trial.

4. Harth's lumberyard was on South Bay Street.

5. On the one hand, the fact that Vesey's Bible included the Book of Tobit could indicate that he had abandoned his earlier Presbyterian faith since Protestant Bibles often omit the fourteen books of the Apocrypha. On the other hand, advertisements in Charleston newspapers indicate that bibles with the Apocrypha were on sale and readily available. The Book of Tobit perhaps appealed to Vesey as it told the story of a righteous Israelite named Tobit who lived in Nineveh after the deportation of the northern tribes of Israel to Assyria in 721 BCE. Since the first translation of the Hebrew Bible was not done until 1851, Vesey, once owned by a Catholic, most likely owned a Catholic Bible. No evidence exists to support the claim made in David Robertson, *Denmark Vesey: The Buried History of America's Largest Slave Rebellion and the Man Who Led It* (New York: Knopf, 1999), 37–40, that he was a Muslim.

6. The "little man" was Jack Pritchard.

7. Colonel John Cordes Prioleau's slave was Peter.

8. In 1822 John Billings (d. 1826) ran the public stables at 122 Church Street and resided at 17 Chambers Street. See *CSCCD,* 71.

9. George Wilson's reference to "my Society" could refer to one of any number of slave and free colored burial societies or "bands" that had formed in Charleston before 1822. City ordinances, dating at least to 1789, had exempted funerals from prohibitions on assemblages of more than seven slaves. See H. M. Henry, *The Police Control of the Slave in South Carolina* (Emory, VA: n.p., 1914), 143–44. William Hasell Wilson, who knew George "very well," describes him as "a dark mulatto of large frame and good appearance, a class leader in the Methodist Church; he could read and write, and bore an excellent character among both whites and blacks." George may have been referring to such associations for persons of partial African ancestry as the Brown Fellowship Society or the Humane and Friendly Society. Although the rules and regulations of both of these societies confined membership to free persons of color, slaves like George Wilson did attach themselves to both groups and were highly visible in their funeral processions. See "To the Honorable the City Council," Charleston *Southern Patriot,* September 19, 1835, and Robert L. Harris Jr., "Charleston's Free Afro-American Elite: The Brown Fellowship Society and the Humane Brotherhood," *SCHM* 82 (1981): 289–310. *Rules and Regulations of the Brown Fellowship Society, Established at Charleston, S.C., 1st November, 1790* (Charleston, SC, 1844), 17, identifies state's witness "William Pinceel" (Penceel), a free person of color, as a member beginning in 1807, but makes no mention of Wilson. Alternatively, "my Society" could refer to a group of religious slaves led by Wilson, who was active as a class leader in both the Methodist and Circular (Congregational) churches.

10. Peter Parlour was a drayman who resided at 5 Magazine Street. See *DSGCC,* 107.

THE TRIAL of JACK, a Mulatto Man, belonging to Mrs. Purcell—Mr. Thomas Smith, the brother of his owner attending.[1]

EVIDENCE.

MONDAY testified as follows:—

I have seen Jack and Vesey talking together before my door—he told me that he was one of those to rise against the whites, and Vesey told me so before—the message that

Frank Ferguson gave to me to give to Vesey, I got Jack to carry to Vesey for me—the message was, that he had just come from the country, that he had there got four plantations of men to join—and to go to Vesey and ask him to be at home to night, as he would call on him—I know he carried it, because Vesey told me so that night—he came to my shop afterwards and said to me he was looking for Vesey, and be sure that I called no name.

FRANK testified as follows:—I know Jack Purcell, but don't know that he is concerned in this business—I did give to Monday Gell a message for Vesey.

CHARLES gave the following evidence:—Jack told me he had been at his Mistress' Plantation and tried to get down the people to join in this business—but could not go again—he said he had joined, and asked me where Lot Forrester lived, that he was the proper person to go into the country to bring the people down.

THE PRISONER asked permission to cross-examine Charles, which was granted; but his questions were such, that no one could well answer them but himself. In the course of this examination he admitted, that a large meeting had been called on Stono[2] by Lot,[3] and that considerable preparations were made to receive him, but that Lot did not attend, and he was requested to reprove him for not doing so.

THE COURT *unanimously* found Jack GUILTY, and passed upon him the sentence of Death.—A few moments preceding his execution, he made the following CONFESSION to the Intendant of Charleston:

If it had not been for the cunning of that old villain Vesey, I should not now be in my present situation. He employed every stratagem to induce me to join him. He was in the habit of reading to me all the passages in the newspapers that related to St. Domingo, and apparently every pamphlet he could lay his hands on, that had any connection with slavery. He one day brought me a speech which he told me had been delivered in Congress by a *Mr. King* on the subject of slavery; he told me this Mr. King was the black man's friend, that he Mr. King had declared he would continue to speak, write and publish pamphlets against slavery the longest day he lived, until the Southern States consented to emancipate their slaves, for that slavery was a disgrace to the country.[4]

1. In 1801 Ann Smith Bonsell Purcell, widow of Joseph Purcell, a surveyor and cartographer, and sister of the planter Thomas Smith, bought a family of slaves that included Jack. See Sale List, Estate of Joseph Purcell, Charleston District Court of Equity, Equity Bill, 1801, no. 64, SCDAH. *CSCCD*, 58, has the "Widow Ann Purcell" residing in 1819 at the corner of Green and Bull streets. She does not appear in the 1822 directory. Hamilton, *Account,* 43, dates Jack Purcell's arrest to Friday, July 12; the Senate transcript indicates that his trial took place on Monday, July 15, and Tuesday, July 16. He was hanged on Friday, July 26.

2. The Stono River is a tidal channel located southwest of Charleston that was also the site of a 1739 slave revolt. The most recent history of that revolt is Peter Charles Hoffer, *Cry Liberty: The Great Stono River Slave Rebellion of 1739* (New York: Oxford University Press, 2010).

3. At the July 17 trial of Lot Forrester, Jack Purcell confirmed that Forrester was asked to attend an organizational meeting at the Stono River, but that work in Charleston prohibited him from doing so.

4. Purcell's confession appeared verbatim in the *Washington Gazette,* September 5, 1822; Richmond *Enquirer,* September 3, 1822; and Hartford *Connecticut Mirror,* September 23, 1822. Michael P. Johnson, "Denmark Vesey and His Co-Conspirators," *WMQ* 58 (2001): 961–62, argues that

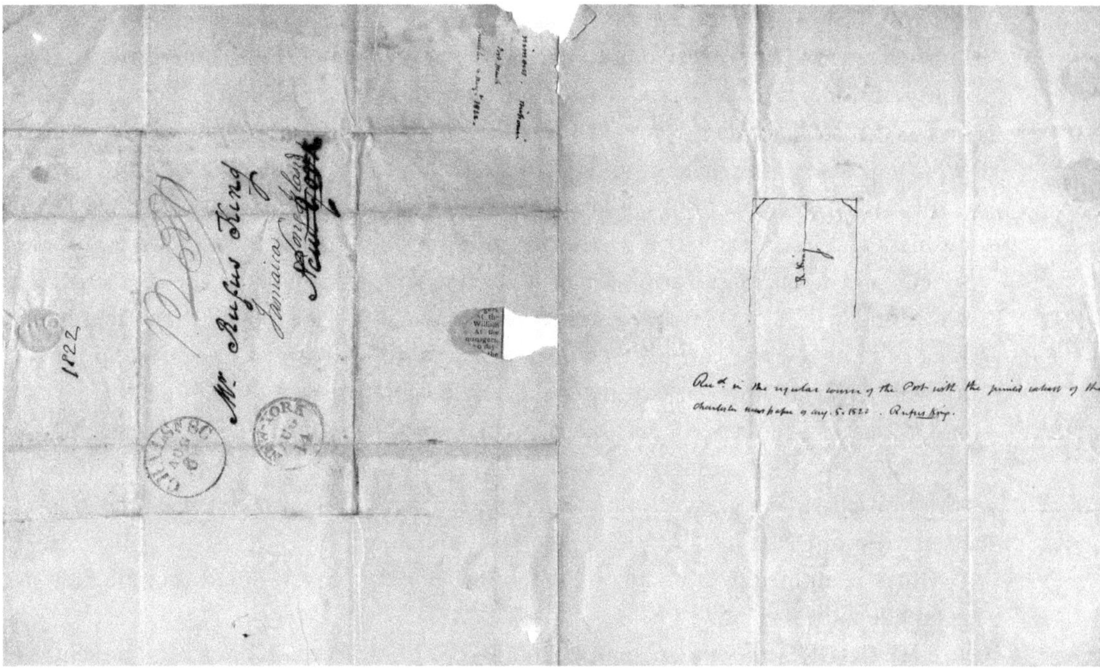

Figure 12. Drawing of a noose sent to New York Senator Rufus King after evidence surfaced that publicized denunciation of slavery during the Missouri debates in 1820 had inspired conspiratorial slaves. Courtesy of the New-York Historical Society.

historians are wrong in suggesting that the Missouri debates played a role in the conspiracy on the grounds that "no witness used the words 'Congress' or 'Missouri' to describe what Vesey said to them." But the references here to both Congress and New York's Rufus King, who delivered a widely reported antislavery speech during the Missouri debates, demonstrate otherwise. See also below, for the trial of Jacob Stagg, in which Monday Gell mentioned the Missouri debates and the letter of Joel Roberts Poinsett, a judge on the second court, to President James Monroe, August 13, 1822, in Part IV.

THE TRIAL of SMART, a Negro Man, the Slave of Mr. Robert Anderson—His owner and M. King, Esq. his Counsel attending.[1]

EVIDENCE.

FRANK testified as follows:—I have seen the prisoner at Vesey's—he told me in the presence of Vesey he had joined and would be ready whenever called on—Vesey sent him one evening to call me.

Cross-Examined by Mr. King—I think at Vesey's there were then present, Monday and Charles and others.

MONDAY gave the following evidence:—I saw Smart at Vesey's in the day—Perault and Peter Cooper were also there—I have often conversed with him on this business, and he seemed to be as much in it as possible—I never asked this man to join—Vesey brought all of us into it—he belongs to the same gang that I did.

Cross-Examined by Mr. King—I was not the first man who spoke to him—I first saw him at Vesey's—he was very much attached to me and called me Pa, and my wife Ma—I don't know that he ever got any one to join, and think he would have told me if he had—he was just such another as myself—I had a list with about forty on it, *but tore it up on the first discovery*—he belongs to the African Church.

PERAULT gave the testimony following:—Smart is a Drayman, and engaged in this business and in the same company, and confessed the same to me—I have met him at Vesey's and at Bulkley's Farm—I met him at Vesey's on Sunday in the day, and there was Monday Gell also, where we talked about the rising—the second time I met him at Bulkley's Farm where were thirteen in all—Smart and I have often spoken and promised to fight by one another against the white people—On Saturday the 15th June, Smart got two *muskets from Mr. Fordham's shop to carry up to Gadsden's Wharf,* they were shortly after taken away from Smart's dray, on which he was carrying them—and he made off with himself—I was present, *one was for me, one for Smart*—we borrowed the muskets from my brother.

Cross-Examined by Mr. King—I met him twice at Vesey's—Smart told me first and got me to join.

THE COURT *unanimously* found Smart GUILTY, and passed upon him the sentence of DEATH.

When Smart was arraigned he pleaded Guilty to the charge, and his Counsel handed to the Court his confession in writing; but the Court advising that the plea of Guilty should be withdrawn, his Counsel did so and pleaded Not Guilty. The CONFESSION handed to the Court was not used against him, but is now given to the public.

"Monday Gell invited me to go up the road to Mr. Bulkley's Farm, on Sunday about three months ago, where there were upwards of thirty persons present, and among them Bulkley's man Billy—I said I would not trust countrymen—I believe Denmark Vesey was there, but did not see him. About four months ago, or going on four months, William Garner, drayman, told me, he expected people from St. Domingo; white people would kill as many as they could. I call Monday Gell Pa, and his wife Ma—About three weeks before going up to the farm, Monday Gell asked me to join him, by telling me that they were in servitude, kicked and cuffed and abused, &c. &c. He spoke to me about St. Domingo people turn and fight the white people. I said we can't do that, but Gell said we could make a contrivance to do it. Monday Gell told me that Gullah wanted to begin when the Negroes of the African Church were taken up in 1818[2]—that if I told any thing they would kill me, and made me hold up my hand and swear not to tell any thing.

I asked when they intended to rise, he said on Saturday night previous to the death of Dr. M'Call. Monday told me the old man said we must begin to night about 10 o'clock—I said to Monday, he must stop it, that Monday must send word to the old man to stop it, that it was a great sin.

I meet at Monday Gell a black man named Jack Glen, a painter.

When at the Farm of Mr. Bulkley, we meet a snake at the gate, which the old man Vesey killed, and one of them says, that's the way we would do them. I seen Monday, and he says, they had better begin about eight o'clock, before the Guard meet, and if they don't do that, meet away on the Green, some where by the lines, march down through the streets, come down to the Guard-House—Monday told me there were three or four gangs—I asked him some questions about the mode of attack, which I consented to—Monday told me that they would have a meeting, or setting up at night, and begin then.

I did not agree to have a fire in the city—At a meeting at Monday Gell's house, Denmark Vesey present, I asked him if he was going to kill the women and children—Denmark answered, what was the use of killing the louse and leaving the nit. I said my God what a sin—Denmark Vesey told me I had not a man's heart, and that I was a friend to Buckra[3]—Monday Gell told me that they sent to several places in the country.

Jack Glen, a black man wanted to borrow my horse to go up the country—I said I had not one to lend—he said he must go in the country that day Sunday, to Goose Creek.

The time I was at the farm they told me they had long things like my arm to put handles to, that they would make contrivance.

Vesey told me one day, after they had taken the place, they would take the money, and he would go in a vessel and put as many as he could, and go back to his own country.

Vesey told me that all the powder was about three miles out of town, and they must take it—could easily get it; and they knew about a place in Queen-street, opposite the Planters' Hotel, where there was arms, &c. The old man, Denmark Vesey, said that they were to attack the Guard House, in three or four ways, and then they would get all the arms.

I never heard about sending the two persons to St. Domingo.

Monday told me they were about to engage some draymen in it, but did not know how to trust them.

Monday told me that they meet every other night, and he would to tell me more about it, when he saw me again. The old man, (meaning Vesey) told me to get some draymen who had horses, and if I was a good rider he would make me a captain of a troop.

When they meet they did not pray at the meeting in the kitchen. I was only at the Neck meeting about one hour—Peter Poyas was not at that meeting. I told Monday not to put my name on the list that they had—Peter was not at that meeting, but was to go with us.—Monday said he expected Peter there. I have no knowlege of any deposit of arms, ammunition or powder—I did not promise to any particular act in the business, or know of any other persons engaged in the business than those I have already mentioned—I never asked any person to join.

1. Smart Anderson was the slave of Robert Anderson. *CSCCD,* 69, identifies in 1822 one person by that name as the owner of a dry-goods store on 294 King Street. His attorney was Scottish-born Mitchell King (1783–1862), who had arrived in Charleston in 1805. King studied law under George Warren Cross, the attorney who counseled Denmark Vesey, and became a highly regarded jurist. In 1822, King resided at 66 Meeting Street with an office near St. Michael's Church. On King, see John Belton O'Neall, *Biographical Sketches of the Bench and Bar of South Carolina . . . ,* 2 vols. (Charleston, SC, 1859), vol. 1: 347–77. Hamilton, *Account,* 43, dates Anderson's arrest to Wednesday, July 10; the Senate transcript indicates that his trial took place on Tuesday, July 16. He was hanged on Friday, July 26.

2. The "Gullah" man referred to here was Jack Pritchard, a member of the African Church. On

the temporary closing of the church, see Charleston *Southern Patriot, and Commercial Advertiser,* Wednesday, June 10, 1818, in Part I of this volume on pp. 26–27.

3. Slaves in the antebellum South and in other slaveholding regions in the Americas used "Buckra" to refer to white persons. Hugh Goldie, *Dictionary of the Efik Language* (Glasgow, UK, 1862), 89–90, traced the word to the Efik "mbakara," meaning "master."

THE TRIAL of PHARO, a Mulatto Man, the prop-[erty] of Mr. John N. Thompson.[1]—His owner and David Ramsay, Esq,[2] his counsel attending.

EVIDENCE.

CHAR[L]ES testified as follows:—Pharo told me himself in Monday's shop that he was engaged in the conspiracy—I met him one day with a scythe in his cart, which he told me he was carrying to a blacksmith's to have made into a sword. About a week after, and previous to the 16th June, he said he was going to meet some young men who could tell him all about it—I have met him several times at Monday's.

Cross-examined by Mr. Ramsay—He bragged of what he could and would do with the white people. I did not hear Pharo tell a man to make a candlestick for him.

MONDAY testified as follows:—I know from our talk about it together that Pharo was one—he said he was making ready for the rising—two days after Peter was taken he told me, that if he could get a ticket, and a $50 bill he would take his horse and run away before he would be taken. On Sunday, about two weeks after Peter was taken up the first time (about 19th June) he pointed to the Archdale Church, where the white people were and said, when shall we be like them, I said when God pleased—Sunday before I was brought here he carried me to his Stable, and said he had told his master he had nothing to do in this business, which was a lie.

Cross-Examined by Mr. Ramsay—Charles told me that Pharo had a scythe which he was going to make into a sword.

PERAULT gave the following evidence:—I know that Pharo is one—one day in the streets we met and conversed on this business, when he told me that he had carried something to a Blacksmith to have a sword made for himself—I know he was just as willing as myself to join.

THE COURT *unanimously* found Pharo GUILTY, and passed upon him the sentence of DEATH.

1. Pharo (also "Pharaoh") Thompson was owned by Jane Thompson (also spelled "Thomson"; died 1840), the widow of John Thompson; her name does not appear in the 1822 *Charleston Directory.* In petitioning the state legislature for remuneration for the executed Pharo, Jane Thompson said that she had reared Pharo, that he had "always demeaned himself in the most orderly submission and Inofensive manner," and that he now supported her in her old age. She believed that Pharo, implicated in the plot by Perault Strohecker, had been led astray by others. See Petition of Jane Thompson to the Senate of South Carolina, November 22, 1822, which appears in Part V of this volume. Hamilton, *Account,* 43, places Pharo's arrest on Saturday, July 13; the Senate transcript indicates that his trial took place on Tuesday, July 16. He was hanged on Friday, July 26. See also the November 20, 1822, deposition of George Thompson, Jane's son, which appears in Part IV.

2. Attorney David Laurens Ramsay (1795–1826), a congregant at Benjamin Morgan Palmer's Circular Church and friend of Mary Lamboll Thomas Beach, resided in 1822 at 109 Queen Street and maintained an office with his partner Thomas John Gantt (1795–1861) at 74 Broad Street. See *CSCCD,* 95, and *BDSCHR* 5: 217–18.

THE TRIAL of SANDY VESEY, a Negro Man, the property of J. J. Schnell—His owner attending.[1]

EVIDENCE.

CHARLES[2] testified as follows:—Sandy had a hand in the rising—he told me that a gentleman had taken him up and asked him if he knew any thing about Jesse, that he said no, as there was no occasion to inform—that he knew how to make cartridges, and would make some—he told me in Monday's shop that he was one of those who had joined and was ready.

Cross-Examined by Mr. Schnell—He did not tell me to what company he belonged—he never gave his name to be put on a list that I know of.

MONDAY gave the following evidence:—Sandy has been in my shop, and he told me he had joined—he said on Sunday the 16th June, in Archdale-street, that he was waiting for Jesse who had gone to get a horse to go into the country—he was frequently in my shop, but only once spoke about this business—he appeared to be anxious and zealous, about it—he belongs to the African Church.

EDWARD P. SIMONS, Esq.[3] deposed as follows:—The day after Jesse was taken up, I examined this fellow, who stated that Jesse had said to him, "Vesey the Guard is too strong to night"—Sandy is a peaceable character—Jesse and himself married sisters.[4]

THE COURT *unanimously* found Sandy Vesey GUILTY, and passed upon him the sentence of DEATH; but recommended to the Governor to pardon him *upon condition that he be transported out of the limits of the United States.*

1. *CSCCD,* 97, identifies John Jacob Schnell, Sandy Vesey's owner, as a grocer who in 1822 lived at 175 Church Street. Schnell presumably purchased Sandy from fellow grocer John Paul, Sandy's previous owner. Hamilton, *Account,* 44, places Sandy's arrest on July 19. The Senate transcript, however, indicates that his trial took place on Tuesday, July 16, which again suggests that the legislative clerk was given disordered documents to transcribe and organize.

2. Charles Drayton.

3. Attorney Edward Peter Simons (1794–1823), of Huguenot descent, resided at 5 Laurens Street. See John Belton O'Neall, *Biographical Sketches of the Bench and Bar of South Carolina . . . ,* 2 vols. (Charleston, SC, 1859), vol. 2: 488–500, and *CSCCD,* 98.

4. Jesse Blackwood was Sandy's brother-in-law.

THE TRIAL OF PARIS, a negro man belonging to Miss Ball[1]—Mr. Minot[2] as the friend of his owner attending.

EVIDENCE.

MONDAY testified as follows:—Paris and Saby Gaillard were frequently in my shop—the week after Peter was taken up he came to me and said, your name is called, be on your guard—He acknowledged he had joined, and frequently came to know how the thing was going on—he belongs to the African Church.

PERAULT testified as follows:—I know that Paris knew of this business—I saw him at Monday's, and heard him speaking of the business—he was as much in it as I am.

THE COURT *unanimously* found Paris GUILTY, and passed upon him the sentence of DEATH, but recommended to the Governor to pardon him *upon condition that he be transported out of the limits of the United States.*

1. Although the "Narrative" of the trials in *OR* refers to a "Miss Ball," the "Calendar" of those arrested identifies Paris's owner as "Mrs. Ball." The woman in question is most likely Anne Simons Ball (1776–1840), the only daughter of Keating Simons, who was married twice: to Thomas Simons (1765–1805) in 1803 and to John Ball Jr. (1782–1834) in 1815. Mrs. Ball split time between the family's Hasell Street residence in Charleston and her Comingtee plantation on the Cooper River. Ancestral lore regarded her as a severe mistress. Paris Ball "was hired out to the city to Williams' Wharf [on the east side of Charleston near the city market], probably as a stevedore. The wharf job put him not far from the carpentry shop of Peter [Poyas], the lead prisoner." See Edward Ball, *Slaves in the Family* (New York: Farrar, Straus and Giroux, 1998), 266. Hamilton, *Account,* 44, places Paris's arrest on July 15. The Senate transcript indicates that his trial took place on Tuesday, July 16.

2. Mrs. Ball's "friend" in attendance was probably William B. Minott, not "Minot" (1777?–1832), a planter who lived at 8 Savage Street. See *CSCCD,* 91.

THE TRIAL of SABY GAILLARD, a free black man—Mr. Wesner[1] attending on his behalf as his friend.

EVIDENCE.

MONDAY testified as follows:—Saby frequently came to my shop and talked on this business—he and Denmark Vesey in my shop talked on this business—he took out one day out of his pocket on the Bay, a piece of news-paper, and asked me to read it—I did so at my shop, and afterwards he asked me if I had read it—I said yes—'twas about Boyer's battle in St. Domingo against the Spaniards,[2] and he said to me afterwards, if he had men he could do the same as Boyer—and that he could whip ten white men himself.

Cross-Examined by Mr. Wesner—he agreed with Vesey's discourse, which was to killed the whites.[3]

PERAULT gave the evidence following:—Saby said to me one day after Peter was taken up "I advise you to have nothing to do with this affair, let the Lord finish it and leave it to those who began it["]—Monday told me before this that Saby was concerned, and had given him a piece of paper to read.

THE COURT found Saby Gaillard GUILTY, and passed upon him the sentence of DEATH, but recommended to the Governor to pardon him *upon condition that he be transported out of the limits of the United States.*

1. The *DSGCC,* 101, lists a Samuel Gaillard, carpenter, at 3 Wentworth Street. The Senate transcript does not mention a "Wesner" attending the trial, but given Gaillard's occupation, Frederick Wesner (1788–1848), carpenter, architect, and city warden, appears the likely candidate. Wesner, a member of the Committee of Vigilance, played a key role in the capture of Denmark Vesey.

Hamilton, *Account,* 44, places Gaillard's arrest on Monday, July 15. The Senate transcript indicates that his trial took place two days later.

2. Jean-Pierre Boyer (1776–1850), a native of French Saint-Domingue, was president of Haiti from 1818 to 1843. When Spanish Santo Domingo became independent in late 1821, Boyer invaded and brought the entire island under his control. See Sara Fanning, *Caribbean Crossing: African Americans and the Haitian Emigration Movement* (New York: New York University Press, 2015), esp. chap. 3.

3. The Senate transcript reads merely "to kill the whites."

THE TRIAL of WILLIAM, a Negro Man, the Slave of Mrs. Colcock[1]—Mr. D. D. Bacot[2] attending as the friend of his owner.

EVIDENCE.

MONDAY testified as follows:—William has often been at my shop and asked me what was going on—I did not tell him any thing—one day he said to me a brother told him, five hundred men were making up for this purpose—he did not say that he was one.

CHARLES' evidence was as follows:—I met William two or three times at Monday's, but did not hear him say he had joined.

PERAULT gave this testimony:—I met William several times at Monday's, but don't know that he joined.

THE PRISONER in explanation of being so often at Monday's, stated to the Court, "when I went to Monday's it was to hear what was going on in Congress, as we expected that Congress was going to set us free, and as what was going on was printed in all the papers,[3] so that black as well as white might read it"—The prisoner had previously stated to Capt. T. H. Jervey,[4] who attended the trial, and one of whose wenches is the prisoner's wife, "Pompey Bryan told me that Mrs. Bryan's coachman held a commission, or was one of the officers of Denmark Vesey—that some hundred Draymen of this city were to act as horsemen. This was about a month ago (early in June.) He also told me that Denmark Vesey had ordered them all out so as to strike the first blow on Saturday night the 15th June. I told him then that I would have nothing to do with it and would go quietly to my bed; he said the same and we parted—One of Col. Cross' wenches about the house, a yellow complection, with a small boy about four or five years old, told me that Joseph, (Joe) the former cook of Col. Cross,[5] said that Morris Brown (the Bishop of the African Church) swore them on the Bible never to divulge the secret, even if they suffered death—Henry Drayton (alias Harry Bull, one of the Bishops or Ministers of the African Church) in crossing the Mall in front of Flinn's Church,[6] told me on a Sunday afternoon "*that the whites wanted nothing but a good spanking with the sword.*" Pompey Haig told me that there were some Frenchmen, blacks, very skilfull in making swords and spears, such as they used in Africa: this was about a month ago. He also told me that there were some Frenchmen determined if those men were hung, to rise and defend them, and that he heard there was a regular army ready in the woods to defend them."

THE COURT *unanimously* found William NOT GUILTY, and discharged him.

1. The "Mrs. Colcock" mentioned as the owner of William Colcock was Milicent (Jones) Colcock (1744–1829), the widow of John Colcock (1744–1782). For decades, Mrs. Colcock ran a

boarding school in Charleston on Lamboll Street. She should not be confused with Miss Susan Colcock (d. 1820), who for a short time also ran a boarding school for girls in Charleston. See "Historical Notes," *SCHGM* 4 (January 1903): 76; A. S. Salley Jr., "Capt. John Colcock and Some of His Descendants," *SCHGM* 3 (1902): 218–20; and *Camden* (SC) *Gazette*, January 28, 1819. Hamilton, *Account*, 46, places Colcock's arrest on July 12. The Senate transcript indicates that his trial took place four days later on Tuesday, July 16.

2. In 1822 Daniel D. Bacot (1799–1838) was a bookkeeper for the Bank of South Carolina and lived at 94 Church Street. See *CSCCD*, 69.

3. The Senate transcript added that this reference "alluded to the Missourie question."

4. Captain Thomas Hall Jervey (1778–1846) was for more than thirty years surveyor and inspector of customs in Charleston. In 1822, he resided at 51 Church Street. See A. S. Salley Jr., "The Jervey Family of South Carolina," *SCHGM* 7 (January 1906): 34–35; *CSCCD*, 84.

5. George Warren Cross (1783–1846), Denmark Vesey's attorney. See Part I, p. 97 n1.

6. Andrew Flinn (1773–1820) was the first pastor of the Second Presbyterian Church. The church still stands on Wragg Square Park, at 342 Meeting Street, close to where Gell ran his harness shop. It once numbered Denmark Vesey among its congregants. See George Reid, *A Sermon Delivered in the Second Presbyterian Church, Charleston, S.C. on the 17th September, 1820, Commemorative of the Life and Character of the Reverend Andrew Flinn, D.D., Late Pastor of Said Church* (Charleston, SC, 1820).

THE TRIAL of POLYDORE, a Negro Man, the property of Mrs. Faber[1]—Mr. C. H. Faber,[2] his owner's brother attending.

EVIDENCE.

BILLY, a negro man belonging to Mr. Bulkley, testified as follows:—Pollydore met once at my master's farm, at which meeting Gullah Jack was—he agreed with the rest to join and raise against the whites. One Sunday early in the morning, when the people were to rise, *Polydore brought to the farm those pike poles* (pointing to the bundle of pike poles found concealed on the farm and then in court) and told me to let them stay there, that Robert was coming—Polydore belongs to the African Congregation.

HARRY, Mr. Haig's slave,[3] gave the following evidence:—Polydore was in Jack's company—I met him at the meeting at Bulkley's farm, where they were talking about rising against the whites, and Polydore agreed to join in it.

Cross-examined by Mr. Faber—Jack was there, and when he made the proposition to join and raise against the whites, all present gave him an answer to join.

THE COURT *unanimously* found Polydore GUILTY, and passed upon him the sentence of DEATH.

1. Catherine Louisa (Clark) Faber, wife of William G. Faber (d. 1816), a Charleston lumber merchant, owned Polydore (also "Polydor") Faber. Although Vesey had a son named Polydore, Polydore Faber does not appear to be the "Polydore Vesey" to whom Bacchus Hammet referred in his July 17 confession. Hamilton, *Account*, 25, says Polydore Faber, "a Gullah" as well as a member of the African Church, provided handles for the pikes made by Tom Russell. The same source, page 43, dates Polydore's arrest to Thursday, July 11, and the Senate transcript indicates his trial took place five days later, on Tuesday, July 16. He was hanged on Friday, July 26.

2. Christian Henry Faber (1777–1828), William's brother, a factor, had purchased Polydore for his widowed sister-in-law to help support her and her five children. Polydore, about thirty-years old at the time of his arrest and appraised at one thousand dollars, possessed numerous skills, including those of sawyer and rope maker. He returned the Widow Faber about twelve dollars per month. See Catharine L. Faber, Petition Asking For Compensation for Her Slave Who was Executed for Participation in the Vesey Rebellion, November 18, 1822, no. 125, series S1655015, SCDAH (which appears in Part VI of this volume). In 1822, C. H. Faber lived at 296 King Street; his sister-in-law resided on Charlotte Street in Mazyckborough, Charleston Neck. See *CSCCD*, 78.

3. David Haig, Harry Haig's owner.

THE TRIAL of ROBERT, a Negro Man, the property of John Robertson[1]—His owner attending.

EVIDENCE.

CHARLES, testified as follows:—I met Robert at Tom Russel's, where he went for the Pikes, and Tom said to him, the pikes are at your house. Tom Russel asked him if he was not to go into the country for the people—he said he had sent word.

Cross-examined by Mr. Robertson—I saw him at Tom's about dark—it seemed to me from the conversation that he was going to fix on the pikes to the poles.

BILLY'S testimony was:—Robert belongs to Gullah Jack's Company—he was at the meeting of Gullah Jack's party at Bulkley's farm—He was at two meetings, and he tried to fire the pistol off but could not. The same day the pike poles were brought he told me not to stir, that the white people had heard of this business—Robert told me that Gullah Jack was the head man in this business—he said Gullah Jack went to Father Morris Brown about this business, and that Father Morris said, I am going to the North, but if you can get men you can try this business, but don't call my name—any thing that Jack wanted he sent Robert for—if any thing happened to Jack, Robert would be the next man. When Polydore brought the poles, he said Robert would know what to do with the poles, and when Robert came he said, let the poles lay there, the whites have found out the business.

Cross-examined by Mr. Robertson—There was no dispute between me and the Rope-walk people.

THE COURT *unanimously* found Robert GUILTY, and passed upon him the sentence of DEATH.

1. Robert Robertson, the slave of John Robertson (1762–1831), a Charleston merchant and banker and United States navy agent, was described as a skilled rope-maker, about thirty-five years of age. See Inhabitants of Charleston, Petition and Supporting Papers Asking Compensation for Their Slaves Who Were Executed for Involvement in a Slave Insurrection, n.d. [ca. 1822], no. 1839, series S165015, SCDAH. *CSCCD*, 59, locates John Robertson's business on Craft's Wharf and his home on 16 Meeting Street. Hamilton, *Account*, 43, dates Robert's arrest, together with two other of John Robertson's slaves to Thursday, July 11. The Senate transcript indicates that Robertson's trial took place five days later on Tuesday, July 16. He was hanged on Friday, July 26.

THE TRIAL OF JACK, a Negro Man belonging to Mr. J. S. Glenn.[1]

EVIDENCE.

CHARLES testified as follows:—Jack is engaged in this business—we have spoken together, and he told me he belonged to the horse company. I have met him once at Vesey's at a meeting about this business; Glenn there quoted Scripture to prove he would not be condemned for raising against the whites—he read a chapter out of the Bible. I have often met him at Monday's, where he was talking of this business—I have often conversed with him, when he always said he was one, and would rather be a horseman—he belongs to the African Church.

MONDAY'S Evidence was:—Jack was engaged in it—he and I talked about it, and he was making every preparation as well as myself about it—I once saw him at Vesey's when we were talking of the plans—He said as he had lame feet he would rather be a horseman—Vesey looked on him as one of his followers or men. I met him on the evening of the 15th June in the street with Benjamin Campbell—he said that Ben belonged to the horse after they had parted—he said he was preparing to rise on Sunday the 16th June—he was often at my shop—Charles Drayton was sometimes present.

PERAULT gave the following evidence:—Jack was concerned as much as myself—I met him at Monday's first, when he said he was one, and the third time I met him at Vesey's, where we met purposely on this affair—Ned Bennett and Peter Poyas were there—Jack agreed to go into the country to bring down the people to fight against the whites—before the 16th June he sent his wife to me to say he wanted to get my horse to go into the country—at the meeting at Vesey's, Jack carried about a hat to get money to pay a man to make pikes—I gave 12½ cents—Jack put in the same—the second time I met him at the Battery, he said he was going into the country to bring the blacks down—he said he had joined as a horseman—at the meeting at Vesey's besides Ned and Peter, Monday, Charles, Bacchus, and Smart Anderson were present, and John Enslow and several others whose names I know not.

BACCHUS[2] testified as follows:—I saw Jack at Vesey's the first time I met there—he was the man who read the Bible—he passed the hat round that night for the contribution—Monday, Charles, Pharo and Smart, and others whom I knew not were there.

THE COURT *unanimously* found Jack GUILTY, and passed upon him the sentence of DEATH.

(*Note.* On the trial of Charles Billings,[3] it was proved, that Jack Glenn intended to sleep at Mr. Billing's Livery Stables on the night of the 16th June, for the purpose of assisting in saddling the horses for the coloured people.)

1. The Senate transcript refers to the accused as "Jacob Glenn alias Jack Glenn." John S. Glen, Jacob's owner, was a planter and member of Benjamin Morgan Palmer's Circular Church. He owned property and slaves in St. James Goose Creek, and in 1822 lived in Charleston at 53 Tradd Street. See *CSCCD,* 43. Inhabitants of Charleston, Petition and Supporting Papers Asking Compensation for Their Slaves Who Were Executed for Involvement in a Slave Insurrection, n.d. [ca. 1822], no. 1839, series S165015, SCDAH, identifies "Jacob" as a carpenter, aged twenty-three. Hamilton, *Account,* 26, refers to the slave Jacob Glen as a preacher and dated his arrest to Tuesday, July 16.

The Senate transcript indicates that Glen's trial was held on Wednesday, July 17. He was hanged on Friday, July 26.

2. Bacchus Hammet.

3. Charles Billings was tried two days later, on Friday, July 19.

THE TRIAL of LOT, a Negro Man, the property of Mr. Forrester[1]—His owner attending.

EVIDENCE.

MONDAY testified as follows:—Lot and I have been talking about this business, and he said he was one engaged in this insurrection and was making ready, this was at my shop where he frequently was, and always talking on this business—he was one of the African Church, but I believe he had been turned out.

FRANK'S evidence was:—I heard Lot tell Vesey that he had gone up to Santee, but before he had got there he met some black persons who told him that the driver had heard it, and told the overseer, and that he is in consequence had to make his escape.

JACK belonging to Mrs. Purcell, gave the following evidence:—Lot was to have gone up to Stono, to a large meeting where they made great preparations for him, but he did not come—I was then up there—I afterwards met him at Monday's and taxed him about not fulfilling his promise—he said his business prevented him.

JESSE before he acknowledged his guilt, requested that Lot, who was not at that time suspected, might be sent for and made to confront him. This being done he first confessed his own guilt, and then charged Lot with being an accomplice, and said in an impressive manner "I am guilty, and so is that man—he is as deep in it as I am—if I am hung he ought to be hung, and if he is passed over no man ought to be condemned by the Court—Lot was the man who said to me on Gibb's & Harper's Wharf, that nothing could be done without fire, and that he had the combustibles for it.*

* Lot denied Jesse's accusations, and as no one at that time but Jesse accused him, against whom Lot volunteered his evidence and was principally instrumental in his conviction, the Court dismissed Lot.[2] After Monday, Jack (Purcell,) and Frank had been arrested, however, Lot, (fearing they would inculpate him) absconded, and was arrested through the vigilance and activity of several gentlemen, who plant in St. James' Santee, as he was attempting to effect his escape across Hibben's Ferry, for the purpose (it is supposed) of getting beyond the limits of the State.

A quantity of *slow match* which was found on Gibb's & Harper's Wharf, and then in Court, was shewn to Captain C. L. BLACK,[3] *Arsenal Keeper*, who testified that the slow match produced to him resembled that in the Arsenal precisely, and he believed it to be a part of the same.

(*Note.* Lot was proved by the next witness to have been in the employment of Mr. Peigne,[4] who is often engaged in the Arsenal, and sometimes has servants with him there.)

NED, a Negro Man belonging to Mr. Piegne, *a witness on behalf of the Prisoner*, testified as follows:—I was at work with Lot on a house in my master's yard, when Vesey came there—Lot told him not to come in, that his master would not allow it—this was about the first of June.

THE COURT *unanimously* found Lot GUILTY, and passed upon him the sentence of DEATH.

1. Alexander J. G. Forrester, a minor, owned Lot Forrester. Alexander was probably the son of deceased parents Captain Alexander Forrester and Susannah Forrester, a seamstress, who married in 1802. See Petition of Jeremiah Yates, John R. Rogers, and A. W. Campbell to the South Carolina Senate, n.d. [ca. 1822] no. 1745, series S165015, SCDAH; "Marriage and Death Notices from the City Gazette," *SCHGM* 27 (1926): 98; Richard Hrabowski, *Directory for the District of Charleston* . . . (Charleston, SC, 1809), 38. Hamilton, *Account,* 25, 43, says Lot Forrester was the "courier" of the plot and indicates that he was initially arrested on Thursday, June 27. The Senate transcript indicates that Lot's trial was held on Wednesday, July 17. He was hanged on Friday, July 26.

2. Since Jesse Blackwood was hanged on Tuesday, July 2, portions of his confession were here read into the court transcript. Hamilton did not indicate the date of Lot's second arrest.

3. Captain Christopher Latell Black (d. 1843) was keeper of the arsenal.

4. "Mr. Peigne" refers to James Laurence Peigne (1784–1839), a Paris-born grocer and artisan who supplied everything from artillery munitions to cabinets. In 1816 he lived at 55 Market Street. The South Carolina legislature received from Peigne a bill "for expenses incurred by the regiment of Artillery in Charleston" during the Vesey affair. See *CSCCD,* 21; Charleston *City Gazette and Commercial Daily Advertiser,* December 18, 1821; E. Milby Burton, *Charleston Furniture, 1700–1825* (Charleston, SC: Charleston Museum, 1955), 111; James L. Peigne to Senate of South Carolina, n.d. [ca. 1823], no. 1887, series no. S165015, SCDAH.

THE TRIAL of ADAM,[1] a Negro Man, belonging to Mr. John Robertson[2]—His owner attending.

EVIDENCE.

HARRY testified as follows:—I met Adam at Bulkley's Farm, at a meeting there for rising against the whites—I know that he belongs to Gullah Jack's company, and that he knew the meetings were for considering on this subject—he did not tell me that he was one, but I heard him agree to be one in this purpose—I heard him acknowledge that he was in Gullah Jack's company—he was one of the African Church.

BILLY gave the evidence which follows:—Adam was twice at Bulkley's Farm, and once at Thayer's, to attend the meetings there—he belonged to the Gullah Company, to rise against the whites—he told me so—I heard him say so more than once.

THE COURT *unanimously* found Adam GUILTY, and passed upon him the sentence of DEATH.

1. About thirty-five years of age, Adam worked as a foreman at a ropewalk along with slaves John and Robert Robertson. Both Harry Haig and Billy Bulkley implicated Adam in the plotting, saying that he attended meetings about the projected insurrection at Bulkley's farm. Harry Haig also said that Adam belonged to Gullah Jack's troop. See Inhabitants of Charleston, Petition and Supporting Papers Asking Compensation for Their Slaves Who Were Executed for Involvement in a Slave Insurrection, n.d. [ca. 1822], no. 1839, series S165015, SCDAH. The second of John Robertson's slaves to be accused, Adam was arrested on Thursday, July 11, with John and Robert

Robertson. See Hamilton, *Account,* 43. The Senate transcript indicates that his trial was held six days later on Wednesday, July 17. He was hanged on Friday, July 26.

2. On John Robertson (1762–1831), Adam's owner, see p. 223 n1, above.

THE TRIAL of JOHN,[1] a Negro Man, the property of Mr. John Robertson—His owner attending.

EVIDENCE.

HARRY testified as follows:—John was engaged in this business—he belonged to Gullah Jack's Company, and was at the same meeting with Adam—he acknowledged that he belonged to the same company that I did—I met him but once at Bulkley's Farm—he belongs to the African Church.

BILLY gave the following evidence:—John belongs to the Gullah Company—I heard him say so once—he was twice at the meetings at the Farm.[2]

THE COURT *unanimously* found John GUILTY, and passed upon him the sentence of DEATH.

1. The last of the slaves of the merchant John Robertson to be tried, the slave of the same name was arrested on Thursday, July 11, and the Senate transcript confirms that his trial was held immediately after Adam Robertson's on Wednesday, July 17. He was hanged with Adam and Robert on Friday, July 26. Michael P. Johnson, "Denmark Vesey and His Co-Conspirators," *WMQ* 58 (2001): 926, asserts that the *OR* "provides no chronology for the various trials and testimony" and "simply listed trials and witness testimonies without indicating who said what when." Johnson is technically correct; since Kennedy and Parker were not writing for posterity, they did not date the trials. But by cross-listing the dates of arrest provided in Hamilton's *Account* with the trial dates provided in the Senate transcript, as we have done here, one can see that with four exceptions only—the trials for Sandy Vesey, Agrippa Perry, and the joint trial of Samuel Guifford and Robert Hadden—the *OR* did present the trials in chronological order. And in the case of Sandy Vesey's trial, the dating inconsistency was probably the fault of the Senate clerk, not the authors of the *OR*.

2. As in the previous case, the slaves providing testimony were Harry Haig and Billy Bulkley. The Senate transcript described them both as using their surnames.

THE TRIAL of BUTCHER, a Negro Man, the Slave of Mr. Gibb's.[1]

EVIDENCE.

CHARLES testified as follows:—Butcher belongs to the Company, and is engaged in this business—I met him at Bulkley's Farm—he is one who acknowledged in my presence that he was to rise against the whites. The object of the meeting at Bulkley's was to consider about this business.—He belongs to the African Church.

BILLY'S evidence was as follows:—Butcher Gibbes belongs to Peter Ward's religious class.[2]

Charles being the only witness against Butcher without any corroborating circumstances; THE COURT found him NOT GUILTY, but suggested to his owner the propriety of sending him away.

1. Butcher was the slave of James Ladson Gibbes (1792–1831), not Gibb's, a planter who in 1819 lived on the corner of George and St. Philip's streets. See *CSCCD,* 43; Richard J. Bryan, "Epitaphs,

the Gibbes Family Cemetery, John's Island," *SCHGM* 50 (1949): 70. Hamilton, *Account,* 46, dates Butcher's arrest to Thursday, July 11. The Senate transcript indicates that his trial was held on Wednesday, July 17.

2. The Senate transcript indicates that Captain Christopher Black testified against Butcher Gibbes as well.

THE TRIAL of SCIPIO, a Negro Man, belonging to Mr. Wm. Simms[1]—His owner attending.

EVIDENCE.

PERAULT testified as follows:—Scipio belongs to those who are to rise against the whites—he hired a horse from me on Saturday, the 8th of June, to go into the country, to get the negroes to come down at the time the rising was to commence. I examined him myself, to see if he was one of my friends to fight against the whites—I met him at Mr. Aiken's lot,[2] after the 8th, when we walked down together, as far as St. Philips' and Wentworth-streets. We talked about this business—the third time I met him near Mr. Murphy's in King-street,[3] on Sunday previous to the execution of Peter Poyas—I then said to Scipio, this thing was all up and now dead; Scipio replied, that all the people he had engaged were cowards and had drawn back, but that he was willing to go on as much as I myself could be.

Cross-Examined by Mr. Simms—Scipio hired the horse, but another man took the horse who paid me $2 in part, and Adam a free man the remaining $1, the hire being $3—I don't know the man who took the horse, but I'd know him if I saw him again.

Re-examined—Scipio hired the horse and said he would send for it, and when the man came for the horse, he said Scipio had sent for the horse—when my horse was brought back the man was on my horse, and Scipio in company with him on another horse—my stable was near Flinn's Church, and they came from towards the lines, this was on Sunday Evening, 9th June. He belongs to the African Church.

MONDAY gave the evidence following:—Jack Purcell told me that Scipio had gone into the country to collect people to come down.

CHARLES testified as follows:—Monday told me pretty much what he has himself stated to the Court.

Mr. WM. SIMMS deposed as follows:—Scipio is an orderly, sober and industrious servant. I raised him, and we have worked together.

Mrs. FICK, *a witness on behalf of the prisoner,* testified as follows:—Scipio never gave to me any arms to keep for him or any thing else—I have always thought him a steady, sober negro, and never heard any thing amiss of him.[4]

Cross-examined by the Court—I never said that Scipio had left a sword or pistol with me*.

* It was reported that Mrs. Fick said that Scipio had left a sword and pistol with her to keep for him.

AGRIPPA, a Negro Man belonging to Mrs. Perry, *a witness on behalf of the prisoner,* testified as follows:—I requested Scipio to hire a horse for me to go into the country with, about the last day of the first week in June, mine being sick—Scipio carried me to the man from whom the horse was hired, I don't know the man—he and I went up on horseback to my mistress' plantation, on Horse-Savannah, where we went for my tools, and returned the next day, Sunday—this was all we went for.

Cross-examined by the court:—The man's name was Perautt, who lives on the green—I paid $2, and when I returned, paid him the $1—when I received the horse, Scipio was not with me—I had a pass—Scipio's name was not in my pass—I brought down my mallet, chisel and axe—I left town on Saturday, about 10 o'clock—about two weeks before this I was in the country.

As soon as Agrippa's examination ceased, Perault was brought into Court, and immediately recognized him to be the man who had hired his horse, though he did not know his name—The Intendant then committed Agrippa for trial. In consequence of this charge against Agrippa, whose testimony was so important to Scipio, Mr. Simms requested the Court not to decide upon Scipio's case until Agrippa was tried, to which request the Court acceeded. Agrippa was not tried until five days after, as his owner asked for time to send into the country and bring down some of the Negroes as witnesses who were on the plantation when Agrippa and Scipio arrived there—Agrippa's trial therefore was not the next after Scipio's; but as in forming their decision on Scipio's case, the testimony given in Agrippa's was considered by the Court, it is thought adviseable, that, in this publication, the report of the one trial should imediately succeed the other.

THE COURT *unanimously* found Scipio GUILTY, and passed upon him the following sentence: "That he be imprisoned in the Work-House of Charleston, until his master, under the direction of the City Council of Charleston, shall send him out of the limits of the United States, into which he is not to return under penalty of death.["]

1. William Sims (1765–1853), not Simms, a planter, who in 1822 lived on Hudson Street in Mazyck borough, Charleston Neck, owned Scipio Simms (also rendered "Sims"). In 1809, William Sims was elected an infantry captain of the Charleston Neck Rangers and in that capacity tracked down and jailed runaway slaves. William Sims testified to Scipio's worth as a skilled slave, sawyer, carpenter, and drayman, and how in his seniority he had become reliant on Scipio. See *CSCCD,* 98; *Charleston Courier,* December 29, 1809; William Sims, Petition to the Senate of South Carolina, n.d. [ca. 1822], no. 1757, series S165015, SCDAH; Wilson Gee, "The Bowles, Anderson and Shelton Families as Related to the Descendants of William Sims (1765–1833), and His Wife, Elizabeth Shelton Sims (1767–1833), of Union County, South Carolina," *WMQ* 16 (1936): 608. Hamilton, *Account,* 45, dates Scipio's arrest to July 13. The Senate transcript indicates that his trial began five days later on Thursday, July 18, and concluded on July 19.

2. William Aiken (1778–1831), a prominent Irish-born merchant, banker, planter, and politician, lived in 1822 on King Street Road, Charleston Neck. In 1816, he ran a store at 128 Queen Street. See *CSCCD,* 69; *BDSCHR* 5: 3–4; *CDSG,* 6.

3. In 1822 Peter Murphy (d. 1827), an Irish-born grocer, resided at 223 King Street. *CSCCD,* 92; "Died," *South-Carolina State Gazette and Columbia Advertiser,* September 15, 1827.

4. "Mrs. Fick" refers to Ruth Fick, the wife of Charles Fick (1754?–1823), a German-born grocer, who in 1822 resided at 57 St. Philip's Street. See *Charleston Courier,* July 24, 1823; *CSCCD,* 79; Petition 21382520, Records of the Equity Court, Bills, no. 1825-14, SCDAH.

THE TRIAL OF AGRIPPA, a Negro Man belonging to Mrs. Perry,[1] Mr. Edward Perry,[2] the Son of his owner, his Counsel Benjamin F. Dunkin, Esq.,[3] Mr. Bartholomew Carrol,[4] the friend of his owner, and Mr. William Simms attending.

EVIDENCE.

PERAULT testified as follows:—On the 8th of June about 10 o'clock, A.M. I met the prisoner, who said he was going into the country on some business, which would be good to me and good to him. On his return, I went to him, when after some conversation, he informed me that he had gone into the country to get men to join this insurrection, and that he had procured some men—He hired a horse from me, for which he paid me two dollars in my hand, and got security for the other dollar, which he afterwards paid through Adam Creighton—the price of the horse was three dollars.

Cross-examined by Mr. Dunkin—I never saw the prisoner before he came for the horse—I saw him the second time after he came from the country, when I examined him particularly, and he confessed that he had got some men to join in the insurrection. Scipio Simms made the contract about the horse, and not the prisoner.

Mr. EDWARD PERRY, *a witness on behalf of the prisoner,* deposed as follows:—My mother allows the prisoner to keep a horse in the country where he usually resides—my mother informed me yesterday that his horse is lame, and has been so for some time. (The general ticket to work out in town or country from his Mistress was produced in evidence.) The mother and father-in-law of the prisoner resides on my plantation, where the prisoner is in the habit of going about once a fortnight—There were not more than four or five able bodied negroes on my plantation when the prisoner went for his tools.

Cross-examined by the Court—I have some near neighbours in the country at whose plantations there are many negroes.

KITT, a Negro man, belonging to Mr. Perry, *a witness on behalf of the prisoner,* testified as follows: I was not present when Agrippa and Scipio arrived at the plantation—on my return home in the evening I met them—Agrippa's horse was so lame, that he once returned home on foot—he returned next day to town—I do not know Scipio—there were only four or five old persons on the plantation, the prime hands had come to town.

ROBIN, a Negro Man, belonging to Mr. Perry, *a witness on behalf of the Prisoner,* testified as follows:—I went into the country with Scipio and Agrippa on Saturday morning—We arrived 'twixt three and four o'clock at Mr. Perry's plantation—we stopped on no plantation, nor to talk with any Negro on the way up—When on the plantation, Agrippa went to his house, and I to my mother's—about eight o'clock Agrippa and Scipio were in bed—Agrippa answered me when I came to the door, that he had gone to bed—I saw Agrippa about seven o'clock next day preparing to start—we started for town directly after breakfast, and did not stop on the way to speak to any one, or at any plantation, and arrived in town about three o'clock—When we got down, I carried my horse from whence I got it—they went to carry their's to the place they got them from—when on the plantation no strange negroes were there, and I don't believe Agrippa or Scipio went off the plantation—they were working together in town, and as one could not go on without the other, as one had to go into the country for his tools, the other accompanied him—there were only about five men on the plantation—I was not all the time with Agrippa and Scipio, that they were on the plantation.

Cross-Examined by the Court—As soon as we arrived on the place, which was about three or four o'clock, we separated, and I did not see the others 'till about eight o'clock, when I called at their house, and found them in bed—from that time to 7 next morning, I did not see them.

Re-Examined—I saw their horses frequently together with mine on the place before 8 o'clock—I saw them together first about an hour after we arrived, and before eight o'clock they were put up—The nearest neighbour is about one mile and three quarters off.

DOLL, a Negro Woman belonging to Mr. Perry, *a witness on behalf of the prisoner,* gave the following evidence:—I was on the plantation when Scipio and Agrippa came up—they came up about an hour before sun-down—I stayed at the big-house—Robin stop't at the big-house, and Agrippa and Scipio went on to Agrippa's mother's house—I did not see them again till next morning—about dusk they sent to me for some clauber[5]—I saw them turn out their horses in the plantation directly after they arrived—and I saw their horses about sun-down—they could not have gone out of the place without passing the big-house, unless they rode or walked through the field, and I did not see them pass—Mr. Singleton's is about a quarter of a mile distant—(Mr. Carroll says about a mile and a half) the driver don't allow a horse to go through the field—I saw them next day after breakfast—there are no prime men on the plantation—all old or boys.

Cross-Examined by the Court—There are about four taskable men on the plantation—Mr. Lee's plantation is not half as far as Singleton's.

LIDY, Agrippa's mother, testified as follows:—I was at home when Agrippa and Scipio came to the plantation, not long before sun-down—they turned their horses loose, then came in and sat down—they did not leave the house that night—Robin came there after they went to bed and called them, but no answer was given him—I got up before either of them next morning—and then I saw them laying as I left them at night—I don't think they could have gone out of the house and I not know it—they had no talk with the people on the plantation—they never left the house further than the door.

Cross-Examined by the Court—I slept but little that night, my grand-child kept me awake—they carried away Agrippa's tools next day—Robin called three times, but no answer was given—they slept in the Hall and I in my room—the tools were some chissels and plains.

Mr. EDWARD PERRY, again examined—The nearest plantation is about three quarters of a mile, but there is but one negro man on it, the next nearest better than a mile.

JACK belonging to Mrs. Purcell testified that Scipio had spoken once to him about the insurrection.

THE COURT *unanimously* found Agrippa GUILTY, and passed upon him the following sentence:—"That he be imprisoned in the Work-House of Charleston until his owner, under the direction of the City Council of Charleston shall send him out of the limits of the United States, into which he is not to return under penalty of death."

1. Widow Ann Drayton Perry, the daughter of John Drayton (1715–1779), owned Agrippa, a valuable wheelwright and carpenter in his late twenties. Ann married Edward Perry Jr. (1775?–1800), a planter, in 1793 and maintained a townhouse at 13 Bull Street, just a few houses from Vesey's rented home at 20 Bull Street. Around November 1822, Ann petitioned the South Carolina's senate, asking that Agrippa, punished by transportation out of the state, be restored to her or that she be remunerated the claimed value ($1,000) of the slave. In the petition, which appears in Part V of this volume, Ann Perry cast doubt on the accuracy of the testimony against Agrippa by Perault Strohecker. Hamilton's *Account*, 45, dates Perry's arrest to Friday, July 19, and the Senate transcript indicates his trial was held on Tuesday, July 23. The two trials above and below Perry's were held on July 18; this appears to be one of the few trials taken out of chronological order in the *OR*.

2. Edward Drayton Perry (d. 1833).

3. Pennsylvania-born, Harvard-educated Benjamin F. Dunkin (1792–1874), kept a law office at 69 Meeting Street. He had a long career in South Carolina politics and would become a successful planter, owning in 1850 several hundred slaves. See *CSCCD*, 77; *BDSCHR* 5: 76–78.

4. Irish-born Bartholomew Carrol (also "Carroll") owned more than fifty slaves and resided on the west end of Boundary Street on Charleston Neck, roughly two blocks from Perry's home. His daughter Rachel married Edward Drayton Perry. See *CSCCD*, 73; *BDSCHR* 4: 102–3.

5. Given the references to tools below, this was probably a craw bar, a crowbar-like instrument used to pull up spikes.

THE TRIAL of DICK,[1] a Negro Man, the Slave of Mr. William Simms—His owner attending.

EVIDENCE.

PERAULT testified as follows:—Dick and I met on a Saturday evening in the Cabinet-Maker's lot, next to Monday's, where were met on this business, Gullah Jack, George Vanderhorst and Charles Drayton—Jack said he was going in his canoe into the country to get people—Dick said he belonged to Gullah Jack's Band, and said he was willing and ready like me—the second time we met at the corner of Market-street, we walked up King-street, and he told me he was ready at any time—the third time I met him between Craft's and Smith's Wharf, and we sat down and conversed on this business—I again asked him, and he again said, he was ready at any time we were ready—I never met him any where else.

HARRY'S evidence was as follows:—Dick belonged to Gullah Jack's Company—I met him at Bulkley's Farm, and he confessed he was ready and willing to join—the meeting was about this business—he joined before I did.

Cross-Examined by Mr. Simms—We all consulted together at the meeting, and all agreed—this was a little before this business broke out.

CHARLES testified as follows:—I saw Dick in the Lot of the Mahogany Shop near Monday's, attending one of the meetings—he was one of Jack's Company—this he said out of his own mouth, and that he was ready.

(*Note.* The prisoner confessed he was at this house, but said he went there to see some one.)

BILLY gave the following evidence:—Dick was at three of the meetings on this business; once at Thayers, and twice at Bulkley's Farm—he was there when they tried to fire off the pistol, and it went off in his hand.

(*Note.* The prisoner confessed he was sometimes at Bulkley's Farm, but said he went there to see Billy.)

Cross-Examined by Mr. Simms—If I had not been there I would not have known of this business.

Re-Examined by the Court—Whenever he came, he came in company with Gullah Jack, they met at the Farm to talk on this business.

THE COURT *unanimously* found Dick GUILTY, and passed upon him the sentence of DEATH.

1. A sworn statement, dated November 20, 1822, by Richard Hart in William Sims, Petition and Supporting Papers, n.d., series S165015, no. 1757, SCDAH, described Dick Sims, the second slave of William Sims to face trial, as a wheelwright and carpenter in his mid-twenties with an appraised value of one thousand dollars. Hamilton, *Account,* 43, dates Dick's arrest to Saturday, July 13, and the Senate transcript indicates that his trial took place five days later on Thursday, July 18. Dick was hanged on Friday, July 26.

THE TRIAL of BACCHUS, a Negro Man, belonging to Mr. Benjamin Hammet[1]—Francis S. Belzer, Esq.[2] his owner's Counsel attending.

EVIDENCE.

PERAULT testified as follows—I engaged Bacchus myself to join in this business; he was one of my recruits—I carried him to Vesey's myself—he was willing to join—Bacchus took one keg of powder from his master and gave it to Vesey, who carried it to Monday's—he promised to give me a sword but did not do so.

Cross-examined by Mr. Belzer—Bacchus told me that he had carried the powder to Vesey.

MONDAY'S evidence was as follows:—Bacchus told me he was one in this business—he has often been at my shop and I there had a keg of powder got by him. I saw him one night at Vesey's.

Cross-examined by Mr. Belzer—Bacchus and Perault brought the powder to my shop.

CHARLES gave the following testimony:—I met Bacchus at Monday's and at Vesey's I was present when he brought the powder to Vesey's—he told me he had got three swords, one for himself, one for Perault and one for Ned Bennett.

THE COURT *unanimously* found Bacchus GUILTY, and passed upon him the sentence of DEATH.

Mr. Hammet, whilst he was not desirous that Bacchus should escape punishment, yet was anxious to save his life, and previously to his trial handed to the Court in writing a confession which Bacchus had made to him, and stated, that he came forward with this candid confession of Bacchus, in hopes of saving his life thereby; but that if the Court thought his case did not admit of a less punishment than death, he then requested that his confession should not be used against him. The Court after consultation determined to proceed to his trial.—The following CONFESSION though not used against Bacchus is now given to the public:

Perault, when hauling cotton from my master's store, told me in the yard, secretly, that he wanted me to go to Society with him. I asked what Society? He told me, never mind what Society, and said he would call for me that night—he did call and I went with him. Perault carried me to Denmark Vesey's house, by Bennett's mill[3]—there I met about twelve men, among whom was Monday Gell, and Smart Anderson. After I got in they fastened the gate—it was before nine o'clock—Denmark and Perault took me to one side, Perault told me they were going to tell me something; this was in another room, not before the gang—Denmark and Perault said that they were going to turn to and fight the white people, and take the country, and that New-Orleans was taken.[4] I considered a long while, and they found me considering, and at last I said to Perault I was very sorry he brought me there, I did not wish to belong to such a Society—Denmark Vesey said to me before Perault, that the one that did not wish to join the Society must be put to death as an enemy—he told all the gang so after he went back with me into the room. Denmark told the gang, that they must meet at his house that night next week. Perault told me to try and get powder, that the gang would *throw in and make it up to me.* They all threw in the night of meeting 12½ cents each, and I also. This money was thrown in to give a man to go into the country and bring down the country negroes when they were all ready. When I asked about arms, and where they were, Denmark recommended to them to look thro' the town for the stores that had the most guns. Perault then jumped up and said "Bacchus don't you know where Capt. Martindale's arms is,"[5] I said, yes, my man, but you can't get them, and you had better drop this thing altogether. About two or three days after this last affair. Perault came to me and told me that they had caught Denmark, and carried me down to Monday Gell. Monday and Perault told me that Denmark said that if they caught him, he would tell no body's name, and that I must not tell his, Perault's name, nor Monday's, and they would not mention mine. I took the keg of powder out of the back store of my master, and carried it in a bag to Denmark, with a man belonging to Mr. Bennett which I believe is a blacksmith—Bennett's man met me at my master's gate—I suppose Pritchard's Gullah Jack and Perault carried the powder to Monday from Denmark's house. In company with Denmark Vesey and Perault, Denmark told me to get what arms I could—I said I could get one horseman's sword in a scabbard, which I took to Denmark's house. I also said I could get a pistol, but was afraid my master would miss it—Perault told me never mind he could make me easy about it—I did take the pistol to Denmark's house with the sword, on Sunday night the 16th June. Denmark told me previously, I must not go home—this Denmark told at the meeting previous, and said they were to go up the road and meet the country negroes. Last night, when I was put in the room in the Work-House with Perault, he told me Gullah Jack had buried the powder, and I think Perault knows where it is. All the negroes engaged in the plot were ordered by Denmark to leave their masters and go up the road.—The night they carried me to Denmark, I was so frightened that I was obliged to say yes; for they threatened to kill every one that did not wish to join. A large book like a Bible was open before them at Denmark's house; but I do not know whether it was to sign names in, or what purpose. At the first meeting at Denmark's, they asked me my name, and Perault answered my name was Bacchus, belonging to Mr. Hammet—Denmark asked me which Hammet? I said Benjamin Hammet, the gentleman who sued Lorenzo Dow.[6]

The week after Denmark was dead, Perault told me to mind and keep myself ready, that they intended to come up at the corner where the arms of the Neck Company is kept; and I said very well; they were to take the arms, and I was to assist them, they were to break open the door—Monday Gell can tell who is at the head of this last arrangement—I believe Perault knows all about it—Gullah Jack was to distribute the Powder amongst us—Perault told me that they had a Blacksmith to make daggers for this party, and that they had made some. On Sunday, 16th June, he told me, *they had three or four hundred daggers*—he told me on the 11th July, the night I was committed, that I must not tell his name or any thing about it—This was the reason I was afraid to tell or make a confession to my master, Mr. Hammet, on this morning, the 12th July—Perault is the fellow that has brought me into this scrape—A fellow about my size, a dark black skin negro, who I believe is called *Charles,* took me up the road just before you come to the forks of the road, on the Meeting-street road, to a Farm—the House on the Farm *has a Piazza on the top;* Charles told the negro man on the Farm, mind next Sunday the business is to be done; meaning to kill the white people; and that the negroes from the country were to stop at this Farm—Denmark Vesey and his party from town was to go there to the Farm to meet the negroes from the country—I solemnly declare as to being brought into this scrape; and that Perault is the one who enticed me into it—At the first meeting at Denmark Vesey's house, on the breaking up of the meeting Denmark said—"Friends you all throw in seven pence a piece, those who have got it, it is to make up for a friend to pay his wages to his master, before he went into the country to bring the people down.["]

At the meeting at Denmark Vesey's the first time I was there, I saw a fat black fellow whom I think was Denmark's son, as he looked very much like Denmark, had a full face, that he could read, as he shewed Monday Gell the large book on the table, and said to Monday, shewing him some of the leaf of the book, "see here, they are making real game at we" and Monday looked at the book and said nothing—Denmark took me a one side and said, "we shan't be slaves to these damn rascals any longer. We must kill every one that we can get hold of, and drive the rest out of the city." No one was with me when I was requested by Charles (whom he calls Charles Drayton now) to go to the Farm at the Forks of the Roads; when Charles set out to go there, he came from Monday Gell's house, met me, and carried me to Monday's—Monday was to go with Charles to the Farm, but put it off on account of having a hog to kill, and said to Charles, let this friend go with you; and I and Charles went to the Farm—when we went to the Farm, Charles asked a negro woman on the Farm, if the old daddy was home, and she called him—this old daddy is an African, marked on both sides of his face—Charles took him in the stable, and also myself, and told him about the country negroes coming there, &c. The fellow who helped me to carry the powder belonged to Bennett I think, because I have seen this man in Bennett's Blacksmith shop at the mill, years before this; Perault told me that they had *two or three hundred bayonets made already*—Perault is a Blacksmith—I believe *Monday* knows as well as Perault where the arms and bayonets are—Monday said they were to have mounted horsemen—that many Draymen belonged to it who had horses—at Denmark's house they all rose up and swore, lifting up the right hand, saying, "we will not tell if we are found out, and if they kill us we will not tell on any one." Denmark said they must all say so, and that they did say so. Denmark told me that he gave the sword to Perault, and Perault gave it to a man named Caesar—I know no other Caesar but a Drayman named Caesar—Smith a tall negro, an African, who is an intimate acquaintance of Perault's, and who is often at the stable where Perault keeps his horses—Perault told me that French negroes were amongst them—Denmark said country born, Africans and all kinds joined—Monday and Perault appeared to be the intimate friends of Denmark, he thought a heap of them—Denmark took the pistol for himself, it was given to him in his own hand—Those meetings were held at Denmark's house, where he had a black wife—two or three women were at the house ironing.

1. Bacchus worked as a porter for his master, Benjamin Hammet (1794?–1826), a merchant who owned a store on King Street Road, Charleston Neck. At the time of the plot, Hammet also served as an officer in the Charleston militia and kept arms and munitions in his store. See *CDSG*, 9; *Charleston Courier*, November 29, 1820; Charleston *City Gazette and Commercial Daily Advertiser*, December 2, 1826. Hamilton, *Account*, 43, dates Bacchus's arrest to Thursday, July 11. The Senate transcript indicates that his trial was held immediately following that of Dick Sims on Thursday, July 18, and that his confession was given to his master on July 12, the day after his arrest. He was hanged on Friday, July 26.

2. The reference is probably to attorney Frederick S. Belser (d. 1851), who in 1825 was residing near Hammet on King Street Road, Charleston Neck. See *CSCCD*, 106.

3. Governor Thomas Bennett Jr. owned several lumber mills at the "w. end of Bull" on the Ashley River. As a result, a number of carpenters, including Vesey, resided on Bull Street. See *CDSG*, 9.

4. The only slave insurrection that ever threatened New Orleans broke out in January 1811. Whether Perault was referring to this event, was repeating a wild rumor based on misheard or misread information, or had concocted the story of New Orleans's capture to serve the plot remains unclear. As with the clearly inflated numbers that Vesey's lieutenants used to recruit followers, Vesey may have played upon these rumors to convince Carolina bondmen that slaves elsewhere were in the process of seizing other cities.

5. James C. Martindale (d. 1823), a militia captain, lived in 1822 on King Street Road, Charleston Neck. See *CSCCD*, 89.

6. On the agitation caused in Charleston by the antislavery itinerant Methodist preacher Lorenzo Dow (1777–1834), see the documents in Part I of this volume.

JOHN, a Negro Man, the Slave of Mr. J. L. Enslow,[1] pleaded GUILTY:—His owner, who was present, stated to the Court, that John was willing to make the only reparation in his power, for his conduct, and would reveal all the information he was in possession of relative to the insurrection. The Court informed John that he might state whatever he had to say, but as they would not make him any promise, he must not make confessions in hopes of pardon.—John said he would state all he knew of the intended insurrection, and proceeded to make the following CONFESSION:

Monday Gell lead me into it, and took me to Vesey's—There was a large meeting—Vesey told the people, the meeting was to rise up and fight the white people for their liberty—we always went to Monday's house afterwards—Monday did all the writing. I heard that they were trying all round the country *from Georgetown and Santee, round about to Combahee,* to get people. Peter Poyas was also there, he was one—Peter named Poyas' plantation where he went to meet—Bellisle Yates I have seen at the meetings, and Adam Yates, and Naphur Yates, and Dean Mitchell, and Caesar Smith, and George a Stevidore—At Vesey's they wanted to make a collection to make pikes for the country people, but the men had then no money—Monday Gell said Perault was one to get horses to send men into the country—I heard that a Blacksmith was to make pikes—Jack M'Neil is engaged—I have seen them all at Monday's—Jack said he was one and would try to get men—The plan was to take the Arsenal and Guard-Houses for arms, and not to fire the town unless they failed—Monday was writing a letter to St. Domingo to go by a vessel lying at Gibb's and Harper's Wharf—the letter was about the sufferings of the blacks, and to know if the people of St. Domingo would help them if they made an effort to free themselves—he was writing this letter in March, I am not certain of the time—Perault was present when Monday wrote the letter, and also a Painter named Prince Righton—I have seen Pompey Haig at Monday's, but he neither assented or dissented—Jerry Cohen was at Vesey's, and said to me he was one—I heard from Vesey and Monday that they had engaged men from the country—Peter Poyas said he had sent into the country to his brother to engage men who would send him an answer[2]—A party was to attack the Guard-House and Arsenal—another the Arsenal on the Neck—another to attack the Naval Store on Mey's Wharf—another to attack the Magazine—another to meet at Lightwood's Alley, and then try to cut off the Companies from meeting at their places of rendezvous—I belong to the African Congregation—On Saturday, the 15th June, a man was to be sent into the country to bring down the people, and Rolla was to command (the country people from Ashley River) at the Bridge—Ned Bennett and John Horry to meet at Mr. Horry's corner, and Batteau to come down with Vesey's party.[3]

The Court having used John as a witness in the subsequent trials, passed upon him the following sentence. "That he be imprisoned in the Work-House of Charleston, until his master, under the direction of the City Council of Charleston shall send him out of the limits of the United States, into which he is not to return under penalty of Death."

1. The slave John Enslow, like his owner Joseph L. Enslow (1790–1866), was a cooper. In 1822 Joseph resided on 89 East Bay Street. See *CSCCD,* 78; *Charleston Mercury,* November 29, 1866. Hamilton, *Account,* 45, dates Enslow's arrest to Saturday, July 13. The Senate transcript indicates that his trial followed that of Bacchus on Thursday, July 18; a similar version of this first confession appeared in the Senate transcript, below, and appears on pp. 324–25. Enslow was confined to the Work-House pending transportation, but he died there before he could be sold outside of the United States. In 1831, Joseph Enslow petitioned the South Carolina senate for compensation, saying that at the time of John's incarceration he was "healthy and able-bodied" and had provided against other slaves "essentially important testimony" for which his death sentence was commuted to transportation. See Joseph L. Enslow, Petition, and Supporting Paper, for Compensation for His Slave John, 1 December 1831, Petitions to the General Assembly, no. 60, series S165015, SCDAH.

2. Hamilton, *Account,* 14–15, describes Peter Poyas as a "first-rate ship-carpenter" and "one of the principal ringleaders in the conspiracy. Edward Ball, *Slaves in the Family* (New York: Farrar, Straus and Giroux, 1998), 265, has Peter raised at Windsor, one of the many Ball family plantations up the Cooper River, and identifies James Poyas Sr. (1790–1872), the brother of Eliza Catherine Poyas Ball (1794–1865), the mistress of Windsor, as Peter's owner. Thus Peter would have become well acquainted with events in Haiti because his owner was the shipbuilder James Poyas, active in the Caribbean trade. He resided at 49 King Street and ran a shipyard at 35 South Bay Street. See *CSCCD,* 95.

3. John Enslow's confession was published verbatim in the *Baltimore Patriot & Mercantile Advertiser,* September 6, 1822.

THE TRIAL of WILLIAM, a Negro Man, the property of Mr. Job Palmer[1]—His owner attending.

EVIDENCE.

MONDAY testified as follows:—William belongs to the association to rise against the whites—he and Vesey, and Jack Glen have been at my shop together—they were talking on this business, and he said he would do as much as any other man, and confessed he had joined.—Vesey seemed to regard him as one of his men, and to feel confidence in him—he and I were to be in the same band under Vesey—he was often in my shop talking on this business, and never shewed any disposition to be off—this was before the first execution.

Cross-Examined by Mr. Palmer—The time that Vesey, Glen and William was at my shop, 'twas when Vesey said there was but one Minister who Preached the Gospel—sometimes he came to my shop alone—the first time he came in he asked for the newspaper—the first conversation he had was about the rising.

CHARLES gave the following evidence:—William is engaged in the Insurrection—he said to Vesey in Monday's shop that Vesey must not think that he would not fight; that he would fight as well an another—I met him opposite to the Circular Church, on Dr. Simons' step,[2] and he then said then it was a shame they should allow the men to be hanged; *that he was ready to join in rescuing them from the gallows*—this was the Sunday previous to Vesey's being hanged, about 2 o'clock, P.M.

Cross-Examined by Mr. Palmer—I knew him long before—I met him just after William Paul was taken up at Vesey's.

See Monday Gell's confession, in which he says, that William promised Vesey to enlist as many men as he could.

THE COURT *unanimously* found William GUILTY, and passed upon him the sentence of DEATH.

(*Note.* His Excellency the Governor has pardoned William, upon condition that his Master transports him beyond the limits of the United States.)

1. Job Palmer (1747–1845), the father of Benjamin Morgan Palmer (1781–1847), Charleston's most prominent Congregational minister, owned William (Billy) Palmer. Benjamin was the first of twenty-seven white signatories to the 1820 petition in support of the opening of the African

Methodist Episcopal Church (called "Zion") created at Hampstead on Charleston Neck. He also visited a number of the accused, including Vesey and Rolla Bennett. Hamilton, *Account*, 44, dates William's arrest to Thursday, July 18, and the Senate transcript indicates that his trial took place the next day, Friday, July 19. See also the reference to "Billy" in Mary Lamboll Beach to Elizabeth Gilchrist, July 23, 1822, in this volume on pp. 408–9.

2. Benjamin Palmer's Congregational Church, located on Meeting Street, also known as the Circular Church. See Walter J. Fraser Jr., *Charleston! Charleston! The History of a Southern City* (Columbia: University of South Carolina Press, 1989), 291. Dr. Benjamin Bonneau Simons (1776–1844), considered to be one of the antebellum South's leading surgeons, lived at 55 Meeting Street. See *CSCCD*, 61; Howard A. Kelly, *A Cyclopedia of American Medical Biography Comprising the Lives of Eminent Deceased Physicians and Surgeons from 1610 to 1910* (Philadelphia: W. B. Saunders, 1912), vol. 2: 377–78.

THE TRIAL OF SEYMOUR, a Negro Man, belonging to Mr. William F. Kunhardt[1]—His owner attending.

EVIDENCE.

PERAULT testified as follows:—I met Seymour once at Monday's with Smart Anderson, where he acknowledged he was one to rise, and that he belonged to Monday's Company—I met him afterwards at the Exchange, where we talked of this business, and he was as much one as myself.

MONDAY gave the following evidence:—Seymour is one in this business—he brought to my shop about two months ago a racoon skin to make a cap of, and he then agreed to join us—he and Joe Jore are particular friends—I met him afterwards in Meeting-street, where he again said he was willing.

THE COURT *unanimously* found Seymour GUILTY, and passed upon him the sentence of DEATH; but recommended to the Governor that he should be pardoned *upon condition that he be transported out of the limits of the United States.*

1. *CSCCD*, 86, identifies William Kunhardt as a factor who ran Kunhardt's Wharf and resided at 34 George Street. From 1820 to 1822, he also served as a lieutenant colonel in a volunteer troop of Charleston cavalry in the Fourth Regiment of the state militia. See H. P. Archer, *Local Reminiscences: A Lecture Delivered by Mr. H. P. Archer before the Mutual Aid Association, No. 1, of Charleston, S.C. in the Hall of the Mechanics Union, at Charleston, S.C. June 6th, 1889* (Charleston, SC, 1893), 12; *Charleston Courier*, June 30, 1820; and Charleston *City Gazette and Commercial Daily Advertiser*, May 25, 1822. Hamilton, *Account*, 44, dates Seymour's arrest to Friday, July 12, and the Senate transcript indicates that his trial took place a week later on July 19. Kunhardt claimed to have owned Seymour for only three months. His previous owner appears to have been John Cordes Prioleau (1772–1825), who also owned Peter Prioleau. Governor Bennett commuted Seymour's death sentence to transportation. See Bill of Sale, John C. Prioleau to William Kunhardt and William Clarkson, April 16, 1822, vol. 4X, p. 52, series S213003, SCDAH; William Kunhardt, Petition Asking Compensation for the Loss and for the Expense of Deporting a Slave, n.d., no. 1841, series S165015, SCDAH.

THE TRIAL of NAPHUR[,] ADAM and BELLISLE, three Negro Men, belonging to the Estate of Joseph Yates[1] deceased—Jacob Axson, Esq.[2] attending as their Counsel.

EVIDENCE.

PERAULT testified as follows:—Bellisle or Blarney was engaged in this business. I met him at Crafts' North wharf—this was the first meeting—the second meeting was at the corner of the scale house, on Smith's wharf—he told me that the night the blacks were to rise, he would engage the people of Mr. Yates to sleep with himself at Mr. Mitchell's, where his people slept on Smith's wharf, where they would commence the fight. Adam and Naphur met at Bulkley's farm where we met on this business; where were Vesey, Monday, Charles and Smart—I there told them they had done the worst thing they could do to engage these people, for that all Charleston would know it next day—the rope-walk people got them to join—Adam and Naphur there acknowledged they had joined—On the 16th I saw Adam in the street, when he said he was going up the road to meet the Country and Neck people, where he intended to remain that night, and come down with those people.

Bellisle belongs to the African Church; they are all Africans.

Cross-Examined by Mr. Axson—Naphur and Adam came up to the Farm about 12 o'clock in the day on Sunday, and stayed there 'till 4 o'clock—this was a Sunday in May—every man in the house agreed to join to rise against the whites—the meeting was for this express purpose—After Peter Poyas and the others were convicted, Bellisle and I came out of the shop together to talk on this business, and I said we must rise and not let these people be hanged, and he said yes, we must do so; this was after he said to me he would get the people to sleep at Mr. Mitchell's shop on 16th June, when they were to rise—Adam told me that Charles Drayton had told him to go up the road on the 16th June, and stay there until the alarm was given, then come down with the Neck and Country people—Adam and Naphur came up to the Farm together—the Sunday was about the middle of May.

CHARLES gave the following evidence:—Naphur, Adam and Bellisle are all in this business—I met Adam and Naphur at Bulkley's Farm, where we met on this business, and where they acknowledged that their hearts were in this business—Bellisle I met in the streets, where he told me he belonged to it—I have also met him often at Monday's, where he talked of it, he said he was one of the army, and ready and willing to go out.

Cross-Examined by Mr. Axson—Napur and Adam at the Farm, said when the rising commenced they were ready—Vesey was there and spoke to the whole, and all who agreed to rise against the whites were to hold up their hands, and Naphur and Adam held up theirs with the others.

JOHN, Mr. Enslow's Slave, testified as follows:—I know the prisoners; they are as much in the plot as I am, and I am in the plot—I have met them all at Monday's—Adam gave to Monday a knife to make a scabbard for it, which he intended to use as a dagger, the knife was such a one as the Riflemen wear—I have heard Naphur at Monday's agree to join—I belong to Monday's company—Bellisle said he was in it—Adam and I have often spoken on the same subject—we all agreed to rise against the whites and fight for our freedom.

Cross-Examined—I saw Adam deliver the knife to Monday, and say make a scabbard if this will do—we all agreed at Monday's to join.

MONDAY gave the testimony following:—The prisoners were in the habit of coming into my shop to talk on this business—I first met Naphur and Adam at Bulkley's Farm—Adam brought to me a long knife to make a scabbard for it, which he intended to use in the business—they belonged to my side which was Vesey's division—I delivered him afterwards the knife.

Cross-Examined by Mr. Axson—Naphur was but once in my shop—Bellisle and Adam often at the Farm—Denmark Vesey explained his plan to all present, and on the proposition to agree, all assented—I met Naphur once at Bulkley's Farm, where as well as at my shop he expressly agreed to join.

(*Note.* Two other witnesses were ready to be produced against the prisoners, but the Court thought it unnecessary to examine them, as they could not testify to any new facts.)

THE COURT *unanimously* found Naphur, Adam, and Bellisle GUILTY, and passed upon them the sentence of DEATH.

1. Joseph Yates (1775–1822), a cooper, resided in 1822 at 23 Meeting Street and had a shop at 83 East Bay Street. Both he and his wife, Elizabeth, were members of the Circular Church. See *CSCCD,* 104; "Register of the Independent Congregational (Circular) Church of Charleston S.C. 1784–1815," *SCHGM* 33 (October 1932): 306–16; Petition of Jeremiah Yates, John R. Rogers, and A. W. Campbell to the South Carolina Senate, n.d., no. 1745, series S165015, SCDAH. Hamilton, *Account,* 43, dates the arrest of all three men to July 18, and the Senate transcript indicates that they were tried together on July 19. The three were hanged on Friday, July 26.

2. Jacob Axson Jr. (1794–1843), a youthful but rising star in Charleston's legal firmament in 1822, would play an active role during the proceedings. Friend of Robert Turnbull as well as Governor Bennett, Axson served as Rolla Bennett's counsel and would cross-examine Joe La Roche and Polydore Bennett. He would also serve as one of two magistrates on the second court. He would eventually hold a wide variety of state and local positions. See John Belton O'Neall, *Biographical Sketches of the Bench and Bar of South Carolina . . . ,* 2 vols. (Charleston, SC, 1859), vol. 2: 338–46; Thomas Curtis, *An Address at the Funeral of the Hon. Jacob Axson, Recorder and Judge of the City Court of Charleston, S.C., Delivered Aug. 26th, 1843, in the First Baptist Church* (Charleston, SC, 1843); *BDSCHR* 5: 8–9.

THE TRIAL OF DUBLIN, a Negro Man, the property of Mr. Thomas Morris—Mr. C. G. Morris[1] attending.

EVIDENCE.

PERAULT testified as follows:—Dublin said to me that Wm. Garner had engaged him to join against the whites—he belongs to the African Church.

CHARLES testified as follows:—Dublin told me one day he heard of it but that was all.

THE COURT *unanimously* found Dublin GUILTY, and passed upon him the sentence of DEATH, but recommended to the Governor to pardon him upon condition that he be transported out of the limits of the United States.

1. Dublin appears to have been the slave of Christopher Gadsden Morris (1788–1848), a merchant who in 1822 kept an office at 80 East Bay Street and resided with his brother Thomas (1790–1857), a notary public, at 2 Wentworth Street. See *CSCCD,* 91; *BDSCHR* 4: 415. Christopher Morris described Dublin as a porter about thirty-nine years of age. See C. G. Morris to the Senate of South Carolina, November 27, 1822, no. 124, series S165015, SCDAH. Hamilton, *Account,* 44, dates Dublin's arrest to Thursday, July 18, and the Senate transcript indicates that he was tried on July 19.

THE TRIAL of CHARLES, a Negro Man, belonging to Mr. Samuel Billings[1]—His owner attending.

EVIDENCE.

JOHN testified as follows:—Charles belongs to this business—we spoke on it at Monday's—he said that when we were ready he would come out and join us—I met him twice at Monday's, and both times he said so—After Peter was taken up, I met him on Edmonston's Wharf, and he said the people were beginning to be frightened, and we had better say as little as possible about it.

PERAULT'S evidence was as follows:—I met him at Monday's where I heard him say he was a horseman—I heard him say he was ready and willing.

MONDAY gave the following evidence:—He told me once that William Garner had spoke to him about a horse, but I don't know that he was one of us—he was frequently at my shop to get harness mended, and he there conversed on this subject, and he appeared willing to join, and said he had joined.

CHARLES testified as follows:—I have met him often, and he acknowledged he was one—Jack Glenn he said was to have slept at his master's Livery Stables the night of the rising, to assist in saddling the horses for the company.

(*Note.* Other witnesses were ready to testify to the same effect, but it was thought unnecessary to examine them as they would testify to no new fact.)

Mr. BILLINGS testified to Charles' general good character.

THE COURT *unanimously* found Charles GUILTY, and passed upon him the sentence of DEATH.

1. Hamilton, *Account,* 43, dates Charles's arrest to Thursday, July 18, and identified his owner as John (not Samuel) Billings. In 1822 John Billings (d. 1826) ran the public stables at 122 Church Street and resided at 17 Chambers Street. See *CSCCD,* 71. His name is rendered "John Billing" in Inhabitants of Charleston, Petition and Supporting Papers Asking Compensation for Their Slaves Who Were Executed for Involvement in a Slave Insurrection, n.d., no. 1839, series S165015, SCDAH. One of the supporting documents, dated November 21, 1822, described Charles as "a coachman and horsier" with "excellent character," in his mid-twenties and valued at eight hundred dollars. He was tried on Friday, July 19, and executed a week later.

THE TRIAL of PRINCE a Negro Man, the property of Miss Righton—Mr. Joseph Righton,[1] attending.

EVIDENCE.

JOHN testified as follows:—I have seen Prince in Monday's shop when Monday was reading the letter to St. Domingo—He must have heard Monday—The brother of the steward of the vessel who was to carry the letter to St. Domingo, was a General as I understand in St. Domingo.

MONDAY gave the evidence following:—I can't say that Prince was engaged—he came once to my shop and then agreed to join, but I have not seen him since, and as he did not come back to say whether he would continue so or not, I therefore did not put his name down to the list—This was long before the 16th June—I then read the list of names to him, but not the letter to St. Domingo—there were three other persons there.

Cross-Examined by Mr. Righton—he came there without any appointment.

CHARLES testified as follows:—I saw him once in Monday's shop, but don't know any thing against him.

HARRY stated that he knew nothing against Prince.

THE COURT *unanimously* found Prince NOT GUILTY—but suggested to his owner to send him away.

1. Prince was most likely the slave of Elizabeth Righton (d. 1828?), who in 1816 resided at 3 Water Street with her brother Joseph Righton (1762–1847), a cooper. Both were members of the Circular Church. See "Death of a Venerable Citizen," Charleston *Southern Patriot,* January 8, 1847; *CDSG,* 72. Hamilton, *Account,* 46, dates Prince's arrest to July 19, and the Senate transcript indicates that his trial took place on the following morning of July 20.

THE TRIAL of PETER, an elderly Negro Man, belonging to Mrs. Cooper—Capt. Sears Hubbell,[1] attending.

EVIDENCE.

JOHN testified as follows:—I have met Peter at Monday's, where he signified his consent, and said he was willing to join; this was about two months ago.

MONDAY gave the following evidence:—Peter said he would join—I met him once at Vesey's, and he there said by word of mouth that he was willing to join; this was previous to the 16th June; (the prisoner is a Guinea Negro)—he has passed my shop driving his cart, but did not come in.

PERAULT, testified as follows:—Vesey told me to tell Peter he wanted to see him; I told him and he said he would go, and did go; but I did not know what passed there; I don't know that he agreed; I came out of Vesey's and left him there; Vesey sent me to him on this business; I only delivered my message.

Cross-Examined by Capt. Hubbell—At Veseys I met Monday there too.

Mr. HUBBELL deposed that Peter has borne a good character, and is an inoffensive man.

THE COURT *unanimously* found Peter GUILTY, and passed upon him the sentence of death; but *in consideration of his age,* recommended to the Governor to pardon him *upon condition that he be transported out of the limits of the United States.*

(*Note.* His Excellency the Governor has pardoned Peter on condition of his receiving twenty lashes.)

1. No source provides the forename of "Mrs. Cooper," although a likely candidate is Mary Cooper, who in 1822 lived on 306 East Bay Street. Sears Hubbell (1777–1838), a sea captain who attended for Mrs. Cooper, lived in 1822 at East End Boundary Street on Charleston Neck, but in 1816 lived on East Bay Street near James Cooper, another sea captain, who may have been married to Mary. See *CSCCD,* 6, 13,75, 83; Walter Hubbell, *History of the Hubbell Family Containing Genealogical Records of the Ancestors and Descendants of Richard Hubbell from A.D. 1086 to A.D. 1915* (New York: Hubbell, 1915), 221. Hamilton, *Account,* 44, dates Peter's arrest to Monday, July 15, and the Senate transcript indicates that his trial followed that of Prince Righton on Saturday, July 20. Governor Bennett reduced Cooper's sentence from transportation to whipping due to his advanced age. See Charleston *Southern Patriot, and Commercial Advertiser,* September 18, 1822.

THE TRIAL of GEORGE, a Negro Man, the property of Mr. Bampfield[1]—His owner attending.

EVIDENCE.

JOHN testified as follows:—I met George at Monday's, where he said, that if all the men in the room was of one mind, he would make a remark—they said we are; he then said, I have spoken to two men who agreed, and mentioned their names; when Monday said for God sake let them alone or they will betray us; (the prisoner on being asked if he belonged to the African Church said, I did belong to the African Church, but they turned me out for keeping a girl.)

MONDAY'S evidence was as follows:—George was once in my shop; the conversation related by John Enslow did not take place; every day there were numbers in my shop on this business; he was often in my shop.

PERAULT testified as follows:—I met George once at Monday's; George did agree to join as much as I did; I did not hear him say any thing about engaging two men to join, this meeting was expressly on this business; I met him afterwards in the Market, when he said the Guards were too strong, let the business lay still; I have not talked to him since any one was taken up on this business.

CHARLES testified as follows:—Monday told me that George was one.

THE COURT *unanimously* found George GUILTY, and passed upon him the sentence of DEATH; but recommended to the Governor to pardon him upon condition that he be sent out of the limits of the United States.

1. George Bampfield's owner, Thomas Bampfield, an accountant, resided in 1822 at 16 George Street. See *CSCCD,* 70. Hamilton, *Account,* 44, dates Bampfield's arrest to Thursday, July 18, and the Senate transcript indicates that he was the third slave to be tried on Saturday, July 20.

THE TRIAL of JEMMY, a Negro Man, belonging to Mrs. Clement[1]—His two young Masters present.

EVIDENCE.

MONDAY testified as follows:—Jemmy is engaged in this business; he belongs to my company, and he agreed in my shop; he said he would like to know when this business would begin, as he had engaged some people in the country where his wife lived, and he would have to bring them down; he has often come to my shop and held conversations on this subject, and confessed he was willing and had joined.

PERAULT gave the following evidence:—I saw Jemmy at Monday's—he knew of it before me, for at that time he was talking on this business, and it was the first time I had heard of it—he was one—he was willing—he belongs to the African Church.

CHARLES testified as follows:—Jemmy told me himself in Monday's shop, that he was one—he one day brought to me on the Market Wharf two or three men, who he said had agreed to join, and belonged to the country—these men said they had joined, and were to carry the news into the country, (Jemmy has a wife at Mrs. Moore's, in St. Thomas' Parish)—this was after Peter was taken up, but before his execution.

THE COURT *unanimously* found Jemmy GUILTY, and passed upon him the sentence of DEATH.

1. Jemmy belonged to the widow Sarah Smith Clement (1754–1831, also rendered "Clements"), wife of John Clement (1744–1801). In 1822 she resided at 101 Queen Street. She described herself in a petition to the South Carolina Senate as a woman "of very slender means and resources" who was supported by Jemmy, "a very valuable slave," appraised at one thousand dollars. See *CSCCD,* 74; Petition of the Widow Clements to the Senate of South Carolina, n.d., which appears in Part V of this volume on pp. 533–34. Hamilton, *Account,* 18, dates Jemmy's arrest to Thursday, July 18, and the Senate transcript indicates that his trial took place two days later on Saturday, July 20. He was hanged on Friday, July 26.

THE TRIAL of JERRY, a Negro Man, the Slave of Mr. M. Cohen.[1]

EVIDENCE.

JOHN testifies as follows:—I met Jerry at Vesey's, and at Monday's—He agreed and said he was one, and joined in the object of the meeting, which was to plan measures against the whites—we have often spoken on this business—at Vesey's where we met, were present, Monday, Charles, Rolla, Ned, Perault, Batteau, Smart, and Jack Glenn, and near 30 men in all they then handed round the hat to make collections to purchase pikes; they were to be provided with dark lanterns to enter stores for arms;—*Vesey said one hundred Pikes were made by a black man who worked by himself*; they also wanted money to pay that black man's wages to his mistress; after Vesey was taken I was afraid to speak on the subject.

MONDAY gave the evidence following;—Jerry was often in my shop, and confessed he was one; his name was on my list with his consent; I did not meet him at Vesey's; he said when we were consulting who should take a lead, said he would be a leader; he was not there when money was collected to procure lanterns; I did not go to the meeting that night 'till eight o'clock.

PERAULT testified as follows:—Jerry was at Vesey's when they made a collection; I am not certain, but think that Monday was present; he Monday *was* there; John Enslow was [a]lso there; the collection was for purchasing spears; Jerry did say we had better stop this business, but still he was willing to go on if we went on.

THE COURT *unanimously* found Jerry GUILTY, and passed upon him the sentence of DEATH.

1. The Polish-born Jewish merchant Mordecai Cohen (1763–1848) became one of South Carolina's wealthiest citizens and most respected philanthropists. He resided in 1822 at 103 Broad Street. See Charleston *Southern Patriot,* July 25, 1848; *CSCCD,* 75. Hamilton, *Account,* 43, identifies the accused as "Mauidore" and placed his arrest on Friday, July 19. The Senate transcript, which called him "Jerry Cohen," indicates that his trial took place the following day, Saturday, July 20, and that he was hanged on Friday, July 26.

THE TRIAL OF DEAN, a Negro Man belonging to Mr. Jas. Mitchell[1]—His owner attending.

EVIDENCE.

PERAULT testified as follows:—I have seen Dean at Vesey's, where he agreed as much as myself—we met purposely to make *a collection for spears*—I heard him say he had joined, and no one would be allowed to enter that house if he was not one—He belongs to the African Church.

Cross-examined by Mr. Mitchell—John Enslow summoned him to attend the meeting.

John testified as follows:

I first told Dean about it—he told me afterwards he saw the thing was going on well, and he was glad of it. I asked him if he would like to go to Vesey's meetings, and he said yes, and went with me. He put in money at Vesey's, I saw him do it; Jack Glenn handed the hat round—we afterwards conversed, and he was always of the same mind. He was on the night of the rising to meet at Vesey's, and march down with his party.

MONDAY confirmed John's testimony as far as it relates to Dean's meeting at Vesey's and as to what passed there.

THE COURT *unanimously* found Dean GUILTY, and passed upon the sentence of DEATH.

1. *CSCCD,* 91, identifies three persons named James Mitchell in 1822. Since Dean Mitchell was a cooper, his likely master was the James Mitchell who ran a cooperage business at 27 East Bay Street and resided a few blocks from there. Hamilton, *Account,* 43, dates his arrest to Friday, July 19, and the Senate transcript indicates his trial took place the following day, on Saturday, July 20. He was hanged on Friday, July 26.

THE TRIAL of ISAAC, a Negro Man, the property of Mr. Wm. Harth.[1] His owner attending.

EVIDENCE.

MONDAY testified as follows:—Isaac was engaged in this business; he told me so himself. After Mingo was taken up, he told me, that Mingo would get clear if Edwin Paul did not testify against him. He said also, that he belonged to the horse company. Mingo told me that his brother was one too.

Cross-examined by Mr. Harth—I conversed with him directly after Mingo was taken up.

WILLIAM testified that Edwin did positively say, all Mr. Harth's people were engaged in it.

CHARLES testified that Monday told him Isaac was engaged.

THE COURT *unanimously* found Isaac GUILTY, and passed upon the sentence of Death; but recommended to the Governor to pardon him *upon condition* that he be sent out of the limits of the United States.

1. Charleston lumber merchant William Harth owned three slaves involved in the proceedings: Mingo, Isaac, and Robert. Harth described Mingo as a twenty-two-year-old "cook and house servant." He was hanged on Friday, July 26. Hamilton, *Account,* 44, dates the arrest of Isaac, a thirty-year-old coachman, to Saturday, July 13, and the Senate transcript indicates his trial was held a week later on July 20. Robert became a significant witness for the state. See *The Seventh Report of the Board of Trustees of the Protestant Episcopal Society for the Advancement of Christianity in South-Carolina Made at the Anniversary of the Society, January 6th, 1817* (Charleston, SC, 1817), 36; and Inhabitants of Charleston, Petition and Supporting Papers Asking Compensation for Their Slaves Who Were Executed for Involvement in a Slave Insurrection, n.d., no. 1839, series S165015, SCDAH.

THE TRIAL of JOHN a Negro Man belonging to Mrs. Taylor[1]:—Mr. James Drummond attending.[2]

EVIDENCE.

CHARLES testified as follows:—John told me one Monday morning, previous to the 16th of June, that all the horses were ready, but the patrol was so vigilant, they could not come out.

Cross-examined by Mr. Drummond—I understood the horses to be intended for the insurrection. This conversation took place at my master's gate—he was as willing as myself and he did not refuse. I only conversed with him but once, and then he told me the horses were ready for the insurrection. William Garner told me that John was engaged in this affair.

THE COURT *unanimously* found John NOT GUILTY, but suggested to his owner to send him away. Mr. Drummond gave John an excellent character.

1. No document provides a forename for John's owner. *CSCCD,* 100, identifies four women named Taylor, including at least two widows, living in Charleston in 1822. Hamilton, *Account,* 46,

dates John's arrest to Saturday, July 13, and the Senate transcript indicates that his trial followed that of Isaac Harth on Saturday, July 20.

2. James Drummond, a shoemaker, resided on 29 State Street. During the Vesey affair, Drummond served as a sergeant in the militia and was held liable by the state for the loss of public arms. See *CSCCD,* 77, and Petition no. 68, November 25, 1822, series S165015, SCDAH.

THE TRIAL of PIERRE LEWIS, a Negro Man, the Slave of Mr. Chappeau[1]—His owner attending.

EVIDENCE.

CHARLES, testified as follows: On Sunday, when the Guards were out, Pierre Lewis told me that something serious would happen, but that I was a country born, and he was afraid to trust me—This was on the 16th June.

THE COURT *unanimously* found Pierre Lewis NOT GUILTY, and discharged him.

1. Lewis's owner, John B. Chapeau (1775–1850), a confectioner born in Saint-Domingue, lived in 1816 at 110 Queen Street in a two-story wooden house that burned to the ground in a major conflagration in February of that year. He reappeared in the city directory in 1829 on 128 Church Street. See *CSCCD,* 5, 140; "Distressing Fire," Charleston *City Gazette and Commercial Daily Advertiser,* February 9, 1816. Hamilton, *Account,* 46, identifies the accused as "Pierre Louis" and dated his arrest to Thursday, July 18. The Senate transcript indicates that his trial was held two days later on Saturday, July 20.

THE TRIAL of JACK, a Negro Man, belonging to Mr. Neil M'Neil.[1]—Mr. M'Kenzie his owner's Co-partner, attending.

EVIDENCE.

MONDAY testified as follows:—Jack belongs to this conspiracy, and with his consent I placed him on my list. He has been frequently at my shop, where Denmark Vesey has often seen him; but he was never at my shop at any appointed meeting—he came here about 7 years of age from Africa, and belongs to the African Church—He is one of my company.

CHAR[L]ES testified as follows:—I have met Jack at Monday's several times, and heard him in his presence acknowledge that he belonged to this conspiracy. After the execution of the first six, Jack appeared to be alarmed, and to regret that he had joined. We had several conversations and he always appeared to exhibit the same feelings.

PERAULT said I know the prisoner, but not that he is engaged.

JOHN[2] testified as follows: I have seen Jack often in Monday's shop and he has acknowledged in his presence and mine, that he had joined; he has spoken to me often on the subject in the streets, and was always willing.

THE COURT *unanimously* found Jack GUILTY, and passed upon him the sentence of DEATH.

1. *CSCCD,* 90, identifies three persons named Neil McNeil living in Charleston in 1822. Since he had a partner named McKenzie, Jack's likely owner was grocer Neill McNeill (also "Neil McNeil"), who in 1822 operated a store at 46 Broad Street in partnership with John McKenzie. In seeking

compensation from the state, McNeill valued the African-born Jack at one thousand dollars, saying that "his value was much beyond the ordinary of negroes being well experienced in the line of business followed" by McNeill. See Neill McNeill to the Senate of South Carolina, November 20, 1822, no. 126, series S165015, SCDAH. Hamilton, *Account,* 43, dates Jack's arrest as July 22, and the Senate transcript indicates his trial took place the following day, on Tuesday, July 23. Jack was one of four slaves to be hanged on Tuesday, July 30.

2. This witness was John Enslow.

THE TRIAL of CAESAR, a Negro Man belonging to Mrs. Smith[1]—Mr. M'Dow[2] attending for his owner.

EVIDENCE.

JOHN[3] testified as follows:—Caesar is engaged and confessed it to me; I have often seen him at Monday's—he is a native of Africa and belongs to the African Church—he told me sometimes in the street he was engaged. After the execution of Vesey he appeared fearful of the consequences.

Cross-examined by Mr. M'Dow—I saw him twice at Monday's before the 16th of June and once after.

MONDAY'S evidence was as follows:—Caesar was one of the party, and I placed his name on my list—He was always willing to join, there was no man more so.

Cross-examined by Mr. M'Dow—He engaged some time before the affair was discovered—he was as zealous as myself—he was at my shop often.

CHARLES testified as follows:—Caesar acknowledged to me at Monday's, that he was engaged, and also several times in the street.

Cross-examined by Mr. M'Dow—I saw him after the execution of Vesey, and he appeared of the same mind.[4]

THE PRISONER, admitted, in his defence, that he had frequent conversations on this subject with the witness, but denied that he had joined.

THE COURT *unanimously* found Caesar GUILTY, and passed upon him the sentence of DEATH.

1. Naomi Smith lived for years with her sister Ann at 36 Coming Street. In seeking compensation for her executed slave, Smith "rejoices at the detection of her servant's guilt" and described Caesar as "a prime healthy able bodied negro, about twenty five years of age." He had supported Smith, who at the time was more than sixty years old and receiving charity from the St. Andrew's Society, by working as a drayman and remitting to her ten dollars per month. See *CSCCD,* 25, 62, 99; Naomi Smith, Petition and Supporting Papers Asking Compensation for a Slave Who Was Executed for Involvement in a Slave Uprising, November 16, 1822, no. 128, series S165015, SCDAH. Hamilton, *Account,* 43, dates Caesar's arrest to Monday, July 22, and the Senate transcript indicates that his trial took place the following day on Tuesday, July 23. He was one of four men hanged on Tuesday, July 30.

2. William McDow (d. 1839?), a teacher, ran an "Academy" in 1816 at 4 Montague Street and in 1822 lived near the elderly Naomi Smith at 29 Coming Street. See *CSCCD,* 18, 89.

3. This witness was John Enslow.

4. The Senate transcript indicates that McDow also cross-examined Gell and Perault Strohecker, who stated only that he knew Caesar.

THE TRIAL of PRINCE GRAHAM,[1] a free black man—Mr. Jones[2] attending as his friend.

EVIDENCE.

MONDAY testified as follows:—Prince Graham is engaged in this conspiracy and belongs to William Garner's company—he acknowledged he belonged to it, but did not wish to have his name down, as he was a free man. He confessed he belonged to William Garner's Company—he was not at my shop.

Cross-examined by Mr. Jones—he said he had a long one, a horseman's sword provided for this purpose—He belonged to the cavalry and was one of the African Church. He never was with Denmark Vesey or attended any of the meetings—he told me he was to be an officer, William Garner had made him one.

CHARLES gave the following evidence—Monday and myself met Prince Graham one night coming out of Dr. Ramsay's yard with Quash Harleston—He said that he was as willing as any body. After Morris Brown had returned from the North, he said he did not wish much to do with it as he was a free man, and had denied it to Morris Brown, who inquired if he was one—this was after Peter was taken up—Morris Brown returned before the 16th of June.

FRANK testified as follows:—Vesey called at the house of Prince Graham one day in my company, and was informed by his wife that he was not at home. I afterwards met him and he asked why Vesey had called on him—I said to go into the country—he replied I cannot go, as I have nothing to do with this conspiracy—this was I think before the 16th of June.

PERAULT['s] evidence was as follows;—I only conversed with Prince Graham once in company with Quash Harleston, when he said, if Monday had told him of it a little sooner he would have joined; but now he had not time to prepare himself for it—this was at Prileau's Wharf.

Prince Graham's Statement and Defence.

I met William Garner who told me he held a commission in the horse, and if I would join, he would resign in my favour; which I refused to do—when in New-York, I first learn't that Denmark Vesey and others were to be hung for an attempt to raise an Insurrection. As I had been spoken to and asked to join in this before I left Charleston, I considered well whether I had ever said or done any thing which could bring me into trouble if I returned; but as I could not reproach myself with having done so, I thought I need not fear to come on. As I was a free man, and could have stayed in New-York if I pleased, I certainly would not have been such a fool as to run myself into such danger if I was in any way engaged in the plot.

THE COURT found Prince Graham GUILTY, and passed upon him the following sentence:—"That he be imprisoned in the Work-House of Charleston for one month, and then be transported by sea out of the State of South-Carolina, by the first opportunity, into which he is not to return under penalty of death."

The prisoner at his own request, was transported to Africa on board of a vessel which sailed from Charleston.

1. Prince Graham was a free colored drayman who resided at 11 Coming Street. See *DSGCC*, 101. Hamilton, *Account*, 45, dates Graham's arrest to Sunday, July 21, and the Senate transcript indicates his trial, which was held on Tuesday, July 23, was the final one heard by the first court. The Richmond *Enquirer*, September 6, 1822, which is reprinted in Part IV, pp. 453, of this volume, reported that Graham sailed out of Charleston on August 13 aboard the *Dolphin* for Liberia, leaving his slave wife Sarah and their children behind. He returned to the United States in the late 1820s and settled in New York City. There he worked as a shoemaker and became a deacon of the AME Church. According to the 1840 census, Graham resided in the Fourteenth Ward with two other "Free Colored Persons," one of them a female above the age of fifty-five. (Born around 1800, Graham was then approximately forty-years old.) See *Daily Albany Argus*, January 22, 1872, and *New York Herald*, February 25, 1872, both reprinted in Part V on pp. 713–14, for Graham's return to New York State as well as Judith Wellman, *Brooklyn's Promised Land: The Free Black Community of Weeksville, New York* (New York: New York University Press, 2014), 16–17.

2. No document provides Jones's forename, and *CSCCD*, 85, identifies more than a dozen white males with the surname, including a John C. Jones, who neighbored Prince Graham on the corner of Wentworth and Coming streets.

THE TRIAL of Billy,[1] a Negro Man, the property of Mr. Robinson—William Crafts, Esq. attending as his Counsel.[2]

EVIDENCE.

PERAULT, testified as follows:—Billy was engaged in this business. On the 16th of June he and I went to Vesey's in the afternoon. This day he said we must raise to day, nothing must put it back. We there met Gullah Jack and Tom Russell—Smart Anderson got him to join. I met him afterwards, on Sunday at his own house. Billy agreed as much as myself.

He, at his house, which was after Vesey and others were taken said, Jack would get more men, and then we would rise. We there spoke of rescuing Vesey and the others, and Billy agreed—he is an African.

Cross-examined by Mr. Crafts—We stopped first at Monday's and then went to Vesey's—on the day of the execution, on the Bay, Billy asked me what I was doing there—why I was not on the green to get men to rescue those to be hung.

The Prisoners Defence.—Mr. Davenport, Mr. Crafts, Mr. Tyler and Mr. Davis testified to Billy's good character.

Mr. TYLER deposed as follows:—I believe that Perault was one of those who were speaking with Billy before my door. At another time, within a few days Perault took away in his dray from before my store some damaged corn sold him by Billy. I have powder in cannisters in my store, which Billy might have stolen if he choose so to do, but I have not missed any.

Mrs. Miller deposed as follows—I live in a house in Elliott-street, there are two rooms on a floor—the first occupied by Mr. Howe, the back by me. Billy occupies a room above my kitchen, and no one can go into his room without passing through my kitchen; I never saw Perault go into Billy's room, or in my yard. Billy has lived in that room for three years.[3]

Mr. Miller, Mr. J. W. Howe, T. Dexter and Mrs. Mitchell, say, (Mr. Crafts) that neither of them ever saw Perault in Billy's house.

PERAULT was called back by Mr. Crafts and examined as to Billy's residence, which he described exactly as Mrs. Miller had done.

SMART, belonging to Mr. Anderson, was examined on behalf of the State and testified as follows:—Billey was engaged in this business—Caesar Smith said to me in Billy's presence, that Billy had joined. Billey told me that he was willing to take a part three or four days after this—he told me after that, that he was one.

Cross-examined by Mr. Crafts—I did not tell Perault I had got Billy to join, but that Caesar had.

Re-examined—I have never been at Billy's house.

THE COURT *unanimously* found Billy GUILTY, and passed upon him the sentence of DEATH.

(*Note.*—His Excellency the Governor has pardoned Billy, upon condition, that his master transport him beyond the limits of the United States.)

1. Billy was owned by Philip Robinson, a merchant and partner in the firm Robinson & Carter, located for years on Crafts' Wharf. In 1816, Robinson resided on Tradd Street and served as vice-consul for Portugal in Charleston. John Quincy Adams appointed him United States consul at Curaçao in 1827. In an official document, Robinson's representatives described Billy as a porter and house servant, thirty-eight years of age, with a value of seven hundred dollars. See *CSCCD,* 23, 59; Charleston *City Gazette and Commercial Daily Advertiser,* March 23, 1815; *New-York Spectator,* May 25, 1827; Samuel Davenport and Dodridge Crocker to the Senate of South Carolina, November 22, 1822, no. 131, series S165015, SCDAH. Hamilton, *Account,* 44, dates Billy's arrest to Tuesday, July 23, and the Senate transcript indicates his trial began on Wednesday, July 24, and concluded the next day.

2. William Crafts Jr. (1787–1826) graduated from Harvard, trained in law in South Carolina, and was elected to a wide variety of public offices. A highly regarded criminal attorney, he counseled Denbow Martin as well as Billy during the proceedings. In 1822, he lived at 52 Beaufain Street and kept an office at 104 Church Street. See *CSCCD,* 75; *BDSCHR* 4: 131–33.

3. Architectural historian Bernard L. Herman, "Slave and Servant Housing in Charleston, 1770–1820," *Historical Archaeology* 33 (1999): 88–101, finds Perault Strohecker's testimony more believable than Billy Robinson's after investigating antebellum Charleston's urban spaces and the typical location of slave quarters.

THE TRIAL of JOHN VINCENT, a Negro Man belonging to Mr. Cruckshanks[1]—Mr. Cornhill, one of the firm of D. Parish & Co. which had for some time hired him attending.[2]

EVIDENCE.

MONDAY testified as follows:—John told me himself he had joined in this business—this was in my shop—I frequently conversed with him on this subject—he once belonged to the African Church—before the 16th June he told me he had a mould, and that he was making balls—this was about three weeks before the 16th—after the 16th he said he was ready still.

Cross-Examined by Mr. Cornhill—He said he would give me some bullets; he said his master, that he was staying with, was going to the North on Monday, the 18th, and if he would go on Saturday before, 'twould be better.

CHARLES[3] gave the following evidence:—I have often talked with John in Monday's shop on this subject, where he said he was willing; he was one; and belonged to the horse company; I have seen him at Monday's three or four times; he said the gentleman he was staying with wanted him to go to the North, but he said he wanted to stay and see the frolic over first.

Cross-Examined by Mr. Cornhill—I think it was in his own room in an Alley from Church-street, viz. Elliott-street, that he told me about his master; this was the Sunday afternoon before Vesey was executed, (30th June)—Mr. Cornhill states that the prisoner did live in Elliott-street.

Mr. CORNHILL gave to the prisoner the very best character.

Mr. KER BOYCE,[4] deposed as follows:—Ker Boyce sworn; I went to D. Parish[5] on Saturday, 15th June, who was going to the North on Monday; Mr. Parish asked John what was the matter, that he looked as if he had lossed his mother? John's looks then were such, that after I heard of this affair next day, I could not but think that John was concerned, I advised Mr. Parish to question him about it.

THE COURT *unanimously* found John Vincent GUILTY, and passed upon him the sentence of DEATH.

(*Note.* His Excellency the Governor has pardoned John Vincent, upon condition that his Master transport him beyond the limits of the United States.)

1. John Vincent belonged to Daniel Cruckshanks (also "Crukshanks"), a shoemaker and tanner, who in 1822 lived at 22 Queen Street and operated a tannery on Hanover Street in Hampstead, Charleston Neck. See *CSCCD,* 76. The Senate transcript indicates that he was in the Work-House courtroom during John's trial. Hamilton, *Account,* 44, dates Vincent's arrest to July 23, and the Senate transcript indicates that his trial began on July 24 and concluded on July 25.

2. The "Mr. Cornhill" here was Jasper Corning (1792–1869). Corning worked for the Charleston merchant firm D. Parish & Co., located on Broad Street, and had hired John to work for the company. Corning, as Mary Beach's letter of September 5, 1822, indicates, came from New York City and the Brick Presbyterian Church there of the Reverend Gardiner Spring (1785–1873); he was a supporter of the American Colonization Society. See George Lewis Prentiss, *The Union Theological Seminary of the City of New York: Historical and Biographical Sketches of Its First Fifty Years* (New York, 1889), 191–92; *Twenty-eighth Annual Report of the American Colonization Society* (Washington, DC, 1845), 55.

3. The witness here is Charles Drayton.

4. Ker Boyce (1787–1854), an affluent merchant, would become president of the Bank of Charleston. In 1822, he worked as a factor on Kunhardt's Wharf and resided at 382 King Street, Charleston Neck. *CSCCD,* 71; *Boston Evening Transcript,* March 23, 1854.

5. Daniel Parish (1796–1880) arrived in Charleston in 1819 as a dry goods merchant and, together with his brothers, built one of New York City's most successful commercial houses. In 1822, Parish's company was located at 56 Broad Street; he resided at 95 Church Street. See *The Parish Will Case, in the Court of Appeals: The Statement of Facts, and the Opinion of the Court* (New York, 1862), 4; Tunis Garret Bergen, *Genealogies of the State of New York: A Record of the Achievements*

of Her People in the Making of the Commonwealth and the Founding of a Nation (New York: Lewis Historical Publishing, 1915), vol. 3: 1192; *CSCCD*, 93.

THE TRIAL of JACOB STAGG, a Mulatto Man, the slave of Mr. J. Lancaster.[1]—His owner and Joseph Clark, Esq.[2] his Counsel, attending.

EVIDENCE.

PERAULT testified as follows:—Jacob and I talked together about April last in Monday's shop on this business, and I found that he knew of it before me; Smart Anderson and George Walker were there. On 15th June, we talked together near Flinn's Church,[3] where I told him that Vesey said, to-morrow the people would come from the country, and we must rise; and he agreed to do so; I have met him frequently at Monday's.

Cross-Examined by Mr. Clark—At Monday's shop on a rainy day he said he was engaged in the business, and belonged to the foot company; near Flinn's Church he said he was ready. *It was agreed to rise in July at first, as at that time the white people go to the North and to Sullivan's Island, and the City would then be thin of men;* but in consequence of the first arrest of Peter Poyas, it was altered and fixed for the 16th June; Monday told me in his shop in Jacob's presence, that he Jacob had joined.

MONDAY gave the following evidence:—Jacob agreed to join with my company in my shop; he asked me for a sword, and when I said I had none to give him, he said, that he would get a scythe and make a sword out of it; Vesey had met him at my shop and talked with him on this business; he sometimes came to my shop and always said he was ready and willing; he first came to my shop about four months ago when it was cold weather; one rainy day he was a long time in my shop talking on this business, when he said he was engaged in painting the house; there were there several persons present; he said he would be ready when they rose.

Cross Examined by Mr. Clark—I don't remember that I told any one that he had joined; Vesey mentioned his plans and arrangements, and what he was going to do, &c. in Jacobs presence; Jacob frequented my shop, and I have known him for four or five years.

CHARLES[4] testified as follows:—I have seen Jacob at Monday's when Vesey was there, but don't know that he had joined; I went out of the shop and left them talking; he said he was tired of paying wages.

Cross-Examined by Mr. Clark—I have known of this about two months.

Mr. LANCASTER and Mr. WHITNEY[5] gave Jacob a good character, and so did Mr. STAGG.

Jacob had a wife at Dr. Ramsay's,[6] and was always at home at night.

THE PRISONER stated that Monday read daily the newspapers, and told him that Congress was going to set them free; alluding to the Missouri question he said, to hear about that carried him to Mondays.

THE COURT *unanimously* found Jacob Stagg GUILTY, and passed upon him the sentence of DEATH.

1. Jacob Stagg was owned by Jacob Lankester, a grocer, who in 1822 lived at 113 East Bay Street. Lankester described Jacob as a mixed-race painter, about twenty-eight years of age. See *CSCCD,* 86; Inhabitants of Charleston, Petition and Supporting Papers Asking Compensation for Their Slaves Who Were Executed for Involvement in a Slave Insurrection, n.d., no. 1839, Series S165015, SCDAH. Hamilton, *Account,* 43, dates Stagg's arrest to Tuesday, July 23, and the Senate transcript indicates that his trial took place on Friday, July 26. He was one of the four slaves to hang on Tuesday, July 30.

2. *CSCCD,* 74, identifies in 1822 an attorney named Joseph Clark at 85 Meeting Street. He appears to be the Charleston attorney Joseph Clarke (1794–1853), who in 1824 married Charlotte Pringle. See Mary Pringle Fenhagen, "Descendants of Judge Robert Pringle," *SCHM* 101 (2000): 304.

3. The Second Presbyterian Church, dedicated on lower Meeting Street in 1811, once numbered Denmark Vesey among its congregants.

4. The witness is Charles Drayton.

5. "Mr. Whitney" refers to Archibald Whitney (1785–1847), a grocer, who in 1822 lived at 36 Market Street. Whitney had been involved in Jacob's sale in 1817 to Jacob D. Stagg, a Charleston merchant with a firm on East Bay Street. *CSCCD,* 63, 103; Bill of Sale, Archibald Whitney to Jacob D. Stagg, January 14, 1817, vol. 4, p. 69, Series S213003, SCDAH.

6. Physician John Ramsay (1768–1828) lived in 1822 at 1 Anson Street. See *CSCCD,* 95.

THE TRIAL of SAM, a Negro Man, belonging to Mr. Henry Barnstile[1]—His owner's friend, Mr. Wadsworth attending.[2]

EVIDENCE.

PERAULT testified that Sam agreed to join, and we have often talked together about it; he often said he was one and was ready.

THE COURT, as they placed great reliance on Peraults veracity, *unanimously* found Sam GUILTY, and passed upon him the following sentence, "That he be imprisoned in the Work-House of Charleston, until his master, under the direction of the City Council of Charleston, shall send him out of the limits of the United States, into which he is not to return under penalty of Death.["]

1. Hamilton, *Account,* 45, identifies Sam's master as "Bainsill" and dated Sam's arrest to Tuesday, July 23. The Senate transcript indicates that Sam's trial took place three days later, on July 26. No one by the name of Henry Barnstile, Barnstille, or Bainsill appears in the Charleston city directories either for 1816, 1819, or 1822, or in the 1820 census for Charleston. One possibility is a man named Henry Barnstein who married in Charleston in 1804 and was involved in a legal case there in 1824. See A. S. Salley Jr., *Marriage Notices in the Charleston Courier, 1803–1808* (Charleston: Historical Commission of South Carolina, 1919), 13; D. J. McCord, *Reports of Cases Argued and Determined in the Court of Appeals of South Carolina* (Columbia, SC, 1826), vol. 3: 162–63.

2. The friend of Sam's master in attendance was William Wadsworth (d. 1827), a grocer, who in 1822 lived at 36 Archdale Street. See *CSCCD,* 102; Charleston *City Gazette and Commercial Daily Advertiser,* July 30, 1827.

THE TRIAL of TOM, a Negro Man, the property of Mr. Wm. M. Scott[1]—His owner attending.

EVIDENCE.

MONDAY testified as follows:—I told Tom of the business, and he joined; he was often at my shop talking on this business; he was willing; had joined, and said he was making ready; *he was of the same mind after the 16th June*; he belongs to the African Church.

Cross-Examined by Mr. Scott—It is about three months since I spoke to him about it; the first time it was fixed to commence on the second Sunday in July, and Vesey afterwards altered it to the 16th June.

PERAULT gave the following evidence:—Tom told me he was engaged in this business with his own mouth, and was willing; he told me the day that Monday was taken of the circumstance and said, *the more we stand still, the more of us will be taken*; he belonged to Monday's company.

CHARLES testified as follows:—I have heard Tom and Monday often in Monday's shop talking on this business, and heard him assent to the business; he spoke boldly.

Mr. HARTH stated that the prisoner had a wife in his yard, and bore a good character; I have examined his trunk but found no arms.

THE COURT *unanimously* found Tom GUILTY, and passed upon him the sentence of DEATH.

1. In 1822, Tom's owner, William M. Scott (also rendered "Scot") worked as a notary public at 183 East Bay Street and resided at 7 Pinckney Street. He described Tom as a young, valuable slave, twenty-eight years of age and worth more than one thousand dollars. Tom worked for wages of "12 to 14 dollars" per month as a laborer and sailor. See Inhabitants of Charleston, Petition and Supporting Papers Asking Compensation for Their Slaves Who Were Executed for Involvement in a Slave Insurrection, n.d., no. 1839, Series S165015, SCDAH; *CSCCD*, 98. Hamilton, *Account*, 43, dates Scott's arrest to Wednesday, July 24. The Senate transcript indicates that Sam's trial took place two days later, on Friday, July 26. He was one of four men hanged on Tuesday, July 30.

THE TRIAL of DENBOW, a Negro Man, the slave of Mr. J. N. Martin[1]—His owner and Wm. Crafts, Esq. as his Counsel attending.[2]

EVIDENCE.

MONDAY testified as follows:—Denbow's name was on my list; he agreed to join about three months ago; Vesey has met him and spoke to him in my shop as one of his men; he was often at my shop; after Peter was taken up he said he was just as much for it as ever; he told me that Stephen Smith told him he belonged to one of the party; none ever told me to put their names down on my list, but those who positively agreed, I put their names down myself.

Prisoner *did* belong to the African Church, but now to the Lutheran.

PERAULT testified as follows:—I met Denbow at Monday's, speaking about this business, about two or three months ago, where he said, that so many persons were knowing of this business, we had better let it alone.

CHARLES DRAYTON testified that he had met Denbow at Monday's, but don't know any thing against him in reference to this business.

Mr. MARTIN stated that Denbow bore a good character.

THE COURT *unanimously* found Denbow GUILTY, and passed upon him the following sentence:—"That he be imprisoned in the Work-House of Charleston until his master, under the direction of the City Council of Charleston, shall send him *out of the limits of the United States,* into which he is not to return under the penalty of Death.["]

1. John N. Martin worked as a "mason and city scavenger" (street cleaner) and in 1822 resided at 15 Hasell Street. In 1820, he was elected captain of a city militia unit. In 1823 Martin petitioned the state senate to be recompensed $41.93, the amount he was billed for the incarceration of Denbow for 105 days before transportation out of the country. See *CSCCD,* 88; *Charleston Courier,* March 8, 1820; John N. Martin, Petition and Supporting Papers Asking Compensation for the Support of a Slave Prisoner Who Participated in the Vesey Rebellion of 1822, n.d., no. 1741, Series S165015, SCDAH. Hamilton, *Account,* 45, dates his arrest to July 25, and the Senate transcript indicates that his trial took place the following day, on July 26.

2. Attorney William Crafts Jr. (1787–1826) also represented Billy Robinson. See p. 6 n2 above.

Upon GEORGE, BILLY, PERAULT, FRANK, and JOHN,[1] *who had pleaded* GUILTY, and had been used as witnesses, the Court passed the following sentence:—"That they be imprisoned in the Work-House of Charleston until their masters, under the direction of the City Council of Charleston shall send them out of the limits of the United States, into which they are not to return under penalty of Death.["]

1. These five slaves were George Bamfield, Billy Bulkley, Perault Strohecker, Frank Ferguson, and John Enslow. See Hamilton, *Account,* 45.

EXAMINATION of BILLY, *taken a day or two after his arrest*[1]—The first meeting was at Mr. Thayer's farm—one Sunday morning I joined them there, but did not learn what was done there, and I left them—After that, they came to Mr. Bulkley's farm—this was in April. At that meeting there were Adam Robertson, Robert Robertson and John Robertson, Dick Simms, and Pollydore Faber.—At that meeting they were consulting about the means of rising against the whites—Gullah Jack was present, he came in company with Adam and Robert—they roasted a fowl, and eat it half raw, as an evidence of union—Robert and Gullah Jack were the principal men.—One day I met Adam, on my return from Market, and he requested me to hide a jug of powder, and I refused to do so. At another meeting, before the 16th June, at which the following persons were present, viz:—Adam, Robert, Pollydore, John Robertson, Dick Simms, and Gullah Jack. A pistol was exhibited, and every one tried to fire it, but no one could discharge it, but Dick Simms. Those, in whose hands it could not go off, were considered as safe. Charles Drayton told me, that the place of meeting for the draymen was to be the farm of Mr. Payne—and Charles also informed me, that they wished to put their horses in my master's farm, which I refused—Charles afterwards told me, that the plot was discovered, and that the blacks must remain quiet, until the whites were off their guard—Robert called and gave me the same caution that Adam had done. Peter Poyas and others, whom I know not, came to the farm, on the night of the 27th of April, about 8 o'clock, PM. and sung and

Figure 13. Charles Manning Furman (1797–1872), son of the Reverend Richard Furman and judge on the Second Court of Magistrates and Freeholders. Courtesy of Special Collections and Archives, Furman University.

prayed until day light—before this time, I asked Robert who was the principal man, he said Gullah Jack—I then asked him, if there were no others; he said that Gullah Jack had gone to Father Morris, (Morris Brown) to ask him, whether he would sanction the insurrection, and MORRIS Brown replied, if you can get men go on, but don't mention my name. I am going shortly to the North—and I shall hear there, what you are about.[2]

Will Bee, told Peter Ward, who mentioned it to me, that all the draymen, without exception, would be light-horsemen. Pollydore belonging to Mrs. Faber, hid more than twenty poles, about 10 feet long, on Mr. Bulkley's farm, under the house. Pollydore said that Bobert would come, and I supposed, that he was coming to fix something at the end of the poles, as Pollydore had said, that Robert was coming.—Robert came in the afternoon and said that it was useless, as the business was discovered.

1. Hamilton, *Account,* 25, describes Bulkley's Farm as a "principal rendezvous" for the plotters and dated the arrest of Billy Bulkley, a rope maker, to Wednesday, July 10. The Senate transcript indicates that Billy began to provide testimony the next day. His owner, Stephen Bulkley (1768–1841), a wealthy businessman, resided in Charleston in 1822 at 261 King Street. He served with Thomas Bennett Jr. on the Charleston City Council's Committee on Contracts and on the board of directors of the Charleston Branch of the National Bank. See *CSCCD,* 72; Charleston *City Gazette*

and Commercial Daily Advertiser, May 18, 1812; Haverhill *Merrimack Intelligencer,* January 25, 1817; "Deaths," Hartford *Connecticut Courant,* October 23, 1841.

2. The Reverend Morris Brown (1770–1849) traveled to the North in early April 1822 to attend an AME conference and meet with Reverend Richard Allen. See Charleston *City Gazette and Commercial Daily Advertiser,* August 10, 1822, in Part V of this volume.

There was a number of other persons charged with the same offence and arraigned by the Court, but the evidence against them being thought insufficient they were discharged without being put upon their trials.

On Friday the 25th July[1] the COURT ADJOURNED, *sine die,* having disposed of every case before them after a session of nearly six weeks.

The following account of the Trials before the second Court, was politely furnished by one of its Members:—

1. This was a typographical error. Friday fell on July 26, not 25, and the Senate transcript indicates that trials, including those of Tom Scott, Sam Barnstile, and Denbow Martin, all took place on Friday, July 26.

IN CONSEQUENCE *of the* DISSOLUTION of the Court over which Lionel H. Kennedy, and Thomas Parker, Esq'rs. Presided. A NEW COURT WAS ORGANIZED for the trial of William Garner, who had recently been apprehended in Columbia, and brought to Charleston, and of such other slaves as might be brought before them.[1]

THE COURT met accordingly, and consisted of the following Gentlemen, viz:

Jacob Axson,[2] *Q.U.* Magistrates.
Charles M. Furman,[3] *J.P.*
Thos. Rhett Smith,[4] Freeholders.
Joel R. Poinsett,[5]
Robert Y. Hayne,[6]
Thomas Roper,[7]
John Gordon,[8]

After a free interchange of sentiments, the Members of this Court were unanimously of opinion, that with respect to capital punishments, enough had been done by way of example, in relation to this conspiracy, and that where the Court might feel themselves compelled by the weight of the evidence to convict, they would punish the offenders by banishment, and that they would only inflict capital punishment where the criminal should appear to have been a leader, or where his case was distinguished by very peculiar circumstances—Fourteen persons were tried by this Court—of these six were acquitted, and eight found Guilty—of the latter seven were sentenced to transportation beyond the limits of the United States, and one (William Garner) was sentenced to death and suffered accordingly. The case of William Garner was one which, in the unanimous opinion of the Court came within the rule established by them. It was fully proved that he *was a leader,* on whom much reliance was placed; he was to have headed a party of the horse, and agreed to enlist men for that service among the Draymen—He stated to the witness that he had made some progress in that service, and when his fears were excited on account of the detection of the conspiracy, he did not seem disposed to abandon the enterprize, though he offered to give up to another his command in the horse. It was fully proved that Garner had entered heartily into the scheme, and was very earnest in his enquires about the extent of the preparations. The Court having resolved to put no questions to any of the prisoners which might induce them to criminate themselves, of course did not question Garner, but on the evidence against him being closed, and on his counsel declaring that he had nothing to urge in his defence, the prisoner requested that he might be permitted to speak for himself. This being granted, he spoke with great fluency for nearly half an hour, and made a defence, which for ingenuity, would have done honor to an educated man. Finding that *four witnesses, separately examined,* had concurred in establishing facts which must lead irresistibly to his conviction, he boldly admitted the whole of the facts stated in evidence, and alledged that his intention from the beginning had been to possess himself of full information concerning the details of the plot—to discover the deposit of arms and ammunition, and then to betray the Conspirators to the white people. He stated that the premature discovery of the plot had alone prevented him from executing this purpose, and finally made an appeal to the Court, and asked "whether a man situated as he was—master of his own time, as good as free, (and as he emphatically expressed it,) "as happy as the days were long," could have any motive to engage in such a scheme"[9]—The Court could not give credit to these *secret intentions* of the prisoner, contradicted as they were by his acts; especially as it would have been so easy for him to have given *private information* to some white person, and thus have put his intentions beyond a doubt. The circumstance of his having fled from Charleston also weighed against him; and though he had a ticket from his indulgent mistress, the Court were not on that account the less convinced, that Garner's journey to Columbia was undertaken by him as the means of escaping from punishment. His being detected and brought back to Charleston, was certainly calculated to make a deep impression on the minds of the Slaves. In every view of the subject, therefore Garner's case seemed to demand the utmost penalty of the law, and it was inflicted accordingly.

In the progress of the trials before this Court one or two circumstances occurred worthy of being noticed. The Court at the commencement of their investigations determined thoroughly to examine into the degree of credit to be attacked to the witnesses, and were very particular in their enquiries in respect to the two principal witnesses, *Monday Gell* and *Perault.* It appeared that the character of these men for veracity and honesty, had been unexceptional through life—Monday indeed seemed to have been distinguished for the candour, sobriety, and integrity of his life, and of Perault, his master declared that his only fault was "that he was sometimes so blunt and free spoken, as to approach to rudeness." The Court were finally of opinion that entire reliance could be placed on these two witnesses, and that every word which came from Monday could be implicitly relied on—Several circumstances occurred during the trials to confirm the favourable impressions of the Court with respect to these witnesses—one or two of them will be here stated. The witnesses were not permitted to have any communications with each other, and they were never informed of the particular prisoner against whom they were to appear. They were brought forth separately and examined. Their *concurrence,* under such circumstances certainly afforded strong evidence of their truth—On

Monday Gills detailing a conversation he had with *Michaw,*[10] (and which was favourable to the prisoner,) Mr. Miller who was present, stated promptly to the Court, that Michaw himself had stated to him the same conversation, in all particulars, as soon as he was arrested; and it appeared that no communication had since taken place between the parties. Of several similar circumstances: but one other will be here noticed. It appeared that Garner, Monday, Peter Poyas, and others, had held a meeting at the house of a blind man named Philip—Monday stated in his evidence before the Court, concerning that meeting, that this man addressed Garner, and asked him, "*why he looked so timorous,*" and quoted a text of Scripture, "*Why should thy heart be troubled,* &c." It appeared so extraordinary, that a blind man should speak of another's *looks,* that some suspicion rested on Monday's statement. The blind man was sent for, and on being brought forward, (though totally ignorant of the statements made by Monday,) stated the remark he had made to Garner about "*his timorous looks, &c.* Garner in his defence, admitted that this remark had been made and said it had greatly alarmed him at the time, knowing that the old man was blind.*

* The name of the blind man had never before been mentioned in the course of these trials, and when he was brought before the Court he exhibited great perturbation. The question put to him by the Court seemed to imply a fear that he was actually on trial for his life, and it is probable if it had been deemed adviseable to investigate his character and conduct, that he would have been found deeply concerned in the Conspiracy. It appeared that some of the Conspirators were in the habit of resorting to his house, that he was a Preacher, said to have been born with *a caul,* and was supposed to foresee events. His influence over the minds of his followers was no doubt therefore very considerable. It is propable that the timid and the wavering were brought to this High Priest of sedition, to be confirmed in *good resolutions.* This would account for the address to Garner about his "looking frightened," and would then shew how applicable the text was "let not thy heart be troubled, neither be afraid." Peter Poyas perhaps had *intimated* to the *Sear* that Garner was timid, and hence the remark and the quotation. *His own account* of the affair, however, was somewhat different. He said he possessed *a Gift*—a species of *second sight*—which came to him *after prayer* or *in dreams*—That the Insurrection had never been mentioned to him, but that he had foreseen something of that sort, and therefore had advised his visitors, *on one occasion* (as he was proved to have done)—"to give up the business," and had told them as a dissuasive "that the white people could fire five times while they fired once." *Thus seeing* Garner's *timid looks*—he resolved (to use his own words) to comfort him with some scriptures."

Two cases were brought before this Court, which furnished incidents worthy of remark. In one of them it was proved that Vesey had forbidden his followers to trust the prisoner, "*because on one occasion he had been seen in a state of intoxication.*" In the other case, that of George (slave of Samuel Parker.)[11] It appeared that Vesey, Monday Gell and the other leaders of the conspiracy came to a resolution that the prisoner should not be trusted. He was an African, but they alledged against him, that he did not associate with his countrymen, and was a babbling fellow, on whom no dependence could be placed. George had heard something about an insurrection, and resolved to have his hand in it. He went about among the conspirators, declared himself one of them, and both by actions and words, manifested a determination to take his part in the contest. He was (notwithstanding his unquestionable good will to the cause) uniformly rejected as a Marplot who could not be trusted. When brought before the Court the levity of manner which distinguished this Negro, convinced the Court of the wisdom and circumspection displayed by the leaders of the conspiracy *in excluding* him from their ranks. . . .

1. On William Garner's attempts to purchase and free his wife and children, and his motivation for joining the plot, see Eliza Smith Garner's petition of July 10, 1834, which appears in Part V, pp. 535–36, of this volume.

2. On attorney Jacob Axson Jr. (1794–1843), who had served previously as counsel for Governor Bennett's Rolla, see p. 167 n2.

3. Charles Manning Furman (1797–1872), an attorney, was the son of Richard Furman (1755–1825), one of the most influential Baptist ministers of his generation and a close observer of the Vesey affair. Charles would become one of Charleston's leading citizens as well as a successful businessman and slaveowner. See *BDSCHR* 5: 96–98.

4. Planter Thomas Rhett Smith (1768–1829) split time in 1822 between his Charleston home at 1 Meeting Street and multiple plantations. During the War of 1812, he had served as Charleston's mayor. In 1820, he owned more than three hundred slaves. See *BDSCHR* 4: 327–28; *CSCCD*, 99.

5. On Poinsett, see Part II, p. 102 n1.

6. See Part II, pp. 148–52, for the letter of Robert Young Hayne (1791–1839), South Carolina's attorney general at the time, who answered Governor Bennett's questions about the proceedings of the first court as well as p. 154 n3. Hayne would sit on the second court.

7. Thomas Roper (1760–1829), a planter, resided in Charleston in 1822 at 163 East Bay Street. A wealthy slaveholder with a philanthropic bent, Roper served in a wide variety of state and local positions and was particularly involved in medical education. See *CSCCD*, 97; *BDSCHR* 4: 488–89; John Hammond Moore, ed., "The Abiel Abbot Journals: A Yankee Preacher in Charleston Society, 1818–1827," *SCHM* 68 (1967): 59–60.

8. Colonel John Gordon (d. 1835), a prosperous builder and brick mason who employed slave artisans, served as director of the State Bank of South Carolina. A militia officer, he was one of five commissioners of the Charleston Work-House about the time of the Vesey affair. He resided in 1822 at 209 Meeting Street. See "Obituary," *Charleston Courier*, March 16, 1835.

9. The imprecise use of quotation marks for this testimony is in the original.

10. "Michaw" refers to Philander Michau, a free person of color, whose case is taken up in the Senate document, below. The Monday "Gills" referred to here is clearly Monday Gell.

11. Samuel Parker (1776–1830), a planter, resided in 1822 at 6 George Street. See *CSCCD*, 93.

Sentence of ten of the Criminals.

The Court, on mature deliberation, have pronounced you guilty; the punishment of that guilt is DEATH. Your conduct, on the present occasion, exhibits a degree of depravity and extravigance, rarely paralled. Your professed objects were to trample not only on the laws of this state, but on those of humanity; to commit murder, outrage and plunder, and to substitute for the blessings we enjoy, anarchy and confusion in their most odious forms. The beauties of nature and of art, would have fallen victims to your relentless fury; and even the decripitude of age and the innocence of childhood, would have found no other refuge than the grave!

Surely nothing but infatuation could have prompted you to enter into a plot so wild and diabolical.—A moment's reflection would have convinced you, that disgrace and ruin must have been its consequence, and that it would have probably resulted in the destruction and extermination of *your race.* But if, even complete success had crowned your efforts, what were the golden visions which you anticipated?—Such men as you, are in general, as ignorant as you are vicious, without any settled principles, and possessing but few of the virtues of civilized life; you would soon, therefore, have degenerated into a horde of barbarians, incapable of any government. But admitting that a different result might have taken place, it is natural to enquire, what are the miseries of which you complain?—That we should all earn our bread by the sweat of our brow, is the decree which God pronounced at the fall of man. It extended alike to the master and the slave; to the cottage and the throne. Every one is more or less subject to controul; and the most exalted, as well as the humblest individual, must bow with defference to the laws of that community, in which he is placed by Providence. Your situation, therefore, was neither extraordinary nor unnatural. Servitude has existed under various forms, from the deluge to the present time, and in no age or country has the condition of slaves been milder or more humane than your own. You are, with few exceptions, treated with kindness, and enjoy every comfort compatible with your situation. You are exempt from many of the miseries, to which *the poor* are subject throughout the world. In many countries the life of the slave is at the disposal of his master; here you have always been under the protection of the law.

The tribunal which now imposes this sen[te]nce through its humble organ, affords a strong examplification of the truth of these remarks. In the discharge of the painful duties which have devolved on them the members of this Court have been as anxious to acquit the innocent as determined to condemn the guilty.

In addition to the crime of treason, you have on the present occasion, displayed the vilest ingratitude. It is a melancholy truth, that those servants in whom was reposed the most unlimitted confidence, have been the principal actors in this wicked scheme. Reared by the hand of kindness, and fostered by a master who assumed many of the duties of a parent—you have realized the fable of the Frozen Serpent,[1] and attempted to destroy the bosom that sheltered and protected you.

You have moreover committed the grossest impiety: you have perverted the sacred words of God, and attempted to torture them into a sanction for crimes, at the bare imagination of which, humanity shudders. Are you incapable of the Heavenly influence of that Gospel, all whose "paths are peace?" It was to reconcile us to our destiny on earth, and to enable us to discharge with fidelity all our duties, whether as master or servant, that those inspired precepts were imparted by Heaven to fallen man.—There is no condition of life which is not embraced by them; and if you had searched them, *in the spirit of truth,* you would have discovered instructions peculiarly applicable to yourselves—"*Servants (says St. Paul) be obedient to them that are your masters according to the flesh, with fear and trembling, in singleness of your heart, as unto Christ; not with eye-service as men pleasers, but as the servants of Christ, doing the will of God from the heart.*"[2] Had you listened with sincerity to such doctrines, you would not have been arrested by an ignominious death.

183

A CALENDAR,

Comprising those Arrested, their owner's names, the time of their commitment, and the manner in which they were disposed of.

Class No. 1.

Comprises those prisoners who were found guilty and executed.

Prisoners Names.	*Owners' Names.*	*Time of Commit.*	*How Disposed of.*
Peter	James Poyas	June 18	
Ned	Gov. T. Bennet	do	Hanged on Tuesday
Rolla	do.	do	the 2d July, 1822
Batteau	do.	do	on Blake's lands,
Denmark Vesey	A free black man	22	near Charleston.
Jessy	Thos. Blackwood	23	
John	Elias Horry	July 5	Do. on the lines near
Gullah Jack	Paul Pritchard	do	Ch.; Friday July 12
Mingo	Wm. Harth	June 21	
Lot	Forrester	24	
Joe	P. L. Jore	July 6	
Julius	Thos. Forrest	8	
Tom	Mrs. Russell	10	
Smart	Rob't. Anderson	do.	
John	John Robertson	11	
Robert	do.	do.	
Adam	do.	do.	
Polydore	Mrs. Faber	do.	Hanged on the lines
Bacchus	Benj. Hammet	do.	near Charleston,
Dick	Wm. Sims	13	on Friday, 26th,
Pharoah	Mrs. Thompson	do.	July.
Jemmy	Mrs. Clement	18	
Jerry	Mordecai Cohen	19	
Dean	Jas. Mitchell	do.	
Jack	Mrs. Purcell	12	
Bellisle	Est. of Jos. Yates	18	
Naphur	do.	do.	
Adam	do.	do.	
Jack	John S. Glen	16	
Charles	John Billings	18	
Jack	N. McNeill	22	
Cæsar	Miss Smith	do.	Do. Tues. July 30.
Jacob Stagg	Jacob Lancaster	23	
Tom	Wm. M. Scott	24	
*William	Mrs. Garner	Aug. 2	Do. Friday Aug. 9

* Tried by the last Court.

Figure 14. Calendar of prisoners identified as "Class No. 1," found guilty and executed. From Kennedy and Parker, *Official Report of the Trials of Sundry Negroes* (1822).

Your days on earth are near their close and you now stand upon the confines of eternity. While you linger on this side of the grave, permit me to exhort you, in the name of the everliving God, whose holy ordinances you have violated; to devote most earnestly the remnant of your days, in penitence and preparation for that tribunal, whose sentence, whether pronounced in anger or in mercy, is eternal.

The following were the Negroes on whom the above sentence was pronounced:—Dick, Bacchus, William, Naphur, Adam, Belisle, Charles, Jemmy, Jerry and Dean.[3]

1. The court references here another Aesop's Fable, the Frozen Serpent, whose moral is ingratitude.

2. Ephesians 6: 5–6.

3. The slaves sentenced here are Dick Sims, Bacchus Hammet, William Paul, Naphur Yates, Adam Robertson, Belisle Yates, Charles Billings, Jemmy Clement, Jerry Cohen, and Dean Mitchell. This information was reprinted nearly verbatim in the Richmond *Enquirer*, September 3, 1822. It claimed to be the SENTENCE OF NINE OF THE CRIMINALS, but did not list Jerry Cohen, and identified Jemmy Clement as "Jeremy." All of the above were hanged on Friday, July 26, with the exception of William Paul, who was transported.

A CALENDAR,

Comprising those Arrested, their owner's names, the time of their commitment, and the manner in which they were disposed of.

Class No. 1.

Comprises those prisoners who were found guilty and executed.

* Tried by the last Court.

Class No. 2.

Comprises those Prisoners who were found Guilty, and Sentenced to Death, but recommended by the Court of Magistrates and Freeholders, to the Governor to be pardoned *upon condition that they be sent out of the limits of the United States.*

They were respited to the 25th day of October, 1822, with a view to the commutation of their punishment to banishment beyond the limits of the United States; but since the respite, the Governor has pardoned Peter Cooper, upon condition of his receiving *twenty lashes*.

Class No 3.

Comprises those prisoners who were found guilty and sentenced to Death, but since respited by the Executive, until the 25th of Oct. with a view to the commutation of their punishment, to banishment beyond the limits of the United States.

Class No. 4.

Comprises those prisoners who were found guilty and sentenced to be transported, beyond the limits of the United States, by their masters, under the direction of the City Council.

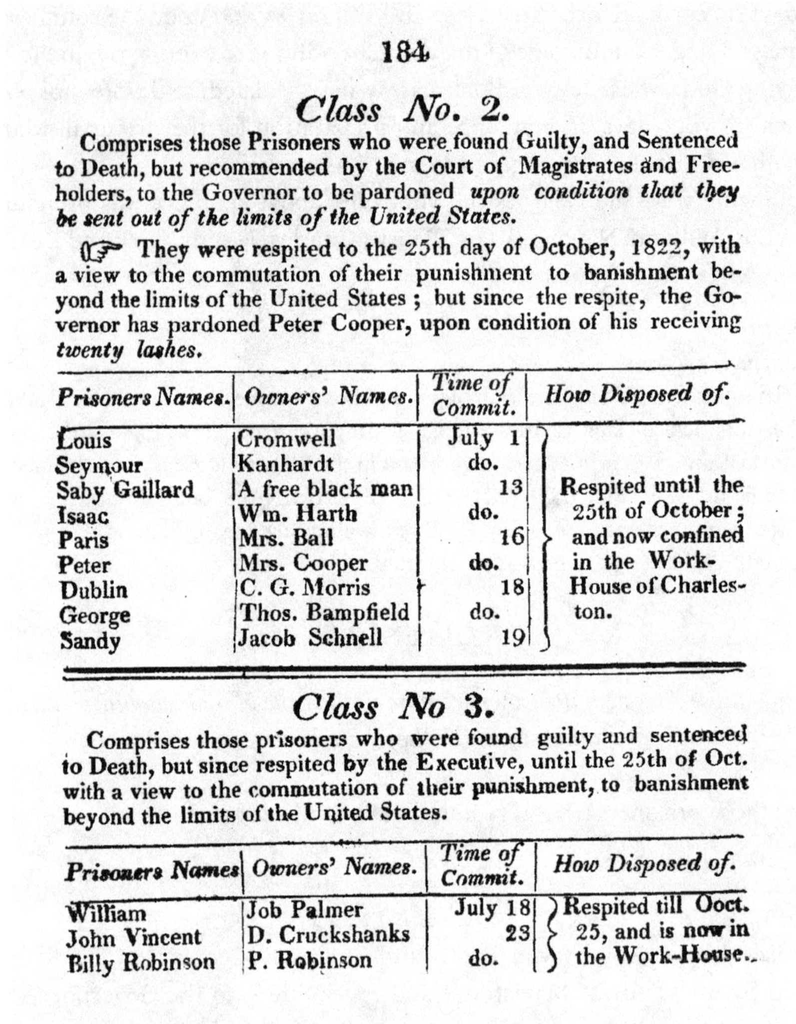

184

Class No. 2.

Comprises those Prisoners who were found Guilty, and Sentenced to Death, but recommended by the Court of Magistrates and Freeholders, to the Governor to be pardoned *upon condition that they be sent out of the limits of the United States.*

☞ **They were respited to the 25th day of October, 1822, with a view to the commutation of their punishment to banishment beyond the limits of the United States ; but since the respite, the Governor has pardoned Peter Cooper, upon condition of his receiving *twenty lashes.***

Prisoners Names.	*Owners' Names.*	*Time of Commit.*	*How Disposed of.*
Louis	Cromwell	July 1	Respited until the 25th of October ; and now confined in the Work-House of Charleston.
Seymour	Kanhardt	do.	
Saby Gaillard	A free black man	13	
Isaac	Wm. Harth	do.	
Paris	Mrs. Ball	16	
Peter	Mrs. Cooper	do.	
Dublin	C. G. Morris	18	
George	Thos. Bampfield	do.	
Sandy	Jacob Schnell	19	

Class No 3.

Comprises those prisoners who were found guilty and sentenced to Death, but since respited by the Executive, until the 25th of Oct. with a view to the commutation of their punishment, to banishment beyond the limits of the United States.

Prisoners Names	*Owners' Names.*	*Time of Commit.*	*How Disposed of.*
William	Job Palmer	July 18	Respited till Ooct. 25, and is now in the Work-House.
John Vincent	D. Cruckshanks	23	
Billy Robinson	P. Robinson	do.	

Figure 15. Calendar of prisoners identified as "Class No. 2" and "Class No. 3," sentenced to death but had their punishments commuted to transportation outside the United States. From Kennedy and Parker, *Official Report of the Trials of Sundry Negroes* (1822).

Class No. 5.

Comprises those who were found guilty and sentenced to be transported beyond the limits of the State of South-Carolina.

(*Note:* * Tried by the last Court)

Class No. 6.

Comprises those prisoners who were acquitted by the Court, their guilt not being fully proved. The Court, however, have suggested to their owners, the propriety of transporting them beyond the limits of the United States.

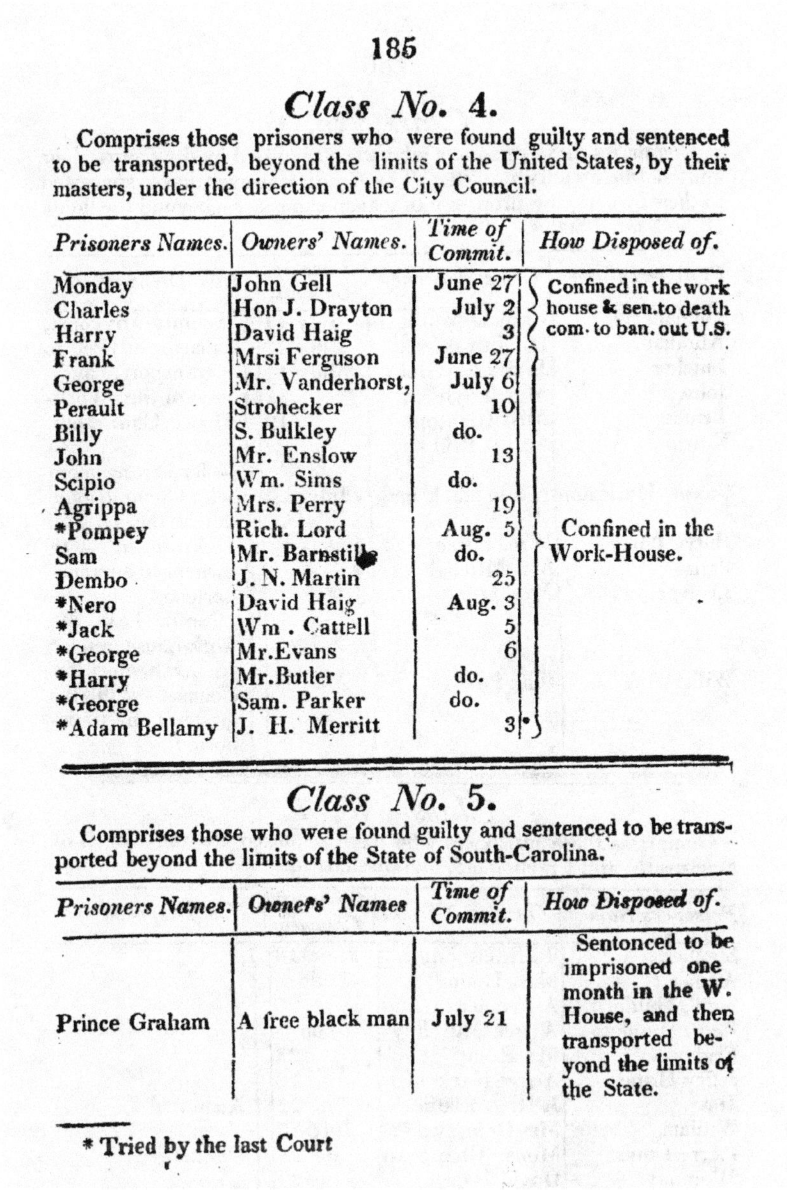

185

Class No. 4.

Comprises those prisoners who were found guilty and sentenced to be transported, beyond the limits of the United States, by their masters, under the direction of the City Council.

Prisoners Names.	*Owners' Names.*	*Time of Commit.*	*How Disposed of.*
Monday	John Gell	June 27	Confined in the work
Charles	Hon J. Drayton	July 2	house & sen.to death
Harry	David Haig	3	com. to ban. out U.S.
Frank	Mrsi Ferguson	June 27	
George	Mr. Vanderhorst,	July 6	
Perault	Strohecker	10	
Billy	S. Bulkley	do.	
John	Mr. Enslow	13	
Scipio	Wm. Sims	do.	
Agrippa	Mrs. Perry	19	
*Pompey	Rich. Lord	Aug. 5	Confined in the
Sam	Mr. Barnstill[illegible]	do.	Work-House.
Dembo	J. N. Martin	25	
*Nero	David Haig	Aug. 3	
*Jack	Wm . Cattell	5	
*George	Mr.Evans	6	
*Harry	Mr.Butler	do.	
*George	Sam. Parker	do.	
*Adam Bellamy	J. H. Merritt	3	

Class No. 5.

Comprises those who weie found guilty and sentenced to be transported beyond the limits of the State of South-Carolina.

Prisoners Names.	*Ownefs' Names*	*Time of Commit.*	*How Disposed of.*
Prince Graham	A free black man	July 21	Sentonced to be imprisoned one month in the W. House, and then transported beyond the limits of the State.

* Tried by the last Court

Figure 16. Calendar of prisoners identified as "Class No. 4" and "Class No. 5," sentenced to transportation outside the United States. From Kennedy and Parker, *Official Report of the Trials of Sundry Negroes* (1822).

Class No. 7.

Comprises those prisoners who were acquitted by the Courts of Magistrates and Freeholders, and discharged.

(*Note:* * Tried by the last Court.)

Class No. 8.

Comprises those persons who were discharged after being arrested, the testimony against them not being sufficient to bring them to trial.

186

Class No. 6.

Comprises those prisoners who werc acquitted by the Court, their guilt not being fully proved. The Court, however, have suggested to their owners, the propriety of transporting them beyond the limits of the United States.

Prisoners Names.	*Owners' Names.*	*Time of Commit.*	*How Disposed of.*
Buonaparte	Francis Mulligan	July 11	Acquitted by court, master advised to transport, and now in the Work-House, Charleston.
Abraham	Dr. Poyas	June 22	
Butcher	James L. Gibbs	July 11	
John	Mrs. Taylor	13	
Prince	Miss Righton	19	
Edwin	Mr. J. Paul	24	
Quash Harleston	A free black man	July 29	—By arrangement with Council, gone out of the U. S.
Harry Purse	Wm. Purse	not arrested	Arranged with owners to be transported.
Panza	Mr. Mitchel		
Liverpool	Mrs. Hunt		
William	John Paul	Mao 31	Confined in the work-house under an arrangemet by Counsel with his master to be transported.

Class No. 7.

Comprises those prisoners who were acquitted by the Courts of Magistrates and Freeholders, and discharged.

Prisoners Names.	*Owners' Names.*	*Time of Commit.*	*How Disposed of.*
Stephen	T. Rhett Smith	June 18	Acquitted and Discharged
Amherst	Mrs. Lining	do	
Saml. Guifford	A free black Lad	20	
Robt. Hadden	A free Mul. Boy	do	
Friday	Mr. Rout	23	
Jeffry Grant	A free black man	20	
Jim	J. H. Ancrum	22	
William	Mrs Colcock	July 12	
Pierre Louis	Mons. Chappeau	do 18	
*Pompey	David Haig	June 23	
*Philander	A free Col. Man	August 8	
*Edw'd Johnson	A free black man	do	
*Stephen Walker	Mr. Walker	do 5	
*James	Do	do	
*Harry	J. Nell	do 6	

* Tried by the last Court.

Figure 17. Calendar of prisoners identified as "Class No. 6" and "Class No. 7," acquitted. From Kennedy and Parker, *Official Report of the Trials of Sundry Negroes* (1822).

187

Class No. 8.

Compris s those persons who were discharged after being arrested, the testimony against them not being sufficient to bring them to trial.

Prisoners Names.	*Owners' Names.*	*Time of Commit.*
Mathias	Thos. Bennett	June 18
Mungo	James Poyas	do
Bram	Jonathan Lucas	20
Richard	Do.	17
John	Do.	do
Hercules	Mr. Clark	20
Sandy	H. P. Holmes	25
Lemon	Mr. Houston	23
Adam	Mrs. Ferguson	27
Pompey	John Bryan	28
Harry	Mr. Harleston	
Robert Nesbitt	A Free Man	July 3
Patrick	Miss Datty	4
Thomas	S. Magwood	5
Charles	F. G. Deliesseline	8
William	Mr. Adger	10
Smart	Mrs. Ward	do
Peter	Do.	do
Sandy	Francis Curtis	11
Isaac	Paul Trapier	do
Charles	Mrs. Shubrick	do
Cuffy	Charles Graves	do
Mungo	Wm. Lowndes	do
Thomas	A. Lord	do
Bob	Mr. Hibben	13
Albert	T. Inglis, a free mullatto man.	15
Jim	Mr. Happoldt	do
John	Mr. Gotes	do
Charles	Mr. Hasell	do
James	Mr. Dowling	17
Prince	Do.	do
Cæsar	Mrs. Parker	19
Billy	Mr. Fordham	20
Ben	Mr. Cammer	22
William	Mr. Cromwell	do
Stephen	Mr. Harper	26
Louis	John Gell	18
Pompey	John Bryan	Aug. 5

B2

Figure 18. Calendar of persons of color identified as "Class No. 8," arrested and discharged. From Kennedy and Parker, *Official Report of the Trials of Sundry Negroes* (1822)

RECAPITULATION.

Number of Prisoners executed—See Class, No. 1.	35
" " respited with a view to their transportation—see Classes, No. 2 and 3.	12
" " sentenced to be transported by their owners, under the direction of the City Council *beyond the limits of the U. States*—see Class, No. 4.	19
" " sentenced to be transported out of the State—see Class, No. 5.	1
" " acquitted, but suggested to owners to transport, &c.—see Class, No. 6.	11
" " Acquitted—see Class, No. 7.	15
" " discharged, &c—see Class, No. 8.	38
Whole number arrested,	131

APPENDIX.

AT A COURT OF SESSIONS

Held at Charleston, on the 7th October, 1822, before his honor Judge Bay,[1] four men were tried and convicted of "*a Misdemeanor in inciting Slaves to Insurrection*[.]" These cases created much interest, in consequence of their connection with the late attempt made by the slaves, to raise an Insurrection in this state. It did not appear that the prisoners were actually concerned in the insurrection, any further than in exciting the Slaves. The plot certainly did not originate with white persons, nor was it ever communicated by any person concerned in it, to a single white man, until the information was given which led to the developement of the scheme.

It has appeared, however, that as soon as *rumours of a Negro Plot went abroad,* some white men of the lowest characters, determined to avail themselves of the occasion, and by exciting the slaves, to hasten an event, which however calamitous to the rest of the community, they vainly imagined might be beneficial to themselves. Whether any of these men would actually have taken part with the slaves in the conduct of the insurrection, and whether the slaves themselves would have permitted white men to act in their ranks cannot be now ascertained. It is presumed that *plunder, and indemnity to their own persons,* were the objects sought for by these offenders. Only four individuals have been detected and brought to punishment for the crime of "inciting slaves to insurrection."—Against these, the testimony of white persons was obtained; but when the nature of the crime, the secrecy that would naturally have been observed, and the incompetency of slaves to give evidence, are duly considered, there is every reason to believe that many other cases perhaps more aggravated) have existed, and which still remain undiscovered. It cannot be doubted, that there are to be found in the city of Charleston, desperate men, (outcasts from countries from which they have been banished for crimes,) who hold themselves in readiness at a moment's warning, to engage in any enterprise of blood and ruin, from which plunder may be gained. It will be the part of wisdom *to mark and profit by,* every fact and circumstance connected with the late Conspiracy. The indictment and conviction of the persons hereinafter named, is an incident in the late transactions in this city, too important to be overlooked; a brief report of their cases is therefore annexed.

1. Elihu Hall Bay (1754–1838) spent almost a half century as a judge in South Carolina, much of it on the Court of General Sessions. See John Belton O'Neall, *Biographical Sketches of the Bench and Bar of South Carolina . . .*, 2 vols. (Charleston, SC, 1859), vol. 1: 53–65; *BDSCHR* 4: 51–52.

The State of South-Carolina, vs. *William Allen.* Indictment for a Misdemeanor, in inciting slaves to insurrection.

This was a tall, stout, fine looking sailor, a Scotchman by birth, about forty-five years of age, and who had recently arrived in Charleston. It appeared that having fallen in company with a free man of color, named *Scott,*[1] at the time when the city was much agitated by the rumors of the late intended insurrection, he enquired of Scott concerning it; and not only urged the execution of the plan, but stated his willingness to be concerned in it.[2] Scott immediately gave information to John Stoney, Esq. an eminent merchant of this city, who directed him to assume an apparent willingness to engage in the plot, and see to what extent Allen would go. In order to identify the man, Scott led him into the store of William E. Snowden, Esq.[3] on the pretence of business, by whom his person was marked. Several interviews took place between Scott and Allen, at all of which he held the same language; and it was finally agreed between them, that they should meet at night, at the house of a free negro man named Joe, the father in law of Scott, where the subject was to be fully considered. Hitherto the evidence against Allen was not such as could have led to his conviction; but arrangements were now made to obtain full information, and decisive evidence of the nature and extent of his guilt. Information having been given to his Honor James Hamilton, jun. Intendant of the City of Charleston, of the contemplated meeting, he summoned Richard W. Cogdell, Esq. one of the Wardens, to his assistance, and they repaired to the house of the negro Joe, and concealed themselves in a small upper room, which was so darkened that they could distinctly see and hear every thing which passed below, without being themselves observed. Allen soon after entered with Scott, and was introduced to Joe. No other persons were present in the room below. As soon as Allen entered the room, he expressed apprehensions that he might be overheard—examined the room, and caused the windows and doors to be carefully closed. He stated also, that he was armed, and threatened vengeance if betrayed. The Negroes soon succeeded, however, in removing his apprehensions—some brandy was produced, and the three sat down together at a table, and entered upon the business of the meeting. During a conversation which lasted nearly two hours, Allen expressed his approbation of the scheme of attempting an insurrection—urged the usual arguments in justification of such a measure, and explicitly declared that he would take part in it. He furnished ready answers to every objection that was urged, and endeavored to remove all the difficulties that were suggested. In doing this, he certainly made *false statements,* intended, however, to give confidence to the blacks. He pretended, for instance, to be acquainted with the plans, & spoke of large parcels of arms secreted near the city. In speaking of the plan of operations, he declared "that it would take 400 men to make the grand stand," and added, "that he would head them as soon as that number was obtained. He added, however, that he knew a Captain of a vessel, whom he named, (who then resided in Elliott-street) who had been *a Pirate for* 15 *years,* and was in all respects qualified to be the leader of the expedition.* He insisted that this man should be obtained, and that he (Allen) would serve under him. He spoke freely of the operations, and declared it to be his opinion, "*that there ought to be an indiscriminate destruction of all the whites, men,* *women and children.*" In the course of the interview, it was objected by the Negroes, that he (Allen) being a white man, could not be safely trusted by them. To this he replied, that "though he had a white face, he was a negro in heart." As the party below stairs continued to drink, Allen, before the end of the interview, became somewhat intoxicated, though he had been sober at the commencement. The Intendant and Mr. Cogdell, from their place of concealment, had a distinct view of every thing which was passing in the room below, and expecting opposition, and finding that Allen was a strong, stout man, and probably armed, they made their arrangements for overcoming him. Allen finally rose to depart, and being immediately followed by the gentlemen above mentioned, was seized in the street by them, and taken to the guard-house. He made no resistance, and seemed so completely subdued by his fears, that no doubt could be entertained that he was by no means qualified on the score of courage, to conduct a dangerous enterprise. In the course of the interview, Allen explicitly declared, that he looked for a *handsome pecuniary reward* for the services he was to render, and hinted that *the freedom of the blacks was an object of no importance to him.*

* The individual named by Allen, was known in this city. He was certainly well qualified on the score of courage and talent, for any desperate enterprise; no reason exists, however, to suppose that he would have engaged in one of a criminal nature.

From this circumstance, and his making false statements in relation to the arms, and pretending that he was one of the initiated, it is clear that Allen was not actually engaged in the conspiracy; that his object was money, and that he would probably have been content in urging on the ignorant blacks to an attempt, which in any event, must have produced the most lamentable consequences. At his trial, Allen made no defence, though his ingenious counsel urged some points of law to the court, as to the legal character of the offence. The Jury found him guilty without hesitation. He was sentenced to be imprisoned twelve months; to pay a fine of one thousand dollars, and to find security for his good behavior for five years after his liberation. This sentence, unless modified by a pardon, will doubtless amount to imprisonment for life, since the circumstances and character of the prisoner, will effectually prevent him from paying the fine, or giving the security. After the sentence was passed, Allen addressed the Court in a clear, distinct voice, and with considerable ingenuity. He gave a brief history of his life, and stated that he had served on board of two American privateers during the late war, and also in the navy of the U.S.—that he had been in several severe actions, and was a pensioner of war in England. His strong Scottish dialect, however, might lead us to doubt his having been so long in this country. Certain it is, that he had never been a resident in Charleston, and had very recently arrived here before the disclosure of the late insurrectionary movements.

1. Existing documents provide no forename for the free person of color named "Scott" whom Charleston officials credited as being "instrumental" in providing evidence that convicted William Allen of spreading "insurrectionary Doctrines in connection with the conspiracy." See Petition, City Council of Charleston, n.d., no. 2059, Series S165015, SCDAH, in this volume. *CSCCD*

identifies no free person of color named Scott in 1822 but does locate one (p. 60) named "Abraham Scot" on Boundary Street in 1819. A free person of color named Isaac Scott lived on 2 St. Philip Street, according to State Free Negro Capitation Records for 1821, SCDAH, but no one with that surname appeared in the *DSGCC.* See the *Charleston Courier,* December 14, 1822, in Part IV, p. 590, of this volume for the state's reward for his services in this case.

2. As this indictment indicates, Allen's crime was in showing solicitude for slaves, a not uncommon view among mariners. Certainly no whites were actively involved in Vesey's plot, and the court documents provide little evidence that Vesey either trusted or liked whites. On the antislavery attitudes of mariners, see W. Jeffrey Bolster, *Black Jacks: African American Seamen in the Age of Sail* (Cambridge, MA: Harvard University Press, 1997), 211–14. For background on the four white men and an analysis of their trials, see Philip F. Rubio, "'Though He Had A White Face, He Was A Negro In Heart': Examining the White Men Convicted Of Supporting the Denmark Vesey Slave Insurrection Conspiracy," *SCHM* 113 (2012): 50–67.

3. William E. Snowden (1790–1841) was a factor who in 1822 resided at 291 East Bay Street. See *CSCCD,* 99.

The State, vs. *John Igneshias.*

This man was indicted for the same offence. He is a Spaniard, a sea-faring man, about forty or forty-five years of age, tall, very athletic, and of a steady determined countenance. He speaks broken English, but so as to be easily understood. The evidence against him was, that he was overheard (by Mr. Joseph Hill, and his sister, Mrs. Silvea,) in conversation with a slave, supposed to be the property of Mr. Lance.[1] There were several other negroes, however, (fishermen,) present. In this conversation, (part of which was overheard by the witnesses,) the prisoner began by declaring that "he disliked every thing in Charleston, but the negroes and the sailors." The slave replied, "that he liked every one who used him well." The prisoner then remarked, "how can you think the white people use you well by keeping you in slavery?" and added, "if you had a favor to ask, would you ask it of a white man or a black man, and will any white man trust you for any thing?" The negro, whose fidelity was not to be shaken, replied, "that he had received many favors from the white people, *that they were his best friends,*" and then specified some instances, particularly one of his having recently bought some articles on credit. The patience of the Spaniard was now completely exhausted, and he exclaimed with anger, "damn them, I would kill them all," alluding, as the witness explained it, to what the negroes ought to do towards the whites.

On this evidence the prisoner was found Guilty of inciting slaves to insurrection, and was sentenced to three months imprisonment, to pay a fine of $100, and to give security for good behavior for five years.

The prisoner at his trial, and on receiving sentence, addressed the Court, and insisted that the witnesses were mistaken as to his identity, and claimed for himself the character of an honest and industrious man.

1. *CSCCD,* 86, identifies a planter named Francis Lance who in 1822 resided at 23 Friend Street.

The State vs. *Jacob Danders.*

This man was indicted for the same offence. He is a German, of low stature, and apparently of dissipated habits; about 45 or 50 years of age. The charge against him was, that he was heard by a most respectable witness (Mr. Joseph Young,)[1] speaking to several negroes concerning the execution of some of the slaves. "Poor creatures," said he, "my heart bleeds for you; the negroes executed were innocent, and have been all murdered, and you (addressing himself to the negroes), *ought not to have permitted it,* and you must rescue those who are still to be hanged," and added, "that he was himself a *Lawyer* and a *Preacher*"

On this evidence the prisoner was found Guilty. The prisoner addressed the Court very fluently in broken German. He did not attempt to deny having spoken the words attributed to him, but said he was intoxicated at the time. Mr. Young, however, declared, that he might have been a little intoxicated, but knew perfectly well what he was about. Danders had been but a short time in Charleston; had been engaged *as a pedlar,* selling trifling articles, and in his course of life was very much of a vagabond. He was sentenced to three months imprisonment, to pay a fine of $100, and to give security for his good behaviour for five years.

1. Joseph Young (1767?–1838), a ship chandler, born in Maine, had settled in Charleston a few years before the Vesey affair. In 1822, he resided at 263 East Bay Street. See "Obituary," *Charleston Courier,* July 20, 1838; *CSCCD,* 104.

The State, vs. *Andrew S. Rhodes.*

This was a tall, fine looking portly man, about 50 years of age, with a fresh complexion, and wearing a light colored wig. He was well known in Charleston, having been a few Courts ago convicted of swindling Mr. Foster Burnet, of this city, by means of a counterfeit letter. The prisoner did not state where he was born and brought up, but said that he had been 30 years in this State, a part of which time he kept a small shop in one of the country parishes in the neighborhood of Charleston.

The testimony against Rhodes was certainly less satisfactory than against either of the other prisoners. A woman by the name of Mary Shievly stated that Rhodes came to the house of Adam Garden (a free man of color,) from whom the witness hires a room, and there in the presence of said Garden, and of two other men of color, then in the house, commenced speaking of *Gullah Jack,* who had been sentenced to be hanged The prisoner, speaking of that event, introduced the name of a respectable gentleman, and said he ought to be hanged in the place of Gullah Jack, and then added, "the negroes ought to fight for their liberty;" "that they had as much right to fight for their liberty as the white people" He stated, "that he would head them in the enterprise, and that in three weeks he would have 2000 men."

The witness here added, that Rhodes then said that "all the white women would soon have black husbands." The three colored men gave no encouragement to the prisoner, and seemed very much frightened. The witness reproached the prisoner with holding such language, and he became very abusive. The free persons of color not being admissible witnesses, were, of course, not examined. Two of the circumstances stated by Mary Shively, were not found in her affidavit before the Magistrates, viz: the statement about the 2000 men and the women having negro husbands. The ingenious counsel for the prisoner, endeavoured on this ground, to discredit the witness, and also submitted some points of law in defence of the prisoner. The Jury however, found him guilty, and he was sentenced to six months imprisonment, to pay a fine of $500, and to find security for his good behavior, for five years. After receiving his sentence, Rhodes addressed the Court in a very clear and ingenious speech, protesting his innocence, and insisting that his whole life had been one of innocence and good conduct, notwithstanding which, he had constantly suffered oppression and injustice.

It is certainly worthy of remark, that none of the slaves or free persons of colour assailed by the seditious language of the prisoners, manifested any disposition to engage in the conspiracy. Scott immediately gave information to Mr. Stoney. Mr. Lance's slave not only combatted the arguments of Igneshias, but acknowledged his obligations to the white people.—None of the negroes to whom Danders addressed himself, gave him the smallest encouragement, and it was proved that Rhodes' auditors displayed great alarm.—These degenerate white men, perhaps, fell in with faithful servants, not to be seduced into crimes; or the proposition, coming from white men, excited suspicion and distrust; or what is still more probable, the *punishments recently inflicted on the Conspirators, had excited a salutary alarm.* [1]

1. For the outcome of this trial, see Charleston *City Gazette and Commercial Daily Advertiser*, Monday, October 21, 1822, which appears in Part IV, p. 459, of this volume.

(*Note.* The Attorney-General indicted these men for *Misdemeanor at common law*, being of opinion that their cases were not embraced within *the letter* of the Act of Assembly of 1805, which inflicts capital punishment on persons connected with slaves in actual insurrection. The Act is in these words, viz. "Be it enacted, That from and immediately after the passing of this Act, every person or persons, who shall, or may be, either directly or indirectly, concerned or connected with any slave or slaves, in a state of *actual insurrection* within this state; *or who shall,* in any manner, or to any extent, *excite,* counsel, advise, induce, aid, comfort or assist, *any slave or slaves, to raise, or attempt to raise an insurrection* within this state, *by furnishing them with any written or other passport,* with any *arms or ammunition,* or munition of war, *or knowing of their assembling for any purpose tending to treason* or insurrection, *shall afford to them shelter* or protection, *or shall permit his, her, or their house,* or houses, *to be resorted to* by any slave or slaves, for any purpose tending to treason or insurrection, as aforesaid, shall on conviction thereof in any court having jurisdiction thereof, by confession in open court, or by the testimony of two witnesses, be adjudged guilty of treason against the state, and suffer Death."

On this Act it must be observed that the first clause punishes with death white persons who shall be concerned with slaves in *actual Insurrection.* All the slaves who have been convicted, were found guilty merely of "*an attempt* to raise an Insurrection;" and it was never pretended that any actual Insurrection existed. The remaining clauses of the act provide for the punishment of offenders *who shall aid and assist slaves* in raising an Insurrection, by one of the following means, viz.

1st. *By* furnishing them with passports.

2d. *By* furnishing them with arms or munitions of war.

3d. *By* affording them shelter and protection when knowing of their assembling for any purpose tending to treason.

4th. *By* permitting his or their house to be resorted to by slaves, for any purpose tending to treason.)

In the cases reported, none of *these specific means* were resorted to, in exciting the slaves. Indeed none of the slaves were engaged in any criminal enterprise; and though Allen *supposed* that the meeting at *Joe's house,* between Scott and himself, was one designed by the negroes for purposes of treason, yet, in point of fact, he was mistaken. That meeting, (as far as the slaves were concerned,) was innocent, and the same remark is applicable to the meeting at Garden's house. Allen was *morally,* though not legally guilty. It is worthy of the consideration of the Legislature, however, whether white persons ought not to be put on the same footing as slaves, with respect to the punishment for Insurrection. The Law, perhaps, ought *in all cases* to be, that "if any person shall raise an Insurrection, or attempt to raise an Insurrection, he shall suffer death."

EXTRACTS, &c.

The following extracts from a Publication in the City Gazette of the 27th of September last, under the Signature of "A South-Carolinian;"[1] are thought interesting, and appropriate, and have been therefore added.

"In the Spanish conspiracy against Venice which partakes the character of this, *three hundred and fifty were put to death.* George II. executed *fifty-four* of the first men in Britain for the rebellion of 1745. Nor are we without domestic precedents. An insurrection occurred in the city of New-York in 1712; as soon as the alarm-gun was fired, and a detachment of the Guards appeared, the insurgents fled to the woods—there they were surrounded, several through desperation *shot themselves,* the rest were captured, and nineteen executed.

"Another was meditated in 1741, when there were two thousand Negroes and twelve thousand Whites in the city of New-York. It was then found necessary to burn *thirteen* and to hang eighteen Negroes with four Whites; to transport eighty Negroes and five Whites.

	In New-York.	In Charleston.
Executed,	35	35
Transported,	85	37
	120	72

"Now, a short period before the Negro Plot was discovered in New-York, an Insurrection broke out in Carolina. Many of the ring-leaders were shot or hanged, but none punished in any other mode.

"Schemes of Insurrection, such as the present, cannot succeed. The white population of each state alone, is adequate to suppress them. From the first settlement of Carolina, we have been accustomed to these abortive efforts. Under our proprietary government, there was a notorious out-law by the name of Sebastian; Governor Gibbes issued his proclamation, and the Indians soon entitled themselves to the reward.

"In 1730, a plan was conceived against Charleston—They were allowed to assemble, were then taken, and proper examples made. Some years afterwards, what we denominate *the Gullah War,* occurred—This was more general—in St. Paul's Parish they appeared in arms; the greater part were killed, and not more than two or three escaped. In St. John's Parish they were discovered by Major Cordes' faithful driver Peter, and in Charleston, they were also discovered, suppressed and punished. The Negro law of 1740, was enacted in consequence of the last, and has proved our security from that period, notwithstanding the occasional effervescences of insubordination. The history of South-Carolina, in this particular, has been the history of every State in the Union.

"Another impediment to the progress of conspiracy will ever be found in the *fidelity* of some of our negroes. The servant who is false to his master, would be false to his God. One act of perfidy, is but the first step in the road of corruption and of baseness, and those who on this occasion, have proved ungrateful to their owners, have also been hypocrites in religion. But it is a reputable TRUTH, that on every such occasion, servants have been found who were worthy the kindness and confidence of their masters.

"Besides, when the moment of trial comes, among large bodies of men, some will tremble, some will be shocked at what they are about to perpetrate, and others will remember that by disclosure, may be obtained more than they seek through perils. Jaffier saved Venice, and most conspiracies own men inferior to Jaffier. We must also remember that the majority of mankind would avoid dangerous enterprises. Therefore, the great body of these people, would prefer safety and quiet with their present comforts, to a hazardous commotion with an issue so fearful as it always has been, and ever will be.

"Superadded to these intrinsic securities, we have the proportion of *two* to *one* in the aggregate population of States situated like ourselves. Our sister and neighbour Tennessee has four to one, and the heroes of Orleans have but to know that we are in danger, to be with us at the first tap of the drum.

"The National Government also can preserve the peace of the country. It was established expressly to ensure domestic tra[n]quility and suppress insurrection. It has been tried, and found efficient. The president may summon upwards of five to one. The old French government with 3000 regulars, protected their largest colony, and a small military force is found adequate in the British West-Indies. Surely the American government could, and would do as much, were it necessary. A change cannot then be effected by force, nor would it be beneficial to the United States. Our roads would swarm with paupers, and every wood be infested with banditti. But, under the existing regulations they contribute to general wealth, and are preserved from want, misery and crime."

1. Benjamin Elliott (1786–1836), a Charleston attorney close to the proceedings, composed the referenced piece in the *City Gazette.* It is reproduced with editorial commentary on pp. 502–7 in Part V of this volume.

POSTSCRIPT.

Since these sheets have been put to press, it affords him, who has been engaged in their preparation, much gratification to be able to correct one mistake, as it places the fidelity of the slave who first gave the intelligence of the intended insurrection, on much higher ground. On conferring with his master and the free man of color, whose advice he sought, it appears that the slave in question[1] communicated the conversation at the Market to his young master, before he consulted his friend (the free man of color,) and that the advice of the latter was that as "his young master was a youth, that it would be best for him *immediately, without delay,* to tell his mistress, that his master might receive the information the instant he came to town."—*Vide* p. 51.

1. This slave was John Cordes Prioleau's Peter.

PRINTED BY. J. R. SCHENCK, BROAD-ST. CHARLESTON.

Senate Transcript

As noted in the Editorial Statement, the trial transcripts requested by Governor Thomas Bennett Jr. for presentation to the state assembly appeared in two versions. The transcription that was presented to the House ran from Wednesday, June 19, to Friday, July 26, and was docketed as "Document B House of Representatives." The longer Senate transcription, docketed simply as "Evidence Document B," includes the trials covered in the House version but runs into August. It concludes with the lengthy sentences read to Denmark Vesey, Jack Pritchard, and "ten of the criminals." As the abbreviations "X exd." And "rexd." in the text indicate, witnesses faced cross-examinations and recross-examinations. The Senate version also contains correspondence between Governor Bennett and state Attorney General Robert Young Hayne (which we have moved to Part II of this volume). Small variations, usually of punctuation or capitalization, exist between the two versions, just as the two transcriptions surely vary slightly from the original fragmentary and now missing court documents. Because of the way the two versions were

Figure 19. Governor Thomas Bennett Jr. (1781–1865). From a daguerreotype, ca. 1820. Courtesy of the South Caroliniana Library, University of South Carolina, Columbia.

microfilmed, scholars using only that format can easily confuse the two transcriptions. The longer Senate version has "Document B 1328-143" inscribed on the top right of the first page, while the shorter version is listed as "Document B House of Representatives 1328-55." The former follows the latter on the microfilm.

Evidence Document B (Senate Copy)

Examination of Pompey a negro man belonging to Mr Bryant.[1]
Denmark Vesey has often spoken to me about the Insurrection and endeavoured to persuade me to join them, he enquired of me if my master had not Arms in his house, and tried to persuade me to get them for him—the blacks stood in great fear of him and I so much so, that I always endeavoured to avoid him.[2]

1. The *OR* indicates that Pompey's owner was John Bryan, not "Bryant." *CSCCD,* 3, identifies a planter named John Bryan at 38 Hasell Street in 1816. No one with that name appears in the 1819 and 1822 directories, although a Jonathan Bryan is located on Hasell Street in 1819 (p. 34) and on King Street in 1822 (p. 72). Pompey's owner appears then to be Jonathan Bryan (d. 1861), a prominent merchant. See Benjamin W. Dwight, *The History of the Descendants of John Dwight of Dedham, Mass.* (New York, 1874), vol. 1: 400.

2. The trials in the Work-House began on Wednesday, June 19, but according to Hamilton, *Account,* 46, Bryan's Pompey was not arrested until Friday, June 28; this discrepancy suggests that the clerk drafting the Senate and House versions simply placed this and the following five undated depositions before the dated trial documents. Hamilton added that Pompey was acquitted and discharged.

Examination of Edwin a negro man belonging to Mr. Paul[1]—Charles belongs to Judge Drayton—he told me that Monday Gell & Denmark Vesey knew about the Insurrection of the Blacks—he said that William Paul in consequence of his having given testimony would run a great risk of his life if he went out—I heard every body, even the women say when several were apprehended that they wondered that Monday Gell & Denmark Vesey were not taken.

1. Edwin belonged to John Paul (1785–1846), a Scottish-born grocer, who in 1822 ran a business with his brother Dunbar (1792–1876) at 47 Broad Street. The slave Charles referenced belonged to John Drayton (1766–1822). See Part II, p. 91 n16. According to Hamilton, *Account,* 45, Edwin was arrested on Monday, June 24; this deposition was given at the July 27 trial of Denmark Vesey. Vesey was arrested on Saturday, June 22, and Monday Gell five days later on Thursday, June 27.

Examination of Frank a negro man belonging to Mrs Ferguson.[1]

The first time I spoke with Monday Gell 'twas one night at Veseys house where I heard Vesey tell Monday, he must send some one round into the country to bring the people down. Monday replied, he had directed Jack[2] to go up & I told him to tell the people to come down and join in the fight against the whites—and to ascertain and inform him how many people he could get to agree. A few days after I met Vesey, Monday & Jack in the street under Mr Duncan's trees at night,[3] where Jack stated that he had been in the country round by Goose Creek & Dorchester and that he had spoken to 6,600 persons who had agreed to join. At Veseys the first time I spoke to Monday, he was going away early and Vesey asked him to stay; when Monday said he expected that night a meeting at his house to fix upon and mature the plan &c. and he could not stay. I afterwards conversed with Monday in his shop, where he asked me if I had heard that Bennett's & Poyas' people were taken up, that 'twas a great pity—he said he had joined in the business—I told him to take care that he was not taken up. Whenever I talked with Vesey, he always spoke of Monday as being his principal and active man in this business. I heard Jack say, he would pay no more wages, he was too busy in seeing about this Insurrection, besides what would the Whites want with wages—they would soon be no more—Monday Gell said to Vesey that if Jack had so many men, they had better wait no longer, but begin the business at once, and others would join

Mr. James Ferguson who was present at Franks examination stated to the Court that the testimony of Frank was in substance what he had before told him

1. Frank was the slave of the widow Ann (Wragg) Ferguson (1756–1835). See Part II, p. 91 n13.

2. Gullah Jack Pritchard.

3. John Duncan (d. 1828), a merchant, lived for years on Bull Street, not far from Denmark Vesey. See *CSCCD,* 8, 40, 77.

Examination of Pharo—belonging to Mr. Thompson.[1]

One evening I overheard two men in the street say that Hales Berry & Denmark Vesey were two principal men—Peirod belonging to Mr. Strohecker said to me last Tuesday that the Black people were not worth any thing, but that there was a French Band which if they could only get 100 men to join with them would attack the work House and take their friends out—I once went to Monday Gells' who had told me he wanted to see me—this was before Mr. Paul's William was taken up. I there met Charles & Mr. Ferguson's Frank frequents Monday's house—Monday said he wanted to say something particular to me, and Charles winked at him, when Monday stopped short—Charles asked me on friday 14th June in the streets to lend him a horse next Sunday evening—I said I could not.

1. The widow Jane Thompson (also rendered "Thomson"), who is identified as the owner of Pharo in the *OR,* 183, claimed that she had reared Pharo from a child, that he was crucial to her support, and that he was "the victim of a wicked combination among his accusers," especially Perault Strohecker. See Jane Thomson, Petition to the Senate of South Carolina, November 22, 1822, which appears on p. 537 in Part V. Charleston city directories for 1816, 1819, or 1822 do not list her, but she may have been the "femme sole milliner" mentioned in Cynthia A. Kierner, *Beyond the Household: Women's Place in the Early South, 1700–1835* (Ithaca, NY: Cornell University Press, 1998), 23. Hamilton, *Account,* 43, indicates that Pharo, the slave of Jane Thompson, was not arrested until Saturday, July 13. This information was provided at the July trial of Louis Remoussin. The House transcript spelled Perault's name correctly; he appeared here as "Peirod."

Examination of Patrick belonging to Miss Datty

I know Charles Drayton—about 5 months ago he met me in the street, when he stopped me, and asked me to join with him—I asked him in what—He said he wanted to make up a company—I said what for he said for some respectable brown man coming here from abroad—I said I did not want death to take me yet—and quit him[1]—

1. According to Hamilton, *Account,* 47, Patrick was arrested on Thursday, July 4, and released two days later. His testimony was given at the July 5 trial of Charles Drayton.

Examination of Y*[1] belonging to Col. George W. Cross.
Peter Poyas first spoke to me and asked me to join—I asked him to join what the Church—He said no, have you not heard that the Blacks are going to try to take the Country from the Whites. I asked him if he thought he had force enough to do it. He said yes aplenty—that he could get aplenty of men and the Society will contribute with which a white man would purchase Guns and Powder for them—He said he would call back and I must consider if I would join them—He called back and asked if I was willing now. Why Peter says I, you have not got force enough—He said if I would not join he would turn all my Country people against me—said I, if so I'll join you when you come out if I find you strong enough, but I will not put my name down—Well said he if you don't join you'll be killed. Peter & Harry Haig called on me afterwards, but I was not at home, the next morning I met Harry, who asked me to put my name down, I refused—He said I would be killed if I did not join I told him I would join when they came out, if they were stronger than the Whites—he called on me again and asked me if I was willing—that the thing would break out soon—I asked him where they would begin—he said in Boundary street—at what hour at 12 oc. at night—or early in the morning as soon as the Patroles were discharged—Jack Pritchard called on me—he is sometimes called Gullah Jack sometimes Cooter Jack—he gave me some dry food consisting of parched corn and ground nuts, and said eat nothing but this the morning it breaks out, and when you join us as we pass, put in your mouth this crab claw, and you cant be wounded—and he said I give the same to all the rest of my troops if said he you drop the large crab claw out of your mouth then put in the small one—I asked him where he intended to break out and have you got arms—he said aplenty, but they are over boundary street, and they could not get them now—but as soon as the Patrols were slack they could get them

* Before the name of this Witness was given to the Court his Master required of the Court a Solemn pledge that his name should never be revealed, under which pledge the Witness was produced and testified[2] this was previous to the 16th June on which day he said they were to break out—On that day he came to me and said, they would not break out that night as the Patrol was too strong—that Sunday fortnight he came to me and said I must lay by still, that they would not break out then, as he had been round to all his company—and found them cowards—I said thank God then—he said give me back my Corn & Cullah (meaning his crab claw) I refused and upbraided him for having deluded so many—He said all the Country borns promised him because he was a Doctor—he said the Whites were looking for him and he was afraid of being taken—that two men came to his masters Wharf and asked him if he knew Gullah Jack, and that he told them no—he said that his charms would not protect him against the treachery of his own colour—He went away and I have not seen him since—Harry Haig has since seen me several times, and told me to hold myself ready—I said I'm ready when called on—He said that all the Draymen came to him at his masters Cooper yard, and said they were ready—but he told him they were

only waiting for Gullah Jack He said he would tell me when they were ready, they were only waiting for the head man, who was a white man, but he would not tell me what was the white man's name, or where the powder and arms were—this was last tuesday the very day the 6 men were hanged[3] about 6 oClock (AM)—this was the last time we spoke though I have seen him since—I have seen Charles Drayton before the 16th June at Monday Gells—I was going to Market & Charles called to me—as I was crossing the street a young man named Joe formerly belonging to my master asked me if I did not know that Monday Gell is at the head of the Ebo company, who are going to fight the white people—Monday is an Ebo. I asked Joe if he was one of that company he said yes he was—I asked him what he could do as he was an invalid he said [he] would take Capt. Remoussin's Sword and Gun (at whose house his wife lives) & tell him to lay down in his bed & be quiet. Previous to the 16th June Monday Gell asked me to go into his Shop. I went in—I told him I heard he was the Captain of his Country mens Company the Ebo's, he said he was a sort of a one. I bid him good morning—he said when you want to hear the news come here—I never saw him afterwards—I met Charles Drayton on the 1st July in the street when he said to me, now get ready we must break out at once, for we will not let 6 lives be taken—I asked him where they would begin, he said at Boundary Street directly as the Patrol and Light horse turned in. I said had you not better wait 'till after the 4th July—he said no because in the mean time the people will be hanged, he said they had force enough—we then parted—I met him in market 'twixt 8 & 9. O.C. on the 2d July & I said to him now the people are hanged, I suppose you are sorry you joined in the business—he said yes & we parted—Peter Poyas told me also that they had force enough—that some would come from the Islands of James & John & some from Christ Church Parish where he generally went over to a meeting to have a talk & that he had some about & about in town, the number of which he could shew me from the Society's books if I would only come to the Society—he said they were to fight the whites & keep on fighting 'till the English came to help them—Harry told me they were to fight the whites & in short told me the same as Peter—Jack being the head man, I asked him about the plan—he said the same thing—that the English were to come & help them—that the Americans could do nothing against the English & that the English would carry them off to St. Domingo—Monday & Charles were very great together—John Mr. Elias Horrys' Coachman, came to me one day & asked me what I thought—are you ready, every one is ready said John to fight the Whites—& he said "I am ready"—This took place some time before the 16th June & every day he asked the same questions—about this time George Vanderhorst who is with Mr. Crawford came to me & said they were going to take the City & he had joined—that he was ready whenever the Blacks broke out—he requested me to let him sleep at my Wife's house in King Street near Boundary Street—I saw him almost every day after the 16th June & he always said he was ready whenever the troops were prepared—Jack also asked me to let 12 men sleep at my Wife's house on the 16th June, as they meant to break out on that night—on being refused he departed in anger & reproached me—George called on me yesterday morning & asked if I knew that Charles Drayton was taken up—He said he was afraid Charles would name him but he was not on his list, but had joined Jacks Company—On Monday the 1st July Charles Drayton told me that there would be a rising on the 6th July early in the morning as soon as the Guards turned in & were dismissed—He also said that he commanded the Country born company—Jack told me on the same day the same thing, & also that they were to rush with the Guns & Swords &c they had got, on the City Guard & take all the arms in the Arsenal—He also said there were some arms in King Street beyond Boundary Street in the possession of a white man[4] which they intended to take—George said he was afraid that Charles Drayton would name him because he had met him at Jack's, but not because he belonged to Charles' Company as he did not, and that when at Jacks' house they were consulting on this subject—he said if he could hear that Charles had named him he would run off—Charles Drayton said that he had prepared for himself a Gun & a Sword—John Horry came to me very often and once said to me, that he had a sword & that as soon as it broke out, he would run up stairs & kill his master & family. On the 17th June John on his carriage box expressed himself to the same effect as before the 16th—I have known Gullah Jack a considerable time, he asked me to go into a house back in the yard by a mahogany shop—This house is about 6 steps from Monday Gells'—They would have risen on the night of the 16th June, if the Guards had not been out so strong—this I know from Harry Haig & Jack, that if the Guards were not too strong they would get the arms near the lines, but if the Guards were out, they could not get them to break out with

Colonel G. W. Cross the owner of Y. being present during the above examination, stated to the Court that the information just given by Y. coincided with that which he had before given to him—that Y. has been twice to the North with him, where he had every reason to believe that attempts were made to induce him not to return—he is a negro in whose honesty & veracity he would confide—that he has owned him since 1806 or 1807 when he bought him out of an African Ship during all which time he has behaved himself well—

1. Witness No. 10 was Yorrick Cross, an African who belonged to the French-speaking attorney George Warren Cross (1783–1836), Vesey's attorney and onetime landlord.

2. Michael P. Johnson, "Denmark Vesey and His Co-Conspirators," *WMQ* 58 (2001): 944, refers to Yorrick Cross, George Wilson, and Joe La Roche as "secret witnesses" and theorizes that "their testimony was given in secret." The court clearly promised the ten witnesses that their names would not be divulged to the public, and they were listed by number in the published *OR*. No source, however, suggests that they did not appear in court or that they gave their testimony in secret, merely that their identities were later shielded from the public to protect them from black persecution.

3. Vesey and five others were hanged on Tuesday, July 2; that places Cross's deposition at some time from the following Wednesday, July 3, to Saturday, July 6, since the court adjourned for Sunday religious services. Michael P. Johnson, "Denmark Vesey and His Co-Conspirators," *WMQ* 58 (2001): 928, note 44, agrees with this dating but then calls Cross's testimony "impossibly prescient." Since the previous testimony, that of Patrick Datty, was given on July 5, Cross's reference to the Vesey hanging was hardly prophetic but rather was a reference to an event that had taken place three days before.

4. Benjamin Hammet (d. 1826) owned a store on King Street Road, just north of the Lines, where the Charleston Neck militia company stored their muskets. As noted above, p. 236 n1, Hammet was also a militia officer who kept arms and munitions in his store.

Examination of George belonging to Mr. Vanderhorst.

Gullah Jack is an enemy against the whites—Charles Drayton told me that he would die with Gullah Jack, this he told me about the time of the execution—I was in the company of Y. he asked me to join & carried me to Jacks house, where they met, Jacks house is next to Monday Gells—Y.[1] said he was ready to join & asked me to join, at Gullah Jacks house I met him Y John Horry, Harry Haig, Julius Forrest. Charles Drayton & more whose names I dont recollect or know—this was long after Mr. Pauls man was taken up & 'twas after the 16th June—It was said there, they would come against the white people—Jack stood at the front of all, that is he was the head man—we all agreed to come against the whites—I said I would join with them—I was begged to do so first by Y. he introduced me to the meeting he was the first person who told me so far about it as to ask me to join—Jack was my leader—He is the head of the Gullah Company—I heard that amongst them, they had charms, & from Y. I heard that they had also parched Corn & ground nuts—Jack is a little man with large black whiskers—I did say after Charles Drayton was taken up, I was afraid he would name me. Jack said if any man betrayed them they would injure him & I was afraid to inform—Peter Poyas asked me long back to join the Band—John Horry & myself have conversed on this business he said he would be ready with these men, whenever they were ready—he spoke much against the Whites & said that he would slaughter them & what & what he would have done—I have conversed with Harry Haig who said he was ready & he would die with them—All the men at Jacks agreed to die together—I said to Julius Forrest once that I did not think we could get over the whites, when he said he would die with his men. I have heard it said all about the streets generally, I cant name any one in particular, that whoever is the white man's friend God help them, by which I understood that they would be killed.[2]

1. The African slave Yorrick Cross.

2. It appears that the clerk here merged testimony given by George at three separate trials. The first section of this examination appears in the *OR* in the July 3 trial of Charles Drayton. The section on John Horry was read at Horry's trial, and the material about Gullah Jack Pritchard was given at his trial on July 9. Since the *OR* indicates that George was nervous about giving testimony in front of conjurer Gullah Jack, yet finally did so, the section on Gullah Jack was clearly not read into the court record. This merger of what were evidently shorter, separate court documents again suggests that the legislative clerk was attempting to make sense of disorganized court documents previously used and discarded by Hamilton, Kennedy, and Parker.

June 19th 1822—

Examination of Mr. John Paul's negro man William made by the Court of Justice and Freeholders on Wednesday the 19th of June 1822—certified as follows (vizt.)[1]

I have heard something about an Insurrection of the blacks but was not concerned in it. Mr. Harths negro man Mingo told me about it & referred me to Peter Poyas for further information who he said had a list with 9,000 names upon it & that he was still taking down names. On the week I was to see Peter I was apprehended. Mingo said that 600 men on the Bay was already down on the list in Peters possession. Mingo would not before the Wardens own what he had told me. I never had any conversation with Peter. [2] Mingo said his name was not yet down & he would not put it down, until he knew all that was to be done—that Ned Bennett knew all about it & told it to all Mr. Bennetts people & that letters were passing between those concerned—I can read & count printed characters but not written. One Saturday afternoon as I was going to market, I met a brown man belonging to Colonel Prioleau in meeting street named I believe Peter. I walked with him down to the market wharf where he called my attention to a pendant on a Vessels' mast & said it was numbered 95: to which I said no 'tis not, 'tis numbered [*blank*] He then showed me a small privateer in the stream & told me of the distress in which she arrived here—I asked him for news & if he had heard any thing strange, when he replied he had heard that there would be a disturbance & interruption shortly between the Blacks & White—I told him I did not understand such talk & stopped the conversation. I did not endeavour to get Col. Prioleaus man to join the rising of the Blacks—On Saturday night Mingo told me as we were going towards his wifes house, that every day at 2 oClock Peter went to Mr. Harth's lumber yard & talked to the other men about this matter to make them sensible of the plan. At Mingos house I took up the Bible & read two Chapters from the Prophet Tobit. Mingo said that all those belonging to the African Church are engaged in the insurrection from the Country to the town that there is a little man amongst them who cant be killed shot or caught, who was to be their General & who would provide them with Arms, that some arms were provided, but did not tell me where they were & that Ned Bennett & Charles Shubrick are Officers. Peter, Ned, & Charles are Class leaders in the African Church. The African association have also a Church in Anson Street near Boundary Street & one in Cow Alley where they have service—I first spoke to Mr. Prioleaus man Peter about the rising—I believe that Mingo was endeavouring to get me to join them in the rising & from his conversation I have no doubt, but that he was engaged in the conspiracy and that all he said to me was to get me to join them—It was also told to me that our colour from the North to the South, had combined together to fight against New Orleans—Mingo was no doubt satisfied that I would join—I never had any conversation with any one about the rising, but with Mingo & Col. Prioleaus man. Mingo said that Peter Poyas would tell me when the rising would take place, that Mr. Bennetts Ned was one of them, that Denmark Vesey was the Chiefest man & more concerned than any one else. Denmark Vesey is an old man in whose yard my masters negro woman Sarah cooks—He was her father in law,[3] having married her mother Beck—They have been parted some time, but he visited her at her house near the Intendant Mayor Hamiltons where I have often heard him speak of the rising—He said he would not like to have a white man in his presence, that he had a great hatred for the Whites & that if all were like him they would resist the whites—He studies all he can to put it into the heads of the Blacks to have a rising against the Whites & tried to induce me to join. He tries to induce all his acquaintances—This has been his chief study & delight for a considerable time. My last conversation with him was in April—He studies the Bible a great deal and tries to prove from it that Slavery and bondage is against the Bible—I beg you wont take up Sarah, for no woman knows anything about it. Mingo said that letters were passing between Peter Poyas, Ned Bennett & Charles Shubrick—I am persuaded that Denmark Vesey was chiefly concerned in this business—Mingo said that the Country places were engaged in the plot & also the Islands—that he knows the little man who cant be shot, who told him that there was a Gullah Society going on which met once a month—that all the orders he got, he got from Peter, Mingo always denied that he was engaged, but yet always talked to me as if he wanted me to join

1. After "Freeholders," the House transcript adds the words: "on Wednesday the 19th June 1822— He stated as follows (vitz)."

2. This portion of William Paul's statement was given at the trial of Peter Poyas on June 19 or 20. Although the *OR* indicates that Paul "testified" at Poyas's trial, it may simply have been read into the record.

3. If Sarah was Beck's daughter by another man, Vesey would have been her stepfather, not her father-in-law.

20th June 1822—

Examination of Joe a negro man belong to Mr. La Roche.

I know Rolla[1] belonging to Mr. Thomas Bennett, we are intimate friends & eat our meals together. All I know of the intended rising I got from him. He asked me about three months ago to join with him in slaying the Whites—I asked him to give me time to consider of it—a week after he put the same question to me & at the end of another week, he again came to me on that subject. I told him take care, God says we must not kill, you are a coward, he said & laughed at me. He said he would tell me how it was to be done—There are white men who have come from off, & who say, that St. Domingo & Africa will assist us to get our Liberty, if we will only make the motion first. I advised him to let it alone, & told him I would oppose them, if they came to kill my mistress, & he again laughed at me as a coward. He summoned me to go to their meetings where said he you will hear what is going on & be better informed. I told him yes I would go. Friday about three weeks ago, he appointed to take me to their meeting. at that night he came to me & again called on me to go. I went away from him—The next day he came to me & said the meeting had been expecting me & I must send my name to be put down, as one of the Band—This thing has been going on for 4 months. He told me that at the meetings 'twas said that some white men said our Legislature had set them free & our people here would not let us be so—that St. Domingo & Africa would come over & cut up the White people, if we only made the motion here first—that last Saturday night might be the last he had to live, as they were determined to break open the thing on Sunday night. I told him it could not be done, it could not succeed, that our parents for generations back had been slaves & we had better be contented. He desired me to tell George Wilson on Sunday last, his & my Class Leader to come up to him, that he wished to see him—George went up after Church in the evening—Rolla told George in my presence what he was going to do—George told him let it alone, he could not succeed & wept. Rolla replied, 'tis now gone too far to stop it. He told George to go out of town on Sunday night as he did not wish him to be hurt—I told George to sound the alarm & if he did not I would—I asked Rolla what was to be done with the women & Children—He said "when we have done with the fellows, we know what to do with the wenches." There are a great many involved in it, in the Country—that Mingo from James Island, was to come over to Charleston with 4,000 men land on South Bay, march up & seize the Arsenal by the Guard House & kill all the City Guard—that another body was to seize upon the Powder Magazine & another body to seize the Arsenal on the neck, then March to town & destroy the inhabitants who could only escape them by jumping into the river—My army he said will first fix my old Buck & then the Intendant. I asked if he could bind his master or kill him—he laughed at me again. I then told him I would have nothing to do with him. He begged me to lend him my Boat to go into the Country & hasten down the Country negroes as he feared they would not come. I lent it to him, but again charged him to let it alone. He was going to Johns Island where he wanted me to go to enlist the people as I knew the Country. He went to Johns Island at Christmas but then this business was not in train, he only went up to get acquainted with the people—I felt that it was a bad thing to disclose what a bosom friend had confided, that it was wicked to betray him—but when I thought on the other hand that by doing so I would save so many lives & preventt the horrible acts in contemplation that 'twas overbalanced, & my duty was to inform. I refused to go to the meetings, as Rolla wished, as I feared if I opposed them there, they might make away with me to prevent me from betraying them. I dont know where the meetings were held, but I believe twas in Bull Street, in which street Denmark Vesey lives. Rolla said that Ned & Matthias were concerned—I am well acquainted with Stephen Smith. I believe him to be a worthy good man & in a conversation with him on this Subject he agreed with me that this was an abominable plot—I have not seen him for the last 4 weeks—I know Denmark Vesey—I was one day on horseback when I met him on foot, he asked me if I was satisfied in my present situation—if I remembered the fable of Hercules' waggon that was stalled, when he began to pray & that God said you fool, put your shoulders to the wheel, whip up the horses & your waggon will be pulled out, that if we did not put our hand to the work, & deliver ourselves, we would never come out of Slavery—that the Legislature[2] had made us free—I know that he is intimately acquainted with Rolla—Rolla said that there had been a sort of disagreement & confusion at their place of meeting & that they meant to meet at Vesey's. Vesey told me that a large Army from St. Domingo & Africa were coming to help us & that we must not stand with our hands in the pocket. He was bitter towards the Whites—Rolla has a wife in my mistress' yard—Sambo the brother of Rolla's wife & who stays at the plantation sent word down by his Sister to Rolla, that he would be in town on Sunday night last—Rolla said that they would have a countersign to be known to their friends & in the action those blacks who could not give it, would be killed—that they would fire the town—Rollas threats are, that if any black person is found out giving information or evidence against them they will watch for them night & day & kill them certainly—that even now the friends of those in the prison are trying about the Streets to find out who has given information—If my name was known I would certainly be killed—I advised Rolla to let it alone, but told him that if they persevered & commenced it, I had no arms but that when they passed by my house I would fall in behind with my line & grains which was all that I had—

1. The *OR* and Hamilton, *Account,* 12, imply that Rolla Bennett's trial took place on Wednesday, June 19, not Thursday, June 20.

2. The *OR* reads "Congress," not "the Legislature."

Examination of Bram a negro belonging to Jon. Lucas.

I knew Batteau, he belongs to Mr. Th. Bennett—Sunday before last he met me &

stopped me & told me something very grievous—he asked me if I would go as one of the army—I told him I could not as I was so bound to my father that I could not go out without his leave—nothing more then took place, as I immediately left him. I have not seen him since. X ex.d.[1] He told me that this Army was to raise the Blacks against the Whites—he said the army was to act last Sunday night[2]—before he commenced speaking to me, he took me [to] one side & then spoke low to me—My brother Richard & myself afterwards spoke together on this business who said Batteau had likewise spoken to him about it.

Examination of Richard a negro belonging to Jon. Lucas.

I know Batteau belonging to Mr. Bennett—he said once to me that he wanted me to agree to join them with as many blacks as I could get to kill the whites—This was last Sunday week in the evening after Church—I said I could not attempt such a thing. He tried to persuade me to join, but I refused—he said he could raise Armies directly—that he was one at the head—that they would put one force at the Bridge & another in town, he expected some aid from the Country—the last time I saw Bram was last Saturday night when he was taken by the Patrol—Batteau said the rising would be on Sunday night—

X ex.d. On Saturday evening as I was going home, I saw Batteau near the Rev.d Mr. Bachmans'[3] near Cannons Bridge talking with a woman: he called to me & took me one side & began the conversation, speaking low so that no one could hear him—he said that if I could raise men enough 'twixt Saturday & Sunday to meet him to kill the White People—he said that they could get arms enough—he is called Batteau & Botteau. My brother Bram & myself afterwards spoke together on this matter & he said that Batteau had spoken to him too

Examination of Mr. John Strohecker one of the Wardens.

The testimony which Bram & Richard have just given is precisely what they some days ago gave before me—

1. The clerk's shorthand term for cross-examined.

2. The Sunday night referred to by both Bram and Richard was June 16. Vesey initially set the date of the uprising for Sunday, *July* 14, Bastille Day, but after the arrest of William Paul, he moved it forward to June 16, a date confirmed by Monday Gell in his second confession. Despite this evidence, Michael P. Johnson, "Denmark Vesey and His Co-Conspirators," *WMQ* 58 (2001): 954–55, claims that slaves deposed in June "focused not on plans made before June 16" but were vague about the date of the rising, whereas July "witnesses routinely referred to June 16 as the date for the burning and killing to start," allegedly evidence for leading questions. Unfortunately for this theory, Hamilton, *Account*, 14, 43, confirms that Batteau Bennett, who was arrested on June 18, was the second slave to be tried. George Wilson's June testimony below also reveals the sort of "crisp memory" Johnson argues was evident only in July.

3. On Lutheran minister John Bachman, see p. 170 n3, above.

Examination of George a negro belonging to Mr. Wilson.[1]

The first I heard was from Joe—he told me that such was the idea of the coloured people—that he was asked to join, but that he asked time to consider—that he was told to tell me to come out of town—that at 12 oClock on Sunday night the rising would take place—I told him I would tell my master & he said he would do the same—On friday myself & Joe told my master everything. I saw Rolla who complained of his hard living—I found he was at something wrong & my heart got so full that I wept—Rolla never told me in express words that he was going to join in a rising to kill the Whites—Joe was present when Rolla & myself were speaking & heard most of what passed—Rollas' last words were "tis gone too far now to be stopped" Though Rolla said nothing expressly to me about insurrection, yet we seemed to understand each other & that such was in contemplation—Rolla told me that on Sunday evening I must go out of town, as he did not wish me to be hurt: he said words to the effect, that he was going to join in the rising—he said that on Sunday night at 12 oClock such & such a thing would take place—Joe said that Rolla told him they were to join & take the Powder Magazine & the Arsenal on the neck & that an Army of 4,000 men from James Island would land at South Bay, march up & take the Laboratory in town & kill all the City guard & then they would kill the Whites &c. Joe is a truly good man and Stephen too—[2]

Examination of Major John Wilson

What George has just said is substantially what he told me some days ago. He is of the best character & every word he says may be relied on. I never heard a complaint against him from White or Black—

1. According to William Hasell Wilson (1811–1902), *Reminiscences of William Hasell Wilson,* ed. Elizabeth Pharo (Philadelphia: Patterson & White, 1937), 6, the grandson of John Wilson (1789–1833), his grandmother, John's wife, Eliza Gibbes Wilson (1787–1853), was the owner of the slave George Wilson. George Wilson and John Wilson provided this testimony at the June 19 or 20 trial of Rolla Bennett, although it here appears after the trial of Batteau Bennett, who was tried second. This again suggests that the transcribing clerk tried to make sense of disorganized, undated documents provided by Kennedy and Parker.

2. Stephen Smith belonged to Thomas Rhett Smith (1768–1829), a wealthy slaveholder with multiple estates, who in 1822 resided at 1 Meeting Street. See *BDSCHR* 4: 527–28; *CSCCD,* 99. Stephen was acquitted.

21st June 1822

Examination of Robert a negro belonging to Mr. Wm Harth.

I know Peter Poyas. In May last Peter & myself met in Legare Street at the corner of Lambol street when the following conversation took place. He asked me the news, I replied none that I know of—He said by George we cant live so I replied how will we do—he said we can do very well, if you can find any one to assist us, will you join—I asked how do you mean—he said why to break the yoke—I replied I dont know—he asked suppose you were to hear that the Whites were going to kill you—would you defend yourself—I replied I'd try to escape—He asked have you lately seen Denmark Vesey & has he spoken to you particularly—I said no—Well then said he that's all now, but call at the Shop tomorrow after knocking off work & I will tell you more—We then parted—I met him the next day according to appointment, when he said to me, we intend to see if we cant do something for ourselves, we cant live so—I asked him where we could get men—he said we'll find them fast enough, we have got enough—we expect men from Country & town—But how said I will you manage it—Why we will give them notice said he & they will march down & camp round the City—But what said I will they do for Arms—he answered they will find Arms enough—they will bring down their hoes and axes &c. I said that wont do to fight with here—He said stop let us get candidates from town with arms & we will then take the guard house & arsenal in town, the arsenal on the neck & the upper Guard house & supply the Country people with Arms—How said I will you approach these Arsenals &c. for they are guarded—Yes said he I know that, but what are those guards, one man here & one man there, we wont let a man pass before us—Well said I how will the Black people from the Country & those from the Islands know when you are to begin, or how will you get the town people together. why said he we will have settings up, that is night meetings for Prayer & there notify them when to start & as the Clock strikes 12 all must move—But said I the whites in the back country, Virginia &c. when they hear the news will turn to & kill you all & besides you may be betrayed—He said well what of that, if one gets hanged we will rise at that minute. We then left his Shop and walked towards Broad Street when he said I want you to take notice of all the stores with arms in them, take down their numbers & give them to me—I said I will see to it & then we parted—About 1st June I saw in the public papers a statement that the white people were going to build Missionary Houses for the Blacks, which I carried & showed to Peter & said to him you see the good they are going to do for us. When he said what of that, have you not heard that on the 4th July the Whites are going to create a false alarm of fire & every black that comes out will be killed in order to thin them—Do you think they would be so barbarous said I—yes said he I do—I fear they have some knowledge of an army from St. Domingo & they would be right to do it to prevent us from joining that army if it should march towards this land. I was then very much alarmed—We then parted & I saw no more of him 'till the guards were very strict about a fortnight ago—As I stepped out of Mr. Peronneaus' gate[1] Peter & Ned Bennett I saw standing & talking together at the corner of Lambol & Legares Streets—They crossed over & met me by Mrs. Myles'[2] & Ned Bennett said to me, did you hear what those boys were taken up for the other day, I replied No, but some say 'twas for stealing—Ned asked me if I was sure I had never said any thing to the Whites about what Peter Poyas had spoken to me about—I replied no—says Peter you never did, no I answered. Says Ned to me, how do you stand—at which I struck the tree box with my knuckles & said as firm as this box—I'll never say one word against you. Ned then smiled & nodded his head & said that will do, when we all separated—Last tuesday or Wednesday week, Peter said to me, you see my lad how the white people have got to the windward of us—You won't said I be able to do any thing—O yes he said, he will, by George we are obliged to. He said all down this way ought to meet & have a Collection to Purchase Powder—what said I, is the use of Powder, the whites can fire three times to our once—he said but 'twill be such a dead time of the night, they wont know what is the matter & our horse companies will go about the Streets & prevent the Whites from assembling. I asked him where will you get horses—why said he there are many butcher boys with horses & there are the Public Stables where we have several candidates & the waiting men belonging to the White people of the horse companies will be told to take away their masters' horses—He asked me if my master was not a horseman—I said yes—Has he not got Arms in his house—I answered yes—Can't they be got at, I said yes—then said he 'tis good to have them. I asked him what was the plan—Why said he after we have taken the Arsenals & Guard houses, then we will set the town on fire in different places & as the whites come out we will slay them: if we were to set fire to the Town first, the man in the Steeple would give the alarm too soon—I am the Captain said he to take the lower Guard house & the Arsenal—but I replied when you are coming up the Centinel will give the alarm—He said he would advance a little distance ahead & if he could only get a gripe at his throat, he was a gone man, for his sword was very sharp; he had sharpened it, & had made it so sharp that it had cut his finger, which he shewed me—As to the Arsenal on the neck, he said that is gone as sure as fate. Ned Bennett would manage that with the people from the Country & the people between Hibbins Ferry & Santee would land & take the upper Guard House—I then said, then this thing seems true—My man said he God has a hand in it, we have been meeting for 4 years & are not yet betrayed—I told him I was afraid after all of the White people from the back Country & Virginia &c.—He said the blacks would collect so numerous from the Country, we need not fear the Whites from the other parts, for when we have once got the City, we can keep them all out—He asked if I had told my boys—I said no—then said he you should do it, for Ned Bennett has his people pretty well ranged. But said he take care & dont mention it to those waiting men who receive presents of old Coats &c from their masters, or they will betray us; I will speak to them. We then parted & I have not since conversed with him. He said the rising was to take place last Sunday night—that any of the coloured people who said a word about this matter would be killed by the others—The little man who cannot be killed &c is named Jack a Gullah negro—Peter said he was to see Monday Gell about expediting the rising. I know that Mingo went often to Mr. Pauls to see Edwin, but dont know if he spoke with William—Peter said, there was a french company in town of 300 men fully Armed—that he had a sword & I ought to get one—he said he had got a letter from the Country. I think from St. Thomas' from a negro man who belonged to the Captain of a Militia Company, who said he could easily get the key of the house where the company's arms were put after Muster & take them all out & help in that way—This business originated altogether with the African Congregation, in which Peter is a leader; when Bennett's Ned asked about those taken up, he alluded particularly to Mr. Pauls William, & asked me if I had said any thing to him about it.

Mr. William Harth. Robert is a good Character, his general conduct is good, he was raised up in the family—I would place my life in his hands

1. On planter William Peronneau, see p. 153 n1.

2. Probably the residence of Mrs. Jane Myles, a midwife, who lived in 1822 at 180 Meeting Street. See *CSCCD*, 92.

Mr. Paul's negro man William.[1]

Edwin is my fellow servant, he brought the first news of the rising into our yard—he has a wife at Mr. Parkers near the Lines. One monday morning when he came from his wifes, he told me that there would be something shortly 'twixt the Blacks & whites that he knew the parties & that the thing was going on & all the African Congregation were engaged in it—& Peter Poyas & Ned Bennett—he told me generally about the matter—every monday morning when he came home, he told us (viz Tom, Toney & myself) what was going on—that Peter knew all & that all who wants to know goes to see him—that Harths Mingo knew all & when I saw Mingo he told me as much as Edwin. Edwin said that Mingo was as much engaged as Peter—Mingo said he was concerned with Peter, but denied having signed his name to the list—Edwin said Harths Robert was engaged in it & all his other negroes except Boston, who was doubting—Edwin & Mingo said Denmark Vesey was concerned. Mingo said they would get horses, which were engaged at 1. 2 or 3 Livery Stables from the Stable boys: two Stables he named in particular viz Mr. Billings' & the one behind the old Church—Mingo said a brown man, the Steward of the Cutter had stolen some of her arms & that Jim a black smith of Mr. Bennetts made Arms.

1. A lengthy space and no punctuation follows the word "William," possibly indicating that the transcribing clerk believed a document was missing. This statement provides the second half of the information William Paul gave against Poyas, which appears as a single deposition in the *OR*. The entire statement was also read into the record at the trial of Mingo. Most likely, in the original court document, this portion was simply the start of a second page of information provided to the court on June 19.

22d June 1822

Examination of Peter a Negro belonging to Thomas Bennett a Witness for and in behalf of Rolla.

I know Joe La Roche—Rolla took away Joes wife from him about 3 years ago—Rolla & his wife quarrelled last summer but have made it up since—They all 3 live in the same yard. I have never seen or heard Rolla and Joe quarrel—

Examination of March a Negro belonging to Thomas Bennett a Witness for and in behalf of Rolla.

I know Joe La Roche—I have never heard Joe & Rolla quarrel. Rolla still goes to Mrs. La Roche's yard.

Examination of Sampson a negro belonging to Thomas Bennett a Witness for and in behalf of Rolla.

I know Joe La Roche. Rolla's wife was once Joe's—I never heard Joe and Rolla quarrel.

Examination of Mrs. La Roche a witness for and in behalf of Rolla.

Rollas wife was once Joes, by whom he had two Children some years ago. Rolla & Joe had a quarrel some time ago, but have since made it up & latterly lived liked brothers. Since Joe gave information against Rolla, he has been distracted—this is the first day he seems composed—he thought & said he had acted like a traitor—there is not the slightest enmity existing between Joe & Rolla—Joe is not jealous on account of Rolla now having his former wife, for he was very glad to get rid of her. Rollas wife Amaritta will do any thing to injure Joe, she is a very blood-thirsty character.

Joe belonging to Mrs. La Roche was called up and cross examined by Mr. Axson for Rolla.

Rolla & myself are very great friends. Rolla did not tell George Wilson all the particulars, but told him of the intended rising & the time—Rolla & myself are like brothers—

Examination of Isaac belonging to Mrs. La Roche a witness for and in behalf of Rolla. Rolla & Joe are not enemies but good friends they eat & drink together.

Examination of Polydore belonging to Mr. Bennett.
Rolla proposed to me to join with the blacks to rise against the Whites—twast last Saturday—He asked me to join him to raise an army against the Whites. I refused & went away—he said I was a fool. X ex.d. by Mr. Axson—When this was proposed August was near me & I told him what Rolla had said—

—24th June 1822—

Examination of Sambo a negro the property of Mrs. La Roche

I reside on my mistress' Plantation on Johns Island. About a month ago Rolla advised me to join the blacks against the Whites. I told him it was vain—he told me to come to town on Saturday week last—his wife is my sister—he said he would let me know what day to be down & sent me word last friday week not to come down on the Saturday, as the thing had been found out—He said the plan was to take the Guard House & the magazine & then get Ammunition & Arms—that a great many were concerned, but no one was named to me—I mentioned it to no one on the Island—

Examination of John Woodworth (on Oath) A white Boy—
I am 14 years old—about a week ago I heard Robert Hadden say to Sam Guifford he was going to join to set fire to the town take the Magazine & kill every white man who did not give up the Country. I do not think he meant me to hear him—Robert Herron, Jefferson Campbell, & Henry Woodworth were also present.

Examination of Robert Herron (on Oath) a White Boy.
I am 12 years old—I heard Robert Hadden say that on the night they raised they would kill the Governor, fire the Magazine and kill every damn white man who would not give up the Country to the blacks—he spoke moderately loud & did not seem to care who heard him. Saml Guifford afterwards repeated to me what Hadden had said—

—June 25th 1822—

Examination of Rolla belonging to Thomas Bennett.

I know Denmark Vesey—On one occasion he asked me what news—I told him none—He replied we are made free, but the White people here won't let us be so—and the only way is to raise up & fight the Whites—I went to his house one night to learn where the meetings were held—I never conversed on this subject with Batteau or Ned—Vesey told me he was the leader in this plot—I never conversed either with Peter or Mingo—Vesey induced me to join—When I went to Vesey's house there was a meeting there, the room was full of people, but none of them white—That night at Veseys we determined to have Arms made & each man put in 12½ Cents for that purpose. though Veseys room was full, I did not know one individual there—At this meeting Vesey said we were to take the Guard house & Magazine to get arms that we ought to rise up & fight for our liberties against the whites he was the first to rise up & speak & he read to us from the Bible how the Children of Israel were delivered out of Egypt from bondage—he said that the rising would take place last Sunday night week—and that Peter Poyas was one—[1]

1. According to the *OR*, 66–67, this confession was made to the court after the evidence was heard but before sentence was passed. It was published in the Hartford *Connecticut Mirror*, September 16, 1822.

Examination of Sally a negro woman belonging to Mr. Alex.[r] Howard.
I know Jesse & heard him speak several times in our yard about it. One day in particular he was anxious to see his brother who has my mother for a wife, & waited until he came when they conversed together. Jesse said he had got a horse to go into the Country to bring down men to fight the white people, that he was allowed to pass by two parties of the Patrol on the road; but that a third party had brought him back & that if there were but 5 men like him they would destroy the City—This was on last Sunday week—he said that before 3 oC. on that night, all the white people would be killed—that if any black person informed or would not join in the fight such persons would be killed or poisoned—he frequently came into the yard to see his brother & I threatened to inform if he came there again & spoke in that way to get us all in trouble—We never had any quarrel—[1]

1. Sally's examination was published in the Hartford *Connecticut Mirror*, September 23, 1822.

Examination of Lot a negro belonging to Mr. Forrester.[1]
I know Jesse, he met me last Sunday week at the corner of Boundary Street as I was coming into town. He said he was going to get a horse to go into the Country to bring down some geese—From what my master had told me the thursday before I distrusted his errand & gave him something of a caution—when as I was going down into town towards Mr. Hibbin's Ferry slip & conversing with him, he said "you shall see tonight when I come down what I am going up for, & if my own father does not assist, I will cut off his head"—he said he was going as far as goose Creek bridge & would get a horse if it cost him $9. The Church Bells were then ringing & at ½ past 11 o.C. of same day I saw him at Mr. Howards & afterwards understood from Sally, that he had sat off for the Country & had been brought down by the Patrol—

1. The Petition of Jeremiah Yates, John R. Rogers, and A. W. Campbell to the South Carolina Senate, n.d., no. 1745, series S165015, SCDAH, indicates that Lot's owner, Alexander G. F. Forrester, was a minor. Hamilton, *Account*, 43, states that Lot was arrested on Thursday, June 27. This testimony was given at the June 28 trial of Jesse Blackwood.

Examination of Mr. Warings negro man Sykes.[1]
Jesse asked me on Sunday week last before breakfast where he could get a horse to go

a little way in the Country with—I told him I did not know—he then went away & did not return before 9 oClock that night—he had a wife at Mr. Warings—

1. This testimony was given at the June 28 trial of Jesse Blackwood. As often appears to be the case, the clerk in charge of the Senate transcription evidently guessed at the date of this undated document.

—26th June 1822—

Batteau was brought before the Court at the request of his Master—Bram & Richard being also present, when they again repeated that he was the individual who had spoken to them as they testified on the 20th instant—and that they had been acquainted with him for some time—

William & Joe were again examined against Denmark Vesey and X examined by Mr. Cross—their testimony was nearly the same as before—Rolla was also re-examined and X examined by Mr. Cross and testified much as before—

Examination of Benjamin Ford a white Lad about 15 or 16 years of age—being first sworn—He stated that Denmark Vesey frequently came into our Shop, which is near his house & always complained of the hardships of the blacks—he said the laws were very rigid & strict & that the blacks had not their rights, that every one had his time & that his would come round too—his general conversation was about religion, which he would apply to Slavery, as for instance, he would speak of the creation of the World in which he would say all men had equal rights, blacks and well as Whites &c. All his religious remarks were mingled with Slavery

—27th June 1822—

Examination of Frank a negro man belonging to Mrs. Ferguson.

I know Denmark Vesey & have been to his house—I have heard him say, that the negroes situation was so bad that he did not know how they could endure it and was astonished that they did not rise and fend for themselves—and advised me to join and rise—he said he was going about to see different people and mentioned the names of Ned Bennett and Peter Poyas as concerned with him, that he had spoken to Ned & Peter on this subject, and that they were to go about & tell the blacks that they were free & must rise and fight for themselves—that they would take the Magazines & Guard houses and the City and be free—that he was going to send into the Country to inform the people there too—he said he wanted me to join them—I said I could not answer—he said if I would not go into the Country for him he could get others—He said himself, Ned Bennett, Peter Poyas & Monday Gell, were the principal men, and himself the head man—He said they were the principal men to go about and inform the people and fix them &c. that one party would land on South Bay, one about Wappoo and about the farms, that the party which was to land on South Bay was to take the Guard House and get arms—and then they would be able to go on—that the attack was to commence about 12 oClock at night—that great numbers would come from all about and it must succeed, as so many were engaged in it—that they would kill all the whites—that they would leave their masters houses and assemble together near the lines, march down and meet the party which would land on South Bay—that he was going to send a man into the Country on a horse to bring down the Country People, and that he would pay for the horse He gave $2 to Jesse to get the horse on Saturday week last about X oClock in the day, and myself and Adam also put in 25 Cents apiece, and he told Jesse if he could not go, he must send some one else—I have seen Ned Bennett at Veseys—I one night met at Veseys a great number of men, and as they came in each handed some money to him—Vesey said there was a little man named Jack who could not be killed and who would furnish them with arms, he had a charm and would lead them—that Charles Drayton had promised to be engaged with them—Vesey said the negroes were leading such an abominable life, they ought to rise—I said I was living well—he said tho' I was, others were not, and that 'twas such fools as I that were in their way, and would not help them, and that after all things were well, he would mark me—He said he did not go with Creighton to Africa, because he had not a Will, he wanted to stay and see what he could do for his fellow creatures—I met Net, Monday Gell and others at Denmark Veseys where they were talking about this business—

Examination of Adam a negro belonging to Mrs. Ferguson.

Denmark Vesey one day at this house asked me for 25 Cents to hire a horse to send up into the Country—I afterwards met the man who was to go into the Country who told me he had set off and had been brought back by the Patrol, that he was going to bring down the black people to take this Country from the Whites—Vesey said the 25 Cents would be for my benefit. I have been at Vesey's house and there saw the man who was to go into the Country—he was a yellowish man—

Jesse Blackwood being brought before him, he said that is the man who was to go into the Country—

Jesse requested to be heard and said I have had several conversations with Denmark Vesey—the first about 4 weeks ago—he asked me if I had heard about the rising, and did I know that the coloured people were going to try and get their liberty—I then could stop no longer & he asked me to call and see him—I afterwards met him on the wednesday before the Sunday that the rising was to take place. We walked up at St Philips Street and were joined by Frank Ferguson opposit[e] Liberty Street and we all three went to Veseys house—Says Frank I am just from the Country—well says Vesey and what success—says Frank I have got two fine men for our purpose on my mistress' plantation, who must be sent up to and informed when the people are wanted in town—Vesey asked me if I would be the man to go—I said yes but I dont know the way—says Vesey Frank will tell you—Frank then told me how to go to Mrs. Fergusons plantation—and that I must ask for John O and Pompey—and gave me other directions—Vesey then gave me $2 to hire a horse and Frank and Adam threw down on the table 25 Cents each—this was about 1 oClock (P.M) on Saturday before last—I promised to go that night—On Sunday I met Lot, who betrayed me—that day I told Vesey I had started, but that the Patrol turned me back—In fact I had not started and only told him to deceive him—The same day I met Charles Drayton at Veseys who said that the business was postponed, Vesey asked

Charles how he knew the business was postponed—Charles said Ned Bennett and Monday Gell told him so—But said Vesey, how could they know it was postponed, as they have not seen me—says Charles, they said they had seen you and you had told them so—As far as I know I believe Vesey and Monday Gell were the Chief men

Peter Poyas was brought before the Court and shewn the Letters of Abraham—he admitted that he had received them from him, and that every word now in them were there when he received the letter—he explained one of them to allude to the negroes in the neighbourhood, who had all agreed that Abraham should be admitted to change his Church and join them, whose Church was of a different persuasion from Abrahams.

Doctor Poyas also stated that subsequent to Abrahams trial, Abraham admitted to him that he had written the words which he previously had denied, and gave an explanation similar to the one given by Peter

Confession of Mr. Hammet's Bacchus on 12th July 1822 to his Master

Perault when hauling Cotton from my store told Bacchus in the yard secretly, that he wanted him to go to Society with him—Said Bacchus asked what Society—he Perault told him that never mind what Society and told Bacchus he would call for him that night—He did call and Bacchus went with him—That Perault carried him to Denmark Veseys house by Bennetts Mills—there he met about 12 men—among whom was Monday Gell and Smart Anderson, after he got in, they fastened the gate—it was before 9-oClock—Denmark and Perault took him to one side, and Perault told him they were going to tell him something—this was in another room, not before the gang—Denmark and Perault said that they were going to turn to and fight the white people, and take the Country—and that New Orleans was taken—That he Bacchus considered a long while, and the[y] found him considering, and that at last Bacchus said to Perault, he was sorry he brought him there, he did not wish to belong to such a Society—That Denmark Vesey said to him before Perault, that the one that did not wish to join the Society must be put to death as an enemy—that he told all the gang so after he went back with Bacchus into the room—That Denmark told the gang, that they must meet at his house that night next week—That Perault told him Bacchus to try and get powder—that the gang would throw in and make it up to Bacchus: that they all threw in the night of meeting 12½ Cents each—and he Bacchus did also—that this money was thrown in to give a man to go into the Country and bring down the Country negroes when they were all ready—That Bacchus asked about arms—Where they were—he Denmark Vesey recommended them to look through town for the Stores that had the most guns—That Perault then jumped up and said Bacchus, dont you know where Capt Martindales arms is—says Bacchus yes my man, but you cant get them—and you had better drop this thing altogether—about two or three days after this last affair Perault came to Bacchus and told him that they had caught Denmark—That Perault came to him and carried him down to Monday Gells—that Monday and Perault told him that Denmark Vesey said that if they caught him, he would tell nobody's name—and that he Bacchus must not tell his Peraults name nor Mondays—That Perault told Bacchus he must not mention his name—nor he would not mention yours—That he Bacchus took the keg of Powder out of the back Store of his master—and he carried it in a bag to Denmark, with a man belonging to Mr. Bennett which he believes is a blacksmith; that he Bennetts man, met Bacchus at his Masters gate—that he supposed Pritchards Gullah Jack and Perault carried the Powder to Monday from Denmarks house—That in company with Denmark Vesey and Perault, that Denmark told him Bacchus to get what arms he could—that he said he could get one horsemans Sword in a Scabbard, which he took to Denmarks house—that he said also he Bacchus could get a Pistol, but was afraid his master would miss it—That Perault told him never mind, he could make him easy about it—that he did take the pistol to Denmark's house with the sword, that on Sunday night the 16th June Denmark had told him Bacchus previously, that he must not go home—This Denmark told me at the meeting previous—and said they were to go up the road and meet the Country negroes—that last night he Bacchus when he was put in the room in the work house with Perault that Perault told him Gullah Jack had buried the Powder and he thinks Perault knows where it is—That all the negroes engaged in the plot, were ordered by Denmark to leave their Masters and go up the road—That the night they carried him to Denmark's that he was so frightened, that he was obliged to say yes—for they threatened to kill every one who did not wish to join—That a large Book like a Bible was open before them at Denmarks house—that he does not know whether it was to sign names in or what purpose—At the first meeting at Denmarks they asked him his name—that Perault answered your name is Bacchus belonging to Mr. Hammet—Denmark asked him which Hammet—Bacchus said Benjamin Hammet the gentleman who sued Lorenzo Dow—That the week after Denmark was dead, Perault told him to mind and keep himself ready that they intended to come up at the corner where the arms of the Neck Company is kept, and he Bacchus said very well that they were to take the arms, and that he Bacchus was to assist them—that they were to break open the door—that Monday Gell can tell who is at the head of this last arrangement—that he Bacchus believes Perault knows all about it—that Gullah Jack was to distribute the powder amongst them—that Perault told him Bacchus that they had a Blacksmith to make daggers for this party—that they had made some—that Perault told him on Sunday 16th June that they had three or four hundred daggers that he told Bacchus on the 11th July the night he was committed that he must not tell his name or any thing about it—That this was the reason he was afraid to tell or make a confession to his Master Mr. Hammet on this morning the 12th July—That Perault is the fellow that has brought him into this scrape—that a fellow about his Bacchus' size, a dark black skin negro, who he believes is called Charles took him Bacchus up the road just before you come to the fork of the road on the meeting street road to a farm, that the house on the farm has a piazza on the top that Charles told him the negro man on the farm—mind next Sunday the business is to be done, meaning to kill the white people and that the negroes from the Country were to stop at this farm—that Denmark Vesey and his party from town was to go there to the farm to meet the negroes from the Country—that he Bacchus solemnly declares as to his being brought into this scrape, and that Perault is the one who enticed him into it—that at the first meeting at Denmark Veseys house, on breaking up of the meeting Denmark said—"friends you all throw in seven pence apiece, those who have got it, to make up for a friend to pay his wages to his Master before he went into the Country to bring the people down

We whose names are hereunto affixed, declare that this confession was made in our presence and hearing this 12th day July 1822.

Signed { B. Hammet (Owner)[1]
J. Tho. Robinson[2]
Duke Goodman[3]

1. Bacchus worked as a porter for Benjamin Hammet (1794?–1826), a merchant with a reputation for "remarkable . . . industry, uprightness and integrity." As mentioned in Part I, Hammet's father William was the Methodist minister whom the antislavery Reverend Lorenzo Dow was convicted of libeling by a Charleston Court of Sessions. See "Obituary," *Charleston Courier,* December 13, 1828.

2. Probably the John T. Robinson (d. 1828) of Robinson & Co., a merchant who, like Hammet, resided in 1822 on Charleston Neck. See *CSCCD,* 82, 96.

3. Duke Goodman (1782?–1841) was a factor who in 1822 resided on Hudson Street, Charleston Neck. See *CSCCD,* 81. Edwin J. Scott, *Random Recollections of a Long Life, 1806 to 1876* (Columbia, SC, 1884), 12, remembered Goodman as a "leading cotton factor and Methodist exhorter."

Further Confession of Bacchus made on the 13th July 1822.

At the meeting at Denmark Veseys, the first time he saw a fat black fellow, whom he thinks was Denmarks son as he looked very much like Denmark, had a full face, that he could read, as he showed Monday Gell the large Book on the table—that he said to Monday shewing him some of the leaves of the book on the table "see how they are making real game at we" and Monday looked at the book and said nothing—that Denmark took him Bacchus one side, and said we shant be slaves to them damn rascals any longer—we must kill every one that we can get hold, and drive the rest out of the City. That no one was with him Bacchus when he was requested by Charles (whom he calls Charles Drayton now) to go to the farm at the fork of the road, that when Charles set out to go there, he came from Monday Gells house—that he Bacchus met Charles and he carried him to Mondays—that Monday was to go with Charles to the farm but put it off on account of having a hog to kill, and said to Charles let thy friend go with you, and that he and Charles went to the farm—When they went to the farm, Charles asked a negro woman on the farm if the old daddy was at home, and she called him, that this old daddy is an African marked on both sides of his face or on his face—that Charles took him in the Stable and also Bacchus, and told him about the Country Negroes coming there &c. that the fellow who helped him to carry the powder belonged to Bennett, he thinks, because he saw this man at Bennetts Blacksmiths Shop at the Mill years before this—that Perault told him they had two or three hundred Bayonets made already, and that Perault is a Black Smith—that he believes Monday knows as well as Perault where the arms or Bayonets are—Monday said they were to have mounted horsemen—that many draymen belonged to it who had horses, that at Denmarks house they all rose up and swore, lifting up the right hand saying "We will not tell if we are found out, or if they kill us, we will not tell on any one—That Denmark said they must all say so, and that they did say so—that Denmark told Bacchus that he gave the sword to Perault and Perault gave it to a man named Caesar—that he knows no other person Caesar, but a Drayman named Caesar Smith, a tall negro an African who is an intimate acquaintance of Perault, who is often at the Stable where Perault keeps his horses—that Perault told him that french negroes were among them that Denmark said Country born Africans and all kind joined—that Monday and Perault appeared to be the intimate friends of Denmark, that he thought a heap of them—That Denmark took the Pistol to himself, it was given to him in his own hand—That their meetings were held at Denmarks house, where he had a black wife—that two or three women are at this house Ironing—

Smart Anderson's Confession delivered to the Court by Mr. King his Counsel his master being also present

Smart says that Monday Gell invited him to go up the road to Mr. Bulkley's farm on Sunday about three months ago—where there were upwards of thirty persons present—Among them Bulkleys man Billy—Smart said he would not trust Country man—believes Denmark Vesey was there—did not see him

About 4 months ago or going on 4 months say William Garner Drayman, he told him expected people from St. Domingo, white people would kill as many as they could, call Monday Gell and his wife may about three weeks before going up to the farm—Monday Gell asked him to join him by telling him they were in servitude, licked and cuffed and abused &c. he spoke to Smart about St Domingo people—turn and fight the white people—Smart said we cant do that, but Gell said we would make a contrivance to do it—Monday Gell told Smart that Gullah wanted to begin when the negroes of the African Church were taken up in 1818—if Smart told any thing they would kill him, and made him hold up his hand and swear not to tell any thing—Smart asked when they intended to raise—On Saturday night previous to the death of Dr. McCall—Monday told him the old man[1] said, we must begin tonight about 10 oClock—Smart says to Monday he must stop it, that Monday must send word to the old man to stop it, that it was a great sin—Smart met at Monday Gells a black man named Jack Glen a painter—when at the farm of Mr. Bulkley met a Snake at the gate which the old man (meaning Vesey) killed, and one of them says thats the way would do them—Saw Monday and he says they had better begin about 8 oClock before the guard meet, and if they dont do that, meet away on the green some where by the lines, march down through the Streets, come down to the guard house—Monday told him there were three or four gangs—asked him some questions about the mode of attack which he consented to—Monday told him that they would have a meeting or setting up at night, and begin then—Smart says he did not agree to have a fire in the City—At a meeting at Monday Gells house, Denmark Vesey present—Smart asked him if you were going to kill the women and Children—Denmark answered what was the use of killing the louse and leaving the nit—Smart said my god what a sin—Vesey told Smart he had not a man's heart, told Smart that he was a friend to the Buckra—Monday told Smart that they sent to several places in the Country—Jack Glen a black man wanted to borrow Smarts horse to go up the Country—Smart said he had not one to lend, said he must go in the Country, that day Sunday to goose creek—the time he was at the farm, they told Smart they had long things like his arm to put handles—that they would make contrivance. Vesey told him one day after they had taken the place, they would take the money, and he would go in a Vessel and put as many as he could and go back to his own Country. Vesey told Smart that all the powder was at the Magazine about three Miles out of town, and they must take it, could easily get it, said they knew about a place in Queen street, opposit[e] Planters Hotel, where there was arms &c. the old man (meaning D. Vesey) said that they were to attack the Guard House, in three or four ways and then they would get all the arms—Smart said he never heard about sending the two persons to St. Domingo—Monday told Smart they were about to engage some Draymen in it but did not know how to trust them—Monday told him that they met every other night, and he would tell him more about it, when he saw him again—The old man (meaning Vesey) told him to get some draymen who had horses, if you hear of a good rider make him Capt of Troop—When they met did not pray at the meeting in the Kitchen—Smart says he was only there about an hour at the neck meeting—Peter Poyas was not at that meeting—Smart told Monday not to put his name on the list they had—Peter was not at the meeting but was to go with us—Monday said he expected Peter there—Smart denied any knowledge (after being repeatedly asked) of any deposit of any arms, ammunition or that he promised to do any particular act in the business, or that he knows of any other person engaged in the business, than those he has already mentioned, and also that he never asked any other person to join in, with this affair

Further Confession of Bacchus taken July 17th 1822

Bacchus states that at the first commencement of the African Church, when the City Guard took up so many negroes on a Sunday (which was when his Bacchus' former master Mr. Feraud was a City Warden[2]) that the meeting of negroes was for the purpose of insurrection—or to use his own words, Monday said to him before Perault "that the time we had the uproar about the African Church, we been after the same thing, but had to put it off, that now they begin to raise all about it" that when Perault took him to Denmarks he told him it was to go to a Class meeting—and he thought so when he first went into Denmarks and saw the big book on the table—that after they called him one side and told him what it was about he was mistaken—Perault told him that they had 3 or 400 men—Monday Gell told him they had 2000 men, so did Denmark—that they had a letter which was placed in the big book, which letter be believes was got from some free Country of black people—may be St. Domingo (he is positive it must be some free Country)—that those people who are at the head of it, will try and get themselves clear, and those who are not, won't be able—that the wise ones cut the root of it, know all about it. If he can see the man he describes as Veseys son, he can identify him (Polydore Vesey old Denmarks son is said to be of the description given) Bennetts fellow he thinks is a blacksmith—and appeared to have more today at the meetings—spoke quite high flown—he is a Country born negro he believes—that the ring leaders, and all who joined were to go up to the farm at the forks and wait for the Country Negroes—that Gullah Jack went up and came down, and told him at Monday Gells house that they must not go up, that the patrol was very strong up there that Perault was very busy and Jack too giving them all notice that Sunday to be ready to join at the farm—That Denmark charged them to be very particular who they got to join—that Perault prevented him from divulging it, by coming after him often by telling him, not to tell, not to tell—That he has not been in it long (according to his description about 2d or 4th May) That Perault tried to get him to get some others to join, but that he never asked any one

1. The "old man" was Denmark Vesey, then roughly fifty-five years of age.

2. Bacchus refers here to the publicized arrest of near 150 blacks, many of them AME Church members, in June 1818. The supplemental "Directory for Charleston Neck," 15, in *The Directory and Stranger's Guide for the city of Charleston, also a Directory for Charleston Neck between Boundary-Street and the Lines: for the Year 1819* (Charleston, SC, 1819), lists Thomas Feraud, a merchant who lived on the corner of Queen and State streets, as a warden of the city. The *New-York Commercial Advertiser,* June 23, 1819, reported Feraud's death and the determination of a coroner's inquest in Charleston that the cause was suicide from "a fit of mental derangement."

William Colcock's Confession to Thomas H. Jervey.
Pompey Bryan told me that Mr. Bryans Coachman[1] held a Commission or was one of the Officers of Denmark Vesey that some hundred Draymen (Horsemen) of this City were engaged this was a month ago—he also told me that Denmark Vesey had ordered them all out, so as to strike the first blow on Saturday night 15th June—I told him then that I should have nothing to do with it and would go quietly to my bed—he said the same and we parted
One of Col. Cross' wenches about house (of a yellow complexion having a small boy about 4 or 5 years old) told me that Joseph the former Cook of Col. Cross said that Morris Brown swore them on the Bible never to divulge the secret, even if they suffered death—Pompey Haig told me that there were some black frenchmen very skilful in making swords and spears, such as they used in Africa—this was about a month ago—he told me also, that there were some frenchmen determined if those men were hung, they were ready to rise and defend them, and he heard there was a regular army ready in the woods to defend them—upon the separation of the Africans from the methodist Church—Henry Drayton in crossing the [*blank*] of Flinns Church told me on a Sunday afternoon that the whites wanted nothing but a good spanking with the Sword

1. This was Pompey Bryan, who was acquitted.

Wednesday July 10th 12 oClock

Present the same Court

Julius Forrest on his Trial began on the 8th Instant[1]—Prudence belonging to Mr. Bussacre—Examined—
I know Julius Forrest I conversed with him first, before the execution of the 6 'twas of a Sunday night, two Sundays ago, that he called at my house—he said he had just come from the Island—He was looking for Harry, but could not find him—that he and Harry were to go up the road on Sunday the 16th June to meet the black Army that was coming to fight in Town—but the White People having got wind of it & turned out too strong they were obliged to go away—I saw him again last Saturday night, he came to my house and said Harry Haig was taken up for the same thing, he was talking to me about, that Sunday night he asked me if I had said any thing to any person about what he had been

talking to me that Sunday night—as they have taken Harry up says he I suppose my turn will come next—if Harry don't call my name I shall be safe—this is our last conversation

Mr. Forrest states he has no questions to ask the Witness that she is like a kind of Mother to Julius—having raised or brought him up—that Harry Haig and Julius are very intimate & are together at his shop every night

Harry Haigs Statement.

I know Julius Forrest—We always worked together—Gullah Jack calls himself a Dr. negroe—He induced me and Julius to join at last—but at first we refused—before the 16th June Jack appointed to meet Julius and myself at Bulkleys farm, when we got there Jack was not there, but Peter Poyas came and asked for Jack—Jack did not come—and Peter took out his book and we all prayed all night and broke up at day light—not a month before the 16th Jack met me and talked to him about war—I asked Jack how he'd do for arms—by & bye said Jack we will have arms—He said he would have some arms made at the Blacksmiths—Jack was going to give me a bottle with poison to put into my masters pump & into as many pumps as he could about town & he said he would give other bottles to those he could trust to—Until Jack was taken I felt as if I was bound up & had not the power to speak one word about it—I refused to poison as I considered that murder and that God would not pardon me 'twas not like fair fighting. Jack charmed Julius and myself at last—& we then consented to join—Tom Russell the Blacksmith and Jack are partners—Jack learn't him to be a Doctor—Tom talked to Jack about the fighting and agreed to join—and those two brought Julius & myself to agree to it—Jack said Tom was his second and when you did not see him and see Tom you see him—Jack said Tom was making arms for the Black people—Jack said he could not be killed, nor could a white man take him

1. Hamilton, *Account,* 43, states that Julius Forrest was arrested on Monday, July 8. The two competing dates here suggest that, while the arrest was on Monday, Forrest's trial began on Wednesday, July 10.

Adjourned to 12 oClock Tomorrow—

Thursday 11th July 1822

The same Court Present—

Billy[1] belonging to Mr. Bulkley.

The first time I heard it, was when I was working at the Rope Walk about middle of March from Gullah Jack—Robert told me that Jack was coming to list hands—there were 5 or 6 people he saw going to Mr. Thayers farm—he asked them what they were going to do—they said they were going to get hands—I asked them for what purpose—They said to fight the whites—as the poor negroes suffer dreadful Slavery—I refused to join, and they told me all who did not join would be put to death—Jack was one of the 5 or 6 and Robert Robertson Adam Robertson and John Robertson.

1. Billy Bulkley was arrested on Wednesday, July 10, the day before this deposition was given. The *OR,* 170, indicates that Bulkley, who pleaded guilty, was transported outside of the United States in exchange for his testimony.

10 oClock Tomorrow

It was with great difficulty that the above Witness could be understood, as he spoke English very badly—The Court therefore postponed a further examination of him until the Agent of his Master Mr. Bulkley would be present, as he understood him with more facility

Friday July 12th 1822

Present the same Court which met at 10 oClock A.M. according to adjournment.

The Court for want of the Presence of Witnesses could proceed on no Trial to day—and adjourned to 10 oClock tomorrow the 13th Instant.

13th July 1822 Present the same Court

The Court found
Julius Forrest Guilty—to be hung on [*blank*]

Mr. James Legare one of the Freeholders composing the Court stated that he was too much indisposed to continue to serve & withdrew—Whereupon a Warrant was instantly issued by the presiding Magistrates to summon Mr. Henry Deas in his stead—who soon appeared and was sworn as one of the Court according to Law

Confession of Monday Gell } I come out as a man who knows he is about to die—Some time after Christmas—Vesey passed my door, and called in and said to me that he was trying to gather the blacks to try and see if any thing could be done to overcome the whites—he asked me to join—I asked him his plan and his numbers—he said he had Peter Poyas, Ned Bennett and Jack Purcell—he asked me to join—I said no—he left me and I saw him not for some time—about 4 or 5 weeks ago as I went up Wentworth Street Frank Ferguson met me and said, he had 4 Plantations of people who he was to go for on Saturday 15th June. How said I will you bring them down—he said through the woods—he asked me if I was going towards Veseys to ask Vesey to be at home that evening and he would be there to tell him his success—I asked Jack Purcell to carry this message, he said he would—that same evening at my house I met Veseys Mulattoe boy—he told me Vesey wished to see me—I went with him—When I went into Veseys I met Ned Bennett, Peter Poyas and Frank Ferguson and Adam and Gullah Jack—they were consulting about the plan—Frank told Vesey on Saturday 15th he would go and bring down the people and lodge them near town in the woods—the plan was to arm themselves by breaking open the stores with arms—I then told Vesey I would join them—after some time I told them I had some business of my own & asked them to excuse me—I went away and only then was I ever there. One evening Perault Strohecker and Bacchus Hammett brought to my shop a keg and asked me to let it stay there 'till they sent for it—I said yes but did not know the contents—the next evening Gullah Jack came and took away the keg, this was before the 16th June—Since I have been in prison I learnt that the keg contained powder—Pharo Thompson is concerned and he told me a day or two after Ned and Peter were taken up, if he could get a $50 bill he would run away—about two Sundays before I was brought here, he asked me in Archdale Street when shall we be like these white people in the Church—I said when it pleased God—Sunday before I was taken up—he met me as I came out of Archdale Church and took me into a Stable in said street and told me he had told his master, who had asked him, that he had nothing to do in this the affair: which was a lie. William Colcock came to my shop once and said a Brother told him that 500 men were making up for the same purpose—Frank said he was to send to Hell=hole swamp to get men—Perault Strohecker is engaged—he used to go of a Sunday on horse up the road to a man he knows, on the same errand—One Sunday he asked me to go with him and I went and Smart Anderson—We went to a small house a little way from the road after you turn into the Ship yard road on its left hand—they two went into the stable with an old man that lived there—I remained in the yard, they remained in [the] Stable about half an hour—As soon as they came out I and Peirault started to town to go to Church and left Smart there—I was told by Denbow Martin who has a wife in Mr. Smiths house that Stephen Smith belonged to some of the gangs—Saby Gaillard is concerned—he met me on the Bay before the 16th June and gave me a piece of paper from his pocket—This paper was about the Battles that Boyer had in St. Domingo—in a day or two he called on me and asked if I had read it and said if he had as many men he could do the same too, as he could whip 10 white men himself—he frequently came to me to speak about this matter—and at last I had to insult him out of the Shop—He and Paris Ball was often together—a week before I was taken up Paris told me that my name was called—Bill Palmer and Vesey were constantly together—there was once in my shop a long talk between them on this same matter, I beg'd them to stop it—Vesey told him to try to get as many as he could, and he said he would—

John Vincent told me that Ed. Johnson a free man, had said as he was a free man he would have nothing to do with Slaves, but the night they began he would join them. I told Charles Drayton what uproar there was about this business and since we have been here we have talked together. Albert Inglis came to me and asked if I knew anything about it I said yes—He asked me if I had joined I said yes. He said he was one also—He said Adam a free man wanted to see me—I went with him one night—Adam asked me how many men had joined—I told him what Frank Ferguson had said—He asked me if I belonged—I said yes—He said if he could only find men behind him he would go before—Previous to the 16th Albert said to me he would quit the business—I told him I was too far into it, so I must stick to it—I never wrote to St Domingo or any where else on this subject, nor kept a list or books, nor saw any such things, but heard that Pauls William had a list—nor did I hear any thing about arms being in possession of the blacks—I dont know that Tom Russell made pikes nor that Gullah Jack had any of them

Lewis Remoussin called at my shop, and asked me to call at his house, he had something to tell me—but I did not go—Jack Glen told me he was engaged—

I met Scipio Simms one Sunday coming from the country who said he had been near the Savannah's to Mr. Middletons place—I heard afterwards that his errand was on this business.

I know John the Cooper who said he was engaged too in this business. William Gardner said he was engaged in it, and had got 12 or 13 Draymen to join—Sandy Vesey told me he belonged to it too—

At Veseys house Frank told Gullah Jack to put one ball and 3 buck shot in each cartridge. Mingo Harth acknowledged to me that he had joined, and Peter Poyas told me so too—he Mingo told me so several times. Mingo said he was to have his masters horse on the night of the 16th. Lot Forrester told me frequently that he was one of a company and I know that he had joined in the business myself—Isaac Harth told me once that he had joined, he knew I was in the business—Maurice Brown knew nothing of it and we agreed not to let him, Harry Drayton or Charles Corr know any thing about it—Yorick Cross told me in my store that he was to get some powder from his master and give it to Peter Poyas—he seemed to have been a long time engaged in it and to know a great deal. Joe Jore acknowledged to me once or twice that he had joined he said he knew some of the Frenchmen concerned, he knew I was in it[1]

1. Monday Gell expanded upon this statement at the trial of Joe Jore. This was Morris Brown, not "Maurice."

Charles Drayton Examined and said—I have seen Perault Strohecker talking with Monday Gell in his Shop—Jack Purcell said to me just before I was taken up that he had gone into the Country to gather the people's mind on this subject, but the overseer was so watchful that he had no chance of speaking to the people

William Palmer—I heard say in Monday Gells shop that he was one—I met Pharo Thompson at Monday Gells—he said what he would do when they commenced—that he had no sword, but that he had a part of a Saw which he would have ground into a sword, that he was one—he bragged of what he would do with his sword—Mingo Harth came once to Monday Gells when I was there and he then spoke to the effect that he was one of them, but I cant recollect his words—his brother also told me that Mingo had joined Lewis the Mattress maker said to me one day that he had something particular to say to me of what was going to happen here, but that as he was a Country born they did not choose him—I took his meaning—Lewis Remoussin told me one day that when it broke out he would be one and in the meantime he would be leagued in it—this was before the 16th June—Sandy Vesey said he knew as much about this business as any one and was engaged in it—this was after Jesse was taken up.

Miss Dattys Cook a french man[1] said to me as I was a Country born I should not know any thing of what was going on 'till the horn blew and it broke out—I heard Tom Russell say in Monday Gells shop that he was to make the pikes—Monday at the time was working and may not have heard him

1. The cook was Patrick Datty, the slave of Julia Datty (1762–1836), a refugee from Saint-Domingue.

Trial of the following Slaves (viz)

Tom Russell, Louis Remoussin, Charles Drayton Perault Strohecker, Monday Gell, Joe Jore, Saby Gaillard Jack Purcell and Mingo Harth.

Notice to the Owners to be given the trial Monday 11 oClock.

Evidence of Billy belonging to Mr Bulkley.

The first meeting was at Mr. Thayer's Farm on Sunday morning—he joined them there, but did not learn what was done there and he left them—after that they came to Mr. Bulkleys farm this was in April—At that meeting there were Adam Robertson, Robert Robertson and John Robertson Dick Sims, Pollydore Faber—At that meeting they were consulting about the means of rising against the whites—Gullah Jack was present, he came in company with Adam and Robert—They roasted a fowl and ate it half raw as an evidence of union—Robert and Gullah Jack were the principal men—One day I met Adam on my return from market, and he requested me to hide a jug of powder and I refused to do so—at another meeting before the 16th June at which the following persons were present vizt. Adam, Robert, Pollydore John Robertson, Dick Sims and Gullah Jack—a pistol was exhibited, and every one tried to fire it but no one could discharge it, but Dick Sims—those in whose hands it could not go off were considered as safe—Charles Drayton told me that the place of meeting for the Draymen was to be the farm of Mr. Payne, and Charles also informed me that they wished to put their horses in my masters farm which I refused—Charles afterwards told me that the plot was discovered and that the blacks must remain quiet until the whites were off their guard—Robert called and gave me the same caution that Charles had done—Peter Poyas and four others whom I know not came to the farm on the night of the 27 April about 3 oClock (P.M.) and sung and prayed until day light—Before this time I asked Robert who was the principal man—he said Gullah Jack—I then asked him if there [were] no others—he said that Gullah Jack had gone to father Morris (Morris Brown) to ask him whether he would sanction the insurrection, and Morris Brown replied if you can get men go on, but do not mention my name—I am going shortly to the north and shall hear there what you are about—Will Bee told Peter Ward who mentioned it to me that all the Draymen without exception would be light horse men—Pollydore belonging to Mr[s]. Faber had more than twenty poles about 10 feet long on Mr. Bulkleys farm under the house, Pollydore said that Robert would come, and I supposed that he would fix something at the ends of the poles as Pollydore had said that something would be fixed on the end—Robert was coming Robert came in the afternoon and said it was useless as the business was discovered

Adjourned to 15th at 11—oClock

Monday 15th July 1822

Present the same Court as on Saturday met at 11 oC[lock].

Tom Russell—arraigned—plea not guilty

Louis Cromwell	Ditto—	Ditto
Mingo Harth	Ditto—	Ditto

Saby Gaillard a free man	Do—	Ditto
Joe Jore	Do	Ditto
Jack Purcell	Do	Ditto

Tom Russell on his trial—Perault Strohecker Examined Tom Russell told me that he had joined the Gullah Band—I know that he belongs to this band, which was Jacks and I belonged to Monday Gells—this he told me at his shop—This Band was to rise against the whites—and he told me himself that he was with them to rise against the whites—I saw 6 pike heads at Monday Gells shop—3 of them were spears of this shape [*see figure 20*] and 3 bayonets of this shape [*see figure 20*] with holes to put poles in—I met the prisoner at Denmarks house when it was agreed that the 16th was the day for the rising at which place Gullah Jack was also—Monday had a list with 42 names on it, mine was one—he burnt this list when Peter Poyas was taken up—

Mr. Gray attended as Counsel for Tom and X examined the Witness[1]—The first time I ever met Tom at Vesey's was on 16th June when I went into Veseys I met Tom there—I knew him long before Tom was willing to agree to all that was adopted there, but did not talk himself—I met at Toms shop Charles Drayton—Smart Anderson was present when the Spears were brought into Mondays shop

re-X examined—I saw Gullah Jack carry those spears to Monday Gells

Charles Drayton—Examined—

Tom told me himself in Monday Gells shop that he was making the pikes for Gullah Jack, which pikes were to be used for fighting according as I suppose X examined I did not meet Perault at Tom's Shop, but at Monday Gells—I never was in company with Tom and Perault together on this business.

Monday Gell—Examined—

Tom Russell and Charles Drayton talked together once in my shop but I did not hear what they said—I had frequent conversations with Perault but not with Tom

Mr. Marks testified—Mrs. Russell the prisoners owner told me that Gullah Jack was constantly with Tom at breakfast dinner and supper—and that she cautioned Tom not to have so much to do with Jack or he would be taken up—

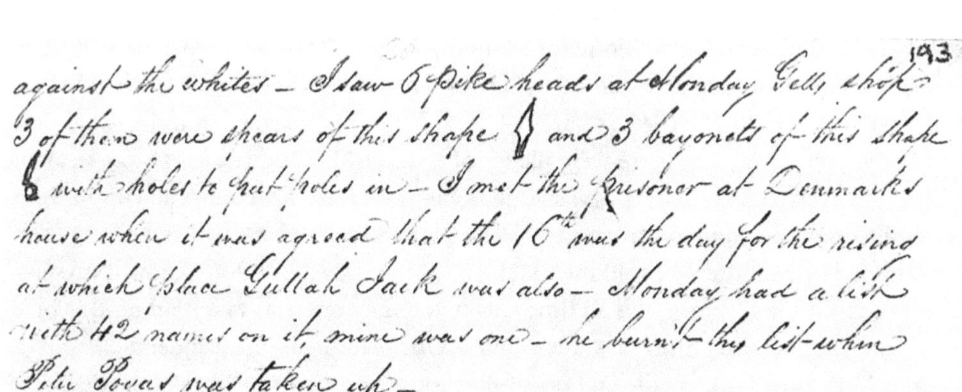
193
against the whites — I saw 6 pike heads at Monday Gells shop
3 of them were spears of this shape and 3 bayonets of this shape
with holes to put poles in — I met the prisoner at Denmarks
house when it was agreed that the 16th was the day for the rising
at which place Gullah Jack was also — Monday had a list
with 42 names on it, mine was one — he burnt the list when
Peter Poyas was taken up —

Figure 20. Drawings of the spear and bayonet pike-heads located in Monday Gell's shop, according to the testimony of Perault Strohecker in the Senate record. "Evidence Document B," RGA, GM, 1328, SCDAH.

James Mall a white man sworn for the prisoner—I was working with Tom from Feb.y to last of March in his shop—I then went into the country and received a message to come down to work with him again and I came down in the last of May when he refused to employ me—One day that I went to his shop I saw him making a knife about a foot long out of a file which he had not finished—he is an edged tool maker. X examined—Gullah Jack was frequently at his shop and they frequently talked together in Gullah so that I could not understand them—he said after the people were taken up that he would not as some had done tell upon one another for money

Louis—on his trial—Cromwells negro Perault examined and said—I know Louis—Louis and Joe and myself met in the street and Joe said to me that Louis was one to join against the whites—Louis did not deny it—this was on the 15th—Louis said he was ready to rise against the white people—Joe said the French Band had been ready [a] long time—this is all I know against Louis—the conversation was in creole french—I understand it (the court required Louis and Perault to speak together in french which they did and Perault evidently understood that language.)

X examined by Mr Cromwell—nothing material

Charles Drayton—Examined and said—Louis met me one day as he came out of the work house and said to me that he had not much to do with the business, but that on the night the attack commenced against the whites he would be ready and he told me to get ready—I understood from his conversation plain enough that he was one of them. X examined by Cromwell—this was the Saturday before the thing was to break out—I met him at his own house—he told me at Monday Gells to come to his house to talk about this business—I have seen him often at Mondays

Monday Gell—Louis came to my shop and told me to go to his house that night that he wanted to see me about something particular—I did not go tho.'

Trial of Joe Jore—Perault examined and said—I met Joe at corner of Boundary and Wall street he said to me how does this business stand now—this affair—I dont want to go home before I see how this business (meaning the rising against the whites) terminates—he was then a run away, and belonged to the man who keeps a shoe shop in King street by Harts.[2] We parted—the next time we met was at Monday Gells when the spears were on the table—Joe said to Monday Gell in my presence that the French people would be ready when they were ready and that he was one of them—the 3d time I met Joe was when we met Louis—after Louis parted Joe said that his masters store in King street was not yet open and that there were plenty of arms at Mr. Duquercrons Store near the Inspection even to Bayonets[3]—he said that when we raised, we must all run in there, break the door open and get arms

X examined by Mr. Jore—he told me that he had run away, but I don't know it myself—this was about the 1st June—the 2d time was before any one was taken up on this business—the 3d time I met him was on 15th June—Our meetings were accidental.

Charles Drayton—Examined—and said I met Joe 3 or 4 times at Mondays—he generally speaks like in a parable, that is gives hints & so forth—he said the French Band was armed through out and were ready and he was ready, but he did not know how to trust country borns—this he said in Mondays presence

Monday Gell—Examined—and said—Joe has been often at my shop and I and he talking of this concern—he said he knew the french who were to join, but as they did not speak to him he did not speak to them—that he was one of those who had joined—this was better than a month ago X examined—he comes to my shop as a friend and to get me to do work for him—he insinuated that he would be an active man.[4]

1. *CSCCD,* 81, identifies James W. Gray (1795–1870) as an attorney who in 1822 resided at 44 Meeting Street.

2. Joe Jore belonged to the shoemaker Peter Louis Jore, who does not appear in the Charleston city directories for 1816, 1819, and 1822, but may be the P. L. Joor identified in the directory for 1825 as living on Cannon Street, Cannonborough, Charleston Neck. "Harts" probably refers to a hardware store run in 1822 by Nathan Hart (1783–1840), a Jewish merchant, at 206 King Street. See Petition, William Sims and Others, Asking for Compensation for Slaves Executed for Participation in an Insurrection, n.d., no. 1743, series S165015, SCDAH; *CSCCD,* 82, 119; Solomon Breibart, *Explorations in Charleston's Jewish History* (Charleston, SC: History Press, 2005), 179.

3. The merchant Francis Duquercron, listed as a "grocer" in the 1819 Charleston directory owned a store on King Street Road, Charleston Neck. See *CSCCD,* 40, 112, 143. James C. Martindale (d. 1823), a militia captain active on Charleston Neck in the aftermath of the discovery of the Vesey plot, armed his corps with muskets and bayonets purchased at his own expense from Duquercron's store. The testimony of Bacchus Hammet makes clear that plotting slaves had their eyes on Duquercron's supply. See Petition of Louisa Martindale to South Carolina House of Representatives, November 20, 1823, no. 54, series S165015, SCDAH.

4. Hamilton, *Account,* 43, states that the court found Joe Jore guilty. He was hanged on Friday, July 26.

Trial of Mingo Harth—Monday Examined and said he told me in my shop that Peter Poyas had told him of this business and that he was to take his masters Horse and act as a horseman in the fight X examined by Mr. Harth—this was before Peter was taken up on the 2d June—he was often at my shop and knows me well—he asked me if I knew Peter I said yes, and that he had spoken to me, he said so too—I sometimes visit the Society he belongs to—George Wilson is his Class leader

Charles Drayton—Examined and said—I have seen Mingo Harth at Monday Gells—He was talking about the rising—he said expressly he was one X exd this was after Wm & Edwin were first taken up.[1]

1. Hamilton, *Account,* 43, states that the court found Mingo Harth guilty. He was hanged on Friday, July 26.

Jack Purcells Trial—Monday Gell says—I have seen him and Vesey talking together before my door—he told me that he was one of those to raise against the Whites—and Vesey told me so before—The message that Frank gave me to give to Vesey I got Jack to carry to Vesey for me—the message was—that he had just come from the country—that he had there got 4 plantations of men to join and to go to Veseys and ask him to be at home to night as he would call on him—I know he carried it because Vesey told me so that night—He came to my shop afterwards and said to me he was looking for Vesey and be sure that I called no name—X exd by Mr. Smith—not material—

Charles Drayton—Examined and said—Jack told me that he had been at his Mistress's plantation and tried to get down the people to join in this business but could not go again—he said he had joined and asked me where Lot lived that he was the proper person to go in the country to bring the people down X examined by the Prisoner, who stated, that a meeting was called by Lot on Stono, but that Lot did not come

Adjourned to 11. oClock

Give notice of the following trials for tomorrow at 5 oClock (PM)
Smart—Robt Anderson
William—Mrs. Colcock
Saby Gaillard a freeman
Jack—Est^e Taylor
Pharo—Thompson
Lewis—Chappeau
Sandy Vesey—
Paris—Mrs. Ball

Tuesday 16th July—Present the same Court

Frank Ferguson Examined and said—I know Jack Purcell but not that he is concerned in this business—I did give to Monday Gell, a message for Vesey.[1]

1. Hamilton, *Account,* 43, states that the court found Jack Purcell guilty. He was hanged on Friday, July 26.

Mingo Harths Defence—George Wilson—Examined and said I never saw Monday Gell at my Society—he would not have been admitted as he was a member of the African Society. X examined he might have been there and I not have known it—there are sometimes 60 or 100 persons present.
Peter Parler a freeman—I have never seen Monday Gell at my Society. X examined—I am generally at meeting unless sick.[1]

1. The *OR,* 116, confirms that George Wilson and Peter Parler spoke at the trial of Mingo Harth, indicating that his trial began late on Monday, July 15, and concluded the following morning. Hamilton, *Account,* 43, states that the court found Mingo Harth guilty. He was hanged on Friday, July 26.

Smart arraigned—plea Guilty—Confession handed to the Court Smart Anderson's Trial—Frank Ferguson Examined and said I have seen the prisoner at Veseys—He told me in the presence of Vesey he had joined and would be ready whenever called on—Vesey sent him one evening to call me X exd. I think at Veseys there were present Monday & Charles & others
Monday Gell Examined and said—I saw him (Smart) at Veseys in the day—Perault and Peter Cooper were also there—I have often conversed with him on this business & he seemed to be as much in it as possible—I never asked this man to join—Vesey bro't all of us into it—he belongs to the same Gang that I did—X examined I was not the first man who spoke to him—I first saw him at Veseys—he was much attached to me & called me

Pa & my wife Ma—I don't know that he ever got any one to join, & think he would have told me if he had—he was just such another as myself—I had a list with about 40 on it—but tore it up on the first discovery—he belongs to the african Church

Perault—Examined and said—He (Smart) is a drayman & engaged in this business & in the same company & confessed the same to me—I have met him at Veseys & at Bulkleys farm—at Veseys on Sunday in the day & there was Monday Gell also—where we talked about the rising 2 time[s] at Bulkeys farm—where were 13 in all—Smart & I have often spoken & promised to fight by one another against the white People. On Saturday the 15th Smart got two muskets from Mr. Fordham's Shop to carry up to Gadsdens wharf[1]—they were shortly after taken away from Smart's dray on which he was carrying them, & he Smart made off with himself—I was present, one was for me, one for Smart—We borrowed the muskets from my Brother. X examd. I met twice at Veseys—he told me first and got me to join

1. Hamilton, *Account*, 43, states that the court found Smart Anderson guilty. He was hanged on July 26.

Pharo—Arraigned—Plea not guilty & put on his Trial

Charles Drayton—Examined & said Pharo told me himself in Mondays Shop that he was engaged in the conspiracy—I met him one day with a Scythe in his cart which he told me he was carrying to a blacksmiths to have made into a Sword—about a week after & previous to the 16th he said he was going to meet some young man who could tell him all about it—I have met him several times at Mondays. X examined by Mr. Ramsay his Counsel—He bragged of what he could & would do with the white people—I did not hear Pharo tell a man to make a Candlestick for him

Monday Gell Examined and said—I know from our talk about it together that he was one—he said he was making ready for the rising—2 days after Peter was taken he told me that if he could get a Ticket & a $50 Bill, he would take his horse & run away before he would be taken—On Sunday about 2 weeks after Peter was taken up the 1st time, he pointed to the Archdale Church where the white people were and said when shall we be like them. I said when God pleased—Sunday before I was brought here he carried me to his Stable & said he had told his master he had nothing to do in this business which was a lie. X exd. Charles told me that Pharo had a Scythe which he was going to make into a Sword

Perault Examined & said—I know that he is one—one day in the street we met & conversed on this business when he told me that he had carried something to a Blacksmith to have a Sword made for himself—I know he was just as willing as myself to join. X examined—I met him in Jim Yeadons yard[1]—

1. Hamilton, *Account*, 43, states that the court found Pharo Thompson guilty. He was hanged on July 26.

Sandy Vesey—owned by J. J. Schnell arraigned—plea not Guilty & put on his Trial

Charles Drayton Examined & said—He (Sandy) had a hand in the rising—he told me that a gentleman had taken him up & asked him if he knew any thing about Jesse—that he said no, as there was no occasion to inform that the men knew how to make Cartridges and would make some—he told me in Mondays Shop that he was one of those who had joined & was ready. X exd. he did not tell me to what company he belonged—he never gave his name to be put on a list that I know of

Monday Gell—Examined and said—He (Sandy) has been in my Shop & he told me he had joined—He said on Sunday the 16th in Archdale Street, that he was waiting for Jesse[1] who had gone to get a horse to go into the country—He was frequently in my Shop, but only once spoke about this business—he appeared to be anxious & zealous about it—he belongs to the african Church. X exd. nothing material

Mr. E. P. Simons sworn—The day after Jesse was taken up I examined the fellow who stated that Jesse had told him "Vesey the Guard is too strong to night"—Sandy is a peaceable character—Jesse & himself married Sisters[2]—

1. Jesse Blackwood, one of the leading conspirators and Sandy's brother-in-law, was hanged with the first group on Tuesday, July 2.

2. Hamilton, *Account,* 44, states that the court found Sandy Vesey guilty but recommended that he be transported outside of the United States.

Paris Ball—Arraigned plea not Guilty upon his Trial.

Monday Examined & said—He (Paris) and Saby Gaillard were frequently in my shop—the week after Peter was taken he came to me & said your name is called be on your guard—He acknowledged he had joined & frequently came to me to know how the thing was going on—he belongs to the African Church.

Perault—Examined & said—I know that he knew of this business—I saw him at Mondays & heard him speaking of this business—he was as much in it as I am.[1]

1. The *OR* indicates that William B. Minott (1777?–1832), a planter who in 1822 lived at 8 Savage Street, sat in on the trial for Ann Simons Ball (1776–1840), Paris Ball's owner. Hamilton, *Account,* 44, states that the court found Paris Ball guilty but recommended that he be transported outside of the United States.

Saby Gaillard on his Trial

Monday Examined & said—Saby frequently came to my Shop and talked on this business—he & Denmark Vesey in my Shop talked on this business—he took out one day out of his pocket on the Bay a piece of news paper & asked me to read it—I did so at my Shop & afterwards he asked me if I had read it—I said yes—'twas about Boyers battles in St. Domingo against the Spaniards—& he said to me afterwards if he had men he could do the same as Boyer & that he could whip 10 men himself. X exd. he agreed with Veseys discourse which was to kill the Whites

Perault Examined &said—Saby said to me one day after Peter was taken up I advise you to have nothing to do with this affair—let the Lord finish it & leave it to those who began it—Monday told me before this that Saby was concerned and had given him a piece of paper to read.[1]

1. Hamilton, *Account,* 44, states that the court found Saby Gaillard guilty but recommended that he be transported outside the United States.

William—Mrs. Colcock—arraigned plea not Guilty on his Trial—Mr. D. D. Bacot attend—
Monday Gell Examined & said—William has often been at my Shop and asked me what was going on—I did not tell him any thing—one day he said to me a brother told him 500 men were making up for this purpose, he did not say that he was one.
Charles—I met him 2 or 3 times at Mondays
Perault—I met him at Mondays several times.
William—The prisoner states that when he went so often to Mondays it was to hear what was going on in Congress, as we the Blacks expected that Congress was going to set us free and as what was going on was printed in all the papers, so that every body black as well as white might read it (he alluded to the Missourie question[1] see his confession to Capt Jervey[2]).
The prisoner was liberated for want of testimony.

1. Michael P. Johnson, "Denmark Vesey and His Co-Conspirators," *WMQ* 58 (2001): 961–62, argues that historians are wrong in suggesting that the Missouri debates played a role in the conspiracy on the grounds that "no witness used the words 'Congress' or 'Missouri' to describe what Vesey said to them."

2. Captain Thomas Hall Jervey (1778–1846) was for more than thirty years surveyor and inspector of customs in Charleston. See A. S. Salley Jr., "The Jervey Family of South Carolina," *SCHGM* 7 (January 1906): 34–35.

Robert, Adam, John } Mr. Robertson	Bounaparte—F. Mulligan
	Sandy—F. Curtis
	Butcher—J. Gibbes
Polydore—Mrs. Faber	Isaac—P. Trapier
Cuffy—Charles Graves	

Arraigned—plea not Guilty & all put upon their trial.
Polydore[1] on Trial—Billy Bulkley Examined & said Polydore met once at Mr. Bulkleys farm—at which meeting Gullah Jack was—he agreed with the rest to raise against the whites—One Sunday early in the morning when the people were to rise Polydore brought to the farm those pike poles & told me to let them stay there, that Robert was coming—he belongs to the African Congregation
Harry Haig Examined & said—Polydore was in Jacks company—I met him at the meeting at Bulkleys farm where they were talking about rising against the Whites & Polydore agreed to join in it. X exd. Jack was there & when he made the proposition to join & rise against the whites all present gave him an answer to join

1. Hamilton, *Account,* 43, states that Polydore Faber was found guilty and hanged on Friday, July 26.

Trial of Robert[1]—Charles Drayton Examined & said I met him at Tom Russells when he went for the Pikes & Tom said the Pikes are at your house—Tom Russell asked him if he was not to go into the country for the people—he said he had sent word. X exd. I saw him at Toms about dark—it seemed to me from the conversation that he was going to fix on the Pikes—

Billy Bulkley—Robert belongs to Gullah Jacks company—he was at the meeting of Gullah Jacks party at Bulkleys farm—He was at 2 meetings & he tried to fire the pistol off but could not—same day the Pike Poles were brought he told me not to stir that the white people had heard of this business—Robert told me that Gullah Jack was the head man in this business—he said that Gullah Jack went to father Morris Brown about this business & that father Morris said he was going to the North—but if you can get men you can try this business, but dont call my name—any thing that Jack wanted he sent Robert for—if any thing happened to Jack, Robert would be the next man—when Polydore brought the poles he said Robert would know what to do with the poles and when Robert came he said let the poles lay there—the whites have found out the business.
X exd. There was no dispute between me & the Rope walk people

1. Hamilton, *Account*, 43, states that the court found Robert Robertson guilty. He was hanged on Friday, July 26.

Charles Shubrick Bacchus Hammet Scipio Sims John Enslow Seamour Kunhardt Dick Sims	Arraigned & plea not Guilty except Bacchus who acknowledges his guilt—see his Confession
John Taylor Pere Louis Chappeau Mungo Lowndes	Arraigned plea not Guilty
Lot Forrester Isaac Harth	Arraigned & plea not Guilty

Adjourned to 11 oClock

Wednesday 17th July

Present the same Court & Col. Drayton.
Jacob Glenn alias Jack Glenn arraigned plea not guilty and on his trial.[1]
Charles Drayton—Examined & said—He is engaged in this business we have spoken together & he told me he belonged to the horse company—I have met him once at Veseys at a meeting about this business—Glenn there quoted Scripture to prove he would not be condemned for raising against the Whites—he read a chapter out of the Bible—I have often met him at Mondays, where he was talking of this business—I have often conversed with him when he always said he was one & would rather be a horseman—he belongs to the African Church.
Monday Gell—Examined & said—He was engaged in it, he and I often talked about it & he was making every preparation as well as himself about it—I once saw him at Veseys when we were talking of the plans—He said as he had lame feet he would rather be a horseman—Vesey looked on him as one of his followers or men—I met him on the evening of the 15th June in the Street with $Benj^{n}$ Cammer—he said that Ben belonged

to the horse after they had parted—he said he was preparing to rise on Sunday the 16th June—he was often at my Shop—Chs Drayton was sometimes present
Perault Examined & said—He was concerned as much as myself. I met him at Monday's first when he said he was one & the 3d time I met him at Veseys where we met purposely on this affair—Ned Bennett and Peter Poyas were there—Jack agreed to go into the Country to bring down the people to fight against the horse[2] before the 16th June he sent his wife to me to say he wanted to get my horse to go into the Country—At this meeting Jack carried about a hat to get money to pay a man to make pikes I gave 12½ Cents, Jack put in the same—2d time I met him at the Battery, he said he was going into the Country to bring the blacks down, he said he had joined as a horseman—At the meeting at Veseys besides Ned & Peter, Monday Charles, Bacchus & Smart Anderson were present, John Mitchell & several others whose names I know not
Bacchus Examined & said—I saw him at Veseys the first time I met there—he was the man who read the Bible—he passed the hat round that night for the contribution—Monday, Charles Pharo & Smart & others whom I knew not were present

1. The *OR* referred to Jacob Glen only as "Jack" and did not indicate that his master, John S. Glen, was in the courtroom. Hamilton, *Account,* 43, states that "Jacob," as he was called in that pamphlet, was among those hanged on Friday, July 26.

2. The *OR* placed the word "whites" here, while the House version simply left a space blank. The Senate version contains an indistinct word, which appears to be "horse."

Lot Forrester on his Trial—Jesse in his confession before sentence was passed on him[1] & in the presence of the prisoner stated, that I am guilty & so is that man, he is as deep in it as I am, if I am hung, he ought to be hung & if he is passed over, no man ought to be condemned by the Court—Lot was the man who said nothing could be done without fire & he had the combustibles for it—(Note—this he said on Gibbs & Harpers Wharf where a quantity of slow match was found secreted.)[2]
Monday Examined & said—He & I have been talking about this business & he said he was one engaged in this insurrection and was making ready—this was at my shop where he frequently was & always talking on this business—he was one of the African Church, but I believe he has been turned out. X exd. not material
Frank Ferguson Examined & said—I heard him tell Vesey that he had gone up to Santee, but before he got there he met some black persons who told him that the Driver had heard it & told the overseer & that he in consequence had to make his escape
Jack Purcell—Examined & said—He was to have gone up to Stono to a large meeting where they made great preparations for him but he did not come—I was then up there—I afterwards met him at Mondays and taxed him about not fulfilling his promise—he said his business prevented him.
Ned Walker belonging to Mr. Peigne on behalf of the Prisoner. I was at work with Lot when Vesey came there & Lot told him not to come in, that his master would not allow it—this was about the first of June—

1. Since Jesse Blackwood was hanged on Tuesday, July 2, portions of his confession were here read into the trial transcript. The *OR* indicates that Lot was arrested on Thursday, June 27, but

released after only Blackwood spoke against him. Lot was arrested again after Monday Gell was arrested; fearing for his life, Lot tried to flee the city. Found guilty, Lot was hanged on Friday, July 26.

2. Despite this comment, Jacqueline Jones et al., *Created Equal: A Social and Political History of the United States* (New York: Longman, 2005), vol. 1, brief 2nd ed., 274, suggests that authorities "never located any material evidence of a planned uprising." A slow match, as the *Oxford English Dictionary* explains, is "A rope-match made so as to burn very slowly."

Adam Robertson—on his trial—
Harry Haig—Examined & said—I met him at Bulkleys farm at a meeting there for rising against the Whites—I know that he belongs to Gullah Jacks company & that the meetings were for considering on this subject—He did not tell me that he was one but I heard him agree to be one in this purpose—I heard him acknowledge that he was in Gullah Jacks company—he was one of the African Church.
Billy Bulkley Examined & said—He was twice at Bulkleys farm and once at Thayers to attend the meetings there—he belonged to the Gullah Company to rise against the Whites—he told me so I heard him say so more than once.
X exd. This business was after I left the rope walk.[1]

1. Hamilton, *Account,* 43, states that the court found Adam Robertson guilty. He was hanged on Friday, July 26.

John Robertson on his Trial.
Harry Haig Examined & said—he was engaged in this business—he belonged to Gullah Jacks Company & was at the same meeting with Adam—He acknowledged that he belonged to the same company that I did—I met him but once at Bulkleys farm—he belongs to the African Church.
Billy Bulkley Examined & said—He belongs to the Gullah Company. I heard him say so once—he was twice at the farm.[1]

1. Hamilton, *Account,* 43, states that the court found John Robertson guilty. Together with Adam and Robert Robertson, John was hanged on Friday, July 26.

Butcher Gibbes[1] on his trial.
Charles Drayton Examined & said—He belongs to the company and is engaged in this business—I met him at Bulkleys farm—he is one who acknowledged in my presence that he was to raise against the Whites—The object of the meeting at Bulkleys was to consider about this business—he belongs to the African Church.
Billy Bulkley [testified that] Butcher Gibbes, belongs to Peter Wards religious Class—
Capt. Christopher Black[2]—Sworn—The match rope produced resembles the rope in the Arsenal precisely, and I believe it to be the same.

1. Hamilton, *Account,* 46, states that the court found Gibbs not guilty but recommended that his owner, James Ladson Gibbes (1792–1831), a planter in Colleton District, transport him outside of the United States.

2. As the *OR* indicates, Captain Christopher Latell Black (d. 1843) brought expert testimony on the match rope since he was keeper of the arsenal.

Peter Ward on his trial—arraigned—plea not Guilty[1]—

1. Peter Ward's case, which appears here only as an arraignment, is not mentioned in the *OR*. Hamilton, *Account*, 46, dates Peter's arrest to Wednesday, July 10. Peter was arrested and discharged for insufficient evidence. Hamilton, like the *OR*, identifies Peter's owner only as "Mrs. Ward." She also owned the slave Smart, who, like Peter, was arrested and discharged. For 1822, *CSCCD*, 102, lists two widows named "Ward": one named Susan and the other the "Widow of Joshua" Ward. The latter refers to Sarah (McCall) Ward, who had married attorney Joshua Ward (1736–1802) and in 1822 lived on 50 Meeting Street. Peter was acquitted and discharged.

The Court decided on the cases of the following Persons & found

Thomas Russell—Guilty	Paris Ball—Guilty
Louis Remoussin Cromwell—Guilty	Polydore Faber—Guilty
Joe Jore—Guilty	Robert Robertson—Guilty
Mingo Harth—Guilty	Jack Glenn—Guilty
Jack Purcell—Guilty	Lot Forrester—Guilty
Smart Anderson—Guilty	Adam Robertson—Guilty
Pharo Thompson—Guilty	John Robertson—Guilty
Sandy Vesey—Guilty	

Adjourned to 11. oClock

Thursday 18th July—1822

Present the same Court

Sentence of death was pronounced against the following Slaves to be carried into execution on Friday the 26th Instant 'twixt 6 & 9 oClock in the morning on the Lines

Julius Forrest	Paris Ball	Louis Remoussin
Tom Russell	Polydore Faber	Pharo Thompson
Joe Jore	Robert Robertson	Sandy Vesey
Mingo Harth	John Robertson	Jack Glenn
Smart Anderson	Adam Robertson	Jack Purcell
	Lot Forrester	

Scipio Simms[1] on his trial

Perault a Witness Examined & Said—Scipio belongs to those who are to rise against the whites—he hired a horse from me on Saturday the 8th to go into the Country to get the negroes to come down at the time the rising was to commence—I examined him myself to see if he was one of my friends to fight against the whites, I met him at Mr. Aikens Lot after the 8th when they walked down together as far as St. Philips & Wentworth Streets—we talked about this business—the 3d time I met him near Mr. Murphys in King Street on Sunday previous to the execution of Peter Poyas—I then said to Scipio this thing was all up & now dead Scipio replied that all the people he had engaged were cowards & had drawn back, but that he was willing to go on as much as I myself could be.

X exd. by his Master—Scipio hired the horse, but another man took the horse who paid me $2 in part & Adam a free man the remaining $1 the hire being $3—I dont know the man who took the horse, but I'd know him if I saw him again.

rexd.[2] Scipio hired the horse & said he would send for it & when the man came for the horse he said Scipio had sent for the horse—when my horse was brought back, the man was on my horse & Scipio in company with him on another horse—My Stable was near Flinns Church & they came from toward the Lines, this was on Sunday evening 9th June, he belongs to the African Church
Monday Gell examined—Jack Purcell told me that Scipio had gone into the country to collect people to come down.
Charles Drayton Examined—
Monday told me pretty much what he has himself stated to the Court
Mr. Sims—Sworn on behalf of the Prisoner—Scipio is an orderly sober & industrious servant. I raised him & we have worked together

1. Hamilton, *Account,* 45, states that the court found Scipio, a slave carpenter and wheelwright, guilty and sentenced him to transportation.
2. The clerk used this as shorthand for "reexamined."

Dick Sims on his trial[1]
Perault Examined—Dick & I met on a Saturday evening in the Cabinet makers Lot next to Mondays where were met on this business Gullah Jack, George Vanderhorst, Charles Drayton. Jack said he was going in his canoe into the Country to get people—Dick said he belonged to Gullah Jacks band & said he was willing & ready like me—2d time we met at the corner of Market Street we walked up King Street & he told me he was ready at any time—the 3d time I met him 'twixt Crafts & Smiths wharf & we sat down & conversed on this business—I again asked him & he again said he was ready at any time, we were ready—never met him any where else
X exd. when I went to the meeting on the Lot Dick was there before me
Harry Haig—Examined—Dick belonged to Gullah Jack's company—I met him at Bulkleys farm & he confessed he was ready & willing to join. The meeting was about this business, he joined before I did. X exd. We all consulted together at the meeting & all agreed—this was a little before this business broke out.
Charles Drayton—I saw Dick in the Lot of the Mahogany shop near Mondays attending one of the meetings—he was one of Jacks company, this he said out of his own mouth & that he was ready—(the prisoner confessed he was at this house but went there to see some one)
Billy Bulkley—Dick was at 3 of the meetings on this business, one at Thayers and twice at Bulkleys farm—He was there when they tried to fire off the Pistol & it went off in his hand (the prisoner confessed he was sometimes at Bulkleys farm to see Billy)

X If I had not been there I would not have known of this business

re X exd. whenever he came, he came in company with Gullah Jack, they met at the farm to talk on this business

1. The *OR* indicated that Dick's owner, William Sims (not "Simms"), attended the trial. Hamilton, *Account,* 43, states that the court found Dick guilty and sentenced him to hang on Friday, July 26.

Bacchus on his trial[1]

Perault—I engaged Bacchus myself to join in this business, he was one of my recruits—I carried him to Veseys myself, he was willing to join—Bacchus gave one keg of Powder & gave it to Vesey who carried it to Mondays—he promised to give me a sword, but did not do so.

X exd. Bacchus told me that he had carried the Powder to Vesey

Monday Gell—Examined—Bacchus told me he was one in this business—he has often been at my shop & I there had a keg of Powder got by him—I saw him one night at Veseys

X Bacchus & Perault brought the Powder to my Shop.

Charles Drayton Examined—I met him at Mondays & at Veseys, I was present when he brought the Powder to Veseys, he told me he had got 3 swords one for himself one for Perault & one for Ned Bennett—add his confession[2]

1. The *OR* indicates that Bacchus's owner, Benjamin Hammet, was in the Work-House courtroom, as was attorney Francis S. Belzer. Hamilton, *Account,* 43, states that the court found Bacchus guilty and sentenced him to hang on Friday, July 26.

2. Bacchus did give three lengthy confessions, dated July 12, 13, and 17, which appeared in both the Senate transcript and the *OR*. The words "add his confession" appears to be the Senate clerk's note to himself. A fourth and undated confession, given to Bacchus's owner, Benjamin Hammet, was not included in the Senate materials but appears in the Hammet Papers at Duke University Library; it appears below.

Fourth Version of Bacchus Hammet's Confession, Undated[1]

Bacchus stated that *Perault,* (Stro[he]ckers man) on or about the 2[nd] May, whilst hauling cotton to the wharf, persuaded him to go to a Society; that he enquired of Perault what society it was, and was told never to mind but pressed earnestly to go. That Perault would call for him that night, which he did.* That they went together to Denmark Vesey's house near Bennets Mills. that they were recd by Denmark when they went into his yard at his house door, and the gate locked upon them.

* About this time Perault was discovered one evening by Bacchus's master as wishing to get into his gate; and on enquiry found, that Perault, wanted to see B and when asked *what for,* after much hesitancy, stated, "*he wanted to give Bacchus a bit of Religion, that Bacchus was a very wicked boy, and he wanted to get him to try and serve God, and try and save his soul and be a better servant to his master.* Mr. H. questioned him as to the liberty he took in attempting such a thing with his servant, and inquired of Perault *if he did not belong to the African Church.* He said *Yes* and when warned about leading his Boy in to such Society as Mr. H. thought them great rascals. Perault replied: *He was sorry but he thought them as good as any other people*: Bacchus no doubt went with him & he was absent at 12 oClock at night.

That Denmark after ascertaining it was Perault & another man (as Perault said to D) he went with them into the house. In a large room I seen ten or dozen men, a table in the midst of the room and a large Book open on it, probably the Bible Denmark asked me who I belonged to and my name, Perault immediately answered "Bacchus belonging to Mr. Hammet," Denmark asked me which Hammet, I said Mr. Benjamin Hammet, the gentleman who put old Lorenzo Dow in jail; and is an officer in Capt. Martindale's company. Perault and Denmark, then took me in a side room; and Perault says to me, "Bacchus I have some particular thing to say to you["]; I asked what it was he said "that they were going to have war and fight the white people" and that I must join them: I said "Perault I am sorry you brought me into this business and you better let it alone," and I considered some time; at last Perault says "*Bacchus you need not fret, you may as well join us.*" Denmark then said "*any person who don't join us must be treated as an enemy and put to death*"; and I said *if that is the case, well I will join you.* We all three then went into the large room, and there I seen Rolla Bennet, Monday Gell, Charles Drayton & Smart Anderson and another who I believe is Denmark Veseys son. They had the large Book open and something like a letter in it, which *believe come from some free Country off, may be St. Domingo*: and Denmarks son says to Monday, shewing him something in the letter, "look here Monday see how they are making fun of we," meaning the people off in the free country. That Denmark said, "Friends we have a friend who is to go into the Country to raise the country negroes to come down, all who can *must* put in money to raise a sum *to pay his master wages while he is gone.*" that they all put in, and I and Perault put in seven pence. Denmark then said they must all swear, that *they all held up their right hand and swore,* and said after Denmark: "*We will not tell on one another, we will not tell on any body, We will not tell if taken by the whites, nor will we tell if we are to be put to death.*" that under the sanctity of this Oath he never told his master. This was the first meeting—Denmark told me and the rest that night the next week, we were to meet again at his House, I believe it was Thursday: at the next meeting, I was asked by Denmark *if I could get any arms,* I told him may be *an old sword*; and he said no matter any arms I can get to bring them to him. Perault told me to try and get arms and powder. I said *my master has pistols, but I am afraid to take them,* and Perault said never mind We *will satisfy your master** on that subject. *That I did at the middle of the day steal out of the Back store of my master when the clerks were busy and the store open one Keg of powder and old horsemans sword.*—that when busy in the house, *I did steal my masters pistol out of the closet of the rooms.* That (Ned Bennet) one of the Bennetts men came and waited in the street for me that night until I came out to assist me in carrying the powder to Denmark's. we carried it in a bag and I gave the sword and pistol & powder to him. He afterwards told me he gave the sword to Perault, and Perault gave it to *Caesar Smith. The powder was carried to Monday Gell house by Perault, where Gullah Jack came and got it. Denmark told me, that on Sunday 16th June we must not go home, that every one must stay out, and go up the road to a farm on meeting Street road, as soon as we hear the noise, and there meet the Country negroes under him, and another—that *I must not join the people where my master lived but join another Gang, and he would send a Gang to*

* No doubt by a murdering argument, as a small hatchet, with a long handle is in possession of the master: a very useful and deadly weapon it is—The Horseman's sword was considered of little value and lay in the Back Store.

* Caesar Smith. Hung 26 July. Capt. M & Mr. H were to be tortured.

take my Master, and to take Capt. Martindale—every one who could was to come out. That morning I went to Monday Gells (the 9th June) and there I met Charles Drayton who was going with Monday to the farm; but Monday seeing me said "Charles here is a friend he will go with you I have a hog to Kill, and can't go. he will go." I went up to a farm on Meeting Street road with a House having a balcony at the top is on it—Here Charles Drayton, called for the old Daddy and some two Women, came to the gate and went back and called him, He came and Charles, and myself, went into the stable with him, and Charles told him, that he must be in readiness as the Country Negroes would be down next Sunday, and he must receive them. we then came away—On the next Sunday the 16th June, Gullah Jack came to Monday Gell, where I was and Charles Drayton, and said you can't go up to the farm, I have been up the road and just come down, and the negroes can't go up *as the *Patrol is out quite strong—That I was to help to get the arms of the Neck Company*—That Monday Gell told me when, the Negroes was taken up (for holding meeting in Anson Street) in 1820, *that the African Church was the people, and that they met for this very purpose but that business, put them back, and now they had began again to try it*—After Denmark was taken, Perault came and told me, and said Denmark said nobody must tell any thing—That Perault said never mind keep yourself in readiness, and when you hear the noise in the street you must come out and help us to *get the Arms of the Neck Company* (6th July) that Gullah Jack was to head this party and then to fight the white people with them. The General plan was to fight the white people and them that were not Killed to be driven out of the City—(That when in prison **Perault told me not to tell as I was put in the same room with him*—He told me when *I asked where the powder was that it was buried by Gullah Jack.*) That Perault told me, "*we have a Blacksmith who is making Baynets or something to stick with,* we have already 2 or 300 Baynets and 3 or 400 (hundred) men—Monday said "We are 2000 (thousand) strong. . . ." When I asked Denmark about how they would be able to do this thing without arms—he said, every one must look out for the different stores that had arms such as guns &c, and take notice to them.—He told me also that all the Ministers* were to be killed except a few who were to be saved and showed the different passages in the Bible* from which Denmark preached (& the rest) and they were to be asked Why they did not preach up this thing (meaning the passages on liberty &c) to them before and that they were to be made to tell—

* The Passages alluded to were Exodus 1st Chap. & 21st Chap & the 16th verse. also, 19th Chap Isiah, and 14 Zechariah 1 & 3 verses &c.

* Corroborated by the Testimony of Jesse Blackwood

Notwithstanding the evidence of guilt against this fellow & from his own confession, yet he went to the Gallows, *laughing and bidding his acquaintances in the streets "good bye."* On being hung, owing to some mismanagement in the fall of the trap, he was not thrown off, but as the board canted he slipped: yet he was so hardened, that *he threw himself forward, and as he swung back he lifted his feet, so that his knees might not touch the Board!*—In prison he was considered very hardened. He told a clergyman the evening before his execution, that "*He never had* any goodness in him, and that Hell was his portion." He was well-used, and had many privileges allowed him—So Hardened was he in fact, that he was seen to laugh a moment or two before the cap was drawn over his eyes. The following is furnished by a friend of the owner who obtained it from the Revd Mr. Backman.

That Revd Gentleman was in the habit of visiting the prisoners; on a visit, of this kind he happened to step into the room where Bacchus was and found him very dejected, apparently in a deep study. He enquired how it was with him, meaning his future state & hopes, Bacchus replied "bad enough," and said "he would go to Hell"; indeed that is bad enough said the clergyman; Bacchus replied "*he was thinking if he ever did a good action,*" and found he never had." He told the clergyman, "*that he was the Devil amongst the women,*" that he believed he would go to Hell, "that his master thought he was a good servant and he had been a very bad boy." He also stated how he was carried to Veseys by Perault, How Vesey sat him along side of him, and when he found he—[*illegible*] to join him He asked him seven queries such as—"*Did His master use him Well—Yes he believed so,* Did He eat *the same* as His master, Yes sometimes not always as well as his master—*Did his master not sleep on a soft bed,* Yes. *Did he Bacchus sleep on a soft a Bed as his master*—No—*Who made his master*—God—*Who made you*—God—*And then ar'nt you as good as your master if God made him & you, ar'nt you as free,* Yes, *Then why don't you join and fight your master. Does your master use you well,* Yes I believe so, *Does he whip you when you do wrong,* Yes sometimes, *Then why don't you as you are as free as your master, turn about and fight for yourself.* Upon this delusive reasoning he joined, and then stated how his name was put down and the mode of swearing &c &c &c already described. After joining (with such delusions) he said would have went as far as any of them in the Business.

1. Benjamin Hammet Papers, Duke University Library.

John Enslow on his trial—Plea guilty & Confession as follows[1]

Monday Gell led me in it & took me to Veseys—there was a large meeting—Vesey told the people the meeting was to rise up & fight the white people for their liberty—We always went to Mondays house afterwards. Monday did all the writing—I heard that they were trying all round the Country to Georgetown, Santee & round to Combahee &c. to get people—Peter was also there he was one—Peter named Poyas plantation where he went to meet—Bellisle Yates I have seen at the meetings & Adam Yates. Nafur Yates—Dean Mitchell[—]Caesar Smith—George a Stevidore—At Veseys they wanted to make a collection to make pikes for the Country people, but the men had then no money—Monday Gell said Perault was one to get horses to send men into the country—I heard a Blacksmith was to make pikes—Jack McNeil is engaged—I have seen them all at Mondays—Jack said he was one & would try to get men—The plan was to take the Arsenals and Guard Houses for arms and not fire the town unless they failed—Monday was writing a letter to St. Domingo to go by a Vessel lying at Gibbes & Harpers wharf—the letter was about the sufferings of the Black & to know if the people of St. Domingo would help them if they made an effort to free themselves—he was writing this letter in March—I am not certain of the time—Perault was present when Monday wrote the letter & also a painter named Prince Righton—I have seen Pompey Haig at Mondays, but he neither assented or dissented Jerry Cohen was at Veseys & said to me he was one—I heard from Vesey & Monday that they had engaged men from the Country—Peter Poyas said he had Sent into the Country to his brother to engage men, who would send him an answer—a party was to attack the Guard house & Arsenal—another the Arsenal on the neck—another to attack the naval store on Meys Wharf—another to attack the Magazine—another to meet at Lightwoods alley and then try to cut off the companies from meeting at the places of rendezvous—I belong to the African congregation On Saturday 15th June a man was to be sent into the Country to bring down the people & Rolla was to command (the Country people from Ashley river) at the Bridge—Ned Bennett & John Horry to meet at Mr. Horry's corner & Batteau to come down with Veseys party

1. This was Enslow's first confession; below is a second, given after he was found guilty; a similar version appeared in the *OR*. The *OR* indicated that Enslow's owner, cooper Joseph Enslow, was in the Work-House courtroom. Hamilton, *Account,* 45, states that the court found Enslow guilty and sentenced him to be transported outside the United States. Before he could be sold away, he died of unknown causes.

Figure 21. Elias Horry (1773–1834), owner of the coachman John Horry, executed on July 12, 1822, for involvement in the Vesey plot. From a photograph of a portrait, undated. Courtesy of the Frick Art Reference Library.

Second Confession of John Enslow

Copy of a Confession made by John the Slave of Mr. Enslow the Cooper, who is to be transported He stated that every black man who was to be attached to the party, was to come out, and assemble at the several places, where the companies, were appointed to meet at the times of alarm; others had their stations assigned to them and where to push for the Guard house and Magazines; The House Servants were to kill their Masters with such instruments as they had or could procure; The house Servants were expected to do most mischief, there was to be no signal, because the principal men said it would excite alarm; at 12 oclock at night they were to take their stations, and act their parts, The people up the road were to take the magazine, and there push for Town, and spare nothing that obstructed them; The Country people were to take possession of Mays wharf, They were to come from the North East and to take the United States Naval Stores at that wharf; This party to be commanded by Gulla Jack; Rolla was to command the Bridge over Ashley River; Ned was to meet at Elias Horry's house, and to command with Horry's man John; They were to go to the Guard house and there meet the main body, Denmark Vesey and Monday Gell were to have the strongest force, and come into the Town, where they had subdued the suburbs, Peter Poyas was to have the most active station, at a large meeting of about Sixty they resolved if they did not succeed to fire the Town and retreat to the Lines, and there fight man to man, if defeated to go to the wood and to do all the mischief they could, he heard them say that they had communications with Santee, Columbia and the Country to the North even beyond Columbia, They had planned to give timely notice to friends at Georgetown, who were to attack on Friday or Saturday, kill the few white people in Georgetown, and between that and Charleston, and then to be in Charleston in time to aid the effects on the night of Sunday the sixteenth day of June—when the general attack was to be made, Peter Poyas as told them, there were many poor white people in Georgetown who would join them from fear, They had resolved at their meeting to exterminate the whites, *men, women* and *Children,* Monday Gell after the confinement of Denmark Vesey was the most active leader, he had determined with Pero (Strohecker's man)[1] to attempt a rescue of the first six that were executed Denmark had several Meetings at different times, he generally opened them by reading the 21st Chapter of *Exodus* and exhorting them from the 16th verse; he that Stealeth a man and Selleth, or if he be found in his hands shall surely be put to death, of 15 against whom this man gave evidence & have been executed, and 2 to be transported. He stated that Peter Poyas had private conferences with many negroes in the suburbs of the Town, but their names are secret; because Poyas died without giving any information, and refused to do so, They made their communications with the Country by messengers who were to go but five miles, to confer with others, who were to go no further, it was done so that none should be missed from their work, He seemed to think that the chief object of the Head, or Leaders of the conspiracy was plunder, which was to be carried off by the Shipping, which were to be saved for that purpose—

Text. Zachariah 14. 1–2–3 Behold the day of the Lord cometh, and thy spoil shall be divided in the midst of thee—

For I will gather all nations against Jerusalem to battle, and the City shall be taken, and

the houses rifled, and the women ravished, and half of the City shall go forth into Captivity; and the residue of the people shall not be cut off from the City—
Then shall the Lord go forth and fight against those nations, as when he fought in the day of battle
Lessons, Exodus/Chapter—Isaiah 19–20 chapters.

1. This was Perault, not Pero, Strohecker.

Confession made by John the Slave of Mr. Enslow, n.d., Henry Ravenel Papers, 11/331, folder 10, SCHS.

Friday 19th July 1822. Present the same Court

Trial of Scipio Sims—Mrs. Fisk on behalf of the prisoner—Examined by the master[1]—He never gave to me any arms to keep for him, or any thing else—I have always thought him a steady sober negroe & never heard any thing amiss of him.
X exd. Never said that Scipio had left a Sword or pistol with me—
Agrippa belonging to Mr. Perry[2]—a Witness for the Prisoner—
I requested Scipio to hire a horse for me to go into the Country with; about the last day of the first week in June, mine being sick—Scipio carried me to the man from whom the horse was hired, I dont know the man—he and I went up on horse back to my Mrs. Plantation on Horse Savannah, where we went for my tools & returned the next day Sunday—this was all we went for—We did not go. X exd. The mans name was Perault who lives on the green—I paid him $2 & when I returned paid him the other $1—when I received the horse Scipio was not with me—I had a pass—Scipios name was not in the pass—I brought down my mallet chisel & axe—I left town on Saturday about 10 oClock—about 2 weeks before this I was in the Country—

1. This testimony concluded the trial that began the previous afternoon. This transcript, like the *OR,* indicates that Scipio's owner, William Sims, was in the Work-House courtroom.

2. As stated above, the owner of Agrippa was not "Mr. Perry" but the Widow Ann Drayton Perry, the daughter of John Drayton (1715–1779).

William Palmer—arraigned—plea, not Guilty—put on his trial—Monday Gell a witness Examined—William belongs to the association to rise against the whites—he and Vesey & Jack Glen have been at my Shop together—They were talking on this business & said he would do as much as any other man & confessed he had joined—Vesey seemed to regard him as one of his men & to feel confidence in him—He and I were to be in the same Band under Vesey—he was often in my Shop talking on this business & never shewed any disposition to be off—this was before the first execution
X exd. by this master—The time that Vesey, Glen & William was at my shop 'twas when Vesey said there was but one Minister who preached the Gospel—Sometimes he came to my Shop alone—the first time he came in he asked for the news paper—the first conversation he had was about the rising
Charles Drayton a Witness exd. William is engaged in the Insurrection—He said to

Vesey in Mondays Shop that Vesey must not think that he would not fight, that he would fight as well as any other—I met him opposite to the circular Church on Dr. Simons' step, that it was a shame they should allow the men to be hanged that he was ready to join in rescuing them from the Gallows—this was the Sunday previous to Vesey's being hung—about 2 oClock (P.M.)
X exd. I knew him long before—I met him just after William Paul was taken up at Vesey's[1]—

1. Hamilton, *Account,* 44, indicates that William (Billy) Palmer was found guilty but was held in the Work-House until Friday, October 25, pending transportation outside the United States.

Seymour Kunhardt—on his Trial—Perault a Witness—
I met him once at Mondays with Smart Anderson—where he acknowledged he was one to rise, that he belonged to Mondays company—I met him afterwards by the Exchange, where we talked of this business & he was as much one as myself X exd by his master[1]
Monday Gell—Seymour is one in this business—he brought to my Shop about 2 months ago a racoon skin to make a Cap of & he then agreed to join us—he & Joe Jore are particular friends, I met him afterwards in Meeting street where he again s[ai]d he was willing[2]

1. The *OR* confirmed that Seymour's owner, German wharfinger William Kunhardt, was in the Work-House courtroom.
2. Hamilton, *Account,* 44, states that the court found Kunhardt guilty and held him in the Work-House until October 25, pending transportation outside the United States.

Naphur, Adam & Bellisle, belong to the Estate of Yates—Plea not guilty & put on their trial[1]—
Perault—Bellisle or Blarney was engaged in this business I met him at Crafts North Wharf—this was the first meeting—the 2d meeting at the corner of the Scale house on Smiths Wharf—he told me that the night the Blacks were to rise, he would engage the people at Mr. Yates' & myself will sleep at Mr. Mitchells when his people slept on Smiths Wharf, where they would commence the fight—Adam & Naphur met at Bulkley's farm, where we met on this business, where were Vesey, Monday, Charles & Smart—I there told him they had done the worst thing they could to engage these people, that all Charleston would know it next day—the rope walk people got them to join—Adam & Naphur then acknowledged they had joined—On the 16th I saw Adam on the Street, when he said he was going up the road to meet the Country & Neck people where he intended to remain that night & come down with those people—Bellisle belongs to the African Church—they are all Africans—
X exd. by Mr. Axson Naphur & Adam came up to the farm about 12 oClock in the day on Sunday & stayed there 'till 4 oC. this was a Sunday in May—every man in the house agreed to join to rise against the whites—the meeting was for this express purpose—after Peter Poyas & the others were convicted—Bellisle & I came out of the Shop together to talk on this business & I said we must rise and not let these people be hanged & he said yes we must do so; this was after he said to me he would get the people to sleep at Mr.

Mitchell's Shop on 16th June when they were to rise—Adam told me that Charles Drayton had told him to go up the road on the 16th June & stay there 'till the alarm was given & then come down with the Neck & Country people—Adam & Naphur came up to the farm together—the Sunday was about the middle of May—
Charles Drayton—They are all in this business, I met Adam & Naphur at Bulkleys farm where we met on this business & when they acknowledged that their hearts were in this business—Bellisle I met in the streets where he told me he belonged to it—I have also met him often at Mondays where he talked of it, said he was one of the army & ready & willing to go out.
X exd. Naphur & Adam at the farm said when the rising commenced they were ready—Vesey was there & spoke to the whole, and all who agreed to rise against the Whites were to hold up their hands—and Naphur and Adam held up their hands with the others.
John Enslow—I know the Prisoners they are as much in the plot as I am & I am in the plot—I have met them all at Mondays Adam gave to Monday a knife to make a Scabbard for him which he intended to use as a dagger—the knife was such a one as the Rifle men wear—I have heard Naphur at Mondays agree to join—I belong to Mondays company Bellisle said he was in it—Adam and I have often spoken on the same subject—We all agreed to rise against the whites & fight for our freedom—
X exd. I saw Adam deliver the knife to Monday & say make a scabbard if this will do—We all agreed at Mondays to join
Monday Gell—They all were in the habit of coming into my Shop to talk on this business—I first met Naphur & Adam at Bulkleys farm—Adam brought to me a long knife to make a Scabbard for it, which he intended to use in the business—they belonged to my side which was Veseys division—I delivered him afterwards the knife. X exd. Naphur was but once in my Shop, Bellisle and Adam often—At the farm Den. Vesey explained his plan to all present & on the proposition to agree all assented. Naphur I met once at Bulkleys farm, where as well as at my shop he expressly agreed to join—2 other witnesses were ready to be produced but twasn't thot necessary.

1. The *OR* indicated that attorney Jacob Axson Jr. (1794–1843) accompanied these three men into the Work-House court, where they were tried together. The highly regarded Axson acted as attorney for Governor Bennett in defending Rolla Bennett during proceedings of the first Court of Magistrates and Freeholders and, like Bennett, was a member of Benjamin Morgan Palmer's Congregational Church. Axson would subsequently serve as one of the two magistrates in the second court that sat in judgment of accused conspirators. See Thomas Curtis, *An Address at the Funeral of the Hon. Jacob Axson, Recorder and Judge of the City Court of Charleston, S.C., Delivered Aug. 26th, 1843, in the First Baptist Church* (Charleston, SC, 1843); John Belton O'Neall, *Biographical Sketches of the Bench and Bar of South Carolina . . .*, 2 vols. (Charleston, SC, 1859), vol. 1: 338–46; *BDSCHR* 5: 8–9. Hamilton, *Account,* 43, states that the court found all three guilty and sentenced them to hang. They were executed on Friday, July 26.

Dublin Morris Arraigned—plea not Guilty—On his trial.[1]
Perault—Dublin said to me that Wm. Gardner[2] had engaged him to join against the whites—he belongs to the African Church—
Charles Drayton—Dublin told me one day he had heard of it, but that was all—

1. Hamilton, *Account,* 44, states that Dublin was found guilty but had his sentence commuted to transportation outside the United States.

2. Hamilton, *Account,* 43, indicates that drayman William Garner was arrested on Friday, August 2.

Charles Billings Arraigned—plea not Guilty—put on his trial
John Enslow—Examd. Charles belongs to this business, we spoke on it at Mondays & he said that when we were ready he would come out & join us I met him twice at Mondays & both times said so—after Peter was taken I met him on Edmonston's wharf & he said the people were beginning to be frightened & we had better say as little as possible about it.
Perault—I met him at Mondays where I heard him say he was a horseman—I heard him say he was ready & Willing.
Monday Gell—He told me once that Wm. Gardner had spoke to him about a horse, but I dont know that he was one of us, he was frequently at my shop to get harness mended & he there conversed on this subject & he appeared willing to join & said he had joined. X exd. not material
Charles Drayton[1]—I have met him often & he acknowledged he was one Jack Glen he said was to have slept at the Stable that night of the rising to assist & saddle the horses for the Company—(Other witnesses were ready to depose to the same effect but 'twas thot unnecessary to do so)
His Master testifies to his general good Character

1. The *OR,* 99, confirms that Charles's owner, Judge John Drayton (1766–1822), was in the Work-House courtroom. As governor of the state in 1800, Drayton had mobilized militia to deal with possible ramifications of Gabriel's plot in Richmond, Virginia. See John Drayton to James Monroe, September 27, 1800, GM, no. 768, SCDAH, and Drayton's General Orders, September 27, 1800, GM no. 768, SCDAH. *BDSCHR* 4: 162–63, delineates Drayton's extensive political career. Hamilton, *Account,* 43, 45, states that the court found Charles Billings guilty and sentenced him to death. Billings was hanged on Friday, July 26; Charles Drayton was transported.

Saturday 20th July—1822—

Present the same Court
No. 1 Prince Righton—Arraigned—plea not guilty, put on his trial.
Jack Enslow Witness examined. I have seen Prince in Mondays Shop when Monday was reading the letter to St. Domingo—he must have heard Monday—The Brother of the Steward who was to carry the letter to St. Domingo was a General as I understand in St. Domingo. X exd. by Mr. Righton—not material
Monday Gell—I cant say that Prince was engaged[1]—he came once to my Shop & then agreed to join, but I have not seen him since & did not come back to say whether he would continue so or not—I therefore did not put his name down on the list—this was long before the 16th June—I then read the list of names to him but not the letter to St. Domingo—there were 3 other persons there.
X exd—He came there without any appointment

Charles Drayton. I saw him in Mondays shop once but don't know any thing against him
Harry Haig—Knows nothing against him—[2]

1. Michael P. Johnson, "Denmark Vesey and His Co-Conspirators," *WMQ* 58 (2001): 945, refers to Gell and Drayton as two "superstar witnesses," who together with Perault Strohecker provided "three-fourths of the July testimony." Johnson neglects to add, however, that in this case and others below, neither Gell nor Drayton implicated the accused. See also the case below of John Enslow, in which Strohecker declined to assert the accused's guilt and was anything but a "superstar" as far as the magistrates were concerned.

2. Hamilton, *Account,* 46, states that, as Righton's guilt was not "fully proved," the court recommended he be transported outside the United States.

No. 2—Capt. Hubbell attends
Peter Cooper—arraigned plea not guilty put on his trial.
Jack Enslow—I have met him at Mondays, where he signified his consent & said he was willing to join—this was about 2 months ago. Monday Gell—Peter said he would join & I met him once at Veseys—he there said by word of mouth that he was willing to join this was previous to the 16th June (Prisoner says he is a Guinea negro) he has passed my shop driving his cart but did not come in
Perault Examined—Vesey told me to tell Peter he wanted to see him, I told him & he said he would go & did go, but I do not know what passed there. I dont know that he agreed. I came out of Veseys & left him there—Vesey sent me to him on this business—I only delivered my message. X exd. at Veseys I met Monday there too
Charles Drayton—Do not know him
Harry Haig—Do not know him
Mr. Hubble—Peter bears a good Character an inoffensive man.[1]

1. Hamilton, *Account,* 44, indicates that Cooper was found guilty and sentenced to transportation. The *OR,* 155, adds that Governor Bennett reduced Peter's sentence to twenty lashes, presumably because of his advanced age.

No 3—George Bampfield—Arraigned—plea not guilty on trial.
John Enslow—I met him at Mondays where he said that if all the men in the room was of one mind he would make a remark—they said we are—he then said I have spoken to 2 men who agreed & mentioned their names—when Monday said for God sake let them alone or they will betray us. (I did belong to the African Church, but they turned me out for keeping a girl)[1]
Monday—He was once in my Shop—the conversation related by John Enslow did not take place—every day there were numbers in my Shop on this business—he was often in my Shop. X exd. by Mr. Bampfield—not material
Perault—I met him once at Mondays—George did agree to join as much as I did—I did not hear him say anything about engaging two men to join—this meeting was expressly on this business—I met him afterwards in the market when he said the Guards were too strong let the business lay still—I have not talked to him since any one was taken up on this business
Charles Drayton—Monday told me that Geo. Bampfield was one.[2]

1. The *OR*, 155, clarifies that Bampfield was answering this question, which was posed to him. It was not John Enslow speaking.

2. The *OR*, 155, states that accountant Thomas Bampfield, George's owner, was present in the Work-House courtroom. Hamilton, *Account*, 44, states that the court found George guilty and sentenced him to be transported outside the United States.

Jimmy Clement arraigned plea not guilty—put on trial
His 2 Young masters Present. Monday Gell—Jimmy is engaged in this business belongs to my company & he agreed in my Shop—he said he would like to know when this business would begin as he had engaged some people in the Country where his wife lived & he would have to bring them down—he has often come to my Shop & held conversations on this subject & confessed he was willing and had joined
Perault—I saw Jimmy at Mondays & he knew of it before me for at that time he was talking on this business & it was the first time I had heard of it—he was one—he was willing—He belongs to the African Church
Charles Drayton—He told me himself in Mondays Shop that he was one—he one day brought to me on the Market Wharf 2 or 3 men who he said had agreed to join & belonged to the Country—these men said they had joined & were to carry the news into the Country (Jimmy has a wife at Mr. Moore's in St. Thomas Parish) this was after Peter was taken up but before his execution[1]

1. The *OR* calls the accused Jemmy Clement, as did Hamilton, *Account*, 43, who states that the court found Jemmy Clement guilty. He was hanged on Friday, July 26.

Jerry Cohen—arraigned plea not Guilty—put on his Trial.[1]
John Enslow—Jerry I met at Veseys & Mondays, he agreed & said he was one & joined in the object of the meeting—which was to plan measures against the whites—We have often spoken on this business—At Veseys were met, were present, Monday, Charles, Rolla, Ned, Perault, Batteau, Smart, & Jack Glenn & near 30 men in all—they then handed round the hat to make collections to purchase pikes they were to be provided with dark lanterns to enter stores for arms Vesey said 100 Pikes were made by a black man who worked by himself—they also wanted money to pay that black mans wages to his mistress—after Vesey was taken he was afraid to speak on the subject
Monday—He was often in my Shop & confessed he was one, his name was on my list with his consent—I did not meet him at Veseys—he said when we were consulting who should take a lead he said he would be a leader—he was not there when money was collected to procure lanterns—I did not go to the meeting that night 'till 8 oClock. X exd. not material
Perault—He was at Veseys when they made a Collection I am not certain but think that Monday was present—He (Monday) was there—John Enslow was also there—the collection was for purchasing Spears—He did say we had better stop this business—but still he was willing to go on if we went on
Charles Drayton—nothing—Harry Haig nothing—Billy nothing

1. Hamilton, *Account*, 43, dates Cohen's arrest to Friday, July 19. The notation below suggests

that the court was done with Cohen's case by Monday, July 22. As Hamilton, 43, and the *OR* indicate, he was found guilty and hanged on Friday, July 26.

Dean Mitchell arraigned plea not Guilty put on his Trial His Master Present[1]
Perault—I have seen Dean at Veseys where he agreed as much as myself—We met purposely to make a Collection for Spears I heard him say he had joined & no one would be allowed to enter that house if he was not one—he belongs to the African Church. X exd. John Enslow summoned him to attend the meeting (prisoner admits he was there)
John Enslow—I first told him of it—He told me afterwards he saw the thing was going on well & he was glad of it—I asked him if he would like to go to Veseys meetings, he said yes & went with me, he put in money at Veseys, I saw him do it—Jack Glen handed the hat round—We afterwards conversed, & he was always of the same mind—he was on the night of the rising to meet at Veseys & march down with his party
Monday Gell confirms in part John Enslows testimony

1. Hamilton, *Account*, 43, dates Dean Mitchell's arrest to Friday, July 19. As mentioned above, he was most likely the slave of the James Mitchell, who ran a cooperage business at 27 East Bay Street. Dean Mitchell, also a cooper, was found guilty and hanged a week later on July 26.

Isaac Harth on his trial—his Master present[1]
Monday Gell—He was engaged in this business he told me so himself—after Mingo was taken up he told me that Mingo would get clear if Ed Paul did not testify against him—he said he also belonged to the horse company—Mingo told me that his brother was one too
X exd. I conversed with him directly after Mingo was taken up
William Paul—Edwin did positively say that all Mr. Harths People were engaged in it.
Charles Drayton. Mingo told me that Isaac was engaged

1. Isaac's owner was lumber merchant William Harth, and Mingo was evidently Isaac's brother. Mingo was hanged six days later on Friday, July 26. Hamilton, *Account*, 44, states that the court found Isaac guilty but sentenced him to be transported outside the United States.

John Taylor on his trial
Charles Drayton—The prisoner told me one Monday morning before the 16th ulto he told me that all the horses were ready, but the Patrols were so vigilant they could not come out. X exd[1]—I understood the horses to be intended for the insurrection—this conversation took place at my masters gate—the Prisoner was as willing as myself and he did not refuse—I only conversed with the Prisoner but once—and then he told me the horses were ready for the insurrection—William Gardner told me that the Prisoner was engaged in this affair
Perault Examined. The prisoner knew nothing of this transaction to my knowledge.
Monday Gell—I do not know that he is engaged.
Harry Haig Says the same thing.
John Enslow Says the same.
Billy Bulkley Says the same.[2]
Mr. Drummond gives the prisoner an excellent Character

1. The *OR*, 159, states that John was accompanied to the Work-House courtroom by white shoemaker James Drummond, who represented John's female owner, described only as "Mrs. Taylor."

2. The *OR*, 159, does not mention the brief testimony provided by Strohecker, Gell, Haig, Enslow, and Bulkley. Hamilton, *Account*, 46, states that as the court found Taylor's guilt "not fully proved" they recommended that his owner sell him outside of the United States.

Piere Lewis belonging to Mr. Chappeau on his Trial
Charles Drayton.

On Sunday when the Guard were out the Prisoner told me that something serious would happen, but that I was a Country born and he was afraid to trust me—This conversation occurred on the 16th of June—all the other Witnesses were called and declared that they knew nothing against the Prisoner[1]

1. The *OR*, 159, mentions no witnesses other than Charles Drayton; the "other Witnesses" may have been the five above who testified in the case of John Taylor. Hamilton, *Account*, 46, states that Lewis was acquitted and discharged.

John Gates—James Happoldt and Charles Hazel were severally arraigned and pleaded not guilty

Monday 22d July 1822 Present the same Court

Dick Sims—	Guilty	Death
Bacchus Hammet—	Do—[1]	Do
William Palmer—	Do—	Do
Seymour Kunhardt—	Do—	Transportation
Naphur } Yates—	Do—	Death
Adam } Yates—	Do—	Do
Bellisle } Yates—	Do—	Do
Dublin Morris—	Do—	Transportation
Charles Billings—	Do—	Death
Prince Righton not guilty suggest to his owner to ship him		
Peter Cooper—	guilty	Transportation
George Bampfield	Do—	Do
Jimmy Clement—	Do—	Death
Jerry Cohen—	Do—	Do
Dean Mitchell—	Do—	Do
Isaac Harth—	Do—	Transportation
John Taylor not guilty suggest to his owner to send him out of the State—		
Piere Lewis Chappeau not guilty		
Butcher Gibbes not guilty suggest to his owner to send him away		
Saby Gaillard—	guilty Transportation	

Friday 26th 'twixt 6 & 9 A.M. to be hung on the Lines and their bodies buried near the gallows or delivered to Surgeons for dissection if required

Lewis Remoussin—Sandy Vesey and Parris Ball recommended to transportation

1. Meaning "ditto."

Tuesday 23d July 1822

Examination and Confession of Monday Gell.[1]

The first time I heard of the intended Insurrection was about last Christmas from Denmark Vesey, who called at my Shop and informed me of it—Vesey said he was satisfied with his own condition being free—But as all his children were slaves, he wished to see what could be done for them—He asked me to join, but I then positively refused to do so—I enquired of him how many he had enlisted and he mentioned the names of Peter Poyas, Ned Bennett Rolla Bennett and Jack Purcell—I enquired if those were all, and he replied yes—He then departed and had no further correspondence with him, until about three months ago—I was then walking in Wentworth Street on my way to a man named Peet Smith up King Street, and was accosted by Frank Ferguson, who told me he had just returned from the Country and had collected four plantations of Negroes—He requested me to inform Vesey, that he would call on him that evening and give him an account of his operations in the Country—I went to Jack Purcells and requested him to carry the message for me being busy—On my return home in the evening, I met Veseys' Son in law at my door, who said that Vesey wished to see me—I accompanied him to Veseys and there found Peter Poyas, Ned Bennett Gullah Jack, Frank and his fellow Servant Adam Ferguson—Frank then informed Vesey he had Collected four plantations of Negroes and said he would start on Saturday the 15th June to bring them to Town on the 16th. He said he would conduct them through the woods and place them about three miles from town until Sunday night Vesey then again urged me to join and I consented—This was about three months prior to the 16th of June—Vesey from that time continued to visit the Shop in which I worked. Peter, Ned, Vesey, Frank, Rolla, Adam, Gullah Jack, Jack Purcell and myself the party at Veseys then agreed to enlist as many men as we possibly could—Vesey even then ceased working himself at his trade and employed himself exclusively in enlisting men and continued to do so until he was apprehended—Shortly afterwards Vesey said he would endeavour to open a correspondence with Port au Prince in St. Domingo to ascertain whether the inhabitants there would assist us—he said he would send letters there and I advised him to do so if he could—Some time after this he brought a letter to me which was directed to President Boyer and was enclosed in a cover which was directed to the Uncle of the Cook of the Vessel by which it was sent—the name of this Cook was William—His Uncle was to open the envelope and present the letter to Boyer—This Vessel a Schooner had been repaired at the Ship Yard at Gadsdens Wharf and was afterwards brought to Vanderhorsts Wharf where she was then lying—I walked with Vesey to the Wharf, Perault was in company with us at the time—Vesey asked William, the Cook if he would carry the letter for him and he consented to do so—We then returned each of us to his respective home—Nothing extraordinary took place after this and I met no other band or association after this time but Veseys particular company—Bacchus Hammett brought a keg of powder to my shop, and said he would procure five hundred (500) muskets from his masters Store on the night of the 16th of June—Bacchus also told me that he could procure more Powder, but did not say where—The plan was to break open all the stores where arms were deposited—and seize them—after they had procured the five hundred muskets above mentioned—Vesey said he would appoint his leaders and places of meeting about one week before the 16th of June, but the meeting for this purpose was prevented by the Capture of some of the principals before that period—Vesey determined to kill both women and Children, but I opposed it and offended him in doing so—Peter and all the rest agreed to the opinion of Vesey in the murder of all—Some time before any discoveries or apprehensions were made, myself & Perault wished to drop the business—but thought we had gone too far to retreat—I knew personally of no arms except six pikes shewn to me by Gullah Jack, which were made by Tom Russell—I knew of no lists except the one which I kept containing about 40 names, and which I destroyed after the first interruption and alarm—It was said that William Paul had a list but I never saw it—William Garner told me that he was to command the Draymen and that he had procured twelve or thirteen horses—Jack Purcell told me that Scipio Sims had been at the Savannah's in the neighbourhood of Bacon's Bridge to obtain men—Dembo Martin belonged to the party and informed me that Stephen Smith acknowledged that he was one—Charles Drayton and Perault have both seen Dembo at my shop—Vesey originally proposed the second Sunday or the 14th of July, as the day for rising, but afterwards changed it to the 16th of June—After the plot was discovered—Vesey said it was all over, unless an attempt was made to rescue those who might be condemned by rushing on the people and saving the prisoners or all dying together—Vesey said that as Peter and Ned were accustomed to go into the Country, they must go there & recruit men—Vesey was in the habit of going to Bulkleys farm—William Palmer and Vesey were very intimate—Jack Purcell knew of the conspiracy before myself—I do not recollect any person who refused when I applied to him—Some took time to consider, but they all finally agreed—Vesey was considered by the whole party as a man of great capacity and was also thought to possess a bloody disposition. He had I am told in the course of his life several wives[2] and had travelled through almost every part of the world, with his former master Captain Vesey and spoke french with fluency Morris Brown, Harry Drayton and Charles Corr, and other influential leaders of the African Church were never consulted on this subject for fear they would betray us to the Whites—Vesey had many years ago, a pamphlet on the slave trade—Vesey said that his eldest step-Son was engaged in this affair—

1. Monday Gell was arrested on Thursday, June 27. His undated confession was almost surely given prior to Tuesday, July 23. Hamilton, *Account,* 19, dates Gell's trial to Monday, July 1, and the *OR* indicated his sentence was read on Tuesday, July 9. Since Gell provided testimony in the trials below, the court presumably referred back to his confession on occasion, and so the Senate's transcribing clerk possibly found it included with these documents.

2. The *OR* transcribes this as "seven wives."

Jack[1]—The slave of Mr. McNeil arraigned and plea not guilty—Mr. McKenzie the partner of Mr. McNeil attended

Monday Gell examined—The prisoner belongs to this conspiracy, and in consequence of his consent I placed him on my list—He has been frequently at my shop and Denmark Vesey frequently saw him at my shop—He was never at my shop at any appointed meetings—He is an African and came here about 7 years of age—he belongs to the African Church and he belongs to my Company

Charles Drayton Examined—I have met the Prisoner at Mondays several times and I heard him in his presence acknowledge that he belonged to the conspiracy—after the execution of the first 6—he appeared to regret he had joined and appeared alarmed—We had several conversations and he always appeared to exhibit the same feelings

Perault Strohecker Examined—I know the prisoner but do not know that he is engaged in this affair

John Enslow Examined—I have seen him often at Mondays Shop and he has acknowledged in his presence and mine that he had joined—He has spoke to me often on the subject in the streets and was always willing.

1. Hamilton, *Account,* 43, states that the court found Jack McNeill guilty. He was one of four slaves to be hanged on Tuesday, July 30.

Ben The slaves of Mr. Cammer arraigned and plea not guilty—David Ramsay Esq. attended as his Counsel[1]

This trial was postponed until tomorrow

1. Ben Cammer was implicated by Monday Gell in the July 17 trial of Jacob Glen. William Cammer (1797–1823), Ben's owner, worked as a carpenter and resided in 1822 at 24 St. Philip's Street. See *CSCCD,* 73; Charleston *City Gazette and Commercial Daily Advertiser,* January 10, 1823. Ben's trial is not mentioned in the *OR,* and this is the only reference to a trial in the Senate transcript. According to Hamilton, *Account,* 47, Cammer was arrested on July 22 and was discharged four days after his brief hearing on July 27 on the grounds of insufficient evidence.

Caesar The Slave of Mrs. Smith[1] arraigned and plea not guilty—Mr. McDow attended for his mistress.

John Enslow Examined—The prisoner is engaged and confessed it to me—I have seen him often at Mondays—He belongs to the African Church, and is a native of Africa and came here a boy (said Mr. McDow). He told me sometimes in the street he was engaged—After the execution of Vesey he appeared fearful of the consequences X I saw him twice at Mondays before the 16th of June and once after—

Monday Gell Examined—The Prisoner is one of the party, and I placed his name on my list—He was always willing to join, there is no one more so—Xd. he was engaged some time before the affair was discovered—He was as zealous as myself—He was at my shop often Charles Drayton Examined—The prisoner acknowledged to me at Mondays that he was engaged and also several times in the street X exd. I saw him after the execution of Vesey and he appeared of the same mind.

Monday Gell was called in at the request of Mr. McDow—he answered none of the questions

Perault Called—He knows nothing against the prisoner—but knows him—

The Prisoner admitted in his defence that he had frequent conversations on this subject with the witness but denied he had joined—

1. Both the *OR,* 183, and Hamilton, *Account,* 43, refer to Caesar's owner, Naomi Smith, as "Miss Smith." Caesar was found guilty and was one of four slaves hanged on Tuesday, July 30.

Agrippa belonging to Mrs. Perry[1] arraigned and plea not Guilty—Ben F. Dunkin Esq. attended as his Counsel and his master Edward Perry Esq.
Perault Examined—On the 8th June 10 oClock (A.M.)—he met the Prisoner, who said he was going into the Country on some business, which would be good to me and him—On his return, I went to him, when after some conversation, he informed me that he had gone into the Country to get men to join in this insurrection and that he had procured some men—He hired a horse from me for which he paid two dollars in my hand and got security for the third, which he afterwards paid through Adam Creighton the price of the horse was three dollars
X exd. I never saw the prisoner before he came for the horse—I saw him the second time after his return from the Country when I examined him particularly and he confessed that he had got some men to join in the insurrection—Scipio Sims made the contract about the horse, and not the Prisoner
Mr. Perry Examined on behalf of the Prisoner.
My Mother allows the Prisoner to keep a horse in the Country where he usually resides—My Mother informed me yesterday that his horse is lame, and has been so for some time—The general ticket to work out in town or Country from his Mistress was produced in evidence—The mother and Father of the prisoner reside on my Plantation, where the prisoner is in the habit of going about once a fortnight—There are not more than 4 or 5 able bodied negroes at my plantation when the prisoner went for his tools—I have some near neighbours in the Country at whose plantations there are many negroes
Kit—The slave of Mr. Perry Examined—
The witness was not present when Agrippa and Scipio arrived. On my return home in the evening I met them—His horse was so lame that he once returned home on foot—he returned next day to town—I do not know Scipio—There were only 4 or 5 old persons on the plantation, the prime hands had come to town

1. Agrippa Perry's owner, widow Ann Drayton Perry, maintained a townhouse at 13 Bull Street. Hamilton, *Account,* 45, states that the court found Perry guilty and sentenced him to transportation outside of the United States.

Prince Graham a free Coloured Person on his Trial—Arraigned and plea not guilty.[1]
Monday Gell—The Prisoner is engaged in this conspiracy, and belonged to the Company of William Garner—He acknowledged he belonged to it, but did not wish to have his name down as he was a free man, but confessed that he belonged to William Garners Company—He was not often at the Shop X exd. Said he had a Sword a long one, a horsemans Sword provided for this purpose—he belonged to the Cavalry—belongs to the African Church—Never was with Denmark Vesey or attended any meetings—He told me he was to be an Officer, William Garner had made him an Officer
Charles Drayton Examined—I met the prisoner one night with Monday Gell in company coming out of Dr. Ramsays with Quash Harleston—He said that he was as willing as any body—After Morris Brown had returned from the North he said he did not wish

much to do with it as he was a free man, and had denied it to Morris Brown, who enquired if he was one—This was after Peter was taken up—Morris Brown returned before the 16th June
Frank Ferguson—Vesey called at the house of the Prisoner, in my company one day, and was informed by his wife he was not at home—I afterwards met the prisoner and he asked me why Vesey had called on him, I said to get him to go into the Country and he replied, I cannot go, as I have nothing to do with this conspiracy—This was I think before 16th of June
Prince on his Statement.
I met William Garner who told me, he held a Commission in the horse, and if I would join the horse, he would resign in my favor, which I refused—I heard in New York that Denmark Vesey and others were to be hung and understood that it was for an attempt to raise an insurrection—This was the first time that I understood it
Perault Examined—I only conversed with him once in company with Quash Harleston—He said if Monday Gell had told him of it a little sooner, he would have joined it—but that now he had not time to prepare himself about it—This was at Prioleaus wharf.

1. The *OR* indicates that a Mr. Jones accompanied Graham to court. Hamilton, *Account,* 45, states that the court found Graham guilty, sentenced him to one month imprisonment in the Work-House followed by transportation beyond the United States. The Richmond *Enquirer,* September 6, 1822, which is reprinted on p. 453 in Part IV of this volume, reported that Graham sailed out of Charleston on August 13 aboard the *Dolphin* for Liberia. See *Daily Albany Argus,* January 22, 1872, and *New York Herald,* February 25, 1872, both reprinted on pp. 713–14 in Part V, for Graham's return to New York State.

—24 July 1822—

Present the Same Court

Edwin Paul—Suggest to his Master to send him out of the State, reasons, believed to be deeply implicated but evidence not sufficient to convict

John Enslow—Postponed until after the execution on friday next

Perault Strohecker—Ditto—Ditto—Ditto—

Prince Righton—See Edwins Case—

Butcher Gibbes—Ditto—

George Vanderhorst—See case of John Enslow—

William Paul—Suggest to be Shipped out of the U.S. as his guilt is fully established—

Frank Ferguson—Suggest to be Shipped out of the U.S. as his guilt is fully established

Resolved that an application be made to the Governor for the pardon of Gell on condition that he be sent out of the United States—also for Charles Drayton—also Harry Haig—

The trial of Agrippa—Continued

Robin Perry a Witness on behalf of the Prisoner—

I went into the Country with Scipio and Agrippa on Saturday morning We arrived 'twixt 3 & 4 at Mr. Perry's Plantation—we stopped on no plantation, nor stopt to talk with any negro on the way up—when on the plantation Agrippa went to his house, and I to my Mothers—about 8. oClock Agrippa and Scipio were in bed—Agrippa answered me when I came to the door, that he had gone to bed—I saw Agrippa about 7. oClock next day preparing to start—We started for town directly after breakfast and did not stop on the way to speak to any one or at any plantation and arrived in town about 3 o'Clock when we got down, I carried my horse from where I got it, and then went to carry theirs to the place they got theirs from—When on the plantation, no strange negroes were there, and I don't believe Agrippa or Scipio went off the plantation, they were working together in town and as one could not go on without the other—as one had to go into the Country for his tools, the other accompanied him—there were only about 5 men on the plantation—I was not all the time with Agrippa and Scipio, that they were on the plantation X exd. As soon as we arrived on the place which was about 3 or 4 oClock we separated, and I did not see the others 'till about 8 oClock when I called at their house and found them in bed—from then to 7 next morning I did not see them—re X exd. I saw their horses frequently together with mine on the place before 8. oClock—I saw them together first about an hour after we arrived and before 8 oClock they were put up—the nearest neighbour is about 1¾ mile.

Doll Perry—On behalf of the Prisoner—

I was on the plantation when Scipio and Agrippa came up—they got up about an hour before Sun-down—I stayed at the Big house—Robin stop't at the Big house and Agrippa & Scipio went on to Agrippas mother's house—I did not see them again 'till next morning—then about dusk they sent to me for some Clabber—I saw them turn out their horses in the plantation directly after they arrived—and I saw their horses about Sun-down—they could not have gone out of the place without passing the Big house, unless they rode or walked through the field, and I did not see them pass—Mr. Singletons is about a quarter of a mile distant (Mr. Carroll says about a mile & a half). The Driver don't allow a horse to go through the field—I saw them next day after breakfast—there are no prime men on the plantation all old, or boys. X exd—There are about 4 taskable negroe men on the plantation—Mr. Lee's plantation is not half as far as Mr. Singleton's.

Lidy—Agrippas Mother—I was at home when Agrippa & Scipio came to the plantation, not long before Sun-down—they turned their horses loose, then came in and sat down—they did not leave the house that night—Robin came there after they went to bed and called them, but no answer was given him I got up before either of them next morning and then I saw them laying as I left them at night—I don't think they could have gone out of the house and I not know it—they had no talk with the people on the plantation—they never left the house further than the door X exd. I slept but little that night—my grand Child kept me awake—they carried away Agrippa's tools next day—Robin called 3 times but no answer was given—they slept in the Hall and I in my room—the tools were some Chissels and planes—

Mr. Perry for Prisoner—the nearest place is about ¾ of a mile, but there is but one negro man—the next nearest better than a mile—

Jack Purcell against the Prisoner—

Scipio spoke to me once about the insurrection[1]

1. Hamilton, *Account,* 45, states that Agrippa Perry was found guilty and sentenced to be transported outside the United States. The "Mr. Perry" mentioned here was Edward Perry.

Billy Robinson arraigned—plea not guilty and put on his trial—Mr. Crafts appears as Counsel[1]

Perault Examined—Billy was engaged in this business On the 16th June, he and I went to Vesey's in the afternoon—this day he said we must raise to day, nothing must put it back—We there met Gullah Jack and Tom Russell—Smart Anderson got him to join—I met him afterwards on a Sunday at his own house—Billy agreed as much as myself He at his house which was after Vesey and others were taken he said Jack would get more men, and then we would rise—We there spoke of rescuing Vesey &c and Billy agreed—he is an African X exd. We stopped first at Mondays and then went to Veseys—the day of the execution on the Bay, Billy asked me what I was doing here, why I was not on the green to get men to rescue those to be hung

Monday Gell—I don't know Billy

Charles Drayton—I dont know that Billy was engaged

The prisoners defence—

Mr. Davenport gives to Billy the best Character and also does Mr. Crafts—great mildness he possesses.

Mr. Tyler—Sworn—Billy [has] a good Character—Before my store I heard a conversation before my door about the Methodist Church—something about damaged corn

Mr. Davis—Gives Billy a good Character—very mild

1. The *OR* indicates that only attorney William Crafts Jr., and not Billy's owner, merchant Philip Robinson, was present in the Work-House courtroom. Hamilton, *Account,* 44, states that Billy Robinson was found guilty and sentenced to death, but that Governor Bennett commuted his sentence to banishment from the United States.

John Vincent—belonging to Mr. Cruckshank[s] arraigned Plea not guilty—put on his trial—his master appeared[1]

Monday Gell—John told me himself he had joined in this business—this was in my Shop—I frequently conversed with him on this subject—He once belonged to the African Church Before the 16th June, he told me he had a mould and that he was making Balls—this was about 3 weeks before the 16th—after the 16th he said he was ready still X exd—He said he would give me some bullets—He said his master that he was staying with was going to the North on Monday the 18th & if he would go on Saturday before 'twould be better

Charles Drayton—I have often talked with John in Mondays Shop on this subject, where he said he was willing—he was one and belonged to the horse Company—I have seen him at Mondays 3 or 4 times—He said the Gentleman he was staying with wanted him to go to the North, but he said he wanted to stay and see the frolic over first

X exd I think 'twas in his own room in an alley in Church Street vizt Elliott Street that

Figure 22. James Reid Pringle (1782–1840), judge on the First Court of Magistrates and Freeholders. From a portrait, 1820. Copyrighted image courtesy of the Gibbes Museum of Art/Carolina Art Association.

he told me about his master, this was the Sunday afternoon before Vesey was executed (30th June)

Mr. Cornhill states that the prisoner did live in Elliott Street.

Mr. Cornhill for the prisoner—gives him a good Character

1. Vincent's trial continued on July 25. The *OR,* 165, states that, in addition to Vincent's owner, shoemaker Daniel Cruckshanks (also "Crukshanks"), Jasper Corning—misidentified here and in the *OR* as "Mr. Cornhill," who while working for the firm D. Parish and Company had hired Vincent's time, appeared in his behalf. Hamilton, *Account,* 44, states that Vincent was found guilty and sentenced to death, but together with Billy Robinson and William Palmer was one of three slaves to be pardoned by Governor Bennett in exchange for banishment from the United States.

Recommendation of Pardon

Charleston 24th July 1822

Sir

We recommend that Monday Gell, Charles Drayton, and Harry Haig be pardoned on condition that they be sent out of the limits of the United States. We feel it our duty to state to your Excellency the reasons which have influenced us in this measure. These men are unquestionably guilty of the offences with which they have been charged, but under the impression that they would ultimately have their lives spared they have made to us disclosures not only important in the detection of the general plan of the conspiracy but enabling the Court to convict a number of the principal offenders. Having used these individuals as witnesses and obtained from them the knowledge they could communicate, we deemed it unnecessarily harsh and amounting at most to treachery afterwards to sacrifice their lives. In addition to this inducement, we regard it to be politic that the negroes should know that even their principal advisers and ringleaders cannot be confided in and that under the conplation [contemplation] of exemption from capital punishment they will betray the common cause.

We remain very respectfully
Yr Excellency's Obdt Sevts.
Lionel H. Kennedy
Thomas Parker
Wm Drayton
Nathl Heyward
J. R. Pringle
H. Deas
Robert J. Turnbull

Court of Magistrates and Freeholders to Governor Thomas Bennett Jr., July 24, 1822, RGA, GM, 1328, SCDAH.

—Thursday 25th July 1822—

—Present the Same Court—

A communication from Mr. Job Palmer relative to the situation of William Palmer under sentence of death was read to the Court—

A communication from Mr. John Robertson relative to his three negroes under Sentence of death was also presented and read[1]

1. These letters appear not to have survived and were not mentioned in the *OR*.

The Court altered the sentence passed on Monday Gell Charles Drayton and Harry Haig—and passed on them the following sentence—That they be imprisoned, in the Work House of Charleston until their masters under the direction of the City Council of Charleston shall send them out of the Limits of the United States—into which they are not to return under penalty of death

Defence of Billy Robinson Continued—

Mr. Tyler testifies—I believe that Perault was one of those who were speaking with Billy before my door—at another time within a few days Perault took away in his dray from before my store some damaged Corn sold him by Billy—I have powder in Canisters in my store which Billy might have stolen if he chose so to do, but I have not missed any

Mrs. Miller Sworn for the Prisoner—

I live in a house in Elliot Street, there are two rooms on a floor the front occupied by Mr. Howe, the back by me—Billy occupies a room above my Kitchen and no one can go into his room without passing through my Kitchen—I never saw Perault go into Billy's room or in my yard—Billy has lived in that room for 3 years—

Mrs. Miller, Mr. J. W. Howe, J. Dexter and Mr. Mitchell say says Mr. Crafts that neither of them ever saw Perault in Billys house—

Perault was called in by the Prisoners Counsel & described Billys residence exactly as Mr. Miller had done

Smart Anderson Examined—

Billy was engaged in this business—Caesar Smith said to me in Billys presence that Billy had joined—he told me that he was willing to take apart 3 or 4 days after this—he told me after that, that he was one

X exd. I did not tell Perault that I had got Billy to join, but that Caesar had—re X exd—I have never been at Billys house[1]—

1. Hamilton, *Account,* 44, states that Billy Robinson was found guilty and sentenced to death, but together with William Palmer and John Vincent was pardoned by Governor Bennett in exchange for permanent banishment outside the United States.

John Vincent's Trial Continued

Ker Boyce Sworn—I went to D. Parish & Co. on Saturday 15th June who was going to the North on Monday Mr. Parish asked John what was the matter, that he looked as if he had lost his mother—his looks then were such, that after I heard of this affair next day, I could not but think that John was concerned, and advised Mr. Parish to question him about it—[1]

1. Hamilton, *Account,* 44, states that Vincent was found guilty and sentenced to die, but was one of the three men whose sentence was commuted to transportation by Governor Bennett.

Court of Magistrates and Freeholders to Governor Thomas Bennett Jr., July 24, 1822

Charleston 24th July 1822

Sir

In deciding on the numerous cases submitted to us, we thought it proper to distinguish between the degrees of guilt of the different offenders and to distribute them into two classes. Under the first were comprehended those who exhibited peculiar energy and activity: under the second, those who did little (if any more) than yield their acquiescence to the proposal to enter into the Plot. Under this second division we included Seymour Kunhardt, Dublin Morris, Peter Cooper, George Bampfield, Isaac Harth, Saby Gaillard a free black man, Louis Remoussin, Sandy Vesey and Paris Ball and therefore recommend to your Excellency that they should be pardoned upon condition that they be transported out of the limits of the United States. The terror of example we thought would be sufficiently operative by the number of criminals sentenced to death; and

Figure 23. Henry Deas (1770–1846), judge on the First Court of Magistrates and Freeholders. From a portrait, 1830. Copyrighted image courtesy of the Gibbes Museum of Art/Carolina Art Association.

therefore without any injury to the community that a measure might be adopted by us which would save the necessity of more numerous executions than policy required.

We remain very respectfully
Yr Excellency's Obdt. Sevts.
Lionel H. Kennedy.
Thomas Parker.
Wm Drayton.
Nathl Heyward.
J. R. Pringle.
H. Deas.
Robert J. Turnbull.

ALS in RGA, GM, 1328, SCDAH.

Governor Thomas Bennett Jr. to Court of Magistrates and Freeholders, July 25, 1822

Executive Department
Charleston July 25. 1822

Lionel H. Kennedy Esqr	Composing court of
Thos Parker Esqr	Magistrates and Freeholders
Wm Drayton Esqr	organized for the trial of Slaves
Nat: Heyward Esqr	and other negroes charged with
James R. Pringle Esqr	an attempt to raise an Insurrection
Henry Deas Esqr	in the city of Charleston
Robert J. Turnbull Esqr	

Gentlemen,

Concurring in the views which you have taken of the degrees of Guilt attached to the convicts Sandy Vesey, Paris Ball and Louis Remoussin and under the most *solemn impression* that the fellow William Palmer is distinctly within that class as well from the consideration that the testimony against him was confined exclusively to convicts under sentence of Death; I have been induced also to include him and to extend a respite to the four slaves.

In preferring this act of executive interposition to that which you have recommended, I am influenced by the opinion, that such further evidence of their guilt may transpire in the investigation of other cases, as to induce me to withhold the clemency recommended. From the same motive, I have preferred a respite to a commutation of punishment in the other six cases and have accordingly included them with a view to an ultimate compliance with your desires.

The cases of Monday Gell, Charles Drayton and Harry Haig would produce to me considerable embarrassment, were you not clothed with authority to carry your recommendation into full effect. In my estimation of the guilt of these men, there is no election in the course I should pursue. It is true they have surrendered to offended justice their associates in this conspiracy but it is *equally true they were the causes of crime in the victims which they have produced.* Availing themselves of the ample opportunities which they possessed, they were eager in the accomplishment of their design and indefatigable in their exertions to involve in the context of guilt all in whom they could confide; beguiling by the most abominable stratagems and falsehood, many whose minds would not otherwise have been tainted by such conceptions. They appear to me at the very "head and front of the offending," without one mitigating circumstance deserving attention. Their evidence has been reluctantly and partially yielded and their concealment of many particulars self-evident. What has been obtained from them, *was obviously elicited by the frankness of Perault,* who furnished the clue and thus supplied (for the greater part) the means of penetrating the mystery.

The policy to which you have adverted can derive an additional force from the course recommended. It is already well known and will be better to that class of persons that they have been betrayed by their "advisers and ringleaders," and if their treachery has not even the excuse of a promise to exempt from capital punishment, the inference will naturally result that when that powerful principle is employed, no hope of escape can exist; while a useful and salutary lesson will be furnished to the prosecutors of similar schemes, that the only prospect of mercy is in a timely and ample confession and that under any circumstances immunity will rarely attend such crimes.

These Gentlemen, you will be pleased to regard as the reasons which in part influence my mind in withholding a compliance with your request; they are respectfully offered for your consideration but with no view to influence your opinions. I would by no means seek to control or give direction to the legal prerogative attached to your judicial character, sincerely happy if the fallibility of my own judgment meets a corrective in yours.

I have the honor to be
with great consideration
and respect. Your obdt Sevt
Tho: Bennett

Governor Thomas Bennett Jr., to Court of Magistrates and Freeholders, July 25, 1822, RGA, GM, 1328, SCDAH.

Friday 26th July [*illegible*]

Present the Same Court

Jack McKenzie	Guilty	Death
Ben Cammer		
Caesar Smith	Guilty	Death
Agrippa Perry	Guilty	transportation & imprisonment as in Gell &c Cases
Scipio Sims	Guilty	transportation & imprisonment as in Ditto

Prince Graham a free man imprisonment for 1 mo. & then transportation out of this State by sea or first opportunity and death for a return

Billy Robinson	Guilty	Death
John Vincent	Guilty	Death

Jacob Stagg The Slave of J. Lankester arraigned—Plea not guilty—Put on his trial—his master with Mr. Clark as Counsel attending[1]

Perault Examined—Jacob and I talked together about April in Mondays Shop on this business—and I found that he knew of it before me, where were Smart Anderson, George Walker—On 15th June we talked together near Flinns Church, where I told him that Vesey said tomorrow the people would come from the Country and we must rise & he agreed to do so—I have met him frequently at Monday's. X exd At Monday's shop on a rainy day he said he was engaged in the business and belonged to the foot Company—Near Flinn's Church he said he was ready[2]—It was agreed to rise in July at first as at that time the white people go to the North and to Sullivans Island and the City would be thin of men—but in consequence of the first arrest of Peter Poyas 'twas altered & fixed for the 16th June—Monday told me in his Shop in Jacobs presence that he Jacob had joined.

Monday Gell—Jacob agreed to join with my Company in my Shop—he asked me for a Sword and when I said I had none to give him, he said that he would get a Scythe and make a Sword out of it—Vesey has met him at my Shop and talked with him on this business—he sometimes came to my Shop and always said he was ready and willing—he first came to my Shop about 4 months ago—'twas cold weather[3]—one rainy day he was a long time in my Shop talking on this business, when he said he was engaged in painting the house—there were there several persons—he said he would be ready when they rose X exd I don't remember that I told any one that he had joined. Vesey mentioned his plans and arrangements and what he was going to do &c in Jacob's presence—Jacob frequented my Shop and I have known him for 4 or 5 years.

Charles Drayton Examined—

I have seen him at Monday's when Vesey was there, but don't know that he had joined[4]—I went out of the Shop and left them talking—he said he was tired of paying wages—

X exd I have known of this about 2 months

Mr. Lankester—Mr. Whitney gives a good Character and so does Mr. Stagg—he has a Wife at Dr. Ramsay's and is always at home at night—he is a good Character

The prisoner states that Monday read daily the papers and told him that Congress was going to set them free—alluding to the Missouri question

1. The *OR,* 166, indicates that both Jacob's current master, Jacob Lankester, and attorney Joseph Clark accompanied the accused into the Work-House courtroom. Hamilton, *Account,* 43, states that Stagg was found guilty and sentenced to die. He was one of the four slaves to be hanged on Tuesday, July 30.

2. On Minister Andrew Flinn (1773–1820), see above, p. 222 n6.

3. The Senate transcript is torn, but the *OR* indicates that the missing word was "cold."

4. Michael P. Johnson, "Denmark Vesey and His Co-Conspirators," *WMQ* 58 (2001): 945, refers to Charles Drayton as one of the court's three "superstar" witnesses who provided "more than 90 percent of the July testimony." As in other cases listed above, however, here Drayton did not argue for the guilt of the accused.

Sam—the Slave of Henry Barnstile—arraigned plea not Guilty—William Wadsworth attends for him and put on his trial[1]—

Perault—Sam agreed to join, and we often talked together about it—he often said he was one, and was ready—

1. Hamilton, *Account,* 45, states that Sam Barnstile—listed as "Bainsill"—was found guilty and sentenced to transportation outside the United States.

Tom—the Slave of William Scott—arraigned—plea not guilty put on his trial—his master attends.

Monday Gell Examined—I told Tom of the business and he joined—he was often at my Shop talking on this business he was willing had joined and said he was making ready—he was of the same mind after the 16th June—He belongs to the African Church.

X exd.[1] 'tis about 3 months since I spoke to him about it—the first time it was fixed to commence on 2d Sunday in July and Vesey afterwards altered it to 16th June

Perault—Tom told me he was engaged in this business with his own mouth, and was willing—[2] He told me the day that Monday was taken of the circumstance and said the more we stand still the more of us will be taken—he belonged to Monday's Company

Charles Drayton

I have heard him and Monday often in his Shop talking on this business, and heard him assent to the business; he spoke boldly

Mr. Harth[3] gives the Prisoner a good Character—I have examined his Trunk and found no arms.[4]

1. The *OR*, 168, indicates that Gell was cross-examined by Tom's master, broker William M. Scott.

2. Several pages are here missing from the Senate transcript, from the word "willing" to the start of trials on August 3. We have here relied upon the transcript provided to the South Carolina House.

3. "Mr. Harth" is the lumber merchant William Harth, whose slave Isaac gave testimony during the proceedings. In the *OR*, 169, William Harth testified that "the prisoner [Tom Scott] had a wife in his [Harth's] yard."

4. The *OR*, 168, indicates that Tom was found guilty and sentenced to die. Hamilton, *Account*, 43, indicates that Tom Scott was hanged on Tuesday, July 30.

Denbow—Arraigned plea not guilty. Put on his Trial, his master John Nicholas Martin and Mr. Crafts as his Counsel attends.[1]

Monday Gell Examined

His name was on my list—he agreed to join about 3 months ago—Vesey has met him, and spoke to him in my Shop as one of his men—he was often at my Shop—after Peter Poyas was taken up, he said he was just as much for it as ever—he told me that Stephen Smith told him, he belonged to one of the party—none ever told me, to put their names down on my list, but those who positively agreed—I put their names down myself—prisoner did belong to the African Church but now to the Lutheran

Perault Examined

I met him at Mondays speaking about this business about 2 or 3 months ago—when he said that so many persons were knowing of this business, we had better let it alone—

Charles Drayton Examined

I have met him at Mondays—but don't know anything against him in reference to this business

Mr. Martin gives him good character

1. Hamilton, *Account*, 45, places Denbow's arrest on Thursday, July 25, the day before his trial. The *OR*, 169, confirms that attorney William Crafts was in the room as well. As the *OR* and their notation below reveals, the court found Denbow guilty and sentenced him to transportation.

Jacob Stagg	Guilty	Death
Sam Barnstile	Guilty	Transportation
Tom Scott	Guilty	Death
Denbow Martin	Guilty	Transportation

Tuesday next the 30th. July 'twixt 6 and 9 o'clock On the Lines

George Vanderhorst	Imprisonment & Transportation
Billy Bulkley	Ditto
Perault	Ditto
John Enslow	Ditto
Frank Ferguson	Ditto[1]

1. The court adjourned *sine die* on Friday, July 26. See *OR*, 171.

Saturday, August 3. 1822

At a Court of Magistrates and Free Holders held at the Work House in Charleston for the trial of William the slave of Mrs. Ann Garner[1] upon a charge of attempting to excite an Insurrection in this State and for aiding and abetting others in a like attempt.[2]

1. At this point in the Senate transcript, a different clerk finished transcribing the original court documents. The handwriting is different, and this clerk tended to underline the names of key witnesses, use apostrophes to indicate possession, and include fewer paragraph breaks between witnesses.

2. The trials are not detailed in the *OR* but are instead collectively summarized on 172–76, most likely because Kennedy and Parker, who published the *OR*, did not serve on this final court. Michael P. Johnson, "Denmark Vesey and His Co-Conspirators," *WMQ* 58 (2001): 942, argues that the *OR* cleaned up and occasionally even manufactured court cases to give the impression that legalistic trials were in fact held; Johnson also asserts that it "is beyond doubt that the *Official Report* falsifies the record of testimony and court procedures documented in the [later] manuscript transcript." In this case, however, the *OR* actually omitted or condensed a series of late trials, and nothing that appeared in shorter form in the *OR* contradicted any testimony that appeared in the Senate transcript. William's owner was Martha Garner, not her widowed mother, Ann.

The Court was organized and composed of the following persons—

Jacob Axson Jr. Q.U. Charles M. Furman, J.P.	magistrates
Thomas Rhett Smith Joel R. Poinsett Robt. Y. Hayne Thomas Roper John Gordon	Freeholders—

The Prisoner[1] was arraigned—plea not guilty—put on his trial[2]—

Monday Gell exd states—He knows the prisoner and that he was engaged in the attempt to raise an Insurrection—ascertained by conversation with himself, that he was engaged—did not know he was engaged until the prisoner called at his shop—he then said, they should be continuing their preparation unless they were attacked before they were quite ready.—he said that he commanded the horse—that he had 12 or 13—that he spoke to them separately and not together—said he was preparing—he first spoke to him in his Shop—does not recollect how the conversation commenced—this was before any person was taken up—Prince Graham told witness that the Prisoner was to give him the command of the horse and to do something else himself—knew the prisoner

Figure 24. Thomas Roper (1760–1829), judge on the Second Court of Magistrates and Freeholders. From an undated portrait. Courtesy of the Waring Historical Library, Medical University of South Carolina, Charleston.

several years and has worked for him—this conversation took place about 2 months before Peter and Ned were taken up. Prisoner never attended a meeting at his shop.—One evening Charles Drayton directed the witness to meet the Prisoner at the gate of Dr. Johnson in Broad Street[3]—witness went there and met him with Peter Poyas and they went together to the house of an old Blind man named Philip in Elliot Street[4]—This was a week before Peter was taken up—This man attempted to dissuade them from the attempt—The old man asked William why he looked frightened—

Charles Drayton—knows the prisoner and that he was engaged in this attempt—prisoner told him he was engaged shortly after Peter and others were first taken up—he said he had a few men and he was to command the horsemen—Saw him once at Monday Gell's [but] heard nothing then said about this business—saw at his own house the Sunday before he left Charleston prisoner said then he was sorry he had any thing to do with this business—heard him say he had spoken with Peter Poyas—saw the Prisoner once at the house of an old man named Philip in Elliott Street—had made no appointment with prisoner to go there—does not recollect that Monday Gell was there—they spoke upon this subject he said he was willing to join and act with the Horsemen—

Perault Strohecker—knows the prisoner and that he was engaged—conversed with him on the subject—he asked the prisoner whether he knew about this business—he said yes—that he had a heap of people and a sword—Saw him a second time—Witness told him to get confidential people lest they should be betrayed—prisoner told him those he engaged were such—These conversations took place some time before any person was taken up—Monday Gell first told Witness that William was engaged in this business—said his were horse.

Prince Graham xd.—knows the prisoner—Monday Gell told witness that the Prisoner had agreed to give him 12 or 13 horses—one day upon the Bay he met William at the time of the disturbance—Wm told him he had an office of the horse but would give up the command to the Witness and to do something else if Witness were engaged—he never saw him after—

The Prisoner and his Counsel Mr. Gantt were here called upon for the defence[5]—Mr. Gantt stated that he had no evidence and had no remarks to make—

The Prisoner Wm Garner then stated to the Court that he was acquainted with the plot for some time before it was discovered—that the proposal to join was first made to him by Peter Poyas and that he also had conversation on the subject with Monday Gell, Charles Drayton, Perault Strohecker and Prince Graham—that he did not expressly agree to join them but always enquired what arms and ammunition they had prepared and told them he would give them an answer when he saw what arms they had—that he was afraid to make a discovery of the plot—as Peter Poyas had threatened him on that subject—the prisoner further admitted that he had met three of the witnesses at the house of Philip the Blind Man and that the Blind man did ask him why he was so timorous—which alarmed him much as Philip was blind—he also admitted that he held out to the witnesses the idea that he was concerned in the Plot and had engaged horsemen (* and also that after the discovery he told Prince[6] that he would give up the command of the horsemen to him.) But the Prisoner [*space left blank*] that he did not engage in the conspiracy and that it was his intention to make a discovery when the arms should be shewn to him—At the commencement of the business Peter Poyas came and told him the whites were about killing every one of the Black People—called again and repeated this conversation and urged him to join—said he wished him to command the Cavalry—said he had abundance of ammunition—Prisoner required to see his arms &c—he promised to permit him to do so, but constantly evaded it—Monday Gell and others also spoke to him—

(*The Prisoner rather evaded than assented to the enquiry made on this subject, so that the words in brackets are doubtful evidence.)

The Court after serious deliberation unanimously found the Prisoner guilty of the charge and sentenced him to be executed on the Public Lines on Charleston Neck on Friday 9th Inst. between the hours of 6 & 9. A.M.

1. The widow Ann Garner was the guardian of her daughter, Martha, owner of William.

2. According to the July 10, 1834, petition of Eliza Gardner, which is included on pp. 535–36 in Part V of this volume, William Garner was a drayman who hired away from his owner, Martha Garner, mostly to Andrew Milne. William had a wife and two children, Sarah and William Jr., all of whom belonged to Daniel Stearns. William had persuaded Milne to buy his family and then

resell them to him at cost. According to the petition, it was unclear whether William had ever completed the transaction, and the agreement may have collapsed due to the 1820 ban on self-purchase, leaving William with no other option but to join Vesey's plot.

3. In 1822 Dr. Joseph Johnson (1776–1862), the brother of Supreme Court Justice William Johnson Jr. (1771–1834), lived near Broad Street at 49 Church Street and operated a pharmacy at 1 Broad Street. See *CSCCD*, 84.

4. See *OR*, 175, on blind Philip. No free black with either the first or last name of Philip appears in the *DSGCC* or in the Charleston city directory for 1822.

5. Probably Thomas John Gantt (1795–1861), an attorney, who partnered with David Laurens Ramsay (1795–1826) at 74 Broad Street. See *CSCCD*, 84, 95.

6. This was Prince Graham. See above, p. 251 n1.

The Court being convened on the Sixth of August 1822.[1] The first person put upon trial was Pompey the slave of Mr. Lord[2] who being arraigned pleaded not Guilty—

Perault Strohecker was produced as a Witness against him He stated that he knew the prisoner and had seen him twice at Gell's Shop. The first time he saw him there they were conversing upon the subject of the insurrection. His second meeting at this place was when Billy Purse carried a Book to Monday Gell, which he stated came from Africa.[3] In the course of the conversation which they had at this shop the Witness understood that pompey had joined tho' he did not hear him say so "with his own mouth." He further stated that no person attended these meetings who was not engaged in the attempt. The Witness had another meeting with Pompey at his (the Witness') stable in the beginning of June, Pompey there asked when they would rise, and said they had better wait until Mr. Brown (meaning Morris Brown, who was then absent from the City) should return.[4] The Witness thought from the circumstances of meeting Pompey at Gell's Shop the first time he attended, that he was *then* engaged At the first meeting at Gells Shop Paris Ball, James Clement, Smart Anderson, Monday Gell the prisoner and the Witness were present. The Witness never heard the prisoner say he had engaged others and never looked upon him as a leader. He further mentioned that those engaged never spoke upon the subject before those persons who were not concerned. Monday Gell was then produced he stated that he knew the prisoner and that he was occasionally at his Shop. That when the business was first mentioned to him he appeared unwilling to join with them, and said that "they should not take it out of the right mans hands" meaning "the Lords." After this he appeared disposed to become a party; he said to the Witness that he was sorry Peter Poyas had been taken up and rather than be treated in that manner "they should do at once what was to be done." When the prisoner was first spoken to at Witness' shop, he was there alone, he was there afterwards with Paris Ball but did not recollect that Peter Poyas, James Clement and Perault Strohecker were ever at his Shop with him. The Witness however here stated that Persons came so frequently to his Shop that he cannot recollect who were there at any particular day or on any particular occasion unless something remarkable had then occurred The Prisoner spoke favourably to this business but once while at his Shop. He never said positively he would join but Witness understood from his conduct and manner, that he was one of the parties to the plot. The Witness considered Perault engaged before he understood that Pompey was concerned with them.

The Prisoner in his defence denied every thing—He was found Guilty

1. The clerk was less clear how long these final trials lasted. James Evans's George and Henry Butler's Harry, whose cases appear below, were not arrested until Tuesday, August 6. See Hamilton, *Account*, 45.

2. The *OR* identifies Pompey's owner as Richard Lord. Although *CSCCD* for 1822 identifies no one by that name, a Richard Lord resided at 54 Beaufain Street in 1825. He appears to have been involved in banking and was a member of the Charleston Grand Jury when in 1826 it applauded the Charleston Work-House for having installed the treadmill as a more humane punishment for slaves. See Charleston *City Gazette and Commercial Daily Advertiser*, May 15, 1826.

3. This may have been a copy of the *Koran*.

4. Morris Brown (1770–1849) had left Charleston for Philadelphia on Monday, April 1, and returned around June 8. See the record of his trial in the Charleston *City Gazette and Commercial Daily Advertiser*, August 10, 1822, on pp. 665–67 in this volume.

Philander Michau (a freeman of colour) was then arraigned and he pleaded not Guilty.[1] Perault was produced as a Witness against him. He knew the prisoner. He never saw him at a Meeting of the conspirators. But one evening in May last, while walking with Smart Anderson, he met with the Prisoner at De Villers' corner,[2] Smart spoke to him and asked what he thought "about the Affair" they then conversed together about the proposed attempt. The Prisoner asked when it would be made It was replied about July. The Prisoner said he was ready and had a sword. Never saw him again upon this subject. When they met the Prisoner, Smart said that he was one of his men. *Monday Gell* was then produced. He knew the prisoner and stated that he had once carried a bridle to his shop to have it mended. Vesey was then there and was conversing upon this subject with the Witness. The Prisoner overheard the conversation and observed that he would have no part in such business as he was already free. The Witness further stated that the conversation was of a general nature and did not allude to the particular attempt then in contemplation. Mr. W. H. Miller[3] stated that the character of the Prisoner was very good and particularly that he had been carried by his Master to England and there offered his freedom which he declined accepting and prefer[r]ed returning to Charleston, & that he has since *purchased* his freedom. This statement was confirmed by Mr. Milliken.[4] Mr. Miller further stated that the prisoner had on his being taken up voluntarily stated to him the circumstances of his going to Gells to have a bridle mended, the conversation of Vesey and the prisoner's remark precisely as above stated by Monday Gell. It also appeared to the Court that there had been no communication between the Prisoner and Monday and this coincidence was regarded as giving much weight to Monday's statements. The Court here thought it adviseable to enquire into Perault Strohecker's character in order to know what weight ought to be given to his evidence. His master John Strohecker one of the Wardens of the City, was called and stated that Perault was a very honest negro, remarkable for his strict adherence to the truth on all occasions. That he had owned him many years—that he was sober—latterly he had worked out and paid his wages with extreme punctuality. He would give full credit to his statements. The only fault he ever had to find with him was his bluntness he was so free spoken as to be occasionally rude—The Intendant was also called on and stated that in the whole course of examination before the former Court Peraults statements had been wonderfully supported and that he considered him as a Witness fully entitled to credit. The Intendant further stated that the Witnesses were kept apart and not allowed to be in the same room except in the presence of an officer who permitted no communication between them and that they never knew the persons against whom they were to testify until they were before the Court. Smart Anderson had been executed before this trial and therefore could not be examined.

He was acquitted.

1. Although free, Michau did not appear in the *DSGCC* or the 1822 Charleston city directory. This case, like all of those below, does not appear in the *OR*. Michael P. Johnson, "Denmark Vesey and His Co-Conspirators," *WMQ* 58 (2001): 934, argues that the *OR* "manifestly creates the illusions of trials by describing separate trials not present in the court record." Here, however, the reverse is true. If the *OR* was crafted to give the appearance of an orderly court, the magistrates would presumably have wished to include a record of these eleven trials.

2. Lewis Devillers (d. 1831) owned a grocery on the corner of King and Church streets. See *CSCCD*, 77.

3. William Henry Miller, a merchant, operated a business on Chisolm's Wharf in 1822 and resided at 33 Anson Street. See *CSCCD*, 90.

4. Thomas Milliken was an auctioneer who lived on Charlotte Street, Charleston Neck.

The testimony in the case of Nero the Slave of Mr. Haig—[1]

Charles Drayton said he met the Prisoner once at Tom Russell's shop—he then talked to the Witness about the Plot of the black people rising up against the whites The Prisoner told the Witness he was one and said he would join in rescueing the negroes who were sentenced to be hanged for their offence. Some time before this the Witness met the prisoner at a Lot in Meeting Street (here the Witness described the place) where Gullah Jacks men always met. Witness did not see Gullah Jack there at that time but he saw several of his party, among them George Vanderhorst, Tom Russel and a fellow of Sims. The Prison[er] did not then speak to the Witness and the Witness did not hear the prisoner say any thing, the Witness made no stay there, not meeting with Gullah Jack as he expected. The Witness did not see, or speak to, the prisoner afterwards, on this business except when he met him at Tom Russells as above mentioned. Then the Prisoner said he was one of the party, and said he would join in making a rescue of Peter Poyas, Vesey and the others who had been condemned to death. He agreed to make one in that business—He is an African. Had known him three years.

Perault Strohecker said the Prisoner was engaged in this conspiracy against the Whites.

The Wit: met him twice at Mr. Haig's cooper's shop. The first time was in company with Gullah Jack, and before Peter Poyas was taken up the prisoner said he was one in this affair. Nero and Jack spoke some time together in the Gullah language. After they had finished the conversation Nero informed Witness, that Jack had said he was going into the country to get people (This was in May)—The Second Meeting at Mr. Haig's shop was on Saturday the 29th of June, the Saturday before Peter Poyas was hung All the people in the Shop then agreed to raise and make a rescue Jack was there, with him again, Nero was present, they consulted about attempting the rescue. Pompey Haig proposed that they should attempt the rescue on Monday in preference to Tuesday as some other present had suggested, as the Guard of Monday night would probably remain under arms on Tuesday Morning. It was then agreed by all to meet at Wharton's on Monday Morning early and it was intended to seize the arms kept there. The Witness did go there at day light, but no one else came. The Prisoner expressly agreed to meet there and join in the rescue.—

Mr. James Haig, here stated that he had a fortnight ago attended the Examination of Perault before the Intendant and Council of Safety that he had taken notes of his evidence and referring to notes then in his hands stated to the Court, that, on that Examination Perault stated that the Second Meeting at Mr. Haig's Shop was on the Monday previous to the Executions and that Nero observed it was too late to attempt a rescue. Mr. H[2] further stated that the notes produced were not those taken at the Examination those were destroyed and these were taken from recollection a day or two after to submit to Mr. Haig but the Witness' memory enables him to speak positively.

The Intendant, Mr. Condy[3] and Mr. Wesner,[4] said they were present at the examination spoken of—They took no notes and cannot speak to what was said. The Examination was brief and cursory—

Mr. David Haig: said Nero was timid and Hypocondriacal and had been long sickly but admitted he was now better and had for the last twelve months been at his work

The Prisoner in his defence stated he *was* at Tom Russell's but it was only to get something he had left to be mended. He admitted also that Perault was at his Masters shop, but denied the conversation stated by the Witness—

The Court unanimously found the prisoner Guilty and Sentenced him to transportation—

1. Nero's trial does not appear in the *OR* and in the Senate document, appears undated at the end. Hamilton, *Account,* 45, states that Nero was arrested on Tuesday, July 23, and was "confined in the work-house," and so the trial has been moved here.

2. James Haig.

3. Thomas Doughty Condy (1779–1858), a prominent attorney, was in 1822 a Charleston city warden who lived at 100 Meeting Street. During the proceedings, he examined both Mingo Harth and Peter Poyas. See *BDSCHR* 5: 52–53; Barnwell Rhett Heyward, "The Descendants of Col. William Rhett, of South Carolina," *SCHGM* 4 (1903): 72; *CSCCD,* 75.

4. On Wesner, see above, p. 93 n45.

Pompey the slave of Mr. David Haig upon his arraignment pleaded not Guilty.[1]

Perault was produced. He knew the prisoner met him at Monday Gells with Pompey Lord and several others. Monday had there a Book which he read to them encouraging them to rebel against the Whites and which stated that the Blacks no more belonged to the Whites than the Whites to the Blacks. He saw him again at Mr. Haigs Cooper's Shop on the twenty ninth of June, they were consulting about an attempt to rescue [*illegible*] who had been condemned and who were to be executed on the following tuesday.[2]

Some one there proposed to make the attempt on the morning of Execution, but the Prisoner objected, and persisted that it should be made the day before, & not on that day, giving for reason that the guard on daily during the night would not be dismissed until the execution was over. At another time at Gells shop, Pompey told the witness that a Gullah man would give them a charm and that he would parch ground nuts so that those who eat of them would join and could not betray them. John Enslow knows the prisoner, had seen him at Monday Gells shop at different times, while there has been in conversation upon the subject. Has seen him there with Denmark Vesey and Peter Poyas Witness never heard the prisoner say any thing upon this subject tho' he was present while others were conversing upon it. Monday Gell was then produced, he knows the prisoner, he was at different times at his shop, but was never present but once when the subject of the insurrection was spoken of. At that time there were several others speaking with him about the business when Pompey called in the witness withdraw from the conversation but the others continued and Witness supposes that Pompey must have heard what they were saying, but Witness did not hear Pompey say anything. He went out after a few minutes. John Enslow was not then in his shop. Enslow was not often at his Shop, does not recollect that he was ever there with Pompey at this time Perault and James Clement were there and Pompey and Harry Nell came in together. The Witness also mentioned that Denmark Vesey had expressly cautioned them not to speak to any of the head leaders of the African Church, Pompey being one, he had not spoken to him, he also stated that Pompey was his Class leader and that he (the witness) acted as secretary or collector, and that Pompey came to his shop to receive the contributions which had been made by his class.

He was acquitted.

1. Pompey Haig's trial is not included in the *OR*. Hamilton, *Account,* 46, places his arrest on Sunday, June 23.

2. The conversation of June 29 with Perault—who was arrested on July 10—evidently referred to Vesey and the other five men, who were hanged on Tuesday, July 2.

Edward Johnson a free black man was then arraigned and he pleaded not Guilty.[1] John Vincent was produced against him, he knew the prisoner and stated that one day while he was riding with Pharo Thompson and two others in a cart they met the prisoner who made a signal to them, a significant sign as if going to strike with his arm Meeting the prisoner shortly after he asked him what he meant by it. the prisoner replied that he would want but twenty men to take the Guard House. Prince Graham who had been riding in the cart at the time the signal was made as above Stated was called and denied the Statement, indeed it was manifest that he was resolved not to give evidence.

He was acquitted.

1. Edward Johnson's case is not included in the *OR*. Hamilton, *Account,* 46, places Johnson's arrest on Saturday, August 3.

Harry,[1] the slave of Mr. Butler[2] was then arraigned and pleaded not guilty. Monday Gell was produced as a witness against him. he was acquainted with the prisoner, and knew that he was engaged in the conspiracy, he has spoken with the witness at his Shop concerning it. Did not recollect whether any persons were present during the conversations, but, they had conversed together several times upon the subject, the Witness did not know when the prisoner became engaged, but thought that he had spoken both with Denmark Vesey and Peter Poyas at his shop. The Prisoner was one of his men. Perault Strohecker was then produced, he knew the prisoner and had met with him twice over at Monday Gells Shop but no conversation occurred there from which he could know that he was engaged. at another time he met him upon the Bay, when he told the Witness that he belonged to Monday Gell's party. the Prisoner mentioned also there that he had just been to Haig's Cooper's Shop to enquire whether Gullah Jack had left a message for him, and that Jack had said that when his people came from the country they would attempt the rescue of those persons under detention. This conversation took place he thinks a week before the first execution.[3] The Prisoner in his defence admitted that he had gone one evening to Mr. Haigs Shop to see Pompey upon some business, but nothing upon the subject of insurrection was mentioned there. That on his return from the shop he met Perault who spoke to him concerning it and mentioned Gullah Jacks intention to attempt a rescue but he refused to join with them. He also stated that Monday Gell had told him that the white people intended to raise an alarm of fire and then destroy all the Blacks.[4]

Mr. Butler purchased the prisoner when he was twelve years of age, he has been sober and honest and has maintained a very good character.—Mr. Bacot mentioned that he has stayed in his yard for some years and has been very orderly and quiet.

He was found guilty.

1. Harry Butler's trial is not included in the *OR*. According to Hamilton, *Account*, 45, Harry was arrested on Tuesday, August 6.

2. In providing a calendar of the arrested slaves, neither the *OR*, 185, nor Hamilton, *Account*, 48, records the forename of the "Mr. Butler" who was Harry's owner, although the *Charleston Mercury, and Morning Advertiser*, August 9, 1822, identified Harry's owner as Henry Butler.

3. The first six men, including Vesey, were hanged on Tuesday, July 2.

4. This testimony suggests that recruiters like Gell played on the murder of slaves by their masters, including widely publicized cases depicted in Part I, to convince bondmen to join the conspiracy.

Stephen[1] and James the slaves of Mr. Walker[2] were then arraigned and pleaded not guilty. Charles Drayton was produced as a witness against them. He knew the prisoners, he stated that when Paul's negroes were taken up, he met the prisoner who told that he was engaged, that Mayor Hamilton had spoken to him upon the subject and enquired whether he knew any thing respecting it, and that he had denied all knowledge of the affair but he assured the witness that he was engaged (it was in evidence that the prisoner had a wife who stayed in Mr. Hamiltons yard) the witness further stated that after Vesey was taken up he again met with the Prisoner who informed him that his fellow servant Stephen was engaged in making bullets and again admitted that he was engaged. the first conversation took place at the market, and was introduced by speaking of the arrest of Pauls fellows. The second took place one afternoon when the prisoner called him out of Gells shop. He never saw the prisoner at a meeting.

He further stated that he one day met Stephen in Monday Gells Shop and they conversed upon the Subject of the insurrection, the prisoner mentioned that he was employed in making Bullets. Never saw him at a meeting, said that George Evans told him that Stephen was making bullets and had them ready. The conversation took place after Vesey and Peter were arrested—Monday Gell was then produced he knew the prisoners but was not aware that they were engaged in the conspiracy. George Evans told him that Stephen was engaged. one day George came to his shop with Stephen witness spoke to George upon the business in the presence of Stephen, but the latter took no part in the conversation. He did not recollect that Charles Drayton was ever in his shop with either of the prisoners. Perault was then produced, he knew both the Prisoners but knew nothing of their being concerned in the attempt at insurrection. George Evans, a prisoner was then examined, knew both the prisoners but denied all knowledge of this attempt. James in his defence admitted having met with Charles Drayton in the market, but stated that they had a dispute upon another subject, and that nothing was said about this business & that he was innocent. Stephen denied all knowledge of any thing relating to this attempt.

They were acquitted.

1. These were the only two slaves tried as a pair; their cases do not appear in the *OR*. Hamilton, *Account*, 46, places their date of arrest as Monday, August 5.

2. Neither the *OR*, 186, nor Hamilton, *Account*, 46, provides the forename of "Mr. Walker," owner of Stephen and James. The *Charleston Mercury, and Morning Advertiser*, August 9, 1822, however, identified their owner to be Scottish-born Thomas Walker (d. 1838), a stonecutter, who lived in 1822 at 149 Meeting Street. Walker knew both John Strohecker and James Evans, since all three were officers in the Charleston Mechanic Society. Walker provided supporting testimony for Evans in the appraisal of the slave George Evans, also a stonecutter, saying he had known George for "Eighteen Years." Monday Gell testified that George Evans had implicated Stephen. See Charleston *City Gazette and Commercial Daily Advertiser*, June 2, 1822, and James Evans, Petition and Supporting Papers Asking for Compensation for the Return of His Slave, December 4, 1822, no. 122, series S165015, SCDAH.

Harry[1] the Slave of Mr. Nell[2] was then arraigned and pleaded not Guilty. Perault was produced as a Witness against him. He knew the Prisoner. Met with him once at Gell's Shop. Pompey Haig, Smart Anderson, James Clement, Pompey Lord, Peter Poyas, Monday Gell and the Witness were there. Smart Anderson spoke to the Prisoner of the necessity of readying themselves in order to accomplish their purpose and told him that he must keep all the old tools he could get, to be made use of upon the occasion. Prisoner said he would do so and mentioned that he could not trust his fellow servants. Never had any other meeting with the Prisoner upon this subject. This took place in April about 8 O'Clock in the evening. Some Scriptures were read to comfort them. Mr. Righton here mentioned that Perault had stated yesterday that it was about the first of May. Monday Gell knew the Prisoner slightly. He stated that one evening while James Clement and Perault were with him in his Shop, Pompey Haig and the Prisoner came in, while they were speaking about this business—Upon seeing them come in the Witness said he drew back, but the others continued the conversation. He did not hear the Prisoner say any thing. That this was about dusk there was no light in his Shop He thought also that it was after Perault was first taken up. Upon being cross questioned he said that if the Prisoner had joined in the conversation he must have heard it, & *that he did not consider him attached to his Band.* The Prisoner admitted that he went one Evening with Pompey Haig to the Shop of Monday Gell He there saw two persons conversing suspiciously together, and perceiving Monday standing alone in a reserved manner he touched his companion and they went away. He denied ever hearing any thing upon this subject. Mr. Haig mentioned that the Prisoner had stayed Eighteen Years in his Yard and was always orderly and quiet and was always at home at night—He was acquitted—

1. Harry's trial does not appear in the *OR.* Hamilton, *Account,* 46, dates his arrest to Tuesday, August 6.

2. Harry belonged to Jesse Nell (1754–1823), a Virginia-born cordage manufacturer who operated a ropewalk on Charleston Neck. See *CSCCD,* 92; Charleston *City Gazette and Commercial Daily Advertiser,* March 21, 1823.

George[1] the Slave of Mr. Evans[2] was then arraigned and he pleaded not guilty—Monday Gell was produced against him. He knew the Prisoner and that he was engaged in this scheme. The Prisoner in company with the Witness has spoken with Vesey upon the subject. He then agreed to become a Party to the attempt and he was attached to the Band under the direction of the Witness—Has spoken with him at different times at his Shop always considered him engaged. Charles Drayton was also produced. He knew the Prisoner but did not know any thing respecting his being engaged in this attempt but the circumstance of his informing him that Stephen was engaged in making bullets to be used on the occasion. Has seen the Prisoner once at Monday Gell's but nothing was then said respecting the insurrection. Monday Gell was the only other Person there at the time. The Prisoner was a Class Leader of the African Church.

Upon being cross examined at the suggestion of the Prisoner who stated that the Bullets were for a Casting Net the Witness stated that the bullets were not for a Casting Net but for the purpose above mentioned the Prisoner offered Witness the loan of the mould that he might make some for himself. The Prisoner in his defence stated that one Evening he saw Denmark Vesey at Monday Gell's shop, while he was passing and that he afterwards asked Gell what Denmark was doing there who replied that he was examining the newspaper for Lottery Reports as he had tickits in one[3]—The Prisoner intimated that this was the only occasion on which he had seen Vesey and Gell together. He also stated that Monday Gell at this time mentioned that he had something to say to him but that he had once seen him intoxicated & on that account Vesey had forbid him to do so and therefore he could not tell it to him—Mr. Evans the Master of the Prisoner stated that Vesey 7 years ago had a wife in his yard but that he had parted from her and taken another—[4]

He was found Guilty.

1. George's case does not appear in the *OR.* Hamilton, *Account,* 45, places his arrest date as Tuesday, August 6.

2. Neither the *OR*, 185, nor Hamilton, *Account*, 45, provides the forename of "Mr. Evans," owner of George. But James Evans, a marble cutter, who in 1819 lived at 37 Wentworth Street, petitioned the state for remuneration for his convicted slave. James Evans describes George as "a good Stone cutter and marble Polisher" and appraised his worth at eight hundred dollars. See James Evans, Petition and Supporting Papers Asking for Compensation for the Return of His Slave, December 4, 1822, no. 122, series S165015, SCDAH. Enslaved stonecutters like George, it should be noted, would have had frequent access to cemeteries since one of their primary jobs was to produce gravestones.

3. This reference suggests that Vesey, who won the city lottery in November 1799, continued to play lotteries. There were numerous lotteries offered each year in Charleston. The Charleston *City Gazette*, June 27, 1822, for example, referred to a "Grand Lottery lately completed" and announced the start of a "Free Mason's Hall Company Lottery."

4. George's master here refers to Beck, Vesey's first wife. Evans's testimony appears to suggest that Denmark and Beck separated around 1815, but since his son John Anthony Vesey, Susan Vesey's child, was born around 1809, it is more likely that they separated around the time she was purchased by Evans, if not before. On September 10, 1808, James Evans purchased a "Negro Wench named Beck and her Son Robert" from John Barker for four hundred dollars. See Bill of Sale, Vol. 4A, p. 97, SCDAH. Robert Vesey would live to become the architect who in 1865 would rebuild the African Church on Calhoun Street.

George the Slave of Mr. Sam Parker[1] was then produced and arraigned, and he pleaded to use his own words "Not Guilty of *Joining* them." He then voluntarily proceeded to state That in the beginning of the year he was walking with Charles Drayton, that the fellow then told him that the White People were about to excite an alarm of fire and then to kill all the blacks, but he said that on that day or night there would be a "Gentleman battle" Prisoner said that he replied he hoped he would be Sixteen feet under Ground when it occurred. He further stated that he had met Perault twice upon the Bay who told him that he had something to say to him and that he the Prisoner should go to his house and he would explain to him. He also saw Perault on Saturday the 16th of June near Flinn's Church, he was on horseback and asked the prisoner if he had a horse upon his replying that he had not. Perault told him to go to his stable *and he would get one for him from Adam Bellamy.* [*blank space*] Charles Drayton a Witness against him was then produced. He stated that the Sunday before Peter was taken up, he met the Prisoner who said to him "how is it." Witness hesitated to reply when the Prisoner observed "you said not be afraid of me for I am as willing as any other man." Prisoner was walking with a Man belonging to Cross[2] and they went into Monday Gell's house. Monday Gell had cautioned Witness not to speak with the Prisoner and that was the reason of his not replying to him when he addressed him in the manner above stated. The Prisoner belongs to Geo: Evans' Class.[3] He never had any conversation with him about the Whites killing the blacks—*Perault* was produced and stated that he never knew the Prisoner to be engaged until he came to the Witness before Mr. J. R. Rogers,[4] and said to Witness "there is going to be war," the Witness replied "No?" he said "yes there is *you need not hide the thing from me, I have a hand in the affair.*" On the 16th June he met the Prisoner in Queen Street, he said to Witness "How will we raise tonight?" Witness replied that if the people come down we will, if they do not come we will not make the attempt. Does not recollect telling the Prisoner to come to his Stable for a Horse. The reason why he did not speak to George at first was that several persons had cautioned them not to do so as he did not associate with his countrymen and they did not think they could trust him.

He was found Guilty.

Monday Gell was produced as a Witness in the case but he stated that he did not know the Prisoner to be engaged he was cautioned against speaking to him. He did one Sunday go to his house with a man of Cross' but heard nothing there said about this affair.—

1. The reference is to the planter Samuel Parker (1776–1830).

2. The man named "Cross" was attorney George Warren Cross (1783–1836). See Part II, p. 97 n1.

3. As Charles Drayton testified in the previous trial, George Evans was a class leader in the African Church.

4. John Ralph Rogers (1785–1857) was a ship chandler who resided in 1822 at 105 East Bay Street. See *CSCCD*, 96.

Adam Bellamy[1] the Slave of Mr. J. H. Merritt[2] was then arraigned and he pleaded not Guilty—

Charles Drayton the first Witness introduced was acquainted with him but did not know that he was engaged in the conspiracy—Monday Gell was then produced He stated that he knew the prisoner and that he was a party to the conspiracy. This man upon going to his Shop upon one occasion said to the Witness "I am your friend" he replied "How." The prisoner answered "In this good cause you have in view." he was asked "What cause." He then explained himself by saying "the rising against the Whites." (It is to be here remarked that the Prisoner was one of the Leaders of the African Church and therefore one of those to whom Monday had been forbidden to communicate the design, the Witness stated this to be the Witness' caution in replying.) The Prisoner was not again at his Shop until Peter and Ned were taken up.[3] He then went there and mentioned "*that he was ready whenever they should turn out for it.*" The Witness was under the impression that there was no one in his Shop when these Visits took place The Prisoner also stated that he had two Horses, that one of them was a good one and he would use it himself but the other was worth but little. The Witness did not know who first spoke to this man—He was a Carter and worked on Williams' Wharf where Paris Ball, Pompey Lord, James Clement and others worked, all of whom were engaged in the Conspiracy. The Witness supposed that Adam had been spoken to by some of these persons. He never was at a Meeting. *John Vincent* was then produced. He knew the Prisoner and stated that while in Company with Pharoah Thompson and several others in a stable It was mentioned that the Prisoner had two horses ready. Perault was then brought forward against him. He stated that he had been informed by Monday Gell that this Man had been to his Shop and had spoken with him about the business and that he was willing to join. He afterwards met the Prisoner who spoke to him about the Black people's rising against the Whites; he said it was too late for him to do any thing, but when it did take place he would have to take care of himself as he could not then get arms; that there would be only two parties as the Whites would kill without distinction and so would the Blacks. He saw the Prisoner again on Sunday the 30th of June, who then said to him, "For God's sake get the People to be done with this business." The Witness said "No, the people *will* rise to prevent the Execution for if those under sentence were executed they would give up all the names" he replied "No hanging was as good a death as any and he did not think they would tell the names." He never saw him at a meeting—

Mr. Blackwood stated to the Court that the Character of the Prisoner was remarkably good

He was found Guilty.

1. Adam's case does not appear in the *OR.* Hamilton, *Account,* 45, dates his arrest to Saturday, August 3.

2. One of the few accused bondmen to be identified by the court with a surname different from that of his master, Adam Bellamy belonged in 1822 to James Harvey Merritt, an English merchant who in 1822 lived at 87 Bull Street and operated a factorage on Kunhardt's Wharf. See *CSCCD,* 90.

3. Having been questioned by authorities as early as Friday, May 31, Poyas was rearrested with Ned Bennett on Tuesday, June 18.

Jack[1] the Slave of Col Cattell[2] was then arraigned and he pleaded not guilty— Monday Gell the first Witness produced stated that he knew the Prisoner that Vesey told him that he had spoken to this man about the insurrection Witness afterwards went upon the Bay to see him they conversed together upon the subject the Prisoner was doubting "he appeared to be of two Minds." In the course of this conversation the Prisoner said it would be well if they could obtain the assistance of the country People and of the runaways of which there were many between this and Savannah. The Prisoner never said positively that he would join them. But he asked will there not be a meeting. He agreed to attend a Meeting at Vesey's but did not as the Witness afterwards informed him that it had been put off. While he was conversing with the Prisoner Perault was sitting near upon a dray. This Man was a drayman. Perault was then produced. He was acquainted with the Prisoner, the first time he spoke to him was upon the Bay opposite Mr. Mitchell's Office door,[3] he then said that he had heard of the affair. The Prisoner asked if they were going to carry on such a business without having meetings. The Witness replied that they did meet and informed him of a meeting at Vesey's, but he did not attend the Witness does not know why he did not. He said that he would come out on horseback. The second time he saw him at his own house sick and in bed, the Prisoner then requested the Witness to tell Monday Gell that he should "take care of himself as many people were talking about it." The Witness recollected seeing this man speaking with Gell near the Exchange upon the Bay. The Prisoner then denied all knowledge of the business he stated that Monday Gell was speaking with him one day upon the Bay but their conversation did not relate to this subject, he came to ask for money due him and he staid but a moment.

Perault was here again called in for the purpose of making some explanation Some altercation had taken place between him and the prisoner during the former examination and was now renewed. Perault then said addressing the Prisoner "Why don't you remember that one day Col. Cattell came down upon the Bay near the place where we were standing and you pointing to him said "Do you see that fellow he is my Master and is the first Man I will kill." The Witness further stated that the first conversation he had with this man was before he saw him speaking with Gell on the Bay— He was found Guilty.

1. Hamilton, *Account,* 45, dates Jack's arrest to Monday, August 5. His case, however, does not appear in the *OR.*

2. Jack belonged to Colonel William Cattell (also rendered "Cattel"; 1776–1842), a prominent planter who resided near Charleston on an estate called Ashley Hill in St. Andrews Parish. In 1822, Cattell commanded an elite militia cavalry unit called the Charleston Hussars. He would become an active member of the South Carolina Association and commissioner of fortifications for Charleston. See *BDSCHR* 4: 103–4; Charleston *Southern Patriot,* April 29, 1842; H. P. Archer, *Local Reminiscences: A Lecture Delivered by Mr. H. P. Archer before the Mutual Aid Association, No. 1, of Charleston, S.C. in the Hall of the Mechanics Union, at Charleston, S.C. June 6th, 1889* (Charleston, SC, 1893), 12; Henry A. M. Smith, "The Ashley River: Its Seats and Settlements," *SCHGM* 20 (1919): 112.

3. John Hinckley Mitchell (1767–1832) was a notary who ran an office in 1822 at 88 East Bay Street and resided at 42 Guignard. See *CSCCD,* 91.

The examination of testimony was here closed.

The Court in every case cautioned each Witness as he was introduced, to be careful to testify nothing but the truth and seriously warned them of the awful responsibility they would be subjected to by bearing *false witness* against the prisoners While the Court were examining one Witness the others were always kept out of hearing.[1]

The Court also as soon as they were organized resolved that no questions should be asked of the Prisoners with the view to occasion them to criminate themselves—[2]

1. Michael P. Johnson, "Denmark Vesey and His Co-Conspirators," *WMQ* 58 (2001): 934, regards the Senate transcript as having "more authority and reliability" than the *OR,* but on p. 946 he discounts his own theory by accusing witnesses Gell and Drayton of "collusion," which the Senate transcript claimed did not happen.

2. Following this closure of testimony, the clerk recopied the case of Haig's Nero; since the House version does not contain the August cases, these pages were perhaps intended for inclusion in the House transcript.

South Carolina At a Court of Justices and free
Horry District holders holden at the Court
House in Conway borough
on the 31st day of July in the year of our Lord 1822
Magistrates Wm Todd
James Singleton
Freeholders John Rogers
James Jordan
Arthur Alfred

The State against a negroe man
Toney the Property of John
Sarvis[1] Esqr

The Court meet and proceeded in the trial of the prisoner agreeable to the act of assembly in that case made and provided, and after Examining the witnesses for and against the prisoner and having his defence the Court found the Prisoner Guilty of trying to raise an Insurrection and threatening the Lives of the whites in said District and passed Sentence of Death on him.[2] But before awarding and ordering the said sentence to be executed appraised and valued the said negro man Named Toney a four hundred and fifty Dollars by the court who tryed him.[3]

1. John Sarvis (1751–1834) served in a variety of public offices in the Georgetown and Horry districts before his death, at which time he owned sixteen slaves. See *BDSCHR* 4: 506.

2. This trial was not held in Charleston, but up the coast in Horry District just above Georgetown. It may not have been related to the insurrection trials in the city, but John Enslow's confession, included on pp. 324–25 in Part III of this volume, indicated that he "heard that they were trying all round the country *from Georgetown and Santee, round about to Combahee,* to get people."

3. Because the Negro Act did not require the state to reimburse masters for hanged property, as did Virginia slave law, the execution of skilled bondmen posed economic hardships on owners like Thomas Bennett Jr., who earned only $875 each year as governor. Toney's value here suggests that Bennett's losses in 1822 far exceeded his salary.

John Sarvis, Petition and Supporting Papers Asking Compensation for a Slave Executed for Attempting an Insurrection in Horry District, ca. 1822, no. 1938, series S165015, SCDAH.

The court met and proceeded in the [illegible] agreeable to the [illegible] of assem-
bly in such [illegible] made and provided, and [illegible] the witnesses for and against
the prisoner and having his defence [illegible] Prisoner guilty [illegible]
as an insurgent and [illegible] and passed
Sentence of Death on him [illegible] present sentence to be
[illegible]
[illegible] the court [illegible]

[illegible]

[illegible]

IV

Eyewitnesses

Charleston officials confined the accused plotters behind the thick walls of the Charleston Work-House, the city jail, and the Charleston Poor-House. Although the trials proceeded deep within the Work-House, numerous eyewitnesses, some of whom like Charleston's white ministers had heard confessions of jailed slaves, reported on the events of 1822. Because of the city's cramped geography and active associational life, residents could not easily have missed the five parades of condemned men as they moved down Meeting Street toward the gallows on Blake's Lands or on the low benches placed against "the Lines," a stretch of earthen fortifications, constructed during the War of 1812, on what were the northern fringes of the city between the Ashley and Cooper rivers (near what is now Line Street). The grim spectacle peaked on Friday, July 26, when authorities executed twenty-two men in a single morning. Having moved the condemned from the Work-House to the former bank vault in the basement of City Hall at the corner of Broad and Meeting streets, the procession moved up Meeting Street, each of the rebels "seated on his coffin [on a] cart, driven by another negro."

In the nineteenth century, hangings were public spectacles that drew large crowds, which came to jeer, mourn, or simply observe what in some cases were destined to be historic events. Far from being something of which to be ashamed and conducted away from the public eye, hangings served as community events, in which whites could assure themselves that elected authorities were maintaining peace and security and, in the case of blacks, the state's racial order. White children watched as well and learned lessons from an early age about what lengths were necessary to protect society from the state's enslaved majority. No evidence exists to demonstrate that Susan Vesey or her children watched as her husband and their father was carted to his death. But as free blacks, they had the choice of attendance. Some masters, thinking of deterrence, herded slaves to the gallows on execution day, so that they might learn the ghastly price of resistance. As the number of executions mounted, Governor Bennett, still chafing at the proceedings, acted to respite slaves from the hangman's noose and succeeded in obtaining for several a commutation of their sentence to a lesser punishment.

The documents in this section speak to the variety of eyewitnesses, the deep impression the Vesey affair made on their minds, and the controversies both local and national generated by the proceedings and the hangings. Some of these eyewitnesses add important information not revealed in the trial documents. Although the two courts closed their doors to spectators, details from the testimony of slaves about Vesey and the design of the plot leaked out and circulated with considerable velocity among men and women, black and white, old and young. Northern newspapers proved particularly eager to excerpt correspondence from eyewitnesses in Charleston. Charleston officials took offense at northern criticism of the way they had handled proceedings and fired back at their critics. In 1822, the story of the Vesey plot had "legs."

Anna Hayes Johnson[1] to Elizabeth Haywood,[2] Friday, June 28, 1822

Charleston

. . . And now my dear Betsey "I will a tale unfold" whose lightest word—Would harrow up thy soul; freeze thy young blood.

Make thy two eyes like stars start from thy spheres
Thy knotted and combined locks to part
Like quills upon the fretful porcupine—list list oh list[3]

In sober phrase, our city is now in the most fearful state. Graceous Heaven when I think what I have escaped & what I may yet suffer my blood curdles—Alas! Sterne too truly said that "Slavery was a bitter draught"[4]—Our Slaves have revolted and the plot was only found out by the noble interposition of a Negro whom they wanted to join them he instantly with the subtlety of his class drew from his acquaintance the design plan time &ca and thus with trembling anxiety informed his master who instantly informed the Intendant & my uncle who is fortunately Governor and by them every means was taken to protect the city—for the information was given only a few days before the insurrection was to have taken place—since which a court of enquiery has been instituted of the most impartial and honourable men of our city who have been sitting now more than a week and the number implicated is incredible—and I blush to own that it has been traced to the whites for this day one or two white men have been taken up and the proofs are so strong as to hang them—for some intelligent negro who acts as a spy for the court found when their nightly meetings were held and carried our Intendant and one or two others there who saw and heard scenes of rapine & murder talked of with the coolness of demons—Thier plans were simply these—they were to have set fire to the town and while the whites were endeavouring to out it, they were to have commenced their horrid depredations[5]—It seems that the Governor Intendant and my poor father were to be the three first victims—the Men & Black Women were to have been indiscriminately murdered—& we poor divils were to have been reserved to fill thier—Harams—horrible—I have a very beautiful cousin who was set apart for the wife or more properly the "light of the Haram" of one of their chiefs—and the old and infirm women were to have shared the fate of our fathers—It is true that in our city the white & Black population are equal 16,000—each but about Georgetown the odds is fearful—16,000—B—to 150 W—I do not know the estimate of the black population thro' the state but I know that it is very great—I am told that the number in the plot is computed to be about 3000—The children were to have been spiked murdered &ca and I am told that the observation heard from the man taken up to day was this—I feel a little sorry for the children, but they must go, as to those already condemned it is no matter some must die for the cause—you have [*illegible*] many brave spirits among you—go on—*booty Beauty & Glory*—this from a free born American—Oh my cousin I thought not to have found such a villain breathing the pure air of free born America—Six of the Chiefs are to be hung the 2nd July. . . .

1. Anna Hayes Johnson (1801?–1871) was the daughter of Supreme Court Justice William Johnson Jr. (1771–1834). In 1823 she married Congressman Romulus Mitchell Saunders (1791–1867) of North Carolina. See S. A. Ashe, "Romulus Mitchell Saunders," in *Biographical History of North Carolina from Colonial Times to the Present,* ed. Samuel A. Ashe, Stephen B. Weeks, and Charles L. Van Noppen, 8 vols. (Greensboro, NC: C. L. Van Noppen, 1905–1917), vol. 3: 392.

2. Elizabeth Haywood (1796–1840) was living in Raleigh, North Carolina, at the time of her correspondence with Anna. Eliza married Edward B. Dudley (1789–1855), who in 1836 would become governor of the state. See Zella Armstrong, *Notable Southern Families,* 2 vols. (Chattanooga, TN: Lookout Publishing, 1922), vol. 2: 154–55; "Died," Keene *New-Hampshire Sentinel,* November 4, 1840.

3. The reference is to William Shakespeare's *Hamlet,* act 1, scene 5.

4. The reference is to Laurence Sterne's *A Sentimental Journey Through France and Italy,* published in 1768.

5. In an attempt to prove that there was no slave conspiracy in 1822, Richard C. Wade, "The Vesey Plot: A Reconsideration," *JSH* 30 (1964): 152–53, hinted that Anna Hayes Johnson may not have believed there was a plot, a theory clearly contradicted by this letter as well as hers of July 18, 1822, which appears below. Indeed, unlike Justice Johnson, her father, Anna obviously did not downplay the content or the magnitude of the plot.

ALS in Haywood Papers, SHC, UNC.

Charleston Mercury, and Morning Advertiser

Saturday, June 29, 1822

The Court of Magistrates and Freeholders, convened for the trial of sundry persons of colour, charged with an attempt to raise an Insurrection in this State, after acquitting several, unanimously found the following *Guilty,* and passed upon them the sentence of death, to be carried into execution on Tuesday next, the 2d July, between 6 and 8 o'clk. in the morning:

Denmark Vesey, a free black man.

Rolla,
Batteau,
Ned, } Slaves of his Excellency Thos. Bennett.

Peter, the slave of James Poyas, Esq.[1]
Jesse, the slave of Thomas Blackwood, Esq.[2]

1. According to the South Carolina Death Records, 1821–1955, SCDAH, on Saturday, June 22, a three-week-old child with the surname of "Poyas" and "no name" listed as a forename, identified as "M[ale], B[lack], S[lave]," died of "Diarrhea."

2. This information was reprinted nearly verbatim in the *Charleston Courier,* June 29, 1822; Savannah *Republican,* July 2, 1822; Philadelphia *National Gazette and Literary Register,* July 6, 1822;

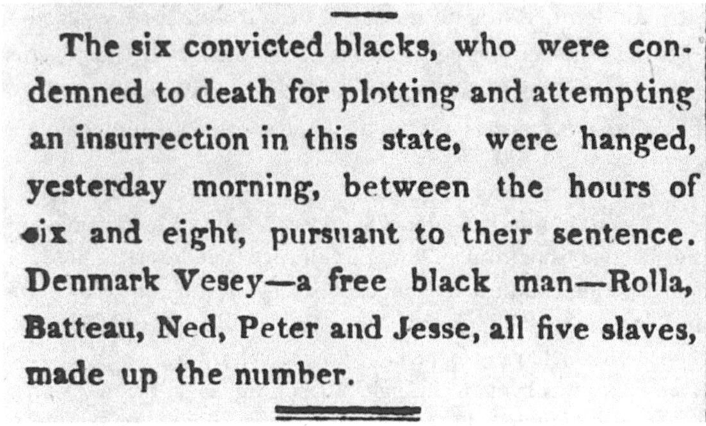

The six convicted blacks, who were condemned to death for plotting and attempting an insurrection in this state, were hanged, yesterday morning, between the hours of six and eight, pursuant to their sentence. Denmark Vesey—a free black man—Rolla, Batteau, Ned, Peter and Jesse, all five slaves, made up the number.

Figure 25. The July 3, 1822, issue of the *Charleston Mercury* reports on the execution the previous day of Denmark Vesey and five slaves, including Rolla, Ned, and Batteau Bennett, all owned by Governor Thomas Bennett Jr.

Baltimore Patriot & Mercantile Advertiser, July 6, 1822; Baltimore *American and Commercial Daily Advertiser,* July 6, 1822; Washington *Daily National Intelligencer,* July 6, 1822; *New-York Evening Post,* July 8, 1822; Philadelphia *Democratic Press,* July 8, 1822; Richmond *Enquirer,* July 9, 1822; Boston *Columbian Centinel,* July 10, 1822; Providence *Gazette,* July 10, 1822; Newport *Mercury,* July 13, 1822; Hartford *Connecticut Courant,* July 16, 1822; *Albany Argus,* July 16, 1822; and St. Louis *Missouri Republican,* August 7, 1822.

Genius of Universal Emancipation

July, 1822

From the New York Gazette. We have seen a letter from Charleston of the 17th inst. of which the following is an extract.—

'You will doubtless hear many reports and exaggerated ones, respecting an insurrection among the Negroes. There certainly was a disposition to revolt manifested, and some preparations made by plantation negroes, to attempt to take the city; but from the arrangements for defence made by us, there is now little *hopes* that the attempt will be made; and, if made, or fear of the result. I say *hopes,* because we did hope they would progress so far as to enable us to ascertain and punish the ringleaders, in an exemplary manner. I was ordered on duty last night, but the orders were afterwards countermanded, we however got very little sleep."[1]

1. In 1821, Quaker Benjamin Lundy (1789–1839) founded in Baltimore the first newspaper, published monthly, devoted to immediate abolitionism. This information was reprinted verbatim in the New Orleans *Louisiana Gazette,* July 30, 1822.

New York *National Advocate*

Tuesday, July 2, 1822

Letters from Charleston announce, that an insurrection of the blacks was in contemplation, and that the principal inhabitants of the city were to have been murdered, on the 29th of June, or the 4th of July. The ringleader[1] was a free black, and the principal actor,[2] was a confidential servant of the Governors. A Court, composed of Freeholders, has been for some time in session, proceeding with great tranquillity, in making discoveries, and tracing the progress of the plot. About twenty negroe[s] have been arrested.

1. Denmark Vesey.
2. Rolla Bennett.

Charleston Mercury, and Morning Advertiser

Wednesday, July 3, 1822

The six convicted blacks, who were condemned to death for plotting and attempting an insurrection in this state, were hanged, yesterday morning, between the hours of six and eight, pursuant to their sentence.[1] Denmark Vesey—a free black man—Rolla, Batteau, Ned, Peter and Jesse, all five slaves, made up the number.[2]

1. On the probable location of the gallows, see Part III, p. 168 n12. No document explicitly indicates where Vesey and the five other men were buried. Nor do Charleston city death records contain any mention of Vesey and the others hanged. Charleston officials wanted to erase this frightening blot on their history. The slaves hanged on July 26 were buried in shallow graves next to the Lines, and the bodies of the four men hanged on July 30 were given to local surgeons for dissection. A memorial to the Charleston City Council, December 3, 1822, excerpted on p. 576 in Part V, indicates that John Jinks Singletary (1777–1857) from St. James, Goose Creek, was paid $9.26 on September 7 "for Expenses on Sullivan's Island on account of Denmark Vesey." Sullivan's Island did have an African American burial ground for blacks who resided there, and although ferrying the bodies to the island would have meant taking them some distance, city authorities may have wished to avoid creating a monument to black martyrs. The African Church owned a burial ground, but fighting to remain open after the affair, the church leaders surely did not want the six men buried there. From 1808 to 1841, the city also maintained a public cemetery, with blacks and whites buried in segregated areas, in the Cannonborough section of Charleston on Thomas and Bee streets. See Michael Trinkley, Debi Hacker, and Nicole Southerland *The Silence of the Dead: Giving Charleston Cemeteries a Voice* (Columbia, SC: Chicora Foundation, 2010), 3–5. White officials suspected slaves involved in the plot of using burial grounds to hide weapons, and perhaps Singletary was sent to Sullivan's Island to find them. On this point, see Robert L. Paquette, "From Rebellion to Revisionism: The Continuing Debate about the Denmark Vesey Affair," *Journal of the Historical Society* 4 (Fall 2004): 307, 329 n47.
2. This information on the five slaves, Rolla Bennett, Batteau Bennett, Ned Bennett, Peter Poyas, and Jesse Blackwood, was repeated nearly verbatim in the *Southern Patriot, and Commercial Advertiser,* July 2, 1822; *Charleston Courier,* July 3, 1822; *Washington Gazette,* July 9, 1822; *Baltimore Patriot & Mercantile Advertiser,* July 10, 1822; *New-York Evening Post,* July 11, 1822; Philadelphia *Democratic Press,* July 11, 1822; Philadelphia *United States Gazette and True American,* July 12, 1822; Baltimore *Niles' Weekly Register,* July 13, 1822; Boston *Commercial Gazette,* July 15, 1822; and *Independent Chronicle and Boston Patriot,* July 17, 1822.

New Haven (CT) *Pilot*

Thursday, Wednesday, July 3, 1822
COMFORTS OF SLAVERY

Extract of a letter from a citizen of Charleston, (S.C.) to his friend in this city, dated "CHARLESTON, 16th June, 1822.

"The last 24 hours have been very anxious ones to our city—this moment two brigades of infantry and one of horse are on duty. Every citizen is provided with 24 rounds, and with arms. About 300 slaves were taken last night, and the deepest plot for an insurrection discovered that was ever planned in this country. All is alarm, and every mind harrowed with anxiety."[1]

1. This information was reprinted verbatim in the Providence *Gazette,* July 6, 1822.

Southern Chronicle and Camden Gazette

Wednesday, July 3, 1822

. . . From very good authority we learn that sixteen Negroes of colour, supposed to have been engaged in the above affair, who fled from Charleston, have been apprehended and lodged in Goal [Gaol] in Columbia.

We are happy to state that our police have taken the necessary steps to secure the citizens from any accident that might occur from such a source. All are on the alert and ready to suppress every similar attempt.[1]

1. This information was reprinted nearly verbatim in the Washington *Daily National Intelligencer,* July 16, 1822.

John Potter to Langdon Cheves, Friday, July 5, 1822

Charleston

My dear Sir,

Since I wrote you[1] our situation here—and investigations made by the Court, which has again been constituted by the same Gentlemen, and are still proceeding in their enquiries—altho' many are implicated in the Crime, for which six have already suffered—I do not know, whether more lives will attone, for their plans of deep laid treachery and murder.

I fear it will have a sad effect, on this kind of property, much depends on what is now adopted for our future safety, and laws that may be adopted at the coming meeting of our legislature—

I do not recollect, whether I mentioned the Circumstances of *Vesey,* (the Chief who was hanged) and others, had wigs and whiskers made, to wear on the occasion—the wretch denied the fact, never had seen the french man who had made them, when confronted together, until this man took one of the wigs from his pocket, and asked him if he knew that—?—[2] when the villian, was abashed—I believe for the first time—as he had denied it totally before—I hear Major Willsons servant,[3] (Gibbes' son in law)[4] was the person who first discovered and divulged the plot of murder, which his mind could not submit to.

I must confess, if one of these fellows, had made his way into my bed room, in the dead of the night, dressed out in his *Whig, whiskers,* and a *whitened* face—that I might have been appaled, not being aware of the circumstances—but probably these precious few—would have had enough to do, out of doors—and the trifling business of *taking care* of *the males* would have fallen to other agents, with the servants of the family many of whom, who are not yet known I fear would have turned traitors on the Occasion—Certainly this discovery has awakened unpleasant feelings, tho' I firmly believe all such danger, is over, for the present—this horror my friend is more than I durst own, before my family, who have been more alarmed, than I have ever been before—nor can I deem it surprising from the horrid aspect of the transactions, and consequences, which might have followed in the event taking place—attended with the smallest success—tho' in the end they could not have succeeded at all.

I have already mentioned, how Judge Johnson was implicated, in foolish ill-timed publications—the minds of the people were exceedingly irritated against him—inclosed is his justification, which came out Yesterday—but which somehow, has not given much relief or satisfaction to the public mind—and his pushing it on Willington, the printer[5] will only involve, I fear, more recriminations.

for a man so well informed it is surprising he does so many I may say weak imprudent acts—Certainly the Anecdote, he first gave the public (as he Calls it) was at any time improper and a libel on his Country—but particularly at such a moment, doubly improper and unfounded. . . .

1. This refers to Potter's letter to Langdon Cheves of Saturday, June 29, 1822, which appears on p. 135 in Part II of this volume, as most of it pertains to Justice William Johnson's critique of the court's methods.

2. Potter left the name of the French hairdresser blank with the question mark in the letter, but the likely candidate is Leon Duplan, who resided at 15 Market Street. See Part II, p. 93 n42.

3. The "servant" was the slave George Wilson, one of the key witnesses for the prosecution. Major John Wilson (1789–1833) worked as South Carolina's chief civil and military engineer.

4. Major Wilson married Eliza Gibbes (1787–1853), daughter of William Hasell Gibbes IV (1754–1834), a Charleston lawyer, planter, and judge with the title in 1822 of "Master of Equity." Although George is often referred to as his slave, Major Wilson's wife, Eliza (Gibbes) Wilson (1787–1853), was probably the legal owner of George. See *BDSCHR* 3: 258–60; *CSCCD*, 80.

5. Aaron Smith Willington (1781–1862), editor of the *Charleston Courier.*

Langdon Cheves Collection, SCHS.

Mary Lamboll Beach[1] to Elizabeth Gilchrist, Friday, July 5, 1822

Charleston

My dear Sister,

We had the pleasure of hearing from you to day by your letter of the 25th (Post mark) to Mary. I find by this letter you had not heard of Miss Huxham's arrival. I am thankful your bill reached you safely, & I am much obliged to you about the offering the use of some of your money for the Taxes. I am sorry to think how unpleasant a subject the most of my late letters have been filled with; but Solomon justly observes out of the abundance of the heart &c[2]—Our thoughts have of late been *so* engrossed with that that it has to my grief shut out (except for short spells) almost *every* thing else. I desire to be truly humble & thankful for the great mercies of our God of which we have been the subjects & have reason to be humbled in the dust on account of my vile impietitude for his *late* mercies as well as *all* those of my past unprofitable life. My heart has been the abode of but a small share of peace or comfort if any at all for some days past; owing to the mournful state of things in our guilty City. I believe *all* danger for the *present* season is over—but to any one at all disposed to reflect, or feel for *others* as well as their *own* interests the events of this week were calculated to excite *much painful* & *bitter* reflection. The execution is over as to us at least for the present & has not been attended with tumult, or resistance as was feared by some of weak nerves. The Military force out that day was so overpowering as to have rendered a rescue a *desperate* attempt. Kitty Ramsay[3] told me that the Negroes were under the impression that Denmark Vesey the free black *would* be delivered & if in *no* other way the Jail doors opened by a Supernatural Power. You will doubtless feel as I did desirous of knowing how the criminals behaved at the execution for I greatly feared they would have made some address to excite further rebellion; but they did not attempt it. Vesey was in a very hardened state in the Jail say *our* people [*illegible*] in *other* places. They will say perhaps he behaved with Magnanimity. M[r] T. Legare[4] says he heard from a white person a gentleman I believe but one who was near enough almost to have touched him that he did not make a single remark but appeared like one to use *his* expression "collecting his thoughts for the scene before him" You can't think what a feeling came for a moment over me when I heard this although he deserved to die for the undertaking he had embarked in. He was said to be a man of superior powers of mind & the more dangerous for it. He asserted in Jail that he had not had a *fair* trial, that his accusers had not been brought before him; the last charge is a fact; but for motives of Prudence & Policy in our present state of affairs it *could* not be allowed, or *was* not at least—but they say his guilt was clearly marked from the testimony of several witnesses examined seperately; but whose testimony fully agreed as to his agency &cc. Poyas's Peter all I have heard speak of, as a very hardened villain & died in a dreadful state of mind. I am told two of them even laughed when first brought out of the Jail & preserved this state of mind to the last. Bennet's fellow Rolla was quite a young man but has been a member for 2 years of our Church he evinced much feeling & penitence even to tears—his Master would not believe I have heard till he heard it from his *own* lips that he had been engaged in it. I do pity Bennet sincerely for he has gained if enemies can be called gained by it—But to a man who has studied his people: (comfort as he has it must be very wounding—I heard he said [*illegible*] was his neighbour Mrs. Townsend[5] who keeps hens (with her bread baking you know & she a woman in easy circumstances & her woman near lying in carrying a load too heavy for a man I should say to come quite here with a great clothes basket of bread) he said working day & night *they* had not *time* for *one* even of them to be engaged in it. [*illegible*] he had 3. And I am afraid this very instance of Bennet's will induce others to be harder with them than they were previous to it; saying it is better to keep them *hardly.* Ah! Slavery is a *hard* business & I am afraid we shall in this country know it to our bitter cost some day or other.

Figure 26. The Reverend Artemas Boies (1792–1844), pastor in 1822 of Charleston's Second Presbyterian Church. From a photograph of a portrait, undated. Courtesy of The Alexander Hamilton Institute, Clinton, NY.

Rolla confessed his being engaged in the business; but said he had felt so much about it that he had resolved to leave the City before the awful event took place as he could not bear to commit Murder & laid the blame on Vesey—Doc[r] Palmer[6] said he appeared to be more cut down when he spoke to him of his sin as a professor than on any other ground—This I thought in his favour poor deluded creature. I hear that Vesey impressed or tried to do it the (professedly serious at least) that *they* ought to engage in the business on account of their abridgement of religious privileges & that he said to them that Doc[r] Palmer even had joined with some of the gentlemen in our Church & made a Catechism *different* for the Negroes. This was the fact; but the good man did it to accommodate it to *their* understanding. Good man he gets it from *all* quarters to think of some person in an office before persons the other day calling him a Rascal with an Oath; for the part he had taken in trying to give them religious instruction; you may recollect the affair when Cogdell[7] & Turnbull[8] had some difficulty with him or rather it was the latter when Doc[r] P.[9] had given some black man a ticket as a class leader or something of that sort. And now the bitterness that is poured out on the dear good Missionaries is enough to make I was going to say Satan triumph. But God can overule it for good as dark as the cloud now is about the increased spread of the Gospel in our state. It seems this business has been of 4 years standing & ever since the affair of their being foiled about the African Church.

There are several still in confinement & it is expected I believe will be transported. They convict none on a *single* testimony. It is said that 500 had given in their names in the City to join them; but this I do not vouch for, for never were more falsehoods perhaps told—It is also said that Vesey & the other ring leaders were to have the pillage of the Banks &c & of which they were immediate to go off with to S[t] Domingo & leave the fools behind to pay the reckoning. Mary Jones[10] I believe (except with the Earthquakes) never went through such a night of Terror as that of the 16th of June—& can you think it *possible* I could have smiled *that* night or rather it was near day yet I did—When she said in a most solemn tone *Oh!* I shall never be able to bear the sight of a Negroe again & if I go (or live to go) to the Northward I *never will* have *one* about me & at present she has almost I may say a *hatred* of them *all.* I have heard it remarked by several that *all* confidence in them now is forever at an end, after the treachery of several in this business. Poor Susan M'Call[11] is in considerable trouble about her Clarissa her children's nurse's, her husband if he is not hanged will be shipped off—She is I think without *any exception* the most superior black female I know—We had an opportunity of seeing her at James Island & the Ramsay's say her husband is as fine a looking black he belongs to Harth.[12] Jesse belonging to Blackwood[13] was a young creature only about 22 I hear he had a most prepossessing countenance & I *have* heard that James Legare[14] wished him pardoned—it seems there was a great openness & candour in his manner & he shewed a very tender & penitent spirit. Doc[r] Furman,[15] Palmer & Mr Boies[16] visited them in Jail, but Vesey & Poyas's fellow[17] would hear *nothing* they had to say; they said they were condemned already & it was of no use to say any thing more. They were executed near the Lines I understand but few blacks attended. The companies on duty were out from 9 at night until 9 the next morning & the City will I understand be strongly guarded for some time to come by the different companies. Whether they think the City Guard not to be trusted I can't say; but I understand they do not patrole the streets at all now; but are kept at the Guard houses & Arsenal. But this won't I expect suit them long to be out of the way of picking up Dollars in addition to their wages. It is said in the voluminous papers found it is astonishing the gain in their knowledge &cc. & they speak of their cause as one they expect the Lord will assist them in as he did the Israelites from their Master's & speak of their deliverance from the hand of the Philistines. I heard that Vesey said in the Jail that it was a Glorious cause he was to die in & the singing of the Psalms &cc in there the night before was carried on to a *great* extent—he said also that his *spiritual* enjoyment never had been as great or greater than that night or the one before it. What do you think of Wigs made by order of the ring leaders being produced before the City Council which they were to wear with their faces painted white when they first were to attack the City Guard. Through mercy we are all well except that Mary has frequently a pain in her limbs which is the case to day. Old Mrs Swinton[18] died of a fit last Sunday (it is supposed so as she had an Apoplectic one a few weeks ago.) She was aged 76 yr & 6 months. Unless any thing of more importance than usual occurs I do not expect to write again untill Cap[t] Bunce[19] sails from here & he has not yet arrived, but if it should be otherwise rest assured I will endeavour to write. It will be time enough to come to any determination what part of the Property to offer for sale I will try to send by the George P. McDonald's statement. I wrote to Holinsby about the interest money; but he has been sick but as soon as better or well enough has promised to call; but I don't know whether it is to pay it or not.

Mary & children all send their love to you both. I was truly concerned to read of the late Mrs R. misconduct on two accounts. With the warmest affection my d^r Sister yours sincerely

M. L. Beach

July 6th 1822
Kitty & several of your friends have at different times lately sent their love to you. Give mine to d^r little Mary

1. Reverend John Thomas (1746–1771), the Welsh-born pastor of Charleston's Circular Church, fathered Mary Lamboll Thomas Beach (1770–1851) and Elizabeth Lamboll Thomas Gilchrist. Mary married Samuel Beach (1761–1793), a Princeton-educated planter; Elizabeth married Adam Gilchrist Jr. (1760–1816), a merchant. In 1822, the widow Beach lived at 23 King Street, was closely associated with Reverend Benjamin Morgan Palmer, and owned a slave named Betty, a literate bondwoman. Betty's class leader was George Wilson, the most important class leader for blacks in the Circular Church. Wilson provided crucial testimony against the Vesey plotters. See David Ramsay, *The History of the Independent or Congregational Church in Charleston, South Carolina, from Its Origin Till the Year 1814* (Philadelphia, 1815), 18–19; William M. Macbean, *Biographical Register of the Saint Andrew's Society of the State of New York*, 2 vols. (New York: printed by the society, 1922), vol. 1: 165; *New-York Gazette and the Weekly Mercury*, October 7, 1771; Jacob Milligan, *The Charleston Directory, and Revenue System* (Charleston, SC, 1790); *CSCCD*, 70; Joanne Calhoun, *The Circular Church: Three Centuries of Charleston History* (Charleston, SC: History Press, 2008), 35–36; *BDSCHR* 4: 232–33.

2. Beach refers here to 2 Chronicles 9:1: "And when the queen of Sheba heard of the fame of Solomon, she came to prove Solomon with hard questions at Jerusalem, with a very great company, and camels that bare spices, and gold in abundance, and precious stones: and when she was come to Solomon, she communed with him of all that was in her heart."

3. Probably Catharine H. Laurens Ramsay (1792–1876), who, like Mary Beach, was a member of Benjamin Morgan Palmer's Circular (Congregational) Church. She never married and was the aunt of the lawyer David Ramsay (1795–1826), who served as attorney for Pharo Thompson. See W. U. Hensel, "Dr. David Ramsay," *Historical Papers and Addresses of the Lancaster County Historical Society* 10 (1905–1906): 366–67.

4. Thomas Legaré (1766–1842), a deacon of the Circular Church.

5. Probably Hepzibah Jenkins Townsend (1780–1847), wife of the planter Daniel Townsend (1759–1842), who in 1822 owned a home on the corner of Boundary Street in Charleston Neck, near Bennett's Mills. See *CSCCD*, 101.

6. Benjamin Morgan Palmer (1781–1847), pastor of Charleston's Independent or Circular (Congregational) Church, played a lead role in missionary outreach to South Carolina's slaves and free persons of color. He was the first of thirty-two white signatories in support of a petition, ca. 1820, of Morris Brown and twenty-five other free persons of color in Charleston to open in the city an independent black church. See John Hammond Moore, ed., "The Abiel Abbot Journals: A Yankee Preacher in Charleston Society, 1818–1827," *SCHM* 68 (1967): 70; Boston *Recorder*, July 15, 1820, and Petition of Sundry Free Persons of Color, Attached to the African Methodist Episcopal Church in Charleston, n.d., no. 1893, series S165015, SCDAH, published on pp. 32–33 in Part I of this volume.

7. Beach probably refers here to John Stevens Cogdell (1778–1847). Trained in law by William Johnson Jr., Cogdell was also an artist, banker, politician, and militia officer. In 1821 President James Monroe appointed him naval officer for the port of Charleston. Cogdell and Robert J. Turnbull (1755–1833) were close friends and fellow Episcopalians. Cogdell resided in 1822 at 46 Meeting Street. The incident Beach describes here helps explain Turnbull's particular interest in formulating the Negro Seamen Act of 1822. See *BDSCHR* 4: 121–23; Charleston *Southern Patriot,* February 25, 1847; John Belton O'Neall, *Biographical Sketches of the Bench and Bar of South Carolina . . . ,* 2 vols. (Charleston, SC, 1859), vol. 2: 215–18.

8. Robert J. Turnbull (1775–1833) served on the first Court of Magistrates and Freeholders that tried those inculpated in the Vesey plot. See Part III, p. 161 n5.

9. Reverend Benjamin Morgan Palmer.

10. Beach probably speaks here of her fellow Congregationalist Mary Jones (1782–1835), resident in 1822 at 1 Guignard Street and the widow of Samuel B. Jones (1780–1813), who at the time of his death worked as a bookkeeper for the Bank of South Carolina. See Joseph Folker, *A Directory of the City and District of Charleston and Stranger's Guide for the Year 1813* (Charleston, SC, 1813), 40; *CSCCD,* 48, 85.

11. Beach refers to Susan Branford Hayne McCall (1789–1875), widow of the attorney Hext McCall (1785?–1821), who in 1819 resided at 48 Church Street. See "Obituary," Charleston *City Gazette and Commercial Daily Advertiser,* August 8, 1821; *CSCCD,* 52; Theodore D. Jervey, "The Hayne Family," *SCHM* 5 (July 1904): 171. Susan Bradford Hayne was the older sister of Robert Young Hayne (1791–1839), South Carolina's attorney general, who would serve on the second Court of Magistrates and Freeholders.

12. The lumber merchant William Harth, who in 1822 resided at 1 Gibbes Street, owned three slaves involved in the proceedings: Mingo Harth was executed; Isaac Harth had his death sentence commuted to transportation outside the state; Robert Harth testified before the first Court of Magistrates and Freeholders.

13. Thomas Blackwood (1771–1836), president, Planters' & Mechanics Bank, owned Jesse. See Charleston *Southern Patriot,* September 15, 1836, and *CSCCD,* 71.

14. James Legaré (d. 1828) served as one of the judges on the first Court of Magistrates and Freeholders.

15. Richard Furman (1755–1825) was in 1822 the South's most prominent Baptist minister. See James A. Rogers, *Richard Furman: Life and Legacy* (Macon, GA: Mercer University Press, 2001); William T. Brantly, *The Saint's Repose in Death: A Sermon Delivered on the Death of the Rev. Richard Furman, D.D., Late Pastor of the Baptist Church, Charleston, S.C.* (Charleston, SC, 1825).

16. Artemas Boies (1792–1844) was pastor of Charleston's Second Presbyterian Church, and like Palmer, had signed the free colored petition for the creation of an African Church in Hampstead. See "Second Presbyterian Church, Charleston County, 1809–1837" (typescript), SCL, and William Buell Sprague, *Annals of the American Pulpit,* 9 vols. (New York, 1857–1869), vol. 2: 664–66. In April 1817, Denmark Vesey was one of "three people of Colour" admitted "to Communion for the first time" at the Second Presbyterian Church, a document reprinted on p. 25 in Part I. See the church's Record of Sessions, 1809–1837, Charleston County, SCL, Columbia.

17. The slave Peter Poyas.

18. Hannah Splatt Swinton (1746–1822), a widow, was also a member of Benjamin Morgan Palmer's Circular (Congregational) Church.

19. Jared Bunce (1759?–1832) captained a packet ship between Charleston and Philadelphia. His daughter Sarah (1787?–1847) married Edward Palmer (1788–1882), brother of the Reverend Benjamin Morgan Palmer the elder and father of the famous Presbyterian Reverend Benjamin Morgan Palmer the younger (1818–1902). Captain Bunce would become a prominent critic of South

Carolina's so-called Negro Seamen Act, passed in the aftermath of the Vesey plot, which required the seizing and jailing of persons of color aboard ships entering the state. See *Documents Printed by Order of the State of Massachusetts during the Session of the General Court, A.D. 1845* (Boston, 1845), 31–32. See "Deaths," *Charleston Courier,* June 2, 1832, and Christopher M. Duncan, "Benjamin Morgan Palmer: Southern Presbyterian Divine" (PhD diss., Auburn University, 2008), esp. 8.

ALS in Beach Papers, SCHS.

Charleston *Southern Patriot, and Commercial Advertiser*

Friday, July 5, 1822

"Executions—It will be seen by our Charleston dates, that they are getting rid of their black population without the aid of the Colonization Society. There are about fifty more in confinement, it seems, who will probably be strung up with as little ceremony as they string up weak fish in the Fulton Market."

We do not know whether the prevailing sentiment of our mind on reading the above paragraph was that of contempt or abhorance for the writer.—That the public of Charleston may know the source of this infamous insinuation against its humanity, it would be proper to mention that the paper from which it is copied, is called the "Commercial Advertiser," printed in New-York, and edited by Mr. STONE.[1] That this man should have penned his atrocious insinuation in the teeth of the information which must have reached him of the character of the Court, and the nature of the offence they were to try, would excite no stronger feeling in our mind than contempt for his understanding, did we not know that he is one of those instruments who has willingly assisted to loosen the ties between master and slave in the Southern States.

Yes! it is to the efforts of this Editor and his co-adjutors at the North that we are to ascribe that discontent and insubordination in our slaves, which leads almost inevitably to insurrection with its attendant crimes—murder, rapine and conflagration. It is well ascertained fact, which the late trials have developed, that the currency given to the sentiments of those who, during the agitation of the Missouri Question, labored together in the humane vocation of rendering the slave discontented with his situation, has assisted to produce the late diabolical plot against our lives. Let Mr. STONE and his allies in this cause, reflect on this fact. Let them consider that to their exertions, in part, is owing the fatal necessity of making those examples which self-preservation dictates, and be the blood of these ill purposed and misguided wretches on the head of him and his co-adjutors.

But to remove all misapprehension as to the kind of trial these negroes have received—to take from libelers all apology for their dark insinuations—it would be proper to state, that, independent of the spotless integrity, enlightened judgement, and distinguished humanity of the gentlemen who composed the Court—the accused were scrupulously tried according to those legal forms and by those legal forms and by those strict rules of evidence which are the land marks of our Courts in all criminal prosecutions. And to shew that the conspiracy had not its origin in the ill-treatment of the conspirators; the fact should be mentioned to the honor of Carolina and to the shame of those who excite discontent and insurrection among us, that the slaves the most deeply implicated in the plot have been the most confidential, the most indulged, and the most humanely treated.

1. Although a number of Charleston editors accused him of involvement, William Leete Stone Sr. (1792–1844), editor of the *New-York Commercial Advertiser,* was not a member of the Hartford Convention, organized in 1814 by more than two dozen New England Federalists disenchanted with the War of 1812 and the so-called Virginia dynasty and speaking openly about the possibility of secession. In 1818, well after the convention, Stone relocated to Connecticut to succeed Theodore Dwight (1764–1846) as editor of the Hartford *Mirror.* In 1821, Stone moved again to New York City to edit the *Commercial Advertiser,* which Dwight published. Dwight served as secretary at the Hartford Convention. As the reference to "Stone" below in the *Charleston Courier* of August 12 indicates, Carolina editors tended to confuse the two men. See essay by Granville Ganter, in *ANB* 20: 874–75.

Henry William DeSaussure[1] to Joel Roberts Poinsett,[2] July 6, 1822

. . . We have been much shocked & grieved here, to learn that the suspicion of Insurrectionary movements among the Blacks were but too true: and that, there has been a necessity to resort to measures of severity. I fear this kind of property is fast losing its value on the Sea Coast; for its vicinity to the W. I. Islands, & the great intercourse with them, must introduce among our people many of those who have been engaged in Scenes of blood in the West Indies, who will beguile our slaves into rebellion with false hopes & sole expectations. We had no indications of any combinations here, tho' the negroes were well apprized of what was passing, in Charleston, certainly as soon as we were, if not sooner—Hamilton and the Council[3] have acted with discretion & firmness, as far as I have learnt; & are entitled to the thanks of the Country—The Court was wisely selected from among the best informed, most reasonable & firm of the Community; men neither to be misled by violent popular rumors, nor deterred from the performance of painful duties, by a false humanity—may God, in mercy, extinguish this rebellious temper. . . .

I am sorry to see Judge Wm J.[4] has been drawn into an unpleasant controversy, on the subject of your distressing events. He certainly meant well, but was indiscreet. Is he clear & decided, as to the proper men & measures on the approaching Contest[5]? When I saw him transiently in Town, he appeared to me to entertain a desire & a vain hope, to remain neutral. Inactive he may be—neutral he cannot be—Be assured that much will depend on y^{r} Elections in Charleston. Tell Hamilton & Hayne, that the vote of the state, & the success of everything depend on Ch^{s}ton. . . .

1. Henry William DeSaussure (1763–1839), a Federalist lawyer, had a long and distinguished career in public service, including the first directorship of the United States Mint in Philadelphia. He helped train John C. Calhoun in law. In 1822 he had an office at 81 Broad Street and a residence at 35 Meeting Street. See *BDSCHR* 4: 154–56; Baltimore *Sun,* April 9, 1839; John Belton O'Neall, *Biographical Sketches of the Bench and Bar of South Carolina . . . ,* 2 vols. (Charleston, SC, 1859), vol. 1: 243–52; *CSCCD,* 77. Within months of the conspiracy's collapse, DeSaussure penned a series of newspaper essays on the need to eliminate skilled urban slaves; it was promptly republished in pamphlet form as *A Series of Numbers,* which is excerpted in this volume on pp. 563–69 in Part V.

2. On Joel Roberts Poinsett (1779–1851), one of five freeholders to sit on the second court in judgment of accused conspirators in the Vesey plot, see Part II, p. 102 n1.

3. Intendant James Hamilton Jr. and the Charleston City Council.

4. Supreme Court Justice William Johnson Jr., whose essay published in the *Charleston Courier* and reproduced on pp. 131–33 in Part II, sparked a controversy with members of the first Court of Magistrates and Freeholders .

5. The presidential election of 1824.

Poinsett Papers, vol. 2, HSP.

Providence *Gazette*

Saturday, July 6, 1822

ANOTHER ACCOUNT.

Extract of a letter from Charleston (S.C.) dated June 16, 1822.

COMFORTS OF SLAVERY.

"The last 24 hours have been very anxious ones to our city—this moment two brigades of infantry and one of horse are on duty. Every citizen is provided with 24 rounds, and with arms. About 300 slaves were taken last night, and the deepest plot for an insurrection discovered, that was ever planned in this country. All is alarm, and every mind harrowed with anxiety." *N. Hav Pilot.*[1]

1. The abbreviated title refers to the New Haven (CT) *National Pilot,* from which the Providence newspaper obtained the story.

Newport *Mercury*

Saturday, July 6, 1822

Insurrection of the Blacks.

The *New-York American* of Monday last, says—"We understand that letters have been just received in town, from Charleston, (S.C) which state, that an insurrection of the Negroes had been planned in that place, but was happily frustrated by the detection of the plot about three days before the period fixed for its accomplishment. About twenty negroes have been arrested, three of which were servants in the family of Governor Bennett, and were to have been his murderers. The eldest of them was to have been the principal chief and leader when the government of the whites should be overthrown; and as a reward for destroying his master, he was to receive in marriage the Governor's daughter, a young lady about 16 years of age.[1]

It is said, on what authority we know not, that the negroes were induced to undertake the project, from hearing repeated an unguarded expression of an eminent Judge,[2] who is reported to have said that a negro had been illegally executed; and these ignorant and deluded wretches, it seems, have thought proper to take the administration of justice into their own hands."[3]

1. This story appears to have circulated widely in Charleston. See the letter of John Potter to Langdon Cheves, June 29, 1822, on p. 135 in Part II of this volume. The "young lady" in question was probably Mary Hayes Bennett (b. 1804), seventeen years old at the time of the conspiracy. Bennett's other daughter, Anna Margaret (1812–1871), was only ten. See Craig Miller Bennett, "Family Records of Governor Thomas Bennett Jr.," *SCHGM* 51 (1950): 51–54. Allegations that rebellious slave men aspired to ravish white women attended many slave conspiracies. For other examples, see Douglas R. Egerton, *Gabriel's Rebellion: The Virginia Slave Conspiracies of 1800 and 1802* (Chapel Hill: University of North Carolina Press, 1993), 77–78, and Martha Hodes, *White Women, Black Men: Illicit Sex in the Nineteenth-Century South* (New Haven, CT: Yale University Press, 1997), 63.

2. Justice William Johnson's article about events of the previous decade, "Melancholy effect of popular excitement," was first published on Friday, June 21, nearly a month *after* William Paul first spoke of the plot to Prioleau's Peter on Wednesday, May 22, and long after Vesey began to organize the conspiracy. 3. This information was reprinted nearly verbatim in the *National Gazette and Literary Register,* July 2, 1822; Providence *Gazette,* July 6, 1822; Boston *Columbian Centinel,* July 6, 1822; Boston *Commercial Gazette,* July 8, 1822; *Albany Argus,* July 9, 1822; Salem *Gazette,* July 9, 1822; Gettysburg *Republican Compiler,* July 10, 1822; Baltimore *American and Commercial Daily Advertiser,* July 14, 1822; Boston *Recorder,* July 18, 1822; and Canton *Ohio Repository,* August 1, 1822.

John S. Cogdell[1] to Langdon Cheves, Saturday, July 6, 1822

My dear Sir,

Permit me to make you acquainted with our very worthy and excellent friend Maj. Alex Garden,[2] who is on a short visit to your City.—

The Maj. will be able to give you some of the many serious and afflicting occurrences NOW disturbing our domestic tranquility. Maj. Hamilton—with whom you are I believe acquainted—has been indefatigable in ferreting out the Leaders of a Plan well conceived to put us all to death.

If this is not effectually subdued the city property will fall in Value very much. My respects attend your Lady & family.

Your obliged Friend
John S. Cogdell

1. On Cogdell, see p. 378 n7.

2. Alexander Garden Jr. (1757–1829) fought in the American Revolution, rising to the rank of major. In 1822 both he and James Hamilton Jr. were officers in Charleston's prestigious Cincinnati Society. See *BDSCHR* 3: 251–53; Charleston *City Gazette and Commercial Daily Advertiser,* July 7, 1821; *Charleston Courier,* March 11, 1829; and Alexander Moore with George C. Rogers Jr. and Stephen G. Hoffius, *The Fabric of Liberty: The Society of the Cincinnati of the State of South Carolina* (Columbia, SC: Home House Press, 2012).

ALS in Langdon Cheves Papers, SCHS.

Martha Proctor Richardson[1] to Dr. James Screven, Saturday, July 6, 1822

Savannah

. . . The people of Charleston have been for some time past in aweful commotion, they had received information that an insurrection was in contemplation, the 16th July the day fixed on for its commencement—the city was to have been set fire to in forty different places—the whites murdered as they left their dwellings—the arsenal to be seized on—the negroes from the country were then to join them—and the shipping in the harbour was to be also taken possession of—This information it is said was given by the coachman of Dr. Simons[2]—The city Council were called together and sat in judgment on those suspected—Six were condemned and executed on 2^{d} July—it is said that the leaders in this conspiracy were class leaders of religious societies—you recollect that in Carolina the blacks are not allowed to preach in congregations of their own—they *must* associate with the white people in the different churches—God knows how all this will end—but I fear such an attempt will one day be made—and of what consequence will it be to those who are killed by them whether they succeed or not—Mr. Harris[3] has just called he brought a letter from Major Hamilton the Intendant of Charleston I will copy the part relating to this unfortunate business as it will enable you to understand it better than I related it—"You may feel some solicitude to learn something of the late threaten'd insurrection in this City—a few of the prominent particulars of which I will relate to you—This plot had its origin among the Black Class leaders of some of the different religious associations of this city—and altho' its causes may be in some degree referable to the temporal inconveniences & suffering unavoidable incident to a state of slavery there are mainly to be attributed to religious Fanaticism—The Ring Leaders of the conspiracy were all of them Class Leaders or Deacons—Six of whom were yesterday executed, and who met their fate with the heroic fortitude of Martyrs—They have been for some time engaged in their preparations for the explosion, which was to have been consummated on the night of 16th. Their plan denoted a fine Military *Tact* and admirable combination. Their forces were to have been divided into Three columns—The first and most important was to carry the main Guard House & Arsenal—This was to have been concentrated at South Bay & to have been composed of the Male Negroes from James Island, led by a determined fellow, full of carnage & sagacity—This body were to have been supplied with arms sufficient to effect their purpose and were to have formed in the centre of the city a junction with the two other divisions from the West & North—on which the Town was to have been fired in Forty different places and the householders murdered at their doors on coming out. This conflagration was to be a signal to the Negroes, from the country to flock in & join their associates in arms in the city.—The discovery of their designs was made by the fidelity of a favorite Slave to his Master—We have been thus far very successful in our developments & have proceeded with great activity & perseverance. I am happy amidst all this excitement to say to you that no excesses of popular feelings & prejudices have disgraced the character of our city—& that a remarkably respectable court has conducted its deliberations with humanity to the accused but with great energy as it regards the public safety—I am sorry to say that our friend judge Johnson has involved himself in an unpleasant controversy with the public authorities & court, by volunteering a very unreasonable & unnecessary admonition by which a great ferment has been excited against him["]—In this place every suspicion appears at rest—and I trust there is no cause for alarm—but I am of opinion that the Blacks knew of this business long before it was known by us. . . .

1. The widow Martha Proctor Richardson was residing in the home of Major John Screven (1777–1830) when she wrote this and other letters to her nephew, Dr. James Proctor Screven (1799–1859), who was in Liverpool at the time. He later became a prominent Savannah rice planter. See the finding aid for the Arnold and Screven Family Papers, 1762–1903, Southern Historical Collection, Louis Round Wilson Special Collections Library, UNC.

2. Richardson probably refers here to Thomas Young Simons (1797–1859), one of Charleston's most esteemed physicians and the brother of the lawyer Edward Peter Simons (1794–1823), who knew Sandy Vesey and testified on his behalf during the proceedings. See "Death of Dr. Thomas Young Simons," *Charleston Courier*, June 9, 1857.

3. "Mr. Harris" refers to Charles Harris (d. 1827), a lawyer and friend of the Screven family, who served three terms as mayor of Savannah and at the time of his death sat with James Proctor Screven as a city alderman. See William Harden, *A History of Savannah and South Georgia*, 2 vols. (Chicago: Lewis Publishing, 1913), vol. 1: 400. Michael P. Johnson, "Reading Evidence," *WMQ* 59 (2002): 196, downplays Richardson's commentary on the Vesey plot as essentially hearsay, but as this letter points out, she had access to sources close to the scene, and, indeed, in this case was in fact quoting to Screven the very words of James Hamilton Jr. himself, who had written to her friend Charles Harris, the former mayor of Savannah, about the plot. See also Robert L. Paquette, "From Rebellion to Revisionism: The Continuing Debate about the Denmark Vesey Affair," *Journal of the Historical Society* 4 (Fall 2004): 314–17.

ALS in Arnold-Screven Papers, SHC, UNC.

New York *National Advocate*

Monday, July 8, 1822

Blacks.—According to the mode pointed out by the legislature of South Carolina, a court of magistrates and freeholders has tried the blacks engaged in the late conspiracy at Charleston. Several were acquitted, and the following were found guilty, and sentenced to be executed on the 2d of July, between 6 and 8 in the morning. . . .

This is a rigid but necessary punishment. The safety of families, from plots thus formed, requires the strong arm of authority. Misguided persons, thus plotting the work of murder and conflagration, may give a fatal blow to a portion of our country. Whatever we may think of slavery, it is not to be denied that the domestics in the south work less and live better than many poor free white men of the north. They are a lazy pampered race, and if they meditate murder when thus indulged they must suffer for it.[1]

1. This information was reprinted nearly verbatim in the *Charleston Mercury*, July 18, 1822, and the Washington *Daily National Intelligencer*, July 20, 1822.

Orders Regarding the Conduct of Troops

Monday, July 8, 1822

HEADQUARTERS, *Charleston, July* 8th, 1822.

THE period of alarm having passed, and the extra Guard being therefore about to be discontinued, the Commander in Chief deems it adviseable to adopt permanent regulations for the conduct of the Troops on all future occasions. The policy and propriety of the measure has been suggested by recent occurrences, the safety and repose of the City of Charleston require it. He, therefore, orders and enjoins that the following Regulations be strictly observed, and carried fully into effect:

In case of Fire, and until the cause of such Fire be ascertained, the *Bells only* will be rung; the beating of the Drum as heretofore, will be discontinued. In this case the Detachment detailed for Guard duty in cases of fire, will instantly repair to their place of Rendezvous, properly armed and accoutered.

In case of Insurrection, and in all cases of resistance to Law, combined with military preparation of any kind, the Drums will beat the Long Roll, or To Arms, and a Field Piece will be fired three times in succession, at or near the City Guard-House. On this signal, every Citizen, as well alarm as effective men, will instantly repair to the place of rendezvous. . . .

General Orders, July 8, 1822, RGA, GM, 1328. See also Permanent Order, Regiment of Artillery, Charleston, July 18, 1822, William Yeadon (1777–1849) MP, SCL; Permanent Regimental orders.—17th Regiment, 1822, 43–266, SCHS.

Norwich (CT) *Courier*

Wednesday, July 10, 1822

Extract of a letter from a gentlemen in Charleston to his correspondent in this city, dated June 22nd, 1822

A few days after you left here, there was an insurrection of the negroes discovered, and the whole town has been in military operation ever since. About 500 troops are kept under arms day and night, and every negro is obliged to be in at eight instead of ten o'clock. There are about 40 conspirators discovered, and are undergoing their trial. Last night a free negro was taken,[1] who is said to be their Major General—he is a very smart, active fellow.—The apprehension of an attack has caused much alarm, and pistols, guns, &. have been in great demand.

1. The writer speaks of the arrest of Denmark Vesey by Captain William Dove.

John Potter to Langdon Cheves, Wednesday, July 10, 1822

(Confidential) . . .

Since I last wrote you, about this most diabolical plot which the mercy of God, prevented on the very eve & very day of destruction—the public mind, has been very much agitated—the first Court resumed its labors—and every step they advanced, it was found that the Conspiracy had spread wider and wider—Confessions were made more freely, and a vast number of slaves were taken up; on yesterday 5 more wretches were Condemned to death, to be hung on friday next—1 belonged to Gill,[1] who kept the stables, 1 to Paul Pritchard (who was the "wizzard"),[2] one to John Drayton his cook[3] who had hitherto behaved well—1 to David Haig,[4] & a favourite servant of Elias Horry's—I believe his coachman!![5]

Indeed it is now well ascertained, that most of the coachmen & favourite servants in the City, knew of it, even if they had not participated, in the intentions & plans proposed—

Mrs. Bryans coachman[6]—as well as Mrs. Fergusons[7]—knew all—but when it came to the murder of their masters (young Bryan and Ferguson) the mind revolted, they say—but as Rolla[8] who is hung, told his master the governor—tho' he would not have done the deed—another had undertaken the Office—it seems—or as reports give it—that Peter Smiths house St[9] Was—a large house newly built opposite Judge Johnson's, R. Cunningham's & several others most conspicuous, at the opposite corner—were to be fired on the night of the 16th Ult. when as the White Males were to appear—even before they Could leave their own doors, the indiscriminate massacre was to take place—the females were to be reserved *for worse than death.* It is believed that Vesey's plans when this had been completed, to have forced the Banks and Carried off as much plunder as he Could to St. Domingo—and leave his blind agents behind (as all could not go) and perish for their crimes—*When your kind,* and *tender hearted Philadelphians,* as *well as Quakers*—preach up emancipation—let them *ponder,* on the deeds of darkness, & misery that would have taken place—had this plot have even in part Succeeded—but such evils are disregarded, if their favourite plan of *philanthropy* had been successful—God in his mercy reward them for it!!! this is the spot from whence our evils spring!! we will throw back on them, all these black free incendiaries—where the wretches who are implicated in Consenting to the deed, will go, I cannot yet say, but here they Cannot remain—a high & steady hand will go forth, where the laws cannot reach—*Your Branch*[10] *here* would no doubt have had the *first preference of plunder*—this is a risk you had not I suppose Contemplated!! Our best respects to all your family & friends—always yrs.

J: *Potter*

1. Monday Gell.
2. Gullah Jack Pritchard.
3. Charles Drayton.
4. Harry Haig.
5. John Horry.
6. Probably Pompey Bryan, who was discharged after giving testimony.
7. Probably Adam Ferguson, who, like Pompey, was discharged after his arrest.
8. Rolla Bennett.
9. Since the reports coming out of the proceedings initially identified Caesar Smith's owner as "Mrs. Smith," Potter may have thought Caesar Smith, the only executed slave with an owner named Smith, belonged to the widow of Peter Smith (1754–1821), a prominent Charlestonian and planter in St. James Goose Creek. Miss Naomi Smith owned Caesar. See her petition for remuneration, November 1822, no. 128, series S165015, SCDAH.
10. In 1822 Cheves served as president of the Charleston branch of the Second Bank of the United States.

ALS in Langdon Cheves Papers, SCHS.

Description of Letter by Reverend Charles Blair Snowden,[1] July 1822

. . . You will pardon an extract from another letter from Charles Snowden to his brother in July, 1822, the preceding year, upon the receipt of the news of the Denmark-Vesey insurrection. He writes in philosophic and pessimistic vein, and doubtless gives the views of some intelligent planters of his class, and he ventures an explanation why slave insurrections are more unlikely in the country than in the cities, which is interesting to students of the slavery régime. "We are henceforth," he writes, "to expect a great deal of such business. The progress of the light of knowledge is such, and the adaptation of man for liberty so constitutional that it will be impossible to keep the negroes utterly in the dark, and utterly tame under the necessary oppression which now weighs them down. It will be long, long indeed, before a completely successful effort will or can be made by them to throw off the yoke of bondage; but efforts and bloody ones, I am afraid, will be continually made until success at last shall crown them. Reflection, the fruit of leisure, will have place with many black people in the city where hard labour for all cannot be found, and reflection will give rise to action, and action once begun will generate action. In the country we are in less danger. Our negroes know that labor is essential to subsistence, and that they have nothing to expect at last but a change of masters, and that for the worse. Hence they will never be generally brought into the scrape until it happens from necessity. On a late search for arms there was nothing found indicating anything like a state of hostile preparation."

1. Charles Blair Snowden (1785–1825) graduated from Yale and trained in law before becoming an Episcopal minister in 1811. Yates Snowden, "The Planters of St. John's," *Transactions of the Huguenot Society of South Carolina* 21 (1915): 25–26.

Charleston Mercury, and Morning Advertiser

Wednesday, July 10, 1822

The Court of Magistrates and Freeholders, convened for the trial of sundry persons of color, charged with an attempt to raise an insurrection in this State, after acquitting several, unanimously found the following GUILTY, and passed upon them the sentence of Death, to be carried into execution on Friday next, the 12th inst. between 6 and 8 o'clock in the morning:

GULLAH JACK, the slave of Paul Pritchard, Esq.
MONDAY, the slave of John Gell, Esq.
CHARLES, the slave of the Honorable John Drayton.
HARRY, the slave of David Haig, Esq.
JOHN, the slave of Elias Horry, Esq.[1]

1. This information was reprinted nearly verbatim in the *Charleston Courier,* July 10, 1822; Savannah *Republican,* July 13, 1822; *New-York Evening Post,* July 15, 1822; Philadelphia *Democratic Press,* July 16, 1822; Philadelphia *National Gazette and Literary Register,* July 16, 1822; Washington *Daily National Intelligencer,* July 16, 1822; *Washington Gazette,* July 16, 1822; *Baltimore Patriot & Mercantile Advertiser,* July 17, 1822; Charleston *United States Catholic Miscellany,* July 17, 1822;

Independent Chronicle and Boston Patriot, July 19, 1822; Boston *Columbian Centinel,* July 20, 1822; Newport *Mercury,* July 20, 1822; *New-Hampshire Sentinel,* July 27, 1822; Providence *Gazette,* July 27, 1822; and *Courier de la Louisiana,* August 7, 1822.

Southern Patriot and Commercial Daily Advertiser

Thursday, July 11, 1822

CORONER'S REPORT.

A Jury of Inquest was impanelled on Monday last [July 8], upon the body of a Negro Woman named BECK, lying in Beadon's Alley; belonging to LIONEL H KENNEDY, Esq who expired in a Fit, the Jury brought in their verdict, that she came to her death by the visitation of God.[1]

J. H. STEVENS,
Coroner for Charleston District

July 10

1. Although this report may have ginned up rumors in both Charleston's white and black communities, the dead woman was most likely not Beck Vesey, Denmark's first wife, who appears to have belonged to James Evans after his purchase of her in 1808. The deceased Beck in this report belonged to Lionel H. Kennedy (1787?–1847), one of the magistrates who tried Vesey and coauthored the *Official Report.*

Boston *Commercial Gazette*

Thursday, July 11, 1822

Charleston papers to the 1st inst. were brought to N. York by the ship President. They contain the first intimation that has been given in the Southern papers, of an attempt among the slaves to excite an insurrection in S. Carolina. Six slaves and one free colored person were sentenced to be executed at Charleston on the 2d inst.[1]

CHARLESTON, JULY 1.—At a moment of no inconsiderable excitement, the citizens of Charleston learn, with great regret, that the members of the court now assembled for the trial of persons suspected of an attempt to excite an insurrection in this State, propose to retire.

1. Five slaves, not six, were hanged on Tuesday, July 2, together with Vesey, the free black alluded to here.

Charleston Courier

Friday, July 12, 1822

AT the request of the Court of Magistrates and Freeholders, his Excellency the Governor, has respited, until Friday the 19th instant, the following Slaves:—*Monday,* belonging to John Gell; *Charles,* belonging to Judge [John] Drayton; and *Harry,* belonging to David Haig:—three of the five persons who were sentenced to be executed this morning.[1]

1. This information was reprinted verbatim in the *Charleston Mercury,* July 12, 1822; *Southern Patriot, and Commercial Advertiser,* July 11, 1822; Richmond *Enquirer,* July 19, 1822; Philadelphia *United States Gazette and True American,* July 20, 1822; and *New-York Evening Post,* July 20, 1822.

Charleston *Southern Patriot, and Commercial Advertiser*

Friday, July 12, 1822

COMMUNICATION.

Mr. EDITOR:—Permit me to express to the gentlemen composing the Court, who are now sitting on a very painful and distressing business, the thanks of I believe the whole community, for their unwearied labors and calm and discriminating investigation of the subject before them.

The combination of talents, respectability and integrity, which are found in those gentlemen, reconciles every man to the awful examples which are making.

To his Honor the Intendant, are justly due the undivided thanks and approbation of his Fellow Citizens, for his able, faithful and zealous discharge of his high and responsible duties.

A Citizen of Charleston.

Newburyport Herald

Friday, July 12, 1822

Slaves in Carolina. Under the mail-head it will be perceived that six blacks have been condemned to death in Charleston for attempting to organize an insurrection among the slaves and free blacks. What may have been the extent of this attempt we know not, as the southern papers have been sedulously silent on the subject; but it was obviously sufficient to excite some alarm at least, if it was not in reality very dangerous, since it is known that it occasioned a considerable military force to be kept under arms some time by the citizens.—The execution of the principal offenders will probably intimidate the rest, and restore tranquillity.

This incident is of a kind which may naturally lead us to reflect on the probable destiny of slave-holding countries—Will slaves exist in them forever, or will the time come when slavery shall be completely abolished? And, if the latter, will slavery cease from a gradual melioration of the habits and feelings of the people, and through the medium of emancipation; or will it not be broken up by some violent national shock in the form of a rebellion of the slaves, or of something else equally terrible? How the situation of Hayti was changed, our own age has seen; her ancient lords expelled from their homes, impoverished, persecuted by the vengeful hand of the slaves whom they themselves had taught to be cruel, and persecuted to the death; her soil fattened by the blood of combatants, which flowed like water for thirty years of civil discord, warfare and revolution; and her present inhabitants slowly recovering from the barbarism in which they were buried for ages, and yet more slowly purifying themselves of the plague-spots which had been eating into their very souls during so long a period of demoralizing and abasing servitude.—Are those numerous and extensive countries, the fairest, the richest, the noblest on earth,—are all those countries which now swarm with negro-slaves to go thro' the same fiery trial with Hayti? The prospect of it is fearful. Yet it seems impossible to prevent or escape from such a consummation.

Mankind are not prone to neglect their present interests for the sake of their future; still less is a generation of men disposed to make great and painful sacrifices for the benefit of their remote or even their near posterity. A nation which contains few negroes may often be honored with acts of generosity in the liberation of one or two or even a whole family of slaves; those acts are then easy, because conformable to the public opinion, and because in no wise injurious to the national grandeur or tranquillity. But where the blacks have already come to exceed the whites, the case is different. There it is most fashionable to be served by slaves, and their emancipation becomes less creditable.—There also it is dangerous to release the blacks from the control of bondage, since freedom enables and prompts them to foment disaffection among the slaves and thereby expose the country to rebellions. Free blacks, in a land where many of their color are held in servitude, are generally given up to vice and lawlessness, because, being treated with contempt and esteemed outcasts, they have neither opportunity nor inducement to become good citizens of a commonwealth.

Much reliance has of late been placed on plans of colonization, either general and immediate, or distant and gradual. The first are opposed by considerations of invincible strength.—Who believes that a whole people will consent to reduce itself to pauperism individually and nationally from motives of benevolence? Where the soil is tilled by slaves, they constitute the riches of the country; universal impoverishment would be the certain consequence of their emancipation. To require or expect a state to descend at once from the height of public prosperity to the lowest depths of littleness is absurd—Projects of gradual emancipation are more plausible, but, we fear, not more sound:—however great might be the blessing to the human race and cause of joy among philanthropists, if such an event as the final abolition of slavery could take place by bloodless means, we confess we do not believe it possible. It is useless to think of gradually liberating slave after slave and thus becoming eventually freed of them all; for in the place of every slave which you emancipate another will spring up from those which remain; so that slavery perpetuates itself; and you must crush him at a single blow; if you desire to kill the many-headed monster. Political economists have demonstrated that colonies, so far from in fact diminishing the population of the country which sends them forth, increase that population; and the same effect would probably follow the gradual colonization of the blacks in slave-holding countries.

Finally, so long as the whites can hold slaves for the cultivation of the soil in warm climates, they will not easily be persuaded to part with them, and thus entirely change their own moral and physical condition. And the case is much worse in America, where slaves are of a different race from their masters, than it was in ancient Greece and Rome, or is now in modern Asia, where, although slaves have been no less abundant than in America, yet they have generally been whites, who were capable of gradually mixing and becoming incorporated with the free population, without debasing its complexion and character. But with us, on the contrary, slaves being of a distinct race & color, a strong line of demarcation, an impassable barrier, seems to be set up between the bond and the free. In Rome, the emancipated slave could silently pass into the condition of liberty, without retaining that indelible mark of former degradation, which is stamped upon the features of the unhappy African. The situation of slave-holding countries on our continent is therefore much more precarious, from this cause, than it is in other warm climates, where the luxury of men prompts them to exact the involuntary service of their fellows.

For these considerations, we cannot but anticipate with anxiety the hour, however distant it may be, when unforeseen accidents should impart an impulse to the blacks among us, as well as in other parts of the new world, and raise them up in arms to vindicate their freedom. If a state, in which the blacks are more numerous than the whites, should be consigned to havoc by victorious enemies; if invaders of it should proclaim liberty and revenge among its slaves, and furnish them with the means of attacking their masters; if chance, or war, or sudden rage, or any cause whatever, should communicate a simultaneous movement to the blacks of that state;—in either case we see nothing to prevent a repetition of the horrors of Saint-Domingo.

Charleston Courier

Saturday, July 13, 1822

Gullah Jack, the property of Mr. PAUL PRITCHARD, and *John,* the property of Mr. ELIAS HORRY, were executed yesterday morning, pursuant to their sentence, between the hours of six and eight o'clock.[1]

1. This information was reprinted nearly verbatim in the *Charleston Mercury,* July 13, 1822; *Southern Patriot, and Commercial Advertiser,* July 12, 1822; Boston *Commercial Gazette,* July 25, 1822; Salem *Gazette,* July 26, 1822; and Newport *Mercury,* July 27, 1822.

Jacob Rapelye[1] to Paul Rapelye, Monday July 15, 1822

. . . The late alarm of the Negro insurrection which threatened distruction to the whole of the white population of this City & the adjoining county, & which has only lately been discovered, has sickened many persons, & disposed those to remove to the North, that can conveniently. they have now sixty negroes in confinement, have condemned 10 to death & hang but will in all probability execute 20 or 30 more. the public mind is greatly excited, and very justly to[o], for by a mere accident this plot was discovered & only one day before it was to be put into execution. they had plenty of Guns, powder & the Dray-man was to act as cavalry. Gov. Bennett has had 3 Negroes hung. it was discovered by a negro confessing to his master. Business very dull, nothing talk of but the negro plot. . . .

1. Jacob Rapelye (1788–1867) moved to Charleston after the War of 1812 and opened a dry-goods business. The 1822 city directory identifies him as an auctioneer with a residence at 38 Broad Street. See Peter Ross, *A History of Long Island, from Its Earliest Settlement to the Present Time,* 3 vols. (New York: Lewis Publishing, 1902), vol. 3: 20; *CSCCD,* 95.

ALS in Paul Rapelye Papers, Perkins Library, DUL.

Mary Lamboll Beach to Elizabeth Gilchrist, Monday July 15, 1822

. . . I am sure our dear Minister[1] has his words twisted & his actions too dear man in the present day. Yesterday he preached two most excellent sermons well worthy of appearing in print from these words in Mark "It must needs be that Offences come but Woe to the world because of Offences."[2] He endeavoured to prove from various places in the old Testament & in later days how God had overruled the actions of men even while they were under a free agency in the business to bring about his intentions both of Judgment & mercy & particularly in the Redemption of the world. & cited some cases where even good men had done wrong & *very* wickedly were. After mentioning cases of the falls of good men & yet their being true children of God & cited the afflictions that God in His righteous Providence followed them up with he made some remarks to show that because there were Hypocrites in the church that yet all religion was not to be rejected no more than all money would be because of counterfeit bills, but he said in the affairs of this life men preferred often their money to their souls & instead of rejecting having any thing to do with that they would be at the pains to examine for the marks that distinguish the one from the other but in religion they would reject the whole often. He said if our Lord had *not* warned them that Offences *would* come then they might expect to see no such cases where religion still existed in a church. I suppose these remarks may have had some allusion on the case of the poor blacks who I fear are in the Community at large All branded as hypocrites for the wicked conduct of some—& some of these guilty ones were perhaps misled by more artful ones—for that wretched Vesey it is said applied his arts to all classes of his tools. I suppose long before this reaches you you will have seen that 5 more were to have been executed on the 12th & that 3 were respited. One that was executed named Gullah Jack was an African a most superstitious creature & apparently one whose figure & whole deportment was of no importance—he gave some of those concerned an idea that he possessed the power of repelling any danger by mixtures he prepared & said that in his own country it had been proved that common bullets could not kill him. It is said that so much ascendancy had Vesey over his superstitious mind that he was filled with dread at the thought of meeting Vesey's spirit at the Gallows. Poor wretched creature he with several others was confined in different cells in the Poor House for want of places in the Jail as I understand they have none in the Work House—Doc^{r} P. G. Prioleau[3] (I don't know what was his errand at the Poor House but he saw this Jack there a day or two before the execution & the creature knowing him said; "Do Massa Doc^{r} beg for me & wept bitterly. Oh! my heart is often I was going to say torn with distress about these people it does appear for the general good they ought to die for there is little or any doubt of their guilt but when we look back on their past sufferings what are we to say the other man executed belonged to Elias Horry[4]—a remarkable pleasant obliging servant previously but of a very enterprising spirit—his Master before he was arrested said to Mrs H^{y} that he hoped he was not concerned in this business for if he was from his enterprising temper he would he thought be deeply so & it has appeared so. Where or when the arrests will stop it is difficult or I should have said impossible to conjecture for on the 13th inst 14 or 15 fresh ones are arrested. I understand there was a meeting of a number of the Citizens either on that or the day before to consult on measures directed to the present state of things. Arthur Haynes[5] told Mary on Sat^{y} when she was at Susan's that there had been a meeting also last week of Military men & they had made such arrangements for present safety that there was no reason for alarm now. Some persons I hear speak of the intention or advisability of making this a Garrison Town in future but all these precautions are yet only in contemplation. Oh! that our God would grant us a spirit of humiliation under this rod & to our rulers Wisdom, forbearance, justice & mercy as well as firmness in their decisions. Through mercy the country in general I believe remains very quiet. There have been some two or three persons it was said a few days ago rather a spirit of dissatisfaction shown but I hear nothing of it more—I was greatly distressed however at hearing it was in more cases but this was *utterly false.* Poor old Mr Jones has had some difficulty at his place which perhaps gave rise to the report. A very young fellow a mere lad joined with 2 or three more of Mrs. Martin's negroes[6] & with fire arms attacked the Stage; but Providentially although they fired twice as there were no passengers in it no hurt was done of course; & at the 2 firing the ball or buck shot passed by the stage drivers hat, only; the last accounts we heard were that Mr. J. lad was in Jacksonborough Jail—but the Negroes in that neighborhood from various accounts so far from having a *daring* spirit were apparently *afraid* to go off their own plantations—& this solely appears to have been only a robbery which business they have been carrying on for some time it seems at the old gentlemans place. . . . Mary & children join love to you both—The Lord Bless you my very dear Sister

M. L. Beach

1. Benjamin Morgan Palmer.

2. The verse comes not from the book of Mark but the book of Matthew 18:7: "Woe unto the world because of offences! for it must be that offences come; but woe to that man by whom the offence cometh."

3. Philip Gendron Prioleau (1776–1844) was an esteemed Charleston physician who in 1822 resided at 220 Meeting Street. See *CSCCD,* 95 and Charleston *Southern Patriot,* June 19, 1844.

4. Elias Horry (1773–1834), the owner of slave coachman John Horry, was one of the wealthiest slaveholders in lowcountry South Carolina, owning hundreds of slaves and several plantations north of Charleston on and near the Santee River. He served three terms as the city's mayor and resided in 1822 on the corner of Meeting and Tradd streets across from the First (Scots) Presbyterian Church. Of Huguenot descent and trained in law by Charles Cotesworth Pinckney (1746–1825), Horry became one of Charleston's leading citizens and one of "the most zealous members and advocates" of the South Carolina Association. See Jasper Adams, *An Eulogium, Pronounced 23d January, 1835, in the Chapel of the College of Charleston, before the Trustees, Faculty and Students; on the Life and Character of the late Elias Horry, Esq.* (Charleston, SC, 1835); Charleston *Southern Patriot,* October 17, 1834; *BDSCHR* 4: 286–88; *CSCCD,* 83. On the trial of John Horry, see the *OR* material reprinted in Part III; the Senate document also in Part III; and the letter of Martha Proctor Richardson to James Screven, August 7, 1822, on p. 438 in this section. Despite these three references, Michael P. Johnson, "Reading Evidence," *WMQ* 59 (2002): 196, argues that there is no proof that Horry ever appeared "before the court."

5. Arthur Peronneau Hayne (1788–1867), the brother of Robert Young Hayne (1791–1839), served with distinction in the US military during the War of 1812. See *A Brief Sketch of the Life and Military Services of Arthur P. Hayne* (New York, 1852).

6. Ann Martin, wife of Jacob Martin of the Colleton District in which Jacksonborough was the county seat, owned slaves convicted of firing on a mail carrier. Two of her slaves, Nashaw and Jim, were executed for the crime. See Charleston *Carolina Gazette,* July 20, 1822.

ALS in Mary Lamboll Beach Papers, SCHS.

John Potter to Langdon Cheves, Monday, July 15, 1822

. . . Since I last wrote you, there has been [*illegible*] of those intended conspirators—three of the five convicts, who were to have suffered on Friday last—were respited a week, and who have since made ample confession—which has implicated many who were before above suspicion—indeed the most confidential servants were first applied to, and many either assisted or else engaged in the plot, who hitherto had irreproachable characters. The Court is [*illegible*] in session and doing its painful but no less necessary duty—on friday. 3 of the Rope Walk negroes; now belonging to Robertson[1] and for many years held as our joint property (about 5 years ago he bought my half) were taken up—and I fear an evidence that will convict them or at least some of [*illegible*], your farms would have been a capital plan of Mutiny, it seems they met at Bulkley's farm on the Meeting Street Road near the fork—and always chose their conferences of *blood* (and I believed poison,) by *prayer* and *psalm singing*!!!

Had it not been for the discovery by Maj. Wilson's servant,[2] and that only three days previous to the intended execution of the plot—we might have been involved in a dreadful time of carnage, particularly if their *well laid plans,* had been brought to bear and put in execution within dead of night on our unprepared, unprovided, sleeping people.

We have been in such a state of apathy & security that few people could believe such an intention could have ever been thought of—I hope it will lead to measures, that such attempts may not be dreaded in future. . . .

1. Potter, writing from Charleston, refers to John Robertson (1762–1831), a merchant who served for years as US naval agent in Charleston. Robertson owned three slaves—Adam, John, and Robert—who were executed for involvement in the Vesey affair. In 1822 Robertson resided at 31 Meeting Street. See *CSCCD,* 96, and Washington *Daily National Intelligencer,* August 31, 1831.

2. George Wilson, class leader in the Circular Church and a literate blacksmith who hired his time, was purchased and liberated by the state on Christmas Day, 1825, for his services. He changed his name to George Watkins, but by 1848 he evidently could no longer live with his actions; he lost his reason and died shortly thereafter, reputedly by committing suicide. See Larry Koger, *Black Slaveowners: Free Black Slave Masters in South Carolina, 1790–1860* (Jefferson, NC: McFarland, 1985), 60, 176; see also undated letter from W. Hasell Wilson to Robert Wilson reproduced on pp. 94–95 in Part II.

ALS in Langdon Cheves Papers, SCHS.

John Potter to Langdon Cheves, Tuesday, July 16, 1822

Charleston

. . . I have sold no further of your stocks. . . . the sensation on peoples minds, seem to occupy their whole attention, as for *negroes*—I do not believe they would bring any price—at present—

I have not heard of the proceedings of the Court yesterday, but they are proceeding, with a firm step, and I apprehend many more will forfeit their lives, new incidents are appearing every day—some pike handles were found at Buckly's farm, and the pike maker is safely housed—but the pikes are not found yet, I believe, as well as powder & arms, that are known, to have been within possession—the Charleston Neck Company had always left their arms and accoutrements at Wharton's[1] on the King St. land and placed in the back store, his negro—or else one he hired, had got the key and agreed to deliver them, at the moment agreed on—Mr. Chanet[2] had a quantity of new Guns, for sale—who lives near the inspection, which were to have been seized also. You cannot think how cunningly devised, the scheme was—and had the execution been as well supported, many of us this day would not have been left, to tell the tale, if it had not been providentially discovered in time—The french Negroes it seems had joined them—a french Negro—a matrass maker ([*illegible*] the very last that could have been suspected) was apprehended on friday or saturday evening[3]—apparently a quiet & most innofensive creature—above all, a fellow[4] of Mrs. Colcock, [*illegible*] pattern of good behavior, has been apprehended—& many such are now coming forward!!! Our best regards to all your family I am always—

Yr obt friend, J. Potter

My Dear Sir—

P:S: Since writing the above I was told by the Intendant Mr. Hamilton that 3 butcher negroes[5] have been apprehended—and many more of that class *suspected*—Dr. Haig's *Harry* who is under condemnation & respited a week to give information—says that *Gulla Jack* who was hanged last friday, wished him to *poison his master's well*—which was it is supposed, to have been general!! Good God, what have we come to. Mr. Hamilton says 50 or 60 more will have to be tried for their lives.

1. Samuel Wharton (1783–1827) ran a store on the corner of King and Mary streets, Charleston Neck. See *CSCCD*, 103.

2. Anthony (Antoine) Chanet (1764?–1839), a French merchant, operated a business on Chisolm's Wharf and in 1822 resided at 19 Tradd Street. See *CSCCD*, 74, and "Obituary," *Charleston Courier*, July 30, 1839.

3. According to Hamilton, *Account*, 47, no slaves were arrested on Friday, July 12, but Pharo (or Pharaoh) Thompson and Dick Simms were both arrested on Saturday, July 13. No other slave was then arrested until July 18.

4. Potter refers here to William Colcock, a slave painter owned by the widow Millicent Colcock (1745–1829), who was acquitted by the court.

5. Of the slaves inculpated in the proceedings, George Bampfield is one who can clearly be identified as a butcher. His death sentence was commuted to transportation outside the state.

ALS in Langdon Cheves Papers, SCHS.

Albany Argus

Tuesday, July 16, 1822

This morning, between the hours of 6 and 8 Denmark Vessey, Rolla, Batteau, Ned, Peter and Jessey, convicted of an attempt to raise an insurrection in this state, will be hanged according to the sentence of the Court of Magistrates and Freeholders. *Fiat Justitia.*[1]

Charleston Gazette, 2d inst.

(A passenger in the sloop Eliza, (who brought the paper containing the above extract) informs that he saw the above mentioned slaves[2] executed previous to his departure. He also states, that there were upwards of 50 others in jail implicated in the same crime, and one *white* man, against whom there were charges of a most serious nature. The particulars communicated by the above informant are deeply interesting—but we deem it imprudent to publish them at present.]—*Ib.*[3]

1. Let justice be done.
2. Denmark Vesey and the five slaves were executed on Tuesday, July 2, 1822.
3. *Ib.* refers to *Norfolk and Portsmouth Herald*, from which the story was obtained.

Charleston Courier

Wednesday, July 17, 1822

A Court of Magistrates and Freeholders having assembled at the Court-House in Jacksonborough, for the trial of four Negro Slaves, charged with having fired at the Mail Driver on the Parker's Ferry Road, after acquitting one, unanimously found the following three guilty, and passed upon them the Sentence of Death, to be carried into execution on Friday next, the 19th inst. between the hours of 10 and 12.—NASHAW, and JIM, the property of Mr. Jacob Martin; and JUPITER, the property of Thomas Jones, Esquire.[1]

1. This information was reprinted nearly verbatim in the Charleston *Southern Patriot, and Commercial Advertiser*, July 16, 1822; *Charleston Mercury*, July 17, 1822; Savannah *Republican*, July 18, 1822; Washington *Daily National Intelligencer*, July 23, 1822; Baltimore *American and Commercial Daily Advertiser*, July 23, 1800; Philadelphia *Democratic Press*, July 24, 1822; Philadelphia *United States Gazette and True American*, July 25, 1822; New York *National Gazette*, July 25, 1822; and Newport *Mercury*, July 27, 1822.

Charleston Courier

Wednesday, July 17, 1822

[COMMUNICATION.]

Mr. Editor.—The public usefulness of a citizen should at no time be overlooked, since if attended with inconvenience and trouble, a grateful acknowledgement for services rendered, is the least reward that can be conferred. Feeling the full force of this conviction, I take pleasure in hearing testimony to Captain MARTINDALE'S[1] unremitting exertions, towards establishing good order among the slaves on Charleston Neck, the importance of which was previously confessed, but more appreciated since a late occurrence. On my removal to said place, the number of blacks frequently assembled, to drink and gamble, was a perfect nuisance to myself and neighbors. So annoyed have I been at night by them, as to be compelled to threaten their dispersion by force of arms. A removal of the evil was perceived and felt immediately after the command of the Rangers was given to that officer. A due organization of this valuable body into nightly patrols, embracing an extensive circuit, has proven so efficient a check, that it is rare to find a slave within their range, unprovided with the owner's written permission to enter or leave the city. The quiet, therefore, of the neighborhood is now undisturbed; and the more serious consequences no doubt prevented from the more secret meetings that otherwise might there be safely held for the worst of purposes. As I feel indebted to Capt. MARTINDALE, principally, for the peace and safety enjoyed by my family, that gentleman will excuse this public expression of my sense of his vigilance, activity, and capacity for the responsible command entrusted to him.

An Inhabitant of Charleston Neck

1. On militia captain James C. Martindale (d. 1823), see Part II, p. 98 n2.

Providence *Gazette*

Wednesday, July 17, 1822

A passenger in the ship Amelia, from Charleston, at New-York, informs, that the negro plot had been entirely quelled, and the principal ringleaders had been secured and confined in prison.

Anna Hayes Johnson to Elizabeth Haywood, July 18, 1822

Charleston

. . . I have been too selfish in my correspondence of late; but my mind has been so much agitated about late occurrences that I could think of nothing else, and not even the dangers that have beset me, have had power to make me feel but I am not always so maussade and hébété[1] as I have been lately and in future I will try to be more entertaining. . . . This time you are anxious to hear more about the unhappy business which has filled with consternation all our city and nothing but the merciful interposition of our God has saved us from horrors equal if not superior to the scenes acted in St. Domingo—the catalogue is not filled up for our thought that it was ended and that the execution of six of the chiefts would suffice. The court had been dismissed and the town was again sinking into its wanted security when information was given that another attempt would be made at such a time, and the states witness gave information of such a nature as to induce the City Council to recall the court and since that period the alarm has spread most widely, and there are now between 50 & 60 of the leaders in our jail. It is said that twenty of them have been convicted & sentenced, and in all probability the executions will not end under 100, but I was told yesterday that the prisoners had been heard to say that even should there be 500 executed there would be still enough to carry the work into execution. Denmark Vesey one of those already executed and who was the instigator of the whole plot acknowledged that he had been nine years endeavouring to effect the diabolical scheme, how far the mischief has extended heaven only knows—I never heard in my life more deep laid plots or plots more likely to succeed, indeed "twas a plot a good plot—an excellent plot"[2] But 'twas a plot that had it succeeded would have told to after ages a most fearful tale—It would be absurd in me to attempt a detail of all the circumstances real or imaginary which I have heard—this much is all that I know of that bears the stamp of truth; That their intention was to take the city and keep it as long as possible and then carry *us* & the common negroes to St D there to be sold as slaves with as much plunder as they could find it seems that this Vesey had been to St. D and made an agreement that at such a time so many Vessels should be hired to assist—It would have been a complete scene of desolation—as yet thank God none of our slaves have been found in the plot, tho there are 20 of them in there in the yard. . . .

1. French for "peevish and dazed."
2. Her reference paraphrases Shakespeare, *Henry IV, Part 1,* scene 3.

ALS in Haywood Papers, SHC, UNC.

Charleston *Southern Patriot, and Commercial Advertiser*

Friday, July 19, 1822

FOR THE SOUTHERN PATRIOT.

Quid Leges sine moribus.[1] The energy that has been displayed by all classes of our citizens during the last month, added to the public spirit of our young and active Intendant, and the unremitted, patient, and enlightened zeal of the Magistrates and Freeholders, who are charged with the dearest interests of the community to which they belong—constitute a subject of admiration and gratitude. I trust, Mr. Editor, that when they, and those who may be united with them in their present labors, (for an additional Court *must* be organized) shall have succeeded in crushing the hydra that once appeared to threaten us, we shall become further indebted to them for their assistance in a most important duty that remains to be discharged: I mean the revision of our present code of police, and the formation of new regulations for the government of our servants.

It is evident, Sir, how much depends upon the provisions of our State and City Laws upon this subject; yet both will be found insufficient, unless they are aided by the regulations of private families. While the City Council are employed in lessening the number of dram shops, and in making them more inaccessible to the victims that now frequent them, let the owners of Negroes shut out, as far as they can, all undue means of furnishing their people with money—the fuel by which the dram shop fire is fed. Locks and keys will do much, and other means will occur to the experienced: I shall content myself with now suggesting a single hint—when Negroes are permitted to work for wages, let those wages be paid by the employer to the owner, without the intervention of the slave. The additional trouble of this arrangement will be amply compensated by the advantages resulting from it to all parties: The owner will be better paid; the employer better served;

the Negro less exposed to corruption and dishonesty. Many a wretch who now skulks for months, because he has spent what he ought to have paid over, will then be ready at the call of his owner, whose reproaches will no longer await him. Arrangements for hire of these persons should provide a reasonable compensation for the master, and stipulate, at the same time, for a peculium to the servant. Money, thus honestly gained, would, probably, be more honestly spent. As it is, the Negro defrauds his master; and the corruption of the moral principle in one way, leads to its deterioration in all. By the plan here proposed, the temptations of those hell-holes (the dram-shops) would end in making the black man cheat himself, and he would discover it, or his wife would discover it for him. She would know that he *ought* to have money, by his master's permission, and would make him account for it, or ring a peal about his ears that no Jerry, black or white, can long support. Under the usual arrangement, he needs only deny the receipt of any wages, and thus silence his wife, however loud may be the voice of his conscience, which, you know Sir, is not heard externally. Upon the subject of dram-shops, I would also suggest that the powers of the City Council be, in some measure, limited by the Legislature. Let an act provide that no licenses shall issue for more than a fixed and moderate number of these negro-traps, in each ward; the population of the ward would suggest the ratio. A dram-shop, with a door in an alley, or any where but in front, (provided the dram-drinker could have access to it) should be subjected to a treble license, or be wholly shut up. Butter, sugar flour, rice, &c find one door quite enough; the purchaser and the goods neither require nor seek concealment. Far different is the case as regards the consumers of rum, gin, whiskey, and brandy; the sneaking countenance of the wretch who sells, and the heavy, bloated, hardened look and air of the wretch who buys, proclaim alike the nature of the transaction and the channel by which it is carried on.

This, Mr. Editor, is one mode, of a thousand that occur, whereby we may attack evil at its source. The moral material is now hot, and may be moulded to good shapes and ends: Let us strike before it is suffered to cool.

EXPERIENCE.

1. The quotation, from Horace's *Odes* 3.28: 35–36, means: "What good do empty laws do without morals (to support them)." The editors are grateful to John M. McMahon of Le Moyne College for this translation.

Charleston Courier

Friday, July 19, 1822

The Court of Magistrates and Freeholders, convened for the trial of sundry persons of color, charged with an attempt to raise an Insurrection in this State, have unanimously found the following GUILTY, and passed upon them the Sentence of Death, to be carried into execution on Friday Morning, the 26th inst. on the Lines, between six and nine o'clock in the morning:—

JULIUS, the Slave		of Thomas Forrest.
TOM,	do.	of Mrs. Russell.
JOE,	do.	of Mr. Jore.

MINGO,	do.	of William Harth, Jun.
SMART,	do.	of Robert Anderson.
PARIS,	do.	of Mrs. Ball.
POLYDORE,	do.	of Mrs. Faber.
ROBERT, JOHN, and ADAM,	do.	of John Robertson
LOT,	do.	of Mr. Forrester.
LEWIS,	do	of Mr. Cromwell.
JACK,	do.	of Mrs. Purcell.
SANDY,	do.	of Mr. Schnell.
JACK,	do.	of Mr. Glen.
PHARO,	do.	of Mrs. Thompson.

The Court still continues assiduously engaged in the trial of others apprehended for the above crime.

At the request of the Court of Magistrates and Freeholders, his Excellency the Governor has extended the Respite already granted, to *Monday,* the slave of Mr. GELL, *Charles,* the slave of the Honorable JOHN DRAYTON, and *Harry,* the slave of Mr. DAVID HAIG, until Friday, the 26th day of July, inst.[1]

[Patriot.

1. This information was reprinted verbatim in the *Charleston Mercury,* July 19, 1822; Charleston *Southern Patriot, and Commercial Advertiser,* July 18, 1822; Charleston *City Gazette and Commercial Daily Advertiser,* July 19, 1822; Savannah *Republican,* July 23, 1822; Charleston *United States Catholic Miscellany,* July 24, 1822; *Darien* (GA) *Gazette,* July 25, 1822; *Washington Gazette,* July 25, 1822; Richmond *Enquirer,* July 26, 1822; Philadelphia *Gazette and Literary Register,* July 26, 1822; Washington *Daily National Intelligencer,* July 26, 1822; Philadelphia *Democratic Press,* July 27, 1822; New York *National Advocate,* July 29, 1822; and Salem *Gazette,* July 30, 1822.

E. M. Starr to Zalmon Wildman, July 19, 1822[1]

. . . This City is very healthy nothing to disturb the quietness (Except the Investigation of the Slaves for an attempt of an insurrection—Seven negroes has been hung. & there is now under sentence of death Ninety and about 60 more confined for trial—owing to this alarm I have been detained about two week thinking that I should not feel very safe to leave our property—The alarm has subsided and the guard increased so that I think this is no longer to be apprehended from the slaves. . . .

1. Ezra Miles Starr (1793–1868) worked as a milliner for the Connecticut-based hat manufacturer Zalmon Wildman (1775–1835). In 1835 Wildman served in the United States House of Representatives as a Jacksonian Democrat. See Hartford (CT) *Patriot and Democrat,* December 19, 1835.

ALS in Zalmon Wildman Papers, folder 1, SCL.

John Potter to Langdon Cheves, Saturday, July 20, 1822

. . . I sent you a newspaper, detailing the sentence of the Court, of the day preceding—and from the numerous arrests daily, there is no knowing how many more will suffer. [*Illegible*] Robertson has three condemned, as you would see[1]—whilst those slaves belonged to us jointly, I never had a Complaint of them for 10 years—one had *then,* a wife in my yard, and when I left the City, I always directed him to sleep in the yard—which I thought safe, under his charge.—

Bennett did the same with Rolla, who had indeed the safety of his family entrusted to him, whilst absent at Columbia—

This Cunningly and deeply devised plot, was much more extensive than you had any idea of, when you wrote on the 11th:[2] nothing Could be better arranged—and would have done Credit, to a better Cause & other means.

all the arms on the Neck were deposited in one place—to which a negro had access, and was to deliver the keys—700 stand of muskets, would also come in their power—& there was enough powder ready at hand—and when the Guard was overpowered—and arsenal taken, the Torch was to give the signal of murder and blood—all those who were to go out on the cry of fire, which was to be multiplied, would meet their fate—the draymen, Carters, and Coachmen to act as Cavalry and scour the streets when the confidential servants in the plot indoors, were to murder every white man of an adult age—many I hope were not implicated. I have no reason to suppose, any of my house servants were guilty—but there were enough to Commence with, and but anyway successfull even for a moment all, or nearly all, would have joined!

it is said by a fellow, in his Confession, that when *Vesey* was inducing him to murder his master, he hesitated—but at length assented—then, what says he, will be done with the children? What says this *arch Villain,* kill the *Lice*—and let the *Nitts,* remain—no—no—never!!! D. Haig's Harry[3] was pressed by Gulla Jack, to poison his masters well—but he says he refused to do that deed, but assented to all the rest—had it taken place two weeks since—as the condemned wretch *Peter Poyas*—wished—the result probably would have been dreadful—we were then all unprepared—Completely so,—this is all private & confidential. . . .

1. Ropemaker John Robertson (1762–1831) owned three slaves, John, Robert, and Adam, who were among those hanged on July 26.

2. Potter sent Cheves a letter on Wednesday, July 10, not July 11.

3. David Haig (1763–1832), a cooper, owned the slave Harry.

ALS in Langdon Cheves Papers, SCHS.

Joel Roberts Poinsett[1] to James Monroe, Saturday, July 20, 1822

. . . Our community has been agitated by the discovery of an intended insurrection of the slaves. The plot had been cautiously and extensively combined and had it not been most providentially discovered almost on the eve of its execution must have been attended with dreadful consequences. . . .

1. Joel Roberts Poinsett (1779–1851) served as one of the five freeholders on the second Court of Magistrates and Freeholders. Governor Thomas Bennett Jr. regarded Poinsett as an "old friend." See J. Fred Rippy, *Joel R. Poinsett, Versatile American* (Durham, NC: Duke University Press, 1935 163.

James Monroe Papers, microfilm, series 1, reel 8, LC.

Providence *Gazette*

Saturday, July 20, 1822

Five more blacks have been tried at Charleston, by the Court of Magistrates and Freeholders, charged with an attempt to raise an insurrection in the State. They were unanimously found guilty, and sentenced to be executed on the 12th inst.—Several others had been tried and acquitted.[1]

1. This information was reprinted nearly verbatim in the Salem *Gazette,* July 19, 1822.

Newbern (NC) *Carolina Centinel*

Saturday, July 20, 1822

Eleven Negro men, one of them free, and the rest slaves, have been executed at Charleston, pursuant to a sentence of death passed on them for being engaged in an attempt to raise an insurrection of the blacks. The plot was a formidable one, and was discovered three days before the time appointed for its accomplishment.

Charleston Courier

Saturday, July 20, 1822

PROCLAMATION.

By his Excellency THOMAS BENNETT, Governor and Commander in Chief, in and over the State of South Carolina.

WHEREAS, I have received information from the Court of Magistrates and Freeholders, organized for, and at present engaged in the trial of Slaves and other Negroes, charged with an attempt to raise an insurrection in the City of Charleston, that a certain Negro man slave, named WILLIAM GARDINER,[1] who appears to have been one of the instigators of the said plot or attempt, has hitherto eluded the effort to apprehend him, and it is supposed has either absented himself from the said City, or is concealed therein.

Now therefore, that the said negro man slave WILLIAM GARDINER, charged as aforesaid, be brought to justice and subjected to the punishment which awaits his crime, I have thought proper to issue this my Proclamation, hereby offering a reward of TWO HUNDRED DOLLARS, to any person or persons who shall deliver him into the custody of any Sheriff within this State.

WILLIAM GARDINER is represented to be about thirty-five years of age, five feet 10 inches in height, stoops a little, but in other respects well made, has a slight impediment in his speech, is light colored and has whiskers. Has for some time pursued the vocation of a drayman in Charleston, where he has a brother, a free man, named Jack Lopez, and is the property of a widow of the name of GARDINER.

Given under my hand and the Seal of the State, at Charleston, this nineteenth day of July, in the year of our Lord One Thousand Eight Hundred and Twenty Two, and in the Forty Seventh of American Independence.

THOMAS BENNETT.

By the Governor.

BEAUFORT T. WATTS, *Secretary of State.*

July 20.[2]

1. Governor Bennett is referring here to slave drayman William Garner, owned by Martha R. Garner (d. 1832).

2. This information was reprinted verbatim in the Charleston *City Gazette and Commercial Daily Advertiser,* July 20, 1822, and the Charleston *Southern Patriot, and Commercial Advertiser,* July 25, 1822.

Charleston *Southern Intelligencer*

Saturday, July 20, 1822

"Who will take shelter under the providence of the Almighty, and whose heart will be hardened by the manifestations of his love.["]

As recipients of his bounty and dependants on his power, we should *always* fly to him for shelter, and bless the hand that feeds us—This should be the conduct of a Christian in the ordinary paths of life—But when the snare of the fowler is set, when the pit of destruction is dug, and we are delivered from the toils of the one and the ruin of the other—ought we not to look to the hand that saved us—To return thanks for his mercy and goodness in discovering by his providence what was shut from human foresight? In averting a storm,[1] which had been collecting for years, and which was ready to burst in ruin and dismay on our devoted heads? Individual and general ruin were contemplated in this scheme of atrocious depravity—The heart was hardened against the influence of tears, of kindness and affection—Every sentiment of gratitude, every remembrance of former indulgence, were to be razed from the memory and blotted out of the heart, and the hand of violence and destruction was to be lifted against the lisping infant, the helpless female and the generous benefactor!—Will not the voice of praise and thanksgiving be heard from every family circle! Will this deliverance be forgotten in the assemblies of the people? And will not the secret chamber witness the throbbings of heart-felt gratitude for mercy so distinguished? And will not the authorities of our city, in the name of the community they represent, recommend to all, a day, to be observed and set apart, for the special purpose of prayer and praise to Him who governs the universe, to Him who gives courage in danger, wisdom in counsel, and eloquence in debate!

The devotion of such a day is peculiarly proper on this occasion, not only that there may be, among the people, a concert of praise and gratitude for our deliverance, but that we may inquire the cause of our visitation, by judgments so awful and tremendous—However the light, the trifling and the profane may consider the subject, the serious and the reflecting, will and must view these judgments as evidences of the anger of Almighty God towards a sinful and disobedient people! It therefore becomes all who believe in the superintendence of a righteous God, and that he has given a holy law for the regulation of their conduct, to inquire whether they have individually obeyed that law and put their trust in that providence?—Both sacred and profane history inform us, that when iniquity has prevailed in a nation, that judgments soon light upon the people—That the blessings of heaven cannot be enjoyed in peace when the laws of God are set at naught—That the spirit of wisdom, of understanding, and of knowledge, can never prevail in the counsels of a nation when the rulers legislate in opposition to the authorities of heaven!

If any one requires proof, let him look to Jacobin France, whose government declared that death was an eternal sleep!—To Spain, involved in the corruptions of a tyrannical government, a putrid luxury, and a grovelling superstition!—What has saved England so long from the dire conflicts of war and the secret attacks of infidelity, but the blessings of heaven dispensed upon her land in answer to the prayers of her saints?—And what delivered our own dear country from the attacks of tyranny and carried her in safety through an unequal conflict? Who but that Being who protected her by his shield from the arrows of impiety and delivered her from the snares of French infidelity? Why were we thus blessed? Because we trusted our affairs in the hands of the Almighty and looked to him for wisdom and strength—because the captain of our armies, who was "first in war, first in peace, and first in the hearts of his countrymen," was not ashamed publicly to return thanks for success and for deliverance—and publicly to petition for blessings in our struggle for independence.

1. The "storm" refers, of course, to the Denmark Vesey plot. Since the Charleston *Southern Intelligencer*, a religious periodical, reflected to a great extent the views of the Reverend Benjamin Morgan Palmer, this article, which expresses no doubt about the reality of a preempted slave insurrection, may well have been written by him, someone who had conversed with at least some of the prisoners.

New York *National Advocate*

Monday, July 22, 1822

From a friend at Charleston, S.C. we have received the following letter:

In addition to the eleven negroes who had been condemned to death, (eight of whom had already suffered the sentence of the law) upwards of fifty more of the principal conspirators in the diabolical plot against the lives and property of the citizens, had been arrested, and were lodged in jail, against many of whom there was sufficient proof of conviction. It appears to have been of a much more serious nature than was at first anticipated, and would undoubtedly have terminated in much bloodshed, if not the total ruin of property both in town and country; their plans were deep, and of long standing, and from the facility the negroes had of obtaining arms and ammunition, but few whites could have escaped

It is to the very able, vigilant, and indefatigable exertions of the Intendant of Charleston, Major James Hamilton, Jun. that the citizens owe their lives and preservation of property; for if ever man deserved the thanks of a community, it is Major Hamilton; possessing activity, intelligence, much presence of mind, great firmness, and in fact every requisite for a public officer, particularly in such times of general consternation and alarm. He has undoubtedly undergone more hardships and privations than any other individual in the city. Commanding one of the most numerous and best company of riflemen in the union, he has already been on duty many whole nights, in addition to his daily unremitted exertions for the public good. Major Hamilton was the first to constitute a court of magistrates and freeholders, composed of gentlemen of the highest respectability in the state, and enjoying the full confidence of their fellow citizens. Their labours have been very arduous and fatiguing, being frequently detained in their examinations till midnight. They are entitled to the thanks and respect of every person who wishes the prosperity of his country; and altho' it may be superfluous to designate any individual of this honorable court, yet I believe you will be happy to learn, that amongst the number is the distinguished Col. William Drayton, whose talents as an eminent lawyer, statesman, gallant soldier, and unimpeachable conduct and general character, is such as to entitle him to every mark of respect and regard, not only in South Carolina, but over the whole union; and through his and Major Hamilton's able management and exertions, the public mind has been much tranquilised.[1]

1. This information was reprinted verbatim in the Baltimore *American and Commercial Daily Advertiser,* July 25, 1822; *Alexandria* (VA) *Herald,* July 31, 1822; and *Independent Chronicle and Boston Patriot,* July 26, 1822.

Baltimore Patriot & Mercantile Advertiser

Monday, July 22, 1822

Account of the Insurrection at Charleston.

The following extract of a letter from a gentleman in Charleston, to the editors of the New York Gazette, is published as giving a faithful account of the rise and progress of the late contemplated rebellion of the blacks in Charleston:

"As you will have heard, ere this reaches you, of a conspiracy in this place among the blacks against the whites, I think proper, as it is now no longer a secret, to state to you the facts, as far as they have come to my knowledge.

"It is now four or five weeks since I first heard a whisper that an insurrection of the blacks was to be apprehended. At first but little attention was paid by the citizens generally to this rumour, but it kept gaining ground by whispers and hints from one to another, till it was known that our City Council had the information from some faithful blacks, which placed it beyond a doubt, that a secret conspiracy was going on, which would very soon, if the conspirators were not apprehended, break out into an insurrection.

"The City Council kept it pretty much to themselves, till they apprehended a number of suspicious slaves, as well as many whose guilt was beyond suspicion. None, I believe, of the citizens, ever thought that the blacks could possibly succeed, were they really to begin to put their nefarious designs into execution, but that they would take some lives; and this would be but a signal for a general massacre of the poor devils.

"The military were all armed, and out every night—this is still kept up.

"A court, consisting of five Freeholders, was organized, being men of talents, and the strictest integrity, to try such as were and might be apprehended. Recently, the ringleader, a free black fellow, has been caught; and the court, after having acquitted several, passed a sentence of death on him & five slaves, who are to be executed next Tuesday, their guilt having been proved beyond the shadow of a doubt. They were all of them leading characters or principals. It is said that they have, or some of them have, acknowledged their object to have been the murder of the white males, the taking of the ladies for their wives, and the plunder of the city: and instead of appearing to feel any contrition, they expressed their regret, that they could not have executed their designs. They will not give the names of any of their accomplices. These are the generally credited reports, which are said to come from head quarters, and I have not a doubt are pretty nearly true. It is also generally believed that they intended to set fire to the city in different places. They were to have commenced carrying their infernal plot into execution last Sunday evening two weeks ago, but the city council having been timely apprized of it, had nearly all the militia of the city out under arms that very night, and even the night before, for some said it was to have been on Saturday night, so that they were deterred from making the attempt—Every day seems to discover more and more of the extent of the plot, or rather of the number of those, who were to have been actors in the tragedy.

Two or three nights since, a white man, said to have been an old pirate, was apprehended by the Intendant of the city. Information that such a man was inciting some blacks to an insurrection, had been given him by a black fellow, who proposed conducting him into an apartment in the house, where this man was in the habit of meeting those blacks as their counsellor. It was in this manner that he was taken, after having been over heard in hellish counsel, by the Intendant and another gentleman. It seems doubtful whether the law will allow this monster to be punished as he deserves. Yesterday a gentleman[1] had his coachman apprehended, as one of the conspirators, and it is said that this monster has since acknowledged it to his master.

"There are many reports going the rounds, which are not to be relied on; but what I have here stated I believe to be true."[2]

1. On Elias Horry (1773–1834), see Part IV, p. 393 n4.

2. This information appeared verbatim in the *Washington Gazette,* July 24, 1822; *New-York Evening Post,* July 27, 1822; Richmond *Enquirer,* July 30, 1822; Salem *Gazette,* July 26, 1822; and Philadelphia *United States Gazette and True American,* July 23, 1822.

Stephen Elliott[1] to William Elliott, Monday, July 22, 1822

. . . I am very glad to find that the machinations of this city did not extend to Beaufort. [2] The leaders boasted of having secured all of the negroes between Santee and Combahee and calculated or pretended to calculate on a very general cooperation. It is certain

Figure 27. Job Palmer (1747–1845), deacon of Charleston's Circular (Congregational) Church, father of the Reverend Benjamin Morgan Palmer, and owner of convicted slave Billy Palmer. From a photograph of a portrait, undated. Courtesy of the Frick Art Reference Library.

that some of their leaders were traversing the country very industriously last winter and spring in the garb of preachers offering to all who were willing to receive them the pure and unsophisticated doctrines of the gospel which they said the whites only garbled to suit their own purposes. This singular[3] notwithstanding how quiet the country has remained, and still more remarkable that no one country negroe has directly been implicated in their plot. If this should be the case at the end of our examinations, I think it will augur favorably for the tranquillity of the country for some time to come. This City can and I think will be very much reformed before our Citizens are permitted again to slumber. . . .

1. Stephen Elliott (1771–1830) wrote this letter from Charleston to his nephew William Elliott (1788–1863). Stephen enjoyed considerable stature in Charleston society as a planter, banker, politician, and intellectual. A Federalist, he owned in 1822 dozens of slaves and multiple properties and resided at 97 Boundary Street. See *BDSCHR* 4: 183–85, 187–89; *CSCCD*, 78.

2. William, a wealthy planter with multiple properties and dozens of slaves, was in Beaufort at the time.

3. Meaning either signal or singular fact.

ALS in Elliott-Gonzales Papers, SHC, UNC.

Mary Lamboll Beach to Elizabeth Gilchrist, Tuesday, July 23, 1822

. . . Oh! God, has a controversy with us. Oh! for his spirit to accompany it. I often think of Mr Newtons lines as applied to our situation, "Sees every day new straits attend's & Wonders where the scene will end"[1] The unraveling of this Awful business is like the chambers in Ezekiel's vision of *greater* & *greater* abominations.[2] On Friday next 26th 29 more people are to be hung & among them Mr Palmer's Billy.[3] *I* don't feel the surprise that *many* do about *him*; for although we often sin in two ways breaking the command of our Savior in *judging* & often in *misjudging* others; yet there was *a something* about him that made me fear it was only a *profession*; but still seeing him so constantly at the Church (& it was only last Wednesday night he was at the Lectern snuffing the candles & arrested the next day) that people feel it sensibly in our Church—his [*illegible*] young Master at first I believe doubted of but are now I understand *fully* convinced of his guilt & he will be a great loss in point of property to that poor old saint. besides the distress of his dying in that way & two other of the communicants besides Billy are to be hanged on Friday. Mrs Purcel's (M^{r}. Smith) man Jack[4] who she used to appear to think a non-such & she was so ridiculous as to say (for she was I may say half a mad woman from what I hear when he was first arrested) "thus they might as well hang Ben Palmer as him" is now convinced of his guilt—Susan McCall's Clarissa's husband is also another of *our* members[5] & the Ramsay's Sarah's husband (he a methodist professor) are of those to die on Friday; the Rmy's feel it a *great* deal & the poor Doc^{r} I never saw look (except about David[6]) as he does about him; they say he feels most sensibly about him—Ours as *yet* have not been implicated as I have heard in the slightest manner; but this is no security that some of them may not perish on the Gallows in ten days; if it should be the case I fear I should be a wretched being to the end of my days for having held them in a state of Slavery to prove a temptation—But Oh! this business I fear is akin to the French revolution to think that many of these people growing up like children as is the case of many of the *condemned* could be brought to such a fiend like temper that they would consent to imbrue their hands in the blood of their Masters & their little sons who never could have shed theirs [*illegible*] that to gratify I don't know what passion, whether it was Lust of Dominion of wealth or revenge; [*illegible*] it is not to[o] hard Master's or the case would be altered widely in its complexion; though I dare say abroad before it is *correctly* known it will be said they could *bear* their oppressions *no* longer—And the bitterness of the men of the world against our poor Church & Dr Pastor is awful; indeed I may say against Religion—I told Mary after hearing of a very bitter speech of Robt Hayne[7] about Missionaries the other day that I don't know but this business may yet end in religious persecution—In conversation with Mr R. Edwards[8] last evening (& he by the by speaks the language of a *Southern* man about [*illegible*] people) I remarked how our poor church & Pastor were vilified [*illegible*] said I hoped there was more religion there than in others by [*illegible*] being so pointed at—he did not say any thing in the affirmative but said the charge or bitterness seemed leveled at *Religion*. These wretched creatures having carried on their seditious Meetings up out of Town under the pretence of their being religious ones has left a sting & bitterness on the minds of the *men of the world that unless* the power of God alone will be applied to the removing of it; an *age* I believe must pass before it *can* be effaced—& the hatred to them so great that I expect and I was going to say *eternal* one will exist reciprocally. The country remains as far as I know perfectly quiet—they only in the City had engaged I suspect a little help from the Islands—Old Mr Jones's man or youth Jupiter I suppose was hung agreeably to his sentence on Friday last & two others belonging to Martin a Black-Smith in that neighbourhood[9]—They had not heard yesterday when Mary dined up there—She says the old gentleman seemed very dull & conversed but little she seemed to feel for him much. We have much cause for thankfulness that the City is very healthy for this season & our family too; except Mary worried with pain in her Stomach which impairs her looks. I believe [*missing*] proceeds partly from bile & the rest from *cares* for the *future* not from *fears* for the *present* as to our *personal* safety. But Oh! this is I believe a *lost* country—I believe she is endeavouring to bring her mind to working for her living for with regard to property being *removed* by sale we can flatter ourselves but little—Negroe men a few days ago when a few were offered could not bring $150—but this is owing to the present uncertainty of *this* property for young Anderson[10] a few weeks or months ago (Mr Blair's son in law I believe) gave 600 for one that is to be hanged this week. One of these Malefactors thinking he could not die in peace without confessing his guilt acknowledged his having set fire to a house in Meeting Street (not his Masters) when a negroe woman was charged with it & he I believe not even suspected. With regard to the report of Miss Bennet (& also D Elliot Huger's daughter)[11] it was in general circulation here but I doubt it for in their various confessions where they hold that all the *male* population even down to *little* boys was to take place I have never heard of their confessing what was to be done particularly with the other sex—The Negroes even had a report that the black women were to be put to death that the men might have white wives, some say all the young ones were to be spared & the old women & children put to death—But this is only one of a thousand lies I believe. . . .

1. Beach refers to hymns by John Henry Newton (1725–1807), although she mistakenly attributes a line from "Remembering All the Way the Lord Has Led Him," by the Baptist minister John Fawcett (1740–1817), to Newton. Beach may also have missed the irony that Newton had recanted his life as a British slave trader to become an antislavery evangelical Anglican minister. His hymns include "Amazing Grace." See Newton, *Thoughts upon the African Slave Trade* (London, 1788); D. Bruce Hindmarsh, *John Newton and the English Evangelical Tradition between the Conversions of Wesley and Wilberforce* (Oxford, UK: Clarendon Press, 1996); and Marcus Rediker, *The Slave Ship: A Human History* (New York: Viking, 2007), chap. 6.

2. The reference is to Ezekiel 8:12–13: "Then said he unto me, Son of man, hast thou seen what the ancients of the house of Israel do in the dark, every man in the chambers of his imagery? for they say, The LORD seeth us not; the LORD hath forsaken the earth. He said also unto me, Turn thee yet again, and thou shalt see greater abominations that they do."

3. William (Billy) Palmer was spared execution through the intervention of Governor Bennett, who along with Beach worshipped at Benjamin Morgan Palmer's Circular (Congregational) Church. Billy, as previously indicated, was owned by Benjamin's father, Job Palmer.

4. The widow Ann (Bonsall) Purcell owned the slave Jack Purcell. His testimony indicated that the national debate about slavery sparked by the Missouri question had influenced the thinking

of at least some of Vesey's coadjutors. In 1792 Ann married Joseph R. Purcell, a surveyor, who died intestate in 1807. Ann and Thomas Smith Jr. acted as administrators of Joseph's estate. See Charleston *City Gazette and Commercial Daily Advertiser,* June 8 and July 3, 1807. *CSCCD,* 99, identifies four men named Thomas Smith in 1822. The most likely candidate appears to be the planter Thomas Smith, who lived near Ann Purcell on Green Street. He may be the Thomas Smith Jr. (d. 1830) described in *BDSCHR* 4: 527. Jack Purcell appears to have been a member of a family of slaves owned by Joseph Purcell and officially purchased by Ann around 1811. See Sale List, Estate of Joseph Purcell, Charleston District Court of Equity, Equity Bill 1801, no. 64, SCDAH. (The editors are indebted to Charles Lesser for this reference.)

5. Beach means "members" of the Congregational Church.

6. Beach speaks of her fellow Congregationalist Dr. James Ramsay (1797–1832), whose father David Ramsay (1749–1815), a celebrated physician and historian, died tragically in 1815 when shot by a madman he was treating. See *BDSCHR* 3: 590–94.

7. On Robert Young Hayne (1791–1839), see Part II, p. 154 n3.

8. Beach was probably speaking to Robert B. Edwards (d. 1824), a Charleston stockbroker, born in Massachusetts, who in 1822 resided at 61 Anson Street. See *CSCCD,* 78; Washington *Daily National Intelligencer,* September 24, 1824.

9. Beach refers to restive slaves inculpated in a case quite possibly related to the Vesey plot. Authorities arrested four slaves who had fired on a mail driver at Parker's Ferry Road. A court in Jacksonborough, a town near Charleston, convicted and executed three of the four: Nashaw and Jim, owned by the blacksmith Jacob Martin, and Jupiter, owned by Thomas Jones (1745–1836). In 1822 Jones was president of the Bank of South Carolina and a member of the Circular Church. He resided at 3 Anson Street. In 1822 Martin resided at 18 Blackford Alley. See Thomas Jones, "Petition for Compensation for a Slave Executed for Shooting at the Mail Driver," n.d., no. 2839, series S165015, SCDAH; *Charleston Courier,* July 17, 1822, which appears on p. 396 in Part IV in this volume; *CSCCD,* 85, 88.

10. Robert Anderson Jr. (1794–1861), who purchased the slave Smart, owned a dry goods store, located in 1822 on 294 King Street. He married Naomi Euphan Blair (b. 1797) in 1813. See *CSCCD,* 69; Elizabeth H. Jervey, "Marriage and Death Notices from the City Gazette and Daily Advertiser of Charleston, S.C.," *SCHM* 38 (April 1937): 66.

11. "Miss Bennet" refers to Mary Hayes Bennett (1804–1844), teenage daughter of Governor Thomas Bennett Jr. Judge Daniel Elliott Huger (1779–1854), patriarch of one of South Carolina's leading families, owned multiple properties, including plantations, scores of slaves, and a residence on Meeting Street. He fathered ten children, including four daughters. The one in question appears to be Mary Middleton Huger (1802–1831). See *BDSCHR* 4: 292–93; Arthur Meredyth Burke, *The Prominent Families of the United States of America* (London: Sackville Press, 1908), 452.

ALS in Mary Lamboll Beach Papers, SCHS.

Salem *Gazette*

Tuesday, July 23, 1822

Three of the five Negroes who were to be hung at Charleston on the 12th have been respited by the Governor until the 19th inst. The other two were hung on the 12th.[1]

1. The two slaves hanged were John Horry and Jack Pritchard. The three respited were Palmer's William, John Vincent, and Billy Robinson. See Hamilton, *Account,* 43–44.

Richmond *Enquirer*

Tuesday, July 23, 1822

Some misguided slaves in Charleston have suffered the sentence of the law.—They had formed the plan of an insurrection which was disclosed by a faithful negro—and the criminals were apprehended, after sufficient evidence of their guilt had been obtained. In the family of Mr. Bennett, governor of South Carolina, "the work of destruction was to have commenced, and a beautiful and accomplished young lady was to have been consigned to a fate which humanity shudders to think of." Troops had been called out to reconnoitre, and guard the town. "Twelve of the unfortunate wretches are said to be the victims of their own temerity." Three of them had been respited until the 19th inst. Four other slaves had been tried at the courthouse in Jacksonborough, for firing at the mail driver on the Parker's Ferry road; one was acquitted and sentence of death passed upon the others.

Charleston Courier

Tuesday, July 23, 1822

THE Court of Magistrates and Freeholders, convened for the trial of sundry persons of color, charged with an attempt to raise an insurrection in this state, have, in addition to those already condemned to be executed, unanimously found the following *Guilty,* and passed upon them the Sentence of Death, to be carried into execution on Friday morning, 26th inst. on the Lines, between 6 and 9 o'clock:—

DICK, belonging		to Mr. William Sims.
BACCHUS,	do.	to Mr. Benjamin Hammett.
WILLIAM,	do.	to Mr. Job Palmer.
JIM,	do.	to Estate of Clement.
JERRY,	do.	to Mr. Mordecai Cohen.
NAPHUS, ADAM, BELLISLE,	do.	to Estate of Joseph Yates.
CHARLES,	do.	to Mr. John Billings.
DEAN,	do.	to Mr. James Mitchell.

Sentence of Death was likewise passed upon the following Negroes, but the Court recommends that their sentence be commuted to transportation beyond the limits of the United States:—

SEYMOUR, belonging		to Mr. William Kunhardt.
DUBLIN,	do.	to Mr. Thomas Morris.
PETER,	do.	to Estate of Jas. Cooper.
ISAAC,	do.	to Mr. William Harth.
GEORGE,	do.	to Mr. Tho[mas]. Bampfield.
SABY GAILLARD,		a Free Black Man.

The Court is still engaged in the trial of others, apprehended for the same crime.[1]

1. This information was reprinted verbatim in the Charleston *Southern Patriot, and Commercial Advertiser,* July 22, 1822; Charleston *City Gazette and Commercial Daily Advertiser,* July 23, 1822; *Charleston Mercury,* July 23, 1822; *Washington Gazette,* July 29, 1822; Baltimore *American and Commercial Advertiser,* July 30, 1822; *New-York Evening Post,* July 31, 1822; Philadelphia *Democratic Press,* July 31, 1822; New York *National Advocate,* July 31, 1822; and *Hartford Courant,* August 6, 1822.

Anna Hayes Johnson to Elizabeth W. Haywood, Wednesday, July 24, 1822

I mentioned in a former letter my dear Betsey to you of my having some articles to send to you which were too bulkey to send by mail. true my packet is large but you must excuse my troubling you about an affair which has *here*[1] caused some very unpleasant moments I allude to the circumstances under which my father[2] has had to contend with his fellow citizens—I am told that letters from No Ca—have been rec'd in which his conduct has been most unmercifully handled and given rise to many tales as unfounded as untrue—I have enclosed a pamphlet written by himself in extenuation of his conduct and which has had the effect of silencing all the impertinent rumors which were set afloat to his disadvantage—perhaps to make you understand the pamphlet better I should give you a sketch of the first publication and the causes of it which caused all the turmoil—I remember perfectly the circumstances which he related for I was in Edgefield with him at the time and tho' I was but a child I remember all the circumstances perfectly.

It was somewhere in the year 1809—or 10 that a Mr Key a most exemplary man had a very faithful servant taken up on the charge of an attempt to raise an insurrection in the state, and hung—the circumstances under which the execution took place rendered it doubly painful to my father from the conviction which his legal knowledge afforded him of the entire innocence of the slave—You know that the leading characteristic of our state is an impetuosity and ardency of feeling which unavoidably lays them open to deception and consequently leads them on to error in action which is sometimes extremely detrimental to them, and you might as well attempt to "fetter tides with silken band" as to make them listen to reason when under this excitement,—The circumstances were these[:] The patrole laws are there most constantly put into force and have rendered them almost a "by word and a proverb thro' the country or district of which I am speaking, one day while the patroles were as usual going their rounds of terror a couple of negro's had stop'd at one of those little scurges of the country—I mean a "dram shop"—to take their Tass to "Auld lang Syne." One was a trumpetor to one of the militia companies belonging to the district—they had purchased a can of grog and had located themselves in the loft of a barn for the purpose of emptying it and then I presume to Sleep off the effects—when they heard the patrole coming—one of them proposed giving them a fright and accordingly sounded his trumpet—the alarm was given and one of them was taken—and whether from private animosity or what—I cannot say but he gave information, that it was Capt. Keys servant blew the horn and told (necessarily) a thousand falsehoods to support his first lie—so true "it is that the first step is the greatest difficulty" and that one falsehood leads the way to a thousand—The unfortunate slave against whom he gave information was taken and upon no other evidence except a bullet mold thro' which there was a hole for casting nets and a congaree horn fill'd with cobwebs, condemned and tho' my father endeavoured to persuade them to wait only until an express could be sent to the Governour he was refused and the negro executed in the day after the sentence was passed upon him—so much for my story now I will tell you how it is connected with the present agitated state of Society—At the time that information was given of the projected insurrection a gentlemen by the name of M'Call—a very promising young man—was so much alarmed at the news that he always slept with a pair of pistols under his head—the morning of which I am speaking he rose early and taking the pistols from his pillow he in putting them into a drawer struck one of them accidentally against the edge of the drawer and it immediately went off and blew out his brains[3]—imagine for one instant, the feelings of his wife when awaking by the explosion she beheld the mangled remains of her husband—this fatal catastrophy by the time it reached us had acquired additional horrors—While going to Church on the same day—my father enquired into it of a gentleman whom he met, and to whom he promised to give the circumstances which I have related he did so, and this gentleman who was the editor of the Courier very *wisely* put it into his paper—thinking that it w[oul]d do no mischief—but the court of Freeholders—now sitting—took up the cudgels—supposing that it was a slur at them—guilty conscience you know the rest—so they thundered their anathemas at him and consequently drew from him the pamphlet in question—So much for that affair which gave rise to another tale which I am told has gained credence in C C[4]—and which is as utterly false as the heart is vicious who invented it—I allude to the *countersign* tale—I am told that it is reported in C C—that my father by fraudulent means obtained the countersign for the purpose of resqueing my Uncles negro's who were then under sentence of death.[5] the circumstances were these A young Scotchman a neighbour of ours—who by the bye deserves to be tied hand and foot and sent back to his own land of "cakes and ale" was at the head of a patrol of which my father was one—and who were stationed at the head of boundary street as we live above that street—this young man "dressed in a little brief authority" thought at last he would "shew the world he was a *man*" and riding up to the sentinel at the opposite side asked him for the countersign in a voice so loud that my father heard it and so did another gentleman who was standing by him, the sentinel reply was "Jackson" and the youth returned to pa and said, have I not got it out of him handsomely my fathers reply was, I think you were wrong to ask him so loud for I heard it—The sentinel became alarm'd and instantly returned to the guard and told what he had done and the countersign was changed and the report raised of which I am speaking—My father returned at 3 oclock and went quietly to bed never suspecting the mischief that had been done the next day it was told him with all the amendments—made to it—his first action was to go to the Intendent of the city and give in his affidavit—stating the circumstances—Hammilton[6] immediately lodged it in one of the offices where thousands flocked to see it—This is the "head and front of his offence" and for a kind and really considerate intention of awakening the fears of a parcel of petticoats and men with the "front of Caesar but a womanly heart" he has been most

Figure 28. Charleston City Hall, first built in 1801 as a branch of the First National Bank of the United States and photographed here in 1865. Convicted slaves were confined to the old vaults prior to their execution on July 26, 1822. Courtesy of the Library of Congress.

unkindly and inhumanely treated—But the fact is that you would be surprised to see the low petty jealousy of my father—exercised and maintained by the generalty of men in this state

I have told a "plain unvarnished tale and if I have failed to bring conviction to your mind—remember mercy" and think that it is a womans pen & head has written and dictated—One thing more—never let [*illegible*] know that I have written this letter. It was written for those [*illegible*] not for the world I have done it with a view of removing any eroneous impression which you may have imbibed, and tell your father not to criticize too severely—On Friday 29 of the unfortunate creatures are to be hung—it is most horrible—it makes my blood curdle when I think of it but they are guilty most certainly I shall write again in a day or two. . . .

1. Johnson was writing from Charleston, and Haywood was in Raleigh, North Carolina.

2. Anna's father was Supreme Court Justice William Johnson Jr.

3. At this juncture, Johnson's letter shifted from 1809 to 1822, since Dr. John Ward McCall accidentally shot himself sometime during the night of June 15–16. See Charleston *City Gazette and Commercial Daily Advertiser,* June 17, 1822, on p. 98 in Part II of this volume.

4. The *Charleston Courier,* which carried Justice Johnson's essay of June 21, 1822.

5. Anna's uncle was Governor Bennett; the slaves in question were Rolla, Batteau, and Ned, all of whom were hanged on July 2.

6. By "Hammilton," Johnson meant Intendant James Hamilton Jr.

ALS, in Ernest Haywood Papers, SHC, UNC.

Mary Lamboll Beach to Elizabeth L. Gilchrist, Thursday, July 25, 1822

My dear Sister,

I have just had the pleasure of reading your letter of the inst & felt indescribably at the wonderful escape you had in your ride along the Skuylkill Canal.[1] Oh! for hearts of gratitude to our Almighty Preserver. After reading it I was stuck with thinking of Mr R. Edwards's[2] remark 3 or 4 even^{gs} ago when on his asking after you I told him how you were but that you were in an anxious state about us at *this* time. He replied either that the same hand did or you should keep in mind (I forget which) preserved us that did you—& how striking is it in this instance I am afraid from some symptoms you mention of the pulsation or beating in the right side of your chest that you are getting nervous pray strive in time against it. Your account of Poor A.G.[3] is most pitiable indeed & none can feel more for him than I do, or *ought* in this respect, for at times *lately* my *horror* at the injections of thoughts I may say directly from Hell or the prince of it; have left me for some moments in despair—Doc^{r} Palmer prayed a few sabbaths ago so particularly for those under temptation that I am sure he had some particular case (though I have not heard so) in view & I told Mary I believed that Satan in a *more* than *common* manner I believed was at work in our community at this time in setting these incendiaries the *Negroes* to work & in the *hearts* of other people with sinful thoughts that our souls must shudder at; for that I had been in a peculiarly tempted state respecting the Magnitude of the suffering for sin in Eternity & not from my old difficulty about the doctrine of Election that I so often have groaned under. I hope the Lord may be preparing Adam by these severe trials for an *instructor* of many other poor Sinners. I got a letter from Mr King of the 12th of June & he mentioned having conversed with A.G. at two or three times & said what discouraging & humbling views Adam had & that *his* (Mr King' s *hopes*) were in proportion to Adam's *fears* of himself; he said that the last time he saw him he was there at the Communion the 1st Sabbath in June & had conversed with A (I think some days before)[.] he then indulged a hope for himself & Mr K—a strong one. With respect to R.G.[4] going off unless very special business carries him; I hardly think he will go at such a time as this; as I suspect from what I hear that it is thought cowardly. The duty of guard is of necessity so heavy that now from 16 to old men are dispensed with; not even if a substitute for their night was offered I understand. I know the Ministers are not for Doc^{r} Palmer had to be out last night & I heard that Bishop Bowen[5] after all his poor health had to *ride* Patrole all Saturday night though he had to preach the next day; he has a nice house on the neck a little above the Arsenal. I am told by *this* arrangement *many* nights pass for each one to rest & then I suppose they will be in a better state [*illegible*] if any serious alarm took place; but before *this* arrangement was made what with many *never* being in the *habit* of turning out, & others (for you know how many Planters there are & they were not liable to City duty owing to their belonging to companies in their own parishes in the country. All but for the Ministers I think it a wise regulation. I think it probable (but I have not heard so) that this was one of the regulations formed by the meeting I told you that had been formed of the Military men that A. Hayne[6] said would place the City in a safe state of defense or security, but this is almost *too* confident a word to use. I trust the Almighty will be ours. I hope it is a time of much prayer here—the Tuesday Afternoon meeting is very full generally, & almost to crowding at times & thus the prayers are under less restraint on account of no blacks being present—for our public ones (at least in our Church) have been very guarded as to the State of things. Mr Boies[7] preached last Sunday Mor[nin]g baptized Doc^{r} P. child (H. Bunce)[8] & I never liked him so well his subject was on the stability & serenity of those who feared God at all hours & in times of trouble particularly & Mr Brown in the Af^{n} preached from these words. Not every one that saith Lord, Lord but he that doeth &^{c} Doc^{r} Palmer a few weeks or short number of months at farthest preached from these words "I will search Jerusalem with Candles" Two most solemn sermons & he has often used those words in prayer since that *our* Jerusalem may be searched; & indeed the search seems now begun—with black professors Old doctor Furman[9] preached a very solemn one about a fortnight ago in the evening from those words Isa[iah]. Chap. 22.14 in Verse "It was revealed in my ears by the Lord of Hosts surely this iniquity shall not be purged till ye be died." I was almost shocked with apprehension when Mary came home & told me lest it was Prophetic; but she said he was rather encouraging at the same time very faithful in shewing *how* the destruction of a community was to be averted or prevented—& she said from all his remarks she supposed thought there ought to be a day of Public Humiliation, but this I suppose is hopeless from the *nature* of the visitation & the young man Hamilton our Intendant who knows not God—You ask if it was not C. U.[10] who made the same remarks about Doc^{r} P. but I am *sure* it was not, but *I* did not nor *Mary* either hear the name. J. Legare[11] I believe mentioned having heard it himself but did not tell the name. I don't know the day I have heard [*illegible*] name mentioned out of our family. And while I speak of the Legare's I will mention to Dr. L.[12] credit what many heard him assert & I believe from what I *used* to know of his arrangements strictly true—T. J. was in conversation about the small profit of money at interest & of Planters profits &^{ca} & D. L. remarked how hard the Negroes work'd in some parts of the country (this not though among those who would ever be called cruel observe)—& he said unless this was practised he did not believe that such *enormous* profits were realized by the Planters, & then from one remark went on to another not boasting though observing "that it had been his constant practice never to as is done in Winter in *many many* places *I* know) have his people at work on his place before the Sun was up nor after dark (I suppose any thing *extraordinary* excepted) for he never could answer to his conscience for any profit to act thus toward his people in serving all he could & spoke of his responsibility &cc. & Mary says for instance about foot Gins he dislikes so much as their labour can be saved by Machines, & in various ways on his place he uses the help of them (though at much expense) to save manual labour, he seems serious & his wife too if they service the old gentleman if removing to the North; he says he has *always* had a predilection for it since spending so much time there. . . . Holinsby[13] yesterday asked me to wait a few days till he sold some Cotton; he has been very sick, & seems dispirited—he paid me a visit that excited some uneasiness about my people—& he has some fears about Quaco being suspected—he says he hears it mentioned by one or two that there have been two meetings held at the old front place that 3 boat loads of black people were said to have gone from town—I begged him to be very still about it & I suppose for his own sake he will—It will be wonderful indeed if there should not in such times some of mine suspected—I suppose the constituted authorities are only waiting to get through their Town business if that *ever* can be done by this set of rulers (or generation perhaps) & then I expect the search for the country conspirators will take place; for I heard when the business first was opened that several on James Island were supposed to be concerned in it. But I must endeavour to leave it with our righteous God. Whether the country is clear of the business or only intimidated by the steps taking in the City it is a great mercy it remains tranquil. In answer to several questions in to day's letter I will answer them in order. Denmark Vesey *was* a Slave to old Mr Vesey (& used to be I think I heard about his store when he & Blake[14] were partners) but whether he was left or he purchased his freedom I can't say—he was gray headed, he told his judges or the Council when interrogated to what Church he belonged with a very firm decisive tone "None"—& I asked Betsy[15] a few evenings ago the same question & she answered with a contemptuous tone of *him* to the same effect—But I believe he was considered the Champion in the African Church business & I believe it is the generally received opinion that *this* church commenced this awful business or at any rate they took this for their rallying point I understand their papers contain allusion to it—But it excites surprise how many things have got out when it is said the Court was under Oath to secrecy. *I* can only account for it in this way; that when different Negroes were trying; their white representatives or friends (I know it was the case with several & I suppose with all) heard the testimony given by the evidences & also the deceased as well as those now under sentence have made disclosures so that I believe the whole of *any* consequence is now out & in possession of the *public.*—I think the *attempt* of keeping their arrangements *secret* was judicious could it have been practicable, & yet perhaps it is more satisfactory to the Public to know it, as our minds must be more satisfied of the awful necessity of such *sanguinary* steps as are now taking place in our City. The Pirates I make no doubt are in safe confinement, but I hear nothing of them; there are two—Wilson & Paull's man[16] & a great many more are to be transported beyond the United States, some say to Africa; & others say to the mines in South America I *hope* not the latter as it is said they had better be put to death & if these are less guilty surely they ought not to have the heaviest punishment as it will at any rate be in the world's eye so. I found in the evening after writing the above about a substitute for others that one was accepted for Doc^{r} Palmer & probably as it was for him it may be in other cases too—but *fines certainly* will not avail for absence & it is right all should bear their share. if the [*illegible*] served but several of his people have offered, & young O'harra went when he heard at late as time nearly for the guard to set) which I thought very praise worthy & the young Ramsay's too have offered; but at first Mr P. thought that *all things* taken together he had best go, I suppose too as Bishop Bowen did—but they took a substitute—& I hope will not again conclude but to go, for he seems truly worn down. It is said not one Episcopalian is among the guilty & only one Baptist.

July 27th, I felt so badly (not sick) my dear Sister & my mind was so tempest tossed yesterday that I was in no suitable state to write if I could help it. You heard before this will reach you that 29 poor miserable culprits were to have been executed yesterday but some were respited till 9th of August & 3 had their sentence commuted for transportation so that 22 were executed—The day before I felt strangely firm about it thinking it *necessary* by evening my distress about the business returned & if giving up every one I own would have made a different state of things that is that they could be freemen with safety to us & themselves I would have done, but this can never be in my day—The night was such as you may picture from a large number of the Cavalry passing back & forth the whole of it—in the middle of it the whole of the criminals for execution in the morning were brought together to the vault under the City Hall[17] where a part of them were before; the others were divided some in the Jail & others in the Cells allotted for the Maniacs in the Poor House & about 6 o'clock the procession moved off up Meeting St. attended with an immense crowd I understand; & a great one of white as well as black were at the awful scene & several Carriages (not with Ladies understand) but such as the Council, Willington & even Docr Palmer in his;[18] who went not in his Official capacity; but by the desire of Docr Leland[19] who accompanied him. With some of the poor Sufferers the business was managed very badly indeed (no doubt owing to the *great* number) as he was shot at *last, said* by accident, but in pity I suppose to end his suffering as it respected one of them I understand they behaved with great firmness—they all died on one or rather a continuation of 3 gallows in one.—A death like silence reigned in the City at the time. Oh! That God in his mercy may have enabled them as the Thief on the Cross by faith to look to this blood which alone can save any of us. Both Docr Palmer & Mr Jones had a very favourable opinion of the state of mind that both Mrs Purcell's man & Pharo Temah's husband were in.[20] I don't wonder that with such an inflamable temper as Mrs Purcel has that she should have gone on as she did on the first surprise, although she had had it hinted to her two or three days before that her Jack had been seen in suspicious company—but he was one of those unassuming civil diligent servants & had a most prepossessing countenance—he sent for Mrs John Holmes[21] (Miss Glover that were) as the intimate friend of his Mistress & told her how the business had been—& observed he could not stand the sight of his Mistress who it seems brought him up from a child & had been so kind to him; but to go on he said when Vesey first proposed it he objected for he said his wife & children were freer & he lived as well as he could wish himself—however Vesey again came to him & with the Bible to quote different passages to prove the lawfulness of it; & told him that if he did not do it for himself or had no reason; he ought to do it for the sake of others—he told Mr Jones he wished he could confess his guilt before the *whole* world. A melancholy accident happened on the ground at the Execution some say some alarm was given; others that a Horse started; but let it have arose from what course it did, a sudden impulse was given & it was then by some called out "a fire in Town" the Troops immediately made a dash or move to clear the ground & of course you may form some idea of such a crowd *falling* back—Mr Perman's carriage[22] either in turning too short; or somehow by the pole of another striking it—but his boy behind it was knocked off from behind & literally trampled to death for his skull was fractured by the Horses that passed over him[23]—& several persons were hurt but none else that we have heard mortally so which I think next to the miraculous: As the Papers I *intend* sending (for they may fail) will inform you about others but they are cramped in their details I will for bear. I send *all* that have *any* thing respecting this. Oh! what sort of business shall I call this sorest judgment *perhaps* it will *prove* that ever our country saw. . . . [24]

1. The Schuylkill Navigation Company, chartered in 1815, undertook to build a canal of more than one hundred miles that would link Philadelphia (near Germantown where Elizabeth Gilchrist was then staying) to the anthracite coal region around Pottsville, county seat of Schuylkill County. The canal was not completed until 1828. See Edward J. Gibbons and Edward S. Gibbons, "The Building of the Schuylkill Navigation System, 1815–1828," *Pennsylvania History* 57 (1990): 13–43.

2. Probably stockbroker Robert B. Edwards (d. 1824). See above, p. 410 n8.

3. "A.G." refers to Adam Gilchrist Jr. (1760–1816), Elizabeth's husband.

4. "R.G." probably refers to Robert Gilchrist, brother of Adam.

5. Nathaniel Bowen (1779–1839) was bishop of the Protestant Episcopal Church of South Carolina. In *A Pastoral Letter on the Religious Instruction of the Slaves of Members of the Protestant Episcopal Church of the State of South-Carolina* (Charleston, SC, 1835), excerpted on pp. 695–96 in Part V, Bowen credited mixed-race communicants of the Episcopal Church with "the discovery of the plot."

6. Arthur Peronneau Hayne (1788–1867), older brother of Robert Young Hayne.

7. Artemas Boies (1792–1844), pastor of Charleston's Second Presbyterian Church.

8. The Reverend Benjamin Morgan Palmer had married Mary Stanley Bunce (1784–1847), daughter of Captain Jared Bunce. In 1822, the Reverend Artemas Boies baptized Benjamin and Mary's child, Harriet Bunce Palmer.

9. Baptist minister Richard Furman (1755–1825).

10. "C. U." may refer to Charles Urquhart, a Scottish merchant who had arrived in Charleston in 1806. In 1822 he resided at 39 Elliott Street. See *Charleston Courier*, September 9, 1832; *CSCCD*, 102.

11. James Legaré (1762–1830), a wealthy planter in St. John Colleton Parish, worshipped with Beach at the Circular Church and in 1822 kept a home in Charleston at 7 New Street. This reference establishes that Beach spoke with someone who had direct knowledge of the court proceedings, since Legaré served as one of the five freeholders of the court until Saturday, July 13, when illness caused him to step down, to be replaced by Henry Deas. See *BDSCHR* 3: 426–27; *CSCCD*, 87; Eliza C. K. Flood, *Biographical Sketches of the Huguenot Solomon Legaré and of his Family* (Charleston, SC, 1886); *OR*, 109n.

12. Thomas Legaré Jr. (1795–1855) studied medicine in Philadelphia under Dr. Benjamin Rush. In 1822 he resided in Charleston at 89 Boundary Street and would become a successful planter on James Island as well as a devout Presbyterian. See *CSCCD*, 87; "Obituary," *Charleston Courier*, July 2, 1855.

13. "Holinsby" may refer to James Hollinsbee, a small slaveholder on James Island, who was apparently working for Beach at the time.

14. Beach refers to a partnership that Captain Joseph Vesey (1747–1835), owner of Denmark, had formed in the late eighteenth century with John Blake (1752–1810), a Charleston merchant who had been active in the Atlantic slave trade. See *BDSCHR* 3: 72–73.

15. In a letter dated September 22, 1823, to Elizabeth Gilchrist, Beach speaks of "Betsy Legaré," who may well be the Betsy referenced here.

16. Slaves George Wilson and William Paul, both of whom provided crucial testimony to authorities about the plot.

17. Charleston City Hall, completed in 1801 and located on the corner of Broad and Meeting streets, began as a branch of the First Bank of the United States. After the bank lost its charter, the city regained the property and turned it into a city hall in 1818. The building's vaults offered ample security for housing conspirators. See Jonathan H. Poston, *The Buildings of Charleston: A Guide to the City's Architecture* (Columbia: University of South Carolina Press, 1997), 157.

18. Beach refers here to the attendance at the hangings by members of the Charleston City Council, as well as by the Reverend Benjamin Morgan Palmer and Aaron Smith Willington (1781–1862), editor of the *Charleston Courier.*

19. Aaron W. Leland (1787–1871) was pastor of the Presbyterian Church on James Island and one of the white ministers who had supported the opening of Morris Brown's Zion Church.

20. The slaves Jack Purcell and Pharo Thompson were hanged on the Lines on Friday, July 26, one day before Beach wrote these words.

21. Beach refers here to Ann Glover Holmes (1785–1868), who married a Johns Island planter named John Holmes. Among the three men named John Holmes identified by *CSCCD,* 87, as living in Charleston in 1822, a planter by that name resided at 117 Tradd Street. See also Henry Schulz Holmes, "The Trenholm Family," *SCHGM* 16 (October 1915): 153.

22. George Perman (1778?–1826), an English-born grocer and merchant, operated a business in 1822 on East Bay Street. See *CSCCD,* 94; *Charleston Courier,* June 6, 1826.

23. See "Coroner's Report," Charleston *City Gazette and Commercial Daily Advertiser,* July 27, 1822, transcribed below on p. 422, for a description of the accidental death.

24. Captain Jared Bunce (d. 1832), father-in-law of the Reverend Benjamin Morgan Palmer, commanded a ship that regularly sailed between Charleston and Philadelphia.

ALS in Beach Papers, SCHS.

Charleston *Southern Patriot, and Commercial Advertiser*

Thursday, July 25, 1822

Such of the citizens of Charleston as witnessed the spectacle, must have been highly delighted in beholding a body of our youthful countrymen, about sixty in number, who are to act as a corps of Cavalry, inspected this morning.—Their dress is a split shirt, and a white hat, turned up in front, with two black plumes; their arms, a double barrelled gun, a pair of pistols, and a sabre. Should the services of this corps be required, we predict that it will be found as formidable as any other body of troops of the same number ever raised within the State. The following gentlemen compose its officers:—

Major GABRIEL H. MANIGAULT, 1st *Leader*
Col. RICHARD W. VANDERHORST, 2*d Leader*
Lieut. Col. JOHN BRYANT, 3*d Leader.*
Adjutant JOHN HARLESTON, 4th *Leader.*

Charleston *Southern Patriot, and Commercial Advertiser*

Friday, July 26, 1822

Accident.—A small black boy, belong to WM. PERRONNEAU, Esq.[1] was unfortunately killed this morning, at the place of execution, by several horses passing over his body.

1. On William Peronneau (1768–1848), who served as acting intendant in 1822 in the absence from Charleston of James Hamilton Jr., see Part II, p. 153 n1. During the executions at the Lines on July 26, an excited crowd caused the death of his teenage slave Sam, when he was accidentally struck by a carriage pole, knocked to the ground, and trampled by horses. See *CSCCD,* 94; "Coroner's Report," Charleston *City Gazette and Commercial Daily Advertiser,* July 27, 1822; Charleston *Southern Patriot,* June 19, 1848.

Charleston *City Gazette and Commercial Daily Advertiser*

Friday, July 26, 1822

The Governor has respited until Friday, the 9th Aug. the following fellows, condemned by the Court of Magistrates and Freeholders, and sentenced to be executed this morning, viz:—*Seymour, Paris, Sandy, Louis, William, Dublin, Peter, Isaac, George, and Saby Gaillard,* a free negro.[1]

1. This information was reprinted nearly verbatim in the *Charleston Mercury,* July 26, 1822. For the owners of the slaves and disposition of the cases, see Part III, pp. 183–84.

Diary of Reverend John England,[1] Friday, July 26, 1822

July 26. On this morning, after having attended a Culprit concerned in the Negro conspiracy to execution, upon my return home I was called upon and informed of the atrocious misconduct of the Revd. Henry Doyle. . . .

1. John England (1786–1842) was born in Cork, Ireland, and in 1820 named first bishop of the Catholic Diocese of Charleston, which included Georgia and North Carolina. Eight years later, England began a Catholic school for free girls of color and female slaves, which was attacked by a mob in 1835. England's diary indicates that he accompanied one of the twenty-two men hanged that day to the gallows erected on the Lines; England heard, as did several other Charleston clergymen, the final words of the accused and was in a position to know whether a plot existed among area bondmen. See Patrick Carey, *An Immigrant Bishop: John England's Adaptation of Irish Catholicism to American Republicanism* (Yonkers, NY: U.S. Catholic Historical Society, 1982).

John England, *Journal of the Right Rev. John England, D.D., First Bishop of Charleston, S.C. from 1820 to 1823* (Philadelphia, 1895), 49.

Anna Hayes Johnson to Elizabeth W. Haywood, Saturday, July 27, 1822[1]

. . . We had yesterday the most aweful tragedy acted in this devoted city that comes with in the recollection of man—22 unfortunate wretches were at one fatal moment sent to render up their dread account. 29 had been sentenced but 7 had their sentence commuted to perpetual banishment—but on Tuesday 6 more are to be executed[2]—Gracious heaven to what will all this lead—certainly it will throw our city back at least ten years—30 have already been executed, and I am told that there are an aweful number yet to be tried, I wish I could act for myself I would not stay in this city another day—for my feelings have been so lacerated of late that I can hardly think speak or act there is a look or horror in every countenance—I wish I was with you, at least I should experience comparative happiness tho' even there what I have seen would pursue me—Do not think I saw them hung, I would as leave be hung my self—tho' it was within sight of our house—But I can imagine & feel. . . . Remember me to all my kith & kin. . . .

1. Johnson sent the letter from Charleston to Haywood in Raleigh, North Carolina.
2. Four, not six, men were hanged on Tuesday, July 30.

ALS in Haywood Papers, SHC, UNC.

Charleston *City Gazette and Commercial Daily Advertiser*

Saturday, July 27, 1822

CORONER'S REPORT.

A Jury of Inquest was held yesterday morning about 9 o'clock, near the lines, on the body of a Negro Boy, named Sam, about 13 years of age, the property of William Peronneau Esq. It appeared that he was knocked down by the pole of a carriage in endeavoring to make his way through a crowd. The Jury brought in their verdict that the deceased came to death by accident.

John Michel, Coroner

For the Parishes of St. Philip and St. Michael.

Charleston Courier

Saturday, July 27, 1822

WILLIAM GARNER, a Slave, for whom a reward of $200 was offered by his Excellency the Governor, was arrested near Columbia, on the 23d inst. by authority of the Intendant of that place. He had just started, in company with his brother JACK LOPEZ, a free colored man, on his turn towards town. These particulars are contained in a letter from the Intendant of Columbia, to the Intendant of this city; which adds, that GARNER will be sent down, as soon as a proper guard can be organized for the purpose.[1]

1. This information was reprinted verbatim in the *Baltimore Patriot & Mercantile Advertiser*, August 2, 1822. On William Garner, see also Petition of Eliza Smith Garner, July 10, 1834, which appears on pp. 535–36 in Part V of this volume.

Charleston *City Gazette and Commercial Daily Advertiser*

Saturday, July 27, 1822

The award of Justice.—Yesterday, about 8 o'clock, *twenty two* culprits expiated, on the gallows, the crime of which they had been convicted—an attempt to raise an Insurrection, not only in this City, but in various parts of the State of South-Carolina.

These slaves were concerned with many others, some of whom have already suffered for their guilt, and some few are reserved for further investigation. Should no new cases be brought to light, we are in hopes the axe has been laid to the root of the evil, and that we have now pretty nearly reached the extent both of the guilt and the punishment.

The gentlemen composing the Court of Magistrates and Freeholders have examined a multitude of cases; forty, we believe, within the last ten days; they have laid aside their private concerns and dedicated their time and talents to the service of the community, in one of the most awful and delicate junctures that has probably occurred since the settlement of Charleston. Some by their habits of legal enquiry and indeed the whole Court, by their patience and intelligence, have rendered a service to this City and this State, that will not soon be forgotten.

The Committee of Vigilance also, as well as the whole City Council, and our active INTENDANT,—who on this occasion has united to the character of a magistrate the ardour of a patriot—shall not sleep in our remembrance.

As we are not over-fond of eulogising, the tribute of respect *WE* tender to such men may therefore wear the better, "for it has been dearly earned."

When the investigation and labours attendant on such a state of things, shall have ceased;—when Justice shall be satisfied, and our city restored to its wonted tranquility—a succinct account of the whole transactions shall be given to the world. It will bring to view a scheme of wildness and of wickedness, enough to make us smile at the folly, did we not shudder at the indiscriminate mischief of the plan and its objects. Those (they were but few) who at first thought we had no cause for alarm, must be overwhelmed with conviction to the contrary.

But there is another object in view, towards which the intended publication more particularly looks—*The character of our City.* The narrative of these trials will evince to our brethren throughout the Union, that such has been the vigilance of our citizens, that they could not be taken by surprise; and such have been the humanity and diligence of the Court, that although some few guilty may escape, not a single innocent slave shall have suffered.[1]

1. This information was reprinted verbatim in the *Washington Gazette,* August 2, 1822; Salem *Essex Register,* August 9, 1822; and *New-Hampshire Sentinel,* August 10, 1822.

Charleston *Southern Intelligencer*[1]

Saturday, July 27, 1822

Yesterday sentence of death was carried into execution, at the Lines, on 22 coloured persons, condemned for attempting to raise an insurrection in this state.

1. The mention of the existence of the preempted plot in the Charleston *Southern Evangelical Intelligencer* is significant because the newspaper was edited by Congregational minister Benjamin Morgan Palmer and Presbyterian minister George Reid, both of whom had access to at least some of those hanged.

Niles' Weekly Register

Saturday, July 27, 1822

South Carolina. Some particulars of the lately projected insurrection of the blacks at Charleston, have been published. The plan was seemingly well laid and extensive; but discovered just before it was ripe for execution by some that were let into the secret.

Another lot of persons, supposed to be leaders, were sentenced to death—some of them were respited, and the rest executed.

Eight negroes, in all, have been executed at Charleston[1] on account of the late insurrectionary plot, and three, sentenced to death, are respited: about fifty more had been arrested as principal conspirators, (so says a letter from Charleston), and lodged in jail, against many of whom there was sufficient proof for conviction. It appears to have been a very serious affair.

Papers of the 20th instant inform us that sixteen more slaves, (whose names, and of their owners are given), have been found guilty and sentenced to death—to have taken place yesterday. It is added, that "the court still continues assiduously engaged in the trial of others apprehended for the above crime"—of an attempt to raise an insurrection. It appears that those respited as mentioned before, were further respited until yesterday.

Three slaves were also hung on the 19th inst. for shooting at a mail driver, on the Parker's Ferry road.

1. News of the twenty-two men hanged the previous day, July 26, had not yet reached Baltimore. The correct total of those executed by this date was thirty.

Charleston Mercury, and Morning Advertiser

Saturday, July 27, 1822

The black fellow, *Wm. Garner,* for whose apprehension the Governor issued his Proclamation offering a reward of two hundred dollars, has been taken and lodged in Columbia jail, until a guard is obtained for bringing him to Charleston for trial.

The Court of Magistrates and Freeholders convened again yesterday, for the trial of sundry persons of colour, charged with an attempt to raise an insurrection in this State, unanimously found the following guilty, and sentenced them to be hanged on Tuesday, the 30th July, between 6 and 9 o'clock in the morning, on the lines, and their bodies to be delivered to the surgeons for dissection, if requested.

Jack,	belonging	to Mr. Neill McNeill.
Caesar,	do	to Mrs. Smith
Billy,	do	to Mr. P. Robinson
John Vincent,	do	to Mr. D Cruckshanks
Jacob,	do	to Mr. J. Lankester
Tom,	do	to Mr. Scott.

Agrippa Perry, Scipio Simms, Sam, Barnstile and *Denbow Martin*—are sentenced to be imprisoned in the Work-House of Charleston, until their owners, under the direction of the City Council, shall send them out of the United States, into which they are not to return under penalty of death.

Prince Graham has been sentenced to be imprisoned in the Work-House of Charleston, for one month, and then to be transported by sea, out of the State of South-Carolina, the first opportunity, into which he is not to return, under penalty of death.

Execution.—The following Slaves were Executed yesterday morning, pursuant to their sentence, for attempting to raise an insurrection in this State.

Julius, belonging		to Thomas Forrest
Tom,	do	to Mrs. Russell
Joe,	do	to Mr Jore
Mingo,	do	to Wm. Harth, jun.
Smart,	do	to Robert Anderson
Polydore,	do	to Mrs. Faber
Robert, *John,* *Adam,*	do	to John Robertson
Lot,	do	to Mr. Forrester
Jack,	do	to Mrs Purcell
Jack,	do	to Mr. Glen
Pharo,	do	to Mrs. Thompson
Dick,	do	to Mr. William Sims
Bacchus,	do	to Mr. Benjamin Hammett
Jim,	do	to Estate of Clement
Jerry,	do	to Mr. Mordecai Cohen
Naphur, *Adam,* *Bellisle,*	do do do	to Estate of Joseph Yates
Charles,	do	to Mr. John Billings
Dean,	do	to Mr. James Mitchell

The subjoined is a list of those who were also sentenced to Death for the above crime, but the Court recommended to the Governor to commute their sentence to transportation beyond the limits of the United States; the Governor has therefore respited them to the 9th of August next, with the intention ultimately, of agreeing to the recommendation of the Court:

Seymour,	belonging	to Mr. Wm. Kunhardt
Paris,	do	to Miss Ball
Sandy,	do	to Mr. Schnell
Louis,	do	to Mr. Cromwell
Dublin,	do	to Mr. T. Morris
Peter,	do	to estate of Jas. Cooper
Isaac,	do	to Mr. William Harth
George,	do	to Thos. Bampfield

Saby Gaillard, a Free Black Man.

WILLIAM, belonging to Mr. *Job Palmer,* sentenced by the Court to be executed yesterday, has likewise been respited by the Governor until the 9th of August.

MONDAY, belonging to Mr. *John Gell,* CHARLES, belonging to Judge *Drayton,* and HARRY, belonging to Mr. *David Haig,* were sentenced to be executed yesterday, but on account of much important information revealed by them, the Court recommended to the Governor to commute their sentence to transportation. The Executive refused to act according to the recommendation, but informed the Court they had the power themselves to commute the punishment. The Court has, therefore, sentenced the above three Negroes to be transported beyond the limits of the United States, under the direction of the City Council.[1]

1. This information was reprinted nearly verbatim in the *Charleston Courier,* July 27, 1822; Philadelphia *United States Gazette and True American,* July 27, 1822; and Charleston *United States Catholic Miscellany,* July 31, 1822.

Charleston *City Gazette and Commercial Daily Advertiser*

Monday, July 29, 1822

FOR THE CITY GAZETTE.

To the Editor of the Southern Patriot.

SIR—In the remarks you were pleased to make on the subject of Garner's apprehension, you observed that "It was not until Mr. M'Cord[1] . . . received a letter from the Intendant of Charleston on the morning of the 23d July that *information* reached *Columbia* of his guilt, *the Governor's Proclamation not having then arrived.*" The facts which can be fully proved, are, that a description of Garner was furnished on the afternoon of the 19th about 4. o'clock; by 6 the P[r]oclamation was in the hands of the Printers, and appeared on the morning of the 20th in both the morning papers of this city. The mail for Columbia closed at half past 12. Copies of the Proclamation were that day sent by mail, to *Columbia,* Cheraw and Georgetown. Letters from the Governor were also sent to the Editors at these places, inclosing the Proclamation. Now, unless the Post-master *suppressed* these letters, unless he kept back the Charleston papers directed to Columbia, (and he is above any such suspicion) the fact cannot be, that the Proclamation did *not* reach Columbia on the morning of the 23d, the time when the Intendant's letter is said to have reached that place. At 10 o'clock on that very morning, the mail containing all the news papers and two private letters from the Governor, was due at Columbia. If the information of the Editor of the Southern Patriot is not *incorrect,* there must have been a suppression of both public and private communications.

But the vigilance of the Executive is not to be questioned, when such stubborn facts put it beyond cavil.

TRUTH.

1. The lawyer David James McCord (1797–1855), son-in-law of Langdon Cheves (1776–1857), was intendant of Columbia in 1822. McCord received considerable acclaim as a legal scholar, compiling and coediting *Reports of Cases Determined in the Constitutional Court of South Carolina* and *The Statutes at Large of South Carolina.* See "Death of D. J. McCord, Esq.," *Charleston Courier,* May 14, 1855; John Hammond Moore, *Columbia & Richland County: A South Carolina Community, 1740–1990* (Columbia: University of South Carolina Press, 1993), 466.

Charleston Courier

Monday, July 29, 1822

On Saturday, after a most laborious and distressing investigation, the Court of Magistrates and Freeholders, organized for the trial of insurgent slaves, adjourned, and was dissolved. Never was public confidence better deserved, and public gratitude more due, than to the respectable individuals who have on this occasion sacrificed their own personal duties and sensibilities, to the public good. Another Court is to be formed for the trial of WILLIAM GARNER, lately apprehended at Granby.

In addition to the sentences already published, sentence of transportation beyond the limits of the United States, and never to return under penalty of death, was passed upon the following negroes, who have served the Court as witnesses:—

GEORGE, the slave of Mr. Vanderhorst.

BILLY,	do.	Mr. Bulkley.
PEIRAULT,	do.	Mr. Strohecker.
JOHN,	do.	Mr. Enslow.
FRANK,	do.	Mrs. Ferguson.[1]

1. This information was reprinted nearly verbatim in the *Charleston Mercury,* July 29, 1822; Charleston *Southern Patriot, and Commercial Advertiser,* July 27, 1822; and Savannah *Republican,* August 1, 1822.

Charleston Mercury, and Morning Advertiser

Monday, July 29, 1822

. . . The Court adjourned, *sine die,* on Friday, having no further business before them.—They have deserved and they receive the grateful thanks of their fellow citizens for their labours. Their humanity has equalled their justice, and their perseverance was not exceeded by their wisdom. Patient, inquiring and firm in the fulfilment of the duties that have devolved upon them, they have discharged their high trust in the spirit of enlightened gentlemen and conscientious Christians. The stream of justice would never be polluted if it always flowed in the channel to which it would be directed by such a tribunal.

The public spirit and well directed zeal of the Intendant and Council, during the late agitation, call likewise for the thanks of the community. After a whole month's incessant vigilance, they at length have reached a period of comparative repose. May the sweets of their labours be found in the satisfaction that exertions like theirs, happily but seldom required, have secured the safety of the city, and the lasting gratitude of its inhabitants!

William Garner, and any other persons accused of the late designs will be tried by a new Court to be organized.

Philadelphia *National Gazette*

Tuesday, July 30, 1822

The Court of Magistrates and Freeholders sitting in Charleston, South Carolina, have unanimously found guilty and sentenced to death, ten more persons of color charged with an attempt to raise an insurrection in the State.

They have likewise passed sentence of death upon six others, but recommended that the sentence be commuted into one of Transportation. The Court, on the 23d inst. still continued assiduously engaged in the trial of others apprehended for the same crime.

Charleston Courier

Tuesday, July 30, 1822

This Morning between the hours of 6 and 9, o'clock, agreeably to sentence of the Court of Magistrates and Freeholders, *Jack,* the slave of Neill M'Neill; *Caesar,* the slave of Mrs. Smith; *Jacob,* the slave of Mr Lankester; and *Tom,* the slave of Mr. Scott, are to be executed on the Lines, for attempting an insurrection in this state. *Billy,* the slave of Mr. P. Robinson, and *John Vincent,* the slave of Mr. D. Cruckshank[s], who were also sentenced to be executed at the same time, have been respited by His Excellency the Governor, until Friday, 9th August.

We understand that, at the suggestion of the Executive of this State, orders have been issued from the War Department, augmenting the force of the garrisons in this harbor.[1]

1. This information was reprinted nearly verbatim in the *Southern Patriot, and Commercial Advertiser,* July 30, 1822, and *Washington Gazette,* August 5, 1822.

Newport *Rhode-Island Republican*

Wednesday, July 31, 1822

Extract of a letter from a gentleman in Charleston, S.C. to his friend in this town, dated July 13, 1822.

"You will no doubt, have learnt that upwards of fifty of the ringleaders of the late infernal conspiracy against the whites, in this place, have been arrested, and that eleven have been condemned to death, eight of whom have already suffered the sentence of the law. Their plans, although deep and of long standing, have been entirely prostrated, through the very able exertions of Maj. James Hamilton, jun. who possess every requisite for an active and intelligent Intendant, and whose constant anxiety has been to discover the principals concerned in the diabolical plot, which had nearly been carried into effect, and which probably would have cost the lives of a great proportion of the citizens and the total [*illegible*] of property. Maj. Hamilton on the first intimation, constituted a Court of two magistrates and five freeholders, consisting of gentlemen of the first standing in society, for talents, integrity, and independence of character; of which number Col. William Dayton[1] is chief one of the brightest ornaments of the Southern States. I trust that from the vigilance that has been shown on this occasion of general alarm and confusion, that but a short time will be necessary to restore every thing to its former tranquility. At present it is necessary to keep up strong night patrols, or military guard, the most numerous and well disciplined of which is a rifle company[2] commanded by the gallant Maj. Hamilton, who on all occasions, as well as his corps, distinguish themselves."

1. On Judge William Drayton (1776–1846), see Part III, p. 160 n1.

2. Riflemen attached to the 1st Battalion, 17th Regiment, South Carolina Militia, elected James Hamilton Jr. their captain on June 8, 1821. See *Charleston Courier,* June 9, 1821.

Providence *Gazette*

Wednesday, July 31, 1822
NEGRO PLOT.

Sixteen slaves, found guilty of an attempt to raise an insurrection in South-Carolina, were ordered to be executed at Charleston, on the 26th inst. Upwards of fifty more of the principal conspirators are in jail. The National Advocate remarks: "It (the conspiracy) appears to have been of a much more serious nature than was at first anticipated, and would undoubtedly have terminated in much bloodshed, if not the total ruin of property both in town and country; their plans were deep and of long standing, and from the facility the negroes had of obtaining arms and ammunition, but very few whites could have escaped."

Philadelphia *National Gazette and Literary Register*

Wednesday, July 31, 1822

The Negro Plot at Charleston.—A letter from that place, dated the 19th inst. gives the following particulars.

"A negro belonging to Col. Prioleau, who was solicited to join the gang, declined, and consulted a friend named Pencell, who advised him to give information thereof to his owners. He did so, and the proper authorities took measures accordingly.

"Their plan appears to have been well digested. They intended to have provided themselves with passes, so as to deceive the guard, and place themselves at certain parts of the city; then a party was to secure the guard at the guard house, and an indiscriminate massacre was to commence on all whites who appeared in the streets, and particularly to prevent any company to form; also to prevent the bells to ring to give any alarm.

"It appears that this was in agitation for a considerable length of time. They formed themselves into a society, and held meetings at a farm that they could approach by water, to avoid being stopped by any patroles, which farm is situated near the fork of the road, on the Meeting street side.[1] Religion and superstition were used by the more cunning to delude the incredulous Africans in the plot.—Gullah Jack was considered invincible; he could not be hurt nor killed by any means whatever, but a blow from him would be instant execution. At one of these meetings they had a fowl dressed and put on the table—Gullah Jack performed some ceremony of witchcraft over it, when he was done an instant scrabble was made for the fowl, every one trying to get a piece; then says Jack, 'do so we pull the buckra to pieces.' But poor Jack has been hung, and satisfied his companions that he could be killed; indeed he showed great fears of death under the gallows."

1. On the attractiveness of Bulkley's farm as a gathering spot for the rebels, see Part II, p. 192 n3. This information on the plot was reprinted verbatim in the *National Gazette and Literary Register,* July 31, 1822; Boston *Commercial Gazette,* August 1, 1822; *Independent Chronicle and Boston Patriot,* August 2, 1822; Salem *Gazette,* August 2, 1822; *Albany Argus,* August 2, 1822; Newport *Mercury,* August 3, 1822; *Providence Patriot,* August 3, 1822; Boston *Recorder,* August 3, 1822; *Baltimore Patriot & Mercantile Advertiser,* August 5, 1822; *Hartford Courant,* August 6, 1822; and London *Times,* August 26, 1822.

Salem *Essex Register*

Wednesday, July 31, 1822

Execution of Slaves.

It has already been mentioned, that an extensive plot among the Slaves at Charleston, South Carolina, to raise an insurrection in that State, and massacre their masters, had been discovered, and a Court of Magistrates and Freeholders organized for the trial of the negroes concerned in the plot, many of whom had been arrested. This Court proceeded in the execution of its duties with the utmost rigor. Ten or twelve of the ringleaders were immediately put upon trial, found guilty, sentence of DEATH pronounced, and the sentence EXECUTED upon several of them without delay. By the last Charleston papers, we are informed, that SIXTEEN more were pronounced guilty, and ordered for execution on the 26th inst. Three others who had been previously sentenced and respited, were likewise to be executed on the same day. The Court was assiduously engaged in the trial of other negroes apprehended for the same crime. It is said there are upwards of fifty still in confinement. Most of these will no doubt be strung up with little ceremony, and thus Charleston is getting rid of her black population without the aid of the Colonization Society. Charleston was in the utmost state of alarm, on the discovery of the plot; and the militia of the city were constantly under arms for patrole duty.[1]

1. This information was reprinted nearly verbatim in the *New-York Commercial Advertiser*, July 27, 1822, and *Pittsfield* (Massachusetts) *Sun*, August 7, 1822.

Philadelphia *Democratic Press*

Wednesday, July 31, 1822

Some interesting particulars of the *Negro Plot* will be found in our paper of this day. Sixteen more negroes are sentenced to death, from seventy to eighty others are in prison, and there are a number yet to be arrested, so soon as there shall be prison room.—When we think of the murder and violence and destruction of property which those deluded wretches might have committed, we cannot but be grateful to the negro who gave the information. We do not doubt but his reward will be commensurate to the services he has rendered. While we shudder at the scenes which might have been acted, and contemplate its origin and progress *in a society,* we cannot but hope that our Southern fellow citizens, will hereafter be permitted to manage their own concerns in their own way. They have as much humanity and intellect and more experience on this sebject, than the people of the non-slave holding states can be supposed to have.

Charleston *City Gazette and Commercial Daily Advertiser*

Wednesday, July 31, 1822

It appears by the Patriot of Monday, that the statement made by the Editor, that the Governor's Proclamation, (a paper in the ordinary official form) did not reach Columbia on the 23d, was an "inference," inadvertently drawn by his informant, from a correspondence, and is now admitted to have been erroneous. If it had been correct, the omission of the Governor to use the earliest means of being auxiliary to the administration of justice in so important a case, might well have incurred censure. A statement of facts proving the error was accordingly made. The object of my first communication is thus accomplished.

The gentleman who gave the information has stated both the cause of the error in his first inference, and his object in making it public thro' the Patriot. After this, it would indeed be idle in me to "catch at straws." Should any one desire a "*private conference,*" there is no impediment, as my address was originally with you, where it remains at the service of any gentleman.

TRUTH.

Charleston Mercury, and Morning Advertiser

Wednesday, July 31, 1822

The following slaves were hanged yesterday morning, agreeably to the sentence of the Court adjudging them to suffer death for their attempt to excite an insurrection in this state.

Jack, belonging to Mr. Neill M'Neill.

Jacob,	do	to Mr. Lankester.
Tom,	do	to Mr. Scott.
Caesar, do		to Mrs. Smith.

Billy, belonging to Mr. P. Robinson, and *John Vincent,* belonging to Mr. D. Cruckshank's, have been respited by his Excellency the Governor, until Friday the 9th of August.

We understand that a new Court of Magistrates and Freeholders will be formed to-day, for the purpose of proceeding in the investigation of the late criminal plot of certai[n] blacks in this city.

Genius of Universal Emancipation

August (Monthly) 1822

CONSPIRACY.

A great sensation has been produced in South Carolina, respecting the conspiracy among the slaves, mentioned in a letter from a gentleman in Charleston to his friend in New York, an extract from which was inserted in the last number of this paper. Many of the miserable creatures have paid the forfeit of their lives. Between 30 and 40 were hung, and as many banished to places beyond the limits of the United States.

The governor of that State has published a lengthy account of the proceedings that took place upon the occasion, which will be noticed in a future period. Some further remarks will also be made upon the subject, probably in the next number.

Baltimore Patriot & Mercantile Advertiser

Thursday, August 1, 1822

The Ex-Governor of East Florida, Col. W. G. D. Worthington[1] and family came passengers in the brig Agent, arrived at this port of Sunday from Charleston. Col. W. left St. Augustine on the 10th inst. in the sch[oone]r. Hero, and stopped in Charleston. The city of St. Augustine enjoyed good health, and there was no apprehension of sickness this season. The city of Charleston was unusually healthy. The Court of Justices and Freeholders were calmly and assiduously progressing in their enquiries respecting the late conspiracy of the people of colour—the plot was fully in possession of the court, and the conspiracy completely annihilated. There would be some further executions, and most likely many involved in a less atrocious degree, would be deported to some distant place of prolonged punishment, not reaching the lives of the culprits—the court were composed of men of the first respectability, who sifted the evidence, and were perhaps, more lenient to the accused than any Jury they could have selected. . . .

1. In 1821 President James Monroe appointed the Maryland-born William Grafton Delaney Worthington IV (1785–1856) governor and secretary of the Territory of East Florida.

Boston *Commercial Gazette*

Thursday, August 1, 1822

Nineteen Slaves were to be executed at Charleston, S.C. on the 26th inst. as being concerned in the late plot.[1]

1. Twenty-two bondmen, not nineteen, were executed on July 26, 1822.

Boston *New-England Galaxy*

Friday, August 2, 1822

AN INSTITUTION FOR ABOLISHING SLAVERY, is now in operation in Charleston, S.C. which bids fair to supersede the necessity of all other Abolition Societies, Colonization Societies, &c. It is called the *Court of Magistrates and Freeholders,* and so *rapid* as well as *certain* are the remedies it proposes, that only a very few seconds of time are necessary to transport the poor negroes from a state of oppression and ignominy to that country where *the small and great are, and the slave is free from his master.*[1]

1. The author appears to be alluding to Shakespeare's characterization of death as "the undiscovered country" (*Hamlet,* act 3, scene 1). This information was reprinted verbatim in the Salem *Gazette,* August 9, 1822.

Richmond *Enquirer*

Friday, August 2, 1822

South Carolina has been compelled to resort to the policy which was forced upon Virginia in 1800. For 22 years we have found it effectual: we trust the example will be equally awful in S. Carolina.[1]

On the 26th July, 22 of the miserable wretches were executed at Charleston. Others have been respited. Some who were less guilty than the rest will exported.—The plan of the insurrection was perhaps wilder in its means and more desolating in its objects than it was in Virginia. Let humanity weep as much as it pleases over such scenes, they are unfortunately inevitable. The elements of our Society are so made up that we must provide against fatal explosions. We must take care, that all the traces of refinement shall not be swept away—that our fair fields shall not be sprinkled with blood; and a howling ignorance shall not usurp the place of the means of civilization. The law of necessity must be applied by judicious legislators and merciful magistrates until some remedy shall be provided for the evils by which we are cursed.

1. This is a reference to the twenty-six slaves hanged in or near Richmond, Virginia, during the fall of 1800 for complicity in Gabriel's conspiracy. On the number of slaves hanged in Virginia, see Douglas R. Egerton, *Gabriel's Rebellion: The Virginia Slave Conspiracies of 1800 and 1802* (Chapel Hill: University of North Carolina Press, 1993), 186–88. This information was reprinted verbatim in the Charleston *Southern Patriot, and Commercial Advertiser,* August 7, 1822.

Washington *Daily National Intelligencer*

Friday, August 2, 1822

On Friday last the 26th ultimo, *twenty-two* Slaves were to be executed in Charleston for being concerned in the late conspiracy among that population; ten others having been respited, and three ordered for transportation instead of death. These persons have been tried and convicted before a high court, and will suffer the punishment which the law decrees against those who conspire against the lives of others. The newspapers furnish no particulars, and it is probable that the safety of the community requires that they should not. We cannot repress, however, the rising doubt whether these extensive sanguinary punishments are *politic*. We suggest the doubt merely, without assigning the grounds of it.

New-York Commercial Advertiser

Saturday, August 3, 1822

"*Charleston, July* 20, 1822.

"Dear Sir—Our authorities are indefatigable in the public good. In addition to the fifteen condemned in Friday's paper, (19th July) there are from ten to fifteen more, against whom there is strong proof; and fifty or sixty others, who are all more or less implicated" (In addition to the above, we have been furnished with the names of the highly respectable gentlemen comprising the Court of Magistrates and Freeholders.)

Col. William Drayton,
Robert Trumbull, Esq.
J. R. Pringle,
Messrs Legard & Hayward,
L. H. Kennedy, and
Thos. Parker, Magistrates.

Charleston Mercury, and Morning Advertiser

Saturday, August 3, 1822

A new Court has been constituted for the trial of such persons of colour as have been engaged in the late plots to raise a disturbance in this State. The following Gentlemen compose the Court:

Hon. JOEL R. POINSETT,
ROBERT Y. HAYNE,
THOMAS RHETT SMITH,
THOMAS ROPER,
JOHN GORDON, } *Freeholders.*
JACOB AXSON,
CHARLES B. FURMAN, } *Magistrates.*

The trial of the black fellow *William Garner,* implicated in the attempt to excite an insurrection, will commence this day. Garner was brought to town yesterday morning.

Charleston Courier

Saturday, August 3, 1822

WILLIAM GARNER, for whom a reward of Two Hundred Dollars was offered by His Excellency Gov. BENNETT, was brought to town yesterday morning, from Columbia.—He is to take his trial this day, before the new Court of Magistrates and Freeholders.

Providence *Gazette*

Saturday, August 3, 1822

Ten more slaves have been sentenced to death, at Charleston, for being concerned in the late conspiracy, and were to be executed on the 26th ult. Five others and a free black man have been sentenced to transportation beyond the limits of the United States. The Court is still engaged in the trial of others apprehended for the above crime.

New Bern (NC) *Carolina Centinel*

Saturday, August 3, 1822

Three negroes were lately sentenced to be hung at Jacksonborough, S.C. for having fired at the mail driver on the Parker's Ferry Road.

The Insurrection.—SIXTEEN more slaves charged with an attempt to raise an insurrection in the state of South Carolina, have been found guilty and sentenced to be hung on the 26th ult. at Charleston. The court still continues engaged in the trial of others apprehended for the above crime.

New-York Commercial Advertiser

Saturday, August 3, 1822

"Charleston, dated July 14, 1822

"You will no doubt hear a variety of reports relative to the unfortunate situation of affairs here, as the daily arrests continue, and it is difficult to say what number of the deluded wretches may yet be taken up. There was certainly considerable cause for alarm, and had not the most active measures been adopted, the consequence, both as to life and property, must have been serious. Too much praise cannot be paid to the vigilance and firmness of Major James Hamilton, Jun. the Intendent of the city, who upon the first discovery of the infernal plot, secured the conspirators, and instituted a Court of Magistrates and Freeholders, consisting of seven of the most respectable gentlemen in the state, and possessing every qualification as eminent lawyers, intelligent men, and in whom there is not an individual in the city but places the most implicit confidence, both as to their sound judgment and decisions. The Court have had a most painful and laborious investigation, and it is hoped that they may soon get through the trials, and that we shall be restored to our former quiet, and peaceful situation. No disposition to mutiny has been shown in the country."

Charleston Mercury, and Morning Advertiser

Monday, August 5, 1822

Sentence of death was passed on Saturday, upon *William Garner*, by the Court of Magistrates and Freeholders assembled for the trial of persons of colour engaged in the late attempt to raise disturbances in this state. He is to be executed on Friday next.[1]

1. This information was repeated nearly verbatim in the Charleston *City Gazette and Commercial Daily Advertiser*, August 4, 1822, and the *Charleston Courier*, August 5, 1822.

Boston *Commercial Gazette*

Monday, August 5, 1822

The discovery of the black insurrection in S. Carolina was indeed most providential and fortunate; for it appears their arrangements were so extensive, that but for the timely disclosure, the whole of that State would, in a few days, have presented the horrid spectacle once witnessed in St. Domingo.—And had the first movement in Charleston been successful, it would probably have been the signal for a general massacre through the slave states. We believe it was Randolph who once said, in debate, that "never does the night bell ring the alarm of fire, but the mother hugs her infant closer to her bosom." If such was the feeling of apprehension and disquietude years ago, what must it be now?

Jacob Rapelye[1] to Paul Rapelye, Monday, August 5, 1822

. . . I have nothing very new to communicate except a contemplated negro plot to rise & murder the whites in this City on the 3 July which was, fortunately discovered in time to prevent any bad consequences—about 200 have been arrested & are now waiting their trial, The Court have condem'd 48 & the Same have been executed, by hanging[2] among them Mrs Anderson's negro man Smart was one—. . .

1. Jacob Rapelye (1788–1867), an auctioneer, resided in 1822 on 38 Broad Street. See *CSCCD*, 95.

2. Rapelye's total for those executed exceeds the actual number, which is thirty-five. Smart Anderson was one of the twenty-two men executed on July 26.

ALS in Napier, Rapelye, and Bennett Manuscripts, SCL.

Harriott Pinckney Rutledge[1] to Edward C. Rutledge, Monday, August 5, 1822

. . . We have had occurrences here lately of a most unpleasant nature About the end of June many reports were circulated of an insurrection of the negroes but from our former security few persons credited what appeared so wild a tale, It soon proved fatally true A servant belonging to Col[l] Prioleau[2] informed his master that on the following 4th of July a party of Blacks were to set fire to the central parts and outskirts of the city, which should be the signal for a general revolt of the negroes and when the whites should rush from their houses to fire on them, & then, (to use their own words) "make a desperate struggle to recover their rights" Col Prioleau's servant had been tampered with, by the chief Conspirator—who told him that by cutting his Master's throat he would acquire liberty & wealth—The faithful negro declared he would rather cut his own and immediately disclosed to his master all he knew of the conspiracy, which Col Prioleau communicated to the Governor & City Council—Proper Measures were taken, the six ringleaders were secured tried & convicted of an attempt to raise an insurrection in the State. They were executed without confessing their guilt Their deluded followers, deprived of the support of these daring master spirits of the plot, fell without resistance into the hands of Justice & made a full confession of their guilt 38 have been hung [*illegible*] sentenced to transportation to the Brazilian mines. Poor wretches! When we consider that they feel slavery to be a state of degradation, can we wonder that they should endeavour to shake off the yoke? Their plan was a well laid one but unhappily for them they did not understand that their total ignorance of the arts of war & their scanty provision of arms & ammunition rendered victory on their side impossible—The ringleaders have had this attempt in contemplation for 9 years, & a great part of the mischief is attributable to the Northern Clergymen, who have distributed incendiary pamphlets among them & as they cannot all read have kindly given them oral instruction on the subject. Do you remember Mr. Sitgreaves[3] & I have no patience when I think of him, or any of his *busy interfering* Bretheren—These sapient observers of the Northern States talk largely of universal emancipation, without being aware that an immense body of people without education, without morals, or the arts of civilized life would form a most disorganized society—They would no more cultivate the fields for themselves than for us of their own accord and as the country affords no spontaneous produce they would rob or murder one another or die of famine—Slavery is certainly an evil entailed on us by our British ancestors but as no remedy can be devised, that would not be worse than the evil, we had better let the matter rest as it is. But this our kind and Conscientious Bretheren of the North have not been disposed to do—they have made known to our Negroes that life & liberty are the natural rights of Man. With this idea & without the Consciousness where one man would [*illegible*] his freedom—ten or twenty would abuse, they have rallied round a standard of rebellion "& grievous had their agitation been." Yet after all we must come to Sir Roger de Coverly's[4] conclusion that much may be laid on both sides of the question. It is indeed an unhappy state of society when we must close our eyes on the right to decree the expedient for it has been ascertained that their frequent meetings on pretense of religious meeting have been for the purpose of planning this horrible scheme. Hence has arrived an important question concerning the propriety of giving them Religious instruction; and perhaps a more dificult one never arose in a Protestant land. We have no right to deprive them of it. "*What I say unto you, I say unto all,*" from the highest, most sacred authority; forbids it and the Christian's own heart revolts at such a scheme of policy. . . .

1. Harriott Pinckney Rutledge (1780–1858) was the mother of Edward Cotesworth Rutledge (1798–1860), who was serving in the United States Navy at the time. Harriott was in Charleston; Edward was in Paris.

2. John Cordes Prioleau owned the slave Peter Prioleau (Desverney). See "Report of the Committee on Military and Pensions on the Petition of Peter Desverny a Free Person of Color Praying for an Increased Pension," November 30, 1857, SCDAH, item 1, series S165005.

3. Samuel Sitgreaves Jr. (1798–1830) was an antislavery Episcopal clergyman from Pennsylvania and son of a Federalist congressman. Sitgreaves visited Charleston and its environs in 1821 and 1822, conversing on slavery and other hot-button political issues with a number of South Carolinian notables, including William Heyward and Charles Cotesworth Pinckney. See P. J. Staudenhaus, "Letters from South Carolina, 1821–1822," *SCHGM* 58 (1957): 209–17.

4. She refers to the words from a fictional character in a popular English daily, *The Spectator*, published in 1711–1712 and subsequently collected in many editions.

Pinckney Family Papers, SCHS.

Independent Chronicle and Boston Patriot

Tuesday, August 6, 1822

The Negro plot recently detected in Charleston, (S.C.) has produced a general alarm in that State. The Democratic Press states, on the authority of information from Charleston, that, in consequence of the plot, a law will be proposed and probably passed at the next session of the Legislature of South Carolina, prohibiting any slave or colored person from being taken out of the state to any of the non-slave-holding states, or any colored person from any of those states from residing in South Carolina.

Philadelphia *National Gazette and Literary Register*

Tuesday, August 6, 1822

The Charleston papers of the 30th ult. state, that at the suggestion of the Executive of South Carolina, orders have been issued from the War Department, augmenting the forces of the garrison in the harbour. "We daily expect," says the editor of the City Gazette, "these forces to arrive, which will fully and completely man our sea-board."

Martha Proctor Richardson to Dr. James Screven, Wednesday, August 7, 1822

. . . Charleston has undergone a dreadful state of things—in my last[1] I gave you an account of what had come to our knowledge of this intended insurrection—it proves to be much more extensive than was at first suspected—Six of the insurgents had suffered when I wrote last—since then, 26 have been hung—and many ordered for transportation out of the limits of the United States—not to return on pain of death—the first court which sat five weeks, had retired from the painful duty—& a new one instituted—they are still going on with trials—The Mail carrier had been fired on in the neigh[bor]hood of Parkers ferry by 4 Negroes—Three of them were executed[2]—we are now fearful some accident has occurred—as it is stated in the papers that the Mail Carrier was pursued by the armed negroes on Tuesday last, near Saltcatcher—since Wednesday we have had no mail from Charleston, this is Sunday—there may be other reasons—such as bad roads—sickness &c., but [*illegible*] always dread the worst that may happen—one white man was found aiding & abetting the Negroes—he has been a pirate[3]—Judge Johnson has published his vindication[4]—but it is very lame—in my poor opinion I should pronounce the writer humbled—at any rate it was too serious a business for jesting—and at his age evinced a degree of levity which takes from the character of a person in his dignified station—We cannot put any other motive on his conduct, than a vanity to appear more wise & resolute than his neighbors—but he should have reflected that strong nerves do not belong to everyone—any more than rectitude & dignity of conduct—the Negroes too who were first convicted belonged to his Brother in law Bennet[5]—therefore delicacy should have kept him silent—It is impossible for me to give a correct account of the proceedings in Charleston—every thing has been kept a profound secret—for reasons which will occur to every one—still enough has transpired to convince us that they had too much cause for alarm—for four years has this business been in agitation—still so secret were they—and prudent also—that no suspicion from their conduct could be entertained—you may judge of their secrecy by what I am going to relate—two negroes belonging to the same Master—both working in the same mill—were ignorant that either was ingaged in the plot until they met in jail—when the constables went into Mr. Horry's yard to take up his Waiting man[6]—he assured them they were mistaken, he could answer for his innocence—he would as soon suspect himself—he accompanied him on his trial convinced still he could not be guilty—on hearing the evidence—he turned round to his Man—tell me, are you guilty for I cannot believe unless I hear you say so—yes replied the negro—what were your intentions?—to kill you, rip open your belly & throw your guts in your face—It is said they were true [*illegible*]—not a single Woman knew a word of their plans In the course of time—the whole proceedings will be published—[*illegible*] told—our [*illegible*] are prepared for an account of the wildest plans engendered by religious enthusiasm—and a [w]rong conception of the Bible—so true it is, "a little learning is a dangerous thing"—I am very fearful this business will not rest here, however we may hope it—and dreadful must be the state of the city [*illegible*] all confidence is lost in our servants—it is to be regretted that almost in every instance, the condemned slaves belonged to the most humane & indulgent owners—some plan must be adopted to subdue them—however repugnant to the feelings—their situation when compared with the poor of other countries was certainly happy—they are clothed, fed & taken care of when sick—and I may venture to say the house servants are not half-worked—had they been more employed—they would have wanted time to plan mischief—I hope the Laws will now force every family to keep but a certain number about them—and oblige all useless ones to be sent into the country—Huxters—day labourers—draymen & all that useless class of Servants—who are only a tax to their owners & a nuisance to the City—I intended to have spent the Summer in the upper country, but circumstances combined with this Charleston business has induced me to remain where I am. . . .

1. See letter of July 6, 1822, reprinted above in this section on p. 382. Richardson is writing from Savannah, Georgia.

2. See *Charleston Courier,* July 17, 1822, reproduced on p. 396 in Part IV.

3. Reference to a pirate who might be recruited to lead an insurrection of Charleston's slaves surfaced in the testimony against William Allen, one of four white men convicted for involvement in the Vesey affair. The *OR,* appendix, iv, notes that the pirate "was known in this city. He was certainly well qualified on the score of courage and talent, for any desperate enterprise; no reason exists, however, to suppose that he would have engaged in one of a criminal nature."

4. [William Johnson Jr.,] *To the Public of Charleston* (Charleston, SC, 1822), excerpted on pp. 137–44 in Part II.

5. Supreme Court Justice William Johnson Jr. married Sarah Bennett (b. 1777), the sister of Governor Thomas Bennett Jr., in 1794. See Craig Miller Bennett, "Family Records of Governor Thomas Bennett Jr." *SCHGM* 51 (1950): 51; Donald G. Morgan, *Justice William Johnson, The First Dissenter: The Career and Constitutional Philosophy of a Jeffersonian Judge* (Columbia: University of South Carolina Press, 1954), 24.

6. The slave coachman John was owned by Elias Horry (1773–1834), one of the wealthiest planters and biggest slaveholders in lowcountry South Carolina.

ALS in Arnold and Screven Papers, SHC, UNC.

Mary Lamboll Beach to Elizabeth Gilchrist, Thursday, August 8, 1822

. . . Through the mercy of God we are all well except Mary who has been very disordered in her stomach too almost exactly as you described yours to have been but she is better now. I hope my dear Sister you have got in a more comfortable state of mind about the state of our affairs here as bad as they *have been*; I trust & *believe* they are not *now* in that state to warrant your fears & anxieties awakened by them & your tenderness for as to destroy your peace Oh! do not indulge such apprehensions; I assure you it is far from being *our* state or experience—& I do not believe me say so merely to quiet you or to put the best gloss on it. With regard to *present* danger I trust by the blessing of God the plans of these deluded creatures are frustrated for a while; some say for 20 & others for 50 years *this,* no one can say, nor do I believe it will be in this age of revolutions as long;

yet I trust that as we have already experienced such a deliverance it has been in answer to the prayers of faith that have been offered up by the people of God here, & who although but few in comparison of the rest of the inhabitants yet have the promise of God to rest on still. Wm Garner[1] for whom $200 reward was offered by the Govr was apprehended near Columbia & is to be hanged to morrow a new Court had to be organized for his trial, as the others declined but not in displeasure to serve any longer; indeed J. Legare gave up serving a fortnight before they did; from the state of his health as he said—& Henry Deas served in his stead. the new Court—are, Poinset, R. Hayne, Gordon, Col Roper, I forget the other one the freeholders, Axon, & Winthop I believe are the Magistrates as the freeholders will not have the trading Magistrates. Kenedy & T. Parker were the Magistrates in the other Court.[2] I understood 3 or 4 days ago that it was hoped or expected no more after Garner would be hung but if others were taken up & found guilty they would be transported as it was thought the *ring leaders were* already hung & the less of death as a punishment the better. And indeed such is the wretched constitution of our vile fallen nature that both black & white are getting familiarized for the Tuesday after the 22 were hung (3 or 4 more were) & actually unless among the immediate friends of them it excited no more sensation in the City than any common event that is in public expression I mean for no doubt many thought of them & prayed for them too—but after the fearful number of 22—4 or 5 more did not carry weight with it—& indeed I felt worse about the first execution I think than I have done since except the night of the 25th for a little while. . . .

1. William Garner belonged to Martha R. Garner (d. 1832) and was the only slave sentenced to death by the second court. In petitioning for compensation, Martha described William "as a Slave [who] had not only been unimpeachable, but highly meritorious" in his conduct prior to his arrest. She had been a woman "in very slender circumstances" who relied on William for support. She appraised his value at the considerable sum of fifteen hundred dollars. It appears that William was indeed an enterprising soul. He worked primarily for Andrew Milne (1783–1857), an affluent merchant who in 1822 operated his business at 66½ East Bay Street and resided on Stoll's Alley. Before 1822, William had accumulated sufficient capital to run a carting business with multiple rigs almost on his own and had worked out a deal with Milne to purchase his enslaved wife and child from another white man so that William might eventually buy them from Milne. See Martha R. Garner, "Petition for compensation for a slave executed for involvement in the Charleston slave conspiracy," n.d., on pp. 534–35 in Part V of this volume; "Death of Andrew Milne," *Charleston Mercury,* December 4, 1857; *CSCCD,* 91.

2. Henry Deas (1770–1846) replaced James Legaré (1762–1830) on the first court after July 13. Beach correctly identifies four of the five freeholders on the second court: Joel Roberts Poinsett (1779–1851), Robert Young Hayne (1791–1839), John Gordon (d. 1835), and Thomas Roper (1760–1829), leaving out only Thomas Rhett Smith (1768–1829). The magistrates were Jacob Axson Jr. (not Axon, 1794–1843) and Charles M. Furman (1797–1870), not attorney Augustus Winthrop (1797–1844).

ALS in Beach Papers, SCHS.

Philadelphia *Democratic Press*

Thursday, August 8, 1822

The articles which we to-day publish from the Charleston papers, are of a most unpleasant aspect. We infer from them that the extent of the NEGRO PLOT, is now only developing itself; and that it was much greater and even more atrocious than had been apprehended. After more than fifty have been executed and the court dissolved, we learn that *another* court is organized, that "several *new* and important cases have arisen," and that at the request of the Governor of South Carolina a reinforcement of the United States troops are sent to Charleston. We look with great anxiety to a complete official exposition of the plot, its discovery, and the facts disclosed on the trial of some of the most active of the conspirators.

Salem *Essex Register*

Friday, August 9, 1822

Twenty-two of the Slaves condemned to death for plotting an insurrection at Charleston, S.C. were executed pm the 26th ult. in pursuance of their sentence. Ten others, sentenced to be executed at the same time, were respited by the governor until the 9th of August.

Charleston Mercury, and Morning Advertiser

Friday, August 9, 1822

The Court of Magistrates and Freeholders, which was formed on Saturday last, for the trial of certain slaves and others, accused of attempting to excite an Insurrection in this State, adjourned yesterday *sine die*, having disposed of all the cases which remained for trial.

The following is the result of the proceedings of the Court—viz:

William Garner, the slave of Mrs. Garner. Guilty—*Death.*

Pompey, the slave of Mr. Lord. Guilty—*Transportation.*

Nero, the slave of David Haig. Guilty—*Transportation.*

Henry, the slave of Henry Butler. Guilty—*Transportation.*

George, the slave of James Evans. Guilty—*Transportation.*

George, the slave of Samuel Parker. Guilty—*Transportation.*

Jack, the slave of William Cattell. Guilty—*Transportation.*

Adam, (otherwise called *Bellamy*) the slave of James H. Merritt. Guilty—*Transportation.*

The following prisoners were found *Not Guilty*, and discharged, the testimony against them not being deemed sufficiently strong to warrant their conviction:

Philander Michau, a free man of colour.

Pompey, the slave of David Haig.

Stephen, the slave of Thomas Walker.

James, the slave of Thomas Walker.

Harry, the slave of Jesse Nell.

Edward Johnson, a free man of colour.

William Garner, slave of MRS. GARNER, and *William,* slave of MR. PALMER,[1] stand over for execution *This Morning* on the lines, between the hours of 6 and 9 o'clock.

John Vincent and *Billy Robinson,* who were erroneously stated to be respited until Tuesday the 9th August, were originally respited, by the Governor, until the 13th inst.

1. Job Palmer (1747–1845), father of the Reverend Benjamin Morgan Palmer the elder (1781–1847) and owner of Billy Palmer, served as deacon in Charleston's Independent or Circular Church. See George Howe, *History of the Presbyterian Church in South Carolina,* 2 vols. (Columbia, SC, 1870–1883), vol. 2: 585. This information was reprinted nearly verbatim in the Philadelphia *National Gazette and Literary Register,* August 12, 1822; Washington *Daily National Intelligencer,* August 12, 1822; and Richmond *Enquirer,* August 13, 1822.

Charleston Mercury, and Morning Advertiser

Saturday, August 10, 1822

William Garner, was hanged yesterday morning, agreeably to the sentence passed upon him by the court for plotting an insurrection in this State. A respite has been extended to *William,* the property of Mr. Palmer.

New-Hampshire Sentinel

Saturday, August 10, 1822

Charleston, July 27. Yesterday morning *twenty-two* black culprits, were executed here for attempts to excite the late insurrection in this city and state. Six other slaves were found guilty yesterday, of the same crime and sentenced to be hung on the 30th inst. Five were also sentenced to be sent out of the United States. The Governor having refused to commute the punishment of death to that of transportation, as prayed for by three culprits; they were among the number executed yesterday. . . .

The discovery of the late insurrection in Charleston, S.C. is represented to have been very providential and fortunate, as it has been ascertained that arrangements were so extensive that but for the timely disclosure, the whole State would in a few days have presented the horrid spectacle once witnessed in St. Domingo.

Joel Roberts Poinsett to James Monroe, Tuesday, August 13, 1822

. . . Our City is again restored to order and tranquillity and the trials of the miserable deluded conspirators are over. The description of the Missouri question at Washington, among other evils, produced this plot.[1] It was considered by this unfortunate half instructed people as one of emancipation. . . .

1. On the question of the resonance of the Missouri debate among the plotters, see Part III, p. 214 n4.

ALS in James Monroe Papers, series 1, reel 8, LC.

Figure 29. Joel Roberts Poinsett (1779–1851), judge on the Second Court of Magistrates and Freeholders. From a photograph of a portrait, ca. 1837. Courtesy of the Frick Art Reference Library.

Charleston Mercury, and Morning Advertiser

Tuesday, August 13, 1822

John Vincent and *Billy Robinson,* who had been respited by His Excellency the Governor unto this day, have received a further respite until the 25th October, with a view to the commutation of their punishment to Transportation beyond the limits of the United States.[1]

1. Both John Vincent, a member of the African Church and a slave of Daniel Cruckshanks, and Billy Robinson, a porter and a slave of Philip Robinson, were transported. This information was reprinted verbatim in the *Southern Patriot, and Commercial Advertiser,* August 13, 1822, and the *Charleston Courier,* August 13, 1822.

Robert Maxwell to Nathaniel G. Maxwell, Tuesday, August 13, 1822[1]

. . . You will have seen by the public prints that we were threatened with Domestic insurrection, an extensive league had been arranging by some of the leading and better informed blacks (almost all Slaves) for some Years—and when the crisis had nearly arrived when it was intended to explode it was revealed almost by mere accident—Those most deeply concerned were arrested. Some gave information of the parties concerned & their disigns—which evidently went to the use of Arms and taking the lives of their masters and employers. Two courts were successively organized for their tryal consisting of the most respectable and intelligent Citizens—Upwards of 30 were found Guilty sentenced to Death and the sentence carried into execution—some have been respited to the last of October who it is probable with some others less deeply engaged than those who have suffered will be sent out of the United States—I consider all cause of apprehension now & for some time to be removed—the severity which has been applied and the thorough knowledge of their plans will prevent for a time a similar attempt—but as their condition has been greatly ameliorated in every respect they have progressed generally in religious & other instruction—Keeping pace in some degree with the march in other countries and with the age—We cannot expect things will go on to an extended period without change. And in my opinion they will do wisely who calculate & regulate themselves by this view.—Remove the Evil of being at the Entire disposal of another and I do not hesitate to say the lot of the majority of slaves in this state is more tolerable and much easier as to *body & mind* than that of the lower classes Elsewhere—Our laws as regards this people it is likely will undergo a revission and be rendered better adapted to the present state of things—and then carried more strictly into execution. of late years there has been great laxity in their enforcement and too many worthless slaves have been suffered to be brought here from the north and disposed of by—their more worthless Dealers and Traffickers:—Providence has kindly vouchsafed its protection so far & will it is to be hoped continue it. . . .

1. Robert Maxwell, a Charleston merchant, residing at 15 Meeting Street, was writing to Nathaniel (d. 1827), who was in Baltimore.

ALS in Redwood Collection, Maryland Historical Society.

Gettysburg (PA) *Adams Centinel*

Wednesday, August 14, 1822

The Charleston City Gazette announces, that when the trial of the blacks, for attempting insurrection, shall have been completed, and tranquility restored, "a succinct account of the whole transaction shall be given to the world. It will bring to view a scene of wildness and wickedness, enough to make us smile at the folly, did we not shudder at the indiscriminate mischief of the plan and its objects."

Charleston *Southern Patriot, and Commercial Advertiser*

Wednesday, August 14, 1822

CITY COUNCIL,

August 13th, 1822.

The Corporation are much gratified in being able to inform their Fellow Citizens that their irksome labors, in relation to the investigation of the causes of the late public disturbance among our colored population, are comparatively at an end, by a result the most satisfactory, arising from a belief that whilst these causes have been most effectually explored, the primary agents in this criminal commotion have expiated their crimes by the most exemplary punishments.

In the course of a few days the Corporation will submit to the public a full statement of the late transactions, which have been so interesting to our community.

By order of Council.

J. HAMILTON, Jun.
Intendant.[1]

1. This information appeared verbatim in the Charleston *City Gazette and Commercial Daily Advertiser,* August 15, 1822, and as part of the much larger report in the *Charleston Mercury, and Morning Advertiser,* August 15, 1822.

Providence Patriot

Wednesday, August 14, 1822

Four more slaves, concerned in the late Insurrection, were executed at Charleston, S.C. on the morning of the 30th ult.[1] A new Court of Investigation had been called—as "several new and important cases had arisen." The Courier states, that orders had been issued from the War Department, at the suggestion of the Executive of S. Carolina, augmenting the force of the garrison in Charleston harbor.

1. The slaves hanged on Tuesday, July 30 were Jack McNeill, Caesar Smith, Jacob Stagg, and Tom Scott. This information appeared verbatim in the Boston *Commercial Gazette,* August 12, 1822.

Charleston Mercury, and Morning Advertiser

Saturday, August 17, 1822

His Excellency, the Governor, has issued his Proclamation, offering a reward of two hundred dollars for the apprehension of some Negroes who attempted to rob the Southern Mail, on the 3d inst. near Saltketcher Bridge.[1]

1. The Saltketcher Bridge crossed the Salkehatchie River, southwest of Charleston, linking the Beaufort and Colleton districts.

Charleston Courier

Monday, August 19, 1822

ALEXANDER HARLESTON, a free black man, with his family, and two or three other free persons of color, were passengers in the schr. *Dolphin,* which sailed yesterday for the Coast of Africa; their intention being to join the settlement of the American Colonization Society at Cape Mesurado.[1] PRINCE GRAHAM,[2] a young black man, one of those implicated in the late plot and sentenced to be transported beyond the limits of the U. States, was sent off in this vessel. A slave belonging to Mr. M'NELLAGE,[3] had clandestinely introduced himself on board, the night previous, with the intention of escaping from his owner, but was discovered, and brought on shore. He had secreted himself in a large pleasure boat, which was upon the deck of the schooner.

1. Cape Mesurado lies on the coast of Liberia, near where the current capital city of Monrovia was founded in 1822, the very year of the Vesey plot.

2. On Graham, see Part III, p. 251 n1.

3. Probably John McNellage (1785–1869), a sailmaker who worked at Kunhardt's wharf.

London *New Times*

Tuesday, August 20, 1822

A letter from Charleston gives the following account of the conspiracy of the negroes lately discovered there:—

"CHARLESTON, JULY 10.

"By the United States papers you will observe that six negroes have been executed, and five more ordered for execution on Friday next, for being concerned in an insurrection to have broken out on the 4th inst. but happily detected by the servant of a Gentleman with whom I am well acquainted. Three of these five have been respited for a week, in consequence of their extreme agitation of body and mind, which has induced them to promise to divulge the whole plan, which, I am informed, was matured in St. Domingo; and the principal agent, a *black Preacher,* one of those executed, had been there on this mission. When the whole is disclosed, I am told it is to be published; in the meantime the utmost secresy is observed, to try and detect the miscreant whites who have instigated these deluded wretches, and who at present escape, because black testimony will not be taken. Several of the Gentlemen's coachmen are registered, who were to have given up their masters' horses for the mounted body; and the Secretary, who superintended a livery stable, a clever fellow, was to throw open the stables to mount the Colonels, composed of a ringleader of influence in each Ward, to concentrate their forces with that from the neighbourhood, murder all the white population, seize upon all the property time would permit put it on board the shipping in the harbor, and proceed for St. Domingo. Such I am told by one of the first characters in this place is the outline: certain it is, a very strong civil and military guard is kept up night and day, which duty your humble servant has been obliged to perform, at the risk of my life from the heavy dews. It is to be feared that, this plot being found out, they will seek for revenge and fire the town. You may rely upon it the people here are very much alarmed."

Charleston *City Gazette and Commercial Daily Advertiser*

Wednesday, August 21, 1822

"An Account of the late intended Insurrection among a portion of the Blacks of this city.—Published by the authority of the Corporation of Charleston."[1]

This is a brief narrative of the facts and evidence attending this important investigation.—It is nevertheless full enough for all the purposes of public information, and embraces every material point in the transactions it undertakes to summarize. The complete *Journal* of these trials can at any time be seen by our citizens, and is kept as an official record for History.

In dwelling upon these interesting pages—to *us* and our brethren of the South painfully interesting—(and we doubt not all our fellow-citizens throughout the Union, who have any feeling, participate in this emotion,) the reader will perceive that the bias has been on the side of MERCY. It was politic to commute the punishment of GELL, though a villain of the deepest dye—because, by his testimony principally, the whole plot was unfolded, and the conspirators brought to justice. Though, during this development, Gell's agency and guilt grew each hour more obvious, still the Court were bound in justice, as much as they were bound in policy, not to deceive those who had relied upon their word. In the case of Palmer, the only case we believe in which we believe the Executive exercised his prerogative, the sin, if any, was on the side of mercy.[2]

In all cases involving such ingratitude to humane owners, such indiscriminate mischief to the unsuspecting, such demonical passion for blood and plunder and conflagration—we confess ourselves to be among the number of those, who deem the punishment cannot be too sudden, sure and final. But the enlightened views of those composing the Court, have made a division of the crime, which would seem to demand a difference in the penalty. Those to be transported will, probably, yet feel *that hour*, when Death would be considered a less evil than the unknown horrors which their fate may still bring down upon their guilty heads.

The task has been accomplished;—accomplished, too, with dignity and singular calmness. The "ACCOUNT" has already been circulated extensively—and a third edition, on the third day of publication, evinces that it will spread "the truth and nothing but the truth," throughout the United States. Any extracts we should make would be superfluous to our readers, and, to those abroad, would convey but an imperfect idea of the history of the Plot, and the characters of those engaged in its execution. . . . [3]

If VESEY was the father of the conspiracy, who, it might be naturally asked, put the original idea into Vesey's susceptible soul? But comment is unnecessary. We only state for the information of certain people, that Denmark (or Telemaque) Vesey was a *free black man*; in his thoughts and actions as free as he should be, and owned property worth above *eight thousand Dollars*.[4] Therefore it was not "resistance of tyranny," but the Prince of Darkness that prompted his develish plan. . . . [5]

The citizens of Charleston, will doubtless express, in some public manner, their sense of the important labours undergone, and the spirit and intelligence displayed by those who conducted the above investigation. The REWARD due to the DISCOVERER of the Plot, is yet to be bestowed. This will be the pleasing business of the Legislature of the State. . . . [6]

It is a remarkable coincidence that the name of Col. Prioleau's faithful servant who felt it his duty to protect his master and family, and our whole city from the late meditated massacre, is, *Peter*, and is the second of the same name and belonging to the same family, who has rendered this service to South Carolina. The remark is trivial, but the facts themselves should be perpetual monitions to all future evil-thinkers that there ever will, as there ever have been, *servants of principle and integrity* who will discover and frustrate such guilty projects. And even should fear prevent them, there are always to be found some partners in iniquity, who to save themselves, will disclose their schemes, so that, after all, good conduct and fidelity will be found the most certain and least perilous road to happiness and that increase of privilege which they would seek in vain by visionary plans of Insurrection.

1. The reference is to James Hamilton Jr.'s pamphlet, which was published in mid-August.

2. Billy, the slave of Job Palmer, was sentenced to death, but Governor Bennett commuted his sentence to banishment from the United States. See *Charleston Mercury, and Morning Advertiser,* September 18, 1822, which appears on p. 456 in this section.

3. The editors here reprinted the confession of Jack Purcell, which appears in both Hamilton's *Account* and Kennedy and Parker's *Official Report.*

4. The editors of this volume have been unable to identify any property that Vesey allegedly owned, and he rented rather than owned his home on Bull Street. The rather snide remark about Vesey's alleged wealth accords with official attempts to portray Vesey and his lieutenants, most of whom were privileged slaves, as ungrateful (hence the reference in the *OR* to Aesop's fable of "The Frozen Serpent"). The remark also seems to suggest miserliness and disinterestedness on Vesey's part, for he did not use his wealth to purchase his yet-enslaved children. Archibald Grimké, the mixed-race activist from Charleston who made it a mission to learn as much as he could about the Vesey affair, said Vesey, a skilled carpenter, "worked with great industry" and "accumulated considerable property." See Grimké's 1903 speech, excerpted in Part VI, pp. 781–82. In 1822, Charleston journalists were certainly in a position to know whether Vesey was black or mixed-race, and throughout the nineteenth century, South Carolina journalists routinely identified African American males as "colored" or "mulatto" in their pieces. The description of Vesey as "black" corroborates Archibald Grimké, *Right on the Scaffold, or The Martyrs of 1822* (Washington, DC: The Academy, 1901), 1, who stated that Vesey was "black but comely," which Philip Morgan, "Conspiracy Scares," *WMQ* 59 (2002): 165–66, erroneously cited as suggesting that Vesey was mixed-race. In the 1903 speech, Grimké spoke of Vesey as a man with "black skin."

5. The *City Gazette* reprints the sentence read to Jack Pritchard by magistrate Lionel Kennedy.

6. The *City Gazette* goes on to include a lengthy extract from the colonial legislature's recording of a reward of ten pounds given to a bondman in 1740 who apprehended one of the Stono rebels.

Stephen Elliot to William Elliot, Friday, August 23, 1822

. . . We have nothing new in town but the dullness of the times if this can be considered new. Even our domestic troubles appear to be forgotten. You will perceive that the Governor by his circular published today makes as little of it as possible. I believe his wish is that it may soon pass into oblivion. . . .

ALS in Elliott-Gonzales Papers, SHC, UNC.

Deborah Norris Logan,[1] Diary

Tuesday, August 27, 1822

Our newspaper filled with melancholy details of the allarming conspiracy of the Slaves in Charleston, and of the execution in consequence, of many of the poor deluded creatures.

I have thought what a benefit it is to have such an Editor as my friend Walsh[2] to represent to the Public in its true light, the view which ought to be taken (and which Posterity will take) of such transaction.

1. The unpublished diaries of the Quaker Deborah Norris Logan (1761–1839) provide an informative glimpse of elite life in antebellum Philadelphia.

2. Robert Walsh (1785–1859) was the editor of the Philadelphia *National Gazette* from 1821 to 1836. See Mary Frederick Lochemes, *Robert Walsh: His Story* (Washington, DC: Catholic University of America Press, 1941).

Deborah Norris Logan Diary, No. 5, November 21, 1821–October 22, 1822, entry for August 27, 1822, HSP.

New Orleans *Louisiana Gazette*

Wednesday, August 28, 1822

Milledgeville, Aug. 6.

A conspiracy of the Negroes has been lately detected at Charleston, S.C.—We at first hoped that it was but a trifling matter; but the following extract of a letter from that city, to a gentleman of this place, shows the alarming extent of the danger:

"Twenty negroes were executed. . . ."

The writer further observes, that even after the execution of the first six, the remainder were still busily engaged in arranging a new scheme, to be carried into execution at a subsequent day.

We know the negroes of Charleston are excessively indulged by their masters. When this confidence has been so grossly abused, they should suffer the penalties of the laws in their utmost severity. But what shall we say of a *white man* who could aid and encourage them in their bloody schemes? *A white man has been detected in conference with the conspirators, encouraging and assisting them with his counsel.* He was formerly a pirate. What punishment is severe enough for such a wretch!

Charleston *City Gazette and Commercial Daily Advertiser*

Tuesday, September 3, 1822

August 17, 1822

The City Council, (on the 17th ult.) *resolved* that their thanks be presented to the Honorable JAMES HAMILTON, junr. (Intendant) for his unremitting attention to the public interest, during his term of service, and more particularly for his vigilance during a late period of uncommon peril. They are also unanimously of opinion, that the conduct of the Intendant during his administration, deserves the thanks of the city. They are also unanimously of opinion, that the conduct of the Intendant during his administration, deserves thanks of the city.[1]

1. This information was reprinted nearly verbatim in the *Charleston Mercury, and Morning Advertiser,* September 3, 1822.

Independent Chronicle and Boston Patriot

Wednesday, September 4, 1822

CHARLESTON, August 23.

Information was received in town yesterday from Coosawhatchie, that five of the negroes who recently attempted to rob the Southern Mail, in Saitketcher Swamp, have been apprehended, and have confessed their guilt. The necessary measures will be immediately adopted for their trial.[1]

1. This information appeared verbatim in the Gettysburg *Republican Compiler,* September 11, 1822, and the Baltimore *American and Commercial Daily Advertiser,* September 15, 1822.

Mary Lamboll Beach to Elizabeth L. Gilchrist, Thursday, September 5, 1822

. . . Through the great goodness of our Heavenly Father *all* our family is in good health except little Diane & she not very sick that I know of & the City in general remarkably healthy although there have been some deaths as must of course take place steadily in our dying world. & our late disturbances are all quieted; business is very dull as it usually is at this season of the year & property much depreciated occasioned as much perhaps from the fall in the prices *all over* the Union (& I should suppose in Europe too as it is a time of peace) as well as from our late difficulties except in the article of Slaves & they would of course have fallen too at least one third from the fall of Cotton, but this property would give me no concern if that had been all to depreciate *them.* The Lord has given us so remarkable a deliverance that it ought still to encourage us to hope that he has yet mercy in store for this sinful community & to hope that in this day of wonders of His grace he may pour out of His Holy Spirit on us too of his own free mercy—Things did appear to me about two months ago to wear the darkest & most mysterious aspect as to the *moral* results of the late unhappy business & viewed now only by the eye of reason it can appear in no other, but when we view the wonder of the Lord's hand in thousands of other cases defeating the Prince of darkness & view the operation of His hand in this day we may yet hope that this may be our experience. I recoil at times when I think of the poor Greeks at this time & also think that this country has a great deal to answer for on the score of Slavery as well as the Greeks for their departure from *real* Christianity—Yet as there are many I doubt not here who may be wrestling Jacob;[1] we may still hope & trust that light may be brought out of all the late darkness—I have no doubt that a spirit of prayer has been in more than usual degree *here* excited by the late events; for christians could not but see the awfully hostile temper shewed by the men of the world against *religion* for actually (as far at least as I have had an opportunity of hearing & observing) there seemed more shewed against it because some of these miserable men who were among the insurgents were professors than because they wished to murder them—for instance where I have heard one remark against the S[t] Domingo people there have been innumerable against the Northward ones who they look upon in general I believe as the secret instigators of the plot, unfortunately you may see their quoting King's speech in Congress mentioned in the case of Jack Purcel[2] yet you see their hope of help was from St Domingo. Now in the case of Vesey until I saw the Pamplet[3] I was under the belief from the report that was afloat & believed generally that he had travelled all over the New England States & also the Western ones within 2 or 3 years; but from this Pamplet it does not appear that he was absent for 20 years. The Tuesday afternoon prayer meeting you ask about has been held for the last year in the school room in Beaufain Street but it has become so crowded that in future (notice was given this week) it is to be held at our Sabbath School room. It will for some time probably be very trying to *me* to go there as there is no way of getting there but going through a part of our church yard that is about 20 or 30 feet from where the Ramsay's yard is to the S. East.[4] I have never yet been in it although the Wednesday evening Lecture has been held there 3 or 4 months & also lately a Sunday evening service steadily either by Docr Palmer or Mr Jones but I have found this meeting so interesting that I must endeavour to stifle my feelings & go for I should feel loth indeed to give up the priveledge. Some of the services there have been truly interesting such fervent supplication & affecting addresses from the good minister & most fervent prayers from old Mr Pilsbury[5] who does indeed seem an old disciple apparently on the very verge of the grave. he formerly was of the Methodist communion but has for some time past belonged to Mr Boies's congregation.[6] And there is another most excellent young member of our Church you may recollect him perhaps as he used to worship there before you left this. he is Mr Corning[7] a Merchant from N. York partner in the house of Parish & Miller he has a young wife & one child—he was from Docr Spring's Church & highly thought of I understand there; I think him a great acquisition to our Church. I wish you could hear his fervent prayers & he is very active in the Mariners Society here too. Poor young man his feelings have been very sorely tried in our late business you may see the name in the Pamplet of John Vincent one of the Culprits this fellow attended in the large store of Parish & Miller & this Mr Corning; & he had a very high opinion of him & as it was only on that villain Monday Gell's evidence M C. having a high opinion of this fellow's honesty appeared at the court to give *his* testimony in his favour & I heard that when sentence was passed the tears rolled down his (Mr Corning's) face & he left the room but soon after this fellow was proven to be a very great villain & a thief too & I understand Mr Corning saw it although afterwards he was not that I know of very deeply though somewhat concerned in the late business & a wretch he tried I hear to bring in every acquaintance he had I heard if he had only spoken once to them; he is to be transported. You ask if none of the Professors offered to be States Evidences—not *one* that I heard of; but this I should not censure them very much for, for I understand that the Oath to secrecy was as solemn as *they* could make it; that was the ringleaders I don't mean the Professors instituted it, but it is generally believed (I believe I have heard it so often) that they swore by the Memorial of the Lord's body. so that every one that did divulge it was guilty of Perjury. I should suppose from Docr Palmer's services last Sunday at the table & again at the Concert for prayer on Monday night that it must be a happy time with him I think he exceeded at the table all I ever heard from him—his Sermon was from these words "Who is he that condemneth it is Christ that died" & he pursued the same words in the most spiritual manner at the table. Urging & encouraging believers to look more at the death of our dear

Redeemer in all their christian warfares & I cannot but hope that it was an interesting theme to many—It is to be lamented that there was not one addition to the Church & only one (Sarah Stevens) the last time. However if in answer to his often & fervent prayers our Jerusalem should be sunshining us with Candles we may hope the graces of its members may be purified & a better state of things produced & I feel a *great* hope *this* will be the case. Mrs Wm Parker (Mr Lightwoods daughter)[8] lost her daughter the 1st inst after a long fever of the nervous class—deprived of her reason nearly the whole of her illness or else in a stupor at other times. I heard but would not wish it mentioned her mother said she would give her up if it was only the body but that she had not a hope for her soul & most *bitterly* reflected on herself for want of faithfulness to her in religious instruction, but I have not heard of her state since her daughter died—I believe as much their [*missing*] for a certain line that it was a very *select* funeral; perhaps however it was only the relatives & communion that were invited; don't tell Miss Huxham of this particular of nor of many things I write, except generals for which I have *no* objection. for Mrs R. told me the other day that Miss H reproached *her* for not writing more *fully* to her about the state of things here & said (whether it was Mrs R's. *way* or Miss Huxham's word I don't know but that I was so *communicative* to you. but I can't help it I have to tell you what interests *me* & what I *know you* would like to hear—Miss H. did it I suppose to *provoke* her sister to write more *fully* to her about the late intended insurrection for this is what I understood Mrs R's she alluded to. Mrs T. Parker her sister in law lost a grown up son at Abbeville about 8 weeks ago too & she has since returned to the City for she had gone to live with this son there. I thank you very kindly my d^{r} Sister for offering about some of your monies for the shingling of this House but unless pressed it won't do to infringe on that for the rent which is *due* on [*illegible*] must pay for it—& Mary & I return you *many* thanks about your *kind* offer about sending the boys if we could not come next year—She says she is as much obliged to you as if she did send them but she says *there* will be the bone of contention with their grandfather: for she supposes she might go to the——& he would not care but these [*illegible*] she thinks he does. she sends her love to you both & the children's theirs too to you both. while I write of the children I will tell of B. the night of the 16th of June in the dead of the night seeing his Mother's agitation (I spent it in her room too) he says Ma don't be frightened don't you know that text in the Bible call on me in the day of trouble & I will deliver thee "& poor fellow his own voice faultering like one in an ague at the same time" he lay awake a great part of that night too but spoke but very little—he nor we (of course [*illegible*] had heard then of the report that only the males were to be destroyed that was afterwards believed; but I believed they would not have regarded had they once [*illegible*] work sex or age; it appears so from the Pamplet & is not natural to be supposed that they would not have burdened themselves with the surplus. . . .

1. Beach, writing from Charleston to her sister in Philadelphia, refers to the lyrical poem "Wrestling Jacob," a meditation on Genesis 32, by theologian John Wesley (1707–1788), the founder of Methodism.

2. During the debate over Missouri's admission to statehood, Federalist Senator Rufus King (1755–1827) of New York unleashed one of the most powerful denunciations of slavery heard in

Congress to that point by seizing on the equality clause in the Declaration of Independence. The testimony of the slave Jack Purcell indicated that he and other slaves in the Vesey plot had heard and read about the debate, which was widely published in southern newspapers, registering the existence of growing northern antislavery sentiment.

3. By "the Pamplet" Beach means Hamilton's *Account*.

4. Beach may be referring to the yard of attorney David Ramsay (1795–1826), who in 1822 resided at 109 Queen Street and had an office at 74 Broad Street. See *BDSCHR* 5: 217–18; *CSCCD*, 95.

5. Beach refers to Samuel Pilsbury (1748–1828), an officer in the United States Customs House in Charleston. In 1822 he lived at 23 Anson Street. See Lorenzo Dow, *The Dealings of God, Man and the Devil; as Exemplified in the Life, Experience, and Travels of Lorenzo Dow in a Period of over a Half a Century*, 2 vols. (New York, 1856), vol. 2: 195; *CSCCD*, 94.

6. Artemas Boies (1792–1844), pastor in 1822 of Charleston's Second Presbyterian Church.

7. Beach refers to Jasper Corning (1792–1869), misidentified in the *OR*, 165, as "Mr. Cornhill," who attended John Vincent, the slave of Daniel Cruckshanks, during the trial. Corning worked for the Charleston merchant firm D. Parish & Co., located on Broad Street, and had hired John to work for the company. Corning, as Beach indicates, did indeed come from New York City and the Brick Presbyterian Church of Reverend Gardiner Spring (1785–1873) and was a supporter of the American Colonization Society. See George Lewis Prentiss, *The Union Theological Seminary of the City of New York: Historical and Biographical Sketches of Its First Fifty Years* (New York, 1889), 191–92; *Twenty-eighth Annual Report of the American Colonization Society* (Washington, DC, 1845), 55.

8. Beach refers to Sarah Peronneau Lightwood, who married the attorney William McKenzie Parker (d. 1802).

ALS in Beach Papers, SCHS.

Richmond *Enquirer*

Friday, September 6, 1822

AFRICAN-AMERICAN COLONY.

Several free persons of color, and one young black man,[1] who had been implicated in the late plot at Charleston, sailed from that place on the 18th inst.[2] in the schr. Dolphin, for Cape Messurado, the seat of the American colony on the African coast.[3]

1. Prince Graham.

2. The editor clearly meant "ult.," meaning the previous month, and not "inst.," a reference to current month, since the newspapers could not have reported that the ship had sailed on September 18. The *Charleston Courier*, August 3, 1822, indicated that the *Dolphin* would sail in August.

3. This information was reprinted verbatim in the Boston *Recorder*, September 7, 1822, and the *Milton* (NC) *Gazette*, September 12, 1822.

The Schooner *Dolphin*

. . . A small vessel named the *Dolphin*, owned and commanded by Benjamin Pearson,[1] a Citizen of The United States of America, arrived at Mr. Lightburne's[2] factory in the month of October last from Charleston, with trade-goods and passengers. These passengers were chiefly persons of colour, Emigrants from The United States, required to remove themselves in consequence of having taken part in some disturbances at

Charleston. Some of the individuals were accompanied by their families. The intention of these Persons in coming to the Rio Pongos[3] has not been ascertained; many of them perished some after their arrival in the River by the fever of the Place and before the commencement of the year 1823, most of the survivors found their way to Sierra Leone. The *Dolphin,* according to the latest accounts, was still at anchor not far from Mr. Lightburne's factory unable to proceed to sea through the loss of nearly all her seamen. . . .

1. Captain Benjamin Pearson owned the schooner *Dolphin,* and in 1830 his widow Ann Pearson petitioned the United States Congress for damages when the vessel was seized by the Navy on suspicion of involvement in the African slave trade. See *Journal of the Senate of the United States* . . . (Washington, DC, 1829), 114.

2. Captain Francis Stiles Lightburne (1773–1826) owned a plantation on Wadmalaw Island near Charleston and was active in the African trade. See "Obituary," *Charleston Courier,* January 17, 1826, and "The Slave Trade—Slave Factories," *Salem Register,* September 29, 1842.

3. The Rio Pongo is an estuary that flows into the Atlantic near Boffa, in what is now the Republic of Guinea.

British and Foreign State Papers, 1823–1824 (London, 1843), 431. See also *Slave Trade Commission Report,* no. 4 (April 29, 1823), FO 84/21.

Baltimore Patriot & Mercantile Advertiser

Saturday, September 7, 1822

THE CHARLESTON NEGRO PLOT. The Philadelphia Press of Thursday states, "that a private letter from Charleston informs that new confessions had been made; several arrests had taken place; many stand of arms been discovered and seized;[1] and a new Freeholders' Court was about to be established."[2]

1. Despite this, Richard C. Wade, "The Vesey Plot: A Reconsideration," *JSH* 30 (1964): 150, argued that "no cache of arms lay hidden in the city." But Governor Bennett admitted the discovery of more than a dozen hoop-poles, which could have been intended for pike handles, as his Circular reprinted in this volume on pp. 467–71, esp. 470, indicates. Thomas Cilavan Brown (b. 1800), a free person of color who had worked in Charleston as a carpenter in 1822, who claimed to know Vesey and traveled with members of Vesey's family to Liberia in 1833, informed the abolitionist Lydia Maria Child (1802–1880), "I heard, at the time, of arms being buried in coffins, at Sullivan's Island. But that is not the negro burying ground. The slaves are buried in a place called the potter's Field, and the colored people have a ground of their own." In response to northern critics who raised questions about weapons, Benjamin Elliott (1786–1836), a Charleston attorney close to the proceedings, responded, "Besides the instruments which many of them possessed as mechanics, villains were engaged in manufacturing arms; several pike-handles were discovered; Pharaoh and Peter had swords; Ned Bennett had a sword to kill wolves but which he designed first to try upon his master." To avoid detection, conspiratorial slaves typically did not stockpile weapons before they revolted; once the proposed uprising got off the ground, they would plunder existing stockpiles whose whereabouts were known. Court testimony reveals that Charleston's slaves knew where arms and munitions in the city were stockpiled. See Circular of Governor Thomas Bennett Jr., August 10, 1822, GM, RGA, 1328, SCDAH; Lydia Maria Child to Thomas Wentworth Higginson, March 17, 1860, William P. Palmer Collection, P-1090, Western Reserve Historical Society; [Benjamin Elliott,] "To Our Northern Brethren," Charleston *City Gazette and Commercial Daily*

Advertiser, September 27, 1822; *BDSCHR* 4: 182–83. For a more detailed consideration of the weapons question, see Robert L. Paquette, "From Rebellion to Revisionism: The Continuing Debate about the Denmark Vesey Affair," *Journal of the Historical Society* 4 (Fall 2004): 306–7.

2. This information was reprinted verbatim in the *Baltimore Patriot & Mercantile Advertiser,* September 7, 1822; Boston *Commercial Gazette,* September 9, 1822; Boston *Columbian Centinel,* September 11, 1822; Providence *Patriot,* September 14, 1822; Philadelphia *Democratic Press,* September 15, 1822; and *Boston Recorder,* September 21, 1822.

Nantucket (MA) *Inquirer*

Tuesday, September 10, 1822

Extract of a letter from one of the gentlemen composing the court of Freeholders in Charleston (S.C.) which was called to try the Negroes who were engaged in the late attempt at Insurrection in that place.

"Being one of the Court, I was incessantly occupied for upwards of five weeks; and a more painful duty I have never been called on to perform. I cannot now exactly say how many were convicted, but probably not less than 60; 34 of whom have already been executed and the remainder ordered for transportation beyond the U. States The example has been awful and terrible, but be assured, very necessary. The Court was composed of members highly respectable for their judgment and humanity, and their proceeding have given universal satisfaction.—We tried these people by the same strict rules of evidence, which govern our criminal courts of judicature; and in every case, the master, assisted by counsel where he desired it, attended to the defence of his slave. By patience and perseverance, we have got at the bottom of the plot; and such has been the example, that we have no fear of the thing occurring again in our lives, if only proper laws are passed, of which all believe there is a necessity."

Martha Proctor Richardson to James Screven, Monday, September 16, 1822

. . . The insurrection in Charleston (the intended one I should have said) has been happily terminated—I will give you an extract from a letter I received last week from Mr. DeSaussure.[1] "I receive Dear Madam your kind congratulations at the successful termination of the recent disturbances in Charleston with much sensibility—The hand of providence was singularly visible in the discovery and developement of the plot, & our gratitude should be commensurate with it—I do not think that the object could have been accomplished to any save a very limited extent, but probably many valuable lives would have been sacrificed before order was re-established—our examples have been written in Blood, but policy & perhaps humanity rendered them indispensable—& will perhaps deter similar efforts for 20 or 30 years"—32 of the poor wre[t]ches were hung—& some shipt for Africa—The trials have been published in a small pamphlet which I have read[2]—it is a history of the wildest plans—engendered by superstition and ignorance—Most of the ring leaders were of the Gullah tribe Mechanics and draymen—of the Methodist religion—You may hear that an attempt has been in agitation here—but it is without foundation—some few have been tried for an attempt to poison their Master—Flourinoy[3] but they have not as yet been sentenced or is it supposed the evidence will be sufficient to criminate them. . . .

1. Richardson's Charleston correspondent was probably Henry William DeSaussure (1763–1839), a notable attorney and politician, who in 1822 kept an office at 81 Broad Street and a residence at 35 Meeting Street. See *CSCCD,* 77; *BDSCHR* 4: 154–55. Richardson was in Savannah at the time.

2. Hamilton's *Account.*

3. A few weeks after the trials of the Vesey conspirators had ended, authorities in Savannah tried three slaves, accused of attempting to poison Robert Flournoy and his family. They were acquitted. Two years later Flournoy and his son were indicted in Hancock County, Georgia, for the gross abuse of seven slaves, who died as a result of their mistreatment. See *Southern Chronicle and Camden* (SC) *Gazette,* September 18, 1822, transcribed in this section on p. 457; Savannah *Republican,* September 21, 1822; "Horrible Barbarity," Philadelphia *National Gazette and Literary Register,* November 25, 1824; and William A. Byrne, "The Burden and Heat of the Day: Slavery and Servitude in Savannah, 1733–1865" (PhD diss., Florida State University, 1979), 269–70.

ALS in Arnold-Screven Papers, SHC, UNC.

Charleston Mercury, and Morning Advertiser

Wednesday, September 18, 1822

LOUIS, slave of Mr. Cromwell; SEYMOUR, slave of Mr. Kunhardt; ISAAC slave of Mr. Harth; PARIS, slave of Mrs. Ball; DUBLIN, slave of Mr. C. G. Morris; GEORGE, slave of Mr. Bampfield, SANDY, slave of Mr. Schnell; JOHN VINCENT, slave of Mr. Crukshanks; WILLIAM, slave of Mr. Palmer; and BILLY, slave of Mr. P. Robinson, who were sentenced to death for their connexion with the late conspiracy, and who were respited from execution until the 25th of October next, have had their punishment commuted by his Excellency the Governor to perpetual banishment from the United States. Their owners are to give bonds with security to the State, in one half the value of these slaves, that they will have them taken out of the limits of the United States in ten days after they are delivered over to them, and the slaves are to be kept in close custody after that delivery until they are sent out of the country. If any of them ever return the penalty is to be the execution of the sentence passed upon them by the Court—to be carried into effect on the Friday following their apprehension; and the same punishment on the slave and the forfeiture of the bond of his owner if he remain after the ten days fixed for his banishment.

SABY GAILLARD, a free coloured man, has had his sentence changed to perpetual banishment out of the limits of South-Carolina; to leave the State within twenty days.[1]

1. This information was reprinted verbatim in the *Charleston Courier,* September 17, 1822; Charleston *Southern Patriot, and Commercial Advertiser,* September 17, 1822; Savannah *Republican,* September 19, 188; *Baltimore Patriot & Mercantile Advertiser,* September 24, 1822; *Darien* (GA) *Gazette,* September 26, 1822; Philadelphia *Democratic Press,* September 26, 1822; *Niles' Weekly Register,* September 28, 1822; and Richmond *Enquirer,* October 1, 1822.

Charleston *Southern Patriot, and Commercial Advertiser*

Wednesday, September 18, 1822

We are requested to say that in addition to the cases in which the Governor has commuted the punishment of certain persons of colour, condemned to be hung (but recommended by the Court to banishment) for attempting to raise an insurrection in this State, is that of the fellow PETER, belonging to the estate of Mr. Cooper, who has had his punishment commuted to receiving twenty lashes on his bare back, and to be discharged.—The punishment of SABY GAILLARD is banishment out of the State of South Carolina.

Southern Chronicle and Camden (SC) *Gazette*

Wednesday, September 18, 1822

The justices of the peace for the city of Savannah closed the examination of the Negroes Dick, Shadrick and Robbin, yesterday forenoon, after a session of two days. After a full and patient hearing, the above named fellows were turned over to the justices of the Inferior Court of Chatham County for trial. The charges alledged against them, are, for attempting to poison their master and family, and for endeavoring to create an insurrection among the blacks. We understand their trial will take place in the course of next week. Should they be found guilty, their lives will be the forfeit.[1]

1. This information, alluded to by Martha Proctor Richardson in her letter to James Screven, September 16, 1822, was reprinted nearly verbatim in the *Southern Chronicle and Camden Gazette,* September 22, 1822; Philadelphia *United States Gazette and True American,* September 23, 1822; Philadelphia *Democratic Press,* September 23, 1822; *Independent Chronicle and Boston Patriot,* September 25, 1822; Boston *Columbian Centinel,* September 25, 1822; and *Washington Gazette,* September 26, 1822.

Catherine Macbeth[1] to John Macbeth, Friday, October 4, 1822

. . . My Dear Brother . . . Our minds were kept in continual agitation as regards the Insurrection which was to take place among the Negroes which I have no doubt you have heard of. I feel hurt that my dear Brother have made no Enquiry after my family or self this summer altho you never had letters from me I always could hear how you all where. . . .

1. Little is known of Catherine Macbeth, who was in Charleston at the time. An advertisement in an 1843 Charleston newspaper identifies her as married and the owner of a tract of land in St. John's Berkley Parish as well as of sixty-five slaves, belonging previously to James Macbeth, a bankrupt. See Charleston *Southern Patriot,* June 20, 1843. *CSCCD,* 88, identifies a grocer named John Macbeth, who in 1822 lived at 132 Tradd Street.

ALS in Macbeth Family Papers, SCHS.

Figure 30. Charleston's Circular (Congregational) Church, ca. 1860, much as it looked after congregants completed a new building on Meeting Street in 1806. The church stands here next to Institute Hall, built in 1854, where the Ordinance of Secession was ratified. Courtesy of the New-York Historical Society.

Mary Lamboll Beach to Elizabeth Gilchrist, Monday, October 7, 1822

. . . Oh! it seems indeed as if the Lord had a controversy with this guilty land. Doc[r] Palmer presented 2 solemn sermons yesterday from those words "Come behold the works of the Lord &[ra] The first sermon he shewed that from the Devastations begining with the Flood & down through the course of sacred History recording these Desolations that they were asserted to be the *immediate* hand of God no matter what Philosophers would say of their *natural* causes & in the 2d sermon he mentioned some of modern times with which we were more familiar & of those of the present year such as the misery of the Greeks the convulsions in Spain, the famine in Ireland, distress in N. York. (for such a population as that City contains to be obliged to abandon their homes or be in most cases certain of death) & then remarked in as couched language as he could to make it prudent in our mixed congregation our late visitation in the Summer & now this sore visitation again & he then urged the duty of beholding the works of the Lord under desolating judgment & the duty of enquiring into their *probable* cause. He then said we were in a remarkable manner guilty of the sin of Omission in this State—& went on to show how peculiarly heavy in the course of a few years the judgments of God had fallen on the planting which was the prevailing interest in this State & our particular sin of omission he endeavoured to prove was in not spreading the Gospel in our own state among our own heathen the mass of which were he said destitute of it as if they were in the "*heart of Africa*" he also spoke very freely of the awful state of the public mind toward religion during or after our late trial about the Insurrection of the Blasphemous sentiments expressed on that occasion. I don't know how it will be received but I do think he is as fearless in the Pulpit as Luther—Three Sabbath's ago he preached a sermon to the servants[1] which by request of some in the Church is published I heard the sermon but have not seen it since printed & in that I suppose he must have given offense to the Blacks & some to our wicked white fornicators & Adulterors too, some expressions about their intercourse I sincerely wished had been omitted—& I suppose is in the printed Sermon. . . .

1. Published as *Religion Profitable: with a Special Reference to the Case of Servants: A Sermon Preached on September 22, 1822, in the Circular Church, Charleston, S.C.* (Charleston, SC, 1822). See Part V, pp. 668–69.

New Orleans *Louisiana Gazette*

Thursday, October 17, 1822

Extract of a letter from South Carolina, dated Sept. 2, 1822.

. . . The late Plot in Charleston was very serious—Had it burst out with any shew of success, it would have blazed forth most destructively over the whole seacoast. This cannot be called an attempted insurrection among the *Slaves.* It originated with free people of color; it began among that class which the abolitionists are most anxious to increase. This fact ought to be borne in mind. It is very important. The slaves engaged in it were principally mechanics, draymen, wharfingers &c. and all those who live much to themselves and with little control from their masters. They were chiefly *Africans.* The non-importation will soon extinguish that race, and those born in the country cannot so easily be induced to revolt. Banish all the free people of colour, exclude colored mechanics from towns and make a few other wise regulations, and there can be little or no danger.—The account published by the city Council should be generally read. It is a faithful and a full account.

Charleston *City Gazette and Commercial Daily Advertiser*

Monday, October 21, 1822

List of Sentences passed on the adjournment day of the Court of Sessions for October Term, 1822, for the District of Charleston,—Judge Bay presiding:

William Allen, indicted for a misdemeanor in exciting an insurrection among the negroes in the city during the last summer,—Sentenced to pay a fine of one-thousand dollars, and to suffer an imprisonment of 12 months.

Andrew S. Rhodes—Indicted for the same offence. Sentenced to pay a fine of five hundred dollars, and to be imprisoned for the space of six months.[1]

Daniel Jacobs, *alias* Dandus,—and John Ignatius, or Spanish John,—These two men were charged with the same offence; but their cases, as made out by the evidence on the part of the state, did not present that dark and atrocious hue, that was exhibited in the two first enumerated instances.—The sentence of the court therefore, was—That they should be imprisoned for the space of three months, and should each pay a fine of one hundred dollars. . . .

1. Rhodes appears to have spent more than six months in jail. On January 10, 1824, he petitioned Secretary of State John Quincy Adams for release from confinement, saying he had served eighteen months of a three-year term of imprisonment. In the petition, which is illegible in a number of places, he claimed to have lived in Charleston for thirty years. Also in the petition, he does not deny the existence of a slave plot but claims his constitutional rights were violated and that Charleston's authorities acted vindictively against him. See Miscellaneous Letters of the Department of State, January 1–April 29, 1824, M179, roll 59, National Archives, Washington, DC.

Charleston *City Gazette and Commercial Daily Advertiser*

Friday, October 25, 1822

We are requested to state, that the Executive of South Carolina has respited Dublin Morris, Billy Robinson and Seymour Kunhardt, until the first Friday in December next; consequent on the owners of these slaves declaring on oath that they could not advantageously comply with the conditions of the pardon recently issued, and pledging themselves to send the said slaves out of the United States as early as practicable. The cases of the remaining seven, who were also conditionally pardoned, are embraced, allowing seven days for the vessels in which they have been shipped to leave the port.[1]

1. The material was reprinted nearly verbatim in the *New-York Evening Post,* November 5, 1822, and *Independent Chronicle and Boston Patriot,* November 9, 1822.

Deposition of George Thompson,[1] Wednesday, November 20, 1822

On the 16th of June Pharo[2] came to me in the morning I asked him if He knew any thing of the intended Insurrection. He Pharo did not know any thing about it further than he had allready stated to me.

That he had frequently heard the Negroes on the wharfe speak about meeting at Denmark Veseys & Hales Berry's[3] but what the meeting was for he could not find out. I asked him if he never attended any of those meetings. He stated that he never did for he did not know where Denmark Vesey lived. I asked him what reasons he had to suspect Denmark as one of the party. He said he had no other than that of hearing the Negroes speak of meeting there so often. This was some time before Denmark was taken. The next day I mentioned it to several of my acquaintance's Mr. John Howard[4] was the first, who said to me, I'm going to the Governors & I will state the case to him. I did not go forward myself thinking he had done so. On the 4th July Pharo came to me a second time & stated that he had some conversation with a fellow belonging to Mr. Strohecker named Perault that he (Perault) came to his stables & said to him what fools the Blacks were. He in reply said he thought they were, but might not mean the same as he did. Perault then stated that because they had taken a few of their leaders they had fell back but if the french band could get One Hundred strong they would come out & he was sure there was a great many would join them

(This I gave information of to the Intendant that afternoon & the next morning to one of the wardens) Previous to his giving me this information I sent for him & told him that as he was amongst the Black's on this wharf to try & get what information he could & let me know which he did as above stated.

I further declare that Pharo Voluntarily communicated Intelligence to me that led to the apprehension of Perault who it was admitted was one of the most Guilty. & I do most solemnly beleive that he had no communication with the conspirators but for the Purpose of discloseing their views to me & through me to the proper authority's and this service was undertaken at my request & at my Suggestion

Sworn to before me
20th November 1822 } George Thompson

1. George Thompson, the son of Jane Thompson and deceased John Thompson, Pharo's original owner, was a bricklayer who resided in 1822 at 24 Blackbird Alley. See *CSCCD*, 101.

2. Pharo was hanged on July 26, 1822. Monday Gell testified against him and indicated that Pharo belonged to his company.

3. In the trial records, Hales Barry is mentioned only by Pharo Thompson, and his surname is spelled "Berry." *The Directory and Stranger's Guide for the city of Charleston, also a Directory for Charleston Neck between Boundary-Street and the Lines: for the Year 1819* (Charleston, SC, 1819) listed Berry as a free person of color who worked as a tailor on 33 Boundary Street.

4. John Howard was a bricklayer who resided in 1819 on 140 Meeting Street. See *CSCCD*, 46.

Series S165015, Petitions to the General Assembly, 1822, no. 132, signed deposition in SCDAH.

Andrew S. Rhodes Sues Unsuccessfully for Trespass, February 1825[1]

. . . It appeared that the plaintiff got possession of a small house in the neighborhood of the defendants, near Monk's Corner[2]; that the defendants were disposed to get rid of him, believing that he was dealing with their negroes and was a troublesome neighbor. To effect this, they issued a distress warrant, whilst the plaintiff was from home, and seized upon such articles as were in the house, which were very few and of little value, being such as were suitable only for the lowest retail grog shop, worth about $5 or $10. . . . Besides evidence was given, that the house was pulled down by the defendants, whose property it was. The house was of no great value. The plaintiff paid tax for no property whatever. He had gone into this house about 18 months before this. The tax for the premises were paid by the defendants. The plaintiff had been committed to jail in Charleston for having been engaged in the insurrection there, a year or two before that. The house was pulled down at the request of the defendant, by defendant and the neighbors, who had been invited there for the purpose. . . . The object in pulling down the house was to prevent plaintiff Rhodes, getting possession again, and to expel him thereby from the neighborhood; as he was trading illicitly with the negroes. The plaintiff was regarded as a nuisance in the parish, and a great vagabond, with whom no white man associated, and who cultivated no land, and owned no other property, than as stated above, which were only fit for negro trading. . . .

1. Although this legal case occurred several years after the Vesey plot and could have been located in Part V of this volume, it remains a crucial source in shedding light on why in 1822 Andrew Rhodes was caught in the dragnet as indicated above.

2. Monk's Corner was located about thirty miles north of Charleston, at a crossroads to the west of the source of the Cooper River.

D. J. McCord, *Cases Argued and Determined in the Court of Appeals of South Carolina, Vol. III* (Columbia, SC, 1826), 66–71.

V

Aftermath

Even as the executions finally ended with the death of William Garner on August 9, and as Charleston gravediggers and surgeons put away their tools, a different sort of struggle ensued both inside and outside South Carolina's borders. Inside the state, Governor Thomas Bennett Jr. battled for his political life and legacy as he defended his view that he had acted quickly and effectively to protect white lives and property. His lengthy Message No. 2 to the state legislature about the Vesey conspiracy so angered the majority of legislators that they voted not to have it published. They hotly disagreed with Bennett's view that the conspiracy was not as widespread and dangerous as Intendant Hamilton claimed it to be. In the public mind, Bennett was also linked to the published opinions of his brother-in-law, Justice William Johnson Jr., who thought the two courts failed to follow the rule of law when it came to the rights of the accused rebels. Neither Bennett nor Johnson denied the existence of the plot; they challenged its seriousness and the fairness of the proceedings. At the same time, Hamilton, while aggressively pursuing his investigation of the plot, sought to maintain public order, calm fears, and restrain white mobs and vigilant associations from excesses that would stain the reputation of the state. Throughout the proceedings, he remained confident that existing laws and courts could control potential black rebels.

Many northern journalists reported on the hangings with little or no commentary. But newspapers, southern and northern, in choosing a headline, excerpting the private correspondence of eyewitnesses, editing official sources, and analyzing the event itself, have left behind a remarkable window into evolving white attitudes about slavery in the immediate aftermath of the great national debate about Missouri's statehood. Never before in the United States had officials in any state spilled so much blood in punishing what was alleged to be a revolutionary plot of rebellious slaves. A minority of antislavery editors denounced the dozens of hangings as a shameful barbarity in a democratic republic. Evidence that domestics and other privileged slaves had numbered among the plot's prime movers challenged the paternalistic narrative emanating most notably from South Carolina's slaveholding intelligentsia, including Judge William Johnson, about the relative benignity of the South's slave system. Carolina journalists and intellectuals, such as Thomas Pinckney and Henry William DeSaussure, fired back at northern attacks in defense of honor and slavery.

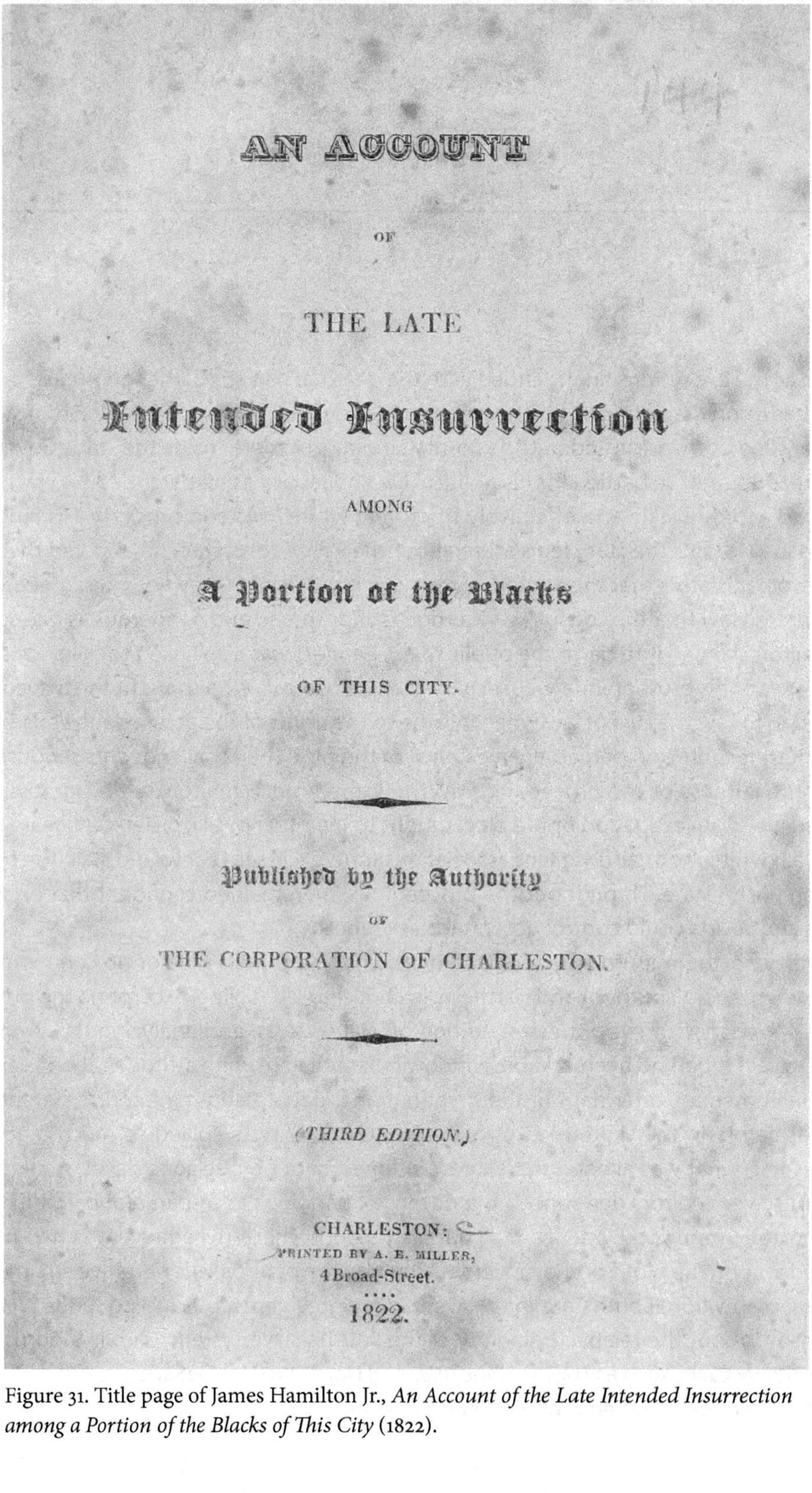

AN ACCOUNT

OF

THE LATE

Intended Insurrection

AMONG

A Portion of the Blacks

OF THIS CITY.

Published by the Authority

OF

THE CORPORATION OF CHARLESTON.

(THIRD EDITION.)

CHARLESTON:
PRINTED BY A. E. MILLER,
4 Broad-Street.
....
1822.

Figure 31. Title page of James Hamilton Jr., *An Account of the Late Intended Insurrection among a Portion of the Blacks of This City* (1822).

What began as newspaper skirmishes quickly escalated into a war of pamphlets, as northern writers criticized unfree labor and the executions and southern writers defended the bloodshed as necessary and just given what was alleged as the magnitude and revolutionary content of the plot. Never much inclined toward the upper South's defense of slavery as an unfortunate but "necessary evil," South Carolina's apologists, both secular and religious, led the way in embracing southern slavery as a "positive good," an institution ubiquitous in history and sanctioned by Scripture. To the extent that writers on both sides of the Mason-Dixon Line were drawn into a debate over slavery's future by the events of 1822, Vesey's failed conspiracy helped to widen the national divide nine years before William Lloyd Garrison launched his Liberator and Nat Turner launched his bloody uprising in Southampton County, Virginia. The Vesey plot would represent for many leading South Carolinians a crossing of the threshold in domestic and national politics. The qualified nationalism of previous years now seemed inadvisable and even suicidal given national and international threats to slavery and the rights of states to order their domestic institutions in ways they deemed fit and proper. The higher law of self-preservation, it was iterated, would trump maintenance of the Union.

The African Church stood at the center of the plot. Although Intendant Hamilton determined Morris Brown and other AME leaders innocent of involvement in the preempted insurrection, Hamilton and other leading Charleston whites still regarded them as negligent and troublesome and thus acted to banish them from the state in the name of their own good. Many of those free blacks, like Morris Brown, who left South Carolina, had to do so under pressure and in great secrecy with Intendant Hamilton interceding in some cases to protect them from white mobs who wanted their heads. The AME connection to the Vesey plot also forced white Carolinians to debate at the highest levels masters' religious obligations to their slaves and the future of missionary outreach in the state to Africans and black Americans.

In the months and years that followed the collapse of the conspiracy, a number of free blacks in the Charleston area—including Susan Vesey—concluded that they had no future in the state and boarded ship for Liberia in West Africa. On the matter of African colonization, however, South Carolina's wealthy planters closed ranks in resisting federal interference with their human property. Slavery, as white South Carolinians readily admitted, was now "woven into the fabric" of the state's social life. The state's leading planters and politicians, with remarkably few exceptions, regarded the border South–based American Colonization Society as a danger to their institutions.

Charleston City Council Minutes

Tuesday, August 6, 1822

Present The Intendant Messrs. Strohecker, Cogdell, Simons, Burger, Condy, Napier, DeLiesseline, Mitchell, Righton, Wesner.

Read the Minutes of the 29th Ultimo. . . .

An Ordinance to amend an Ordinance passed the 28th October 1806 entitled "the Negro Ordinance"[1]

And an Ordinance to increase the duties of the Intendant of the City of Charleston and to fix an annual Salary as a compensation for his services and for other purposes therein mentioned being engrossed,

Were Ratified in due form.

The Bill to provide for the appointment of Assistant Marshalls & for other purposes, was taken up for a 2nd reading.

Mr. Wesner moved that the Bill be postponed, and called for the yeas & nays which were as follows.

Yeas Messrs. Wesner, Strohecker, Mitchell.

Nays The Intendant, Messrs. Napier, Cogdell, Righton, DeLiesseline, Burger, Simons, Condy.

Yeas 3. Nays 8. . . .

Adjourned

Sine Die.

1. On October 28, 1806, the Charleston City Council passed "An Ordinance for the Government of Negroes and Other Persons of Colour within the City of Charleston." The ordinance had twenty-eight sections, most of which aimed at regulating the residence, assemblage, and economic activity of slaves and free persons of color. Section eight prohibited slaves from owning boats unless properly licensed as "fishermen or fisherwomen." Charleston newspapers published the ordinance in its entirety. See, for example, *Charleston Courier,* November 4, 1806.

Charleston County Public Library.

Negro Ordinance, Tuesday, August 6, 1822

An Ordinance, to amend an Ordinance; passed October 28th, 1816, entitled the Negro Ordinance. (*Ratified August 6, 1822.*)

Whereas, the eighth section of that Ordinance makes no provision for granting Licenses to free persons of colour, as fishermen and fisherwomen.

1. *Be it ordained,* That from and after the passing of this Ordinance, no free person or persons of colour shall hereafter own any boat or other vessel, without first obtaining a licence from the Commissioners of the Markets, under the rules and regulations required by the eighth section prescribed for slaves, except as to the correction, which may be commuted, by the parties paying a fine of not more than ten dollars, nor less than five dollars, as the Commissioners of the Markets may determine.

A Collection of the Ordinances of the City Council of Charleston: from the Twenty-Eighth of September, 1818, to the Twelfth of August, 1823 (Charleston, SC, 1823), 31.

New York Commercial Advertiser

Thursday, August 8, 1822

Four more blacks have been executed at Charleston for being concerned in the late conspiracy; and the first Court of Freeholders (whose names have already been given in this paper) has been dissolved. A new court has now been nominated, consisting of the following gentlemen: Hon. Joel R. Poinsett, Robert Y. Hayne, Thos. Rhett Smith, Thos. Roper, John Gordon, Jacob Ax[s]on, and Charles H. Furman. A number of cases yet remain to be investigated. Have there not been executions enough to satisfy the stern demands of justice?

Circular of Governor Thomas Bennett Jr.

Saturday, August 10, 1822

EXECUTIVE DEPARTMENT.
Charleston, August 10th, 1822.

SIR:

AFTER a prolonged and almost uninterrupted session of six weeks, the first Court organized for the trial of Slaves charged with an attempt to raise an Insurrection in this City, was dissolved on the 20th ult. Another Court was subsequently convened, and, after a session of three days, closed the unpleasant investigation with which it was charged, and adjourned on the 8th instant, *sine die.*

During the interesting period occupied by the Court first organized, the public mind was agitated by a variety of rumors calculated to produce great excitement and alarm. These had their origin in the nature of the transaction, and the secrecy and seclusion observed in the incipient stages of the inquiry; as but few of the circumstances were known to the community, and the number apprehended and sentenced to the severest punishment, beyond any former example. Certainty gave place to exaggeration, and the general impression sustained the rumor of a very extensive conspiracy.

The effects resulting from these reports, if uncontrolled by an exhibition of the facts, are too obvious to require comment. The reputation of the State must suffer abroad, and a rapid deterioration of property occur within; while suspicion and anxiety will continue long to mar the public tranquillity. It becomes, therefore, a duty imperiously obligatory on me, to represent the occurrences as they have transpired, and thus evidence to you that the attempt has not only been greatly magnified, but as soon as discovered, it ceased to be dangerous.

A servant[1] prompted by attachment to his master, communicated to him, that he had been requested to give his assent & subscribe his name to a list of persons already engaged in the conspiracy. The Intendant immediately received the information, and caused the arrest of three slaves of Mr. Paul:—one of whom was subsequently identified by the servant making the communication.[2] The City Council was convened, and after a very close and attentive examination, a general impression was produced, that but little credence could attach to the statement. A prudent caution was nevertheless exercised, and the fellow charged committed to solitary imprisonment. A few days after his confinement, he made many disclosures to a member of the Council, but so amplified the circumstances, that the utmost credulity was requisite to the belief of his tale.

Some consternation was obviously produced amongst a few of the conspirators by the arrest of these slaves, and I cannot doubt led to a detail more plausible and deserving of attention. Another servant,[3] whose name is also concealed, from prudential motives, stated generally, that such a combination actually existed, and mentioned the names of several who were most conspicuous in their exertions, adding, with great confidence, that the explosion of their schemes would occur on the ensuing Sunday Night. This confession was given on Thursday, the 13th June, and contained the recital of several occurrences which would precede the attempt and evidence the intention. This suggested the propriety, while it sanctioned the effort to conceal from the community the intelligence thus received for the intervening time; during which, extensive and efficient preparations were made for the safety and protection of the City. Saturday night and Sunday morning passed without the predicted demonstrations; doubts were again excited, and counter orders issued for diminishing the guard. The facts communicated were generally known to our fellow citizens on Sunday; producing a night of sleepless anxiety. But no one of the predicted (or any other) occurrences presented itself to disturb the general tranquility.

On the 18th June, ten slaves were arrested, and on the 19th the court was organized for their trial. Investigation was retarded by the difficulty of procuring authentic evidence, and it was not until the 28th that the sentence of death as pronounced against six of the persons charged with the offence. Denmark Vessey, a free negro, was arrested on the 21st, and on the 22d put on his trial.—Although he was unquestionably the instigator and chief of this plot, no positive proof of his guilt appeared until the 25th. This grew out of the confession of one of the convicts, and on the 27th, his guilt was further established by a servant of Mr. Ferguson.[4]

The progress made, and the expectations of immunity from punishment by confession, gradually developed the plot, and produced the arrest of several others, fortunately two who were principals, Monday Gell, and Gullah Jack. These with three others, John Horry, Charles Drayton and Harry Haig were convicted and sentenced to die on Friday the 12th July last; but at the suggestion of the Court, that important communications were expected from them, Monday Gell, Charles Drayton and Harry Haig were respited.

The arrest of Perault, a servant of Mr. Strohecker,[5] which took place the day previous to the respite and the general and very important discoveries made by him, enabled the Committee of Vigilance, not only to elicit the confirmation of his statement from the three convicts, but to apprehend a great number of persons engaged in the plot. Among others, William Garner, reputed to be one of the principals, the only one not then apprehended.

The number of persons at this period under arrest evinced the necessity of such arrangements of the testimony, as would enable the Court to progress with more rapidity. This duty devolved on the Committee of Vigilance: and principally from the general information of Perault, and of the convicts Monday Gell and Charles Drayton, facility was given to the further proceedings of the Court.—In the short space of seven days, thirty-two Negroes were convicted; twenty-two of whom were executed on Friday, the 20th July; and within four days after, eleven others were convicted, four of whom have also been executed.

Having established the existence of a plot and the places of rendezvous, all that was deemed requisite for conviction, was to prove an association with the Ringleaders, and an expression of their assent to the measure. On such, generally, the sentence of death has been executed. Others, who without actually combining, were proved to have known of the conspiracy, and to have given their sanction by any act, have been sentenced to die, and their punishment commuted to banishment from the United States; or sentenced in the first instance to banishment from this State, or from the United States. In this manner, the whole number, seventy-two, have been disposed of; thirty-five executed, and thirty-seven sentenced to banishment. With these we may reasonably conclude, that we have reached the extremities of this conspiracy, and this opinion, if not conclusive, is entitled to great weight, when we advert to the extraordinary measures pursued to effect the object and the motives which influenced the accused.

No means which experience or ingenuity could devise were left unessayed, to eviscerate the plot. In the labors of investigation, the Court was preceded by a Committee formed by the City Council, whose intelligence, activity and zeal were well adapted to the arduous duties of their appointment. Their assiduity, aided by the various sentiments which influenced the prisoners, produced a rapid developement of the plot. Several of the conspirators had entered into solemn pledges to partake of a common destiny, and one at least, was found, who, after his arrest, felt no repugnance to enforce the obligation, by surrendering the names of his associates. A spirit of retaliation and revenge produced a similar effect with others, who suspected that they were the victims of treachery; and this principle operated with full effect, as the hope or expectation of pardon predominated. To the last hour of the existence of several, who appeared to be conspicuous actors in this drama, they were pressingly importuned to make further confession.

Among the conspirators, the most daring and active was Monday, the slave of Mr. Gell.[6] He could read and write with facility, and thus attained an extraordinary and dangerous influence over his fellows. Permitted by his owner to occupy a house in a central part of the city, hourly opportunities were afforded for the exercise of his skill on those, who were attracted to his shop by business or favor. It was there that his artful and insidious delusions were kept in perpetual exercise. Materials were abundantly furnished in the seditious pamphlets brought into this state, by equally culpable incendiaries; while the speeches of the oppositionists in congress to the admission of Missouri, gave a serious and imposing effect to his machinations. This man wrote to Boyer[7] (by his own confession) requesting his aid, and addressed the envelope of his letter to a relative of the person who became the bearer of it, a negro from one of the Northern states.—He was the only person proved to have kept a list of those engaged; and the court considered his confession full and ample. From such means and such sources of information, it cannot be doubted that all who were actually concerned, have been brought to justice. There is no exception within my knowledge; it has, however, been stated, that a plantation in St. John's was infected, but I do not know on what authority.

This plain detail of the principal incidents in this transaction will satisfy you, that the scheme has not been general nor alarmingly extensive. And it furnishes a cause for much satisfaction, that although religion, superstition, fear and almost every passion that sways the human mind, have been artfully used by the wicked instigators of this design, so few have been seduced from a course of propriety and obedience. Those who associated were unprovided with the means of attack or resistance. No weapons (if we except 13 hoop-poles) have been discovered; nor any testimony received but of six pikes, that such preparations were actually made. The witnesses generally agree in one fact, that the attempt was to have taken place on Sunday night the 16th June, differing a little as to the precise time; 12 o'clock appears to have been the hour.

From the various conflicting statements made during the trials, it is difficult to form a plausible conjecture of their ultimate plans of operation; no two agreeing on general definite principles. That the first essay would be made with clubs against the State Arsenal is inferrible, from their being unprovided with arms, and the concurrence of several witnesses. But whether the attack would be made simultaneously by various detachments, or whether the whole, embodied at a particular spot, would proceed to the accomplishment of their object, is very uncertain. Upon the whole it is manifest, that if any plan had been organized, it was never communicated by the principal conspirator to the leaders or the men, as they were wholly ignorant even of the places of rendezvous; although within two days of the time appointed, and but one man arrested prior to the day fixed on for the attempt.

When we contrast the numbers engaged with the magnitude of the enterprize, the imputation of egregious folly or madness is irresistable: and supposing the attempt to have been predicated on the probability, that partial success would augment their numbers, the utmost presumption would scarcely have hazarded the result. Servility long continued debases the mind and abstracts it from that energy of character, which is fitted to great exploits. It cannot be supposed, therefore, without a violation of the immutable laws of nature, that a transition from slavery and degradation to authority and power, could instantly occur. Great and general excitement may produce extensive and alarming effects; but the various passions which operate with powerful effect on this class of persons, impart a confident assurance of detection and defeat to every similar design. While the event is remote, they may listen with credulity to the artful tale of the instigator, and concur in its plausibility; but the approach of danger will invariably produce treachery, the concomitant of dastardly dispositions. In the fidelity and attachment of a numerous class of these persons, we have other sources of security and early information; from both of which, it is reasonable to conclude, that in proportion to the number engaged, will be the certainty of detection; and that an extensive conspiracy cannot be matured in this State.

I have entered with much reluctance on this detail, nor would it have been considered requisite, but to counteract the number of gross and idle reports, actively and extensively circulated, and producing general anxiety and alarm. And, although their authors may have no evil design, and may really be under the delusion, it is easy to perceive what pernicious consequences may ensue from not applying the proper corrective. Every individual in the State is interested, whether in relation to his own property, or the reputation of the State, in giving no more importance to the transaction than it justly merits. The Legislature have wisely provided the means of efficient protection. If the citizens will faithfully perform the duty enjoined on them by the Patrol Laws, I fear not we shall continue in the enjoyment of as much tranquility and safety, as any State in the Union.[8]

I have the honor to be,
Very respectfully, Sir,
Your obedient servant,

1. Peter Prioleau (also "Peter Desverney") communicated to his master John Cordes Prioleau (1772–1825), a wealthy planter in St. John Berkeley Parish with a townhouse located in 1822 at 50 Meeting Street.

2. Peter Desverney identified William Paul, a slave owned by John Paul (1785–1846), a prosperous Scottish-born merchant. Although listed in the 1822 directory as a "grocer," located at 47 Broad Street, John Paul served for years on the board of directors of Charleston's Planters' and Mechanic's Bank. See *CSCCD*, 94; *Charleston Courier*, May 2, 1820.

3. The slave George Wilson.

4. The slave Frank Ferguson.

5. The slave Perault Strohecker, owned by the blacksmith John Strohecker.

6. Monday Gell belonged to John Gell Jr. (d. 1824), who in 1822 ran Charleston's livery stables at 127 Church Street. See *CSCCD*, 80.

7. Jean-Pierre Boyer (1776–1850), president of Haiti.

8. Joseph Kelly, *America's Longest Siege: Charleston, Slavery, and the Slow March toward Civil War* (New York: Overlook Press, 2013), 147, erroneously argues that "Governor Bennett was skeptical from the beginning and grew more and more doubtful" of the plot's reality.

Circular of Governor Thomas Bennett Jr., RGA, GM, 1328, roll 7. This information was reprinted verbatim in the *Charleston Courier*, August 23, 1822; *Genius of Universal Emancipation* (monthly), August 1822; Connecticut *Courant*, September 3, 1822; *Niles' Weekly Register*, September 7, 1822; Gettysburg *Republican Compiler*, September 11, 1822; and Louisville *Public Advertiser*, September 18, 1822.

Charleston Courier

Monday, August 12, 1822

We are happy to state that the tranquillity of the city is now restored. The legal investigations of crime have ceased. The melancholy requisitions of Justice, as painful to those who inflicted, as to those who suffered them, have been complied with; and an awful but a necessary, and, it is hoped, an effectual example has been afforded to deter from further occasions of offence and punishment.

We have not been inattentive, in this distressing period, to the notice which might be taken of our situation by the journals in our sister states. It is grateful in the extreme to mark the tenderness and sympathy which, with the exception of one solitary print in New-York, have been universally manifested towards us. We are not in a state of mind to use language of acrimonious asperity. We regard with pity the individual who could deliberately sneer at our misfortunes—we leave him to the consolations of his conscience—his nightly dreams on his pillow—and hope he may always enjoy that security, which he so much rejoices that our city has been deprived of.

Yet, as an historical fact, worthy to be remembered, particularly at this time, and which Mr. STONE,[1] of the N. York *Commercial Advertiser,* appears to have forgotten, we would remind him, as we had occasion once before to remind another editor of New-York, that in the year 1741, in the city of New-York, *thirteen Negroes were* BURNT ALIVE *for insurrectionary efforts.*[2]

During the whole of this momentous inquiry, the utmost confidence has been felt in the State and City authorities, and in the two successive Courts organized to award justice, and acting under the most painful responsibilities. The Militia have with alacrity performed the unusual and laborious duties assigned them;—and now let us hope that the God of goodness and of mercy, who has guarded and protected us in the hour of peril, will continue to us his benevolent care, and frustrate always the evil designs of our enemies, and of those who conspire against our happiness and their own.

1. William Leete Stone Sr. (1792–1844), editor of the *New-York Commercial Advertiser.*

2. The reference is to an alleged slave conspiracy uncovered by authorities in New York City during the summer of 1741. Of the several hundred persons brought to trial, thirty-four were executed. See Graham Russell Hodges, *Root and Branch: African Americans in New York and East Jersey, 1613–1863* (Chapel Hill: University of North Carolina Press, 1999), 83–99.

Charleston City Council Minutes

Tuesday, August 13, 1822

Present The Intendant Messrs. Burger, Condy, Wesner, D'Oyley, Mitchell, Cogdell, Napier, Strohecker, Simons, Righton.

Read the Minutes of the 6th Instant.

(d) An Ordinance to provide for the appointment of Assistant Marshals and for other purposes therein mentioned being engrossed,

Was ratified in due form.

(d) Resolved that the Intendant be requested to prepare for publication an Account of the late intended Insurrection in this City with a Statement of the Trials, and such other facts in connection with the same as may be deemed of Public interest. . . . [1]

(d) A Communication was received from Major Manigault relative to the Magazine in Cumberland Street belonging to his mother & now used by the City.[2]

Referred to Messrs. Cogdell, Strohecker & Wesner. . . .

Mr. Simons asked and obtained leave to bring in a Bill to amend an Ordinance entitled an Ordinance for the government of Negroes and other persons of Color within the City of Charleston and for other purposes therein mentioned.

Ordered that the reading thereof be postponed.

(d) On Motion of Mr. Condy Resolved, that the thanks of this Council be given to Aeneas S. Reeves[3] for his exertions and attention during the sittings of the Courts for the trial of persons of Color for exciting an Insurrection in this State, and that the sum of $200 be granted to Wm. E. Gordon[4] for his labours and extraordinary services at the Work House on the same occasion.

(d) Resolved that the sum of $70 each be granted to Sergeants Street[5] & Rogers,[6] Corporals Varner[7] & McCullum[8] for their services during the late alarm.

On Motion of Mr. Cogdell,

(d) Deeply impressed with the important services rendered the Public at large by the recent investigation by the Two Courts for the trial of Persons of Color engaged in an attempt to raise an Insurrection in Charleston,

Resolved that the thanks of Council be tendered the gentlemen composing said Courts for their able impartial & patient trial of said persons.[9]

(d) The Committee appointed to enquire into the conduct of Captain Wm. Dove of the City Guard[,] charged with improper behavior towards a Warden[,] made a report.

The same being considered was concurred in.

Resolved that the investigation of the charges to take place on Saturday next at ½ past 3 O'Clock.

(d) Resolved that in future no person be suffered to see any of the Convicts now confined in the Work House the Wardens of the City excepted, and that no provisions be suffered to be brought from outdoors.[10]

Adjourned
Sine Die.

1. Intendant James Hamilton published his *Account* in late August. Page 2 of his pamphlet referred to the council's request, and Hamilton's statement of compliance on the same page was dated August 16.

2. The powder magazine dated to 1712 and remained in private hands. Ralph Izard (1742–1804) left it to his daughter, Margaret Izard (1768–1824), the wife of Gabriel Manigault (1758–1809), and to her son Charles Izard Manigault (1795–1874). See *Charleston News and Courier,* March 6, 1967, and March 9, 1936.

3. Aeneas S. Reeves (1787–1822) was "master of workhouse" and in 1822 lived at 1 Lynch Street. See *CSCCD,* 96.

4. William Edward Gordon (1781–1832) served in 1822 as "Deputy Keeper" and later superintendent of the Work-House. See *CSCCD,* 81; "Board of Health," *Charleston Courier,* September 4, 1823.

5. "Sergeant Street" was probably Joseph Street. Listed in 1822 in the city directory as a wheelwright, he retired as a Charleston constable in 1831. See *CSCCD,* 106; Charleston *City Gazette and Commercial Daily Advertiser,* August 4, 1831.

6. Of the four men surnamed Rogers in the 1822 directory, "Sergeant Rogers" most likely refers to John Ralph Rogers (1785–1857), a ship chandler who resided at 105 East Bay Street. See *CSCCD,* 96.

7. Henry Varner, a member of the Charleston City Guard who was active in 1822 tracking down runaway slaves, appears a likely match for Corporal Varner. See "Committed," Charleston *City Gazette and Commercial Daily Advertiser,* April, 18, 1822; *CSCCD,* 65.

8. "Corporal McCullum" probably refers to Robert McCullum, who resided in Charleston in 1822 at 33 South Bay Street. See *CSCCD,* 89.

9. This formal resolution of gratitude may be partly in response to the innuendo created by Justice William Johnson's essay, "The Melancholy Effect of Popular Excitement," which was published in the *Charleston Courier,* June 21, 1822, and appears here in Part II, pp. 131–33.

10. The City Council here overruled Intendant Hamilton, who on July 10, in a statement to Frederick Beard (in Part II of this volume), had directed Beard to allow "Wives, Masters, Children & such clergymen as they may be desirous of communicating with" to visit the accused slaves held in the Charleston Poor-House (also known as the Alms House), permission that Hamilton presumably extended to the Work-House.

Charleston County Public Library.

Charleston *City Gazette and Commercial Daily Advertiser*

Wednesday, August 14, 1822

From the "New-York Daily Advertiser."

"BLOODY SACRIFICE.

"Twenty-two human beings, blacks, were executed at *Charleston* on the morning of the 26th ult. Ten more were respited to the 9th of August, instant; and three were ordered to be sent out of the limits of the United States, never to return under penalty of death."

In the opinion of the community of Charleston, Mr. Dwight,[1] the Blue-light Editor of the "New-York Daily Advertiser" might invent some other way of edyfying his readers, than in groaning over the execution of a score of Culprits upon whose fate Justice and Humanity alike pronounced their sentence. The "bloody sacrifice" of which he insolently speaks, might have been prevented by a few peace offerings of such *lambs* as he and his faction can produce.

They may talk of Philanthropy, &c. but the Missouri poison is still "garnered" in their bosoms; and although they may never have dreamed of the awful consequences of those wild and foolish doctrines which have gone abroad—they begin already to feel in New-York, Philadelphia, and Boston, how very agreeable is the extension of the rights of Citizenship to those whom they *pretend* to regard as equals. We say *pretend,* for the Blacks in those cities are neither citizens nor aliens. There are few or no places (particularly in New-York) where they are admitted to amusement or instruction; little or no moral education by which they can be rendered virtuous members of society; little or no interest in their *temporal* welfare—though some specious shew of interest in their *spiritual* happiness;—no master or patron by whom they are protected, as was the case of the Freedman in ancient Rome, and as is frequently exhibited in South-Carolina.

What then is there in the destiny of these people and of the innumerable white poor who infest these cities, comparable in real protection, in plenty, or in intrinsic worth, to the faithful slave of a just master in the South? Nothing. We answer from the very statements made in the New-York papers. The class of people which we speak of exhibit vice without refinement, and ignorance without simplicity. They oppress, not enrich the soil, on which they are cast.

"'Tis an unweeded garden
That grows to seed; things rank, and gross in nature,
Possess it merely.'"

When we make this sketch, let it not for a moment be supposed, that we insinuate aught against the activity or intelligence of the city authorities of New-York. We are well aware that in so vast a population they have immense difficulties to contend withal. The good and the wise, the citizens who regards each and every state of our happy Union, from Maine to Georgia, as the land of his brothers, cannot but feel and think correctly on this delicate subject; whether it regards the prevention or the punishment of crime. The sympathy of these we did not expect, and do acknowledge. But there are a few—very few, thank God—who love to rant about what they either cannot or will not understand; and in the words of the Republican MILTON,

"That brawl for freedom in their senseless mood,
And still revolt when TRUTH would set them free.
Licence they mean when they cry Liberty;
For who loves THAT must first be wise and good."

1. Theodore Dwight (1764–1846).

New-York Commercial Advertiser

Thursday, August 15, 1822

The Charleston Southern Patriot has attacked us unhandsomely, unjustifiably and wickedly. But we have not time nor room for a formal reply. All that we have said of the executions at Charleston, was simply to express the opinion that they were too prodigal of life. The first ten or twelve executions were perhaps called for as an example. But was not the execution of twenty-two at one time, soon afterwards, going farther than was necessary? The poor negroes had only plotted a crime—they had not shed blood. And why should not a little mercy be meted out to them, as well as whole measures of it to the pirates, who, crimsoned with blood, have been pardoned at different times at Charleston, and other places at the south. When five or six pirates were sentenced to expiate their crimes on the gallows, it was said in some of the southern papers, that the moral feelings of the community would revolt at such a sacrifice of human life. But with the poor, misguided ignorant blacks, a different feeling seems to prevail. We hope every time we express a feeling of humanity, the Charleston Patriot, for the talents and moderation of which we have hitherto entertained a great degree of respect, will not fly in a passion at us.

Charleston *City Gazette and Commercial Daily Advertiser*

Thursday, August 15, 1822

A WORD OF ADVICE

To the Editor of the Philad. "Franklin Gazette."

Whenever you wish to write an essay upon "The insurrection of the Blacks," take any other model than the Editor of the *New-York Daily Advertiser.*[1] A man who has been illuminated with *blue lights,*[2] and been innoculated with the virus of the Hartford Convention, is a very unsafe guide to a good meaning Republican!—He tells you, "As nothing has appeared that has met *our view* to justify the great sacrifice of human lives that has taken place!" Something, as you perceive above, will soon meet "his view," but whatever inferences he draws, do not think with him; for treason will naturally be defended by a Hartford Conventionist. He also tells you, "Certain it is that *neither the spirit nor letter of the law* under which these executions have taken place, sanctions the enormous sacrifice!" Yet he immediately under quotes the *letter* of the law which has been in operation in this Country from the Proprietary to the Royal, and from the Royal to the Independent Government. The *spirit* of this law exists in every civilized society. It is the same spirit which detected and punished the Conspirators in the Cato-street plot, against the British Government[3]—the conservative spirit which preserves all organized Governments.

He *knows* this, yet is he *wicked* enough to keep it out of view; and you are *weak* enough to write about "striking for liberty," and "hailing" the victims of sedition as "patriots and martyrs"!—Yet, not contented with this rant, you make an exception which is ludicrous enough as it confounds all your fine sentiments, "*but for the atrocious mode of executing their purpose*"! Go, my friend, go—reflect more—read more, and you may probably come across the story of the *Stork* who was taken with the Cranes and Geese infesting and destroying a farmer's field. The silly Stork insisted he was neither Crane nor Goose, but, for all that, his neck was twisted for being found in *bad company.*

1. William Leete Stone.

2. "Blue light" was a pejorative term used to describe a New Englander disloyal during the War of 1812, particularly someone who had supported the Hartford Convention.

3. The reference is to the Cato-Street conspiracy (1820), which aimed at the assassination of members of the British cabinet. See George Theodore Wilkinson, *An Authentic History of the Cato-Street Conspiracy: With the Trials at Large of the Conspirators for High Treason and Murder* (London, 1820).

Charleston Mercury, and Morning Advertiser

Thursday, August 15, 1822

We have, hitherto, purposely abstained from noticing any of the remarks made in some Northern journals upon the late necessary decrees of justice that have been executed here upon convicted offenders of the laws. It did not appear to be necessary to exhibit any strictures upon the cold and unfeeling jests that have been sported in a manner that indicates a callousness of heart both to the culprits who fell under the laws, and the society for whose benefit those laws were enacted. We were willing that the authors of such jibes should enjoy them in undisturbed satisfaction.

There was a hope, also, that the Editors of other journals at the north, who have spoken like sensible and reasonable men upon the proceedings of the Court of Freeholders and Magistrates in this city, would have defended their fellow-countrymen upon the spot where they were attacked and put their accusers to shame—but these gentlemen have been contented with giving us their own approval.

Before a man sets down to write upon a subject he should ask himself if he is acquainted with it. Ignorance breeds error, and our own misconceptions, harmless if kept silent in the bosom, become mischievous when they are thrown before the world. It caused therefore sensations of mingled regret and resentment in us to observe [*illegible*] from which arose from the total ignorance of the writer of the matter he was discussing. He quotes a part of a law of South-Carolina, which he found in one of our newspapers, and applies that law to punishments that were inflicted under the sanction of other enactments of the law—and says that he cannot find, either in the letter or the spirit of the law, a sufficient reason for the extent to which the executions of the offenders were carried among us.

This is shocking injustice to say the least of it—a commentary upon a section of a law, without an acquaintance with the whole law can be nothing but the gloss of ignorance and mistake—it leads the public astray and touches the good name of a people, whose whole conduct, throughout the late proceedings, has been strictly conformable to statutory provisions and was regulated by a sense of justice and duty tempered by mildness and humanity.

The Editor in New-York conveys an implied censure upon the citizens of this place in remarking, that the justification of the punishments inflicted upon the offenders against our peace must appear from future disclosures, if indeed any justification can be offered for such a number of victims being handed over to the rigour of the law.

It became this gentleman, in decency, not to pronounce these words until he knew what justification there was for the acts which we had done. We are upon the spot and know what that justification was, and our knowledge is something on which to ground an opinion, but he who is ignorant of every thing relating to the late events in this city is not worthy of being listened to when he prates about them.

As to the numbers of those who have expiated their villainy, hypocrisy, and ingratitude, by an ignominious death, they have no relation whatever to any thing but the justice of their fate. In a wide spread conspiracy, wherein hundreds were implicated, the leaders and the most heinous offenders engaged in it were detected—they were doomed to death, and if two hundred or two thousand had been found as guilty as they were they too would have suffered. Justice is not to be disarmed because she is called upon to strike among a multitude of convinced plotters of assassination and barbarian horrors.

The people of this city are as humane, as pious, as obedient to the calls of charity and to the dictates of mercy and christian foregiveness as are the citizens of New-York, or any other place. They want no newspaper lectures—they have nothing to do with a grave doctor, in his broad phylactery, who would teach them their duty in matters of which he knows nothing, and with which they are intimate—they know what conscience is and what deeds are fair and what are foul; they know what is required of them in the state of society in which they live, and that which is required they have done and would do again—they did it without fear, and they hoped that their fellow countrymen would have unanimously suffered them to do it without reproach.

CITY COUNCIL.

Charleston City Council Minutes

Saturday, August 17, 1822

Present The Intendant Messrs. Wesner, Mitchell, Burger, Strohecker, D'Oyley, Cogdell, Condy, Simons, Napier, DeLiesseline.

Read the Minutes of the 13th Instant. . . .

(d) A Letter was received from Lionel H. Kennedy Esquire enclosing certain suggestions for the consideration and revision of Council by the Members composing the late Court of Magistrates and Freeholders as drawn out by Colonel Drayton.[1]

Referred to Messrs. Simons, Cogdell, Napier and DeLiesseline.

Council proceeded to investigate the Charges preferred by Mr. Simons against Captain Dove of the City Guard.[2]

And after hearing evidence, came to the following conclusion.

Under Specification 1st.

That Captain Dove is not guilty of saying that he would offer Mr. Simons personal violence, or of challenging him, but guilty of an impropriety in conversing with his Officers, as to our explanation with Mr. Simons which looked pointedly to that result.

2nd Specification. Withdrawn on the explanation & disavowal of Captain Dove of any intentional disrespect to Mr. Simons.

Charge 2nd, Involving the same degree of *impropriety* as the 1st specification.

Charge 3rd, Guilty in permitting a gross error in the Pay Roll he certified although Council acquits him of all implication of Fraud.

Mr. Wesner moved that Captain Dove be reprimanded by the Intendant in private.

Mr. Simons moved to strike out the word private and insert "the presence of Council," and called for the Yeas & Nays as follows.

Yeas The Intendant, Messrs. Wesner, Strohecker, Napier, Simons.

Nays Messrs. Cogdell, D'Oyley, Burger, DeLiesseline, Mitchell.

Yeas 6. Nays 5.

So the same was stricken out and the words "the presence of Council" inserted.

The Question was then taken on the Resolution as amended and carried in the affirmative.

Captain Dove was immediately sent for and reprimanded by his Honor the Intendant.

The Intendant having left the room Mr. Simons was requested to take the Chair.

When the following Resolution was offered by Mr. D'Oyley and concurred in.

Resolved that the thanks of Council be presented to the Honorable James Hamilton Junior for his unremitting attention to the Public Interest during his term of Service, and more particularly for his vigilance during a late period of uncommon peril and danger, at a Season of extraordinary commotion and alarm the Council feel happy when they reflect, that the efforts of Chief Magistrate of the City were distinguished by an activity and energy suited to the public emergency.[3]

The Council are unanimously of opinion that the conduct of the Intendant during his administration deserves the ardent and lasting thanks of this City.

Resolved that this Resolution be published at the expiration by the Intendant's term of service for the Year.

Adjourned
Sine Die.

1. This letter, which clearly predated Kennedy's extant letter of July 24 to Governor Bennett regarding court procedures and pardons, seems not to have survived. The Colonel Drayton referred

to here is William Drayton (1776–1846), a lawyer and close friend of Hamilton. Drayton served on the first Court of Magistrates and Freeholders.

2. See the City Council Minutes of July 8 for the first mention of this near-duel between Captain William P. Dove and councilman Edward P. Simons.

3. Given the intendant's differences with groups of citizen vigilantes, together with the council's disagreement with Hamilton regarding visitors for accused and condemned slaves, this resolution of thanks may have been designed as much to smooth over public differences as it was to praise his handling of the crisis.

Charleston County Public Library.

Charleston Mercury, and Morning Advertiser

Monday, August 19, 1822

FOR THE MERCURY.

The Civil Authorities of the City have at length announced that their labours, as connected with the late conspiracy among our coloured population, have nearly or entirely closed.

While we rejoice in the event, and congratulate our fellow citizens on its annunciation, we think some duties, on the part of the inhabitants of this City and State, remain yet to be performed. We owe to the Public Authorities of this City, and to the many citizens connected with them in the development and prosecution of these offences against our laws, public acknowledgements for the eminent services they have rendered to their country.

This act is due to them and to ourselves.—It is due to them, for their zeal, their vigilance, their firmness and the cautious and scrupulous regard to justice with which severe but necessary laws have been carried into execution. It is due to ourselves to express the gratitude we feel for their services, to show the undivided opinion of our citizens, to manifest our determination to support and maintain the municipal regulations of the State; and to protect from aspersion the characters of those who have acted in our behalf.

And it may, also, merit consideration whether this is not a proper moment to have the Municipal and State laws, on the subject of our Domestics, submitted to the revision of a respectable Committee of our citizens. Public attention has now been forcibly drawn to this subject; many suggestions are already in circulation; much information has been gained during the late trials of the guilty, and no one can doubt that it will be beneficial to have a well digested system, if such can be obtained, prepared and offered to the Legislature at their next session.

Our laws may not require amendment, if this is the case it ought to be understood.—But if additions to the provisions of our present code are necessary it will, surely, be better to have them presented at an early period to the attention of our citizens, than to leave them to the chance of recollection and examination during the short period of our Legislative sessions. It should be our object not so much to provide for the punishment of offences; this perhaps has been already done so as to prevent their recurrence, but it must be to the habitual police of our country, if I may use such an expression, that we are to look for its future tranquility. This is an important subject and deserves at present an almost undivided attention.

It is therefore recommended, that a public meeting of the citizens of Charleston should be convened, at an early day, to take this subject under their consideration. This at least is the wish of

MANY CITIZENS.

Baltimore Patriot & Mercantile Advertiser

Monday, August 19, 1822

Mr. Stone[1] of the *New-York Commercial Advertiser,* with some other northern Editors, have made several remarks on the necessary and every way proper example set, in the execution of insurgent blacks at Charleston. The Editor of the *Charleston Courier*[2] keenly rebukes this ill-judged interference; and adds the following:

Yet, as an historical fact, worthy to be remembered, particularly at this time, and which Mr. STONE, of the N. York *Commercial Advertiser,* appears to have forgotten, we would remind him, as we had occasion once before to remind another editor of New-York, that in the year 1741, in the city of New-York, *thirteen Negroes were* BURNT ALIVE *for insurrectionary efforts.*

1. William Leete Stone.
2. Aaron S. Willington.

Charleston Mercury, and Morning Advertiser

Tuesday, August 20, 1822

To the Editor of the Mercury.

SIR,

In common with all the inhabitants of this city, with whom I have conversed upon the subjects of the hint published in your paper yesterday signed "Many Citizens," I cordially approve of the objects therein stated. It appears to me to be the duty of every one among us to promote the purposes recommended, and this is the time for doing so effectually. Something is certainly due from the collective body of the citizens, as an honourable testimony that they appreciate the value of the services rendered by those gentlemen, who have devoted their days and nights to secure the peace of the city, and the Courts of Magistrates and Freeholders should not be suffered to silently dissolve without a full expression of public gratitude for the exemplary manner in which they have discharged the trust confided to them.

Let us also, by a well chosen committee, examine into the police laws of the state and city. If additions or alterations are unnecessary it is well—if they are wanted, we have now a body of experienced men, whose familiarity with the operation of the present system, its merits and its deficiencies is such that we can hardly ever expect to find again among us & whose counsel is invaluable. While this is fresh let it be applied to secure a lasting benefit. The public may not yet have gathered all the good that these gentlemen are capable of affording to them in matters so essential to the community.

This is a time of leisure. In a few weeks business of various kinds will draw off the attention of the citizens to immediate personal concerns. Gentlemen will be dispersed in the country, and those who are always in the city will be occupied with their own affairs and thus the benefits of combination, and the lights that arise from consultation and intercourse will be lost.

I hope that some gentlemen of influence in society will see the necessity of urging this important business immediately.

A CITIZEN.

Philadelphia *United States Gazette and True American*

Thursday, August 22, 1822

FROM THE NEW YORK NATIONAL ADVOCATE.

Insurrection.—We have received several letters from Charleston, relative to the insurrection of the blacks, all tending to release the citizens from a charges of cruelty, which they imagine the people to the north impute to them. Really no such feelings exists, and no defence of their just and proper measures is necessary.

One of our correspondents writes:

For evidence of this, it was ascertained that the letters of the conspirators were forwarded through New York to St. Domingo. The principal of this dreadful conspiracy was a free black man, and in the enjoyment of every comfort that he could wish; yet this troubled spirit could not rest satisfied, and after visiting St. Domingo once or twice,[1] returned to this place to accomplish his hellish designs. He suffered with five others at the first execution, and frequently alluded in the course of his trial to the sanction their conduct would meet with from a most enlightened Senator[2] from your state—a gentleman who once dwelt in the heart of every good man here, and even those who were opposed to him in politics. Pray tell him to reflect in the goodness of his heart, how many innocent women and children were on the eve of being butchered by this delusion, and entreat him, as he holds the union of these states sacred, to use his means in removing the evil which he perhaps has innocently been instrumental in creating.

If the northern and eastern section of our union are determined that slavery should be abolished in the south, we ask how these states (southern) can be cultivated. It is very evident, from the unhealthiness of the climate, that white laborers cannot be employed, whereas the others, during the summer season, enjoy the best health. We must either abandon our homes and property to seek a living elsewhere, or be allowed to retain them in more tranquility.

Another correspondent gives the following intelligence:

We shall have a complete revisal of the laws, applicable to colored persons; it is full time that the lives and property of the citizens should be put under no apprehension of a return of the horrid scenes that have just been exposed; and without a most Providential interference, would have been murdered and destroyed. Two *mulatto bishops*[3] have been tried before a magistrate, and being guilty of having returned to the state, contrary to the act of 1820 against free persons of color, have been ordered away in 15 days, or be liable to be sold for five years servitude. They have appealed to the court of Common Pleas, and very animated arguments are made, pro and con. The Judge, seeing the importance of the case, has deferred giving his decision, although it is generally thought it will be against the mulattoes.[4] It is not supposed there will be any more trials for the attempt to raise any insurrection. A new ordinance of Council grants to the Intendant a salary of $3,500 from October next. His duties are amply defined, and will add much to the improvement of our city, police and law.

1. Denmark Vesey was actually a freedman, not a freeman, having purchased his freedom in 1799. As a boy, Vesey lived in French Saint-Domingue from the fall of 1781 until late April 1782. There is no evidence that he revisited Saint-Domingue after the start of the slave revolution in 1791, or visited Haiti after it became independent in 1804.

2. Senator Rufus King (1755–1827) of New York was publicly critical of slavery. He called for an end to the internal slave trade in 1817 and denounced its extension into Missouri during the debates of 1819–21. See Robert Ernst, *Rufus King: American Federalist* (Chapel Hill: Published for the Institute of Early American History and Culture at Williamsburg, VA, by University of North Carolina Press, 1968). Denmark Vesey referred to him as "the black man's friend." See Confession of Jack Purcell on p. 214 in Part III of this volume.

3. Morris Brown (1770–1849) and Henry Drayton (d. 1837) appeared in the Court of Common Pleas before Judge John Blake White (1781–1859) and were sentenced to leave the state. Drayton appealed his sentence, without avail, to the Court of General Session before Judge Elihu Hall Bay (1754–1838). Drayton's petition, filed on August 8, 1822, is transcribed on pp. 667–68 in Part V.

4. Morris Brown's son Malcolm evidently did not leave the state with his father, who relocated to Philadelphia. On April 11, 1871, Malcolm Brown Jr., who listed his father as "Malcolm, dead," opened an account with the Charleston branch of the Freedman's Savings Bank. See Bank Records, Microfilm Roll 23, NA, Washington, DC.

Charleston City Council Minutes

Saturday, August 24, 1822

Present The Intendant P.T. Messrs. Cogdell, Napier, Condy, DeLiesseline, Strohecker[,] Wesner[,] Mitchell[,] Simons.

Read the Minutes of the 17th Instant. . . .

(d) The Committee to whom was referred the Accounts of John J. Singletary[1] report,

That they have examined the same and find them to be correct and recommend they be ordered for payment.

Frederick Wesner

Edward P. Simons

Thomas D. Condy.

Agreed to.

(d) Resolved that the sum of $125.45 be appropriated to defray the expenses of a Corporation Dinner and refreshments furnished at the Work House during the late Investigation by the Courts of Magistrates.

Adjourned to Tuesday ½ past 4 O'Clock.

Tuesday August 27th 1822.

Present The Intendant P.T. Messrs. Burger, Condy, Simons, Righton, Strohecker, D'Oyley, Cogdell, DeLiesseline, Napier, Wesner, Mitchell.

Read the Minutes of 24th Instant.

The Treasurer's Statement of Cash for August 1822 was presented.

Received as information.

(d) The following Accounts were passed and ordered for payment.

Mark Marks	$18.00
Committee of Vigilance	9.25
Doct. John M. Righton	*40.00*[2]
	$67.25

(d) Read a Letter from the Chairman Commissioners Cross Roads stating a Complaint had been made by many persons residing within the vicinity of the Lines of an alarming nuisance occasioned by the slight and offensive manner in which many of the Culprits lately executed have been interred.[3]

Resolved that the Intendant Pro Tempore be requested inform the Commissioners that the nuisance complained of was attended to immediately on the receipt of the Communication from their Chairman.

A Communication was received from Jared R. Bunce acknowledging to have received on Board the Ship Georgia Packet a Colored Man named John Parker who was committed as a runaway, and afterwards proved to be free & ordered to be sent out of the State by Council. . . .

Received a Letter from John & D. Paul respecting their Slaves Wm. & Edwin[4] who were committed of attempting to raise an Insurrection in this City.

Ordered to lie on the Table. . . .

(d) Read a Petition from Mary Roddy praying to be refunded a Fine paid by her on Account of her Negro working out without a Badge.

Referred to the Committee on Relief. . . .

A Report was received from the Committee on the Letter of G. H. Manigault Esquire requiring rent for the old Arsenal in Cumberland Street now in the use of the City as a repository of Powder & attached to the Engineer's Department.

Consideration postponed. . . .

(d) A Petition was received from Jack Lopez[5] stating he was arrested on the cause of a suspicion to raise an insurrection in this City and put to considerable expense & praying Relief.

Resolved that the Petition cannot be heard unless it be made by a White Guardian.

. . .

Adjourned

Sine Die.

1. John Jinks Singletary (1777–1857) was from St. James Goose Creek Parish. The Charleston City Council in 1822 paid Singletary $100 for "bringing down" to Charleston the slaves Abram and Sambo. He was paid an additional $9.26 "for Expenses on Sullivan's Island on account of Denmark Vesey." See Petition of the City Council, December 3, 1822, no. 130, series S165015, Petitions to the

General Assembly, SCDAH. In a letter dated March 17, 1860, reproduced on pp. 749–53 in Part VI, the abolitionist Lydia Maria Child pulled information from her personal papers for Thomas Wentworth Higginson, who had solicited what she knew about slave insurrection for an article he was writing for the *Atlantic Monthly.* When turning to the Vesey affair, she quoted Thomas Cilavan Brown, a free colored carpenter whom she had met. He had lived in Charleston in 1822 and claimed to know Vesey. "'I heard, at the time,' Brown told Child, 'of arms being buried in coffins, at Sullivan's Island. But that is not the negro burying ground. The slaves are buried in a place called the potter's Field, and the colored people have a ground of their own.'" There was, however, an African American graveyard on the island for local residents.

2. Dr. John McCulloch Righton received his medical degree from the New-York College of Physicians in 1816. In 1822 he was appointed "Physician of the Work House" and attended sick and injured slaves there from July to December 1822. Typically, he received his fees from the owners of the slaves, but the state legislature paid him $353.43 for his services during the Vesey affair. In 1822, he resided at 15 George Street. See Charleston *City Gazette and Commercial Daily Advertiser,* May 21, 1816, and October 22, 1822; Petition of John M. Righton, ca. 1823, no. 1736, series S165015, Petitions of the General Assembly, SCDAH; Thomas Cooper and David J. McCord, eds., *The Statutes at Large of South Carolina* (Columbia, SC, 1839), vol. 6: 232; *CSCCD,* 96. In 1830, Righton owned twenty-six slaves, an increase of fourteen from the census of 1820. See 1830 US Census, Christ Church, Charleston, South Carolina, roll 170, p. 197, NA.

3. This reference to the manner of internment suggests that many of those executed on July 26 were buried in shallow graves along the Lines and that their bodies attracted vermin. This may be one of the reasons why the court began to turn the bodies of the executed over to local surgeons for dissection. See *Charleston Mercury, and Morning Advertiser,* July 27, 1822, which appears on p. 424 in Part IV.

4. Both William and Edwin were transported. Hamilton, *Account,* 45, lists both slaves as the property of John Paul, a prosperous Scottish-born merchant. *CSCCD,* 94, identifies "John & Dunbar Paul" in 1822 as "grocers," working at 47 Broad Street.

5. Jack Lopez was a freeman and the brother of William Garner, the last of the slaves to be hanged. See *Charleston Courier,* July 20, 1822.

Charleston County Public Library.

Baltimore Patriot & Mercantile Advertiser

Wednesday, August 28, 1822

NEGRO INSURRECTION.

We give, in this paper, a detail of a part of the circumstances, which transpired on the examination before the Intendant and Council of Charleston, (S.C.) relative to the projected revolt. We are no advocates for severity towards this class of people; but the lesson furnished by this alarm should not be forgotten. It is a remarkable fact, that not a single slave concerned in it, had the slightest complaint to make of ill-treatment. It originated and was prosecuted by those, who werein judiciously pampered and patronized—in a common phrase, by those, who were allowed to get *out of their place* in society. One faithful and grateful fellow, however, forms an exception to the general rule; and it is principally to him, that our sister city is indebted for exemption from the most serious calamities.—It is to a *free negro,* DENMARK VESEY, who appears to have been in the words of *Prospero,* [1]

"A devil, a born devil, in whose nature,

Nurture could never stick,"

That this most diabolical of all projects, the promiscuous massacre of the white men, and a worse fate for the white females, is to be traced.

The authorities of Charleston appear to have acted with great precaution, with deliberate impartiality and discriminating severity.

The pretended necromancy of the native of Angola,[2] and the fanatical appeal following, are exactly of a piece.

"*Dear Sir,*—With pleasure I give you an answer. I will endeavour to do it. Hoping that God will be in the midst to help his own. Be particular and make a sure mark. Fear not, the Lord God that delivered Daniel, is able to deliver us. All that I inform agree, I am gone up to Beach-Hill."

Abraham Poyas."[3]

When superstition is inculcated upon minds, without the guidance of intelligence, it is but a means of producing the direst evils; and the plea of *good intentions,* should not avail those who neglect to instruct, before they pretend to convert.

1. The protagonist in Shakespeare's *The Tempest,* a play that speaks to issues of slavery, imperialism, and colonialism.

2. This was a reference to Gullah Jack Pritchard.

3. Abraham Poyas, the slave of Dr. John Ernest Poyas Jr. (1759–1824) and a member of the African Church, was transported. This letter, which was presented into evidence and appears in this volume on p. 181 in Part III, was found in the trunk of Peter Poyas.

Charleston City Council Minutes

Thursday, August 29, 1822

Present The Intendant P.T. Messrs. Righton, Burger, DeLiesseline, Strohecker, Napier, Mitchell, Simons, Wesner, Condy, Cogdell, D'Oyley.

Read the Minutes of 27th Instant. . . .

X[1] The Letter from J. & D. Paul respecting their Slaves Wm. & Edwin who were committed, and now confined in the Work House on suspicion of attempting to raise an insurrection in this City; the consideration of which was postponed on the 27th Instant was taken up. Resolved that the Negroes of Messrs. J. & D. Paul be retained until the return of Major Hamilton. . . . [2]

Adjourned

Sine Die.

1. Council Minutes editors Bennett and Butler write: "The following paragraph is written vertically in the right margin of page 103, preceded by an 'X' indicating that it is to be inserted into the text at this point."

2. Both William and Edwin were transported. See Hamilton, *Account,* 45.

Charleston County Public Library.

William Peronneau to Governor Thomas Bennett Jr., Friday, August 30, 1822

Charleston 30th August 1822.

His Excellency
Governor Bennett
Dear Sir

As an individual, I hope you will do me the justice to believe, that no one can regret more than I do, that any difference of opinion should ever exist between your Excellency and the Council; but as the organ of that body, it has become officially my painful duty to inform you, that the Council have directed that no person but your Excellency, shall be permitted for the future to see any of the Culprits.

I have the honor to be
With the greatest respect
y Excellency's most obt Sert

Wm. Peronneau. J. P.

ALS in GM, no. 1328, SCDAH.

New Orleans *Louisiana Gazette*

Friday, August 30, 1822

Governor Bennett's detail of the late conspiracy among the blacks of South Carolina, appears to be ingenuous and undisguised, and we certainly hope it may have the effect to quiet the alarm, which the conspiracy produced, and "to prevent that rapid deterioration of property," which the chief magistrate of that state foresaw would be a consequence, unless the tranquillity of the public mind was restored.

Several circumstances are developed in this official account of the plot, which furnish new proof to justify the remarks we made a few day[s] since on the evils of slavery, and the anticipations in which we indulged of the future condition of the slave-holding states. It seems a letter was addressed by Gell, one of the ring-leaders, to President Boyer, of St. Domingo, soliciting his alliance and co-operation in the conspiracy. Although this proposition, in the present instance, was not accepted, or did not produce its desired effect, the fact is scarcely the less alarming, since it shows that the blacks understand fully the situation of their brethren in that island, and the relation that may by possibility exist between them and the slaves of the South. It manifests intelligence and skill on the part of Gell, with regard to the measures necessary for the execution of the conspiracy, which under different circumstances might prove successful.—The letter, it appears, was with a good deal of sagacity, directed to a third person, that the address might not give alarm and expose the writer to detection

Another important fact disclosed by Governor Bennett's statement, is the use that has been made of the speeches in Congress, against the admission of Missouri. If the blacks of the south are capable of reading and understanding the argument or even the passionate appeal on that question, they are more ripe for conspiracies, than we had been led to suppose. It was believed that the great mass were yet too ignorant to read, and to be excited by inflammatory pamphlets. If they are capable of being excited to insurrection by such means, it will be extremely difficult to interpose barriers, which shall prevent future conspiracies.

Charleston *City Gazette and Commercial Daily Advertiser*

Friday, August 30, 1822

The approaching election for Intendant and Wardens, is particularly interesting. The present Council until within a few days, have received constant marks of public approbation. . . . It is understood, however, that great dissatisfaction exists in the minds of some persons, and that a strenuous opposition will be made to the re-election of Mr. Hamilton and some of his colleagues who are supposed to be friendly to him. . . . [A] lthough we disclaim the language of eulogy, we have a right to examine the objections and charges that are brought forward against the Council, and against the Intendant more particularly, and these seem principally to concern the Ordinance respecting the duties and compensation of the Intendant's office.[1] . . . There is another consideration that deserves the attention of impartial men.—The events which have lately taken place in this city are the subject of discussion all over the union, and our own character is intimately connected with the justification of those acts, in which the City Council had so large a part. If the late Intendant was not a fit person to fill the place he has lately held, this consideration would not alone induce us to support him: but while his qualifications, his integrity and public spirit are unimpeachable, we will not concur in a vote of censure, which cannot fail to be gratifying to the enemies of this country. . . .

1. James Hamilton Jr. ultimately ran unopposed in 1822 for the position of intendant. A controversy surfaced about the payment of a salary for what had previously been an unpaid post. Friends of John Geddes (1777–1828), a former governor of the state, circulated the possibility of his candidacy, but when Hamilton announced publicly that he would take no salary, Geddes's name was withdrawn. See *BDSCHR* 4: 224–25.

Independent Chronicle and Boston Patriot

Saturday, August 31, 1822

THE NEGRO PLOT IN S. CAROLINA. Gov. Bennett's Circular in relation to this plot is evidently intended to allay the apprehensions, that every planter and slave-owner in South Carolina must have entertained, especially after the various rumors that had been put into circulation in respect to its magnitude and the progress which it had made. The Governor states, that the first intelligence of its existence was obtained from a favorite servant, who, prompted by his own feelings of attachment, informed his master that he had been solicited to join a number of persons already engaged in the conspiracy. Three slaves were upon this information, immediately arrested and confined; one of whom shortly after made some confessions to the city authorities. The arrest of these slaves and the fear of disclosures that they might make, evidently produced much consternation among the conspirators, and induced another slave to come forward and make a disclosure of the names of several of the most conspicuous conspirators. He also stated that their plans would be matured and their attempt made on the night of June 16th. This night however passed and no attempt was made. On the following 18th, ten slaves were arrested, upon whom sentence of death was pronounced on the following 28th of June—Denmark Vesey, a free negro, was arrested June 21st, and by the confession of one of the abovementioned ten convicts, his guilt was established. . . .

Hartford *Connecticut Mirror*

Monday, September 2, 1822

EXTRACT OF A LETTER.

The Late Black Plot, at Charleston, S.C.

It was ascertained that the letters of the conspirators were forwarded through New York to St. Domingo. The principal of this dreadful conspiracy was a free black man, and in the enjoyment of every comfort that he could wish; yet this troubled spirit could not rest satisfied, and after visiting St. Domingo once or twice, returned to this place to accomplish his hellish designs. He suffered with five others at the first execution.

"We should have a complete revisal of the laws, applicable to coloured persons; it is full time that the lives and property of the citizens should be under no apprehension of a return of the horrid scenes that have just been exposed. Two mulatto bishops have been tried before the magistrate, and being guilty of having returned to the state, contrary to the act of 1820 against free persons of color, have been ordered away in 15 days, or be liable to be sold for five years' servitude. They have appealed to the Court of Common Pleas, and very animated arguments are made pro and con. The judge,[1] seeing the importance of the case, has deferred giving his decision, although it is generally thought it will be against the mulattoes. A new ordinance of Council grants to the Intendant, a salary of $3,500, from October next."

Another says, we tried these people by the same strict rules of evidence, which govern our criminal courts of judicature; and in every case, the master, assisted by counsel, where he desired it, attended to the defence of his slave. By patience and perseverance, we have got at the bottom of the plot; and such has been the example, that we have no fear of the thing occurring again in our lives, if only proper laws are passed, of which all believe there is a necessity.—*Mer. Adv.*

1. John Blake White (1781–1859).

Philadelphia *Democratic Press*

Tuesday, September 3, 1822

For the Democratic Press.

I observe in the New York Statesman of the 21st inst. an editorial piece, headed "*Evils of Slavery*" which I consider highly injudicious on the part of the learned editor, and calculated to 'irritate without producing any good effect.' The motive that produced it I have yet to learn—the consequences it leads to are too evident to be mistaken. If the same train of reflection had been published in a foreign country, where the sentiments would never reach the region of rebellion, it might be innocent. If Mr. Carter[1] had expressed himself in the same language to a friend, it might have been harmless, but to give *publicity* where advantage may be taken of every word, constitutes the highest indiscretion. If any good were deducible from the piece, it might be its justification, but I do not think it susceptible of being tortured into any thing of the kind. Then, why publish such sentiments upon a subject too delicate to be handled, and too proximate in all its consequences; about which no thought should have a tongue. I will not ascribe to the author, any sinister design, or culpable motive, but I do not hesitate to say that his piece inculcates the doctrine of insurrection and tends to stimulate the poor, deluded, blacks to persevere in their scheme of cruelty and blood. I will quote his own words to sustain me in my assertion. "The late conspiracy and the measures deemed necessary to deter others from other attempts, form merely a prelude to horrors of the same kind, which must hereafter occur in the slave holding states." "Such events must inevitably take place." "The progress of knowledge among the blacks, and the proximity of St. Domingo will probably hasten the bloody catastrophe." It seems by no means to follow as an 'inevitable' consequence, because these attempts have been made, that they must be made again. If the state of society be daily giving into amelioration of the condition of the slave if to the feelings of humanity, we superadd the principle of interest on the part of the master to work his slaves with moderation, to feed them plentifully, to clothe them well, to have them comfortably housed, to nurse them attentively in sickness and to teach them the necessity and advantage of obedience, are we to consider these as so many provocatives to conspiracy—if their minds are capable of rational reflection, and their principles susceptible of gratitude, we may hope for better results. But the "progress of knowledge will hasten the bloody catastrophe." What "knowledge" let me ask? Is it to know that they have means commensurate to their ends? Then what has Mr. Carter told them? Has he not communicated a most essential stock of "knowledge" by taking a survey of the relative increase of the white and black population within a given period and thereby shewn that the ratio of increase is decidedly in favor of the blacks; that they have a numerical superiority in some of the states, and growing physical advantages in all the slave holding states. Not content with alone stating these particulars, he draws his deductions; which purports just so much *advice.* This is his language, "the moment therefore that the blacks get an idea of their superiority in point of numbers and strength over those who hold them in bondage, endless scenes of conspiracy, violence and mutual destruction will be expected to ensue." Again, "nothing will be wanting but a knowledge of the fact and a disposition to avail themselves of it"—"It is unreasonable and improbable to suppose, that intelligent and adventurous leaders will not be found with sufficient talents to project conspiracies, persuade others to enrol themselves under their standard, and carrry their plans into execution."—Had Mr. Carter been a *professor* in the school of insurrection, or a colleague in their sanguinary schemes of midnight murder, he could not have given a more forcible lecture, or a more encouraging address. If he had been threorising upon the ultimate prospects of Greece or reasoning upon the present condition of Spain, he might have used such language; but there is no justification for it shaped and addressed as it is. To a people who are labouring under a mistaken infatuation, who have already had too much of this le[a]ven thrown into their midnight orgies, such language amounts to criminal encouragement. Predisposed as they already are to believe that a living interest is felt for them in this part of the country, may they not infer from the doctrine of Mr. Carter that the people of the middle and eastern states are with them, either openly to espouse their cause, or that neutrality will be their course in the hour of trial. Let no such delusion be indulged, though some few have dared to intimate as much, it is a libel upon the general feeling.—There is a community of interest, there are ties of propinquity, there are recorded warnings, there is a resistless impulse arising from the identity of our race, throughout our common country, that will forever forbid the white population sanctioning the rule of any part, to the dominion of blacks. If for a moment we were to admit the premises assumed by Mr. Carter, we should unhesitatingly deny his conclusions that they can never "carry their plans into execution." No scheme of general insurrection in the south can ever succeed—the situation of the blacks are too dispersed, their means too limited, their views and feeling, too discordant, their intellectual capacities too narrow, and their physical resourses too ineffectual, to produce a well organized plan, or simultaneous operation, upon which would depend their success. But were we to admit that they might succeed in one or two of the states, it would be only a momentary victory, the national arm would be immediately extended for their subjugation, and foreign succour could not stay the issue. It would then either eventuate in the entire extermination of the race of blacks from this continent, or else consign them to an aggravated bondage that might at first shock the best feelings of humanity, but that would have to yield to that paramount impulse of our nature—self preservation. I take this for granted that the white population can at all times suppress insurrection, and coerce the blacks to a state of bondage—that as society is now organized, it is to the interest and it behoves every part of the country to enforce this principle, and that any attempt in contravention of this truth, would only increase the privations which now belong to slavery. Let no enthusiast for liberty, let no fanatic in religion, think that he is promoting the one, or serving the other, by holding out the language of insurrection to the slaves of the south.—To such, I would point to the sanguinary and memorable catastrophe of St. Domingo and ask if we are prepared to rehearse that direful tragedy. No, let mercy and humanity plead for the least evils—If pure, permanent and rational liberty could wave its banner over the wide spread theatre of southern insurrection, it might plead in extenuation of the long catalogue of cruelties that would stain and deform its consummation: but, who would approve the policy, or sing an anthem to the birth of its fruition. Should these few remarks reach the eye of Mr. Carter, may they convince him that it would have been more judicious to "have cautiously abstained from making any remarks on the bloody scene," and to reflect how much more commendable it would have been if he had imitated the example of the illustrious Apostle who said, "Servants, be obedient to them that are *your* masters."[2]

PHOCION.

1. Nathaniel Hazeltine Carter (1787–1830), editor of the *New York Statesman.*
2. Ephesians 5:10.

Charleston *City Gazette and Commercial Daily Advertiser*

Thursday, September 5, 1822

The papers from the North which we have received for some days past, are uncommonly barren of *News.* Most of them are filled with the official account of the late insurrection in this city. Only *one* Editor as yet has attempted to animadvert upon that publication—we do not envy his disposition.

If the editor of the "Washington City Gazette" will calmly read the passing remark we hazarded upon Jack Purcell's confession, he will find that it does not admit the construction he puts upon it. A man (black or white) standing upon the confines of eternity, is not apt to utter a deliberate falsehood. Purcell's confession stands recorded. He was one of Vesey's deluded victims. We are sincerely averse to mention the respectable name of Mr. King, as connected with this affair; but as the BIBLE has been profaned in the service of guilt, where is there any thing improbable, or even remarkable in the fact that extracts of speeches on the Missouri question were circulated to promote insurrection?[1] 'The Devil can quote scripture'—and propositions about liberty and equality (particularly when made to bear upon a particular class) suited exactly the ends of those who grasped at the brightest names, and even tore the inspired page, to sanction deeds of darkness.

Considering the subject, and more particularly the *manner* of Mr. Walsh's remarks, in his paper of the 27th August, we deem it unnecessary to make any comment. This gentleman has been at variance with himself on several occasions—unfortunately so on the late attempt to excite a *bellum servile* in this city. He has *proved* nothing in favour of the agitators of liberty in the Missouri question; he has *disproved* nothing in the moderate and authentic account published by order of the corporation of this City. 'Tis time for this writer (whose reading we respect, but whose inconsistency is somewhat laughable) to cho[o]se a more agreeable, as he can easily a more innocent subject, for the occupation of his pen.

1. The author refers to Federalist Senator Rufus King (1755–1827) and his ferocious denunciation in Congress in February 1820 against extending slavery into Missouri. King relied on the Declaration of Independence and natural law—which he defined as God's law—to argue for slavery's extinction. For a revealing document on the inflammatory impact of King's speech, see Senator John Williams Walker to Charles Tait, February 11, 1820, Alabama Department of Archives and History, Montgomery.

Boston *New-England Galaxy*

Friday, September 6, 1822

THE NEGRO PLOT AT CHARLESTON. People in the northern states have read with some degree of sensibility the late accounts from Charleston, of the trial and execution of a number of negroes for a projected insurrection; but it has generally been supposed that the court which was organized for the purpose was in possession of facts, necessarily unknown here, which justified the course pursued. The court has at length completed its work, and the governor of the state has issued a circular, detailing the principal incidents connected with the attempted insurrection. We saw this document in several papers, before we ventured to read it, presuming that it developed a series of ungrateful, nefarious, and, perhaps, bloody, transactions on the part of the negroes, with which we had no desire to become acquainted. If any others have been induced, from similar feelings to turn aside from the perusal of the governor's "plain detail of the principal incidents," we assure them, their anticipations are entirely unfounded. They may peruse it, without being called to exercise their sympathies for ravished women or murdered infants—no houses were burnt, no excesses of any kind committed,—nor can we find from this elaborate document that any proof of an intention to attempt any very flagitious act was intended. "No means, (says the governor) which experience or ingenuity could devise, were left unessayed, to eviscerate the plot;" and his excellency acknowledges, that "the scheme was not general nor alarmingly extensive. Those who were associated (he adds) were unprovided with the means of attack or resistance. No weapons, if we except THIRTEEN HOOP-POLES, have been discovered; *nor any testimony received but of six pikes, that such preparations were actually made.* (This passage which we have printed in Italics, is *above* our comprehension.) Upon the whole it is manifest, that if any plan had been organized, it was never communicated by the principal conspirator to the leaders or the men, as they were wholly ignorant even of the places of rendezvous; although within two days of the time appointed, and but one man arrested prior to the day fixed on for the attempt." Yet—(will it be believed?)—it is true, for the governor of the state has declared it in his official account, that, for attempting an insurrection, *the plan of which had never been communicated even to the leaders,* and which was to be effected with no other weapons than THIRTEEN HOOP-POLES, seventy-two of these miserable wretches, *unprovided with the means of attack or resistance,* have been tried, and, as the governor says, "disposed of"—thirty-seven sentenced to banishment, and THIRTY-FIVE EXECUTED!

Keene *New-Hampshire Sentinel*

Saturday, September 7, 1822

The City government of Charleston, S.C. have published an official *expose* of the late attempt at insurrection amongst the negroes. From a perusal we have no doubt of the guilt imputed to the principals in this business; but it does not appear they had any organization, or any efficient means to accomplish their dreadful purpose, that of seizing the arsenal and massacreing the white inhabitants. No attempt was made, nor no movement observed at the hour it was ascertained by previous confessions, the work was to begin. The trial Court established the correctness of the principle, that all should suffer death who had acceded to the plan proposed by the few desperate negroes who instigated the revolt. About 60 or 70 were hanged, and others banished.[1] The sacrifice was certainly ample in proportion to the extent of danger. The city authority might have found, we think, causes sufficient without reference to "certain discussions assumed in Congress" on the Missouri question![2] No set of men have heretofore been more profuse in "beautiful propositions of civil and natural freedom," than the Slave-holders of the South. Religious fanaticism is assigned as another cause, and it is asserted that a majority of the conspirators belonged to the African Church. The report, however, absolves the head of that church, and the association has since been voluntarily dissolved.—The report speaks of the "misguided benevolence" of some slave owners, who have not only permitted their slaves to be *instructed,* but have lent aid to such efforts.

1. The number of slaves who were hanged numbered thirty-five, not sixty. Another thirty-seven slaves were transported outside the United States.

2. The reference to the Missouri debates may be found in the confession of Jack Purcell, in Part III, p. 214. Nor, according to the Charleston *Southern Patriot,* August 29, 1822, was Purcell alone among the accused slaves in mentioning the Missouri debates as influencing the Vesey plot. Despite this evidence, Michael P. Johnson, "Denmark Vesey and His Co-Conspirators," *WMQ* 58 (2001): 961, argues that the trials contained no allusions to the Missouri debates.

New-York Evening Post

Saturday, September 7, 1822

Extract of a letter to a gentleman in Boston, dated Charleston, Aug. 19. "You may feel desirous to know the actual truth in relation to a late attempt to disturb us, by some of the blacks, and I wish our friends at the north should be satisfied that severe as has been the retribution which the law has awarded, it was due to justice, and consistent with humanity. Those who are at a distance cannot judge correctly of our situation. Our slaves are the labouring class, and such a class exists every where, and is always the majority in numbers. A negro cannot by marriage mingle with the whites; he cannot as a soldier or a magistrate command a white man. In a word, in our country the pride and ambition of a negro has no room to act. His colour is an insurmountable barrier to actual equality. This is equally true in the north as in the south. In every community of white men, negroes are a degraded cast, and are therefore incited to vent in crime those feelings which lead the whites to the pursuits of worldly ambition. The state prisons of the north verify this remark. A vast proportion live in idleness, and support themselves by plunder. A slave in the southern states enjoys perfect freedom from the cares of life. His food and clothing are provided, and his master identifies him with his domestic establishment—his labour is light, and he has no anxiety for his future support. It would thus be taking from them the protection of a kind master to liberate the blacks, if it were even practicable; but none but a mad man can contemplate it—it would fill the community with men degraded by their colour, and exasperated by the reflection, that their liberty was only nominal. The slaves concerned in the late plot were almost without exception substantially free. They were mechanics, who consumed a great part of their earnings, much more than a taxed Englishman ever retains.—There were many the property of ladies who exercised little control over them, and in two instances, had been actually nursed and reared by them. With no reason to rebel, these deluded creatures, partly from religious fanaticism, and partly from the instigation of base incendiaries, who from a pretended humanity interfered in our domestic concerns, actually planned and concerted to desolate our city with conflagration, rapine and indiscriminate murder—and yet some unprincipled editors have stated they saw no justification for the severe punishment inflicted. The plot was one which could only have ended in the utter extermination of its authors, although it would have been productive of many afflicting scenes. The citizens when suddenly called on, would have required a little time to act efficiently, but all efforts, like the late intended insurrection, are utterly hopeless of success. The late example has produced a wholesome effect. Never was Charleston more quiet, and centuries will hardly witness another attempt. The plantations are unaffected. The scheme was confined to less than one hundred, most of whom have been tried and variously punished. They were with scarce an exception, Methodists, who had seceded from the white Methodists, and the "class leaders" were the instigators and leaders in the plot. Proving satisfactorily that religion, in the hands of the ignorant and uninstructed, is the fruitful source of delusion; while under the direction of pious and learned men, it produces nothing but peace and good will. We believe humane and intelligent men in every quarter of our common country will rejoice that the hand of desolation has been arrested, and that a community that delights in affording its hospitality to them, is once more in the enjoyment of domestic tranquility.[1]

1. This information was reprinted verbatim in the *Providence Patriot*, September 11, 1822, and the Richmond *Enquirer*, September 17, 1822.

Boston *Recorder*[1]

Saturday, September 7, 1822

THE NEGRO PLOT. The Charleston papers have published a detailed account of the late conspiracy among the blacks in Charleston. It appears by a letter from the Governor of South Carolina, that the plot was first disclosed by a servant who was prompted by attachment to his master. The number of persons arrested were seventy-two, thirty-five of whom were executed, and thirty-seven sentenced to banishment. . . .

1. The Boston *Recorder*, published by Nathaniel Willis (1780–1870), the son of a newspaperman who had apprenticed under Benjamin Franklin, is considered one of the first religious newspapers published in the United States.

Portland *Eastern Argus*

Tuesday, September 10, 1822

The Negro Plot at Charleston.

It appears from the confession of the criminals that this plot has been agitating about 4 years; during the whole of which time, the conspirators have been cautiously increasing their numbers by inveigling the slaves and free negroes of the city and of the neighboring plantations, and have actually maintained a correspondence with certain persons in St. Domingo. The author and master spirit of the conspiracy was a free black, named Denmark Vezey. This person is said by the Intendant to have been distinguished for his great strength and activity; his temper was impetuous, his passions fierce and ungovernable, and he was looked upon by all his brethren with the utmost respect and veneration. [1] Monday Gell, a Slave, appears to have been second to Vezey; he was remarked for uncommon knowledge and sagacity, acted as scribe at their meetings, and is known to have written several letters to St. Domingo for succors. Peter, the slave of Mr Poyas, was one of the most efficient ringleaders of the plot. He was a slave of great value, and a first rate ship carpenter; 'he had enjoyed the confidence of his master in a remarkable degree, and had been treated with indulgence, liberality and kindness.'

Gullah Jack was another active agent in the conspiracy. It seems that Jack was *born* a *physician* and a *necromancer*—for in his own country the properties qualifying for these important offices are inheritable, just as those which fit men to be lawgivers and judges, are elsewhere. The influence of this negro over his fellows, particularly the native Africans, on account 'of their credulous superstition and clannish sympathies,' is stated to have been extensive and powerful. Such, remarks the Intendant, 'was their belief in his invulnerability, that his charms and amulets were in request; and he was regarded as a man who could *only* be harmed by the *treachery* of his fellows.'

These with two or three others appear to have been the ringleaders of the plot; with them it commenced, by them it was fomented, and they were to have headed the conspirators in the daring enterprise in which it was to have been consummated.

The *outlines* of the plot are well enough defined, but nothing more. The leaders appear to have taken the alarm, before they had settled the details of their operations.—The 16th of June last, at midnight was the time fixed for the explosion. At that silent hour, the conspirators were to have assembled, and commenced operations by seizing upon the State Arsenal, and to have provided themselves with arms, of which it appears, they were entirely destitute; but in what manner this attack was to have been made whether by distinct detachments simultaneously, or by the whole body of conspirators under a single leader, Gov. Bennett thinks was not determined.

Had they been successful in this attempt, their intention was to fire the city in as many different places as possible, and then joined by several bands of Slaves from the neighboring plantations, to have committed indiscriminate massacre upon all the white inhabitants.

Their plan then was to seize some vessels in the harbor, and to embark with the plunder of the banks and warehouses for St. Domingo.

We leave it to the reader's imagination to picture the horrible scene which *must* have ensued, had the enterprise even *commenced.*

But Charleston was not destined to experience at this time the horrors of a Negro Insurrection.

On the 30th of May, (but a fortnight before the night fixed on by the conspirators for the explosion of their plot) a servant, prompted by gratitude and affection to his master, informed him that he had been requested to take part in the conspiracy, and to subscribe his name to the roll of those engaged. Information was instantly given to the civil authorities, and several suspected persons were arrested. Throughout the city, every thing was now alarm and excitement. That a deeply laid and extensive conspiracy was on foot, whose only aim was plunder and indiscriminate murder, was rendered certain;—but the numbers, the agents, the means to be adopted, and almost every other particular remained still a profound mystery. We cannot conceive a more agonising situation!

The course pursued by the City Council was prompt and efficacious. All suspected persons were imprisoned, the military force of the city was put in requisition, a committee of vigilance was appointed and a Court organized for the trial and punishment of the offenders.

All these proceedings were successful. The Conspirators were alarmed, and became jealous and distrustful of each other, so that very shortly, nearly their whole number was detected, and a speedy and decisive punishment followed their conviction. In explaining the cause of so much success in detecting the guilty persons, Gov. Bennet says "Several of the conspirators had entered into solemn pledges to partake of a common destiny, and one at least, was found who after his arrest, felt no repugnance to enforce the obligation, by surrendering the names of his associates. A spirit of retaliation and revenge produced a similar effect with others, who suspected that they were the victims of treachery; and this principle operated with full effect, as the hope or expectation of pardon predominated."

The whole number of conspirators convicted, is seventy-two; of these, thirty-five have been executed, and thirty-seven banished without the territories of the U.S.

1. This information was taken from Hamilton, *Account*, 17, who used many of the same words to describe Vesey.

Philadelphia *Democratic Press*

Thursday, September 12, 1822

Extract of a letter from South Carolina,

dated, Sep. 2.

. . . "The late Plot in Charleston was very serious—Had it burst out with any shew of success, it would have blazed forth most destructively over the whole seacoast. This cannot be called an attempted insurrection among the *Slaves*. It originated with free people of color; it began among that class which the abolitionists are most anxious to increase. This fact ought to be borne in mind. It is very important. The slaves engaged in it were principally mechanics, draymen, wharfingers &c. and all those who live much to themselves and with little control from their masters. They were chiefly *Africans*.[1] The non-importation will soon extinguish that race, and those born in the country cannot so easily be induced to revolt. Banish all the free people of colour, exclude colored mechanics from towns and make a few otherwise regulations, and there can be little or no danger.—The account published by the city Council should be generally read. It is a faithful and a full account. . . ."

1. In 1822 African-born slaves amounted to a substantial minority of the slaves in and around Charleston. Available evidence does not permit a precise reckoning of the proportion of African-born relative to creole or country-born slaves in the plot. Although African-born slaves were clearly a minority among the thirty-five alleged ringleaders who were executed, African-born leaders such as Gullah Jack and Monday Gell stood out in importance to whites during the proceedings. Thomas Cilavan Brown, the free colored carpenter who knew Vesey, claimed that he was a "Corromantee negro," that is, born in the Gold Coast region of West Africa. See Brown's quoted words, reproduced on p. 749 in Part VI of this volume, in Lydia Maria Child to Thomas

Wentworth Higginson, March 17, 1860, William P. Palmer Collection, P-1090, Western Reserve Historical Society.

Charleston *Southern Patriot, and Commercial Advertiser*

Thursday, September 12, 1822

. . . If you will look into Grimke's justice in (Article XL) the Negro Act (if I mistake not, as I quote from memory) you will find a law of the Assembly regulating the dress of Negroes and Mulattoes; it was to be confined to *oznaburghs, checks* and *calicoes,* of certain price and quality—to a certain description of Woolens except for livery servants. [1] Has this law been repealed, or has it become like many other good and wholesome laws obsolete? . . . No doubt to many, this subject may appear trifling, ridiculous, and unworthy serious notice, (but they must not forget that often from trifling causes great events arise. . . . Let any one disposed to think so, walk out on Sunday, or any other public day, and he will soon satisfy himself of the appearance, impudence, and bold effrontery of this class. . . . Far be it from me to recommend despotic laws; but I certainly do think that after our *late warning* we should not suffer *this class,* to continue their encroachments towards that level which our good nature and liberal dispositions towards them, are advancing daily. We may be kind and indulgent masters without *assimilating them to us.* A line of distinction in *every respect* should be drawn, and that so broad, that there shall be no incroachment. . . .

RUSTICUS[2]

1. Article XL of the Negro Act of 1740 (reproduced in Part II) did indeed contain the sumptuary provision restricting the dress of slaves as Garden remembered.

2. "Rusticus" was the pseudonym of Alexander Garden Jr. (1757–1829), whose father, a Scottish-born physician, immigrated to Charleston and became famous as a naturalist for whom the gardenia is namesaked. The younger Garden was a planter and soldier, residing in 1822 at 8 Short Street. He wrote *Anecdotes of the Revolutionary War in America* (1822) and was a founding member of the South Carolina Association. In a visit to Philadelphia in July 1822, Garden was introduced to Langdon Cheves in a letter (excerpted in Part IV) by John S. Cogdell as someone well versed in what was going on in Charleston with respect to the Vesey affair. See Alfred N. Hunt, *Haiti's Influence on Antebellum America: Slumbering Volcano in the Caribbean* (Baton Rouge: Louisiana State University Press, 1988), 111; *BDSCHR* 3: 251–53; *CSCCD,* 80.

Salem *Gazette*

Friday, September 13, 1822

From the New-York Statesman.

THE NEGRO PLOT.

We this evening publish Gov. Bennet's statement of the late conspiracy among the blacks of South Carolina, and tomorrow we shall give the more full account, published by the authority of the Corporation of Charleston. Governor Bennet's detail of the circumstances appears to be ingenuous and undisguised, and we certainly hope it may have the effect to quiet the alarm, which the conspiracy produced, and "to prevent that rapid deterioration of property," which the chief magistrate of that state foresaw would be a consequence, unless the tranquillity of the public mind was restored.

Several circumstances are developed in this official account of the plot, which furnish new proofs to justify the remarks we made a few days since on the evils of slavery, and the anticipations in which we indulged of the future condition of the slave-holding states. It seems a letter was addressed by Gell, one of the ringleaders, to President Boyer, of St. Domingo, soliciting his alliance and cooperation in the conspiracy.[1] Although this proposition, in the present instance, was not accepted, or did not produce its desired effect, the fact is scarcely the less alarming, since it shows that the blacks understand fully the situation of their brethren in that island, and the relation that may possibly exist between them and the slaves of the South. It manifests intelligence and skill on the part of Gell, with regard to the measures necessary for the execution of the conspiracy, which, under different circumstances might prove successful. The letter, it appears, was, with a good deal of sagacity, directed to a third person, that the address might not give alarm and expose the writer to detection.

Another important fact disclosed by Governor Bennet's statement, is the use that has been made of the speeches in Congress, against the admission of Missouri. If the blacks of the south are capable of reading and understanding the arguments, or even the passionate appeals on that question, they are more ripe for conspiracies, than we had been led to suppose. It was believed that the great mass were yet too ignorant to read and to be excited by inflammatory pamphlets. If they are capable of being incited to insurrection by such means, it will be extremely difficult to interpose barriers, which shall prevent future conspiracies.

An indirect censure seems to be cast upon the members of Congress, who opposed the admission of Missouri, and furnished the materials for incendiary publications. But it is futile to complain of the evil effects resulting from a free discussion of the slave question on any particular occasion, when inflammatory materials of the same kind, sufficient to fill volumes, might be drawn from other sources. We conclude these hasty remarks, with expressing hope, that the prompt and decisive measures, which have been adopted at Charleston, may prove effectual in restoring tranquillity, and that it will be long, very long, before such energetic proceedings shall again be found necessary.

1. The reference to Monday Gell's attempted communication with Jean-Pierre Boyer, president of Haiti, appeared in many newspapers that reported on events in Charleston. Although Bishop Richard Allen (1750–1831), founder of the African Methodist Episcopal Church, adamantly opposed the American Colonization Society, he and other leaders of the AME Church did support emigration of blacks in the United States to Haiti. Before the Vesey affair, agents of President Boyer, a revered figure among blacks in the United States, were encouraging black emigration from the United States to Haiti. In addition to the documents presented in Part I, see Boston *Colombian Centinel,* February 28, 1821, and February 23, 1822; "Commemoration by the African," *African Repository, and Colonial Journal* 3 (July 1827): 155–56; Daniel A. Payne, *The Semi-Centenary and the Retrospective of the African Methodist Episcopal Church in the United States of America* (Baltimore, 1866), 28; Richard Newman, *Freedom's Prophet: Bishop Richard Allen, the AME Church, and the Black Founding Fathers* (New York: New York University Press, 2008), 246–57.

Niles' Weekly Register

Saturday, September 14, 1822

THE GREAT CURSE OF OUR LAND. . . . Thousands of Europeans who arrive on our shores, and tens of thousands of white persons born and brought up among us, have less intelligence, less honor, less of every estimable quality of the head or heart, than many of the blacks—but there is no impediment to their progress in society, and they, or their children, may arrive at eminence, through honest industry and steady perseverance in well doing, form alliances with the most reputable families, and lose the character and condition of their ancestors, or shake off a bad one of their own, by good behavior; while the black must retain his station, and continue a degraded being. And hence, perhaps, it is that, hopeless of being better off in the future, they are careless of the present—and the result commonly is, that the best treated among them, whether slaves or freemen, are as worthless as any. Cases of this sort are daily presented to us, and the fact appears to have been established at Charleston, that the leaders of the late contemplated insurrection were chiefly of those who were most indulged by their masters. Unpleasant as the fact may appear, there seems to be *reason* in it—we must admit that the slaves have a *natural right* to obtain their liberty, if they can; and hence those who best know what indulgence is, are the most desirous of being masters of their own conduct. The just man cannot blame the slave for seeking his freedom, though self-preservation may interpose to check his proceedings to obtain it. If, when captain Bainbridge[1] and the crew of the Philadelphia frigate, were held in slavery at Tripoli, they had acquired their liberty by a conflagration of that city and the slaughter of every one who opposed them, even to the amount of tens of thousands of persons, *we* should have hailed them as *heroes "covered with glory"*—and, surely, the dey had a better claim on them as slaves than we can pretend to in imported negroes: they had crossed the ocean to attack him. . . .

Thirty-five have been hung and others remain for execution at Charleston, and many were sentenced to transportation, &c. yet it appears that the trials are not over. The plot seems to have been well devised, its operation was extensive, and its intent terrific. The conspirators were associated in a sort of a society, and held frequent meetings. It was agreed that each slave should first kill his own master and the males about the house, then repair to a certain rendezvous, rush upon the guard, fire the city in various places, seize upon certain ships and laden them with plunder, and then proceed to Hayti, having secured a sufficiency of seamen to conduct them thither. When the plan was nearly ripe, the conspiracy was made known, and a large number of the supposed principals were arrested—twenty-two of whom were executed in one day! It is thought that some severe laws will be passed for the preservation of the whites, and to guard against such attempts in future. The system of slavery involves in itself a state of dreadful severity, for it is sustained only by force—and about 60 years ago, thirteen blacks were burnt alive in then colony of New York for insurrectionary movements. Sanguinary punishment always has been and ever will be the attendant of slavery every where. We neither approve of the one nor the other—but all that we can do is, to disapprove of them.

1. The article refers here to William Bainbridge (1774–1833), who was captured during the Barbary Wars by pirates in 1803 and imprisoned with his crew in Tripoli for almost two years.

Boston *Columbian Centinel*

Wednesday, September 18, 1822

NEGRO PLOT.

JUST published, by JOSEPH W. INGRAHAM,[1] Franklin Avenue, and No. 90, Court street, and for sale by him, and at the Bookstores,

An Account of the late intended Insurrection among a portion of the Blacks of the city of Charleston, South Carolina. Published by authority of the Corporation of Charleston.

1. When republished in a second edition in Boston, James A. Hamilton's *Account of the Late Intended Insurrection* was retitled *Negro Plot: An Account.* Joseph W. Ingraham (1799–1848) was an educator, a friend of Horace Mann, and one of Boston's most eminent book publishers. The choice of Ingraham to publish Hamilton's *Account* suggests the importance he and other prominent South Carolinians attached to the state's honor and to countering northern criticisms of how the proceedings and executions in Charleston were handled. See John Woart, *An Address Delivered in Christ Church, at the Funeral of Joseph W. Ingraham* (Boston, 1848).

Louisville *Public Advertiser*

Saturday, September 21, 1822

The Governor of South Carolina has been censured for having partly attributed the late attempt of the blacks of that state, at insurrection, to the discussion of the Missouri Question. That the arguments of the restrictionists, were of a nature to excite insurrections, among the blacks, can scarcely be doubted. The Missouri Question, was not discussed by most of the eastern and northern members of Congress, as a question involving an important state right, or as one of mere national policy. By them, it was converted into a question of *freedom* or *slavery.* The news-papers followed the example of the members of Congress, in some instances; in others, they gave tone to their arguments, and even exacted of the candidates previous to their election, an explicit declaration, that they were or were not opposed to *slavery.* If a candidate replied that he was opposed to the admission of slaves into the then proposed state, it was not esteemed sufficient. He had to "go the whole" (as we backwoodsmen would say;)—he had unequivocally to declare that he was hostile to *slavery.* With these admonitions they entered Congress, where the *horrors* of slavery were *horribly* depicted by them They used every argument in their power, to prove the injustice and the cruelty of the southern and western slaveholder. The right of the slave to freedom, was frequently and boldly asserted, and on their side the restrictionists said all that could have been said, with this single exception:—they did not declare that the British entailed this heavy curse upon the American people; but whether this omission was the result of forgetfulness or of extreme *delicacy,* we have never been able to learn. At all events, such of the negroes as could read, (and there are many who can,) must have been highly delighted with the impassioned appeals of the advocates of their rights and liberties in Congress.

Charleston *Gazette and Commercial Daily Advertiser*

Monday, September 23, 1822

By letters received yesterday from Beaufort, on this subject of the arrest of certain slaves, charged with attempting to excite an insurrection, it appears that a highly respectable court had been organized for the trial of eight slaves, accused of that offence. After a patient investigation of two days, they were acquitted, the court being perfectly satisfied of their innocence.—It appeared, however, to the court, that the fellow who implicated the others had been attempting to involve them in treasonable acts. The court held his case still under advisement. It did not appear that these transactions had any connection with the recent conspiracy in this place.

It is highly gratifying to find that there is no just ground for uneasiness on account of our friends in Beaufort, while the result of these proceedings afford additional evidence of the calmness, deliberation and perfect justice, with which cases of this nature are investigated in South Carolina.[1]

1. This material was reprinted verbatim in the Savannah *Republican,* September 24, 1822; *Charleston Mercury, and Morning Advertiser,* September 24, 1822; *Washington Gazette,* September 26, 1822; Richmond *Enquirer,* September 27, 1822; *New-York Evening Post,* September 28, 1822; *United States Gazette and True American,* October 1, 1822; Boston *Columbian Centinel,* October 2, 1822; Providence *Gazette,* October 1, 1822; *Independent Chronicle and Boston Patriot,* October 2, 1822; Salem *Gazette,* October 4, 1822; Newport *Mercury,* October 5, 1822; Philadelphia *Democratic Press,* October 2, 1822; and *Darien* (GA) *Gazette,* October 3, 1822.

Charleston *Southern Patriot, and Commercial Advertiser*

Monday, September 23, 1822

To the Editor of the Southern Patriot.

Allow me to suggest to our Fellow-Citizens, as candidates, LIONEL H. KENNEDY and THOMAS PARKER, Esquires. These gentlemen, exclusive of their general merits, have, I think, peculiar recommendations to the favor and high opinion of our community at this period. They have already rendered us services of a most delicate and important nature, and I am satisfied, as representatives would act with equal fidelity and judgment.

A VOTER.

Charleston *Southern Patriot, and Commercial Advertiser*

Tuesday, September 24, 1822

The Negroes SHADRICK, ROBIN and DICK, who were apprehended in Savannah for the crime of attempting to raise an insurrection in that state, were tried on Thursday last; and after the court had been occupied nearly the whole day in the examination of witnesses, &c. they were pronounced *not guilty* by the Jury.

Letters from Beaufort state that the eight slaves who had been arrested there on suspicion of being engaged in an attempt of the same nature as the above, had been acquitted after a laborious investigation of two days. The case of a fellow who had implicated the above negroes, was still under advisement for attempting to involve them in treasonable acts.[1]

1. This material was reprinted nearly verbatim in the Philadelphia *United States Gazette and True American,* October 2, 1822; Charleston *City Gazette and Commercial Daily Advertiser,* September 25, 1822; and Boston *Commercial Gazette,* October 7, 1822.

Savannah *Republican*

Tuesday, September 24, 1822

CHARLESTON, Sept. 20.

Insurrection.—A letter from Beaufort dated 16th inst. states, that on the night previous, Ten Negroes, belonging to as many of the most respectable families in that place, had been apprehended as concerned in attempting to raise an Insurrection of the Blacks in this State. When the letter was written, the town Council were in secret session on their examination. The mail from Beaufort due here on Sunday, will probably furnish us with more particulars. We trust it is only a *branch* of the same plot detected here (which by some has been considered *nothing*) and not the sowing of new seeds of mischief, which must and shall be exterminated.[1]

1. This information was reprinted verbatim in the *Charleston Mercury, and Morning Advertiser,* September 24, 1822; *Washington Gazette,* September 26, 1822; Richmond *Enquirer,* September 27, 1822; *New-York Evening Post,* September 28, 1822; Philadelphia *United States Gazette and True American,* October 1, 1822; *Independent Chronicle and Boston Patriot,* October 2, 1822; Providence *Gazette,* October 2, 1822; Boston *Columbian Centinel,* October 2, 1822; Salem *Gazette,* October 4, 1822; and Newport *Mercury,* October 5, 1822.

Charleston *City Gazette and Commercial Daily Advertiser*

Friday, September 27, 1822

"TO OUR NORTHERN BRETHREN"

FELLOW-CITIZENS—

Were we to misjudge you from the vile paragraphs of some of your editors, we should almost believe that you would delight to see Charleston another Wyoming, and could behold without emotion Virginia and Kentucky smoking like the first Isle of the Antilles.[1] We however, hold no such unworthy opinion of you. It is the lot of all countries to produce beings, who, like the depredators in the diseased district of the City of New-York, would prosper on the affliction of their fellow-creatures. But, while we must expect to find characters who would foment commotion to advance themselves, we should be satisfied that the American people are too sound to inculcate treachery and justify assassination. It is, therefore, I would suppose, that you were not aware of the deep atrocity of the late machinations in our city, or you would declare that we have felt, as you would have felt, and in our proceedings have but obeyed the dictates of nature and of wisdom. We would therefore invite you temperately to survey the various circumstances of this event.

This description of our population had been allowed to assemble for religious instruction.—The designing leaders in the scheme of villainy availed themselves of these occasions to instil sentiments of ferocity, by *falsifying the Bible.* All the severe penal laws of the Israelites were quoted to mislead them, and the denunciations in the prophecies, which were intended to deter men *from* evil, were declared to be divine commands which they were *to execute.* To confirm this doctrine, they were told that Heshbon, that Bashan with its sixty cities had been destroyed, man, woman and child; that in the desolation of Midian, only the males were destroyed, at which Moses was displeased, and deliberately ordered the death of the boys and their mothers. That Joshua levelled the walls of Jericho, and regarded neither age nor sex; and that David vanquished empires and left not man, woman or infant alive. Not content with this execrable perversion—with exhibiting the God of Mercy as another Jaggernaut, they were informed of what their colour had perpetrated abroad. Such was their religion, such the examples to be imitated.

After having rendered them fiends in principle, they were prepared to be fiends in action. A regular plan was formed to annihilate us and our abodes; the arsenal and strongholds were to have been seized, and the leaders were nominated for each attack. Besides the instruments which many of them possessed as mechanics, villains were engaged in manufacturing arms; several pike-handles were discovered; Pharaoh and Peter had swords; Ned Bennett had a sword to kill wolves, but which he designed first to try upon his master, of whom he had received only indulgence. The places of rendezvous, the night, the hour were determined—and the imps of rebellion were to have made Charleston one scene of flames and carnage, had they been able. It is no diminution of their crime to say they were not able;—guilt is in the intention and not in the act.

Under such circumstances of just exasperation, what did the citizens of Charleston? Did they yield to their passions and commit an indiscriminate massacre, as would have been done in many places under less excitement? Nothing like it. A court was organized of distinguished integrity, respectability and intelligence; the members of which felt their own high reputation involved with the untarnished reputation of their State and Country. So far from being precipitate they were occupied several days in investigating the nature of the conspiracy, before they put the individuals accused upon their trials.—The causes of the criminals were conducted with that liberality, justice and impartiality which characterise American jurisprudence, which is no where more conspicuous than in South-Carolina, and was never more pure than on this painful occasion. Their guilt was demonstrated, and what ought to have been done? Disregard the law, let them loose upon society, and encourage a repetition of their projects? No one, I hope, in our extensive empire, would intimate such a wish. What was done?—That which duty enjoined and precedent justified.—These culprits meditated against us, fire, pillage, treason, treachery to their masters, with outrages not to be named. Thus they blended four capital offences in one crime. Ought not capital punishment then to have been awarded? It is certainly not unexampled.—In the Spanish conspiracy against Venice which partakes the character of this, *three hundred and fifty were put to death.*[2] George II, executed *fifty-four* of the first men in Britain for the rebellion of 1745.[3] Nor are we without domestic precedent: an insurrection occurred in the city of New-York in 1712; as soon as the alarm-gun was fired, and a detachment of the guards appeared, the insurgents fled to the woods—there they were surrounded, several through desperation *shot themselves,* the rest were captured, and nineteen executed.[4]

Another was meditated in 1741, when there were two thousand Negroes and twelve thousand Whites in the city of New-York. It was then found necessary to burn *thirteen* and to hang eighteen negroes with four whites; to transport eighty negroes and five whites.[5]

	In New-York,	*In Charleston.*
Executed	35	35
Transported	85	37
	120	72

Now, a short period before the negro plot was discovered in New-York, an insurrection broke out in Carolina. Many of the ring-leaders were shot or hanged, but none punished in any other mode.[6] There can then be no ground to imagine that we ever, under the same circumstances, would be more severe than our Northern brethren. Every measure essential to our self-protection, will be, and I think you will not dispute, ought to be adopted. It would, therefore, be philanthropy to impress upon the more intelligent portion of this population, the wisdom of good conduct. Schemes of insurrection, such as the present, cannot succeed. The white population of each State alone, is adequate to suppress them. From the first settlement of Carolina, we have been accustomed to these abortive efforts. Under our proprietary government, there was a notorious out-law by the name of Sebastian;—Governor Gibbes[7] issued his proclamation, and the Indians soon entitled themselves to the reward.

In 1730, a plan was conceived against Charleston. They were allowed to assemble, were then taken, and proper examples made.[8] Some years afterwards, what we denominate *the Gullah war,* occurred. This was more general—in St. Paul's Parish they appeared in arms; the greater part were killed, and not more than two or three escaped.[9] In St. John's Parish they were discovered by Major Cordes' faithful driver Peter, and in Charleston, they were also discovered, suppressed and punished.[10] The negro law of 1740, was enacted in consequence of the last, and has proved our security from that period, notwithstanding the occasional effervescences of insubordination.[11] The history of South Carolina, in this particular, has been the history of every State in the Union.

Another impediment to the progress of conspiracy, will ever be found in the *fidelity* of some of our negroes. The servant who is false to his master, would be false to his God. One act of perfidy, is but the first step in the road of corruption and of baseness, and those who on this occasion, have proved ungrateful to their owners, have also been hypocrites in religion. But it is a reputable TRUTH, that on every such occasion, servants have been found who were worthy [of] the kindness and confidence of their masters.

Besides, when the moment of trial comes, among large bodies of men, some will tremble, some will be shocked at what they are about to perpetrate, and others will remember that by disclosure may be obtained more than they seek through perils. Jaffier saved Venice, and most conspiracies own men inferior to Jaffier.[12] We must also remember that the majority of mankind would avoid dangerous enterprizes.—Therefore the great body of these people would prefer safety and quiet with their present comforts, to a hazardous commotion with an issue so fearful as it always has been, and ever will be.

Superadded to these intrinsic securities, we have the proportion of *two* to *one* in the aggregate population of States situated like ourselves. Our sister and neighbour Tennessee has four to one, and the heroes of Orleans have but to know that we are in danger, to be with us at the first tap of the drum.

The National Government also can preserve the peace of the country. It was established expressly to ensure domestic tranquility and suppress insurrection. It has been tried, and found efficient. The President may summon upwards of five to one. The old French government with three thousand regulars, protected their largest colony, and a small military force is found adequate in the British West Indies. Surely the American government could, and would do as much, were it necessary. A change cannot then be effected by force, nor would it be beneficial to the United States. Our roads would swarm with paupers, and every wood be infested with banditti. But under the existing regulations, they contribute to general wealth, and are preserved from want, misery and crime. The States in which they are located, have been fully as instrumental in originating and defending our political independence, as those without them; and at every crisis have equally illustrated the valor and power of our common country. During the Revolution, we frustrated and repelled the enemy for four years, from 1776 to '80; during which period our Northern brethren were over-run and under their feet. What nation—what *portion* of this great nation has surpassed in splendor and in conduct, the victories of MOULTRIE and of JACKSON[13]? In civil talents, in devotion to the Republic, in the most ennobling sentiments of the heart, in charity, in hospitality—when has the South or the West been deficient? Never—you will voluntarily acknowledge.

From these observations, then, I trust you will feel that our Court have done their duty, and merit the gratitude not only of their immediate fellow-citizens, but of their fellow-citizens throughout the Union. You will also, I think perceive, that the happiness of this population will be measured and decided by their own good conduct, and that to support subordination, is a duty enjoined by philanthrophy, patriotism, and the best interests of America.

I submit the above facts and observations to my fellow-citizens generally; and trust that the voice of animadversion will be forever hushed, in the universal good feeling of our sister States.

A SOUTH-CAROLINIAN.[14]

1. The author refers here to the French colony of Saint-Domingue, not an island, but the western third of the island of Hispaniola.

2. The author compares the response of Charleston's whites during the Vesey conspiracy to the ferocious repression of a suspected Spanish plot against Venice during the rule of Doge Antonio Priuli (1548–1623). See Horatio Forbes Brown, *Studies in the History of Venice,* 2 vols. (New York: E. P. Dutton, 1907), vol. 2: 245–95.

3. The second Jacobite Rebellion, also called the Forty-five, failed in its attempt to restore the

Stuart line to the throne of Scotland. See W. A. Speck, *The Butcher: The Duke of Cumberland and the Suppression of the 45* (Oxford, UK: Blackwell, 1981).

4. Twenty-one slaves were condemned to death in the aftermath of the 1712 insurrection in New York City; eighteen were actually executed, most by hanging. See Kenneth Scott, "The Slave Insurrection in New York in 1712," *New-York Historical Society Quarterly* 45 (1961): 43–74; Graham Russell Hodges, *Root and Branch: African Americans in New York and East Jersey, 1613–1863* (Chapel Hill: University of North Carolina Press, 1999), 63–68.

5. Jill Lepore, *New York Burning: Liberty, Slavery, and Conspiracy in Eighteenth-Century Manhattan* (New York: Knopf, 2005), xvii, 246, places the total number of executed at thirty-four, including fourteen slaves burned to death, sixteen slaves hanged, and eighty-four slaves transported.

6. The largest slave insurrection in the history of colonial British mainland North America broke out in 1739 near the Stono River, about twenty miles from Charleston. More than twenty whites and more than forty slaves perished as a result. The author neglects to mention that executed slaves had their bodies mutilated and heads piked. See Peter Wood, *Black Majority: Negroes in Colonial South Carolina from 1670 through the Stono Rebellion* (New York: Knopf, 1974), 308–23; Robert Olwell, *Masters, Slaves and Subjects: The Culture of Power in the South Carolina Low Country, 1740–1790* (Ithaca, NY: Cornell University Press, 1998), 21–28.

7. In 1711, South Carolina's Governor Robert Gibbes (1644–1715) identified a slave named Sebastian as the source of slave unrest in the colony. An Indian auxiliary eventually tracked down and killed Sebastian. See Herbert Aptheker, *American Negro Slave Revolts* (New York: Columbia University Press, 1943), 171.

8. In August 1730, colonial officials uncovered in Charleston what they thought was an insurrectionary plot, designed to break out on the Sabbath. According to one eyewitness, the slaves "soon made a great Body at the back of the Town, and had a great Dance, and expected the Country Negroes to come & join them; and had not an over-ruling Providence discovered their Intrigues, we had been all in blood." See *Boston Weekly News-Letter,* October 15, 22, 1730.

9. In 1706, South Carolina's Commons House of Assembly passed the Church Act, which created St. Paul's Parish and nine other ecclesiastical parishes. The Stono uprising of 1739 erupted in St. Paul's Parish. By the time of the Vesey plot, South Carolinian notables had come to refer to the Stono uprising as "the Gullah War." Scholars have debated the etymology of the word "Gullah," but its usage here strengthens the argument that it derives from a compression of the word Angola, a region in West-Central Africa. Eighteenth-century English speakers involved in the Atlantic slave trade used "Angola" to demarcate a region that included the Kingdom of Kongo, and the Stono uprising amounted to an ethnic uprising of African-born slaves from the Kingdom of Kongo. As John Thornton, a historian of precolonial Africa, has pointed out, "the 'Angolans' of the Stono Rebellion" most likely came not from the Portuguese colony of Angola but "from Kongo." Advertisements in South Carolina newspapers published as early as the 1780s refer to the Angola-Congo region of West-Central Africa as "Gullah country." See John K. Thornton, "African Dimensions of the Stono Rebellion," *American Historical Review* 96 (1991): 1101–13; Charleston *South-Carolina Gazette and General Advertiser,* July 24, 27, 1784.

10. Little is known about the alleged plot that followed the Stono uprising in St. John Berkeley Parish in 1740, although it is briefly mentioned in several colonial newspapers and appears to have resulted in the executions of more than a dozen slaves. The newspapers say the plot was uncovered "but Two days before it was to have been put into Execution." Major Thomas Cordes (1697?–1748?) owned a plantation in the parish called Whiskinboo, where the loyal driver may have worked. See J. H. J. H. Easterby, ed., *The Journal of the Commons House of Assembly, September 12, 1739–March 26, 1741* (Columbia: Historical Commission of South Carolina, 1952), 364, 377–78; *Boston Weekly News-Letter,* July 3, 10, 1740; *Boston Evening-Post,* July 7, 1740; Emma B. Richardson, "Dr. Anthony

Cordes and Some of His Descendants," *SCHGM* 43 (1942): 136–37; Suzannah Smith Miles, *East Cooper Gazetteer: History of Mount Pleasant, Sullivan's Island and Isle of Palms* (Charleston, SC: History Press, 2004), 121.

11. "An Act for the Better Ordering and Governing Negroes and Other Slaves of This Province," passed on May 10, 1740, remained the fundamental slave law in South Carolina until the end of the Civil War (see pp. 110–31 in Part II). The emphasis that the author places on the plot of 1740 as the precipitant of the so-called Negro Act parts company with most modern scholars, who have emphasized the Stono rebellion of 1739 as the decisive factor in passing South Carolina's first major slave code. A particularly intense period of slave restiveness, sufficient to be called a "war" and related to the recent importation of thousands of West-Central African slaves at a time of war and imperial rivalry with Spain, may reconcile the conflicting positions. Before his invasion of Florida in 1740, General James Oglethorpe (1696–1785) justified his campaign by referring to persistent efforts by the Spanish "to foment and countenance the Slaves in rebellion, burning of Houses, Murders, & other Cruelties." See Charleston *South-Carolina Gazette,* March 29, April 4, 1740. The Negro Act is published in its entirety in Thomas Cooper and David J. McCord, eds., *The Statutes of South Carolina,* 10 vols. (Charleston, SC, 1836–41), vol. 7: 397–417.

12. Jaffeir in the play *Venice Preserv'd* by Thomas Otway, a tragedy familiar to the English stage during the Restoration. It centers on the so-called Spanish Conspiracy to capture Venice during the rule of Doge Antonio Priuli.

13. William Moultrie (1730–1805) led the successful defense of Charleston against the British in 1776; Andrew Jackson (1767–1845) led American forces to victory over the British at the Battle of New Orleans in 1815.

14. [Edwin C. Holland,] *A Refutation of the Calumnies Circulated against the Southern & Western States Respecting the Institution of Slavery among Them . . .* (Charleston, SC, 1822), 79–82, republished this essay verbatim and identified "A South-Carolinian" as Benjamin Elliott (1786–1836), a prominent Charleston attorney. Portions of it were reprinted in the Salem *Gazette,* November 15, 1822, and *Providence Patriot,* November 23, 1822.

Philadelphia *Democratic Press*

Monday, September 30, 1822

It is suggested that most of the desperate Ruffians who are transported from South Carolina, will find their way to Philadelphia. What can be done to prevent it?[1]

1. Because of the size and strength of the AME Church in Philadelphia, many free persons of color from Charleston did indeed flee to Philadelphia in the wake of the Vesey affair, only to face intensifying racial resentment. See Julie Winch, *Philadelphia's Black Elite: Activism, Accommodation, and the Struggle for Autonomy, 1787–1848* (Philadelphia: Temple University Press, 1988), 14–15, 57, 131.

Darien (GA) *Gazette*

Thursday, October 3, 1822

FROM THE PHILADELPHIA NATIONAL GAZETTE,
AUGUST 15.

"Strictly speaking, nobody can blame the servile part of the population (the blacks) for attempting to escape from bondage, however their delusion may be regretted.—*Boston Ev. Gazette.*"

"We by no means would be understood to justify *any* attempts in slaves to regain their liberty in any other mode than by manumission. We warn them of the awful consequences inseparably connected with an enterprize which would in all probability produce a war of extermination against them in this country or at least be the means of riveting the galling fetters tenfold more firmly on the unhappy captives. If ever their emancipation be effected, it must be through the Divine agency of the light of reason, not by the sword, bloodshed, and rapine.—*Camden (N.J.) Star.*"

The first of these quotations is made from a considerable paper of Boston—the second from a respectable one published at the village opposite to this city. The writers of both refer particularly to the insurrection concerted among the negroes of South Carolina. We think the views of the Camden Gazette far more just and reasonable than those of the Boston paper. . . .

There are large associations, and multitudes of individuals, in the non-slave holding States, who avowedly desire, and seek the gradual emancipation of all people of color held in bondage on our soil; who would timely prepare them, by religious and lettered instruction, for the temperate and beneficial use of the freedom to be imparted to them by a regular legislative system. But we have never heard that any Abolition Society, or any individual cherishing the same wishes, looked with complacency upon the idea of a sudden general liberation; or would hesitate to condemn, both as impolitic and as wicked, machinations or attempts to gain freedom forcibly and bloodily.—The negro slave is no where, in the United States, situated in such manner as to possess the le[a]st chance of remaining, after an insurrection of whatever immediate issue, like the Haytien, lord of the soil, or even co-partner with the white. Ultimately he must perish, or be subjected anew to the yoke rendered more galling and weighty, in consequence of his abortive endeavors to shake it off. If he were not, in the end, overpowered by the energies and resources of the collective white population of the theatre of revolt, he must be by the armed force of the Free States, whose duty and interest it would be to aid and avenge their fellow-citizens.

It seems to us that there is scarcely any black of common intelligence who would not of himself discover that schemes of general insurrection, though prosperous for the moment, could not fail to involve all concerned in final ruin or greatly to aggrevate their servitude. Hence, and independently of the claims of the whites to security and sympathy, the philanthropist must deprecate such schemes as baneful, and the moralist reprehended them as culpable. They include, almost necessarily, the design of a war of extermination against the whites: a servile war is proverbally horrible and relentless.—With regard to the present case, it is understood, that the most dreadful havoc and carnage and the most abominable cruelties and crimes were meditated. Regret, indignation, and abhorrence are, then, the proper sentiments to be entertained and expressed by us all. We must not be surprised if those who were marked out as victims, should exercise great severity in making examples of the conspirators, in order to protect themselves from future danger and to maintain the established order of things: And we ought to presume, from the characters of the individuals who compose the inquest and court at Charleston, that they proceed according to the forms and principles of law, and temper justice with mercy as far as is compatible with *their* sense of what is due to public safety and to the ends of the penal code.

Philadelphia *Democratic Press*

Thursday, October 10, 1822
INSURGENTS AND INCENDIARIES.

On Monday, September 30, we put the following note in the paper, not thinking that we should so soon be called upon to notice it in the manner we are about to do.

"It is suggested that most of the desperate Ruffians who are transported from South Carolina will find their way to Philadelphia. What can be done to prevent it?"

Unacquainted with the laws of *South Carolina* we cannot examine whether any, and if any, what provisions are made to punish any of her citizens, who may transport their slaves to other states, nor do we know whether any indemnification is granted by law to the owners of slaves who may legally be found guilty and sentenced to the punishment of death. In *Pennsylvania* great care has been taken by her Legislators to prevent her slaves or servants from being obtruded upon any other state; and in case a slave should be sentenced to death, the jury who try him appraise and declare his value, and the owner receives an order from the Court on the State Treasurer for the amount. We are not called upon to point out the justice and regard for the rights of others which enacted those provisions; it is enough that they are of record, on our statute book, and in full force: their existence, ought in a special manner, to guard us against injustice, wrong or outrage from any portion of the Union.

Our readers have anticipated that we are about to say that our apprehensions have been realized and that some of the insurgents from South Carolina, have actually found their way to Philadelphia. The fact is so. A magistrate of this city told us that he had two or three days ago, some conversation with a gentleman from Charleston, who said he had seen in Philadelphia and spoken with some of the Negroes who had been sentenced to death in Charleston, and that they told him they were come to settle here and had sent to South Carolina, to get their wives and families sent on to them.[1]

We pass over the outrage of sending *such* Negroes to dwell among us, and the injustice of making Pennsylvania a Botany Bay, to receive the convicts of the Southern States; these are grievances which we ought, and which we trust, we will, ourselves redress.—We would now appeal to the interest of the slaveholding states and ask whether they hope to deter other slaves from conspiring by manumitting the conspirators and sending them to live, at their ease, in a non-slave-holding state? Is not this a bounty for conspirators and an encouragement to those who associated together for the purposes of Rape, Rapine and Murder? Is it for their own safety to have it known, that the ringleaders of a contemplated Insurrection have not only been bettered in their condition and emancipated, but that they are within 36 hours sail of Charleston, ready to join in any future scheme to burn it and destroy its inhabitants?

For obvious reasons we have no disposition to say more than is necessary to call the attention of our constituted authorities, and those of the south, to the facts we have placed before them. They can see the probable consequences of such a course of conduct, and it rests with them to do that which justice, and a respect for the rights of others, shall require.

1. The Carolina blacks mentioned here were probably Morris Brown and Charles Corr, who were not found guilty of insurrection, but only of violating the 1821 statute that banned free blacks from leaving and returning to South Carolina.

Hartford *Connecticut Mirror*

Saturday, October 12, 1822

We have read with deep interest the official communication of the Intendant of Charleston, on the subject of the plot of the slaves and free blacks of that city to massacre the whites. It affords most abundant evidence of the extreme danger to which they were exposed, and from which, by the most trifling accident, they were relieved. Notwithstanding many parts of the publication very injudiciously intimate, that the blacks have been encouraged to these measures by the language held in Congress, on the subject of the Missouri Question, yet the inhabitants of that city, and all the slave-holding states, may rest assured, that a deep sympathy is felt for them on this occasion, as well as on account of the dangers to which the nature of their population *constantly* exposes them, and must forever expose them. It is, however, illiberal to intimate, that measures truly and sincerely intended to check the evil of slave cultivation, to prevent the extension of that evil to states, at present, little, if any, afflicted with it, were calculated to produce, and did produce, a feeling of resistance, and afford encouragement to their slaves. It was still more unjustifiable to sneer at them, as *pretty displays* of a *love of abstract liberty.* No such design was entertained, we are assured. And surely, there were causes enough deeply founded causes, and causes we deplore, to account for the effects produced without resorting to this. The example of St. Domingo, within ten days sail of Charleston, and the constant intercourse with that Island would alone account for it. We may be also permitted another remark—which is, that we doubt the policy of the present publication in the present form. If intended to awe the blacks, it would seem that the executions and banishments *silently* made, would be more *terrible*—but if really designed as an appeal and a justification to the American people and the world, as to the justice of the sentences, it appears either too much or too little. The historical part is too loose—too declamatory. It would have been more satisfactory if we had possessed, as in the appendix, all the *actual* testimony. Not that we doubt the fact of a most alarming conspiracy, or that there was as much clemency exercised, as is consistent with a state of slavery—but we must still doubt, whether a public trial by Jury, a Jury of white men, and in the common forms of law, would not be as useful in repressing such attempts as such an anomalous tribunal grounded on a law of 1748.[1] The alarm was natural, inevitable,—but after perusing the whole evidence, with great care, it would seem that the project had never extended so far as greatly to endanger the safety of the white population of Charleston, though undoubtedly much suffering must have been felt, if the conspiracy had taken effect. This we infer from the assertion that the punishments have reached *all* the guilty. The whole case teaches but *one lesson,* and that a very solemn one, which is, that no kindness, no indulgence, no ties, however long continued, can ever reconcile even *black men* to a state of slavery, nor to the degradation of a despised caste even after they are free; and of course, points us to the only remedy,—the gradual extinction, instead of the spread of slavery.—*Rep.*[2]

1. The procedure for the trial of slaves accused of capital offences was established by Section IX of the Negro Act of 1740, not "a law of 1748." James Hamilton Jr. referenced repeatedly the Negro Act of 1740 in his *Account* to persuade others that legal procedures were properly followed.

2. This story was copied from a newspaper with the word "Republic" in the title, but which paper is unclear.

Charleston *City Gazette and Commercial Daily Advertiser*

Tuesday, October 15, 1822

PRESENTMENTS OF THE GRAND JURY.

State of S. Carolina, Charleston District In the Court of General Sessions, His Hon. Judge BAY,[1] presiding.

. . . 5th. We present as a grievance the number of slaves working out and bringing wages to their owners; and recommend the number to be limited which each owner may thus employ in the city. We earnestly recommend to the Legislature to take into consideration the number of licences issued by the City Council, to individuals who open small dram-shops, which we consider injurious in the extreme to our slaves, enticing them to plunder their owners.

6th. We present as a dangerous and growing evil, the frequent introduction of slaves from other states in this state. . . .

1. Elihu Hall Bay (1754–1838).

New Orleans *Louisiana Gazette*

Thursday, October 17, 1822

Extract of a letter from South Carolina, dated Sept. 2, 1822. . . . "The late Plot in Charleston was very serious—Had it burst out with any show of success, it would have blazed forth most destructively over the whole seacoast. This cannot be called an attempted insurrection among the Slaves. It originated with free people of color; it began among that class which the abolitionists are most anxious to increase. This fact ought to be borne in mind. It is very important. The slaves engaged in it were principally mechanics, draymen, wharfingers &c. and all those who live much to themselves and with little control from their masters. They were chiefly *Africans.* The non-importation will soon extinguish that race, and those born in the country cannot so easily be induced to revolt. Banish all the free people of colour, exclude colored mechanics from towns and make a few other wise regulations, and there can be little or no danger.—The account published by the city Council should be generally read. It is a faithful and a full account.

Richmond *Enquirer*

Friday, October 18, 1822

CHARLESTON. . . . Extracts from Northern papers, relating to the late negro plot in this city, are inserted in the English Gazettes without any remarks.

Philadelphia *United States Gazette and True American*

Monday, October 21, 1822

A letter from Savannah, dated Sept. 20, informs that the three negroes who had been arrested for an attempt to destroy their masters and excite an insurrection among the blacks, were the day preceding brought up for trial, and all acquitted, no proof whatever appearing against them.

Charleston Mercury, and Morning Advertiser

Wednesday, October 23, 1822

[COMMUNICATION]

One of the late convicted Negroes, whose capital punishment was commuted to "transportation beyond the limits of the United States," was sold on the 15th inst by the former owner, to a Horse dealer; on condition that the above terms should be complied with. Information having been received that the said Negro had left town to accompany his master through the country to Beaufort and Savannah, without being secured in any manner: he was pursued by several public spirited gentlemen, and found as above mentioned, totally unguarded—the means of escape fully within his power. He was accordingly secured and brought back to the city. It being deemed a highly dangerous precedent, that a felon, convicted of exciting insurrection, should be carried openly and unguarded through the interior of the State, with all the facilities necessary to evade the sentence of the Court, and again to expose the community to the contamination of his principles and example. The above measure appeared suggested by necessity, and no doubt will receive the approbation of the community. We feel assured that the owners of the remaining convicts, confined under similar circumstances, will adopt some other mode of carrying the sentence of transportation into effect.[1]

1. This information was reprinted verbatim in the *Washington Gazette,* October 31, 1822, and the *Baltimore Patriot & Mercantile Advertiser,* November 11, 1822. Fear among white inhabitants in Lower Louisiana that New Orleans would be used as a dumping ground for criminal slaves preceded the Louisiana Purchase in the aftermath of Gabriel's Plot of 1800 in Richmond, Virginia, and of slave conspiracies detected in Virginia and North Carolina two years later. Just after the Vesey plot, the Louisiana state legislature passed a law that required slave traders to certify the good character of the slaves brought for sale from other southern states into the New Orleans market. See Juan Ventura Morales to Carlos Delassus, May 24, 1802, Pierre Choteau Collection, Missouri Historical Society; Walter Johnson, *Soul by Soul: Life Inside the Antebellum Slave Market* (Cambridge, MA: Harvard University Press, 1999), 145–46.

St. Francisville (LA) *Asylum and Feliciana Advertiser*

Thursday, October 24, 1822

By the following article from the Louisiana Advertiser, it would seem that the Mayor of New Orleans has detected and arrested seven slaves concerned in the contemplated insurrection in South Carolina.—Others have doubtless been introduced into other parts of the State. It behoves every good citizen to be vigilant to detect these enemies of our peace and safety. The alarming fact that *seven* have found their way into our state calls loudly on our legislature to prevent the further introduction of slaves into our state as merchandize, unless under severe restrictions.

"It must afford sincere pleasure to every well wisher of this state, to be informed, that the Mayor of our city has detected and arrested seven of the slaves, who were concerned in the late insurrection at Charleston, S.C. and who were brought to this port a few days ago, for sale. These culprits were pardoned, on condition their owners would send them out of the state."[1]

1. The material was reprinted nearly verbatim in the *Darien* (GA) *Gazette,* November 21, 1822.

Edwin C. Holland[1] Defends the Courts

Tuesday, October 29, 1822

. . . The people of the North and East will . . . take the liberty of interfering in the designing of some of our most important local regulations and of directing the steps of our constituted authorities. We are not only distated to, but we are slandered in their public prints, denounced in their pulpits, and calumniated in pamphlets and orations. We are exposed to still greater perils, by the swarm of MISSIONARIES, white and *black,* that are perpetually visiting us, who, with the Sacred Volume of God in one hand, breathing peace to the whole family of man, scatter, at the same time, with the other, the firebrands of discord and destruction, and *secretly* disperse among our Negro Population, the seeds of discontent and sedition. It is an acknowledged fact, that some of these religious itinerants, these apostolic vagabonds, after receiving the charities which the philanthropy and open-hearted generosity of our people have bestowed, have, by the means of *Tracts* and other modes of instruction, all professedly *religious* in their character, excited among our Negroes such a spirit of dissatisfaction and revolt, as has, in the end, brought down upon them the vengeance of offended humanity, and given to the gallows and to exile, the deluded instigators of a most diabolical and unholy INSURRECTION. Those who are intimately acquainted with the efficient causes of the late intended Insurrection in Charleston and the districts adjoining, which, from the testimony as well of many of those who have been executed, as from that of the hundreds who either knew of or were engaged in the plot, was to have been conducted with a ferocious barbarity, at which humanity shudders and turns pale; those, we repeat, who are acquainted with the rise and progress of that nefarious plot, know how blasphemously the word of God was tortured, in order to sanction the unholy butchery that was contemplated, and what a powerful agency was put into operation by the dispersion among our Negroes, of *religious magazines, news paper paragraphs* and *insulated texts of scripture*; all throwing such a delusive light upon their condition as was calculated to bewilder and deceive, and finally, to precipitate them into ruin. Religion was stripped of her pure and spotless robe, and, panoplied like a fury, was made to fight under the banners of the most frightful Conspiracy that imagination can conceive, and her voice was heard instigating the midnight ruffian and coward, to creep silently to the pillow of his unsuspecting master, and at one "fell swoop" to murder *him* in the unconscious hour of sleep, prostitute the partner of his bosom, violate the child of his affections, and dash out the brains of his innocent and unoffending infant. The measure of desolation was not even yet full; after robbing our banks, and seizing on our shipping, killing all but the *captains,* who were to be reserved as *pilots,* their atrocious footsteps were to have been lighted from our shores by a *general conflagration,* and our city, that proudly swells with life and with wealth, was to have been left an awful monument of the most ferocious guilt. Such are a few of the barbarities to which we would have been exposed had the late intended Insurrection been crowned with success. . . . Let it never be forgotten, that "our NEGROES are truely the *Jacobins* of the country; that they are the *anarchists* and the *domestic enemy*; *the common enemy of civilized society,* and the barbarians who would, IF THEY COULD, become the DESTROYERS *of our race.*

1. Edwin Clifford Holland (1794–1824) was a twenty-eight-year-old lawyer, poet, and essayist when he published the volume from which this excerpt was extracted. He had served a few years before the Vesey plot as editor of the Charleston *Times.* Although the title page of the book listed no author, the publication page revealed that "on the twenty-ninth day of October . . . Edwin C. Holland, Esq. deposited in this office the title of a book, the right whereof he claims as author and proprietor." In "Pro-Slavery Testimony Examined," *Quarterly Anti-Slavery Magazine* 1 (1835): 93, Elizur Wright Jr. (1804–1885), one of the founders of the American Anti-Slavery Society, quoted from Holland's *Refutation* to underscore in the first issue of his journal that southern masters themselves claimed absolute dominion over their slaves.

[Edwin C. Holland], *Refutation of the Calumnies Circulated Against the Southern & Western States Respecting the Institution and Existence of Slavery among Them* (Charleston, SC, 1822), 11–13, 86.

Nicholas Herbemont[1] on Indulgent Masters and Domestic Slaves

. . . It is among these idle pampered fellows that we must ever expect to find discontent, and it is a well known fact that all blacks concerned in the late attempt at an insurrection belonged to very indulgent masters, and were, almost without exception, fully in the enjoyment of their masters' confidence. Many of them were, or pretended to be, very religious, and several were preachers. In the revolution of St. Domingo, it is almost without an exception also that the most indulgent masters were the first sacrificed. . . .

1. The French-born Nicholas Herbemont (1771–1839) arrived in Charleston in 1801, advertising himself as teacher of the French language to ladies and gentlemen of quality. He went on to become South Carolina College's first professor of French as well as a celebrated viticulturist. He translated into English Louis Dubroca's polemical *The Life of Toussaint Louverture Late General in Chief and Governor of the Island of Saint Domingo: with Many Particulars Never before Published:*

to which Is Subjoined, An Account of the First Operations of the French Army under General Leclerc (Charleston, SC, 1802). See also Charleston *City Gazette and Daily Advertiser,* October 7, 1801; David S. Shields, ed., *Pioneering American Wine: Writings of Nicholas Herbemont, Master Viticulturist* (Athens: University of Georgia Press, 2009), 1–30.

Nicholas Herbemont, *Observations Suggested by the Late Occurrences in Charleston* (Columbia, SC, 1822), 6–7.

Charleston *Southern Intelligencer*

Saturday, November 2, 1822
A PROCLAMATION
By James Hamilton, Jun. Intendant

Whereas, the Corporation in City Council assembled, have instructed me to proclaim that THURSDAY, the 7th of November next, will be set apart as a period of *Thanksgiving, Humiliation and prayer.*

In conformity with which, I do hereby announce the same, inviting the Reverend Clergy of the City, to assemble their respective Congregations for Public Worship, and earnestly soliciting the universal participation of our fellow citizens, in the solemnities of an occasion peculiarly calculated to inspire the feelings of Piety, Gratitude, and Devotion. . . .

A Citizen from Charleston Neck Puts Forth a Petition

Saturday, November 9, 1822

The following petition is respectfully submitted to the consideration of the inhabitants and owners of properties on Charleston Neck, and after a few days will be offered to them for signatures. . . . That from the large and increasing population and property on Charleston Neck, and the various temptations held out to our domestics to depart from the line of their duty, an efficient Guard under proper command and discipline is becoming absolutely necessary, for the security and protection of the lives, property and peace of the citizens; and, whereas, the present patrol guard is found by experience to be ineffective, distressing and oppressive; ineffective, inasmuch as it is not kept every night, and all night, but generally every fifth night, by which the citizens remain unprotected from the machinations of evil, designing persons; distressing and oppressive, as this duty is performed oftener by poor mechanics, who are obliged to toil all day for the honest support of their families, who perhaps look up to their labour alone for existence &c. . . . To such, an exposure to the night air, on many parts of the Beat district, where they are called to perform their duty in July, August, and September, must end in sickness or death. . . . For these and many other reasons which the wisdom of you honorable body[1] will suggest, we pray that you will authorize the Commissioners of Cross Roads,[2] to levy and raise a tax, on the inhabitants and owners of property on the Neck, such as will enable them to raise and organize a guard of—Cavalry, to do duty every night for the protection of Charleston Neck. . . .

1. The South Carolina House of Representatives.

2. The commissioner of roads was an elected position created by the South Carolina state legislature to maintain public order over Charleston Neck, the area above Boundary Street.

Charleston *City Gazette and Commercial Daily Advertiser*, November 9, 1822.

Charleston *Southern Patriot, and Commercial Advertiser*

Monday, November 11, 1822

"*An official Report of the Trials of sundry Negroes charged with an attempt to raise an Insurrection in the State of South Carolina.*"

A pamphlet with the above title has been issued by the Magistrates,[1] with the sanction of the Freeholders that composed the Court on the occasion of the late trials to raise an insurrection in this State. The account published under the authority of the City Council, was necessarily brief and condensed in its statements. As it was written and published to gratify public curiosity, the most material circumstances of the conspiracy and an outline of the evidence were all that was necessary for this purpose. But it is perhaps desirable that the plot, in all its parts, from its first inception until the moment of discovery, as it is unfolded in the evidence, should be minutely described and better known. The public have now, in the present pamphlet, all the links in the chain of evidence which the compilers of the former account, from the nature of their more limited plan, could only present somewhat broken and interrupted. The irresistible conviction on our minds, from an attentive perusal of the present account and a full comparison of the evidence, is not only the guilt of each and every one of the accused who have been convicted, but of the perfect fairness of the proceedings and the equity of the rules which the Court laid down for its government in the trial of the conspirators. Annexed to the account of the Magistrates, as regards their own proceedings, is a report of the trial, before the Court of Sessions of four White Men, accused and convicted of exciting certain Slaves to insurrection. With the tone and style of this pamphlet, we are much pleased. There is no exaggeration or intemperance in the statements. They are strictly deducible from the testimony, and are expressed in language both plain and perspicuous.

1. Lionel H. Kennedy and Thomas Parker.

Charleston *Southern Patriot, and Commercial Advertiser*

Monday, November 11, 1822

We understand that persons who are compelled to travel along the road over the New Bridge,[1] are continually robbed by the gang of armed runaway Negroes, who, as we mentioned a few days past, are hovering about that place. Several depredations were committed on Saturday last by these fellows. Eleven of them were seen near the 8 mile post, armed with muskets, cutlasses and hatchets. We trust that prompt measures will be adopted to put a stop to these shameful robberies.[2]

1. The New Bridge was only a few miles from Charleston. See the advertisement "By William Payne & Sons" in Charleston *City Gazette and Commercial Daily Advertiser,* February 17, 1823.

2. This information was reprinted verbatim in the Savannah *Daily Republican,* November 14, 1822; *Baltimore Patriot & Mercantile Advertiser,* November 19, 1822; *New-York Evening Post,* November 21, 1822; *Washington Gazette,* November 21, 1822; and *Niles' Weekly Register,* November 23, 1822.

Gettysburg *Republican Compiler*

Wednesday, November 13, 1822

When we first read the communication signed "Crispus," we were somewhat at a loss to know how to dispose of it—but at length concluded to publish it. We hesitated for several reasons:

In the first place—It might have a tendency to excite sectional jealousies, and thus have an effect upon the question of who shall be the next President, (whether intended by the author or not.) Secondly—Crispus ascribes improper motives to the Court, and ridicules the idea that there was any danger to be apprehended—when we are assured that the Court was composed of the most respectable men; and we are satisfied, from reading some of the testimony, (which we have not now at hand) that an insurrection was contemplated, and that, in all probability, an attempt would have been made to set Charleston on fire, and murder the inhabitants, had it not been prevented.—Again—it is, perhaps, rather unfair to attack the proceedings of the court here, because it is not likely that there will be any person to defend their cause.—One of the conspirators stated, in substance, that he had been encouraged by reading some of the speeches in Congress in opposition to the admission of slavery in Missouri; which was probably the reason why the subject was alluded to by Governor Bennet[t].

Though we are opposed to slavery in principle and in practice—yet as it is recognized by the Constitution, and the southern states cannot get rid of it, we are unwilling to condemn the citizens of those states, and encourage feelings which might possibly, lead to a dissolution of the Union. . . .

FOR THE COMPILER.

MR. LEFEVER—

I saw a statement of the transaction in South Carolina, relative to the Negro Plot, in a letter from Thomas Bennet, Governor of that State, contained in your paper of the 11th September, which placed that circumstance in a most ridiculous light, in my mind, and chilled my very soul with horror.

Seeing that the evidence and circumstances, there related, made an impression on my mind very different from what they must have made on the minds of the Carolinians, I did not know whether my impressions were peculiar to myself—or whether they might not agree with every northern constitution. I determined, therefore, to ask the opinion of a friend of mine, who was so obliging as to send it to me in writing: and which I found, upon examination, perfectly to correspond with my own.

That Monday Gell, who, it is said, could read and write with facility, and was considerably enlightened, entertained sentiments favourable to the liberty and emancipation of his race, is altogether probable—and, that he was industrious in disseminating these sentiments, may also be true; but, that there was any thing like a regular plot organized, for the purpose of insurrection, we think they have entirely failed to establish—and, indeed, the Governor seems to be of the same opinion. That it was created and subsisted by their fears and apprehensions, and existed only in the minds of the Court and people, we think will amply appear from the evidence contained in the Governor's relation—and must be obvious to any one who reads this account. With this view of the subject, we think the proceedings against the blacks unprecedented, unjustifiable, barbarous and reprehensible, in the highest degree.

Enclosed I send you the letter; by giving it a place in your paper, if you do not aid the cause of humanity and gratify all your readers, you will, at least, confer a favor on one of your Subscribers. *A SUBSCRIBER.*

The Governor says—no means, which experience or ingenuity could devise, were unessayed to eviscerate the plot: That expectations of immunity from punishment, by confession, were encouraged: That a committee was formed by the City Council, to assist the Court in the labours of investigation, whose intelligence, activity and zeal, were well adapted to the arduous duties of their appointment—and whose assiduity, aided by the various sentiments which influenced the prisoners, produced a rapid developement of the plot: That, to the last hour of the existence of several who appeared to be conspicuous actors in the drama, they were pressingly importuned to make further confessions: That a solitary one was induced, through cowardice, the expectation of immunity from punishment, the persuasions or importunity of the committee, or some other motives, to surrender the names of associates: That a spirit of retaliation and revenge produced a similar effect with others, who suspected that they were the victims of treachery—and this principle operated with full effect, as the hope or expectation of pardon predominated.

He says, that investigation was retarded by the difficulty of procuring authentic evidence: That, although Denmark Vesey was unquestionably the instigator of this plot, no positive proof of his guilt appeared until the 28th, when it grew out of the confession of one of the convicts: That, principally from the general information of Perault, and of the convicts Gell and Drayton, facility was given to the further proceedings of the Court.

So that it appears, that all the means which the experience, ingenuity, activity, zeal and ardor of a committee of prejudiced, frightened, incensed individuals, aided by the various sentiments of hope, expectation, fear, suspicion, retaliation and revenge, could devise, were practiced upon these poor, ignorant creatures, in order to extort evidence of their guilt. And nothing appears to have been wanting but the rack and the torture, to enable this committee, court and jury, of free men and citizens of the United States, to rival the inhuman barbarity of a Spanish Inquisition in the days of a Peter.

The proceedings of the court were slow, and the investigation much retarded, until the passions of the poor victims were excited and thrown into a ferment, and they were induced, through hope, fear, jealousy, revenge, &c. to tell tales on each other—all of which were seized with the utmost avidity, and converted into conclusive evidence, without any regard to its truth or probability, by these persecutors of sable misery: Yet a considerable length of time elapsed, before a train of evidence could be constructed, which could satisfy even the prejudiced minds and smothered consciences of these human vultures. The train once laid, every thing went on swimmingly, and human lives were never more lavishly disposed of by the most ignorant and arbitrary tyranny.

Of the kind of evidence, and its truth or probability, you will be enabled to judge from further extracts from the Governor's letter. He says—"a servant, prompted by attachment to his master, communicated to him, that he had been requested to give his assent and subscribe his name to a list of persons already engaged in the conspiracy." "The city council was convened, and, after a very close and attentive examination, the general impression was produced, that but little credence could attach to the statements." That "another servant stated, generally, that such a combination actually existed; adding, with great confidence, that the explosion of their schemes would occur on the ensuing Sunday evening." "Saturday night and Sunday morning passed without the predicted demonstration." That, from the various conflicting statements made during the trials, it is difficult to form even a plausible conjecture of their ultimate plans of operation, no two agreeing on general definite principles. That, if any plan had been organized, it was never communicated, by the principal conspirator, to the leaders of the men; as they were wholly ignorant of the place of rendezvous, altho' within two days of the time appointed—and but one man arrested prior to the day fixed on for the attempt. That no weapons were discovered, except thirteen hoop-poles, nor any testimony received that such preparations were actually made, but of six pikes. He says, that, having (from such evidence,) established the existence of a plot and the places of rendezvous, all that was deemed requisite for conviction, was, to prove an association with the ring-leaders, and an expression of their assent to the measure. On such, generally, the sentence of death has been executed. Others who, without actually combining, were proven to have known of the conspiracy, and to have given their sanction by an act, have been sentenced to die, and their punishment commuted to banishment from the United States. In this manner, he says, the whole number, Seventy-two, have been disposed of—thirty-five executed, and thirty-seven sentenced to banishment.

Although there was but one man arrested prior to the day fixed on for the attempt; although but two days before the pretended time appointed, there was no plan organised, and even the ringleaders knew nothing of the place of rendezvous, or the precise time; although it was difficult, from all the evidence that could be elicited or extorted from these poor ignorant beings, by the "ingenuity" of enlightened men, to form even a plausible conjecture of their plans of operation; although no two of them agreed in their evidence; although all the weapons discovered or heard of were thirteen hoop-poles and six pikes—and although the pretended time appointed, passed over without the least symptom of insurrection or disturbance: Yet the ingenuity of the committee and court found means to establish the existence of a plot, and the places of rendezvous—and this done, all that was deemed requisite for conviction, was, to prove them to have associated with the ringleaders, or to have known of the plot. GOOD HEAVENS! Is this the manner in which the lives of human beings are disposed of in the Southern States!

Is it possible that any man, or set of men, in a civilized country, could '*infer*,' from the fact of men being without arms, that it was their intention to attack a public arsenal, with "clubs"! Can it be, that any man in America could so far deviate from the path of reason, as to imagine that half a dozen poor, starved negro slaves, could take it into their heads to subjugate the United States with THIRTEEN HOOP-POLES, (for even the six pikes were not discovered)—and that without any plan of organization! and can it be true, that upon a suspicion, reared upon such a slight foundation and supported by such flimsy evidence, SEVENTY-TWO HUMAN BEINGS have been deprived of their *rights, liberties* and *lives!*

All the annals of the long night of tyranny and bondage, ignorance, error and superstition, which involved mankind for centuries, afford not an instance which discovers a greater abuse of power, or more bigotry, prejudice and barbarity—nor has the *united fears* and *jealousies* of *Legitimate tyranny,* ever sanctioned a more horrible scene of injustice and oppression, on such a pitiful pretext.

Yes, it is too true, it is a lamentable fact, that upon such grounds THIRTY-FIVE of our fellow creatures have been butchered in cold blood—and THIRTY-SEVEN buried alive in the mines of South America, to endure a living death: and all this, by *enlightened, free,* and *republican citizens* of the *United States!*

Pnoo! no matter, they were nothing but Negroes!

Crispus.

Charleston Courier

Thursday, November 14, 1822

The authorities at New-Orleans appear to have taken the alarm, lest the Convict Negroes, ordered to be transported from this state, should find their way to that city. A letter from Capt. MESSERVEY,[1] of the brig *Commerce,* of this port states that his vessel had been detained in the river by the Sheriff of New-Orleans, under a misapprehension that the slaves he had on board, were some of those sentenced to be transported. They may quiet their apprehensions on this score, as these convicts were condemned, and are only allowed to be taken away from Charleston, on bonds being given that they shall be taken without the limits of the United States. We know that none of the slaves on board the *Commerce,* were of this description. The following is the section of the act concerning the introduction of slaves into Louisiana, under which the brig has been detained:—

"*Section* 6th—And be it further enacted, that in all cases within the meaning of this act, the burthen of proof shall be on the person who imports, or brings, or claims the said slaves or free persons; provided, that in all cases the production of the certificate of the clerk of the county from whence they are imported or brought, accompanied with the certificate of the Governor of that state, shall be received as prima facia evidence."[2]

1. In 1822 Captain Philip Messervey (d. 1828; also rendered as "Messervy") resided at 120 Meeting Street. See *CSCCD,* 90.

2. This information was reprinted verbatim in the *Washington Gazette,* November 21, 1822.

Charleston *Southern Patriot, and Commercial Advertiser*

Thursday, November 14, 1822

. . . We have admitted it, for the sake of argument, to be a possible case, (though we have no other ground for believing it to be so, than the *credo quia impossible est,* of an old Ecclesiastical writer)[1] that by force or by compact, the black population might not only be emancipated, but placed on the footing of a perfect equality of rights, civil and political, with the whites. That state of equality would include the right of exercising their industry in every department and walk of public and private life. They might not only be cultivators of the earth, day labourers, artisans, and manufacturers, but merchants and professional men. They might according to the law, glide into our families as physicians in the perfect confidence of that delicate relation; they might vindicate or violate our rights as advocates; sit in judgment upon our lives and property as jurors and judges; and instruct and guide our consciences as pastors. They might vote and control the popular elections; be themselves elected to state legislatures, and to Congress; command our armies and navies; preside over our councils, as presidents and Ministers of state; and represent the dignity and interests of the nation as ambassadors in foreign countries. . . .

This would be the legitimate fruit of equal rights between the whites and blacks. If it be said that this could not take place because our prejudices would counteract the exercise of the right, let it be answered how these prejudices could produce that counteraction in the sea coast districts of Virginia, North Carolina, South Carolina, Georgia, and Louisiana, where the blacks greatly exceed the whites in number? Many of the blacks would acquire wealth by industry, or other means; and wealth would bring education and ambition.—They would certainly be elected in the districts spoken of, and the heterogeneous mixture would take place, which has been described. . . . The wealthy and the powerful among the blacks would find multitudes among the poorest and most ignorant whites, and perhaps even among some in moderate circumstances, who would bow down and worship these Idols. . . .

Thus some of the blacks, who inherit the cunning as well as the punic faith of the ancient Carthaginians, their predecessors, and countrymen, would find ways and means to advance themselves, to mingle with many of the whites, to create a new race, in violation of nature, of vile complexion and odious character, who would tarnish the national reputation, as well as colour, and humble it in the dust. . . .

A COLUMBIAN

1. The saying "*credo qui impossible est*" ("I believe because it is impossible") is attributed to Tertullian (d. ca. 220), an Early Christian theologian.

Certification of Execution for William Garner

Charleston:

We Certify, that at a Court of Magistrates and Freeholders, Consisting of Jacob Axson and Charles M. Furman Esq. Justices, and the Hon: Joel R. Poinsett, Thomas R. Smith and Robert Y. Hayne Esquires, Col. Thomas Roper and Col. John Gordon assembled in

Charleston on the 3rd day of August last, a negro man called William Garner, said to be the Slave of Martha R. Garner, was tried and convicted of an attempt to raise an Insurrection among the negroes of Charleston—for which he was sentenced to be executed on the 9th August 1822, at which period the Sentence was carried into effect—

15. November 1822

Justices	Freeholders
Jacob Axson	Tho. Rhett Smith
Charles M. Furman	Robt. Y. Hayne
	Thos Ropers
	John Gordon

Certification of Execution for William Garner, November 15, 1822, series S165015, Petitions to the General Assembly, no. 234, SCDAH.

Charleston *Southern Patriot, and Commercial Advertiser*

Friday, November 15, 1822

. . . Are the slaves, it is again asked, possessed of the qualities necessary to convert them with safety at once into freemen, with all political privileges? Are they trained and brought to that state of mind, which feels a proud obedience to the laws, though it would disdain submission to any other power? The answer must be the negative. . . .

It is vain hope to expect that these two races of people can blend and assimilate, and live in harmony together. It would be perpetual struggle for power, and then for existence itself. When the French Convention in its madness emancipated the slaves of St. Domingo,[1] and its orators pronounced the dreadful dogma, let the earth and its inhabitants perish, rather than a principle, (the principle of universal freedom) it little imagined that this decree would produce the extermination of the whites, the utter destruction of that fine colony, and the ruin of the best commerce which France enjoyed—yet such were the fruits—and such would be the case in the southern states in the struggle and civil wars which would inevitably follow, if the blacks were emancipated unless the whites, feeling that their existence depended on it, put forth their strength vigorously, and subdued them promptly. There could indeed, be no doubt of the issue, if they did justice to their own strength and talents unless the interposition of foreign powers, the active energy of the Haytians in aid of their black brethren, (to whom these last have already turned their eyes, and addressed their letters as their natural allies;) and the apathy of the northern states, should overwhelm the southern states. . . .

A COLUMBIAN

1. The Jacobin ascendancy in the National Convention during the French Revolution led to the ratification on February 4, 1794, of a decree that emancipated slaves in the French colonies. Slavery in France's colonies did not finally end, however, until 1848.

Charleston Courier

Friday, November 15, 1822

. . . (From the Boston Recorder.) We were not aware that the late proceedings of the people in Charleston, in regard to the Insurrectionists, had been regarded by the people of the north as "unlawful, unjust and cruel." Here and there an uninformed individual, or an enthusiast in "Freedom's cause" may have felt and expressed such an opinion; but we believe that with scarcely an exception, the whole northern population have deeply sympathized, both in the danger and the deliverance of their brethren at the south.—EDITOR RECORDER)

For the Boston Recorder

Mr. EDITOR—I was highly gratified in reading an extract from the *Charleston Courier,* punished in the Southern Intelligencer of the 17th August, and solicit the favor of reciprocating our views and sentiments with its author, through the medium of your excellent paper. The sentiments contained in this article, respecting the late difficulties in Charleston, are those of a liberal and enlightened mind. . . .

There are those in the north who condemn the late proceedings of the people of Charleston as unlawful, unjust and cruel; who contemplate all the horrors of the intended insurrection without one sympathetic emotion, and who extend their indifference to the peace and safety of all their southern brethren. They view them as answerable for the existence, and all the evils of slavery, and of course deserving the judgments of heaven. This arises from a limited knowledge of facts, and is unjust and unchristian. On the contrary there are those in the south who consider the northern people as mean, ignorant and depraved. They believe them devoid of every generous feeling; hypocritical in their professions of morality and religion; selfish in all their political measures, and devising plans to deprive them of their property, or to involve them in difficulty. . . . [T]he system of slavery is not a local but a national evil; that it has been handed down from one generation to another, and that the southern people, or the present generation, are not accountable for its existence; that the recent difficulties in Charleston, arising from this unhappy system, originated in the ambition of free negroes, and that the plans were to have been executed by those treated, (in most respects) more like gentlemen than servants; that the people of Charleston have acted just as every other enlightened and humane people would have acted under similar circumstances, and that it is unjust for those unacquainted with those circumstances to suspect their motives, or condemn their proceedings. . . .

Charleston *Southern Patriot, and Commercial Advertiser*

Saturday, November 16, 1822

. . . The great fundamental principle, it is believed, should be that the slaves should be kept as much confined as possible to agricultural labors. These so employed are found to be the most orderly and obedient of the slaves. And now that the foreign admixture of native Africans is absolutely and permanently prohibited by law, and almost wholly so in practice, and that leaven of barbarism which was heretofore continually infused into the mass is thus withheld, there may be a reasonable hope that descendants, born and bred in the country, may gradually become docile, and in some degree a civilized people.

There should be no black mechanics or artizans, at least in the cities. These are placed by the nature of their employments, much more from under the eye and inspection of their masters, and they acquire vicious habits injurious to themselves, as well as their owners, and of evil example to other slaves. In the sea coast towns, often filled with so many worthless and idle strangers from the West India Islands, the black mechanics, artists, draymen and wharfingers, are thrown into bad company who infuse false notions and delusive hopes into their minds, which render them dissatisfied with their condition and prepare them for plots and other mischiefs.

It is true as it is trite, that knowledge is power. Education therefore on no account be permitted. . . . The gospel was taught and spread over the whole world by preaching and not by reading; for there were no printed books in those days, and not one man in ten thousand could purchase manuscript books. The slaves also should have no separate place of worship; a station should be appropriated for them in every place of worship used by the whites, where they should be able to see and to hear, and they as well as their masters should be taught the mild doctrines of the gospel. . . .

A COLUMBIAN

Petition of Naomi Smith,[1] Saturday, November 16, 1822

The State of South Carolina.

To the Honorable the president of
members of the Senate.

The petition of Miss Naomi
Smith respectfully sheweth.

That in the late insurrectionary efforts among the slaves of Charleston, a negro fellow named Caesar, belonging to your petitioner was implicated, & after a full & fair investigation before a Court of Magistrates & freeholders, was sentenced to be executed, & pursuant to said Sentence, on the 30th day of July in this year 1822 was executed. The case of your petitioner being somewhat peculiar, she respectfully begs leave to state some of its Circumstances not only to manifest the propriety of this application: but also to obtain, if practicable some remuneration proportionate to her loss.

The fellow Caesar above mentioned was a prime healthy able bodied negro, about twenty five years of age, with a boy about fourteen & a Child of four years old, were all the slaves & constituted all the property, except a little furniture, belonging to your petitioner. That Caesar was an active drayman, & besides Clothing & supporting himself at his own Expense paid her regularly ten dollars per month: That her boy of fourteen years old paid her four dollars per month; which with a small annual Charity of one hundred dollars gratuitously given her by the St. Andrew's Society, constituted her only means of living: That since the execution of Caesar, in consequence of the loss of so great a proportion of her little income, she has been obliged to give up house keeping & depends for support on the munificence of her friends: That your petitioner is upwards of Sixty years of Age and very infirm. She deplores the existance; but rejoices at the detection of her servants guilt, & this discomfiture of the plot, in which it appears he was concerned. And for her peculiarly severe personal loss, throws herself upon the liberality of of your honorable body.

Novr. 16th 1822 Naomi Smith.
City of Charleston

Council Chamber

Nov 16th 1822.—

By the instruction of the Corporation, I do hereby certify that the facts set forth by Miss Smith are true & that her situation is one peculiarly hard, and well entitled to the compassionate consideration of the Legislature.—

J. Hamilton Jun
—Intendant.—

I do hereby certify, that I verily beleive from authentic information, that all the facts set forth in the foregoing Petition; are true—

Lionel H. Kennedy
Presidg. Justice of the first Court of Mag. & Freeholders
Robert J. Turnbull—Freeholder
Jas Legare
Wm Drayton
J. R. Pringle
Nath. Heyward

1. On Naomi Smith, the owner of the slave Caesar Smith, see Part III, p. 249 n1.

Naomi Smith, "Petition and Supporting Papers Asking Compensation for a Slave Who Was Executed for Involvement in a Slave Uprising," November 16, 1822, no. 128, series S165015, SCDAH.

Charleston *Southern Intelligencer*

Saturday, November 16, 1822

EMANCIPATION.

. . . If a colony could be formed where the people would be saved from the pressure of immediate want and have the means of providing for future necessities, there would then be no objection to emancipation, as fast as it could be produced by voluntary act; by partial remuneration, or by full satisfaction, as the feelings and situation of different individuals should require or demand.

Provided there was such a colony, the legislature could then, consistently with justice and humanity, compel the free people of colour gradually to leave the State. Where can they now go, with a hope of finding a permanent home or place of safety? With what justice can we remove from ourselves an evil, a source of danger, and throw it upon a sister state? . . . [P]ass a law providing that every free black shall leave the state after arriving at a certain age. This would to a certainty stop the increase of their numbers, and probably produce a great decrease, by causing the emigration of whole families. . . .

Charleston *City Gazette and Commercial Daily Advertiser*

Saturday, November 16, 1822

COMMUNICATIONS.

Mr. Editor—I have read with interest the Memorial left at the State Bank[1] for the signatures of the Citizens, and I am pleased at the boldness and energy of the measures recommended to the consideration of the Legislature. Many plans have been suggested by my friends, to remove causes of future disquiet. But my objection to them all has been, that they merely profess to diminish existing grievances, and to *postpone an evil day.* To legislate thus far, is to do nothing. There is, Mr. Editor, a leprosy in our system, whose causes are deeply fixed, and must be removed before they become more so. How this is to be done, is the only question. The Memorial points to the means, and if from any false sensibility, we do not resort to these, we may bid adieu to any permanent security for South Carolina. Some of my neighbours say, the measure is a strong one. Certainly, it is a strong measure, and let me ask, where is the country that ever was preserved in times of peril, but by strong measures. It is your politicians who look forward to a few years only; these are they who bring distress upon some countries, and ruin others.

I know from good authority, that a Document on this important subject was submitted to the City Authorities, by the first Court of Magistrates and Freeholders, unanimously signed by its Members; developing by accurate tables of our population at different periods, and other data, such a view of the danger of retaining amongst us an intermediate class between the owner and the slave, as would satisfy any reader, and to have induced the City Council to submit it to the Charleston Delegation as worthy of their deepest concern and reflexion. From the intelligence, talent, and humanity, which we all know belong to the members of that court, we may presume, that they would not deliberately recommend such a measure without good grounds; and though each of us is entitled to have this opinion, yet such a recommendation ought to have at least so much weight as to make us ponder the subject well, before we object to the Memorial. I lament that this document did not meet the public eye.

Some object to the memorial because there are no exceptions. The aged, for instance—I presume it is not the intention even of the memorialists to include them, for they may be permitted to remain, and yet the main object be attained, viz the *rooting out* of a permanent evil. To make any other exceptions, is to *perpetuate* the evil. The memorial embraces no details; these must rest with the wisdom and discretion of the Legislature and who but knows our country, can for a *moment* believe, that all harshness will not be avoided; the removal of these people may be by *gradual* means; sufficient time will no doubt be given them to make all necessary arrangements for their emigration; months and perhaps years may be given them. But let the time be known, when there must be an end to anxiety and apprehension from this source. *Halcyon* days indeed will those be, when our slaves shall have removed from their eyes, these constant sources of jealousy and disquiet, and the master indulge in safety his disposition to ameliorate still further the condition of his slave.

But, Mr. Editor, to what place are these people to go? To a wilderness, and to starve? No.—They are to have the liberty to go where they please, and may choose their residence in other sections of these happy States, where, if they are industrious, they may live and amass wealth, and enjoy in common with every white citizen, the blessings guaranteed by the Constitution of the United States; and where, if the people are sincere in what they say, they must meet with many friends, and much aid from their societies, and where if they are not so, they are free from the restraints which our laws of necessity impose on them, and from that degraded state, which, as their intelligence increases, and their industry is rewarded, must forever be a subject of mortification and misery to them.

In throwing together these hints, my only object is peace, and *permanent* security for myself and my children. All my fellow citizens have the same interest. If we now act with energy, and support the memorial, our society (chiefly as regards our daughters), will be rendered more delightful; our rich inhabitants will be doubly secure in their possessions, and the poor industrious mechanic and labourer, whom want often drives from his home here, to seek employment elsewhere, will have no competition but from his own colour and may thereby be tempted to stay with us, giving us one more arm to defend us in a time of trouble.

SENEX.

1. The said "Memorial of the Citizens of Charleston to the Senate and House of Representatives of the State of South Carolina" is reprinted below, pp. 577–83.

Charleston *Southern Patriot, and Commercial Advertiser*

Monday, November 18, 1822

TO THE INDEPENDENT VOTERS *of Colleton and Beaufort District*. . . . As Intendant of Charleston, Major HAMILTON, during the last summer, was *principally instrumental* in saving our State from the horrors of *insurrection*: He is perhaps better acquainted than any other man with the nature and extent of that plot, and is admirably qualified *to vindicate South-Carolina on the floor of Congress,* when our late disturbances shall become the subject of discussion. Unless we send such men as Major HAMILTON to Congress (uniting the qualities of *firmness* and *manly courage,* with the *habit of public speaking*) we will have to submit to the taunts and sarcasms of our Northern brethern. . . .

JEFFERSON.

John Potter[1] to Langdon Cheves, Wednesday, November 20, 1822

. . . A much fatter edition of the late intended plot has been published, by the sitting magistrates,[2] on that matter this was judged necessary, to meet the Governor's *statements,* which it is supposed he will make!! I have sent a copy to Joseph Dulles[3]—and requested him to send it to you—as the first edition was all out—until more are printed—there will be some warm words, I expect, at Columbia—I do not believe *Bennett,* would fit the office of a Constable in this City—Kind regards to all Yr family—in haste. . . .

1. Potter sent this confidential letter to Cheves from Charleston.

2. Potter referred to Lionel Kennedy and Thomas Parker, *The Official Report on the Trials of Sundry Negroes.*

3. Joseph Heatly Dulles (1795–1876), Langdon Cheves's brother-in-law, split time between Philadelphia and Charleston. He owned a plantation near the city. See Charles W. Dulles, "Extracts from the Diary of Joseph Heatly Dulles," *Pennsylvania Magazine of History and Biography* 35 (1911): 276

ALS in SCHS.

Gettysburg *Republican Compiler*

Wednesday, November 20, 1822

FOR THE COMPILER. Mr. Lefever.—As you have stated your objections to the letter of Crispus, and appear to have entertained doubts of the propriety of publishing it; we shall endeavor to answer those objections, and justify its publication. With regard to its effect upon the selection of a President, we can assure you it was not the intention of Crispus, nor do we think it can have any.

As to the respectability of the Court—we shall only observe, that respectability of character has nothing to do with right or wrong—with justice or injustice; because respectable men are liable to error and the influence of prejudice, and therefore, never should be made a cloak of, to screen error from detection, or shield wickedness from punishment.

He did not "ridicule the idea that here was any danger to be apprehended"—it was only the extent of that idea. That there was growing danger we admit; but we think it could have been prevented without the loss of so much human blood—and we do think that such strong measures could only have been warranted, and such severe punishments justified, by an open and actual insurrection—and that, when there was only danger to be APPREHENDED, and not a single act of hostility, violence or outrage committed, the measures adopted and punishments inflicted, were unjust and barbarous in the highest degree; and merit the reprobation of every man, possessed, in the least degree, of the principle of Justice, inspired with one particle of freedom, or animated with one spark of humanity.

We do not reflect on our Southern brethren for the evil they inherit, or the misfortunes of Slavery. Although we reprobate Slavery, both in practice and in principle, yet we are fully sensible of the difficulty of getting rid of it in the Southern States. But, at the same time that we, as Christians, extend our charity and sympathy toward their misfortune, we must, as free men, stamp with our decided disapprobation, their arbitrary and unjust exercise of power over this oppressed and miserable part of our species.

That it is unfair, we deny. It is just and fair to send the antidote with the poison. That transaction has been published here: it may have a tendency to prejudice many honest people against the Blacks. Justice to the defenceless Slaves demands of the philanthropist, that it be investigated and set in its true light. The investigation has not been instituted in private, but in the public papers—and, if erroneous or untrue, can be corrected or refuted.

A SUBSCRIBER.

Darien (GA) *Gazette*

Thursday, November 21, 1822

Seven of the slaves who were concerned in the late insurrection in Charleston, and pardoned on condition that they should be sent out of the state, arrived at New-Orleans about the 20th ult. and were immediately arrested by the mayor,[1] on his own responsibility, as it appears there is no law in that state to prevent the importation of felons. Much credit is given the mayor for the prompt manner in which he acted, and it is proposed by a writer in the Louisiana Advertiser, that as the law is defective, the citizens should rally round him and supply the deficiency.

1. This is Louis Philippe de Roffignac, a French-born merchant and banker who served as mayor from 1820 to 1828.

Charleston *Southern Patriot, and Commercial Advertiser*

Thursday, November 21, 1822

GEORGETOWN, (S.C.) Nov. 20.

The Murderer Joe[1]—The following extract from a letter of a gentleman of respectability was put into our hands yesterday, by his correspondent; the writer states that he has been requested to inform the citizens in this neighborhood, "That *Joe*, the murderer of Mr. Ford,[2] had gone back to his old range—Mrs. Horry's plantation.[3] He was pursued in Clarendon, a short time ago, and followed as far as Vance's ferry; two of his companions were taken, who stated it was their intention to go to the plantation of Mrs. Horry. *Joe* is armed, and is quite lame, from the wound he received when shot at over the river of which you have no doubt heard."—*Winyaw Intelligencer.*

1. Although no hard evidence has surfaced to link the fugitive slave named Joe (also called "Forest") directly to the Vesey plot, he created a legend for himself in lowcountry South Carolina before, during, and after the proceedings. Joe ran away from a plantation owned by a "Mr. Carroll of the Richland District," near the state capital of Columbia. Joe moved east to the Georgetown district. In the lowcountry, Joe formed a small band of runaway slaves who terrorized whites by traversing the swamps to carry out depredations. He escaped numerous pursuers and was not hunted down and killed until October 1823, when a fellow slave betrayed his location. See "Petition to the South Carolina Senate, ca. 1824," in John Hope Franklin and Loren Schweninger, *Runaway Slaves: Rebels on the Plantation* (New York: Oxford University Press, 1999), 303–5; "The Murderer Joe Destroyed," Charleston *City Gazette and Commercial Daily Advertiser,* September 10, October 8, 1823.

2. George Ford (1776–1821) was a wealthy planter. See *Columbia* (SC) *Telescope,* June 12, 1821; *BDSCHR* 3: 240.

3. Probably the property of Harriott Pinckney Horry (1748–1830), the wife of Daniel Horry Jr. (d. 1785).

Benjamin Hammet[1] to William Crafts, Thursday, November 21, 1822

Dear Sir

Having had the misfortune to loan one of my slaves, who was hung in July amongst the twenty two conspirators, and feeling that loss sensibly,[2] I have signed a memorial to the Legislature in company with Capt Sims & others; Who have informed me that you have charge of the said memorial, Not being able from a great press of business to get my appraisement ready until now. I respectfully take the liberty of inclosing it to your care as an accompanying document, as it relates to my petitioning as an individual. Capt Sims has assured me that you have cheerfully, accepted of the charge entrusted to you, I regret I should be so troublesome, to a stranger. But you being in a public station to whom we must apply I pray you to excuse my occupation of your time.

I will merely remark, that my slave was named Bacchus; a valuable porter in a store; in which capacity he was generally employed about me—*He was committed by myself*, on 11th July, when I had my suspicions of his being concerned in the diabolical plot strongly excited without waiting for any demand from Legal Authority. Every succeeding exertion of mine was such, as I shall not regret, as a citizen, and master. I communicate these facts, lest a contrary impression should be made than they would have

With considerations of the highest respect

I am
Dr Sir
Yr obet Servt
B Hammet

1. On the merchant Benjamin Hammet (1794?–1826), see Part III, p. 236 n1.
2. Bacchus Hammet was one of the twenty-two slaves hanged on Friday, July 26.

Report to the General Assembly, no. 25, series S165029, SCDAH.

Twelve Inhabitants[1] Petition for Compensation, November, 1822

. . . Your petitioners and memorialists would by no means wish to be understood, as casting the slightest reproach upon the tribunal before which the slaves were tried and condemned. On the contrary, if the [*illegible*] of approbation could add any thing to the universal sentiment on this subject, they would say in the most decided and unqualified manner, that they believe a more wise, discrete, humane and intel[l]igent Court was perhaps never formed for the trial of criminals. They have so full a confidence in their virtue and impartiality, that if it should ever be the misfortune of any of the undersigned, to be accused of any offense they would infinitely prefer being tried before such a tribunal, to that of a court and jury, notwithstanding all the boasted superiority of jury trial. . . . They neither pretend that their slaves were innocent, or that they had not an impartial trial, but the foundation on which they rest their expectation is one growing naturally out of the policy of the country. It is one vitally concerning the dignity and honor of the State. There is no principle better established both in law and morality than this, that if one man take the property of another he should give him in return the value of said property. . . . Your petitioners and memorialists so far from attempting to shield or protect any of their culprit slaves have been the most vigilant and active to bring them among others to condign punishment. Many of your petitioners and memorialists have actually took their own slaves in person and delivered them up for trial, without the intervention of any civil authority. Much might be said relative to that arch-demon Monday Gill.[2] Your petioners and memorialists believe that he in conjunction with Judge Drayton's and Mr. Strohecker's slaves[3] swore away the lives of many, not actively, if in any degree concerned in the conspiracy, but they forbear any comment on that subject, as their slaves have been condemned and executed. . . .

1. John Robertson (1762–1831), owner of the executed slaves Adam, Robert, and John. Robertson identified them all as "about 35 years." They worked in Robertson's rope-making business, with Adam in the position of foreman. William M. Scott, a notary public, owned Tom and described him as "about 28 years a labour[er] and sailor." The grocer Jacob Lankester, owner of Jacob, said he was a painter "about 28 years" old. John Billings (d. 1826), owner of a Charleston stable, put the age of his executed slave Charles at "about 24 years" and listed his occupation as coachman and hostler. The lumber merchant William Harth, who owned Mingo and Isaac, described Mingo as a cook and house servant, twenty-two years old. Isaac, who was transported, served as Harth's coachman and was thirty years old. John S. Glen, a planter, described his executed slave, Jacob, as a carpenter, twenty-three years of age. William Wightman and Thomas F. Purse, not Thomas Forrest, claimed ownership of the executed slave Julius. Julius was a cooper, twenty-seven years old. Paul Pritchard Sr. described Gullah Jack as a "caulker," "about 29 years" of age. The other signatories to the petition were Sarah Russell, owner of Tom; James Poyas, owner of Peter; Mordecai Cohen, owner of Jerry; and A. Forrester, owner of Lot. See the *OR*, 183; Inhabitants of Charleston, Petition and Supporting Papers Asking Compensation for Their Slaves Who Were Executed for Involvement in a Slave Insurrection, n.d. [ca. 1822], no. 1839, series S165015, SCDAH.

2. Monday Gell.

3. Judge John Drayton's enslaved cook Charles had his death sentence commuted to transportation outside the United States. Blacksmith John Strohecker's slave Perault, also a blacksmith, was punished by transportation as well. See the *OR*, 186.

Inhabitants of Charleston, Petition and Supporting Papers, n.d., no. 1839, series S165015, SCDAH.

Petition of Ann Drayton Perry, Saturday, November 23, 1822[1]

To the Honorable President and the other Members of the Senate:
Humbly Sheweth,

THAT your petitioner is the mistress and owner of a Negro Man Slave, called *Agrippa*, condemned to Transportation, by the Court, organised for the Trial of Slaves and others, charged with attempting to raise an Insurrection. She wishes not to screen her Negro from just punishment; but, conceives his case a singular one—Amongst the many trials reported, (to which she calls the attention of your Honorable House.) His name was never mentioned nor given in, in any of the lists made out by the Conspirators that gave evidence in behalf of the State; he was required by Capt. SIMS[2] to appear as a witness in favor of his Fellow *Scipio*; at whose trial *Perault* was the accusor; and with which request (*conscious of his innocence*) he willingly complied. Here, and not before, *Perault* becomes his accusor, and he is hurried from the Court into confinement. The attention of your Honorable House is craved to examine the nature of the charge, made by *Perault*, (a fellow possessing intelligence and understanding above the generality of Negroes, glorying in the part he was to act, and boasting he would do it again, if an opportunity offered) he charges *Agrippa* with this conversation—that, on his going to get the Horse, he asked him what he wanted the Horse for; *Agrippa* said, "*to do a thing good for you and good for me*;" which, he said, he understood was to go to raise men for the Insurrection. He asked the price of the hire of the Horse; Perault said three dollars; Agrippa replied that was too much, as he wanted him only a part of two days; Perault replied *that is my price, if you don't pay it you leave the Horse.* Agrippa then replied, I have but two dollars, will you let me have the Horse on paying that? I will pay you the other dollar when I come down. Perault said, "*No, the Horse dont move without the money.*" Will you take Sims as security? *Perault* answered, *no!* Then *Adam* (a free man,) was offered, and accepted for the dollar.

When we recur to the declaration made by *Agrippa*, to such a conspirator, as *Perault* avows himself to be, either his *truth* suffers or the *conspiracy* falls below contempt. Yet, on this single inconsistent evidence of a desperado swearing for his life, (although disproved by the clearest testimony of five witnesses—to which the attention of your Honorable Body is referred in either of the reports) an unfortunate fellow creature is torn from his children and family; and your petitioner from a Negro invaluable to her, but, in estimation, of freeholders worth $1,000 Your petitioner craves the interposition of your Honorable Body in this hard case; and that you will be pleased to restore her the Negro; or if, in your justice and wisdom, you should deem the sacrifice necessary, that you will give her the value of the slave. . . . [3]

Personally appeared William Sims who being duly sworn—deposeth and sayeth, that he has been acquainted with a Negro man named Agrippa for ten or twelve years, the property of Mrs. Ann Drayton Perry and now confined in the work-house of Charleston, under sentence of Transportation out of the limits of the United States under the direction of the City Council of Charleston, Said Negro man has been frequently in my Employment. he is a good Wheelwright and House-Carpenter between twenty five and thirty years of age, and of a remarkable good orderly behaviour and in my opinion is worth one thousand Dollars

Wm. Sims

Sworn to Before me
this 23 Nov[r] 1822

Personally appeared J. C. Morgan who being duly sworn, deposeth and Sayeth, that the above named Negro Agrippa hath worked for him at his trade as a Carpenter and that he found him deserving the Character above set forth and thinks him richly worth the Sum of One thousand dollars

JC Morgan

Sworn to before me this 23 Nov. 1822
B. Carroll

1. On Ann Drayton Perry, see Part III, p. 232 n1.

2. On Captain William Sims, see Part III, p. 229 n1.

3. Apart from Perault's testimony, the other slaves who testified at Agrippa Perry's trial said only that the enslaved wheelwright had traveled outside the city to obtain his tools, not to recruit followers. See Part III of this volume. Despite this plea, Charleston authorities declined to overturn the court's recommendation of transportation in Agrippa's case.

Ann Drayton Perry, Petition and Supporting Papers Asking that Her Slave Agrippa, in Confinement. Due to the Testimony of Another Slave, Be Restored to Her, n.d. [ca. November 1822], no. 1840, series S165015, SCDAH.

Petition of William Sims, 1822

. . . I beg leave to observe to your Honorable Body, that the Magistrates and free-holders have imposed a duty on me, in requiring of me the transporting, my Negro Man (Scipio) into the dominions of some foreign Prince, or Potentate, which no existing Treaty between Nations in amity with the United States will permit. I am therefore at a loss to know how to proceed, and therefore have determined to submit my Case to the discretion of your Honorable Body.—Praying that you will Return him to me, or take him for the rise of the State, at the price he has been appraised at, (by Gentlemen of information, and of the first Respectability) One thousand dollars, which is below his worth, he is a good House-Carpenter, can frame a three story–house and finish it in the completest manner, can make a good Waggon, Cart or Dray, can make as good a Saw-Gin, or Roller-Gin, as any man in the State, has always been an orderly honest negro, my dependence for support, in the Evening of Life, (which has overtaken me, I am 60 years of age) was on him. . . .

William Sims, Petition to the Senate of South Carolina, n.d. [ca. 1822], no. 1757, series S165015, SCDAH.

Petition of Sarah Clement,[1] 1822

To the honble the Senate of South Carolina

The humble Petition of the Subscriber sheweth,

That she is a widow of very slender means and resources. That her servant named Jemmy, a very valuable slave was during the late afflicting calamity at Charleston executed for conspiracy. That in common with the other residents of Charleston and perhaps in as great a degree as any, she shared the alarm, peril and horror of that period, but unconscious herself of any offence against the State she cannot believe that the State will punish her for the treachery of her slave

That the said Slave at his appraised value was worth one thousand dollars.

Your Petitioner humbly requests of your honble Body such remuneration, as the character of the State and the suffering of your Petitioner may authorize and require[2]

Clements. by
W. C.[3]

1. On Sarah Clement, whose name was frequently rendered as "Clements" (1754–1831), see Part III, p. 245 n1.

2. Jemmy was one of the twenty-two slaves hanged on July 26.

3. Charleston attorney William Crafts (1787–1826).

Petition of the Widow Clements to the Senate of South Carolina, n.d., no. 1758, AD 1302, series S165015, SCDAH.

Charleston Mercury, and Morning Advertiser

Saturday, November 23, 1822

. . . The saving to the community if a Stepping-Mill were erected in our Work-House as has been done in many large European cities, would be considerable, as the grists now advertised for could be ground there, not only for the Poor-House, but for the Orphan-House also. . . . But it is chiefly for the advantage to be derived from it, by its application as a *punishment amongst our domestics,* that I would earnestly call your attention, and that of every owner of town negroes, to the consideration of the subject. If the popular notion prevalent here is correct, that white people work more willingly than blacks, and if the punishment now pointed out is so eminently successful when used for their reformation, the introducing it into our Work-House would also be attended with the happiest effects, for in proportion to the greater dislike which Negroes have to labour, will be the additional benefit attending their employment in the Stepping-Mill. To the female owners of Slaves,[1] whose humanity but too often stands between the Negro and the well merited visit to the Work-House, the good effects to be derived from this excellent invention would be incalculable. No lady even would hesitate to send a lazy insolent waiting-man, or a sulky seamstress, to the refreshing exercise of a week's walk in the Stepping Mill; and our male and female dandies, and even some ladies who are not dandies, would find their silk stockings and corsets considerably more lasting through its influence. . . .

A CITY RUSTIC

1. Of the thirty-four slaves executed as a result of the Vesey trials, ten were either owned by women or, in the case of Elizabeth Yates, part of the estate of her deceased husband. See the "Calendar," Part III, p. 264.

Petition of Martha R. Garner, 1822

South Carolina.

To the Honorable the President and members of the Senate of the State aforesaid—

The Petition of Miss Martha R. Garner of the City of Charleston,

That your Petitioner being possessed in her own right Sheweth, of a very valuable negro man named William, whose character as a Slave had not only been unimpeachable, but highly meritorious, discovered, in July last, with the deepest mortification and sorrow that he was implicated in the late Conspiracy of the Slaves in Charleston, and being apprehended, tried and convicted, the said William was executed on the lines, pursuant to his sentence on the 9th day of August 1822;[1] That while your Petitoner most readily acquiesces in the Justice of the Sentence passed upon her Slave by the Court before whom he was tried, she cannot but hope your Honorable House will deem it expedient and proper to make her some adequate compensation for the loss of so valuable a Slave, of whom she has been deprived by the laws of the State.

Your Petitioner further shews, that she is in very slender circumstances, and by the execution of the said Slave is now deprived of her principal support. That as touching the value of the said Slave, your Petitioner begs leave to assure your Honorable Body, she has heretofore been offered as high as Fifteen Hundred Dollars for him; and the members of the Court who tried and sentenced him, appraised him "as high as the law allows"

Your Petitioner therefore prays your Honorable House to take her peculiar case into Consideration and grant her such relief and such compensation for the loss she has sustained, as in the wisdom of your Honorable House, she may be deemed justly entitled to receive—

And your Petitioner will ever pray, and so forth

Martha. R. Garner.

1. William Garner, a drayman, was the last slave to be hanged in 1822 and the only slave who was sentenced to death by the second court.

Petition of Eliza Smith Garner, Thursday, July 10, 1834[1]

The State of South Carolina
Charleston District

In Chancery

To the Honorable the chancellors of the said state.

Humbly complaining sheweth unto your honors your exetrix, Eliza Smith Garner, of Charleston in the District and State aforesaid Spinster, that the sister of your exetrix, Martha R. Garner, departed this life on the 3d day of November AD. 1832, without an issue, but having some property to which your exetrix has succeeded as the sole surviving heir at law, consisting chiefly of certain legacies, and more especially of a claim to two negro slaves, named Sarah and William, for the money of which slaves your exetrix now solicits the aid of this honorable court. On the [*blank*] day of February 1834 your exetrix took out letters of administration of the goods, chattels, rights, sundries, and personal estate of her sister Martha and in proceeding to prosecute her claims whereas there is a reasonable prospect of this [*illegible*]. The ground upon which she claims the negroes Sarah and William is as follows, William, their father, was the property of Martha the sister of your exetrix and worked out in this city in the capacity of drayman, and was more or less in the employ of Andrew Wilson, the Defendant. The defendant, upon the application of William, purchased his wife and child, then the property of Daniel Stearns, for the sum of six hundred dollars or thereabouts, upon the understanding that William should be permitted to repurchase his wife and children for the amount of the original purchase money whenever he was able to do so William accumulated money by his skill and industry and was able in the [*illegible*] of five years to purchase and drive about town six or seven drays. but William never for his labor and service paid his mistress any wages, she being a lone woman, living in the country, was able to possess little or no control over him. William repurchased his wife and children from the defendant, taking receipts for the money which was due, and shortly after forfeited his life in the insurrection in 1822. His wife died about eighteen months ago. Your exetrix, as the heir of her sister, now claims the surviving children of William[:] Sarah and William,[2] on the ground that the property of the slave rights in her sister, the issue of the slaves, and more especially on the ground that the proceeds of the labor and service of the slaves, to which her sister was entitled and of which she was deprived, was appropriated to the purchase of property to which your exetrix, as her sisters heir, now, and, she thinks, strongly lays claim. . . .

1. This petition reveals that William Garner planned to purchase himself and his family, a hope ended by the legislature's "An Act to Restrain the Emancipation of Slaves," passed on December 20, 1820. Following that ban on private manumissions, Garner appears to have entered Vesey's plot. The petition, filed by the deceased sister of Garner's owner, Martha Garner, intended to re-enslave William's two children on the grounds that he had not paid his owner a proper share of his earnings as a slave for hire; no document reveals the outcome of this petition. Because it pertains to the executed William and his children, we have placed this document here.

2. That is, William Garner Jr.

Petition of Martha R. Garner for Compensation for a Slave Executed for Involvement in the Charleston Slave Conspiracy, n.d., no. 234, series S165015, SCDAH.

Constable M. P. Belknap Requests Compensation[1]

. . . That during the late unfortunate attempt of the Negroes to encite an insurrection in this part of the State your petitioner was called upon by the competent authorities to attend with extreme vigilance, to the apprehension of those individuals concerned or suspected to be concerned in the plot and that he did so attend at his own costs and charged, not only to such apprehensions, but in various other ways and in the performance of different services contributed to the successful termination of this affair. That on the first day of July last past he was called upon and required as one of the State constables in and for Charleston District by Isaac Jackson[2] then being High Constable for the same to assist him the said Isaac in the execution of the six negroes then under sentence of death, and also to hold himself in readiness to attend to and assist at all executions that might be afterwards directed, and that we did so attend to and assist at the execution of the said first mentioned negroes and all those subsequently executed except that of William Garner. That at these different executions he rendered all his time and services to the calls of the public—both by night and by day—in assisting at the preparation of the Gallows, the digging of the Graves, and in various other offices connected with the execution—much to his own personal inconvenience, the derangement of his private business and the exposure of his own health at late and unseasonable hours. . . .

1. *CSCCD*, 70, identifies Moses P. Belknap in 1822 as a saddler and trunk maker who resided at 9 Pin Alley.

2. Although *CSCCD* lists no resident named Isaac Jackson in any of the directories from 1816

to 1829, the name does appear in Charleston newspapers in 1822 in reference to serving papers for the jailing of runaway slaves. An Isaac Jackson from Charleston married Catherine Fredericks from New York in 1822, and it may be that Jackson left Charleston soon after the Vesey affair. See "Committed," Charleston *City Gazette and Commercial Daily Advertiser,* April 1, 1822; "Married," New York *Spectator,* May 3, 1822.

M. P. Belknap, Petition and Supporting Papers, Requesting Compensation for Services Rendered in the Execution of Slaves for Attempting an Insurrection, n.d., no. 728, series S165015, SCDAH.

Jane Thompson to the Senate of South Carolina[1]

. . . Your petitioner would further humbly represent to this Honorable house that she has every reason to believe & doth Verily Believe that the said slave Pharaoh was the victim of a wicked combination among his accusers and that if he ever entered at all into the views of the conspirators it was done at the express Suggestion of the Person under whose controul he was and with the Laudable Intention to expose their machinations. But having excited their suspicion was accused by Perault the Slave of Mr. Strohecker whom he had previously accused before the Intendant & wardens—all which mite now fully appear by Reference to the affidavit accompanying this Petition. But wether he was Guilty or Innocent she has been deprived of her Support to appease Publick Justice and humbly Prays that such relief may be granted to her. . . . [2]

1. On Jane Thompson (also rendered "Thomson"), see Part III, p. 218 n1.
2. Pharo (or Pharaoh) Thompson was among those hanged on the Lines on Friday, July 26.

No. 132, series S165015, n.d., SCDAH.

Charleston *City Gazette and Commercial Daily Advertiser*

Monday, November 25, 1822

Persons concerned in the preservation of good order on Charleston Neck, are requested to notice the riotous conduct, the blasphemous language, and obscene songs that are sung by the Negro Butchers when driving their master's carts, particularly through St. Philip-street, into the city, just before daylight. Gentlemen owning slaves of that description, are particularly solicited by their timely interference and orders, to put a stop to the outrage against decency of which we complain, and which we firmly believe need only be made know to them, to receive their marked disapprobation.

A Resident of St. Philip Street.

Charleston *City Gazette and Commercial Daily Advertiser*

Tuesday, November 26, 1822

"COMMUNICATION."

Mr. EDITOR,—The Corporation having lately appointed additional Officers to assist the City Marshall in his varied duty, it is now expected that more attention will be paid to overlooking the *Dram Shops.* These sinks of corruption appear to put the laws at defiance; but as we now have four Officers, whose vigilance and industry are beyond suspicion, we may reasonably expect the happiest results from their labours. Let them take *a round* in their respective *Wards* every night *after* 8 *o'clock,* and they may make a capital haul. You must know Mr. Editor, that the keepers of the shops above noticed, are so intent in trafficking with slaves, that the late regulations respecting the *hour limited* are utterly disregarded! Let these Deputy Marshals be particularly vigilant on Sundays—it is on the Sabbath that these Dram Shops are most crowded with Negroes—aye, from sunrise to 9 o'clock! Some of these places have entries and *side doors* which are fastened inside, and it would be well to keep a sharp look out under these circumstances. Of all the streets in the city, none requires such attention as Elliott-street.

AN OBSERVER

Governor Thomas Bennett, Jr., Message to the State Legislature, Thursday, November 28, 1822

Message No. 2

Executive Department
Columbia Nov[r]. 28. 1822.

To the Senate and House
of Representatives of the
State of South Carolina
Fellow Citizens,

A brief narrative of the principal circumstances which developed, and attended the investigation of a Plot, lately formed within the Parishes of St Philip and St Michael, by a number of evil disposed negroes, will be found in the accompanying document marked A. The proceedings of the Court, and the testimony received on the trials of those; charged as principals or accomplices, are also transmitted and marked B

A scheme for organizing an Insurrection in those parishes, had been for several months covertly agitated, and was eventually discovered and communicated, by a servant the property* of Mr. Prioleau[1]; to which act he had been counselled with great earnestness and decision, by a Free man of Color.[2] To that communication, although detailing very indistinctly, some immaterial circumstances, and referring to but one individual, we are without doubt particularly indebted for the full developement, which eventually followed. The recompense of such service has hitherto been so liberally awarded by the Legislature, that it would be an act of supererogation, to urge it here. I would nevertheless distinctly state, that independent of the policy, which suggests a liberal reward of such deeds, they are entitled to commendation, for the promptitude and fidelity, which characterized their conduct.[3]

* I would refer to several honorable members of your house for the names of these persons.

The person accused, a slave of Mr. Paul,[4] was apprehended with two other fellows the property of the same gentleman, and although the investigation of these persons, was unattended with the results which were anticipated; many of the conspirators experienced all the apprehension, incident to detection. One of them, who subsequently acknowledged a participation in their scheme . . . at the suggestion of another, revealed many of the circumstances, to a servant of Mr. Wilson,[5] who with praiseworthy promptitude, made a full disclosure to his master. *The fellow of Mr. Wilson,* is also entitled to the liberality of the Legislature. This statement, which was immediately communicated to the Hon: James Hamilton, Intendant of Charleston, exaggerated the means of the conspirators, and gave an extent to the plot, calculated to deprive it of credibility. He represented, that a majority of the Slaves in Charleston had concurred; that 4,000 from James Island,[6] and a great many others within several miles of the City had confederated, and under various arrangements, would arrive within the City on Saturday night, and the ensuing Sunday the 16th of June; that the boats ordinarily used by the neighbouring planters, would be employed to effect their descent, and continue during that period actively employed, in transporting the disaffected. At 9 o'clock on Thursday night the 13th of June, the Intendant and Mr. Wilson informed me of these particulars, and at 10 on the same night, the Field Officers of the Charleston Regiments were convened by my order, at the Intendant's. Although doubts were entertained generally by this Board, of the magnitude of this conspiracy, the reality of some design of that character, was fully assented to. After several private consultations, it was resolved, to watch the development of the plot, and to detach for that night, a military guard adequate to the emergency. Whatever opinions I privately entertained, my duty suggested a line of conduct, which was not equivocal. The information on which I was called to act, was admitted to a certain extent; it may have been wholly true, and the responsibility which rested on me, required the organization of a force, not only sufficient to defeat the enterprize in its declared extent, but to give entire security and confidence to the citizens. The order No. 1 was therefore issued on Saturday, and the Quarter Master General[7] directed to place in the Charleston Arsenal, 20,000 Ball Cartridges, and have ready for delivery, 300 muskets, in addition to those in the hands of the militia, for the use of Rifle Corps, and others who required them; the inspection of the muskets having been previously confided to a skilful gunsmith, and the cartridges which were made during the war, subjected to such tests, as satisfied me that they were not impaired. My personal attention was given to these arrangements.

Having from sources entitled to implicit confidence, as well as from personal observation, established the falsity of that part of the statement, which referred to the use of Boats, for the transportation of the conspirators; I issued on Sunday Morning a Counter Order, also submitted and marked No. 2. By this order, the Guard being reduced to less than a Regiment, it was at my particular instance, that Col: Hayne[8] took command; all the arrangements having been previously made, in concert with that officer. The companies embraced in the last order, repaired at the hour appointed, with extreme punctuality, to their respective places of Rendezvous. Measures had been previously taken, to remove some arms from the United States' Arsenal, to a place of more security; the other military depots were efficiently guarded, and at every assailable point, the City was amply protected. The utmost tranquillity prevailed. An extraordinary nightly guard was immediately after organized, pursuant to the order No. 3 which was occasionally augmented and continued during the investigation. Simultaneously with this order, a Board of Field officers was convened, for the purpose of organizing permanently, that part of the 4th Brigade, comprehended within the two parishes; no measures having been previously adopted, to regulate the conduct of the troops, or give alarms in case of an extraordinary character. This Board concurred in my suggestions generally, but as the public mind was excessively agitated, and as the means already employed were efficient, it was deemed prudent to delay issuing the order, until it could be published, without producing further excitement. This was effected on the 8th of July, (order No. 4) but not without some of the consequences deprecated. These arrangements were severally communicated to the Intendant.

As the City Council of Charleston, were deeply interested in the result of this investigation, and as a course of proceeding variant from that, which usually regulates judicial enquiry, would from the nature of the transaction, become expedient; I suggested to an influential member of that body, the propriety of appointing a select number of judicious persons, to precede the state courts, as a Court of Investigation. Such a Court, untrammelled by the usual forms, could pursue fearlessly the mazes of the labyrinth, dissipate the obscurity which concealed alike the conspirators, and their wicked machinations, and every irregularity in the proceedings of the Court of Magistrates, prevented. The suggestion appeared to be favorably received, and when the names of the gentlemen were communicated, I was gratified in the selection of the Council, which had so happily drawn into the public service, distinguished talent and great decision of character. It was not until a day or two after, that I was informed *that the corporate authorities, had organized a court of ultimate jurisdiction.* . . . In every sense, this was an usurpation of authority, and a violation of the Law. It was in vain to justify it, on the ground of expediency, or to urge the celebrity of the gentlemen, composing that Court. The lives of individuals, and the property of the Citizens, were subjected to a tribunal illegally constituted, and however definite the line which separated the Executive and Judiciary, I felt imperatively the obligation, which required, that I should not obey the mandate of a Court, which did not derive its existence and authority, from Legislative sanction. The Council I believe, were governed by the purest motives, the error was accidental, but its effect as related to myself officially, was to be deprecated. The situation in which I was unhappily placed, was extremely delicate; a majority of those, subjected to this tribunal, were my property, and the confidence I felt in the Court, induced me to wave the objection, until they were disposed of. Immediately after which, I communicated to Thomas Parker Esq,[9] one of the Presiding Magistrates, this objection to the Court, with two others to their proceedings, on which I subsequently consulted the attorney general;[10] *distinctly stating to these gentlemen, that they were not designed to apply to the cases adjudicated.* The Court was reorganized on the 1st of July, immediately after this communication. . . . The Letter and Answer marked D & E, are those referred to. In these it will appear, that the evils at first anticipated, had actually occurred. That it should be deemed expedient, in a Court exercising criminal jurisdiction, to close its doors upon the community, to shut out those accidental rays, which occasionally illuminate the obscurity, in which innocence and guilt are indistinguishable, was to be deeply lamented. At a moment too, when the highest exercise of human intelligence, minds elevated above the ordinary standard, and beyond the reach of prejudice, were requisite, in the multiplied and intricate cases which admitted no testimony, but such as was equivocal, the offspring of treachery or revenge, and the hope of immunity. This course of proceeding, incidentally, produced other consequences, peculiarly affecting. The public mind had been raised to a pitch of excitement, which sought relief in an exhibition of truth, but unhappily it was increased in many, to little less than a prostration of Law and authority, by idle and weak suggestions, indistinct details of testimony, or direct assertions of an alarmingly extensive, and deeply concerted plan, and voluntary compacts to enforce the laws,—these admitted of no restraint. Nor was it less a source of embarrassment and concern, that testimony should be received, under pledges of inviolable secrecy; and that the accused should be convicted, and sentenced to death, without seeing the persons, or hearing the voices of those, who testified to their guilt. On the ground of expediency, the first was unnecessary, as subsequent events have fully demonstrated. The person who discovered the plot, and others to whom this pledge was given, pass unmolested, though distinctly and generally known; with the exception of trifling insults, which have been punished. Besides, the State was competent to protect those, who administered to her welfare; and that protection was the only shield, which could be effectually interposed, when danger menaced. The rules which universally obtain among civilized nations, in the judicial investigation of crime, are not merely hypothetical, or simply matter of opinion, but the result of the highest intelligence, instructed and matured by experience. They are given as guides, to assist the imperfections of human reason, and to enable it to combine and compare the various circumstances and probabilities, which occur in every case. Few minds are competent without these aids, to develope the intricate affections of the heart. The presence of the innocent, will sometimes fetter the tongue of guilt, and dissolve the best concerted schemes of falsehood. The profound intelligence of this Court may be urged, as the best security against the occurrence of evil—it may be so;—but it must be recollected, that at the moment of which I speak, rumour had extended the plot, to all the adjacent parishes. Other Courts were to be organized, and while the example of this, would operate with dangerous influence, the corrective which emanated, from the luminous understandings of those gentlemen, could not in every instance, be applied. To my interrogatories embracing these objectives, the Attorney General gave an elaborate opinion; in which with sentiments honorable alike to his understanding and benevolence, he sought to remove the embarrassments, to which this course of proceeding had given birth. From this, it would appear, that these persons had no civil rights, not derived from the Statutes; and that the Executive was not bound to correct errors, in judicial proceedings. If a reluctant acquiescence was yielded to the opinion of this enlightened Jurist, it was because if these persons have no civil rights, not deducible from the Law, I conceived it my duty, in the exercise of a constitutional prerogative, to test the extent of their guilt, by principles familiar to the commonest understanding. Deprived of these by the act of the Court, the authority of the Executive could not be exercised, either for the protection of the life of the Individual, or the property of the Citizen, without involving his decisions, in all the uncertainty of chance; for a rigid adherence to rule, governs as essentially the decision of the Executive as of the Court. He is bound to correct their aberrations as they affect individuals, *where they manifestly appear*; or the constitutional power of pardon, is erroneously founded on the range of uncertainties, which usually attend the investigation of crime.

If the disquietude, which had arisen from these cases, rendered my official duties painful and perplexing, it is difficult to pourtray the effect, which was produced by the knowledge, that three of the Conspirators, on whom sentence of death had already been pronounced, were used as witnesses, while they were under the impression, that they would ultimately have their lives spared. Under this impression, their testimony was not only regarded important, in the detection of the general plan of the conspiracy, but enabled the Court to convict a number of the principal offenders. . . . add to this that two of these were sometime closeted together, and it will not be difficult to imagine, that when the testimony of one alone, (See the case of Saby Gaillard[11]) was deemed sufficient, and actually produced conviction; my situation in regard to the persons thus implicated, became excessively distressing. Of the Court itself my opinions were in unison with the great majority of the Citizens. To one of the gentlemen, long before I had the pleasure of a personal acquaintance, those sentiments of respect and admiration were elicited, which are called forth by extraordinary endowments. It was with painful reluctance, that these objections forced upon me, the course of conduct, which I was officially bound to pursue, in extricating several thus implicated, from the effects of their sentence.

The Court having used these persons, Monday Gell, Charles Drayton and Harry Haig as witnesses, recommended that a pardon should be conditionally extended. This, under the views previously taken of their guilt, was wholly incompatible with that line of conduct, I had invariably pursued. Monday, the servant of Mr. Gell, was if not the projector of the plot, (which was doubtful) the most active partizan. He had seduced a greater number than any other; his shop was the depot of their offensive preparations, and he alone enrolled them. The others, though less conspicuous, were equally decisive. It was admitted by the Court, that their only claim to mercy, was founded on their confession and testimony. But Bacchus, the servant of Mr. Hammett[12] had the same claims; Smart, the servant of Mr. Anderson,[13] and Pharo, the servant of Mrs. Thompson,[14] but little inferior. The two first confessed generally, and all of them were used as witnesses, and subsequently executed. Impartial justice urged the rejection of the claim; besides, what was an "act of spontaniety" in others, was extorted from Monday. Stratagem had been employed, and the confession of Perault, the servant of Mr. Strohecker,[15] enabled the Committee of Vigilance[16] to relate to him, a tissue of facts, which were assented to, and eventually produced his confession. The recommendation of the Court was not concurred in; and the embarrassment occasioned by a refusal, to comply with the desire of so enlightened a tribunal, was wholly obviated by the knowledge, that they originally possessed full authority, to carry their recommendation into effect. . . . Nor could I comply with their desire, to commute the punishment of nine others; as the removal of the sentence of death pronounced against them, would have prevented me from carrying into effect, the ulterior measure of transportation, to which their owners could be coerced, only while I could exercise the alternative. Subsequent to this, the Court having commuted the punishment of the first-mentioned convicts, delegated *to the Corporate Authority of Charleston,* the care and superintendance, of carrying their sentences of transportation into effect; which as relates to one individual, (Prince Graham)[17] had been exercised, *in the commutation* of his punishment. The remainder of these persons (21) twenty one in number, are still in the custody of the City Officers, and the interference of the Legislature, (which is respectfully recommended) will be requisite, to enforce the mandate of the Court. Those who were submitted to my discretion, have left the United States, with the exception of three (who will shortly be removed[)] and an old and very infirm man, whose union with the conspirators, being (*as I conceived*) equivocal, was pardoned and his master requested to send him from the State; to which he consented. Saby Gaillard had been sentenced to be hung; the Court recommended a commutation of punishment, to transportation from the United States, which has been complied with; although an examination of his case (Monday being the only evidence against him, and wholly unsupported by circumstances, or the knowledge of any other), had induced a commutation, to banishment from the State.

The punishment of William, the slave of Mr. Palmer,[18] was changed from death to banishment from the United States. This man having been convicted exclusively, on the testimony of two of the persons under sentence of death; his solemn declarations of innocence, made under circumstances of peculiar terror; no evidence of his attendance at their meetings, or personal exertions to promote the general object; and his previous unexceptionable character, induced a short respite. Availing myself of the intervention of time; an examination of the witnesses fully satisfied me, that he was distinctly an object of mercy. Independent of a tissue of contradiction, in the Statements of these men, it was obvious to me, that Charles Drayton had predicated his claims of escape, on the number of convictions he could make. Nothing could exceed the chilling depravity of this man. William has been sent from the United States.

Jack, the slave of Mrs. Purcell,[19] would from the causes of being convicted on the testimony of Monday Gell and Charles Drayton only, have shared the Executive clemency. But his confession evidenced, an early participation in the plot, a particular association with Vesey, and a zealous effort to promote its successful accomplishment; this confession forbade it. The trial of Jack, the slave of Mr. Glenn,[20] will fully exemplify the reasons, why his punishment was not commuted. These three men would not thus have been brought to your view, were it not forced on me, by the remarks of the Corporate Authority of Charleston, in relation to them.

The punishment of John Vincent, was commuted from the same cause, and Billy Robinson from collision of testimony. In addition to which, all the executions were closed, and I conceived that I consulted the best feelings of my fellow-citizens, in arresting these dreadful punishments, which were become but too familiar, ceased to produce a salutary terror, no longer served for example, and at which humanity wept.

From a very early period after the discovery of the plot, I held communication with the surrounding country. The perfect tranquillity which every where prevailed was the strongest evidence of their having no participation, with the disaffected of the Metropolis.[21] The Patrols were nevertheless, with the exception of one or two parishes, very active. Cols. Lauton,[22] Thompson[23] & Mallard[24] discharged their respective duties, with great zeal and fidelity. The first named officer incurred some expense, with two detachments of his Regiment; should he present his claim for remuneration, permit me to request your liberal attention to it.*

* In executing the Health Laws of the State, I acquired in the early part of the summer correct information of the number of United States' troops stationed near Charleston, and discovering the inability of their Commander to detach a sufficient number of men to enforce the Quarantine Regulations, I availed myself of this emergency to request its augmentation from the Secretary of War. A prompt compliance was accorded by Mr. Calhoun[25] and the garrison increased by the addition of another Company.

It would be expected, that a minute account of the particular circumstances which led to, and the class of persons among whom, this plot originated, should be laid before you; but I could procure no documentary evidence of these facts. Having informed myself of many particulars, touching on the rise and progress of this conspiracy; the clue was furnished to several respectable gentlemen, with a request that they would prosecute the enquiry, but they were arrested in the attainment of their object, by an order emanating from the City Council, interdicting any communication with the prisoners, by my authority. . . . Nor is it practicable, to impart correct information of the number concerned. Beyond the City of Charleston, with the exception of a single plantation (Mr. Ferguson's) it does not appear, that any were engaged.[26] This Gentleman waited on me, and with obvious anxiety stated his impression, that the slaves on his Plantation were infected, and while he deprecated the ruinous consequences to himself, with great propriety offered to surrender the whole number, and personally aid in delivering them, into the hands of justice. He required to know, whether as Chief Magistrate, I would cause their arrest; to his remarks I replied generally, that the responsibility of arresting persons charged with crimes, did not devolve on me, but on the Justices of Peace, in the respective parishes; that should he deem it requisite, a military detachment would aid in the execution of the warrants, which should issue, but advised a careful investigation of the charges alledged, previous to the adoption of a measure, so pregnant with evil consequences to himself. He appeared to be solicitous that it should be distinctly known, that he had made this proposition, and in avoiding the Course suggested, he was actuated by a desire, that the Court, organized in Charleston should try his negroes. A compliance with this requisition would have been attended with serious loss to this Gentleman, and excessive distress and alarm to the inhabitants of that, and the contiguous parishes. Great discretion was requisite; and subsequent events have happily illustrated the propriety of the course pursued. But the motive by which I was particularly influenced, emanated from my own and the general confidence in the Court. They were charged with the investigation, had extended their jurisdiction to slaves in the surrounding parishes, and would as was presumed, not act with partiality; and as they had incidentally closed every avenue, through which I could derive a knowledge of the facts submitted, were bound to communicate *to me,* every point of information, that should immediately or eventually involve, the peace or security of the State.

Admitting the guilt of all who were convicted in the City, the number may a little exceed eighty (80). Of that number, from an attentive perusal of the evidence, it would appear that several were not conspirators, in the sense here implied, but had united for the purpose of self preservation. With other arts of seduction, the fears of such were assailed—the tale often repeated, of an intention on the part of the whites, to create a false alarm, and in the general consternation, to attack and destroy them, eventually gained credit; and they yielded to suggestions, which promised protection. The most conspicuous actors in this drama, were deceived or affected to believe, that their physical resources were adequate to the object—that Gullah Jack had enlisted 6,000 men;—Mingo Harth, 4000;—Frank Ferguson, four plantations;—Peter Poyas, a great number;—and that there was within the City, a French Band of 100 men, trained, armed and impatient for the conflict—this argument was addressed to the disaffected. The influence of several wicked men, who professed religion, and were leaders of religious associations, was exerted with some effect. They referred to the sacred oracles, to justify their sanguinary intentions; and to evidence the protecting care of Heaven, asserted, that they had been four years engaged in the project. The standing and respectability of character of a few, who countenanced the plan, gave an imposing effect to the enterprize. Such were the materials and delusions, brought into action against a weak and inconsiderate multitude, under adventitious circumstances, peculiarly favorable in promoting such an object—unrestrained intercourse—a perfect acquaintance with the tempers and defection of each—and opportunities and time to consummate their wicked purposes, by the most artful and insinuating addresses. Four months appear to have been sedulously devoted, by men lauded for some particular trait of character, in selecting from thousands, all whom they could corrupt or delude, by persuasion and artifice, and appeals to passion and affection; and less than one Hundred are found in their ranks: a great majority of whom are declared by an enlightened Court, to have done little if anymore, than acquiesce in the proposal to join in the Plot, and this established, upon proof peculiarly unfavourable to the accused. It is scarcely possible to compare the means with the result, without admiring that Fidelity, which successfully resisted the artful insinuations of the Conspirators, or awed them into cautious silence.

It is concomitant on such events, that we are unhappily forced from that equanimity of temper, by means of which alone, the lessons of misfortune are of inestimable value. The circumstances of this plot, taken in connection, furnish many useful hints, on which I am persuaded you will calmly deliberate, and judiciously act; and in adopting measures of prevention, attentively guard against those, which may produce excessive coercion. It has been said, had the attempt been made by the small number who had confederated, thousands would have joined in the revolt. This is at the least problematical, and opposed by the weight of circumstances; the conspirators had no confidence in such a contingency; they had refused to communicate their secret, but with the most jealous caution; whole classes were the objects of suspicious vigilance; they saw in thousands a Fidelity, which they dared not tamper with, and in units only, could discover a suitable defection. To that fidelity we are indebted for the present, and all previous discoveries; it should not be rebuked or destroyed, *by unnecessary* rigour. In the total absence of that genius and intelligence, which is fitted for such enterprizes, and which was palpable in the details of this plot, we may safely predicate ulterior arrangements. It is scarcely possible to imagine one, more crude or imperfect. They were unprovided with arms, and if we except a few cents occasionally subscribed, to pay the wages of a blacksmith who is said to have furnished six pikes; no effort whatever was used to procure them. Yet several of the Conspirators were represented to possess property, which they were unwilling to adventure, in so hazardous a project. They exhibit no confidence in each other. A debt was incurred in promoting the plan, and the crediting conspirator required ample security for future payment. Their leaders were not appointed—no different plans of attack concerted; nor place of rendezvous fixed—yet the whole plot is represented as mature, and within a few hours of consummation. The Conspirators were in many instances unknown to each other—their enterprize was predicated, as was generally asserted, on a force included in the surrounding parishes; yet without any communication with their main body, or devising the means of collecting this force, scattered over a great extent of territory; or directing their movements to the scene of action; they resolve on the night. Their prime mover Vesey has been represented as a man of intrigue, and fitted for command; yet it does not appear, that he ever tested the truth of those assertions, on which mainly depended, the successful result of the enterprize; for on the day of the contemplated attack, he appears to have discovered, that he was himself the victim of deception; and that the host engaged by his sanguine associates, were the creation of an ardent fancy. Such implicit confidence had been placed on these assertions that he directed a servant of Mr. Blackwood[27] to repair to the plantation of Mr. Ferguson and hasten down the men of Frank (the servant of that Gentleman). His incapacity is strikingly exemplified in this act; this boy is represented as extremely simple, and assures him that he neither knows the place or the people; yet Vesey enjoins the duty, and as an outfit supplied him with two Dollars: he is to travel a distance of twenty two miles from the City, and without any evidence of his mission, to deliver a message to two persons, who are at his bidding to assemble the males of four plantations and march them to the City, by 12 o'clock that night; the suspicion to be excited by this movement, or the vigilance of Patrols, form no part of his care. At 11 o'clock on Sunday morning, the boy is seen in the streets of Charleston, alledging to one that he did not intend to go, and to another that the Patrols were too strict. But it does not appear that Vesey subsequently evinced the slightest solicitude for his success; for on Sunday, he is represented shivering with fear, and in a paroxysm of phrenzy accusing Gullah Jack, as his destroyer. It was in vain, that this conspirator sought to encourage and pacify his panic-struck leader, with the assurance that he had 250 men, in the adjacent woods. Vesey and his associates doubt the adequacy of this force. It is therefore not only probable, that the attempt would not have been made with 72; but obvious that they do not possess the requisites, for an extensive and deeply concerted scheme of insurrection.

This detail is submitted, with a view to furnish the information requisite, in a revision of the Laws governing that class of our population. It is an event, which will necessarily attract your attention to the subject; of much importance that your deliberations should be guided, not only by a knowledge of the leading incidents, but unbiassed by those views of the extent and danger, which have unhappily existed in the public mind. Another motive arises, from an earnest desire which has influenced my official conduct, throughout the transaction, of opposing the weak and dangerous proceeding, of exciting the public apprehension, and exhibiting to these people, a distressed and agitated community. The inference thus forced on them, is not sanctioned by a wise or sound policy, and is to be deprecated as an indiscretion, inviting to more serious ills. It may be ascribed to the forces of early prejudice, but the most deliberate convictions of my mind, lead to the conclusion, that successful rebellion cannot occur in this State. The liberal and enlightened humanity of our Fellow-Citizens, produce many attachments, that operate as checks on the spirit of insubordination. Their habitual respect for, and obedience to the authority of their owners; their natural indolence, and want of means and opportunities to form combinations; their characteristic cowardice and treachery, excited by a knowledge of the positive ability of the State, to crush in an instant, their boldest enterprizes; are insurmountable obstacles, to the completion of any general effort. Yet late occurrences clearly demonstrate, that such principles are latent in the minds of some of them, and we must admit, that evils limited in their extent and duration, would result from their best concerted schemes, if consummated. To guard against every such attempt, is the peculiar province of Legislation.

In making this communication, I am also actuated by the necessity, which exists for a more distinct expression of your will, in relation to the trial of Negroes. If it be your object, in the organization of Magistrates' Courts, to establish tribunals, which shall exercise the power of life and death, and the most absolute controul, over an immense and valuable property, unlimited by those rules, which ordinarily govern judicial enquiry; unrestrained by any regulations, but such as those Courts may adopt or reject, and guided solely by the dictates of conscience; an unequivocal and full avowal should distinctly manifest that will. It is essential, to curb the asperities, which such a course of proceeding, is apt to engender, and requisite, to guide the Executive decision. The argument will not always apply correctly to these Courts, that the Executive is not bound to supervise judicial proceeding; a recurrence to the palpable errors committed by these, during the short period of my administration, will evince the necessity.—Humanity, not less than the solemn obligations of his high appointment, imperiously require the interposition of Executive authority; where it is manifest that the sentence of death has been pronounced under the misapplication of a term or the misconstruction of a Law; and particularly, as time is seldom allowed in such cases, to suggest causes of prohibition, a course of proceeding not generally countenanced. The indistinctness of the provisions of that Law, is also manifest in the construction, recently obtained of the words "Corporal Punishment." If they include banishment from the State and the United States, that property is held under a very precarious tenure; as the whole class of offences, not extending to life are thus punished; and for minor offences the owner and not the offending slave under this construction, may incur the heaviest penalty. It is also dubious, whether the clause providing for the punishment of Slaves charged with insurrection, includes Free Negroes. It cannot admit of doubt that such was the intention of the Legislature, and should have been the provision of the Law, but the construction is forced, which extends it to them.

In reviewing generally the Laws, which relate to the government of Negroes, we are disposed to admire the penetration and intelligence, which produced a system so wisely adapted to the object. In these, although crimes are imperfectly defined, (which is perhaps the most conspicuous defect); they are with much propriety, subjected to a summary and expeditious adjudication; when abroad, or separated from the superintending care of their respective owners, the most rigorous, yet salutary provisions restrain their conduct. Sumptuary regulations curb dispositions to licentiousness, and forcibly inculcate suitable views of their condition; they cannot under its provisions, assemble beyond a very limited number; for any purpose, without the presence of a white person; nor are they permitted to use offensive weapons or receive instruction, beyond what is requisite for their spiritual and eternal welfare. Under such regulations rigidly observed, it would appear wholly impossible, that dangerous combinations could exist. The fault is chargeable therefore, rather on the maladministration, than the insufficiency of the Law; Hitherto, it has been regarded the duty of every individual in society, to enforce its mandate. Without infringing the general privilege, it is worthy of your consideration, whether it may not be more distinctly made the duty of the State Officers. It is appurtenant to the office of Conservator of the Public Peace, and to render it obligatory, should be incorporated in the oath of office. To constitute a Board in each Parish, in aid of the duties thus required of Justices, under special Legislative provisions, with authority to inspect generally, the conduct and dwellings of these persons, and the economy of each plantation, would conduce to the general security. Indolence, the bane of society, acts with pernicious influence over the minds of these persons; the effect is obvious on those plantations, which seldom partake of the superintending care of the proprietor; or when his presence is withdrawn, and either through prejudice or neglect, he refuses or omits to employ overseers. This in a peculiar manner deserves Legislative attention; for while it tends to depopulate such districts, by exiling the less fortunate, it deprives them of the vigilance, essential to the preservation of order. The rule hitherto adopted, is partial in its effect, and easily evaded; it is partial, because the planter of ten negroes or of five hundred, is required to have one overseer; and easily evaded, as informers are contemned by the community. No planting interest should be deemed too small, to remain wholly without the superintending care of a white person; and those embodying a greater number of negroes, should be required to provide an overseer for every fifty workers. The Planter in making his Tax return, should testify to his compliance with such requisition, or be subjected to a penalty, proportioned to the danger the State incurs, by such delinquency. The wisdom of the law regulating traffic with slaves, would be conspicuous, if enforced by the means first mentioned; but it is submitted for your consideration, whether it should extend to authorize slaves to trade generally under my license. The convenience to the farmer and the community, of thus sending the produce of his farm, or the fisherman the results of his pursuit, are not designed to be embraced; but there is an intermediate class, who prey upon every community, which they are permitted to infest, by a monopoly of the necessaries of life. This severely affects the necessitous, procures time and means for exciting discontent, and presents an example of mischievous tendency; these I conceive should be wholly interdicted, even under corporate sanctions.

Nor should slaves be permitted to carry on, or conduct any mechanical trade or other pursuit, under any circumstances of character or favour. In the City of Charleston, the encouragement given to these persons, has impoverished or exiled a great many of that class of our Fellow-Citizens. It would in general be a salutary provision, to prevent the owners of slaves, from suffering them to work abroad, but under a particular contract with a white person. To subject the owners of Runaway slaves and others, who are absent for more than one week, to the payment of a specific sum, as a compensation to those who will apprehend them, making the person of the slave liable for the amount thus allowed, and to forfeit every such slave after an absence of one year, unless redeemed by the owner; who shall pay One Hundred Dollars for the recovery of such runaway, would be highly beneficial and tend to diminish the number of idle and dissolute, in every district. The convenience or profit to the planter, of permitting his slaves the use of a Gun, is not commensurate with the risk, which the State incurs, by the privilege thus extended and knowledge thus acquired; to interdict them wholly by the use of fire arms, and embrace in this inhibition all persons of colour, would be productive of salutary effects. I would also recommend that each proprietor of a public bridge or ferry, be subjected to a penalty for every slave he permits to pass, without a ticket or license from his owner or employer. These in addition to the regulations heretofore adopted, would tend to render the system more perfect; but the most perfect system of laws, will be ineffectual, if they are not enforced by wise regulations, resulting from the provident care of the Legislature.

The rapid increase of the Free colored population of Charleston has been the subject of serious reflection and great anxiety and in ascertaining the property remedy, it will doubtless attract your profound consideration. The accumulation complained of has been the result of those Laws which the States contiguous to us have seen proper to enforce rather than the effect of natural increase or the facility with which the Slave could heretofore obtain his manumission. The course dictated by obvious policy will lead you to throw off that part of the Free Colored population which the prohibitory Laws of other communities or their own vices have forced on us. The natives of that description and those who have accepted their freedom under the guarantee of our own Laws may then with safety be protected in their persons and property. From them little danger may be apprehended as their numbers will be greatly reduced, while the property they hold and the privileges they enjoy afford the best guarantee for their proper demeanor.

Slavery abstractedly considered will perhaps lead every mind to the same conclusion; but the period has long passed by, when a corrective may have been applied. The treasures of Learning, the gifts of ingenuity and the stores of experience have been exhausted in the fruitless search of a practicable remedy. The institution is established; the evil is entailed and we can now do no more than steadily pursue that course indicated by stern necessity and not less imperious policy. The energy of the State must be exerted; we should frown indignantly on every project of partial and general emancipation, as destructive of their happiness and subversive of our own. We must be true to ourselves and just to them; watch over their welfare with kind solicitude but tenaciously protect our own; rigorously enforce the salutary restraints of the Law, without permitting its inhibitions to diverge into cruelty or wanton infliction. Such a course of conduct will afford the best answer to the uncharitable rebukes heaped on us by those who cannot appreciate our motives or estimate the difficulties which surround us; check the vituperative spirit which tends to the dissolution of our happy compact and disarm our unkindest enemy of every reproach. The world will cease to chide us for evils we did not originate and cannot remedy and the reflecting and virtuous of every community will sympathize with us.

Tho: Bennett

1. Peter Prioleau (Desverney), the slave of John Cordes Prioleau (1772–1825).

2. William Penceel (also rendered "Pinceel") was a member of Charleston's Brown Fellowship Society, established by "free brown men, natives of the city of Charleston." See *Rules and Regulations of the Brown Fellowship Society, Established at Charleston, S.C., 1st November, 1790* (Charleston, SC, 1844), 3, 17.

3. The Charleston City Council petitioned the state legislature to reward three individuals for providing valuable state's evidence: Peter Prioleau (Desverney), William Penceel, and a free person of color surnamed Scott. See the petition of the City Council of Charleston, n.d., no. 2059, series S165015, SCDAH, reproduced on pp. 573–74 in this section.

4. William Paul, the slave of merchant and grocer John Paul.

5. George Wilson, the slave of Major John Wilson, although George may have been legally owned by the Major's wife, Eliza (Gibbes) Wilson. See Part II, p. 103 n3.

6. The Sea Island closest to Charleston, located just across the Ashley River, to the south.

7. Colonel Benjamin Arthus Markley (1787–1841), also an attorney, who in 1822 lived on Thomas Street. See *CSCCD,* 88.

8. Robert Young Hayne (1791–1839), who at the time was also the state's attorney general.

9. This was evidently a verbal communication, since no letter on this matter from Bennett to Parker exists.

10. See Bennett's letter to Robert Young Hayne of July 1, 1822, in Part II, pp. 147–48.

11. Bennett spoke of the testimony of both Monday Gell and Perault Strohecker against Saby (Samuel) Gaillard, a free black carpenter, who lived in 1822 at 3 Wentworth Street. Monday Gell testified that Gaillard had shared news with him of Jean-Pierre Boyer's triumphs over the Spanish in eastern Hispaniola. Confined to the Charleston Work-House for an extended period, Gaillard had his death sentence commuted to transportation outside the United States. See *CSCCD,* 80; Hamilton, *Account,* 44; *OR,* 125, 184.

12. Benjamin Hammet. See Part III, p. 236 n1

13. Robert Anderson. See Part III, p. 217 n1.

14. The widow Jane Thompson.

15. The blacksmith John Strohecker.

16. The Committee of Vigilance was composed of members of Charleston's City Council and formed during the proceedings to support Intendant James Hamilton Jr. in his investigation of the plot. See Hamilton, *Account,* 11–12.

17. Prince Graham, a free colored drayman, who was sentenced to imprisonment in the Work-House for one month and then transportation outside the United States. See Part III, p. 251 n1.

18. The carpenter Job Palmer, father of the Reverend Benjamin Morgan Palmer. See Part III, p. 238 n1.

19. The widow Ann Smith Purcell.

20. Planter John S. Glen owned Jack (also "Jacob") Glen, who was executed on the Lines on Friday, July 26.

21. The inclusion of the letter, James Ferguson to Thomas Parker, September 16, 1822, published

in the *OR*, 28, appears designed to refute the claim that Governor Bennett had previously made in a circular that the Vesey plot had no ramifications in the countryside. On Ferguson, see Part II, p. 109 n1.

22. In 1822, John C. Calhoun was secretary of war.

23. Probably Winborn Lawton Jr. (1778–1861), a wealthy planter of James Island.

24. Colonel William N. Thompson, a slaveholding planter of Colleton District, served in the Twenty-fourth Regiment, South Carolina Militia. See *BDSCHR* 5: 267–68; Charleston *City Gazette and Commercial Daily Advertiser*, September 15, 1819.

25. Colonel William Mellard (1791–1860), of St. James Goose Creek, commanded the Eighteenth Regiment of Fourth Brigade, South Carolina Militia, in 1822. See Charleston *City Gazette and Commercial Daily Advertiser*, September 6, 1822.

26. The "infected" plantation was owned by James Ferguson. Bennett's words here seem discordant with his previous assertion that "perfect tranquility" prevailed in the countryside. So does his acknowledgment of the three militia commanders whom he had muster forces in Charleston's surrounding countryside to preempt slave unrest.

27. The slave Jesse owned by Thomas Blackwood (d. 1837), president of the Planter's and Mechanics' Bank, who in 1822 resided at 18 Pitt Street. See *CSCCD*, 107.

RGA, GM, no. 1328, series S165009, SCDAH.

New Orleans *Louisiana Gazette*

Friday, November 29, 1822

Some of the blacks who were implicated in the attempted insurrection in South Carolina and banished from that state, have found their way to the city of Philadelphia. "A magistrate of this city," says the Democratic Press[1] of the 10th Oct. "told us that he had two or three days ago, some conversation with a gentleman from Charleston, who said he had seen in Philadelphia and spoken with some of the Negroes who had been sentenced to death in Charlestown, and that they were come to settle here and had sent to South Carolina to get their wives and families sent on to them."

1. The Philadelphia *Democratic Press*, one of the leading newspapers in the state in 1822, was published by the Irish-born John Binns (1772–1860).

Charleston *Southern Patriot, and Commercial Advertiser*

Saturday, November 30, 1822

A letter received yesterday from Columbia, states that the Petitions of various owners of the slaves executed for being engaged in the late intended insurrection have been referred in the House of Representatives, to a Special Committee, consisting of Messrs. Hamilton, Lee, Myrieck, and O'Neal.[1]

1. The "special committee" was composed of James Hamilton Jr., Littleton Myrick (d. 1838), Thomas Lee (1769–1839), and John Belton O'Neall (1793–1863). See *BDSCHR* 4: 345–46; *BDSCHR* 5: 118, 193, 198–200.

Governor Thomas Bennett Jr. to John Lyde Wilson,[1] November 30, 1822

Executive Department
Columbia Novr 30. 1822

The Hon: John L. Wilson
President of the Senate
Sir

Permit me to request through you of the Senate, the obliteration of the words "usurpation of authority" in that paragraph of my second Message which refers to the organization of the Court. It will manifestly appear that those words were undesignedly retained, by referring to other parts of the sentence. No intention or opinion existing to induce a representation to the Legislature of a wilful violation of rule or Law, on the part of the Corporate Authorities or the Court arranged by them; the course pursued by either (I never doubted) arose wholly from honest convictions of propriety.

I have the honor to be
Very Respectfully Sir
Your Obt Sert
Tho: Bennett

1. John Lyde Wilson (1784–1849), an attorney who would enjoy a long career in public service, followed Thomas Bennett Jr. as governor of South Carolina. Wilson composed *The Code of Honor; or Rules for the Government of Principals and Seconds in Duelling* (Charleston, SC, 1838), which became the most authoritative dueling manual in the antebellum South. See *BDSCHR* 4: 605–6.

RGA, GM, 1327, SCDAH.

Thomas Pinckney[1] Reflects on the Causes of the Vesey Affair and Its Remedy

The following Reflections are from the pen of a Soldier and a Patriot of the Revolution; whose name (did we feel ourselves at liberty to use it) would stamp a peculiar weight and value on his opinions.

They were written after the public disturbances in this place, during an excursion into the interior, and have been transmitted to a few friends for their perusal, who have deemed them worthy of a more comprehensive dissemination than a single manuscript copy could possibly have afforded.—It will be sufficiently obvious that these Reflections are the result of much patient thinking on a subject well calculated to arouse the anxieties of patriotism, and to invoke all that the maturity of experience is capable of yielding. . . .

THE vigor and decision which marked the conduct of the City Authorities in preventing the late meditated Insurrection of the Negroes in Charleston; so ably supported by the patient investigation, sagacious conduct, and inflexible justice of the Court of Magistrates and Freeholders appointed for the trial of the criminals, has for the present terminated all cause of alarm: and the example made of those infatuated miscreants who had rendered themselves obnoxious to the severity of the law, will, probably, for sometime, preclude the danger of similar conspiracies. It is not to be doubted that the Legislative body, and the Magistrates, to whom the care of the public welfare is confided, will adopt such measures as their wisdom and patriotism can devise, to prevent forever the recurrence of such enormities. Hence it becomes the duty of every one, who has maturely reflected on the subject, to suggest, in aid of their consultations, such measures as may appear reasonable, and likely to be attended with success.—If these measures have already occurred to the minds of those whose duty it is to provide for the public safety, the suggestion may tend to corroborate their opinion; if it offers any thing new, the plan will be considered, and adopted or rejected according to its merit. Being deeply interested in whatever concerns the welfare of my native city, and tremblingly alive to the danger which may threaten the amicable and defenceless part of the community, who have, by their exemplary conduct at every crisis of our history, so richly merited all the protection which duty and affection can afford, I may probably mistake the desire for the ability to propose measures competent to promote that welfare and avert that danger. I will, notwithstanding, venture to offer my view of the subject.

Previous to the proposal of any plan for preventing the recurrence of similar danger, it may be useful to advert to the causes which produced the late conspiracy. The following may be assigned as some of the most obvious:—1st, The example of St. Domingo, and (probably) the encouragement received from thence.—2dly, The indiscreet zeal in favor of universal liberty, expressed by many of our fellow-citizens in the States north and east of Maryland; aided by the Black population of those States.—3dly, The idleness, dissipation, and improper indulgencies permitted among all classes of the Negroes in Charleston, and particularly among the domestics: and, as the most dangerous of those indulgencies, their being taught to read and write: the first bringing the powerful operation of the Press to act on their uninformed and easily deluded minds; and the latter furnishing them with an instrument to carry into execution the mischievous suggestions of the former.—4th, The facility of obtaining money afforded by the nature of their occupations to those employed as mechanics, draymen, fishermen, butchers, porters, hucksters, &c.—5th, The disparity of numbers between the white and black inhabitants of the City. No effort of ours can remove some of these causes, but over others we may exercise control.

1. Nothing effectual can be done by us to obviate the influence of the example of St. Domingo, so long as it retains its condition. It would be difficult also to prevent encouragement being offered from thence, because we cannot cut off the direct communication, neither, if this were practicable, would it avail while the circuitous intercourse through the Northern States must remain open.

2d. Still less can we prevent evils arising from injustice, impolicy, and indiscriminating cruelty of many citizens of the Northern States, who directly or indirectly instigate our Black population to such scenes as they lately meditated. It is termed injustice, because it is a violation of the Federal compact. Impolicy, because if there be a single cause which can dissolve the Union, it would be the attempt to reverse the conditions (and no other alternative could in our situation take place) of the present master and slave. It would be, moreover, impolicy as it respects their own interest; because if they could, even without bloodshed, effect a general emancipation, the influence of the Southern States in the General Government would be augmented, and that of the Northern States comparatively depressed, in the ratio of five to three. It is indiscriminately cruel, because, from the nature of the contest their measures tend to excite, if the party they favor should succeed, it would be a war of extermination to their white fellow-citizens, their wives and children; as was the case in St. Domingo. If detected, as in the present instance, they see how many of those whose conditions they wished to ameliorate, must necessarily be the victims of the law of self-defence;—victims of their misguided interference! But such is the state of political enthusiasm among many of the less informed inhabitants of those States, extended by the agitation of the Missouri question to some who formerly held more moderate opinions, and had taken juster views of our situation, that all we can now do is to be vigilant to detect any emissaries, and to stop all incendiary publications which may be sent from that quarter.

3d. Over the indulgences which have so pampered the enormous number of domestics, entertained by the inhabitants, the State Laws and City Ordinances may have considerable control; but the execution of these laws may be so frustrated by public inattention, and more by the particular way of thinking and weakness of many proprietors, that it is to be feared this evil will not be effectually checked, particularly as it respects the dangerous instrument of learning, which many of them have acquired; for it is not only impracticable to deprive them of what they have attained, but as it is easily communicated, it is probable that, spite of all endeavors to the contrary, this evil will rather increase than diminish.

4th. Neither will it be practicable to prevent those who are permitted to engross the occupations of draymen, fishermen, hucksters, butchers, barbers, porters, &c. from coming into the possession of much money, which being almost invariably spent in drunkenness and debauchery, prepares them to be willing instruments of any delusive plan of mischief which may be presented to them; while the instruments of their employments with which they are usually intrusted, such as horses, tools, &c. and the knowledge they acquire by their occupations, increase their ability to do mischief. It seems evident, therefore, that we cannot effectually obviate the ill effects of the causes assigned. Hence it is the more urgent that we should apply the remedy, which appears to be completely within our control, to the remaining cause, the disparity of numbers.

5th. If we examine the last census, and refer to that taken twenty years previous, we shall find that this evil is rapidly increasing; for at the former period the white population of Charleston exceeded the other, while in the last census the black population was to the white nearly as 22 to 14.—Now, as it must be admitted that this excess of physical force does diminish the great superiority which their means and qualifications give to our citizens, a reliance on this circumstance must have formed the principal encouragement to the late attempt; for without it, mad and wild as they appear to have been, they would not have dared to venture on a contest of force. How imperative is then the policy of removing this rapidly increasing evil—this *sine qua non* of insurrection!

The next questions then, which naturally occur, are, to what degree will it be necessary to extend the reduction? And what substitute can be obtained to occupy the employments now filled by the Negroes?

With respect to the degree, some previous investigation may enable us to arrive at a just conclusion. It would, perhaps, appear sufficient, on a slight examination, to reduce the number of their effectives something below that of the active citizens; because the various advantages of the latter, would, in time of action, give them a decided superiority over their adversaries; but it should be considered that plots of this kind are always intended to be executed by treachery and surprise; and that the case is not similar to that of an openly opposing adversary, whose attempts at surprise, or insidious aggression, might by proper precautions be averted. But this is an intestine enemy, who by availing himself of his advantageous situation, and properly selecting the time of attack, might render it extremely formidable.—That in this case, or even in the case of his being greatly superior in numbers, he must ultimately fail, is certain; but the mere rumor of a conspiracy would occasion distressing alarm, and the attempt, though ultimately unsuccessful, would produce incalculable evils. It would be, therefore, prudent not only to reduce their force below what, upon a fair calculation, would afford no prospect of success to rational persons, but to place it so low as to deprive even the rash and desperate of all hope. Another consideration also points to the propriety of very considerable reduction, which is the great repugnance felt by freemen to be placed in any respect on the same footing with the slave; whereby many industrious white men, who cannot brook either the concurrence or the association of the blacks, are deterred from settling among us: wherefore, if we desire to see the places of journeymen in the various mechanic arts, occupied by a superior class, we must have no blacks in the same rank of society. And that it would be highly advantageous, in other respects also, to have this class occupied by freemen, will be evident from the following considerations: All the business of these occupations would be better performed. In the first place, from the emulation to excel; a strong motive among freemen, but scarcely felt by the slave:—next, because the rate of wages is necessarily in proportion to the skill and good conduct of the workman; whence in the case of the freeman, a direct appeal is made to his interest; while the slave, whose master receives his wages, has no inducement of this kind to exertion. Another spur to the industry of the freeman, is the hope that his earnings may be sufficient to support himself in time of sickness; and, if he has a family, to assist in their maintenance. The slave knows that both himself and his family, in sickness and in health, must be supported by his master; he is, therefore, perfectly indifferent on this score: the continuance of the industry and good conduct of the freeman, is cherished by the expectation that persevering success will advance him in the ranks of his occupation; that from a journeyman he may in time become a master workman:—the slave can have no such expectation. A further advantage in the employment of freemen is, that with them much business may be executed by job work, a mode which of late years has been productive of great satisfaction and utility; being found profitable to both parties; because while the employer has his work completed according to his direction, without further superintendance, and in general, at a cheaper rate; it operates as a stimulus to exertion by the workman whose earnings are in proportion thereto. Job-work by the slave who has no inducement either to greater accuracy or expedition, would be of no advantage. In drawing the above comparison, no stress is placed upon the superiority of natural ingenuity, and comprehension of the white man over the black, although it is believed to be considerable; for, though good imitators may be found among the blacks, it is very rare to find one who can plan or invent, even in the business in which he has been educated, and carefully instructed.

Enough has, probably, been adduced to convince our fellow-citizens, who are master-mechanics, that the employment of white men would, upon the whole, be more to their advantage than hiring at a lower rate of wages, these inferior workmen. Long experience has also proved to many owners of black tradesmen, who are not themselves mechanics, that they are not so profitable to them when hired out in town, as when working in the field, or at their trades, when required, in the country. The nominal rate of wages in town seems much in favor of employing them there; but the sick days, the idle days, the doctor's bills, the work-house and guard-house fees, which are the results of that intemperance and debauchery so generally prevalent, diminish in an extraordinary degree the profits of his labor, while it ruins the constitution and morals of the slave. And if the master-mechanics who own any of this property were accurately to calculate the interest of their capital, the insurance of life, and the various draw-backs of the nature of those above enumerated, they would find it not much to their advantage, to employ this species of workmen even as owners. Reasoning analogous to the above would show also that the employment of draymen, porters, fishermen, hucksters, butchers, barbers, &c. would be more advantageously filled by white men. It will likewise apply, with equal force, to the house-servants, or those employed immediately about the persons, and in the dwellings of the inhabitants. But it must be admitted, that these would be given up with more reluctance, and could be replaced with less facility; they are, however, certainly the most dangerous; their intimate acquaintance with all circumstances relating to the interior of the dwellings; the confidence reposed in them; and the information they unavoidably obtain, from hearing the conversation, and observing the habitual transactions of their owners, afford them the amplest means for treacherous bloodshed and devastation. The success, therefore, of servile conspiracies, mainly depends on this class, for taking off by midnight murder their unsuspecting owners; and the late trials, by exhibiting so large a proportion of this description among the ringleaders of the conspiracy, afford a melancholy proof of their promptitude to become prominent actors in such scenes. A conviction of the truth of these remarks would, probably, induce a disposition more willingly to relinquish the services of these dangerous dependants, if an adequate substitute could be procured: and this leads to a consideration of the probability of our being able to procure substitutes for these several classes, whose disadvantages, as it respects pecuniary interest, has been shown, and from whom the danger is too manifest.

That, if we get rid of the blacks, who now occupy these employments, we may easily supply their places by free white men, will be evident when we reflect that the advantages of commerce are become so extensively beneficial, that wherever it has a free course, the supply of all transferable articles is equal to the demand; so that if it be once known, that

Charleston requires any number of mechanics, draymen, &c. who will be liberally paid for their services, as many as can be so remunerated will find their way thither, provided there be no impediment to their exercising their business with safety and satisfaction to themselves. Two objections have hitherto formed this impediment;—the reported unhealthiness of the climate; and the competition of the blacks.—This last, which is believed, for the reasons assigned, to be the most powerful, will of course cease with their removal. With respect to the climate, the frequent recurrence of the yellow fever within the last thirty years, has undoubtably given an unfavorable impression of the salubrity of our City; but, as its ravages have not been so extensive, nor so certainly fatal, in its last accessions, as it has not appeared here for several years; and as the increased attention to cleanliness may, by Divine permission, avert for a protracted period, this scourge of the cities of hot summer climates, we may reasonably hope that it will not be an insuperable objection in the emigration of the persons required; but that they will readily offer their services, when they are informed, as they may be with truth, that a considerable portion of our population consists of acclimatised foreigners; that the general salubrity of Charleston is scarcely surpassed by any city of great population, when not visited by yellow fever; and when they learn the superior encouragement given to industry in active employments.—Who that contemplates the unhappy condition of Ireland, where impolitic regulations, and the enormously unequal distribution of property have reduced a brave, industrious, and honest peasantry to perish by famine in a fruitful country, when at the time there is no real scarcity of provisions, can doubt that from that ill-fated Island alone an accession might soon be received, of active, industrious mechanics and labourers, to a City, where are already comfortably established, so many of their countrymen, who having passed through their seasoning, and now understanding the precautions necessary to be taken on change of climate, would with their accustomed benevolence and hospitality, effectually advise and assist the new-comers to establish themselves with safety and advantage.—Nor is Ireland the only part of the globe whence indigence and oppression compell the industrious to emigrate; but we might reasonably expect to see the destitute of various countries, resorting to a place where they would be certain of profitable employment.

Nor would the supply be limited to foreign countries, for in this part of the United States, encouragement to industrious occupation is so great, that we every autumn witness the importation of a considerable number of industrious mechanics and fishermen from the Northern and Eastern States, where neither oppression nor regulations tending to create inequality of property exist. And it is probable, that many of them would bring their families and establish themselves among us, were it not for the humiliating consideration, that they would, in some respects, be placed so nearly on a level with the slave. Their present practice of returning home in the summer, proves how encouraging must be that reward of industry, which can profitably defray the expense of two sea voyages in a few months. That no climate will deter from emigration to it, is proved by the disregard daily shown to the dangers arising therefrom; a disregard founded on the hope of individual exemption, so natural to the human mind. Hence the immense population of Constantinople, the head-quarters of the plague; and of Havanna, Batavia, and other cities, which, though the constant seats of fatal disease, are so thickly inhabited, that their population seems to be in an inverse ratio to their salubrity. It may, therefore, be fairly concluded, that no fear of our climate will prevent us from receiving as large a supply as our exigencies may require, of industrious mechanics, draymen, &c. That a sufficient number of white persons would readily come to undertake also, the domestic or menial offices, were the blacks totally dismissed, must be evident from there being no scarcity of such persons, wherever their services are required; but repeated experiments have proved that they cannot, with advantage, be mixed with the black domestics.—It is true, also, that the habits of our inhabitants render them averse to employing such domestics; having seen these offices constantly occupied by slaves, they would, with reluctance, exact similar services from those whom nature, as well as the law, have made their equals: and, it must be admitted, that this same perception of equality renders hired domestic servants less obsequious, and in some measure, more independent in the United States, than those occupying similar stations in Europe. In order, therefore, to command the services required, it will be necessary that they should be liberally remunerated. With this incitement to obedience and orderly conduct, aided by the desire of insuring good employment, by keeping a good character; and encouraged by that humane consideration for their condition, which will be here generally prevalent, it is probable that the essential part of their services would be more efficient than that of those now employed. The expense, also, of liberal encouragement, would not be beyond the present rate; for, although the wages paid to each hired servant might exceed the interest of capital, insurance of life, and maintenance of a slave in the same situation, yet, it should be considered, that the families of the hired servants would be no incumbrance on the employer; that he would not have to maintain the superannuated, the infirm, or the indolent, who are now so heavy a tax on the proprietor; he would then contract for efficient service, which, if the person employed, should be incapable or unwilling to perform, he would be discharged, and a more suitable subject engaged. It may be fairly presumed, from what has been adduced, that hired service would be most efficient; considerable saving would result from the reduction which might be made in the number of servants employed:—and on examining the domestic establishments of persons of similar property and stations in society, in the Northern Cities of the United States, we shall find that the domestics there are not so numerous, by one half, as those in Charleston; and as persons of the same description might be employed here, no good reason can be assigned why the same reduction in number should not take place in Charleston; in which case, the employment of white servants would be more economical than the work of the slaves.

If the proper authorities should be of opinion that it will be advantageous and practicable, to make for the City, this exchange of the black for a white population, they will, of course, proceed with that prudent deliberation, which will ensure its execution to be attended with as little loss and inconvenience to the proprietors as possible; time being allowed for the sale, hire, or other disposal, out of town, of the coloured people; and notice given, in proper places, of the employments for which occupants will be required. The details for the execution of such a plan will require much practical information, sound judgment, and discretion: and even when conducted in the most judicious manner, will, probably, be attended with much temporary inconvenience and expense. The question then, to be decided is, whether the object be worth the cost? To solve the doubt, it may be proper to review some of the most prominent disadvantages of the present system, and the benefits to be expected from the change.

The disadvantages are principally the result of the condition of the slave, which depriving him of all interest in the success of his exertions, removes the most powerful stimulus to industry and good conduct. The terror of punishment is not an adequate substitute for this all-powerful motive. That may be easily eluded by falsehood and cunning, and is often averted by compassion; indeed the infliction of corporal punishment is so repugnant to human feelings, that its effect is the reverse of "twice bless'd mercy," punishing him who inflicts as well as him who receives. It is, therefore, rarely applied with effect. Hence every thing consigned to the management of the slave, who has neither the incitement of interest, nor the fear of certain punishment, is neglected or abused,—Horses, and all inferior animals left to their charge, are badly attended; their provender finds its way to the dram-shops, and they are used frequently without discretion or mercy; their cariages and harness are slightly and badly cleaned; the tools of the mechanics are broken and lost through neglect; their very clothing becomes more expensive through their carelessness, arising from the knowledge that they must be supplied with all these articles, as well as their subsistence, at their master's expense; and waste, that moth of domestic establishments, universally prevails.

Another disadvantage is, that the morals of the slave, from the want of education, and the absence of self-respect, are more depraved than those of the freeman in similar stations: it cannot be denied, that the latter, in some situations, are at a low ebb; but it will always be found where that is the case, that the depravity is the result of great inequality of conditions, and other unjust political institutions, where the lower order are reduced more nearly to the condition of slaves.—But, it is in the nature of things, that any class of white men, possessing the privileges enjoyed by all in the United States, must, generally, be exempt from the degrading vices of the slave. Hence, in addition to the various other benefits to be derived from this superiority, the morals of our children would be more safe, and less liable to contaminaton by that intercourse with servants, which, in early youth, is unavoidable: and this objection to a continuance of the use of black domestics, must alone have a preponderating influence with considerate parents. But, the greatest of all their disadvantages, is, certainly, that of which Charleston has lately experienced the terror.

The above are some of the disadvantages of the present system: the benefits which will be derived from the change, will be, in the first place, security: not merely that we and our families shall be safe from these horrors, but, that we and they shall feel, and be perfectly assured that we are so; that we may retire to our repose at night, with the certain knowledge of our immunity from the dagger of the treacherous internal assassin, and all the horrors which were so fatally exhibited at St. Domingo, and were distinctly threatened here. Another advantage is, that all the labor and domestic business of the City, will be better performed, and all articles committed to the charge of subordinate agents more carefully preserved.

But, it is not merely exemption from the disadvantages attending the employment of slaves, that will result from the change of system, but great positive benefits will attend the introduction and employment of so many white inhabitants. The most obvious, is the effective force which will thereby be added to the militia of the City. If, in the place of 22,432 coloured persons now maintained there, only half the number of white inhabitants were introduced; as all the mechanics, the draymen, the fishermen, and the porters, would of course be males, more than five thousand effective men would be added to our muster-roll; whereby, not only Charleston would be perfectly secure, but all thoughts of servile insurrection in the country, would be forever banished: for with a militia force of seven or eight thousand men, well armed and accoutred, which would then compose the militia of Charleston, on one side, and the numerous white population of the upper country, on the other; it would be more than madness for any portion of the country slaves to meditate an insurrection, destitute as they are of most of the advantages and facilities for such an enterprize, of which those in Charleston might have availed themselves.

What an additional protection to our City, also, in time of war, would this augmentation of force afford? Little occasion would then exist to harrass our fellow-citizens of the interior, to come down as militia-men to our assistance; nor would there be any reason for distressing those of the low country, by the incessant duties of the patrol, now so indispensably necessary for safety, but which then would have only for its object the prevention of minor irregularities.—Charleston would also acquire an increase of political importance, both in the State and in the Union; her pure population would, probably, in a few years, exceed the number of mixed inhabitants she now possesses; for the slow progress that has been made both in number of people, and value of property, when compared with other cities of the United States, may fairly be attributed, in a great measure, to the nature of her lower population; to a residence among whom, such general and well-founded repugnance is prevalent.

It is generally admitted, even in these Southern States, that the slavery which here prevails, is an evil entailed upon us by our former British rulers, and difficult to be averted from its extensive influence, being amalgamated with most of the property of the country; as well as on account of the nature of our climate, and a part of our soil: but all must agree, that it would be compatible, both with our interest and our principles, to get rid of it where it can be done without endangering the welfare of the community. Here then, is the place, where this desirable purpose may be effected, without material injury to the interests of any party, and not only with safety, but, where it will be the parent of security. The interests of the owners will not be injured, because they may, by sale, by hire, or by employment on their own lands in the country, obtain nearly an equal interest on their capital, to what it now produces. It may, also, be fairly assumed, that it would, in some points of view, be beneficial to the slaves; for by annihilating all prospects of success, every temptation to revolt would be removed, and they could never be again subjected to the horrors and calamities, in which an attempt at insurrection, whether at first successful or not, must inevitably involve them. Besides, while they continue in any degree, objects of apprehension to their proprietors, which in their present position must be the case, it is in human nature that they will be viewed with distrust, and considered as hostile to their safety; and the benevolence and humanity, which their services and situation would otherwise command, will be repressed. But place them where, not being dangerous, they cannot give rise to unfriendly emotions, and they will again be considered as the victims of former policy, as the unfortunate instruments of our comforts and our prosperity; and the kindlier feelings of nature will freely operate in ameliorating their condition. For the probability of this result an appeal may be made to the recollection of those who have observed the favorable alteration in the condition of these people, since the termination of the revolutionary war. But an excess of these humane feelings, combining with other causes, accumulated in Charleston, but which can never exist in the country, rendered them in the late instance, instead of a blessing, a curse to both parties. If then, the existence of the present system be attended with inconveniences so great, with dangers so formidable; and the alteration proposed will not only avert them, but be productive of further benefits; if all experience proves that nothing good and valuable can be obtained without exertion and expense, no reasonable person will object to the price or inconvenience attending the exchange. The expense will be nothing more than the difference of price between the labour of freemen and of slaves; the inconvenience will only be severely felt, while the alteration is carying into effect. It is to be lamented that the greatest part of this will be experienced in the domestic line, and fall heaviest on that class whom every man would wish to exempt from the burden.—But, when it is considered that they, and the objects of their tender solicitude, their young children, will be, in some respects, the most benefited by the measure; and that habit and judicious treatment, will render their future domestics more suitable to their views; while they will themselves, by custom, become reconciled to such deficiencies as may be found in their new attendants; it is hoped they will, with their accustomed self devotion, make the sacrifice which their own and the public welfare so urgently requires.

The foregoing considerations are the result of much anxious reflection on the late occurrences in Charleston; this reflection has convinced the writer that, as most of the causes of the late misfortune are beyond our control, the best way to remove the evil is to abolish that which is completely within our power:—He has endeavored to show that this total substitution of a free white population, for that now employed, will not only afford security, but will be attended with other important advantages. For the purpose of showing to every description of the employers of slaves, the benefits which will probably result to them respectively, from the substitution proposed, he has enumerated the most obvious disadvantages of several classes of the black population, contrasted with the advantages to be derived from freemen in the same vocation: it has also been shown that while the change cannot be materially detrimental to the owners, it will, in some respects, benefit the slaves themselves.

The calculations made in this investigation, relate merely to the pecuniary interest of the proprietors or employers, independently of the great objects of security, strength, and importance; the value of the first of these objects cannot easily be made the subject of calculation; it will be best appreciated by those who have felt the apprehension of its absence: no effort has been made to depict in glowing colors the blessings of its presence, or the horrors of the reverse; for on a subject so serious, attempts at eloquence would be misplaced. The appeal is made to the sober reason and judgment of those who have so valuable a stake in the decision. An attempt has been made to show that the measure recommended is not only highly beneficial, but, that it is also practicable; and the whole is, with due deference, submitted to the consideration of those to whom are confided the safety and the welfare of the public.

ACHATES.

NOTE.

AS some persons, interested in the decision of this question, may not be accurately informed of the expense attending the employment of Negro Slaves, the following statement is submitted:

The average annual expense of plantation slaves in the lower country of South-Carolina, extracted from the account of several executors and attornies, for four successive years, amounts to $35 per head. The chief items of expense are provisions, clothing, taxes, overseer's wages, medicines, doctors bills, sugar, molasses, spirits, tobacco, salt-fish, ploughs, tools, nails, locks, hinges, fish-hooks, pipes, salt, &c. &c. The average value of such slaves, rated at what they have usually sold for at auction, during many years preceeding 1820, may be stated at $500, *annual interest* $35.—No charge is made for the insurance of life, because, with attention and good usage, the natural increase will about keep up the numbers, even on rice plantations, which are considered the most unhealthy.

The average expense, therefore, of each negro, being $35, and the interest of capital, also $35; the whole charge against each head is $70. But it is found, that in general, not more than one half the number are effective workers; that is, that the daily tasks which are performed on each plantation do not exceed in number one half the negroes maintained thereon; so, that for every worker, the interest and expences of two persons must be charged, which will make the annual cost of each working-hand amount to $140.

In Charleston, the expense must be considerably greater, because there are, in general, clothed more expensively, and more daintily fed. In the above expences of country negroes, the provisions purchased do not usually form a charge for more than two-thirds of the year, because on every plantation, where a full market crop is planted, about one-third of the provisions is raised thereon: in Charleston the whole must be purchased.—The City tax forms an additional charge against the town slave. The average price of tradesmen and others, bought and sold in Charleston, is also considerably higher than that of field slaves, whereby the interest on capital is proportionably enhanced.—Where they have not families to keep up the stock, the maintenance of two, for one efficient workman, should not be charged against them, but the insurance on life must be substituted, which, it is presumed, would there be very high. Sufficient data are not at hand to form a precise estimate of the whole expense of a Charleston black mechanic or house servant. But from the above statement, it must greatly exceed that of the field slaves. And when the draw-backs from his efficiency are considered, it is probable that the labour of white men will, on the whole, be as cheap as that of the slave.

FINIS.

1. Thomas Pinckney (1750–1828) was a Charleston-born soldier, diplomat, and politician. Following military service in the Revolution, Pinckney was elected governor of South Carolina in 1787, serving for two years before taking a seat in the state legislature in 1791. Like his brother Charles Cotesworth Pinckney, a staunch Federalist, Pinckney served President George Washington as minister to Great Britain in 1792. While in Europe he negotiated the popular Treaty of San Lorenzo with Spain in 1795. The fame of that treaty helped bring him the Federalist Party nomination for vice-president in 1796, although he lost that position to Thomas Jefferson. He then served in the national House of Representatives until 1801. As the burial petition reproduced in Part I points out, Thomas's brother Charles knew Morris Brown and many other prominent free persons of color in Charleston. Achates, the pen name that Thomas Pinckney gave himself, was the confidant of Aeneas in Virgil's *Aeneid.* On this pamphlet, which was completed on November 4, 1822, and published in December, see Lacy K. Ford, *Deliver Us from Evil: The Slavery Question in the Old South* (New York: Oxford University Press, 2009), 240–45.

Achates, *Reflections, Occasioned by the late Disturbances in Charleston* (Charleston, SC, 1822).

Henry William DeSaussure on the Futility of Emancipation and Colonization[1]

. . . We have shown in the preceding number, that the domestic slavery of the Africans was not brought upon this country by her own act, but by the policy of Great-Britain, in spite of the opposition and remonstrances of several of the northern and southern colonies. It should have been added that in the year 1794, within five years after the formation of the new federal government, with real Legislative power, Congress commenced that system of measures restraining the slave trade, which terminated in the act of the 2d March, 1807, absolutely prohibiting the slave trade forever, directly or indirectly, after the first day of January, 1808. This act was passed without opposition from the southern states, and it is believed nearly with unanimity, by both houses of Congress. And this act has been followed up by a succession of others, with additional severe sanctions, which have effectually prevented the importation of slaves into the southern states.—All these acts had the entire concurrence of the southern states. The result is that they did not originate the trade, and got rid of it as soon as they could.

We arrive now at the consideration of the question, what can or ought to be done with the slaves, now in the United States? That domestic slavery is an evil is not denied by intelligent persons in the southern states; and the citizen would be entitled to civic crowns and everlasting gratitude, whose wisdom could devise a plan for getting rid of the evil, which was just to others, and practicable in itself. It will be found, however, infinitely easier to point out what plans will not be safe or just than to indicate any one which is.

Revolving this subject maturely in the mind, there do not appear to be any other than three modes in which the slaves can be disposed of:

1st. By being sent out of the country to Africa, or elsewhere.

2d. By being emancipated and permitted to remain in the country, with or without the civil and political rights of other citizens.

3d. By being retained in their present condition.

We will treat of all three briefly. Let us now consider the first proposition, the removal of the slaves to Africa or elsewhere.

Would this be just to the rights of others? These slaves are unquestionably the property of the present owners, as much so as the lands, and houses, ships and personal property in other states are the property of their several owners. The money of the present holders, or of their ancestors, has been paid for these persons, or their progenitors. The fortunes and the prosperity of about three millions of citizens, from Maryland, south and west, are deeply implicated in this subject. A vast portion of the country is cultivated by those slaves; and many families who have no lands, subsist by hiring out their slaves to landholders. It seems therefore to be a fair claim of the owners that these slaves should be paid for at a reasonable price, before the nation could ask their consent to their transportation from this country. It is possible indeed that this right to compensation may be denied by some who insist that slavery is not founded in right, and that the owners have no just title to hold their persons in servitude. We are not however going into the question of abstract right. That might well be a subject of discussion, between a government and individuals asking authority to import slaves, but not between individuals who hold them under the authority and almost by the compulsion of its supreme government, as in the case we are considering. Now, as the government of the United States has succeeded to the obligations as well as to the authority of the British Government, (modified by our constitutions) which forced the trade in slaves, it can never justly deny the right of the citizen to compensation for the privation of property, acquired under its laws, without any regard to the question of abstract right. The question of conscience is an affair between the individual and his Creator, with which the government has nothing to do; and if it had, it would be difficult to prove that to be immoral which was expressly permitted to the Jews under their theocracy—and which was not prohibited by the Saviour or his successors, to their followers. In pursuance of the system of universal benevolence, preached under the new dispensation, the Apostles strenuously recommended gentle treatment by the owners of slaves, but they never expressed one word on the duty of emancipation. . . .

In our last number, we endeavoured to shew that the purchase of the slaves, held by an unquestionable title in the southern and western states, for the purpose of transporting them from this country, would be attended with an enormous expense, exceeding in amount the sums cost by the revolutionary war, and by the late war waged in self defence, and in vindication of our outraged rights. But this is not all. The cost of transporting so great a number of persons as 1,500,000 slaves, and 250,000 free people of colour, (for they too should be ejected, if the policy is adopted at all) would amount to a great sum of money. For it would require 7000 ships of 500 tons burthen, each, to transport 1,750,000 persons even crowded to an extreme degree. The hire of the ships, and of seamen, and the provisioning the ships for a long voyage with such a freight, would amount to at least 100,000,000 of dollars. . . .

Having shewn in the preceding number the utter hopelessness of being able to get rid of the slaves, by transporting them out of the country, we are next led to inquire into the praticability and effect of emancipation.

It must be obvious that this measure can never be adopted and carried into execution, but with the consent of the southern and western states, and by compensation to the slave holders, for the privation of their property. The government of the United States has no authority to touch the subject; and are even bound by the constitution to ensure domestic tranquillity, and to protect the several states from domestic insurrection: It is bound also to protect the citizens in the secure enjoyment of that species of property, as well as every other, and it has heretofore done so faithfully. In negociating the last peace with Great-Britain, the American ministers took care to obtain a clause to be inserted in the treaty, for compensation to be made to the proprietors of slaves, who had been plundered of them on the land, by the British naval marauders. That very claim has been since zealously urged by the government of the United States, and upon some difficulties of construction, a reference was made by both parties, under the treaty, to the Emperor of Russia, who has recently decided in favour of the American claims.

Thus our government, and those with whom it transacts the most important affairs, treat this species of property as sacred as any other, and concur in opinion that the proprietors are entitled to compensation for any illegal violation of their rights.

It will not then be denied that if the interests or policy of the United States should require the emancipation of the blacks, the government which asks that concession of the states, (for it cannot enforce it of right) will be bound to make compensation to their owners. The enormous amount which that would cost, for the whole mass, has been shewn to exceed the financial powers of this country in so overwhelming a degree, as to render that scheme impracticable.

If a different plan should be adopted, and those only should be purchased for emancipation, who might be born after this period, this also is full of difficulties. The number of births must be very great, from 1,550,000 persons, who never suffer from famine, who have the best medical attendance, without cost to themselves, and who have no apprehensions of marrying very early, and having children in abundance, because they know they will be taken care of, and cloathed and fed at all events.—The increase in South-Carolina, was so great, between the census of 1810, and 1820, as to give, upon an estimate founded in the usual proportion of deaths and births, such a result, as would make the whole of the annual births of slaves in the United States amount by the same calculation to upwards of 70,000.

But, if we make larger allowances than usual for deaths and casualties, and put them at 50,000, the cost of these would be enormous:—at 300 dollars, for each person, it would amount to fifteen millions of dollars annually. It may be said that the price above named would be much too great. That is true; but it must be considered, that if the government purchased and paid for the children at the birth, it would be obliged to provide for them until they could maintain themselves by their own labour, and that could not be at a lower age than 12 or 14 years. The expense of that would greatly exceed the calculation made on another principle, to-wit: That the government should purchase and pay for them at the age of 14 years, when they could maintain themselves; at which time the reasonable price would certainly be 300 dollars for each of them. . . .

It cannot be doubted that if the blacks should be emancipated and put on a footing with the whites, as to civil rights, but excluded from political rights, their course would be precisely that of all who have preceded them in that situation and career.—They would never cease to contend for a participation of all political privileges. Denmark Vesey, the head and animating spirit of the late plot in Charleston, was free, at ease in his circumstances, protected in his rights of person and property, and unoppressed: But he was excluded from political rights, and was disconte[nte]d: he sought them through appalling difficulties, and in the pursuit of his object, disregarded the dangers which confronted him, and defied the death which he encountered.—The emancipated blacks of the southern and western states, would bear a portion of one to two, or about 1,500,000 blacks to 3,000,000 whites. They would acquire property, obtain education, become ambitious, and aspire to share in the government. This would lead to fierce contentions, and ultimately to civil wars, inhuman, desolating to individuals, and ruinous to the country within, and weakening it against foreign powers without. If their claims were successfully repelled, we should have a discontented population, always ready for a change, always eager for an opportunity to rebel, and to acquire the long coveted right of participating in the government.

Should they succeed by force, or by solicitation acting on the fear, or on the policy of the whites, in acquiring the object of their desires, they would then be put on a footing of perfect equality with the whites. . . .

Should the blacks subdue the whites, it would be a war of extermination. Men accustomed to freedom and to superiority, could not submit to the domination of their former slaves. They would fight to the last extremity; and when hope was gone, the few who survived would abandon the country, and take refuge among their brethren in the northern states.

What sort of neighbors, what kind of friends the black empires of the south and west would be to the north, is left to the calm and deliberate consideration of the northern statesmen. It will be for them to decide whether they would prefer the present race, who are masters, and who are united to them by every tie which binds men together—a common origin and colour, a common religion and language, similar habits and feelings, laws, governments and institutions of all kinds—to be their friends and associates in peace and in war; or to have the blacks, descendants of the barbarian Africans, who have never in any age or under any circumstances been distinguished by virtues or talents—to be their neighbors and their allies or their enemies.

It cannot be doubted for one moment, which they would choose. It would be a gross injustice to their well known judgment, to entertain the smallest doubt. But, the argument is put to them in this shape, in order to bring them to reflection. Without intending to do a real injury, or to produce any lasting ill consequences, many of the northern citizens, indulge even in the public prints in reflections and reasonings which, if followed out into their consequences, must produce all the ill effects of discontent and rebellion in the minds of these slaves. They are thus sporting with inflammable substances. Let them reflect seriously where that would end, and then pause. The wise and the good should then interpose, and prevent fools from casting about firebrands, which may light up a conflagration, that could not be extinguished without torrents of blood. . . .

If, as we have attempted to show, the slaves can neither be purchased, and transported to other countries, nor emancipated with advantage to themselves, or safety to the whites, there remains no other course, than to retain them in their present condition. Some alterations and improvements can and ought to be made in the plan of treating and managing them.

The present code contains many harsh enactments which are never enforced, and have no other effect than to excite prejudices against us among those who can judge of us only by the provisions of the statute book. It should be revised and adapted to the feelings and habits of the present times; that is, it should be a humane code. The slaves should be put more effectually under the protection of the laws, against abuse and cruelty; and secured absolutely in the enjoyment of an abundant supply of food and cloathing adapted to their condition, with moderate labour, not above their strength. The system, having secured these essential points, should be one of strictness, and of steady superintendance. It is in vain to expect to maintain subordination, without the strong hand of power; and that should be exhibited steadily and uniformly. It must be left to the wisdom of the Legislative body, combining the experience and the judgment of many minds, to prepare, digest, and complete a code adequate to all these objects. But it may be permitted to a private citizen to suggest a few hints for the consideration of others. The great fundamental principle, it is believed, should be, that the slaves should be kept as much confined as possible to agricultural labours. These, so employed, are found to be the most orderly and obedient of the slaves. And now that the foreign admixture of native Africans is absolutely and permanently prohibited by law, and almost wholly so in practice, and that leaven of barbarism which was heretofore continually infused into the mass is thus withheld, there may be a reasonable hope that the descendants, born and bred in the country, may gradually become a docile, and in some degree a civilized people.

There should be no black mechanics or artizans, at least in the cities. These are placed by the nature of their employments, much more from under the eye and inspection of their masters, and they acquire vicious habits injurious to themselves, as well as their owners, and of evil example to other slaves. In the sea-coast towns, often filled with many worthless and idle strangers, from the West-India Islands, the black mechanics, artists, draymen, and wharfingers, are thrown into bad company who infuse false notions and delusive hopes into their minds, which render them dissatisfied with their condition, and prepare them for plots and other mischief.

It is as true as it is trite, that knowledge is power. Education therefore should on no account be permitted. I am aware that this may be considered a hard measure, to close the book of knowledge on the human mind, and shut it out from the delights of learning: Nor would I insist upon it, if it were possible ever to incorporate the black race with the white race, and make one people of them. But as that is impossible, it is a favour to them to keep them in ignorance, and contentment, with their lot. It should be remembered too, that this was the case with the great bulk of mankind from the creation, until the discovery of the art of printing, a few centuries ago; for when all books were manuscript, and were sold for a great deal more than their weight in silver, education was con[f]ined chiefly to the wealthy. The gospel was taught and spread over the whole world by preaching and not by reading; for there were no printed books in those days, and not one man in ten thousand could purchase manuscript books. The slaves also should have no separate place of worship; a station should be appropriated for them in every place of worship used by the whites, where they should be able to see and to hear, and they as well as their masters should be taught the mild doctrines of the gospel, which, whilst they instruct the slave to be obedient, and to serve industriously, for conscience sake, and not as eye servants,[2] teach the master also that he is bound to treat his slaves with gentleness and kindness, and to provide for their comfort, in sickness as well as in health, in infancy, and old age, as well as in the vigor of useful life. Many other regulations will doubtless be framed by the wisdom of the legislature for the double purpose of ensuring kind treatment and complete protection, on the one hand, and for maintaining on the other hand the proper subordination of the slaves. And when our northern brethren are fully satisfied that all has been done which can be done, to ameliorate the condition of these people, consistent with their station, and that no other system can be devised, which is practicable and safe, then they will cease to throw out those reproachful remarks which can do no good, and may do much harm. For we are quite sure that even enthusiasts, who are led away by a morbid feeling of false humanity, would not do evil for its own sake; nor even venture to act on the vile maxim ascribed to the Jesuits, that evil may be lawfully done, that good may come of it,—a maxim which Paschal triumphantly refuted, and which the good feeling and common sense of mankind has banished from society.[3]

We will conclude these hasty sketches of this important subject, by summing up the *argument,* in a few words.

We state then, that the importation and slavery of the blacks was imposed upon us by the British Government, which refused to listen to the petitions of the Colonies against such importations.

That slavery, when the blacks were reduced to that state in this country, was universally considered lawful; and the scriptures no where prohibit slavery. Every power which now denounces it, encouraged and practised it, and particularly Great Britain, France, Spain, and Portugal. Northern capital and shipping were also employed in the trade.

That the slaves cost an enormous sum of money, and are as much the property of their holders, as any other property, of any other owners—and that they cannot be justly or lawfully deprived of this property, but by their own consent, and at a fair and full price.

That the price of 1,500,000 slaves would amount to so enormous a sum of money, as to preclude all hope of the government of the United States being able to pay it, or to provide for the payment of the usual interest of it. And that if it be attempted to make a gradual reduction by annual purchases, the natural annual increase would exceed the annual number and amount which they could purchase.

That if it were possible for the government to purchase and pay for the slaves, they could not be transferred to Africa, but at an enormous and overwhelming expense: and experience shows that such a body of people could not be transported across the ocean without great sufferings, miseries and destruction on the passage, and probably utter annihilation on their arrival in Africa. And that locating them on any part of the North American continent, would not remove the difficulty in any degree.

That the agriculture of the southern states, and the commerce of the northern states, would be deeply injured by the subduction of so much labor from the country.

That emancipation (even admitting the government to be able to purchase the slaves for that purpose) could not be permitted with safety to the whites, and would not in practise, be found beneficial to the blacks. That it would produce jealousies, discontents, civil wars, and the extermination of the one race or the other, who could not live together in amity on terms of equality.

Finally, that as no plan can be devised for getting rid of them, or of emancipating them, they must of necessity remain in their present condition, improved by humane regulations, and wise provisions, adapted to their state. Any other course would be vain and useless, and might be dangerous if not ruinous.

A COLUMBIAN.

1. Henry William DeSaussure (1763–1839), a Federalist attorney, served as mayor of both Charleston and Columbia. In 1803 he helped found the *Charleston Post,* which still exists today as the *Charleston Post and Courier.* Always a Unionist, DeSaussure defended slavery but was publicly critical of Nullifiers, although he remained personally friendly with sectionalist John C. Calhoun, who mentored him in the law. Shortly after the *Chesapeake-Leopard* affair of 1807, DeSaussure was named aide-de-camp to General Thomas Pinckney, and the ideas advanced in his *A Series of Numbers* so resemble those in Pinckney's *Reflections* that historian Lacy Ford suspects that the two pamphleteers corresponded during the writing of their essays. See Lacy K. Ford, *Deliver Us from Evil: The Slavery Question in the Old South* (New York: Oxford University Press, 2009), 240–45.

2. An "eye servant," derived from Colossians 3:22, was a favorite of slaveholders: "Servants, obey in all things your masters according to the flesh; not with eye service, as men pleasers; but in singleness of heart, fearing God."

3. "Paschal" is a variant spelling of "Pascal." DeSaussure appears to be referring to the arguments of the French intellectual Blaise Pascal (1623–1662) in letter XIV of *Lettres provinciales* (1656–57).

Henry William DeSaussure, *A Series of Numbers Addressed to the Public, On the Subject of the Slaves and Free People of Colour* (Columbia, SC, 1822).

Genius of Universal Emancipation

December 1822

"SERVILE CONSPIRACY."

Review of the Letter of Governor Bennett, of South Carolina, relative to the meditated insurrection of the Blacks, near Charleston, in that State.

The Letter of the governor of South Carolina, relative to the late conspiracy among the blacks in that State, was evidently intended to answer a two-fold purpose. The object was, 1st, to allay the fears and anxiety of the white people in the slaveholding States, & more particularly in that section of the country—& 2d, to remove the apprehensions of Foreigners as to the propriety of settling there.

His excellency professes to have given us a true representation of "the occurrences as they have transpired," and assures us "that the attempt has not only been greatly magnified, but as soon as discovered, it ceased to be dangerous."

It will readily be admitted, that, as the plot was discovered in time to secure the ringleaders before it was ripe for execution, it *then* ceased to be dangerous.—But unless we are to suppose, (which for my part I am unwilling to do) that the court proceeded upon the plan of the British government, and created an alarm for the purpose of an excuse to draw the cord of oppression tighter, we must yield to the belief that a great deal of danger really existed. Why were so many executed, & so many banished from the society of their relatives, if this was not the case?—He will, doubtless say that *some cause* existed for such measures, and that to *prevent danger*, an unusual degree of severity was necessary. But I would wish to impress it on his mind, as well as all slaveholders, that this is a very unsafe ground to go upon. It might be supposed that he is sensible of this, for he commences his account of the developement of the plot by saying, that "*A servant prompted by attachment to his master,* communicated to him," &c.—Here is *prima facia* evidence that the safety of the master, in many cases, consists in securing the attachment of the slave; and this we all know can only be done by kind and merciful treatment.

That there was much more danger than the governor would have us to suppose, I infer from the great anxiety manifested upon the occasion, from the relative situation of the different classes, and from the very nature of the system of slavery. The slaves in that section of country are exceedingly numerous; and the mistaken opinion has been generally entertained that to keep them in ignorance, and treat them with severity, is the only means of preserving a proper subordination among them. Shut out from the means of religious or moral improvement; reduced to the lowest and most humiliating state of degradation; compelled to labour without the hope of reward, save the scanty pittance which barely serves to sustain life; and often scourged in the most brutal and unfeeling manner for trivial offences; how could it be expected that under such circumstances they would rest contented?—Although they are debased nearly to a level with brutes, still there is a something in them which cannot be extinguished. It has existed in the human breast ever since the day that "God created Adam." A Nimrod, a Nero, a Caligula, and a thousand others, have strove, in vain, to eradicate it, and it ill becomes a petty tyrant, *professing republicanism,* to make the silly attempt.[1] It is the intellectual vision—the vital spark emanating from Deity, and has its residence in the soul. It is connected with the body in such a way, that neither the inventions of earth or hell can destroy it. Possessed of this, it is impossible for them to be reconciled to their abject condition. They hear, and *understand the meaning,* of the words Liberty, Freedom, &c. which are in every white man's mouth. Many of them are permitted to hear our Fourth of July Orations; and some of them can sing the songs, aye, the *battle songs,* of American warriors. It would be strange indeed, if these things should not have some effect in producing discontent among them; and nothing can prevent its baleful tendency as long as they are denied the benefits of religious instruction, and deprived of the inalienable rights that nature gave.—Hence, I consider it reasonable to suppose that the plot alluded to was extensively and deeply laid, and that its timely discovery, alone, prevented a scene of bloodshed and massacree, at the bare thought of which, humanity would have shuddered. And I further believe, that there will always be more or less of danger, in many parts of our country, on account of the dreadful vassalage of a portion of the inhabitants, until a radical change is effected, and the hell-born monster oppression is completely exterminated. It may be laid down as a maxim, that the bosom of a man who has been deprived of his natural rights, is the seat of enmity, and that he is ever ready to embrace the opportunity of revenging the outrage, unless he is acquainted with the rules of Christianity, and has been taught to "forgive his enemies."

Leaving that part of the letter that is confined to a narration of the circumstances, we come to a passage of rather extraordinary import, and which is particularly calculated to arrest the attention. Speaking of the conduct of one of the conspirators, the governor says:—"Materials were abundantly furnished in the seditious pamphlets brought into this State, by equally culpable incendiaries; while the speeches of the oppositionists in congress to the admission of Missouri, gave a serious and imposing effect to his machinations."—Here we are told that "*seditious pamphlets*" have been published, and "*incendiaries*" employed in distributing them. And further, that certain speeches delivered in Congress, (which are of course also considered *seditious* no doubt) were made use of to promote the insurrection. Why did he not also tell us, that the Declaration of American Independence, (which some of the Europeans think a horribly *seditious* thing) as well as the thousands of speeches, orations, toasts and songs, that are echoed and re-echoed from hill to hill, were used for the same purpose?—This was no doubt the fact; and a particular passage in the venerable Jefferson's Notes on Virginia, was likewise very probably made use of, all of which, together with the writings of Franklin, Rush,[2] and hundreds of others, on slavery, are now to be viewed as *vile,* "SEDITIOUS," and TREASONABLE!!!—But it would not have answered the gentleman's purpose to have brought these things into view. It was his desire to cast a reflection upon some of our Statesmen, in order to counteract the effects of their patriotic exertions relative to the *Missouri Question,* and the occasion was so extremely opportune that he could not let it pass without indulging his favourite wish.

With respect to the "seditious pamphlets" of which he speaks, he has not been sufficiently explicit to enable us to form an idea of their character. So various are the sentiments of different persons, that what some would view in that light, by others is frequently considered quite the reverse. That there may have been unworthy persons employed in circulating mischievous publications, is possible; but we never heard any thing of it until his excellency's vision was brightened by the discovery of a negro plot: consequently it is doubtful whether that occurrence did not magnify, and even transform certain objects, as they passed under his review. It may not be amiss, however, to observe, and I wish every one to lay it to heart, that wherever oppression prevails, there will not only be plottings and insurrectionary efforts, but that there will also be individuals of daring enterprise, in other places, ready to embark in the work of revolution, whenever it may commence. Many will do it in the hope of enriching or aggrandizing themselves, regardless of every tie, religious or moral, that binds man to man, or promotes a feeling of charity and brotherly love. Others will proceed from what they believe to be a sense of duty—from a desire to uphold the principles of liberty; and though the means they use may be in direct violation of Chirstian maxims and precepts, still, they will reconcile it to their consciences as well as they can. This state of things may be looked for until the true light of Christianity shall be more generally shed abroad in the hearts of men. When this shall be the case, the occasion will no longer exist; for not only wars and fightings, but tyranny and oppression of every kind, must then cease.

Before I dismiss the subject, I would advise his Excellency to look *nearer home* for the cause of the meditated insurrection. What, I would ask him, was the cause of a similar attempt, a few years since, near the city of Richmond in Virginia, and also of a still later date, at Petersburgh?—At the former place, so well had they matured their plot, and so completely had they organized their system of operations, that nothing but a seemingly miraculous intervention of the arm of Providence was supposed to have been capable of saving the city from pillage and the flames, & the inhabitants thereof from butchery.[3]—So dreadful was the alarm, and so great the consternation produced upon that occasion, that a member of Congress [John Randolph] from that State was sometime afterwards heard to express himself in his place as follows:—"The night bell is never heard to toll in the city of Richmond, but the anxious mother presses her infant more closely to her bosom."[4]

It will be found, that notwithstanding "Servility long continued, debases the mind, and abst[r]acts it from that energy of character which is fitted to great exploits," still, the combined efforts of such as are verging on the border of despair, and those instigated by motives of avarice, ambition, or revenge, may be productive of the most deplorable consequences; and it becomes a wise man to assist in taking measures to obviate them. This, as I have shewn, can only be completely effected by a general dessemination of the principles of Christianity, and a final eradication of the servile system.

1. Nimrod, according to the Book of Genesis, was the ruthless and power-hungry third son of Noah, who was the first man after the flood to name himself emperor. Nero ruled Rome from 54 to 68 CE and allegedly set fire to Rome in 64 CE. The Roman Emperor Caligula, who governed from 37 to 41 CE, was a megalomaniac given to capricious cruelty.

2. Benjamin Lundy (1789–1839), the Quaker abolitionist who founded the *Genius of Universal Emancipation,* refers to a "particular passage" in Jefferson's *Notes on the State of Virginia.* In response to Query XVIII on "The particular customs and manners that may happen to be received in that state?" he described the relation of slavery as "a perpetual exercise of the most boisterous passions, the most unremitting despotism on the one part, and degrading submissions on the other." Benjamin Franklin (1706–1790) signed the Quaker petition to Congress in 1790 that called for an immediate ban on involvement in the Atlantic slave trade. The physician Benjamin Rush (1746–1813), also of Philadelphia, was an early pamphleteer against slavery and one of the founders of the Pennsylvania Abolition Society. See Richard S. Newman, *The Transformation of American Abolitionism: Fighting Slavery in the Early Republic* (Chapel Hill: University of North Carolina Press, 2002), chaps. 1 and 2.

3. Slaves organized by the enslaved artisan Gabriel (1776–1800) planned to seize Richmond in 1800, but their plan collapsed following a deluge on August 30. Two years later, a less coherent conspiracy begun by Sancho attracted a number of slaves around Petersburg and Virginia's southern counties. For both plots, see Douglas R. Egerton, *Gabriel's Rebellion: The Virginia Slave Conspiracies of 1800 and 1802* (Chapel Hill: University of North Carolina Press, 1993).

4. John Randolph (1773–1833) of Roanoke, Virginia, who was both antislavery and a states' rightist, uttered these words on the floor of the House of Representatives in a memorable speech

on December 10, 1811. See "Foreign Relations," *Annals of Congress,* Twelfth Congress, First Session, 1811–12, esp. 451.

Memorial of James Hamilton Jr. to the Charleston City Council, 1822[1]

To the Honorable the President of the Senate
The Memorial of the City Council of
Charleston respectfully

Sheweth,

That Your memorialists from the opportunities which have been afforded them, of being cognizant of the events of the late conspiracy to raise an insurrection among a portion of the black population of Your Metropholis, are deeply sensible of the many interesting considerations growing out of this transaction, and the various obligations which will arise for the prompt and effected interposition of that supreme authority of which You are possessed in Your Legislative capacity. That you will adapt to the Crisis, those measures which are required for the public safety and its future tranquility and prosperity is an expectation which they feel conscious will not be disappointed,

They beg leave however, respectfully to suggest the policy of Your passing a Law which shall embrace the following provisions—

1 That all free persons of Color who are not natives of the State, and who have come within its limits within ten Years should be compelled to leave the State on such terms and under such modifications as shall be the least oppressive

2 That Slaves and free persons of Color should be interdicted from returning to this State who may hereafter visit any of the non Slaving holding States.

3 That by some wise enactments the number of male slaves be greatly diminished within the Lines comprehending as well our Domestics, handicraft persons and all those who hire themselves out or are hired by their owners,

4 That the Laws now in force be so far amended as to subject to the punishment of Death all white persons who shall be principal Advisers or abettors in any actual projected insurrection of Slaves or free persons of Color, the evidence to substantiate the offence to be the same as in the crimes of Murder Arson & Burglary

5 That as our City is entirely destitute of Buildings capable of affording protection to the arms which belong to it or any means of protected resistance in case of a sudden attack a Citadel ought to be constructed within the Lines for securing the arms, and Capable of Containing a competent force of its defence,

That a Military force of not less than two hundred Men under Martial Law should be organised commanded by experienced Officers, and that their duties and distribution be regulated by such authorities as the Legislature may see fit to appoint

6 That the Legislature appropriate the Land now so comparatively useless as a Tobacco inspection, as a scite for the projected Citadle

In reviewing the incidents of the late plot, Your Memorialists, as a measure obviously connected with the soundest considerations of policy would recommend that those Slaves and free persons of Color who by their fidelity or attachment to the best interest, of the State made important disclosures should be liberally remun[er]ated, that to such previous examples the most distinguished notoriety should be given

It is with this view Your memorialists would beg leave to present the following cases well worthy of Your generous appreciation

Peter the Slave of John C. Prioleau Esquire of Charleston communicated to his master the first intimation of the intended conspiracy and through out the whole transaction has evinced a veracity which has been only equaled by the admirable fidelity which dictated his inestimable Disclosures[2]

Pencel a free Colored Man of the City was consulted by Peter, as to the course which he ought to pursue when burtherned with such a momentous secret, and altho Pencels advice was given at intermediate period previous to the return of Mr. Prioleau to the City but after Peter had communicated to the Son of Mr. Prioleau what he had learnt of the intended insurrection. Your Memorialist conceive that Pencels Counsels were so praiseworthy by so emphatically enforcing the best lessons of fidelity to the Country and attachment to his master and family that he has abundant claims to your generosity and Justice,

A free Colored Man of the name of Scott[3] was principally instrumental in the detection of William Allen[4] who at the late Court of Sessions in Charleston was convicted of having endeavoured to disceminate insurrectionary Doctrines in connection with the conspiracy, but for the disclosures of Scott to the City Authorities and his well executed stratagems by which the Testimony of white persons was procured to the Guilt of Allen his detection could not have taken place and we should have been deprived of the salutary example which flows from his conviction

These three individuals are warmly recommended as fit subjects for Your wise munificence

Your Memorialists further recommend to Your Notice the remaining Criminals in the work House under sentence of Transportation that some Measures may be promptly taken withe the view of carrying ultimately their sentences into effect,

Your Memorialists would beg leave to refer You to Your Board of Public Works for the particulars of the sale made to the state by this Corporation of a most eligable and beautiful Lot for the erection of the Fire proof buildings You have directed to be built in Charleston and ask Your Honorable Body to ratify the Conditions of the previous contract made by Your Memorialist[s] with the Board which is in every respect so advantageous to the State

All of which is respectfully submitted and Your Memorialist[s] as in duty bound will ever pray

By Order of the City Council of Charleston
James Hamilton Jr.
Intendant of the City of Charleston

1. Section 10 of the state constitution of 1790 required the annual meeting of the state legislature to begin "on the fourth Monday of November," which in 1822 would have been November

22. Although undated, the memorial clearly was presented to the General Assembly at the start of their legislative session, and many of the recommendations included here were turned into law.

2. For William Penceel, see Part II, p. 94 n53.

3. On Scott, see Part III, p. 272 n1, and Part V, p. 590 n2.

4. For the trial of Allen, a white man, see Part III, pp. 271–72.

Petitions to the General Assembly, n.d., no. 2059, series S165015, SCDAH.

Charleston *Southern Patriot, and Commercial Advertiser*

Tuesday, December 3, 1822
COLUMBIA, (S.C.) Nov 26

South-Carolina Legislature

SENATE—*Tuesday November 26.*

Petition[s] were presented as follows, viz.—by Mr. Crafts,[1] from Wm. Sims[2] and others, praying compensation for slaves executed for a conspiracy—by the same, from the executors of Joseph Yates,[3] with the same prayer; both referred to a select committee consisting of Messrs Ramsay, Crafts and Moser . . . [4] by Mr Ramsay, from Elizabeth Martin, praying compensation for two slaves executed; referred to the committee on the petitions of Wm. Sims and others, on the same subject—by Mr. Moser, from David Haig, from Neil M'Neil, from Martha R. Garner, and from C. L. Faber, (widow) all praying payment for slaves executed; all referred to the last mentioned committee—by Mr Crafts, from John Robinson, praying payment for slaves executed, referred to the last committee—by the same, from Wm Sims, praying that the state would assume the transportation of his slave, condemned to banishment, and award him his value; referred to the same committee. . . . [5]

1. Attorney William Crafts (1787–1826). See Part III, p. 144 n2.

2. On William Sims, see Part III, p. 229 n1.

3. Joseph Yates, a slaveholding cooper, had died in 1822. In 1820, his wife, Elizabeth, wrote from Charleston to Federalist Senator Harrison Gray Otis (1765–1848), a conspicuous critic of slavery during the Missouri debate, pleading for continued action against "the Evil of Slavery." See letter of September 30, 1820, on pp. 51–55 in Part I.

4. Members of the Senate committee were physician John Ramsay (1768–1828), attorney William Crafts, and Philip Moser (1770?–1835), an antislavery physician who had studied under Benjamin Rush. See *BDSCHR* 5: 216–17; *BDSCHR* 4: 130–31, 415–16.

5. William Sims was the owner of Dick Sims, a wheelwright who was hanged on Friday, July 26, and of Scipio Sims, a carpenter who was transported. Joseph Yates lost three slaves, Bellisle, Naphur, and Adam, all of whom were hanged on July 26. Elizabeth Martin petitioned in behalf of her husband's estate for Denbo. David Haig's Harry died in the Work-House, and Haig's Nero was transported. Neil McNeil's Jack was hanged on Tuesday, July 30, and Martha Garner's William was hanged on Friday, August 9. Catherine Faber's Polydore was hanged on July 26, and John Robinson lost three slaves, John, Adam, and Robert, all of whom were executed on July 26. These petitions are reprinted elsewhere in this volume on pp. 530–35.

Memorial of the City Council, Tuesday, December 3, 1822

TO the Honorable Speaker and House of Representatives
The Memorial of the City Council of Charleston
Respectfully sheweth—

That your memorialists during the late public disturbances in Charleston in relation to the Conspiracy to raise an insurrection among a proportion of our black population were under the necessity of expending sundry sums of money for the apprehension of the conspirators and other contingent expenses which will more ever fully appear by reference to a document herein inclosed marked A. They were likewise constrained to direct that the individuals so apprehended should be held in confinement to await their trials, which confinement in many instances has been continued by sentence of two respectable courts of Freeholders & Magistrates which were convened for the trial The expense attending these confinements in the Work House of Charleston is specifically set forth in exhibit marked B also herein

As these expenses were incurred in the execution of the State Laws, and for purposes in which the whole of our country had an equal concern your memorialists refrain from any further comment on the obvious and irresistible justice of their claim but respectfully request that the amount so expended and for which they are pledged may be refunded and paid to them.

Wm Roach Ju^r^[1] J. Hamilton, Ju^r^
Clerk of Council Intendant of the City of Charleston

Statement of Money expended by the City Corporation of Charleston on Insurgents, in the Months, June, July August & September 1822–Vizt
1822
June 18 p^d^ Col. Prioleaus Man Peter for secret services rendered[2] $200. . . .

1. In 1822, William Roach Jr. (1799–1838) lived at 13 Society Street. He served for years as clerk of the Charleston City Council and would have had an intimate knowledge of the evidence against the Vesey plotters. William Roach Sr. (1759–1823) was not only Charleston's city treasurer, but a deacon in Benjamin Morgan Palmer's Circular Church. See *CSCCD,* 96; *BDSCHR* 4: 482; "Died," Boston *Weekly Messenger,* March 8, 1823.

2. This document reveals that Peter Prioleau (also "Desverney"; ca. 1787–1861), a trusted domestic slave and person of partial African ancestry, not only "communicated to his master the first intimation of the intended conspiracy," but was paid to gather additional information about it. For his role in uncovering the Vesey plot, Peter obtained his freedom and would eventually own slaves himself. Larry Koger, *Black Slaveowners: Free Black Slave Masters in South Carolina, 1790–1860* (Jefferson, NC: McFarland, 1985), 156, 178–79, contends that the free colored elite in Charleston "viewed Peter Desverney as a hero" for disclosing the plot. The view that Charleston's browns betrayed Charleston's blacks in the Vesey affair also found favor with black activist Martin Delany when, as a Union officer, he addressed Charleston's people of color at the end of the Civil War. On Delany's speech, see *New York Herald,* May 22, 1865.

Petition of the City Council of Charleston, December 3, 1822, no. 130, series S165015, SCDAH.

Charleston Mercury, and Morning Advertiser

Wednesday, December 4, 1822
FOR THE MERCURY
NO. 1

MR. EDITOR—In the *City Gazette* of the 11th November, I observe a writer under the signature of *A Planter,* with whom, as to that part of the subject which relates to the City Guard, I do not at all agree; but shall defer answering that part of his essay for the *moment,* it being of minor importance, and proceed to the other part, in which I agree with him so far as I think it absolutely necessary for the safety of our lives and fortunes that this place be secured, in some way or another, from a recurrence of any such evil as that which we have lately witnessed; and therefore, I have no doubt the Legislature will take the subject into their immediate consideration, and grant, forthwith, a levy of a Standing Army, for the protection of the low country in general; and the head-quarters will be fixed at Charleston.

It will, therefore, become necessary to make provisions for lodging them; but as to the Inspection for this purpose, 'tis out of the question. What have barracks, a garrison, a fort, a citadel, or what not, in the very heart of a city? Who ever heard of such a thing? It may be very well to have a Guard-house in Broad-street, another at the Inspection, and a third at the lines; but as to a Fort, a Citadel, in the very heart of a City, 'tis preposterous. . . . [M]y principal subject . . . is the Standing Army; or that part of the Standing Army which it is probable the Legislature will find necessary to raise, and have stationed at Charleston, and the Barracks in which they are to be lodged, or in other words, the Citadel, recommended by the Planter, which is to serve not only for lodging the army, but as a place of refuge for citizens. A CITIZEN

Memorial of the Citizens of Charleston Demanding Harsher Laws

At a moment of anxiety and in a season of deep solicitude, resulting from the recent discovery of a projected insurrection among our colored population, your Memorialists submit to you the following considerations:

Under the influence of mild and generous feelings, the owners of slaves in our state were rearing up a system, which extended many privileges to our negroes; afforded them greater protection; relieved them from numerous restraints; enabled them to assemble without the presence of a white person for the purpose of social intercourse or religious worship; yielding to them the facilities of acquiring most of the comforts and many of the luxuries of improved society; and what is of more importance, affording them means of enlarging their minds and extending their information; a system whose establishment many persons could not reflect on without concern, and whose rapid extension, the experienced among us could not observe but "with fear and trembling," nevertheless, a system which met the approbation of by far the greater number of our citizens, who exulted in what they termed the progress of liberal ideas upon the subject of slavery, whilst many good and pious persons fondly cherished the expectation that our negroes would be influenced in their conduct towards their owners by sentiments of affection and gratitude.

The tranquility and good order manifested for a time among the slaves, induced your memorialists to regard the extension of their privileges, in a favourable light, and to entertain the hope that as they were more indulged, they would become more satisfied with their condition and more attached to the whites.

But in the midst of these promising appearances, whilst the citizens were reposing the utmost confidence in the fidelity of the negroes, the latter were plotting the destruction of the former. A plan was perfected—a corps was organized—arms were collected, and everything arranged to overwhelm us with calamity—a calamity from which we were preserved by the fidelity of a single slave, who disclosed to us a plot, which in its origin, extent and design, may well bear comparison with the most atrocious of the West Indian insurrection schemes. No regard was to be paid to age or sex—no discrimination to be made between the benevolent master and the severe slave-holder, without even respecting the sacred character of our Clergy, who had been assiduous in instructing them in the duties of life, and encouraging them in the pursuit of Heaven; the slaves had resolved to seize on the arsenals, destroy the guard, murder the citizens, and envelope the town in one extended conflagration. The discovery of the plot, but a few days before the period resolved on for its execution, fortunately preserved us from these horrors, and brought many of the conspirators to justice. But although the immediate danger has passed away, yet the causes from which it originated your memorialists conceive to exist in full vigor and activity, and will, as they conscientiously believe, produce, before many years, a series of the most appealing distresses, unless speedily removed by the most resolute and most determined laws. To the enacting of such laws, the attention of the Legislature is solicited by your memorialists, who, after the most attentive investigation into the origin, design and extent of the late projected insurrection—after careful inquiry into the existing evils of our slave system, and after mature reflection on the remedies to be adopted, humbly recommend that laws be passed to the following effects:—

1st. To send out of our State, never again to return, all the free persons of color.

In considering this subject, it naturally resolves itself in two parts: 1st. the evils to be expected from the movements of the free people of color from themselves, and 2nd. those which arise from the influence which the existence of such a class of persons must produce upon our slave system.

In considering first, the evils to be apprehended more immediately from the free people of color themselves, we must consider the relation in which they stand both to the whites and the slaves. They form a third class in our society, enjoying more privileges than the slaves, and yet possessing few of the rights of the master; a class of persons having and exercising the power of moving and unrestrained over every part of the State; of acquiring property, of amassing wealth to an unlimited extent, of procuring information on every subject, and of uniting themselves in associations or societies—yet still a class, deprived of all political rights, subjected equally with slaves to the police regulations for persons of color, and sensible that by no peaceable and legal methods can they render themselves other than a degraded class in your society. Thus it appears that they have sufficient of liberty to appreciate the blessings of freedom; and are sufficiently shackled to be sensible they enjoy comparatively few of those blessings. But it is the very constitution of the human mind, that it desires progress in a ratio proportioned to the increase of its acquisitions; and in no respect is this more observable than in its efforts after freedom. Restraints are always irksome, but restraints on one portion of the community, from which the other are exempt, become doubly so from comparison; it therefore follows from the very nature of things, that the free people of color must be discontented with their situation, and will embrace the first favorable opportunity of attaining all the privileges enjoyed by the whites, and from which, with deep regret, they see themselves cut off. The efforts of men to obtain any given object are always proportioned to the animation of their hopes or the energy of their despair. The negroes will increase with their numbers, and when they shall have equalled the whites, which it can easily be shown will happen before many years have passed, they will expect and claim all the privileges, rights and immunities of citizens, which if denied them, as they must be, they will be driven by despair to obtain by force what cannot be effected in any other way; and then, indeed, will the evil have become of such magnitude as will render it almost impossible to remove it. This naturally leads us to the inquiry of what is the actual, and what is the relative increase of the free persons of color. To simplify the calculation, let us take the increase for the last ten years; In eighteen hundred and ten, there were one thousand six hundred (1680) and eighty free persons of color in the Parishes of St. Michaels and St. Phillips; in eighteen hundred and twenty, but ten years afterwards; they had increased to three thousand (3062) and sixty two; in the same period, the whites had only increased from 13,007 to 14,958, so that whilst the whites increased only a little more than 14 per cent, the free people of color increased about 85 per cent. or, in other words, the whites in ten years have increased about (1/7) one seventh, and the free people of color have nearly doubled—Should the free people of color increase for the next thirty years as they have done for the last ten, in the year one thousand eight hundred and fifty, they will amount to 18,402, whilst the whites will only have amounted to 21,824; so that in thirty years, the whites in the Parishes of St. Philip and St. Michaels will exceed the free persons of color only by 3,422, whilst at this moment they exceed them by 11,896.[1]

This calculation, however, is made upon the most favorable principles for the whites—for if we judge from the evidence afforded by the last ten years, the ratio of increase among the whites is diminishing, whilst that of the free persons of color is increasing.

But there are other causes which must operate upon these relative numbers, and must render the free persons of color in a few years more numerous than the whites—at the same time evincing how dangerous this class must prove, if suffered to remain among us.

The Free people will never emigrate; they have so little to hope for, and so much to dread, from any change of place, that they will adhere to the spot of their nativity, under the pressure of any inconvenience, rather than seek to improve their condition in distant countries. As they multiply, they are bred up to the mechanical arts, or perform such labor as is usually performed by the poorer class of whites; of course they must come in competition with this class, and before the lapse of many years, the quantity of labor will greatly exceed the demand, and employment must be sought where the demand is greater—one class must therefore emigrate; but the free people of color will not emigrate; consequently the whites must; so that as the free people of color are extending their lines, the whites are contracting theirs. This is not mere speculation, but a fact sufficiently exemplified already. Every winter, considerable number of Germans, Swiss and Scotch arrive in Charleston, with the avowed intention of settling among us, but are soon induced to emigrate towards the west, by perceiving most of the mechanical arts performed by free persons of color. Thus we learn, that the existence of this class among us, is in the highest degree detrimental to our safety.

But in another point of view, the residence of free negroes among us, is pregnant with evils, evils arising from the influence which the existence of such a class of persons must have upon our slave system.

The superior condition of the free persons of color, excites discontent among our slaves, who continually have before their eyes, persons of the same color, many of whom they have known in slavery, and with all of whom they associate on terms of equality—freed from the control of masters, working where they please, going whither they please, and expending their money how they please—the slave seeing this, finds his labor irksome; he becomes dissatisfied with his state, he pants after liberty! A liberty he can never hope to acquire by purchase or faithful services, for the Legislature has deemed it expedient to close the door against emancipation, his only chance for freedom is to combine with others and endeavor to incite an insurrection; an insurrection which offers to the free colored man as many temptations as to the slave—for as the slave is desirous of being on equality with him, so he likewise is desirous of being placed on the same footing with the whites. It is therefore the interest of the free persons of color, to cherish the spirit of discontent among the slaves, as they hope to avail themselves of their assistance to promote their own schemes of ambition. There is identity of interest between the slave and the free person of color, whilst there is none between the latter class and the whites; but there is not only an identity of interest, but also an identity of feeling among the colored people of both descriptions—they are associated by color, connected by marriages, and by friendships, Many of the free negroes have parents, brothers, sisters and children, who are slaves; should an insurrection occur, they would have every inducement to join it; they would be distrustful of the whites, and the whites would be naturally distrustful of them; they would therefore carry over to slaves their intelligence and numbers, and would serve as channels for communication between slaves of the different portions of the state. But it may be remarked, that in the late projected insurrection, very few of the free people of color were engaged—let it however, not be forgotten, that Denmark Vesey was a free person; he who projected and planned the insurrection; who was the leader of the conspirators, and the most active in collecting the materials.—Had he not been free, it would have been impossible for him to communicate so extensively with the slaves in the country, without whose co-operation, the slaves in the city would not have dared to make the attempt to emancipate themselves.

But it is said, great inconvenience will result to the free persons of color, and we ought not to inflict so much distress on an innocent race of persons. Your memorialists are aware of the inconvenience to which the free persons of color will be subjected if compelled to emigrate. But they are sensible that a partial evil must frequently be tolerated for the promotion of the general welfare, and the only inquiry to be made is, whether the good to be received by the state, exceeds any evil which can possibly arise to the free people of color. Now your memorialists conceive there is no comparison between them; the evils which the free people of color will experience, must in its very nature, be temporary. In a few years they will have acquired new habits, found out new channels of industry, and formed new connections—whilst those remaining amongst us, will be a source of continual apprehension to the whites; of continual discontent to the slaves, and sooner or later, the inevitable cause of disastrous and bloody commotion in our state.

It becomes us, however painful it may prove, to sacrifice feeling to reason, and mistaken compassion to a stern policy, and expel from our territory every free person of color, that we may extinguish at once every gleam of hope which the slaves may indulge of ever being free—and that we may proceed to govern them on the only principle that can maintain slavery, the "principle of fear."

2nd, your Memorialists are decidedly of opinion, that the number of negroes to be hired out, should be limited by law, and that no negro should be allowed to work as a mechanic unless under the immediate control and inspection of his master.[2] By far the greater portion of negroes who work out, are released in a considerable degree from the controul of their masters—laboring or forebearing to a labour, as their interest or inclination prompts, rendering unto their owners, only a monthly account; and provided they but settle the wages with punctuality are permitted to regulate their own conduct; the consequence is, they assemble together whenever they wish, and having their time at their own disposal, can be convened at any given and fixed period, and having regular and stated meetings, can originate, prepare and mature their own plans for insurrection. Whereas, the slaves who are kept in the yards of their masters, are immediately under their eyes, and cannot fix upon a period of assembling—they know not at what hour they may be called for by their owners, or for how long a period they may obtain leave of absence—they cannot, therefore, act in concert and "concert is the very life of a conspiracy."

But there is another consideration. The facility of obtaining work is not always the same. At one period the demand for labor is considerable; at another the demand is comparatively small; the consequence is, the labor of the slaves hired out is very irregular, and a quantity of time is consumed in idleness. Irregularity of habits is thus acquired; this irregularity produces restlessness of disposition, which delights in mischief and detests quiet. The same remarks will apply to the negro mechanics, who having a stated portion of labor to perform, are masters of the remainder of the day, when the work is ended. The time in the evenings, and on the Sabbath is so entirely at their disposal, that the most ample opportunity is afforded of forming combinations and devising schemes. Should a law be passed limiting the number of slaves to be hired out and confining the exercise of the mechanical arts to white persons (except in the case above specified) the result will be that a large portion of the black population now in the city, will be removed into the country, and their places be supplied by white laborers from Europe and the

Northern States. In this manner we will exchange a dangerous portion of our population for a sound and healthy class of persons "whose feelings will be our feelings, and whose interests our interest."

The late intended Insurrection forcibly proves the truth of the above remarks; for with a very few exceptions, the negroes engaged in that conspiracy were mechanics or persons working out. Great inconvenience, perhaps even considerable misery, may be experienced by many worthy citizens, who at present are maintained by the hire of their slaves. But to obtain important objects by effecting considerable change or reform, great sacrifices must be made, and great difficulties encountered. This is an affair in which temporizing expedients will avail nothing. We must meet the difficulties with resolution, and overcome them by the most vigorous and determined course of action. They are difficulties which, if eluded now, will meet us again in their progress, multiply and crowd upon us until we are involved in confusion and disorder.

3rd. Your memorialists also recommend to the Legislature to prescribe the mode in which our persons of color shall dress.—Their apparel had become so expensive as to tempt the slaves to dishonesty; to give them ideas not consistent with their conditions; to render them insolent to the whites, and so fond of parade and show as to cause it extremely difficult to keep them at home. Your memorialists therefore recommend that they be permitted to dress only in coarse stuffs, such as coarse woolens or worsted stuffs for winter—and coarse cotton stuffs for summer—felt hats, and coarse cotton handkerchiefs. Every distinction should be created between the whites and negroes, calculated to make the latter feel the superiority of the former. It is not the intention of your memorialists to embrace in these sumptuary regulations "livery servants," as liveries however costly, are still badges of servitude. The object is to prevent the slaves from wearing silks, satins, crapes, lace, muslins, and such costly stuffs, as are looked upon and considered the luxury of dress.

4th. The next topic to which your memorialists would invite the attention of the Legislature, is the organization of a regular, efficient military force, in lieu of the City Guard, as at present constituted. The City Guard, as now organized, are of little benefit to the city. Most of them are shop-keepers or retailers of spirituous liquors to the negroes. It is therefore their interest and it is notorious that this interest induces them to permit such of the negroes as are their customers, to pass unmolested through our streets after the bell has rung, and the watch has set. Independently of this circumstance, the members of the Guard are employed in some occupation throughout the day, and when night comes are totally incapacitated from serving at sentinels. In such a city as ours, where there is a large slave population, we should be extremely vigilant; a regular well disciplined force, well officered, and distinct from the body of the citizens, generally, should be kept on duty night and day. It is of equal importance to the city and country that such a body be organized, for insurrections, though they may break out on the plantations, must necessarily have their origin in the city. We should always act as if we had an enemy in the very bosom of the State, prepared to rise upon and surprise the whites, whenever an opportunity be afforded.

5th. It is further recommended by your memorialists that a law be passed, preventing persons of color from holding real property. Many of them are becoming rich, and some of them are already owners of plantations. It is impossible to calculate the evil which may arise from any number of these people possessing extensive plantations. Living in the country, they must, in a great measure, be removed from the vigilance of the whites. They can harbour any number of runaway negroes; their plantations may become the rendezvous of the desperate and discontented among the slaves, and having within themselves the means of support, they may carry on their schemes of destruction, without any likelihood of detection. Neither should they possess real estate in the city, as it will enable them to become landlords to many white persons, who lease from them lands and houses. *Now* the laws respecting landlords and tenants are such, that unless the tenant be punctual in the payment of his rents, it places great power in the hands of the landlord,—a power which should never be permitted to those who, by the laws and policy of our State, are considered a degraded and inferior class.

6th. Your memorialists have viewed with deep regret the influx into Carolina of slaves from the middle states. These slaves are of the most worthless and abandoned characters, taken out of the jails and houses of correction; the greater portion are criminals, whose punishments are commuted into banishment. Yet this degraded and villainous body of negroes are continually pouring in upon us—mingling with our colored population, and contaminating the minds of our most valuable domestics. Your memorialists therefore most earnestly entreat the Legislature to make the bringing of slaves into our state highly penal.

7th. It is deemed requisite to prevent negroes from residing upon premises where no white persons reside. It is our policy to place the slaves under the inspection of their masters as much as possible, and every care should be taken to prevent their association and leagueing together.

8th. Your memorialists consider the laws now in force, so far as they relate to white persons concerned in insurrections of the slaves, extremely defective, as those laws only extend to white persons assisting the negroes in a state of actual insurrection—whereas it is equally criminal to incite the slaves to insurrection. Your memorialists therefore recommend that the laws now in force be so far amended as to subject to the punishment of death all white persons who shall be principals, advisers or abettors in any actual or projected insurrection of the slaves.

And we recommend that a law be passed, prohibiting under severe penalties, all persons from teaching negroes to read and write.

With these observations and recommendations, it remains only to add the hopes of your memorialists, that on a subject of such deep and extensive concern, such measures may be adopted as are calculated to afford protection to our property and security for our lives.

1. According to US Census data from 1790 to 1820, South Carolina's free colored population was growing, but only as a tiny percentage of the total population. In 1790, 1,801 free persons of color amounted to 0.7 percent of the state's total population of 249,073. In 1820, 6,826 free persons of color amounted to 1.4 percent of the total population of 502,741. In Charleston in 1790, 586 free persons of color amounted to 3.6 percent of the city's total population of 16,359. In 1820, 1,475 free

persons of color amounted to about 6 percent of the total population of 24,780. See E. Horace Fitchett, "The Origin and Growth of the Free Negro Population of Charleston, South Carolina," *JNH* 26 (1941): 435.

2. Contrary to law but in accord with custom, many slaves, whether hired by the day, month, or year, enjoyed the freedom to negotiate their own deals as long as they resulted in the return to the master of a stipulated sum at an agreed upon time. Before 1822, a number of laws dating as far back as the Negro Act of 1740 had attempted to regulate the practice of slave self-hire. See Harlan Greene, Harry S. Hutchins, and Brian E. Hutchins, *Slave Badges and the Slave-Hire System in Charleston, South Carolina, 1783–1865* (Jefferson, NC: McFarland, 2004).

"Memorial of the Citizens of Charleston to the Senate and House of Representatives of the State of South Carolina [Charleston, 1822]," in Ulrich B. Phillips, ed., *Plantation and Frontier Documents: 1649–1863 Illustrative of Industrial History in the Colonial & Ante-Bellum South,* 2 vols. (Cleveland: A. H. Clark, 1909), vol. 2: 103–16.

Charleston *City Gazette and Commercial Daily Advertiser*

Wednesday, December 4, 1822

THE GOVERNOR"S MESSAGE.—We have been asked several questions concerning the nature, spirit, and final disposal of the Executive MESSAGE, No. 2.—We can only answer that we understand, its nature was (as implied in the Message No. 1.) a detail of the late insurrection among our slaves; and its *spirit* pretty nearly that of the *Circular*[1] which was published some time ago in Georgetown. Its language and the opposition it displayed to the acts and publication of the Court of Magistrates appointed upon that interesting occasion by our City Council, gave great offence not only to those members of the Legislature whose conduct was immediately involved, but to the body generally. After its being read, a profound silence ensued; when, upon a suggestion made that the Message, No. 2, should be printed, it was moved and seconded that it should remain unpublished, as being unsupported by the feelings and opinions of the house, as reflecting unworthily on the honorable Court representing the City of Charleston in the affair alluded to: and as containing a view of the late unfortunate transaction not borne out either by law or the evidence. In this motion the house concurred. The Message No. 2 accordingly remained on Thursday, Friday and Saturday *sub silentio.* It is uncertain what order the House will hereafter take upon a document possessing such electoral materials.

1. Governor Bennett's circular of August 10, 1822, is reproduced on pp. 467–71 above.

Providence *Gazette*

Wednesday, December 4, 1822

The interested slave holders in Charleston (S.C.) have prepared a memorial addressed to the State Legislature, praying for remuneration for the loss of their slaves, who were executed for the late attempted insurrection in that State!

Claims Against the State, Friday, December 6, 1822

. . . The Committee on Claims to whom was referred the memorial of the City Council of Charleston, asking to be refunded a sum of money expended by it in the apprehension of certain persons charged with attempting to raise an insurrection in Charleston.

Beg leave to report that they have had the memorial and documents under consideration and find that there were many free persons of colour and slaves in Charleston, under a charge of attempting to raise an insurrection in that city. That great delay was unavoidably attendant on this investigation of the charge against [*illegible*] many individuals implicated [*illegible*] expense occurred [*illegible*] and the apprehension of all such as were supposed to be aiding & abetting in the said conspiracy.

The Committee therefore respectfully recommend that the account of the Master of the Work house[1] for receiving & keeping in confinement such of the said conspirators as were committed & his charge amounting to Eight Hundred and ninety four dollars, thirty one and one quarter cents be paid. . . .

Thomas Carr[2]

1. During the Vesey proceedings, Aeneas S. Reeves (1787–1822) was master of the Work-House. He resided at 1 Lynch Street. The *Lineage Book National Society of the Daughters of the American Revolution* (Washington, DC, 1897), vol. 22: 295, errs in dating Reeves's death in 1824. See "Notice," Charleston *City Gazette and Commercial Daily Advertiser,* January 13, 1823, and *CSCCD,* 96.

2. Thomas Carr (d. 1827), a planter with more than forty slaves in 1820, represented Prince George Winyah (Georgetown) in the twenty-fifth state assembly. See *BDSCHR* 5: 44–45.

Report of Legislative Committee, December 6, 1822, no. 159, series S165005, SCDAH.

Governor Thomas Bennett Jr. to State Legislature, Friday, December 6, 1822[1]

Message No. 10

. . . An uncertainty as to the constitutional power of the Executive to appoint a day of thanksgiving and prayer to Almighty God, has alone induced me to delay what has been as feelingly urged by my own sense of duty as by the highest recommendation. It would now be acceptable to our fellow citizens, accord with our sacred obligations, and meet the approbation of Him, whose infinite majesty can be estimated only by the boundless creation. If the preservation of health, and the inestimable blessings of uninterrupted prosperity and security ought to elicit gratitude, the debt is ours, I earnestly recommend the appointment of this grateful day.

In the distressing exigencies which have given a peculiar character to the period of my administration, I guarded with anxiety the welfare of the State. The terrible example cannot fail to convince the world that we have within ourselves energy to arrest sedition, and sufficient force to put down anarchy. The avenging sword was not returned into its sheath, until by the most irrefragable evidence, I saw that Justice herself was satisfied. When it became evident that public and ignominious punishment had exhausted its terrors, the exercise of mercy was at once consistent with duty and policy. I well know that even then my motives were impugned, my conduct injuriously arraigned, and the worst dispositions imputed to me: but the consciousness of having discharged my duty to God and my country efficiently, persuade me, that at that tribunal where the searcher of hearts will expose and I trust vindicate my motives; it will be found that I have done justice and loved mercy. . . .

1. Bennett's valedictory message to the state was published in its entirety in the *Washington Gazette*, December 20, 1822.

Message No. 10 to the State Legislature, December 6, 1822, RGA, GM, 1324, SCDAH.

Charleston Mercury, and Morning Advertiser

Saturday, December 7, 1822

Extract of a letter from Columbia, dated December 3, 1822.

"A petition was presented to the Lower House this morning by Mr Dunkin[1] from Amos Cruckshanks, a free man of colour, of Charleston, when an objection was made against receiving a petition from a free man of colour and after some debate it was thrown out. . . ."[2]

1. In 1822 Benjamin Faneuil Dunkin (1792–1874), a Harvard-educated teacher who became an attorney, operated a law office at 69 Meeting Street.

2. *CSCCD*, 76, identifies Amos Cruickshanks (also "Cruckshanks") as a free colored painter, who lived at 67 Boundary Street. He was one of the leaders of Charleston's AME Church and in late 1822 emigrated to Philadelphia with Morris Brown, Charles Corr, and Henry Drayton. Cruickshanks's petition to the state house caused a stir as legislators debated whether they should even receive a petition from a free person of color. The petition was eventually thrown out. See *Charleston Mercury, and Morning Advertiser*, December 7, 1822, and Daniel Alexander Payne, *History of the African Methodist Episcopal Church* (Nashville, TN, 1891), 14, which is excerpted later in this section on pp. 703–4.

Governor Thomas Bennett Jr. to the Senate of South Carolina, Monday, December 9, 1822

. . . I hasten to comply with your request calling for information relative to the detachment of State Militia ordered out for the purpose of arresting several runaway slaves in the Parishes adjacent to Charleston.

It appears from various communications made by respectable citizens of John's Island[1] that a number of armed fugitive slaves were infesting that Parish, destroying the cattle, breaking into and robbing the dwellings, and threatening the lives of their most faithful domestics. On receiving this information I deemed it expedient to order Capt Jos: Jenkins[2] who commanded that Beat to attempt their apprehension. The order was promptly obeyed, and with as much secrecy as the nature of the service permitted, Capt Jenkins arrived at their camp before their fires were extinguished and but a few moments after they had left it. This vigilant officer continued the pursuit for two days and nights and until he had received information that they had fled from his precinct. Col:

Cattell[3] minutely acquainted with the topography of St Andrew's where it was represented that they had resumed their depredations was requested to institute an enquiry into the facts and suggest a more successful mode of apprehending them. . . .

Another detachment under the command of Capt: Huggins[4] were in obedience to the Militia Laws of this State engaged in a similar service. The daring and atrocious murderer of Mr. Ford[5] of Georgetown had fled for concealment to the swamps of the Santee. . . .

1. Johns (also "John's") Island, South Carolina's largest sea island, lies to the southwest of Charleston, separated from James Island by the Stono River. See Charles F. Kovacik and John J. Winberry, *South Carolina: A Geography* (Boulder, CO: Westview Press, 1987), 23–24.

2. Joseph Daniel Jenkins commanded the Beat Company of John and Wadmalaw Islands. See Jenkins's 1824 petition, no. 61, series S165015, SCDAH.

3. Colonel William Cattell (1776–1842) was a wealthy planter from St. Andrew Parish. See *BDSCHR* 4: 103–4; Charleston *Southern Patriot,* April 29, 1842.

4. Captain Charles Huggins (1792?–1849), a planter in lowcountry Georgetown, had been elected sheriff of the district during the summer of 1822. See Camden (SC) *Southern Chronicle,* June 11, 1822; *BDSCHR* 5: 131.

5. On the killing of planter George Ford in 1821 by a runaway slave, see p. 529 n2, in this section.

RGA, GM, 1325, SCDAH.

Justice William Johnson to Thomas Jefferson, Tuesday, December 10, 1822

. . . I have now passed my Half-century, and begin to feel lonely among the Men of the present Day. And I am sorry to tell you, particularly so in this Place. This last summer has furnished but too much cause for shame and anguish. I have lived to see what I really never believed it possible I should see,—Courts held with closed Doors, and Men dying by scores who had never seen the Faces nor heard the Voices of their Accusers. I see that your Governor[1] has noticed the alarm of insurrection which prevailed in this Place some Months since. But be assured it was nothing in comparison with what it was magnified to. But you know the best way in the World to make them tractable is to frighten them to Death; and to magnify danger is to magnify the claims of those who arrest it. Incalculable are the evils which have resulted from the exaggerated Accounts circulated respecting that Affair. Our Property is reduced to nothing—strangers are alarmed at coming near us; our slaves rendered uneasy; the confidence between us and our Domestics destroyed—and all this because of a trifling cabal of a few ignorant pennyless unarmed uncombined Fanatics, and which certainly would have blown over without an explosion had it never come to light. Our Governor has so represented it in his Message No. 2 but the Shame of Some & the Interest of Others I expect prevent its Publication.

When the Court of Magistrates and Freeholders who tried the Slaves implicated, were pursuing that course of sitting in conclave and convicting them upon the secret ex parte Examination of slaves without oath, whose names were not I believe revealed even to the

Owners of the accused, the Governor, whose feeling revolted at this unprecedented & I say illegal mode of Trial, consulted the Attorney General (the Gentleman lately elected Senator)[2] on the legality of their proceedings, and you will be astonished to hear that he gave a direct Opinion in favour of it. If such be the law of this country, this shall not long be my country. But I will first endeavor to correct the Evil. . . .

1. Thomas Mann Randolph Jr. (1768–1828), the twenty-first governor of Virginia, was also Jefferson's kinsman and son-in-law, having married his eldest daughter, Martha. See Noble Cunningham, *In Pursuit of Reason: The Life of Thomas Jefferson* (Baton Rouge: Louisiana State University Press, 1988), 134. Randolph recalled Gabriel's plot (1800) in Richmond, and the recent events in Charleston led him to express his "determination" to meet the threat of insurrection in his state in a message to the state legislature. See "Governor Randolph," *Portsmouth* (NH) *Journal of Literature and Politics,* December 14, 1822.

2. Robert Young Hayne.

Thomas Jefferson Papers, Series 1. General Correspondence, 1651–1827, LC.

Dr. John Righton[1] to South Carolina House of Representatives, December 10, 1822

. . . That your Petitioner in consequence of his Office had been in attendance on the convicts in the Work House of Charleston who were engaged in the late insurrection. That from the twentieth of July to the thirtieth of November he has given his time and professional services to them without receiving any compensation. . . . Your Petitioner would beg leave to call your attention to the annexed accounts—the first from the twentieth of July to the thirtieth of September amounting to One Hundred and thirty Nine Dollars—and the second from the first of October to the thirtieth of November amounting to One Hundred and forty Dollars Eighty Seven Cents. . . .

1822		
July 20	to a visit and mixture for *Billy Bulkley*	$2.00 . . .
November 1st	. . . bleeding, and powder for *Pero Strohecker*	$2.50 . . . [2]

1. In 1823 the state legislature authorized the payment of $353.43 to Dr. John M. Righton, physician of the Work-House, for his medical services while attending incarcerated slaves during the Vesey trials. His petition describes surgical and medicinal treatments of various kinds to twenty-four slaves: Billy Bulkley, Sam Barrestine, John Vincent, Henry Butler, Lewis Cromwell, Adam Merrill, Nero Haig, Scipio Sims, Frank Ferguson, George Vanderhorst, Seymour Kundhardt, Agrippa Perry, Paris Ball, George Bampfield, Monday Gell, Dublin Morris, "Pero" (Perault) Strohecker, Jack Cattel, Abraham Poyas, Charles Drayton, John Enslow, Billy Robertson, Harry Haig, and "Dumbow" (Denbow) Martin.

2. Billy Bulkley, a rope maker owned by Stephen Bulkley, and Perault Strohecker, a blacksmith owned by John Strohecker, were both transported out of the state.

No. 121, series S165015, SCDAH.

Charleston Mercury, and Morning Advertiser

Tuesday, December 10, 1822

FROM COLUMBIA . . . "The Citadel and Guard Bill will probably have a hard struggle. No order has been made on the negroes to be exported. The Governor's second Message[1] has been disposed of by an indefinite postponement—there was some warm language upon the occasion."

1. The reporter here refers to Governor Thomas Bennett Jr.'s message to the state legislature of November 29, 1822, which appears in this section on pp. 538–50.

Charleston Courier

Wednesday, December 11, 1822

PRIVATE CORRESPONDENCE.

"COLUMBIA, DEC. 7.—A Bill has been reported by the Charleston Delegation, for the purpose of rewarding three of the Negroes who gave information of the late intended insurrection. A Bill has also been reported, which provides for the sending away all Free Negroes and Persons of Color, who have come into this State within the last five years.—A joint committee of both houses agreed on the evening of the 6th inst. to recommend the sum of $100,000 to be appropriated towards erecting an Arsenal and Citadel at the Tobacco Inspection, for the further protection of Charleston. . . ."

New-York Commercial Advertiser

Thursday, December 12, 1822

Legislature of South Carolina—the late meditated insurrection of the Blacks.—A letter from Columbia, S.C. of the 27th of November, published in the Charleston Mercury, states, among other things, that Gov. Bennett's second Message, upon the subject of the late insurrection in that city, was considered by many as touching harshly upon the citizens of Charleston, and especially upon the characters of the gentlemen of the Court, who were organized for the trial of the insurgents—much excitement in the House was the consequence, and we learn that the warmth of the several parties had not abated when the last advices left Columbia. It was hoped, however, that moderation and propriety would soon become ascendant, and full harmony be restored.

Charleston *City Gazette and Commercial Daily Advertiser*

Thursday, December 12, 1822

LEGISLATIVE. A BILL . . . *To establish a competent Military Force for the protection of Charleston and its vicinity and the preservation of the Arms and Munitions of War, there located.* . . . That the house and buildings now used as a Tobacco Inspection in

Charleston be, and the same are hereby appropriated for an arsenal and guard house, and that the same be forthwith fortified according to the rules of military art, so as to be proof against any probable force that may be brought against it: that it be so constructed as to contain a garrison of two hundred men, and in emergencies, of one to two thousand, including quarters for officers. Also, an arsenal and workshops for the safe keeping and preservation of five thousand stand of small arms, and other weapons and equipments for infantry and cavalry, and a due proportion of artillery; and also, a magazine sufficient to contain ammunition for any ordinary occasion. . . .

Charleston Courier

Saturday, December 14, 1822

S. CAROLINA LEGISLATURE

IN SENATE.

Friday, December 6.

. . . The report of the joint committee, to whom was referred the petition of Wm. Sims and others, praying payment for slaves executed, was then considered and agreed to, and ordered to be sent to the House of Representatives, as follows:—That they have met with the committee of the House of Representatives, had a conference with them, and have agreed on the following joint report: That in all cases where executions have taken place, that the owners of said slaves receive the sum now allowed by law. . . . [1]

HOUSE OF REPRESENTATIVES, Friday, December 6

. . . Mr. HAMILTON, from the same committee to whom was referred the memorial of the City Council of Charleston, on the late disturbance in that place; reported a bill for the remuneration of Peter, of George, of Pincell, and of—Scott,[2] and for the compensation of the owners of certain slaves now under sentence of transportation; and to provide for the expense of sending said slaves beyond the U. States.

Mr. HAMILTON, from the special committee to whom was referred sundry petitions from Charleston, for compensation for slaves executed for being concerned in the attempted insurrection at that place, reported a bill to provide for the compensation of those persons whose slaves have been executed, and of certain other persons whose slaves have suffered by the judgment of the law; read the said bills severally a first time, and ordered to a second reading to-morrow. . . .

The report of the special committee on the subject of negro slavery, was ordered to lie on the table, and be printed.

1. William Sims (1765–1833), a planter, was the owner of Dick, a wheelwright who was hanged on Friday, July 26, and of Scipio, a carpenter who was transported.

2. "Peter" refers to Peter Prioleau (Desverney); "Pincell" refers to William Penceel. "Scott" was a free black who gave testimony in the trial of Scotsman William Allen. According to the *OR*, he was known only by that name. No free black with that surname appears in the *DSGCC*.

Charleston *Southern Intelligencer*

Saturday, December 14, 1822

Legislature of South-Carolina . . . Nothing more than the renumeration now allowed by law, can be obtained from the legislature, for the slaves executed in this city last summer.

. . . A bill is before the Legislature for rewarding three negroes, who gave information of the late intended insurrection, and another, for sending away all free negroes, who have come into this state within the last five years.

It is as yet uncertain whether the State will assume, the transportation of the slaves condemned to exile. . . .

Charleston Courier

Tuesday, December 17, 1822

HOUSE OF REPRESENTATIVES.

Monday, December 9.

. . . The House having proceeded to the special order of the day, took up for a second reading, a bill to prohibit the bringing of slaves into this state, for sale, barter or exchange, and for the better regulation and government of free negroes and persons of color, and for other purposes.

On the question, will the House agree to the first clause of the said bill, the yeas and nays were required, and were as follows, viz:

YEAS . . . 52.

NAYS . . . 61.

So the clause was rejected. . . .

Salem *Gazette*

Tuesday, December 17, 1822

Gov Bennett, of South Carolina, in his message to the Legislature,[1] speaks of the late insurrection among the Blacks in such terms, as to give great offence, so that a vote was passed not to publish it.[2]

1. This refers to the governor's Message No. 2, delivered on November 29, 1822.
2. This information was reprinted verbatim in the Providence *Gazette*, December 21, 1822.

Charleston Courier

Wednesday, December 18, 1822

Extract of a Letter to the Editor of the So. Patriot. "Columbia, Dec. 14.—We have now entered seriously into business, and the House continues in session every day until a late hour. We were engaged the whole of yesterday in discussing the "Bill to prohibit the introduction of slaves in this state, for sale, barter or exchange, and for the better regulation and government of free persons of color in this state." The second clause, preventing slaves being brought in, when acquired by inheritance or devise, was lost by a large majority; and the third clause, which prevents any slave who may have left, or may hereafter leave the state, from returning, was stricken. . . . Mr. Dunkin[1] introduced a clause, affixing a tax of $50 per annum on all free negroes and persons of color, within this state, who may not be natives of the state, and shall not have resided therein five years next before the passing of this act; the yeas and nays being taken, it was lost by a majority of two—and the House adjourned. This morning the House resumed the consideration of the bill to prohibit slaves, &c. and on motion of Mr. Warren,[2] seconded by Mr. Steedman,[3] (both having previously voted with the majority) the House agreed to re-consider the clause introduced by Mr. Dunkin, when Mr. Mason[4] moved to amend it, by introducing the words "Males, between the ages of 15 and 50"[5]—which was agreed to. Mr. Steedman moved to amend, by adding after the word act, "And in default of payment, the said free persons of color shall be dealt with in the same manner as free persons of color emigrating into this state, as prescribed by the act passed in this year 1820."[6] Thus amended, the clause was agreed to by a vote of 72 to 35. . . .

1. Lawyer Benjamin F. Dunkin (1792–1874) represented the Perry family in the trial of the slave Agrippa. See Part III, p. 230.

2. Colonel Samuel Warren (1761–1841) lost a leg in the American Revolution. In 1822, he owned a plantation with dozens of slaves in the Pendleton District. See *BDSCHR* 3: 747–49, and "Death of Col. Samuel Warren," *Charleston Courier*, December 5, 1841.

3. Charles John Steedman (1783–1838), a big planter in St. James Santee Parish, would likely have known Denmark Vesey because his father-in-law Captain John Blake was Captain Joseph Vesey's partner. See Part I, p. 6 n2, and *BDSCHR* 4: 538–39.

4. Archy Mayson (1777?–1823) represented the Edgefield District, where at the time of his death he owned more than twenty slaves. See *BDSCHR* 4: 388–89.

5. During the early republic and beyond, the age of fifteen was often seen as a marker for the coming of age of young men, a time when they crossed into maturity and were capable of bearing arms. The Federalist Alien Enemies Law (1798), for example, made "males of the age of fourteen years and upwards" liable for removal. Soon after the Louisiana Purchase, the Territory of Orleans territorial legislature prohibited free colored males aged fifteen years or older from entering the territory.

6. On the law of 1820, see Part I, pp. 61–63.

Charleston Mercury, and Morning Advertiser

Wednesday, December 18, 1822

. . ."To-day[1] the House adopted two amendments to the bill for the regulation &c. of free persons of colour—the one enacts that all free male negroes or persons of colour, between the ages of 15 and 50 years, shall be liable to a tax of fifty dollars—the non-payment of which will subject them to the penalties of the act of December 1820, relative to free negroes, &c. The other amendment enacts, that all free persons of colour, &c. brought into the State, on board of vessels, serving as cooks, mariners, &c. shall be confined in jail until the vessels depart. The House refused to agree to a clause restricting the number of slaves to be hired out. The clause prohibiting male slaves being hired to negroes was adopted; also one compelling free male negroes, &c. above the age of 15 to have guardians, and to give security for their good behaviour, on or before the first day of June next. Aiders, &c. of Slaves and others to raise an insurrection in the State are to be liable to the punishment of death. . . .

1. Saturday, December 14, 1822.

Charleston Mercury, and Morning Advertiser

Thursday, December 19, 1822

House of Representatives. *Monday, Dec. 9.* . . . By permission, pursuant to notice Mr. Harrison[1] introduced a bill to repeal so much of an act passed in the year 1740,[2] as allows compensation to the owners of slaves executed.

1. Thomas Harrison (1790–1835) was a slaveholding attorney who represented the Pendleton District in the northwestern upcountry of South Carolina. See *BDSCHR* 5: 123.

2. The Negro Act of 1740, see Part I, pp. 110–131, esp. 116.

George Logan[1] to Caesar A. Rodney,[2] Thursday, December 19, 1822

. . . I wrote to you in July last, at a period when much agitation prevailed, in consequence of a contemplated insurrection of the blacks in this City—of the distressing circumstances connected with its suppression, you have already been informed, a more painful degree of anxiety has never before, been experienced here; our Legislature now in session will adopt every measure suited to the Crisis but I fear sometime will elapse before the threatened evil will be ef[f]aced, and confidence restored between our wretched Slaves & their owners. . . .

1. George Logan Jr. (1778–1861), a Charleston physician, resided in 1822 at 22 Beaufain Street. See *CSCCD,* 87; George William Logan, *A Record of the Logan Family of Charleston, South Carolina* (Sacramento, 1874), 26, 30–32.

2. Logan's correspondent, Caesar Augustus Rodney (1772–1824), was at the time an antislavery Democratic-Republican US senator from Delaware. He had previously served as attorney general under both Thomas Jefferson and James Madison. See William Plumer, "Caesar A. Rodney," *Delaware History* 4 (1951): 369–73.

Gratz Manuscripts, HSP.

Charleston Courier

Friday, December 20, 1822

HOUSE OF REPRESENTATIVES . . . The House proceeded to give a second reading to the bill to provide for the compensation of those persons whose slaves have been executed in Charleston for the late attempt to raise an insurrection in this state, and certain

other persons whose slaves have suffered, &c. And on the question to agree to the first clause thereof, allowing the sum of $122 44 for each slave so executed, the yeas and nays were required, and are as follows, viz:
YEAS . . . 94.
NAYS . . . 24.

So the same was decided in the affirmative, and the clause agreed to, and the bill ordered to the Senate.

A bill for the remuneration of Peter, of George, of Pincel, and of Scott, was then taken up for second reading. The following clause being under consideration:

"*And be it further enacted,* That if the said John C. Prioleau, refuses to emancipate the said slave Peter, or the said Peter refuses to accept his freedom, that then the sum of $[*blank*] per annum be paid to the said Peter during his natural life."

A motion was made to fill the blank with the words *one hundred,* and on the question to agree thereto the yeas and nays were required, and were as follows, viz:—Yeas 67—Nays 42.

The question having been decided in the affirmative, the blank was consequently filled with the words one hundred, so as to allow the said Peter $100 per annum during his natural life.

The bill was then ordered to the Senate, and the House—adjourned.

An Act for the Better Regulation and Government of Free Negroes and Persons of Color;

Saturday, December 21, 1822

I. *Be it enacted* by the honorable the Senate and House of Representatives, now met and sitting in General Assembly, and by the authority of the same, That from and after the passing of this Act, no free negro or person of color, who shall leave this State, shall be suffered to return; and every person, who shall offend herein, shall be liable to the penalities of the Act passed on the twentieth day of December, in the year one thousand eight hundred and twenty, entitled "An Act to restrain the emancipation of slaves, and to prevent free persons of color from entering into this State; and for other purposes."

II. *And be it further enacted,* that every free male negro or person of color, between the ages of fifteen and fifty years, within the State, who may not be a native of this State, or shall not have resided therein five years next preceding the passing of this Act, shall pay a tax of fifty dollars per annum; and in case said tax shall not be paid, the said free male person of color shall be subject to the penalties of the Act against free persons of color coming into the State, passed on the twentieth day of December, one thousand eight hundred and twenty.

III. *And be it further enacted* by the authority aforesaid, That if any vessel shall come into any port or harbour of this State, from any other State or foreign port, having on board any free negroes or persons of color, as cooks, stewards, mariners, or in any other employment on board of said vessel, such as free negroes or persons of color shall be liable to be seized and confined in jail until said vessel shall clear out and depart from this

State; and that when said vessel is ready to sail, the captain of said vessel shall be bound to carry away the said free negro or free person of color, and to pay the expenses of his detention; and in case of his neglect or refusal so to do, he shall be liable to be indicted, and, on conviction thereof, shall be fined in a sum not less than one thousand dollars, and imprisoned not less than two months; and such free negroes or persons of color shall be deemed and taken as absolute slaves, and sold in conformity to the provisions of the Act passed on the twentieth day of December, one thousand eight hundred and twenty, aforesaid.

IV. *And be it further enacted* by the authority aforesaid, That the sheriff of Charleston district, and each and every other sheriff of this State, shall be empowered and specially enjoined to carry the provisions of this Act into effect; each of whom shall be entitled to one moiety of the proceeds of the sale of all free negroes and free persons of color that may happen to be sold under the provisions of the foregoing clause; *provided* the prosecution be had at his information.

V. *And be it further enacted,* That it it shall be the duty of the harbor-master of the port of Charleston, to report to the sheriff of Charleston District, the arrival of all free negroes or free persons of color, who may arrive on board any vessel coming into the harbor of Charleston, from any other State or foreign port.

VI. *And be it enacted,* That from and after the passing of this Act, it shall be altogether unlawful for any person or persons to hire to any male slave or slaves, his or their time; and in case any male slave or slaves be so permitted by their owner or owners, to hire out their own time, labor or service, the said slave or slaves shall be liable to seizure and forfeiture, in the same manner as has been heretofore enacted in the Act in the case of slaves coming into this State contrary to the provisions of the same.

VII. *And be it further enacted,* That from and after the first day of June next, every free male negro, mulatto or mestizo in this State, about the age of fifteen years, shall be compelled to have a guardian, who shall be a respectable freeholder of the district in which said free negro, mulatto or mestizo shall reside. And it shall be the duty of the said guardian to go before the clerk of the court of the said district, and before him signify his acceptance of the trust, in writing; and, at the same time, he shall give to the clerk aforesaid, his certificate, that the said negro, mulatto or mestizo for whom he is guardian, is of good character and correct habits; which acceptance and certificate shall be recorded in said office, by the clerk, who shall receive for the same fifty cents; and if any free male negro, mulatto or mestizo shall be unable to conform to the requisitions of this Act, then, and in that case, such person or persons shall be dealt with as this Act directs for persons of color coming into this State contrary to law; and the amount of sale shall be divided, one half to the informer, and the other half for the use of the State.

VIII. *And be it further enacted* by the authority aforesaid, That if any person or persons shall counsel, aid or hire any slave or slaves, free negroes or persons of color, to raise a rebellion or insurrection within this State, whether any rebellion or insurrection do actually take place or not, every such person or persons, on conviction thereof, shall be adjudged felons, and suffer death without the benefit of clergy.

IX. *And be it further enacted* by the authority aforesaid, That the commissioners of the cross roads for Charleston Neck, be, and they are hereby declared to be, justices of the peace, ex-officio, in that part of the parish of St. Philip's without the corporate limits of Charleston, for all purposes, except for the trial of causes small and mean.

In the Senate House, the twenty-first day of December, in the year of our Lord one thousand eight hundred and twenty-two, and in the forty-seventh year of Independence of the United States of America.

Jacob Bond I'ON,[1] *President of the Senate.*
Patrick Noble,[2] *Speaker of the House of Representatives*

1. Jacob Bond I'on (1782–1859), a wealthy planter, owned multiples estates, including Clayville plantation in Christ Church Parish. He had an extensive career of public service. See *BDSCHR* 4: 304–30.

2. Patrick Noble (1787–1840), a slaveholding attorney, represented the Abbeville District in the state's twenty-fifth General Assembly. See *BDSCHR* 4: 423–24.

Thomas Cooper and David J. McCord, eds., *The Statutes at Large of South Carolina* (Columbia, SC, 1840), vol. 7: 461–62.

Charleston Courier

Wednesday, December 25, 1822

S. Carolina Legislature.

IN SENATE.

Monday, December 16.

. . . The report of the special committee to whom were referred sundry petitions from the owners of slaves who were sentenced by the late court of magistrates and freeholders in Charleston, to be transported by their owners under the direction of the city council of Charleston, was then taken into consideration, amended and agreed to as follows:

That it is their unanimous opinion the state ought to assume the transportation of said negroes, under the direction of the Governor, and that the owners of each slave or slaves, be paid the sum allowed by law for slaves executed, viz: $122.86, for each slave, on the owners assigning to the state, all right of property in said slaves, and that a bill be introduced to that effect by the chairman.

Tuesday, December 17.

Mr. Moser, from the joint committee, on the petition of Wm. Sims and others, reported,

A bill to provide for the transportation of such slaves as have been convicted of an attempt to excite an insurrection in this state, who are now confined in the Work House of Charleston, and for other purposes; which was read a first time and ordered to a second reading to-morrow. . . .

A bill to impose a tax on slaves brought into this state, for sale, barter or exchange, and for the better regulation and government of free negroes and persons of color, and for other purposes, reported the engrossed bill; and on the question, shall the bill be sent to the senate? the yeas and nays were required, and are as follows, viz:—

YEAS, 64—NAYS, 51.

The question having been decided in the affirmative, the bill was sent to the senate. . . .

Charleston Mercury, and Morning Advertiser

Wednesday, December 25, 1822

FROM COLUMBIA. The Legislature adjourned on Saturday last at a late hour. They have passed twenty-six Acts. . . . A law has passed allowing the enlistment of 150 men, to serve as a standing body for the protection of this city, the suburbs and Charleston neck. . . . The owners of slaves executed for the late negro plot are to receive the usual compensation for such losses under the law, $122. The owners of slaves condemned to transportation out of the U. States are left to carry the sentence into execution at their own expense. Pinceel is to receive $1000 and to be exempt from taxation, and Scott is to receive 500 with a like exemption. Col. Prioleau's and Major Wilson's slaves are to be freed with the consent of their masters, and to receive $50 per annum for their lives.

Charleston Mercury, and Morning Advertiser

Tuesday, December 31, 1822

SOUTH-CAROLINA LEGISLATURE

SENATE

Saturday, December 21. . . . The house of representatives sent to the senate, a report on the memorial of the city council of Charleston, praying to be reimbursed expenses incurred in suppressing the late attempt at insurrection; ordered to be laid on the table. . . .

HOUSE OF REPRESENTATIVES. . . . An act to establish a competent force to act as a municipal guard for the protection of Charleston and its vicinity; ordered that the bills be delivered to the engrossing committee. . . .

The house considered and agreed to a favorable report of the committee on claims on the memorial of the city council of Charleston, praying for the relief of the keeper of the work house and their contingent account for apprehending and keeping in confinement the negroes concerned in the late insurrection.

Read a third time, a bill for better regulation of free negroes and persons of color; while under consideration, a motion was made to postpone the said bill, and on the question, shall the house agree thereto, the yeas and nays were required.

YEAS, 22—NAYS, 68.

The question being decided in the nega[t]ive, the bill was not postponed.

The bill was then passed into an act, and sent to the senate.

Read a third time the following bills from the senate. . . .

The senate returned to this house a bill for the better regulation of free negroes and persons of color, which had three readings in this house—delivered to the engrossing committee. . . .

[A] bill to provide for the compensation of those persons whose slaves have been executed in Charleston during the summer of 1822, for an attempt to raise an insurrection in this state; and

A bill for the remuneration of Peter, of George, of Pinceel, and of Scott, were severally read a third time, passed into acts, and sent to the senate. . . .

Genius of Universal Emancipation

January 1823

The Legislature of South Carolina has given to Purcell,[1] the free man of colour, who gave information of the late intended insurrection, in that state, 100 dollars a year for life, and exempted himself and family from taxation.

Southern Paper.

(An *incontrovertible* argument in favour of the principle maintained in this work, and by true philanthropists generally, that where slaves are numerous the safety of the masters consists in treating them kindly. Else why not *punish* this man instead of *rewarding* him?—Answer me this, ye aspiring and avaricious nabobs, who are fain to use *any pretext* to perpetuate your usurped authority.—*Gen Univer. Eman.*)

. . . *Look*!—A bill has been introduced into the Legislature of South Carolina, for the purpose of imposing a tax of $50 on all free male negroes, or persons of colour, between the age of 15 and 50 years; and to imprison all such persons brought into the state on board of vessels, serving as cooks, mariners, &c. until the vessels depart.

1. This was the freed mixed-race William Penceel, not Jack Purcell, who was hanged on Friday, July 26. The assembly awarded Penceel the sum of one thousand dollars and exempted him from the Free Black Tax.

Charleston *City Gazette and Commercial Daily Advertiser*

Wednesday, January 1, 1823

COMMUNICATION.

To the Citizens of Charleston and others, of this State.

Citizens, owners of Carts, Drays, and Hackney Carriages, who suffer them to be driven by their slaves, which slaves hire their services to any person requiring them in such occupation, and to all others who suffer their slaves to hire their time and services as employment offers, will, by a law passed at the late session of the Legislature of this State,* forfeit the said negro slaves so continuing to hire their own time; one half of the amount of sale to go to the informer, and the other to the State. This extends to all male slaves, who are suffered by their owners to hire their own time—no matter of what occupation or trade.

Seeing the advertisement of the City Treasurer, to grant yearly licenses for Carts, Drays, Hackney Coaches, and City Badges, on and after the 2d of January next, I feel it a duty owing to the citizens, to make this public statement for their information and reflection; and as a warning against the consequences of permitting their male slaves to work in such manner. A City Badge, or City Licence, or written Ticket, is the only protection under the *City* ordinance; but it is no protection against the operation of the *State* law—which compels every owner, guardian, &c. to hire his or her slave *personally.* Perhaps *Proxy* may do, if an adult white person. Let owners look to this.

A Representative of the People.

* *Title*—"An Act for the better regulation and government of Free Negroes and Persons of Colour, and for other purposes."

New Bedford Mercury

Friday, January 10, 1823

S. CAR. CHARLESTON, Dec. 25. Our State Legislature rose late on Saturday night, after passing 26 acts. The most interesting of them are those to prevent future insurrections of the blacks. By one of them the city is authorised to raise a standing military force of 150 men to carry into effect the laws against slaves, instead of the City Guard. Part of the expense of this force is to be raised by a tax on negro tenements, and negro mechanics. All free native blacks are to have guardians, and those not natives and who have migrated since five years, to pay a tax of $50 per annum.—Whites who excite or attempt to excite negro insurrections are to suffer death. The blacks who discovered the late insurrection have been rewarded by public grants. Pencil,[1] a free black, is to have $1000, and be exempted from taxation.

1. William Penceel.

Salem (MA) *Gazette*

Friday, January 10, 1823

SLAVERY.

The city of Charleston is about raising a little standing army of 150 men for its own defence; at this ratio the United States will have on foot a standing army of 50,000.

Charleston will probably expend in supporting this force 6000 dollars a year, just about as much as it costs this state to maintain our State Prison. Application will probably be made to Congress for permission to levy and keep these troops, as the constitution of the United States prohibits a state from keeping troops, except in case of invasion or imminent danger of it. . . .

While slavery exists, the fearful apprehension of massacre and insurrection will be inevitable; and for the causes of turbulence our brethren need not look to the north, but nearer home, at their own doors. The household slaves, who are numerous, are treated with kindness and familiarity, and from their association acquire much knowledge, and of course a relish for the sweets of liberty, and an abhorrence of their servile condition. Some of them are very intelligent as well as enterprising and fearless. Denmark Vesey and Gullah Jack shewed that they possessed the qualities and powers to be formidable and terrific foes. In a free community these slaves will of necessity imbibe notions of liberty. From household slaves the contagion of liberty cannot but spread among the plantation slaves. Unless the masters seal up the avenues of knowledge among the blacks, unless they close their eyes that they see not, and stop their ears that they hear not, they certainly will be prone to fancy that liberty is a blessing worth the hazard of their lives to obtain.

City Council on the Work-House Prisoners, 1823

City Council

January 21st 1823.

Resolved that the Owners of Slaves now confined in the Work House shall from and after this date have free communication with them, and that the Resolution prohibiting access, shall be, and is hereby repealed.

Entered from the Minutes

Wm. Roach Junr.[1]
C.C.

D. Haig, Esq.[2]

1. William Roach Jr. (1799–1838) was the clerk of the Charleston City Council.
2. David Haig (1783–1832) operated a cooperage in Charleston at Craft's Wharf.

City Council's Permission to See Negroes in W. House, January 21, 1823, series S165015, Petitions to the General Assembly, 1823, no. 72, SCDAH.

Francisco de Valderrama (Baracoa) to Governor of Santiago de Cuba, March 7, 1823[1]

In my official communication of the 7th of last month, I informed your Excellency about the expulsion of people of color from the United States of America about which that government had forewarned. The captain of a boat, anchored in this port, of that very same nation had so informed me, and without a doubt this news had been communicated to various local businessmen. Subsequently, another boat from another destination has arrived, and its captain and owner Mr. [*illegible*] has assured me that the said order of expulsion is effective, although so only for the Province of Charleston where the conspiracy against the whites was hatched. Nevertheless, it will be my intent to exert my authority over any novelty that occurs in this instance, by the boats that appear in these places so that your Excellency will be opportunely advised as to object and so that in conformity with your Excellency's previous official communication of the 7th of this same month, no individuals of this sort will be introduced into this territory.

1. Valderrama was writing from Baracoa, a port town in Guantánamo Province near the eastern tip of Cuba. In 1823 Gabriel de Torres y Velasco held the post of governor of Santiago de Cuba. He ranked as the second-highest executive official in colonial Cuba behind the captain-general. See Emilio Bacardí y Moreau, *Crónicas de Santiago de Cuba,* 2 vols. (Barcelona: Tip. de Carbonell y Esteva, 1908–1909), vol. 1: 18. The editors would like to thank Professor Manuel Barcia for providing a copy of this document, which was translated by Paquette. In 1825, during one of the largest slave insurrections in the history of Cuba, the island's chief executive received information that slaves transported from Charleston to Cuba in the aftermath of the Vesey affair might be involved

in the unrest on one of the Cuban estates afflicted by the 1825 insurrection. See Captain-General Dionosio Vives to governor of Matanzas, June 21, 1825, Escoto Papers, Houghton Library, Harvard University.

ALS in Francisco de Valderrama to governor of Santiago de Cuba, March 7, 1823, Archivo Nacional de Cuba (Havana), Asuntos Politicos, legajo no. 113, signatura 58.

Charleston *Southern Intelligencer*

Saturday, March 15, 1823

Mr. Editor—It is known to many of your subscribers, that some months since, a meeting was called to consider the expediency of forming an association, for the purpose of giving aid to the civil authorities in enforcing the laws against various immoralities. At that meeting a committee was appointed, with instructions to draft a constitution, and call a second meeting whenever they were ready to report. As some of your readers may be curious to know what progress has been made, I have taken some pains to be informed on the subject. I will take the liberty to state what follows, hoping that some member of the committee will add any thing else worth knowing, or correct any mistake here made.

The committee having agreed on the form of a constitution, thought it a proper mark of respect for the City Council, to lay it before them for their approbation. After considerable delay, occasioned by an extraordinary pressure of business, that body returned it with a verbal message, importing that they did not feel at liberty to act on it officially, but had no objection to it. At this crisis several important laws were passed, some of which removed by their wise and energetic provisions much of the evil the intended association was calculated to check, and induced an expectation that if not rendered quite needless, its operations would be facilitated and guided to the best purpose. The organization of the City Marshal's department then engaged the deliberations of a committee of council for a considerable time, during which the chairman of the committee, as I understand, left the city. The business seems then to have remained at a stand, probably, because the committee were willing to see, whether the new regulations would fully produce the desired effect, but at length the infernal plot of 1822 broke out, and every thing else was forgotten in the anxieties of that unhappy period. Nor has the subject apparently been recalled to this day, though I fear there is as much need of exertion for the improvement of morals among us as ever. I am informed that some of our churches in view of the present state of things, have begun to use some influence by means of committees consisting of some of their respectable members, to check the very general profanation of the Sabbath. . . . ALIQUIS

Abolitionist Reflections on the Plot, Friday, March 28, 1823

For the Genius of Universal Emancipation

OBSERVATIONS ON THE LATE PLOT AT CHARLESTON

I have read some account, in a late paper, of an insurrection at Charleston, S.C. by the negroes of that place. The writer mentioned that certain black men, by the names of Vessey, Monday, &c. were the "ring-leaders" in the plot; and after expressing some pleasure in its being in the power of the people of Charleston, to punish, with death, the principal offenders, goes on to glory in the consideration, that "We are powerful enough to *punish*, whatever THEY are vile enough to plan!"[1] I do not wish it to be understood that I am about to justify the conduct of these negroes; I by no means approve the plot, but have the utmost aversion to any thing of the kind; yet I must confess that this expression struck me with some weight, and introduced me into serious consideration on the subject; and believing that my fellow citizens, as well as myself, may take a useful hint from the circumstance, I have noted down the results of my reflections.

I immediately turned to the declaration of independence, in 1776; and, on perusing it, I found that the united Colonies complained of the King of England, as a tyrannical oppressor, in that of appointing rulers of his own choosing; deciding causes of himself; neglecting a proper attention to their complaints; imposing heavy taxes, without consent of the people, &c. &c.—They said, moreover, that he was a prince who was not fit to bear rule over such a people. I found that in consideration of these, and other things of a similar nature, they felt themselves fully justifiable in taking up arms, and FIGHTING for their LIBERTY. Fighting against whom? against their brethren, in every sense of the word; brethren of the same blood, of the same colour, of the same professions, of the same religion. For what reason did they thus break through the laws of moral rectitude? Because they declared, that "FREEDOM *is the* NATURAL *right of* ALL *men,*" (the truth of which I have never heard disputed by any reasonable authority). Well, I thought, are we republicans, possessed of the same love of liberty, that we were possessed of in 1776? for, after several years' conflict, and the loss of much blood and treasure, freedom was obtained, and the negroes who fell a sacrifice for the country, or who distinguished themselves by their good policy in warfare, were renowned by the historians; poets sung their praises; and great firing and parade was made in every part of the Republic, where they chanced to make their appearance; and yet because a few black men, mostly under greater oppression from individuals, now in these days, made some arrangements for gaining their liberty, they were executed, with very little consideration.

Perhaps some may think their slaves in as happy situations as though they were free. But the proper way to discover the error of this opinion may be to suppose ourselves enslaved by some inhumane pirates, and sold to the Algerines or Arabs, who might think themselves pretty clever fellows: in this situation we should reflect, that we, and our offspring perhaps, were doomed to drag out wretched lives of miserable slavery, and that of this there was not likely to be an end unless the righteous interposition of Heaven should take place. We will go on to suppose, that, accordingly, we should wear out a short life of the greatest human wretchedness; and death itself would be a relief. Our offspring grow up, and in the greatest degree of ignorance; and having never seen any of their description in the possession of any thing that was real enjoyment, they would, in that debated situation, readily conclude, that if their iron-hearted oppressors would only use them well, that is, hide their nakedness, give them a moderate portion of victuals, and not oppress them too much with labour, they would as willingly be slaves as free:

especially as their masters had found it to their interest to persuade them that they were better off in that situation than in a state of freedom. In this situation of things, suppose the Congress of the United States to take these poor creatures, whom we have supposed in Africa, to the country of their forefathers, give them a moral and christian, as well as scientific education; and suffer them to enjoy, amongst men, the liberty of men; and if one in ten thousand would prefer slavery in Africa to this state, then I am ignorant. In the same manner, let any master in the U. States educate his slave, transport him to a region where he can enjoy the common liberty of a free country; and if after being placed in this situation, he prefers a state of ignorance and servitude, I shall again confess my ignorance.

But to return to the plot: I have no doubt that Moses was considered a very disadvantageous personage by the Egyptians, and if he had undertaken a scheme for the relief of the Israelites, similar to that which the negroes of the south undertook, he would, in all probability, have been executed with as little ceremony as those negroes were. But, as the time appointed by Providence for the release of the Israelites *had come*; and, as he went about it in a way ordered by Providence, he succeeded. So, as Providence is pleased to indulge wonderful sinners a while longer, who hold his children in bondage, and as the conspirators did not go about it in the right manner, the citizens of the South were *permitted, once more,* to escape the impending destruction, and to punish the *offended*; and not only to punish them with death, but to glory in the consideration, that "*We are powerful enough to punish whatever them are vile enough to plan!*"

If the reports of the Marshalls be correct, the blacks are in some places, more numerous than the whites; and as the climate suits their constitutions better, their increase will, likely, be greater. So it appears that it will not be long before the negroes will lack nothing but another "ring-leader" to massacre us all on the spot. It is said by some, in objection to this sentiment, that there are always some slaves, whose attachment to their owner is so great, that no plot can ever go into effect without discovery; and that a state of long servitude has debased them in such a manner, that they are not qualified to ascend into power; thus indulging a vain hope, that their safety is fully established. But they who reason thus, argue as if there was no God in the world. Do we expect, that by debasing the minds of the slaves, and confining them to hard servitude, in such manner as to prevent any improvement, we can prevent the judgments of the Almighty from overtaking us? If so, then it would be good policy for all to pass laws, as some of our slave states have done, to prevent scientific knowledge. But such unreasonable restrictions as these, go only to increase our own guilt, and hasten the day which we may wish never to see! Do we expect that the justice of God will sleep forever? or do we think him unable to punish us? In either case I think we shall be mistaken; and, unless a speedy repentance, and a great change in the conduct of slaveholders towards their slaves, take place, they will, if they escape the punishment of an insurrection during their short stay on earth, not escape the horrors of a guilty conscience in an Eternal World! JOHN.

1. "John" extracted the quote from Hamilton, *Account,* 2.

Certification of William Roach, Saturday, March 29, 1823

Council Chamber

March 29th 1823.

I do hereby certify that an Account due to the Corporation for the apprehension, dieting and expenses incurred on account of certain persons who were concerned in the late insurrection was by the authority of the City Council sent to the Legislature to obtain an order for payment of the same.

William Roach.
Clerk of Council.

Series S39 008, General Assembly and other Miscellaneous Records, 1823, no. 17, SCDAH.

Not content merely to pass new legislation tightening controls over slaves and free blacks, a number of influential Carolinians banded together formally in July 1823 to create the South Carolina Association, a vigilant organization designed to ensure that city and state authorities did not drop their guard once the dangers of 1822 had passed. Comprised of many of the men who had been involved in the trials the previous summer or who even owned some of the accused bondmen, the impressive roster of politicians, businessmen, and planters meant that the association could be ignored by officials only at their peril, a point made publicly by Governor John Lyde Wilson in opposing the group. (As the City Council Minutes suggest, Mayor James A. Hamilton also opposed the vigilantism of the group and, tellingly, did not join it.) With branches outside of Charleston, the association would serve for decades as the most prominent of its kind in South Carolina and, indeed, throughout the South. Among its members were Colonel John Cordes Prioleau, whose slave Peter first broke news of the plot; Robert J. Turnbull, a member of the first court; merchant Benjamin Hammet, whose slave Bacchus was a leading conspirator; and Elias Horry, whose coachman John provided explosive courtroom testimony. Members James Poyas and John Strohecker both had slaves either hanged or transported, and proslavery pamphleteer Edwin C. Holland signed the memorial below, as did "Rusticus" essayist Alexander Garden and court member and *Official Report* coauthor Lionel Kennedy. Even George Warren Cross, Vesey's attorney and sometimes landlord, and Frederick Wesner, who had arrested Vesey in June of 1822, joined the group. Association members helped prepare the groundwork for the Negro Seamen Act, and they believed themselves justified when Scipio Simms, who had been sentenced to transportation, somehow found his way back to Charleston. The association was instrumental in bringing that fact to the Charleston press, and Simms was eventually recaptured.

On the Need to Control Slaves, 1823

. . . It may easily be understood, that the relation in which we stand to the negro population, their number, employments, habits, and peculiar characters, require of us an extended, well defined, and efficient system of laws, and also, some attention on our part to the due enforcement of those laws; but it seems to have escaped the observation of many persons that the enactment of important and determined Rules, without a correspondent, determined vigilant, and steady spirit to carry those Rules into effect, is worse than no legislation, being destructive of the end proposed, rather than productive of any good effect whatever. . . .

Events, which recently excited our alarm, and roused our attention to the immediate protection of life and property, have passed away, and left us in the same unsuspecting and inactive state we had fast been settling into before their occurrence. Legislative acts passed from awful experience, and a full conviction of their necessity have been suffered to lay dormant on the statute book; the spirit of insolence and insubordination among the negroes, so far from being subdued, appears to have grown with increased vigour and activity; the raising of an efficient military force, to act as a permanent guard, has not even been resolved upon, whilst all the methods of corrupting our negroes are as operative now as ever. . . .

Rules of the South-Carolina Association Adopted in the City of Charleston on the Fourth Thursday in July Being the 25th Day, A.D. 1823 (Charleston, SC, 1823), 11. On the creation of the organization, see Alan F. January, "The South Carolina Association: An Agency for Race Control in Antebellum Charleston," *SCHM* 78 (1977): 191–201.

Memorial of the South Carolina Association to the Senate, November 1823

To the HONOURABLE the Members of the SENATE of the State of SOUTH CAROLINA;

THE MEMORIAL

Of the Officers and Members of the SOUTH-CAROLINA ASSOCIATION;

SHEWETH,

That a complaint amongst our citizens, being of late years very prevalent, that the laws enacted against free persons of colour, were not executed; your Memorialists have recently formed themselves into an Association, for the purpose of aiding in their enforcement, by giving to the constituted authorities, the earliest information of their infraction. The fundamental principle of their Society, being, OBEDIENCE TO THE LAWS, and reverence for the civil magistrate, and their labours being felt, to be evidently beneficial to the State at large, they have had the good wishes of their fellow-citizens generally, and their Association has increased, in numbers and respectability, beyond their most sanguine expectations.

In the prosecution of their object, your Memorialists have had ample opportunities, from the personal experience of their Standing Committee, of perceiving the defects in some of these laws: and they have thought it their duty, with the utmost deference to the Legislature, to notice a few of the most prominent, and to petition for redress.

In the first place, there can scarcely exist in our southern community, an evil of greater magnitude, to the country at large, than the constant intercourse, which is maintained between the blacks of the North and the South. The means of communication has been confined, principally to the City of Charleston: and hence it is, that in the interior, there is not the same knowledge of the danger to the State at large, from this intercourse. Not only are the greatest facilities afforded, to such as would inveigle away our slaves, by the employment of blacks on board of the passage vessels and packets, whereby this evil has increased of late to an alarming degree; but abundant opportunities are offered these people, for introducing among our slaves, the moral contagion of their pernicious principles and opinions. These evils are the more to be dreaded, because, there appears every prospect of this intercourse increasing. The difficulty on the part of the free negroes at the North, in procuring employments suited to their habits and inclinations, and the consequent low wages at which they may be procured, has induced many ship owners there, to employ them, in preference to whites. In one instance the Liverpool Line Ship Canada arrived here from New York (in June last) with her whole crew, fifteen in number, all black, and the Brig Maine from Boston, has also since come into this port, with her crew also black. There is scarcely a vessel which arrives in our port from the North, which has not two or three, or more black persons employed, as stewards, cooks, or mariners; and the belief is general, that were it not for the obstacles, offered by the informations and prosecutions of your Memorialists, most of the vessels coastwise, would, in a few years, be manned principally by free negroes and persons of colour from the Northern and Eastern States. The consequence of this, to our slave property, and to the peace and quiet of the State, must be obvious to all. Now too, that so many different lines of packets are established, between this port and New-York, and the opportunities for embarking are occurring almost every day in the year, there can be no security, that our slaves, will not be seduced from the service of their masters, in greater numbers than heretofore, and that the Abolition Societies of the North, will not be encouraged to persevere in their designs, to intrigue, through this class of persons, with our slave population. Heretofore the societies there, have confined their views, to the abolition of slavery in the particular State, or section of the Union, in which they originated. But of late, their views have been greatly extended, [*illegible*]. To permit a free intercourse to exist, under such circumstances, between our slaves and *their* free persons of colour, would be, to invite new attempts at insurrection. To your Memorialists, who, from the agents which they employ, have the best knowledge of the proceedings of the blacks at the North, and of the projects of their adherents and friends there, the evil presents itself, in a form truly appalling, to every owner of lands and negroes.

But it is not from the North alone, that we are threatened with doctrines subversive of our peace. In all the British West-India Islands, with scarcely an exception, there is, at this moment, considerable inquietude, in consequence of the desire of a strong party in the British Parliament, to interfere with the regulations of their slaves.[1] In the Island of *Grenada,* a memorial was presented by the free persons of colour, setting forth, "that as loyal and dutiful subjects, they ought to be admitted into a participation, in the rights and privileges to which every Englishman is entitled, under the British Constitution." The Committee to whom the House of Assembly referred this memorial, have reported, "that a bill should be brought into the House, to repeal an existing law in that colony, so far as the rights and privileges of the free coloured inhabitants are affected thereby, and also that the elective franchise ought to be extended, to free persons of colour, possessing the qualification required by law."[2] In *Antigua* and *St. Christophers*, similar petitions have been presented to their Colonial Assemblies, the fate of which is not known.[3] In the Island of *Jamaica*, a similar question was intended to be made, and such has been the uneasiness in some of the Islands, that some persons, it is said, have actually removed into the United States with their families. But, in *Demerary*, as appears by the Governor's proclamation of the 19th August, the United Colony of *Demerary and Essquebo*, was put under martial law, in consequence of a very serious attempt, at a general insurrection.[4] From the official documents, it appears, that on the East coast of Demerary, near one thousand armed negroes were embodied, but afterwards defeated and dispersed by the military, with the loss of about one hundred and fifty negroes; and by the Royal Gazette of that Colony of the 28th August, it also appears that the convictions were numerous, and the examples prompt and terrible. In the Island of *Barbadoes*, the Governor in August last, was obliged to issue his proclamation, to contradict a report, that the slaves were to be emancipated; and later accounts represent, that they were then in alarm, in the expectation of an insurrection.[5] From other Islands, other reports on the same subject, entitled to great credit, have from time to time reached different parts of the United States; but, as they come to your Memorialists in no official form, they forbear to mention particulars. Your Memorialists, however, repeat with the utmost confidence, that at no period of the history of the West-Indies, has there been such uneasiness and excitement, and angry feeling on the part of the whites, and such insubordination amongst the slaves, as has been experienced of late in that quarter, attributable altogether to the proceedings of the African Associations in London, and to the influence of Mr. WILBERFORCE[6] in Parliament, whose object is now open and avowed, that the work of abolishing slavery in the Colonies, ought immediately to be commenced. The conductors of the public journals in all the Islands, unhesitatingly charge the intemperate enthusiasts in and out of the British Parliament, as the sole, and immediate cause of all the disturbances, and from several of the Colonial Assemblies, remonstrances and addresses have been forwarded to the Mother Country, in spirit and feeling, not greatly inferior to a Declaration of Independence.

With such proceedings in these Islands, and with the known habits and sentiments, of the coloured people of the North, aided and encouraged as they are, by a portion of their white population, your Memorialists cannot conceive a measure, which can give greater security to the State in general, than to prevent ANY FREE COLOURED PERSON FROM ANY PART OF THE WORLD *ever entering again into the limits of the State of South-Carolina*, by LAND OR BY WATER.

It has been the most anxious desire of your Memorialists, to avail themselves of the existing laws for the purpose of stopping an intercourse, which they feel to be so ruinous to the country; and defective as the laws are, by reason of the mildness of their penalties, your Memorialists have, nevertheless, at considerable expense to their Society, greatly succeeded. Many masters of vessels begin to bring white seamen into our port, and with a little aid from the Legislature, your Memorialists are confident, that by the excellence of their organization, and by means of their incessant informations, and prosecutions, it would be in their power, to bring to justice all violators of these laws, and to suppress the intercourse for *ever hereafter.* They confidently hope, that every man who has a family, or property to protect, would rejoice at such an event.

That the Legislative body may be apprized, of the extent, to which this intercourse may be maintained, your Memorialists beg leave to submit, that since the organization of their Society, which is not much more than two months, they have on one subject alone, caused the Act of the Legislature to be executed against *one hundred and fifty-four* coloured persons, who have entered the State, in defiance of its enactments. Of these, there were

From Northern Ports,	118
the West-Indies,	15
Europe,	*21*
	154

If in so short a time, and principally during a season, when there is little or no trade, so many have arrived here, some idea may be formed, of the number which must enter into our limits, in the course of the year.

In entering upon their important duties, your Memorialists have had to struggle, with a great and an increasing difficulty. This arises from the inadequacy of the law, to prevent its re-iterated infraction, by some who have already been subjected to its penalties. Amongst those who have entered the State contrary to law, some have been confined in jail *twice,* and some *thrice* for the same offence. The penalty of mere confinement during the stay of the vessel in port, which in the case of Northern vessels, generally does not exceed a few days, seems to be disregarded by many, who would cheerfully submit to this temporary deprivation of liberty, rather than forego the irresistible temptation which these people have to come to a Southern country. As the act now stands, there is no penalty upon the captain, who brings into the State a person of colour. The penalty only occurs if the master refuses or neglects to carry him away; your Memorialists would, therefore, respectfully suggest, that an adequate fine be imposed upon the master of the vessel in the first instance; and that, for the *first* offence, the seaman should be confined in jail, during which confinement he should receive regular notice from a magistrate, never to enter again into the State; and that if he shall ever return to the State, after being regularly warned and sent away, that he should be liable to corporal punishment, or to be sold for a term of years. With these alterations in the law and by extending the act to all the descendants of negroes, whether on the father's or mother's side, your Memorialists believe, the evil would be at once suppressed, whilst as the law stands at present, it can never be enforced, so as to be productive of the good, contemplated by the Legislature.

The intercourse being so far stopped, that no person of colour from abroad shall ever again land on our shores; your Memorialists would pray to have the law revised, which prohibits free persons of colour from visiting the Northern and Eastern States; nor is it less essential to extend the provisions of the act, so as to prevent slaves who are carried out of the State by their masters, from being returned again into it, if at any time during their absence, they have been in the West-Indies, or in any part of Europe, or within the limits of States North, of the Potomac, or the Susquehana.

Your Memorialists lastly, most respectfully pray your honourable body, that you would give your earliest attention, to the state of our laws, respecting slaves and free persons of colour generally. Most of these laws were passed, prior to the adoption of our State Constitution,[7] and when we were a Colony of Great-Britain. Some of their provisions are useless, some obsolete, and many require modification. To adapt them to the present state of society, and to the new relations in which we stand to the rest of the world, would be productive of great public good. Passing from the dependency of a Colony, to the rank of a sovereign State, and at liberty to resort to any measures which may be necessary for our own security, Your Memorialists cannot but hope, that the dangers which menace our prosperity as a Slave-holding-State, will be met by a corresponding energy in the laws. Your Memorialists, without presuming to point out the alterations which may be necessary and proper, most respectfully suggest and pray your honourable body, that a general revision of these laws should take place, with all the assistance, that time, deliberation and research, and experience and talents can give to the subject; so that our magistrates and citizens hereafter, instead of being compelled to look into hundreds of acts and parts of acts passed in the course of a century, may be presented by the Legislature, with one CONSOLIDATED NEGRO ACT, or code, for the government of this class of people; embracing the provisions of every previous act, which may heretofore have been enacted, and which policy requires to be continued, and repealing, at the same time, every other act or part of an act, in relation to the subject which is to be found on the Statute Book. An act of this nature and character, drawn up with great care and with the subject well distributed and arranged, and in which the framers of it, shall avail themselves, as well "of the reproaches of our enemies, as the suggestions of our friends," and having in view at the same time, every regulation or plan of discipline, which is essential to our own preservation, will give security to the master, without taking away from the protection of the slave; and whilst it shall enable every planter and citizen, at one glance to see his rights and his duties, and thus be a public convenience, it will, in the humble opinion of your Memorialists, give more confidence to the capitalist, and more permanency to the quiet and good order of our slave population, than can be expected, under our present system.

And your Memorialists, as in duty bound, will ever pray.

Keat Simons President

On behalf of the Officers and Members[8] of the South-Carolina Association. OFFICERS,[9]

KEATING SIMONS, *President.*
Col. JOHN C. PRIOLEAU, *Vice-Presidents.*
Gen. THOMAS PINCKNEY,
STEPHEN ELLIOT,
HENRY DEAS,
JOSEPH MANIGAULT,
ROBERT J. TURNBULL, *Recording Sec.*

Major J. S. COGDELL, *Corresponding Sec.*
JOHN BAY, *Treasurer.*
ISAAC E. HOLMES, *Solicitor.*
Col. JOHN BRYAN, *Stewards*
JAMES FERGUSON,
JOHN MIDDLETON, *Chairman*
SEDGWICK L. SIMONS, *Standing Committee*
Col. R. W. VANDERHORST,
Col. RICHARD CUNNINGHAM,
Col. WILLIAM CATTEL,
CHARLES PARKER, and
Col. JOHN GORDON,

MEMBERS . . .

1. The memorialists presented their petition to the state legislature on Wednesday, November 26, 1823. By this time, they were well aware of the intensifying efforts of the British antislavery movement, led by William Wilberforce (1759–1833) and Thomas Fowell Buxton (1786–1845), to persuade Parliament to enact legislation to emancipate slaves in Britain's colonies. In a widely reported development in May 1823, Buxton presented a motion in Parliament demanding the expeditious end of slavery throughout the empire. See "Legislature of South Carolina," Charleston *Carolina Gazette,* December 6, 1823; *Substance of the Debate in the House of Commons, on the 15th May, 1823, on a Motion for the Mitigation and Gradual Abolition of Slavery Throughout the British Dominions* (London, 1823); Philadelphia *National Gazette and Literary Register,* July 10, 1823; Charleston *City Gazette and Commercial Daily Advertiser,* July 18, 1823.

2. Baltimore *Niles' Weekly Register,* September 20, 1823, reported on the free colored petition in words that appear verbatim in the memorial. The petition is discussed in Edward L. Cox, *Free Coloreds in the Slave Societies of St. Kitts and Grenada, 1763–1833* (Knoxville: University of Tennessee Press, 1984), 101–4.

3. Notices on these petitions, like the one composed by Grenada's free persons of color, appeared in US newspapers. See, for example, "Latest Foreign Intelligence," Philadelphia *National Gazette,* November 21, 1821; Hartford *Connecticut Mirror,* November 26, 1821. Edward L. Cox, *Free Coloreds in the Slave Societies of St. Kitts and Grenada, 1763–1833* (Knoxville: University of Tennessee Press, 1984), 101–4, compares the St. Kitts petition with the Grenadan.

4. Demerara (also "Demerary") and Essequibo were British plantation colonies located in what is today Guyana. The slave insurrection in Demerara in 1823 involved thousands of slaves and ranks as one of the largest in the history of the British Empire. Emilia Viotti da Costa, *Crowns of Glory, Tears of Blood: The Demerara Slave Rebellion of 1823* (New York: Oxford University Press, 1994), remains the best study of the insurrection.

5. Rumors of a general emancipation that was somehow thwarted or denied by local planters and officials proved to be a powerful trigger for slave plots and revolts throughout the Americas in the late eighteenth and nineteenth centuries. How such rumors affected the Vesey plotters in light of both the Missouri debate and South Carolina's manumission law of 1820 is discussed in Robert L. Paquette, "From Rebellion to Revisionism: The Continuing Debate about the Denmark Vesey Affair," *Journal of the Historical Society* 4 (Fall 2004): 319–21. See also David Patrick Geggus, "Slavery, War, and Revolution in the Greater Caribbean, 1789–1815," in David Barry Gaspar and David Patrick Geggus, eds., *A Turbulent Time: The French Revolution and the Greater Caribbean* (Bloomington: Indiana University Press, 1997), esp. 8–10. 6. A voluminous literature exists on the

crucial role of William Wilberforce (1759–1833) in the history of British emancipation. A good starting point is Christopher Leslie Brown, *Moral Capital: Foundations of British Abolitionism* (Chapel Hill: Published for the Omohundro Institute of Early American History and Culture, Williamsburg, VA, by the University of North Carolina Press, 2006).

7. The memorialists referred to South Carolina's constitution of 1790, the state's third.

8. Information about the nineteen officers and 316 members of the South Carolina Association who affixed their signatures to this printed memorial to the state legislature were derived largely from *CSCCD*; *America's Historical Newspapers* database, http://www.readex.com/content/americas-historical-newspapers; SCDAH database, http://www.archivesindex.sc.gov/onlinearchives/Search.aspx?br=1; *Find A Grave*, http://www.findagrave.com/; and volumes 1–5 of the *Biographical Directory of the South Carolina House of Representatives.* Unless otherwise stated, location of residence comes from the 1822 directory. For convenient searching, the names of members were placed here in alphabetical order according to first letter of surname. Titles affixed to names in the original document are retained. Naming information in addition to that provided by the signatories is here enclosed in brackets.

Members:

Adams, William (1762–1825), planter, corner of Pinckney and Cannon streets, Charleston Neck.

Aikin, William (1778–1831), merchant and planter, King Street Road, Charleston Neck.

Alexander, Samuel (1787–1866), proprietor Bank Coffee House, 129 East Bay Street.

Allan, William (1763?–1827), factor, 46 Tradd Street.

Annely, Thomas (1802?–1834), cooper, 54 East Bay Street (1825 directory).

Anthony, J. C., probably Captain Israel Church Anthony (1767–1836), tallow chandler, Mary Street, Mazyckborough, Charleston Neck.

Ashe, John, probably John Ashe Sr. (1760–1828), planter, 8 South Bay Street (1825 directory).

Ashe, John Jr. (1796–1868), planter, 8 South Bay Street (1825 directory).

Axson, John (d. 1840), planter, Charlotte Street, Mazyckborough, Charleston Neck.

Bacot, Daniel D[eSaussure] (1799–1838), bookkeeper, Bank of South Carolina, 94 Church Street.

Bacot, Peter (1788–1836), Cashier, Bank of Discount & Deposit, 22 Society Street.

Bacot, Thomas W[right] (1765–1834), cashier, Bank of South Carolina, 94 Church Street.

Bacot, Thomas W[right] Jr. (1795–1851), Assistant Postmaster, 94 Church Street.

Baker, Barnard E[lliott] (1792–1850), planter, St. George Parish.

Ball, Isaac (1785–1826), planter, 1 Vernon Street.

Ball, John (1782–1834), planter, 27 Hasell Street.

Barksdale, Thomas (d. 1850), planter, 13 Washington Street.

Bell, William, probably the planter William Bell (1788–1853), Berkeley County.

Berry, Alexander (d. 1836?), clerk, D'Oyley's Wharf, residence 16 Water Street.

Black, Alexander (d. 1849), merchant, 172 King Street.

Black, James (d. 1847?), merchant, 130 East Bay Street.

Blackwood, John, Major (1790–1833), merchant, King Street Road, Charleston Neck.

Blamyer, William (1784–1857), factor, Alexander Street, Mazyckborough.

Boag, William [S.] (1798–1840), wholesale druggist, 355 King Street (1825 directory).

Bonneau, William H[enry] (1799–1890), planter, Christ Church Parish.

Bonnell, John (1773–1854), ship chandler, 14 Lynch's Lane.

Bounetheau, Henry [Brintell] (1797–1877), clerk and artist, 34 Cumberland Street.

Brodie, Robert H. A Robert Howard Brodie, Mazyckborough, Charleston Neck, was involved with William Henry Evans in slave trading.

Brown, Charles, possibly Charles Tennent Brown (1795–1840), planter, who in 1829 resided on the corner of Anson and Georges street.

Bulow, J[ohn] J[oachim], Major (1768–1844), planter, 14 Montague Street.

Campbell, A[lexander] W., factor, 63 Beaufain Street (1825 directory).

Campbell, John, commission merchant, 171 Meeting Street.

Carew, Edward (1780–1850), pump & block maker, corner Wall and Laurens Street (1819 directory).

Carmile [Carmille], John (d. 1833), butcher, Meeting Street Road, Charleston Neck.

Carson, William A[ugustus] (1800–1856), planter, 90 Tradd Street.

Carston [Carsten?], John, city scavenger, Elizabeth Street, Wraggsborough, Charleston Neck.

Cheeseborough, John W[eaver] (1787?–1845), commission merchant, 7 Water Street.

Chisolm, George (1772–1835), factor, 25 East Bay Street.

Chisolm, George Jr. (1796–1837), 25 East Bay Street.

Chisolm, John A., possibly the son of John Chisolm, a Beaufort rice planter.

Claiborn[e], James H[eyward] (d. 1840), planter, Colleton District.

Cobia, F[rancis] J[oseph], Col. (1785–1842), butcher, Reed Street, Charleston Neck.

Cochran, Charles B., Col. (1766–1833), banker, 24 Society Street.

Cogdell, Richard W[alpole] (1785–1867), bank teller, 7 St. Michael's Alley.

Corrie, Samuel (d. 1846), wheelwright, corner King & John streets (1819 directory).

Cross, George W., Col. (1783–1836), attorney, 44 Meeting Street.

Cuthbert, James (1794–1838), planter, 6 Smith Street (1825 directory).

Cuthbert, John A., Gen. (1760–1826), planter, 32 Society Street.

Davis, John N[orvelle] (1785–1851), lawyer and planter, St. James, Goose Greek Parish.

Dawes, Hugh P. (d. 1858), grocer, 19 Hasell Street.

Dawson, Lawrence E[dwin] (1799–1848), attorney, law office on Meeting Street (1825 directory).

Deas, Thomas H[utchinson] (1781–1859), commission merchant, 8 King Street.

Dewees, Joseph (d. 1835?), factor, corner of Alexander and Charlotte streets, Charleston Neck.

Dewees, William (1749–1827), factor, corner Alexander and Charlotte streets, Charleston Neck.

Dewees, William Jr. (1790–1843), factor, Wall & Minority streets.

Dobson, O[liver] L. (1790?–1850), grocer, 65 East Bay Street.

Doughty, James, Dr. (1790–1831), physician, Pinckney Street, Charleston Neck.

Douglas, Campbell (b. 1782?), grocer, 141 Meeting Street.

Dukes, William C. (1794–1867), merchant, King Street Road, Charleston Neck.

Eason, Robert (1778–1838), shipwright, Reaper's Alley.

Edmondston, Charles (1782–1861), factor, 75 Church Street.

Edwards, Charles Lee, Dr., planter and physician, St. Thomas and St. Dennis Parish.

Edwards, Edward H[olmes] (1796–1843), attorney, 4 Meeting Street.

Edwards, James F[isher] (1793–1844), planter, 27 Wall Street.

Elfe, Benjamin Jr. (d. 1828?), Deputy Secretary of State, Amherst Street, Hampstead, Charleston Neck (1825 directory).

Elliot, Benjamin (1786–1836), attorney, 20 Legare Street.

Elliot, Samuel P. (d. 1825?), planter, St. Andrews Parish.

Elliot, Thomas O. (d. 1859), attorney, 4 New Street.
England, Alexander (1771?–1849), baker, 54 Tradd Street.
Evans, William, probably William Henry Evans (1794–1831), businessman, 33 Laurens Street (1825 directory) and not the watchmaker located on 299 King Street in 1822 directory.
Faber, H. J. [F] (d. 1839), factor, Charlotte Street, Mazyckborough, Charleston Neck (1829 directory).
Fordham, Richard, either the blacksmith, 6 Gillon Street or the planter (1785?–1857), St. Thomas Parish
Fraser, Frederick G[rimké] (1794–1852), planter, 99 Tradd Street.
Fraser, John (1777–1854), factor, 4 East Bay Street.
Frierson, John (1777?–1833), planter, Doughty Street, Charleston Neck.
Fuller, Benjamin (1766–1832), planter, corner Boundary & Comings streets, Charleston Neck.
Gadsden, John (1787–1831), attorney, 11 Meeting Street.
Gaillard, Alfred S[amuel] (1796–1830), planter, Lynch Street (1825 directory).
Gaillard, Augustus T[heodore] (1799–1837), factor, 6 New Street (1829 directory).
Gaillard, Bartholomew (1776–1849), planter, Hudson Street, Cannonborough, Charleston Neck (1825 directory).
Gaillard, Peter (1757–1833), planter, 300 East Bay Street.
Gantt, Thomas J[ohn] (1795–1861), attorney, 75 Broad Street.
Garden, Alexander, Major (1757–1829), planter, 8 Short Street.
Gates, John, butcher, Cannon Street, Cannonborough, Charleston Neck (1825 directory).
Gibbes, Peter Smith (1802–1825), planter, Johns Island.
Gibbes, Robert [Reeve] (1769–1831), planter, Johns Island.
Gibson, William H. (1791–1862), tanner, 228 Meeting Street.
Gibson, William Jr. (probably the William Gibson (d. 1849?), listed as a factor, residing on 22 Mazyck Street.
Gilchrist, Robert B[udd] (1799–1856), attorney, 18 Cumberland Street (1819 directory).
Gitsinger, John R. (d. 1830?), businessman and appraiser, 6 Tradd Street.
Glover, Joseph, Dr. (1778–1840), physician, Wentworth Street.
Graves, Charles (1769–1845), factor, 103 Meeting Street.
Green, Thomas P. (1794–1863), druggist, 187 East Bay Street.
Gregson, Thomas (d. 1830), assistant clerk, State Bank, 28 Magazine Street.
Grimball, P[aul] C[haplin] (1788–1864), planter, Vanderhorst Street, Charleston Neck.
Haig, H[ezekiah] M[aham] (1786–1836), physician, St. John, Berkeley.
Hall, George (possibly Dr. George Hall) (1771–1829), 9 Meeting Street (1819 directory).
Hall, William, Dr. (1789–1867), physician, 297 East Bay Street.
Hammet, Benjamin (d. 1826), merchant, King Street Road, Charleston Neck.
Happoldt, C[hristian] D[avid] (1789–1841), butcher, Bridge Street, Charleston Neck.
Happoldt, Christopher (1787–1836), butcher, Cannon Street, Charleston Neck.
Harleston, Edward (1761–1825), planter, 91 Boundary Street.
Harleston, Edward Jr. (1794–1871), planter.
Harleston, James B[urn] (1795–1828), planter, Berkeley County.
Harleston, John (1797–1831), planter, St. Thomas & St. Dennis Parish.
Harleston, Nicholas (1768–1832), planter, Alexander Street, Mazyckborough, Charleston Neck.
Harleston, Nicholas Jr. (1800–1853).

Harvey, Thomas P[inckney], sheriff, 54 Society Street (1825 directory).
Hayne, William A[braham] (1787–1841), accountant, 20 George Street.
Hazlehurst, George Abbot (1797–1858), factor, 55 East Bay Street.
Henry, Alexander (1771?–1836), carpenter, 77 Anson Street.
Heyward, Charles (1802–1866), planter, corner Society and East Bay streets (1829 directory).
Heyward, Nathaniel (1766–1851), planter, 275 East Bay Street.
Holland, Edwin C. (1794–1824), editor Charleston Times, 7 Legare Street (1819 directory).
Holmes, Charles Rutledge (1800–1840), surveyor, 9 East Bay Street.
Holmes, Henry [McCall], Dr. (1790–1854), physician and planter, Berkeley County.
Holmes, Henry P[eronneau], planter, 10 West Street.
Holmes, William H[enry] (1792–1874), factor, Washington Street, Mazyckborough, Charleston Neck (1825 directory).
Hopkins, James S. (1783?–1826), planter, St. James Goose Creek Parish.
Horlbeck, Henry (1776–1837), bricklayer, 241 Meeting Street.
Horlbeck, John (1771–1846), bricklayer, 241 Meeting Street.
Horry, Elias (1773–1834), planter, Meeting Street.
Horry, Elias Lynch (1774–1831), planter, 124 Broad Street.
Hort, Benjamin S[immons] (1791–1825), millwright, Hudson Street, Cannonborough, Charleston Neck.
Howard, John, probably the bricklayer John Howard, 140 Meeting Street (1819 directory).
Huger, Alfred (1788–1872), planter, 114 Broad Street (1825 directory).
Huger, John (1786–1853), planter, 3 Meeting Street (1825 directory).
Hume, Alexander (1795–1848), planter, 96 Wentworth Street (1825 directory).
Hume, John (1763–1841), planter, 17 Wentworth Street.
Hume, Robert (1790–1871), planter, Lynch Street (1825 directory).
Hunt, Benjamin F[aneuil], Col. (1792–1854), attorney and planter, 1 State House Square.
I'On, Jacob Bond, Col. (1782–1859), planter, Christ Church Parish.
Jenkins, Micah (1754–1830), planter, 11 Legare Street.
Jervey, Thomas H[all] (1778–1846), surveyor and inspector of customs, 51 Church Street.
Johnson, William A., possibly the William Johnson listed as a planter, Pinckney St., Cannonborough, Neck, although a planter named William A. Johnson also lived in Georgetown at the time.
Jones, Edward, Dr. (1775–1836), physician, 37 St. Philip's Street, Charleston Neck.
Jones, Elias (d. 1842), Charlotte Street, Mazyckborough, Charleston Neck.
Jones, John S. (1794?–1857), wire worker, 92 Church Street.
Keckley, George (1765–1829), merchant and planter, King Street Road, Charleston Neck.
Keckley, Michael (d. 1830), planter, corner of Boundary and Coming Street (1825 directory).
Keenan, George, merchant, King Street Road, Charleston Neck.
Kennedy, Lionel H[enry], Maj. (1787?–1847), attorney, 7 St. Michael's Alley.
Kiddell, Charles (1777–1844), merchant, 35 Broad Street.
Kirkland, William L[ennox] (1797–1828), physician, 118 Church Street.
Knox, John F. (d. 1845), shipwright, Pritchard & Knox's Wharf.
Kunhardt, William, Col., factor, 34 George Street.
Laborde, Francis, liveryman, corner King and Society streets (1825 directory).
Laurens, Frederick (1802–1827), planter, probably resided at 290 East Bay Street with widowed mother and brother.

Laurens, John B[all] (1799–1827), planter, 290 East Bay Street (1825 directory).
Lazarus, Michael (1786–1862), merchant, 103 Broad Street.
Lee, William, Col. (1778–1848?), teller, Bank of South Carolina, 46 Coming Street.
Legaré, Daniel, Dr. (1781–1854), physician, 3 Guignard Street (1825 directory).
Legaré, Francis Y[onge] (1789–1834), planter, St. Paul's Parish.
Legaré, James (1762–1830), planter, 7 New Street.
Legaré, J[ohn] D[aniel] (d. 1860), planter, Christ Church Parish.
Lesesne, Charles (possibly Charles King Lesesne) (1750?–1840), planter, Georgetown or Charles Lesesne, farmer, Cannonborough, Charleston Neck (1825 directory).
Levy, Elias (1791–1856), accountant, 11 West Street (1825 directory).
Linsser John L[ewis] (d. 1839), butcher, Cannon Street, Cannonborough, Charleston Neck.
Lord, Archibald B., porter, Bank of Discount & Deposit, 2 State Street.
Lothrop, Samuel H. (d. 1827), merchant, East Bay Street.
Lowndes, James (1769–1839), planter, 14 Meeting Street.
Lucas, William (1789–1878), planter, corner Wentworth & Smith streets (1825 directory).
Lynah, James (1793–1877), planter, Colleton District.
Magwood, Simon, Col. (1763–1836), planter, 122 Queen Street.
Manigault, G[abriel] H[enry] (1788–1834), planter, 16 Meeting Street (1825 directory).
Manigault, Joseph Jr. (1801–1829), planter, corner Meeting & John streets, Charleston Neck.
Margart, John H[enry], Deputy Commissary of Ordinance, Military District #6, King Street Road.
Marion, Francis Jr. (1777–1833), planter, Pinckney Street, Cannonborough, Charleston Neck (1825 directory).
Marion, Theodore S[amuel] (1764–1827), planter, East Bay Street, Hampstead, Charleston Neck (1825 directory).
Marsh, James, probably James Marsh Sr. (1777–1852), shipwright, Marsh's Wharf (1825 directory).
Marsh, James Jr. (b. 1802).
Martin, Robert (1790–1852), merchant, King Street Road, Charleston Neck.
Mathewes, Benjamin, Tradd Street, Commander of the US Revenue Cutter *Gallatin*.
Mathewes, William (d. 1848), planter, Charlotte Street, Mazyckborough, Charleston Neck.
Mathews, John Ward (1794–1831), planter, 12 New Street (1825 directory).
Mathews, William, possibly the William Mathews who ran a mill St. James Santee Parish.
Maxwell, William R[ivers] (1794–1873), planter, Cannon Street, Charleston Neck.
Maybank, Joseph (1799–1844), probably planter, Christ Church Parish.
Mazyck, Nathaniel B. (1777–1830), factor, 7 Archdale Street (1825 directory).
Mazyck, P[hilip] P[orcher] (1792–1860), physician, 50 Wentworth Street.
Mazyck, William Jr. (1792–1863), factor, 50 Wentworth Street.
McCartney, Samuel (d. 1849), merchant, 18 Broad Street.
McClary, Samuel (d. 1831), merchant, King Street Road, Charleston Neck.
McInnes, Joseph (1772–1851), wheelwright, Charlotte Street, Charleston Neck.
McNellage, John (1785–1869), sail maker, Kunhardt's Wharf.
Mennar, Louis.
Michel, John (1791–1854), notary public and coroner, 173 Meeting Street (1825 directory).
Middleton, Arthur (1785–1837), planter, 294 East Bay Street.
Middleton, Thomas (1797–1863), factor, 11 George Street.
Miller, Abraham, Col. (1793–1839), clerk, State Bank, 53 Society Street.

Miller, George, probably dry goods storekeeper, King Street Road, Charleston Neck.
Miller, William H., merchant, 33 Anson Street.
Milliken, Thomas, auctioneer, Charlotte Street, Charleston Neck.
Moisson, John (1775–1830), gunsmith, 16 State Street.
Moore, James (d. 1836?), carpenter, Meeting Street Road, Charleston Neck (1825 directory).
Moore, Philip B. (1768–1857), lumber merchant, corner of Montague and Gadsden Streets.
Morford, Edmund (1782–1833), bookseller, 8 Broad Street.
Morris, George W[ashington]. (1799–1834), planter, Edisto Island.
Morris, William E. (1788–1828), planter, St. Bartholomew's Parish.
Mortimer, Edward (1766–1827), appraiser, 63 Anson Street.
Mortimer, Edward (1766–1827), US appraiser, 63 Anson Street.
Muggridge, Matthew (d. 1837?), blacksmith, Hudson Street, Cannonborough, Charleston Neck.
Murray, William, possibly planter, Lynch Street (1825 directory), though not William C. Murray (d. 1856), English merchant.
Murrell, Jonah (d. 1854?), planter, 23 Middle Street.
Mynott[,] William, probably William B. Minott [also Minot] (1777?–1832), planter, 8 Savage Street.
Nelson, James, probably butcher, St. Philip's Street, Charleston Neck.
Newton, William, merchant, Cannon Street, Cannonborough, Charleston Neck (1825 directory).
Norris, James C. (1792–1854), cabinet maker, 119 King Street.
North, Edward W[ashington], Dr. (1778–1843), physician, 89 Meeting Street.
Ogier, Thomas (1755–1833), broker and commission merchant, 188 East Bay Street.
O'Hara, Henry (1775?–1833), broker and vendue master, Mazyck Street.
O'Hear, James (1791–1861), factor, 7 Smith Street.
O'Hear, Joseph F., planter, 7 Smith Street.
O'Neale, James (1791–1871), carpenter, 26 Magazine Street.
Osborne, Richard (d. 1832?), factor, 32 South Bay Street.
Parker, Samuel (1776–1830), planter, 6 George Street.
Parker, William Henry (d. 1828?), factor, 61 Meeting Street.
Patrick, Casimir (d. 1849?), tanner, King Street Road.
Patrick, Philip, planter, 106 Meeting Street (1819 directory) also a Philip Patrick who was a notary public and lived on 37 State Street (1829 directory).
Patterson, Samuel, Major (1786–1839), 2 Hasell Street.
Patton, William (1794–1858), merchant 108 Church Street.
Paul, Dunbar (1792–1876), grocer, 47 Broad Street.
Payne, Josiah Smith (d. 1859), worked in father William's firm, 2 Friend Street (1825 directory).
Payne, William (d. 1833?), broker and vendue master, 28 Broad Street.
Perry, Edward D[rayton] (d. 1833), planter, Vanderhorst Street, Charleston Neck.
Peronneau, Henry W[illiam] (1798–1859), planter, 4 South Bay Street (1819 directory).
Peronneau, William (1768–1848), planter, 34 South Bay Street.
Phelon, Col., E[dmond] M[eade] (1758?–1833), grocer, 88 Meeting Street.
Pinckney, C. C. Jr., probably Charles Cotesworth Pinckney (1746–1825), 223 East Bay Street (although the "Jr." is curious).

Pinckney, Henry L[aurens] (1794–1863), planter and founding publisher and editor *Charleston Mercury*, 4 New Street.

Pinckney, Robert Q[uash] (1802–1860), surveyor, 5 State Street, Canonborough, Charleston Neck.

Poyas, James (1790–1872), shipwright, 4 Gibbes Street (1825 directory).

Price, O'Brien Smith (1795–1843), planter, King Street Road, Charleston Neck.

Price, Philip S. (b. 1801), planter, corner St. Philip and Radcliffe Streets (1829 directory).

Price, Thomas W[illiam] (d. 1827), planter, 12 George Street.

Price, William Jr. (d. 1831?), planter, 116 Broad Street.

Price, William Smith (1797–1848), physician, King Street Road, Charleston Neck.

Pringle, Edward Jenkins (1796–1838), planter, 62 Tradd Street (1829 directory).

Pringle, William Bull (1800–1881), planter, All Saints Parish.

Prioleau, Philip G[endron], Dr. (1776–1844), physician, 220 Meeting Street.

Quash, Francis D[allas] (1793–1857), planter, 307 East Bay Street.

Quash, Robert H[asell] (1786–1846), planter, 108 Broad Street.

Ramsay, David (1795–1826), attorney, 109 Queen Street.

Ramsay, James, Dr. (1798–1832), physician, 74 Broad Street.

Read, John Harleston (1788–1859), planter, corner Wentworth & Rutledge streets, (1825 directory).

Read, William, Dr. (1754–1845), physician, 14 Logan Street.

Reid, George B. (1793–1876), bookkeeper for Bank of South Carolina, 49 East Bay Street.

Reid, William, 104 Meeting Street (1825 directory).

Richardson, Henry, Dr. (d. 1829?), physician, 210 Meeting Street.

Righton, Joseph (1762–1847), cooper, 5 Water Street.

Rivers, John (1786–1857), planter, James Island.

Robertson, John T. (1799–1836), merchant and naval agent, 31 Meeting Street.

Robinson, John, probably (1776–1849), merchant, John Street, Wraggsborough, Charleston Neck.

Robinson, Randal (1785?–1854), merchant, 94 Tradd Street.

Rogers, John R[alph] (1785–1857), ship chandler, 105 East Bay Street.

Roper, Robert W[illiam] (d. 1845), merchant and planter, East Bay Street.

Routledge, John, merchant, King Street Road, Charleston Neck.

Rowand, Charles Elliott (1771–1835), planter, 93 Meeting Street.

Rutledge, Frederick (1771–1824), planter, 111 Tradd Street.

Rutledge, John (1792–1864), planter, 292 East Bay Street.

Rutledge, States (1783–1829), planter, 303 East Bay Street.

Schirer, John (1774–1827), gunsmith, 188 Meeting Street (1816 directory).

Schmidt, Wilbrandt, planter, North Edisto.

Schnierle, John M[ichael] (1778–1844), carpenter, 11 Friend Street.

Schutt, John G. (d. 1840?), hardware merchant, 89 East Bay Street (1825 directory).

Seigling, John (1789–1867), music business, 69 Broad Street.

Shoolbred, James (1776–1847), planter, 46 Montague Street.

Shoolbred, John G[ibbes], Dr. (1796–1860), physician, Radcliffborough, Charleston Neck (1829 directory).

Simons, Edward (1778–1842), 2 Brownlee's Row, King Street, Charleston Neck.

Simons, Maurice (1786–1845), factor, 1 Middle Street.

Simons, Thomas G[range] (1789–1863), factor, 48 Bull Street (1825 directory).

Sinkler, William (1787–1853), planter, St. Johns Parish.

Smith, F. C.
Smith, Richard D. (b. 1798), probably Richard Downes Smith of Georgetown.
Smith, Thomas Jr. (d. 1830), probably planter from St. Paul Parish, resided 10 Green Street (1825 directory).
Smith, William, possibly Judge William Smith (1762–1840), 73 Queen Street.
Smith, William J., factor, Mazyckborough, Charleston Neck.
Smith, W[illia]m Mason (1788–1838), planter, 10 Lamboll Street.
Spring, John (1775?–1827), mechanic, Wraggsborough, Charleston Neck.
Stevens, Daniel (1746–1835), planter, 28 George Street.
Stewart, Angus (d. 1849?), proprietor coffee house, 20 Tradd Street.
Stoney, John (1780–1838), merchant, 293 East Bay Street.
Strohecker, John (1776?–1849), blacksmith, 18 Cumberland Street.
Taylor, Josiah (1780?–1847), factor, 4 Lamboll Street.
Teasdale, George, bricklayer, 218 Meeting Street (1825 directory).
Teasdale, Richard (1789–1857), factor, 54 East Bay Street.
Thayer, Ebenezer Jr. (1767–1824), teacher, 62 Wentworth Street.
Timmons, William (1773–1838), proprietor hardware store, 165 East Bay Street.
Toomer, Anthony V[anderhorst], Dr. (1775–1856), physician and planter, Chapel Street, Wraggsborough, Charleston Neck.
Toomer, Joshua W[ashington] (1789–1840), attorney, 290 East Bay Street.
Tovey, Henry (1797–1844), block maker, 285 East Bay Street.
Trescott, Joseph (1788–1828), merchant, 19 Maiden Lane.
Vance, William (d. 1824), planter, Pinckney Street, Cannonborough, Charleston Neck (1819 directory).
Vanderhorst, Elias (1791–1874), planter, Kiawah Island.
Venning, Nicholas (1788–1855), planter, Christ Church Parish.
Vinyard, John (1778–1851), planter, Hampstead, Charleston Neck.
Walker, Robert (1772–1833), cabinet maker, 139 Church Street.
Waring, Horatio S[mith], Dr. (1789–1868), physician, 74 Wentworth Street.
Waring, Morton A[lexander] (1783?–1863), factor, 36 Meeting Street.
Wesner, Frederick (1788–1848), carpenter, 138 Queen Street.
Westendorff, C[harles] P. L. (1787?–1863), merchant and Portuguese consul, 230 East Bay Street (1819 directory).
Weston, Paul, Dr. (1779–1837), planter and physician, Hampstead, Charleston Neck (1819 directory).
Weyman, Joseph T[urpin] (d. 1834), merchant, corner King and Vanderhorst streets, Charleston Neck.
Wharton, Samuel (1783–1827), merchant, corner King and Mary streets, Charleston Neck.
White, John, possibly the factor, 216 Meeting Street or the planter, Smith's Lane.
Wigfall, Thomas (1768–1843), planter, Washington Street, Mazyckborough, Charleston Neck.
Wigfall, Thomas Jr. (1799–1840), planter. Wilkes, John (d. 1857?), merchant, 18 Meeting Street.
Williman, Christopher (1787–1864), planter, Pinckney Street, Charleston Neck.
Wilson, Hugh (1786–1864), planter, Pinckney Street, Charleston Neck.
Wilson, John H. (1793?–1843), planter, 12 Pitt Street.
Wilson, Samuel Jr., Dr. (1763–1827), physician, 6 New Street.
Wilson, William H[andy] (1793–1849), commission merchant, 100 Meeting Street.

Winthrop, Charles (1799?–1833), factor, 105 Tradd Street (1829 directory).
Wragg, Samuel, Major (1770–1844), cashier, State Bank, Meeting Street (1825 directory).
Yates, Jeremiah A[tmar] (1773–1846), planter, Ladson's Court.

9. Officers of the South Carolina Association:
President Keating Simons (1753–1834) was a wealthy slaveholder with multiple properties in and around Charleston. The slave Paris Ball, punished for involvement in the plot, probably belonged to Simons's only daughter, Anne Simons Ball. See Part III, p. 220 n1. Keating Simons had an extensive career of public service. A prominent factor and planter, he owned estates in St. James Goose Creek and St. John Berkeley parishes and scores of slaves. He had served during the American Revolution as an officer in the Charleston militia and under the command of the legendary Francis Marion. In 1822 he resided at 5 Orange Street.

Vice-President 1: Col. John Cordes Prioleau
On Prioleau (1772–1825), who owned Peter, the first slave to reveal the plot, see Part I, p. 44 n1.

Vice-President 2: Gen. Thomas Pinckney
On Pinckney (1750–1828) and his anonymously published pamphlet on the Vesey affair, see above, pp. 552–63.

Vice-President 3: Stephen Elliott
On Elliott (1771–1830) and his thoughts on the Vesey affair, see Part IV, pp. 406–7.

Vice-President 4: Henry Deas
On Deas (1770–1846), one of Vesey's judges on the first Court of Magistrates and Freeholders, see part III, p. 161 n6.

Vice-President 5: Joseph Manigault
Manigault (1763–1843), a big planter with multiple estates and several hundred slaves, resided in 1822 on the corner of Meeting and John streets, Charleston Neck. He was the brother-in-law of Nathaniel Heyward, one of Vesey's judges on the first Court of Magistrates and Freeholders. See *BDSCHR* 3: 473–75.

Recording Secretary: Robert J. Turnbull
On Turnbull (1775–1833), one of Vesey's judges on the first Court of Magistrates and Freeholders, see Part III, p. 161 n5.

Corresponding Secretary: Major J. S. Cogdell
On Cogdell and his response to the Vesey affair, see Part IV, p. 378 n7.

Treasurer: John Bay
Bay (1785–1845), a prominent merchant as well as an active Episcopalian and Freemason, resided in 1822 at 72 King Street.

Solicitor: Isaac E. Holmes
Isaac Edward Holmes (1796–1867), attorney and planter, was a close friend of Robert J. Turnbull. In 1822 he resided at 9 East Bay Street.

Steward 1: Col. John Bryan

Bryan (1791–1848), a planter, served in 1822 as an officer in the Charleston cavalry and resided on Hasell Street.

Steward 2: James Ferguson

On Ferguson (1784–1874), who had several slaves inculpated in the Vesey plot, see Part II, p. 109 n1.

Members of the Standing Committee

Chairman: John Middleton

In 1822 Middleton (1784–1826), a planter, owned property on Sullivan's Island and resided in Charleston at 42 Bull Street. He was the stepson of Thomas Pinckney. See *BDSCHR* 5: 183; *CSCCD,* 90.

Sedgwick L. Simons

Sedgwick Lewis Simons (1788–1834), the son of Keating Simons, was a factor who resided on Montague Street. See *BDSCHR* 5: 243; *CSCCD,* 130.

Col. R. W. Vanderhorst

On Vanderhorst (1786–1832), who in 1820 owned several hundred slaves, including George, convicted of involvement in the Vesey plot, see Part III, p. 200 n4.

Col. Richard Cunningham

Cunningham (1785?–1837), planter, politician, and militia officer, resided in 1825 on Charlotte Street, Mazyckborough, Charleston Neck. See *BDSCHR* 3: 140–41; *CSCCD,* 111.

Col. William Cattell

On Cattell (1776–1842), whose slave Jack was convicted of involvement in the Vesey plot and transported out of the state, see Part III, p. 364 n2.

Charles Parker

Parker (1797–1859) was an engineer and Charleston's city surveyor, who, in 1822, resided at 2 New Street. See *CSCCD,* 93.

Col. John Gordon

On Gordon (d. 1835) who served on the second Court of Magistrates and Freeholders, see Part III, p. 262 n8

Petitions to the General Assembly, n.d. [ca. September 1823], no. 1415, series S165015 SCDAH.

Charleston Courier

Monday, August 25, 1823

PROCLAMATION.

By JOHN GEDDES, Intendant of the City

of Charleston,

WHEREAS, at a Court holden at Charleston during the last year, a Negro Man slave, named SCIPIO, then the property of Capt. Simms, was tried and sentenced to death, for being concerned in a projected insurrection; which sentence was commuted on the express condition of his being sent out of the limits of the United States; and whereas information has been received by me that the said fellow named Scipio, was discovered on the evening of the 22d inst. to have returned; and on being pursued, made his escape: And, whereas the safety and good order of society require that those who violate the laws should meet the punishment due to their offences:

Now, therefore, I deem it proper to issue this *Proclamation*, calling on all officers civil and military, and on all good citizens, to be active and vigilant in apprehending the said fellow named Scipio, so that the ends of justice may be satisfied. And I do hereby offer a reward of *One Hundred Dollars* to any person or persons who shall apprehend said culprit, and lodge in confinement, to be dealt with according to law. And all persons are hereby forewarned from harboring, or in any wise aiding and abetting the said fellow named Scipio, under the penalties of the law in such cases made and provided.

Given under my hand, and the seal of the Corporation, this twenty-fifth day of August, in the year of our Lord one thousand eight hundred and twenty-three, and in the forty-seventh year of the independence of the U. States of Ame[r]ica.

JOHN GEDDES, *Intendant.*

Charleston Courier

Monday, August 25, 1823

BE ON THE ALERT!

MR. EDITOR—You will confer a favor on the public by inserting the following:

"A Negro Fellow, who calls himself *Scipio*, belonging to Capt. SIMMS, who was transported to the back states, was on his way to Charleston, and stopt at the Twenty-Five M[il]e House, on the Wasmasaw Road, where he was taken up by a widow lady, who lives at the same, and put into confinement, from whence he made his escape the same night he was taken up, being the 18th day of August. He had with him, in cash, ten dollars and twenty-five cents, three vests, one round jacket, one coatee, one blanket, one sheet, two shirts, three pairs of pantaloons, one pair of shoes, two cravats, two pocket handkerchiefs and one pillow case. It is expected he is now in Charleston, as he was on his way thither. He had with him a free pass, that he said was given him by his master, and afterwards acknowledged that he wrote it himself. He had several newspapers, with some tickets, written by himself, the first dated August 16, 1823."

The Standing Committee of the "South-Carolina Association," being on Friday informed that this notice was sent to the "City Gazette" for insertion, requested the Editor to defer its publication until a search could be made for the man therein mentioned. A search was accordingly made on Friday night by the Patrol on Charleston Neck, for the said Negro *Scipio*. He was found out and pursued, and escaped only by leaping from the kitchen of Mr. SIMMS into the garden of Mr. BROWNLEE, where the Patrol were unable to pursue him. He made his escape into the city.

N. B.—*Scipio* belonged to Capt. WM. SIMMS, was last year sentenced to death by the Court of Magistrates and Freeholders, for being concerned in the projected insurrection;

which sentence was commuted on the express condition of his being "sent out of the limits of the United States."

Newburyport Herald

Tuesday, September 9, 1823

A fresh alarm is excited at Charleston S.C. on account of the negroes—a leader in the late conspiracy was banished, under penalty of forfeiting his life if he returned. He had the audacity to show himself in the city; a hue-and-cry was set up, but Scipio was secreted, and could not be found; this showed he had friends and abettors. The police were on the alert, and strict guards set at night.

Providence *Gazette*

Wednesday, September 10, 1823

Scipio, a black who had received sentence of death, but was afterwards banished from the State of South-Carolina for his participation in the plot formed by the negroes in Charleston some months since, has recently returned to that city and occasioned a general alarm among the inhabitants, by eluding their pursuit from the 22d ult. when he returned, to the 25th, when he was apprehended and imprisoned.

Charleston *City Gazette and Commercial Daily Advertiser*

Wednesday, September 10, 1823

September 1st, 1823.

. . . The inhabitants of Clarendon having been induced to believe it to be the wish of the South-Carolina Association to become the depository of all information on this highly interesting subject, hasten to state facts in illustration of their opinion of its importance and value.

It will be recollected that three years since Mr. Ford[1] of Georgetown was cruelly murdered by a negro fellow (Joe) then fugitive. . . .

He uses the most dense and impervious swamps, places himself at the head of fugitive slaves . . . (their number is various and uncertain). . . .

Of his influence over fugitive slaves and of the utter impossibility to obtain information from others respecting him, there are too many proofs.

It may here be well to state, that Scipio Simms has long been at large and perfectly unmolested in this neighbourhood. It is possible he may have had communication with Joe. . . .

1. On the fugitive slave Joe and the death of planter George Ford (1776–1821), see pp. 66, 529.

New Bedford Mercury

Friday, September 12, 1823

A black man, named Scipio, who was convicted at Charleston, S.C. of being concerned in the conspiracy in that State, and sentenced to death, was pardoned on condition of leaving the State, and never returning. But he came back to Charleston a few weeks since, and skulked about for sometime; at length he was discovered and after being once caught and escaping, he was by the information of a slave, and the efforts of many spirited individuals again taken into custody—and will probably suffer under the first sentence. . . .

Newbern (NC) *Carolina Centinel*

Friday, September 12, 1823

Considerable excitement appears to have been produced in Charleston, by the return to that city of a negro man by the name of Scipio, concerned in the late conspiracy, who had been sentenced to perpetual banishment. After an active search of two days, he was found in a privy, completely exhausted, and exclaiming that *he was at last hunted down,* surrendered without resistance. He will probably suffer death.[1]

1. This information appeared verbatim in the Providence *Gazette,* September 10, 1823; *New Bedford Mercury,* September 12, 1823; and *Newburyport Herald,* September 9, 1823.

Newport *Mercury*

Saturday, September 13, 1823

SOUTH CAROLINA

CHARLESTON, AUGUST 28.

At a Court of Magistrates held yesterday, the fellow Scipio, who was last year sentenced to banishment from the State, but had returned, was arraigned, and called upon to show cause why sentence of death should not be passed upon him, when his counsel requested time to confer with his master, and three weeks were allowed by the Court.

Charleston *City Gazette and Commercial Daily Advertiser*

Wednesday, September 24, 1823

The Court of Magistrates and Freeholders, has decided that the Negro Fellow SCIPIO shall be confined until his original sentence is complied with—transportation beyond the limits of the United States.[1]

1. This information appeared verbatim in the Charleston *Carolina Gazette,* September 27, 1823, and the Camden *Southern Chronicle,* October 1, 1823.

Camden (SC) *Southern Chronicle*

Wednesday, October 22, 1823
MORE NEGROES DESTROYED.
Extract of a letter, dated Pineville,[1] *Oct.* 13.

"A party went out on Tuesday last, and routed the remainder of Joe's gang. They fired on two of the men and wounded one. One of the Negroes wounded Evance Cordes in the shoulder and one finger, with duck shot. The wound is very slight, and he is entirely recovered. On Wednesday, some of the same party went out, and came up with two men and three women. One of the men fired on John Ravenel,[2] but without effect, and made his escape. They took one fellow and the wenches, and we have them now in confinement in this place. One of the women having a man's cloak on was fired upon, and I am sorry to say was wounded—her chance of recovery is doubtful.

"On Tuesday when the party were routed, they left a child about three years old in the camp, and a chance shot struck it in the back of the head, and it has since died. The fellow taken and the woman wounded, (who is the wife of Joe) belongs to Dr. Roual; a Girl, the mistress of Joe, belongs to Mr. Ballard; and the other woman, the wife of Anderson who was killed, belongs to Mr. Bates. Two of the most desperate and one woman, are not yet taken.

A Court of Magistrates was sitting for the trial of those taken, and others suspected. An Acting Committee of the Association are very active in gaining information."

1. Established in 1795 in St. Stephen's Parish, Pineville is now in the northern part Berkeley County, fifty-plus miles from Charleston.

2. Probably John Ravenel (1793–1862), the son of Daniel Ravenel (1762–1807) and Catherine Cordes Prioleau Ravenel (1769–1849).

Governor John Lyde Wilson in the Camden *Southern Chronicle*

Wednesday, November 12, 1823
EXECUTIVE DEPARTMENT

Charleston, 3d Nov. 1823.

To John S. Cogdell,[1] *Esq. Corresponding Secretary of the South Carolina Association.*

SIR—I have received your circular covering the proceedings and constitution of the South-Carolina Association, wherein the countenance of the Executive is solicited, to support the general principles for which the Association has been formed.

I have given the best consideration to the subject of which I am capable, and regret, that I cannot, consistently with the dictates of my judgment, approve of the Association. I have heretofore considered it among the many blessings we enjoy, that we live under a government of laws. No Association can add strength or energy to the rules prescribed by the supreme authority of the State, and it is a reflection upon the laws to suppose it. I can readily see that many and serious inconvenience may arise out of these voluntary Associations. They are to be dreaded from the character and standing of those that compose them. The press is already enlisted in behalf of the one in question. All magistrates will be deterred from acting, until the feelings of the Association in the particular case be known; and whenever stability is imparted on the institution, what guarantee is left to the coloured population, that a moment of excitement may not prostrate all law, and produce scenes at which humanity will weep. It may be answered, the standing and character of the members forbid such a suspicion. I have the most profound respect for the intelligence and patriotism of the Presiding Officers of the institution. Yey I would confide with more security in the wisdom of the Law, and its correct administration by the proper officers of the Government, unaided by any authorized body of citizens, unawed by powerful Associations. But who can predict with certainty, that the members who succeed the present Association will be entitled to implicit confidence? What guarantee is there, that other and far different objects may not be essayed? Politics and party feelings have found their way into almost every association of men; *even within the walls of the sacred sanctuary they have intruded*; and as long as human nature remains as it is, this and every similar institution will be subject to the same prejudices and partialities, which are inseparable from our frailty. The South-Carolina Association is bottomed upon strong affections of the heart; "*deep concern* for the non-enforcement of the laws enacted IN RELATION TO FREE PERSONS OF COLOUR and the laxity which prevails as regards our BLACK POPULATION, an evil which threatens the most serious results, to the peace and prosperity of South-Carolina." I cannot imagine a case where any one of the Association, aided by the Law, may not fearlessly enforce it against the coloured population of the State, whether they are bond or free. Let incompetent police officers be removed or punished by the authority to which they are amenable. If the Laws with respect to this species of population, be so imperfect as to threaten the peace and prosperity of the State, let them be amended. To this end I would be the willing organ of communication to the proper authority, and would receive the suggestion of any one of my fellow-citizens with pleasure. Our constitution wisely commits the peace and prosperity of the state to the Legislature composed of the representatives of the people, an independent Judiciary, and elective Executive. These are all responsible for any neglect of the general, and to these co-ordinate branches of the government, let the happiness of the people be confided. . . .

1. On John Stevens Cogdell (1778–1847), see Part IV, p. 378 n7. In his position as naval officer for the port of Charleston, Cogdell, friend of proslavery firebrand Robert J. Turnbull, would have known better than most South Carolina notables of the threat posed by black seamen from outside the state in providing information to Charleston's persons of color about events in the wider world.

Edisto Island Auxiliary Association[1] on the Dangers of Antislavery Doctrines

Thursday, November 18, 1823

. . . That a sacred regard for the safety of their property, and the welfare of the State, have forcibly induced them to establish a Society, in aid of the constituted authorities, with respect to the regulation of the Coloured Population. Altho' it is their peculiar boast and pride, that they do live under a government of laws yet, it must be conceded that in the execution of an edict, the assistance of individuals is oft times not only required, but imperiously demanded. Experience has clearly demonstrated the fact, that notwithstanding the activity and vigilance of our Police officers, the mid-night incendiary has escaped with impunity, and the assassin perfected his scheme of horror. The history of the times too warrants the conclusion, that the period is rapidly approaching, when the sober dictates of reason on the subject of slavery, must yield to the hypocritical feelings of a misguided philanthropy. To avert so serious a calamity to remove the misty veil which obscures the light of truth and justice, and forever to crush the spirit of insubordination and revolt, it is not necessary only that the civil authorities should display their customary alertness and devotion to the public weal, but that the zealous aid of every patriotic citizen should be freely offered. If our constitutional rights are in imminent peril of being forever lost; if the tenure by which our most valuable privileges are held, is dubious and uncertain; surely, the laws of God and Man invoke us not to behold a scene so dear to the human heart, unconcerned and free from serious apprehensions. The crisis is indeed assuming a critical and an imposing aspect. The ties of consanguinity and interest are insufficient to prevail over our neighbours from publicly thundering their anathema against the holders of Slaves; neither moral considerations or political motives can restrain their demagogues from infusing into the bosoms of our credulous and superstitious colored people, the most dangerous and revolting doctrines.

With our mixed and peculiar population, it is vitally important not only that the provisions of the Legislature relative to the government of our Slaves, should be strictly and rigidly enforced, but that no aberrations from the line of policy, marked out by the State should ever be permitted. To effectuate so laudable a purpose, and *to inform and assist* the legal powers, are the sole motives which induce your petitioners now to beg the countenance and support of your Honorable Body. Independently of the other general arguments which could be advanced, your petitioners would call the attention of the House to one consideration peculiarly local. The white population of Edisto Island is to the Black as 200 to 3000, or as 1 to 15. This fact speaks volumes. . . .

1. Whitemarsh Benjamin Seabrook (1793–1855), a major planter on Edisto Island, forty-plus miles southwest of Charleston, led the Edisto Island Auxiliary Association. A graduate of Princeton, trained in law and a prominent voice for agricultural reform, Seabrook composed *A Concise View of the Critical Situation and Future Prospects of the Slave-holding States in Relation to Their Coloured Population* (Charleston, SC, 1825), an essay that was deeply informed by the Vesey affair. See *BDSCHR* 4: 511–12.

Officers of the Edisto Island Auxiliary Association to South Carolina House of Representatives, November 18, 1823, no. 151, series S165015, SCDAH.

Appraisal of Peter and George Wilson

Executive Department
Columbia, Nov. 27th 1823

. . . Agreeably to the act of Assembly passed last session I appointed John Geddes, William S. Smith and Francis G. Deliesslines, Esquires as appraisers of the value of the slave named Peter, the property of John C. Prioleau Esqr[1] and George, the property of Mrs. Wilsons. And the said appraisers did on the twelfth day of April last value the said Negro slaves, at one thousand Dollars each; which said sum has been paid to the owners of the said Slaves agreeably to the act aforesaid. The warrant of appointment and the said appraisement are herewith enclosed.

Your fellow citizen
John L. Wilson

1. Upon becoming free, Peter (1787?–1860) adopted the name of "Peter P. Desverney." Peter was evidently the son of an enslaved woman and the white "Citizen Peter Francis Desverney," identified by Robert Goodloe Harper in 1798 as a "native of France" who had settled in Charleston and worked as a gunsmith. See William Cobbett, ed., *Porcupine's Works* (London, 1801), 327–30. The Charleston *City Gazette,* May 6, 1800, reported the death of a "Francis Desverney," age sixty-eight and a resident of the city for two decades. Judith Rollins, *All Is Never Said: The Narrative of Odette Harper Hines* (Philadelphia: Temple University Press, 1995), 25, provides a genealogy of the Desverney family. Hines confided to Rollins that family lore held that her great-great-grandfather, Peter Desverney, "was the man who betrayed Denmark Vesey to the whites. I've never tried to verify that story; I guess, I don't want to find out for sure that it's true."

According to two accounts opened with the Freedman's Savings Bank, Charleston branch, on June 28, 1868, and May 11, 1869, by his sons Anthony K. Desverney (1831–1892) and Francis Desverney, respectively, Peter died in 1860 at approximately age seventy-three. (Francis, presumably, was named for his grandfather.) The two sons, ages thirty-seven and fifty-seven when they opened their accounts, had different mothers, who evidently had different complexions. Anthony was listed in the bank records as "Light," and his mother's name was Sarah Claussen. Francis was born in 1812 (thus ten years old at the time of the Vesey conspiracy) and listed as "Dark Brown." His mother's name was Clara. Thus the desire to elevate his son into freedom may have played into Peter's motivation for revealing what he knew. In 1852, Francis Desverney ran a livery stable at Broad and Friend streets and lived at 5 Magazine Street. See James W. Hagy, *Directories for the City of Charleston, South Carolina: for the Years 1849, 1852, and 1855* (Baltimore: Clearfield, 1998), 63. In 1878, Frank, then a "colored policeman" in the city of Charleston, lost his position after "redemption." See John Oldfield, "Black Policemen in City of Charleston, 1869–1921," *SCHM* 102 (2001): 153–68.

Peter Desverney joined the Friendly Union Society, founded in Charleston on September 4, 1831, as a mutual-support association for persons of partial African ancestry, the self-styled "browns." See *Constitution and By-Laws of the Friendly Union Society of Charleston, S.C.* (Charleston, SC, 1889), 24.

In 1847, the Charleston City Council remitted a fine imposed on Peter for employing a boy to work as drayman in violation of a city ordinance. A decade later, Desverney, then approximately seventy years old, petitioned the state to increase his annual stipend from $50 to $150, in a document reprinted in this section, pp. 639–40. Because of his information in 1822, the state legislature passed an act to give Peter his freedom and awarded him an annual sum of $50. See "Proceedings of the Council," Charleston *Southern Patriot,* May 18, 1847; "Report of the Committee on Military and Pensions on the Petition of Peter Desverny a Free Person of Color Praying for an Increased Pension," November 30, 1857, no. 1, series S165005, SCDAH.

According to the Freedman's Savings Bank records, the two boys had three sisters—Rebecca Snead, Sarah Robertson, and Isabella Desverney—and one brother, John C. Desverney. Curiously, Robert Vesey Sr., son of the hanged abolitionist, and John C. Desverney, son of the informant, both served on the 1865 Charleston Mechanics' Association. Desverney was the group's president, and Vesey served on the eight-member Committee on Charity. See Charleston *South Carolina Leader,* December 9, 1865. Richard C. Wade, *Slavery in the Cities: The South, 1820–1860* (New York: Oxford University Press, 1964), 229, misidentified Peter as "Devany Prioleau."

Message Regarding the Appraisal of John C. Prioleau's Slave Peter, and Mrs. Wilson's Slave George, November 27, 1823, no. 1343, series S165009, SCDAH.

Memorial Regarding Slave Patrols, Tuesday, December 9, 1823

. . . The petition of the President and Members of the Black Swamp Association humbly sheweth.

That your petitioners have associated their selves together, under the name and style of the Black swamp Association, for the purpose of enforceing the laws of this State, against the violators thereof; and for the better governing and managing negroes and other persons of colour, in conformity to a similar association established in Charleston, for a similar purpose. . . .

Petition of the Black Swamp Association, December 9, 1823, 147, series S165015, SCDAH.

Charleston Mercury, and Morning Advertiser

Wednesday, June 23, 1824

Yesterday, Amos Daley, a free man *of color,* who hails from Rhode Island, was tried before a Court of Magistrates and Freeholders, for having recently *entered the State a second time,* contrary to the Act of the Legislature, he having in April last received official warning, under the provisions of the Act, never again to appear within the limits of the State.

Messrs. COURTENAY[1] and MCCREEDY[2] appeared as counsel for the prisoner, and Mr. HOLMES,[3] Solicitor of the South Carolina Association, on behalf of the prosecution.

The defence of the prisoner was, that he was an Indian and therefore not subject to the operation of the act; but the Court being satisfied from the evidence that he was of negro descent, (and a mulatto he indubitably is from inspection) sentenced him to corporal punishment by whipping, which was promptly inflicted on him under the direction of the Sheriff at five o'clock in the afternoon of yesterday at the work-house.

Should he, after leaving the State, again return he will be liable to be again tried and whipped, and so on as long as he continues to violate the act.

1. Charleston attorney Edward S. Courtenay (1795–1857) was a close friend of William Crafts Jr. (1787–1826), who counseled Billy Robinson and Denbow Martin during the Vesey trials.
2. "McCreedy" may refer to Charleston attorney Edward McCrady (1802–1892).
3. Isaac Edward Holmes (1796–1867), attorney and planter, was solicitor for the South Carolina Association.

Resolution of the Senate of South Carolina

. . . Resolved that it is as much the duty of the State, to guard against insubordination or insurrection among our colored population as to control and regulate any cause which might excite or produce it, as to guard against any other evil political or physical which might assail us. This duty is paramount to all *laws,* all *treaties,* all *constitutions:*—it arises from the supreme and permanent law of nature, the law of self-preservation; and will never by this State be renounced, controled, or participated with any power whatever. . . .

Resolution of the Senate of South Carolina, December 8, 1824, no. 8, series S165018, SCDAH.

Memorial Regarding the City Guard

. . . That in and by an Act of Assembly passed on the 21st day of December 1822 entitled an "Act to establish a competent force to act as a Municipal Guard for the protection of Charleston and its vicinity["] it was enacted "that for the purpose of defraying the expenses of the said Guard a Tax of Ten dollars should be imposed on all houses within the limits so guarded inhabited by negroes or persons of color either as Tenants or owners." And also "a Tax not exceeding 20 per cent tax upon all property within the limit aforesaid to be assessed by the Municipal Board and a Tax of Ten dollars upon all free male persons of color who exercise any Mechanick trade within the said limits." That after the passing of the said act . . . the owners of houses assessed for payment of the said tax applied for a prohibition to restrain the collecting of the same on various grounds, among which were urged the inequality of the Tax as the Guard was intended for a general benefit: it would then be an injustice to render only certain land owners liable who had already paid their General Tax, the more especially in the case of those who had leased to free persons of color lots of land many years before the imposing of this tax, which leases had not expired. That against persons so situated this Tax operated as a penalty for having done what was not by Law forbidden to be done when such leases have been made. . . .

Memorial of Sundry Citizens to South Carolina State Legislature, n.d. [ca. 1825], no. 1798, series S165015, SCDAH.

Francis Kinloch[1] to Thomas Waties,[2] Friday, April 29, 1825

. . . I find by Ogier's and Carter's letter, that though field negroes had risen very much in price, previously to the late improvement in the sale of cotton, yet servants had not, owing I believe, to the bad conduct of great numbers of that description, at the time of the intended revolt in Charleston. They therefore thought the price offered by Mr. Waterman, as much as I could get for Charlotte and her children, if I sent them to Charleston. . . .

1. Charleston-born Francis Kinloch (1755–1826) owned multiple estates and several hundred slaves in the late eighteenth century before turning to absenteeism and a life of travel toward the

end of his life. See "Obituary," *Rhode-Island American and Providence Gazette,* March 7, 1826; *BDSCHR* 3: 402–5.

2. Thomas Waties (1760–1828), lawyer, judge, and planter, owned dozens of slaves on an estate in Prince George Winyah in the Georgetown district. See *BDSCHR* 3: 753–55.

ALS in Waties Papers, box 1, folder 12, SCL.

Committee on Claims, 1825

. . . About the time of the contemplated Insurrection of Slaves in the city of Charleston, the petitioner[1] with certain others seized some horses on the plantation of Mr. Blake[2] which they believed to be the property of certain slaves, and with which it was apprehended they intended making their escape. The horses were carried before a Magistrate, condemned, and sold, and the money still remains in the hands of the Magistrate who holds himself bound to pay it over to the state.

Mr. Clark was then tried by Mr. Blake in an action of Trespass for entering his plantation; and carrying off his horses, and on the Trial obtained damages to the amount of Two hundred dollars from where it appears the whole was a high-handed and Illegal proceeding. . . .

1. George S. Clark (also rendered "Clarke") resided in the Colleton District, neighboring the Charleston District to the southwest.

2. The English-born Daniel Blake (1775–1834) owned "large estates" in the region. See "Blake of South Carolina," *SCHGM* (April 1900): 164.

Committee on Claims, Report and Resolution, no. 253, December 2, 1825, series S165005, SCDAH.

Memorial Regarding Schools and Employment for Persons of Color, 1826

. . . That the Grand Jury of Charleston District have presented the number of Schools publickly kept for the instruction of persons of Colour in reading and writing as injurious to the Community. Your Memorialists concur fully with their opinion. To be able to read and write is certainly not necessary to the performance of those duties which are usually required of our Slaves, and on the contrary is incompatible with the public safety. The facility with which the knowledge of the art of writing will enable persons of this class to carry on illicit trafic, to communicate privately among themselves and to evade those regulations that are intended to prevent confederations among them, renders it important that the Law prohibiting their being taught should be rigidly enforced. . . . It is impossible to distinguish between the free and the slave of our colored population and therefore it is extremely difficult to detect violations of the Law. We know of no remedy so effectual and at the same time so little liable to objection as the absolute prohibition of all Schools for the instruction of Colored persons. . . . It has been the policy of some evil minded persons to publish inflammatory writings and to circulate them among their people. . . .

There is another subject relating to our Coloured population which your Memorialists would bring to your attention. It has been ascertained that Slaves and free persons of

Colour have been employed by their owners and others, as salesmen in stores and shops, and generally as Clerks to traders of different descriptions. This is an increasing evil and it is impossible to determine where it will stop. It not only drives a white population from employment, which have hitherto afforded a support to many, but introduces the Coloured population and especially slaves, into situations which are inconsistent with their Condition. Your memorialists respectfully suggest that as the system of slavery is so interwoven with the constitution of our Society that even if our interests permitted it would be impossible to eradicate it. . . .

Memorial of the City Council of Charleston to South Carolina House of Representatives, n.d. [ca. 1826], no. 1799, series S165015, SCDAH.

Charleston *City Gazette and Commercial Daily Advertiser*

Monday, October 9, 1826

To the Emigrants and Northern People, now Citizens of Charleston and of the United States.

GENTLEMEN—You will, by perusing the underwritten communication extracted from the Mercury, of the 7th inst. find a piece signed by HENRY IZARD,[1] in explanation of the motives which induced him to make use of the liberal and high-minded expression two years since, and which sentiment by mature reflection, has become more *strong and energetic* upon his mind, that "about to depart for the Legislature, he would rather leave his family under the same roof with Denmark Vesey, with all the crimes proved upon his head, than with any white man who came to this city for the purpose of occupying the place of a menial in our community."—THE WORD MENIAL ALLUDES TO SERVICES IN ANY CAPACITY.—He says, "where is the white man in this city willing to place himself by the side of the black slave, and share with him the menial character?" Does he suppose that the application of the word menial here is not understood? I would ask where is the white man, *mechanic, merchant, or laborer,* that would not (possessing both a moral and religious obligation) prefer work, of whatever kind, in preference to becoming *a pauper, and a slave to his high and honorable sentiment*?

Mr. HENRY IZARD may have been one of those few that fortune smiles upon—but *fortune is a slippery jade,* and as much as she may have smiled upon him, may yet leave him in that situation to prefer brushing of boots, cleaning of a coat, or using some other mechanical instrument in preference to becoming a charge upon the city.—I would remind him of Pope's Essay.[2]

"Honor and shame from no condition rise,
Act well your part, there all the honor lies;
Fortune has some small difference made,
One flaunts in rags, another in brocade."

AN ADOPTED CITIZEN

Oct 9

To the Electors of St. Philip's and St. Michael's.

FELLOW CITIZENS—I have made no secret of my opinions and wishes with regard to the great questions which agitate the community as the election approaches. In so doing, I have incurred the resentment of some who wish differently from me. An old charge has been brought up against me, which I rejoice in as opportunity of repelling—I am accused of entertaining contemptuous feelings, and having used contemptuous expressions towards the poor strangers who have sought a refuge in this country from the Northern States and from Europe. An expression of mine has been misunderstood by some, and purposely garbled and misrepresented by others, to injure me in the favor of that portion of my fellow-citizens. As this game was played immediately after I had used the terms, I took a note of them, as I foresaw the possibility of my being called upon to defend them. I pledge myself for the accuracy with which I here repeat them.

Immediately after Denmark Vesey's plot, a meeting of the Charleston Delegation, of which I was one, was called, to deliberate on some plan to be pursued at Columbia, with regard to our slave policy. Among other expedients, it was proposed that a law should be passed to effect, either by express prohibition, or severe taxation, the exclusion of black male slaves from the families of their proprietors in Charleston, in order that their places might be filled by poor white men, who would thus be induced to come here for the purpose. I was opposed to the measure, I even thought the remedy worse than the disease, and I purposely used a strong expression to explain and enforce my opinion I said that "About to depart for the Legislature, I would rather leave my family under the same roof with Denmark Vesey, with all his crimes proved upon his head, than with any white man who might come to the city for the purpose of occupying the place of a *menial* in our community." I have not repented of that expression. Every moment's reflection from that day to this, has confirmed me in the correctness of that opinion. And who is there, that it is calculated to offend? Where is the white man, in this city, willing to place himself by the side of the black slave, and share with him the *menial* character? For my part, I recognize but one broad distinction in our society—that of the white man and the black—the free man and the slave. From the latter, I exact implicit, prompt, respectful and cheerful obedience. I desire not that he should reflect, that he deliberate, but that ge [he] should obey—and that he should be strongly impressed with the conviction that doubtless his master has sufficient motives to justify his orders. The white man, whatever may be the depression of his circumstances, the poverty by which he is for the moment weighed down, I meet as my equal; as engaged in the same career, the same pursuits with myself, and frequently more likely than myself to be a successful competitor in those pursuits. I recollect the numerous instances of his having reached the highest stations in the various departments of our government. I have seen him influencing the Legislatures of the States, occupying the multiplied offices in the executive, the legislative, judicial, the fiscal department of our government. I remember him in the halls of Congress taking the lead with natives of the country, and quieting envy and jealousy by his merits. It is without any affectation that I declare myself mortified at seeing men entitled to these high pursuits reduced to the station of slaves, of *menials*. It is with a most uncomfortable sensation that I ever receive *menial* services at their hands; that I ever behold them behind my chair and table, or employed in brushing the dust from my coat or the mud from my boots. These occupations belong to the slaves of our community, who exercise them without degradation. No native Carolinian will deign or resort to such means of livelihood—a thousand times rather would he repair to the most sickly swamp and encounter fever and death, than live as a *menial,* and consort with slaves. No foreigner, however humble his habits, or broken his spirit, will have breathed the air of Charleston for three days without acquiring a similar aversion; if he be not utterly destitute of that honest pride which is at the bottom of all the virtues which characterize the white population of this country. There are it is true, in all large communities, in all cities, particularly seaports, individuals, few in number it may be hoped, who from some hard dispensation of nature, from bad education, from the severity of fortune, or unfortunate associations in their youth, are destitute of such honest pride, and are willing to take *menial* stations by the side of slaves. In the published trial of that very Denmark Vesey, they have pronounced their own character, when they avow, that although their faces are white, their hearts are black; they have the hearts of slaves. They are capable of seizing an introduction to the lowest stations of our families, for purposes the most flagitious. Now, who would blame me for preferring Denmark Vesey to an inmate of this description? With Denmark Vesey in my house, I would say to my servants, this is a murderer, he has mischief in his heart; watch him, and if he utters a word, or puts on a look which threatens injury to the family, seize him, drag him to instant punishment. My fear would be, that such servants would construe his words or his looks with too much severay [severity]. In the other case, where could I hope for safety or redress? Should a slave attempt to protect the family of his absent master against a white miscreant; whips and gibbets would be his portion, while the culprit would be protected by all the formalities and the delays of justice. Volumes might be written on this subject. My object is only to correct an error and disarm calumny. To my fellow-citizens of all descriptions, a plain statement of my language and my opinions is all that is necessary. In vain should I have passed my life in this community, if any defence of my motives could be necessary.

HENRY IZARD

1. At the time of the Vesey affair, Henry Izard (1771–1826) served the city of Charleston as a representative in the South Carolina House of Representatives. Although he resided in 1822 at 3 Meeting Street, he owned multiple plantations and scores of slaves in lowcountry South Carolina. See *BDSCHR* 4: 306–7. He died a few months after this publication.

2. To chastise Izard for his elitist condescension, the author draws lines from *An Essay on Man,* a poem published in 1734 by Alexander Pope (1688–1744).

South Carolina Association, Request for Incorporation, November, 1828

To the Honourable The Speaker and Members of the House of Representatives of South Carolina

We the Officers and Members of the South Carolina Association respectfully request of your Honourable body the passage of an act incorporating us under the style and Name of The South Carolina Association an association of gentlemen not for private emolument or individual advancement, not to acquire exclusive privileges or procure for themselves important benefits at the expense of other classes; But a Society for the more humble but not less honourable purpose of enforcing the Laws and aiding the constituted authorities in executing those peculiar regulations, deemed so essential for the protection of our property and the safety of our families. Those who now address your honourable body were induced by the events of the summer of 1822 to form themselves into a temporary association; a common danger brought them together, a common interest has thus long preserved them; and a thorough conviction of the necessity and utility of their continuing united has induced the Members to form a permanent connection, to obtain a corporate name and the legal privileges incident thereto. This has become the more essential inasmuch as their numbers have increased with the increasing conviction of the utility of the Society—whilst their friends likewise have accumulated by the voluntary contributions of those whose best interests are connected with the true policy of the State,—all our efforts have been hitherto directed to obtain of your honourable body the passage of acts rendering more consistent and energetic the laws for the regulation of our coloured population, and assisting the Officers constitutionally appointed to carry those laws into effect—to keep a vigilant eye directed to that quarter where danger is to be expected, to defeat the machinations of our enemies abroad and finally to paralyze the exertions of our enemies at home—To effect these purposes our time and our money have been freely rendered up—We have been instrumental in obtaining the passage of three most important Laws—We have in a great measure restrained the coloured population of other states from mingling with and contaminating our own slaves—We have discovered the first openings of insurrectionary schemes and without creating any alarm among the citizens have been enabled to crush those schemes before they had fully developed themselves and poured out all their horrors over an unsuspecting community—As our object therefore is consonant with the policy of the State—as the means employed are at our own expense whilst the benefit derived therefrom extends over all—as we can have no interests but such as are common to our fellow citizens in every portion of the State we respectfully but with confidence pray your honourable Body to grant a charter of Incorporation to the Subscribers[1]

In and on behalf of the South Carolina association

H. Deas
President
Joseph Manigault
Stephen Elliot
Robert J. Turnbull
Jacob Bond Ion } vice presidents
Fred[k] A. Ford Secy. & Treas.

I E Holmes Sol:
John B. Irving—Chairman of the Standing Com[te]
R. W. Vanderhorst
Barnard E. Bee
D. Jennings Waring
Wm Newton
S B R. Finley

1. The state senate received the petition on Wednesday, November 26, 1828. See *South-Carolina State Gazette and Columbia Advertiser,* November 29, 1828. Of the thirteen subscribers, eight

(Deas, Manigault, Elliott, Turnbull, I'on, Holmes, Vanderhorst, and Newton) had signed their name to the memorial of 1823 and are thus identified above. Of the remaining five, Frederick A. Ford (1805–1880) is listed in the 1829 city directory as an attorney; John Beaufain Irving (1800–1881) was a physician; Barnard Elliott Bee Sr. (1787–1853) was an attorney and planter; Daniel Jennings Waring (1795–1832) was an attorney; Samuel Benjamin Rush Finley (1801–1833) was a physician.

Petition of the South Carolina Association, n.d. [1828], no. 4757, series S165015, SCDAH.

Petition of David Haig,[1] Monday, November 17, 1828

To The Honorable The President & Members of The Senate of The State of South Carolina

The petition of David Haig

Respectfully Sheweth

That in the year of 1822 his Negro Slave Harry[2] was convicted & sentenced to death by a Court of Magistrates & Freeholders then sitting in Charleston upon the charge of having been concerned in a projected insurrection of the colored population of the City. That agreeably with the said conviction & sentence, the said Slave was to have been executed on the 12th day of July of that year—but that in consequence of his testimony having been used by the Court "very efficaciously to the ends of public justice," his sentence of death was reconsidered & commuted to transportation beyond the limits of the United States. That he was thereupon retained in confinement in the Workhouse of Charleston by order of the aforesaid Court, and out of the control & care of Your Petitioner. That the said confinement occasioned the death of the said Slave—and your Petitioner was thereby deprived of his Services as effectually as if the originall sentence of the Court had been carried into execution.

Your Petitioner further sheweth unto your Honorable Body, that he would have been entitled, in the event of the execution of the said Slave, to compensation under an Act of the General Assembly of this State. He cannot therefore, consider the subsequent decision of the Court as in any wise impairing his right to that compensation. The review of its proceedings and the alteration of its sentence were certainly beyond his control & without his concurrence, and gave him no advantages whatever. He remained as deeply affected in his interests as before—and the Law under this View, applies in its spirit, if not in its letter, to his claim, *not,* with as much force as it could do under the supposition of his Slave having suffered capital punishment.

With regard to the amount of compensation to which he is entitled, he leaves it under the peculiar circumstances stated, wholly to the liberality & justice of Your Honorable Body to determine. The Court which was organized in the name & under the authority, & whose proceedings have subsequently received the sanction of the State divested him of his property for public purposes—and he therefore cannot be considered upon an inferior footing to that of any other claimant upon the State for individual property taken from him for the use & benefit of the public

And calling your Attention to the annexed certificates—shewing the exclusive control assumed by the Court over the said Slave & his having died from the effect of confinement—Your Petitoner as in duty bound will ever pray

Charleston 17 Nov 1828

David Haig

Office of The WorkHouse
Charleston So Carolina

I do hereby certify that I was acting as Deputy to A. S. Reeves[3] my predecessor as Master of the WorkHouse, during the period of the trial of the Negroes in 1822, and that Harry the Slave of Mr David Haig, confined in the said WorkHouse under the sentence of the Court, died therein on the nineteenth day of December 1822—

I also certify, that the said Slave Harry when first committed was to all appearances a healthy & able bodied person

Witness W. E. Gordon[4]
James Haig Master W House

Copy of a letter from Wm E Gordon to H Haig

WorkHouse 19 Dec 1822

David Haig Esq

Dr Sir Your Servant Harry which was confined in this Institution for attempting an insurrection expired this day & I was desired by his Honor the Intendant to give you immediate notice so that you should take the necessary steps. I am Dear Sir your[s] very respectfully

W E Gordon

N.B. Please send me an answer so that I may know how to Ac[t].

Copy of a Resolution of the City Council

City Council
Jany 21—1823

Resolved that the owners of Slaves now confined in the WorkHouse shall from and after this date have free communication with them & that the resolution prohibiting access shall be & is hereby repealed.

Extract from the Minutes

Wm Roach Junr

C. C.

Addressed D Haig Esq

1. On the cooper David Haig (1783–1832), see Part II, p. 94 n59.

2. Harry Haig, like his master, was also a cooper and provided key testimony against Gullah Jack. See Part III.

3. On Aeneas S. Reeves (1787–1822), master of the Work-House, see this section, p. 473.

4. On William E. Gordon (1781–1832), Reeves's deputy, see this section, p. 473 n4, above.

Petition of David Haig to the Senate of the State of South Carolina, November 17, 1828, no.71, series S165015, Petitions to the General Assembly, SCDAH; see also Petition of David Haig to the Senate of the State of South Carolina, no. 131, series S165015, SCDAH.

Memorial Regarding Free Blacks and Runaway Slaves, 1829

. . . That Your Memorialists Planters of South Carolina, from the vicinity of their property to Charleston, from their Parish being surrounded by Navigable water leading directly to and occasioning much intercourse with that city, and from the great Northern road passing through their parish in its whole length, are peculiarly exposed to the great evil of absconding slaves and their serious depredations. . . .

Prior to the passing of the Law of 1821 entitled an act to increase the punishment inflicted on persons convicted of murdering any Slave, and *for other, purposes therein mentioned,* it is asserted by your Memorialists without fear of contradiction, the Slaves of this part of South Carolina were in every respect more obedient and better servants, and infinitely more trustworthy and faithful than they have been subsequently—Since the passing of that law changes in the prices of our crops and consequently in the fortunes of many of our fellow citizens have taken place, and these changes have carried to Charleston for sale, large bodies of negroes. The unrestrained intercourse of these with free blacks and low and worthless white people, during their sojourn there has infused into the minds of the negros ideas of emancipation and insubordination, which they carry with them when sold into every part of the state. . . .

Your Memorialists therefore deny most unequivocally the policy, much less the necessity, of such a law as that of 1821, unless to satisfy the morbid feelings of those who wish to interfere with our slaves; and they further assert that the negroes of South Carolina were better protected by the Laws and penalties which were founded by our forefathers, on the dictates of common sense and the nature of the property than by the law of 1821, for the old laws, were practical, reasonable and therefore carried into execution, while the new law which inflicts death without benefit of clergy on a white man for killing a slave, apparently admits of no mitigation or exception even if the slave should have ravished his daughter, attempted to kill him, or burnt his dwelling, and is therefore only productive of injury to the slave, to his owner and to the country. . . .

Inhabitants of the Parish of Christ Church to Senate of South Carolina, n.d. [ca. 1829], no. 1563, series S165015, SCDAH.

Petition of the Georgetown Town Council after a Slave Plot Is Uncovered, November 16, 1829

. . . That upon the discovery of a Plot of Insurrection in July last;[1] a great number of commitments followed the Several Orders of a Court of Magistrates and Freeholders, and Such was the Excitement among the negroes of this and adjoining districts that there were very properly fear entertained for the Safety of the Town and district, It was known to the Town that one Connected with the plot in Charleston in 1822 had looked to the day of Execution as the proper one, and the Gallows the proper place at which to rally their force and rescue the Culprits. To thwart any attempt of this Sort in this place and more particularly to Keep Secure a great number of prisoners in Jail your petitioners were called upon, as with One Voice to supply the services requited. . . .

1. The 1829 slave plot uncovered in Georgetown remains understudied. Newspapers in South Carolina published almost nothing about it. James Louis Petigru, *Life, Letters, and Speeches of James Louis Petigru, the Union Man of South Carolina,* ed. James Petigru Carson (Washington, DC: W. H. Lowdermilk, 1920), 66, remembered that, in response to the plot, "[t]roops and arms were sent from Charleston, and for a time great alarm was felt throughout the state." See also *New-York Evening Post,* August 28, 1829; William W. Freehling, *Prelude to Civil War: The Nullification Controversy in South Carolina, 1816–1836* (New York: Harper & Row, 1966), 62–63.

Petition of the Georgetown Town Council, November 16, 1829, Petitions to the General Assembly, no. 98, series S165015, SCDAH.

Petition of Joseph L. Enslow, Thursday, December 1, 1831

To The Hon[ble] The President & Members of the Senate of the State of So: Carolina

The petition of Joseph L. Enslow

Respectfully Sheweth

That your Petitioner was the Owner of a Slave named John[1] convicted before a Court of Magistrates and Freeholders convened in Charleston in the year 1822, of being engaged in a conspiracy and projected insurrection of the Negroes, and sentenced to be "imprisoned in the Work House of Charleston until his Master under the direction of the City Council of Charleston shall send him out of the limits of the United States into which he is not to return under penalty of death." That said sentence was in fact a commutation of the punishment of death, to which his offence subjected the said Slave, and was so intended, upon a tacit understanding, the said Negro having pleaded guilty and his confession having afforded essentially important testimony against other slaves.—That according to said sentence, the said slave was imprisoned—That during said confinement he died—

It is therefore respectfully suggested to Your Honorable Body that it is the same both as relates to the State and to your petitioner whether the said Slave died in confinement or had been executed under the sentence of the Court, in either case the property of Your Petitioner being taken from him by the public authority, and in the present, the sentence being dictated by a consideration of the public good. Your Petitioner has also been informed that a precedent for this application is to be found in the case of the Petition of Mr David Haig relative to his slave Harry. Wherein the usual compensation was granted by your Hon[ble] Body, altho the slave was not executed, but had his sentence commuted to a similar punishment with that of the slave of Your Petitioner. Wherefore Your Petitioner prays Your Hon[ble] Body to take his case into consideration & to grant him the compensation allowed by Law in case of a slave executed under sentence of a Court

Sworn to before me

Charleston 1 Dec 1831 Joseph L. Enslow

James Haig

Your Petitioner further declares upon oath that the aforementioned Slave when put under confinement was a healthy and able-bodied person, and died therefore as he verily believed and as far as he can possibly know from the effects of it

Sworn to before me
1 Dec 1831 Joseph L. Enslow
James Haig

I do hereby certify that I was acting as Deputy of A S Reeves my predecessor as Master of the Work House during the period of the trial of the Negroes in 1822 for a projected insurrection and that John the Slave of Mr J L Enslow then confined in said Work House under sentence of the Court died there on the [*blank*] day of 1822 during said confinement

Charleston 1 Dec 1831 W. E. Gordon
Witness M. W. House
James Haig

1. On the cooper Joseph Enslow (1790–1866) and his slave John, see Part III, p. 237 n1.

Petition of Joseph L. Enslow, December 1, 1831, Petitions to the General Assembly, no. 60, series S165015, SCDAH.

Charleston Courier

Saturday, April 13, 1839

"Right of Free Colored Persons to hold Real Estate" . . . From all these legislative provisions, it follows that so far from these people being considered as aliens, they are taken under the special protection and controul of the law, and although the station assigned them is a degraded one, yet that they are recognized as forming a part of the body politic, and if not citizens, they are subjects. Subjects of that power which is exercised over man, under various modifications, by all the Governments of the world, and by one country over another race of beings, inhabiting a portion of our territory, but yet forming a distinct class. But to conclude this opinion, I refer to the acts of 1822 and '23, which impose a tax on the real property of free people of colour, in so many words, all, which of course, must remove every doubt which may hitherto have existed on this subject. The act has for its object to establish a competent force to act as municipal guard for the protection of the City of Charleston and its vicinity. . . .

Petition of Peter Desverney, 1857

The Committee on Military & Pension to whome was refered the Petition of Peter DesVerny, a free person of colour for an increase of the anual bounty of the state, for meritorious services rendered the citizens of Charleston in the year 1822, have had the same under consideration, and beg leave to Report,

That they find that the Petitoner was in 1822 the confidential slave of one of the most respectable gentlemen in the city of Chrleston, Mr. Hamilton Prileau.[1] That he was the person who revealed to his master the first intimation of the intended insurrection by the portion of the blacks of Charleston, that this insurection was intended to have commenced on Sunday night the 16th June 1822, headed by one Denmark Vesey; but through the loyalty of this slave to his master, and the revelations he made, the city of Charleston was saved from being laid in ashes and the citizens from a horrid butchery.

That in consequence of these meritorious services, the Legislature passed an Act in December 1822 manumitting Peter, and remunerating him with an anual pension of $50.00 per annum. That he is now advanced to the age of about seventy years, and very much enfeebled by the failure of health, That from the testimony of some of the most respectable citizens of Charleston, he has always conducted himself uprightly and maintained a good character for honesty.

Your committee in view of his past services, and his advanced age and enfeebled health, think that he is a fit and proper object, for the fostering care and protection of the State and would therefore recommend the adoption of the following Resolution,

Resolved, That the Treasurer of the Lower Division be and he is hereby authorized, to pay to Peter DesVerny a free person of colour the sum of one hundred and fifty dollars anually in lieu of the sum he now receives by law, and payment to commence on the first day of January 1858

Respectfully submitted
J. Foster Marshall Chm.

1. In 1822, Peter Prioleau (Desverney) was owned by Colonel John Cordes Prioleau (1772–1825), son of Samuel Prioleau Jr. (1742–1813), not "Hamilton Prileau," whom the committee may have confused with James Hamilton Prioleau (1812–1854), son of Samuel Prioleau (1784–1839).

"Report of the Committee on Military and Pensions on the Petition of Peter Desverny for an Increase of the Annual Bounty of the State," November 30, 1857, "Reports to the General Assembly," no. 1, series S165005, SCDAH.

Seeking to isolate the state's slaves from the intellectual currents washing about the Atlantic, South Carolina legislators passed the Negro Seamen Act on December 22, 1822. Mindful that Vesey had once been a mariner and that black seamen carried word of Caribbean freedom struggles into Charleston harbor, the legislators imposed a quarantine on any vessel from another "state or foreign port, having on board any free negroes or persons of color." In an attempt to halt any conversation between black sailors and enslaved dock workers, the state required that all African American seamen had to be "confined in jail until [their] vessel departs." If the ship's master refused to pay the cost of incarceration, or tried to evade the law altogether, the foreign seamen were deemed "absolute slaves" and auctioned into bondage to defray expenses. The law precipitated a crisis that roiled diplomatic relations between Britain and the United States for decades. South Carolina's behavior, the British insisted, violated federal treaty obligations. The situation came to a head in 1823 when Henry Elkison, a British seaman from Jamaica, challenged the validity of the Negro Seamen Act in court. Supreme Court Justice William Johnson Jr., already in hot water with the planting elite for his behavior during the Vesey affair, heard the case. Although Johnson threw out Elkison's claim for a writ bailing him from confinement, Johnson launched a blistering opinion defending the supremacy of the federal government in regulating such matters. The hostility to Johnson in Charleston became such that he eventually left his native state. Not only did

South Carolina's legislature renew the Negro Seamen Act in 1823, it became a model for other slaveholding states and even other slaveholding countries. Georgia passed a similar law in 1823, Louisiana in 1830, Florida in 1832, and the Spanish colony of Cuba in 1837. In the legal arguments to sustain the law and the debate about the meaning and locus of sovereignty, lawyers for South Carolina argued that the highest law of nature—self-preservation—trumped the federal government's treaty obligations with respect to foreign seamen of color. The jousting between the federal government and South Carolina on the fate of colored seamen foreshadowed the nullification movement, in which white officials prominent in the Vesey affair would take a lead role.

Joel Poinsett to John Quincy Adams, Friday, February 28, 1823

Washington 28th Feby. 1823

Dear Sir,

The act of the Legislature of South Carolina, to which Mr. Canning's[1] letter refers, was passed immediately after the detection of an intended insurrection of the Slaves in Charleston—It appeared in evidence on the trial of those deluded men, that the coloured stewards, cooks & mariners on board the coasting vessels were in the practice of bringing into the country, inflammatory publications, and of disseminating them among the slaves of Charleston, and that, by the same means, a constant correspondence had been carried on between them, and the Negroes of San Domingo—

With the knowledge of these facts, the Legislature of South Carolina was bound to take such measures as would protect the country from the contagion of rebellious principles, which might involve it in the horrors of a servile War—

But while they exercised a right, which they possessed as undoubtedly, as they do that of passing laws to prevent the introduction of contagious diseases, they have overlooked the operation of this Act, as it respects the subjects of foreign Powers—I have no doubt that, on a proper representation being made, they will immediately repeal so much of the Act as violates the treaty of commerce between the United States and Great Britain, which provides for a reciprocal liberty of commerce between the two countries, and that the inhabitants of each respectively, shall have liberty to come into any ports and to remain, and reside in any parts of the said territories respectively—

In the event of any further attempt being made to enforce the Act, before such an alteration can be made, Mr. Canning may be assured, that the courts of Law in the City of Charleston, will do ample justice to H:B: Majesty's subjects, who may be aggrieved by its operation.—

Very respectfully,
Your obedt. Servt.,
Signed–J. R. Poinsett.[2]

1. Stratford Canning (1786–1880) served as the British minister in Washington from 1819 to 1823, a position he owed to his cousin, Foreign Secretary George Canning. John Quincy Adams (1767–1848) was then secretary of state. For the act, see Thomas Cooper and David J. McCord,

eds., *The Statutes at Large of South Carolina* (Columbia, SC, 1840), vol. 7: 461; the *Charleston Mercury, and Morning Advertiser,* December 18, 1822; and W. Jeffrey Bolster, *Black Jacks: African American Seamen in the Age of Sail* (Cambridge, MA: Harvard University Press, 1997), 202–3.

2. Poinsett (1779–1851) sat on the second court that tried the Vesey conspirators. See Part II, pp. 102–103 n1.

ALS in MHS.

John Quincy Adams to Stratford Canning, Tuesday, June 17, 1823

The Right Honourable Stratford Canning, Envoy Extraordinary and Minister Plenipotentiary from Great Britain

Department of State
Washington 17 June 1823.

Sir,

With reference to your Letter of the 15th of February last, and its enclosure, I have the honour of informing you that immediately after its reception, measures were taken by the Government of the United States, for effecting the removal of the cause of complaint set forth in it, which, it is not doubted, have been successful, and will prevent the recurrence of it hereafter.

I pray you, Sir, to accept the renewed assurance of my distinguished Consideration

John Quincy Adams.

ALS in MHS.

Supreme Court Justice William Johnson to Thomas Jefferson, Monday, August 11, 1823

. . . I acknowledge to you my dear Sir, that I have sometimes some gloomy Doubts crossing my Mind respecting the Destiny of our beloved Country. Those who cannot govern us may perhaps succeed in dividing us. That greatest of Evils Disunion, appears to be losing its Terrors. My Ears are shocked at Times by Expressions that I hear on the subject. I enclose you a Copy of an Opinion which I had to deliver a few days ago[1] which will excite some Surprise. The very Men who not long since made such an Outcry against self-created Society are now heading a most formidable one in this Place. How they will go God knows. I hope there may be temperate Men enough among them to control the furious Passions and false Policy which govern most of them.

That unhappy Missouri discussion shewed its Effects in Blood the last year and will shew them in Persecution for many a Year to come. If it be true that "*quem Coelum perdere vult prius dementat*"[2] I have received a Warning to quit this City. I fear nothing so much as the Effects of the persecuting Spirit that is abroad in this Place. Should it spread thro' the State & produce a systematic Policy founded on the ridiculous but prevalent Notion—that it is a struggle for Life or Death, there are no Excesses that we may not look for—whatever be their Effect upon the Union. They are really exemplifying your Observations on their general Principles of Government. They now pronounce the Negros the real Jacobins of this Country,[3] and in doing so shew what they meant when they honored us with the same Epithet. . . .

1. Johnson delivered his opinion in the Elkison case three days before he wrote Jefferson.

2. "Those whom the gods would destroy, they first make mad." Attributed to Greek playwright Euripides.

3. This phrase appeared in Edwin C. Holland's pamphlet *Refutation,* which appears on pp. 513–14 in this section.

"Letter From William Johnson to Thomas Jefferson," *SCHGM* 1 (1900): 211–12.

Richmond *Enquirer*

Tuesday, September 2, 1823
FREE PEOPLE OF COLOUR.

A memorial was laid before the last Congress, from sundry masters of American vessels lying in the port of Charleston, complaining of a law of the state of *S. Carolina,* touching certain *free people of colour.*[1] The substance of this is contained in the following paragraphs from the "Charleston Gazette" of the 5th August.

"*Interesting Notice*—We understand that the Harbour-Master of this Port, is directed to require all masters of vessels to report immediately on their arrival, the names of all passengers, whether they be whites or free persons of colour, and the names of all free negroes or persons of colour, in any capacity on board.

"The law is highly penal, and directs that no free negro or person of colour, who shall have left this state, shall be suffered to return. That no vessel shall come into any port, or harbor of this state from any other state or foreign port, having on board any free negroes or persons of colour as cook, stewards, mariners, or in any other employment on board, without being liable to be seized and confined in gaol, until said vessel is ready to sail; the captain shall be bound to carry away the said free negro or free person of colour, and pay the expenses of his detention. . . ."

1. For the petition of masters of vessels, see "Free People of Colour," *Trenton Federalist,* March 31, 1823.

John Quincy Adams, Diary, Thursday, September 4, 1823

. . . 4th, Dined at General H. A. S. Dearborn's, at Brinley Place, Roxbury. There was a company of about thirty men, among whom Colonel Hayne, the Senator,[1] and Mr. Archer—Crowninshield, Silsbee, and Sprague, of Salem. There was at table a conversation, chiefly between Colonel Hayne and George Blake, upon a decision of Judge Johnson's, of the United States Supreme Court, pronouncing an Act of the Legislature of South Carolina unconstitutional, in which Hayne discovered so much excitement and temper that it became painful, and necessary to change the topic. It was the Act prohibiting free persons of color from coming or being brought into the State as sailors, upon penalties, among which are their being sold as slaves. . . .

1. Before election to the Senate, Colonel Robert Young Hayne (1791–1839) had served as the state's attorney general at the time of the Vesey affair and as one of the five freeholders on the second court.

John Quincy Adams, *Memoirs of John Quincy Adams, Comprising Portions of His Diary from 1795 to 1848*, ed. Charles Francis Adams, 12 vols. (Philadelphia, 1874–77), vol. 6: 176.

Daniel Brent to John Quincy Adams, Thursday, September 4, 1823

. . . I have thought that it might be agreeable to you to receive, with the Enclosed news-paper, copies of Mr. Poinsett's[1] letter to you and yours to Mr Canning, on the Subject of the law of S.C. which produced the opinion of Judge Johnson, that is commented on in that Paper; and they are sent, accordingly.

Daniel Brent.[2]

4 September 1823

1. On Poinsett (1779–1851), a judge on the second Court of Magistrates and Freeholders, see Part II, p. 103 n1.
2. Daniel Brent (1770–1841) was chief clerk in the US Department of State from 1822 to 1834.

ALS in MHS.

Niles' Weekly Register Reports on the Elkison Case

Saturday, September 6, 1823

. . . A friend has favored us with the opinion lately delivered by judge Johnson,[1] of the United States district court, to which we referred two days ago; which, notwithstanding its length, we are induced to publish entire.

It appears that the case was that of a British seaman, who, (being a colored man), was arrested and confined in prison. From the form of the state act which authorizes such arrests, it appears that all free negroes, the subjects of foreign governments as well as our own, are liable in this manner, which sets the infraction of the constitution in so clear a light, that it cannot be doubted for a moment by any impartial mind. Judge Johnson remarks that this single measure, by which a British subject is seized without any alleged crime, is tantamount to a declaration of war against Great Britain.

It is gratifying to learn that the execution of this act was, for a certain time, suspended, under an apprehension of its constitutionality, or at least of its impropriety, and that, as judge Johnson states, its revival is more a personal than a public measure, as might have been inferred, from the fact that the attorney general did not appear in the defence. That a high state of excitement exists among a portion of the community, may, however, be easily discovered from the remarks made by Mr. Holmes[2] and col. Hunt,[3] who opposed the discharge of the prisoner.

The opinion of the honorable William Johnson, delivered on the 7th August, 1823, in the case of the arrest of the British seaman, under the 3d section of the state act, entitled "an act for the better regulation of free negroes and persons of color, and for other purposes," passed in December last.

Ex parte--HENRY ELKISON,
A Subject of his Britannic Majesty,
vs.
FRANCIS G. DELIESSELINE,
Sheriff of Charleston District. } U. States District Court

The motion submitted by Mr. King[4] in behalf of the prisoner, is for the writ of *Habeas Corpus ad subjiciendum*; and if he should fail in this motion, then for the writ *de Homine replegiando*; the one regarding the prisoner in a criminal, the other in a civil aspect; the first motion having for its object his discharge from confinement absolutely, the other for his discharge on bail, with a view to try the question of the validity of the law under which he is held in confinement. . . .

The act is entitled, "An act for the better regulation of Free Negroes and persons of Colour, and for other purposes." And the third section is in these words: "That if any vessel shall come into any port or harbour of this state from any *other state,* or *foreign port,* having on board any free negroes or persons of color, as cooks, stewards, or mariners, or in any other employment on board of said vessels, such free negroes or persons of color shall be liable to be seized and confined in gaol until such vessel shall clear out and depart from this state: and that when said vessel is ready to sail, the captain of said vessel shall be bound to carry away the said free negro or free persons of color, and to pay the expenses of his detention; and in case of his neglect or refusal so to do, he shall be liable to be indicted; and on conviction thereof, shall be fined in a sum not less than one thousand dollars, and imprisoned not less than two months; and such free negroes or persons of color shall be deemed and taken as absolute slaves, and sold in conformity to the provisions of the act passed on the 20th December, 1820, aforesaid."

As to the description or character of this individual, it is admitted, that he was taken by the Sheriff, under this act, out of the ship Homer, a British ship trading from Liverpool to this place. From the shipping articles it appears that he was shipped in Liverpool; from the captain's affidavit, that he had known him several years in Liverpool as a British subject, and from his own affidavit that he is a native subject of Great Britain, born in Jamaica. . . .

Two questions have now been made in argument, the first on the law of the case, the second on the remedy.

On the unconstitutionality of the law under which this man is confined, it is not too much to say that it will not bear argument; and I feel myself sanctioned in using this strong language, from considering the course of reasoning by which it has been defended. Neither of the gentlemen has attempted to prove that the power, therein assumed by the state, can be exercised without clashing with the general powers of the United States, to regulate commerce: but they have both strenuously contended, that, *ex necessitate,* it was a power which the state must and would exercise, and indeed, Mr. Holmes concluded his argument with the declaration, that if a dissolution of the union must be the alternative he was ready to meet it. Nor did the argument of Col. Hunt deviate at all from the same course. Giving it in the language of his own summary, it was this: South-Carolina was a sovereign state when she adopted the constitution—a sovereign state cannot surrender a right of vital importance—South-Carolina, therefore, either did not surrender this right, or still possesses the power to resume it—and whether it is necessary, or when it is necessary to resume it, *she is herself the sovereign judge.*

But it was not necessary to give this candid exposé of the grounds which this law assumes; for it is a subject of positive proof that it is altogether irreconcilable with the powers of the general government; that it necessarily compromits the public peace, and tends to embroil us with, if not separate us from our sister states: in short, that it leads to a dissolution of the union, and implies a direct attack upon the sovereignty of the United States.

Let it be observed that, the law is, "if any vessel" (not even the vessels of the United States excepted) "shall come into any port or harbor of this state," &c. bringing in free coloured persons, such persons are to become absolute slaves, and that, without even a form of trial, as I understand the act, they are to be sold. By the next clause the sheriff is vested with absolute power, and expressly enjoined to carry the law into effect, and is to receive the one half of the proceeds of the sale.

The object of this law, and it has been acknowledged in argument, is to prohibit ships coming into this port from employing coloured seamen, whether citizens or subjects of their own government or not. But if this state can prohibit Great Britain from employing her colored subjects (and she has them of all colours on the globe), or if at liberty to prohibit the employment of her subjects of the African race, why not prohibit her from using those of Irish or of Scottish nativity; if the colour of his skin is to preclude the Lascar or the Sierra Leone seaman, why not the colour of his eye or his hair exclude from our ports the inhabitants of her other territories? In fact, it amounts to the assertion of the power to exclude the seamen of the territories of Great Britain, or any other nation, altogether. With regard to various friendly nations, it amounts to an actual exclusion in its present form. Why may not the shipping of Morocco or of Algiers cover the commerce of France with this country, even at the present crisis? Their seamen are all coloured, and even the state of Massachusetts might lately, and may perhaps now, expedite to this port a vessel with her officers black and her crew composed of Nantucket Indians, known to be among the best seamen in our service. These might all become slaves under this act. . . .

[T]he right of the general government to regulate commerce with the sister states and foreign nations is a paramount and exclusive right; and this conclusion we arrive at, whether we examine it with reference to the words of the constitution or the nature of the grant. That this has been the received and universal construction from the first day of the organization of the general government is unquestionable, and the right admits not of a question any more than the fact. In the constitution of the United States—the most wonderful instrument ever drawn by the hand of man—there is a comprehension and precision that is unparalleled, and I can truly say that, after spending my life in studying it, I still daily find in it some new excellence.

It is true that it contains no prohibition on the states to regulate foreign commerce. Nor was such a prohibition necessary; for the words of the grant sweep away the whole subject and leave nothing for the states to act upon. Wherever this is the case, there is no prohibitory clause interposed in the constitution. Thus, the states are not prohibited from regulating the value of foreign coins, or fixing a standard of weights and measures, for the very words imply a total unlimited grant. The words in the present case are "to regulate commerce with foreign nations, and among the several states, and with the Indian tribes." If congress can regulate commerce, what commerce can it not regulate? and the navigation of ships has always been held up by all nations to appertain to commercial regulations.

But the case does not rest here. In order to sustain this law, the state must also possess a power paramount to the treaty-making power of the United States, expressly declared to be a part of the supreme legislative power of the land; for, the seizure of this man on board a British ship, is an express violation of the commercial convention with Great Britain in 1815. Our commerce with that nation does not depend upon the mere negative sanction of not being prohibited. A reciprocal liberty of commerce is expressly stipulated for, and conceded by that treaty; to this the right of navigating their ships, in their own way and particularly by their own subjects, is necessarily incident. If policy requires any restriction of this right with regard to a particular class of the subjects of either contracting party, it must be introduced by treaty. The opposite party cannot introduce it by a legislative act of his own. Such a law as this could not be passed even by the general government without furnishing a just cause of war.

But to all this, the plea of necessity is urged, and of the existence of that necessity we are told the state alone is to judge. Where is this to land us? Is it not asserting the right in each state to throw off the federal constitution at its will and pleasure? If it can be done as to any particular article, it may be done as to all; and like the old confederation the union becomes a mere rope of sand. But I deny that the state surrendered a single power necessary to its security against this species of property. What is to prevent their being confined to their ships if it is dangerous for them to go abroad?—This power may be lawfully exercised. To land their cargoes, take in others and depart is all that is necessary to ordinary commerce, and is all that is properly stipulated for in the convention of 1815, so far as relates to seamen. If our fears extend also to the British merchant, the supercargo or master being persons of colour, I acknowledge that, as to them, the treaty precludes us from abridging their rights to free ingress and egress, and occupying houses and warehouses for the purposes of commerce. As to them, this law is an express infraction of the treaty. No such law can be passed consistently with the treaty; and unless sanctioned by diplomatic arrangement, the passing of such a law is tantamount to a declaration of war.

But, if the policy of this law was to keep foreign free persons of color from holding communion with our slaves, it certainly pursues a course altogether inconsistent with its object. One gentleman likened the importation of such persons to that of clothes infected with the plague, or of wild beasts from Africa; the other, to that of fire-brands set to our own houses only to escape by the light. But surely if the penalty inflicted for coming here is, in its effect, that of being domesticated, by being sold here, then *we,* ourselves inoculate our community with the plague, *we,* ourselves turn loose the wild beast in our streets, and *we* put the fire-brand under our own houses. If there are evil persons abroad that would steal to this place, in order to do us this mischief (and the whole provisions of this act are founded in that supposition), then this method of disposing of offenders by detaining them here, presents the finest facilities in the world for introducing themselves lawfully into the very situation in which they would enjoy the best opportunities of pursuing their designs.

Now, if this plea of necessity could avail at all against the constitution and laws of the United States, certainly that law cannot be pronounced necessary which may defeat its own ends; much less when other provisions of unexceptionable legality might be resorted to, which would operate solely to the end proposed, viz. the effectual exclusion of dangerous characters. On the fact of the necessity for all this exhibition of legislation and zeal, I say nothing: I neither admit nor deny it. In common with every other citizen, I am entitled to my own opinion, but when I express it, it shall be done in my private capacity. . . .

1. Supreme Court Justice William Johnson Jr. delivered his opinion in the Elkison case on Thursday, August 7, 1823.

2. Colonel Benjamin Faneuil Hunt (1792–1854), attorney and planter, was one of the charter members of the South Carolina Association.

3. Isaac Edward Holmes (1796–1867) was the first "solicitor" or designated attorney of the South Carolina Association.

4. Scottish-born Mitchell King (1783–1862) studied law under George Warren Cross (1783–1836), the attorney who counseled Denmark Vesey during the proceedings. King acted as Smart Anderson's attorney, delivering his confession to the first court.

William Johnson Jr. to John Quincy Adams, July 3, 1824

Charleston . . .

SIR: I know not from whom the Government expects communications such as the present, but I am daily made sensible that the eyes of the community are turned most particularly to the judges of the Supreme Court for protection of their constitutional rights, while I feel myself destitute of the power necessary to realize that expectation. Hence, although obliged to look on and see the Constitution of the United States trampled on by a set of men who, I sincerely believe, are as much influenced by the pleasure of bringing its functionaries into contempt, by exposing their impotence, as by any other consideration whatever, I feel it my duty to call the attention of the President to the subject, as one which may not be unworthy of an official remonstrance to the Executive of the State.

In the envelope which encloses this, I have taken the liberty to enclose three documents. The first is an act of the Legislature of this State, passed at their last session, from which you will perceive how very far your expectations are from being realized, as you expressed them to Mr. Canning in your letter of June 17, 1823. The second is a paragraph from the Charleston Mercury of the 23d ultimo, from which it will be seen how pointedly the South Carolina Association, as it is called, are pressing the execution of that law. And the third is an article from the Charleston Courier of the 29th, which contains a report of the case of Amos Daley,[1] from which it appears that he was a citizen of Rhode Island, and an articled seaman on board of an American vessel.

The ground of defence taken for him will also appear, and, in the disregard of them, the principles acted upon by the people who are pressing these measures.

This man has come off with twelve lashes, because "he could not help himself in returning to this port;" but you will see from the law that this summary court possesses the power of inflicting, in the most summary manner, twelve thousand lashes, should they think proper.

I am wholly destitute of the power of arresting those measures. Both the writs of habeas corpus and injunction I am precluded from using, because the cases assume the form of State prosecutions; and, if I could issue them, I have nobody to call upon, since the district attorney is himself a member of the association; and they have, further, the countenance of five other officers of the United States in their measures. To this fact I attribute much of the confidence with which these measures are prosecuted.

In fact, the law itself was passed under the influence of a memorial from the association, who, I am informed, actually had it drawn up here, in pursuance of their own deliberations, in order to be submitted to the Legislature. It is emphatically their law. The only resource of the masters for having their men taken from them, or of the men, and the only mode of bringing up the subject to the Supreme Court, is by an action for damages. But, without friends, without funds, and without time, mariners cannot resort to suits at law.

I must again apologize for troubling you with this communication, and there are many private considerations that would have deterred me from making it. But I am perfectly sure that I am the only public functionary here by whom it would have been made. The society has the countenance and support of some men who cannot openly join it; and, although I am confident there is a decided majority against them, yet there are many wealthy and distinguished men in it, and some whose rank in life ought, in my opinion, to have prevented them from taking part with it.

A copy of Mr. Poinsett's letter to you on this subject has been shown among his friends here, and I have perused it. At the same time that I am well convinced Mr. Poinsett believed all that he there urges in excuse of the measure, yet I am well persuaded that it is in the power of no one to establish the facts there stated. Indeed, I do not hesitate to express the opinion, that the whole of the alarm of 1822 was founded in causes that were infinitely exaggerated.

A few timid and precipitate men managed to disseminate their fears and their feelings, and you know that popular panics spread with the expansive force of vapor. The rest of the State, I am well persuaded, takes no interest in these measures, but rather yields them to the fears of the city representation, where their chief operation is felt, than adopts them from an opinion of their necessity or utility.

With very great personal and official consideration, I have the honor to subscribe myself, sir, your very humble servant,

WILLIAM JOHNSON.

Hon. JOHN QUINCY ADAMS,
Secretary of State United States.

Figure 32. Robert James Turnbull (1775–1833), judge on the First Court of Magistrates and Freeholders. From a portrait, ca. 1830. Copyrighted image courtesy of the Gibbes Museum of Art/Carolina Art Association.

1. On the case of Amos Daley, a free colored seaman from Rhode Island, whipped by authorities for violating the Negro Seamen Act, see Michael Schoeppner, "Peculiar Quarantines: The Seamen Acts and Regulatory Authority in the Antebellum South," *Law and History Review* 31 (2013): 559–86.

United States Twenty-seventh Congress, Third Session, House of Representatives, Report no. 80, Free Colored Seamen, Majority & Minority Reports, January 20, 1843.

Robert J. Turnbull[1] Replies to Justice William Johnson Jr., 1824

. . . I do aver, that the free and uninterrupted ingress of a colored population into this State, from the North, and elsewhere, with their known habits, feelings and principles, animated and emboldened as they are, by the philanthropy of the day, and by the events, which Europe in its throes and convulsions casts upon mankind, is the most formidable evil, which South Carolina has to look upon in these her days of apparent quiet. To permit such persons, with such principles, to have a footing on our soil, is to introduce a *moral* pestilence, which must destroy subordination in the slave, and with it the State itself. . . .

What was the situation of South Carolina when she accepted this Constitution? To use a familiar phrase, lately introduced, she was a *slave-holding* State, a term by no means unappropriate to our present purpose. She was *then,* and is *now,* a State, whose prosperity and existence depends upon the labor of her slaves. From time immemorial, all her institutions, and her whole domestic jurisprudence, have been founded upon the principle, that negroes and mulattoes in her land, whether *slave* or *free,* had no civil or political rights. That, as to the regulation of a colored population, she was, and ought to be, the best and only judge. . . .

If she did not at that day, make an express provision for the exercise of this power over blacks, which might come into her limits, it was because no man at that day doubted her right, or her power to exercise such a right. She did not then feel, that it would so soon become necessary, to exclude from her territory, even black seamen from abroad. There were then afloat no doctrines of African emancipation. If they existed at all, they existed only in the minds of a few pseudo-philanthropists. These doctrines had not stalked abroad as now, "shaking from their hair horrid pestilence." The *Abolition Society* of Philadelphia, the *British Association* in London, and the *Amis des Noirs* in Paris, had not then been formed. The National Assembly of France, had not yet promulgated their decree, to give privileges to their colored colonists, and the Abbe GREGOIRE had not written that celebrated letter, which was afterwards the torch, which lighted up the insurrection in St. Domingo. Why do I say, that these things had not then happened? I forget the French Revolution itself. This memorable event, from which came licentiousness, as well as liberty—irreligion, atheism, and every species of madness, and every wrong principle of enthusiasm; this volcano, which vomited from its crater, every doctrine which was calculated to overturn all governments, and to unsettle the principles of obedience, and subordination in the minds of men, whether bond or free—this political *Vesuvius* was then quiet and harmless. Not even those who were peaceably cultivating their vineyards around its fertile boarders, heard any rumbling or noises, which could portend the dreadful irruptions of fires, which so soon succeeded, and which have at intervals, continued to amaze the nations. . . .

That in the year 1800, our Legislature passed a bill, prohibiting masters of vessels from bringing into this State, any free persons of color. In 1803, our ports were opened to the importation of slaves, but the provisions of the Act of 1800, so far as respects free colored persons, were rendered perpetual; the reasons for which, are familiar to every one acquainted with the history of those times. St. Domingo was in the possession of the negroes, and of course those negroes were free. Some of them had gone over to France for education, and were disposed to claim the same privileges as the European whites—to mingle in our commerce, navigate vessels, and settle among the people of these states for the purposes of trade; one of the principal chiefs, had some years previously, visited this very State, on his return from France—and a few years afterwards, a vessel, officered and manned by black people, arrived at Hartford, in the State of Connecticut. Among the officers, was Boyer, now President of Hayti, a smart, sagacious, and intelligent fellow, well skilled to devise any scheme, or perpetrate any mischief. . . .

1. Attorney Robert J. Turnbull (1775–1833) sat on the first court during the summer of 1822. For more on Turnbull, see Part III, p. 161 n5 of this volume. Turnbull, once a neo-Federalist, composed

the Negro Seamen Act and would become one of the driving forces behind the nullification movement. See William W. Freehling, *Prelude to Civil War: The Nullification Controversy in South Carolina, 1816–1836* (New York: Harper & Row, 1966), 126.

Caroliniensis [attributed to Robert J. Turnbull], *A Series of Articles Discussing a Pamphlet Entitled "The Opinion of the Hon. William Johnson"*... (Charleston, SC, 1824), 41, 44, 45, 69.

Portland *Eastern Argus*

Thursday, December 30, 1824

SENTIMENTS OF THE SOUTH.

Dr. John Ramsay,[1] of the Senate of S. Carolina, has recently offered the following resolutions, which were to be called up and discussed on the 7th instant:

Resolved, That the state of South Carolina is desirous of complying with any measure necessary to promote harmony between this state and the government of the United States, and foreign nations, and will cheerfully comply in all cases which do not involve a surrender of the safety and inherent rights of the state.

Resolved, That the Legislature of this state has carefully considered the documents transmitted by the President of the United States, being a correspondence with the British Minister, relative to a law passed December, 1822, regulating free negroes and persons of colour, and yet can perceive no departure from the duties and rights of this state, or the United States, in that law.

Resolved, That the Legislature see with profound regret the alarming symptoms of an unconstitutional interference with her coloured population, whose condition, as it existed at the establishment of the present constitution of the United States, is expressly recognized, (paragraph 3 of Sec. 2 of Art. I) and distinctly guaranteed by that instrument.

Resolved, That it is as much the duty of the state to guard against insubordination or insurrection among our coloured population, or to control and regulate any cause which might excite or produce it, as to guard against any other evil, political or physical, which might assail us. This duty is paramount to all *laws,* all *treaties,* all *constitutions.* It arises from the supreme and permanent law of nature, the law of self-preservation—and will never by this state be renounced, compromised, controlled or participated, with any power whatever

Resolved, That this Legislature is aware of the dangerous and insidious conduct of a party in Great Britain and the United States, who are ever ready to indulge their benevolent propensities at the expense of their neighbours, and who seem to reflect with complacency on the scenes of carnage and cruelty, which must be the result of their inconsiderate and mischievous machinations.

Resolved, That this Legislature sees with surprise, that the attention of the British minister was not directed to the numerous acts which have been passed by the Parliament of Great Britain, within the last twenty years, for the expulsion of Aliens, and for the repeal of the Habeas Corpus act, founded on the suspicion that foreigners were interfering with the domestic tranquillity of the country, and justified in Great Britain by the very law of self-preservation to which we now appeal.

Resolved, That this Legislature having received a very strange and ill-advised communication from the Legislature of the state of Ohio,[2] approves of the reply of the Governor of Georgia[3] to a similar communication, and will, on this subject, be ready to make common cause with the state of Georgia, and the other southern states similarly circumstanced in this respect.

Resolved, Therefore, that the Legislature of South Carolina *protests* against any claims of right of the United States to interfere in any manner whatever with the domestic regulations and preservatory measures, in respect to that part of her property which forms the coloured population of the state; and which property they will not permit to be meddled with, or tampered with, or in any manner ordered, regulated, or controlled by any power, foreign or domestic, other than this Legislature.

The subject of the foregoing resolutions is an act of the Legislature of South Carolina, passed in the year 1822, the third section of which provides, that "if any vessel shall come into any port or harbor of this State, from any other State or foreign port, having on board any free Negroes or person of Colour, as cooks, stewards, mariners, or in any other employment on board said vessels, such free negroes or persons of colour shall be liable to be seized and confined in gaol, until said vessel shall clear out and depart from this State; and that when said vessel is ready to sail, the captain of said vessel shall be bound to carry away the said free negroe or person of colour, and pay the expenses of his detention; and in case of his neglect or refusal so to do, he shall be liable to be indicted, and on conviction thereof, shall be fined in a sum not less than one thousand dollars, and imprisoned not less than two months; and such free negroes or persons of colour shall be deemed and taken as absolute slaves, and sold in conformity to the provisions of the act passed on the twentieth day of December, one thousand eight hundred and twenty, aforesaid."

To give our readers a fair view of the matter at issue, it is necessary to call their attention to a fact which is no doubt still fresh in their memories. We allude to the contemplated insurrection of the slaves in Charleston two years ago, which was fortunately discovered in time to prevent the execution of its object, which was the massacre of the white inhabitants & the enfranchisement of the slave population. Several of those who were concerned in the conspiracy for an insurrection were tried and executed, and one or more, we believe, were banished. Such was the terror that seized upon the minds of citizens of Charleston, that they established at no inconsiderable expense to themselves, an armed patrol, subject to regular military duty every night, to guard against surprise, from any secret combination among the slaves, for a like bloody purpose. The Legislature of South Carolina, convinced that a spirit of insubordination among the blacks and people of colour was fomented by freemen of their own complexion, and that these, entering the territories of the State in various guises, but chiefly in the character of mariners or persons employed on board merchantmen, might, in fact, be emissaries, sent with the evil design of producing a servile war, which would be fraught with frightful disasters to the white inhabitants, enacted, in the month of December 1822, a law, from which the above extract is taken, it being the third section thereof. It appears from the document lately communicated by the Gov. of South Carolina[4] to the Legislature of that State, that in Feb. 1823, Mr. Canning the British minister to the U. States, addressed a note[5] to Mr. Adams, Secretary of State, remonstrating against the principles and practical operation of the act. The case which occurred is detailed in a letter from Mr. Petrie,[6] of Liverpool to the President of the Board of Trade, under date of Jan. 1824, by which it appears, that four persons of colour, belonging to the crew the ship Marmion were arrested and imprisoned according to the provisions of the act above cited, notwithstanding the earnest remonstrances of Capt. Petrie, and the British Consul at Charleston.[7]

On the ninth of April, 1824, Mr. Addington[8] the British Charges d'Affaires at Washington addressed a note to the President of the United States, remonstrating once more against the provision of the above-mentioned act and reminded the Executive of his verbal and written assurance to the British authorities to use every effort to remedy the grievances complained of, and to prevent a recurrence of them. The subject was referred by the Secretary of State to Mr. Wirt,[9] the Attorney General of the United States, who gave the following opinion, as to the constitutionality of the act of South Carolina:—

The question which you propound for my opinion on this section is, "whether it is compatible with the rights of nations in amity with the United States, or with the national constitution."

By the national constitution, the power of regulating commerce with foreign nations, and among the states, is given to Congress; and this power is, from its nature, exclusive. The power of regulating commerce is the power of prescribing the terms on which the intercourse between foreign nations and the United States, and between the several states of the Union, shall be carried on. Congress has exercised the power; and among these terms there is no requisition that the vessels which are permitted to enter the ports of the several states shall be navigated wholly by white men. All foreign and domestic vessels, complying with the requisition prescribed by Congress, have a right to enter any port of the United States and a right to remain there, unmolested in vessel and crew, for the peaceful purposes of commerce. No state can interdict a vessel which is about to enter her ports, in conformity with the laws of the United States, nor impose any restraint or embarrassment on such vessel, in consequence of her having entered in conformity with those laws. For the regulations of Congress on this subject being both supreme and exclusive, no state can add to them, vary them, or touch the subject in any shape whatever, without the concurrence and sanction of Congress.

By the regulations of Congress, vessels navigated by black or coloured men, may enter any port of the Union for the purposes of commerce, without any molestation or restraint in consequence of having so entered; but the section of the law of South Carolina which we are considering, declares, that if any vessel shall enter one of her ports, navigated in whole or in part by negroes or persons of colour, they shall be immediately seized and imprisoned at the expense of the captain, with various other contingent and severe penalties, both on the captain and his imprisoned crew. Here is a regulation of commerce, of highly penal character, by a state, superadding new restrictions to those which have been imposed by Congress; and declaring in effect that what Congress has ordained may be freely and safely done, shall not be done but under heavy penalties. It seems very clear to me, that this section of the law of South Carolina is incompatible with the national constitution, and with the laws passed under it, and is therefore void. All the nations in amity with the United States have a right to enter the ports of the Union for the purpose of commerce, so long as by the laws of the Union commerce is permitted; and so far as it is permitted and inasmuch as this section of the law of South Carolina is a restriction upon this commerce, it is incompatible with the rights of all nations which are in amity with the United States.

There is another view of this subject. By the national constitution, the power of making treaties with foreign nations is given to the general government, and the same constitution declares that the treaties so made shall constitute a part of the supreme law of the land. The national government has exercised this power also, of making treaties. We have treaties subsisting with various nations, by which the commerce of such nations with the United States is expressly authorized, without any restriction as to the colour of the crews by which it shall be carried on. We have such a treaty with Great Britain, as to which nation this question has arisen. This act of South Carolina forbids, or what is the same thing, punishes what this treaty authorizes.

I am of the opinion, that the section of the law under consideration is void, as being against the constitution, treaties and laws of the United States, and incompatible with the rights of all nations in amity with the United States.

On the 6th July last, the Secretary of State, by the order of the President, addressed a note to the Gov. of South Carolina, enclosing the opinion of the Attorney General, together with the several documents above alluded to, and expressing the hope of the Executive, "that the inconvenience complained of will be remedied by the Legislature of the State of South Carolina itself."

Governor Wilson, in his message communicating the documents, remarks:

"I deem this subject worthy your serious attention. My continued indisposition prevents me from presenting such views as I otherwise would have done. The reflection, however, which I have given the matter, brings my mind to the conclusion, that South Carolina has the right to interdict the entrance of such persons into her ports, whose organization of mind, habit and associations, render them peculiarly calculated to disturb the peace and tranquillity of the state, in the same manner as she can prohibit those afflicted with infectious disease to touch her shores. The law of self preservation derives its authority from a higher source than any municipal or international law—and it should be the first policy of government to prevent, if possible, such encroachments as eventually would lead to the injury and destruction of all the citizen holds most dear. This necessity of self-preservation is alone to be determined by the power to be preserved; it therefore rests with those whose rights are to be affected, to judge how long such laws shall exist, as were enacted for the peace and security of the community."

From this extract, and from the spirit of the resolutions, on which we have no space for comments at present, there is a prospect that the Legislature of South Carolina will be at issue with the general government on this question.

1. John Ramsay (1768–1828), a physician, resided in Charleston in 1822 at 1 Anson Street, but he also owned a plantation with more than sixty slaves in St. Paul Parish. See *CSCCD*, 95; *BDSCHR* 4: 466–67.

2. In 1824, the Ohio legislature passed a resolution, applauded by several northern states, calling slavery a "national evil" that required a national remedy of gradual emancipation. By implication, the resolution indicated that the federal government had the right to take action against what South Carolinians and other southerners regarded as a subject of state sovereignty, protected by the Constitution. See William W. Freehling, *Prelude to Civil War: The Nullification Controversy in South Carolina, 1816–1836* (New York: Harper & Row, 1966), 116–17.

3. Georgia Governor George Michael Troup (1780–1856), at the request of Georgia's state legislature, responded directly to the Ohio Legislature, defending slavery and state sovereignty in an annual message. Charleston *City Gazette and Commercial Daily Advertiser,* November 13, 1824, published extracts of the key passages.

4. John Lyde Wilson (1784–1849) had succeeded Thomas Bennett Jr. as governor of South Carolina.

5. The letter, Stratford Canning (1786–1880) to John Quincy Adams, February 15, 1823, can be found in *British and Foreign State Papers, 1824–1825* (London, 1846), 639–40.

6. For Captain Peter Petrie's complaint to the Board of Trade, see *British and Foreign State Papers, 1824–1825,* 641–42.

7. Benjamin Moodie (1755?–1823) was the British consul in Charleston at the start of the Negro seamen controversy.

8. Henry Urwin Addington served as British chargé d'affaires.

9. President James Monroe appointed his fellow Virginian, lawyer William Wirt (1772–1834), attorney general of the United States in 1817.

Boston *Recorder & Telegraph*

Friday, September 30, 1825

. . . While on this topic, Messrs. Editors, permit me to dissent from a position, which northern writers on slavery seem to have assumed, as possessing the certainty of a maxim. The amount of it is this, that the legislative acts of any State are a fair criterion, by which to judge of the opinions, the spirit and the feelings of a people. This sentiment cannot be admitted without, in any case, very much qualification. Many laws, severe in their aspect, owe their origin to certain emergencies, which produce great excitement at the time. Such laws, tho' remaining on our statute books, become obsolete in fact afterwards, and pass away with the occasion that gave rise to them. What would be thought of the character of South Carolina for example, if we[1] judged of it by an existing law which enacts, that all assemblages of blacks for religious worship are unlawful, unless a majority of whites are present. . . . But the intention of the law was to counteract insurrectionary schemes, which have almost always been engendered and cherished at meetings professedly religious. The object of the law therefore is completely gained, and the spirit of it complied with, if three or four white persons, possessing the confidence of the community, are found in an assembly of 2 or 300 slaves. Such is the language of fact *now,* even in that state, which has so recently been agitated with apprehensions of an insurrection. . . .

1. The letter was signed "Hieronymous," who was almost certainly a Charlestonian. Alice Adams, *The Neglected Period of Anti-Slavery in American History (1808–1831)* (Boston: Athenaeum Press, 1908), 282–83, believes Hieronymous was the Reverend Benjamin Morgan Palmer

(1781–1847) of Charleston's Congregational Church. Another possibility is the antislavery Episcopalian Thomas Smith Grimké (1786–1834), an attorney, who had joined the debate about slavery and was one of the few leading Charlestonians to support the American Colonization Society.

James Hamilton Jr. in Congress on the Recognition of Haiti, Monday, April 10, 1826

The House having again resumed the consideration of the Report of the Committee of Foreign Relations, approving the Mission to Panama,[1] with the amendments proposing a qualification to the general expression of approbation thereto—

Mr. HAMILTON took the floor. . . .

Sir, it is proper, that, on this occasion, I should speak with candor, and without reserve; that I should avow what I believe to be the sentiments of the Southern People on this question; and this is, that Haytien Independence is not to be tolerated in any form. Our opinions are derived from a solemn conviction that the consequences of this recognition would be fatal to our repose; that the perilous examples on our own shores, and in our own harbors, of the ensigns of the sovereignty of this People, would involve a condition of danger which would bring home, for our adoption, the law of a supreme necessity, in its most potent and insuperable form. The municipal laws of many of the Southern States would conflict with the provisions of a treaty containing such a recognition, and produce a concussion which must end either in the annihilation of these States, or the destruction of the power of the General Government. A People, Sir, will not stop to discuss the nice metaphysics of a federative system, when havoc and destruction menace them in their doors. The law of necessity is the most imperious, because it is the most ultimate and the most urgent of all laws. . . .

1. "Mission to Panama" refers to United States participation in a meeting called by Simón Bolívar (1783–1830), Latin America's foremost revolutionary leader, to promote hemispheric solidarity and a unified policy against the possibility of European intervention to overturn the results of the Latin American revolutions. That the question of Haiti's official recognition by other American states might be placed on the table in an assemblage that might also include the presence of Haitian delegates themselves sparked a heated debate along sectional lines in Congress.

Register of Debates, House of Representatives, Nineteenth Congress, First Session, 1250.

Charleston Merchants Protest the Negro Seamen Act, 1830

To the Hon. the President and other Members Of the Senate of South Carolina.

The Memorial of the Charleston Chamber of Commerce and other Citizens, respectfully sheweth,—That, by an Act passed in December, 1823, "in case any vessel shall arrive in any port of this state, from any other State, or from any foreign port, having on board colored persons as Cooks or Stewards, it is made the duty of the Sheriff to apprehend such persons, and keep them in custody until the vessel shall be ready to proceed to sea; and that in case of the refusal of the Captain to pay the expenses of their confinement, he shall forfeit the sum of $1000, and suffer imprisonment for a period not exceeding six months—And that no person shall be allowed to bring back into this state any slave who has been carried out of the same, if, during his absence, such slave hath been in places situated in Europe, the West Indies, Mexico, South America, or in States north of the Potomac or the city of Washington, under the penalty of a fine of $1000, and the forfeiture of the slave." And also, that by an Act passed in December, 1825, amendatory of the Act of 1823, vessels arriving in any port of this state, from any other state or foreign port, having colored persons on board as Cooks or Stewards, are required to lay in the stream at the distance of 150 yards from the wharves, and to load and unload by lighters, under the penalty of the forfeiture of $1000 by the captains of such vessels.

Your Memorialists are perfectly aware of the circumstances in which the above enactments had their origin. No class of our citizens can feel more sensibly than they do the peculiar nature of those circumstances, nor deprecate more sincerely the possibility of their recurrence. They appreciate, therefore, in all their force, the purity and patriotism of the motives by which the Legislature was governed in passing those acts, and, in common with the rest of their fellow citizens, feel grateful for the active zeal and paternal supervision which it has always displayed, upon the interesting points which form the subject matter of those laws, at the call of its constituents. But at the same time that your Memorialists acknowledge the general patriotism and wisdom which characterize those laws, they deem it their duty to represent the grievances to which the mercantile community is subjected by their operation. Your memorialists would not obtrude upon your time by a statement of those grievances, if they did not believe that such an alteration may be made of those laws, as, without impairing their general utility, will not only remove the inconveniences alluded to, but even render the acts themselves more salutary and efficient. Deeply impressed with the conviction that such an alteration may be made, and anxious equally to preserve the domestic tranquillity, and promote the commercial welfare of the State, your Memorialists respectfully solicit your attention to the following considerations:

First, The laws above mentioned have proved extremely detrimental to the commerce of Charleston, and of the state at large: they operate injuriously in a variety of ways—they drive away vessels from our ports—they subject our own masters of vessels to the necessity and consequent very heavy expense of employing white cooks and stewards in the place of blacks—and they harass and impede the operations of trade by the obligation they impose upon vessels from other ports to lay in the stream, and load and unload by lighters. In the Northern and Eastern states, and particularly in the Southern, in which, for very obvious reasons, the services of coloured persons, as cooks and stewards, can be more cheaply and readily procured than those of whites, a preference is naturally given to persons of that description. But our laws prohibit their appearance in our harbours. As a necessary consequence, therefore, numerous vessels, which would otherwise have come to Charleston for the disposal of their cargoes, and for supplies repairs, etc, have, rather than submit to the operations of our laws, gone on to Savannah, or to some other port in which no such interdictions are enforced. If, indeed, there existed among all the Southern states, a uniform system of prohibition, the evils, perhaps, would not be so severe as they are at present. The same impediments being equally opposed by all, vessels from other ports would not, of course, be governed by the strong inducements which now exist to give a preference to other Southern places over Charleston; but there is no such uniformity of system—No such restrictions are known in Virginia, North Carolina, or Georgia. A system, indeed, somewhat similar to ours was, a few years ago, of force in Georgia, but the Legislature of that state, sensible of the injuries which it inflicted upon its trade, very soon repealed it. South Carolina, instead of benefiting by this lesson, has committed the very error which Georgia so wisely corrected. As the matter now stands, therefore, seeing that this is the only State in which such laws prevail, it is scarcely possible to regard them in any other light, than as laws, whose natural tendency and inevitable consequence are, to depress the commerce of South Carolina, and to establish upon its ruins the trade and prosperity of a rival port. But this is not all. The interests of this community are not only injured by thus compelling vessels to carry their cargoes to ports in our neighbouring states, but our own masters of vessels are subjected to very heavy inconveniences, arising from the prohibition to employ slaves in the trade carried on to the West Indies, and the consequent obligation to employ whites as cooks and stewards. It is impossible to represent these inconveniences too strongly. From the nature of our society, menial occupations are necessarily confined to coloured persons. White men disdain and are unwilling to undertake them. Very few, if any whites, consequently, are qualified to act as cooks and stewards, whilst numerous person of colour have been regularly bred to those offices and are capable of performing them with great dexterity. Not only, therefore, are passengers dissatisfied with the change which the law compels, but the whites themselves, who are thus substituted as cooks and stewards, enjoying a complete monopoly, are extravagant and extortionate in their demands, and so extremely wilful in their conduct as to have frequently abandoned vessels at the very moment of their departure.

Your Memorialists earnestly hope that your Honourable Body will give to these facts the serious consideration which they merit. It is unnecessary, they trust, to enlarge upon the vital importance of commerce to the state, or upon the propriety of giving to it every assistance and facility compatible with the personal safety of our citizens. Commerce and agriculture depend vitally and reciprocally upon each other. In exact proportion to the facilities afforded to trade, are the correspondent advantages enjoyed by Planters. Shackle the commerce of Charleston, and you paralyze the industry and destroy the profits of your farmers. The principal sea-port of the State, Charleston, bears the same relation to the state at large, which the heart does to the human system—If prosperous itself, it diffuses wealth and vigour to every other section—if depressed, there is no portion, however remote, which will not experience the effect of its embarrassments. The station of South Carolina, moreover, in the scale of the union depends upon its commerce. Its relative rank and importance are regulated by its contributions to the general government, and those, of course, by the condition of its trade. In this respect our state has hitherto held a high and enviable rank. Whether it will continue to occupy that rank, will mainly depend upon the measures which may be devised to promote its welfare. Laws such as ours, therefore, severe and burdensome as they would be even under circumstances of comparitive prosperity, are particularly oppressive at the present unexampled period of commercial depression. Dependent, then as we are, upon the markets of Europe, and suffering severely as we have done, and still do, under the influence of European embarrassment, is it not incumbent upon the Legislature to extend such relief to the commerce of the State, as may be consistent with the great objects of its policy in regard to its coloured population? Ought it not to foster trade, instead of throwing factitious and unnecessary impediments in its way? Ought it not to invite intercourse, rather than repel it? And to encourage the industry and enterprise of our citizens rather than destroy them?

The next great point to which your Memorialists solicit your attention, is that these laws themselves, as they now stand, are totally useless and inefficient. Your Memorialists, perhaps, would not so earnestly urge their alteration, if they effected the purposes for which they are intended. But experience has proved that they are liable to perpetual evasion and infractions. While they embarrass commerce, they cannot prevent the enterance of colored persons by land—it is also useless as regards their ingress on board of vessels. The severity of the law defeats itself. As long as human nature continues as it is, juries will be governed by their own ideas of the expediency of a law, and of the adaptation of the punishment to the nature of the crime. So has it happened with these laws. The humanity of our Juries has revolted at them. In almost every instance in which attempts have been made to prosecute under them, the grand Juries have refused to find bills of indictment, regarding the penalty as too disproportioned to the offence—and in the only instance in which a bill was found, the Court, giving a particular construction to the act, directed the jury to acquit the accused. These laws, therefore, unless relaxed, will in all probability never be executed. Now no laws ought to be continued which cannot be enforced; nor ought the Legislature to suffer statutes to remain unaltered, which, while they have not answered and cannot answer the particular ends for which they were designed, operate evils they never were intended to produce. These laws, as far as they do operate, militate against our commerce; in every other respect they are mere dead letters in the statute book.

Your Memorialists, having thus presented this subject in its two most important lights, do not deem it necessary to dwell upon others in which it may be incidentally considered. They therefore say nothing of the great division of sentiment which exists in the community in regard to the constitutionality of these laws. Certain it is, however, that such division does exist, not only in regard to their constitutionality, but also to their expediency in their present shape. While many of our best and most enlightened men consider them as directly infringing that provision of the Federal Constitution which gives to Congress the exclusive power to "regulate commerce with foreign nations and among the several States," others again, confining their views altogether to their policy, consider them too severe, and calculated to defeat themselves, as indeed they have done, by their excessive vigour. Our own State Constitution also says, that "excessive fines shall not be imposed"—and it may be a question worthy of the attention of your Honourable Body, whether, in the cases of Captains of vessels, generally speaking, a fine of $1000 is not extremely disproportioned to their ability to pay. But, whatever weight may be given to these suggestions, your memorialists deem it their duty to press particularly upon your notice, that the same necessity does not now exist to continue these laws in their present shape, which induced the Legislature originally to enact them. Since the unfortunate occurrence which gave rise to these laws, a highly respectable and very numerous association of our citizens has been formed, for the sole and exclusive purpose of detecting attempts at disturbance, and of preserving order and good government among our slaves. This association, distinguished by its vigilance and by the excellence of the system it has organized, (so much so indeed that it is morally impossible for a seditious movement to remain a moment undiscovered) almost of itself supersedes the necessity of the laws in question. Under all these circumstances then, seeing that these laws drive away commerce and impoverish our city, that they subject our citizens to great and unnecessary personal inconvenience and pecuniary loss—that they prevent masters of vessels from employing colored persons and slaves in the line of business in which they would be most useful and profitable, at the same time that they compel them to employ whites at a very heavy expence and consequent loss—and that they subject our trade to all the delays, damages, and vexations arising from the obligation upon vessels to load and unload by lighters—seeing also that these laws defeat themselves by their own excessive severity—that great doubt is entertained of their constitutionality and even of their policy in their present shape—that the occasion which produced them has in some degree passed away—Your Memorialists earnestly solicit your serious attention to the following points.

First.—Whether so much of these Laws, may not be repealed, without injury to the public safety as compells Vessels arriving in our ports, having on board, coloured persons as Cooks and Stewards to load and unload in the stream—and whether, other and more salutary provisions and enactments may not be adopted by which our trade, will be benefited, and the communications between such colored persons and our Slaves more effectually prevented.

Second.—Whether so much of these laws may not be repealed, without injury, as prohibits the employment of slaves as mariners, Cooks and Stewards, in our trade with slave holding Colonies, in the West Indies.

Your Memorialists would beg leave respectfully to make one more suggestion—By the late arrangement between our General Government and the British Ministry, our trade with the British West Indies will shortly be renewed. And your Memorialists cannot but express the hope, that your Honourable Body will therefore perceive the encreased propriety of so modifying the aforesaid Laws, as to permit the producers and merchants of South Carolina to enjoy their due proportion of this advantageous branch of Commerce.

And your Memorialists will pray &c.

Charleston	In behalf of the Charleston
19th November 1830	Chamber of Commerce
R Heriot[1]	David Alexander[2]
Secretary	President

1. Although *CSCCD*, 147, identifies the Scottish-born Roger Heriot (1769?–1849) as merely a notary public, he joined the export firm of Heriot & Tucker in 1787 and became a prosperous merchant. See "Obituary," *Charleston Courier*, March 10, 1849.

2. David Alexander (d. 1840), president, Union Insurance Company, in 1830 would serve as president of the Charleston Chamber of Commerce. See "Charleston Chamber of Commerce," Charleston *Southern Patriot,* January 29, 1840.

Memorial of the Charleston Chamber of Commerce, November 19, 1830, Petitions to the General Assembly, no. 124, series S165015, SCDAH.

Memorial Regarding Black Seamen, 1851

. . . The law which we[1] are invited to surrender, was originally introduced soon after the detection and suppression of an insurrectionary movement, devised and set on foot by a free negro who had been for some time in the habit of leaving the State, and returning to it at pleasure, and whose frequent excursions were proved to be connected with his bloody designs. The law has existed for nearly thirty years, and during that time no similar conspiracy has occurred. How far it has contributed to this result we cannot pretend to estimate. But we know that the experience of our predecessors led them to adopt it, and there is certainly nothing in our experience to induce us to abandon it. . . .

It was originally enacted and has been continued solely and exclusively with a view to own internal good order and security, and without the remotest intention to trespass upon the rights or obstruct the commerce of any other people. . . .

1. This memorial appears in handwritten form in Special Committee, "Report and Resolutions on a Governors Message Transmitting Communications from British Consul George B. Mathews Regarding the Law Affecting Black Seamen," December 2, 1851, Report of Legislative Committee, no. 79, series S165005, SCDAH. Alexander Mazyck (1801–1894), a prominent Charleston attorney, composed it.

[Alexander Mazyck], *Law of Colored Seamen* (Charleston, n.d.).

Liberator

Friday, December 12, 1845

. . . The following is an extract from the recent message of the Governor of South Carolina[1] to the legislature of that lawless state.

I herewith lay before you, the Protest of the Legislature of Massachusetts against South Carolina and the laws, which she has in, the high duties of self-preservation, and in the exercise of her undoubted rights, seen fit to enact, prohibiting the ingress of free persons of color, who are dangerous to the peace and safety of her own population. . . . The simple history of the legislation, and the circumstances of the controversy which has been unhappily fomented by Massachusetts, is the best vindication of South Carolina. It is briefly this.

In 1822, a most dangerous and extensive conspiracy of the black population in and about Charleston was discovered. It had been chiefly planned and devised by foreign free persons of color, who had seduced and corrupted the native free blacks and slaves. The schemes of their operation embraced the burning and plunder of the city, destruction of life and other enormities. The trial of the culprits elicited the most irrefragable evidence of their active agency, and of the dangers arising from the intermingling of the foreign blacks with our slaves, and humanity demanded, both for the slave and the master, that they should be protected from these seductions. The Act of 1822 was therefore passed by the Legislature, which is the beginning of this Legislation; it was revised and reenacted with some immaterial alterations in 1836. The reasonableness, the humanity, the propriety of this act, was not questioned by any American State for fourteen years; when the first resolutions of Massachusetts were levelled against it. It is true that Great Britain did complain, at an early date after the passage of the act, to the general government . . . and it is equally true that Mr. Wirt, then attorney General of the United States, did give the opinion which is quoted in the protest, against the constitutionality of the law—but South Carolina never for one moment "yielded" her convictions that she was right nor her determination to maintain her position, as Massachusetts erroneously asserts. . . .

South Carolina has never interfered with the institutions or people of other States; she has indulged in no speculations dangerous to the peace of her sisters in the confederacy; she has given no countenance to measures or doctrines, which could stimulate insurrection, desolate States, or lead to the carnage of men, women and children. She has simply taken such precautions, as would to her best judgment prevent all these, and other accumulated horrors of servile war, from visiting her domains; of guarding a happy and peaceful race, from crimes and punishments at which humanity shudders. . . .

1. William Aiken Jr. (1806–1887), a prominent planter, was governor of South Carolina in 1845.

Report on Black Mariners, Thursday, December 7, 1854

HOUSE OF REPRESENTATIVES,
Columbia, Dec. 7th, 1854.

THE COMMITTEE ON COLORED POPULATION,

To whom was referred so much of the Message No. 1 of His Excellency the Governor as relates to the imprisonment of Free Persons of color employed as mariners or otherwise on board of vessels trading with our ports, ask leave to

REPORT:

That they have given the subject that careful consideration which the high authority from which the recommendation proceeds, and its own intrinsic importance seemed to them to demand. The Statute of 1835, now in force, was enacted under circumstances which induced a belief that those who were opposed to our domestic peace might have in their employment this class of persons, as emisaries, in carrying out their designs against our safety. There can be no doubt as to the right of the State to enact laws of this character. It is not the right we propose to consider, but the mode and manner of enforcing it. All nations have the right of protecting themselves by police laws and provisions excluding from their borders those who may be regarded as dangerous to their internal peace and security. . . . We cannot deny that the operation of our law is particularly harsh in some of its features. Whether entering our ports voluntarily or driven there by accidents beyond their control; whether designedly or by the act of God, no discrimination is made; all alike come under its operation, and are immediately, on touching our soil, incarcerated in our common jails and treated as malefactors. It is surely a spectacle not to be desired, nor do we believe our safety requires it, that on the arrival of any vessel, whether trading intentionally with our ports or compelled to seek shelter there, either by tempest or disease, that this class of persons be at once hurried into prison. Such a course would seem to indicate a sense of insecurity on our part which we pursuade ourselves does not exist. . . .

Your Committee are of the opinion that the present regulations of our law are not only unnecessarily harsh, but that they are to a great extent inefficient for the purposes designed. They are fully convinced that they may be modified with entire security, and think that this is called for as well by our experience of their inefficiency as from a desire to exhibit that spirit of comity which we would wish to cultivate with foreign powers. With these views your committee would report the accompanying Bill, and recommend its adoption by the House.

Respectfully submitted.

J. HARLESTON READ, JR.,[1]
Chairman of the Committee of Colored Population.

1. John Harleston Read Jr. (1815–1866) was a prominent planter from Georgetown. For an analysis of his defense of free persons of color, see Michael P. Johnson and James L. Roark, *Black Masters: A Free Family of Color in the Old South* (New York: Norton, 1984), 279–81.

Great Britain, Public Record Office, Kew, England, FO 5/601.

The forced exile of the Reverend Morris Brown and the destruction of the African Church dealt a devastating blow to Charleston's black community. Several of the documents in this subsection, although they could have been located in other parts of the volume, are published here for the light they shed on the fate of Charleston's AME Church and the resonance of the Vesey affair in African American communities outside of Charleston. The Reverend Henry Highland Garnet encountered a Vesey "betrayer" in New York City. The Reverend Daniel Alexander Payne, a Charleston-born free person of color who served as Morris Brown's private secretary and spared no effort in writing the first history of the AME Church, speaks clearly about the existence of a plot led by Vesey and the subsequent flight of AME Church leaders from Charleston.

Following the failure to implement class leader Vesey's Old Testament brand of revolutionary theology, enslaved Charlestonians instead continued to adapt Christian teachings to ameliorate the harshness of bondage. At the same time, a number of white ministers, many of whom had known the condemned and had visited them in the Charleston Work-House prior to their executions, continued to argue that Christianity, if properly taught and sanitized by elite churchmen, could produce a godly, subservient, and more productive labor force. They faced both support and opposition in their efforts from elite planters. Some members of the African Church, including Morris Brown, had close ties to white ministers. Since leaders of the Vesey plot belonged to the African Church, some elite planters blamed evangelical outreach by white ministers to slaves for stoking unrest. The ministers countered by arguing that those slaves who had not broken away from established denominations had not only remained loyal, but had contributed to the plot's discovery. In that regard two documents in this section stand out in importance: the exchange during fall 1822 between the Charleston Bible Society and Governor Bennett. Precipitated by the desire of the leadership of the Bible Society to have Bennett declare a statewide day of thanksgiving to the Lord for His saving Charlestonians from blood and fire, Bennett in his response demurs. Given how close the principals in these exchanges were to the conspirators, with most of the ministers in the Bible Society having visited inculpated slaves in their confinement, information furnished about the plot underscores that, whatever reservations Bennett had either about its seriousness and magnitude or about the fairness of the judicial proceedings, he did not deny the existence of a plot.

In attempting to mediate the master-slave relation, Charleston's divines charted a complex political course. On the one hand, they defended the humanity of slaves, pushed missionary work among slaves, and sought to get masters to run their households according to Christian precepts. On the other hand, as the Reverend Richard Furman's influential *Exposition* on slavery, published in the immediate aftermath of the Vesey affair, evidences, Charleston's theologians took a leading role in moving the defense of slavery in the South away from the soft ground of necessary evil or temporary expedient to a much firmer, more sophisticated biblical and historical defense of the institution as a positive good. Furman intended his *Exposition* for multiple audiences: antislavery northerners, elite slaveholders, his fellow theologians, and the slaves themselves. It marked a significant advance in the proslavery argument, particularly in the use of serious biblical exegesis to assert that slavery was divinely sanctioned. In religion as well as politics, South Carolina would set the tone in the soul-searching to come on slavery as the South responded after 1831 to Nat Turner's insurrection and the rise of immediate abolitionism.

Charleston *City Gazette and Commercial Daily Advertiser*

Saturday, August 10, 1822

FOR THE CITY GAZETTE.

MR. EDITOR,

Having been favoured with the perusal of the following decision, which appears to accord both with the policy of the State, and the opinion of the Law; we deem the publication of the same, as useful and beneficial to those whom it may concern, and doubtless will be acceptible to your readers:

A SUBSCRIBER.

THE STATE,
vs.
MORRIS BROWN
and
HENRY DRAYTON
Free Negroes

The act under which the present proceedings are had against Morris Brown and Henry Drayton, free persons of color, for coming into this State contrary to law, was passed 20th December, 1820. The act states, "That from and after the 1st day of March next, (1821) it shall not be lawful for any free negro or mulatto to migrate into this State, except any free person of color being a native of this State, who shall return within the limits of this State within two years after the passing of this act, or who shall leave this State as a servant of any white person, and shall return with any white person in such capacity."

The facts of the case are, that Brown and Drayton being free men of color, and natives of this State, were here at the passing of the act, and that on or about the 1st of April last, they went to Philadelphia, New-York, &c. &c. and returned, the one about the 8th, the other about the 29th June last to Charleston. That they went away on their private concerns, with a view to return, not as servants to any white person, nor did they return in that capacity.

It is well known that the interest and policy of the State required, at the passing of this act, that some efficient measures should be adopted, to prevent, in the language of the preamble, "free persons of color from entering into the State." It therefore became necessary for the Legislature so to provide, as that the citizens of this State should be protected, while at the same time there should be as little violation of the rights of the free persons of color as possible. It was then manifest, that there were three classes of such persons to be protected from the rigor of this act. 1st. such as were within the State at the passing of the law. 2d. such as were away from the State, and 3d. such as were within the State after the 1st March, 1821, and might leave it with an intention to return. For the benefit of the first class, it was no doubt considered, that sufficient time was given until the 1st March, 1821, a term of some thing better than two months, during which time there is no restriction whatever upon their going or returning as they might think proper.

With regard to the second class, a greater allowance of time was deemed reasonable. It was considered possible that some might be engaged in distant voyages, and two years was a reasonable term for such to receive notice of the law. With regard to such, it is to be remarked, that the law went into operation, as it were, immediately; the two years commencing not from the 1st March, 1821, but from the 20th December, 1820, the very date of the act.

On behalf of the defendants, it is insisted (with force, and certainly with great ingenuity) that the term of two years is given to all native free persons of color, to go and return at pleasure. That these persons have now *returned* within the time allowed, and therefore have not violated the law. But if this reasoning be correct, then why did not the act go into operation immediately on its passage? Who were intended to be saved harmless between the date and operation of the law, if not those who were in the State, and who might have necessary arrangements to make against their final settlement here. The construction contended for, might be more reasonably insisted upon, had not the Legislature expressly provided for such as should leave the state with an intention of returning into it.

Under which class then do these defendants come? It is not pretended that they are embraced within the last; they having neither gone away, nor returned as servants to any white person. They are not embraced within the first, they having gone away after the 1st March, 1821. I am at a loss to conceive how they can expect to be included within the second class. They were here at the passing of the act, they knew of the law, they departed of their own free will and accord, and have now returned within the limits of this State, contrary to what I consider the intention, as collected from the context, and even the letter of the act.

It therefore becomes my duty to order, and I do hereby order the said Morris Brown and Henry Drayton, to leave this State within fifteen days from this date, under the pains and penalties which await them in case of their disobedience.[1]

JOHN B. WHITE, Q.U.[2]

August 6, 1822.

1. This document firmly fixes Brown and Drayton in Charleston during the Vesey proceedings, and both men would surely have used sources within the AME church that they headed to investigate the reality of the plot. It is unclear whether Reverend Brown's son Malcolm emigrated north with his father. On April 11, 1871, thirty-six-year-old Malcolm Brown Jr. opened an account with the Charleston branch of the Freedman's Savings Bank. He listed his father, "Malcolm [as] dead," but he had a son named Morris. See Freedman's Savings Bank Records, Roll 23, NA.

2. John Blake White (1781–1859), attorney, dramatist, and artist, was serving in 1822 as a justice of the peace in Charleston when asked to hear this case by Morton A. Waring (d. 1863), the city's federal marshal. See *BDSCHR* 5: 280–81; William Griffith, *Annual Law Register of the United States,* 2 vols. (Burlington, NJ, 1822), vol. 4: 823 [volumes 1 and 2 never published].

Charleston Courier

Wednesday, August 14, 1822

By Wm. A. Caldwell. On Friday afternoon, at four o'clock, will be sold by the order of the Trustees of the African Church, on their Lot in Hampstead, ALL THE LUMBER, Which comprised the said Church, in lots to suit purchasers.

Conditions: cash, and the Lumber, to be taken charge of immediately, after the sale and removed the next day.

August 14.[1]

1. This advertisement, coming eight days after the trial and banishment of Reverends Brown and Drayton, suggests that the African Church was not burned by a mob, as popularly supposed, but ordered razed by city authorities. The remaining trustees, evidently, hoped to sell the lumber and perhaps use the money to rebuild in the future. William A. Caldwell was a "Vendue Master" who lived at 58 Meeting Street. See *CSCCD,* 4.

Petition for Prohibition, 1822

Be it remembered that on the sixth day of August in the year of our Lord one thousand eight hundred and twenty two in the court of common pleas and General Sessions comes Henry Drayton a free man of colour and gives the court to be informed that whereas he is a native of the city of Charleston in which he has resided from his infancy, he has always before the 20th of December 1820 by the law of the said State been permitted to go abroad on his lawful business and return to the State: and whereas by an act of assembly: and whereas by an act of the General Assembly made on the day before mentioned it was intended that after the first day of March ensuing it shall not be lawful for any free negro or mulatto to migrate into this State; and by the 4th section of said Act it is also expressly provided that nothing in said act contained shall affect any free person of colour being a native of the state who shall return within the limits of this State within two years after the passing of this act; and whereas in April last the said Henry Drayton having occasion to go as far as Philadelphia, consulted counsel learned in the law, to know whether it would be lawful for him to return, if he should go away with a view to a temporary absence, and was advised that no law would be violated thereby; and therefore without any apprehension of offending he the said Henry Drayton returned to the city of Charleston sometime in June last: and so is not guilty of any violations of the aforesaid act, and no justice has by the law of the land jurisdiction or authority to drive him from his family and home: Nevertheless Col. Morton A. Waring hath caused him the said Morris Henry to be taken before John Blake White Esquire, a justice of the peace for the city of Charleston, and accused him the said Henry of violating the said act by unlawfully coming into the state: and the said John Blake White well knowing the premises has condemned him the said Henry of violating the said act, and ordered him to leave the State, to the end that he may proceed further against him unless he the said Henry shall obey the said order within fifteen days against the laws of the State: & to the great injury of the said Henry and this he is ready to verify. Wherefore the said Henry most humbly imploring prays remedy by the writ of Prohibition to be directed to the said John Blake White to prohibit him from holding plea of the premises in putting in force the said order. . . .

Henry Drayton
V
John B. White
Morton A. Waring
Filed 8 August 1822

Upon consideration of the matters contained in the within Suggestion, and on hearing Counsel fully on both sides for and against the Prohibition prayed for I am of opinion that there are no grounds of Law to warrant me in granting the Said Writ and is therefore ordered that the Rule be discharged.

E. H. Bay
13 Augt. 1822

Charleston District Court of General Session, Petition for Prohibition, 5A, SCDAH.

Reverend Benjamin Morgan Palmer Preaches on Slavery, Sunday, September 22, 1822

. . . Paul, in saying "Masters, give unto your servants that which is just and equal," never could have meant, that his injunction should be so construed and extended, as in its influence and effects to tend to subvert the very relations themselves, the mutual duties of which he was carefully pointing out. Owners may be very kind, indulgent and even affectionate to their domestics, without so conducting towards them, as to make them forget their station and their duty, and create, in their hearts an aspiring disposition, which tends only to their own unhappiness and the unhappiness of all connected with them. . . .

We find, we have, in our discussions on this subject, insensibly glided, from the consideration of the duties of servants in general, into a view of the state of things amongst ourselves, and, almost before we were aware, have slipped along from the Apostles' times down into our own. It was however not an unnatural course. But, having now got into our own times, we have one further remark to make on the obstructions which the Gospel has to meet with in our own community: it is the *licentious intercourse of the whites*, respectable whites too. A significant remark of a person who is in the habit of periodically visiting our city is in point here. Arriving at the period, when the late iniquitous and murderous plot was discovered, he spoke to a friend who gave him the account of it, to the following effect "Do you know the reason of it. It is owing, more than to any other cause, to the criminal and illicit commerce with the whites." This is no doubt the root and source, the deep root and the fertile source of man[n]ers, if not of most of the natural and moral mischiefs, that we have so just reason to complain of and is particularly the source of *the dressing system.*[1] It is a fact susceptible of proof in more instances than one, that some of the best and most valuable, as well as most kindly treated servants in the city, have been corrupted and ruined by temptations from this quarter. And, if those who have uttered their vociferations most loudly and issued their rage and blasphemy against religion, its professors and its ministers, most copiously during the late disturbances, would employ but half their noise and half their strength and zeal in tracing out the source and drying up the streams of moral corruption in the midst of us; if a committee of vigilance were compelled to aid the regular authority of the city, in the execution of the laws particularly those which go to enforce God's fourth command, and his 3d 7th and 8th commandments too, if such laws there be; or if there is morality enough in the community, and concord enough among the different denominations of Christians that belong to it, to form an Association to remedy the defects of the law under the name, or at least possessing the character of *a moral society*; institutions that have been found highly useful in other cities and places, there would be much less occasion for religion to be blamed and abused for things, with which it has nothing to do, other than to condemn them utterly. . . .

1. Palmer complains here of slaves in extravagant dress and calls for enforcement of existing sumptuary laws that date back to the Negro Act of 1740. Since he entered places where inculpated slaves were confined and conversed with some of them, including his father's own slave Billy Palmer, about the plot, the Reverend's unequivocal emphasis on its existence and seriousness in this sermon and his attempt to explain causes are especially noteworthy. Palmer had a reputation for integrity in Charleston that crossed the color line.

Benjamin Morgan Palmer, *Religion Profitable: with a Special Reference to the Case of Servants. A Sermon Preached on September 22, 1822 in the Circular Church, Charleston, S.C.* (Charleston, SC, 1822), 16–17.

Figure 33. General Charles Cotesworth Pinckney (1746–1825), founder and president in 1822 of the Charleston Bible Society. From a portrait, ca. 1819. Copyrighted image courtesy of the Gibbes Museum of Art/Carolina Art Association.

The Charleston Bible Society[1] Asks Governor Bennett for a Day of Thanksgiving

---

Charleston, September 23rd 1822.

Sir

As Individuals, deeply concerned, and as the Board of the Charleston Bible Society, to whom our Constituents have confided an important Trust, analogous, in its nature & design, to the great Principles & interests of Religion, Morals, Government & Social Happiness at large, our Attention has been turned with Seriousness to the recent, merciful Interposition of Divine Providence, by which the Inhabitants of this City, and, not improbably, of a great part of the State, have been preserved from the Execution of a ferocious, diabolical Design, which privy Conspiracy had formed, in the Councils of Domestic Barbarians, among us: A Design fraught with every Principle of premeditated Wickedness, and calculated to open, in an unexpected moment, on the astonished view of our unsuspecting Citizens, and to bring home to their tortured feelings horrid Scenes of Anarchy, Desolation, Violence and Massacre. And, in the Contemplation of this Subject, we have been induced to conclude, conscientiously, that it is incumbent on the Citizens of this State, at large, to make grateful acknowledgments to our Heavenly Preserver, by a Strong Expression of their Sentiments & Feelings, for the signal Display of his Goodness & Mercy toward them, made on this memorable occasion.

We therefore take the Liberty of recommending, to your Excellency, the Exercise on this occasion, of that discretional Power, which by common consent & usage, if not by Law, is vested in you, as our Chief Magistrate, in favour of Religion; by appointing, at some proper time, a Day of Public Thanksgiving to Almighty God, for the Instance of his Goodness here recognized; And that it be recommended to our Citizens throughout the State, to be observed by them in the Manner which becomes a People who acknowledge God's Superintending Providence, feel their obligations to his Goodness, & live under the governing Influence of pious Affections—Unless, indeed, countervailing Reasons, with which we are unacquainted, exist, to render, in the Judgment of your Excellency, the Measure ineligible. Such Reasons, however, if just, we conceive, must be, not only very weighty, but of an uncommon character. Those of which we have been informed, do not, to us, appear sufficient.

That the Conspiracy was confined to a few, & the Evil, therefore, to be considered as of no great magnitude, as to its Extent, & the Probability of Success; though it is a position admitted by some liberal Minds, which are inclined to think favourably of mankind; yet, to us, it appears to be, at least, problematical. Many of our discerning Citizens, not in the habit of indulging Suspicions, did observe symptoms, both in Spirit & Conduct, among the class of Persons designed to be drawn into the Measure, of what appeared to be the Spirit of Conspiracy & Revolt in exercise, or the Effects of Guilt, extensively operating among them, about the Time the Work of Darkness was to have been perpetrated; or when the Ministers of Justice were prosecuting in their Investigation. Among the Reasons why more of the Conspirators have not been discovered, this no doubt is one of weight: Artful Measures were pursued to preserve Secrecy; so that Many, though Acquaintances, while actually engaged in Plot, did not know that they were mutually so concerned. It appears, by different confessions, that they had the Address to keep their Design concealed from Discovery more than three years; which proves that they were deeply versed in the Arts of Concealment. And if three Years ago (which has been also confessed) they had the Prudence to defer the designed Attack, from an Apprehension that they had not then a sufficient Force engaged to secure their object; there seems to be just Reason to conclude that having had so long a Time to prepare; having held Communications, by Messengers, with the Country; carefully formed their Plan, and fixed upon the very day and hour for its Execution; that they were then well assured they had large Numbers on their side; and that their Associates in the Country would have been in Motion, as soon as the prime Movers had taken the lead in the City. But their Plan was disconcerted. A Kind Providence interposed & frustrated their Designs. A disclosure was made; & they knew it. The Measures taken by your Excellency, & the subordinate Constituted Authorities, for counteracting their Operations which did not escape their Observation, intimidated them: These seem to have been the True Reasons why they did not appear in Arms, resort to the Places of Rendezvous, or begin the Work of Death.

Though an Attempt, when made, should have proved abortive, as to the main object; yet being made in a Time of general Security, which was their Plan, it can hardly be supposed that no partial Success would have attended it; at the very Idea of which, [*illegible*] even in a low Degree, the Mind recoils with horror. Thought here will not bear

Expression!—But if from such Evils, as cause Humanity, Purity & Virtue to shudder, the most Merciful Providence of God has preserved us—How cordial, fervent, public & general should our Thanksgivings be? Even tho the City should have been their only object, how deeply must success have affected the State at large? And how pernicious must the Example have proved to Slaves throughout the Country?—

Some Cautious, & highly respectable Characters, who gratefully acknowledge the Divine Interposition on this Occasion; yet think, that from Political Considerations it would be best to have no Day of Publick Thanksgiving appointed: As it would spread the Knowledge of the Fact extensively, & produce such an Idea of its importance in our Estimation, of our Fear and Danger, as would prove an Excitement to such Villains as have been concerned in the late Plot to engage in a Similar Enterprise.—On this Sentiment we would remark that scarcely can more publicity be given to a subject than that to which this has already attained. The Legal Proceedings, & the Executions have been of such notoriety that, by the ordinary Channels of private Conveyance, Information of them must have gone, or will go to every part of the State. But the Publick Prints have teemed with this Information, not only in this State, but through the whole of the United States; Your Excellency's Communication[2] on this subject appears in this Open Manner before the World; and the City Magistrates have sanctioned a Publication,[3] which exhibits a Historical View of the Conspiracy, of their own, & of the Courts' Proceedings on the Occasion.

If merely political, or Social Considerations, furnished just and sufficient motives for these Publications; and if no Evil is to be apprehended from them, while yet the Fact they disclose, its Magnitude, Criminality, and dangerous Nature, are by them exhibited in a Strong Light to the public View; it seems natural to ask, Why should so much Danger be apprehended from a pious, devotional reference to these subjects in the manner here contemplated; & especially, when already well known; & when every Mind capable of the least Reflection must be sensible of the Reasonableness & Importance of gratefully recognizing the Divine Interposition, by which we have been preserved? But, if gratefully acknowledging the Divine Goodness, on this occasion, as a People, is our Duty; should we not, though certain Danger attended it, be willing to encounter that Danger? And, may we not then, with confidence, look up to Heaven for that protection which is a better Defense than numerous Armies, or Fortresses of Adamant?—May not, also, our Silence & Remissness on this Occasion, operate powerfully, in an indirect manner, to produce the very Effect we would avoid & Will they not be attributed, by the Persons from whom our Apprehensions arise, to our Consciousness of being in the Wrong; to our Fear, & Sense of Weakness; and thus by fixing on the true Principle on which the Policy is founded, as it exists in the Minds of many, with the superceded Idea of our being irreligious, & therefore the more vulnerable; will they not, the rather from this View of the subject, be induced to renew their Machinations and Efforts? That there are many of them in every Part of the State who have Discernment, & the Faculty of Reasoning is evident.

But, Sir, we beg leave to observe, that in respect to the Black Population among us not Concealment, but Information on this subject, appears to be, at least to us, the Policy which the true Interests of the Community call for. We have no doubts Concerning the Moral & Religious Right of holding slaves, lawfully obtained; when they are treated with Justice & Humanity. And whatever Apprehensions we entertain, respecting the Evils which might be produced, partially and for a time, by an Insurrection of the Slaves, we have no Fear with Respect to the Result, as their general object, & Causes of Excitement would be concerned. Rightly informed, the Great body of them, & especially the more enlightened & virtuously disposed, will see just cause for joining in General Thanksgiving to the Almighty; for frustrating the late scheme of Madness & Folly, as well of Wickedness, which was calculated to pull down, in its Results, general Misery & Ruin upon the Heads of the Innocent as well as the Guilty among them: When they learn what was the Design of those villains who took the lead in the late scheme of Massacre; that it was to go off with their Plunder, in a Case of Extremity, & leave their deluded Followers, to bear alone the Indignation of an Injured Country, & to inherit Guilt, Shame & Remorse, united to legal Punishment, as the proper Fruits of their mutual Delusion & Madness; Nor, do we believe, they would entertain a thought of succeeding, at any Time, in such an Enterprise, were they brought to know, the comparative Paucity of their Numbers, when Contrasted with that of the White Population in the United States; to consider, their general Ignorance, particularly in the use of arms, & their being generally destitute of them; the stupid, inactive Condition of a large proportion of those upon whom they must rely; their liability to be betrayed; the Strong Inducement the well-disposed, and cautious, would have to discover their Designs; & the equally Strong probability, that success in such an undertaking, would not better their condition.

To our benevolent Citizens, the Preservation of the Negroes themselves, as a Body, furnishes pleasing Matter of Thanksgiving to the Almighty; especially while they possess Strong Evidence, that many of them were not only free from any just Charge of Guilt in respect of the Insurrection, but are in general influenced by a Spirit of uprightness & Religion—

As these Considerations obviate, in our view, the objection we have heard advanced against the Appointment of a Day of General Thanksgiving, on this occasion, & as the Reasons for it, originating in Principles of Piety & Gratitude, are of a commanding nature, we have taken the liberty to lay them with deference, but also with freedom, before your Excellency; hoping that they will meet with your concurrence.

But before we close this Address, we feel it incumbent on us, to invite your attention, Sir, to another Subject; a Subject which though not included in this, is related to it; and in which we, as Agents of the Bible Society, are particularly concerned. This is the apprehension we have, from intimations, that in consequence of the late projected Insurrection, & the claims laid to a Religious Character by several of those who ranked as Leaders in the nefarious Scheme, ideas have been produced in the minds of many Citizens, unfavourable to the Use of the Bible among the Negroes; and that attempts will, probably, be made to obtain Legislative Interference, to prevent their learning to read it, or to use it freely.—Though we are sensible that the Power of Direction & Control, in this important Concern, does not rest with the Chief Magistrate of our State; Yet, we are also sensible, that his Sentiments & Recommendations have a powerful Influence, in giving Tone to Publick Opinion & Feeling; and think, that in cases of delicacy, when the Cause of Truth, Righteousness, Humanity & Religion are to be advocated, they may be advantageously and laudably employed.

The Sentiment, Sir, that the Doctrines of Holy writ are unfavourable to the holding of Slaves, is we grant, a sentiment which many, & some very worthy Men have advanced; and which some still advocate; but, as we conceive, without just foundation. Its lawfulness is positively stated in the Old Testament, & is clearly recognized in the New. In the latter a luminous Exhibition is given of Slaves, & their Masters, enjoying Membership together in the Christian Church; while under the immediate Care & Government of the Inspired Apostles: Their Respective Duties also, are taught, explicitly, and enforced by eternal Sanctions. By these Rules the former are not directed to claim a Right to Liberation, not encouraged to use Fraud, or Force to effect it; but to be faithful, good, & obedient: The latter are required, not to emancipate their Slaves, but to give them the things which are just, and equal, forbearing Threatening, & remembering that they also have a Master in Heaven.

The Bible, Sir, as well as all other Things, good and Sacred, which have come into the hands of men, may be, & has been abused. But to argue against its use, from the abuse it has suffered, is to adopt a Mode of Reasoning which is not logical, just, nor pious.

The Scriptures are given to Man (without respect of Persons) to make him wise unto Salvation; and all are required, by Divine Authority to read them; because they contain the Words of Eternal Life. To prohibit the use of them therefore, in respect of any man or class of men, is to contradict & oppose the Divine Authority; and to suppose that the regular use of them will naturally lead to Conspiracy, Rebellion & Blood, is a reflection of the Divine Wisdom & Goodness, bordering on Blasphemy. But we have seen that, instead of encouraging Slaves to engage in Schemes of this Nature, they establish Rules of a directly contrary character, & enforce them by considerations which far transcend all that Human Munificence can offer as reward; or that the Punishment of Human Laws can inflict.—Were we only reasoning from the cause to its Effect, on this subject, we should naturally arrive at this conclusion; that wherever the Truths of the Bible are received in an honest Mind, even by Persons in a State of Servitude, they must & will produce happy Effects in favour, not only of Piety & Devotion; but of willing subordination to lawful Authority, & Conformity to the Principles of Truth, Justice, Good-order, Peace & Benevolence—But in adverting to matters of fact, many can & do testify, that they have seen these Effects produced among the Class of People in Question, really and extensively.

Though it is true, that a considerable Number of the Persons who were concerned in the late Conspiracy professed to be a religious character; yet it is also true, that the most leading Characters among them, & the chief of the rest, were members of an irregular Association, which called itself the African Church, & was intimately connected with a similar Body in Philadelphia, from which their sentiments & directions in Matters of Religion were chiefly derived: Whose Principles are formed on the Scheme of general Emancipation, for which they are zealous advocates; & which they endeavour to support, by a misconstruction, or Perversion of the Scriptures. Very few, indeed, of the religious Negroes, in regular Churches among us, were drawn into the Plot; & in some Churches there were not any on whom a charge of Criminality has been proved. The Individuals composing the Great Body, of the well-known, regular, & esteemed Members, of Churches, have not been impeached. It would indeed seem that the Conspirators were afraid to trust them. For since the Plot has been discovered, voluntary Information has been given, that Attempts, not then understood, were made to feel the Pulse of some of them, by artful, distant approaches, which not being countenanced were laid aside.

Vesey, the prime Mover in this Plot, was, as we are informed, notorious for his libidinous & petulant Conduct. Glen,[4] though a Preacher among them, and, for one of his opportunities, of extraordinary Talents, was generally considered as a Sharper, & one commonly chargeable with Falsehoods.

Nothing that we can discover, has transpired to make appear that the Meetings of the religious Negroes, approved by the Churches to which they belong, for reading the Scriptures, learning their Catechisms, & the general Purposes of Devotion & religious Improvement, have been in anywise instrumental in producing or advancing the late horrid Design to which we refer; but on the contrary, we have reason to believe, they had a good Influence on the general state of Society, by the promotion of good Morals, as well as Piety among that Class of People.

This Circumstance corroborates a Sentiment which has long been entertained by some who have been careful in making observations, as well as in reasoning on this subject, with the true Interests of Society in view: It is this, that one of the best securities we have to the domestic Peace & safety of the State, is found in the sentiments and correspondent dispositions of the religious Negroes; which they derive from the Bible.—If this sentiment is just, it would seem, that instead of taking away the Bible from them, & abridging the truly religious Priviledges they have been used to enjoy, to avoid Danger; the better way would be, to take Measures for bringing them to a more full & just acquaintance with the former; and to secure to them the latter, under Regulations the least liable to abuse. That strict Care should be taken to prevent abuses, & the Influence of designing Wicked Men among them is unquestionable, & highly important: And should be seriously regarged by Churches & Ministers, as well as by the Civil Government.

Should Confidence, Respect, & some special Privileges be considered as generally attached, under prudent Regulations, to the character & State of those who manifest in Religion, a uniform, faithful regard to just Sentiments, upright Conduct, the due subordination of Servants, and the general Peace & Good-order of Society, it is believed that such Regard manifested toward them, which is but reasonable, would have a happy Effect; not only on the Mind & conduct of the Slaves, but on the General Interests of the Community.

But should a Course of Policy, contrary to that which is here advocated, be pursued, with respect to the Negroes, either by a Law of the State, or the common consent of the Citizens, in reference to what some Wicked Men among them have done; not only, would the Innocent be made to suffer for the Guilty; but the Sufferers, feeling themselves deprived of what they esteem a great Priviledge, connected with their Spiritual & Eternal Interests, would, of course, feel unhappy, and be brought under the Influence of a Strong

Temptation to become indifferent to the Interests of their Masters, if not to hearken to the voice of Seduction; the State, it is feared, would lose an important security for its domestic Peace; & the Gospel would suffer Obstruction in its operations & benign Influence, by that Arrest which Benevolence & Piety would experience, while employed in disseminating the Word of Life among the Poor, & promoting the Use of those Means of Grace which are designed by Heaven for the Conversion & Salvation of Sinners.

We submit these considerations to your Excellency, & remain with high respect, Sir

Your Obedient
Humble Servants

His Excellency
Governor Bennett.

^{x}1 ὑπὸ ζυγὸν δοῦλοι Bondservants, or Slaves under the yoke. 1 Tim^{y} V1.1.2. (6:1).[5]

1. At the time of the discovery of the Vesey plot, the Charleston Bible Society had as its highest ranking officers some of the most respected men in the state and beyond. Charles Cotesworth Pinckney (1746–1825), president; Baptist minister Richard Furman (1755–1825), senior vice-president; Congregationalist minister Benjamin Morgan Palmer (1781–1847), vice-president; Lutheran minister John Bachman (1790–1874), vice-president; Thomas Lowndes (1766–1843), vice-president; Presbyterian minister Arthur Buist (1799–1843), corresponding secretary; Episcopalian minister Allston Gibbes (1793–1851), corresponding secretary; Thomas Smith Grimké (1786–1834), recording secretary. "Managers" of the society included Presbyterian minister Artemas Boies (1792–1844), Daniel Ravenel (1789–1873), and James Legaré (1762–1830), judge on the first Court of Magistrates and Freeholders . Although the letter clearly has a collective authorship, Richard Furman played a central role in its composition. See *Charleston Courier,* July 3, 1822. All of these ministers had contact with inculpated slaves; Furman, Palmer, Boies, and Bachman conversed with some of those who were confined. Allston Gibbes was the older brother of Eliza (Gibbes) Wilson, and thus would have had to know slave George Wilson, a key witness for the state. For an analysis of this letter and the response by Governor Bennett, see Robert L. Paquette and Douglas Egerton, "Of Facts and Fables: New Light on the Denmark Vesey Affair," *SCHM* 105 (January 2004): 7–47.

2. The reference is to Governor Bennett's circular of August 10, 1822. See pp. 467–71.

3. Kennedy and Parker's *Official Report.* See Part III.

4. Jack (also "Jacob") Glen was the slave preacher. He belonged to planter John S. Glen. Hamilton, *Account,* 26, refers to the slave Jacob Glen as a preacher and dates his arrest to Tuesday, July 16. The Senate transcript indicates that Glen's trial was held on Wednesday, July 17. He was hanged on Friday, July 26.

5. Considerable debate about biblical sanction for slavery centered on the Greek word *doulos* which, Furman pointed out, does mean slave. See Elizabeth Fox-Genovese and Eugene D. Genovese, *The Mind of the Master Class: History and Faith in the Southern Slaveholders' Worldview* (Cambridge, UK: Cambridge University Press, 2005), 508–9.

Governor Bennett Responds to the Charleston Bible Society, October 1, 1822

Executive Department
Charleston Octr 1. 1822.

Genl. Charles C. Pinckney Pres^{t} &
the Members of the Board of the Charleston Bible Society.

The recommendation of a Board so respectable, as that which represents the Bible Society of Charleston, will ever command the most respectful attention; and on a subject so intimately connected with the cause of Religion (which it is essentially their object to cultivate, by a charitable distribution of the Holy Scriptures) my reverence and utmost consideration. With these sentiments, Gentlemen, your communication of the 23rd was received on the 25th, and perused with unusual interest. If the remarks contained in that address, derived additional weight from any circumstances, abstracted from its bearing the stamp of a deliberate act, maturely and solemnly adopted by the Board, they are manifest in the force of those impressions, which could prompt you to pass the bounds which limit the purpose, and determine the objects of your institution, and in the sanction of a name which so happily unites to an elevated character, long experience, profound talents, and a thorough acquaintance with the history and policy of the State. The potency of these considerations, the character of your association, and the reasons with which your recommendation is supported, cannot fail to produce a considerable influence, on the decision required of me, relative to the subject which they embrace.

I shall not conceal from you, Gentlemen, that my early impressions were directly adverse to this measure, and in opposition to the views you have taken, of the cause, which should induce it; nor are those objections removed by the most deliberate reflection. So far from conceiving that it would be acceptable to the people of this State, that a day of thanksgiving to Almighty God be specially set apart for this particular instance of his goodness, and to which it is your desire *that it be exclusively devoted,* I have been induced to believe that even within this vicinity so directly and deeply interested, a majority of the Citizens question its propriety. The grounds on which this doubt is predicated, may be traced to a laudable desire, tenaciously to protect the character of the State, against imputation morally and politically affecting it, and some fearful consequences, which are neither remote nor contingent. They would not have the world believe, that the slightest insurrectionary movements inspire general terror; that the public sensibility thus excited, is founded in impressions that in every slave, his master contemplates an incensed and implacable enemy, and that from a combination of such, he conceives the State is physically impotent to save him. They would not communicate such fears to their domestics; it is a mistaken policy, which should inform them, that the slightest apprehension of their power is entertained, or that we believe that any effort they can possibly make, would be attended with even partial success. I do not myself believe it, and I am convinced that nine tenths of the State do not believe it. They would not excite in the minds of the timid who are slaveholders, those prejudices and passions, which lead directly to measures of coercion and restraint, and to acts of severity and cruelty, at which a sensibility abroad vitally affecting the interests of the Slaveholding States, might be excited. My judgment may be warped and my reasoning powers feeble, but I do fear that if the present moment is pregnant with danger, we shall give birth to it. Much discretion is requisite. We must put ourselves in opposition to every course of proceedings, which shall conduce to prolong the public panic, or acknowledge its existence.

It will not be expected by you, that in reply to the reasons you have urged, predicated on isolated points of testimony*, entitled to but little weight, and discredited by a development of facts too formidable to leave them a resting place, in the mind of any one acquainted with all the circumstances, that I should fully pourtray my own views of that painful transaction, or seek to counteract the force of your arguments, by an effort to shew that it was a plot, originating in the falsehood of an Individual, and depending for its ultimate effects, on a combination of circumstances, which were conceived in folly, wholly impracticable, and quite as visionary as the expected aid from St Domingo and Africa. It has been my misfortune (perhaps), essentially to differ from those who anticipated a calamity, extending to the most horrid scenes, which a warm, vivid, and excited imagination could pourtray. I then expressed, and still repose the utmost confidence in the belief, that a formidable conspiracy cannot be matured in this State, and admitting (what is barely within the scope of possibility) that such as could be formed, might pass undiscovered to the moment of its accomplishment, the evils resulting would be limited and transient.

* The various isolated points of evidence here adverted to are—that the conspiracy has been contemplated four years—that their plans were fully organized—leaders appointed—a *place* of rendezvous fixed—the *hour* of attack determined—aid expected from Africa, the West Indies, or Great Britain—an army of Gullah Jack of 6 or 9000 men—of Mingo Harth of 4000—of Peter Poyas comprising all Santee & St. Thomas—and of Frank Ferguson four plantations—or that all the negroes between this and Columbia were engaged—and that all the wells were to be poisoned. All of these things, have been stated, and no doubt may have been employed by the conspirators, as means of seduction, but are certainly not entitled to belief, and positively denied by those, who were the principal witnesses and most conspicuous actors.

Human power is impotent in preparing the mind, and disposing the heart to offer an acceptable oblation to a just, wise and merciful Being. Short experience with some observation fully assures me, that it is not the recommendation of those in authority, which can produce that devotional state of feeling, not only essential, but indispensable in the observance of a day, set apart, to express our gratitude for benefits conferred, or to deprecate the wrath of Almighty God. Such a state of the public mind, can only be produced by Him, whose manifestations of favor, or intimations of anger are exhibited to those, whom he loves or those whom he would chide. When therefore a people rejoice, "beneath the light of his countenance," or "are sorrowful when it is withdrawn," the duty of a ruler is manifest. His invitation to the altar, will be accepted by hearts predisposed to acknowledge with Gratitude, that it is God who blesses; or with contrition and humility, the justness of his displeasure. Unaided by the impulse of such sentiments, he may "gather them, in the consecrated places of the most High," but a cold, listless, and unacceptable offering will be laid before him. Nor is the duty less incumbent on rulers, to appoint days of religious observance, when occasions call for them, than it is to designate particularly the most conspicuous causes and which immediately affect the whole community. If I am correct in this, with what propriety can I ask the people to offer thanks to Almighty God, for his preserving and protecting care of the City, when such causes for thankfulness are every where found, in the health which has blessed and the uninterrupted industry which clothed their families, and the fruitful abundance which fills their habitations with gladness? Are we certain, that there is not a more positive cause for rejoicing, at the extraordinary health with which this city has been favoured during the past summer, than in the escape from *a probable evil*? This at least is my deliberate opinion, that under existing circumstances, we may with equal propriety appoint a day of thanksgiving throughout the State, for *the health of the city exclusively,* as for the occasion to which you have confined it.

It is the peculiar and happy attribute of our government, that the feelings and desires of the people, are annually expressed through their immediate representatives. To no tribunal with more propriety, can such subjects be referred, than to the Legislature. Associated from every part of the State, they are enabled successfully to effect those objects, which promote the general welfare and advance the general happiness. They bring together a knowledge of the sentiments, of the whole people, and are fully competent to adopt and determine such measures, as shall subserve the cause of Religion, morality and good government. I persuade myself, that as the representatives of a virtuous, intelligent and religious people, they will neglect no opportunity which suitable occasions present, to remind their constituents of the obligations, which they owe, to their Creator and Preserver; and should they deem this, a suitable subject for general thanksgiving, your desires will be crowned with success. Besides, it is a matter of some doubt and surely at variance with a wise policy, that the appointment, of such days, should be with the Executive. It is impossible that he can know minutely and distinctly, what is the will of the people, and in my opinion, it is conclusive that such appointments should emanate from their will. The usage too, supports this position, whether we refer for precedent, to the General State or City Governments. With but a few exceptions *in our own State,* the rule obtains. If it be the duty of the Executive, it is a censure on his conduct that the Legislature should supply the omission; if of the Legislature, the Executive should not interfere with their privilege. While a doubt on this point exists, I would prefer removing it by a reference to usage, which vests it in the Legislature.

I have endeavoured Gentlemen rather to assign the reasons which govern me, than to answer to arguments you have adduced, and although I have little hope of satisfying your minds, on the propriety of the grounds taken, they are submitted to you with entire respect.

The subject involved in the closing remarks of your address, becomes peculiarly interesting, from the view you have taken of it. Yet I cannot persuade myself, that there are in this community, or any other on earth professing the Religion of the Gospel, those who would close that sacred volume, to any being for whom its instructions were designed; nor can I conceive that there is a beleiver, devoutly founding his faith on those inspired pages, who could look for the justification of his conduct, to an all-righteous Judge, while denying to a supplicant for divine grace, the consolations which it affords, and the hopes which it inspires. This among others, is one of the consequences which as a Citizen of this State, I have most dreaded. Under the influence of strong excitement, we are the easy victims of dangerous errors. It is therefore the part of wisdom, to check the impulse which influenced the passions, before we decide those questions, which involve the privileges or happiness of others, or the glory and honour of our Country.

The measure which you have recommended, of appointing a day of thanksgiving, would, I fear produce the unhappy effect, to continue that excitement, and thus defeat the important object of your last recommendation, by attaching to the event an importance to which it has no just title.

The character of the Southern States, has been somewhat freely attacked, by our Northern brethren. They have said of us, in the asperity of rebuke, "that we deprived our slaves of the means of cultivating their mental powers, of enlightening their understandings, of improving their affections. That they were incapacitated from raising their minds to the source of intelligence, their hearts to the fountain of good; of acquiring the principles, learning the promises, practicing the duties, and enjoying the consolations of Religion. That they were cut off from the knowledge and hopes of that future and blessed state of existence, which crime and misery can never reach." What Carolinian, feeling indignant at this calumny, did not rejoice that he could oppose it, by the simple exhibition of truth? Who is it, cherishing a love for his native state, that would consent to brand her character; with so infamous a reproach? I believe and may venture to assert, that her Legislature will not. Can the advocates of these opinions (if indeed there be any, who seriously entertain such) believe, that the doctrine, "which subjugates the most powerful genius by its sublimity, and adapts itself by the clearness of its light, to the most feeble intellect," is a more fruitful source of those passions, which subvert social order and riot in scenes of revolt, confusion and carnage, than the wild illusions, the gloomy incantations, and horrible superstitions of mental darkness: or can they believe in contradiction to the evidence furnished by every nation and tribe on earth, that there is a placability in the mind and heart of man, which inclines him to be content with his present state, and indisposed to seek a knowledge of that Being, whose works fill all creation. If indeed these opinions are maintained, we may enter on that stern policy, and if possible, *enjoy a security* against *anticipated dangers,* at the price of all considerations of charity, and state reputation.

The leading circumstances of the late conspiracy in my mind, fully establishes the narrative of one of the conspirators, whose veracity was unimpeached by the Court, and supported by the Intendant and his master, "that its birth place was the mind of Gullah Jack and not of Vesey[1]; and that the lure which he held out to some was the assurance, that he had 6000 men engaged, while he attracted others by promises of invincibility, founded on the potency of his incantations. Attaching to himself Monday Gell, and subsequently Denmark Vesey, who were both inclined to admit the influence of his supernatural powers, the nefarious project progressed under their patronage. That professors of religion were seduced, was the natural consequence of their being first assailed by the insidious arts of those men, who knew the confidence they reposed, was less liable to be betrayed by such, when once entangled in their snares, and the pledge of secrecy solemnly given. It was not the religion of these men that they invoked; it was those passions which were unsubdued by her mild precepts, and to suppose that they were invincible to the wicked machinations or evil devices of these men, because they had received some religious instruction, is to estimate human nature beyond the standard which human actions indicate. [*illegible*] made to participate in their guilt, the transition from propriety of conduct to the most diabolical intentions, was natural, easy and inevitable. But as it does not follow, that all are thus easily won, and as we have the most substantial evidence, that others were enticed who did not follow, it would be an instance of injustice to which the temperate and enlightened of this community will never submit, that the severest chastisement which can be inflicted by man on his fellow, *that of being cut off from the* hopes and consolations of scripture, should fall on the innocent.

With these sentiments Gentlemen, I shall use the little influence which I possess, to avert the evil which so justly excites the deep concern you have expressed.

I have the Honor to be Gentlemen
With considerations of the highest respect
Your Ob[t] Se[t]
Tho: Bennett

1. There is no closed quotation mark in the original.

Blacks Return to White Churches, 1822

. . . Thursday evening 10 October 1822 the Session met at House of Mr. Flemming—present Revd. Mr. Boies, John Todd, Tho: Flemming, James Black, David Bell, the attention of the Session on this occasion, principally occupied by a number of coloured persons heretofore attached to the African Church, wishing to be admitted into ours & who at the desire of the Session were present this evening—concluded with an address and prayer by Revd. Mr. Boies. . . . [1]

1. On Artemas Boies (1792–1844), pastor of the Second Presbyterian Church, see Part I, p. 34 n1. *CSCCD,* 70, 71, 79, 101, identifies those with Boies in the session as John Todd, a teacher; Thomas Flemming, a merchant; James Black, a bootmaker; and David Bell, an accountant.

Records of Sessions, Second Presbyterian Church, Charleston County, 1809–1837 (typescript), SCL, Columbia.

Reverend Arthur Buist[1] on the Vengeance of God, Thursday, November 7, 1822

. . . Those blessings which we have enjoyed, have been rich and numerous. The past Summer had been indeed eventful. During its revolution, we were called to witness scenes which excited alternately our hopes and fears, and upon which the eyes of the most aged inhabitant in our community never before gazed. The first display of the Particular Providence of God which we are required this day to recognise, is that which led to the detection of privy conspiracy. The view I am to take of this civil commotion must be exclusively of a religious kind. To the interposition of God we are to look for the disclosure of this atrocious combination. His Providence, you have seen, brethren, is particular. He brings to pass every event. And on this occasion, when the storm which had been long gathering, was about to burst upon our unconscious community, the vengeance of God against these workers of iniquity could no longer be restrained; and by the occurrence of an event, in itself trivial, but highly important, when viewed with regard to its results, he made us acquainted with our situation, and left the suppression of this savage enterprise to our instrumentality. Yes! The Lord of Hosts was with us; the God of Jacob was our defence. He interposed, and by the use of those means which were within our controul; this barbarous design—this projected attempt, in which a blasphemous disregard to the laws of God, to every feeling of gratitude and every principle of humanity, appeared—was overthrown. But there are none in whose bosoms the emotions of gratitude should beat more intensely, than that class of our population to which the chiefs in this conspiracy belonged. It becomes them in a very peculiar manner, on the present occasion to render thanksgivings unto the Lord for his interposing goodness, and, by the instrumentality of man, preventing a scheme which must have ended in their own extermination. It becomes us all, my brethren, to sing unto the Lord this day with thanksgiving, to sing praise on the harp unto our God, for his mercy endureth forever. . . .

1. Arthur Buist (1799–1843) became pastor of the First (Scots) Presbyterian Church on January 5, 1822.

Arthur Buist, *A Sermon Delivered in the First Presbyterian Church, on Thursday, Nov. 7, 1822, Being the Day of Thanksgiving, Humiliation & Prayer* (Charleston, SC, 1823), 19–20.

Reverend Richard Furman's *Exposition* on Slavery, Tuesday, December 24, 1822

. . . The Convention[1] are aware, that very respectable Citizens have been averse to the proposal under consideration; the proposal for appointing a Day of Public Thanksgiving for our preservation from the intended Insurrection, on account of the influence it might be supposed to have on the Black Population—by giving publicity to the subject in *their view,* and by affording them excitements to attempt something further of the same nature. These objections, however, the Convention view as either not substantial, or overbalanced by higher considerations. As to publicity, perhaps no fact is more generally known by the persons referred to; for the knowledge of it has been communicated by almost every channel of information, public and private, even by documents under the stamp of Public Authority; and has extended to every part of the State. But with the knowledge of the conspiracy[2] is united the knowledge of its frustration; and of that, which Devotion and Gratitude should set in a strong light, *the merciful interposition of Providence,* which produced that frustration. The more rational among that class of men, as well as others, know also, that our preservation from the evil intended by the conspirators, is a subject, which should induce us to render thanksgivings to the Almighty; and it is hoped and believed, that the truly enlightened and religiously disposed among them, of which there appear to be many, are ready to unite in those thanksgivings, from a regard to their own true interests: if therefore it is apprehended, that an undue importance would be given to the subject in their view, by making it the matter of public thanksgiving; that this would induce the designing and wicked to infer our fear and sense of weakness from the fact, and thus induce them to form some other scheme of mischief: Would not our silence, and the omission of an important religious duty, under these circumstances, undergo, at least, as unfavourable a construction, and with more reason?

Figure 34. The Reverend Richard Furman (1755–1825), president in 1822 of the South Carolina Baptist State Convention. Courtesy of Special Collections and Archives, Furman University.

But the Convention are persuaded, that publicity, rather than secrecy is the true policy to be pursued on this occasion; especially, when the subject is taken into view, in connexion with other truths, of high importance and certainty, which relate to it, and is placed in a just light; the evidence and force of which truths, thousands of people, when informed, can clearly discern and estimate. It is proper, the Convention conceives, that the Negroes should know, that however numerous they are in some parts of these Southern States, they, yet, are not, even including all descriptions, bond and free, in the United States, but little more than one sixth part of the whole number of Inhabitants, estimating that number which it probably now is, at Ten Millions; and the Black and Coloured Population, according to returns made at 1,780,000: That their destitution in respect to arms, and the knowledge of using them, with other disabilities, would render their physical force, were they all united in a common effort, less than a tenth part of that, with which they would have to contend: That there are multitudes of the best informed and truly religious among them, who, from principle, as well as from prudence, would not unite with them, not fail to disclose their machinations, when it should be in their power to do it: That, however, in some parts of our Union there are Citizens, who favour the idea of general emancipation; yet, were they to see slaves in our Country, in arms, wading through blood and carnage to effect their purpose, they would do what both their duty and interest would require; united under the government with their fellow-citizens at large to suppress the rebellion, and bring the authors of it to condign punishment: that it may be expected, in every attempt to raise an insurrection (should other attempts be made) as well as it was in that defeated here, that the prime movers in such a nefarious scheme, will so form their plan, that in a case of exigency, they may flee with their plunder and leave their deluded followers to suffer their punishment, which law and justice may inflict: and that, therefore, there is reason to conclude, on the most rational and just principles, that whatever partial success might at any time attend such a measure at the onset, yet, in this country, it must finally result in the discomfiture and ruin of perpetrators; and in many instances pull down on the heads of the innocent as well as the guilty, an undistinguishing ruin. . . .

Had the holding of slaves been a moral evil, it cannot be supposed, that the inspired Apostles, who feared not the faces of men, and were ready to lay down their lives in the cause of their God, would have tolerated it, for a moment, in the Christian Church. If they had done so on a principle of accommodation, in cases where the masters remained heathen, to avoid offences and civil commotion; yet, surely, where both master and servant were Christian, as in the case before us, they would have enforced the law of Christ, and required, that the master should liberate his slave in the first instance. But, instead of this, they let the relationship remain untouched, as being lawful and right, and insist on the relative duties. In proving this subject justifiable by Scriptural authority, its morality is also proved; for the Divine Law never sanctions immoral actions. . . .

The Christian golden rule, of doing to others, as we would they should do to us, has been urged as an unanswerable argument against holding slaves. But surely this rule is never to be urged against that order of things, which the Divine government has established; nor do our desires become a standard to us, under this rule, unless they have a due regard to justice, propriety and the general good. . . .

The Convention are particularly unhappy in considering, that an idea of the Bible's teaching the doctrine of emancipation as necessary, and tending to make servants insubordinate to proper authority, has obtained access to any mind; both on account of its direct influence on those, who admit it; and the fear it excites in others, producing the effects before noticed. But it is hoped, it has been evinced, that the influence of a right acquaintance with that Holy Book tends directly and powerfully, by promoting the fear and love of God, together with just and peaceful sentiments toward men, to produce one of the best securities to the public, for the internal and domestic peace of the State.

It is also a pleasing consideration, tending to confirm these sentiments, that in the late projected scheme for producing an insurrection among us, there were very few of those who were, as members attached to regular churches, (even within the sphere of its operations) who appear to have taken a part in the wicked plot, or indeed to whom it was made known; of some Churches it does not appear, that there were any. It is true, that a considerable number of those who were found guilty and executed, laid claim to a religious character; yet several of these were grossly immoral, and, in general, they were members of an irregular body, which called itself the *African Church,* and had intimate connection and intercourse with a similar body of men in a Northern City, among whom the supposed right to emancipation is strenuously advocated[.]

1. The Reverend Furman refers to the recently held Baptist Convention of the State of South Carolina.

2. Mary Lamboll Beach's letter of July 5, 1822, in Part IV, pp. 373–77, indicates that Furman was one of three white ministers who visited Vesey in his cell on the night before his execution.

Richard Furman, *Exposition of the View of the Baptists Relative to the Coloured Population in the United States in a Communication to the Governor of South-Carolina* (Charleston, SC, 1823), 4–7, 9, 16–17.

Charleston *Southern Intelligencer*

Saturday, January 4, 1823

A PROCLAMATION.

Whereas the Baptist Convention of the State of South Carolina, by the Rev Richard Furman their President, and the Presbytery of Harmony, by Robert Means their Moderator, in behalf of themselves and the various religious denominations of this State, have petitioned that the *first Wednesday in February next, may be set apart as a Day of Thanksgiving, Humiliation and Prayer,* and be sacredly regarded by all the different churches throughout the same; and whereas it well becomes us, who are in the enjoyment of such great privileges, religious and political, to bow down before the Author of our existence, and with pure hearts, humbly beseech a continuance of His favor.

NOW KNOW YE, That I have appointed and set apart the first Wednesday in February next, to be observed throughout this state, as a Day of Public Thanksgiving, Humiliation and prayer, by all the citizens of South-Carolina; and the Reverend Clergy are earnestly solicited to attend at the Altars of HIM, who makes the clouds his chariot, and walks with awful majesty upon the wings of the wind, and there by their precept and example point out to man his weakness and dependence upon his Maker, open on him that vista through which the only real happiness is to be found, and with gentle chiding and parental solicitude lead all into that fold, where none can molest, and where the Creator only is superior to the creature.

Given under my hand and seal of the State, at Columbia, this 17th day of December, 1822, and in the forty-seventh year of American Independence.

JOHN L. WILSON.

Reverend Frederick Dalcho[1] on Blacks Meeting without Supervision, 1823

. . . Upon a late afflicting occasion in Charleston, one of the convicts, the day before his execution, was overheard expounding to his wife, the beginning of the 14th chapter of St. John,[2] and applying it to himself. It was necessary, he said, that he should go to prepare a place in heaven for his wife! Thus abusing the gracious words of our blessed Saviour to his immediate disciples.*

* The celebration of the *Fourth of July,* belongs exclusively to the white population of the United States. The American revolution was a family quarrel among equals. In this the *Negroes* had no concern; their condition remained, and must remain, unchanged. They have no more to do with the celebration of that day, than with the landing of the Pilgrims on the rock at Plymouth. It therefore appears to me, to be improper to allow these people

> to be present on these occasions. In our speeches and orations, much and sometimes more than is politically necessary, is said about personal liberty, which Negro auditors know not how to apply, except by running the parallel with their own condition. They, therefore, imbibe false notions of their personal rights, and give reality in their minds, to what has no real existence. The peculiar state of our community, must be steadily kept in view. This, I am gratified to learn, will, in some measure, be promoted by the institution of *The South-Carolina Association.*[3]

This leads me to advert to a circumstance connected with the unhappy event which gave rise to these remarks. The circumstance is this: *None of the Negroes belonging to the Protestant Episcopal Church were concerned in the late conspiracy.* To what cause is this to be attributed? . . . Is it because in the sober, rational, sublime and evangelical worship of the Protestant Episcopal Church, there is nothing to inflame the passions of the ignorant enthusiast; nothing left to the crude, undigested ideas of illiterate black class-leaders? Is it because the coloured leaders in that Church, were not permitted to expound the Scripture, or to exhort, in words of their own; to use extemporary prayer, and to utter at such times, whatever nonsense and profanity might happen to to come into their minds? Is it because the order and language of worship of that Church, being precomposed and arranged, cannot be perverted or abused? These questions deserve serious reflection. . . .

The event which gave rise to these "considerations," had its origin and seat, chiefly in the *African Church,* which was entirely composed of negroes, under preachers of their own colour; but it involved a few individuals belonging to other Churches. And I write it with feelings of the deepest regret, that some of the conspirators were preachers, classleaders, and communicants; thus verifying the truth of a remark which teachers have, too often occasion to make, that there is but little confidence to be placed in the religious profession of negroes. I speak generally. Much animal excitement may be, and oftentimes is, produced, where but little real devotion is felt in the heart. I sympathize, most sincerely, with the very respectable and pious Clergyman, whose heart must still bleed at the recollection, that his confidential class leader,[4] but a week or two before his just conviction, had received the Communion of the Lord's Supper, from his hand. This wretch had been brought up in his Pastor's family, and was treated with the same Christian attention, as was shown to their own children!

To us, who are accustomed to the base, and proverbial ingratitude of these people, this ill return of kindness and confidence is not surprising; but they who are ignorant of their real character, will read and wonder.

1. Born in the English borough of Holborn, Frederick Dalcho (1770–1836) emigrated to Baltimore as a young man. Trained as a physician, he joined the army in 1792, becoming a "surgeon's mate" and was later stationed in Savannah and Charleston. Upon leaving the military, he settled in Charleston. After publishing a number of theological works, Dalcho, a freemason as well as an Episcopalian, was named assistant minister at St. Michael's Church. See Walter Lynwood Fleming, ed., *The South in the Building of a Nation: A History of the Southern States Designed to Record the South's Part in the Making of the American Nation* (Richmond, VA: Southern Historical Publication Society, 1909), vol. 11: 251; Howard A. Kelly and Walter L. Burrage, *American Medical Biographies* (Baltimore: Norman, Remington Co., 1920), 278.

2. John 14:1–4:
Let not your heart be troubled: ye believe in God, believe also in me.
In my Father's house are many mansions: if it were not so, I would have told you. I go to prepare a place for you.
And if I go and prepare a place for you, I will come again, and receive you unto myself; that where I am, there ye may be also.
And whither I go ye know, and the way ye know.

3. The placement of the asterisk in the text and Dalcho's fulmination against slaves in attendance at Fourth of July celebrations suggest that the executed slave had combined religious and secular themes to formulate a liberationist message.

4. Dalcho was probably referring to the Reverend Benjamin Morgan Palmer and the slave Billy, who was owned by Benjamin's father, Job Palmer.

[Frederick Dalcho,] *Practical Considerations Founded on the Scripture, Relative to the Slave Population of South-Carolina* (Charleston, SC, 1823), 5, 33, 36–37.

Reverend John Holt Rice[1] on Black Preachers, 1825

. . . Now it is well known that there is a large and increasing part of our population, whose ignorance is almost absolute. Their spiritual interests have been very generally neglected; and attempts to afford them religious instruction have often been frowned on by men of power and influence. But have they thus been able to suppress the workings of the religious principle? That is impossible. It would be easy to exclude the light of the sun by a leaf of the statute book. What then has been the result of this very general negligence? Why, thousands of this race have a set of religious opinions of their own in many very important respects at variance with the religion of the New Testament. They have long shown a most observable preference for those meetings by whomsoever conducted, where there is most noise and vociferation, most to strike on the senses, and least to afford instruction. While some among them are, no doubt, true Christians, many unquestionably are rank fanatics.—They are chiefly under the influence of ignorant spiritual guides. It is most obvious to the careful observer that they are withdrawing more and more from those ministrations, where they can learn the true character of christianity; and insist, with increasing pertinacity, on holding meetings in their own way, and having preachers of their own colour. The profession of religion among them is becoming perceptibly less beneficial: so that in some neighbourhoods, this very thing generates suspicion of the professor, rather than confidence in his integrity. The preachers among them, although extremely ignorant (often unable to read a verse in the Bible, or a line in their Hymn book) are frequently shrewd, cunning men. They see what influence misdirected religious feeling gives them over their brethren, and they take advantage of it. Many of them feel their importance, and assume the post of men of great consequence. This thing is growing in the southern country. And while efforts to afford these people salutary instruction have been repressed or abandoned, a spirit of fanaticism has been spreading, which threatens the most alarming consequences. Without pretending to be a prophet, I venture to predict, that if ever that horrid event should take place, which is anticipated and greatly dreaded by many among us, some *crisp haired* prophet, some pretender to inspiration, will be the ringleader as well as the instigator of the plot. By feigning communications from heaven, he will rouse the fanaticism of his brethren, and they will be prepared for any work however desolating and murderous. The opinion has already been started among them, that men may make such progress in religion, that nothing they can do will be sinful, even should it be the murder of those whom they are now required to serve and obey! The present state of the country presents a prospect truly alarming: and when the rapid growth of our population both black and white is considered, it requires a man of a stout heart indeed, to view the scene without dismay. It is appaling, when such a mighty power as that afforded by the religious principle, is wielded in most cases by ignorant and fanatical men. Shall we, then, let this matter alone? . . .

1. The Reverend John Holt Rice (1777–1831) was first professor of Christian Theology in the Union Theological Seminary in Virginia. Southern Presbyterians interested in missionary outreach to the slaves frequently referred to Rice's remarks in this essay, and Nat Turner's insurrection in Southampton County, Virginia, in 1831 made him appear prescient. See Philip B. Price, *The Life of Reverend John Holt Rice* (Richmond: Library of Union Theological Seminary in Virginia, 1963).

John Holt Rice, "The Injury Done to Religion by Ignorant Preachers: A Sermon Delivered before an Education Society, in Sept. 1825," *Evangelical and Literary Magazine* 8 (November 1825): 603–4.

Assemblyman Whitemarsh Benjamin Seabrook[1] on Black Christianity, 1825

. . . Our history has verified the melancholy truth, that one educated slave and, or coloured freeman, with an insinuating address, is capable of infusing the poison of insubordination into the whole body of the black population. Possessing our means of information, it cannot be supposed, that he will be unacquainted with our domestic and political transactions. Is it not likely too, that he will intentionally misrepresent facts, and draw with a deeper colouring the lineaments of those baneful pictures, with which he may be furnished? Was not this really done by the leaders of what is termed the Gullah war in this State—of the insurrection at Stono in 1740 and of the contemplated risings of the negroes, at Camden in 1816, and in Charleston in 1821?—Did not the unreflecting zeal of the North and East, and the injudicious speeches on the Missouri question animate Vesey in his hellish efforts? Were they not indirectly tendered to him for a guidance, by self styled patriots, and by those whom we have been accustomed to respect as the faithful expounders of the word of God, the "most wild and frantic ideas of the rights of man, the mis-conceived injunctions and examples of Holy Writ?"[2] This manifestly indiscreet conduct of the abolitionists constitutes an evil, against which from its essential nature, we cannot guard. If then such are the anticipated results attendant on the discussion of any question incidentally relating to slavery, what have we not to expect, when our right to our slaves shall be disputed, And can this ever be done? The abolitionists have said, that the dictates of truth and of justice, precede all the enactments of man. They might turn to the 8th Sec. of the 1st Article of the Constitution of the United States, as confirmatory of the power of Congress to extirpate slavery, should the welfare of the nation demand it.—This remark is not an idle chimera of the brain. . . .

1. From 1848 to 1850, Seabrook (1793–1855) served as South Carolina's sixty-third governor. He owned Gun Bluff plantation on Edisto Island, where he was born and raised. In 1814, at the young age of twenty-one, he was elected to the state legislature, a position he retained until his election to the state senate in 1826. In 1823, he took a lead role in establishing the Edisto Island Auxiliary Association, a vigilance organization similar to the South Carolina Association. In seeking incorporation by the state, the petitioners noted, "The white population of Edisto Island is to the Black as 200 to 3000, or as 1 to 15. This fact speaks volumes." See Petition of the Officers of the Edisto Island Auxiliary Association, November 18, 1823, no. 151, series S165015, SCDAH. See also Eric H. Walther, *The Fire-Eaters* (Baton Rouge: Louisiana State University Press, 1992), 100; *BDSCHR* 4: 511–12. Seabrook misdated both Vesey's conspiracy and the Stono revolt, one year off in each case.

2. Seabrook is quoting Edwin C. Holland *Refutation of the Calumnies Circulated Against the Southern & Western States Respecting the Institution and Existence of Slavery among Them* (Charleston, SC, 1822), 76.

Whitemarsh Benjamin Seabrook, *A Concise View of the Critical Situation, and Future Prospects of the Slave-holding States, in Relation to Their Coloured Population* (Charleston, SC, 1825), 14–15.

A German Traveler[1] on the Danger of Black Ministers, 1825 and 1826

. . . Charleston has a population of forty thousand inhabitants, about twenty-five thousand of these are free. . . . I took up my abode in Jones's Hotel,[2] a well supported and finely situated house, whose host was a mulatto. . . . I received visits from a number of the distinguished inhabitants. . . . Some extremely interesting strangers were also in the hotel, so that I did not lack entertainment. The following was related to me:—Some years previous, the negroes of the country engaged in a conspiracy to murder all the white males, and spare none but the females. This design was found out, and it was discovered that the original projectors were free negroes out of the limits of the state, who travelled in the northern section of the union, and in part were become Methodist preachers.[3] They had returned home and preached freedom to the slave population. Since that period the legislature of this state has adopted very severe precautionary laws against free negroes and mulattoes. One of them is, that no individual of this description, if he have once left the state, shall be permitted to return. The wife of our host, Jones, found herself in this predicament. She had undertaken a voyage to New York, her native city, and now dared not to attempt a return. On this account, I was informed, had I brought a free black servant with me, he would have been taken from me, and put in custody till I should have left the state, or I must deposit a considerable security for him. . . .

1. Carl Bernhard, Duke of Saxe-Weimar Eisenach (1792–1862), a commander of Dutch troops at the Battle of Waterloo, visited Charleston December 11–19, 1825.

2. Jehu Jones Sr. ran a tailoring business with his son, Jehu Jones Jr. (1786–1852), before owning several boarding houses. The duke stayed in the one located on Broad Street, next to St. Michaels Church. Jehu Jones Jr. became a Lutheran minister. In the late 1820s, he briefly settled in Liberia and then returned to Charleston. The elder Jones had family in New York City, and like Morris Brown and Henry Drayton, was charged with breaking the 1821 law against free black return to the state. See Charleston *City Gazette and Commercial Daily Advertiser,* May 4, 1809; William C. Nell, *The Colored Patriots of the American Revolution with Sketches of Several Distinguished Colored*

Persons to Which Is Added a Brief Survey of the Condition and Prospects of Colored Americans (Boston, 1855), 245; Loren Schweninger, ed., *The Southern Debate Over Slavery, Volume I, Petitions to Southern Legislatures, 1778–1864* (Urbana: University of Illinois Press, 2001), 87.

3. Although Morris Brown and Henry Drayton were forced to leave the state, no other source identified them as active conspirators, and certainly not as being among the "original projectors" of the plot.

Carl Bernhard, Duke of Saxe-Weimar Eisenach, *Travels through North America during the Years 1825 and 1826,* 2 vols. (Philadelphia, 1828), vol. 2: 5.

Jeremiah Evarts[1] to H. Hill, Saturday, February 18, 1826

. . . Before taking leave of Carolina, I would say that there are some things of a discouraging nature, in regard to the character of slavery and the treatment of slaves. It is now more difficult, than it was a few years ago, to instruct the blacks. Many legal impediments are thrown in the way. Sabbath schools for their benefit cannot be maintained. When they attempt separate worship, with teachers of their own color, they are dispersed, sometimes in the most barbarous and cruel manner. The discussions in the northern papers on the subject of slavery, irritate the people of Carolina (South) and Georgia beyond what you would suppose. The paper in the Christian Spectator[2] more than a year ago, excited a great flame here. There is a passage in the paper alluded to, which I was sorry to see at the time. I am persuaded, however, that the southern people must make up their minds to have northern people speak rashedly, unadvisedly, and ignorantly on this subject. . . .

1. Jeremiah Evarts (1781–1831), the editor of the *Panoplist,* was a Vermont-born missionary, reformer, and critic of federal policy toward Native Americans. See John A. Andrew, *From Revivals to Removal: Jeremiah Evarts, the Cherokee Nation, and the Search for the Soul of America* (Athens: University of Georgia Press, 1992).

2. *The Christian Spectator,* published in New Haven, Connecticut, had theological connections to Yale University. In 1825, someone with the initials "S.F.D." published a two-part essay, "People of Color." It called for a national remedy to extinguish slavery and made a passing reference to "the Charleston insurrection."

E. C. Tracy, *Memoir of the Life of Jeremiah Evarts* (Boston, 1845), 231–32.

Charles Cotesworth Pinckney[1] on Black Churches, 1829

. . . As usual, the Methodists were the pioneers of this enterprize.[2] It was not without hesitation that they were employed by some planters, who had heard their black congregation accused of being deeply implicated in the affair of 1822. On investigation, it appears that all concerned in that transaction, except one, had seceded from the regular Methodist Church in 1817, and formed a separate establishment, in connexion with the African Methodist Society, in Philadelphia: whose Bishop, a coloured man, named Allen,[3] had assumed that Office, being himself a seceder from the Methodist Church of Pennsylvania.[4] At this period, Mr. S. Bryan,[5] the local Minister of the regular

Methodist Church in Charleston, was so apprehensive of sinister designs, that he addressed a letter to the City Council, on file in the Council Chamber, dated 8th November, 1817, stating, at length, the reasons for his suspicion. . . .

1. The planter Charles Cotesworth Pinckney (1789–1865) was the son of Thomas Pinckney (1750–1828) and the nephew of Charles Cotesworth Pinckney (1746–1825), both of whom were keen observers of events in Charleston in 1822, with close connections to some of the persons of color involved. His argument about the religious implications of the Vesey affair resonated, and he was quoted, for example, by the influential Presbyterian minister William Swan Plumer (1802–1880) in *Thoughts on the Religious Instruction of the Negroes of This Country* (Savannah, GA, 1848), 4–5.

2. Pinckney was a close friend of the Methodist preacher William Capers (1790–1855), one of the leaders in the "enterprize" of instructing slaves in Christianity.

3. The Reverend Richard Allen (1760–1831), founder of the African Methodist Episcopal Church.

4. St. George's Methodist Church in Philadelphia.

5. F. A. Mood, *Methodism in Charleston* . . . (Nashville, TN, 1856), 203, names Solomon Bryan as one of four white Methodist ministers on duty in Charleston in 1817. For the legal implications of white fears of the African Church in the wake of Vesey's conspiracy, see Nicholas May, "Holy Rebellion: Religious Assembly Laws in Antebellum South Carolina and Virginia," *American Journal of Legal History* 49 (2007): 250.

Charles Cotesworth Pinckney, *An Address Delivered in Charleston, before the Agricultural Society of South-Carolina, at Its Anniversary Meeting on Tuesday, the 18th August, 1829* (2nd ed.; Charleston, SC, 1829), 20.

Abolitionist David Walker[1] on Southern Camp Meetings, 1829

. . . Yes, I have known small collections of coloured people to have convened together, for no other purpose than to worship God Almighty, in spirit and in truth, to the best of their knowledge; when tyrants, calling themselves *patrols,* would also convene and wait almost in breathless silence for the poor coloured people to commence singing and praying to the Lord our God, as soon as they had commenced, the wretches would burst in upon them and drag them out and commence beating them as they would rattlesnakes—many of whom, they would beat so unmercifully, that they would hardly be able to crawl for weeks and sometimes for months. . . . I remember a Camp Meeting in South Carolina, for which I embarked in a Steam Boat at Charleston, and having been five or six hours on the water, we at last arrived at the place of hearing, where was a very great concourse of people, who were no doubt, collected together to hear the word of God, (that some had collected barely as spectators to the scene, I will not here pretend to doubt, however, that is left to themselves and their God). Myself and boat companions, having been there a little while, we were all called up to hear; I among the rest went up and took my seat—being seated, I fixed myself in a complete position to hear the word of my Saviour and to receive such as I thought was authenticated by the Holy Scriptures; but to my no ordinary astonishment, our Reverend gentleman got up and told us (coloured people) that slaves must be obedient to their masters—must do their duty to their masters or be whipped—the whip was made for the backs of fools, &c. Here I pause for a moment, to give the world time to consider what was my surprise, to hear such preaching from a minister of my Master, whose very gospel is that of peace and not of blood and whips, as this pretended preacher tried to make us believe. . . .

1. David Walker (1785–1830) was a North Carolina–born freeman who became a member of the African Methodist Episcopal Church and settled in Boston, where he wrote his celebrated antislavery jeremiad. Peter P. Hinks, *To Awaken My Afflicted Brethren: David Walker and the Problem of Antebellum Slave Resistance* (University Park: Pennsylvania State University Press, 1997), 32–42, builds a compelling case that Walker had lived in Charleston, witnessed there the persecution of religious slaves and free persons of color, knew Vesey, and carried his incendiary message north.

[David Walker], *Walker's Appeal in Four Articles* . . . (3rd ed., Boston, 1830), 42–44.

James Osgood Andrew[1] on Black Churches, 1830

. . . [W]hen, some years afterward, an insurrectionary plot was discovered in which these people had a very considerable share, it was very confidently asserted that it originated in the Methodist Church; whereas the fact was that not a solitary member of this Church, in regular standing, had the slightest concern in the business. There are certain men in this community who esteem themselves *somewhat,* and who withal are quite *too dignified* to inquire into the *truth* or *falsehood* of any charge against *Methodism,* or *Methodist preachers,* who have been quite lately in the habit of laying this sin at the door of the Methodist Church. It is, indeed, surprising to observe the tendency there is among a certain class of men, to credit any evil report against Methodism, or Methodist preachers. I remember some years ago, when there was an insurrection among the blacks in Demarara, it was reported confidently that a Methodist preacher was an active agent in the business.[2] The intelligence flew to our shores on the wings of the wind. Our industrious editors soon had it in print, and hastened it with the speed of the mail to every corner of the land. After some time, when the true state of the facts was disclosed, and it appeared that neither the Methodist missionary, nor any of his flock, had had any participation in the business, and this was announced by the Methodist Magazine, I looked that the corps editorial, who had so cheerfully and industriously cast in their mite to aid in *spreading* the *important news,* would have been equally ready to set the matter right. But whether they were slow of heart to believe, I know not. One thing I observed, they were very slow of type to correct their former statements.

Amidst all the shocks and hinderances above mentioned, Methodism here has continued still to live. There have been periods in its history when its prospects were exceedingly dark; times when the tempest has swept fearfully through its branches, and broken not a few of them off. But the trunk has remained full of sap, and has continually been putting forth vigorous shoots, laden with precious fruit. Its enemies have often been ready to exult over it, as dead or dying. Some *gifted seers* have predicted that its end was nigh. Yet it has risen with fresh vigour from all the blows which have been inflicted on it. And perhaps at no period in its history has it manifested more of the vigour of youth, than at present. We have every reason to believe '*God is with us;*' and we are content to abide by the doctrine of the apostle, 'If God be for us who can be against us.' I have dwelt longer on this article than I intended, and must postpone some additional remarks to a future letter.

1. This excerpt continues Minister James Osgood Andrew's discussion of Methodism in Charleston as backdrop to the plot in Part I, p. 18. A considerable literature exists on the Georgia-born Osgood (1794–1871). His ownership of slaves precipitated a denominational schism along sectional lines in 1844. A good place to start is George G. Smith, *The Life and Letters of James Osgood Andrew, Bishop of the Methodist Episcopal Church, South* (Nashville, TN, 1882).

2. On the 1823 Demerara conspiracy and the alleged involvement of Methodist minister John Smith, see Emilia Viotti Da Costa, *Crowns of Glory, Tears of Blood: The Demerara Slave Rebellion of 1823* (New York: Oxford University Press, 1994), esp. 125–68.

Letter II, James Osgood Andrew, January 1830, in "Letters on Methodist History," *Methodist Magazine and Quarterly Review* 12 (1830): 22–25; see also Charles F. Deems, ed., *Annals of Southern Methodism for 1856* (Nashville, TN, 1857), 212–13.

Charles Colcock Jones[1] on Religious Control, 1832

. . . It has been said, that religious instruction tends to create insubordination, and that religious meetings of the Negroes are nurseries for every sort of irregularity, and we have been pointed for an example to the affair in Charleston of 1822. But the example adduced, refutes the very point it was intended to prove. Those meetings which were held in Charleston for the purpose of exciting the colored population, *were not religious meetings*. They were meetings held under *color* of religion; but religion, properly speaking, had nothing to do with them; nor had the Negroes composing them any connexion with any white church or congregation.

Supposing that it was religion itself that excited those people? (which we deny with all our might) men are religious beings. They will meet for religious purposes again. And in what way shall we prevent the recurrence of the same consequences? Only by being present in their meetings ourselves. If our plan of sending a white instructor into every assembly of Negroes for religious purposes, had been in operation in Charleston in 1822, there would never have existed any difficulty. As we said before, our plan [for the religious instruction of the slaves] seems to carry our security in it. . . .

1. Charles Colcock Jones (1804–1863), a Georgia-born Presbyterian minister, was one of the principals in the antebellum southern mission movement to Christianize slaves. See Donald G. Mathews, "Charles Colcock Jones and the Southern Evangelical Crusade to Form a Biracial Community," *JSH* 41 (August 1975): 299–320.

Charles Colcock Jones, *The Religious Instruction of the Negroes. A Sermon, Delivered before Associations of Planters in Liberty and M'Intosh Counties, Georgia* (4th ed.; Princeton, NJ, 1832), 27.

Liberator

Saturday, December 14, 1833

SUPERSTITION OF AMERICAN SLAVES.—The 'Journal of a missionary to the negroes of Georgia,' publishing in the Charleston Observer, has this notice of their credulity: not confirmed, by the way, to the ignorant negro.

They believe in second sight, in charms, and visions, and voices and dreams, &c. Designing men, men who wish to gain an ascendancy over them, avail themselves of their ignorance and superstition. This was the course pursued by Denmark Vesey, in Charleston, by Nat Turner in Virginia, and others within our knowledge on a smaller scale. They begin by giving out themselves to the people as great ones in the earth. Their pretensions to courage, to divine protection, the exercise of peculiar power in consummating their own plans, or the plans of others; to invulnerability, &c. are boldly insisted on; and, of course, without any regard to truth wherever facts are appealed to for confirmation. Then they avail themselves of the passions and prejudices of the poor people and thus fit them for their own purposes. They proceed to predict events or to see visions and dream dreams, or to give out *charms* of various kinds and for various purposes; some charms that buried in the path, or under the door of an enemy will exert a fatal influence over him; some that will enable the possessor to make free use of any part of his owner's property without detection, and others which will remove sickness or the meditated revenge of enemies, or in the midst of dangers, preserve the person invulnerable. The charms are for any and all uses. They that make them know that they are as good for one use as for another. And then the *composition* of these charms is singular. A bunch of negro or animal hair, or wool, crooked sticks, glass of bottles, rusty nails, roots, &c. &c. prepared in size and quality and with various incantations, suitable to persons and circumstances. One or two *coincidences* are sufficient to establish the pretensions of one of these deliverers, or doctors; for they go by different names. And the consequence is, they are feared. Their power is dreaded, and a *threat* is sufficient to produce trembling and obedience.

Whitemarsh Benjamin Seabrook[1] on Black Ministers, 1834

. . . Shall we adopt improvidently any and every measure which our Christian duty inculcates? In our evangelical labours, ought not the circumstances of society and the dangers that encompass it, to be duly weighed? Although the proper imparting of religious information to negroes might not endanger the public peace, still it must be conceded, that where prudence and circumspection are not scrupulously observed, there may be reverence to the Lord in the face, but the malignity of the fiend in the heart. Were not many of the blacks who distinguished themselves in the contemplated conspiracy of 1822, "catechists," and proverbially faithful ["]disciples of Christ?" Nat Turner, it is said, was a professor, if not promulgator of the Scriptures, and so was Touissant[2] of St. Domingo. It was not true religion that influenced the minds of those deluded persons, but a maddening zeal brought about by men in high places. Again: The South are not, and I trust never will be prepared to establish among our servants a system of ecclesiastical preferment. They cannot allow any slave or free negro to assume an authority and influence, in derogation of the right, which, in this community, should be the exclusive property of the whites. Coloured preachers, lecturers, and catechists, have been the instruments of positive evils to society; apparent good they might have rendered; of real benefit, they never have been to any one. . . .

1. At the time of this publication, Seabrook (1793–1855), a major Edisto Island slaveholder, was lieutenant governor of South Carolina, on his way to becoming governor in 1843. See p. 626 n1.

2. Toussaint Louverture (1743–1803), the foremost leader of the Haitian Revolution, openly professed to be a devout Catholic, although scholars continue to debate the depth and content of his religious beliefs. See Philippe R. Girard and Jean-Louis Donnadieu, "Toussaint before Louverture: New Archival Findings on the Early Life of Toussaint Louverture," *WMQ* 70 (January 2013): 65–66.

Whitemarsh Benjamin Seabrook, *Essay on the Management of Slaves and Especially on Their Religious Instruction: Read before the Agricultucal* [*sic*] *Society of St. John's Colleton* (Charleston, SC, 1834), 19–20.

Reverend Nathaniel Bowen[1] on Religion and Rebellions, 1835

. . . An appeal to facts will confirm the assertion, that whenever the Gospel is preached in all its purity to these people, and religious instruction afforded, immense good has resulted, both to the master and the slave.

. . . In the insurrection of 1712, in New-York,[2] only two of the scholars of the Catechist of the Episcopal Church, were even accused of being engaged. One of them was proved innocent, and the other (not a baptized person), was not engaged in the murder committed. At the time of the contemplated insurrection in Charleston in 1822, there were 316 coloured persons, communicants in our Episcopal Churches in that city, and a large, not ascertained number of worshippers not communicants, not one of whom was implicated; and indeed the discovery of the plot is to be attributed to the just sense of duty entertained by individuals of that class, who were Episcopalians. The experience of your Committee, warrant them to assert, that the best ordered, and most prosperous plantations, are those where true religion flourishes among the slaves. . . .

On this subject, I may be permitted to adduce the testimony of one, who though dead, is well entitled, from his long and extensive experience of it, to be heard: I mean the late venerable Minister of the Baptist Church in this city. It is a matter of painful regret, that I have not his written words, in which to convey the effect of his experience on the mind. It is, however, perfectly recollected, that when, some few years, before his death, he had expressed to me his concern for the existence of a prejudice against the religious instruction of our slave population, in the minds of respectable fellow-citizens, as seeming to find its justification in unhappy facts which had brought to light the crimes of some professing Christian people, long successfully concealed from Ministers and masters by the plausible guise of religion, he declared it (the delusion of fanaticism among these people admitted, for which others were more in fault than they, and the treachery and deceit natural to the slave, allowed for) to be the result of the long experience and observation of his Ministry, that the practical influence of Christian profession and communion, was not by any means less, among them, than among those with whom, under other circumstances, he had so extensively been conversant. I adduce the testimony of Dr. Furman as that which is, on every account, eminently entitled, on this subject, to carry with it. . . .

1. Nathaniel Bowen (1779–1839) served for more than twenty years as rector of St. Michael's Episcopal Church and was the third bishop of the Episcopal Diocese of South Carolina. He remained critical of laws designed to inhibit black spirituality, which he believed safe if guided by white ministers. See Lacy K. Ford, *Deliver Us from Evil: The Slavery Question in the Old South* (New York: Oxford University Press, 2009), 472–75.

2. In 1712, a revolt of primarily African-born slaves broke out in New York City. About two dozen rebels were executed, mostly by hanging. Charlestonians, in defending themselves against northern criticism of their handling of the Vesey affair, would reference this event and the repression of a subsequent slave plot in New York City in 1741. See Kenneth Scott, "The Slave Insurrection in New York in 1712," *New-York Historical Society Quarterly* 45 (January 1961): 43–74.

Nathaniel Bowen, *A Pastoral Letter on the Religious Instruction of the Slaves of Members of the Protestant Episcopal Church of the State of South-Carolina* (Charleston, SC, 1835), 8, 13.

New-York Spectator

Monday, April 27, 1835

Letters from the South—No. V.

Charleston, April 17, 1835.

I expressed an opinion, in my last, against the policy . . . of the laws just enforced here against the instructing of the colored people—including the free, *free* including, of course, the brown people as well as the blacks. Now, setting aside altogether the question of policy, as regards all the rest, it does seem to me most manifest, that as regards *these,* it admits of no sort of debate; and that measure must not only fail of its end, but inevitably furnish a very considerable source of the kind of evil it was intended to prevent. There is a broad distinction between the free blacks and the free mulattoes. Their condition and character, and their relations to the whites, respectively, are widely variant: and, of course, their relation to each other is a marked one. I suppose it cannot be denied that the free blacks, here, are, almost, without exception, the most contemptible population, which ever infested a civilized community. . . . The effect of the existence of such a population any where and particularly here, among the slaves of the same color, is obvious enough. The case of the brown people differs from theirs, *toto caelo. Their* color is as complete a distinction from the slaves, as it is from the whites. As I have remarked before, a great many of them are not very easily distinguished from the whites. In intelligence, education, enterprise, comfort of condition, and character in general, they differ as widely from the one class, and approximately as nearly to the other. They may be considered sub-whites, in fact; or whites, number two. Their entire interest lies in unison with that of the whites. They have always taken sides with the whites, and against the slaves and free blacks, in case of collision; and always would, under the same circumstances. . . . Black and white are not half so hostile to each other, as black and brown—and that for plain reasons which need no explanation;—it is the dictate of human nature. Hence these brown men have never engaged, to any observable extent, in the numerous conspiracies, with which Carolina has always been rife from the days of 1739, (when there were three) and even earlier, down to 1822. Hence, too, they have been most active in discovering and disclosing these insurrections; you will remember that they were so in the *last,* and it is notorious that some of them were employed in the police of the city during that period of peculiar alarm. . . .

Reverend Whiteford Smith[1] to Dr. M. T. Mendenhall, Saturday, November 10, 1849

. . . With regard to the free colored people, of whom many have been under my charge in this city, I can bear a most favorable testimony, having found them equally as subordinate as the slaves. . . .

In the year 1817, being five years before the insurrection of 1822, some of the members of the Methodist Church in this City manifested a spirit of dissatisfaction and insubordination. The first man to detect and report this disposition was Castile Selby[2] (recently deceased) a free black man and *leader* among the negroes. He made known the fact to the Rev. Mr. Bryan, then the minister in charge of the Methodist churches here. An occasion was soon made by the disaffected, to withdraw from our Church, and these formed the noted African Church, afterwards the cause and instrument of so much mischief. *The Rev. Mr. Bryan addressed a letter to the City Council informing them of his apprehensions, but the warning was unheeded.*

I doubt if a more loyal body of colored people can be found than those belonging to the M. E. Church. . . .

In the insurrection of 1822, no colored members of the Methodist Churches in Charleston, were implicated. This is a fact which deserves to be known. . . .

1. Whiteford Smith (1812–1893) was the eloquent minister of the Cumberland-Street Methodist Episcopal Church. He would later teach English at Wofford College. See "Called to His Reward," Columbia (SC) *The State,* April 28, 1893.

2. *CSCCD,* 24, identifies Selby as a drayman who resided in 1816 at 12 Swinton's Lane. Mood, *Methodism in Charleston,* 187–88, describes Selby as a "humble carter," who was "eminent for his humility, holiness, and unbending character."

Public Proceedings Relating to Calvary Church, and the Religious Instruction of Slaves. With an Appendix, Containing the Reports of the Sub-committees, and the Answers of Different Persons Interrogated (Charleston, SC, 1850), 41, 43.

Reverend Daniel Alexander Payne[1] on the AME Church and Vesey, 1866

. . . About 1817, Rev. Morris Brown, at the head of about 1,000 souls, resigned from the M.E. Church in South Carolina, and united with the Connection—now 1822, the number had swelled to 3,000, including Charleston, and the Circuit immediately surrounding it. When we take into consideration the intolerant laws, and police regulations, which were made to restrain the movements of the slave and free colored people of South Carolina, that was a large increase. Among these were the eleven preachers whose names we have already given, who would, if they could, have been members of the Convention of 1816.

This little band of Christians had to suffer great persecutions on account of their *independent spirit, their opposition to colorphobia,* and *their desire to worship God in their own house consecrated to His* service—in which no one could say, "*Away to the seats and galleries for Negroes,*"—for this simple desire, this determination, prompted by the purest motives, for which white men would have been commended throughout the country—they were *repeatedly arrested,* while *in the act of public worship,* and driven like a flock of sheep before the civil authorities, who punished them by fines and stripes according to their ability to pay or not pay, or their condition as free or bond. In the case of slaves, sometimes a humane master did interfere, and save the trembling flesh of his favorite servant from the bloodly lash.

After repeated arrests and punishment, they were allowed to worship God in their own house, but under the most humiliating restrictions, till 1822, when the civil authorities of the State, maddened by the incipient efforts of the heroic, but luckless Denmark Vesey, to overthrow the infernal system, ordered their organization to be suppressed. The safety of their leader, Morris Brown, being threatened, General James Hamilton[2] interposed, and after secreting Elder Brown in his own house for a certain time, gave him a safe passage to the glorious North—that land of the free—that home of the brave. Thus was this little band of Christians broken up; some of whom joined the Independents or Circular Church, under Dr. Benjamin Palmer, of blessed memory—others joined the Scotch Presbyterians, under Dr. Buist. "I will smite the Shepherd and the sheep shall be scattered." Thus was the African M.E. Church in South Carolina doomed to destruction till *that generation of persecutors, and the persecuted should meet in the spirit-world*—when she was to be *resuscitated* by the voice of holy Freedom, and, *endued with a vigor, an activity and a tact, which no earthly power can crush,* and *which we believe destined to continue with increasing volume and power—till the Great Head of the Church himself shall see fit to change its form, for a changing field of action. . . .*

1. As a young free person of color in Charleston, Daniel Alexander Payne (1811–1893) opened a school for blacks. It was closed in 1834 because of legal prohibition on the teaching of slaves to read and write. Encouraged by his friend and patron, the Lutheran minister John Bachman (1790–1874), Payne moved northward to enter the Lutheran ministry. Payne met Morris Brown in Philadelphia in 1837. Payne eventually moved into the AME Church, served for years as Morris Brown's private secretary, and devoted much of his adult life to compiling information that would result in the first published history of the AME Church. He was appointed official historian of the church in 1848. After the Civil War, he ranked as one of the country's most conspicuous and respected black ministers. Payne knew intimately many Charleston whites and persons of color involved in the Vesey affair; his Charleston roots and intimacy with Morris Brown make him a vital source on the events of 1822. See his *Recollections of Seventy Years* (Nashville, TN, 1888).

2. Michael P. Johnson, "A Conversation with Michael Johnson," Centre for the Study of the United States, University of Toronto, online newsletter, January 12, 2004, argues that "the mayor [James Hamilton Jr.] has a big political agenda to make himself famous." Yet in this instance, as with his opposition to the South Carolina Association, Hamilton risked his political career to

shield a man threatened with hanging by a Charleston mob. Hamilton was many things, but never a coward. (He drowned in 1857, trying to save a mother and her child.) According to his unique code of honor, he was every bit as obliged to protect the innocent Brown as he was to hang the guilty Vesey. Payne had obviously kept abreast of Hamilton's career, indicating his rise in rank as a militia officer from a major in 1822 to a general at the time of his death.

Daniel Alexander Payne, *Semi-Centenary . . . of the African Meth. Episcopal Church in the United States of America* (Baltimore, 1866), 23–24; Nelson T. Strobert, *Daniel Alexander Payne: The Venerable Preceptor of the African Methodist Episcopal Church* (Lanham, MD: University Press of America, 2012).

Henry Highland Garnet[1] on a Vesey "Betrayer" in New York City, Saturday, March 6, 1869

. . . Those South Carolinians, fully understanding the situation, in 1818 if I mistake not, cast their lot with the young African M.E. Church. Surely God approved and blessed those fearless men, and future generations will venerate their names. Four years after this Southern accession to the Church, followed the dark and bloody days of affliction, and disaster to our people in South Carolina. Denmark Vesey whose true history to this day remains unwritten, arose and shook the wide dominions of slavery. Slaveholders and men-stealers, who hitherto, were proud and boastful of their strength, grew pale and trembled in their strongholds, when one black man, and a few followers raised the cry, "give us liberty, or give us death." The well meant, and grandly conceived plans of Vesey were frustrated by traitors of his own race, and he suffered a felon's death, but history has snatched his name from oblivion, and inscribed it among the heroes and martyrs of his age and race.

In my youth, I remember seeing in the city of New York, a singular looking and wretched old colored man, who used to drive a heifer harnessed to a rickety cart, which was evidently built with his own, not very skillful hands. This wretched being seemed to carry a load of guilt and shame in his heart, and no one pitied him. Crowds of boys usually followed him, crying, "*Old Cush! Old Cush*!" One day this modern Calu was missed from the streets. His cart stood before his miserable hut, and his poor heifer, his sole companion, was found bellowing in her hovel. Old Cush was dead. The manner of his death was thus described by the coroner's jury: "Came to his death by blows inflicted by the hands of some person or persons to the jury unknown."

Now for the sequel; it was currently reported that, "Old Cush" was one of the betrayers of Denmark Vesey.[2] The insurrection of 1822 culminated in the butchery of Vesey and twenty-two of his compatriots, and the banishment from the State of South Carolina of all suspected persons, and negro preachers in particular. Chief among the banished negro clergy were Morris Brown and Henry Drayton. The former was a man of solid judgment, and glowing piety, and the latter was as brave as Paul, and as eloquent as an angel. These brethren with others were saved as by "the skin of their teeth" through the instrumentality of some of their personal slaveholding friends, and in consequence of their Masonic connections. Driven out from home and kindred, the magnets of their souls pointed Northward, and hither they came. "Therefore, they that were scattered abroad, went everywhere preaching the word." . . .

1. Henry Highland Garnet (1815–1882), son of runaway slaves, settled with his parents in New York City in the 1820s and remained there until the mid-1830s before becoming one of the United States' most militant abolitionists. Although Garnet was ordained as a Presbyterian minister, his father, George, served as a class leader at Bethel, the African Methodist Episcopal Church on Mott Street in New York. There Henry came into contact with many persons of color who had fled Charleston and other areas of the South. Garnet clearly had an interest in Denmark Vesey, and by the 1840s he was referencing Vesey in public speeches. See James McCune Smith, "Sketch of the Life and Labors of Rev. Henry Highland Garnet," in Henry Highland Garnet, *A Memorial Discourse by Rev. Henry Highland Garnet, Delivered in the Hall of the House of Representatives, Washington City, D.C. on Sabbath, February 12, 1865 . . .* (Philadelphia, 1865), 20, 26; and Garnet, "An Address to the Slaves of the United States of America, Buffalo, N.Y." (1843), in John L. Thomas, ed., *Slavery Attacked: The Abolitionist Crusade* (Englewood Cliffs, NJ: Prentice-Hall, 1965), 99–104. That Garnet initially had tied into an oral tradition about Vesey is suggested by his rendering Vesey's surname "Veazie" in the address (102). According to Garnet, Vesey "formed a plan for the liberation of his fellowmen. In the whole history of human efforts to overthrow slavery, a more complicated and tremendous plan was never formed." Garnet also intimated that a black-mulatto divide had caused Vesey's betrayal to white authorities. See also Joel Schor, *Henry Highland Garnet: A Voice of Black Radicalism in the Nineteenth Century* (Westport, CT: Greenwood Press, 1977), 4–12.

2. Of the four likely "betrayers" of Vesey, Peter Prioleau (Desverney) and George Wilson died in Charleston in 1860 and 1848, respectively. The other two, both already free, were William Penceel and the man identified in public documents only by the name of Scott. Larry Koger, *Black Slaveowners: Free Black Slave Masters in South Carolina, 1790–1860* (Jefferson, NC: McFarland, 1985), 23, found that the light-skinned Penceel, who already owned slaves, bought two more with the thousand-dollar reward given him for his role in revealing the conspiracy. Old Cush, therefore, may have been Scott.

Henry Highland Garnet, "Pioneers of the A.M.E. Church—No. II. Bishop Morris Brown," Philadelphia *Christian Recorder,* March 6, 1869.

Reverend Daniel Alexander Payne on the Exiled AME Leadership, 1883

. . . I was born of free parents in the city of Charleston, S.C., on the 24th of February, 1811, in what was then known as Swinton Lane, now called Princess Street. My parents were London and Martha Payne. I remember that my father was a man of brown complexion, of slender frame, and about five feet eight inches high. He was an earnest Christian and a class-leader, having two classes under him—what used to be called the Seekers' Class and the Members' Class. He was a faithful observer of family worship; and often his morning prayers and hymns aroused me, breaking my infant sleep and slumbers. He taught me the alphabet and my monosyllables, and I remember that once he whipped me for neglecting my lessons. After the war of 1812 the city of Charleston was illuminated, and, in order that I might have a clear view of every object, he carried me through the streets with my feet straddling over his shoulders. . . .

The effect of this dream was to settle my mind on the determination to seek a field of

Figure 35. The Reverend Daniel Alexander Payne (1811–1893), sixth bishop and first historian of the African Methodist Episcopal Church. From Payne's *Recollections of Seventy Years* (1888).

usefulness as a teacher in the free North, where I believed I could teach without let or hinderance. So I called upon Dr. William Capers, Dr. Benj. W. Palmer, Dr. John Bachman, Bishop Gadsden, and Rev. Kennedy, my pastor, all of whom I consulted.[1] But chief of all, I sought the advice and counsel of my beloved class-leader, Mr. Samuel Weston,[2] who is still living in Charleston, a venerable, intelligent, holy man—intelligent then beyond most men of his age and opportunities; venerable now on account of his great age, sanctity, and usefulness; then only a class-leader because *slavery decreed him to the condition of half man and half brute*; now an elder in the itinerant ministry of the M.E. Church because freedom has recognized his genuine manhood and restored him to the normal position of a child of God (1881). I say him above all others I consulted, and he, with the others, approved my determination to seek a field of usefulness in the free regions of the North. From all but him I received letters of introduction to their Northern friends. . . .

Before I entered upon the work which was to occupy me for so long a time I was called to assist in performing the last sad rites for Bishop Morris Brown, who died in

May, 1850, after having lain helpless for nearly five years, having been struck by paralysis while attending a Conference in Canada.*

* Bishop Brown was a man of mixed blood, and on the father's side of Scotch descent. He grew up without any chance of intellectual development; therefore he was illiterate. I often served him as private secretary.[3] Though illiterate, he was by nature sagacious, and therefore large-hearted; so that without education his common sense always led him to give a hearty indorsement to it. The man who does otherwise proclaims himself a fool; if a fool, then is he wicked, for every wicked man is a fool, and challenges our firm opposition. If an idiot, then is he to be pitied and let alone.

I preached his funeral sermon, as I did that of Bishop Waters two years before. . . .

As might be expected, the data of first importance to be gained for the Church history was regarding the formation of the A.M.E. Church. The first general convention was held in 1816, with the following persons present: Rev. Richard Allen, President; Rev. Richard Williams, Rev. Morris Brown, Rev. Henry Harden, Charles Pierce, James Towsan, Jerry Miller, Shadrach Bassett, Henry Fox, William Cousins, Don C. Hall, David Smith, James Cole, Jacob Richardson, Joseph Cox, Edward Waters, William Quinn (not as a member, but as an observer), Abner Coker, Daniel Coker.

On the 9th of April, 1816, an election took place for bishop, and Daniel Coker[4] was elected on account of his superior education and talents. An objection was immediately made by the pure blacks, led by Jonathan Tudas, a friend in council with Richard Allen. This objection was on account of his color, his mother being an Englishwoman and his father a pure African. Daniel Coker, being a man of high feeling, resigned on the spot in favor of Richard Allen, who was then absent in the country, but arrived on the 10th, and hearing the facts of the case accepted the nomination to the bishopric. There is not a scrap of paper in existence relative to this important era of the A.M.E. Church.

It was the desire of conciliating the opposing factions which led Bishop Allen later to name Morris Brown (who was not a black man) for the office of bishop, and the same cause led the latter to name Edward Waters (a dark man) for the same office. But the last-named bishop served, simply bearing the title without exercising any of the functions of the office. . . .

1. Payne's close association with both Benjamin Morgan Palmer and John Bachman suggests how close Charleston's black and white religious communities were, even after the founding of the city's AME congregation. As Mary Beach's letter of July 5, 1822, included on pp. 373–77 in Part IV, reveals, Palmer, Boies, and Furman visited Vesey on the night before his execution, yet none of these ministers indicated that they believed the accused to be innocent.

2. Samuel Weston (1804–1882), a freedman, worked as a tailor in Charleston for decades, owning a few slaves for much of that time. See Ruliff Vancleve Lawrence, E. H. Stokes, and George Hughes, *The Centenary Souvenir: Containing a History of Centenary Church, Charleston, and an Account of the Life and Labors of Rev. R. V. Lawrence, Father of the Pastor of Centenary Church* (Charleston, SC, 1885), xv; Larry Koger, *Black Slaveowners: Free Black Slave Masters in South Carolina, 1790–1860* (Jefferson, NC: McFarland, 1985), 64, 71, 148–49.

3. Working as the illiterate Brown's secretary, Payne was in a position to hear what Brown knew about the Vesey conspiracy, and about the exiled minister being protected and housed by Mayor

Hamilton. Although not part of the plot itself, Brown intimately knew most of those involved, yet the passages here indicate that Brown believed that there had been a conspiracy among his parishioners. Joseph Kelly, *America's Longest Siege: Charleston, Slavery, and the Slow March toward Civil War* (New York: Overlook Press, 2013), 162, theorizes that Hamilton "ransacked the church buildings and homes of its leaders in a dogged search for evidence." If anything, Payne's story suggests just the reverse.

4. Born a slave in Maryland, Daniel Coker (d. 1846) returned to the state as pastor of Bethel AME Church in Baltimore. Unlike Richard Allen, Coker supported the American Colonization Society and settled himself and his family first in Liberia and then in the British colony of Sierra Leone in the early 1820s. See Mary F. Corey, "Daniel Coker," in *African American Lives*, ed. Henry Louis Gates Jr. and Evelyn Brooks Higginbotham (New York: Oxford University Press, 2004), 177–78.

Daniel Alexander Payne, *Recollections of Seventy Years* (Nashville, TN, 1883), 14, 34–35, 94–95, 100–101.

Reverend Daniel Alexander Payne on the Loss of Charleston's AME Church, 1891

. . . On the morning of the eighth of June, 1822, the first Conference for this district was opened by Bishop Allen in accordance with the resolution passed at the May Conference in Philadelphia. The members present were Rev. Richard Allen, Henry Harden, Thomas Webster, George White, Richard Williams, Samuel Ridley, Charles Corr, Henry Drayton, Joseph Cox, Stephen Dutton, Jeremiah Miller, Jacob Matthews, Thomas Miller, Isaac Cropper, Joseph Harvey, Edmund Crosby, Peter Croger, Benjamin Croger, James Thompson, Charles Spicer, Titus Rosarett, Henry Davis, Michael Parker, Thomas Jones, Charles Butler, James Scott, John Morris. . . .

The loss of South Carolina was occasioned by a terrible civil excitement in 1822, which was produced by the discovery of a contemplated insurrection on the part of certain slaves for the overthrow of slavery in that State. The ringleaders, six in number, were arrested, tried and convicted, and hung on a single gallows at a single blow. Chief of these were Denmark Vesey and Gullak Jack. Subsequently twenty-two of the conspirators were convicted of the same offense, to-wit: a combination to overthrow the most villainous system of oppression beneath the sun. They, too, were hung on the same gallows, and at the same moment. They had not shed a drop of their so-called master's blood, nor had they taken up arms or committed one act of violence, but they had conspired against the infernal system, and that was a crime in itself sufficiently heinous to be punished with death.

But slavery is a system based upon injustice, born of violence and blood, hence it knows not what is mercy nor justice. But how terribly has the blood of these helpless victims been avenged by the punitive visitation of indignant Heaven during the Civil War and Rebellion against the American Union! How differently has the spirit of Liberty dealt with the blood-stained leaders of the Rebellion of 1860–65! Their conspiracy against Liberty and the American Union resulted in the death of about two hundred and seventy-nine thousand three hundred and seventy-six men, and a National debt of ten billions three hundred and sixty-one millions nine hundred and twenty-nine thousand nine hundred and nine dollars; yet they were allowed to go unpunished.

The slaveholders of South Carolina were not satisfied with punishing with death the conspiracy against slavery in that State; they did not stop their proceedings till our Church in that State was entirely suppressed. Being an independent ecclesiastical organization, it gave the idea and produced the sentiment of personal freedom and responsibility in the Negro. . . .

Daniel Alexander Payne, *History of the African Methodist Episcopal Church* (Nashville, TN, 1891), 37, 45.

The repression that followed in the wake of the discovery of the Vesey plot combined with long-standing discrimination and oppression to direct the attention of many free black Carolinians toward emigration to West Africa. Founded in Washington City in December 1816, the "American Society for Colonizing the Free People of Color in the United States" was a curious blend of evangelicals, conservative reformers, and border-South entrepreneurs. The brainchild of Virginia Federalist Charles Fenton Mercer, the American Colonization Society, as it quickly came to be known, enjoyed the support of some of the most prominent politicians of the post–War of 1812 era. House Speaker Henry Clay and Treasury Secretary William Crawford were two of the most visible members, and Supreme Court Justice Bushrod Washington served as its figurehead president. In South Carolina, especially after the Vesey affair, however, few members of the state's ruling elite endorsed the ACS because it raised the specter of federal interference in a matter reserved to the states and because in no other state was slavery more deeply woven into the fabric of life. To the extent that the ACS began to receive federal funds in 1819—indeed, the organization was literally founded in the House of Representatives chamber—it was the only branch of the broad antislavery movement to properly regard itself as a division of the US government.

The founding of the ACS, followed shortly thereafter by the Missouri debates and the Vesey conspiracy, forced many leading South Carolinians—like James Hamilton Jr., Robert Young Hayne, and John C. Calhoun—out of their post–War of 1812, neo-Federalist spirit of national unity into a more calculated, intertwined defense of slavery and state sovereignty. As the Missouri debates had revealed in the votes cast on the antislavery Tallmadge Amendments in the House of Representatives, the South had become a minority within the federal union. With South Carolina leading the way after the Vesey affair, the argument for states' rights would cross a threshold in the 1820s, becoming an essentially southern argument, one taken to "the outpost," to paraphrase James Hamilton Jr., in order to protect "the citadel."

Although free blacks remained deeply divided about the ACS, a higher proportion of them supported its efforts than was the case among South Carolina's ruling elite. Liberia, purchased at gunpoint for less than three hundred dollars of federal funds, remained a colony of the United States until its independence in 1847. Although free blacks in the northern states were generally hostile to the ACS, a large number of southern freedpeople, weary of oppressive racism and state laws that limited their economic opportunities, proved more willing to emigrate. Denmark Vesey himself considered sailing for Sierra Leone in 1818 with his old friend James Creighton, a wealthy freeman, at the time when city authorities briefly closed the African Church. After her husband's death, Susan Vesey took two of her children and a daughter-in-law and briefly relocated to Liberia's capital city of Monrovia.

The part Thomas Smith Grimké (1786–1834) played in financing the *Hercules*, and aiding those who wished to emigrate from Charleston during the winter of 1832 and 1833 also reveals much about the Vesey affair. Grimké was a member of the wealthy and well-connected Carolina family, but he was also an original thinker and a member of the Colonization Society. His sisters Sarah and Angelina would become noted abolitionists, and his brother Henry later fathered activist Archibald Grimké with his enslaved mixed-race nurse Nancy Weston. Historian Dickson D. Bruce Jr. suggests that Archibald's 1901 biography of Vesey—excerpts of which may be found in Part VI of this volume—was based both on documents and on stories told to him by his aunts, and that is undoubtedly true. But Thomas Smith Grimké's 1832 letters reveal that he knew a great deal about the *Hercules* passengers, from ages to genders to occupations. There was a long history between the two families, and so Vesey's earliest biographer clearly got his information from a wide variety of first-hand, oral sources.[1]

These letters also remind us what a tight, inbred society the Carolina lowcountry was, and how intimately—and in how many ways—these men and women knew one another. Among those who supported the ACS were the Reverends John Bachman and Benjamin Morgan Palmer, both of whom visited the condemned slaves just prior to their executions in 1822.

1. Dickson D. Bruce Jr., *Archibald Grimké: Portrait of a Black Independent* (Baton Rouge: Louisiana State University Press, 1993), 88–89.

Salem *Gazette*

Friday, November 9, 1821

A black man by the name of Creighton,[1] who has accumulated considerable property as a barber, in Charleston, S.C. sailed from that port on the 17th inst. in his own schooner, the *Calypso,* for Sierre Leone, where he and his family, and several other free persons of color, have gone for the purpose of settling, and spending the remainder of their days.—Creighton was the owner of several slaves, to all of whom he offered the choice, either to accompaay him in his expedition, and have their freedom, or to be sold and remain in this country; yet, only one could be prevailed upon to proceed with him.—*N.Y. pap.*

1. On freedman James (also "John") Creighton, see Part III, p. 186 n6. The June 27 examination of Ferguson's Frank, printed in Part III of this volume, indicates that Vesey briefly considered "go[ing] with Creighton" to Africa. Like many emigrants to Africa, Creighton may have returned to the United States.

Wilmingtonian, and Delaware Register

Thursday, July 22, 1824

EMIGRATION TO HAYTI.—A large number of the coloured people of Philadelphia assembled at Bethel Church in that city on the 6th inst. and passed unanimously the following resolutions, the Rev. R. Allen[1] being in the Chair.—

Resolved, That we do approve of the proposals of President Boyer: also, heartily concur with him in the belief that the emigration to the Island of Hayti will be more advantageous to us than to the Colony in Africa.

It was also on motion.

Resolved, That a Committee of twenty appointed to devise and adopt, such measures as shall or may be deemed most expedient for the promotion of the above object which accordingly was done.

1. The Reverend Richard Allen (1760–1831) founded the African Methodist Episcopal Church. Although a ferocious opponent of the American Colonization Society, he voiced support for black emigration to Haiti.

Thomas S. Grimké to Ralph R. Gurley, Thursday, June 14, 1832[1]

Charleston
14 June 1832

My Dear Sir,

. . . I have been asked when it is likely that a vessel will be ready anywhere else, earlier than the contemplated voyage from this port;—as some are desirous of leaving here as soon as they can. I have been also asked what is the [*illegible*] fall of the tide, whether there are any medical men at Liberia, and whether there is employment there for Draymen, Cartmen & if saws and Carts can be got there.

The number of Emigrants expected to depart in October may be safely estimated at 200. It will be [*illegible*] preferable for these people, that the vessel should sail from Charleston: and the sooner you begin to make the arrangements the better—leaving the exact time of the Vessel's coming here uncertain—My reason is this. I have told some of these people, to whom I could speak confidentially, that the coming of the vessel to this port would depend much on the situation of our state politics at the time. Now, as at present advised, I should say, that the Vessel must not come before the elections are over—say not till the 20th of October and possibly it may become important to postpone its coming till after the Legislature shall have commenced it's [meeting] at Columbia, which will be the 4th Monday in November, at which time all, who might be disposed to give us any trouble will be absent. I hardly anticipate any after the election; tho it is not unlikely that one party might endeavor to turn the circumstances to account, before that, against the others—

In the meantime, I shall see how much I can raise here for this good cause & shall be glad to know what amount it may be expected to cost the Society, as that will be a guide to me, in getting aid. . . .

You will observe by the list of names every particular as far [as] they could be furnished, and quite sufficient, I believe to enable you to form a very good judgment as to every thing connected with the matter. . . .

Yours Very Truly
Thos. S. Grimké

1. The Reverend Ralph Randolph Gurley (1797–1872), the son of a Connecticut Congregationalist minister, served as secretary for the ACS. This letter reveals how deeply unpopular the society was in South Carolina in 1832 since many proslavery theorists regarded any interference in their black population as highly dangerous. The fact that Mayor James Hamilton was a supporter of the movement as late as 1824 raises questions about historian Michael Johnson's assertion that Hamilton was an early nullifier who used the Vesey plot as a "wedge issue" against more progressive political opponents like Bennett. If anything, Hamilton's political opinions were anathema to his planter-politician brethren. See Robert S. Tinkler, *James Hamilton of South Carolina* (Baton Rouge: Louisiana State University Press, 2004), 81–82, and on Gurley, see Eric Burin, *Slavery and the Peculiar Solution: A History of the American Colonization Society* (Gainesville: University Press of Florida, 2005), 23–24.

American Colonization Society Papers, LC.

Benjamin Morgan Palmer to Ralph R. Gurley, Monday, July 9, 1832

Charleston

My dear Sir,

. . . I perceive in the last number of the African Repository[1] that I have received, mention made of the colony being overstocked with traders & [*illegible*] unless some turn their attention to Agriculture, there may be difficulty in obtaining a livelihood. I fear that scarcely any of those expecting to go from Charleston, are much, if at all acquainted with agriculture. They are mostly mechanics. It would be a very unhappy circumstance, if this company of colonists should become dissatisfied, or should be embarrassed in obtaining the means of living: since it would retard if not prevent future emigrations from this quarter, whereas a universally favourable report sent back by this company, would probably give a powerful impulse to the cause—especially among those *already free*. How it would operate toward increasing instances of emancipation I cannot say.

The colony, going from this quarter are intelligent and pious in a high degree, and the expectation of doing good in a religious way appears, as far as I can learn to be a prominent motive. One of them is the holder of a few slaves himself, but says he cannot think of either leaving them [*illegible*] them to slavery, and thinks he would not be prosperred if he did. . . .

I am, my dear Sir Truly Yours
B M Palmer

1. The *African Repository and Colonial Journal* was the ACS's official publication; the first issue came off the press in March 1825. The Reverend Benjamin Morgan Palmer (1781–1847), the

minister of the Circular Church and a member of the Charleston Bible Society, visited Vesey in his cell on the night before his execution.

American Colonization Society Papers, LC.

Jehu Jones Jr.[1] to Ralph R. Gurley, Saturday, July 14, 1832

We are acquainted with Jehu Jones Junr. We believe him to be a temperate, industrious and religious man, and from his education & character well qualified to fill the situation for which he applies in the above letter.

Jn. Bachman[2]

1. Jones applied to Gurley for transportation to Liberia, and the letter was endorsed by Thomas S. Grimké and John Bachman. For more on Jehu Jones the younger and elder, see p. 689 n2.

2. John Bachman (1790–1874) served as pastor of St. John's Lutheran Church in Charleston and was friend and patron of Daniel Alexander Payne. A member of the Bible Society, he visited many of the condemned in the city's Work-House during the summer of 1822.

American Colonization Society Papers, LC.

Thomas S. Grimké to Ralph R. Gurley, Tuesday, September 11, 1832[1]

Charleston
11 Septr. 1832

My Dear Sir,

. . . The number of Emigrants on my list now is nearly two hundred—The list formerly promised to you contained 160—Add now Jesse Scott & Patience his Wife 57 and 53—Sawyer & Washer. . . . Thomas Brown 50 Carpenter & farmer. . . .

1. The letter reveals Grimké's detailed knowledge of the passengers of the *Hercules,* from their ages to their occupations. Although the earlier list mentioned in this letter does not appear in Gurley's correspondence, this document suggests that Grimké knew Susan Vesey, whose name does not appear on this second list. A document labeled "Applications for Emigrants" reveals that on "Jan 17" Grimké wrote "In behalf of several persons desirous of emigrating from C[harleston]."

American Colonization Society Papers, LC.

Thomas S. Grimké to Ralph R. Gurley, Thursday, September 13, 1832

Charleston
13 Septr. 1832

My Dear Sir,

I hasten to inform you that I have just received a letter from Mr. G. S. Milles under date of 1st. Septr of which the following is an extract: being an extract from a letter of his Charleston Correspondent to him. "We must decline putting the advertisement as not only our own interest [*illegible*] principles are opposed to the measure. We thought it our duty to submit the leter to one of our friends in this city, who concurr with us in opinion that it would be highly improper that such an advertisement should be published here."

This confirms the view presented by me two or three days since and I can only say the more I have thought of the matter, the more I am convinced of the correctness of the view then taken.

Many of the passengers you have observed will provide their own provisions. Is it requested that they do this, by contributing in money the value of their share of that they can contribute in kind? If the latter, will they have an opportunity of purchasing their own food, or must it be brought into the common stock—and then share as the others do. If they must contribute in kind, do you decide the dispensation of the provisions & the quantity?

Yours Truly,
Thos. S. Grimké

American Colonization Society Papers, LC.

Peter Ward, Daniel Johnston, and Thomas C. Brown[1] to Ralph R. Gurley, Saturday, October 6, 1832

Charleston October 6th 1832

Dier Sir We have heatherto addressed the colonization Society through you by our honorable friend T. S. Grimky but are compeled at this late period to lay fully open our situation at present,—and the causes that led us into this dilemah, Viz in February last we enquired weather an expadition would be filed from Charleston. If we could raise sixty persons, secondly would we in consideration of paying three hundred dollars in and of said expedition be allowed the privilage of taking in said vesel three horses and cart 60.000 ft of lumber and other articles therein mentioned,—and before these our questions reached you, a leter was received by our friend and and handed to us proposeing to us the very questions we asked, and in a few days after received a communication from you in answer to our several questions declaring that yours was a work of charity that you have allways aimed to acommodate all emigrants and that we should be allowed to carry the things named on the conditions we mention accordingly we closed our affairs under expectation of going out in April Last—but unhappily for us it was concluded by Mr. T. S. Grimky and the Society beter to send a vesel in Octobr for one hundred and fifty or more, and during all this interval we have been out of Bisiness consequently rendered ourselves unable to take more than 30.000 ft and that in hopes of going directly from Charleston to Liberia on or about the 15th of Octob, according to all information that we could get and more than all it was sanctioned by an extract we have seene in Several publick prints taken from the African Repository, but to our great disappointment on 5th we Learned that we will have to go to Savannah to meet the vesel on the first of Novr. . . .

We are yours respectfully
Peter Ward
Daniel Johnson
Thos C Brown

1. This is the same Thomas Cilavan Brown (b. 1800), a Charleston carpenter, who provided Lydia Maria Child in the 1830s with information about Denmark Vesey. Child drew on notes she had taken of Brown's words in responding to a request in 1860 from Thomas Wentworth Higginson for information on slave resistance. For the letter, see Part VI, pp. 749–53. See also *Examination of Mr. Thomas C. Brown, a Free Colored Citizen of S. Carolina, As to the Actual State of Things in Liberia in the Years 1833 and 1834* (New York, 1834).

American Colonization Society Papers, LC.

Ship *Hercules*'s company, arrived at Monrovia January 16, 1833[1]

Thomas C. Brown, jr.	32	South Carolina	Monrovia	Writes	Carpenter	US	1835
Mary Brown	27	South Carolina	Monrovia	Writes	Mantuaker	US	1835
Samuel Brown	4	South Carolina				US	1835
Thomas C. Brown	2	South Carolina					1833 Fever
. . .							
Susan Vesey	45	South Carolina	Monrovia		Laundress	US	1835
Diana Vesey	14	South Carolina	Monrovia	Writes		US	1841
John Anthony	24	South Carolina	Monrovia	Writes	Carpenter		1833 Fever
Eliza Anthony	22	South Carolina	Monrovia				1833 Fever

1. This printed chart listed all 180 people aboard the *Hercules,* as well as their age, whether they were "free born or otherwise," whether they had been emancipated so that they might emigrate to Liberia, where they located in the colony, the extent of their education, their profession, date and cause of death, and whether they subsequently left Liberia and, if so, to what destination. Thomas Cilavan Brown (b. 1800), the free carpenter and lay minister who worked in Vesey's shop, is most likely the son of the Thomas Brown, identified in Thomas S. Grimké's letter of September 11, 1832, who was then a fifty-year-old carpenter and farmer. The Thomas C. Brown who died of a fever in 1833 was clearly the grandson of the eldest Brown.

Although the 1830 census listed Susan Vesey as "age 35–36," which would put her birth year around 1795, the census takers were most likely guessing as to her age. If forty-five in 1833, Susan was instead born around 1788.

Information Relative to the United States Squadron on the West Coast of Africa, Twenty-eighth Congress, Second Session, Senate Document 150, Serial 458, p. 231.

Emigration Register, 1833[1]

Ship Hercules from Charleston S.Ca.			
Vesey, Susan	45	Washer	Charleston
Vesey, Jo. Antonio	24	Hou[se]. Carpenter	Charleston
Vesey, Eliza	22	Pastry Cook	Charleston
Vesey, Diana	16	Mantua Maker	Charleston. . . .

1. This handwritten document, in which families are grouped together, clarifies the previous document. Here Diana Vesey is sixteen rather than fourteen, but the ages and occupations for "John Antonio Vesey" and "Eliza Vesey" makes it clear that they are the "John Anthony" and "Eliza Anthony" listed above. John, most likely a son to Susan and Denmark, was born around 1809, at which time Susan was roughly twenty-one. He would have been just thirteen at the time of his father's execution, too young to have been involved in the conspiracy. Eliza, who in both documents appears just below John, was almost certainly his wife, while Diana, born around 1819, was approximately three years old in 1822.

Emigration Register, American Colonization Society Papers, LC.

Barque *Hercules* Emigrants, 1833[1]

Thomas C. Brown	32	teachr. Reli & H. Carpenter	
Mary Brown	27	Mantua maker	Wife of T. C. Brown
Samuel do	4		Son " "
Thomas J. do	2		" "
. . .			
Susan Vesy	45	Washer &c.	
John Anthony	24	House Carpenter	
Eliza do	22	Pastry Cook &c.	
Dianna do	14	Mantua Maker	

[Origin of emigrants]

Charleston, S.Ca.	145
Beaufort, "	11
Savannah, Geo.	9
Augusta, "	11
Florida	4
Total	180

74 [?] Children

Manumitted Slaves 23

[Occupation of emigrants]

3 Presbyterian Preachers	25 Seamstresses & Mantua Makers
2 Baptist Ditto	4 Nurses
16 Tea. Of Rn. & Sunday School Teachers	1 Cabinet Maker
1 Sawyer—4 Tailors	1 Mason
16 Carpenters 2 Blacksmiths	1 Painter

4 Wheelwrights 3 Millwrights	1 Boatsman
3 Pastry Cooks	4 House Servants
3 Shoemakers	14 Washers & Ironing
1 Tanner	1 Drayman
6 Farmers1 Schoolmaster	1 Laborer

1. Here too, emigrants are listed in family groups, but John and Eliza once more are given the surname of "Anthony," as is Diana, whose name is misspelled. Curiously, given the notoriety surrounding the Vesey name in Charleston, Susan's surname is also misspelled.

Thomas Cilavan Brown's appearance in this document, as well as in the first, as a carpenter indicates that he is the same craftsman of that name who worked with Vesey. Brown's comments about Vesey under questioning from Lydia Maria Child were recorded by her in a journal and then quoted subsequently in a letter to Thomas Wentworth Higginson. See the March 17, 1860, letter of Child to Higginson on pp. 749–53 in Part VI of this volume. The fact that this document also reveals him to be a lay minister suggests he may also have had access to the Charleston Work-House in 1822, although his comments indicate he was not someone who had heard Vesey's response in the courtroom to his sentence of death on the scaffold. See the Charleston Poor-House records and instructions regarding inmates in Part II of this volume for information on ministers being allowed into the buildings where the accused were held.

Barque *Hercules* Emigrants, American Colonization Society Papers, LC.

African Repository and Colonial Journal

December, 1834

THE HON. THOMAS SMITH GRIMKE.[1] The death of this distinguished and most virtuous man is a public calamity. . . . Mr. Grimke was an eminent lawyer, a profound scholar, and enlightened statesman, philanthropist and Christian. With manners unassuming, and a meek and childlike spirit, he united independence of thought and force of character. He was a warm and efficient friend of all the great and benevolent institutions of our country. . . . Africa has by the death of Mr. Grimke been deprived of an active and devoted friend. Through his efforts, principally, was the expedition sent from Charleston to Liberia, in December 1832, and the amount of time and labour which devoted to correspondence in behalf of the emigrants, to the arrangement of their affairs, and to all matters connected with their embarkation, was very great.

1. Thomas Smith Grimké (1786–1834) was a Yale-educated attorney who once partnered in Charleston with Robert Young Hayne. A devout Episcopalian and Christian moralist with pronounced antislavery leanings, Grimké became one of the very few prominent whites in Charleston to support the American Colonization Society. He was the older brother of the famous abolitionists Angelina and Sarah Grimké. See John Belton O'Neall, *Biographical Sketches of the Bench and Bar of South Carolina . . .* , 2 vols. (Charleston, SC, 1859), vol. 2: 378–89; Adrienne Koch, "Two Charlestonians in Pursuit of Truth: The Grimké Brothers," *SCHM* 69 (July 1968): 159–70.

Concord *New Hampshire Patriot and State Gazette,* Wednesday, April 11, 1860

TAX-PAYERS AND FREE NEGROES IN CHARLESTON.—A correspondent of the N.Y. Spirit of the Times, writing from Charleston, South Carolina, says:—

"The most notable feature in the list of taxpayers of Charleston, is the tax on property paid by 'free persons of color.' The number of colored persons taxed is three hundred and fifty-five, and of these, three hundred and four are owners of real estate, while two hundred and twenty-six of them own real estate to the amount of $1000 or more—some of them nearly $50,000 worth; the entire amount owned by the two hundred and twenty-six above referred to is about $717,495! In addition to this, I may as well inform you that the three hundred and fifty-five 'persons of color' who are free, own two hundred and seventy-seven slaves. There is one free 'gentleman of color' still residing, as we are informed, in Charleston, an owner of property, who is honored above any white citizen in the Union in being exempt from taxation; he is the negro (then a slave) who gave the information that led to the discovery of the insurrection of 1822.[1] For his faithful services, the corporation granted him his freedom, and the immunity above referred to."

1. The writer speaks of Peter (Prioleau) Desverney (1787?–1860).

Daily Albany Argus

Monday, January 22, 1872

A very important suit. Damage Awarded to Property in Albany, Troy, Rochester, and Brooklyn. January 20.—At a special term of the King's County Supreme Court, an action was brought by Sarah Graham against Daniel A. McDonald and others, to receive dower in twenty-six lots in Albany, Troy, Rochester, and Brooklyn. This is one of a series of suits brought by the plaintiff, the widow of Francis P. Graham, who was banished to Africa for taking part in the Denmark-Vesey insurrection in South Carolina, and who subsequently settled in New York. His fourth wife attempted to recover dower, but failed in consequence of his previous marriage with the present plaintiff. Judge Pratt decided yesterday in favor of the plaintiff, but reserved the question of the value to the property.[1]

1. On Prince Graham, see Part III, p. 251 n1.

New York Herald

Sunday, February 25, 1872

The Prince Graham Estate Again—The Prince's First Wife After the Dower. Before Judge Gilbert. Sarah Graham vs. N. B. La Bau and Others.—This is nearly the last of some twenty-five suits brought by plaintiff against different parties. The defendant La Bau is son in-law of Commodore Vanderbilt, and plaintiff brought suit against him and the other defendants to recover her dower in a trace of land—five acres in extent—near the Ninth Ward Boulevard. The husband of plaintiff, Prince Graham, was a slave,[1] and left her in Charleston, S.C., at the time he was banished to Africa for the part which he took in the Denmark Vesey insurrection, and on his returning to the states he married at various times three other women. It was by these last wives he came into possession of the property in suit, and the first wife and widow now coming on from Charleston sues for her dower. The property is valued at $20,000, and was left to La Bau by the will of Prince Graham. La Bau had been the attorney for Graham during his lifetime. Some time after Graham's death he sent word to the heirs to come over and hear the will read. The paper purporting to be a will was drawn in the handwriting of La Bau, and after giving a life estate to his nephew and sister the estate was given in fee to La Bau. The property covered several valuable plots of land in the Ninth ward of the city of Brooklyn.

When the will was offered for probate before Jesse C. Smith, then Surrogate of Kings county, it was rejected. All the circumstances surrounding it seem very suspicious. La Bau appealed, had the question of its validity tried before a jury, and again the will was defeated. A new trial was obtained, and on a technical question of law the jury was charged to bring in a verdict for defendant. The heirs at law had no money to appeal or bondsmen to offer, and, therefore, they had to let the case rest. The attorneys, Judge Nelson of New York, and also Judge Gilbert and others, had given their time and money to sustain the heirs at that time in setting aside the will.

Graham brought a suit against his third wife for divorce on the ground of adultery, but while the trial was proceeding in the Brooklyn Supreme Court, he met his wife and made all up with her again, whereupon they both went home and left Court and jury waiting for them.[2]

After hearing the argument in the present suit, Judge Gilbert decided in favor of plaintiff, the form of judgment to be settled by the Court.

1. This was in error. In 1822 Prince Graham was a freeman, but his first wife, Sarah Graham, was enslaved.

2. For the abortive divorce trial between Graham and his wife, who was allegedly forty-one years his junior, see the *Daily Sandusky Register,* November 21, 1851, and the *New-Hampshire Patriot,* November 26, 1851. According to the New York *Weekly Herald,* February 19, 1853, Graham died on February 11.

Charleston Daily News

Monday, March 28, 1873

A REMARKABLE WILL CASE. A LEGAL FIGHT OVER A DEAD WOMAN'S PROPERTY—The Relatives of Denmark Vesey in Court. Auditor Bennett as a Will Maker.

A curious and complicated will case was decided yesterday in the Court of Common Pleas, to which court it had been taken by an appeal from the decision of Probate Judge Buist. The decedent was an old colored woman by the name of Hannah Vesey, relict of one Denmark Vesey, a son of the notorious Denmark Vesey, who was the leading spirit in the famous negro insurrection of 1822, and who, with twenty or thirty of his followers, paid the penalty of his rash attempt upon the gallows during the administration of Governor Bennett. She was always free, and before the war was well known to most of the residents of Charleston as a thrifty, well-to-do market woman, occupying a stall in the city market, where she drove a flourishing trade in butter, cheese, eggs and poultry, in the course of which she amassed a very respectable competence, her property being estimated to be worth, at the beginning of the war, some twenty thousand dollars. She never had any children, and she appears to have long ago bestowed her affections upon the four children of a sister of hers, named Binah Gadsden, who was then a slave belonging to Mrs. Ann S. Smith. In 1837 she purchased this sister and her four children, who are now grown up and named respectively Ann Matthews, Rosanna Holmes, Betsy Price, and Titus Gadsden, and brought up the children, giving them some degree of education, although still keeping them in nominal servitude, because it was impossible for her, under the then existing laws, to make them free by a deed of emancipation. She always manifested a considerable degree of affection for these nieces, and she appears to have endeavored, some time before the war, to provide for their comfort and support after her death. It was, of course, at that time impossible for her to bequeath her property to them either directly or through trustees, for being slaves, they were not competent to hold any property, and a will was drawn out at her request by Colonel Wm. Whaley, in which she left all her real and personal estate, including the nieces, her slaves, to Messrs. John Y. Stock, William C. Bee, and the late Dr. Edward North, three prominent and wealthy gentlemen of this city, and in whom she had every reason to place the utmost confidence. It is hardly to be supposed, however, that this bequest from the humble market woman to these three wealthy gentlemen was intended for their own enrichment, and the more natural theory is that Mrs. Vesey meant thereby to place her nieces in kind hands and thus to provide for their comfort and support after her death. Another will of a similar nature was drawn for her by the same gentleman, Colonel Whaley, during the early years of the war, somewhere about the time of the battle of Secessionville, for the old woman appeared to have had a penchant for will-making, but as neither of these wills have been produced, the supposition is that she destroyed them after the war, when the emancipation of the slaves and the consequent changes in the laws left her more free to follow her own inclinations and affections in the posthumous disposal of her property. She then appears to have taken again to will making, this time entrusting her instructions to the new crop of legal luminaries of her own color who sprang up after the war, and have flourished apace ever since upon the proceeds of just such cases as this. In 1866 she called in General W. J. Whipper, to whom she gave instructions for a will, which he prepared and read over to her, she being unable to read or write, and which she signed by her mark and preserved.[1] This will gave the principal portion of her property to her husband, Denmark Vesey (since dead), and her nephew and niece, whom she had bought and brought up, and left the remainder to Whipper. This will, however, was never produced, and the supposition is that the old woman, probably after getting some better educated neighbor to read it over to her, destroyed this will, as she had her two former ones.

At this time, Mrs. Vesey was the matron of the Old Folks' Home, a worthy institution where feeble or aged colored people are cared for at the expense of the city, and she was thus brought into official relations with Samuel L. Bennett, a colored man, who was then connected with the Freedmen's Bureau, and who is now well known as the present county auditor of Charleston County.[2] She became well acquainted with him, and he soon became her general advisor, factotum, and man of business. In March, 1870, Mr. Bennett, who was then a trial justice, having his office in Military Hall, Wentworth street, called in to his office three neighbors, Messrs. Wm. Robb, Thomas McCarthy, and R. M. Alexander, asking them to step in for a moment to witness a signature. There they found Mrs. Vesey seated with a paper lying on the table before her, which she said, in answer to a question from Bennett, was her will, and which she signed by a cross mark, after which the three gentlemen affixed their signatures as witnesses, not doubting but that everything was correct and in due form.

On January 1st, 1872, the old woman died, and was buried and dutifully mourned by her loving relatives and expectant heirs, and as soon as a respectable time had elapsed they dried their tears and proceeded in a body to the office of Trial Justice Bennett to attend the ceremony of reading the will.[3] They were received by Bennett with all due respect and sympathy, and furnished by him with a paper they were told to take to the probate judge, George Buist, Esq., who would acquaint them with the contents of their affectionate relative's last will and testament. They accordingly proceeded to that gentleman's office, presented the document with which they were armed, and seated themselves in a little semicircle, with their clean handkerchiefs up to their eyes, ready, at the proper moment, to bewail the loss of their generous and beloved aunt. The will was read, but their lamentations turned to astonishment and their white handkerchiefs were crammed back into the pockets of their alpaca [*illegible*], when they found that to each of the nieces was given a life use of two rooms in certain small shanties in Hasel street, and to the nephew the sum of twenty dollars in cash, while Mr. Samuel L. Bennett, who was made sole executor, was bequeathed a valuable residence on Spring street, which constituted the [*illegible*] portion of their venerable relative's estate. They departed from the office of the probate judge speechless with consternation, but finding their tongues by the time they returned to Bennett's office, they demanded of him, with no small agitation and vehemence, what was the meaning of the extraordinary will. Mr. Bennett blandly required what were the contents of the will, and they retorted by asking how it was that he hadn't known all about the will all the time. All this amounted to nothing, however, and the disconsolate nephew and niece then proceeded to pour their sad recital into the professional ears of Messrs. Whaley & Minott, who undertook to conduct their case before the courts, and to restore them to their heritage.

The case was then tried and argued before Probate Judge Buist, and his decision was in favor of the will. An appeal was taken from this decision to the Court of Common Pleas, the grounds of the appeal being as follows:

The paper propounded at the will of Hannah Vesey ought not to be admitted to probate—

1. Because it appears that the decedent could neither read nor write, and there is no evidence of knowledge of the contents.

2. Because the proponent is sole executor and principal legatee, and had the conduct of the execution of the paper propounded.

3. Because the proponent, who is executor, and was the attorney, principal legatee and man of business of the deceased, and that the paper was either drawn by him or one of his clerks, and there is no proofs of instructions, reading over or knowledge of contents.

4. Because in the cases above mentioned the *onus probandi* is on proponent to show something beyond the ordinary execution and attestation of the paper.

5. Because the acknowledgement on the part of decedent that it was her will, if proved would be insufficient.

6. Because the paper was obtained by undue influence, which may be inferred from the facts mentioned in the first three grounds.

7. Because the will is unnatural and inofficious, and the *onus probandi* of knowledge of contents and of fairness is on the proponent.

8. Because so far as any evidence of knowledge appears it is inconsistent with the will, and the contestants have shown, so far as the ruling of the court admitted, declarations of the decedent showing an entire want of knowledge of the contents.

9. Because the circumstances of suspicion developed in this case, unexplained, are evidence that the will in this case was obtained through fraud.

10. Because the decedent was advanced in years, and her capacity was doubtful, and the proponent and legatee having drawn the will, it was incumbent on him to prove knowledge of the contents of the will.

It will be seen that the theory of the contestants was that the will was drawn up by Bennett; that the old woman had little or no knowledge of its contents, and that he had taken good care to appropriate to himself the most valuable part of the property. The case came on for trial last Tuesday, and Bennett, who was represented by Messrs. Whaley & Mitchell, of course denied all these surmises and assertions of the contestants. The trial lasted two days, and a very large number of witnesses were examined. Bennett swore positively that he did not draw up the will, but, on the other hand, several experts gave it as their opinion, after examining many papers written by him, that the whole will was in his handwriting. The history of the old woman's life, her relations to the contestants, her former wills, &c., were all elicited in the testimony, and, after elaborate arguments by counsel on both sides, and a clear and impartial charge by Judge Graham, the case was given to the jury on Wednesday evening. Yesterday morning they rendered a verdict to the effect that the paper propounded was not the last will and testament of Hannah Vesey, and judgment was entered accordingly. The effect of this decision will be to restore the property to the nephew and nieces, who are the heirs-at-law, and who, after all their troubles, will now come into possession by the due course of law.[4]

1. Although never a general, Philadelphia-born William J. Whipper served as a noncommissioned officer in the Thirty-first US Colored Troops. After the war, he bought a home in Hilton Head, taught school with the Freedmen's Bureau, and practiced law in Columbia and Beaufort. See Eric Foner, ed., *Freedom's Lawmakers: A Directory of Black Officeholders During Reconstruction*, rev. ed. (Baton Rouge: Louisiana State University Press, 1996), 226.

2. Samuel L. Bennett was a mixed-race Charlestonian who was born free around 1820. Formerly a shoemaker, he served as a delegate to South Carolina's black convention of 1865 before becoming a supervisor of the state's orphan asylum in 1870. See Eric Foner, ed., *Freedom's Lawmakers:*

A Directory of Black Officeholders During Reconstruction, rev. ed. (Baton Rouge: Louisiana State University Press, 1996), 17. On March 22, 1872, he opened a bank account for the "Estate of Hannah Vesey" with the Charleston branch of the Freedman's Savings Bank; the entry did not list an amount deposited. See Freedman's Savings Bank Records, NA.

3. Hannah Vesey appeared in the 1870 census, which listed her as seventy years old and a black native of Charleston. She died on January 1, 1872. See US Census, South Carolina, Charleston, series M593, roll 1487, p. 601, NA, the Charleston City Death Records, 1821–1914. In the 1860 census, however, she was listed as Hannah Nelson, a sixty-year-old mixed-race female who resided with Betsy Price. See series M653, roll 1216, p. 506, NA. Her husband, Denmark Vesey Jr., was the son of Dolly, Vesey's second wife.

4. The case also appeared, without mention of either Denmark Vesey, in J. S. G. Richardson, ed., *Report of Cases Heard and Determined by the Supreme Court of South Carolina* (Columbia, SC, 1876), vol. 5: 478–85.

VI

Recollections and Memorializations

In the history of slave plots and insurrections in the United States, Denmark Vesey's conspiracy set no records for the shedding of blood. Rebellious slaves killed about two dozen whites, and whites killed about forty slaves during the Stono uprising (1739), part of what white South Carolinians at the time of the Vesey affair referred to in the context of a close succession of acts of slave resistance in those bygone colonial years as the "Gullah War." Although only two whites lost their lives in the German Coast insurrection (1811) in the territory of Orleans, about one hundred slaves were killed in battle or in the summary executions that followed. Nat Turner's revolt (1831) in Southampton County, Virginia, led to the death of about sixty whites and more than sixty slaves. But these acts of collective rebelliousness that reached the stage of open violence took place in colonial frontier societies, or on the periphery of the young republic, or in rural Virginia. Vesey's revolutionary plot extended to the dense slave populations of the South Carolina lowcountry from the heart of one of the nation's busiest port cities during the so-called Era of Good Feelings, a time when most white Americans felt buoyant about their country's future.

Those who lived in and around Charleston during the summer of 1822 never forgot the conspiracy and remembered how it had changed their lives and the laws and politics of their state. In explaining over time what had been done to themselves and the outside world, they alternated between defensiveness and bravado. Families, black as well as white, passed down stories that became part of folklore and legend. Residents of Charleston and visitors to the city had the event seared into their minds, to be discussed in detail for a variety of purposes when the occasion called for it. As various antislavery organizations rose in the 1830s and 1840s to challenge the "peculiar institution," the names of Denmark Vesey and Nat Turner surfaced increasingly in abolitionist oratory. Especially after the passage in 1850 of a stricter federal fugitive slave law, black and white abolitionists reassessed their thinking about how to bring slavery to an end. Frederick Douglass openly broke with pacifist William Lloyd Garrison and his followers on the question of means beyond moral suasion in effecting emancipation. Some white abolitionists did so as well and joined former slaves and black activists in becoming much more willing to embrace and celebrate violence against slaveowners.

In the 1850s, a burgeoning northern antislavery movement proved more receptive to the use of violence against slaveholders as the broadening abolitionist indictment of slavery zeroed in on the corrupting nature of the master-slave relation. The private ownership of human beings, it was alleged, fostered a lording spirit in masters, making them brutal, corrupt, and aristocratic. By extension, they posed a dire threat to democratic civil rights and the future prosperity of the nation. In print and voice, abolitionists employed the sacrifice of Vesey and his followers to incite northern audiences into action. John Brown's attack on the federal arsenal at Harpers Ferry in 1859, the first act of an intended drama to unleash a chain of slave insurrections in the South, bespoke the extremist wing of the new militancy and sparked a burst of national interest in the history of slave rebellion. Indeed, Thomas Wentworth Higginson, a gifted intellectual and Unitarian minister, one of the Secret Six who supported Brown, had been investigating the subject of slave rebelliousness for some time in order to think through strategies of how best to bring slavery to a quick end. He conducted pioneering research that culminated in a series of published essays on Denmark Vesey and other rebellious slaves throughout the Americas. Denmark Vesey's name also cropped up during and shortly after the election of Abraham Lincoln to the presidency. A number of newspaper articles sought to inform the public about the history of slave rebellion in the United States in light of a flood of reports, similar to those in 1856 (only this time from every southern state) of uncovered instances of slave conspiracy.

During the Civil War, black leaders called on the memory of Vesey as a symbol of black manhood to help efforts in mustering black recruits into the war effort. By late 1862, Union commanders fighting in the South began to make sporadic use of black soldiers. As 1863 dawned and the Emancipation Proclamation went into effect, President Abraham Lincoln and Secretary of War Edwin M. Stanton, acting in conjunction with Massachusetts Governor John A. Andrew, sought to recruit black soldiers in the northern states. The first such regiment raised was the Fifty-fourth Massachusetts Volunteer Infantry, a unit that included freemen from across the North. Among those who served in the regiment were Charles and Lewis Douglass, and their father, abolitionist editor and speaker Frederick Douglass, used the memory of Vesey and Turner to recruit young men into the military.

Because none of these writers had actually known Vesey and because of the cut-and-paste style of antebellum journalism in which essays and stories were reprinted, repeated, and then used by others in their own writing and oratory, a number of errors crept into the storytelling. Many speeches and essays drew heavily on data extracted from either Hamilton's *Account* or Kennedy and Parker's *Official Report*, suggesting just how widely disseminated those publications had become, even though as abolitionist Thomas Wentworth Higginson contended in an essay excerpted below, southern owners of these works took care to shelter them from the prying eyes of their slaves.

For antebellum southern whites, the circulation of stories about the events of 1822 helped to justify stricter methods of managing and controlling slaves and in certain cases to rationalize outright brutality. On the one hand, white storytelling over the years tended to pronounce Vesey a mulatto, perhaps because he had obtained his freedom, perhaps because mulattoes had emerged in a favored narrative as the prime instigators of the slave revolution in Saint-Domingue, or perhaps because the very sophistication of the revolutionary plot could only admit into prejudiced minds the notion of a worthy foe who was only partly of African ancestry. On the other hand, for antebellum people of color, particularly in the North, the Vesey affair fitted revealingly into evolving discussions of color consciousness among themselves. No person of color who can be placed in Charleston in 1822 or had access to the eyewitness testimony of persons there ever claimed that Vesey was a mulatto. To the contrary, Vesey's betrayal fitted into a didactic narrative of the need for racial solidarity: lighter-skinned persons of color, after all, had betrayed the darker-skinned Vesey to white authorities. It is hard to believe that the victorious Major Martin Delany, one of the highest-ranking black officers in the Union Army, would have spoken to throngs of blacks and browns in Charleston in 1865 about the moral lessons to be drawn from the Vesey affair without knowing, for sure, that Vesey was not a mulatto. In addition, the written testimony of Charleston carpenter Thomas Cilavan Brown, who claimed to have worked with Vesey and, without question, knew members of his family, indicates that Vesey was black and in origin a "Corromantee negro," that is from the Gold Coast region of West Africa.

Modern writers, in dipping too quickly into the well of readily available sources, have often repeated mistakes: about Vesey's color and names, origin, relative wealth, and the adopted surname of the man who first leaked word of the conspiracy, to name a few examples. Whatever the mistakes, however, Denmark Vesey, with the passing of generations, would become for certain groups for varying reasons a swelling symbol of pride, a lowly, intelligent, daring disrupter of the status quo, martyred on the gallows to the cause of human freedom and dignity.

A British Traveler Remembers, 1830

. . . The last and most deep laid plot to throw off the yoke of their masters, and at the same time to glut their revenge, took place, or rather was brought to light in 1822. The ringleaders of this scheme were some of them men of considerable talents, who conducted their secret machinations with a good deal of ingenuity, but certainly no very great share of foresight or prudence; for even had they succeeded in overwhelming the white population of Charleston for a time, they could have stood but for a short period indeed, against the whole force of the United States, which would have been inevitably directed against them. The intentions of the conspirators were discovered to be of the most desperate nature; on a certain day they were to set fire to the city in many different places at once, attack the guard house, and after possessing themselves of all the arms they could lay their hands on, then to commence an indiscriminate slaughter of every *white* male, and every *black* woman, reserving all the choice *young white ladies* as companions to their sable conquerors. Amongst the papers of the conspirators, lists were discovered containing the names of many of the most accomplished young ladies in the city, who were reserved to a fate ten thousand times more horrible than death in its worst form. A fellow who was coachman to one of the highest authorities in Charleston, had his master's daughter designated as his intended wife, and it was his intention to save the life of his master, as he said that excepting himself, "Massa was the best whip hand in the city, and would answer extremely well to drive *his* coach."

The plot was discovered by one of the conspirators, who was determined upon saving his master from the general massacre, but as his comrades would not consent to this, he gave the information to a proper quarter, when the whole affair was instantly blown up, and about three hundred Negroes arrested and tried forthwith; about forty of these were executed without delay. Twenty-two were led to execution one morning, and this operation was performed with very little ceremony. The chief amongst them addressed his fellow Negroes who came to witness the scene, conjuring them to remain true to the cause of freedom, and to prosecute their plans against their white tyrants, to the death; those who suffered seemed to take the matter quite easy. One fellow who thought the executioners were very dilatory, and did not seem to relish the idea of standing so long with the rope about his neck, bawled out to the captain of the city guard, "Massa D—you take us here for hang, why you keep us waiting all day, do hang us Massa or let us go home for work." The request of this poor sinner was speedily complied with, but that in a very bungling manner, the plank upon which the wretches stood not descending low enough, several of them were kept for some minutes with their feet dangling on it.[1]

The discovery of this plot caused much consternation in Charleston, especially amongst the fair sex, who differ very much in opinion from Desdemona. . . . [2]

1. Peter Neilson (1795–1861) settled in Charleston around 1816. See his *The Life and Adventures of Zamba, an African Negro King; and His Experience of Slavery in South Carolina. Written by Himself. Corrected and Arranged by Peter Neilson* (London, 1847). Although no other source contains this quotation, the words of this unnamed slave sound similar to those attributed to Bacchus Hammet, who was one of the twenty-two slaves hanged on July 26. The "Massa D" referred to here was presumably William Dove (1789–1828), captain of the guard, who attended the hangings that day and shot those slowly strangling to death. On this point, see the comment of Mary Lamboll Thomas Beach, July 25, 1822, Part IV, p. 415.

2. Neilson refers here to the beautiful Venetian lady from an elite family who married the darker-skinned Othello in one of Shakespeare's most famous plays.

Peter Neilson, *Recollections of a Six Years' Residence in the United States of America . . .* (Glasgow, 1830), 295–97.

A Planter[1] on Vesey and Free People of Color

December 1832

. . . By far the greatest evil . . . which slave-holding communities have to contend with, is an intermediate population, without, whose presence and daily association with our slaves very little regard would be paid to insurrectionary movements among the slaves themselves, and still less to foreign interference. . . .

There is an identity of interest between the coloured persons of both classes, which associated as they are by cast[e], and connected as they are by intermarriages and friendships it were in vain to attempt to dissolve, it is the interest of the free-coloured population to cherish a spirit of discontent among the slaves, as they would hope to avail themselves of their assistance in promoting their own schemes of ambition—or, if this broad assertion be denied, it is certainly the interest of those who have wives and children, and other relatives, in slavery, to throw themselves, upon an emergency, into the ranks of the slave, and "to carry over to their unhallowed cause their intelligence and their numbers, and to serve them as channels of communication through different parts of the State." Here, again, I am speaking on proved authority, and not from idle speculation. Denmark Vesey, with whom the conspiracy of '22 originated, was a free man, and the partial liberty he enjoyed gave him an opportunity of collecting and preparing the materials for that plot, and of communicating so extensively as he did with the country slaves, without whose co-operation those in the city, mad as they appear to have been, would never have dared to make an attempt at emancipation.

To abate this nuisance (an intermediate population) many projects have been, from time to time, advanced, but they are all liable to the same fault, that of tending immediately to create the very excitement which they are ultimately intended to obviate. The true policy, although it be a stern one, is the entire extinction of the class; and in consideration of the political influence which they indirectly possess through the means of their patrons and guardians, and the yet more hateful power which many of them have over their tenantry among the poorest class of whites, the sanatory remedy—banishment—should be applied, before they shall have too firmly engrafted themselves upon the country. . . .

1. Edward Rutledge Laurens (b. 1806), the author of this published address, was a lowcountry planter. His father-in-law, Elias Horry (1773–1834), had owned John, the coachman executed in 1822.

Edward R. Laurens, "An Address Delivered before the Agricultural Society of South-Carolina, September 18, 1832," *Southern Agriculturist* 5 (December 1832): 617, 621–22.

Scottish Traveler James Stuart[1] on Slave Trials, 1833

. . . Charleston has long been celebrated for the severity of its laws against the blacks, and the mildness of its punishment towards the whites for maltreating them. . . .

A dreadful case of murder occurred at Charleston, in 1806. A planter, called John Slater,[2] made an unoffending, unresisting slave be bound hand and foot, and compelled his companion to chop off his head with an axe, and to cast his body, convulsed with the agonies of death into the water. Judge Wild[s], who tried him, on awarding a sentence of imprisonment against this wretch, expressed his regret that the punishment provided for the offence was insufficient to make the law respected,—that the delinquent too well knew,—that the arm, which he had stretched out for the destruction of his slave, was that to which he alone could look for protection, disarmed as he was of the rights of self-defence. But the most horrible butchery of slaves which has ever taken place in America, was the execution of thirty-five of them on the lines near Charleston, in the month of July, 1822, on account of an alleged conspiracy against their masters. The whole proceedings are monstrous. Sixty-seven persons were convicted before a court, consisting of a justice of the peace, and freeholders, without a jury. The evidence of slaves not upon oath, was admitted against them, and, after all, the proof was extremely scanty. Perrault, a slave, who had himself been brought from Africa, was the chief witness.[3] He had been torn from his father, who was very wealthy, and a considerable trader in tobacco and salt on the coast of Africa. He was taken prisoner, and was sold, and his purchaser would not give him up, although three slaves were offered in his stead. The judge's address, on pronouncing sentence of death on this occasion, on persons sold to slavery and servitude, and who, if they were guilty, were only endeavouring to get rid of it in the only way in their power, seems monstrous. He told them that the servant who was false to his master would be false to his God,—that, the precept of St. Paul was to obey their masters in all things, and of St. Peter, to be subject to their masters with all fear,—and that, had they listened to such doctrines, they would not now have been arrested by an ignominious death.

The proceedings of this trial made some noise at the time. An official account of it was published, in which the execution of so great a number of persons was justified by the precedent of George the Second, who executed fifty-four of the first men in Britain for the rebellion of 1745. . . .

1. James Stuart (1755–1849), born in Edinburgh and trained in law, was an antislavery Whig politician. See Ursula R. Q. Henriques, "An Early Factory Inspector: James Stuart of Dunearn," *Scottish Historical Review* 50 (April 1971): 20–23.

2. On the Slater case and Judge Wilds's sentence, see Part I, pp. 41–42, esp. note 1. Slater appears to have been a ship captain and not a planter. He may have been the John Slater who died near Nassau, the Bahamas, in 1807. See *Charleston Courier,* August 19, 1807.

3. At the trial of Russell's Tom, the court identified blacksmith Perault Strohecker as born in "Jumba in Africa, about a week travel from Goree," Senegal.

James Stuart, *Three Years in North America,* 2 vols. (Edinburgh, 1833), vol. 2: 145–47.

Charleston Mercury

Friday, September 11, 1835

NORTHAMPTON. (Mass.) Sept. 3. 1835.

Gentlemen—Yours of the 25th ult. I have just received, informing me that some of my fellow-citizens of your place, have charged me with being an Abolitionist, and having contributed to their aid. I regard this information, so faithfully and promptly given, as an evidence of friendship, which I shall ever remember with gratitude. It is a duty which I believe I owe to my God—to myself—to my friends, and to the best interests of my fellow-men of all nations and of all colors, to denounce every principle and feature of Abolitionists; and that such has been my views and feelings, and principles, I think I may say every respectable inhabitant of this town, as well as many others throughout the Northern and Middle States, *can* and *would* be willing to testify. They know as well as many in your State, that I have opposed the Abolition Society in public in large assemblies, as well as in private. The year 1822, (being then honored by my fellow-citizens of your city with a seat in your Council,) I shall never forget, as I then had an opportunity of seeing something of the fruits of Abolitionists. After such a sight, any man that could advocate their principles, is, in my opinion, the worst enemy of man, and destitute of every christian principle.

I am not disposed to take any advantage of excited feelings, (knowing how much the feelings of your city have been taxed;) but the man or men, (be who they will) who have charged me with being an abolitionist, if they do not contradict the same in a public manner, will do me great injustice. I can assure you, though I am in some measure separated from my brethren of the South, at no period of my life have I felt a deeper interest in their happiness and prosperity than I have done since I came to the North; and I hope and believe that I shall carry these feelings to my grave. It is utterly false that I ever gave a cent to the aid of any abolition society in this or any other land. In very great haste, very respectfully, yours truly,

THOMAS NAPIER.[1]

1. Thomas Napier (1777–1860), a Charleston resident with business interests in Northampton, Massachusetts, was a warden who served on the Charleston City Council at the time of the Vesey trials. See Part V, p. 466 n1.

Lydia Maria Child[1] on Charleston Controls, 1836

. . . A lady, who had been in South Carolina when an insurrection was apprehended,[2] related several anecdotes concerning the alarm that prevailed there at the time: and added, "I often wish that none of my friends lived in a slave State." "Why should you be anxious?" rejoined the Southern gentleman; "You know that they have built a strong citadel in the heart of the city, to which all the inhabitants can repair in case of insurrection." "So," said I, "they have built a *citadel* to protect them from their happy, contented servants—a citadel against their *best friends*!" I could not but be amused at the contradiction that occurred during this conversation. . . . [3]

1. Lydia Maria Child (1802–1880) ranks as one of the foremost abolitionists of the antebellum period. For a biography that centers on her wide intellectual, literary, and reformist connections, see Carolyn L. Karcher, *The First Woman in the Republic: A Cultural Biography of Lydia Maria Child* (Durham, NC: Duke University Press, 1994).

2. By 1836, Child would have had multiple conversations about the Vesey affair with fellow abolitionists Sarah and Angelina Grimké, South Carolina–born sisters of Thomas Smith Grimké (1786–1834).

3. Following the Vesey affair, in late 1822 a guard of 150 men was established in Charleston. Half the guardsmen were stationed in a castle-like arsenal dubbed "the Citadel," a building that was later turned over to the South Carolina Military Academy. See William H. Buckley, *The Citadel and the South Carolina Corps of Cadets* (Charleston, SC: Arcadia, 2004), 9. The building still stands and is today the Embassy Suites Charleston hotel.

Lydia Maria Child, *An Appeal in Favor of that Class of Americans Called Africans* (New York, 1836), 140.

Liberator

Friday, August 25, 1837

Dr. Palmer[1] of Charleston S.C., relates the story of a pious black, who was forward in plotting an insurrection against the whites and was detected and sentenced to death. The church sent an elder to remonstrate with him on his conduct and to urge him to repent of this great sin of which he had been guilty.—'Sin,' exclaimed the astonished black, 'what sin? You applaud the leaders of the American revolution, who resisted a small tax on tea; and rather than pay it killed tens of thousands, but what was that tax to our sufferings? Washington was a white man and you idolized him; but I, alas am a black man, and you hang me for the very act you applauded in him.'

1. As the letter of Mary Lamboll Beach to Elizabeth Gilchrist, July 5, 1822, which appears on pp. 373–77 in Part IV, demonstrates, the Reverend Benjamin Morgan Palmer visited the Charleston Work-House and spoke to Rolla Bennett, Vesey, and Peter Poyas. Beach, however, indicates that neither Vesey nor Poyas would speak with Palmer, so this may have been Rolla Bennett, whom Beach claimed "confessed" to Palmer.

Harriet Martineau[1] on Governor Thomas Bennett Jr., 1837

. . . What, again, is to be thought of the freedom of citizens who are liable to lose caste because they follow conscience in a case where the perversity of the laws places interest on the side of conscience, and public opinion against it? I will explain. In a southern city, I saw a gentleman[2] who appeared to have all the outward requisites for commanding respect. He was very wealthy, had been governor of the State, and was an eminent and peculiar benefactor to the city. I found he did not stand well. As some pains were taken to impress me with this, I inquired the cause. His character was declared to be generally good. I soon got at the particular exception, which I was anxious to do only because I saw that it was somehow of public concern. While this gentleman was governor, there was an insurrection of slaves. His own slaves were accused. He did not believe them guilty, and refused to hang them. This was imputed to an unwillingness to sacrifice his property. He was thus in a predicament which no one can be placed in, except where man is held as property. He must either hang his slaves, believing them innocent, and keep his character; or he must, by saving their lives, lose his own character. How the case stood with this gentleman, is fully known only to his own heart. His conduct claims the most candid construction. But, this being accorded as his due, what can be thought of the freedom of a republican thus circumstanced? . . . [3]

1. Harriet Martineau (1802–1876), a celebrated author and antislavery critic, spent about two years in the United States, arriving in 1834.

2. Thomas Bennett Jr.

3. As the letters of Mary Lamboll Beach to Elizabeth Gilchrist, July 5, 1822, and John Potter to Langdon Cheves, July 10, 1822, both reprinted in Part IV, pp. 373–77, 385–86, indicate, once Rolla confessed his guilt to both the court and to Bennett, the governor ceased to believe his slaves innocent.

Harriet Martineau, *Society in America*, 3 vols. (New York, 1837), vol. 2: 347–48.

New York *Emancipator*

Thursday, December 6, 1838
REMONSTRANCE.

To the Rev. Mr. Turpin:[1]

Sir:—A portion of the citizens of the districts of Abbeville and Edgefield are informed that you have been nominated a Missionary by the S C. A. Conference, to preach to the black population especially. It seems that you assemble the negroes at places which you regularly appoint, where you give them a course of exclusive and especial instruction on religious subjects; and if invited, you attend negro quarters, where you give similar instruction and teach the Catechism; but if not invited, you ask this permission. We conceive it our duty to address the Remonstrance to you, explaining the impropriety of such a course. . . .

We will take another view of the subject, showing the *dangerous tendency to the peace of the white community, of permitting black congregations to assemble alone for religious purposes.* We will select two insurrectionary movements for illustration: The first we shall mention occurred in the city of Charleston, we think in the year 1822. The citizens manifested a disposition of the liveliest sympathy towards the black population, in allowing them the privilege to hold prayer meetings, and to establish a church of their own, where they had separate worship. They assembled on such occasions under the pretence of devotional exercises, and concocted a plot for the massacre of the white population of the city of Charleston. Mock interments at their burying ground, with funeral ceremony, were performed, but the coffins which were interred, instead of inclosing the dead, were filled with military materials for an insurrection.[2] The plan of attack was consummated, and every preparation made for the arrival of the appointed hour. A few days previous to the concerted time, the conspiracy was disclosed. . . .

1. The remonstrance, signed by James S. Pope and 352 others, is probably addressed to the Reverend Thomas D. Turpin (1805–1838), a Methodist pastor quite active in preaching to slaves in the South. See *Minutes of the Annual Conferences of the Methodist Episcopal Church, for the Years, 1829–1839* (New York, 1840), vol. 2: 665.

2. On the use of burial grounds to hide weapons, see the testimony of Thomas Cilavan Brown, quoted in the letter of Lydia Maria Child to Thomas Wentworth Higginson, March 17, 1860, reproduced in this section, pp. 749–53.

Sarah M. Grimké[1] Remembers South Carolina, 1839

. . . It will be recollected that the testimony of Sarah M. Grimké, and Angelina G. Weld,[2] was confined *exclusively* to the details of slavery as exhibited in the *highest* classes *of society,* mainly in Charleston, S.C. . . . The former has furnished us with the following testimony in addition to that already given.

"Nathaniel Heyward of Combahee, S.C., one of the wealthiest planters in the state, stated, in conversation with some other planters who were complaining of the idle and lazy habits of their slaves, and the difficulty of ascertaining whether their sickness was

Figure 36. Nathaniel Heyward (1766–1851), judge on the First Court of Magistrates and Freeholders. From a portrait, 1829. Copyrighted image courtesy of the Gibbes Museum of Art/Carolina Art Association.

real or pretended, and the loss they suffered from their frequent absence on this account from their work, said, 'I never lose a day's work: it is an *established rule* on my plantations that the tasks of all the sick negroes *shall be done by those who are well in addition to their own.* By this means a vigilant supervision is kept up by the slaves over each other, and they take care that nothing but real sickness keeps any one out of the field.' I spent several winters in the neighborhood of Nathaniel Heyward's plantations, and well remember his character as a severe task master. *I was present when the above statement was made.*"

The cool barbarity of such a regulation is hardly surpassed by the worst edicts of the Roman Caligula—especially when we consider that the plantations of this man were in the neighborhood of the Combahee river, one of the most unhealthy districts in the low country of South Carolina; further, that large numbers of his slaves worked in the *rice marshes,* or 'swamps' as they are called in that state—and that during six months of the year, so fatal to health is the malaria of the swamps in that region that the planters and their families invariably abandon their plantations, regarding it as downright presumption to spend a single day upon them 'between the frosts' of the early spring and the last of November.

The reader may infer the high standing of Mr. Heyward in South Carolina, from the fact that he was selected with four other freeholders to constitute a Court for the trial of the conspirators in the insurrection plot at Charleston, in 1822. Another of the individuals chosen to constitute that court was Colonel Henry Deas, now president of the Board of Trustees of Charleston College, and a few years since a member of the Senate of South Carolina. From a late correspondence in the "Greenville (S.C.) Mountaineer," between Rev. William M. Wightman, a professor in Randolph, Macon, College, and a number of the citizens of Lodi, South Carolina, it appears that the cruelty of this Colonel Deas to his slaves, is proverbial in South Carolina, so much that Professor Wightman, in the sermon which occasioned the correspondence, spoke of the Colonel's inhumanity to his slaves as a matter of perfect notoriety. . . .

1. Sarah Moore Grimké (1792–1873), younger sister of Charleston attorney Thomas Smith Grimké (1786–1834), was raised among slaves in Charleston and the Carolina lowcountry. After the death of her father, John Faucheraud Grimké (1752–1819), a prominent planter and politician, Sarah left South Carolina, converted to Quakerism, and became one of the country's most conspicuous abolitionists. See *BDSCHR* 3: 290–92.

2. Angelina Grimké (1805–1879) married the abolitionist Theodore Dwight Weld (1803–1895) one year before the publication of his famous abolitionist tract, which quoted her sister.

Theodore Dwight Weld, *American Slavery as It Is: Testimony of a Thousand Witnesses* (New York, 1839), 174–75.

William Gilmore Simms[1] on Vesey, 1840

. . . The year 1822 was distinguished in Charleston, by a bold but unsuccessful attempt at insurrection, by a small portion of the slave population. The conspiracy was planned by one Denmark Vesey, a mulatto from Saint Domingo, who had been a spectator of the insurrection in that island, and brought with him a taste for its horrors to Carolina. His plans were marked by considerable intelligence and judgment. By the fidelity of native slaves, the plot was discovered and the design defeated. Vesey, the ring-leader, with thirty-four of the more prominent conspirators, was hung; a like number were transported from the state, and about twice the number, who had been arrested, were acquitted. The whole number arrested was one hundred and thirty-one. Four white men, foreigners, were indicted as privy to, and participants in, the conspiracy. They were indicted for misdemeanor in inciting slaves to insurrection, found guilty, and sentenced to fine and imprisonment. . . .

1. William Gilmore Simms (1806–1870) was a Charleston-born poet, novelist, and amateur historian. Sixteen years old at the time of Vesey's execution, Simms was evidently the first writer to suggest that Vesey was mixed-race or was born in Saint-Domingue. Although as a child Vesey briefly labored in the French colony, he had settled in Charleston by 1783 and so was neither born on the island nor present during the insurrection of 1791. Despite this, Philip Morgan, "Conspiracy Scares," *WMQ* 59 (2002): 165–66, cites Simms as evidence that Vesey was mixed-race. On this point, both Joseph Kelly, *America's Longest Siege: Charleston, Slavery, and the Slow March toward Civil War* (New York: Overlook Press, 2013), 133, and Morgan also cite Archibald Grimké, *Right on the Scaffold, or The Martyrs of 1822* (Washington, DC: The Academy, 1901), 6, a page that actually makes no mention of Vesey's color. Grimké, on page 1, identified Vesey only as "black." In at least one subsequent speech, excerpted here on p. 780, Grimké referred to Vesey's "black skin." (Curiously, Kelly, 272, also confused black abolitionist Frederick Douglass with Democratic Senator Stephen Douglas.) On Simms, see Jon L. Wakelyn, *The Politics of a Literary Man: William Gilmore*

Simms (Westport, CT: Greenwood Press, 1973) and the impressive *Simms Initiatives* project undertaken by the University of South Carolina, http://simms.library.sc.edu/.

William Gilmore Simms, *The History of South Carolina, from Its First European Discovery to its Erection into a Republic* (Charleston, SC, 1840), 328.

Philadelphia *Pennsylvania Freeman*

Wednesday, July 14, 1841

REMINISCENCES OF SEVERAL YEARS' RESIDENCE AT THE SOUTH. . . . I arrived at Charleston late in the autumn of 1822, soon after the detection of a deep-laid and extensive plot for the destruction of the whites, by the colored population. It was not contrived by slaves alone, for they were aided by the superior knowledge of the free blacks and mulattoes. . . . The deadly hatred which is felt by slaveholders towards the free blacks at the south and elsewhere, is not without a cause, and it should inspire that class of our countrymen with hope, and with a firm resolution never to desert their brethren who are in bonds, by emigrating to another country.

A gentleman, to whom I carried letters, made me acquainted with the circumstances connected with the discovered conspiracy and as he pointed to the gallows on which some twenty poor creatures had been executed, he expatiated upon their amazing "*ingratitude*" towards their masters and mistresses. I could hardly believe him in earnest, but his enkindling wrath, as he proceeded, gave me too convincing proof that oppression had steeled his heart and perverted his understanding.

It seems that the conspirators had held frequent meetings, and that the Bible, that enemy to the tyrant's peace, had been quoted and explained by such as could read it. Other texts were found in it besides "that standing one (as the shrewd fellow observed) for all preachers whom his master permitted to address his slaves, 'Servants obey your masters.'" The Bible proved to the hearers of it in those meetings, that they were men, and, as such, entitled to liberty, though it does not approve of assassination as a means of securing it. . . .

As I intend that my communication shall be of a miscellaneous character, I will here record an interesting circumstance, connected with the suppression of the conspiracy, which my friend told me, and, to do him justice, with no little feeling of, I may say, *respect,* for one of that race to whom it is not unusual, in that part of the country, to deny the dignity of man!

He said that one of the slaves who were tried for their lives had, not long before, been brought from Africa, that he was the son of a king, and that he had arrived at maturity before his importation. On his being arraigned at the bar, another slave alleged against him, that he was the one who proposed the measure of firing the town in the night, and massacreing the white inhabitants. Upon hearing this testimony, the prisoner turned upon him with an eye darting fury, while assuming an attitude of great dignity, and with a tone of thunder, he thus addressed him: "Wretch, how dare you thus accuse me? Was I not always opposed to that cowardly measure? Did I not denounce it in our assemblies, and declare that I, who had led my father's troops to battle on the open plain, and before the sun, would never attack my enemy in the dark? Yes, I disdained the act, and scorned to join you in such a cowardly massacre." . . . While repelling dishonor, he had conceded the point of his connection with the conspiracy, though he had not liked the manner of conducting it. . . . And, although the trial was over, and the judge had to pass sentence of death, yet this penalty was commuted afterwards for banishment, I think, to Haiti.[1]

My stay in Charleston was short. It was a time of anxiety. It was feared that a second act of the plot was yet to be performed. Every sound, at night, was alarming. The citizens slept upon their arms. . . .

1. This inculpated slave may have been Billy Robinson, a porter and house servant owned by Philip Robinson (d. 1828), a Charleston merchant. Perault Strohecker identified Billy as a fellow African. Described in a petition as "remarkable for honesty & integrity," Billy was nonetheless found guilty but had his death sentence commuted to transportation outside the United States. See Samuel Davenport and Dodridge Crocker to the Senate of South Carolina, November 22, 1822, no. 131, series S165015, SCDAH.

Henry Highland Garnet[1] Appeals to Slaves, 1843

. . . Fellow men! patient sufferers! behold your dearest rights crushed to the earth! See your sons murdered, and your wives, mothers, and sisters, doomed to prostitution! In the name of the merciful God! and by all that life is worth, let it no longer be a debatable question, whether it is better to choose LIBERTY or DEATH!

In 1822, Denmark Vesey, of South Carolina, formed a plan for the liberation of his fellow men. In the whole history of human efforts to overthrow slavery, a more complicated and tremendous plan was never formed. He was betrayed by the treachery of his own people, and died a martyr to freedom. Many a brave hero fell, but History, faithful to her high trust, will transcribe his name on the same monument with Moses, Hampden, Tell, Bruce, and Wallace, Toussaint L'Ouverture, Lafayette and Washington. That tremendous movement shook the whole empire of slavery. The guilty soul thieves were overwhelmed with fear. It is a matter of fact, that at that time, and in consequence of the threatened revolution, the slave states talked strongly of emancipation. But they blew but one blast of the trumpet of freedom, and then laid it aside. As these men became quiet, the slaveholders ceased to talk about emancipation; and now, behold your condition today! Angels sigh over it, and humanity has long since exhausted her tears in weeping on your account! . . .

1. On Henry Highland Garnet (1815–1882), his AME connections, and his interest in Vesey, see Part V, pp. 699–700.

"Speech by Henry Highland Garnet Delivered before the National Convention of Colored Citizens, Buffalo, New York, 16 August 1843," in *The Black Abolitionist Papers, Volume III: The United States, 1830–1846*, ed. C. Peter Ripley (Chapel Hill: University of North Carolina Press, 1991), 409.

Boston *Emancipator*

Wednesday, June 16, 1847

AN EXTRAORDINARY TRIAL.[1] We make no apology for publishing the following long report of an extraordinary trial in Charleston, South Carolina. . . .

Before this witness left the stand, B. F. HUNT, Esq.,[2] one of the counsel for the prisoners, rose and opened the defence before the jury in substance as follows:

. . . He said that the scene before them was a very novel one; and, whether for good or evil, he would not pretend to prophesy. It was the first time, in the history of this State, that a lady of good character and respectable connections stood arraigned at the bar, and had been put on trial for her life, on facts arising out of her domestic relations to her own slave. It was a spectacle consoling, and cheering perhaps, to those who owned no good will to the institutions of our country; but calculated only to excite pain and regret among ourselves. He would not state a preposition so revolting to humanity, as that crime should go unpunished—but judicial interference between the slave and the owner was a matter at once of delicacy and danger. It was the first time he had ever stood between a slave owner and the public prosecutor; and the sensations were anything but pleasant. This was an entirely different case from homicide between equals in society. Subordination is indispensable, where slavery exists; and in this there is no new principle involved. The same principle prevails in every country—on shipboard and in the army a large discretion is always left to the superior. Charges by inferiors against their superiors were always to be viewed with great circumspection at least, and especially when the latter are charged with cruelty or crime against subordinates. In the relation of owner and slave there is an absence of the usual motives for murder, and strong inducements against it on the part of the former. Life is usually taken, from avarice or passion. The master gains nothing, but loses much, by the death of his slave; and when he takes the life of the latter deliberately, there must be more than ordinary malice to instigate the deed. The policy of altering the old law of 1740,[3] which punished the killing of a slave with fine and political disfranchisement, was more than doubtful. It was the law of our colonial ancestors—it conformed to their policy and was approved by their wisdom, and it continued undisturbed by their posterity until the year 1821. It was engrafted on our policy in counteraction of the schemes and machinations or in deference to the clamors of those who formed plans for our improvement, although not interested in nor understanding our institutions, and whose interference led to the tragedy of 1822. He here adverted to the views of Chancellor Harper[4] on this subject, who, in his able and philosophical memoir on slavery, said: "It is a somewhat singular fact, that when there existed in our State no law for punishing the murder of a slave, other than a pecuniary fine, there were, I will venture to say, at least ten murders of freemen for one murder of a slave. Yet it is supposed that they are less protected than their masters." . . .

1. In 1847, Eliza Rowand stood trial in Charleston, indicted for whipping to death one of her female slaves. The jury acquitted her. In addition to the detailed article in the *Emancipator,* see *Charleston Courier,* May 5, 1847; "Trial of Mrs. Eliza Rowand," Charleston *Southern Patriot,* May 7, 1847.

2. Colonel Benjamin Faneuil Hunt (1792–1854), charter member of the South Carolina Association, planter and lawyer, acted as attorney for the defense. Massachusetts-born and Harvard-educated, Hunt settled in Charleston in 1810. He acted as attorney for the state in the volatile Elkison Case (1823), defending the Negro Seamen Act, discussed in Part V, pp. 644–48. See *BDSCHR* 5: 132–34.

3. Hunt references the Negro Act of 1740, particularly article thirty-seven, which punishes whites guilty of "wilfully murder[ing]" slaves with a fine. See Part II, pp. 124–25.

4. Born in the British Leeward Island of Antigua, Chancellor William Harper (1790–1847) enjoyed a distinguished career in South Carolina as a lawyer, judge, and proslavery intellectual. His essays had considerable influence on southern statesmen like John C. Calhoun. The quote is drawn from Harper's "Memoir on Slavery," *Southern Literary Messenger* 4 (October 1838): 617. See also *BDSCHR* 5: 119–21; Elizabeth Fox-Genovese and Eugene D. Genovese, *The Mind of the Master Class: History and Faith in the Southern Slaveholders' Worldview* (Cambridge, UK: Cambridge University Press, 2005), 492, 708.

Philadelphia *Pennsylvania Freeman*

Thursday, July 29, 1847

. . . In the summer of 1822, just 25 years ago this month, and the 3d day after the "glorious 4th," we took our departure from Savannah for the north, intending to stop for a short time in Charleston, for the purpose principally of greeting once more, and as we then thought and as it has since proved, for the last time, those friends and familiars to which a three years residence in the Queen City of the South had somewhat endeared us. Rumors had reached Savannah, on the eve of our departure from that place, that an alarming insurrection had occurred, or was about to break out in Charleston, and we were strongly advised not to touch there, but make our way by sea directly to the north. This circumstance, however, excited youthful curiosity and confirmed rather than weakened the intention of visiting the infected city, for our apprehensions of evil refused to be excited, and although our convictions with regard to slavery were, that it would eventually terminate in blood and violence, yet we could not feel that the beginning of that end had come, or that any other than a partial and abortive attempt had been, or was about to be made. and such proved to be the fact. If any serious intention of revolt was entertained by any one or more of the black population, which I did then, and have ever since doubted, it was certainly abortive. The white population were however most thoroughly alarmed, and it would have been little short of treason to express any skepticism on the cause of their fear. The first alarm had in a measure subsided, but yet the most extravagant rumors were afloat, which men whispered into each other's ears in the street, first casting about with a hurried look to see if there was a clear coast, free from dangerous eaves-droppers. This, however, soon wore off, and then people boasted how promptly and easily the insurrection (which had never existed) had been put down, and how impossible it was for the negroes ever to succeed in any attempt of the kind. During the fortnight passed in Charleston, I believe the first and the last executions for participation in this insurrection took place, and the number of victims amounted to about thirty. How many were whipped and otherwise tortured I had no means of knowing, the executions, only, being public. One of these I attended, the first and last I ever went to see; I went for the purpose of noting how the colored population were moved by the spectacle of the sacrifice of three of the[i]r fellows, one of whom was a reputed ring leader in an attempt to secure for themselves those "inalienable rights" which in our national creed are so strongly insisted upon as the birth-right of every human being, and which, by our national practice, are so grossly outraged. The victims, however, perished without eliciting any sign or sympathy on the part of their colored brethren, who witnessed the sacrifice.

What evidence there was to found or sustain the charge of an intent to raise the standard of revolt among the slave population, we of course never knew, nor were the public any wiser than ourselves, on this point; of course no one doubted it then, whatever they may have done since, and it is no less true, that no one except the Court of magistrates and freeholders which tried the negroes had any evidence whatever on the subject.[1] My own impression then, and conviction since, was and has been that no insurrection or violence was intended or thought of, certainly by any half dozen in the whole city; possibly two may have entertained such an idea, or they may not have done so.

Many circumstances tended to create and strengthen this opinion, and not among the least was the fact that the court especially created to try the accused in such cases, consisted of, I think, three magistrates, (justices of the peace) and four freeholders, held their sessions with closed doors, and elicited testimony by threat and torture. Another circumstance which excited suspicion was the pertinacity with which Gen. Hamilton, then Intendant of the City, and since of much notoriety in Texan affairs and history, sought to elicit a confession from Gullah Jack, a reported leader of the insurrection, while he stood upon the drop with a comrade on either hand with ropes about their necks and ready to be launched into eternity.[2]

Hamilton besought him, long and earnestly to make a full confession, reminding him of his offended God whose *justice he had violated,* and before whose judgment he was soon to appear; and the only reply was "Massa Hamilton I don't know anything about it—I am innocent." After a pause, in this horrid situation, Hamilton again approached the gallows, and again urged a confession. The negro again protested his entire ignorance of the whole affair, and his innocence of any design of wrong, in words of sober earnestness, and with a calm, though depressed manner; and thus he died, and during a fortnight, about every other morning were such scenes enacted on Charleston neck, and thus ended the so-called insurrection of 1822. . . .

1. The writer was incorrect on this point. See the Charleston Poor-House Records, Part II, pp. 99–100, which indicate that both white and black ministers were allowed into both the Poor-House and the Work-House to hear final confessions from the accused.

2. This statement suggests that the writer, contrary to claims made in the essay, did not actually witness this alleged conversation, since the only slave beside Gullah Jack Pritchard to die on July 12 was John Horry, who neither claimed to be innocent nor died penitent. The writer also claims that he witnessed the execution of three bondmen, but on no day in 1822 was that number executed; one would assume that nobody could be mistaken on whether they witnessed the death of two or three men. In addition, the Court of Magistrates and Freeholders had two magistrates and five freeholders.

"A Colored American"[1] on the Events of 1822, in 1850

. . . [T]he beginning and ground work for modern persecution against the free colored American people . . . began in the latter part of 1819, and has continued to operate with demoniac ferocity upon defenceless, innocent free colored Americans, up to the present day. Perhaps it was about three years after this period that the philanthropic and patriotic Denmark Vesey, well known for his industrious habits as a carpenter, and moral pursuits in life as a Christian, in full communion in one of the Established churches in Charleston,[2] with his coadjutor, Peter Poyas, a ship carpenter of some eminence, a holy and devout man, and four other equally worthy patriots, suffered martyrdom, merely for an oral review of their grievances, in their outraged rights and privileges, perpetrated on them and their enslaved brethren by the enactment of new and cruel laws for that express purpose, without any justifiable cause, and, as it had been alleged, for a contemplated insurrection o[f] the slaves in Charleston in the month of June, 1822.

As I have already stated, the recommendation of the Governor, with reference to ameliorating the condition of the free colored people, appeared to be just the thing that was wanted as an excuse for those of the new school party to foist themselves into public favor, on a substantial platform; that is, to commence a fresh and unprovoked public persecution against the orderly, well-behaved, free colored people in Charleston, who at that time appeared to be growing into affluence and respectability. The subject of the recommendation of the Governor was referred to the Judicial Committee, of which Mr. Prioleau,[3] a gentlemen of great influence and respectability, and deservedly popular with all parties of citizens, was, I think, chairman—a new party man, a quid,[4] who reported recommendations of laws adverse, not only towards free colored foreigners, but against native born South Carolinians—denying to that useful and industrious class of citizens many privileges and rights they had heretofore enjoyed. Besides this gross innovation on liberty and the rights of man, the Committee reported the propriety of the Legislature to enact laws forbidding slaves in future, no matter how enterprizing, industrious, or meritorious their moral character might be, from being manumitted, except by special law of the Legislature when in session in Columbia; and then the manumitted slave be expelled immediately beyond the limits of the State, never to return within its precincts under severe penalties: which Report was accepted and adopted as a part of the fundamental laws of the State of South Carolina.[5]

Hence the prospects of the slaves for freedom were blasted; many of whom had toiled anxiously at night to earn sufficient means to purchase freedom for themselves; all of whom aspired to the manly boon of freedom, the declaration of their masters to the contrary notwithstanding. Freedom many of the slaves resolved to have at all hazards. Many of them, in confidence reposed in their masters, in addition to their wages, paid large sums of money to their masters—hard earnings at night work, for the express purpose of purchasing their freedom; all of which, by the enactment of erroneous and cruel laws, was lost to the poor slaves forever.

Several years after the enactment of laws to cut off entirely all hopes, and to prevent the slaves from acquiring their liberty by purchase . . . it is probable that a party of these disappointed slaves, justly incensed with the cruel passage of such uncivilized laws, which were a great and intolerable hinderance to their peace and happiness, had conspired to free themselves from the yoke of the most unholy bondage ever invented by man in that liberty-loving country—to become owners of their own sacred persons, over the bodies of their masters.[6] In this matter, however, they failed owing to one of the party who was found to be a traitor[7] to their supposed righteous cause, who communed with a free colored man[8] on the subject of their intention to make an attempt to liberate themselves, who in turn communicated the whole subject matter to the constituted authorities of the city of Charleston; which timely information saved the city from a bloody servile contest. But it resulted in the capture of the entire band of patriots, and in their subsequent execution—the most barbarous on record in that day—notwithstanding the sanctity of their cause, made holy by the American Revolution.

The mock and summary trial of those brave men, after the alleged plot was discovered and the party taken prisoners, exceed credence, and will ever blight the escutcheon of the Palmetto State. A Court was summoned for the express purpose of trying the contemplated conspirators, composed of gentlemen slaveholders, upon the plan of Judge Lynch, for which the South is peculiarly celebrated. The proceedings were, as usual when slave interests are supposed to be interfered with, a solemn farce; and in this form the business was conducted. Freeholders were readily selected, pre-disposed to condemn and hang every prisoner brought before them on the charge of insurrection ("as a terror to the slaves, to keep them in awe for a quarter of a century," as one of the prosecutors said, and that there was "nothing too bad for the slaves to contemplate doing, but the masters had to punish them for it,")[9] without sufficient lawful evidence that was necessary to convict anybody except in the Slave States. The prisoners were arraigned in the most despotic form of the darkest gone-by age, where they were truly forlorn. No lawyer dared to defend them fairly or professionally. I think the Governor and one of the Judges of the Supreme Court were threatened with violence for expressing an opinion adverse to the ruling party of the city at that time.

Under such charges as were brought against the accused, one of the prisoners, whose name was Pharo,[10] acted as States-evidence on the promise of rewards, with security for his life; which promise the honorable Court failed to keep, and Pharo was condemned and hung with twenty-one others of the so-called conspirators, at the lines of Charleston, after every information was extracted from him, and, as it was alleged, he proved himself to be a false witness. . . .

In this horrible situation he was led out of prison to be executed, without friend or relative to assuage or console the culprit in his overwhelming calamity. Nay, the endearing ties of nature were ruthlessly sundered by the demon "office-hunter;" neither wife nor children, ah, no! no colored persons whatever were allowed to manifest the slightest grief for affliction in their family. . . . [N]or were the free colored people allowed to wear a bit of crape to mourn the loss of father, mother, brother, sister, daughter or son, but the act was construed into sympathy for the contemplated conspirators. . . .

The matter of hanging the contemplated conspirators, and whipping and stripping the peaceable colored people of their black dress, crape, &c., continued for several weeks, and would perhaps have continued much longer . . . but some of the citizens who had already suffered great loss in having their slaves hung without full remuneration for their value, and the fears of others who were surfeited in seeing, and having their property in human flesh sacrificed in order to gratify and pave the way of a few young men to office, without sufficient pay for their loss of property in the condemned slaves (Governor Ben——tt, the then executive of the State, perhaps would have hesitated to take $10,000 for two of his slaves[11] that were executed for being declared leaders of the contemplated conspiracy. They were men above the ordinary standing of first-rate slaves, of deep piety and experience—ingenious engineers and millwrights; indeed, it was said of them they were above mediocrity); when one of the freeholders, as I have been informed, devised the following plan to rid themselves of the odious measures:—

A rash youth had, by his advice and zealous counsel, put the city under. He sent into the interior of the country, beyond the residence of any of the reported contemplated conspirators, and had two of his slaves brought before the august assembled Court, to discover what effect their appearance would have on the secret evidence, dressed as they were in their country rags. The secret witnesses, after reviewing carefully the persons brought before them for inspection, declared that there was no accusation against them, and they were discharged free from blame into the hands of their owners: the identical slaves were washed and dressed fashionably, and again presented before the Court for examination, on charges pretended to be preferred against them, when the same disinterested, pure witness, who had previously declared these men innocent of any criminal charge against the State, without hesitation, on their second and improved appearance before the Court, pronounced these very men participants in the scheme of the contemplated conspiracy.

The success of this method on the part of the Court to detect false witness was complete, for they had become surfeited of their own abominable work; and stayed the execution of more than a hundred valiant victims prepared by their order for the scaffold, as the court themselves declared in a publication issued by authority from one of the public presses in Charleston, the contents of which has escaped my memory. . . . Some of the honorable members of the Court owned slaves who were implicated in the affair of the contemplated insurrection.[12] That circumstance, perhaps was one of the chief motives of humanity that influenced the court to stay their hand and authority. . . .

The day on which twenty-two of the patriots were hung, or rather sacrificed to the wicked principles of slavery, at one time, owing to some bad arrangement in preparing the ropes—some of which were too long, others not properly adjusted so as to choke effectually the sufferers to death, but so as to give them the power of utterance, whilst their feet could touch the ground—they, in their agony of strangulation, begged earnestly to despatched; which was done with pistol-shot by the Captain of the City Guard,[13] who was always prepared for such an emergency; i.e. shooting slaves.

I recollect seeing him shoot down dead a colored man,[14] who did not give him the slightest offence, in Bull street, Charleston, opposite the residence of Major Hamilton, sen. . . .

Denmark Vesey, according to the printed report, by the authority of the city of Charleston, if my memory is correct, was a native of Africa,[15] from whence he was taken . . . in his youth, and carried to St. Domingo. . . . It is there, in that country, perhaps, the seed of patriotism was sown in the heart of Vesey, the head and front of the alleged contemplated conspiracy, which might have had an influence on him, nobly to hazard his valuable life against such odds, the army of the Northern States, in arranging and developing a plan upon the most extensive scale for the attempted emancipation of his enslaved brethren. It was said, also, of the blind man, whom the Court of Freeholders had seen fit to excuse from sharing the fate of thirty-six of his less fortunate brethren on the scaffold, owing to his blindness—his name I do not recollect[16]—but of whom it was said, that he was a West India Frenchman, of the Haytian Republic; it was also said that he gave considerable aid with his judicious council and advice to that patrician band of worthies, in the movements of the alleged contemplated conspiracy, the matter of which plan was nearly or quite consummated, only waiting the proper period for concentrate action. The arrangements, it was said, were more extensive for a general attack upon the city, with prospects of successful execution than any heretofore contemplated insurrection meditated by the slaves, the entire body of whom were men of great respectability and intelligence in their respective spheres of life, many of whom were head men, entrusted with the entire control and management of their owners' business. They were well aware of the importance and magnitude of the hazardous contemplated enterprize. Indeed, had the affair riped into execution, nothing short of Uncle Sam's long and ponderous arm, and that from the Northern States, would have availed the South much good in a contest for Liberty brought about by a determined revolutionary spirit of her slaves, led on by such patriotic bravery as Denmark Vesey, Peter Poyas, and other martyrs in the art of Freedom, eminently possessed. . . .

1. Scholars have speculated about the authorship of this curious pamphlet. Herbert Aptheker, "Militant Abolitionism," *JNH* 26 (October 1941): 463n59, appears to have been the first to make Henry Bibb (1815–1854), a runaway slave from Kentucky who escaped to the North to become a prominent abolitionist, a strong possibility. Bibb clearly had an ardent interest in the Vesey affair, publishing *Slave Insurrection in 1831, in Southampton County, VA., Headed by Nat Turner, also a Conspiracy of Slaves, in Charleston, South, Carolina, in 1822* (New York, 1849). In this work, however, Bibb essentially quotes at length from James Hamilton Jr.'s *Account of the Late Intended Insurrection.* The New York Public Library's copy of the rare pamphlet by "A Colored American" has "[Hamilton, T]" scratched onto it, leading other writers, such as David Robertson, *Denmark Vesey: The Buried History of America's Largest Slave Rebellion and the Man Who Led It* (New York: Knopf, 1999), 122, to add Thomas Hamilton (1823?–1865) as another candidate for authorship. Hamilton, a free black from New York City, published the *Weekly Anglo-African* and had strong connections to the AME Church. Whoever the author was, "A Colored American" claimed to have spent time in Charleston and witnessed the person who was captain of the City Guard when slaves were being hanged in 1822 shoot a slave in the city. William Pritchard Dove (1789–1828) occupied that post as far back as 1818. Given the birth dates of both Bibb and Hamilton and the absence of evidence placing either man in Charleston from 1822 to 1828, the likely identity of "A Colored American" is probably someone other than Bibb or Hamilton. Free black abolitionist Robert Purvis (1810–1898), who often referred to himself in his writings as a "colored American," remains a

possibility. He left Charleston in 1819 to settle, as did many other free colored Charleston émigrés, in Philadelphia. See Margaret Hope Beacon, *But One Race: The Life of Robert Purvis* (Albany: State University of New York Press, 2007), esp. 7–9.

2. Denmark Vesey did, indeed, become a member of an established church in Charleston, the Second Presbyterian Church, in 1817. See Part I, p. 25.

3. "Colored American" correctly remembered that Samuel Prioleau (1784–1840), brother-in-law of James Hamilton Jr., was a member of the Judiciary Committee at the time of the passage of the 1821 restrictive manumission law. See "Legislature of South-Carolina in Senate," Charleston *City Gazette and Commercial Daily Advertiser,* December 20, 1820, and *BDSCHR* 5: 214–15.

4. By "quid," Colored American" refers to various factions within the Democratic-Republican Party whose particulars varied from state to state. Samuel Prioleau, like James Hamilton Jr., was, in 1821, a neo-Federalist or, as some newspapers called him, a Federal Republican. See *Hallowell* (ME) *Gazette,* November 17, 1819.

5. For the law itself, see Part I, pp. 61–63.

6. Modern scholarship has tended to discount or ignore the manumission law as a significant contributor to slave unrest before the Vesey affair. "Colored American," however, clearly had strong links to members of Charleston's slave community in the 1820s. Michael P. Johnson, "Denmark Vesey and His Co-Conspirators," *WMQ* 58 (2001): 962–63, suggests that Vesey and Charleston's slaves may have read the language of the manumission legislation as a general emancipation, given the state legislature's use of the word "emancipation" in the 1821 law. "Colored American's" pamphlet casts doubt on that argument, indicating that Charleston's slaves had a basic understanding of the law's intent.

7. Peter Prioleau (Desverney).

8. William Penceel.

9. The writer's second quotation paraphrases part of the last line in Hamilton's introductory statement "To the Publick" in *An Account,* 2: "[T]here is nothing they [the slaves] are bad enough to do, that we are not powerful enough to punish."

10. Pharo Thompson belonged to the widow Jane Thompson (d. 1840). See Part III, p. 218 n1.

11. Actually Governor Bennett lost three slaves to Judge Lynch: Ned, Rolla, and Batteau, all hanged along with Denmark Vesey on July 2.

12. The calendar in *OR* indicates that only one member owned a slave who was tried by either of the two courts. Stephen belonged to Thomas Rhett Smith (1768–1829), freeholder on the second court, and was acquitted and released by the first court.

13. William Pritchard Dove (1789–1828) was elected to the position of captain of the City Guard as early as 1818 and remained in that position at the time of the Vesey affair. See "Election of City Officers," Charleston *City Gazette and Commercial Daily Advertiser,* October 20, 1818.

14. This statement and the paragraph above it indicate that "Colored American" had spent time in Charleston and had observed the summary execution of a person of color by a captain of the City Guard.

15. Neither Hamilton's *Account* nor the *OR* suggest that Vesey was born in Africa, although the testimony of "Colored American" accords with that of Thomas Cilavan Brown. See Part V, pp. 496–97 n1, and Part VII, p. 749.

16. As the court record included on p. 352 in Part III indicates, this was a blind man identified only by the name of Philip.

A Colored American, *The Late Contemplated Insurrection in Charleston, S.C. with the Execution of Thirty-Six of the Patriots . . .* (New York, 1850), 4–9.

Reverend Moses Stuart[1] Remembers the Executions, 1850

. . . Our brethren of the South tell us, in conversation and in their journals that they have not the least fear in the world of the negroes. . . . They are not afraid, forsooth! So said a gentleman from the South, not long since, to a friend of mine, who asked him, whether he did not sometimes fear that danger was nigh. Not in the least, said he. . . . Had I been there, I could have suggested to the gentleman from the South, some reasons for abating the confidence which he manifested in his last reply—reasons drawn from what I personally witnessed, some 25 or more years ago, in Charleston. I arrived there a few weeks after the plan of an insurrection of the blacks had been concerted, and was within one day of being executed. The plan was, to set the city on fire in all parts simultaneously, in the dead of night; to massacre the whites in detail, as they came out of their houses; and then to take possession of all the shipping in the harbor, and compel or bribe the masters on board of the vessels, to carry them off to St. Domingo. A servant, who had been treated as a child, out of compassion to his master and his family, betrayed the secret of the conspirators. The leaders were forthwith apprehended, and speedy execution followed. Some 20 or 25 were hung before I left the North. But, for some two weeks before I left home, the papers had ceased to give us any more intelligence respecting the conspirators. When I arrived at Charleston, one of the magistrates of that city took me to his home, with the noble hospitality which characterizes the inhabitants of that city. From a room where we sat conversing, the next day after my arrival, there were visible some hillocks of sand, of considerable height and extent.[2] Pointing to them my friend said: Do you see that highest hillock? Yes, said I. There, said he, were executed our insurgent blacks. Well, I rejoined, and how did the black population behave, who went to witness the execution; and how did the criminals demean themselves? Behave? said he, why they marched by my house by thousands, in perfect triumph. They sung; they danced; they shouted, so as to make the welkin ring. And the criminals? said I. As to them, replied he, they considered themselves as martyrs to the glorious cause of liberty; and so did all the procession. They ascended the scaffold exultingly, and shouting as if their masters were within hearing, they said: Now we are going to have *freedom*, the glorious liberty of the children of God, and you can no more deprive us of that. But how is it, said I, that not a word has been said in your journals, for these three weeks, about the conspirators? For a very cogent reason, replied he, for we found that all the best servants in the city, male and female, were coming forward, and accusing themselves as partners in the conspiracy, even those who were as innocent of it as the child unborn. The spirit of martyrdom had got among them, and they had a burning thirst for the honors of a martyr's death, who perishes in the cause of liberty. The gentleman himself, i.e. my friend, had two slaves, man and wife, who were *inherited* by the mistress of the house, and who had been tempted to go to Liberia by offering to them their freedom and $500 besides, and yet they would not look at the offer. "Massa," said they, "you better care for us, than we for ourselves; we cannot go." I doubt not, from what I saw myself, that there are many such masters and mistresses in the South.

During all my stay in the city, not a black man could appear in the streets, after evening twilight commenced, without a permit in his hand from his master. The city-guard was trebled and quadrupled. No man could exempt himself from the duty of a watchman; not even the ministers of the gospel or the magistrates. Dr. Palmer, a highly respectable minister of the first Presbyterian church[3] there, told me that the magistracy would not suffer him to hire a substitute. Gov. Hayne himself went the rounds of a watchman's duty, and supervised the whole.

1. According to Mark A. Noll, *America's God: From Jonathan Edwards to Abraham Lincoln* (New York: Oxford University Press, 2002), 93, Moses Stuart (1780–1852), a Congregationalist theologian at the prestigious Andover Seminary, ranked as the foremost American "biblical scholar" of his time, a "pioneer of modern academic biblical scholarship." Although staunchly antislavery, he had a very high opinion of the intellectual quality, hospitality, and character of South Carolina's elite.

2. Stuart refers to the Lines, a string of fortifications that ran from the Ashley and Cooper rivers above the Charleston suburb of Hampstead. See Part II, p. 103 n3.

3. Stuart appears to have confused Benjamin Morgan Palmer the elder, a Congregationalist, with Benjamin Morgan Palmer the younger, a Presbyterian.

Moses Stuart, *Conscience and the Constitution with Remarks on the Recent Speech of the Hon. Daniel Webster in the Senate of the United States on the Subject of Slavery* (Boston, 1850), 92–94.

Abolitionist Edmund Jackson[1] on "Servile Insurrections" in 1851

. . . It was my fortune, or fate, to be in Charleston during the *quasi* insurrection of 1822, and certainly the scenes I witnessed, and the declarations of the impending danger that met us, at all times and on all occasions, forced the conviction that never were an entire people more thoroughly alarmed or more seriously affected by their fears, than were the people of Charleston at that time, and in view of such an event. No actual outbreak or overt act on the part of the blacks, however, occurred, and we had our doubts then, which after events and circumstances strengthened, that any insurrection was impending or seriously designed on the part of the accused negroes. But the city authorities and the people universally thought otherwise, and acted in accordance with their faith in the matter; for they arrested, according to rumor, some two or three hundred, and according to verity, hung about forty; and in proportion to their fear of the impending danger, so was their gratulation at so *cheap* an escape from it.

During the excitement and the trial of the supposed conspirators, rumor proclaimed all (and doubtless more than all) the horrors of the plot. The city was to be fired in every quarter, the arsenal in the immediate vicinity was to be broken open and the arms distributed to the insurgents, and a universal massacre of the white inhabitants to take place. Nor did there seem to be any doubt in the minds of the people that such would actually have been the result, had not the plot fortunately been detected before the time appointed for the outbreak. It was believed, as a matter of course, that every black in the city would join in the insurrection, and that, if the original design had been attempted and the city taken by surprise, the negroes would have achieved a complete and easy victory. Nor does it seem at all impossible that such might have been or yet may be the case, if any well arranged and resolute rising should take place.

The scenes I then witnessed impressed me with the opinion that the Slaveholders do actually believe in the liability of insurrection, live in the fear, greater or less according to circumstances, of an outbreak; and do think that under favoring influences, an insurrection of the Slaves may prove successful to an extent which would appall the stoutest, and involve a sacrifice of life and property to a terrible extent. . . . [2]

1. Edmund Jackson (1795–1875) was, indeed, in Charleston in 1822, operating a soap and candle manufactory on St. Philip's Street, Charleston Neck. He left the city to establish a similar business in Boston and became a committed abolitionist and educational reformer with a particular interest in the study of slave rebellion. See *CSCCD,* 84; Andrew Kull, *The Color-Blind Constitution* (Cambridge, MA: Harvard University Press, 1992), 35–37.

2. *The Liberty Bell, by Friends of Freedom,* a literary miscellany published in Boston and strongly committed to abolitionism, ran from 1839 to 1857 under the organizational and editorial guidance of Maria Weston Chapman (1806–1885). See Ralph Thompson, "The Liberty Bell and Other Anti-Slavery Gift-Books," *New England Quarterly* 7 (1934): 154–68.

Edmund Jackson, "Servile Insurrections," *Liberty Bell* (1851): 160–62.

William Cooper Nell[1] on African American Patriots, 1855

. . . During the Revolutionary War, Captain Veazie, of Charleston, was engaged in supplying the French in St. Domingo with slaves from St. Thomas. In the year 1781, he purchased DENMARK, a boy of about fourteen years of age, and afterwards brought him to Charleston, where he proved, for twenty years, a faithful slave. In 1800, DENMARK drew a prize of $1500 in the lottery, and purchased his freedom from his master for $600. From that period until the time of his arrest, he worked as a carpenter, and was distinguished for his great strength and activity, and was always looked up to by those of his own color with awe and respect.

In 1822, DENMARK VEAZIE formed a plan for the liberation of his fellow-men from bondage. In the whole history of human efforts to overthrow slavery, a more complicated and tremendous plan was never formed. A part of the plan matured was, that on Sunday night, the 16th of June, a force would cross from James' Island and land on South Bay, and march up and seize the Arsenal and guard-house; another body, at the same time, would seize the Arsenal on the Neck; and a third would rendezvous in the vicinity of the mills of Denmark's master. They would then sweep the town with fire and sword, not permitting a single white soul to escape.

The sum of this intelligence was laid before the Governor, who, convening the officers of the militia, took such measures as were deemed the best adapted to the approaching exigency of Sunday night. On the 16th, at 10 o'clock at night, the military companies, which were placed under the command of Col. R. Y. Hayne, were ordered to rendezvous for guard.

The conspirators, finding the whole town encompassed, at 10 o'clock, by the most vigilant patrols, did not dare to show themselves, whatever might have been their plans.

In the progress of the subsequent investigation, it was distinctly in proof, that but for these military demonstrations, the effort would unquestionably have been made; that a meeting took place on Sunday afternoon, the 16th, at 4 o'clock, of several of the ringleaders, at Denmark Veazie's, for the purpose of making their preliminary arrangements, and that early in the morning of Sunday, Denmark despatched a courier to order down some country negroes from Goose Creek, which courier had endeavored in vain to get out of town.

The conspirators, it was ascertained, had held meetings for four years, without being betrayed. The leaders were careful to instruct their followers not to mention their plans to "those waiting men who received presents of old coats, &c., from their masters," as such slaves would be likely to betray them.

DENMARK VEAZIE was betrayed by the treachery of his own people, and died a martyr to freedom. The slave who gave information of the projected insurrection was purchased by the Legislature, who held out to other slaves the strongest possible motives to do likewise in similar cases, by giving him his freedom.

The number of blacks arrested was one hundred and thirty-one. Of these, thirty-five were executed, forty-one acquitted, and the rest sentenced to be transported. Many a brave hero fell; but History, faithful to her high trust, will engrave the name of DENMARK VEAZIE on the same monument with Moses, Hampden, Tell, Bruce, Wallace, Toussaint, Lafayette, and Washington. . . .

1. Boston-born William Cooper Nell (1816–1874) knew David Walker and worked for William Lloyd Garrison's *Liberator.* Nell performed pioneering research into African American history, foreseeing that it would be vital in the struggles ahead against slavery and racial prejudice. See Robert P. Smith, "William Cooper Nell: Crusading Black Abolitionist," *JNH* 55 (July 1970): 182–99.

William C. Nell, *The Colored Patriots of the American Revolution with Sketches of Several Distinguished Colored Persons: To which Is Added a Brief Survey of the Condition and Prospects of Colored Americans* (Boston, 1855), 253–55.

New York *National Anti-Slavery Standard*

Saturday, October 25, 1856
SAFETY OF THE INSTITUTION OF SLAVERY
MILITARY STRENGTH OF THE SOUTH.

It is a wide-spread, but as widely erroneous an opinion at the North, that there is in the South a sense of insecurity and a constant apprehension of outbreaking insurrection. There never was a greater or more unfounded mistake. Our sense of security is perfect; we go to our slumbers, with our slaves, as our watchers and guardians, to protect us and our property from violence or spoliation. My servants lock me up at night, keep the key of my door, and unlock me in the morning, and *ex uno disce omnes*. . . . [1] Besides, in all the time that slavery has existed in the Southern States, the worst and the only serious insurrection which has ever occurred was that of Nat Turner, in Virginia, in 1831, when but sixty white lives fell a sacrifice to the mad and easily crushed *émeute.*[2] Why, accidents on railroads and steamboats, steam car and steam boiler explosions, and collisions of railroad cars on land, and of ships or other vessels on the water, destroy more lives, at a time, than are here chargeable to insurrectionary account; and Northern mobs are far more frequent and destructive to life and property than slave disturbances in the South. In Charleston and in South Carolina, my own native city and State, there has been no serious or well authenticated attempt at insurrection, since the commencement of the Revolution, and for a long time before that event, except the seasonably detected and easily frustrated one of 1822, which was of very limited extent. History records no previous one; although tradition does dimly shadow forth one, in an early period of our colonial existence when the African slave was fresh from his barbarian home. . . . [3]

Richard Yeadon,[4] *Ed. Charleston Courier*

1. "From one we can judge the rest," was taken from Virgil's *Aeneid,* book 2, lines 65–66. The editors thank John McMahon of Le Moyne College for identifying the source of this quotation.

2. Riot.

3. The author refers here to the Stono uprising of 1739, part of the so-called Gullah Wars and the crucial backdrop to the Negro Act of 1740.

4. Trained as a lawyer and a respected elder of Benjamin Morgan Palmer's Circular Church, Richard Yeadon (1802–1870) began work for the *Charleston Courier* in 1833. He came out of retirement in 1856 to once again serve as editor in large part because of the threat of Republicanism during the presidential election year. See Carl R. Osthaus, *Partisans of the Southern Press: Editorial Spokesmen of the Nineteenth Century* (Lexington: University Press of Kentucky, 1994), 72–76.

New York Daily Tribune

Wednesday, December 10, 1856

We have to record accounts of slave conspiracies in the South,[1] overtaken before they burst forth, but terrible as indications of an unfortunate state of society. History is philosophy teaching by example, and all history but proves that the enslavement of man by man has been accompanied by the fiercest reactions on the part of the oppressed. It was so in antiquity, when the light did not shine as now, and when letters were denied to but few. It was so when, at a later period of the old empires, the number of educated slaves had become the harbingers to the abolition of the system in Italy. It was so when the local jacqueries of France foretold the most exciting period of human annals—the servile uprising of the year 1793. It was so in St. Domingo when the African overcame the white man. What right, then, have we to expect that as we go on multiplying the slave population, mixing his blood with that of the white man until millions of "human brutes" and "human chattels" have the fire, the pride, the intellect and genius of the whites—no longer, as of old, the humble Guinea negro with his fetich, but the man bleached like his master—what right have we to expect that our history so outworking shall form an exception to the world's and be exempt from insurrections by the enslaved?

Will not the South learn? Will not Charleston remember the year 1820, when she was on the brink of being handed over to fire and sword, when the American-African population were under the influence of religious ecstacy as well as reactionary hate—when the negro leaders called on their brethren in secret to remember that God delivered

Daniel out of the lion's den, and Shadrach, Meshach and Abednego out of the fiery furnace? . . .

1. During and after the presidential election of 1856, whites in a majority of southern states uncovered what they believed were slave plots to rise in rebellion. Reporting on these plots, real and perceived, generated renewed interest in the history of slave insurrection, even if the reporting, as in this case, did not get all the facts correct. See "Negro Insurrections," *Richmond Whig*, December 16, 1856; Kenneth M. Stampp, *America in 1857: A Nation on the Brink* (New York: Oxford University Press, 1990), 35–36; Douglas R. Egerton, "The Slaves' Election: Frémont, Freedom, and the Slave Conspiracies of 1856," *Civil War History* 61 (March 2015): 35–63.

Charleston Mercury Reports on the Death of James Hamilton Jr.

Wednesday, July 22, 1857

. . . On his return to Charleston he commenced the practice of the Law, in co-partnership with the late Judge HUGER.[1] But his decided proclivity for public life and personal popularity did not allow him to remain long at the Bar, and he soon became a candidate for the Mayoralty of the city, was elected, and in the year 1822 greatly distinguished himself by his extraordinary activity, vigilance and executive ability, in detecting and defeating a deep laid and extensive plot for a negro insurrection, and in bringing to prompt and condign punishment the conspirators. His exertions were at that time esteemed of such signal ability and merit as to command the admiration and commendation not only of the citizens of Charleston, but of the entire State. He was, during this dangerous crisis, constantly in the saddle throughout every night for six weeks, and acted with a degree of energy and vigor in bringing the guilty to execution which has, beyond a doubt, given security for a century to the city of Charleston. . . .

1. Judge Daniel Elliott Huger (1779–1854).

Southern Literary Messenger

26 (1858): 53–55

THE LATE GEN. JAMES HAMILTON OF SOUTH CAROLINA

The tidings of the dreadful death of this great and good man, which fell from the telegraph upon his afflicted friends "like a thunderbolt from Heaven," were soon too bitterly confirmed. In the stillness of the midnight waste of waters and in the deep hush of his quiet slumbers, this noble spirit was, without a moment's warning, by an act of murderous negligence, hurled, amid the tumultuous rush of waters, into the presence of his eternal Creator. . . .

Gen. HAMILTON was born at Charleston, South Carolina, in the year 1789. His maternal grandfather, Thos. Lynch, not only signed the Declaration of Independence, but was the author of the first address and remonstrance to the British House of Commons in the first Congress of the Colonies after the passage of the stamp act. His father, the late venerable Major Hamilton, of the old continental line, was a favorite aid of the great Washington; commanded one of the regiments of Wayne's brigade, and was gallantly distinguished in almost every important battle of the Revolution. The invincible love of liberty and elevated spirit of patriotism for which his ancestors were so eminent, were inherited by himself in their highest vigor. In the war of 1812 Gen. (then Major) Hamilton served with great distinction throughout the Canadian campaigns. At the termination of the war he returned to the practice of the law in Charleston, in copartnership with the late eminent Judge Huger; and was soon after elected mayor of the city, the duties of which office he discharged with signal ability, and especially in the year 1822, when he exhibited remarkable energy, sagacity, and courage in suppressing a most dangerous [slave] insurrection. In the following year he was elected to the State Legislature, and was there also highly distinguished for the power, eloquence, and ability of his speeches on many important occasions. . . .

New York *Journal of Commerce*

Wednesday, October 26, 1859

INSURRECTIONS AT THE SOUTH—From the nature of the case, these outbreaks must ever be impotent to effect the object aimed at. The organizations of the land are too strong, and the resources of insurgents too feeble, even to command success. Besides, conspirators have some conscience left, and cannot always be reliable. Their dreadful secret cannot be kept long. It leaked out in Charleston, in 1822, and the Secretary of War was informed of the late plot in good time, though he chose to disregard it.[1] The very name of the ringleader in the Charleston plot was made known to the Secretary of War, and some of the movements were pointed out. The ringleader of the plot bore the name of Denmark Vezey. He was a free mulatto, cunning, active, restless, and possessing a talent of influencing negroes, which he plied with great dexterity. The negroes, long indulged, held secret meetings, some of which were professedly religious, and the exhorters among them participated in them. The could not be said to complain of oppression, for many of them were trusted and even petted servants in the households of their masters, carrying the keys, and enjoying the largest liberty compatible with their station; yet they devised one of the most diabolical plots of blood and murder that ever stained the annals of insurrection. The progress of their trial by a court of magistrates and freeholders was fearful, and fruitful in the disclosures. It was in evidence that the plan was to murder the masters, appropriate the desirable females to their own brutish uses, burn the city, and in the midst of the panic and conflagration, seize the ships in pier, and push for the island of St. Domingo. One of the praying negroes, smitten probably by his conscience, for he had been greatly indulged in the pious and respectable family of his master, gave the clue to the conspiracy, and after a long and full trial, some thirty or forty were sentenced to death, which sentence was thoroughly carried into execution by hanging. We have never heard of any subsequent attempt in that quarter to repeat this style of self-emancipation. We suspect the tradition of that awful retribution had been faithfully handed down to this generation, and that the example has been powerful to deter all like-minded servants from adventuring upon the repetition of the crime. . . . [2]

1. John C. Calhoun was secretary of war in 1822, and as the documents presented in Part II, pp. 101–7, point out, he most certainly did not disregard the Vesey plot.

2. Much of this story was reprinted in the Philadelphia *Public Ledger,* November 7, 1859.

A Black Pastor[1] Looks to the Heavens, November, 1859

. . . In the darkest night of our history in this land, a few stars of hope and promise have shone forth, like Phillis Wheatly and Benjamin Banneker—minds which stirred up thought for the race in Washington and Jefferson. The past has given, as a people, a Richard Allen, an Absolom Jones and a John Gloucester, a Theodore S. Dwight, a David Walker, to say nothing of a Denmark Veazy, or a Nathaniel Turner—names significant, and inspiring all. Among these millions are there not a host of others, which await only fair culture's genial hand? . . .

1. Connecticut-born abolitionist Amos Gerry Beman (1812–1874) was active in the Middletown Anti-Slavery Society and was pastor of the Temple Street African Church in New Haven. See R. A. Warner, "Amos Gerry Beman, 1812–1874, A Memoir of a Forgotten Leader," *JNH* 22 (1937): 200–221.

Amos Gerry Beman, "The Education of Colored People," New York *Weekly Anglo-African* 1 (November 1859): 338.

Buffalo *Morning Express*

Tuesday, December 13, 1859

. . . JOHN BROWN is the first white American citizen upon whom has been inflicted the penalty for treason, by due process of law. The highwayman MURRELL[1] was arrested for attempting to create an insurrection among slaves—but he was hung by Lynch process upon the charge of murder and other crimes. DOMINICK VESEY and the other leaders in the projected Charleston insurrection, of 1822, were many of them free persons of color; but none were entitled to citizenship under the laws of the State. JOHN BROWN is the first citizen, entitled to the right of suffrage, upon whom has been visited this final penalty. And the previous extended reputation, well-known character and severe sufferings of the unfortunate man, will make this, then day of his execution, a memorable one in the annals of the country.

1. John Murrell (d. 1844) led a notorious band of thieves and cutthroats in the Southwest. In 1835, in Hinds and Madison counties in Mississippi, rumors bruited about that Murrell intended to stoke a slave insurrection. A panic resulted; vigilant associations formed; both blacks and whites were lynched. See David J. Libby, *Slavery and Frontier Mississippi, 1720–1835* (Jackson: University Press of Mississippi, 2004), 104–15.

New York Herald

Friday, January 6, 1860

. . . THE INSURRECTION OF 1822 AT CHARLESTON. This was one of the most formidable conspiracies which ever was concocted in this country for the liberation of the slaves, and, had it not been discovered in time, would, in all probability, have been attended with the most terrible consequences. It appeared from the confessions of some of the ringleaders that the rising was to take place on Sunday, the 16th of June, at twelve o'clock at night, and that it was *their intention to burn the town and massacre the inhabitants.* The whole plan of the intended insurrection was, however, revealed by a favorite and confidential slave of a resident of Charleston, by whom it was made known at once to the Mayor of that city. This slave, according to the statement made to his master, and subsequently to the Mayor and Corporation of Charleston, had been informed of the plot by another slave named William, the property of Messrs. Paul. In the course of a conversation which took place between them in a fish market, William told him that the slaves had resolved on shaking off their bondage, and that if he would join them he would go with him to the man who had the list of names down, and who would enter his upon it. Alarmed at the design which had thus been made known to him, and in which he refused to have any part, he resolved, after consulting with a free man of color, to tell his master all he had heard.

It was in this way that the plot finally came to the ears of the city authorities, who immediately took measures to arrest the guilty parties and to prevent the uprising. William was accordingly taken into custody and examined, but refused at first to give information of the affair. He admitted having a conversation with the other slave, but denied all knowledge of the conspiracy. On a further examination, however, he admitted all that had been related to the authorities, and gave the name of the man who had the muster roll of insurgents. This man was called Mingo Harth, who, with another named Peter Poyas, was examined; but they preserved such an appearance of innocence of the charges made against them that they were discharged. Spies, however, were set to watch them while at large. William, who had meanwhile been subjected to solitary confinement, made a complete confession. His statement was corroborated by others, and the revelations that were made were, as we have stated, of the most horrible character. The disclosures showed that the negro insurgents expected to receive assistance from St. Domingo and England, and that some Frenchmen would also join them. Denmark Vesey, who was the ruling spirit, and who was a free negro of superior abilities, had stated to another negro that they (the blacks) *were fully able to conquer the whites if they were only unanimous and courageous as the St. Domingo people were.* He had intended in the event of his success to set the mills and dwellings on fire, and when the bells began to ring to kill every man as he came out of his house. *This should be done by negro servants with axes and clubs, and when they had accomplished their bloody work they were to murder the women and children, for that God had so commanded it in the Scriptures.* When he was told that it was cruel to kill women and children, he answered that it was for their own safety to do so, and *not to spare one white skin, for this was the plan they pursue in St.*

Domingo. In fact they seem to have decided on adopting the same fiendish and bloody course that marked the progress of revolution in that island. The design of Vesey was to induce the slaves in the country parts to co-operate with those in the city, and *then, after a general massacre of the unsuspecting inhabitants, to take possession of the forts and ships, to kill all on board of the latter except the captains, and then, having plundered the banks and the stores, to set sail for St. Domingo*. . . .

The public, after reading the foregoing historical accounts of negro insurrections, will be better qualified to judge of the results of a negro insurrection in this country. Those we have described were on a comparatively small scale, and can give us, after all, but an inadequate idea of the bloody and fearful consequences of a general insurrection in the South, where the negro population numbers four millions. The facts we have presented will enable them partially to realize the sanguinary results which must attend the designs of the Sewards, the Greeleys and the Garrisons should they prove successful in exciting to rebellion four millions of men whose instincts and passions are of the most brutal character. The inevitable conclusion is, that if these dreamers, politicians and fanatics are successful, it would result in a war of annihilation, which would present scenes the most revolting and terrific that the imagination can picture, and which would end in the extermination of the black race in the United States. . . .

Lydia Maria Child[1] to Thomas Wentworth Higginson,[2] Saturday, March 17, 1860

Wayland, March 17th, 1860

Dear Friend,

Such information as David or I have is most heartily at your service. But if you ever speak again of paying us for anything we can do in the Anti Slavery cause, or anything we can do for *you*, I shan't forgive it in a hurry.

In Philadelphia, some years ago, David became acquainted with Thomas C. Brown,[3] a free colored man, who was born in Charleston S.C. in 1800, and left the South in 1832. He was there at the time of Vesey's Insurrection; and we have a journal in which is written down some of his statements about it, as follows:

"In 1822, a slave,[4] brother of Mr. Devany,[5] now in Liberia, told of the projected insurrection to another colored man named Pensil;[6] and he communicated it to a white man. Pensil received a thousand dollars; and Devany had his freedom, and was set up in business with two or three drays and horses. Six slaves were executed first; afterward 22; and still later 13. I cannot recollect how many in the whole; but I do not think these were all. I was a young man then, and owing to the policy of preventing communication between free colored people and slaves, I had little opportunity for ascertaining how the slaves felt about it. I know several of them were abused in the street, and some put in prison, for appearing in sack-cloth. There was an ordinance of the city that any slave who wore a badge of mourning should be imprisoned and flogged. They generally got the law, which is 39 lashes; but sometimes it was according to the decision of the court. Denmark Vesey, sometimes called Telemachus, was a Corromantee negro.[7] He was brought from the coast by Capt Vesey, and bought himself for a low price, on account of his good conduct. He was a large, stout man.[8] He was called the leader of the insurrection, and it was said arms were collected in his house. I was a carpenter, and worked with Vesey who was also a carpenter; and I knew of his plan. I knew that several persons were in the habit of meeting at his house, who were afterward convicted and executed. I heard, at the time, of arms being buried in coffins, at Sullivan's Island.[9] But that is not the negro burying ground. The slaves are buried in a place called the Potter's Field,[10] and the colored people have a ground of their own. In the time of the insurrection, the slaves were tried in a small room, in the jail where they were confined. No colored person was allowed to go within two squares of the prison. Those two squares were filled with troops, 5000 of whom were on duty day and night. I was told Vesey said, to those that tried him, that *the work of insurrection would go on*; but as none but white people were permitted to be present, I cannot tell whether he said it."

The Thomas C. Brown, from whom the above is quoted, went to Liberia in 1832, but returned to Philadelphia. I don't know whether he is now living.

You will recollect that in Mrs. Stowe's Dred,[11] there is something about Vesey. See Vol. 1st from page 248 to 254.

A gentleman (I cannot remember whom) told me that he had talked with a South Carolinian about Dred, and that *he* said Mrs. Stowe ought to have chosen Peter Poyas[12] as the hero of the Insurrection; for his character was much stronger and sterner than Vesey's. He said that Peter was remarkable for a kind of magnetic power in his eye, which gave him great control over the colored people. If he fixed his eye upon one of them, he was sure to subdue him to his purpose. After his arrest, he was chained to the floor, in a cell with another of the conspirators. White men came and by promises and threats tried hard to ascertain the names of their accomplices. His companion, wearied out with fear and suffering, and stimulated by the hope of saving his life, at last began to confess. Peter rose up from the floor, leaned on his elbow, and fixing his powerful eye on the poor fellow's face, said "Die like a *man*!" and immediately laid down again. The scene was bright as a flash of lightning, but no promises, and no threats could extort another word from the prisoner. What *tortures* were applied we shall never know.

Mrs. Loring[13] was with her brother Dr. Gilman,[14] in Charleston when the executions were going on. Perhaps she could tell you something about it. Joshua Coffin[15] has written a Tract on Insurrections, recently published.

In New York, David and I were acquainted with a very interesting old colored woman, who had been a slave in Edenton N.C. on the borders of Virginia. Her name was Charity Bowery, and I told her story in one of my N. York Letters.[16] She had a vivid recollection of the excitement at the time of Nat Turner's insurrection. She sang to us some portions of a Methodist Hymn. "I has some friends has gone before me;

And I must try and go to meet them;
There's a better day a coming!
O, Glory! Hallelujah!"

Charity gave us a roguish look, as she said: "The whites would not let us sing *that.* They said, 'You want to kill your masters.' They thought we was going to *rise,* cause we sung 'A better day is coming.' At the time of the old Prophet Nat, the colored folks was afraid to pray loud; for the whites threatened to punish 'em dreadfully, if the least noise was heard." ["]The patrols was low drunken whites; and in Nat's time, if they heard any of the colored folks praying or singing a hymn, they would fall upon em and abuse 'em and sometimes kill em afore massa or missis could get to 'em. The brightest and best was killed in Nat's time. The whites always suspect such ones. They killed a great many at a place called Duplon.[17] They killed, Antonio, a slave of Mr. J. Stanley, an eminent lawyer, and a great friend of the colored people. Antonio was chained with another, whom they shot; then they pointed their guns at him, and told him to confess about the insurrection. He told 'em he didn't know anything about any insurrection. They shot several balls through him, quartered him and put his head on a pole, at the fork of the road leading to the Court. It was there but a short time. He had no trial. They never do. In Nat's time, the patrols would tie up the colored people, flog 'em, and try to make them lie against one another, and often killed them before anybody could interfere. Mr. James Cole, High Sheriff, said if any of the patrols come on his plantation, he would lose his life in defence of his people. One day, he heard a patroller boasting how many niggers he had killed. Mr. Cole said, 'If you don't pack up, as quick as God Almighty will let you, and get out of this town, and never be seen in it again, I'll put you where dogs won't bark at you.' He went off, and wasn't seen in them parts again." "If Polly McNiel was here, she could tell you about a great deal of shooting in Wilmington, (N.C) just before the Prophet Nat's time. The reason of it was this. A colored Baptist preacher, named Spaulding had one of Walker's books.[18] He lent it to another, and his master saw him reading it. The white folks got together and read the book, and they had the colored folks up in no time. The slave that was found reading the book said Brother Spaulding lent it to him. John Spaulding was a cooper, and was busy at his work when a crowd of people took him prisoner and put him aboard a vessel in chains. He never see his home again. He lives in New York now, and gets a living by blacking boots. I believe they shot eight slaves in Wilmington at that time. They shot Polly McNiel's husband; and she has been a poor broken hearted woman ever since. She has been here in New York; but I believe she is in Canada now. Her husband was the best carpenter in Wilmington. His name was Billy McNiel."[19]

In the Liberator Vol 2. 1832 there are some accounts of the Southampton Insurrection. In the Richmond Whig (Va.) there is also a narrative by the editor, who was on duty, in the militia. In one or the other of those papers, there is the following statement: "A party of horsemen started from Richmond with the intention of killing every colored person they saw in Southampton County. They stopped opposite the cabin of a free colored man, who was hoeing in his little field. They called out, 'Is this Southampton County?' He replied, [']Yes, sir; you have just crossed the line, by yonder tree.' They shot him dead, and rode on."

I think you would do well to consult with colored people, who have lived at the South. I heard Rev. Stella Martin[20] say, in a public address, that when he was a slave in Georgia, scarcely a month passed without *some* attempt at planning an insurrection, but the newspapers were very *silent* about it. He told of one case within his knowledge, where I think he said *nine* slaves were hung. He had learned to read, previous to this time, and he watched for the papers, to see if any account was given of the affair; but there was not the slightest allusion to it.

The only authentic account of Nat Turner's Insurrection, that I know of, is in Abdy's "Residence and Tour in the U. States" Vol. 3. page 391.[21]

A strike for freedom occurred in the jail or workhouse, Charleston, S.C. which is described by a Mr. Adams, an exile from S. Carolina. It was in the Tribune about 4 years ago.[22]

There were, as you recollect, attempts at insurrection during the Fremont campaign, owing to the Southerners railing against the Republican Party as enemies of their "peculiar institution."[23] I wish the charge were True. There were many slaves executed at that time. But, according to their usual policy, everything was kept from the public as much as possible.

Mrs. Adams, in her letter to John Adams, in Congress, says that the slaves in Massachusetts (in 1775) threatened to join the British unless they had their freedom.[24]

There was a conspiracy of slaves in the city of Lima for a general rising throughout the Vice-Royalty in 1809.[25]

Insurrection in Jamaica 1795. See "History of Maroons."[26] Another in Jamaica 1832; alluded to by Bleby, with some interesting details, in his First of Aug. Address.[27]

There was an insurrection in Barbadoes in 1816,[28] and I think one in Antigua,[29] not far from the same date.

See "Stedman's Narrative of a five Year's Expedition against the Revolted Negroes of Surinam."[30]

See the Oasis, page 113, for an account of Three Colored Republics formed of slaves.[31]

I do not at present think of anything else; but if anything comes to our memories, or "turns up" in the source of our reading, I will inform you.

I don't remember whether I wrote to tell you how much I liked your Rationale of Spiritualism. I sent it to Miss O[s]good of Medford,[32] saying it seemed to me the best thing that had been said on the subject; and she returned it with word that she thought so also.

I have a favor to ask of you. I have heard extraordinary things about a Mr. Foster, who is a medium in New York. If he is ever about in this region, and you happen to know of it, I wish you would inform me, that I may obtain an interview with him.

Oh, how disappointed I was in Seward's Speech![33] It seems to me such a falling off from the commanding position he had taken. My soul has been fretted all winter, by the goings on of Republican leaders in Congress; but always I solaced myself with the idea that when Sumner and Seward spoke, we should have something manly and direct. But Seward's Speech is nothing but a cold, cautious, diplomatic baiting for a nomination. How I wish there were virtue enough in the party to refuse him a nomination, for that very reason! But there is *not.* His adducing the "African in bondage," as one who would uphold this Union, made me gnash my teeth. There are some American[s], who are self-conceited from ignorance; but Mr. Seward *knew* he lied, when he said the lowest of our states was superior to any country in Europe. I wonder what old England will say to *that,* in view of the doings in Kansas, the presentations of canes in S. Carolina,[34] the lynchings in Virginia,[35] and the expulsion of free colored citizens from Missouri and Arkansas?[36] I wish Punch[37] would get hold of it, and serve it up in his best style.

I felt exceedingly heavy of heart, yesterday. Poor Stevens![38] what a sad reward for the rash generosity of his noble young heart! And he had not the sympathy and the glory to sustain him, that John Brown had. I had written to him often, and so felt somewhat as if I were acquainted with him.

I do not see the Atlantic Monthly, and have had no chance to read the articles to which you refer.

Yours cordially,

L. M. Child.

1. On Child, see p. 725 n1, above.

2. Thomas Wentworth Higginson (1823–1911) was a Massachusetts-born abolitionist who was to soon serve as colonel of the First South Carolina Volunteers, a federally authorized black regiment, from 1862 to 1864. When Child received this letter, Higginson was in the process of publishing a series of essays on black rebels in the *Atlantic Monthly.* No antebellum writer would investigate the subject of collective slave resistance more thoroughly. His *Atlantic* essays would be republished in book form in 1889 as *Travelers and Outlaws: Episodes in American History.* Excerpts from the *Atlantic* essay on Vesey appear below in this volume on p. 758. See Mary Thacher Higginson, *Thomas Wentworth Higginson: The Story of His Life* (Boston: Houghton Mifflin, 1914), 408.

3. On Thomas Cilavan Brown (b. 1800), the free colored carpenter from Charleston who emigrated to Liberia with members of Denmark Vesey's family and returned to give testimony about the colonization movement, see Part V, pp. 454 n1, 483–84 n1.

4. The "slave" mentioned here is none other than Peter Prioleau (Desverney).

5. Francis Devany (1797?–1833), the brother of Peter Prioleau (Desverney), once belonged to Langdon Cheves (1776–1857), a wealthy lawyer, planter, and banker who split time between Charleston and Philadelphia. Devany, once freed, lived in Philadelphia, and became a successful businessman, active in the colonization movement to Liberia. See "Examination," *African Repository and Colonial Journal* 6 (June 1830): 97–105; "Death of F. Devany, Esq.," *African Repository, and Colonial Journal* 10 (May 1834): 90.

6. "Pensil" is William Penceel. See Part II, p. 94 n53.

7. The designation "Corromantee" would have placed Denmark Vesey's origin in the Gold Coast region of West Africa. See Part I, p. 2 n3.

8. Michael P. Johnson, "Denmark Vesey and His Co-Conspirators," *WMQ* 58 (2001): 918, errs in writing that "no source documents Vesey's physical size."

9. Sullivan's Island borders the entrance to Charleston Harbor on the north. In 1822 it contained not only Fort Moultrie but white residences and an African American burial site, perhaps dating from the days when the island was used to quarantine imported African slaves. Brown's recollection challenges the contention of Richard C. Wade, "The Vesey Plot: A Reconsideration," *JSH* 30 (1964): 150, that "no cache of arms lay hidden about the city." Indeed, Brown suggests the authorities were looking in the wrong burial ground.

10. Potter's field, where the Citadel would be located, was a "common burial ground" for slaves and others of low status. See H. L. Pinckney, *Remarks Addressed to the Citizens of Charleston on the Subject of Interments and the Policy of Establishing a Public Cemetery, beyond the Precincts of*

the City (Charleston, SC, 1839), 4, and Michael Patrick Hendrix, *Down & Dirty: Archaeology of the South Carolina Lowcountry* (Charleston, SC: History Press, 2006), 53.

11. In Harriet Beecher Stowe's *Dred: A Tale of the Great Dismal Swamp* (New York, 1856), the main character was Denmark Vesey's runaway son.

12. James Hamilton Jr. regarded Peter Poyas, a ship carpenter, as "one of the principal ringleaders in the conspiracy, on whose courage and sagacity great reliance was placed" and "the most efficient of all the ringleaders . . . one who possessed the largest share of the confidence of Denmark Vesey, who was, in every sense of the term, the father of the plot." See Hamilton, *Account,* 6, 14.

13. Abolitionist Louisa Gilman Loring (1797–1868) was the wife of Ellis Gray Loring (1803–1856), one of the founders of the New England Anti-Slavery Society.

14. Samuel Gilman (1791–1858), brother of Louisa Gilman Loring, arrived in Charleston in 1819 to become pastor of the city's Unitarian Church. A Harvard graduate, Gilman would become one of Charleston's and the antebellum South's most respected divines, known for both his intellect and amiability. See John Macaulay, *Unitarianism in the Antebellum South: The Other Invisible Institution* (Tuscaloosa: University of Alabama Press, 2001), esp. 69–71.

15. Joshua Coffin (1792–1864) was an American abolitionist and essayist. In 1860, Coffin published *An Account of Some of the Principal Slave Insurrections,* which contained two brief mentions of Vesey.

16. Lydia Maria Child met Charity Bowery, a freedwoman from Edenton, North Carolina, in New York City and told her story in Letter V, January 20, 1844, in *Letters from New York: Second Series* (New York, 1845).

17. Duplin County, North Carolina, is about one hundred miles southwest of Edenton. Bowery is speaking of slaves in that county caught up in the repression associated with Nat Turner's revolt in 1831.

18. Rumors of slave plotting and insurrection swept several counties in North Carolina during the last months of 1830. White officials in Wilmington, North Carolina, arrested John Spaulding, a free black cooper and Baptist preacher. Spaulding had in his possession a copy of David Walker's incendiary *Appeal to the Colored Citizens of the World* (1829). Upon investigation, authorities discovered that a slave named Jacob Cowan had in his possession two hundred copies of the pamphlet for distribution. Both Spaulding and Cowan were removed from the state. See Peter Hinks, "David Walker's *Appeal,*" in *Encyclopedia of African American History, 1619–1895: From the Colonial Period to the Age of Frederick Douglass,* ed. Paul Finkelman (New York: Oxford University Press, 2006), vol. 2: 370.

19. Billy McNeil and six other slaves were executed in Wilmington in November 1831 for "conspiracy to make insurrection." See New York *Spectator,* November 22, 1831.

20. Reverend J. Sella, not "Stella," Martin (1832–1876) was born a slave in Charlotte, North Carolina, and sold eight times while still a child. After escaping north in 1856, he became a minister in Boston's First Independent Baptist Church. See *Lift Every Voice: African American Oratory, 1787–1900,* ed. Philip S. Foner and Robert Branham (Tuscaloosa: University of Alabama Press, 1998), 452.

21. Edward Strutt Abdy (1791–1846) actually had little new to say about Nat Turner's revolt in *Journal of a Residence and Tour in the United States of North America, from April, 1833, to October, 1834,* 3 vols. (London, 1835), although an appendix in volume 3 contains a transcription of Nat Turner's *Confessions* to Thomas Gray.

22. Child refers to an attempt by slaves to break out of the Charleston Work-House. At least three of the jailbreakers were executed. See "The South Carolina Work-House Insurrection," Rochester *North Star,* August 24, 1849.

23. During and after the 1856 presidential election, when one-time College of Charleston

student John C. Fremont was the first candidate of the Republican Party, whites in Arkansas, Georgia, Kentucky, Mississippi, North Carolina, South Carolina, Tennessee, Texas, and Virginia uncovered alleged slave plots.

24. Abigail Adams to John Adams, September 22, 1774, in *Letters of Mrs. Adams: the Wife of John Adams,* 4th. ed. (Boston, 1848), 24.

25. Child may have been thinking of the involvement of slaves at the beginning of the Spanish American revolutions, but Lima, Peru, was not the site of either a slave plot or slave insurrection in 1809.

26. Henry Bleby (1802–1882) worked decades as a Methodist missionary in the British Caribbean. He was in Jamaica at the time of the so-called Baptist War, the largest slave insurrection in the history of the British Caribbean. The insurrection erupted during the Christmas holiday in 1831 and continued for months before suppression. Bleby knew a number of the principals inculpated, including Sam Sharpe, one of the prime movers. His *West India Emancipation Vindicated* (1858) derived from an address he had delivered to the Massachusetts Anti-Slavery Society in July of that year.

27. R. C. Dallas, *The History of the Maroons, from Their Origin to the Establishment of Their Chief Tribe at Sierra Leone,* 2 vols. (London, 1803).

28. Child refers to the largest slave insurrection in the history of Barbados, involving thousands of slaves, in 1816. See Hilary Beckles, *Black Rebellion in Barbados: The Struggle against Slavery, 1627–1838* (Bridgetown, Barbados: Antilles Publications, 1984), 87–117.

29. Newspapers reported that in 1817, at about the time of an earthquake, authorities in the British Leeward Island of Antigua had mobilized forces in response to concerns about an impending slave insurrection. See, for example, *Newburyport* (MA) *Herald and Commercial Gazette,* January 27, 1818.

30. John Gabriel Stedman, *Narrative of a Five Years' Expedition against the Revolted Negroes of Surinam, in Guiana, on the Wild Coast of South America, from the Year 1772 to 1777* (London, 1796).

31. "The Three Colored Republics of Guiana," in *The Oasis,* ed. Lydia Maria Child (Boston, 1834), 113–26.

32. Probably Lucy Osgood (d. 1873), a close friend of Lydia Maria Child. See Carolyn L. Karcher, *The First Woman in the Republic: A Cultural Biography of Lydia Maria Child* (Durham, NC: Duke University Press, 1994), 5–6, 445, 576–77.

33. Senator William Seward (1801–1872), of New York, delivered an important speech on the admission of Kansas as a state on February 29, 1860.

34. In the aftermath of the caning of Massachusetts Senator Charles Sumner (1811–1874) by South Carolina Congressman Preston Brooks (1819–1857) in 1856, white southerners congratulated Brooks by presenting him with new canes to replace the one he had splintered over Sumner's head.

35. By "lynchings in Virginia," Child means the hangings of John Brown and others captured with him during the attack on Harpers Ferry.

36. In 1859, in the aftermath of John Brown's assault on Harpers Ferry, free persons of color in Missouri were being encouraged to emigrate to Haiti, and the state legislature passed a law to expel free persons of color. It was vetoed by the governor. In 1859, the Arkansas legislature passed legislation that gave free persons of color a choice between removal from the state or enslavement within it. *Boston Semi-Weekly Courier,* April 4, 1859; "Free Negroes in Arkansas," *New York Herald,* January 22, 1857; Ira Berlin, *Slaves without Masters: The Free Negro in the Antebellum South* (New York: Pantheon Books, 1974), 372–79.

37. *Punch* is the popular British satirical magazine founded in 1841.

38. Aaron Dwight Stevens (1831–1860) accompanied John Brown in his attack on the federal arsenal at Harpers Ferry. Captured along with Brown, Stevens was executed by hanging on March 16, 1860, one day before Child wrote her letter to Higginson. See David S. Reynolds, *John Brown, Abolitionist: The Man Who Killed Slavery, Sparked the Civil War, and Seeded Civil Rights* (New York: Knopf, 2005), 459–60.

William P. Palmer Collection, P-1090, Western Reserve Historical Society.

George Francis Train[1] on Slave Revolts, 1860

. . . These Maroons[2] ruled supreme in St. Domingo for eighty-five years. The French and Spanish combined to subdue them. These runaway negroes liked their African mode of bloodshed, Barbados can also testify to the brutality of the negro character. Had not the plot of 1649 been discovered,[3] all the whites would have perished, and the hanging of forty of the ring-leaders in 1689 saved the island a second time.[4] Then the "handsomest of the white women were to be reserved for their desires," says the historian. In 1702 they were equally unsuccessful.[5]

Martial law, organization of the militia, hanging of the chiefs, was the only salvation to this island in 1816. Parliamentary speeches started it, and on Easter day the destruction was to commence.[6] The fires swept over the plantations, burning down sugar-mill and cottage in all directions all for the Wilberforcean theory, that a negro is equal to a Caucasian![7]

The slave States are not barren of negro insurrections. In 1712 the negroes prepared to burn down New York, and nearly succeeded in 1741, "all the white men were to be killed, and the negroes were to take their wives." Fourteen blacks were burned at the stake and eighteen hanged for this little piece of mischief, when New York had only 10,000 population.[8]

Sunday is the day of massacre for this barbarous race—it's always on the Sabbath.[9]

The better the day, the better the deed, guides the negro assassin. The Nat Turner affair in Southampton County, Virginia, in 1831, was on Sunday.[10] Three hundred mounted negroes, armed to the teeth, cut down all before them. "Whole families, mothers, fathers, daughters, sons, sucking babies and school-children, were butchered by them, thrown into heaps, and left to be devoured by hogs and dogs, or to putrefy on the spot."

In Charleston, S.C., the whites were all to have been murdered on the 16th June, 1822. As usual the plot was to ripen on Sunday: but William, the slave of Mr. Paul, peached[11] and saved the city. Dominick[12] Vesey was the leading ruffian of this infernal plot. Thirty-five leaders were hung and a hundred sent out of the State. Only three years ago the people of Arkansas, Louisiana and Tennessee were alarmed at rumors of an insurrection to come off on Christmas Eve.[13] So long as there are negroes and whites in the same country, so long may we expect these periodical revolutions.

1. George Francis Train (1829–1904) was born in Boston and grew wealthy trading with Australia and Britain. Like many conservative northern businessmen, Train feared that antislavery agitation would disrupt the Union and endanger his business interests. See James McCague, *Moguls and Iron Men: The Story of the First Transcontinental Railroad* (New York: Harper & Row, 1964).

2. "Maroons" refer to runaway slaves.

3. Richard Ligon, *A True & Exact History of the Island of Barbados* (London, 1657), 46–47, remains the best starting point for the Barbadian plot of 1649, the first major act of collective slave resistance in the island's history. Investigations sparked by the betrayal of one of the plotters led to the execution of more than a dozen slaves.

4. Barbadian planters preempted no plot in 1689. Train may be referring to one that allegedly combined slaves and Irish indentured servants a few years before. See Jerome Handler, "Slave Revolts and Conspiracies in Seventeenth-Century Barbados," *New West India Guide* 56 (1982): 20–21.

5. Whites blamed slaves for fires that ravaged Bridgetown, Barbados, around Christmas Day, 1701. See Jerome Handler, "Slave Revolts and Conspiracies in Seventeenth-Century Barbados," *New West India Guide* 56 (1982): 29–30.

6. On other references to this conspiracy, see p. 755 n28.

7. Rumors that emancipation by royal decree was being thwarted by Barbadian planters helped spark the insurrection of 1816 on Easter Sunday, April 14. Train directs his sarcasm at William Wilberforce (1759–1833), one of the decisive political forces behind the ending of the slave trade and slavery in the British Empire. See Eric Metaxas, *Amazing Grace: William Wilberforce and the Heroic Campaign to End Slavery* (New York: HarperSanFrancisco, 2007).

8. On the New York slave insurrection of 1712 and the plot of 1741, which Charleston whites referenced in 1822 to fend off northern criticism, see Part III, p. 161 n10 and Part V, p. 504.

9. South Carolinian whites and other masters throughout the Americas recognized their vulnerability to slave unrest on Sundays, a time of greater mobility for slaves and of leisurely distraction for whites. Many acts of slave violence did indeed erupt on Sunday evenings. See Section XXXVI of the Negro Act of 1740, p. 124, in Part II and Sally E. Hadden, *Slave Patrols: Law and Violence in Virginia and the Carolinas* (Cambridge, MA: Harvard University Press, 2001), 140.

10. Nat Turner and six followers met to plot rebellion and have a feast in the woods on Sunday, August 21, 1831. The insurrection itself began in the early morning hours of Monday, August 22.

11. "Peached" meant to tell on.

12. Train may have read the Buffalo *Morning Express*, December 13, 1859, which also referred to Vesey as "Dominick."

13. Reports of slave unrest and plotting in the 1856 presidential year, which featured the first Republican candidate, John C. Frémont, circulated widely in newspapers. Genuine slave unrest at the Cumberland Iron Works in Tennessee received considerable attention. Whites in St. Martin and neighboring parishes in Louisiana claimed to have discovered plots as well. A story entitled "Servile Insurrections," which appeared in such publications as the *New Orleans Delta*, December 18, 1856, and Washington *National Era*, January 8, 1857, spoke of the three affected states together and may have been the source on which Train drew for his publication. See also Douglas R. Egerton, "The Slaves' Election: Frémont, Freedom, and the Slave Conspiracies of 1856," *CWH* 61 (2015): 35–63.

George Francis Train, *The Facts; or, At Whose Door Does the Sin (?) Lie? Who Profits by Slave Labor? Who Initiated the Slave Trade? What Have the Philanthropists Done?* (New York, 1860), 15–17.

Charleston Mercury

Monday, November 12, 1860

A WORD TO THE LADIES. . . . *Trials must come*—but let them come in the right way, and all will be well. Secede—put ourselves in a state of defence—be ready for any emergency, should the Government coerce and our sister States come not to the rescue. Let it be so. Better to perish beneath the shock than to live degraded!

Arming the State will also keep the negros in check. They are arrant cowards, these dear, dark friends of ours. Some of you remember how, in '22 they would shrink away at the gleam of their master's sword, as he armed for the nightly patrol. And the creaking of the horsemen's saddles, as they paraded the streets, sent them hiding every hole and corner. I was a very little child then, but I remember it all. We children knew more than the old folks the state of the mind in those alarming days. Our negros love us—they love our children, and will do us no harm if we are true to ourselves.

O women of Carolina! Mothers, sisters, wives, do not wear the white feather now unless, like that gallant king of old, it waves *on our men* to the van! A DAUGHTER OF SOUTH CAROLINA.

November 9, 1860.

New York *Weekly Anglo-African*

Saturday, April 27, 1861

"One man in the right, is a majority." Frederick Douglas crystalized the heroism that animates practical Abolitionists, in those ringing words. They were forcibly brought to our minds, by hearing a prominent orator say, that, being in the minority, it was no use trying, for colored men to attempt stemming the current. We wonder if he thought *that,* when, but a few years since, as a slave, he fled the land of bondage. Five hundred black men, divided into guerrilla bands, and working their way through the mountain Ranges of Virginia, Kentucky, Tennessee, Arkansas, and the swamps of the Atlantic Coast, can do more to destroy slavery, than five thousand Regulars. It only wants men determined to do or die. White men had this spirit at Harper's Ferry, on that memorable October morn. We want Nat. Turner—not speeches; Denmark Vesey—not resolutions; John Brown—not meetings.

Thomas Wentworth Higginson on Denmark Vesey, June, 1861

. . . My friend David Lee Child[1] has kindly communicated to me a few memoranda of a conversation held long since with a free colored man[2] who had worked in Vesey's shop during the time of the insurrection, and these generally confirm the official narratives. "I was a young man, then," he said, "and, owing to the policy of preventing communication between free colored people and slaves, I had little opportunity of ascertaining how the slaves felt about it. I know that several of them were abused in the street, and some put in prison, for appearing in sackcloth. There was an ordinance of the city, that any slave who wore a badge of mourning should be imprisoned and flogged. They generally got the law, which is thirty-nine lashes, but sometimes it was according to the decision of the Court. "I heard, at the time, of arms being fed into coffins at Sullivan's Island." "In the time of the insurrection, the slaves were tried in a small room, in the jail where they were confined. No colored person was allowed to go within two squares of the prison.

Those two squares were filled with troops, five thousand of whom were on duty, day and night. I was told, Vesey said to those that tried him, that the work of insurrection would go on; but as none but white persons were permitted to be present, I cannot tell whether he said it." . . . [3]

The first official report of the trials was prepared by the Intendant, by request of the city council. It passed through four editions in a few months,—the first and fourth being published in Charleston, and the second and third in Boston. Being, however, but a brief pamphlet, it did not satisfy the public curiosity, and in October of the same year (1822), a larger volume appeared at Charleston, edited by the magistrates who presided at the trials, Lionel H. Kennedy and Thomas Parker. It contains the evidence in full, and a separate narrative of the whole affair, more candid and lucid than any other which I have found in the newspapers or pamphlets of the day. It exhibits that rarest of all qualities in a slave-community, a willingness to look facts in the face. This narrative has been faithfully followed, with the aid of such cross-lights as could be secured from many other quarters, in preparing the present history.

The editor of the first official report racked his brains to discover the special causes of the revolt, and never trusted himself to allude to the general one. The negroes rebelled because they were deluded by Congressional eloquence, or because they were excited by a Church squabble, or because they had been spoilt by mistaken indulgences, such as being allowed to learn to read, "a misguided benevolence," as he pronounces it. So the Baptist Convention seems to have thought it was because they were not Baptists, and an Episcopal pamphleteer because they were not Episcopalians. It never seems to occur to any of these spectators that these people rebelled simply because they were slaves and wished to be free.

No doubt, there were enough special torches with which a man so skillful as Denmark Vesey could kindle up these dusky powder-magazines; but, after all, the permanent peril lay in the powder. So long as that existed, everything was incendiary. Any torn scrap in the street might contain a Missouri-Compromise speech, or a report of the last battle in St. Domingo, or one of those able letters of Boyer's which were winning the praise of all, or one of John Randolph's stirring speeches in England against the slave-trade. The very newspapers which reported the happy extinction of the insurrection by the hanging of "the last conspirator." William Garner, reported also, with enthusiastic indignation, the massacre of the Greeks at Constantinople and at Scio; and then the Northern editors, breaking from their usual reticence, pointed out the inconsistency of Southern journals in printing, side by side, denunciations of Mohammedan slave-sales and advertisements of Christian ones. . . .

More than a third of a century has passed since the incidents of this true story closed. It has not vanished from the memories of South Carolinians, though the printed pages which once told it have been gradually withdrawn from sight. The intense avidity which at first grasped at every incident of the great insurrectionary plot was succeeded by a distaste for the memory of the tale; and the official reports which told what slaves had once planned and dared have now come to be among the rarest of American documents. In 1841, a friend of the writer, then visiting South Carolina, heard from her hostess for the first time the events which are recounted here. On asking to see the reports of the trials, she was cautiously told that the only copy in the house, after being carefully kept for years under lock and key, had been burnt at last, lest it should reach the dangerous eyes of the slaves. The same thing had happened, it was added, in many other families. This partially accounts for the great difficulty now to be found in obtaining a single copy of either publication; and this is why, to the readers of American history, Denmark Vesey and Peter Poyas have been heretofore but the shadows of names.

1. As the letter of Lydia Maria Child to Thomas Wentworth Higginson, March 17, 1860, reproduced in this section, pp. 749–53 indicates, she, not her husband, David (1794–1874), provided Higginson with information about Vesey. Shortly after the publication of this essay, Higginson would become first a captain of the Fifty-first Massachusetts Infantry and, a year later, a colonel in the all-black First South Carolina Volunteers.

2. Higginson refers here to Thomas Cilavan Brown (b. 1800), the Charleston-born free black carpenter, mentioned by Lydia Maria Child.

3. According to the instructions given to the Poor-House director, black ministers, including lay preachers like Thomas Brown, may have been allowed to see the prisoners.

Thomas Wentworth Higginson, "Denmark Vesey," *Atlantic Monthly* 7 (1861): 728–44.

Philadelphia Inquirer

Thursday, June 27, 1861

A Terrible Reminiscence for To-Day.

In this month of June, in the year 1822, the people of Charleston were intensely excited and alarmed by the discovery of a widespread plot among their slaves to rise in revolt; and this day, the twenty-seventh of June, is the anniversary of that on which the leader of the insurgents was condemned to be hanged. As the Charleston *Mercury* is vehemently protesting against sending any more troops away from that State to Virginia, and as there are many indications of restiveness among the slaves throughout the South, this coincidence of time and of circumstance may give a reference to the more notable particulars of that conspiracy instructiveness as well as curious interest. . . .

As we have said, the plot never came to a head. It was exposed by one faithful slave to a free colored man, and this latter, acting upon a high sense of duty, caused it to be made known by the slave to his master, and thus, through the fidelity of these two men, Charleston escaped a scene of horrors. Though it is thirty-nine years to-day since VESEY'S condemnation, Charleston still shudders at the recollection of him and his conspiracy. Let us hope that richly as Charleston and the South merit the severest punishment for the calamities they have wantonly brought upon the country, that the avenging NEMESIS may never visit them in the horrid form of a servile insurrection.

Osborne P. Anderson[1] on John Brown, Gabriel, and Vesey, 1861

. . . There is an unbroken chain of sentiment and purpose from Moses of the Jews to John Brown of America; from Kossuth, and the liberators of France and Italy, to the untutored

Gabriel, and the Denmark Vesey's, Nat Turners and Madison Washingtons of the Southern American states. The shaping and expressing of a thought for freedom takes the same consistence with the colored American—whether he be an independent citizen of the Haytian nation, a proscribed but humble nominally free colored man, a patient, toiling, but hopeful slave—as with the proudest or noblest representative of European or American civilization and Christianity . . .

To go into particulars, and to detail reports current more than a year before the outbreak, among the many in the United States and Canada who had an inkling of some "practical work" to be done by "Osawattomie Brown," when there should be nothing to do in Kansas,—to give facts in that connection, would only forestall future action, without really benefiting the slave, or winning over to that sort of work the anti-slavery men who do favor physical resistance to slavery. Slaveholders alone might reap benefits; and for one, I shall throw none in their way, by any indiscreet avowals; they already enjoy more than their share; but to a clear understanding of all the facts to be here published, it may be well to say, that preliminary arrangements were made in a number of places,—plans proposed, discussed and decided upon, numbers invited to participate in the movement, and the list of adherents increased. Nine insurrections is the number given by some as the true list of outbreaks since slavery was planted in America; whether correct or not, it is certain that preliminaries to each are unquestionable. Gabriel, Vesey, Nat Turner, all had conference meetings; all had their plans; but they differ from the Harper's Ferry insurrection in the fact that neither leader nor men, in the latter, divulged ours, when in the most trying of situations. Hark and another met Nat Turner in secret places, after the fatigues of a toilsome day were ended; Gabriel promulged his treason in the silence of the dense forest; but John Brown reasoned of liberty and equality in broad daylight, in a modernized building, in conventions with closed doors, in meetings governed by the elaborate regulations laid down by Jefferson, and used as their guides by Congresses and Legislatures; or he made known the weighty theme, and his comprehensive plans resulting from it, by the cosy fireside, at familiar social gatherings of chosen ones, or better, in the carefully arranged junto of earnest, practical men. Vague hints, careful blinds, are Nat Turner's entire make-up to save detection; the telegraph, the post-office, the railway, all were made to aid the new outbreak. By this, it will be seen that Insurrection has its progressive side, and has been elevated by John Brown from the skulking, fearing cabal, when in the hands of a brave but despairing few, to the highly organized, formidable, and to very many, indispensable institution for the security of freedom, when guided by intelligence. . . .

1. Osborne Perry Anderson (1830–1871) participated with John Brown in the attack on Harpers Ferry and lived to tell about it. Born free in Pennsylvania, Anderson worked as a printer before joining up with Brown in Canada. In Virginia, Osborne attempted to arm slaves into rebelliousness by distributing pikes to them. See Hannah N. Geffert, "John Brown and His Black Allies: An Ignored Alliance," *Pennsylvania Magazine of History and Biography* 126 (October 2002): 600–603.

Osborne P. Anderson, *A Voice from Harper's Ferry: A Narrative of Events at Harper's Ferry, with Incidents Prior and Subsequent to Its Capture by Captain Brown and His Men* (Boston, 1861), 5, 7–8.

Moncure Daniel Conway[1] on the Goals of Rebel Leaders, 1861

. . . Let it be remembered that up to this time there were no "fearful scenes" in St. Domingo, except such as were occasioned by a mad rebellion of the white planters against the just decrees of their government. And each fresh horror came of their mad conspiracy to transfer the island to foreign powers. The slaves, after their manumission by the French Commissioners, went on for the most part working patiently, as before, seeking no political privileges, until this quiet was changed by the conspiracies of the planters to betray them, now to this nation, now to that,—to any that would re-enslave them. When their liberties were assaulted, eight years after they were legally gained, by Napoleon, these men showed themselves worthy of those liberties, by defending them as brave men have done in every age and land; and instead of such defence being attended with barbarities on the part of the Negroes, the whole history of the Haitian Republic down to this day is a continuous record and attestation of French and English and Spanish treacheries and cruelties,—perfidies and cruelties persistent and almost incredible,—and of heroism, patience, and only too much generosity, on the part of the Negroes.

Indeed, there never was a siege or campaign of one of these white nations which was not followed by outrages for the cruelty of which the records of insurrection furnish no parallel. In even the insurrection of Nat Turner, in Virginia, the violation of woman formed no part.[2] In the plan of Denmark Vesey, in South Carolina, there was a stern prohibition against any wanton outrage, and not a blow was aimed but would have been essential to liberation.[3] No woman or child was ever slain, except it was certain they would be able to alarm neighborhoods, and defeat the plan of insurrection; and the blow, wherever it fell, was swift, the death instant, where in other lands vindictive tortures have been resorted to. The motto of the Negro, in the few instances where he has struck for his freedom, has always been *Liberty,* never *Vengeance.* In this regard, the mildest race in the world has been most infamously slandered, or absurdly misunderstood. . . .

1. Moncure Daniel Conway (1832–1907) was born in Stafford County, Virginia, into a slaveholding family. After education at Dickinson and Harvard, Conway turned to antislavery and became a Unitarian minister. At the time this pamphlet was written, Conway lived in Cincinnati, where he also edited a liberal journal called *The Dial.*

2. Conway speaks here of rape; of the sixty or so whites killed by Nat Turner, the majority were women and children.

3. Contrary to Conway's claim, the trial record indicates "outrages" were intended. See also John Potter's letters to Langdon Cheves, July 10 and July 20, 1822, Part IV, pp. 385–86 and 401.

Moncure Daniel Conway, *The Rejected Stone; or, Insurrection vs. Resurrection in America* (Boston, 1861), 124–25.

Robert Morris[1] on Vesey and Turner, Thursday, September 18, 1862

. . . The presentation of the portrait of JOHN T. HILTON[2] to the Prince Hall Grand Lodge was an interesting occasion, and the following sketch of some of its features will, it is thought, prove acceptable to the readers of the *Liberator.* . . .

Dr. DeGrasse was followed by ROBERT MORRIS, Esq., in addition to what specially concerned the Order, submitted these remarks, which found ready acceptance with the audience:—

"This is our first effort to transmit to posterity a portrait of any of our public men; I trust it may not be the last.

"I wish we could point to well executed likenesses of those old colored heroes of revolutionary memory, who so nobly, patriotically and willingly side by side with their white brethren, fought, bled and died to secure freedom and independence to America.

"It would be a source of continual pleasure could we have in some public room pictures true to life of those intrepid heroes, Denmark Veazie and Nat. Turner, whose very names were a terror to oppressors; who, conceiving the sublime idea of freedom for themselves and their race, animated by a love of liberty of which they had been ruthlessly deprived, made an attempt to sever their bonds; and though in such attempts to open the prison doors of slavery and let the oppressed go free, they were unsuccessful, their efforts and determination were none the less noble and heroic. In the future history of our country their names to us will shine as brightly as that of the glorious old hero who with his colored and white followers so strategically captured Harper's Ferry, and touched a chord in the life of our country that will vibrate throughout the land, and will not cease until the last fetter has been struck from the limbs of the last bondman in the nation; and though the bodies of these heroes mouldering in the clay, their souls are marching on. . . .

1. Robert Morris (1823–1882) was a Massachusetts-born African American attorney. Admitted to the state bar in 1847, Morris was active in abolitionism and other reform causes, and in 1848 he joined with Charles Sumner to challenge segregated public schools in the case of *Roberts v. Boston.* See Stephen Kendrick and Paul Kendrick, *Sarah's Long Walk: The Free Blacks of Boston and How Their Struggle for Equality Changed America* (Boston: Beacon Press, 2004).

2. John Telemachus Hilton (1801–1864), a free black businessman and abolitionist, born in Pennsylvania, organized the Prince Hall Lodge, a black Masonic organization, which in 1826 had admitted David Walker. See Peter P. Hinks, *To Awaken My Afflicted Brethren: David Walker and the Problem of Antebellum Slave Resistance* (University Park: Pennsylvania State University Press, 1997), 70–78.

Henry Highland Garnet on the Emancipation Proclamation, Wednesday, February 4, 1863

. . . [A] large number of the inhabitants of the village of Weeksville[1] and vicinity turned out to join in the general rejoicing of the issuing of the great proclamation. . . . The new John Brown song was then sung, Rev. H. H. Garnet expressed much pleasure in being present. . . . He hoped that our poets and orators would remember our own heroes.

Nat Turner and Denmark Vesey were the forerunner of John Brown and are to be honored as such. He hoped yet to see erected to the memory of these men a monument in Greenwald Cemetery, the apex of which should be crowned with a wreath of laurel.

1. Weeksville, Long Island, emerged in the early nineteenth century as one of first important communities of free persons of color in the United States. Weeksville covered in Brooklyn what are today parts of Bedford-Stuyvesant and Crown Heights. On Garnet, see Part V, p. 700 n1.

"Emancipation Jubilee Meeting at Weeksville, L.I.," New York *Weekly Anglo-African*, February 14, 1863.

Wisconsin *Appleton Motor*

Thursday, March 19, 1863
Men of Color, to Arms!
A CALL BY FREDERICK DOUGLASS[1]

Massachusetts now welcomes you to arms as her soldiers; but she has a small colored population from which to recruit. She has full leave of the General Government to send one regiment to the war, and she has undertaken to do it. Go quickly and help fill up this first colored regiment from the North. I am authorized to assure you that you will receive the same wages, the same rations, the same equipments, the same protection, the same treatment and the same bounty secured to white soldiers. You will be led by able and skillful officers—men who will take especial pride in your efficiency and success. They will be quick to accord to you all the honor you shall merit by your valor, and see that your rights and feelings are respected by other soldiers. I have assured myself on these points, and can speak with authority. More than twenty years unswerving devotion to our common cause may give me some humble claim to be trusted at this momentous crisis.

I will not argue. To do so, implies hesitation and doubts and you do not hesitate, you do not doubt. The day dawns; the morning star is bright upon the horizon. The iron gate of our prison stands half open. One gallant rush from the North will fling it wide open, while four millions of our brothers and sisters shall march out into liberty! The chance is now given you to end in a day the bondage of centuries, and to rise in one bound from social degradation to the plane of a common equality with all other varieties of men. Remember Denmark Vesey, of Charleston! Remember Nathaniel Turner, of South Hampton! Remember Shields, Green and Copeland, who followed noble John Brown, and fell as glorious martyrs for the cause of the slave. Remember that in a contest with oppressors the Almighty has no attribute which can take sides with oppression. The case is before you. . . .

1. Douglass later learned more about Vesey from Thomas Wentworth Higginson. See his letter of January 17, 1893, to Richard J. Hinton, in "Two Letters of Frederick Douglass," *JNH* 33 (1948): 471. His call to arms, which first appeared in Rochester, New York, was published widely by newspapers in the North.

Recollections of Charlotte Forten Grimké,[1] April 5, 1863

Sunday, April 5. . . . Was much interested in listening to an old man whom Mr. P(ierce), the unwearied, was questioning. This man, Don Carlos, by name, was a slave, originally from Vir(ginia) and living here in the family of the Allston's. He knew the Gov(ernor) Allston whom Aaron Burr's daughter married, and was well acquainted with her mournful story. He also knew Mr. Pierpont when he was teaching in the Gov(ernor)'s family—teaching the sons of his second wife. Carlos has been taught to read by (him) and seems to be a man of considerable intelligence. He, and afterwards, Dr. B(risbane), gave us some interesting reminiscences of the Denmark Vesey Insurrection. . . .

1. Charlotte Forten Grimké (1837–1914) was a Philadelphia-born black activist who taught freed slaves in South Carolina after the war. In 1878 she married Francis J. Grimké, the brother of Archibald Grimké, whose pioneering essay on Vesey is excerpted on p. 780 in this volume. See Mark Perry, *Lift Up Thy Voice: The Grimké Family's Journey from Slaveholders to Civil Rights Leaders* (New York: Viking, 2001).

Charlotte Forten, *The Journal of Charlotte Forten: A Free Negro in the Slave Era*, ed. Ray Allen Billington (New York: Collier Books, 1953), 198.

Liberator

Friday, April 17, 1863

. . . Mr. Coffin,[1] in his valuable tract on Slave Insurrections, enumerates nineteen risings throughout the United States between 1712 and 1831, inclusive. Of these, South Carolina claims nine, (and a tenth might be added,) of which one was dignified by the name of "war"—that of 1780[2]—and three others occurred in one and the same year. . . .

All of these nineteen insurrections antedate the abolition movement, and all but one were primarily the work of slaves. Yet, to the slaveholders, this is not the only ground for alarm. Denmark Vesey, who almost annihilated Charleston in 1822, was a freedman whose children were slaves; and his attempt was the occasion of the law imprisoning colored seamen who arrive at that port, just as Gabriel suggested to the Virginians the idea of colonizing freed and otherwise dangerous blacks. With Vesey were also implicated certain of the poorer whites, not, of course, from a regard for the rights of the slaves, but from a willingness to participate in the plunder of their haughty superiors. . . .

1. The author refers to the abolitionist Joshua Coffin (1792–1864) and his *An Account of Some of the Principal Slave Insurrections*, published in 1860.

2. The date is an error. The author speaks of the so-called Gullah War around the time of the Stono uprising in South Carolina in 1739.

Edward L. Pierce[1] in Port Royal, South Carolina, 1863

The tax-commissioner[2] before referred to, who was a resident of Charleston during the trial and execution of the confederates of Denmark Vesey, relates that one of the native Africans, when called to answer to the charge against him, haughtily responded,—"I was a prince in my country, and have as much right to be free as you!"[3] The Carolinians were so awe-struck by his defiance that they transported him. Another, at the execution, turned indignantly to a comrade about to speak, and said, "Die silent, as I do!" and the man hushed. . . . [4]

1. Edward L. Pierce (1829–1897), an antislavery attorney, fought in the US Army and was appointed to supervise the transition of emancipated slaves into free laborers in Port Royal, South Carolina. Pierce is a central character in Willie Lee Rose, *Rehearsal for Reconstruction: The Port Royal Experiment* (Indianapolis: Bobbs-Merrill, 1964).

2. William H. Brisbane (1803–1878) was a slaveholding South Carolina planter who after his ordination as a proslavery Baptist minister in 1831 converted a few years later to abolitionism. He took his slaves northward and emancipated them; he preached in the Sixth Baptist Church in Cincinnati, Ohio. After leaving South Carolina for the North, he returned to his native state during the Civil War to help educate the freedmen, holding the federal post of tax commissioner. See "Obituary," *Boston Daily Advertiser*, April 8, 1878; Rose, *Rehearsal for Reconstruction*, 196, 280–81, 287–89.

3. Probably African-born Billy Robinson. See pp. 443 n1 and 731 n1.

4. According to Hamilton, *Account*, 19, and the *OR*, 46, this was Peter Poyas.

Edward L. Pierce, "The Freedmen at Port Royal," *Atlantic Monthly* 12 (September 1863): 301.

Philadelphia Inquirer

Monday, November 2, 1863

. . . The late insurrection of the slaves in Hancock county,[1] Northern Georgia, is acknowledged now by the Rebels, as we first published some days ago, to have been a very serious affair. These slaves, numbering some ten thousand, had completed a military organization, and chosen officers, from a Major-General down to a corporal. Their plan was to join Rosecrans' army[1] when he arrived and captured Atlanta. Through the treachery of some of their number, the plot was discovered and the ringleaders placed in close confinement to await "summary justice."

Although the Rebels discovered this conspiracy in time to prevent its consummation, still their minds have been made very uneasy by it. It proves to them that their slaves can no more be trusted now than in the days of DENMARK VESEY, and NAT TURNER. Surely the cornerstone of the Confederacy is not resting easily, at least in Northern Georgia. . . .

1. The story is exaggerated. In October 1863, thirty-four slaves were arrested in Hancock County for conspiring to raise an insurrection. See Jonathan M. Bryant, *How Curious a Land: Conflict and Change in Greene County, Georgia, 1850–1885* (Chapel Hill: University of North Carolina Press, 1996), 87.

2. By November 1863, Ulysses S. Grant had relieved General William Rosecrans (1819–1898) of his command of the Army of the Cumberland after his defeat at the battle of Chickamauga, in Tennessee, near the northwestern part of Georgia.

William Wells Brown[1] on Denmark Vesey, 1863

. . . No class of persons in the world, who have the name of being free, are more sorely oppressed than the free colored people of the Southern States. Each state has its code of black laws, which are rigorously enforced, and the victim made to feel his degradation at all times and in all places. An undeveloped discontent pervades the entire black population, bond and free, in all the slave states. Human bondage is ever fruitful of insurrection, wherever it exists, and under whatever circumstances it may be found. Every community the other side of "Dixon's Line" feels that it lives upon a volcano that is liable to burst out at any moment; and all are watchful, and fearfully in earnest, in looking after the colored man's affairs, and inventing sterner enactments to keep him in subjection. The most oppressive of all the states is South Carolina. In Charleston, free colored ladies are not allowed to wear veils about their faces in the streets, or in any public places. A violation of this law is visited with "*thirty-nine lashes upon the bare back.*" The same is inflicted upon any free colored man who shall be seen upon the streets with a cigar in his mouth, or a walking stick in his band. Both, when walking the streets, are forbidden to take the inside of the pavement. Punishment of fine and imprisonment is laid upon any found out after the hour of nine at night. An extra tax is placed upon every member of a free colored family. While all these odious edicts were silently borne by the free colored people of Charleston in 1822 there was a suppressed feeling of indignation, mortification, and discontent, that was only appreciated by a few. Among the most dissatisfied of the free blacks was Denmark Vesey, a man who had purchased his freedom in the year 1800, and since that time had earned his living by his trade, being a carpenter and joiner. Having been employed on shipboard by his master, Captain Vesey, Denmark had soon a great deal of the world, and had acquired a large fund of information, and was regarded as a leading man among the blacks. He had studied the Scriptures, and never lost an opportunity of showing that they were opposed to chattel-slavery. He spoke freely with the slaves upon the subject, and often with whites, where he found he could do so without risk to his own liberty. After resolving to incite the slaves to rebellion, he began taking into his confidence such persons as be could trust, and instructing them to gain adherents from among the more reliable of both bond and free. Peter Poyas, a slave of more than ordinary foresight and ability, was selected by Vesey as his lieutenant; and to him was committed the arduous duty of arranging the mode of attack, and of acting as the military leader. . . .

Gullah Jack, Tom Russell, and Ned Bennett. The last two were not less valuable than Peter Poyas; for Tom was an ingenious mechanic, and made battleaxes, pikes, and other instruments of death, with which to carry on the war. All of the above were to be generals of brigades, and were let into all the secrets of the intended rising. It has long been the custom in Charleston for the country slaves to visit the city in great numbers on Sunday, and return to their homes in time to commence work on the following morning. It was therefore determined by Denmark to have the rising take place on Sunday. The slaves of nearly every plantation in the vicinity were enlisted, and were to take part. . . .

The secret and plan of attack, however, were incautiously divulged to a slave named Devany, belonging to Colonel Prioleau, and he at once informed his master's family. The mayor, on getting possession of the facts, called the city council together for consultation. The investigation elicited nothing new, for the slaves persisted in their ignorance of the matter, and the authorities began to feel that they had been imposed upon by

Devany and his informant, when another of the conspirators, being bribed, revealed what he knew. Arrests after arrests were made, and the Mayor's Court held daily examinations for weeks. After several weeks of incarceration, the accused, one hundred and twenty in number, were brought to trial: thirty-four were sentenced to transportation, twenty-seven acquitted by the court, twenty-five discharged without trial, and thirty-five condemned to death. With but two or three exceptions, all of the conspirators went to the gallows feeling that they had acted right, and died like men giving their lives for the cause of freedom. . . .

The excitement which the revelations of the trial occasioned, and the continual fanning of the flame by the newspapers, were beyond description. Double the guard in the city, the country patrol on horseback and on foot, the watchfulness that was observed on all plantations, showed the deep feeling of fear pervading the hearts of the slaveholders, not only in South Carolina, but the fever extended to the other Southern States, and all seemed to feel that a great crisis had been passed. And indeed, their fears seem not to have been without ground, for a more complicated plan for an insurrection could scarcely have been conceived. And many were of opinion that, the rising once begun, they would have taken the city and held it, and might have sealed the fate of slavery in the south. The best account of this whole matter is to be found in an able article in the Atlantic Monthly for June, 1861, from the pen of that eloquent friend of freedom T. W. Higginson, and to which I am indebted for the extracts contained in this memoir of Denmark Vesey.

1. William Wells Brown (1814–1884) was a Kentucky-born African American abolitionist, novelist, and historian. Brown escaped to the North in 1834 at age twenty and spent most of his life in Massachusetts. His 1853 novel *Clotel,* loosely based on allegations that Thomas Jefferson had fathered a mixed-race daughter, was one of the first published by an African American. After the passage of the 1850 Fugitive Slave Law, Brown fled to Britain, where his liberty was purchased by an abolitionist couple. See Ezra Greenspan, *William Wells Brown, An African American Life* (New York: Norton, 2014).

William Wells Brown, *The Black Man, His Antecedents, His Genius, and His Achievements* (New York, 1863), 142–48.

New York *Weekly Anglo-African*

Saturday, March 18, 1865

"*Delenda est Carthago!*"[1] The mother of nullification, secession and disunion, the fiery torch which first lighted up rebellion in the South and Union in the North, the home of the chivalry and far famed beauty of the South, the stronghold which laughed to scorn all the force which modern military science and skilful military daring could bring to bear against it, the fated city wherein the inhabitants grew as familiar with raining shot and shell as with the rain which falls from the heavens—Charleston at once the boast of the rebellious and the execration of the loyal, the last ditch of the chivalry and the winning goal of the loyal yeomanry, has fallen into our hands almost without bloodshed.

As an act of poetic justice, rather than a mark of ignominy, the military authorities gave the colored troops the post of honor, in taking possession of the captured-city. *Harper's Weekly* gives a lively and telling picture of the 55th Mass. marching through the ruined city, singing the "John Brown Song," and cheered on all sides by their redeemed brethren; the toppling walls and shattered doors of the "old" resounding with the glad *Alleluiahs* of the new. To the right of the picture, a little in advance of the regiment, two little colored boys, in the most approved style of dress on such occasions, are "letting themselves go" in their proud and earnest step to the music; who knows, but that, in the good time coming, one or both of those boys may find their way into the United States Congress?

. . . Another distinction, glorious in the history of our people, belongs to Charleston. In 1821–2 a most formidable plan of insurrection was laid out, and nearly carried into action by DENMARK VEASEY, and a number of other slaves and free people of color. Within forty-eight hours, had it not been discovered by the betrayal of an accomplice, Charleston would have been in the hands of the insurgents. A poor wretch of a slave, whose love for or gratitude towards a kind master was greater than his love of liberty, betrayed the plot. . . .

1. Translates as: "Carthage must be destroyed."

Martin R. Delany[1] with Robert Vesey at Fort Sumter Ceremony, April 14, 1865

. . . Major Delany embarked to witness the ceremony on the historical steamer Planter, with its gallant commander, Robert Small[s],[2] whose deeds will live in song and story, whose unparalleled feat and heroic courage in the harbor of Charleston, under the bristling guns of rebel batteries, bearing comparison with the proudest record of our war, will remain, commemorative of negro strategy and valor.

On the quarter-deck of the steamer the major remained an interested witness. Beside him stood one, whose father, believing and loving the doctrine that all men were born free and equal, and within sight of the emblem of freedom as it floated from the battlements of Sumter, dared to aim a blow by which to free his race. Betrayed before his plans were matured, the scaffold gave to Denmark Vesey and his twenty-two slave-hero compatriots in Charleston, South Carolina, in 1822, the like answer which Charlestown, Virginia, gave John Brown in 1859. . . .

1. Born free in Virginia, Martin Robison Delany (1812–1885), physician, journalist, novelist, abolitionist, and soldier, rose to become one of the most prominent black leaders of his generation. After the Emancipation Proclamation, Delany actively recruited blacks into the cause. Thanks in large part to Abraham Lincoln, he received near war's end a commission that elevated him to the rank of major, the highest rank for any black soldier at the time, in the 104th United States Colored Troops. See Robert S. Levine, *Martin Delany, Frederick Douglass, and the Politics of Representative Identity* (Chapel Hill: University of North Carolina Press, 1997).

2. Robert Smalls (1839–1915), born a slave in Beaufort, South Carolina, worked as a crewman aboard the Confederate steamer *Planter* at the beginning of the Civil War. In the darkness of early morning, May 13, 1862, Smalls commandeered the craft and navigated it out of Charleston harbor into the waiting arms of the Union fleet off shore, making him a northern hero. During

Figure 37. African American children at the foot of a column that once formed part of the porch of Charleston's Circular (Congregational) Church at the end of the Civil War. Courtesy of the Library of Congress.

Reconstruction he would serve South Carolina as a Republican Congressman. See Okon Edet Uya, *From Slavery to Public Service: Robert Smalls, 1839–1915* (New York: Oxford University Press, 1971).

Frank A. Rollin, *Life and Public Services of Martin R. Delany, Sub-assistant Commissioner, Bureau Relief of Refugees, Freedmen, and of Abandoned Lands, and Late Major 104th U.S. Colored Troops* (Boston, 1883).

New-York Tribune

Monday, May 22, 1865

... CHARLESTON, May 12, 1865.

There was a large meeting of the loyalists of Charleston to-day—over 4,000 of them—in Zion's Church,[1] convened in less than twelve hours, to welcome and to listen to our honored Chief-Justice.[2] At least two thousand persons went away unable to obtain an entrance to the church. The Chief-Justice had purposely remained over in Charleston one day, to have the opportunity of seeing the loyalists of the city. The proceedings of the previous day, it is understood, did not tend to increase his respect of the old ruling class, who profaned their ballots and showed themselves unfit to be intrusted with the rights of suffrage four or five years ago, and who now seek to resent any attempt to invest with the political franchise the only class here who are loyal alike to the flag and the principles it represents. . . .

Mayor Delaney[3] next spoke and sought to show that the ill-feeling between the blacks and mulattoes arose out of the betrayal of Denmark Vesey by a mulatto!

While Major Delaney was speaking, Chief-Justice Chase entered the church. Instantly the vast multitude arose, and cheer after cheer of the most heartfelt enthusiasm showed how well they knew and how deeply grateful they were to their illustrious visitor for his life-long services to their cause. . . . [4]

1. Built before the war by Presbyterians, Zion Church, called "Big Zion," by Charleston's slaves, stood on the corner of Calhoun and Meeting streets. It could house several thousand worshippers and became the most important place of worship for persons of color in South Carolina. See Erskine Clarke, *Our Southern Zion: A History of Calvinism in the South Carolina Low Country, 1690–1990* (Tuscaloosa: University of Alabama Press, 1996), 159, 219–20.

2. Salmon P. Chase (1808–1873) was the sixth chief justice of the Supreme Court.

3. Major Martin R. Delany.

4. A slightly different version of this story appeared in the *Charleston Courier,* May 13, 1865, and in the New York *Weekly Anglo-African,* May 27, 1865. No copy of Delany's speech has ever been found. Because Major Delaney had previously met Robert Vesey Sr. at the Fort Sumter ceremony, it is hard to credit that he would have spoken to throngs of blacks and browns in the city about the moral lessons to be drawn from the Vesey affair without knowing, for sure, that Vesey was not of mixed race.

Philadelphia *Christian Recorder*

Saturday, June 3, 1865

CHARLESTON CORRESPONDENCE. . . . MR EDITOR:—The new era has dawned, the sun has lit up the horizon, and humanity is rising to a just appreciation of the crisis. Monday, May 15th, 1865, marks an epoch in the history of our race in this country. Forty years ago the African M.E. Church was established in this city. Morris Brown, the second Bishop of our connection, was one of the founders. A house was erected, in which the lovers of Christ and of religious liberty, bowed in humble acknowledgment of God's mercy to them. For six years the little church continued to prosper, under the benign influence of the Lord, when the hell-hatched demon, slavery, conspired to sweep it from the earth.

Denmark Vessey, (immortal name,) conceived the mighty idea of liberating his race. The consonance of his great thought of liberty with the ultimate end and workings of the A.M.E. Church, placed her in juxta position to his plans, and her destiny was sealed with the fate of his enterprise. He suffered, and all who had any thing to do with him, as martyrs to human liberty. Our Church was demolished and blotted out of existence, and from that day to this our people have had to wear the accursed yoke of religious bondage; paying for all the church property belonging to the Methodists, and supporting the bloody-handed ministers, who have administered unholy doctrines.

The fall of this city opened the way for the return of Joseph, in the person of Bishop Daniel A. Payne,[1] to his brethren, he having been made ruler over all the Church *in the land of Abraham.* He returns to establish Zion in his native city. . . . R.H.C.[2]

1. AME Bishop Daniel Alexander Payne (1811–1893), born in Charleston and the former private secretary of Morris Brown, returned triumphant as the inaugural president of Wilberforce University. See Part V, p. 698 n1.

2. Richard Harvey Cain (1825–1887) was a Virginia-born freeman, ordained in 1844 as a minister in the African Methodist Episcopal Church, and educated at Wilberforce University. After the war, he settled in Charleston as superintendent of AME missions. Elected to the state senate in 1868, he served until 1872, when he was elected to two terms in Congress, where he was instrumental in passing the Civil Rights Act of 1875. See Philip Dray, *Capitol Men: The Epic Story of Reconstruction through the Lives of the First Black Congressmen* (New York: Mariner Books, 2010).

Philadelphia *Christian Recorder*

October 14, 1865

CHARLESTON CORRESPONDENCE. . . . On Monday the 25th of September, at 4 o'clock, the corner stone of the first African church was laid with appropriate ceremonies. Rev. Mr. Randolph of the 26th Regiment, read the opening prayer. The choir rendered an appropriate chant. Rev. E. J. Adams read the fourth chapter of first Kings in a clear and distinct voice, after which Rev. R. H. Cain delivered an appropriate address from 1 Kings vi. 12, 13: "Concerning this house which thou art building, if thou wilt walk in my statutes, and execute my judgments, and keep all my commandments to walk in them, then will I perform my word with thee, which I spake unto David thy father, &c."

Over three thousand people listened with marked attention to the delivery of the discourse. The choir pealed forth one of those enchanting anthems, appropriate for such an occasion. . . .

The building is of yellow pine, 95 feet long, 45 feet wide, 18 feet ceiling, gallery on both sides and at the end, 8 feet on sides, 13 feet front, and is calculated to seat at least 2,500 people. It is situated on Calhoun St. between Meeting and Elizabeth Sts. nearly opposite Zion church. It will cost about $10,000, and every man who is working on it is a colored man. Robert Vesey,[1] son of Denmark Vesey, is the architect. The building is progressing very rapidly, and we expect to raise the frame on the second of October, and to dedicate the house on the second Sunday in November. . . .

1. Before constructing the Emanuel African Methodist Episcopal Church in Charleston, the oldest AME Church in the South, Robert Vesey Sr. had remained an active churchgoer in Zion Presbyterian. See Erskine Clarke, *Our Southern Zion: A History of Calvinism in the South Carolina Low Country, 1690–1990* (Tuscaloosa: University of Alabama Press, 1996), 340 n1.

William Wells Brown[1] on Failed Resistance, 1880

. . . The great struggle for our elevation is now with ourselves. We may talk of Hannibal, Euclid, Phyllis Wheatly, Benjamin Bannaker, and Toussaint L'Overture, but the world will ask us for our men and women of the day. We cannot live upon the past; we must hew out a reputation that will stand the test, one that we have a legitimate right to. To do this, we must imitate the best examples set us by the cultivated whites, and by so doing we will teach them that they can claim no superiority on account of race.

The efforts made by oppressed nations or communities to throw off their chains, entitles them to, and gains for them the respect of mankind. This the blacks never made, or what they did, was so feeble as scarcely to call for comment. The planning of Denmark Vesey for an insurrection in South Carolina, was noble, and deserved a better fate; but he was betrayed by the race that he was attempting to serve. . . .

1. On Brown, see p. 768 n1.

William Wells Brown, *My Southern Home: Or, the South and Its People* (Boston, 1880), 243–44.

New York Globe

Saturday, August 12, 1882

THE NATIONAL CAPITAL. DEATH OF MRS. FREDERICK DOUGLASS—REMARKS OF BISHOP T. M. D. WARD. From Our Staff Correspondent.

WASHINGTON, Aug. 8—At the residence of her husband, Cedar Hill, Uniontown, surrounded by her affectionate companion and their devoted children, grandchildren and a few very intimate friends, at five o'clock Friday morning, the 4th instant, Mrs. Anna Murray, beloved wife of Hon. Frederick Douglass, 'gave her honors to the world again, her blessed part to Heaven, and slept in peace.'

Three weeks ago Mrs. Douglass was stricken with paralysis, from which she never sufficiently rallied to give hope of her final recovery. She had been a constant sufferer from the effects of rheumatism for years; but the last twenty days of her life were attended by the most excruciating pain, which rendered her for the most part unconscious up to the time of her demise.

Mrs. Douglass was born in the State of Maryland, of free parents, in 1813, and was consequently sixty-nine years of age. She is said to have first met Mr. Douglass at church in their native State, of the Baptist denomination, for which he had organized a choir, of which he was leader. He soon became betrothed to Miss Anna Murray, but he vowed that he would never marry her as a slave. Seizing his first opportunity, he made his escape from bondage in 1838. Arriving at New York, he notified the object of his affection of his successful flight to liberty, and bade her join him as had been agreed. She came forthwith and they were immediately united in holy matrimony in the great emporium. This was forty-four years ago. Since that time they had lived happily together as man and wife. . . .

When Mr. Douglass began his public career he had nothing to depend upon but a brave heart, a massive brain and skillful hands. These were tempestuous times. Prominent anti-slavery men were everywhere denounced and traduced. Often was the husband of this wife hunted down by a blood thirsty mob who clamored for his life. Frequently did poverty stare him in the face. Did she repine? Did she upbraid him? Did she charge him with neglect when perhaps their little ones asked for bread when there was but a scanty allowance in the larder? No! she taxed her women's wit, made an old coast look like a new one; passing by a piece of wool she was not too proud to pick it up. She said: 'My husband is battling with the minions of oppression, why not I endure hardship that my race may be free? I will do my duty as a wife towards him and our children; they shall look neat and spruce on the street, in the house, in the school room.' . . .

She has gone up to meet the illustrious host who fought and won the battle of equal rights for all men in America and throughout the world—Lundy, Torry, Nat Turner, Denmark Vesy, Allen, Lovejoy, Garrison, John Brown, Ward, Stephens, Giddings, Beman, Shaw, Sumner, Lincoln, Gerritt Smith, Garnet, Garfield and a long line of unnamed and unknown heroes who died that men of all races for all coming time might remain forever free on the Continent of America, on the face of the globe. . . .

Douglass Family Scrapbook, No. 2, Walter O. Evans Collection, Savannah, GA.

New York Globe

Saturday, August 18, 1883

THE VIRTUE OF AGITATION.

. . . In our own country the conflict of wrong and right has been long and bloody. Around the battle-fields of Bunker's Hill and Yorktown, and Manassas and Appomattox the masses contended and conquered, and so they will always, if they fight on the side of right.

Agitation does not always lead to an appeal to arms. Peace has its triumphs, and often they are more substantial than those that follow the victorious car of Napoleon or Wellington. Our history in this country dates from the moment that restless men among us became restless under oppression and rose against it. From Denmark Vesey to Nat Turner, from the flight of Frederick Douglass and Henry Highland Garnet from the blood hounds of Maryland to the present time the voice of the race has been heard on the lecture platform and on the field of battle protesting against the injustice heaped upon the race. . . .

Charleston News and Courier

Sunday, December 13, 1885

THE VESEY INSURRECTION. A history of the great conspiracy of sixty years ago. Narrow Escape of Charleston from the Horrors of a Rising of the Slaves—An Interesting Narrative of One of the Most Thrilling Event[s] in the History of the State.

The opponents of Southern slavery have reiterated again and again that our people were in constant dread of slave insurrections. In spite of the loyalty and devotion of the negroes to their masters' families during the civil war, when every opportunity was afforded the negro for insurrection, none took place. But the old charge is still trumped up, and an account of the only attempted insurrection of any importance which took place in South Carolina will be of interest. It is timely, too, as showing how quickly and thoroughly stern justice was visited upon the leaders of the insurrection, and how idle and wicked was the threat of the negro ministers of Charleston in their recent address, that the scenes of St. Domingo might be reenacted in this state should their fancied grievances be disregarded. . . . [1]

1. The remainder of the lengthy front page story was drawn, as the editor indicated, from a copy of Kennedy and Parker's *Official Report.* The story was inspired by a mass meeting of black ministers at Charleston's Morris Brown AME Church, where speakers denounced attacks on African American political and economic rights. This introduction to the story appears designed to praise passive blacks while reminding activists of the power of white retribution. For the "immense meeting" of black clergymen, see *Charleston News and Courier,* November 3, 1885.

Reverend William J. Simmons[1] on Vesey's Conspiracy, 1887

. . . NINETEEN years before the opening of this century, on the island of St. Thomas, was born a child who was destined to become a martyr for his race. Men may differ as to what makes a martyr, and believe it comes through the flesh or the wicked one; but martyrs are made of such material as fit men to attempt great things for what they believe to be right. Denmark was purchased by a man named Veazie, after whom he takes his name. He was fourteen years old when he was purchased. In 1800 he drew a prize of fifteen hundred dollars in a lottery. Of course we do not approve of his playing lottery by any means, but he made good use of six hundred dollars of the money, securing his freedom thereby. He was a carpenter by trade, and was the admired of all his companions, because of his strength and activity. Twenty-two years later he formed a plan to liberate the slaves of Charleston, South Carolina. His plan was to put the whole city to fire and the sword on June 16. He had particularly objected to any slave joining the conspiracy who was of that class of waiting men who received presents of old coats, etc., from their masters, as such slaves would be likely to betray them. At 10 o'clock at night, the governor having been informed of the conspiracy by the treachery of some of the Negroes, had military companies thrown around the city, and no one was allowed to pass in or out.

The slaves who were to come from Thomas Island, and land on the South bay, and seize the arsenal and guardhouse, failed to do so. Another body that was to seize the arsenal on the Neck, was also thwarted in its plans. All the conspirators, finding the town so well protected, did not attempt that which they intended. On Sunday afternoon, Denmark Veazie, for the purpose of making preliminary arrangements, had a meeting and dispatched a courier to inform the country Negroes what to do, but the courier could not get out of the city, and thus the project was a failure, but the leader died a martyr upon the gallows, and the slave who had betrayed him was purchased by the Legislature, thus putting a premium upon the betrayal of any one who should attempt an insurrection of this kind. From William C. Nell's 'History of the Colored Patriots of the American Revolution,' we take the following:

The number of blacks arrested was 131: of these 35 were executed, 41 acquitted, and the rest sentenced to be transported. Many a brave hero fell, but history, faithful to her high trust, will engrave the name of Denmark on the same monument with Moses, Hampden, Tell, Bruce, Wallace, Toussaint L'Ouverture, La Fayette and Washington.

I have stood in the arsenal yard and seen the place where these men were executed, and the memory of their attempt will never fade from the history of the Negroes of South Carolina. . . .

1. Born a slave in Charleston, William J. Simmons (1849–1890) escaped with his parents to Philadelphia at a young age. He would fight in the Civil War, become a Baptist minister, graduate from Howard University, and serve as second president of Simmons College in Louisville, Kentucky. See Rayford W. Logan and Michael R. Winston, eds., *Dictionary of American Negro Biography* (New York: Norton, 1982), 556–57.

William J. Simmons, *Men of Mark: Eminent, Progressive and Rising* (Cleveland, OH, 1887), 231–33.

Recollections of the Ravenel Family, 1898

. . . Mrs. Mary McCall's history had a tragic cast. During the negro insurrection in 1822 the gentlemen in Charleston kept arms about their bedrooms. Mr. McCall had arisen before his wife one morning and was aroused by the report of a pistol, to find shot dead by his own weapon, the blood being sprinkled over the bed. How the accident happened no one will ever know. She never married again, but lived a widow more than sixty years, dying in 1886. . . . At the time of the insurrection of 1822, or just prior thereto, Peter, a servant of Mr. John Cordes Prioleau, informed Mr. John Ravenel that the negroes were planning it, and Mr. Ravenel conveyed the intelligence to General Hamilton, mayor of the city, but the mayor would not believe it. The loyalty of the servant to the whites is an interesting bit of family history. . . .[1]

1. Mary Ravenel (1800–1886) married John Ward McCall (1793–1822), the Charleston physician who accidentally killed himself in June 1822 while putting away one of his pistols. (See Part II, p. 98.) Mary was the daughter of Daniel Ravenel (1762–1807) and Catharine Cordes Prioleau (1769–1849). Catherine and John Cordes Prioleau (1772–1825) were siblings. John Ravenel (1793–1862) and her sister Mary (Ravenel) McCall were thus the nephew and niece, respectively, of the man who owned Peter Prioleau (Desverney). According to the 1860 US Census, Charleston Ward 1, Charleston, South Carolina, roll M653-1216, p. 212, Mary McCall was born around 1802. Among those who lived in this household was an Eliza P. Ravenel, probably Mary's sister.

Henry Edmund Ravenel, *Ravenel Records: A History and Genealogy of the Huguenot Family of Ravenel, of South Carolina; with Some Incidental Account of the Parish of St. Johns Berkeley, Which Was Their Principal Location* (Atlanta, 1898), 60, 69–70.

Thomas Wentworth Higginson Recalls What Black Soldiers Said, 1898

. . . Comparing notes in later years, I never have encountered a really good and successful officer of colored troops who had not become attached to his men, while attaching them to him. . . .

One would think it would have occurred to all observers that the only race which systematically organizes women as warriors could certainly produce men fit for soldiers, and that the apparent subjection produced by centuries of slavery was perfectly comprehended by the negroes themselves. When I asked the ablest men why there had been so few slave insurrections, they always made the same answer—that they had neither the knowledge, nor the weapons, nor the mutual confidence to make any such attempt successful. Even they knew by tradition what history shows, that the really daring insurrections of the Southern blacks—those of Gabriel, of Nat Turner, of Denmark Vesey—had all been betrayed by confederates, after they had accomplished enough to leave a tradition of terror for many years. . . .

Thomas Wentworth Higginson, "The First Black Regiment," *Outlook*, July 2, 1898, 527–28.

Reverend John Bailey Adger[1] Looks Back on His Boyhood in Charleston, 1899

. . . Before I close this chapter let me go back and give some account of occurrences in Charleston during the year 1822, which very greatly excited our good city, and fixed impressions on the public mind, which lasted many long years in full vigor. On the 30th of May a faithful slave communicated to his master that an attempt at insurrection by the negroes against the whites was to be made very shortly. He had learned this from one of the conspirators, who wished him to join in the attempt. That man was immediately arrested, and by degrees all the leaders came to be known, taken up and imprisoned. A few of them proved to be men of remarkable energy and daring. But even they showed themselves to be very ignorant and utterly incompetent to plan or carry out such a movement. The most remarkable of these few men was Denmark Vesey. During the Revolutionary war, in the year 1781, he was brought as a slave boy, aged about fourteen, from Africa to San Domingo by one Captain Vesey, who commanded a ship in the slave trade. On the voyage the captain and his officers were struck with his beauty, alertness and intelligence. They made a pet of him by taking him into the cabin, changing his apparel, and calling him, by way of distinction, Telemaque, which appellation was, by gradual corruption among the negroes, changed to *Denmark*, or sometimes *Telmak*. Subsequently he was brought to Charleston by Capt. Vesey, who retained possession of the boy, and he was his most faithful slave for twenty years. In 1800 Denmark drew a prize of $1,500 in a lottery in Charleston called "East Bay Street Lottery," and he then purchased his freedom from the captain at the low price of $600. From that time he continued very successfully, for about twenty-one years, his trade as carpenter in Charleston. Among his color, he had unbounded influence. His temper was impetuous and domineering in the extreme. All his passions were ungovernable and savage, and to his numerous wives and children he displayed the haughty and capricious cruelty of an Eastern Bashaw. This man, it was abundantly proved, was the sole originator of the plot of insurrection. He had revolved the subject in his mind for many years, and had succeeded in uniting with himself a considerable number of others. It was at his house that the leaders continually assembled to take counsel together. And there it was, he, who encouraged the timid, removed the scruples of the religious by gross prostitution of the sacred oracles, and inflamed the resolute by all the savage fascinations of blood and booty.

The 16th of June, at midnight, was the time appointed for the insurrection. Under the several leaders, different companies were to attack the arsenal in the northwestern part of the city, and another depot where arms were kept in King street, besides other places of a like kind. Different parts of the city were to be simultaneously set on fire, and when the fire bells were rung and white men rushed out from their houses, they were all to be put to death, and then the women and children were to be disposed of, and not one white skin was to be left alive. These poor creatures seemed to imagine that this was all to be done with the greatest ease, and without any white resistance. Such was the ignorance even of the leaders and of Denmark Vesey himself. They counted on all their race in Charleston rising at once to get free, forgetting how many of them were too faithful to their masters and how few of them had any arms or capacity for such a contest. They counted on whole armies coming in from the immediate neighborhood of Charleston, as if any such widespread cooperation were a thing conceivable. They were even made to believe that as soon as they began to fight with the whites of Charleston, the English, against whom there had been war a few years before, would come to their assistance. They were even made to believe that the San Domingo people, who had lately made a successful insurrection, would "march an army" to aid their struggle; and Vesey had proclaimed amongst them that as soon as they had robbed the banks of their specie and the King street shops of their goods and got everything on board ship, they should then sail away to San Domingo to enjoy their treasure.

In conformity with the act of Assembly passed in 1740, when South Carolina was a province under the British government, a court was immediately convened, consisting of "Magistrates and Freeholders," to try all the accused. The penalty prescribed by this act for insurrection was death. There was a careful consideration of the evidence in every case. The whole number of the accused was one hundred and thirty-one, of whom thirty-five were hanged, thirty-seven banished beyond the limits of the United States, the rest were discharged as not being found guilty. On the 2d of July Denmark Vesey and five others of the ring-leaders suffered death by hanging. Immense crowds of whites and blacks were present at the scene. On the 26th day of July I saw distinctly, from the third-story window of my father's house in upper King street,[2] not far from the scene, a long gallows erected on "The Lines," and on it twenty-two negroes hanged at one time. I might say that the whole city turned out on this occasion, and this was certainly a sight calculated to strike terror into the heart of every slave. Among these twenty-two, there was one of the leaders, whose name was Jack Pritchard. Being a gullah negro, he was commonly known as Gullah Jack. In Africa he had been known as of the family of conjurers inheriting by descent the powers belonging to his forefathers. With all these he was still accredited after being brought to Charleston as a slave. It was his claim no white man could arrest him, nor was he liable to death at any white man's hand.[3]

All these facts which I have here stated I get from an old pamphlet, in my possession, published at the time, which appears to be, in some sense, an official account of the whole matter.

I must quote a paragraph from its pages, as I draw to a close. In speaking of the negroes, who were led to engage in this attempt, the writer says, "It was distinctly proved that with scarcely an exception they had no individual hardship to complain of, and were amongst the most humanely treated negroes in our city. The facilities for combining and confederating in such a scheme were amply afforded by the extreme indulgence and kindness, which characterizes the domestic treatment of our slaves. Many slave-owners among us, not satisfied with ministering to the wants of their domestics by all the comforts of abundant food and excellent clothing, with a misguided benevolence have not only permitted their instruction, but lent to such efforts their approbation and applause. Religious fanaticism has not been without its effect on this project, and, as auxiliary to these sentiments, the secession of a large body of blacks from the white Methodist church, with feelings of irritation and disappointment, formed a hot-bed, in which the germ might well be expected to spring into life and vigor. Among the conspirators *a majority* of them belonged to the '*African Church,*' and among those executed were several who had been class-leaders. It is, however, due to the late head of their church (for since the late events the association has been voluntarily dissolved) and their deacons to say that, after the most diligent search and scouting, no evidence entitled to belief has been discovered against them. A hearsay rumor in relation to *Morris Brown* was traced far enough to end in its complete falsification." . . .

But the real ground of the opposition which I encountered on the part of many in the Charleston community, had a history which I have already given, and to which I must now again allude. Twenty-five years previously a plot had been discovered among the negroes for a murderous insurrection against the white people. Many negroes were arrested and tried, but most of them found innocent, were released, yet some thirty-five or forty of them were executed. Of these, I myself, when a boy eleven years old, saw twenty-two hanged on one gallows. A very profound impression was made by these occurrences upon both the black and white population of the city. Unfortunately, whether justly or not, a separate colored church, which had existed some years, with a most excellent negro man for its minister, was accused of some complicity in the plot. The storm that arose wrecked the church. He moved to Philadelphia, and he became subsequently a bishop in some negro denomination, and the members of his Charleston church and congregation were all glad to house themselves from the tempest in the colored membership of the different white churches. The consequence of all these events was that the idea of a separate church for negroes, which was the plan proposed, could not be thought of by hundreds of people in Charleston without horror. . . .

1. The Reverend John Bailey Adger (1810–1899), son of James Adger (1777–1858), a wealthy Charleston merchant, ministered to blacks in the city's Second Presbyterian Church. In *My Life and Times,* the Reverend Adger mentions that he was mentored by Benjamin Morgan Palmer (47) and knew James Hamilton Jr., describing him as "very intelligent" (54). Adger energetically pursued Christian outreach to South Carolina's slaves, which effort drew down upon him white hostility. Adger neglected to mention in his account that a slave named William, owned by his father, was arrested during the Vesey affair and released. See the calendar in Part III, class of prisoners no. 8. See "Religious Instruction of the Colored People," Philadelphia *Pennsylvania Freeman,* July 22, 1847; George A. Blackburn, ed., *The Life Work of John L. Girardeau, D.D., LL.D.: Late Professor in the Presbyterian Theological Seminary, Columbia, S.C.* (Columbia, SC: State Company, 1916), 31–105.

2. *CSCCD*, 69, does, indeed, locate the Adger residence on King Street Road, Charleston Neck.

3. Adger's memory was incorrect here. Pritchard was not one of the twenty-two slaves to die on July 26; he and John Horry were hanged at the gallows on Blake's Lands on July 12. Since Adger was but twelve years old at the time, much of what he wrote here was perhaps based less on memory than on written sources. Since the "old pamphlet" to which Adger alluded had, as he indicates, a sole author, he derived much of the material in his book from Hamilton's *Account*. That he and other Charleston whites retained such documents decades after the fact is telling.

John Bailey Adger, *My Life and Times, 1810–1899* (Richmond, VA, 1899), 50–54, 165.

Archibald H. Grimké[1] on Denmark Vesey, 1901

. . . He was black but comely. Nature gave him a royal body, nobly planned and proportioned, and noted for its great strength. There was that in his countenance, which bespoke a mind within to match that body, a mind of uncommon native intelligence, force of will, and capacity to dominate others. His manners were at once abrupt and crafty, his temper was imperious, his passions and impulses were those of a primitive ruler, and his heart was the heart of a lion. He was often referred to as an old man, but he was not an old man, when he died on a gallows at Charleston, S.C., July 2, 1822. No, he was by no means an old man, whether judged by length of years or strength of body, for he was on that memorable July day, seventy-eight years ago, not more than fifty-six years old, although the hair on his head and face was then probably white. This circumstance and the pre-eminence accorded him by his race neighbors, might account for the references to him, as to that of an old man. . . .

Like many of his race he possessed the gift of gab, as the silver in the tongue and the gold in the full or thick-lipped mouth, are oftentimes contemptuously characterized. And like many of his race he was a devoted student of the Bible to whose interpretation he brought like many other Bible students, not confined to the Negro race, a good deal of imagination, and not a little of superstition, which with some natures is perhaps but another name for the desires of the heart. Thus equipped it is no wonder that Vesey, as he pored over the Old Testament Scriptures, found many points of similitude in the history of the Jews and that of the slaves in the United States. They were both peculiar peoples. They were both Jehovah's peculiar peoples, one in the past, the other in the present. And it seemed to him that as Jehovah bent his ear, and bared his arm once in behalf of the one, so would he do the same for the other. It was all vividly real to his thought, I believe, for to his mind thus had said the Lord.

He ransacked the Bible for apposite and terrible texts, whose commands in the olden times, to the olden people, were no less imperative upon the new times and the new people. This new people was also commanded to arise and destroy their enemies and the city in which they dwelt, "both man and woman, young and old, & & & with the edge of the sword." Believing superstitiously, as he did, in the stern and Nemesis-like God of the Old Testament, he looked confidently for a day of vengeance and retribution for the blacks. He felt, I doubt not, something peculiarly applicable to his enterprise, and intensely personal to himself in the stern and exultant prophecy of Zachariah, fierce and sanguinary words which were constantly in his mouth: "Then shall the Lord go forth, and fight against those nations, as when he fought in the day of battle." According to Vesey's lurid exegeisis "those nations" in the text meant, beyond a peradventure, the cruel masters, and Jehovah was to go forth to fight against them for the poor slaves, and on which ever side fought that day the Almighty God, on that side would assuredly rest victory and deliverance.

It will not be denied that Vesey's plan contemplated the total annihilation of the white population of Charleston. Nursing for many dark years the bitter wrongs of himself and race had filled him, without doubt, with a mad spirit of revenge, and had so given him a decided predilection for shedding the blood of his oppressors. But if he intended to kill them to satisfy a desire for vengeance, he intended to do so also on broader ground. The conspirators, he argued, had no choice in the matter, but were compelled to adopt a policy of extermination by the necessity of their position. The liberty of the blacks was in the balance of fate against the lives of the whites. He could strike that balance in favor of the blacks only by the total destruction of the whites. Therefore, the whites, men, women and children, were doomed to death. "What is the use of killing the louse and leaving the nit?" he asked coarsely and grimly on an occasion when the matter was under consideration. And again he was reported to have, with unrelenting temper, represented to his friends in secret council, that, "It was for our safety not to spare one white skin alive." And so it was unmistakably in his purpose to leave not a single egg lying about Charleston, when he was done with it, out of which might possibly be hatched another future slave-holder and oppressor of his people. "Thorough" was in truth, the merciless motto of that terrible man. . . .

1. Archibald H. Grimké (1849–1930) was the Charleston-born son of Nancy Weston, a mixed-race slave, and her owner, Henry W. Grimké (1801–1852), the younger brother of Thomas, Sarah, and Angelina Grimké. At the time of his death, Henry, a prominent lawyer known for his court battles with Benjamin Faneuil Hunt (1792–1857), resided at the corner of Amherst and East Bay streets in Charleston and owned a plantation in St. Paul's Parish. Although Archibald's brief biography was clearly based in part on Hamilton's *Account*, Grimké also grew up hearing about Vesey from both black and white Charlestonians, including his two abolitionist aunts, Angelina and Sarah Grimké, who were born in 1805 and 1792, respectively, and who well remembered Vesey's execution. See Dickson D. Bruce Jr., *Archibald Grimké: Portrait of a Black Independent* (Baton Rouge: Louisiana State University Press, 1993). On Henry Grimké, see John Belton O'Neall, *Biographical Sketches of the Bench and Bar of South Carolina* . . . , 2 vols. (Charleston, SC, 1859), vol. 2: 542–43.

Archibald H. Grimké, *Right on the Scaffold, or The Martyrs of 1822* (Washington, DC: The Academy, 1901), 3, 11–12.

Archibald H. Grimké on Vesey in Springfield, Illinois, May 8, 1903

. . . . This attempted slave uprising of which I am to speak occurred in Charleston, S.C., in the year 1822. Denmark Vesey was its leader. He had been a slave, but had bought his freedom, was able to read and write, and spoke with fluency the French and English languages. He had traveled extensively over the world in his master's slave vessel, and had thus acquired a stock of experiences and a range of knowledge of men and things possessed by but few of the inhabitants of Charleston at this time. He was a carpenter by trade, and worked with great industry. He accumulated considerable property and was one of the solid men of the community, in spite of his color and previous condition of servitude. Notwithstanding these facts, his unquestioned ability and efficiency as an industrial factor in that city, he was in legal and actual ownership of precious little of that right to "life, liberty and the pursuit of happiness" which the most ignorant and worthless white man enjoyed as a birthright.

This man was conscious of the possession, notwithstanding his black skin and blacker social and civil condition, of longings, aspirations, which the slave code made it a crime for him to satisfy. He felt the sting of forces and faculties within him which, under the heaviest pains and penalties, he was forbidden to exercise. Thus robbed of freedom, ravished of manhood, what was he to do? He resolved to make a strike for freedom.

It is impossible to fix exactly the time when the bold idea of resistance entered his brain. Before embarking on his perilous enterprise he seemed to have reckoned on time as an essential factor in its success. He certainly took time, years, in fact, in the work of preparation. He was thoroughly acquainted with the immense difficulties which beset an uprising of the blacks. Not once did he underestimate the strength of his foes. He was a past grand master in the art of intrigue and dissimulation. In the underground agitation which, during a period of three or four years, he conducted in Charleston and over a hundred miles of the adjacent territory, went, with his great passion of hate and his great purpose of freedom, this untiring founder of sedition. . . .

"The Birthday of John Brown. Tributes at Local Meeting," *Springfield* (IL) *Daily Republican*, May 8, 1903.

Samuel Wragg Ferguson[1] Remembers His Family's Slaves

. . . Here I will digress to tell of Adam,[2] who was a great favorite with me, in early youth and from whom I learned a great many lessons. Born my fathers slave and taken by him at an early age as a body servant, he served as such all through the War and afterwards had charge of the stables particularly of the race horses which father kept. He was a most daring and beautiful rider . . . a fine hunter and he kept fathers beautiful pack of hounds in the most perfect order. . . . In the year 1822, a great insurrection was plan[n]ed, to take place in Charleston and adjacent country. At a certain hour the City was to be fired in several places and as the men ran out of their houses to go to the fire they were to be killed and the city given over to the blacks, the plot was discovered only a few hours before its intended execution and happily frustrated, in the investigations which followed, it was found that Adam was implicated, but that he had stipulated that he should be allowed to save his masters life. The leaders were regularly tried by the legal tribunals, and those found guilty, received appropriate sentences. Twenty two were sentenced to death, and were hung on the same gallows, together. Henry Barker writes thus about it "my father S. W. Barker was a boy at school at the time, the school house was on the lot now occupied by the Fire Proof buildin[g], corner of Meeting and Chalmers Streets and the ghastly procession passed by, each negro seated on his coffin which was in a cart, driven by another negro. Father often spoke to me of it, and particularly of one poor devil[3] who bowed and smiled and grinned in the most horrible fashion, evidently so overcome with fright that he knew not what he did."

Others were sentenced to Banishment, among these was my fathers "driver" o[r] head man[4] on the plantation. . . .

1. Samuel Wragg Ferguson (1834–1917) wrote this unpublished, undated memoir in the years after the Civil War, in which he served the Confederacy as a brigadier general. Hired by the Mississippi Levee Board as treasurer and secretary, Ferguson was suspected of embezzling up to forty thousand dollars in missing funds in 1894. He returned first to Charleston and then moved for a time to Ecuador. See Bertram Wyatt-Brown, *The House of Percy: Honor, Melancholy, and Imagination in a Southern Family* (New York: Oxford University Press, 1994).

2. Legally, Adam belonged to Ann Wragg Ferguson (1756–1835), the widow of Thomas Ferguson (1726–1786). In 1822, she lived at 5 Liberty Street. See *CSCCD*, 79. Adam was acquitted, perhaps in exchange for his testimony.

3. This "poor devil" was Bacchus Hammet. As the notation attached to Bacchus's confession suggests, however, his behavior on the morning of his execution was based more on bravado than on fear.

4. The first court found Frank Ferguson guilty and sentenced him to transportation. On the role of drivers in slave insurrections, see Robert L. Paquette, "The Drivers Shall Lead Them: Image and Reality in Slave Resistance," in *Slavery, Secession, and Southern History*, ed. Robert L. Paquette and Louis A. Ferleger (Charlottesville: University Press of Virginia, 2000), 31–58.

Samuel Wragg Ferguson Memoirs, typescript, SCHS.

Harriott Horry Ravenel[1] Presents the Dunning School Interpretation of Slavery, 1931

. . . In 1822 occurred the only really serious threat of servile insurrection which had threatened Charleston since that incited by the Spaniards at St. Augustine in 1739.

By this time the disputes consequent upon the admission to the Union of the new States of the Louisiana Purchase were raging.

The abolition party was violent. It was proved that certain negroes who had gone to the North had there become so perverted that upon their return to Charleston, they proposed a plot of insurrection to their friends.[2]

They asserted that in this scheme they had the support of a large and influential body of sympathizers at Boston and elsewhere.

The negroes—or some of them—lent ear. The plot thickened, and the consequences might have been too terrible for words, had not two faithful servants told their masters of the startling tale. These gentlemen at once informed the Intendant, Colonel James Hamilton, and the Governor, Mr. Bennett.

Upon examination it was found that the originator of the scheme was a free mulatto named Denmark Vesey, who had been much in the North in communication with the abolition party, and had brought in and disseminated their publications.[3] His chief colleague was an African called "Gullah Jack, an hereditary conjurer," supposed by the negroes to be immortal and able to work miracles by magic. These and others were the ringleaders. Their chief followers were the mechanics, carpenters, blacksmiths, carters, mill-hands, wheelwrights, etc. Very few were house servants, and it was two of these who had, "for love of their masters," told the story. It is impossible to say how far the field-hands had entered into the conspiracy; but it was known from the Santee to Port Royal.

Their plan was that at midnight on Sunday, June 12, a large body of negroes should cross from the islands to the town, and those from the adjacent country march in. They were to seize the arms in the armouries, particularly those in one known to be carelessly guarded on "the Neck." The Intendant and Governor were to be instantly killed; the town fired in many places; all white men to be massacred, the women kept; all possible booty to be secured. There was much talk of St. Domingo, to which place they were to go with their plunder.

On learning this, the authorities immediately took the necessary measures. There was horrible anxiety and few people slept on the night of the 12th of June; but the guard was doubled, the militia was in readiness, the arms secured. The negroes, seeing the preparations which it was impossible to conceal, kept perfectly quiet. All suspected were arrested. Vesey showed great courage, and could not be brought to confess until confronted with a barber from whom he had ordered a wig made of "white man's hair" as a disguise. Then he broke down.

They were all brought to trial, the trials being conducted with the greatest care by courts of freeholders, men of the first character. It was found that many implicated were too ignorant and stupid to be worthy of punishment; they were dismissed. Of the guilty, twenty-nine were transported and thirty-five executed—twenty-two at one time in the jail yard in the presence of many spectators.[4] Never since the days of the pirates had such a thing been seen.

There was not the least attempt at rescue or even any great excitement on the part of the crowd; but the impression left on many minds was most painful. Henceforth their compatriots might be their foes. . . .

1. Harriott Horry Ravenel (1832–1912) was the author of a number of popular works about early Charleston, including *Eliza Pinckney* (New York, 1896). She was the daughter-in-law of John Ravenel (1793–1862), whose uncle owned Peter (Prioleau) Desverney. See p. 795 n4.

2. Ministers Morris Brown and Henry Drayton, as the documents included in Part V demonstrate, had been to Philadelphia to meet with other AME leaders, but they were neither the instigators of the plot nor actively involved.

3. Although Vesey allegedly owned a cache of smuggled antislavery pamphlets, he had never been to the North nor met with white abolitionists.

4. The twenty-two slaves who were hanged on July 26 died on the Lines on the northern edge of the city, not within the walled Jail–Work-House compound.

Harriott Horry Ravenel, *Charleston: The Place and the People* (New York: Macmillan, 1906), 437–40.

Savannah Tribune

Saturday, May 4, 1907

. . . Last Friday Prof. Pearson[1] lectured on "Negro Insurrection for Freedom." He showed from facts of history that the Negro made many insurrections for freedom some recorded and some merely referred to in a general way, that only by keeping the Negro in complete ignorance were insurrections prevented, that as soon as the Negro understood the situation civilly, morally and physically he was ready to make a dash for liberty at the risk of his own life. Gen. Gabriel, Nat Turner and Drumark Vesey were fully discussed. He stated that the proposed insurrection of Gen. Yabrill and Drumark Vesey were planned with considerable skill resourcefulness and wisdom. Commencement next!

1. Henry Pearson, an African American graduate of Claflin University, taught at Georgia State College for Colored Youth, Savannah. See "Claflin Graduates and What They Are Doing," *Christian Educator* 22 (February 1912): 9.

Reverend George Sherwood Dickerman[1] Hears from an Eyewitness, 1907

. . . In the spring of 1822 the conspiracy of Denmark Vesey was discovered; this was a crude scheme for a Negro insurrection, wild and unlikely of execution, but none of the less portentous to excitable imaginations. Vesey was a Negro who had bought his own freedom by working over hours; he had been owned by a sea captain with whom he had sailed over the seas to many ports and learned much of the world; then after his emancipation, he had settled in Charleston as a carpenter and put his mind to the problem of emancipating all slaves. When his operations were found out he and thirty-four others were tried, convicted and hanged. These events put the free colored people in general in a very delicate position and worked much to their injur[y]. They came under the most painful suspicion, were closely watched, restrictions were put upon their movements, and laws were enacted to forbid meetings and to debar any who left the state from ever returning. . . .

There is still living in Charleston—or was a few months ago—an aged man who was born September 13, 1809. He is the patriarch of the Brown Fellowship Society which he joined in 1830, seventy-six years ago. He was once brown of complexion, but now his skin, like his hair, has become singularly white. But of more consequence than this his mind has continued clear, and when I saw him last he could recall distinctly the incidents of more than eighty years. He was present at the execution of Denmark Vesey and his companions and describes their behavior; he was in the turmoil of the years that followed, was early made President of the "Fellowship," and piloted it through the troublous events that culminated in the war between the states, and on into wholly changed conditions of the present time. This venerable man, Thomas Holmes,[2] tells of an interview with Senator Hayne in 1836 when a law had been passed forbidding more than seven negroes to meet together in any place by themselves. . . .

1. Connecticut-born George Sherwood Dickerman (1843–1937), a graduate of Yale Divinity School, became a Congregationalist minister. He spent much of his adult life in the South, pursuing a variety of sociological and literary interests, including black education and land tenure. He served as general field agent of the Southern Educational Board. See Kansas City *American Citizen,* February 20, 1903. The editors are indebted to Harlan Greene, College of Charleston, for directing them to this source.

2. The Holloway Family Scrapbook, Avery Center, Special Collections, College of Charleston, contains scattered information about Thomas McPherson Holmes (b. 1809) and membership in the Brown Fellowship Society.

G. S. Dickerman, "A Glimpse of Charleston History" *Southern Workman* 36 (1907): 20–21.

Dr. W.E.B. Du Bois[1] on Gabriel, Vesey, and John Brown, 1909

. . . John Brown, even as a child, saw the puzzling anomalies and contradictions in human right and liberty all about him. Ever and again he saw this in the North, leading to concerted action among free Negroes, especially in cities where they were brought in contact with one another, and had some chance of asserting their nominal freedom. Just at the close of the eighteenth century, first in Philadelphia and then in New York, small groups of them withdrew from the white churches to escape disgraceful discrimination and established churches of their own, which still live with millions of adherents. In the year of John Brown's birth, 1800, Gabriel planned his formidable uprising in Virginia, and the year after his marriage, 1821, Denmark Vesey of South Carolina went grimly to the scaffold, after one of the shrewdest Negro plots that ever frightened the South into hysterics. Of all this John Brown, the boy and young man, knew little. In after years he learned of Gabriel and Vesey and Turner, and told of their exploits and studied their plans; but at the time he was far off from the world, carrying on his tannery and marrying a wife. Perhaps as a lad he heard some of the oratory that celebrated the act of 1808, stopping the slave trade, as the beginning of the end of slavery. Perhaps not, for the act did little good until it was reenforced in 1820. All the time, however, John Brown's keen eyes were searching for the way of life and his tender heart was sensitive to injustice and wrong everywhere. Indeed, it is not unlikely that the first black folk to gain his aid and sympathies and direct his thoughts to what afterward became his life-work, were the fugitive slaves from the South. . . .

1. Voluminous scholarship exists on William Edward Burghardt Du Bois (1868–1963) and his intellectual and political activities. The subject of slave resistance held considerable interest for him, and he contemplated writing his Harvard dissertation on the Nat Turner insurrection, which he claimed was "the most successful and bloody of slave uprisings since Hayti." See W.E.B. Du Bois, *John Brown* (Philadelphia: G. W. Jacobs & Co., 1909), 85; Scot French, *The Rebellious Slave: Nat Turner in American Memory* (Boston: Houghton Mifflin, 2004), 177–85; David Levering Lewis, *W.E.B. Du Bois, Volume I, Biography of a Race, 1868–1919* (New York: Henry Holt, 1993), 356–57.

W.E.B. Du Bois, *John Brown* (Philadelphia: G. W. Jacobs & Co., 1909), 82–83.

Booker T. Washington[1] on Vesey and Turner, 1909

. . . The most important, because the most far-reaching in their effects, of these efforts of Negro slaves to gain their freedom by force, were the attempted insurrection of Denmark Vesey in 1822 and the outbreak under Nat Turner in 1831. . . . Vesey was known among his people as a deep student of the Bible and exerted a marked influence over them, particularly through their religious meetings which then as now, were of the nature of popular assemblies for the discussion of all questions relating to the welfare of the race. Vesey's plot failed of its purpose, and he was caught, duly tried, and, with thirty-four others, put to death. . . .

1. Born in slavery in Virginia, Booker Taliaferro Washington (1856–1915) became the most prominent black leader in the United States before the end of the nineteenth century. Like W.E.B. Du Bois, with whom he competed, Washington has engendered a voluminous scholarly literature. Like Du Bois, Washington studied the history of slave resistance, and his differences with Du Bois on the subject can be discerned perhaps most clearly in Washington's biography *Frederick Douglass* (Philadelphia, 1907), a book that the publisher, George W. Jacobs & Company, had originally asked Du Bois to write. It also dissuaded Du Bois from writing as an alternative topic a biography of Nat Turner.

Booker T. Washington, *The Story of the Negro: The Rise of the Race from Slavery*, 2 vols. (London: T. Fisher Unwin, 1909), vol. 1: 172–73.

Charleston Historian Yates Snowden[1] on Slavery and Vesey, 1915

. . . The relations between master and slave in St. John's and St. Stephen's were generally kind for over 100 years. There were cruel slave owners as there are now cruel husbands—and cruel wives!—and cruel slave owners were despised by the community and were known of all men. With the negro race largely preponderant, naturally the laws bore harshly on the subject population. I would be the last to defend all legislation passed for the subjection of negro slaves—and yet I believe, and shall always contend, that in St. John's and St. Stephen's, there was a minimum of cruelty, and that the relations of the master and slave were, on the whole, ideal for that time. . . . I would remind you that 1822 was the year of the celebrated Demark-Vesey–Gullah Jack slave insurrection, when Charleston and the plantations along Cooper River barely escaped a frightful massacre, which would, if successful, have rivaled the horrors of St. Domingo! The only echo of that attempted insurrection I have found in St. John's and St. Stephen's, is in this letter from the Rev. Charles B. Snowden[2] to his brother in Charleston. . . ."The taking up of the crop required my presence at the plantation. I had also to go with the patrol into the swamp after the remnant of Joe's party,[3] and then I had to spend two days attending the court pleading for one of the negroes." . . . On Friday the 17th Strephon a slave of Dr. Ravenel's[4] was executed near the Canal (Santee) bank, just at the foot of the bridge at Big Camp. He was one of the party which lately infested the neighbourhood of the mouth of the Canal. He appeared under the fatal tree unappalled. He acknowledged that his sentence was just; that he should have been glad if he could have been saved, but must submit to his fate with resignation and with no ill will towards any one. He professed . . . that he had never attempted the life of any person and had strenuously advised Joe in more instances than one not to commit murder. He knelt under the tree, and was engaged in silent prayer for some time, and was twined off almost inaudibly singing a hymn. The Court I believe, gave all due consideration to the circumstances of his case, and delayed the passage and execution of the sentence for several days. The rest of the party being women are to be dismissed, I believe, without punishment. Whether "Joe," the ringleader, was ever apprehended, and what his fate,[5] I do not know . . . You will pardon an extract from another letter from Charles Snowden to his brother in July, 1822, the preceding year, upon receipt of the news of the Denmark-Vesey insurrection. He writes in philosophic and pessimistic vein and doubtless gives the views of some intelligent planters of his class, and he ventures an explanation why slave insurrections are more unlikely in the country than in the cities, which is interesting to students of the slavery régime. "We are henceforth," he writes, "to expect a great deal of such business. The progress of the light of knowledge is such, and the adaptation of man for liberty so constitutional that it will be impossible to keep the negroes utterly in the dark, and utterly tame under the necessary oppression which now weighs them down. It will be long, long indeed, before a completely successful effort will or can be made by them to throw off the yoke of bondage; but efforts and bloody ones, I am afraid, will be continually made until success at last shall crown them. Reflection, the fruit of leisure, will have place with many black people in the city where hard labour for all cannot be found, and reflecting will give rise to action, and action once begun will generate action. In the country we are in less danger. Our negroes know that labor is essential to subsistence, and that they have nothing to expect at last but a change of masters, and that for the worse. Hence they will never be generally brought into the scrape until it happens from necessity. On a late search for arms there was nothing found indicating anything like a state of hostile preparation." . . .

1. Born in Charleston and a graduate of the College of Charleston, Yates Snowden (1858–1933) worked as a journalist for the *Charleston News and Courier* and taught history at the University of South Carolina. He coedited a *History of South Carolina,* 5 vols. (Chicago: Lewis Publishing, 1920). See Theodore D. Jervey, "Yates Snowden," *SCHGM* (July 1933): 175–76.

2. Charles Blair Snowden (1785–1825), Yates Snowden's grandfather, was an Episcopalian minister who served as rector of St. Stephen's Parish near Charleston. See "Obituary," *Churchman's Magazine* 4 (1826): 320.

3. On the runaway slave Joe and his band of fugitive slaves, see Part V, pp. 529, 622, 624.

4. Yates Snowden may have misread his grandfather's script. Strephon belonged not to Dr. Edmund Ravenel (1797–1871) but to the French-born physician Jean Louis (also "Lewis") Raoul de Champmanoir. See Raoul's "Petition for compensation," 1823, no. 174, series S165015, SCDAH, and Camden (SC) *Southern Chronicle,* October 22, 1823.

5. A hunting party of whites killed the legendary Joe near the Santee Canal, upriver from Charleston, in October 1823. See "The Murderer Joe Destroyed," Charleston *City Gazette and Commercial Daily Advertiser,* October 8, 1823.

Yates Snowden, "The Planters of St. Johns," *Transactions of the Huguenot Society of South Carolina* 21 (1915): 24–26.

Carter G. Woodson[1] on Vesey, 1924

. . . In 1822, Charleston, South Carolina . . . was the scene of a better planned effort to effect the liberation of the slaves by organizing them to assassinate their masters. The leading spirit was one Denmark Vesey, an educated Negro of Santo Domingo, from which he had brought his new ideas as to freedom.[2] It was observed that these Negroes in Charleston had been reading the slavery debate of the Missouri Compromise and were emboldened by the attacks on the institution to effect its extermination. In all of these cases the plans of the Negroes were detected in time to foil them, and the conspirators were promptly executed in such a barbarous way as to serve as a striking example of the fate awaiting those who refused to be deterred from such efforts. . . .

1. Historian Carter Godwin Woodson (1870–1950), the son of Virginia sharecroppers, received a PhD from Harvard. He founded and served as editor of the *Journal of Negro History* from 1915 until his death. No journal in the United States in the twentieth century contributed more to the study of slave resistance.

2. Although Vesey briefly lived in the French colony of Saint-Domingue (not Spanish Santo Domingo) from fall 1781 to spring 1782, he was not technically "from" the colony. Woodson evidently got this erroneous data from *The History of South Carolina,* coedited by William Gilmore Simms, which is excerpted on p. 729.

Carter G. Woodson, *The Negro in Our History,* 3rd ed. (Washington, DC: Associated Publishers, 1924), 93.

Chicago World

Thursday, October 29, 1925

. . . A smoke-filled room, decorated with tritely worded placards. A room hung with banners bearing the words of the great socialist philosopher Karl Marx, a room [*illegible*] where hang oil paintings of Saklatvala, Sun Yat Sen, Abd-el-Krim, Denmark Vesey, Nat Turner and Toussaint L'Overture. A room filled with eager and attentive listeners—black and white. This is the scene at the opening of the American Negro Labor Congress,[1] whose purpose in the word of its sponsors, is to promote unity and harmony between the workers of all races. The locale is the Metropolitan Community Center, 3118 Gates avenue. . . .

1. The American Communist Party established the American Negro Labor Congress in 1925.

Reed Smith[1] on Jack Pritchard, 1926

. . . Both the word Gullah and the Negroes so named came from the West Coast of Africa, but exactly where has not been agreed upon. There are two widely-held conjectures. One is that Gullah is a shortened form of Angola, the name of an African West Coast district lying south of the Equator and the mouth of the Congo River. A small but positive bit of evidence to this effect is found in an entry of the Charleston City Council, under the year 1822, in which reference is made to "Gullah Jack" and his company of "Gullah or Angola

Negroes." This indicates that rightly or wrongly, as far back as 1822 the official governing body of the city of Charleston regarded Gullah as a corrupted form of Angola. . . .

1. Reed Smith (1881–1943) performed pioneering work on the Gullah language and culture as a professor of English at the University of South Carolina. See Henry H. Lesesne, *A History of the University of South Carolina, 1940–2000* (Columbia: University of South Carolina Press, 2001), 10. Of the more than sixty thousand African slaves entering Charleston from 1804 to 1808, when the state had reopened the traffic, the majority of those imported were from Kongo-Angola region of West-Central Africa.

Reed Smith, *Gullah* (Columbia: Bureau of Publications, University of South Carolina, 1926), 7–8.

Resolutions of the National Negro Congress

February 14–16, 1936

Randolph's Speech.[1]

. . . Greetings and felicitations upon this great Congress. Though absent in the flesh, I am with you in the spirit of the deathless courage of the 18th and 19th century black rebels and martyr[s] for human justice, in the spirit of Frederick Douglass and Nat Turner, of Gabriel and Denmark Vesey, of Harriet Tubman and Sojourner Truth—those noble rebels who struck out in the dark days of slavery that Negro men and women might be free. . . .

1. A. Philip Randolph (1889–1979), son of an AME preacher, served as the first president of the National Negro Congress, a Communist-front civil rights and labor organization, founded in 1935.

Speech of A. Philip Randolph, in *Resolutions of the National Negro Congress. Held in Chicago, Ill., February 14, 15, 16, 1936* (Washington, DC, 1936), 1.

Benjamin Brawley[1] on Black "Heroes," 1937

. . . Even more carefully planned was the effort of Denmark Vesey in Charleston in 1822. The Christian name of this man was originally Télémaque, but this was corrupted to Telmak and then to Denmark. Vesey was the slave and personal attendant of a sea-captain of the same name who commanded a trading vessel going chiefly between Charleston and the West Indies. In 1800, at the age of thirty-three, he won $1,500 in a lottery, and with $600 of this amount he purchased his freedom. Meanwhile he worked diligently at his trade, that of a carpenter. Of striking appearance, handsome, alert, magnetic, he came to have unbounded influence over the slaves, understanding well their superstitious nature and having just the domineering temper needed to make his conquest complete.

Vesey conceived an insurrection that aimed at the annihilation of the white population of Charleston. His assistants he selected with the utmost care. Peter Poyas was intrepid and resolute, cautious, and not easily deterred by obstacles. Rolla Bennett was plausible in address and had uncommon self-possession. Gullah Jack was feared as a sorcerer and was thought to bear a charmed life. Others were hardly less capable. "Take care," said Poyas, in speaking to a recruit about the plan, "and don't mention it to those waiting men who receive presents of old coats from their masters, or they'll betray us." In course of time Negroes within a radius of seventy or eighty miles about Charleston were brought into the plot, and the date set was the second Sunday in July. The plan was for Poyas to lead in the seizure of the Arsenal in Meeting Street opposite St. Michael's Church, and the other leaders, coming from six different directions, were to converge upon this center. Meanwhile a body of horse was to keep the streets clear. "Eat only dry food," advised Gullah Jack as the day approached, "parched corn and ground nuts, and when you join us as we pass, put this crab claw in your mouth and you can't be wounded."

Late in May a slave spoke to his master about some things he had heard, and the arrest of some of the men followed. Poyas and Mingo Harth, a leader of one of the companies of horse, were cool and collected; they ridiculed the whole idea and were discharged. Ned Bennett, brother of Rolla, hearing that his name had been mentioned, voluntarily went before the officials and succeeded in baffling them further. By Friday, June 14, however, another informant had spoken to his master, and this man had the facts well in hand. He said that the original plan had been changed and that the night of Sunday, June 16, was the time now set for the insurrection. A messenger moving about on Saturday night found sentinels on guard, and arrests soon followed. As a result of this effort for freedom thirty-five Negroes were executed and forty-three banished. Vesey was hanged on July 2 with five of his chief associates. He made no confession, and Poyas was similarly resolute. "Do not open your lips," he said; "die silent as you shall see me do." . . .

1. Benjamin Griffith Brawley (1882–1939), born in Columbia, South Carolina, taught at Howard University and published numerous works on African American culture and history. See John W. Parker, "Benjamin Brawley and the American Cultural Tradition," *Phylon* 16, no. 2 (1955): 183–94.

Benjamin Brawley, *Negro Builders and Heroes* (Chapel Hill: University of North Carolina Press, 1937), 43–44.

Israel Nesbitt on Great-Grandfather Robert Nesbitt

. . . Israel Nesbitt, 1315 McDuffie Avenue, Columbia, S.C., says he is a great-grandson of Robert Nesbitt,[1] a Negro who was acquitted of insurrectionary charges at Charleston, S.C., in 1822, when Denmark Vesey and 34 of his rebels were hanged. Israel, who is a bricklayer and carpenter, says he had to content himself with an education barely sufficient to enable him to read, write, and cipher. His one big gift is a memory which retains much of the history of early day slavery, now little more than a tradition.

"My great-granddaddy was a son of Robert Nesbitt and he tell me 'bout de Vesey uprisin' as his daddy tell it to him. He say 131 Negroes, 'cludin' his daddy, was brung to trial as a result of de secret plan of Vesey and his friends, to take over de city and kill off de white folks. Denmark Vesey come to Charleston from de West Indies wid his owner, Cap' Vesey, a rich, white importer of Charleston. For many years, probably fifteen or twenty, Vesey was a faithful slave of Cap' Vesey, at Charleston.

"Bout 1800, when Denmark was 33 years old, he win $1,500 in a lottery. Wid dis money he buy his freedom, from Cap' Vesey, for $600. De other money, he invest. He work every day at de trade of carpenter. He talk French and English good and soon become much 'spected by slaves and esteem by de white folks. De most of dis time he was sowin' de seeds of discontent 'mong Charleston Negroes and in de districts 'round it. But he was so sly 'bout it, de white folks do not 'spicion him.

"Vesey hold meetin's at his house at midnight and he swear his members to secrecy. My great-granddaddy attended a meetin' one night. He and Vesey both was property owners and friends. But my great-granddaddy never take no part in de plannin,' 'cause he tried all de time to show Vesey he was ridin' to a fall and was playin' wid dynamite. He tell Vesey he was takin' too big a dare and dat de plan was too dangerous and a wrong step wid it.

"After my great-granddaddy tell them dis, Vesey smile and stand up and tell them: 'Take care. Don't mention dis plan to no waitin' slave who git old coats and such things from deir masters, or they will betray our secrets!'

"De meetin' break up and de slaves scatter out to deir quarters, and sho' as you born, it was one of dese same waitin' men dat tattle de secret to de masters. De revolt was squelched and de leaders was tried before a special court, in which Robert Y. Hayne 'peared, then risin' to 'stinction.

"Vesey take hand as his own lawyer, but wid all his skill, him and 34 others of de rebels, was convicted and hanged.

"De court find dat de Negro leaders plan to kill all de white folks and put de Negroes in de saddle. My great-granddaddy say he never see so much tumult in his born days, as dere was when de Vesey crowd was hanged, near Charleston. De court go right 'long. Of de 131 'rested, 35 was hanged, 28 found not guilty and acquitted, and de rest deported from South Carolina.

"Granddaddy say dat de loyalty of dc slave to his master was so deep under de skin of de slave, dat it was even stronger than de long dream of freedom. He say dere was three kinds of slaves. De first, was de slave who was just plain bad, by choice. De second, was de slave who would rather endure de ills he bear, than fly to others dat they don't know 'bout. De third, was de one who was always waitin' for de big change, to make a getaway. But down in deir hearts, all slaves hopin' and prayin' for de day dat freedom may dawn.

"My great-granddaddy was de leader in de prisoners who was acquitted in de Vesey case. He was fairly big property owner in Charleston. My own granddaddy was pretty well fixed, but, generally speakin,' Jordan road has been pretty stumpy for de rest of us. I tells my chillun to get all de schoolin' they can, trust in God, and they won't go very far wrong. Don't you think so?"

1. The calendar of the *OR* lists "A Free Man" of color named Robert Nesbitt, arrested on July 3 and released. The State Free Negro Capitation Tax Book, Charleston, South Carolina, 1821, SCDAH, contains the name of "Bob Nesbit."

George P. Rawick, ed., *The American Slave: A Composite Autobiography,* Supplement, *North Carolina and South Carolina Narratives* (Westport, CT: Greenwood Publishing, 1972), ser. I, vol. 11: 261–63.

Daniel Goddard[1] on Vesey and Turner

. . . "My name is Daniel Goddard. I was born in Columbia, S.C. Feb. 14, 1863, to slave parents. . . . The Nat Turner insurrection in Virginia and the Vesey uprising in Charleston was discussed often, in my presence, by my parents and friends. I learned that revolts of slaves in Martinique, Antigua, Santiago, Caracas and Tortugas, was known all over the South. Slaves were about as well aware of what was going on, as their masers were. However the masters made it harder for their slaves for a while. . . .

I once talked with Frederick Douglass, perhaps the most eminent Negro to appear so far in America. . . . He was United States Minister to Haiti at the time I met him and was eminent as an orator. . . . [2]

1. Goddard was born in 1863, and at the time of his undated interview he was seventy-four, placing this exchange sometime in 1937. Goddard, who had been educated at a Freedmen's Bureau school, then lived in Columbia.

2. Frederick Douglass was minister to Haiti from 1889 to 1891.

Slave Narratives: A Folk History of Slavery in the United States from Interviews with Former Slaves, Volume XIV: South Carolina Narratives, Part 2 (Washington, DC, 1941), 149.

Kurt Singer[1] on the tale of Denmark Vesey

. . . Denmark Vesey resolved to lead his followers to Haiti. His plan called for the seizure of ships in Charleston harbor, stocking them with provisions and arms to take an expedition in safety to Toussaint L'Overture's Negro Republic.

Denmark gathered his followers, man by man, approaching only those he was sure he could trust. To his new recruits his first order was: "Learn to read and write." He organized Bible classes and religious study groups.

"Don't say we cannot do anything. Go and buy a spelling book and read the fable of Hercules and the Wagoner."

Not many of his speeches have been recorded, but here is one which survived and can be found among old manuscripts in a Charleston Library.[2]

"Remember how you are wronged every day. Remember how you and your mothers and sisters, your wives and children were wronged. Remember the generations weeping and clanking heavy chains from the cradle to the grave. Remember the oppression of the living who, with heartbreak and death wounds, are treading their mournful way in bitter anguish and despair across burning desert sands and with parched souls and shriveled minds, with piteous thirsts and terrible tortures of body and spirit. Weep for them, weep for yourselves too, if ye will, but learn to hate, aye, to hate with such hatred as blazes within me, the wicked slave system and the wickeder white men who oppress and wrong us thus."

Although Vesey, who drew upon the Gospels for inspiration, had begun only with compassion, he had now learned to hate. Like many great rebels he had discovered that there was no more potent force than hatred to weld together a revolutionary movement. . . . [3]

1. Vienna-born Kurt Singer (1911–2005) was a prolific journalist and author, whose books included studies of World War II espionage and a biography of entertainer Danny Kaye. See Myrna Oliver, "Kurt Singer, 94; Espionage Writer and Biographer Spied on Nazis in World War II," *Los Angeles Times,* December 14, 2005. *This Month* was a short-lived progressive magazine based in Montreal, Canada.

2. A story about Singer's piece in the Baltimore *Afro-American,* October 5, 1946, also noted that he had "utilized all manuscripts in the Charleston, S.C. library as sources." Neither Singer nor John Jasper, the author of the short piece in the *Afro-American,* indicated what this source was and in which Charleston library Singer conducted research. As Nicholas Butler, manager of Charleston Archives in the Charleston County Public Library, observed, in 1946 the Charleston Library Society did not collect "black history" materials, while the Charleston County Public Library, then known as the Charleston Free Library, maintained a "Negro branch" called Dart Hall, which dated back to the early twentieth century. Dr. Butler noted that Dart Hall "had a good collection of primary source materials related to Charleston black history," some of which were lost or already missing when transferred to the Avery Research Center in the 1980s (letter of Nicholas Butler to editors, March 5, 2010). Certainly no black congregant would have written down Vesey's "speech," and no contemporaneous source suggests that such testimony was read into the trial record in 1822. Joe La Roche, however, did testify that Vesey used the story of Hercules and the wagoner to recruit followers, and the angry tone of the sermon corresponds to what others testified about Vesey's tough, cold demeanor. If such a document did exist, most likely it constituted second-hand testimony.

3. The remainder of Singer's essay, which ran to roughly three thousand words, appears to be taken from the *Official Report* as well as Grimké's *Right on the Scaffold.* Although the framework for the essay was largely biographical, Singer, usually a respected journalist, invented dialogue and misspelled the names of some of the key conspirators. Only when alluding to the sermon, however, did Singer claim to be transcribing an "old manuscript."

Kurt Singer, "America's First Underground," *This Month* (October 1946): 34–40.

New York Times

Wednesday, November 3, 1948

PREMIER TONIGHT OF HEYWARD PLAY. . . . Motivated by broad-minded principles, the Theatre Guild abhors hard and fast rules. For instance, back in 1941 it was seriously thinking of doing "Set My People Free." Written by Dorothy Heyward, co-author with her late husband of such Negro shows as "Porgy," "Porgy and Bess" and "Mamba's Daughters," "Set My People Free" deals with Denmark Vesey's abortive slave uprising of 1822 in Charleston. . . .

The project was dropped for the following reasons: The war came along and it wasn't considered advisable to do the play then. Moreover, in its original form the venture would have been saddled with a budget of at least $125,000. . . .

Recollections of Rose Pringle Ravenel[1]

. . . I have often heard my father[2] discuss the slave conspiracy and insurrection that was part of a plot conceived by Denmark Vesey, a free mulatto, which was to take place the night of June 16, 1822. The plan was to murder the whites in Charleston and establish a regime analogous to that in Santo Domingo. My father's version of the story was that Peter Desvernays,[3] Uncle John Prioleau's servant, betrayed the existence of the plot to Uncle John Ravenel.[4] The latter went in company with another gentleman, and with Peter, to one of the Negro meetings in a stable loft where the servant hid them in the hay. They listened to the speech of the conspirators and satisfied themselves of the truth of Peter's story. . . .

1. Rose Pringle Ravenel (1850–1943), of Huguenot descent, grew up on Farmfield plantation in St. Andrew's Parish. In her seniority she suffered from blindness, and her stories, compiled by "many hands," were published posthumously. Her aunt was Mary (Ravenel) McCall, who was widowed in 1822.

2. William Ravenel (1806–1888), Rose's father, builder of Farmfield plantation, was a wealthy businessman and banker. See Henry Edmund Ravenel, *Ravenel Records: A History and Genealogy of the Huguenot Family of Ravenel, of South Carolina* (Atlanta, 1898), 55–56.

3. Upon becoming free, Peter took the surname of "Desverney," not "Desvernays." By "Santo Domingo," Ravenel meant Haiti. No document suggests that Vesey planned to establish a black republic in South Carolina.

4. John Ravenel (1793–1862) was a merchant and railroad executive. Since he was the nephew of John Cordes Prioleau (1772–1825), Rose Pringle Ravenel's great-uncle and the owner of Peter Prioleau, it is possible that John had some role in investigating the truth of the plot, although no hard evidence has yet surfaced to substantiate Rose's claim. That said, the Henry Ravenel Papers at SCHS do contain a document with the testimony of John Enslow.

Rose Pringle Ravenel, *Piazza Tales: A Charleston Memory*, ed. Anthony Harrigan (Charleston, SC: Shaftesbury Press, 1952), 9.

Los Angeles Tribune

May 15, 1959

Concerteer." Waldemar Hille,[1] concert pianist, known to the locals for his leadership of the choir of the First Unitarian church . . . has held teaching posts in several colleges and has appeared in piano recitals in Steinway and Town halls, is also well known as a composer and arranger. Notable among his works are choral settings to the "Blues," "Freedom's Plow," and "Let America be America Again," by Langston Hughes, and the oratorio "Denmark Vesey," based on poems about the South Carolina Negro who led slave insurrections in South Carolina. . . .

1. Waldemar Hille (1908–1995), pianist, composer, and activist, performed on several occasions as an accompanist for Paul Robeson (1898–1976). Hille joined the Communist Party in 1942 and edited *The People's Song Book* (New York, 1948), a collection of protest musical scores. See David King Dunaway, *Singing Out: An Oral History of America's Folk Music Revivals* (New York, 2010), 205.

New York Times

Monday, July 22, 1963

CHARLESTON TORN BY RACIAL UNREST.

. . . A riot Tuesday night, following a Negro demonstration, prompted Gov. Donald S. Russell to dispatch 125 state law enforcement officers here to aid the city police. He also alerted the National Guard.

Officials of the National Association for the Advancement of Colored People were imprisoned on riot charges. . . . The prospect is for continued demonstrations by the Negro teen-agers and children who filed out of the Emanuel African Methodist Episcopal Church day after day this week to march through the business district.

Emanuel Church has known other Negro revolt. An earlier building on the same site served as a stop on the Underground Railroad. Loosened flooring gave access to basement trenches in which fugitive slaves found sanctuary.

Preparations for an abortive slave insurrection were made in the church in 1822 by Denmark Vesey, a sea captain's slave who had bought his freedom with $600 of the $1,500 he had won in a Charleston lottery. The plot was discovered, Vesey and 34 of his associates were hanged and the church was closed for a time.[1]

Mayor J. Palmer Gaillard and many other whites believe that outsiders rather than city Negroes are largely responsible for the present unrest. . . .

1. Charleston authorities razed the first AME Church in the northeastern suburb of Hampstead in 1822. At the end of the Civil War, Robert Vesey Sr. designed a new wooden structure for worship on the corner of Calhoun and Meeting streets. An earthquake severely damaged this building in 1886. The current Emanuel AME Church at 110 Calhoun Street, the one featured in this 1963 story, was completed in 1892 and is the oldest AME church in the South. After Bethel AME Church in Philadelphia, it is the oldest in the world.

Chicago Metro News

Saturday, February 13, 1982

Yaphet Kotto and Cleavon Little in "Denmark Vesey Rebellion."

In 1822, a prosperous free Black man named Denmark Vesey risked his life to free his enslaved brothers in Charleston, South Carolina.[1]

Denmark Vesey's story, which took place over 40 years before the Emancipation Proclamation, becomes a powerful 90-minute drama when public television presents A HOUSE DIVIDED: DENMARK VESEY'S REBELLION on Wednesday, February 24th at 8 pm CT.

The pilot for a proposed series on slavery in America, the program reveals both the human urgency and the historical context in this troubled period in American life.

An outstanding cast, including Yaphet Kotto, Tony award–winner Cleavon Little, Ned Beatty and Antonio Fargas star in the film, which was shot in authentic period locations recreated in Charleston. . . .

1. The final title for the PBS drama was simply *Denmark Vesey's Rebellion*. Filmed during a writers' strike, the movie has never been released commercially and is not available today in any

Figure 38. The artist Ed Dwight relied on his imagination in creating this controversial monument to Denmark Vesey, unveiled in Charleston's Hampton Park, February 15, 2014. Photo by Daron Lee Calhoun.

format. Vesey also appeared in a 1991 television film for adolescents, "Brother Future." In this telling, a rowdy street youth from Detroit is hit by a car and wakes up in 1822 Charleston. Vesey, who has several cameos in the film, was played by a far-too-young Carl Lumbly, who was forty at the time. Curiously, the far more appropriate sixty-two-year old Moses Gunn, who made a career out of playing tough characters, was cast as a meek plantation hand.

Charleston Post and Courier

Saturday, February 15, 2014

"Denmark Vesey Monument Unveiled in Hampton Park Before Hundreds."

In 1799, Denmark Vesey won $1,500 in the East Bay Lottery. He spent part of the money, $600, to purchase his freedom.

Vesey would go on to help start Hampstead AME Church downtown and agitate for others' education and freedom. The violence perpetrated by whites against blacks—attacks both legal and physical, including assaults on the church—convinced him that rebellion was justified.

Vesey and his co-conspirators plotted insurrection but were exposed by informants. The repercussions were fierce: Vesey and 34 others were publicly hanged, 37 more were banished, four whites were fined and the church building was destroyed. The rebellion struck such fear into the hearts of the white minority at the time, they insisted on answering it with brutality and newly organized militias to keep the city's blacks under control.

That history was recognized Saturday in Hampton Park when a monument to Vesey was unveiled before several speakers and hundreds of appreciative onlookers. It was a long time coming. The monument committee was formed in 1996 by Charleston County Councilman Henry Darby and Curtis Franks of the Avery Research Center; it took 18 years to see the effort through to completion.

The city provided critical support, including a corner of the park and careful landscaping that began three years ago. The monument, a life-size rendering of Vesey, was made by Ed Dwight, a Colorado-based artist. Committee members and speakers all said the monument was an important step taken to fill in the historical gaps—to widen recognition of slavery's terrible legacy and the full cost of freedom. Vesey's actions of 1822 can inspire anyone who cares about liberty, Franks said. "The spirit of freedom is so pervasive."

Mayor Joe Riley, admiring the site, said it was neither hidden nor too prominent, affording people a contemplative spot to pay their respects to an important historical figure. "The undeniable fact is this: Denmark Vesey was free," Riley told the assembly. "He was a free black man, No one owned him. . . . He risked his life and gave his life to make enslaved people free."

The Rev. Joe Darby, speaking as a leader of the AME Church, was perhaps the most outspoken about the controversies surrounding Vesey and the effort to memorialize him. "Some people see Denmark Vesey as a dangerous terrorist," Darby said. "Most see him as a freedom fighter. My hope is that this monument will add to the full story of our southern heritage."

Committee member Dorothy Wright echoed the need to tell the whole story of America's history. "We did not come to glorify or complain, we came to notate and explain," she said.

College of Charleston history professor Bernard Powers said too many people don't know about Vesey. "Today, many people are still unable or unwilling to grasp the pertinence of slavery and freedom," he said. "They don't have the conceptual framework or proper vocabulary to understand Denmark Vesey."

Vesey had known what it was like to be someone else's property, and he had known about the suffering experienced by captured Africans during the Middle Passage: he had been sold at 14 to the captain of a slave ship and accompanied him on many trading voyages.

In 1783, Vesey relocated to Charleston where he remained enslaved for another 17 years—until luck set him free and outrage at injustice led to doom. He had hoped liberated blacks, in the wake of insurrection, would escape to Haiti, which was the only place in the world where a slave revolt had been successfully accomplished, Powers said. Years later, as blacks were recruited to fight in the Civil War against the Confederacy they were implored to remember Vesey. In this way the links of history form a chain, Powers said.

Henry Darby, chairman of the monument committee and member of City Council, was recognized as the main force behind the effort. He, in turn, acknowledged Franks and many others who persevered, often against the odds. "Frequently bewildered, we never relented, frequently disappointed, we pressed forward," he said.

And now, finally, one of Charleston's most important historical figures has found a prominent place under the oaks of Hampton Park.

Echoes of the Past in Emanuel AME

Not long after the founding of the United States, the white establishment of Charleston, S.C., had much to fear. A slave revolt had swept the French colony of Saint-Dominque, now Haiti, in 1791. Charlestonians read of slaves who slaughtered whites indiscriminately, carrying as their standard "a pike with the carcass of an impaled white baby."

Could such horrors come north?

"I am afraid if not checked in time it is a flame which will extend to all the neighbouring islands, & may eventually prove not a very pleasing or agreeable example to the Southern States," Charles Pinckney, South Carolina's governor, wrote to President George Washington that year. "The conflagration . . . the general destruction of property, & a probable famine are particularly unpleasant to us who live in Countries where Slaves abound." . . . [1]

Into this charged atmosphere came Morris Brown, a free mulatto, and Henry Drayton, a former South Carolina slave. Both were members of the Bethel Methodist Church, a majority black church in Charleston nonetheless run by whites, as was common at the time. In 1818, Brown and Drayton discovered the church's white trustees had decided to build a hearse house on top of the black cemetery adjoining the church. In protest, more than 4,300 African American parishioners walked out and formed their own congregation, which soon associated itself with the newly-formed African Methodist Church in Philadelphia.

This was the beginning of what is now the Emanuel AME Church of Charleston—the one allegedly invaded on June 16 by Dylann Roof, who is charged with gunning down nine people gathered for Bible study and prayer. The dead included the Rev. Clementa Pinckney, most likely a descendant of slaves owned by the vast Pinckney family that included Charles Pinckney, who wrote the letter to President Washington worrying about insurrection. . . .

Just forming the church that would become Emanuel AME was, to Charleston's whites, a form of . . . insurrection. For the first time in that city, blacks could worship and conduct classes on their own despite "religious assembly" laws expressly banning just that. . . .

In June 1818, 140 members of the church were arrested. Five ministers, including founder Brown, were given the choice of leaving South Carolina or serving a month-long jail sentence. Brown elected to do his time and stay in Charleston.

So did the church. But that wasn't the end of its troubles.

In 1820, congregants were arrested for holding late night services—a crime. Two years later came allegations of a worse one: Members of the church led by a free black named Denmark Vesey plotted a slave insurrection. Authorities said up to 9,000 slaves were to mobilize with stockpiles of pikes and other weapons; none were ever found, and other physical evidence was thin. . . .

Still, this could not stand. Southerners saw themselves as good Christians, but when it came to teaching the word of God to slaves, they were conflicted. On one hand, they felt it was their duty; on the other, they understood the Gospels threatened their twisted moral justification for slavery—and perhaps even threatened white lives. . . .

Vesey and 34 others, all associated with the church, were hanged in July, 1822. Thirty-seven were transported outside the United States.

This, said the authorities, is the consequence of letting blacks worship on their own, with their own leaders. Meetings of any kind by "held solely by slaves" were dangerous. Worse: The congregation—Brown's church, Vesey's church—"was not only composed altogether of coloured persons, but their Ministers of the Gospel. . . . The influence which such men and class leaders must necessarily acquire over the minds of the ignorant blacks is evident."

Especially, as the tribunal wrote, "if a disposition exists in them to obtain for their own colour and themselves, the freedom and privileges enjoyed by the whites."

Discovery of Vesey's purported plot destroyed the church for decades. It was razed by order of the city, but reopened with a new building after the Civil War. The building was designed by architect Robert Vesey—yes, Vesey's son.

Whatever the extent of the Vesey insurrection, his heroism stands. He could not be broken. Nor could the church, which lives on. Today, a monument to Vesey stands in Charleston, and his memory stirs passion.

Ironically, the court's portrayal of Vesey, intended to illustrate his capacity to execute such a vast conspiracy, has contributed to his mystique: "He was remarkable throughout his trial, for great presence and composure of mind," the proceedings said. He exhibited "no signs of fear." . . .

[W]ord of Roof's arrest came. . . . [T]he words reportedly uttered by the alleged killer—"You're taking over our country"—and his apparent fear of African Americans eerily echoed the sentiments of white Charleston in the first days and years after the seed that would grow into Emanuel AME was planted.

As the South's great novelist William Faulkner wrote: "The past is never dead. It's not even past."

1. Charles Pinckney (1757–1824), cousin of Charles Cotesworth Pinckney (1746–1825), was governor of South Carolina three times, 1789–92, 1796–98, and 1806–8. Both Pinckneys signed the US Constitution. The referenced letter, dated October 6, 1791, about a month after the Saint-Domingue slave revolution began, can be found in Mark A. Mastromarino and Jack D. Warren, eds., *The Papers of George Washington: Presidential Series*, vol. 9: *September 1791–February 1792* (Charlottesville: University Press of Virginia, 2000), 55–56.

INDEX

Douglas R. Egerton has taught history at Le Moyne College since 1987; he has also held visiting appointments at Colgate University, Cornell University, and the University College of Dublin. He is the author of eight books, including *He Shall Go Out Free: The Lives of Denmark Vesey*; *The Wars of Reconstruction: The Brief, Violent History of America's Most Progressive Era*; *Year of Meteors: Stephen Douglas, Abraham Lincoln, and the Election that Brought on the Civil War*; *Gabriel's Rebellion: The Virginia Slave Conspiracies of 1800 and 1802*; and *Death or Liberty: African Americans and Revolutionary America*. His essays and reviews have appeared in the *New York Times*, the *Nation*, and the *Boston Globe*. He lives near Syracuse, New York, with his wife, historian Leigh Fought.

Robert L. Paquette, president and executive director of The Alexander Hamilton Institute in Clinton, New York, is coeditor of *The Oxford Handbook of Slavery in the Americas*. His *Sugar Is Made with Blood* won the Elsa Goveia Prize. His essay "Of Facts and Fables: New Light on the Denmark Vesey Affair" (coauthored with Douglas Egerton) won the Malcolm C. Clark Award given by the South Carolina Historical Society. With Seymour Drescher and Stanley Engerman, he coedited *Slavery*.With Mark M. Smith, he coedited *The Oxford Handbook of Slavery in the Americas*. In 2005, he received the Mary Young Award for distinguished achievement from his alma mater, the University of Rochester. In 2014, he received the Jeane Jordan Kirkpatrick Prize for Academic Freedom. He lives in Clinton, New York, with his wife, Zoya.

SOUTHERN DISSENT

Edited by Stanley Harrold and Randall M. Miller

The Other South: Southern Dissenters in the Nineteenth Century, by Carl N. Degler, with a new preface (2000)

Crowds and Soldiers in Revolutionary North Carolina: The Culture of Violence in Riot and War, by Wayne E. Lee (2001)

"Lord, We're Just Trying to Save Your Water": Environmental Activism and Dissent in the Appalachian South, by Suzanne Marshall (2002)

The Changing South of Gene Patterson: Journalism and Civil Rights, 1960–1968, edited by Roy Peter Clark and Raymond Arsenault (2002; first paperback edition, 2020)

Gendered Freedoms: Race, Rights, and the Politics of Household in the Delta, 1861–1875, by Nancy D. Bercaw (2003)

Civil War on Race Street: The Civil Rights Movement in Cambridge, Maryland, by Peter B. Levy (2003)

South of the South: Jewish Activists and the Civil Rights Movement in Miami, 1945–1960, by Raymond A. Mohl, with contributions by Matilda "Bobbi" Graff and Shirley M. Zoloth (2004)

Throwing Off the Cloak of Privilege: White Southern Women Activists in the Civil Rights Era, edited by Gail S. Murray (2004)

The Atlanta Riot: Race, Class, and Violence in a New South City, by Gregory Mixon (2004)

Slavery and the Peculiar Solution: A History of the American Colonization Society, by Eric Burin (2005; first paperback edition, 2008)

"I Tremble for My Country": Thomas Jefferson and the Virginia Gentry, by Ronald L. Hatzenbuehler (2006; first paperback edition, 2009)

From Saint-Domingue to New Orleans: Migration and Influences, by Nathalie Dessens (2007)

Higher Education and the Civil Rights Movement: White Supremacy, Black Southerners, and College Campuses, edited by Peter Wallenstein (2008)

Burning Faith: Church Arson in the American South, by Christopher B. Strain (2008; first paperback edition, 2020)

Black Power in Dixie: A Political History of African Americans in Atlanta, by Alton Hornsby Jr. (2009; first paperback edition, 2016)

Looking South: Race, Gender, and the Transformation of Labor from Reconstruction to Globalization, by Mary E. Frederickson (2011; first paperback edition, 2012)

Southern Character: Essays in Honor of Bertram Wyatt-Brown, edited by Lisa Tendrich Frank and Daniel Kilbride (2011)

The Challenge of Blackness: The Institute of the Black World and Political Activism in the 1970s, by Derrick E. White (2011; first paperback edition, 2012)

Quakers Living in the Lion's Mouth: The Society of Friends in Northern Virginia, 1730–1865, by A. Glenn Crothers (2012; first paperback edition, 2013)

Unequal Freedoms: Ethnicity, Race, and White Supremacy in Civil War–Era Charleston, by Jeff Strickland (2015)

Show Thyself a Man: Georgia State Troops, Colored, 1865–1905, by Gregory Mixon (2016)

The Denmark Vesey Affair: A Documentary History, edited by Douglas R. Egerton and Robert L. Paquette (2017; first paperback edition, 2022)

New Directions in the Study of African American Recolonization, edited by Beverly C. Tomek and Matthew J. Hetrick (2017; paperback edition 2022)
Everybody's Problem: The War on Poverty in Eastern North Carolina, by Karen M. Hawkins (2017)
The Seedtime, the Work, and the Harvest: New Perspectives on the Black Freedom Struggle in America, edited by Jeffrey L. Littlejohn, Reginald K. Ellis, and Peter B. Levy (2018; first paperback edition, 2019)
Fugitive Slaves and Spaces of Freedom in North America, edited by Damian Alan Pargas (2018; first paperback edition, 2020)
Latino Orlando: Suburban Transformation and Racial Conflict, by Simone Delerme (2020)
Slavery and Freedom in the Shenandoah Valley during the Civil War Era, by Jonathan A. Noyalas (2021; paperback edition, 2022)
The Citizenship Education Program and Black Women's Political Culture, by Deanna M. Gillespie (2021)